Encyclopedia of

CREATIVITY

VOLUME 1
A-H

Editors-in-Chief

MARK A. RUNCO
California State University, Fullerton

STEVEN R. PRITZKER
Luminescent Creativity, Greenbrae, California

Executive
Advisory Board

Howard Gardner
Harvard University

Ravenna Helson
University of California, Berkeley

Ruth Richards
Saybrook Graduate School; University of California, San Francisco;
and Harvard Medical School

Tudor Rickards
University of Manchester

Dean Keith Simonton
University of California, Davis

Robert J. Sternberg
Yale University

Encyclopedia of

CREATIVITY

Editors-in-Chief

MARK A. RUNCO
California State University
Fullerton, California

STEVEN R. PRITZKER
Luminescent Creativity
Greenbrae, California

VOLUME 1
A-H

San Diego   London   Boston   New York   Sydney   Tokyo   Toronto

RECEIVED

AUG 2 4 1999

MSU - LIBRARY

Ref.
BF
408
.E53
1999
v.1

This book is printed on acid-free paper.

Copyright © 1999 by ACADEMIC PRESS

All Rights Reserved.
No part of this publication may be reproduced or transmitted in any form or by any
means, electronic or mechanical, including photocopy, recording, or any information
storage and retrieval system, without permission in writing from the publisher.

Academic Press
a division of Harcourt Brace & Company
525 B Street, Suite 1900, San Diego, California 92101-4495, USA
http://www.apnet.com

Academic Press
24-28 Oval Road, London NW1 7DX, UK
http://www.hbuk.co.uk/ap/

Library of Congress Catalog Card Number: 99-61534

International Standard Book Number: 0-12-227075-4 (set)
International Standard Book Number: 0-12-227076-2 (Volume 1)
International Standard Book Number: 0-12-227077-0 (Volume 2)

PRINTED IN THE UNITED STATES OF AMERICA
99 00 01 02 03 04 MM 9 8 7 6 5 4 3 2 1

Contents

Contents of Volume 2

T

U

V

W

Z

About the Editors-in-Chief

MARK A. RUNCO, Ph.D., is Professor of Child and Adolescent Studies at California State University, Fullerton. He is founder and continuing editor of the *Creativity Research Journal* and acts as senior editor of the *Perspectives on Creativity* book series. Author of over 120 books, chapters, and articles in the area of creativity, he is a fellow and past president of the American Psychological Association's Division 10 (Psychology and the Arts). Dr. Runco is recipient of a Spencer Foundation Research Grant and also of the Early Scholar Award from the National Association for Gifted Children.

STEVEN R. PRITZKER, Ph.D., is a writer and creativity consultant who has worked with companies such as Fox, MTM, Paramount, Time-Warner, Disney, Eastman Kodak, The Museum of Creativity Project, and Sara Lee. He has taught writing, creativity, and Educational Psychology at UCLA and at the University of Southern California.

Dr. Pritzker has written over 75 network television episodes for series, including Emmy winners *Room 222* and *The Mary Tyler Moore Show*. He worked as a writer or writer/producer on over 200 network episodes including such popular shows as *The Partridge Family, The Loveboat, Maude, Fish, Silver Spoons,* and *Valerie.* He has been nominated for the Writers Guild of America Award and received an award from Parents Anonymous for a show written about child abuse. Dr. Pritzker received his Ph.D. in Educational Psychology from the University of Southern California. He writes both academic and popular press articles and books about creativity. In addition, Dr. Pritzker is President of Luminescent Creativity, which consults with corporations and individuals about ways they can improve their creativity.

About the Executive Advisory Board

HOWARD GARDNER is the John H. and Elisabeth A. Hobbs Professor in Cognition and Education at the Harvard Graduate School of Education. He also holds positions as Adjunct Professor of Psychology at Harvard University, Adjunct Professor of Neurology at the Boston University School of Medicine, and Co-Director of Harvard Project Zero. Among other honors, Gardner received a MacArthur Prize Fellowship in 1981 and has been awarded eleven honorary degrees—most recently from Princeton University and from Tel Aviv University. In 1990, he was the first American to receive the University of Louisville's Grawemeyer Award in education.

The author or 18 books and several hundred articles, Gardner is best known in educational circles for his theory of multiple intelligences.

RAVENNA MATHEWS HELSON is a professor at the Institute of Personality and Social Research at the University of California, Berkeley. She conducts studies of creativity in women and of gender differences in cognitive and affective styles in creative work. Her studies have identified "patriarchal and matriarchal" styles of creativity in men and women. She has also studied the development of creativity longitudinally, and creativity as analyzed in children's literature.

In 1984 Helson received the Henry A. Murray Award, primarily for her work on creativity, from Division 8 (Personality and Social Psychology) of the American Psychological Association, and in 1994 she received the Rudolph Arnheim Award from Division 10 (Psychology and the Arts).

RUTH RICHARDS is a Board Certified psychiatrist and professor of psychology at Saybrook Graduate School; associate clinical professor at the University of California, San Francisco; research affiliate in psychology and psychiatry at McLean Hospital in Belmont, Massachusetts; and lecturer in the Department of Psychiatry at Harvard Medical School.

Dr. Richards is on the editorial board of the *Creativity Research Journal* and *Journal of Humanistic Psychology*. She is on the Advisory Board of the Manic-Depressive Illness Foundation, established in cooperation with Johns Hopkins University School of Medicine to increase public awareness and understanding of affective disorders. Dr. Richards is also active in the American Psychological Association and was elected At-Large Representative for 1999–2002 for Division 10 (Psychology and the Arts).

Dr. Richards' research has focused on everyday creativity, health, and the higher development of human potential, including issues of coping, aesthetics, altered states, and social responsibility.

TUDOR RICKARDS is Professor of Creativity and Organisational Change at the Manchester Business School, England, from where he directs the Creativity Research Unit. He has published over a hundred articles and 12 books related to creativity, innovation, and the management of change. He has held visiting professorships at the University of Kiel and at SUNY, Buffalo, is holder of a personal professorial chair at the Victoria University of Manchester, and is a Fellow of the Royal Society of Arts.

Dr. Rickards' research interests include epistemological and methodological issues in the study of creativity, assessment of factors that block creative performance, application of creative problem-solving techniques to industrial problems and to challenges involved in creativity training, and evaluation and development of models of creative and innovative processes.

Dr. Rickards has received many awards, including the Philips and Drew first prize for an expert system assisting young entrepreneurs, the Alex Osborn Visiting Professor, State University of New York, Buffalo, and the UK Partnership Trust award for innovative contributions to the teaching of creativity at graduate and post experience levels.

Dr. Rickards is also the current editor of *Creativity and Innovation Management* and is an editorial advisory board member of *Journal of Managerial Accounting, Creativity Research Journal,* and *International Marketing Review.* He is former editor of *Leadership and Organisation Development Journal.*

DEAN KEITH SIMONTON is a professor of psychology at the University of California, Davis, and former Fellow of both the Danforth Foundation and the National Science Foundation. His research program is distinctive for its application of historiometric methods to the study of genius, creativity, leadership, and aesthetics. This research program has produced over one hundred articles in journals of psychology, education, sociology, anthropology, the natural sciences, and the humanities. In addition, he is the author of seven books on genius, leadership, and creativity. Simonton is the editor of the *Journal of Creative Behavior* and serves on the Editorial Boards of the *Creativity Research Journal, Empirical Studies of the Arts, Leadership Quarterly,* and *Political Psychology.*

Among his many honors are the Rudolf Arnheim Award for Outstanding Contributions to Psychology and the Arts, the Sir Francis Galton Award for Outstanding Contributions to the Study of Creativity, the George A. Miller Outstanding Article Award, the Award for Excellence of the Mensa Education and Research Foundation, and the UC Davis Prize for Teaching and Scholarly Achievement.

ROBERT J. STERNBERG is IBM Professor of Psychology and Education in the Department of Psychology at Yale University. Dr. Sternberg is a Fellow of the American Academy of Arts and Sciences, the American Association for the Advancement of Science, the American Psychological Association, and the American Psychological Society. He is currently editor-elect of *Contemporary Psychology* and is past editor of *Psychological Bulletin.* He has been associate editor of *Child Development* and of *Intelligence,* and is currently associate editor of the *Journal of Theoretical and Philosophical Psychology.*

Dr. Sternberg has won a number of awards, including the Early Career Award and McCandless Awards from the American Psychological Association; the Outstanding Book, Research Review, and Scribner Awards from the American Educational Research Association; the Cattell Award of the Society for Multivariate Experimental Psychology; and the Distinguished Scholar Award from the National Association for Gifted Children. He has been an NSF Graduate Fellow as well as a Guggenheim Fellow.

Dr. Sternberg is the author of over 650 articles, book chapters, and books in the fields of creativity, intelligence, thinking styles, and love.

Preface

Creativity is increasingly important on personal and social levels. Life has become highly complex and challenging, and many individuals are therefore searching for ways to understand more about their own creativity. Organizations must now constantly reinvent themselves because change occurs at an increasingly rapid pace. The educational system is coming to recognize the need to prepare students for a future that is not foreseeable.

The need for a deeper understanding of creativity has inspired a great deal of research. Since 1960, over 10,000 research articles in creativity have appeared in hundreds of journals and periodicals. Over 600 books about creativity have been published in the 1990s. These confirm that creativity is a concern in numerous fields, including all of the arts and sciences. The research is being conducted by individuals in many different disciplines, including psychology, the health sciences, education, and business.

The quantity and diversity of research have made it difficult to locate and understand the wealth of material available. The *Encyclopedia of Creativity* is a source book, the first of its kind, comprehensive, and written for a wide audience. Here everyone from the casual newcomer to the seasoned researcher can find a broad cross section of information and even guidance about creativity.

One of the axioms in creativity research is that many breakthroughs occur when information or concepts from one field are applied to a different one. Darwin's theory of evolution was partially inspired by his reading Malthus' theory of population growth and Lynell on geological change. Jean Piaget, noted developmental psychologist, borrowed heavily from biology and epistemology. Freud used a medical model to understand the psyche. Our hope is that practitioners of creativity research will similarly benefit by looking at work done in fields other than their own. The comprehensive nature of the encyclopedia will offer readers the opportunity to find a new perspective, which we hope will suggest new insights about themselves, their work, and their place in the world.

This book is designed to inspire further recognition in both the general public and the academic community that the study of creativity is a field in itself. Enough is now known about creativity that it can be integrated into every level of our educational system. Perhaps over the next decade more universities throughout the world will join the pioneers who have developed degree-earning programs in creativity at the graduate level. We also expect to see the teaching of creativity and the creative process integrated into many more professional schools, such as business and medicine. It is our hope that teachers at the elementary and high school level will learn about their own creativity and how to value and encourage creative students. It is not always an easy task, but it is very worthwhile.

CONTENTS

Creativity is multifaceted and manifested in different ways in different domains. Moreover, there are different processes that can each lead to creative work. Thus a comprehensive *Encyclopedia of Creativity* required many different kinds of articles. There are articles that present overviews of the different theories and perspectives about creativity. There are reviews of a number of domain-specific areas, such as the arts, acting, architecture, and dance. Creativity and education are examined in articles about thought processes, such as the enhancement of creativity, intelligence, and memory. Programs and courses in creativity are discussed as well as strategies, tactics, techniques, and tests of creativity. Those interested in business and organizational creativity can view articles about advertising, brainstorming, corporate culture, creative climate, group creativity, innovation, leadership, and teams, among others. Many articles examine the creative process across domains, covering how we come to be inspired, work methods, individual differences, and other factors that may impact creativity, be they psychological, physical, or sociological. The complex interrelationship between society and creativity is explicitly examined in articles about censorship, conventionality, conformity, consensual assessment, cross-cultural differences, and several others. Because this encyclopedia focuses on scientific information about creativity, there are also articles that discuss research methodology, definitions, and even the concept of creativity itself. Finally, there are selected biographical studies conducted with creativity as the key concern. The sampling of biographical subjects represents eminent individuals in different domains, including inventors, writers, scientists, psychologists, and painters.

As is apparent from the breadth of articles included, the study of creativity is a vast subject. Several topics required more than one perspective and more than one article. The *Encyclopedia of Creativity* is alphabetically organized with extensive cross-referencing that will allow the multitude of bridges and relationships to be easily found and explored.

AUDIENCE

The encyclopedia is designed for use by students of creativity as well as by researchers and professionals who utilize creativity in their work. Anyone who is interested in learning more about their own creativity and the creative process can benefit from the articles presented here. Readers are encouraged to follow their own interests and inclinations in exploring these volumes.

A FINAL INTRODUCTORY COMMENT

More than any other kind of book an encyclopedia is a collaborative effort. We thank our eminent panel of editorial advisors: Howard Gardner, Ravenna Helson, Ruth Richards, Tudor Rickards, Dean Keith Simonton, and Robert Sternberg. We also thank each of the distinguished contributors to this work. In addition, we appreciate the efforts of our editor, Nikki Levy, and her assistant, Barbara Makinster, who kept this sizable project organized. We hope this encyclopedia will not only inform but inspire readers to become more creative in their personal and professional lives.

Mark A. Runco
Steven R. Pritzker

How to Use the Encyclopedia

The *Encyclopedia of Creativity* is intended for use by students, research professionals, and interested others. Articles have been chosen to reflect major disciplines in the study of creativity, common topics of research by professionals in this domain, and areas of public interest and concern. Each article serves as a comprehensive overview of a given area, providing both breadth of coverage for students and depth of coverage for research professionals. We have designed the encyclopedia with the following features for maximum accessibility for all readers.

Articles in the encyclopedia are arranged alphabetically by subject. Complete tables of contents appear in both volumes. The Index is located in Volume 2. Because the reader's topic of interest may be listed under a broader article title, we encourage use of the Index for access to a subject area, rather than use of the Table of Contents alone.

Each article contains an outline, a glossary, cross-references, and a bibliography. The outline allows a quick scan of the major areas discussed within each article. The glossary contains terms that may be unfamiliar to the reader, with each term defined *in the context of its use in that article*. Thus, a term may appear in the glossary for another article defined in a slightly different manner or with a subtle nuance specific to that article. For clarity, we have allowed these differences in definition to remain so that the terms are defined relative to the context of each article.

Each article has been cross-referenced to other related articles in the encyclopedia. Cross-references are found at the first or predominant mention of a subject area covered elsewhere in the encyclopedia. Cross-references will always appear at the end of a paragraph. Where multiple cross-references apply to a single paragraph, the cross-references are listed in alphabetical order. We encourage readers to use the cross-references to locate other encyclopedia articles that will provide more detailed information about a subject.

The bibliography lists recent secondary sources to aid the reader in locating more detailed or technical information. Review articles and research articles that are considered of primary importance to the understanding of a given subject area are also listed. Bibliographies are not intended to provide a full reference listing of all material covered in the context of a given article, but are provided as guides to further reading.

A select number of biographies have been included. These biographies discuss the lives of individuals famous for their creative endeavors. Only those individuals whose lives had already been studied by specialists in creativity were included. Hence, although there are many individuals famous for their creative pursuits, you may not find coverage of your favorite here. Inclusion is not intended to be a judgment on the impact or value of these individuals or their creations.

Acting

Jill Nemiro

California School of Professional Psychology, Los Angeles

Acting Pretending to be a character (someone other than one-self) in the context of a drama; the process whereby an actor conceives of a character and reveals that character to the audience.

Actor The individual who acts.

Character That which a person or thing really is; the physical expression of a person in a play or drama.

Imagination The ability to create one's own ideas of how things should be.

Improvising Setting out to solve a problem with no preconception as to how it will be done; permitting everything and everyone in the environment to work with you in solving the problem.

Pretending Substituting for reality.

Spontaneity A state in which an actor is open, lives in the moment, becomes an instrument for the work, and allows his or her own instincts to take over; a moment of explosion; a free moment of self-expression.

All of us have at one time or another watched a movie, television show, or theatrical performance. Central to each of these types of performances are actors. Thus, the art of ACTING is not unfamiliar to us. But what actually is acting? Where did it start? How has this art form developed over the ages? What is involved in the actor's creative process? What is the relationship between an actor's personal identity and that of the characters he or she portrays? And finally, what contextual factors enhance or undermine the realization of an actor's creativity? The present article addresses each of these questions and emphasizes the Western histrionic tradition of acting in the theatre. The expressive art of the East, and acting for film and television, a more recent phenomenon, are not discussed.

I. ACTING DEFINED

Actors strive to perform in such a manner as to make fiction believable, not as facts, but as a pleasurable, entertaining theatrical experience. Good acting demands that an actor is convincing in the part, and convinces the audience that she is the character being portrayed. Thus, acting is more than mere simulation or pretending. Acting is the process whereby an actor con-

Copyright © 1999 by Academic Press
All rights of reproduction in any form reserved.

ceives of a character and portrays that character to the audience.

II. THE HISTORY OF ACTING

A. The Birth of Acting

As far back as 4000 B.C., the Egyptians may have had religious dramatic events in which an actor-priest worshiped the memory of the dead. It was, however, in ancient Greece that Western histrionic tradition originated during the sixth century B.C. The genesis of tragic drama and acting lay in the ritual choral dances honoring Dionysus, the god of wine and fertility. In 535 B.C., the ruler Pisistratus introduced competitive performances at the Dionysian festival in Athens. At these performances, Thespis, who was the first actor, introduced impersonation, accompanied by musical narration performed by a chorus and a leader. In these early performances, there was only one actor—the poet himself. The actor was assisted by a chorus and a leader. The actor-poet wore a mask which enabled him to play many parts. The importance of the chorus diminished when the poet Aeschylus added a second actor, and then Sophocles added yet a third actor. The three actors took on specific roles: protagonist, usually the major roles; deuteragonist, more minor roles; and tritagonist, usually a tyrant, monarch, and someone who spoke the prologues. During the fourth century, actors replaced actor-poets. Several famous Greek tragic actors performed in this century—Neoptolemus, Thettalus, Athenodorus, Polus, Theodorus, and Aristodemus. The large stylized mask was a marked characteristic of these actors, as was the cothurnus, a thick-soled boot.

In ancient Rome, drama and acting were modeled after the Greek Theatre. Roman plays were performed on various holidays. However, these performances did not have the same ritual significance as that of the Greek contests. Dramatic performances shared the stage with chariot races and gladiatorial shows, and the latter two were more popular. Needless to say, Roman actors did not enjoy the same high social and religious position that Greek actors did. Most of the actors were slaves without legal or religious rights. Only a few, such as Roscius and Aesop, who both lived in the first century, attained high status.

B. The Anonymous Amateur Actors of the Middle Ages

By the fifth and sixth centuries, A.D., acting in formally staged tragedies and comedies had become a lost art. The Christian church had condemned these theatrical performances, and during the Dark Ages, written drama and regular theatres ceased to exist. During this era, it was the mime artist who kept alive the tradition of professional acting. Most of these mime artists lived poorly, were considered outcasts and vagabonds, and wandered from town to town providing entertainment. These wandering mime artists narrated heroic deeds, chanted bawdy songs, danced comic steps, and engaged in sarcastic jests. They were both popular in the village streets and the courts of great lords, and thus won a permanent place in the medieval world of acting.

Oddly enough, it was within the church itself that formal acting and drama were reborn in the Middle Ages. Priests, chanting brief Latin dialogues, became the first medieval actors. However, these actor-priests were soon replaced by laymen who breathed local humor and comic elements into the plays. Throughout Europe in the 14th and 15th centuries, vast numbers of anonymous amateur actors performed in dramatizations based on the Bible, and on the lives of saints and Christ's Passion.

Morality plays were also popular in the 15th century. Here, the lively dramatizations of the bible were abandoned for the presentation of "everyman" in his struggle between good and evil. Essentially, the plays were dramatized sermons, and the characters were personifications of human vices and virtues. Of course, interspersed throughout these religious plays was a spirit of lively comedy and crass realism.

By the 16th and 17th centuries these medieval dramas performed by anonymous amateur actors were replaced by secular, national dramas written and acted by professional actors. Thus, the professional actor emerged once again, leaving behind vast numbers of anonymous amateur actors who had paved the way for the rebirth of professional acting.

c. Italy's Commedia dell' Arte

For the true actor during the Renaissance period, we must turn to the unique Italian commedia dell' arte. These players were, for the most part, performing on street corners, in squares, and at festivals. Without a theatre or aid of elaborate scenery, these actors performed an improvised drama with skill and style. Groups of trained, astute actors performed a repertory of conventional dramatic forms with only a skeletal script. They played from a scenario usually provided by the director of the group. Individual actors supplied their own dialogue based on the theme of the play. However, it was not the plot of these performances that set them apart. It was the characters who gave these performances life and color. There were stock types in each play (e.g., a pair of young lovers; *Capitano,* a braggart warrior; *Dottore,* a foolish old jurist or medical man; *Pantalone,* usually a mean, greedy, lascivious or silly and doting character; and *zannis,* masked, comic servants). An individual actor usually became identified with one of these characters and spent his entire professional life perfecting the role. It was in the commedia that women for the first time in theatrical history assumed an important position. Commedia actors were commanded to play in the courts of great lords in many lands (e.g., Austria, England, France, and Spain). In the middle of the 17th century, the commedia reached its peak. During the next hundred years, its inspiration waned and by the second half of the 18th century, the commedia had disappeared.

D. The Elizabethan Actor of England

During the reign of Queen Elizabeth, dramatists constructed plays for the pleasure of Elizabeth and her noblemen. These plays were given in private halls before royal audiences, and were performed by boy actors trained by schoolmasters and choirmasters. Professional players also emerged, and when they were not needed by the lords, they also performed in and around London in inn-yards and village squares.

This short period between 1580 and 1620 was the greatest era in English dramatic history. Poets like Christopher Marlowe, William Shakespeare, and Ben Jonson emerged. Two professional companies stood out in this lively period—"The Chamberlein's Men" boasting of such players as Richard Burbage, William Kemp, and actor-poet William Shakespeare; and the "Admiral's Men," whose leading actor was Edward Alleyn, known for playing heroic figures in Christopher Marlowe's plays. These professional companies were composed of a fairly stable group of leading actors

who owned their theatres. Performing with them were a number of hired actors, and young boy apprentices who played the female roles. Women were not seen on the English stage until 1656. The poet-dramatists created their plays specifically for their companies. Shakespeare, for example, was not only a leading dramatist for "The Chamberlein's Men," but also an actor and sharer in the financial profits of the troupe as well.

The public theatres in which Elizabethan professional acting companies played resembled the inn-yards used by the earlier actors of this period. London's first theatre was built in 1576 by James Burbage and was called The Theatre. It had no roof, was circular, and had a simple platform stage. There was no curtain or proscenium to separate the actors from their spectators.

The typical Elizabethan actor was also a clown, entertainer, and writer, who was part minstrel and part professional actor. Actors possessed more of a formalistic acting style, and were known for dancing, ability of the body, memory, skill with a weapon, and wit. The Elizabethan actor was primarily distinguished by an excellent voice. Players were frequently in elaborate dress. These actors were sometimes criticized for directing their attention to the spectators instead of their fellow players.

E. The Restoration of the New English Theatre

As a war measure, the theatres in London were closed in 1642 and were kept officially shut by the Puritans who were in power. In 1660, Charles II was returned to the throne, and the theatre came back to life.

During the Restoration period of the 17th and 18th centuries, the bare platform of the Elizabethan stage disappeared and a more modern picture stage with a proscenium arch, curtain, and scenery appeared. Outdoor theatres vanished as well, and new, indoor theatres were built, primarily to house aristocratic, upper-class audiences. Women, for the first time, graced the English stage. Interestingly, the actor became more important than the playwright, as the plays of this time were little more than vehicles for the great actors of this period.

In Restoration tragedies, actors spoke to each other in rhymed couplets. Love was the most familiar word in the titles of Restoration comedies. These plays had their brand of stereotypes—the fashionable playboy whose success was measured by the number of his conquests and the witty, attractive young lady who was willing to be wooed and enjoyed the elaborate ritual of seduction.

Thus, from 1660 to the beginning of the 19th century, an evolution in the histrionic tradition occurred to which each of the outstanding actors of this period contributed. For 50 of those years, from 1660 to 1710, Thomas Betterton dominated the stage.

F. The Romantic Theatre

The romantic movement, as it was called, actually began in Germany, but it was in France that the movement generated the greatest intensity. The end of the 18th century was a period of violent change in national governments. Two major revolutions occurred—in the American colonies in 1776, and in France in 1789. Monarchical rule was abolished in favor of republican systems. During this period, the theatre in France also underwent a revolution. This was a period of explosion, revolt, and shock to the senses. Playwrights, actors, and audiences were forced to look at the theatre from new perspectives. A battle was waged between the rules of classic theatre and the lack of rules in the romantic performances.

In the classic dramas, duty won over desire, and the will of the individual was controlled by forces greater than himself. In these new romantic dramas, the will of the individual dominated. The hero in these plays tended to be a revolutionary fighting the tyranny of a corrupt political establishment.

From 1680 to the French Revolution, every actor of importance made his way to the Cómédie Française. It was here, in 1830, that the romantic movement in France was ushered in with Victor Hugo's production of "Hernani." The play was long and packed with sensational melodramatic incidents such as duels, forced marriages, and an attempted assassination.

It appeared that the romantic movement catered to those who found life dull, who mourned vanishing high ideals, and who longed for a flag to follow and a rallying cry. On stage, actors re-created stirring passages from colorful periods of history, providing excitement for their audiences.

G. 19th Century Realism

The 19th century found the actor searching for the illusion of reality on stage. Acting was transformed from elocution and standardized gestures to realistic characterizations. This new realism was most prominent on the Russian stage. Stanislavski, who was an actor, director, and teacher of acting, was motivated by a search for truth, reality, and serious theatrical activity. He and Vladimir Nemirovich-Danchenko agreed on this new realistic focus and outlined the structure for the Moscow Art Theatre, which opened in 1898. It became one of the most long-lasting, productive, and significant modern theatres.

Stanislavski was basically interested in what actors did to calm and focus themselves. He studied what great performers did, and, as a result, created the only known complete system for building a character. Even today, the Stanislavski System is used in some form by most reputable acting companies. (This system is discussed in detail in Section III.)

The American version of the Stanislavski System was called "The Method." Lee Strasberg was instrumental in the development of The Method. Strasberg co-founded the Group Theater in 1931, with Harold Clurman and Cheryl Crawford. In the early 1940s, the Group Theatre began to unwind and the now famous Actors Studio was formed in 1947. Strasberg joined the Actors Studio in 1949 and remained there for 35 years, where he was often referred to as *the high priest of The Method*. A key element of The Method was Stanislavski's emotional or affective memory technique, in which actors were encouraged to summon up their own emotions that paralleled a particular moment in their character's life.

H. 20th Century Experimentation

The advent of the movies made realism less important in the theatre. Robert Benedetti characterized the transition of acting in the 20th century as a general movement "away from mere representation and toward the creation of independent reality on the stage; that is, away form seeming and into being" (1976, p. 76).

With the turn of the century, a wave of experimental theatre came about. German born Bertolt Brecht (1898–1956) was one of the experimentalists. In Brecht's productions, actors were asked to create both consistent and believable characters and force a detachment on the audience (called the verfremdungeffect or the alienation effect) by stepping out of their characters, to remind the audience that they were actors and that this was only a play. Usually, these moments of alienation occurred in the songs that punctuated the dramatic action. Brecht also used a projection screen as a backdrop on the stage, on which he could project titles, slogans, or photo montages that would both relate to the play and serve as another form of alienation. In this way he was limiting the audience's empathy with the play's characters by showing them as mere components in the larger scheme of things.

French actor and director Antonin Artaud (1896–1948) formulated a "Theatre of Cruelty," that had the intent of embracing the audience in a collective experience. The text of these performances, if there was any, was only a starting point for the theatrical event. Actors were free to depart from and improvise on it. The old distinction between the acting space and the audience disappeared as actors were encouraged to find ways of drawing the audience into the dramatic action, and to have spectators abandon their inhibitions and become participants in the collective experience. For these actors, physical gesture, mime, dance, and gymnastic movements were more important than eloquent speech.

In the United States and Europe, the best-publicized champion of this approach has been The Living Theatre, which was founded by Julian Beck and his wife, Judith Malina. This experimental theatre, which lasted for over 20 years until in 1970 it was broken into a series of smaller groups, dispensed altogether with characterization, as actors confronted the audience in their own personas. Performances were unrehearsed segments. The actors of the Living Theatre had no plot, no characterizations, nothing but themselves.

Benedetti suggested that these experimental theatre artists of the 20th century helped to restore the theatre to its ancient spiritual beginnings. He wrote,

The once degraded art of the actor is being made moral again in the deepest, most human sense of the word. Young artists are returning to ancient impulses not to destroy current conventions, but to forge their own ideas, to drink, as it were, from the original well (1976, p. 76).

III. THE ACTING PROCESS

Several contemporary acting theorists have tried to characterize the stages of the creative process of actors. Most mention, in one form or another, at least four major stages. First, in *general preparation,* actors build the working knowledge and skills to do their craft. To accomplish this, actors take acting classes to develop necessary skills and to have a place to work through personal deficiencies; they observe the work of other actors to learn what works and what does not work; and they observe people in general to build a knowledge of human behavior for use in characterization. The general preparation stage actually continues throughout the creative process.

Second, actors build a *knowledge of the play.* Once actors are cast in their roles, they first familiarize themselves with the entire play, reading it several times over. During this stage, the actor begins to see the play as truth, not fiction. Or perhaps, more appropriately, the actor believes the fiction, accepting that the characters are people and incidents are real. The actor begins to believe in this imaginative truth, and the acting rehearsal process can now proceed.

It is during the *rehearsal* period, where actors work in conjunction with a director to experiment, improvise, and practice. This is a period in which alternatives are explored and choices are made about the direction of how the play will unfold. It is during this period that the actor's character is built.

The outcome of all the previous stages is the final stage of *performance,* in which actors engage in a theatrical experience with the audience; spontaneity is needed to keep the performance alive, and constant adaptation is needed to adjust to fellow actors and the audience. The creative process of acting does not end with the first performance. During each performance, the actor develops new impressions of the character and situations from her or his interaction with the audience.

A. Stanislavski's Approach to Building A Character

As stated earlier, Stanislavski was responsible for creating the most complete system of building a character. Central to Stanislavski's approach were three propositions. The first proposition states that the actor does pretend, but does so in a state like a normal person in life. To accomplish this, the actor's body and instrument must be physically free and controlled; the actor must be alert and attentive, in a state of relaxed readiness; the actor must listen and observe and be in genuine contact with her or his fellow actors in the play; and the actor must believe, accept, and live inside the reality of her or his character.

The second proposition states that the actor, now in the place of the character, can only achieve honest action on stage by combining psychological action, strong motives that drive the character forward toward his other objectives; and physical action, movement which expresses and supports feelings and psychological action. This has sometimes been referred to as "the method of physical actions," meaning that using physical action is the most reliable way to summon up feelings for emotional expression. (As an example, if an actor needed to be angry in a scene, the action of grabbing onto the back of a chair would assist in calling up that emotion.)

The third proposition states that organic action results from the combination of psychological and physical action, and in turn, gives rise to sincere, believable feelings on the part of the actor. An actor's thorough preparation through researching and analyzing the role ensures this believability.

Stanislavski clearly laid out specific steps for the actor in researching, analyzing, and building the character. In the first step, the actors search out all the relevant facts or given circumstances that influence the character's behavior. Second, actors use the given circumstances to place themselves inside the character to experience life from the character's perspective. This is referred to as the *magic if*. Third, the actors establish, from the character's point-of-view, what the character wants most out of life, the super objective; and also determine the character's range of lesser goals, the objective hierarchy. Fourth, the actors search out the connection between all the moments when a psychological motive prompts a physical response until a pattern emerges, and thus creates a through-line of actions. Fifth, the manuscript of the play is scored, marked and separated into workable units of action. Sixth, the actors bring life to the people and objects in the play by projecting qualities from their own imagination and experience, referred to as endowment. Seventh, all five senses are used by the actor to awaken memories of both physical sensations and emotions that can be filtered through the character's feelings, referred to as recall. Eighth, actors visualize through images the words they are hearing. Ninth, actors examine and make external adjustments in their own mannerisms to suit those of the character. Finally, in the tenth step, the actors use all of the above work to free themselves for entry into a creative state that allows for both discovery and control simultaneously.

B. The Importance of Spontaneity

In both the rehearsal stage and the performance stage of the acting process, there is an emphasis on spontaneity. Actors need to improvise, be spontaneous, and "live in the moment" to truly co-create with the author and director. Herein lies the true creative portion of acting, where the actor brings her or his own novel and appropriate interpretation to the role to make it live. This does not imply that the actor improvises new lines or business delineated by the director. On the contrary, the given lines and business are the bases on which the actor must and does develop his improvisations. Improvisations assist actors in developing a better understanding of the reality of the character, circumstances, time and place, emotions, and the possibilities of varied action. For actors in an interview study by Jill Nemiro, the need for spontaneity in the creative process was strongly emphasized. Spontaneity was defined as keeping oneself open, living the moment, letting go, becoming an instrument for the work, and allowing one's instincts to take over. One of the actors explained,

> you had to just clear yourself as completely as you could so you could be really present to whatever wanted to show up. You know what I mean, not plan it every step of the way, but see what was going to happen (1997, p. 236).

IV. THE DELICATE BALANCE

Actors face an interesting challenge in that they bring to their creative process two separate identities—their own and that of the characters they are portraying. Remember, Stanislavski's concept of the *magic if* suggests that the actors imagine themselves in the character's place. Actors are constantly asking the question, What would I do if I had experienced this person's entire life up to this moment?

Brian Bates studied the relationship of the actor's and character's identities, through exploration of actors' experiences with what he termed *possession*. Among the actors he interviewed, Charlton Heston's experience best illustrated the process of possession during performance. In the role of Commander Queeg in *The Caine Mutiny Court Martial,* Heston described how he lost control: "That moment when Ben gives Queeg a chance to escape, the emotion built up, and the last night it frightened me, as Queeg. To the point where there was, in my judgment, too much emotion. I couldn't control it" (1991, p. 13). Bates described Heston's experience: "At the crucial moment in the scene, the character took full possession and Heston realized it was his own emotion being expressed. He had allowed the character Queeg to possess him" (1991, pp. 13–14).

This tension or delicate balance between the actors' own personal identities and that of the characters they are portraying was also explored in the interview study of actors conducted by Nemiro. Actors in this study suggested four ways in which the experiences of their character affected their own personal identities. The first effect, scary or dangerous, suggested that actors feared taking on too much of a character's identity, feared going mad or losing themselves in their characters' identities. Second, actors suggested that a character's identity could be cathartic for them personally, allowing them to release or get out their own personal feelings through their characters. Third, actors actually avoided certain roles because these roles would involve experiencing emotions that would be too painful. Fourth, actors sometimes felt physically and emotionally drained after experiencing a character's emotional life. Fatigue, and loss of energy followed a performance.

So, how, then, during performance can actors achieve the creative outcome of portraying a believable character and still maintain their own personal identities? Although Stanislavski encouraged emotional memory—the summoning up by actors of feelings from their own past in order to achieve emotion on stage—he recommended this only for experiences that were not so raw

that they threatened an individual's own sanity and control. In Nemiro's study, the actors suggested that balance was maintained by developing a "third, objective eye" to stand outside the performance and objectively monitor the tension between the character's and their own personal identities.

V. CONTEXTUAL INFLUENCES

Even with all the previously discussed elements in place—a fine-tuned system for building a character, an appropriate balance between one's own identity and that of the character's—the creative process of actors can be either undermined or enhanced depending on the context of the actor's interaction with others. The process of acting involves interaction with other actors, directors, and the audience; and actors are affected by this interaction. The interview study by Nemiro was the first study to look into contextual influences specific to actors' creativity.

Eight contextual influences served to promote an actor's creativity. First, a high degree of collaboration was essential. Actors felt highly creative when they felt part of a group that was working together to serve something bigger than oneself; and when they assisted, interacted with, and adapted to fellow actors. Establishing a unity with the audience, an energy exchange between the actor and the audience, was characteristic of situations in which actors felt highly creative. Clear direction—decisive, forceful, and concrete—assisted actors in being creative. Trust between the actor and the director was essential. The actor needed to be able to rely on the director to function as an objective eye and to offer feedback on how honest or believable the actor's work was. With this trust in place, the actor could experiment, take risks, and reach high levels of creativity. Freedom, having the opportunity to develop one's own interpretation of the character and not be forced into a preconceived interpretation enhanced an actor's creativity. Lack of evaluation pressure, not being overly concerned with impressing someone, whether it be the director or members of the audience, was characteristic of the actors' highly creative performances. An actor needed respect for and recognition of her or his own special gift and talent in order to be creative. And finally, actors needed to be challenged, dared, baited, or pushed to go as far as possible, to reach high levels of creativity.

Six contextual influences served to inhibit an actor's creativity. It is no surprise that poor direction, characterized as rigid, inflexible, vague, overly cerebral, or no direction, severely limited an actor's creativity. Feeling interchangeable, a lack of appreciation for the actor's individuality, undermined creativity. Evaluation—having someone in the audience who is there to judge one's work, trying to impress that someone, worrying about what the audience thinks—can make an actor self-conscious, unfocused, and uncreative. In addition, acting primarily for the reward, specifically money to financially survive, while practical for survival, can sometimes hamper creativity. Actors who have stopped listening, interacting, or adjusting to one another do not encourage highly creative performances. And finally, distrust, a lack of faith or trust in the director to give appropriate feedback or a situation in which the actor does not feel the director trusts his or her abilities, can lead to low levels of creativity.

VI. THE FUTURE OF ACTING

What lies ahead for the young actor of the future? Benedetti suggested that actors of the future will be able to look forward to a diversity of acting styles, a theatre of variety and multiplicity of forms. Actors will continue to create, as the 20th century experimentalists did, a theatre centered around their own visions. Actors can look forward to "a life in the theatre motivated by meaningful moral and social purpose, a life in a deeply ethical profession of immediate importance to his culture" (1976, p. 76). However, along with the diversity and variety that may make up the theatre of the future, an actor will need

self-discipline to form his own aesthetic vision and moral objectives. He must then pursue the agonizing search for the practical techniques which will bring his vision to fruition. These are heavy dues, but the young artist willing to pay them will be repaid with a measure of artistic freedom and a sense of personal dignity unique in the entire history of our theatre. It is a wonderful time to be an actor (1976, p. 77).

Bibliography

Adler, S. (1988). *The technique of acting.* Toronto: Bantam Books.

Barton, R. (1989). *Acting: On stage and off.* Fort Worth, TX: Holt, Rinehart and Winston.

Bates, B. (1991). Performance and possession: The actor and our inner demons. In G. D. Wilson (Ed.), *Psychology and performing arts.* Amsterdam: Swets & Zeitlinger.

Benedetti, R. (1976). *Seeming, being and becoming: Acting in our century.* New York: Drama Book Specialists.

Cole, T., & Chinoy, H. (Eds). (1970). *Actors on acting.* New York: Crown.

Kirby, M. (1995). On acting and not-acting. In P. B. Zarrilli (Ed.), *Acting (re)considered* (pp. 43–58). London: Routledge.

Nemiro, J. (1997). Interpretive artists: A qualitative exploration of the creative process of actors. *Creativity Research Journal, 10,* 229–239.

Stanislavski, C. (1948). *An actor prepares* (translated by E. Hapgood). New York: Theatre Arts Books.

Adaptation and Creativity

LeoNora M. Cohen

Oregon State University

Don Ambrose

Rider University

Accommodation The act of modifying or adjusting the knowing structures in order to deal with discrepancies or conflicts with them.

Adaptation To adjust the self to fit environmental conditions through conformity, agreement, or compliance; to acclimatize or apply experience to the use or selection of an environment to personal advantage; to modify or transform the environment to suit the individual.

Assimilation The act of bringing in elements or aspects to the systems or knowing structures that conflict with those structures.

Complexity Theory A theory that focuses on subtle, mutually shaping adaptive behaviors of complex systems.

Continuum of Adaptive Creative Behaviors A continuum of seven levels of creative behaviors that explains the shift in adaptation from individual-to-world to world-to-individual.

Discontinuity A break between the old and the new, involving construction of relationships not inherent in the elements themselves.

Equilibration The act of restoring a balance when conflicts to the knowledge systems occur through the processes of assimilation and accommodation; the linking mechanism between adaptation and the mental organization of the individual; the mechanism by which the individual moves from one developmental stage to the next.

Mature Creativity The products or performances of individuals who have mastered a field or fields at very high levels, normally associated with adulthood; creativity by extension or transformation of a field.

Mundane Creativity (Creativity in the Small) Creativity that is new to the individual or perhaps to peers, but does not result in products or performances that are rare or of value to the world.

Structure The mental organization(s) of the individual based on what has been previously assimilated and accommodated.

*Depending on the situation, **ADAPTATION** can hinder creativity or support it. In some cases, adaptation means tightly conforming to a confining environment that stifles creativity. In other cases, it means creatively adjusting to the subtle nuances of a changing environment. Adaptation also occurs when an individual forces the environ-*

Copyright © 1999 by Academic Press
All rights of reproduction in any form reserved.

ment to change in response to his or her needs and desires. Adaptation even may mean that an individual moves out of one environment into another better suited to his or her abilities or preferences. In most cases, creative adaptation in our highly complex world involves most or all of these mutually shaping influences between person and environment. The dynamic interplay between person and environment is one of the most important issues in analyses of creativity. The focus of this article is on who does the adapting. On one hand, some definitions and theories related to creativity and adaptation focus on conforming to or fitting in to an environmental situation by the individual. Those who do not "fit" into prevailing values and mores are considered weird or maladaptive. "Crazy" artists and "mad" scientists typify this view. However, when adaptation is viewed as modifying or transforming the environment, particularly when the created products or ideas are valued by a culture, the creator is considered to be the epitome of human development and health. This article explores a wide range of issues and concepts relevant to creative adaptation. These include (a) definitions and theoretical perspectives on adaptation, (b) research on adaptation and creativity, (c) facilitation of adaptation for creative individuals, and (d) a developmental continuum of creative behaviors in which there is a shift from individual adaptation to the environment to adaptation by the world to the individual. This developmental continuum accounts for creativity in both young children and eminent adults. Variables that influence development along the continuum include purpose, novelty, value, speed, and structure.

I. DEFINITIONS OF ADAPTATION

The term "adaptation" is derived from the Latin *adaptare*, meaning "to fit." The dictionary definitions for adapt are "to adjust to environmental conditions," or, "the modification of an organism or its parts that makes it more fit for existence under its environmental conditions." However, there are three distinct shades of meaning for this term. As described in the dictionary definition, the first and most common is adaptation as fitting in—conformity, agreement, compliance, or yielding to the environment or situation. Essentially, this is modification of self to fit environment. For ex-

ample, a new bank employee quickly adapts by dressing like other employees to "fit in." In this view of adaptation, individuals who do not conform to prevailing values, mores, and practices of a given culture often are considered maladaptive outsiders or even lunatics. Early definitions of creativity, in fact, focused on the pathology of creators. Such definitions portrayed creators as neurotic or mentally ill, partly because they were unable or unwilling to adapt to the styles and customs of the times. This may explain the origin of the crazy artist or mad scientist stereotypes. But groundbreaking, paradigm-shifting creators do not make their greatest impact by conforming to the prevailing belief systems of their eras. [*See* CONFORMITY; CONTRARIANISM; CONVENTIONALITY.]

On a smaller scale, a creative young person who does not conform to the prevailing fashions worn at school, or who does not hang out with the "in" students, is likewise often ostracized. This failure to adapt may or may not be a sign of mental instability. But when a little child says, "Look how the moon is following me!" this unusual and delightful use of words is hardly a sign of neurosis. Instead, it is a creative-adaptive attempt to understand the world. In like manner, the young student who bucks the system may be demonstrating a healthy sense of self.

A second definition of adaptation emphasizes the role of experience in successful orientation to an environment or situation. Adapting to the heat and humidity by resting in the afternoon when living in a tropical country is an example. One type of intelligence involves rapid "reading" of an environment and selection of responses that provide the greatest benefit to the individual. For example, a politician who sizes up a crowd and delivers a speech tailored to that audience could be considered contextually creative because she successfully uses experience to adapt to a given situation. Experience also might help the individual select an environment best suited to his full development, or even reject a detrimental environment. Examples of this kind of adaptation include moving to a setting that is aesthetically invigorating, enrolling in a school that offers a program in which the young person has deep interest, or leaving a job when it becomes debilitating or toxic. Such selection of an environment based on experience might prevent maladaptive situations where individuals do not feel they belong. It also may prevent high-potential people from feeling inferior and developing a poor sense of self based on the mismatch between self and setting. [*See* CONDITIONS AND SETTINGS/ENVIRONMENT; CREATIVE CLIMATE.]

A third definition of adaptation suggests something different; that is, the individual acts on the environment to modify, change, translate, or transform it. For example, some creative employees make their work environments more fulfilling and challenging by initiating innovative and interesting projects in otherwise barren, stifling offices. On a larger scale, some highly creative people modify their environments by developing profound ideas or products that affect many people for long time periods. For example, Thomas Edison's inventions and Albert Einstein's theories made high-impact long-lasting transformations in the modern era. In considering the dynamics of creative adaptation, the issue is directionality. Eminent adults must adapt to their environments, but they also encourage the world in which they function to adapt to their ideas and products. In contrast, children and adult novices concentrate on adapting to their environments, and exert little influence on those environments. Both of these forms of adaptation involve creative thought and action; but what is creativity?

II. DEFINITIONS OF CREATIVITY

The most common definition of creativity involves the production of something new or rare that has value in the world. However, this definition applies only to creativity in eminent adults because children are unlikely to produce something truly new or valued by people other than their families or peer groups. Hence, this definition is not very helpful to those concerned with creativity in the classroom, nor does it apply to "mundane creativity," or "creativity in the small"—the less than earth-shaking variety of creative products or ideas made by adults as well as children. [*See* EVERYDAY CREATIVITY.]

J. P. Guilford's conception of divergent thinking is probably the second most common definition of creativity. Divergent thinking involves production of ideas from given information, with an emphasis on variety and quantity of output. "How many different uses can you think of for a cup," is a typical classroom prob-

lem based on this definition. Divergent thinking encompasses several forms of creative thought, including (a) the number of ideas generated (fluency); (b) changes in category, from container to ornament to noise maker (flexibility); (c) uniqueness or divergence from typical answers, such as using the cup as a snout for a noseless pig (originality); and (d) extensions or improvements to ideas (elaboration). The definition of creativity as divergent thinking is used extensively in classrooms, and is commonly assessed through Torrance's *Tests of Creative Thinking*. It appears to apply to both childhood and adulthood. [*See* DIVERGENT THINKING; APPENDIX II: TESTS OF CREATIVITY.]

Jonathan Plucker of Indiana University recently reanalyzed research on Paul Torrance's tests of divergent thinking, finding that these instruments strongly predicted later-life creative achievement. However, developmental psychologist Howard Gruber pointed out that divergent thinking has inherent problems when applied to creativity at the highest levels. He found that highly creative people rarely use divergent thinking. Rather than generating many ideas, they concern themselves with the correctness, appropriateness, and social relevance of ideas, moving parsimoniously and efficiently to one or a few "good fits" with their problem. Although tests of divergent thinking may measure divergent thinking abilities in several major creativity-training programs as well as predicting moderate levels of creativity in later life, there appears to be little relationship to the highest levels of creativity in the real world. Therefore, divergent thinking does not span the gap between children's creativity and mature, eminent creativity. It may relate more to some forms of successful problem solving.

Definitions of adaptation are influenced by differences between problem solving and creativity. Both creativity and problem solving share a common starting point—incongruity in a problem. Both also require knowledge, motivation, repetition, and discovery of unique combinations. But problem solving and mature creativity are different in duration and effect, both externally and internally. Problem solving is generally a short-term process while creativity at higher levels is lifelong. Creativity also focuses on a larger unit of analysis, more on a totality rather than a specific answer, and it usually involves a greater impact on the world. Additionally, in problem solving the problems are usually externally set, with the focus more on resolution. By contrast, mature creativity involves problem finding in which both problems and innovative solutions are generated internally and intrinsically, although there certainly are both external stimulations and parameters. [*See* PROBLEM SOLVING.]

Mature creativity involves a discontinuity with what was before, while problem solutions can be explained by more continuous, straightforward processes. For example, solving the problem of how to get kids to use more toothpaste might involve researching children's flavor preferences in coming up with grape-flavored toothpaste. Creativity, on the other hand, involves a shift in context, which allows the creator to see the world in a new way. In this process, the direct connections between the new and the old perspectives on the situation are not directly discernible. For example, in coming to understand the inner world of individuals, Freud created new perspectives with his concepts of id, ego, and superego. These new concepts produced a discontinuity with the knowledge that had prevailed previously in the field. Such discontinuities are consistent with Howard Gruber's conclusion that mature creativity involves the construction of a point of view while problem solving does not. Gruber came to this conclusion during his analyses of the lives of highly creative individuals such as Charles Darwin and Jean Piaget. [*See* DARWIN, CHARLES; PIAGET, JEAN.]

Mature creativity, then, involves both external transformation of a field and internal transformation of self. Adaptation is evident in both aspects. External transformation involves sensitivity to a context as well as awareness of the limitations of a field and the desire to work hard to transform it. This is primarily adaptation by external transformation although there are certainly internal aspects, such as the zeal to put forth effort. Internal transformation involves sensitivity to one's self and the openness and willingness to modify one's present ways of thinking in order to construct a unique point of view. Thus, mature creators adapt in both ways, modifying the environment to fit their schemes and theories and modifying themselves to be able to accommodate to the environment. This is not a meek or passive attempt to fit in. Rather, according to Howard Gruber, it involves the active construction of a way of looking at the world. It is not always conscious, but it is dynamic and effortful. In both external and internal transformation, adapting means being tolerant of uncertainty or ambiguity from the outside and being willing to not have answers, to be wrong, and to try alternatives on the inside.

III. THEORETICAL PERSPECTIVES RELATED TO ADAPTATION

Returning to the three definitions of adaptation, early definitions of creativity focused largely on the fitting of individual to the environment, sometimes by equating mental instability with creativity. For example, Freud believed that creativity arises from attempts to sublimate libidinal or sexual impulses into more socially acceptable forms; in short, adapting to the values or mores of the times. For him, creativity and mental illness have identical origins, both arising from conflict within the unconscious. According to Freud, creative individuals blend productive abilities with neurotic tendencies.

The first theorist who suggested a direct relationship between creativity and adaptation, however, was Otto Rank, a disciple of Freud. Rank broke with his mentor over the issue of sexual sublimation as the motivating force in behavior. Instead, Rank believed that motivation came from the dynamic tension between the wish to depend on and unite with others, and the wish to separate from others in order to assert one's individuality through the will. For Rank, the will is a life-shaping force that includes a sense of self and a sense of what the individual wishes to accomplish. As a positive force, it is the urge to create; as a negative force, it manifests itself in repression and control.

If the parents have a healthy regard for the child as an individual and grant the child autonomy and the chance to assert his or her own will, the child moves toward a secure sense of self. This enables the child to establish independent individuality through force of will without feeling rejection from the parents. When the child is not accepted as separate and different, the will becomes a source of guilt instead of ego strength. Rank's definitions of three distinct personality types—adaptive, conflicted, and creative or artistic—clearly portray adaptation as fitting into an environment and as counter to creativity.

Rank called the "adapted type" the creativity-inhibiting personality of the "average man." Very early on, the child identifies with and adapts to the will of the parents, and later to the will of society in order to avoid the pain of guilt. This form of adaptation produces harmony and reduces the potential for conflict, but it also works against creativity. Rank's "conflicted type" is characterized by divisions in the personality. These divisions involve moral struggles against the compulsion of the outer world as well as inner conflicts between the will of the child and the will of the parent. The individual attempts to form personal goals, ideals, and standards, rather than those sanctioned by society, but remains conflicted, guilty, and unable to move to the third level of creativity and productivity. For Rank, the third and ideal personality type is the creator or artist. This is the ideally functioning person who has accepted and integrated two conflicting fears: the fear of being a separate individual and the fear of union and dependency. Acceptance and integration of these fears produces ideal mental development and healthy behavior. The creative impulse comes from the artist's desire for immortality. In Rank's theory, therefore, adaptation is antithetical to creativity because it exclusively involves fitting into the environment. Creativity requires the individual to resist adaptation.

Psychologist Jean Piaget generated a constructivist-developmental theory that portrays intelligence as adaptation. His theory explains how individuals adapt by modifying their knowledge structures to fit the environment. Piaget also links intelligence to creativity, calling the period of early childhood the most creative period in life because young children must construct their understandings of the world. According to Piaget, intelligence develops through the child's actions in and on the social and physical environment. Using the mechanism of reflective abstraction, the child projects new concepts to a higher plane of understanding and reorganizes them at that higher level, thereby creating ever-more complex relationships among actions, objects, ideas, and social experiences. Piaget believed that this mechanism is the same in both child and eminent creator.

For Piaget, individuals evolve through distinct levels or stages of organization, actively assimilating and accommodating concepts that relate to their idiosyncratic learning structures. Individuals develop higher levels of organization through the process of equilibration in which they accommodate new concepts that do not fit current knowledge structures by modifying those structures. [*See* DEVELOPMENTAL STAGES.]

Through these processes, growth in understanding arises from environmental stimuli that cause gaps, conflicts, or disturbances in current mental structures. These discrepancies provide the impetus for reorganization of these structures. Thus, individuals adapt to the environment by modifying themselves. Each equilibration leads toward higher and broader levels of understanding, and hence stronger adaptation.

In Piaget's theory, the concept of discontinuity provides the first glimmerings of adaptation of environment to individual. Discontinuity occurs because the construction of relationships is not inherent in the elements themselves, but is brought about through mental action. It is the individual's construction and imposition of orderly rules and patterns on environmental objects or events that make this adaptation of the environment to the individual, at least to some extent. This is the case even if the same rule has been constructed for centuries by other learners. For example, the little boy who is arranging sticks from smallest to largest and constructs the idea of putting all the ends against a baseline has constructed the rule for seriation discovered by every child who does so. This child has imposed order on the environment that is not inherent in the sticks themselves (a discontinuity) as he modifies his structures to create the rule for seriating.

Except for statements about the period of early childhood, Piaget said little about creativity, with the exception of his three rules for being creative. First, after becoming knowledgeable in a field, read widely around it, in order to cross-fertilize that field with new ideas. Second, have an adversary in mind, something against which you react. Third, believe in yourself and distrust influences from the outside. From these rules, it appears that Piaget was going beyond merely adapting to the world to protecting the self from the world and even to shaping it.

Developmental psychologist David Feldman proposed another perspective on adaptation. Feldman claimed that universal cognitive development moves the individual toward competence with the general adaptive abilities that are needed for getting along in the world. From this viewpoint, adapting is finding a satisfying, useful way to live. This is similar to Piaget's notion of intelligence as adaptation. But Feldman also described nonuniversal development, which takes place in creative individuals and child prodigies. Not everyone attains this type of development. It requires specific instruction and sufficient development within a field in order to reach very high levels. This domain-specific development can be thought of as talent that enables the individual to excel if the right niche is found.

Feldman described a Universal–Unique Continuum that portrays both how an individual moves through different levels of development in a given domain and how his or her creative product affects the world. There are five levels in this continuum: *universal, cultural, domain specific, idiosyncratic,* and *unique. Universal development* is the type of cognitive growth that emerges without instruction and across all cultures, such as learning to conserve liquid and substance. *Cultural development* is the result of growing up in a given context. For example, most children brought up in the United States share cultural learning about the Thanksgiving holiday. Subcultural experiences, such as specific manners, dress, or habits of speech, also fit here. Adults in the environment teach children this information by offering them encounters with cultural events, values, or practices, but without formal instruction. *Domain-specific development* requires instruction by skilled teachers whose pedagogical skills and familiarity with a field help the new learner become competent within that field. Learning to play the flute, use a computer, play chess, or ski are examples.

Idiosyncratic development occurs when a learner is reaching high levels of accomplishment in a given domain. At this point, the individual may develop distinctive movements in skating, characteristic phrasing in piano playing, or mastery of a surgical technique that is different from the repertoire of most other surgeons. Finally, at the *unique level,* the individual has mastered a field so completely and created such original products or performances that his or her influence on a field requires new learners to learn the field in its transformed state. A performance by pianist Vladimir Horowitz or dancer Judith Jamieson, or Einstein's theory of relativity are examples of accomplishments that emerge from the unique level of development. The more the influence of a unique accomplishment works its way back down the Universal–Unique Continuum toward cultural or even universal levels suggests its value to the world. At this level, Feldman emphasizes adaptation by the world to the individual.

From yet another theoretical vantage point, psychologist Robert Sternberg provides an extensive and integrative definition of adaptation. Sternberg's Triarchic Theory of Intelligence portrays integrative relationships among three subtheories: the *componential,* the *experiential,* and the *contextual.* The *componential subtheory* relates intelligence to three types of information-processing components within the mind of the individual. These include metacomponents (higher-order executive thought processes), performance components (lower-order processes that serve as tools for the metacomponents), and knowledge-acquisition components that enable the individual to learn how to do what the metacomponents and performance components eventually do.

The *experiential subtheory* connects intelligence to experience. Effectively dealing with novelty and automatically processing information (automaticity) are signs of intelligence. An individual who can automatize efficiently, conserves mental resources that can be allocated to dealing with novelty. Conversely, a person who effectively deals with novelty can apply more intellectual resources to automatization. Thus, adaptation can improve through experience.

The contextual subtheory relates intelligence to a person's external world. People may choose to exercise their contextual intelligence in one or more of three ways. They may adapt to an existing environment, shape that environment to better suit their needs, or leave the environment in favor of one that better suits their abilities and aspirations. For example, if workers feel trapped in a confining work setting, they can adjust their own beliefs and behaviors to fit in with the system, they can unionize to force the system to adapt to their needs, or they can quit and seek more rewarding employment elsewhere. In Sternberg's theory, we begin to see intelligence and adaptation linked by these three emphases on context: fitting in to, modification of, and selection of an environment.

IV. INTELLIGENCE AND CREATIVITY: A CONVERGENCE OF PERSPECTIVES AROUND ISSUES OF ADAPTATION TO NOVELTY

In these theoretical approaches linking creativity and adaptation, discussions of intelligence have been necessary. Theories of intelligence deal with the ability to adapt successfully to the environment and to solve problems related to one's particular setting. Art Costa describes intelligent behavior as what one does when one does not know the answers. Facing a new situation in the environment, what types of responses would be appropriate?

This is an important starting point for a comprehensive understanding of creative adaptation, as theories of intelligence have been evolving in an interesting direction in recent years. Theories developed by psychologists Howard Gardner and Robert Sternberg emphasize multiple abilities and modes of information processing, modified by cultural context They also focus on modification of the environment to meet the individual's needs rather than merely the reverse: the individual adapting to the environment. [See INTELLIGENCE.]

It becomes evident that theories of intelligence and theories of creativity are converging. Recent theories of intelligence are moving toward including creativity because they are concerned not only with the individual's capacity to adapt to the world, but also the ability to shape or transform it. Theorists now are recognizing the pivotal role of creativity in intelligent adaptation.

Moreover, older theories of intelligence focused on adaptation to the environment. In recent theories of creativity, the adaptation is mutual. The creative person must master a field sufficiently to be able to see the problems or gaps at the "edges" of the field. As Howard Gruber explained, "It is safe to say that *no case* of early achievement occurs without a long apprenticeship." (Gruber, 1989, p. 15.) This is adaptation to the world. But when the creative individual extends or transforms the domain in which he or she functions, that world of endeavor adapts to him or her. For example, when Freud described the workings of the unconscious mind, he changed the way new psychology students learned the knowledge base in their field.

Such creative transformation of the world requires an ethical commitment to its betterment. It also involves a transformation of self that enables the individual to grasp the edges of a field, and that provides the courage and will to construct a point of view. The most recent theories of intelligence incorporate creativity by acknowledging this shaping of the world aspect of adaptation, but they do not address the transformation of self.

V. RESEARCH AND SCHOLARSHIP ON ADAPTATION AND CREATIVITY: STYLE, EXPERTISE, AND CHANCE

A. Creative-Adaptive Styles

The research literature connecting adaptation and creativity is meager with the exception of the work of Michael Kirton and his colleagues. Kirton hypothesized that there are two distinct types of creative people. He developed a scale to distinguish cognitive style preference, the *Kirton Adaption–Innovation Inventory*. Numerous studies have been done using this scale.

The pattern emerging from this research suggests that creative adapters and creative innovators are two types of creative people with quite different cognitive styles. Adapters and innovators both have distinct attributes that can be disadvantageous or advantageous, depending on the context. Structure is a key to the style differences. Those who prefer more structure are adapters while those who prefer less are innovators. However, either too much or too little structure inhibits generation of new thought or action.

The appropriateness of a given style is totally dependent on a specific context and a given situation. When faced with a difficult context that demands other than the preferred style, the individual must use coping behavior to bridge the gap between his or her preferred style and what is perceived as necessary to achieve goals. Coping behaviors can be used as long as needed or tolerated. Excessive demand for a different cognitive style usually results in the individual wanting to leave the situation.

Innovators prefer situations that allow them to do things differently while employing looser cognitive structure. Innovation has a meaning of breakthrough

TABLE I
A Comparison of Creative Adapters and Creative Innovators

Attribute	Adapters	Innovators
Structure	Tight.	Loose.
Group conformity	Seek consensus; fit with group.	Loner, isolated.
Number of ideas generated	Sufficiency: produce fewer original ideas, but those produced are sound, useful, relevant.	Originality: proliferation of original ideas, toying with ideas; less attentive to their relevance to problem.
Brain laterality	Left-brained.	Right-brained.
Personality traits	More intolerant of ambiguity, inflexible, introverted, humble, conscientious, controlled, subdued, emotionally tender; more anxious, less self-confidence; take fewer risks; prefer efficiency and attention to details; satisfied with smaller changes within a system.	Less resistant to change; prefer long-range effectiveness; less tolerant of rules; want quantum changes in a system for satisfaction.
Self-esteem	Lower.	Higher.
Learning style	Reflective; learn in detailed, sequential, linear mode.	Active. Learn in holistic, here and now approach, with hands-on experiences.
Types of solutions	Pose solutions applying accepted, normal procedures. Problem solution involves effective application of known principles to produce predictable outcomes.	Offer novel solutions that change context in which problem is embedded. See problem solving as opportunity to try something different with unpredictable consequences.
Paradigms	Create within old paradigms.	Seek new paradigms.

Note. Adapted from Kirton (1994) and Goldsmith (1994).

change, or breaking out of a paradigm into another structure. But Kirton makes clear that innovation is not the "best" nor the highest form of creativity. Adapters prefer structured situations. They are interested in refinements of existing products, processes, or ideas. Their focus is on redefining, elaborating, modifying, and improving a paradigm. Table I provides a comparison of these two styles. [*See* INNOVATION.]

B. Creative Adaptation and Expertise

Bruce Shore, Gillian Resjkind, and Lannie Kanevesky used recent findings in cognitive research to illuminate linkages among various conceptions of giftedness, creativity, and expertise. This work relates to creative adaptation because the cognitive abilities and habits of experts usually make them much better adapters than are neophytes or novices. Experts have mastered the knowledge base and skills of a field; hence,

the thought processes necessary for efficient problem solving, adaptation, and innovation have become automatic, or automatized. This makes the expert quite efficient when it comes to adaptation within the field. By contrast, neophytes, who are new to a field, and novices, who have some rudimentary knowledge of the field, have not developed automaticity nor the necessary knowledge and skills. Consequently, they are not efficient adapters within that field. [*See* EXPERTISE.]

However, questions arise about the degree of automaticity an expert can muster when confronted with a profound paradigm shift in a field. Standard knowledge and practices could become hindrances that lock an expert into ineffective actions when a paradigm shift changes the operational rules of a profession. In most situations, however, the experts' large accumulation of knowledge and skills provides them with strong adaptive advantages, including (a) problem-solving flexibility, (b) effective use of prior knowledge, (c) strong associative and interdisciplinary connection-making capacities, (d) the ability to develop and follow effective action plans, (e) the ability to understand and use the context of a problem, and (f) metacognitive strength, or the ability to monitor the effectiveness of one's own thought and actions. [*See* PARADIGM SHIFT.]

C. Creative Adaptation and the Element of Chance

Abraham Tannenbaum described a dynamic interplay between chance and ability in the fulfillment of one's potential. According to Tannenbaum, chance is one of five factors that combine to influence the development of potential. There is a static element of chance, which includes things the individual cannot control, such as the accidents of genetic inheritance, or birth into a family of privilege or deprivation. There is also a dynamic element of chance, which includes things the individual can influence. For instance, rather than merely accepting their lot in life, people can actively and/or randomly explore new ideas or work processes. Although randomness of motion may be inefficient, it can lead to "lucky" breaks. Those who actively prepare their minds according to perceived trends in their environmental contexts are likely to be even more "fortunate" than those who simply employ random activity. Those who are most fortunate, however, are the few who develop a facility for luck through highly individualized action. They develop unique perspectives from which to view problems and their environmental contexts. These perspectives enable them to encounter opportunities more frequently than those who lack unique, individualized vantage points.

Recent developments in the emerging science of complexity add new dimensions to the influence of chance on creative adaptation. Complexity theory involves interdisciplinary studies of complex adaptive systems. Of most interest to complexity theorists such as Stuart Kauffman and Doyne Farmer are the ways in which order spontaneously emerges from apparent chaos. Complex adaptive systems, such as human minds or international political and economic systems, can be strongly influenced by minor environmental fluctuations; yet these systems seem to settle into patterns of order that enable them to adapt and thrive in changing conditions. High-powered computers and mathematical analyses are helping these theorists discover metapatterns in the activity of complex adaptive systems. Given the existence of these patterns, it is likely that pattern finding in the midst of apparent chaos enables individuals to survive and thrive in complex, changing conditions. If so, "good fortune" may be more dependent on intuitive pattern perception than on the elements of chance, at least in some conditions. [*See* CHAOS THEORY IN CREATIVITY.]

Whether people are blessed with socioeconomic status or earn more opportunities through activity, preparation of mind, or development of useful perspectives and pattern-finding abilities, the element of chance can affect creative adaptation. Those who are more fortunate are more likely to adapt successfully to problems, or to force adaptations in the environment that better suit their needs and desires.

VI. ASSISTING ADAPTATION: FACILITATIVE CONTEXTS AND ENVIRONMENTAL SUPPORT

According to Lev Vygotsky, a Russian psychologist, mediation is needed to help the individual become adaptive and creative. Vygotsky, working over 60 years ago, posited that caring individuals are needed to help young learners interpret new knowledge. The "zone of proximal development" is the conceptual space in which such interventions are most effective. This zone is the discrepancy between the child's actual mental age and the problems she or he can solve with assistance. Vygotsky found that instruction leads development and assists in the ripening of knowledge structures. Therefore, the adult plays an important role in mediating the learning process by providing hints, guidance, and correction. Through interactions with the mediator, the child internalizes problem-solving processes, thereby becoming better adapted to dealing with problems in the environment. Ideally, as the child becomes more able to generalize and transfer what is learned, the adult becomes less of a guide and more an encourager.

Psychologist Reuven Feuerstein also believes that mediation plays an important role in adaptation. Feuerstein believes that intelligence is dynamic and modifiable, not static. In efforts to help the Israeli army find ways to improve the intelligence of "retarded performers," he posited that direct intervention in an individual's cognitive development through mediation by an adult optimizes the effectiveness and efficiency of that development. He also suggested that lack of mediation can result in retarded performance. The intelligent person is able to effectively gather needed information and use that information to solve problems, or to generate new information. Through the benefit of mediation, the individual becomes more open to experience and more adaptable to new situations.

Both Vygotsky and Feuerstein focused on the role of the adult in interpreting both the inner and the outer worlds for the child in order to assist in the adaptive process. For instance, when a parent says to her 3-year-old son, "You are really angry that Sammy took your bucket. Could you think of another way of getting it back, instead of hitting him with a shovel?" the description of the child's feelings and experiences helps him adapt to both the specific situation and to other similar situations. Such early mediation appears to promote successful adaptation to the world, and may even promote creative development.

Mediation provided by caring others also may support the work of mature creative people. Gruber's studies of highly creative individuals suggest that social support is essential for full development of creative ideas. For example, in his study of Charles Darwin, Gruber found that Darwin's concerns about contradicting the social values of his time, as well as his desire for social support, inhibited completion of *The Development of Species* for some 20 years. This can be interpreted as a desire for mediation—the need to discuss and share with like-minded others, or with those more knowledgeable who can facilitate thinking. It may be that mediation early in life prepares the individual for adaptation to the environment while allowing the individual the internal freedom to modify that environment.

VII. PROCESS, PRODUCT, CONTEXT: A CONTINUUM OF ADAPTIVE CREATIVE BEHAVIORS

In the previous two sections, one emphasis has been on adaptation and the creative person, with particular focus on cognitive style. Another emphasis has addressed a contextual aspect—the facilitation needed to fully nurture both adaptation and creative development. In this section, we explore another continuum, one that addresses adaptation in context, as well as the creative process and product. Linkages are needed to connect childhood creative adaptation to the type of creativity seen in eminent adults. Another bridge is needed to explain the more mundane creativity found in the everyday lives of adults. LeoNora Cohen suggested that one way to build these bridges is to think of creativity as a range of adaptive behaviors along a continuum of seven levels or developmental stages. This continuum can help explain the processes and progress of creativity itself.

A. The Common Element in the Continuum: Discontinuity

Common to all levels on this continuum is the notion of a discontinuity between what was before and the new. It is what Gregory Bateson, Bertrand Russell, and Alfred North Whitehead described as a "jump in logical types" from the particular to the general that results in a new context. Piaget defined this leap as "reflective abstraction," a process of reflection and putting events or thoughts into relationship, which leads to new understandings not inherent in the thoughts or events themselves.

In the Continuum of Adaptive, Creative Behaviors, the variables hinge on six aspects related to context, process, and product, as described in Table II.

B. The Seven Levels of the Continuum of Creative Behaviors

At one end of the Continuum is Level One, Learning Something New: Universal Novelty. This type of creativity occurs in infants and children as they deal with novelty in the world. Experienced as insight, this kind of creativity remains in adults who are able to stay open to the world, curious, joyful in pursuit of interests, and tolerant of disequilibria (imbalances to their systems). We see it in ourselves when we attempt to master a new field or skill; for example, when we "get the hang" of pushing off against the ice the first time we skate or when we grasp the secret of a perfect chocolate chip cookie. It is our own construction of the relationships

TABLE II
Variables in the Continuum of Adaptive Creative Behaviors

Aspect	Variable	Description
Context	Adaptation	Initially, creativity involves adaptation of the individual to the world. At the highest levels, it involves adaptation of the world to the individual. This shift occurs between Levels 4 and 5.
Process	Purpose	The creator's purpose shifts from mastery to extension, and finally to transformation.
Process	Speed	Creativity is rapid in early levels, involves more time in each increasing level, and involves living a creative life at the highest levels in which one's major focus is on creating, often requiring many years of effort.
Process	Structure	Initially, the mental structures are very incomplete and creativity involves construction of these structures. At the opposite end, the structures are very well developed, and the individual sees gaps, lags, and conflicts—limits to the present level of understanding. Early levels of creativity involve simple structures, a single domain or scheme. Later creativity involves major structural reorganization and transformation. The goal is to push out the edges and to transform the structures.
Product	Novelty	In the first level, creative products or ideas are new to the individual. They become rare compared to age-peers, offer new combinations of others' ideas, and finally are considered new and transformational to the world.
Product	Value	The creative product is of value initially to the self, then to others, and finally to the world.

among variables involved in getting across the ice or keeping the cookies crisp. This Level 1 end of the Continuum is similar to Sherri Heller's concept of "creativity in the small," or mundane creativity. Creative-adaptive activity at this level helps us modify ourselves when we try to assimilate aspects of the environment that do not fit our existing systems. The construction, which usually remains in the realm of thought, is of value to the individual but not of value to others.

At the opposite end of the Continuum is Level Seven, Creating by Transforming a Field. This is a level of creativity found only in a few individuals: those who society labels geniuses. It is the type of creativity that revolutionizes a field or creates a new one by combining aspects of different areas of endeavor. According to David Feldman, the transformation is passed on to new learners as part of the knowledge base of the field, thereby creating a paradigm shift. Howard Gruber suggests that at this level, the individual constructs both a unique point of view and transforms the field in which he or she works, requiring that field to accommodate the new point of view. The creative product, developed over long time periods with many insights along the way, is highly valued by those both within and outside the field. It is primarily an adaptation of the world to the individual rather than of the individual to the world. Society is changed by such creative efforts.

Between Levels One and Seven are stages that bridge the two ends of the Continuum. In Level Two, Making Connections That Are Rare Compared to Peers, the individual develops products, ideas, or approaches that are unusual compared to peers but are not new to the world. Such efforts are valued by the individual and may be considered interesting or charming by others. For instance, a 4-year-old stops her preschool class on a city walk to focus on a pile of broken glass. "Look," she says, "here is a city with all the buildings and busy people. And see this piece? (pointing to a single fragment) This is a lonely child." This little girl sees the world in a fresh, open way, which is different from most children her age. Elements not ordinarily associated are assimilated to schemes (e.g., glass fragments to a city scheme), or there may be playful assimilation without accommodation, a trying out of new possibilities before accommodating reality. In an adult, this might emerge in the use of images and metaphors to understand complex material. The process is usually rapid and is demonstrated in a variety of endeavors. When a child develops such unusual ways of understanding, some adults appreciate the child's uniqueness while others may scorn the child's refusal to conform to the "right way" of doing things. When connections are made that are rare compared to others, that inventiveness and autonomy should be encouraged.

Likewise, the employee who has fresh ways of looking at a situation should be encouraged to share that vision, rather than being thought of as a kook or troublemaker. Often the best solutions come from those who make unusual connections.

Levels Three and Four may develop simultaneously, one focusing on mastering a field, and the other on developing strategic ways of thinking. In Level Three, Developing Talents, the individual develops skills in one or more domains. According to psychologist David Feldman, this is essential to creativity, because people are creative in a particular field of endeavor. The child becomes a craftsperson, moving through a series of stages in which skills are honed and the accumulated knowledge that has been developed throughout the history of a field is learned. The child may demonstrate talents in a specialty such as athletics, music, chess, art, mathematics, or writing. Level Three also includes the adult who becomes good at a specialty, such as fixing old cars, computing, or French cooking.

At times, a child's products or abilities may approach adult levels. The child who plays violin with a major symphony orchestra at age 11, writes a moving story about the holocaust at age 10, or beats a world chess master at age 12 is considered a prodigy. There is both vertical skill and knowledge growth as the interest develops, as well as horizontal development through assimilation to a wide range of schemes. The interest is applied broadly to every new experience as well as being linked to different interests and areas of knowledge. [*See* PRODIGIES.]

At Level Three, the individual experiences an overwhelming compulsion to work hard in the area of interest, setting a variety of challenges to the self. The individual may attain a state of "at-onement" in effort toward achievement, or what psychologist Mihalyi Csikszentmihalyi calls "flow." Great involvement and internal motivation characterize this level, which involves a purposeful and joyful movement toward mastery of one's field. There is a "clicking" or "rightness of fit" between the individual and the field.

Heredity and environment are interwoven inextricably in this level of creative development. The individual has a genetically endowed capacity to be very good at something. The environment must offer the opportunity and the support for that development to occur. In order to reach mastery levels in a domain, talents must be recognized and nurtured with appro-

priate instruction, materials, and family support. Even with strong support, what appeared to be remarkable in a child of 10 may be more commonplace among 16-year-olds. David Feldman pointed out that there must be an exquisite coincidence of historical and environmental factors for the young prodigy to become the mature artist or athlete. Whether or not such children become mature creators and reach Levels Six and Seven also depends on (a) the evolution of their strength of purpose (the intent to create), (b) emotional-affective influences, (c) environmental, chance, and historical factors, and (d) the success with which the young person integrates an intuitive approach to the field with his or her evolving formal thinking. [*See* CONDITIONS AND SETTINGS/ENVIRONMENT.]

At Level Four, the individual is involved in Developing Heuristics through instruction in a wide range of strategies. Examples of these strategies include developing alternatives using fantasy and imagery; thinking flexibly, fluently, originally, or elaboratively; constructing remote associations; using critical thinking; making transformations; and systematically using problem-solving and problem-finding processes in a variety of areas. These are the techniques typically taught in creativity training programs, several of which are based on divergent thinking notions. The true value of such training may emerge from the habits and dispositions they encourage and from the supportive environments they typically provide. For instance, most creativity training programs encourage original thinking, risk taking, and exhaustive exploration of topics. Most importantly, they help participants develop a set of heuristics for use in problem solving. [*See* HEURISTICS.]

In addition to these types of heuristics, development of aesthetics is important. Individuals need to learn how to engage their senses to develop stronger awareness of the beauty, harmony, and patterns around them, and to enrich their experiencing of the world. Finally, metacognitive awareness is an important development at Level Four. The individual must recognize her own preferred strategies and styles for working and thinking, as well as different approaches to solving problems. She must gain control of mental processing by learning to select appropriate procedures or heuristics for specific problems. Problem solving and products developed at Level Four may be of limited value to others, but more importantly, the individual develops strategies and approaches for dealing with problems and for constructing novelty. [*See* LEARNING STYLES; METACOGNITION.]

Level Five engages the individual in Producing Information. At this level, the individual discovers and investigates his own real problems related to areas of interest and developing knowledge. Joseph Renzulli and Abraham Tannenbaum point out that new information is produced at this level, but it is of limited scope. For example, a fourth grader goes beyond consuming information from an encyclopedia article on dogs to becoming a producer of information by keeping a log for eight weeks of weights, measurements, behaviors, and daily photographs of the changes in her husky's litter of puppies. In another example, an elderly citizen, deeply moved by the plight of the homeless, single-handedly rallies a community to help.

At this level, the individual pursues a "burning question," with purpose, zeal, and commitment, while building up a considerable knowledge base. This deep, passionate involvement begins to change the way that individual views the world. These changes go beyond the cognitive restructuring that takes place at Level Four, because the individual engages in a purposeful and emotion-driven, all-consuming focus on the problem. It may take several weeks or months to generate a product. Problem-solving heuristics are exercised, but the individual begins to develop his own way of working. The product is of value to both self and others, although the scope likely is limited to an arena "close to home." The individual's views begin to be imposed on the world. Adaptation starts to shift from making self fit the world to changing the world a little by one's ideas and efforts.

What most people consider creativity—production of something new or very rare to the world that is of value—is reserved for Levels Six and Seven on the Continuum. Creativity at these levels is called "mature" because it involves well-developed, extensive, and intricate knowledge systems representing mastery of a field or fields. Usually 10 years or more of effortful study and practice are required to reach such levels, according to Mihalyi Csikszentmihalyi. In addition, this type of creativity involves the regular solving of problems, not a one-time occurrence, according to Howard Gruber.

In Level Six, Creating by Extending a Field, the creator constructs a partial point of view and adds a new dimension or valuable new information to a field, thereby extending that domain of endeavor. The creator must have mastered the knowledge base in the field in order to be aware of its gaps, needs, problems, and pressing issues. This internally motivates him to create a solution for one or more of these gaps or needs. Creativity at this level remains within a paradigm. Support in Levels One through Five can lead to this level of mature creativity.

Level Seven, the highest level of the Continuum, Creating by Transforming a Field (already described), involves the revolution of a field of endeavor or creation of a new field. At this level, the field, and possibly even the world, adapts to the creator. The well-developed construction of a point of view occurs at this level, and this contributes to the paradigm shift. Both the individual's internal knowledge structures and the external environment in which she works are transformed.

Ethical thought becomes very important at Levels Six and Seven. Creativity involves choices, some of which may have a profound effect on others. Creative products such as nuclear power or genetic engineering may be valuable when they are produced, but their long-term effects are unpredictable and potentially disastrous. Those with the most creative potential carry the greatest moral responsibility for the ultimate effects of their creative thought.

In this Continuum of Adaptive Creative Behaviors, the shift in adaptation occurs between Levels Four and Five. Prior to this point, the individual has been adapting to the world. In Level Five, the world begins to adapt a bit to the individual. To make such a shift usually requires facilitation from knowledgeable and supportive adults, as well as the building of a knowledge and experience base. School and work settings that encourage autonomy, freshness of vision, and originality; the development of talents and multiple strategies for thinking; and purposeful, self-set effort help individuals make the shift.

VIII. CONCLUSIONS AND ISSUES

Creative adaptation involves highly complex dynamics that depend on a wide range of situational constraints. It involves both short- and long-term thought, action, and development. It brings forth transformations within the individual as well as modifications, or even paradigm shifts in the environmental context. It also involves a wide range of cognitive, emotional, and motivational elements. In short, virtually all human faculties are called into play during creative adaptation to environmental problems and opportunities. Ultimately, adaptation is one of the most important issues relevant to the development of creativity.

Successful creative adaptation involves a number of paradoxes. Creators need to destroy existing structures while maintaining safety and harmony within the environmental context. They must make major transformations to their own cognitive structures while remaining resilient in the face of the inevitable attacks that accompany creative work. They must perceive pressing and immediate problems and opportunities in the environment while staying focused on a long-term sense of purpose. To do so requires creative balancing of self in the environment. If one merely adapts to the will and the world of others, it is unlikely that highly creative products can result. If on the other hand, the distance between the world and the individual's created product or performance is too great, "pearls may be cast before swine" and the world will not recognize the breakthroughs. Bucking prevailing paradigms is always difficult if not dangerous. Individuals have been relegated to mental institutions and even tortured or killed for such differences in perspective. Although such penalties were more prevalent in the past, anyone who has tried to get major research funding for a "far out" idea faces the problem of critics who simply cannot escape their own world view.

It is the long-term development of the individual along the Continuum of Adaptive Creative Behaviors that enables the resolution of these paradoxes. The broader, more integrative cognitive structures and the stronger sense of purpose one develops through progress along the Continuum help to provide the resilience and competence necessary for successful adaptation of both self-to-world and the world-to-self, even in the face of the difficulties imposed by creative work.

All of this raises one final issue relevant to considerations of creative adaptation. To what extent should the creative adaptation of one individual or group impinge on the opportunities for success of another individual or group? This question brings into play profound issues such as individual freedom, social Darwinism, class conflict, exploitation, and the moral-ethical implications of creative products and processes. In a post-industrial era of rapid, unpredictable change our answers to this question may determine our chances for successful creative adaptation as a species.

Bibliography

Cohen, L. M. (1989). A continuum of adaptive creative behaviors. *Creativity Research Journal, 2,* 169–183.

Cohen, L., & Ambrose, D. (1993). Theories and practices for differentiated education for the gifted and talented. In K. A. Heller, F. J. Monks, and A. H. Passow (Eds.), *International handbook for research on giftedness and talent* (pp. 339–363). Oxford, UK: Pergamon.

Feldman, D. H. (1980). *Beyond universals in cognitive development.* Norwood, NJ: Ablex.

Feldman, D. H., Csikszentmihalyi, M., & Gardner, H. (1994). *Changing the world.* Westport, CT: Prager.

Goldsmith, R. E. (1994). Creative style and personality theory. In M. Kirton (Ed.), *Adapters and inventors: Styles of creativity and problem solving* (pp. 34–50). New York: Routledge.

Gruber, H. E. (1981). *Darwin on man: A psychological study of creativity.* Chicago: University of Chicago Press.

Gruber, H. E. (1989). The evolving systems approach to creative work. In D. B. Wallace & H. E. Gruber (Eds.), *Creative people at work* (pp. 3–24). New York: Oxford University Press.

Kauffman, S. (1995). *At home in the universe: The search for laws of self-organization and complexity.* New York: Oxford University Press.

Kirton, M. (Ed.). (1994). *Adapters and innovators: Styles of creativity and problem solving* (revised ed.). New York: Routledge.

Piaget, J. (1980). *Adaptation and intelligence: Organic selection and phenocopy.* Chicago: University of Chicago Press. (Originally published in French, 1974)

Piaget, J. (1981). Creativity: Moving force of society [talk presented at 1972 Eisenhower Symposium, Johns Hopkins University, Baltimore, MD]. Appendix to J. M. C. Gallagher & D. K. Reid, *The learning theory of Piaget and Inhelder.* Monterey, CA: Brooks/Cole.

Sternberg, R. J. (1990). *Metaphors of mind: Conceptions of the nature of intelligence.* New York: Cambridge University Press.

Advertising

Sandra E. Moriarty and Brett A. Robbs

University of Colorado, Boulder

Brainstorming A creative-thinking technique using free association in a group or team environment to stimulate inspiration.

Creative Concept The "big idea" that is original, dramatizes the selling point, and makes the creative leap from the strategy to an attention-getting and memorable idea.

Creative Directors Executives who manage the creative work of copywriters, art directors, and producers.

Execution The form taken by the finished advertisement.

Portfolio Also called "the book," a compilation of work samples used by copywriters and art directors to present to potential employers.

Visualization The ability to imagine how an advertisement or commercial will look when executed.

ADVERTISING *creativity is the practice of developing original, attention-getting, and memorable ideas that meet strategic objectives that promote products and services as well as ideas. Effective advertising creativity, in other words, is measured not only by originality but also by its strategic contributions. To understand how advertising works, it is important to understand basic principles of creative thinking and how they are applied in advertising.*

Advertising is perhaps the only industry with staff designated as "creatives," people who are responsible for developing the creative concepts and executions that bring creative ideas to life as advertisements. They are grouped in a creative department in which creative directors manage the work of teams of art directors and copywriters. This creative team analyzes and critiques advertising ideas in terms of their strategy, as well as the originality and impact of the creative concept in its various executions. [*See* TEAMS.]

I. THE DEVELOPMENT OF ADVERTISING CREATIVITY

Advertising messages have been posted on walls since the days of Pompeii; however, the creative dimension of advertising art became obvious in the late 18th century, particularly in France where posters were used to promote the ideals of the French Revolution.

Advertising posters focused on products and perfor-

Copyright © 1999 by Academic Press
All rights of reproduction in any form reserved.

mances appeared in the early 1800s. The period from the 1890s until 1914 was considered the golden age of the poster with work by artists such as Jules Cheret, Eugene Grasset, and Henri de Toulouse-Lautrec in France; Audbrey Beardsley in England; Alfons Mucha in Czechoslovakia; and Will Bradley, Maxfield Parrish, and Edward Penfield in the United States. Their work introduced the genre of Art Nouveau.

War and revolution dominated the advertising posters during and between the two world wars and created some distinctive visual propaganda styles in Germany under the Nazis and in Russia under Stalin. The International Style of Design, with its emphasis on functionalism, from the Netherlands and the Bauhaus style that originated in Germany ushered in the new century. Art Deco celebrated the short era of peace in the 1920s and 1930s after World War I and before the Depression, and was reflected in the work of James Montgomery Flagg and J. C. Leyendecker in the United States.

In the 20th century, the focus shifted to mass media, and visual imagery, while still important, lacked the impact of the 19th century posters. Although in politically controlled societies, such as Hungary during the communist rule, creatives like Pocs designed posters that were political satire; in capitalist economies words became more important as advertising was defined by legendary copywriter John E. Kennedy as "salesmanship in print." The emphasis on salesmanship and persuasion brought in an era of strategic development leading to contemporary approaches to advertising as both art and science.

II. THE CREATIVE CONCEPT

Effective advertising is built on a strategy that is a carefully reasoned analysis of the audience, its needs, and the appeal of the product. The strategy, however, is developed in business language and the job of the creative people is to make what advertising giant Otto Kleppner called "the creative leap" which translates the strategy into a big creative idea. In other words, the creative team strives to dramatize the strategy in a novel and unexpected way that showcases the selling premise.

Advertising has to be both strategic and creative. The strategy is the springboard; however, there is usually a big difference between the creative concept and the strategic brief with its marketing and business language, which describes such things as objectives, markets, targets, and positions. The difference between the two represents the "leap." The creative concept is a central idea, a thought, or a theme that expresses the selling premise in a way that is both attention getting and memorable. The long-running Energizer Bunny is an example of a creative idea that delivers on the brand's strategy, which is to position itself as a long-life battery. The difference between the idea of a long-life battery and the long-running bunny represents the creative leap made by the campaign's creators at the TBWA/Chiat Day agency.

The objective of the creative concept is to deliver communication impact that is measurable using standard copytesting methods that evaluate awareness, recall and recognition, attitude change, comprehension, and likability. Another example of a creative concept that achieves those objectives is the "milk mustache." The strategy developed by the milk producers' association was to reposition milk from a children's drink to one that adults also drink, thereby broadening the market for milk. The "mustache" (and the people found sporting it) was the creative concept that delivered the leap from a child's drink to an adult drink.

In addition to big creative ideas for individual advertisements and campaigns (a series of advertisements in different media using a central theme across a specific period of time), creatives also develop "big brand ideas." For example, one of the most effective brand icons of all time is the Marlboro cowboy, which associates the cigarette brand with Western ideals of independence. Other enduring big brand ideas include the Maytag repairman, the Jolly Green Giant, and the Absolut campaign which identified the bottle and hence the product with a variety of cultural icons.

"Unless your advertising contains a big idea," as advertising legend David Ogilvy once remarked, "it will pass like a ship in the night." Ogilvy is referring to the context in which advertising messages are delivered. People watching, listening to, or reading the ad may be busy, distracted, too tired to concentrate, or disinterested in the product. Much advertising just "washes over" its audience without making much, if any, impact. Furthermore, the environment in which the advertisement is delivered is usually cluttered with other messages—commercial, entertainment, and personal. The concept or big idea is what allows the advertisement to break through the clutter and indifference, and register an impact that touches the target audience's minds and emotions.

Bill Bernbach, founder of the renowned Doyle Dane Bernbach advertising agency, observed in *Bill Bernbach's Little Book,* "Finding out what to say is the beginning of the communication process. How you say it makes people look, listen, and believe." But "how you say it" not only includes the big idea but all of the executional details that bring that idea to life.

Advertising creative people are also responsible for all of the details and decisions involved in the production of the advertising—such as the writing of headlines, body copy, and dialogue; the ad layout with its art and typography; and the casting, staging, setting, action, lighting, props, music, and audio track for broadcast advertisements. In executing an idea, the writer and art director team usually works with an agency producer who in turn hires the photographers, illustrators, and all of the other people necessary to take the idea from conception to reality. How all these elements are combined to create a coherent whole is called the *execution* of the advertisement and refers to the process of bringing the creative concept to life.

III. CREATIVE THINKING AND THE IDEATION PROCESS

The creative process in advertising is not unlike that in other areas of ideation. Ideation, the process used to come up with an original or creative idea, has long been a topic of study by advertising experts. Some of the earliest writings on ideation were produced by advertising people such as James Webb Young and Alex Osborn.

The ideation process is based on the notion that ideas do not always come easily. Disciplined procedures have been developed to help creative people move through a fairly predictable process. Various agencies may approach the steps differently, but one such process that was identified many years ago by Osborn includes the following steps:

1. Orientation: identifying the problem to be solved.
2. Preparation: gathering background information.
3. Analysis: breaking apart the relevant material and seeing relationships and importance.

4. Ideation: compiling a bank of alternative ideas.
5. Incubation: putting the problem aside and letting it gestate until there comes a point of illumination.
6. Synthesis: putting the pieces together and seeing the relationships and connections.
7. Evaluation: judging the resulting ideas.

Although there have been a number of different models proposed to describe the creative process, most contain these similar stages: a preparation stage where information and material are gathered; a phase when initial rough ideas are generated; a kind of hiatus period when the idea and materials are allowed to percolate in the mind; a period of illumination and insight; and a verification stage when ideas are elaborated and evaluated. While such descriptions of the creative process are extremely useful, they may be overly linear and so fail to account for the element of serendipity that often seems involved in the production of creative advertising ideas.

Young defined a creative idea as a new combination of thoughts. He suggested that a creative idea is a thought that is stimulated by placing two previously unrelated concepts together. A wide variety of critics ranging from Arthur Koestler to James Marra have also argued that creative ideas involve "bisociation," or the connecting of disparate thoughts to form a new and relevant idea. In fact, there appears to be a consensus that creativity is the ability to see new relationships or connections. These juxtapositions set up new patterns and new relationships, and create new and surprising ways of looking at things. For example, an ad for the Altoids breath mints shows a muscular body builder holding the product's little red-rimmed tin with a headline that says, "Nice Altoids." Instead of commenting on the man's body as expected, the headline compliments the mints. This mind-shift phenomenon has been described as making the familiar strange and the strange familiar.

These new relationships are frequently formed by drawing parallels between the product and some aspect of the world in general. By working in teams, advertising creative people expand their potential for discovering such new relationships, as together they have more information about the world than separately and so have more material with which to work.

To facilitate the creative process, writers and art directors working as teams use free association, divergent thinking, analogies, and brainstorming. Association, where one thought stimulates another, is particularly important since some scholars identify association as an underlying theory of how advertising works. Divergent thinking is used by advertising creatives to search for all possible alternatives (in contrast to convergent thinking, which uses a linear logic to arrive at the "right" conclusion). Although most creative people in advertising have probably never heard of this term, they use the technique naturally and without thought. Analogies and metaphors are composed of patterns and contain within them the juxtapositions that advertising creatives search for to create unexpected ideas. [*See* ANALOGIES; DIVERGENT THINKING; METAPHORS.]

Brainstorming, however, is central to the ideation process in advertising. Brainstorming uses associative thinking in a group context to stimulate inspiration. With 6 to 10 people working together to develop ideas, one person's comments will stimulate someone else to have a different thought. The combined power of the group associations produces far more ideas than any one person can think of alone. The rule in this type of brainstorming is to remain positive and defer judgment since negative thinking during a brainstorming session ("it won't work," "it's not on strategy") can destroy the supporting atmosphere necessary to achieve good ideas. [*See* BRAINSTORMING.]

Recent research on ideation in advertising has found that creatives have redefined brainstorming to mean "kicking ideas around," something that can be done alone as well as in a group. Generally they are not real fond of group creativity and will say things like, "Great creativity doesn't happen in committees." The most common application of brainstorming in advertising is found in the work of creative teams—the copywriter and designer—working together to develop a concept and execute it. [*See* GROUP CREATIVITY.]

Some agencies have special places or procedures for brainstorming—rooms, for example, with no distractions such as telephones and walls that can be papered over with tissues covered with ideas. These are sometimes called "war rooms," particularly if the agency is locked in a battle with competitors to win or retain an important client. If such a space is not available in house, then agencies may move their brainstorming group to a hotel suite. [*See* CONDITIONS AND SETTINGS/ ENVIRONMENT; CREATIVE CLIMATE.]

The purpose of such idea-generating techniques is to produce a large number of concepts. Researchers have consistently found that increasing the quantity of ideas also increases the overall quality. Once a large number of rough concepts have been generated, the problem is set aside and the initial ideas allowed to incubate until illumination occurs. But this is not a passive period. The creative team continues to be ready and alert, viewing the world with a soft focus that enables connections to continue to be made. The writer and art director allow the world to move by and are completely open to what is passing in front of them. At times an event in the external world will trigger a "eureka" experience. At other times, illumination is achieved through additional brainstorming or through the interaction of the incubating ideas in the creative people's unconscious.

A description of how Ed Biglow created the Volkswagen "Mass Transit" ad suggests how this process works. The ad was meant to convey the Volkswagen's roominess. After carefully reviewing the strategy and creating a number of rough ideas, Biglow set the problem aside. As he was driving down the freeway, he passed a car full of nuns. Suddenly, the idea hit him. But the incident on the highway triggered the headline "Mass Transit" only because Biglow had already done his work and focused on the problem.

IV. THE ROLE OF VISUALIZATION

Obviously, advertising is a highly visual medium and frequently uses powerful images like the "mass transit" visual to convey its messages. In fact, there is an important connection between visualization and creativity. Definitions of creativity usually include imagination, the ability to form a mental image. Research has found that creative people are more likely to represent, recall, and reconstruct images from their environment in novel and original ways. Visualization is the ability to imagine how an advertisement or commercial will look when produced. In addition to being able to imagine a product, people, scenes, and action—or see it in their "mind's eye"—advertising creatives also must be able to visualize the finished ad while it is still in the talking, or idea, stage. [*See* IMAGERY; IMAGINATION.]

James L. Adams argues that the ability to see new relationships and make relevant combinations can be maximized only when both verbal and visual thinking skills are employed. In order to maximize the interplay between the two elements, in the early 1950s Bill Bernbach decided that at his agency the art director would no longer simply draw the writer's ideas, but would instead be a full creative partner. The practice was soon adopted throughout the advertising business. As writers and art directors began working closely together, their talents began to mingle and soon creative teams were composed of writers who doodle and designers who scribble.

Today, art directors suggest headlines and campaign themes, and write radio commercials while writers think in pictures and suggest graphic treatments. Modern advertising creatives no longer think of themselves as writers and art directors but as ad makers. Visualization not only helps them develop fresh concepts but to imagine in detail how those concepts will look when finally produced.

In advertising, visualization has another dimension. An effective creative concept is a clever package of verbal and visual elements. All media use both words and pictures—including radio, where the visual is created in the listener's mind. Both the visual and the verbal elements are important, but what is more important is that these elements are integrated as a concept with one reinforcing the other. That does not mean they have to say the same thing, but they do have to work together in concert to create a coherent creative concept. Often, in fact, the words may deliver a surprise or twist by contradicting an expected relationship or connection set up by the visual. The "Nice Altoids" headline is an example of how the words twist the associations conjured up in the imagery. Likewise, copywriters, as well as art directors, must be able to marry the verbal with the visual elements to create an effective advertisement.

V. DISCIPLINED CREATIVITY

Unlike fine artists who seek only to express themselves, advertising creatives must express the product benefit called for by the strategy. Bill Bernbach is quoted in *Bill Bernbach's Little Book* as saying,

Merely to let your imagination run riot, to dream unrelated dreams, to indulge in graphic acrobatics and verbal gymnastics is not being creative. The creative person has harnessed his imagination. He has disciplined it so that every thought, every idea, every word he puts down, every line he draws, every light and shadow in every photograph makes more vivid, more believable, more persuasive the product advantage.

Far from being a hindrance, strategic focus is a distinct advantage. The advantage of such strategic boundaries is that they concentrate attention in one area. The strategy, then, enables the creative team to mine a small plot in great depth rather than explore a much wider territory somewhat superficially. By concentrating their efforts, the writer and art director can push beyond more expected solutions and generate a richer variety of creative ideas.

Ultimately, these options must be evaluated against the objectives. Such evaluation is an integral part of the creative process described by Osborn and a fact of daily life in an advertising agency. Like fine artists, advertising creatives must examine their work in terms of such aesthetic issues as memorability and originality. But they must also judge their work in terms of its strategic soundness, message clarity, and simplicity of expression.

Advertising creativity also requires another kind of discipline—the ability to create on deadline. Unlike fine artists, copywriters and art directors do not have the luxury of waiting for a creative idea to appear. As former advertising executive and long-time advertising professor Gordon White has said, "It is creativity on demand." Somewhat surprisingly, deadlines are viewed as an advantage by those who work under them. Douglas West reported in the *Journal of Creative Behavior* that a survey of 900 advertising creative people from around the world found that most believed that realistic deadlines helped teams focus.

Finally, advertising creativity requires that copywriters and art directors be able to evaluate the effectiveness of their work. One recent study of creative directors found that copywriters and art directors need first to be able to recognize an idea as original, and second, they need to be able to judge their own concepts as well against this internalized standard of orginality.

VI. DEVELOPING AND MANAGING CREATIVE TALENT

Unlike fine artists, advertising creatives do not work alone in their studios. Instead, they work together as part of the creative department. How successful and productive individual copywriters and art directors are depends on how well that department is managed. That task falls to the creative director and is no easy one. The creative director's job is a balancing act that calls for him or her to be both a traditional manager concerned with time schedules, profits, and workloads and also a socioemotional leader who can provide the support and criticism needed to inspire creative teams to do their best work.

To nurture creative ability and help writers and art directors achieve their full potential, David Ogilvy argued many years ago that a good agency executive should be a father figure, offering understanding, consideration and affection. But both Osborn's and West's descriptions of the creative director as "a good coach" suggests that in addition to understanding, the department leader must also set high standards and provide advice, criticism, and direction. Such direction, of course, must be applied with a light touch since creative people are innately rebellious and resent being given orders. Controlling the amount of time creative people invest in a project is particularly difficult because writers and art directors are perfectionists who are willing to spend many extra hours on a project to improve it by a very small percentage. That places them in conflict with management whose job it is to keep accounts on schedule and profitable. But since the creative flame only burns in a sympathetic environment, it is not simply a matter of watching the numbers. Managers must balance the need for profitability against the need to provide creative people with the time and resources to execute ideas to their satisfaction. That is not an easy balance to strike.

For creative talent to flourish, it is also critical for the creative director to establish an atmosphere in which risk taking is encouraged. Unlike the fine arts where a creative risk that does not pay off only produces disappointment, in advertising such failure can also have severe business consequences. Only when writers and art directors believe they can fall short without be-ing sharply penalized will they be willing to take the chances that can produce truly memorable work.

Finally Osborn has suggested that of all the qualities needed to successfully manage and inspire a creative department, a creative director must have above all else a high regard for the power of the idea. It is upon ideas that both agencies and individual creative teams base their reputations, but original ideas are fragile and can be easily destroyed by either lack of support or direct attack. That is why the creative director must protect the integrity of that original idea from all comers.

VII. A CHANGING INDUSTRY CREATES NEW DEMANDS

Getting a job on the creative side of advertising is tough, but recent changes in the industry have made the task even more challenging.

During the 1980s, the advertising industry was convulsed by a series of downsizings and mergers. These organizational changes had an unexpected impact on junior people who were seeking to enter the business. In the past, there had been layers of middle managers who helped develop entry-level creative talent. But with the elimination of those layers, agencies no longer had the staff to train beginning writers and art directors.

That caused the requirements for entry-level creative people to change. They are now expected "to hit the ground running." Junior writers and art directors are still required to have a broad liberal arts background in order to have a wealth of material to draw upon for ideas. But now they must also have highly sophisticated portfolios which demonstrate their ability to produce effective ideas from their very first day at work. Furthermore, they are expected to be up on all the new technology, especially art directors.

Because agencies are having to get more work out of far fewer people, they are no longer willing to take a chance on junior creative talent with exciting but unpolished ideas. To find people who can measure up to these new creative demands, agencies have come to depend more and more on exclusive professional portfolio schools which creative people now attend after graduating from college. But at a time when agencies are striving to become more diverse, reliance on these professional schools may be turning creative departments into elite preserves primarily open to those who can afford the training. In other words, good creative talent may be lost to advertising as the price of entry goes higher and higher.

Bibliography

Baker, S. (1979). *A systematic approach to advertising creativity.* New York: McGraw-Hill.

Bendinger, B. (1993). *The copy workshop workbook.* Chicago: The Copy Workshop.

Bernbach, B. *Bill Bernbach's Little Book.* New York: Doyle Date Bernbach.

Felton, G. (1994). *Advertising: Concept and copy.* Englewood Cliffs, NJ: Prentice Hall.

Fletcher, W. (1990). The management of creativity. *International Journal of Advertising, 9,* 1–37.

Jewler, A. J. (1992). *Creative strategy in advertising* (4th ed.). Belmont, CA: Wadsworth.

Marra, J. (1990). *Advertising creativity: Techniques for generating ideas.* Englewood Cliffs, NJ: Prentice Hall.

Moriarty, S. E. (1991). *Creative advertising: Theory and practice* (2nd ed.). Englewood Cliffs, NJ: Prentice-Hall.

Ogilvy, D. (1985). *Ogilvy on advertising.* New York: Vintage Books.

Osborn, A. F. (1963). *Applied imagination* (3rd ed.). New York: Scribners.

Young, J. W. (1975). *A technique for producing ideas* (3rd ed.). Chicago: Crain Books.

Affective Disorders

Ruth Richards

Saybrook Graduate School,
University of California, San Francisco,
and Harvard Medical School

Acquired Immunity A biological model, with potential psychological parallels. Early exposure to diseases such as whooping cough or measles can provide a milder experience than in later years, and provides an ongoing immunity. Certain psychological exposures have been proposed to have similar, although potentially more complex, effects.

Bipolar Affective Disorders A group of related mood disorders with explicit criteria, found in the American Psychiatric Association's *Diagnostic and Statistical Manual of Mental Disorders,* 4th edition (*DSM-IV*). These can be very serious, but can also be effectively treated. Bipolar disorders are characterized primarily by mood elevations and depressions; these frequently alternate with periods of normality. The following types may be distinguished, although these can only approximate any individual's unique pattern and experience: bipolar I disorder, bipolar II disorder, and cyclothymia. Among other criteria, bipolar I disorder involves major mood elevations, as well as depressions. Bipolar II disorder involves severe depressions, along with relatively mild mood elevations. Cyclothymia involves milder mood elevations and depressions, but

may be characterized by more rapid alternation of mood swings. One should note that these disorders tend to run in families, and a familial liability to bipolar disorder may manifest even more frequently in a unipolar depression than a bipolar disorder, involving lowered mood from mild to severe degrees, with no clinically significant periods of mood elevation (although subclinical elevations have been postulated).

Compensatory Advantage Another biological model for which a psychological parallel has been suggested. In biology, there are inherited liabilities which run in families, which not only increase vulnerability to illness, but are also tied to positive characteristics which run in the same families. An example is sickle cell anemia, which can be devastating as a full-blown syndrome, but mild in the carrier state. At the same time, there is the compensatory advantage: resistance to malaria. In psychology, a compensatory advantage involving everyday creativity has been suggested in connection with bipolar disorders and familial liability.

Eminent Creativity This regards creators, creative efforts, and creative outcomes (persons, process, product) in situations where recognition for creativity has been given by society or by relevant professional organizations in forms including prizes, awards, honors, publication, and other forms of recognition. The quality of originality or novelty is generally part of what is recognized. Individuals and accomplishments are generally thought to have exceptional qualities or importance in their cultural context—although a different culture or generation would not necessarily agree in every case.

Everyday Creativity This regards creators, creative efforts, and creative outcomes (persons, process, product) which pertain

31

Copyright © 1999 by Academic Press
All rights of reproduction in any form reserved.

to day-to-day activities at work or leisure, and tend to be characterized by both originality (involving new and unusual aspects) and meaningfulness to others (rather than being random or idiosyncratic). A great many types of outcomes qualify, be they concrete products, behaviors, or ideas. The creativity has more to do with *how* a task is done than *what* it is. Possible examples include making home repairs, designing kids' activities, reorganizing an office, counseling a friend, doing gourmet cooking, charitable work, and replanting a garden.

Inverted-U Effect A curvilinear relationship between two variables, in which a high or low level of a predictor is associated with lower levels of the criterion, but where an intermediate level of the predictor can be optimal, and predict for the maximum values of the criterion. It has been suggested that certain characteristics related to bipolar liability, when they are neither too strong nor too weak, may be associated with higher creativity, following an inverted-U association.

Unipolar Affective Disorders A range of disorders involving explicit criteria, found in the *DSM-IV*. These can be serious, but effective treatments are available. Unipolar disorders are characterized primarily by periods of low mood, alternating with periods of relative normalcy. Multiple other functions can be affected, including sleep, appetite, and energy. Disorders range from major depressions to milder ones, but sometimes more pervasive or long-lasting dysthymias.

Modern studies and older evidence support the popular notion of a connection between **AFFECTIVE DISORDERS** *and creativity. Evidence is strongest around a personal or family history of bipolar disorders. However, the relationship is not simple, nor does it apply to everyone with a mood disorder (or everyone who is creative). Factors to be considered include* family as well as personal and psychiatric history, *particular place on the* wide spectrum of bipolar and unipolar mood disorders, state vs. trait effects, *issues of* everyday vs. eminent creativity, *particular* field of creative endeavor *(especially the arts vs. other areas), and availability of a constellation of* supports, resources, opportunities, and other personal qualities *that allow realization of creative potential more readily for some than others within a clinical designation. Related to this is the possibility that treatment can at once diminish suffering and free more creative potential. The creative advantage of interest may involve all of thought, affect, and motivation. It may occur in connection with different clinical pictures, and may range even to relatives of bipolar individuals who have been diagnosed psychiatrically normal. An evolutionary significance is addressed for liability to bipolar disorders in particular (which can manifest as a range of both unipolar and bipolar mood disorders), based on factors including its genetic contribution, and high ongoing prevalence in the population. Patterns linking creativity and psychopathology are discussed in terms of biological models of* compensatory advantage *and* acquired immunity. *Varied social roles in an evolving culture are also addressed—including that of creative instigator—that it behooves society to keep filling. Creative and healthy social effects may potentially be amplified through qualities such as "expanding the acceptable limits of normality," recalling that* abnormality *does not necessarily mean pathology, and by looking beyond symptoms to strengths, and diagnostic labels to individuals.*

I. INTRODUCTION

Throughout history, one finds the notion of a link between creativity and psychopathology, going back to pre-Grecian myth, and to Plato's "divine madness." As will be discussed, there is indeed scientific support for this long-standing popular belief about creativity and psychological disturbance. Particularly among eminent creators in the arts, there is a higher than average risk of major mood disorders, both bipolar and unipolar. This fits with varied older literature as well. Among eminent creators in non-arts fields, the discussion is more complex.

Among everyday creators, researchers have started with people chosen for clinical reasons and not for creativity, a key difference, and a design feature to be discussed. Evidence so far supports an advantage for everyday creativity—for the originality of everyday life—in conjunction with a personal or family history of bipolar disorders. The creative individual him- or herself may not be the most severely disordered, in accordance with an inverted-U hypothesis. She or he at times may even be psychiatrically normal. In the latter case, what is important may be something positive and subclinical that runs in the family, more than the pathology of a creative individual. [*See* EVERYDAY CREATIVITY.]

It is hopeful indeed if creative advantages are not necessarily linked directly to the pain and suffering that can accompany mood disorders, but to a potentially more neutral factor. One may ask if there are creative advantages that, in themselves, could heal or even protect against developing the full mood-disordered syndrome. These are exciting questions for the future—all the more so because of sheer numbers. By some accounts, as much as 4–5% of the population may end up developing one of a number of "bipolar spectrum disorders," ranging from mild to quite severe in degree. If each of these affected people had even one non-mood-disordered relative who also carried a familial risk, as much as 10% of the population could have a heightened potential for everyday creativity and for all that this might bring.

Finally, a note of caution. Here are considered some serious and painful mood disorders, including major depressions, and manic-depressive illness. It is important not to romanticize these just because creativity might at times be involved. The morbidity and mortality are serious. Without treatment, one out of five people with a bipolar disorder will end up taking his or her life. This is all the more tragic because treatment can be highly effective. Further, it appears treatment may often increase creative potential and actual creative activity. Treatment options should be well understood by any person at risk for a mood disorder.

A. "Spectra" of Mood Disorders

There is not just one depression, nor one manic-depressive illness. Mood swings appear to fall along a broad continuum. Indeed, they may even affect the population at large, as in one clinical study in which 40% of the control group showed cyclical mood swings, similar in periodicity to those of a clinical sample. The difference: control subjects' mood swings were less intense. Another major study showed a great many people suffer at least a few minor symptoms of "winter blues" or seasonal affective disorder (SAD).

Nonetheless, people often think of two types of syndrome, major depression and manic-depressive illness, which are said to affect roughly 5 and 1% of the population, respectively. Even here, though, there is a further spectrum which ranges into milder variants. The underlying risk typically runs in families, and displays a genetic influence, as shown by adoption and twin studies although there is also a large (but poorly understood) environmental component. Bipolar risk or liability involves a more marked genetic component than a unipolar risk. The high density of bipolar mood disorders in families is shown by one study of over 500 relatives of manic-depressive individuals, in which over 23% had a major bipolar or unipolar disorder (or, less commonly, a schizoaffective disorder). Despite the bipolar family history, over half of all these cases were unipolar depression.

As will be further discussed, there are possible implications for creativity in relatives of persons with bipolar disorders, even including the psychiatrically normal relatives of people with bipolar disorders. Hence, it is important to consider both personal history and family psychiatric history.

In reviewing the spectrum of mood disorders, one should note that there are many additional features required for diagnosis than the few given here and these are listed in the *Diagnostic and Statistical Manual,* 4th edition (*DSM-IV*), of the American Psychiatric Association. In a family carrying risk for bipolar disorders, depressive manifestations can range from dysthymias and milder depressions, to severe major unipolar depressions (all of these without clinically significant periods of mood elevation). Then there are bipolar disorders of varying severity, including bipolar I disorder or manic-depressive illness (with severe mood elevations and depressions), bipolar II disorder (with milder, or hypomanic, elevations but severe depressions), and cyclothymia (with milder mood swings but which may be rapidly alternating). There may be long periods of normalcy between such mood swings. A smaller number of individuals in such families may show "schizoaffective" disorders, characterized by both ongoing mood pathology and thought disorder. Hence a bipolar liability may manifest in a variety of ways.

The course of mood disorders may vary dramatically, in both quality and quantity. There are people who have only one episode of depression, for instance, in their whole life. In addition, people who have recurrent mood swings or depressions may also spend a great deal of their time in relative euthymia or normalcy. Thus, we are not talking about people who have an ongoing chronic and unchanging condition—indeed a factor which may be important to creativity.

As it occurs, both temporary "state" factors and ongoing "trait" factors may be significant.

B. Bipolar–Unipolar Disorder Distinctions

At this time research is more plentiful on creativity in families with bipolar compared to unipolar disorders. It is worth repeating that pure depression is an even more common outcome with a bipolar family risk than are bipolar mood swings—that unipolar depression is what one sees most often.

Yet one depression may also not be the same as another. One preliminary study suggests that creativity may be higher in depressed persons with bipolar disorder in the family than in people without this family history. Perhaps there are subtle and subclinical reflections of a bipolar liability—even ones which are adaptive and positive—along with the more debilitating symptoms. This needs careful study. Clinicians can be so intent on sniffing out illness and dysfunction that they fail to notice when something is going right or unusually well.

The four sections which follow concern issues of: (a) eminent creativity and mood disorders; (b) everyday creativity and mood disorders; (c) mood disorders, creativity, and evolution; and (d) three related biological models in which illness and health may be intertwined, with psychological applications to mood disorders and creativity, and the generation of resilient creative strengths.

II. EMINENT CREATIVITY AND MOOD DISORDERS: CONSIDERATIONS

There is evidence for an association between creativity and bipolar disorders, but the answer depends upon the way the question is asked.

A. Defining Creativity, Defining the Question

People often identify creative outcomes using a minimum of two criteria involving the presence of (a) originality and (b) meaningfulness to others (versus randomness or idiosyncrasy). When one speaks of eminent creativity, there is the additional consideration of social recognition; the achievements and their creator

have been recognized and won acclaim, either from society at large or from people in particular professions or other relevant subpopulations. Many people think of creativity largely in terms of such eminent people's accomplishments—the works of the best-selling author, the prize-winning playwright, the Nobel-prize-winning scientist, and the artist whose work went for millions at an auction. One may ask if these eminent creators are unusually able, or motivated, to offer creations we will accept as a culture and respond to overwhelmingly. Such creators, or creativity, should have some different ingredients than those found for everyday creativity. [*See* DEFINITIONS OF CREATIVITY; EMINENCE.]

A critical caution: With mood disorders, the question you ask helps determine the answer. It depends whether one is studying (a) eminent versus everyday people; (b) people chosen for mood disorders rather than creativity (the second can be an overall better functioning group); (c) patterns across families instead of just within individuals (where one finds both creativity and mood disorders, but not necessarily in the same person); or (d) one versus another field of endeavor (e.g., the arts versus the sciences).

B. Are the Rumors about Artists True?

Several studies, using modern methodology, are particularly notable, and gave new credence to a range of older and less rigorous studies, which nonetheless pointed in the same direction. In Nancy Andreasen's study of 30 well-known creative writers teaching at the renowned Iowa Writers Workshop, a remarkable 80% had had a history of a major mood disorder (compared to 30% of controls). If they were not ill at that moment, they had been sometime in their past. In addition, over half of those affected had a form of bipolar disorder, and a little over half of that number, a bipolar II disorder, showing milder mood elevations.

Compare the finding when Kay Jamison asked 47 highly distinguished British artists and writers if they had been treated for a psychiatric disorder—a full 38% said that they had been so treated, with mood disorders again highly prominent. This is surely a significant underestimate of the rate of mood disorders in this eminent group, since only about one out of three mood-disordered persons currently tends to seek help at all (indeed, a sadness, considering the efficacy of treatment). Furthermore, a full 89% of these eminent persons had had intense creative episodes (of modal length 2 weeks), which showed many of the symptoms of clinical hypomania. Finally, these rates may be compared to the lifetime prevalences of bipolar and unipolar disorders in the population at large, which are substantially lower, in the range of 1 and 5%.

Further support comes from Arnold Ludwig's psychobiographical study of more than 1,000 deceased figures whose biographies were reviewed in the *New York Times Book Review,* and covering 18 different professional fields. Almost two-thirds of the poets had had bouts of depression after age 40, with expository and fiction writers, visual artists, and musical composers up there in the 40–50% range. Mania occurred in as much as 13% of poets before age 40, and 5–10% of several other artistic groups. This suggests an even higher rate of more subtle bipolar spectrum disorders, including clinical hypomania and bipolar II disorder, which could not be differentiated by this biographical method.

Results support a range of older studies from the 19th century to the early 20th century indicating a creativity–psychopathology connection, and particularly in the arts, where most of the work had been done. Despite varied research design flaws, these tended to point in the same direction, supporting a connection between artistic creativity and psychopathology, and particularly creativity and mood disorders. [*See* WRITING AND CREATIVITY.]

C. A Different Story for Scientists?

The sole older study which included scientists, showed them to be a healthier group, with nonpsychotic disorders about half as common as for artists. More modern work supports this. Across 18 occupational groups, there was a much healthier picture generally for nonartists than for artists—or else, the illness of scientists was less obvious or less likely to be reported. Social scientists showed rates of depression in the mid-20% range, and physical scientists showed rates in the low teens. Other groups showing lower psychopathology included businesspersons, explorers, athletes, military figures, social activists, and social figures. [*See* SCIENCE.]

This method did not provide comparable information on the more subtle bipolar disorders, or family history. Still, it shows quite clearly, where overt mood disorders are concerned, that the best predictor is not being an eminent creative person but, rather, an eminent creative artist. Yet clearly, there are many mood-disordered people who do not become eminent, or even highly creative. One may ask what other factors might combine to make the achievement of eminence in Western culture more likely.

D. Eminence Revisited: A Complex Equation

Robert Albert identified a finite number of early personal and family dimensions which may together yield a "multiplier effect," including certain parental and sibling characteristics, and family birth order. Many positive forces combine to provide personal strength, support, opportunity, and expertise. Albert also found that long-standing family interests or capacities were frequently transmitted or made available to the individual, allowing a channeling of interests and a long-term immersion in a subject, and one with support from both the family and the culture. [*See* BIRTH ORDER.]

Strong motivation is important for creativity especially for the creator with a bipolar disorder. Ruth Richards and Dennis Kenney have shown a definite preference for work-related over leisure-related creativity among bipolar subjects in a sample of everyday creators. (By contrast, the relatives of schizophrenics showed greater preference for leisure-ated creativity.) Extracreatvity factors linked with bipolar mood disorders have been proposed which may raise the chance of eminent recognition when creative talent is already present. These include a driven work orientation, ability to think in broad (and at times grandiose) terms, altruistic and socially concerned motives that may accompany mood elevation, a sense of "standing apart" from the mainstream, and a need for external validation.

Results have been similar for individuals in arts or non-arts areas. Important personal characteristics have included: contrariness, capacity for solitude, physical illness or disability, drive for supremacy, production of work with a personal seal or signature, and a psychological "unease" or drive. Mental disturbance is included in this "unease." Research on eminent individuals has shown that psychopathology was four times as common among the most eminent relative to the lesser eminent individuals. The same research indicated that 78% (vs. 55%) of the most eminent individuals developed a psychiatric problem.

E. Contexts of Eminence: Creative Insight, Systems, and Chaos Theory

Eminence is a pattern in time and space which emerges around a creative person in a context. The eminent creator may be viewed as an open system, in tune with a culture, which can express where it wants (or needs) to go. In serving the culture, the creator can serve as a symbol, as well as an enabler, of a new trend of meaning that becomes socially useful. He or she can even alter fundamentally how we think about and organize reality.

The creative person may conceivably sit on a real or metaphorical edge of chaos—related to new creative insights about to erupt. A creative insight may reorganize the mental field in a dramatic new way (a mental "butterfly effect," or an irreversible avalanche of new awarenesses and mental reframing). This self-organizing process shows the nonlinear, irreversible, and dramatic sensitivity to initial conditions which is characteristic of chaotic systems. People with mood swings and mild mood elevation might find such an "edge-of-chaos" effect, or mental shift, particularly available, as Richards proposes, in association with tendencies toward overinclusion (or looser associations).

Physical illness may also provide an opportunity for creative (and chaotic) reorganization and transformation, as Zausner has proposed. [*See* CHAOS THEORY IN CREATIVITY.]

Here is one societal role for a cadre of creative initiators—the seeding of culture with new ideas, some to be kept and some to be rejected. Eminence may be conferred if a large enough audience has their own mental reaction, or creative insight, on assimilating the innovation, and if they like the idea. The creation can bring on similar mental shifts—avalanches of new ideas, or mental reframings—in an appreciative public. But a reframing is not always welcome in an era or it may impact a cultural taboo. Then, the creator may be ostracized, and even pathologized. Among those

most apt to take such risks may be people who already "stand apart" and are seen as deviant. [*See* CONTRARIANISM; ECCENTRICITY.]

III. EVERYDAY CREATIVITY AND MOOD DISORDERS: CONSIDERATIONS

A. Subjects Chosen Using Clinical versus Creative Criteria

Let us turn things around and start with psychopathology. If all creative writers had mood disorders, one would not expect everyone with a mood disorder to be a creative writer. One still does hear people making these equations of mood disorders with creativity as if the statement was (a) always true and (b) reversible. It is not so. We are talking about predictors and probabilities (they are directional). Beyond this, creative writers, or people in any field who have achieved a measure of success, bring together a constellation of intellectual and personal qualities and strengths. This might not be the case for the average person on the street, or someone with a severe mood disorder. We are not at the less-productive extremes of an inverted-U relationship between symptomatology and creativity, but are somewhere into the more functional middle (raised) segment of the inverted U.

B. Special Abilities or a Way of Being?

One also needs to consider area of endeavor. Special ability factors may be one ingredient in creativity, and cognitive style another. Researchers at IPAR produced broad evidence of a preference for originality, which appears in well-known creators across fields. In fact, if a link with mood disorders involves adaptive factors showing genetic influence, one would expect such adaptation to be general, and not to be constrained, for example, to a limited area such as verbal ability. [*See* COGNITIVE STYLE AND CREATIVITY; INSTITUTE OF PERSONALITY ASSESSMENT AND RESEARCH.]

There is confirming family data for this. Relatives of creative persons, say, in the arts, were not necessarily in the arts themselves, even though they showed higher than average creativity. Findings are consistent with

IPARs general finding of a "disposition toward originality." Whether or not one holds a unitary view of intelligence or leans toward multiple intelligences, the secret ingredient for creativity may involve a superimposed style of living and working that brings originality to one's efforts. Artistic or other special skills may be necessary for some work, but not sufficient. It is one thing to copy a Rembrandt,and another thing to be Rembrandt. [*See* INTELLIGENCE; MULTIPLE INTELLIGENCES.]

C. Compensatory Advantage? A Key Study and Method

The phenomenon of compensatory advantage may be a factor in creative ability. In sickle cell anemia, a gene from each parent leads to serious disease, but one gene (or the carrier state) may yield only a mild anemia, while providing the compensatory advantage of resistance to malaria. Although the genetic model may be more complex, it seems plausible that certain psychiatric disorders may carry a compensatory advantage involving creativity. The numbers are important; with mood disorders, one is addressing a benefit not only for a handful of highly eminent people, but for millions of individuals in everyday life. This may also involve a more complex variant of genetically based selection, favoring people who may contribute to our memetic evolution, as well as genetic evolution. They facilitate growth in the units of information (or memes) which reflect creativity in our world, and may subsequently effect genetic survival, as in the discovery of fire or of penicillin.

Accordingly, an inverted-U association has been postulated between creativity and degree of bipolar symptomatology. Richards, Kinney, and colleagues compared manic-depressives, cyclothymes, and their normal relatives to each other, to normal control subjects, and to controls with another type of diagnosis. The criterion involved a "peak" measure of real-life broad-based everyday creativity at work and leisure, from the Lifetime Creativity Scales, consistent with evidence of a disposition toward originality. Results showed everyday "peak" creativity higher among the clinical sample (bipolar, cyclothyme, and normal relative) than controls, with the intermediate cyclothyme group showing high creativity—higher than

the manic-depressives. However, another group was also high: the psychiatrically normal relatives of bipolars.

This is a critical finding, since severe pain and suffering and overt pathology were not necessary to the purported creative advantage. Nor did normalcy explain the findings, since the normal control subjects were not so distinguished. Interestingly, other researchers have found advantages on achievement in general in relatives of bipolar individuals. Results may support the inverted-U effect, if a subclinical hypomania or other mild effect is what raised the odds for creativity. They are also consistent with the finding of creativity being linked to intermediate, rather than high or low, levels of Eysenck's psychoticism variable and of subtle findings of thought eccentricity found in the normal relatives of bipolars, and in creative college students who, in the work of Schuldberg and others, were also somewhat elevated on a clinical hypomania scale.

D. State Effects: Is a Good Mood a Good Thing?

When asked directly, bipolar subjects reported experiencing greater creativity during mild mood elevations than during major elevations or depressions. They gave characteristics associated with this, such as a spontaneous exuberance and a cognitive facility (including rapid thinking and fluent associations). Eminent artists and scientists gave similar reports and the great majority had also experienced "intense creative periods," with many characteristics of mild hypomania. The prominence of bipolar II disorder in a sample of writers, rather than bipolar I disorder, with the more extreme mood elevations, is also notable. Mechanisms involving cognitive, affective, and motivational advantages have been proposed.

Even in the general population, mild mood elevation—say, from watching a comedy film—can directly enhance creative problem solving. It can also enhance cognitive style factors relevant to creativity, such as unusual associations and the creative style factor of overinclusion. For example, in classifying things as "flat," the overinclusive person might mentally stretch a little further, and pull in more imaginative possibilities (or some might say "loose," or inappropriate ones). Flat things, then, might include items such as a piece of paper, a dinner plate, a postage stamp, a body of water, the crown of the head of a person with a "crew cut," the nose of a professional boxer, and the surface of the ancient earth. Certainly, thought as well as affect is relevant to this cognitive style factor. Notably, evidence has been found of overinclusive thinking in creative samples, and linked with a psychoticism dimension.

Of key importance are studies of overinclusion comparing patients and creators directly. Beginning with Andreasen's work in the 1970s, similarities have been found between writers and manics in particular, along with some key differences. These related to whether or not one had adaptive use of overinclusive thought, as did the writers. This relates to what is called "regression in the service of the ego," and to the finding that eminent creators were high on many MMPI psychopathology scales, yet alongside this showed an uncharacteristic superiority in ego strength. [*See* INSTITUTE OF PERSONALITY AND RESEARCH.]

There is an important implication for health: with treatment, certain mood-disordered people may not only show decreased symptomatology but increased creative potential. If it is not so much what one says as why one says it, it becomes all the more important to value eccentricity, defer judgment, and not pathologize creative people. Abnormality does not necessarily mean pathology.

E. State Effects: What about Negative Mood?

Unipolar patients have reported a heightened sensitivity in connection with depressed moods. They do not necessarily report advantages ascribed by bipolar subjects to other mood states. Although there is preliminary evidence that people with a history of depression may show higher everyday creativity if there is a family history of bipolar disorders, one cannot necessarily conclude the depressions are different for this group. One must consider subclinical hypomanic "highs" which may occur in the first group.

Bodies of work suggest negative affect does not make a particular contribution to creativity. An inverse relationship has been shown between negative affect and creative personality patterns. However, others have linked negative mood with greater creative problem solving.

Research on children's play has shown that negative affect, experienced as part of a mixed affective state—in which one is overcoming a troubling difficulty and is triumphing—can also carry a positive affective charge. Indeed, much creative work in the arts deals with gaining perspective on, expressing, and transforming hardship and adversity. Along related lines, it has been suggested that an alternation of negative and positive mood states in bipolar individuals may enhance (a) creativity ability (enriching the interconnection of positive and negative mood-linked schemas in memory storage—schemas which might otherwise be stored separately in a mood-congruent structure), and (b) creative motivation (where an inevitable succession of negative and positive mood states enhances conviction that mood will change, and activity may help, as with a hypomaniac response to depression). Hence, faced with adversity, one is able to learn a style of approach, rather than a style of avoidance. [*See* CHAOS THEORY IN CREATIVITY.]

F. State and Trait Effects: What about the "Normal Relatives" of Bipolars?

For manic, schizoaffective, and schizophrenic patients, a related (though muted) form of thought disorder was found in the first-degree relatives of these individuals. This included the relatives who were not themselves clinically ill. This is consistent with findings of elevated creativity in, for instance, the normal relatives of bipolars, and in depressed individuals with a bipolar family history, and suggests operation of some subtle factors. In fact, there are particular qualitative patterns of thought abnormality which differentiate mania from schizophrenia, and might yield higher creative potential. These include a quality called *combinatory thinking,* including incongruous combinations and playful confabulation related to Holzman and Johnston's *Thought Disorder Index.* There are loosely tied together ideas and often a playful quality to their production.

IV. EVOLUTIONARY SIGNIFICANCE

In October 1996, there was an invitational conference at the Banbury Center, Cold Spring Harbor Laboratory, in New York, on "Manic-Depressive Illness: Evolutionary and Ethical Issues," convened by Kay

Jamison of Johns Hopkins and Robert Cook-Deegan of the National Academy of Sciences. Participants came from throughout the country, as well as the United Kingdom and Italy, to discuss genetic and environmental factors, social costs, and the adaptive value of bipolar disorders, as well as evolutionary perspectives of this complex situation. The group ultimately made strong recommendations for further study on multiple fronts, as well as issuing a caution, in this burgeoning era of genetic engineering, against any precipitous thought about altering a syndrome and familial liability which is complex, not fully understood, and has demonstrated advantages for individuals and society.

A. Everyday Creativity and Survival

Over time, multiple authors have noted that a link between bipolar risk and creativity (and perhaps also leadership) could help explain why the spectrum of bipolar mood disorders has not been selected against, down through history. A reproductive advantage would presumably keep this syndrome around. According to Robert Albert, (a) any form of human development and behavior with a substantial degree of heredity may well involve an evolutionary process, and (b) both genetics and environment are apt to be involved, providing flexibility toward changing environmental conditions.

One must ask whether such an advantage would operate at the level of eminent or, more likely, everyday creativity. This is a critical point. A handful of eminent people, however dramatic their reproductive power, could not generate this subpopulation in society, and maintain bipolar spectrum disorders in at a rate as high as 4–5% of the population. Everyday creativity is key. The liability for bipolar disorders must play out in everyday life so as to maintain its adaptive value and reproductive advantage. Prevalence of eminent creativity may be linked in as well. Receptive ground for everyday creativity may provide (a) a greater openness to the innovations of our eminent and exceptional leaders, and (b) an ability to produce more such leaders than would a conservative culture—individuals symbolizing for all of us new trends and ideas.

Candidates for a reproductive advantage include traits related directly to mood elevation or even a sometimes-associated hypersexuality. There are also the creative behaviors themselves, either of bipolar spectrum individuals or of nonaffected relatives, who show more subtle effects. Creative style or accomplishments could directly enhance interpersonal appeal, or indirectly increase personal desirability through mechanisms such as social favor, status, or economic reward.

B. Genes and Memes

This explanation demands that one ask not only about genes, or biological units of heredity, but of memes, or units of information or culture. Examples of memes are an equation, an idea, or a song. Indeed, we know that the producers of ideas help the survival of society, both at the everyday and at the eminent level and that society may help such contributors to survive. Here is a critical interaction between biological and cultural evolution.

Within our evolving cultures and subcultures, creativity is especially important. It can advance the most radical, and the fastest, evolution of our ways of life and our human personalities. With memes, we do not just have a joining of genes (or chromosomes from mother and father) at one point in time, but the repeated joining, day by day as needed, of vast quantities of information from around the world, and throughout recorded time, in whatever complex combinations are most appropriate to a need. When new combinations of memes (information) are both original and meaningful, this is precisely what many of us mean by creativity. Whether of personal or societal value, such information can be made available, duplicated endlessly (letters, internet, telephone, books and magazines), and distributed in seconds around the world. Be it the latest news, or a cure for cancer, this can radically change our lives.

There is a dialectic between the innovators and more conservative forces in culture. For changes to occur, there needs to be a seeding of new ideas—sometimes a little bizarre or a little radical—in an ongoing metabolism, to keep change happening. It has been suggested that individuals or families with bipolar disorders may be particularly adept at the formation of new linkages—at the production of seeds of originality—within a great many aspects of life, and carry such a leavening effect within the culture. This contribution may advance our survival and be duly rewarded, such that its effects will be perpetuated.

V. WHEN ILLNESS YIELDS CREATIVITY: TWO MODELS

There is more than one way in which illness and health may be intertwined, such as to have immediate, as well as ongoing, evolutionary effects. Here, first, a five-part general typology of direct and indirect relations between creativity and psychopathology is summarized (see Table I) using examples from mood dis-

orders. Next, this is used as a framework for two biological models, showing how creativity and illness can be intertwined, as well as to draw from more than one of these five possibilities simultaneously. The biological examples are linked to psychological models involving mood disorders and creativity, involving (a) compensatory advantages (relevant to the inverted-U effect), and (b) acquired immunity (regarding response to adversity).

TABLE I
Typology of Creativity and Psychopathology with Applications to Mood Disorders

1. *Direct relationship of pathology to creativity* (P → C)
Aspects of psychopathology (P) can contribute directly to creative outcomes or processes (C). Consider Kay Jamison's *An Unquiet Mind*, a remarkable first-person account of manic-depressive illness by an internationally known expert. Personal experience is relevant both to the content of the book and to aspects of creative process in writing it.

2. *Indirect relationship of pathology to creativity* (P → T → C)
Here, a third factor (T) intervenes between pathological and creative factors. Consider a person who does journal writing about mood states or conflicts, for personal reasons of catharsis, but comes to discover a greater creative potential and rewards. Nobelist John Cheever, who suffered from depression, did youthful writings about family and school situations which are thought to have helped him personally. Such expression can free one up psychically; enhance perspective, empowerment, and general health; and, at best, put one in touch with more universal themes and altruistic motives. Individuals like Cheever may end up writing or creating for the benefit of others.

3. *Direct relationship of creativity to pathology* (C → P)
Humanistic psychologist Rollo May, among others, wrote about the anxiety that may at times attend creative expression. Especially in the arts, one must be open to whatever comes up. The heightened sensitivity reported by people with unipolar or bipolar mood disorders could raise the odds at times of distress. In the best circumstances, such psychological discomfort and anxiety during the creative process can be an important step along the way to a more healthy and open personality. Hence, if creativity leads to such pathology in the short term, it can ultimately lead to greater creativity and health.

4. *Indirect relationship of creativity to psychopathology* (C → T → P)
Here, the third or intervening factor is the emergent conflicts that come to consciousness during the act of creation. Consider problems with substance abuse as a less healthy response to conflict than the working through in 3 above. Substance abuse occurs more often with individuals with mood disorders than in the general population. Another example is the creative and outspoken schoolchild who is ostracized by peers, and misunderstood by teachers. Sometimes a seeming hyperactivity is an early indicator of later bipolar disorder. Reticence, withdrawal, or clowning around and behavior problems may occur with creative children, and should the child have familial tendencies toward depression, this too might become activated under the stress. With more supportive environmental conditions, a better outcome can be possible.

5. *Third factor which can affect both creativity and psychopathology* (C ← T → P)
An important potential third factor is a familial liability for bipolar or manic-depressive illness. Having this may raise the odds of (a) problems related to mood swings, but also of (b) positive qualities related to creativity or leadership. These may occur separately or together in individuals, or across different family members, as found for instance by Andreasen, Karlsson, and Richards and Kinney. This third factor could involve cognitive, affective, and/or motivational factors—thus bringing along with mood elevation, for example, a more overinclusive cognitive style (original thinking versus thought disorder), heightened emotional sensitivity (depth of appreciation versus emotional instability), and inspired motivation (energetic confidence versus grandiosity).

A. Creativity and Psychopathology: Five-Part Typology

Factors connecting creativity and psychopathology can involve all biological, psychological, and social factors—and not surprisingly, the patterns can be complex. Here one may simplify the possibilities a bit through a classification scheme. Factors affecting both ability and motivation for creativity also occur, as do direct and indirect effects. (Factors affecting motivation may be classified as indirect—as background enhancers of the application of creative abilities.) There are also directional issues—for example, times when creativity can lead to problems, and ways illness can impact creativity. These relationships can be multiple and overlapping. The five-part typology helps simplify the conceptualization of these. P and C are used for psychopathology and creativity respectively (or some aspect of these. T refers to a third factor (or factors) which may independently influence aspects of both creativity and psychopathology. Examples relating to mood disorders are given below (see Table I) for each pattern. [*See* FIVE-PART TYPOLOGY.]

B. Three Biological Models, and Psychological Applications

Two biological models follow which may be linked to mood disorders, and which may also be viewed in terms of a combination of categories in this typology. One may therefore consider a varied number of ways in which creativity may appear in relation to mood pathology, and which can intertwine health and pathology.

1. Compensatory Advantage

Existence of a problem—if at an attenuated level—can carry an advantage and a low-enough cost–benefit ratio that there may be adaptive, and even evolutionary, advantages overall in a population. Sickle cell anemia, both in the disease state (two genes) and carrier state (one gene) was mentioned earlier. The carrier suffers little but holds the compensatory advantage: resistance to malaria. In typology category 5 in Table I, sickle cell genes represent the third factor (T) which can separately influence both illness and health, and in the same person, at the same time.

The linked psychological model involves creativity as the compensatory advantage. In the typology, familial liability (which includes genetic risk) is the third factor which stands between the pathological and creative effects (P ← T → C). This may manifest in terms of cognitive, affective, and/or motivational effects. some people—for example, normal relatives of bipolar individuals—might show only the creative effects and not noticeable mood pathology. Other individuals might show only pathology, and be too debilitated or distraught to manifest what might, with greater modulation, support, and opportunity, become heightened creative potential. Others, or indeed the same people already discussed, might additionally harvest a creative advantage directly (P → C) or indirectly (P → T → C) from the disorder itself or related experience, as in the typology above.

2. Acquired Immunity

This biological model can be exemplified by infectious illnesses such as whooping cough. Childhood infection with whooping cough is relatively mild compared to the adult form of the illness. Early exposure (and immunization) is therefore useful as protection against adult illness. With an adult disease like flu, getting a yearly flu shot is also useful, as a more controlled means of exposure to a changing pathogen. With such manageable exposure, a resilient capacity can be developed, in this case through one's immune system. The immunized organism knows what to expect and how to respond, and is stronger and more capable than before. In the typology above, this situation connects first to the mediated relationship (P → T → C), in which pathology leads to personal strength which enhances healthy function.

The psychological parallel is the large number of people, particularly eminent creators in the arts, who have suffered early adversity and high rates of mental illness. Notably, when a child has a mood disorder, a parent is more likely to have one as well, and this can lead to many sequelae, including emotional distance, inconsistency, and early stress.

A great many people with early difficulty to not thrive. The important question is to find "what makes the difference"—what intervening or "third factors" (with P → T → C), may further a resilient outcome or a creative coping and survivor strategy. Personal and family supports and advocates, role models, high intelligence and other individual characteristics, personal opportunities, and other advantages may all contribute to the psychological "immunization." This route might be particularly fertile for people with personal sensitivity to mood swings and mood disorders—both decreasing pain and increasing creative potential and a positive feedback loop leading to further coping, growth, and self-esteem.

Indeed, those willing to confront adversity through psychological inquiry and the arts (P → T → C) may gain advantages (and further "immunization") for both creative ability and motivation. This involves (a) affective integration and access to a rich reservoir of emotionally coded information and building strategies for making it conscious, rather than suppressing it. Included here is the painful pathology that may directly provide content for creative work (P → C). The creator becomes increasingly adept at circumventing our usual limiting patterns of positive mood maintenance ("That's great," "Everything looks fine," "I remember a good time last week") and negative mood repair ("I'm not going to think about that," "Forget it!") in order to draw from whatever part of memory is useful. A mixed affective quest can end up an overall positive experience.

Allied with this is (b) creative courage, the conviction that one can confront adversity creatively, and can do so again. It is "fight, not flight!" When creation reactivates difficult memories and distress (C → P), there can be growing confidence that this may yet pay off, both in the work and in a further "immunization"—a greater psychological openness and well-being that can continue to grow.

VI. CONCLUSIONS AND RECOMMENDATIONS

A. Links with Mood Disorders: Yes, but They Are Complex

There is support for links between creativity and bipolar and unipolar mood disorders, and perhaps more importantly, with psychiatric family history and the underlying risks one carries, which might manifest in different ways. The manifestations of this risk differ in nature and intensity between eminent and everyday creators. For eminent creators, there is a high prevalence of mood disorders in the arts in particular, and particularly of bipolar disorders. Mild mood elevation seems particularly conducive to creative insight, potentially offering cognitive, affective, and motivational advantages. Outside of the arts, major mood disorders are less common, although more information is needed about mild or subtle mood swings or possible family psychiatric history. Perhaps aspects of a familial liability to bipolar disorder also help influence a drive toward eminence.

For everyday creators, it appears that relatively well-functioning individuals are most apt to display higher creativity at work or leisure, showing more intermediate levels of bipolar pathology, and sometimes even normalcy, against the background of a bipolar family history. (Do note that eminent mood-disordered artists may also represent relatively well-functioning persons within the group of people with a particular diagnosis—although, of course, there are always exceptions, and certain people may be high-functioning in some mood states and not in others.) One must again differentiate state from trait, noting, for instance, advantages of mild mood elevation. Then there are potential benefits for creative ability and motivation, involving (a) for ability, more mindful awareness of one's own personal states and one's world, including the ability to link and access diverse affects in memory storage, and (b) for motivation, a growing sense—at last for some people who are properly "immunized"—that one can face adversity and transform it creatively, rather than defend against it.

B. Resilience and Creative Confrontation—Some Special Roles?

There are interesting people—and interesting families—in which psychological problems are more apt to occur, but perhaps with some freshness of vision as well. There is support for an evolutionary basis for this, and suggestion of some adaptive value for society (if not always for individuals), conceivably on the basis of a compensatory advantage.

Regarding personal or family history of bipolar disorders, the following are partly supported patterns in the literature which are worthy of further study. Some individuals may be more apt to (a) stand apart from the mainstream, due to differences including identified illness and its effects; (b) come up with new ideas as a behavioral norm, as well as challenge old ones, and often in the world of work and social contributions; (c) be more aware at times of what is going on in their immediate environment or in the world, (d) as well as be more sensitively attuned to input in general; (e) include a subset of people more willing and able to face certain adversities head on, as per the model of acquired immunity; (f) at times be more altruistically inclined in their creative intentions.

C. Evolutionary Shift—and Broadening the Acceptable Limits of Normality

The evolutionary hypothesis, that the spectrum of bipolar disorders (including unipolar disorder where there is a family history of bipolar disorders) have been favored down through evolution, could draw on multiple advantages, as related to a "reproductive advantage." With compensatory advantage, a genetically influenced advantage may relate to, and rise above, the morbidity of mood disorders. With acquired immunity, the creative twig may be bent in a positive way for later personal resilience and creative coping.

A memetic shift may be necessary for successful survival in a changing world. To further memetic shifts, we may need a different form of valuing that will embrace deviant seers and creators, as well as tolerate ambiguity in a rapidly evolving culture that must welcome new ideas. It is important not to pathologize abnormality simply because it is different—when it may lead to creative, and healthful, possibility.

Bibliography

Friedman, H. S. (Ed.). (1998). *Encyclopedia of mental health.* San Diego: Academic Press.

Goodwin, F. K., & Jamison, K. R. (1990). *Manic-depressive illness.* New York: Oxford Univ. Press.

Gruber, H., & Wallace, D. (Eds.). (1993). Creativity in the moral domain. [Special issue]. *Creativity Research Journal, 6* (1/2).

Ludwig, A. (1995). *The price of greatness.* New York: Guilford.

Richards, R. (1981). Relationships between creativity and psychopathology: An evaluation and interpretation of the evidence. *Genetic Psychology Monographs, 103,* 261–324.

Runco, M., & Richards, R. (Eds.). (1997). *Eminent creativity, everyday creativity, and health.* Greenwich, CT: Ablex.

Russ, S. W. (Ed.). (1993). *Affect and creativity.* Hillsdale, NJ: Erlbaum.

Russ, S. W. (Ed.). (1999). *Affect, creative experience, and psychological adjustment.* Philadelphia: Brunner/Mazel.

Shaw, M., & Runco, M. (Eds.). (1994). *Creativity and affect.* Greenwich, CT: Ablex.

Special issue. (1993). *Psychological Inquiry: An International Journal of Peer Commentary and Review, 4* (3). (Target article by H. J. Eysenck, Creativity and personality: Suggestions for a theory: plus 17 commentaries, and response by H. J. Eysenck).

Aging

Becca Levy

Yale University

Ellen Langer

Harvard University

Creativity The ability to transcend traditional ways of thinking by generating ideas, methods, and forms that are meaningful and new to others. It exists on a continuum both within and between individuals.

Life Span Developmental Model Creativity does not increase or decline but rather changes in quality across the life span.

Old Age Style A term used in art history to describe the style practiced by many artists over the age of 60. It includes selecting dramatic subjects and painting images in the foreground with few distracting background details.

Peak and Decline Model Creativity increases in adulthood until the late 30's and then begins to decline.

Theory of Optimization with Compensation Those who are aging optimize their functioning by finding ways to compensate for any loss they might experience.

The United Nations Demographic Office recently announced that the average global life span has soared to 80 years. People around the world are living almost 30 years longer now than their ancestors lived a century ago. In this article we will examine what happens to creativity in these added years.

*Two competing models about the relationship between creativity and **AGING** exist. According to the Peak and Decline Model, creativity increases in adulthood until the late 30's and then begins to decline. According to the Life Span Developmental Model, creativity does not increase or decline, but rather different types of creativity are expressed in different stages of the life span. We will first define creativity and discuss the conditions which promote it. Then we will outline the two models, and argue that the second model is best supported by existing research on creativity. In the last part of this article, we will discuss how creativity may influence health and even longevity in old age.*

I. THE NATURE OF CREATIVITY

Creativity in this article is defined as the ability to transcend traditional ways of thinking by generating ideas, methods, and forms that are meaningful and new to others. It exists on a continuum both within and among individuals. That is, creativity not only differs over time as individuals develop, it also differs between individuals due to differences in personality and how they interact with their environment. [*See* DEFINITIONS OF CREATIVITY.]

Copyright © 1999 by Academic Press
All rights of reproduction in any form reserved.

As a person ages both the nature and the degree of creativity vary. Young children at play tend to be very creative. They have not yet internalized many of the societally transmitted rules that can limit creativity. Thus, they can easily apply their imagination to their surroundings. [*See* PLAY.]

Those who remain creative in later life have already internalized many social norms. Therefore, unlike children, they must deliberately reject some of these norms. It may be easier to be creative after completing the relevant training in one's discipline. At this point one knows the principles to reject and change. As we will come back to in the second part of this article, in later life developmental changes may lead to new perspectives that foster creativity.

A. Openness to New Ideas

One characteristic that helps promote creativity is an openness to new ideas, which includes an ability to question surroundings and a tolerance for uncertainty. Essentially uncertainty leads to choice, and choice fosters mindfulness, which paves the way for creativity. Certainty makes individuals believe they know all there is to know and thus feel complacent. This state is at odds with the motivation to explore the target of uncertainty and to create something new.

The openness to new information may arise from childhood experiences. Researchers have found that more creative children, as measured by the ability to give novel responses, had parents who are more uncertain, and therefore probably less dogmatic, about child raising practices. Still other research has found that children presented with more choice and control over their surroundings, by being able to choose the material to work with, tended to produce more creative art as judged by outside raters.

Just as adherence to mindsets can prevent creativity, mindfulness or finding ways to think flexibly about one's surroundings can promote creativity. In a 1987 study to test this idea, Langer and Piper presented a series of objects to all their participants. They told half of their research participants that each object had one use, for example, "This piece of rubber is a dog chew toy." When talking to the other half of the participants, they implied that these same objects could also have other uses, for example, "This piece of rubber could be

a dog's chew toy." After the experimenters presented the objects, they expressed a need to use an eraser or the study could not continue. As expected, only those in the second group thought to use the piece of rubber as an eraser.

A naturally occurring group of people that tend to think flexibly about their surroundings and be creative are those with dyslexia. Dyslexia causes difficulty with perception. Thus, those with dyslexia can never take their environment for granted. When Piper and Langer repeated their study with dyslexic and normal students, they found that the dyslexic students tended to give more creative responses than the nondyslexic group regardless of how the objects had been described by the experimenters. For them the world stays uncertain.

B. Assertiveness and Focusing Attention

To generate creative ideas it helps if individuals are open to new ideas. On the other hand, to translate their creative ideas into products, whether it be an elegant mathematical equation or a dramatic sculpture, it is necessary for these individuals to focus their attention. This often requires that individuals be assertive when it comes to guarding their time. [*See* ATTENTION.]

A longitudinal study that demonstrates the importance of assertiveness to creativity was conducted by Ravenna Helson and colleagues. They traced the lives of 30 Mills College women who while still in college were nominated by the faculty as most outstanding in creative potential. Three decades later, the researchers found that the women who were judged best at actualizing their creative potential in their careers had scored higher on measures of extroversion and social dominance when they were still in college than their less successfully creative peers.

In a study of 91 exceptionally creative people (almost all of whom were over the age of 60 years), Mihaly Csikszentmihalyi found that a majority of the people he studied showed an ability to become single-minded, specialized, and guarded with their time. For example, Albert Einstein insisted that his wife serve him his meals in his home office so he would not be distracted by her or their children. Csikszentmihalyi points out that this tension between the ability to come up with creative ideas and then put them into action, and thus avoid obstacles, is captured in the Roman expression "libri aut liberi" (children or books). Interestingly, to the outside world Einstein may have appeared single-minded. His ability to mindfully approach his discipline and draw subtle and novel distinctions may have left him without need to explore much else. [*See* EINSTEIN, ALBERT.]

C. Supportive Environment for Creativity

The third way that creativity can be promoted is through societal expectations and institutions. One needs the proper environment to create. As Dean Rodeheaver and colleagues have pointed out, the underrepresentation of women in art history books may be due in part to a bias of authors, but to a greater degree it is due to the environmental obstacles to creative careers of women. Historically, women have been denied formal art training and access to drawing nude models. Although these obstacles no longer exist, a stereotype remains that women should get married, have children, and put their families before their careers. This stereotype may cause those in the male-dominated art industry to minimize the representation of women in galleries and museums. It also may cause women artists to put aside their artistic careers.

Guerrilla Girls is a protest group of women artists that formed in the mid-1980s in response to the low representation of women at the Modern Museum of Art in New York. They frequently don monkey masks and adopt guerrilla tactics, such as hanging up manifestos in art galleries and public places. Their manifesto jokingly declares that the advantages of being a woman artist include: (1) working without the pressure of success; (2) having an escape from the art world in one of your four freelance jobs; and (3) not having to undergo the embarrassment of being called a genius. That is, the artists try to make the point that in today's society women artists are still not given the respect of their male counterparts. [*See* WOMEN AND CREATIVITY.]

It seems that some of these dynamics between stereotypes about women and women's career aspirations also exist between stereotypes of aging and career trajectories of older artists. A stereotype persists that senility increases and creative potential declines in old age. This stereotype may contribute to the decline in cre-

ative productivity with age. Research by Becca Levy and Ellen Langer has demonstrated that stereotypes of old age as a time of loss, can worsen memory performance and self-efficacy of older adults. A survey found that many older artists doubt their abilities. This may lead to a drop in motivation and an increase in obstacles for creative productivity. For example, funding may be harder to obtain for older artists.

II. PEAK AND DECLINE MODEL

The Peak and Decline Model fits into the general belief that aging is a time of decline and loss. According to this model, named by Martin Lindauer, creativity increases in early adulthood and then starts to decline starting in one's 30's. This assumes that creativity is the same construct across the life span. Any changes that take place are thought to be due to the quantity, not the quality, of creativity. Therefore, studies within this tradition operationalize creativity consistently throughout the life span. The studies supporting this model have operationalized creativity in two ways.

The first way creativity is operationalized is with psychometric tests. These tests were originally given as paper-and-pencil tests. More recently, psychologists have developed computer programs. Psychometric creativity tests are designed to tap divergent thinking, which is defined as the ability to come up with many different associations. An example of a test item that might appear on a creativity test would be to list as many uses for a brick as you can. Divergent thinking is believed to differ from intelligence, which tends to be based on convergent thinking or the ability to come up with one correct response to a question. This is thought to be tapped by IQ tests that include grammar questions and fact questions, such as the distance between two cities. [*See* DIVERGENT THINKING; APPENDIX II: TESTS OF CREATIVITY.]

The second way that studies supporting this model have operationalized creativity is by productivity measures. According to the reasoning behind these measures, creativity can be assessed by the number of creative products. [See PRODUCTIVITY AND AGE.]

The underlying assumption of the Peak and Decline Model can be seen operating in a variety of decisions and policies. For example, the committee that gives the most prestigious mathematical honor, the Field Award, has decided to only consider mathematicians under the age of 40 years. Many of the academic institutions that employ those who make a profession of creative endeavors have traditionally imposed retirement in the late 60's. Also, Sigmund Freud argued that psychoanalysts should not give therapy to patients over the age of 50 because they tend to lack both personal insight and the ability to make meaningful changes. This was his belief despite the fact that he was over the age of 50 when he made this point and he considered one of the greatest plays to be *Oedipus at Colonus,* which was written by Sophocles at the age of 89.

A. Critique of the Peak and Decline Model: Psychometric Tests

There are numerous problems with this model. We will divide our comments into the two types of data used as evidence for this model: psychometric tests and productivity data. In terms of the psychometric tests, the studies that show decline tend to be cross sectional and do not take into account cohort changes, such as the fact that older individuals tended to receive less formal education than those born decades after them. One might argue that declines in tests of divergent thinking is not due to creativity, but to the confound of education with age. Second, although these tests are highly reliable, they tend to have little construct validity. That is, people judged as highly creative by society often perform poorly on tests. Also, people who score highly on creativity tests tend to not display high degrees of creativity in other areas of their lives.

Part of the reason for the lack of validity of psychometric tests is that they do not capture the creativity process. According to Howard Gardner, creative individuals tend to engage in a process that includes finding the best match between their strengths and a particular discipline, evaluating the discipline to identify spaces that appear promising, evaluating their progress, and cutting losses if sufficient progress is not being made. This active process is not tapped by paper-and-pencil tests in which the research participant passively responds to questions selected by the test designer.

Another reason for the lack of validity of these tests is that divergent thinking, which creativity tests tend to measure, may be less emphasized in later life. In youth,

many individuals try to distinguish themselves from others as they attempt to strengthen their identity. In old age, however, individuals have already developed their identity. Thus, they may turn their focus to integrating their many experiences. Integration may also be creative. In youth it may be easier to come up with numerous responses for a question or it just may be more desirable for that age group to do so. As individuals get older, research suggests that often there is a shift to a more mature way of thinking where the benefits come from contrasting and integrated ideas in light of one's own experiences. Thus, studies which contrast older and younger adults' scores on psychometric tests may be inappropriately comparing two very different content areas and not creative ability at all.

B. Critique of the Peak and Decline Model: Productivity Tests

Although the studies that chart a loss in the productivity of prominent creative individuals avoid many of the validity problems raised by the psychometric measures of creativity, they have their own problems. First, productivity is not equivalent to quality. Although there are individuals, such as Shakespeare and Beethoven, who have managed to be both extremely prolific and creative, these constructs are not equivalent. As Martin Lindauer discovered, (1) in a study of 100 well-known artists who lived until they were 79 years or older, 21 reached a productivity peak more than once, and (2) a lot of variation exists in the patterns of creative productivity of individuals. For example, although Marcel Duchamp showed a productivity decline early in life, Man Ray did not reach his peak until his 60's. Moreover, evaluating artists is not independent of evaluating their audience. As the population ages we may find artistic works produced by artists in their late life are the ones that are valued. [*See* SHAKESPEARE, WILLIAM.]

Furthermore, productivity may decline with age for a number of reasons not related to the quality of creativity. These reasons are both internal and external to the creator. As individuals get older, their income and social networks frequently decline, which could limit their ability to produce creative works. As careers progress, there is often an increase in professional obligations, such as committee work, teaching, and public lectures. After achieving success in a field, it is not uncommon for some of the initial passion and motivation to lessen.

The Peak and Decline Model may be perpetuated by a bias in which older creators are "youth judged." That is, many researchers and judges of creativity are younger than the older creators. This age discrepancy may lead to several dynamics that make the works of older creators appear less novel. Researchers have found that people tend to make more distinctions when judging the members of an ingroup than an outgroup (i.e., they are all the same). Thus, younger audiences may draw more distinctions between younger artists than between older artists and thereby judge the younger artists as more creative. Moreover, research has found that the more distinctions made in judging an object, the more an individual will like that object. Thus, the younger observers may better appreciate the works of younger artists because they consider them outputs of their ingroup.

It is the earlier work that makes us take notice of an artist's creative ability. After the initial attention the artist receives, it may take a big change in style for the audience to become equally impressed. When artists enter a field it is easy for the public to notice the ways in which their art is distinct since their work is compared to other artists. Subsequently, artists' later works are compared to their own earlier works. This within-person comparison that tends to take place at the end of an artist's career may also make the young appreciate the work of older artists less. By drawing fewer distinctions they are less likely to notice the subtle ways in which the artists have grown.

C. Simonton's Model of Creative Careers

According to a model developed by Dean K. Simonton, age does not predict one's creative productivity. Instead, the predictors he uses are when the creative career begins; the process of coming up with creative ideas; the process of transforming one's ideas into products; and the domain of creativity. In creative domains in which one deals with a finite array of concepts, such as math, creativity tends to peak and decline early, whereas in domains that deal with complex and associative-rich concepts, such as history, the cre-

ative productivity tends to peak and decline later. Simonton believes the timing of the creative peak is due to the fact that creative careers tend to be much shorter when there is little delay between coming up with ideas and elaborating them into creative products. This leads to an early consumption of creative potential. [*See* DOMAINS OF CREATIVITY.]

Simonton's model suggests that those with a later start date should have a career peak later than their peers. His model also suggests that individuals may experience multiple career peaks if they find ways to relaunch their career by taking on a new problem, medium, or discipline. This is an especially effective strategy if one begins a creative career in an area with an early peak and then switches to a discipline with a later peak. For example, William Wordsworth accomplished this by starting his career in poetry, and then switching to criticism and philosophy later in life. [*See* WORDSWORTH, WILLIAM.]

More important, Simonton found that the ratio between high-quality works and total number of works does not change over time. In one study of 10 eminent psychologists, he tracked the ratio of major articles that were highly cited to the overall number of articles published. Those who produced many highly cited works early in their career also produced many infrequently cited works during that period. Again, those who produced few highly rated works later in their career tended to produce few infrequently cited works during that period. He found the same pattern with composers. Thus, one could argue that the quality of creativity remains constant over one's career.

III. LIFE SPAN DEVELOPMENTAL MODEL

The Life Span Developmental Model, in contrast to the Peak and Decline Model, assumes creativity and productivity are not equivalent. It also assumes that creativity changes with development as a result of the underlying cognitive processes that changes with one's life stage, as well as one's experiences. The studies that support this model tend to operationalize creativity as the products judged by society to be novel and significant. For example, in painting, researchers have identified the most creative artists by looking for the number of references to their works that appear in major art history books.

This model is based on the qualitative analysis of creative individuals over time. As Martin Lindauer has pointed out, there are many advantages to using art as a way of examining creativity across the life span, including: (1) these data are valid, because professional artists have produced publicly recognized manifestations of creativity; (2) often artists translate complex ideas, such as their feelings about mortality and death or society's reactions to aging, into images and text; (3) they provide case studies of how various handicaps, such as the cataracts suffered by Monet, can be overcome; and (4) artists provide longitudinal records of their work. Many of the better known artists started producing in their youth and continued until their death.

It is particularly instructive to track artists who approached the same subject matter at different times in their lives. Thus, they serve as their own controls. For example, Michelangelo sculpted a Pieta at age 22 and then again at age 90. Similarly, Francis Bacon produced a series of paintings in which he tried to depict a cry. He painted the first image when he was 35 and continued to paint cries until the age of 79. As Gene Cohen points out, Bacon believes that it was not until the last painting that he finally got it right.

A. Why Creativity Changes in Later Life

In this section we will first discuss why creativity may change in later life, and then we will examine the way in which creativity changes. There are a number of theories about late-life development that seek to explain the evolution of creativity within individuals. These include the psychodynamic theories. For example, Erik and Joan Erikson felt that old age is a time of psychodynamic development that could change the quality of creativity. In old age, individuals can undergo dramatic changes as they try to resolve conflicts of previous stages as well as new conflicts raised by trying to maintain wisdom despite the factors that can lead to despair, such as trying to come to terms with their approaching death.

Some believe that as individuals approach death they try to find a way to make a lasting mark on the world.

This can lead to a surge of creative energy, sometimes called "the swan song." This phenomenon is exemplified by the career of Henry Roth, considered to have been one of the greatest American writers of this century. When he was 28 his first novel, *Call it Sleep,* was published. For the next 45 years he suffered from writer's block. Then, between the ages of 73 and 89, despite suffering from severe rheumatoid arthritis, he produced a series of six autobiographical novels entitled *Mercy of a Rude Stream.* Roth felt that as he approached his own death writing allowed him to come to terms with the acts of his life that he regretted and his mortality. In thinking about the creative process, the protagonist in one of Roth's later autobiographical novels, *From Bondage,* declares that writing is "a window into my remaining future . . . (it) is my survival, and a penance."

There are also cognitive changes in old age that could contribute to a change in creativity style. Whereas some cognitive qualities that may be associated with creativity do not seem to change, such as the ability to use imagery, others seem to change. For example, whereas fluid intelligence or the abstract capacity for problem solving may decline, crystallized intelligence or the acquisition of knowledge from experience, such as vocabulary may increase. [*See* IMAGERY; PROBLEM SOLVING.]

In addition, changes in physical functioning may lead to a new perspective that can fuel creativity. Paul and Margaret Baltes have developed a theory called Optimization with Compensation which suggests that those elderly who face physical or cognitive decline must find ways to change their style to compensate. For example, when Degas began to lose his eyesight he changed his medium from oil paints to the more tactile wax and oily chalk. In a different creative realm, physicist Hans Boethe explained that although he made more mistakes in old age, he became more alert at catching mistakes.

B. How Creativity Changes in Later Life

Art historians have identified an Old Age Style of creativity that is also referred to as "Altersstil." Its elements include an increased sense of drama; a more profound interpretation of human nature; a more instinctual, less studied approach; looser, freer brush-work; more amorphous corporeal forms; a compression of space such that figures loom close to picture plane; a lessening of emphasis on setting and background details; a theme of death; and an emphasis on unity and integration.

In support of the observation that older artists may use a less studied style with looser, freer brushwork, many of those who have become known as folk artists began painting in their later life. Gene Cohen reported that 60% of artists in a recent exhibition of contemporary folk art were over the age of 60. One of the most famous and most prolific folk artists, Grandma Moses, started painting in her 70's.

An example of the Old Age Style can be seen in Winslow Homer's painting entitled "Left and Right." He painted this at the age of 73, soon after recovering from a stroke and the year before his death. It is a dramatic image of two ducks right after one has been shot and the moment before the second is likely to be shot by the shell in the hunter's other barrel. The birds are pressed up against the foreground. The background lacks details. It depicts an abstract sea and sky. A balance exists between the female bird on the right who is dying and the male bird on the left who holds on to life. This painting has a completely different style than Homer's earlier paintings featuring sun-filled pictures of people.

A style particular to old age has been reported in other fields besides painting. For example, as Csik-szentmihalyi writes, scientists "in old age . . . seem to throw all caution to the wind, break out of disciplinary boundaries and start concerning themselves with the big problems of existence" (1997, 232). Elderly writers often become more philosophical and cynical, and tend to use more metaphors and older characters.

In his study of seven creative people that he thinks helped change the direction of this century, Howard Gardner describes late life changes in styles of creativity. Albert Einstein in later life turned from a focus on theoretical formulas to public policy. Sigmund Freud also switched his style in later life from writing about medical case studies to broader ideas about civilization and culture. At the end of her life Martha Graham made a dramatic switch. In her younger life she choreographed dances for herself. Then at the age of 73 she reemerged as director of her own troupe, and started to tour the country giving lecture demonstrations to educate the masses about her vision of modern dance.

Although these patterns have been observed in many creative works, the difficulty with generalizations is that they are based on particular instances. One could argue that the art historians who have noted these trends are selecting the older artists who fit their hypothesis and ignoring two groups: the many older artists who do not fit this trend and the many young artists who do. In response to these criticisms, Lindauer conducted a study to see if raters blind to the age of artists could identify a style for older artists. He had undergraduates rate the work of 24 artists when they were older and younger. Consistent with the descriptions of the Old Age Style, he found that students tended to rate the older art works as more holistic and less detailed. It seems important to repeat this study with older judges, however, before making any conclusions about the pervasiveness of the old age style. Lindauer's study conducted with college-aged students also supports our earlier hypothesis about young viewers making less distinctions in the art of older artists since they are members of an outgroup. [*See* OLD AGE STYLE.]

IV. INFLUENCE OF CREATIVITY ON HEALTH AND LONGEVITY IN OLD AGE

Thus far in this chapter, we have discussed how aging influences creativity. Several studies suggest that the reverse also occurs: creativity influences aging and longevity. For example, Lindauer discovered that many of the great artists lived longer than the general population. Another study found that individuals who attend more creative events (vicarious creativity) have extended longevity. This study conducted in Sweden of over 12,000 individuals found that those who were more culturally active tended to outlive those who were less cultural. The authors measured cultural activity by counting reports of attending events such as plays and concerts, and visiting institutions such as museums and art galleries. Participants were interviewed and then their survival rates were monitored over the next 8 years. The authors controlled for eight possible confounding factors including social networks, income, and long-term diseases.

Several factors may contribute to the extended life span of the accomplished artists described by Lindauer and the Swedes who participated in creative activities. When individuals vary their environment and take in new information they tend to become more mindful. Two studies suggest that increased mindfulness can contribute to increased longevity. Langer and Judith Rodin found that increasing mindfulness of nursing home residents, by giving them more control over such activities as when to attend a movie, extended their life spans. In another study, Langer and her colleagues encouraged nursing home residents to gather information about their environment by asking them to find out such information as the names of the nurses. Two and half years later, only 7% of this group had died as compared to about 30% of the comparison group.

In addition, directly or vicariously experiencing the emotions of the art may lead to venting of anxiety and emotional arousal. To examine the health effects of expressing emotions, James Pennebaker has conducted a series of studies. In one study he found that when college students were asked to write about a traumatic event for 15 minutes on 4 consecutive days, they significantly reduced their number of visits to the student health services and showed enhanced immune functioning over those college students asked to write about superficial topics such as the types of shoes they were wearing.

Creativity may also enhance the structure of the brain, even in later life. Diamond demonstrated that older rats exposed to complex environments with challenging toys in later life increased their ability to solve mazes and showed numerous kinds of growth in brain cells. Also, PET scans show increased blood flow to the brain during periods of creative thought. And levels of the neurotransmitter serotonin increase with satisfying creative activities. The more creative activities engaged in, at any age, the better off one may be.

While much research and theories of creativity focus on youth, the Life Span Developmental Model and intrapersonal career analyses reveal that creativity continues and changes in content and style. With the gray-ing of the world population, we should see a historic increase in creativity in the elderly due to the growing numbers of older artists and the aging of those evaluating the art. Most people's evaluations of those in with whom they share some aspect of identity, whether it be sex or age, tend to be more favorable than their evaluations of those without this shared quality. This changing context of creativity in the next few decades will provide numerous examples of aging artists that will strengthen the theories of how creativity develops with time.

Bibliography

Bygren, L., Konlaan, B., & Johansson, S. (1996). Attendance at cultural events, reading books, periodicals, and making music or singing in a choir as determinants for survival: Swedish interview survey of living conditions. *British Medical Journal,* 1577–1580.

Csikszentmihalyi, M. (1997). *Creativity: Flow and the psychology of discovery and intervention.* New York: Harper Collins.

Feldman, F. (1996). *I am still learning: Late works by masters.* Washington, DC: National Gallery of Art.

Gardner, H. (1993). *Creating minds: An anatomy of creativity seen through the lives of Freud, Einstein, Picasso, Stravinsky, Eliot, Graham and Gandhi.* New York: Basic.

Langer, E. (1996). *The power of mindful learning.* Reading, MA: Addison-Wesley.

Langer, E., & Piper, A. (1987). The prevention of mindlessness. *Journal of Personality and Social Psychology, 53,* 230–287.

Levy, B. (1996). Improving memory in old age through implicit self-stereotyping. *Journal of Personality and Social Psychology, 71,* 1092–1107.

Levy, B., & Langer, E. (1994). Aging free from negative stereotypes: Successful memory in China and among the American deaf. *Journal of Personality and Social Psychology, 66,* 989–997.

Lindauer, M. (1998). Artists, art and arts activities: What do they tell us about aging? In C. Adams-Price (Ed.), *Creativity and successful aging: Theoretical and empirical approaches.* New York: Springer.

Pennebaker, J. (1997). *Opening up: The healing powers of expressing emotions.* New York: Guilford Press.

Sasser-Coen, J. (1993). Qualitative changes in creativity in the second half of life: A life-span developmental perspective. *Journal of Creative Behavior, 27,* 18–27.

Simonton, D. K. (1997). Career paths and creative lives: A theoretical perspective on late life potential. In C. Adams-Price (Ed.), *Creativity and successful aging: Theoretical and empirical approaches.* New York: Springer.

Alcohol and Creatvity

Steven R. Pritzker

Luminescent Creativity, Greenbrae, California

what creativity researchers have found about the use of alcohol among eminent creative people and how it influenced their work.

Alcoholism Repeated intake of alcoholic beverages to an extent that causes repeated or continued harm to the drinker.

There has been a romanticized connection between AL-COHOL AND CREATIVITY. Alcoholic drinks predate history so it is not surprising that references to alcohol are threaded through notable art and literature dating back to the time of Homer and Seneca. Alcohol has also been the subject of many creative artists. There have been countless blues, country and western, and jazz songs that have references to alcohol. These often reflected the lifestyles of the writers and musicians who wrote and performed them and the "lovable drunk" was a staple in comedy for many years. Creative works about alcoholism reflected the serious underlying issues and long-term effects of drinking. Plays like The Iceman Cometh, *novels such as* Under the Volcano, *firsthand reminiscences of drinking like Jack London's* John Barleycorn, *and Oscar-winning movies* The Lost Weekend, The Days of Wine and Roses, *and* Leaving Las Vegas *are just a few examples. This article will review*

I. USE OF ALCOHOL BY EMINENT CREATIVE PEOPLE

A. Extent of Use among Eminent Creative People

Alcohol and creativity have been linked by the fact that many eminent creators have been heavy users and alcoholics. Table I is a partial list which is impressive because there are numerous great writers, artists, performers, and musicians.

The largest scale attempt to identify the level of alcoholism in eminent creative people was done by Arnold Ludwig, who in 1995 reviewed the lives of 1,004 eminent people who had a biography reviewed in *The New York Times Book Review* between 1960 and 1990. He assessed alcohol dependence or abuse on the basis of physical problems, work interruption or poor performance, personal and interpersonal problems, and arrests. He found,

among our eminent people 26% experience alcohol-related problems during their lifetime, 23% for women and 27% for men. . . . Actors or directors, musical

Copyright © 1999 by Academic Press
All rights of reproduction in any form reserved.

TABLE I
Eminent Creative People Thought to Be Alcoholic

Sherwood Anderson	Ring Lardner
John Barrymore	Charles Laughton
Bix Beiderbecke	Sinclair Lewis
Robert Benchley	Jack London
John Berryman	Robert Lowell
Mathew B. Brady	Malcolm Lowry
Robert Burns	Dean Martin
William Burroughs	Carson McCullers
Richard Burton	Edna St. Vincent Millay
Truman Capote	Robert Mitchum
Raymond Chandler	Modigliani
John Cheever	Mary Tyler Moore
Eric Clapton	Modest (Petrovich) Mussorgsky
Stephen Crane	Nick Nolte
e. e. cummings	John O'Hara
William de Kooning	Eugene O'Neill
Theodore Dreiser	Charlie Parker
T. S. Eliot	Dorothy Parker
William Faulkner	Edith Piaf
W. C. Fields	Edgar Allan Poe
F. Scott Fitzgerald	Jackson Pollock
Gustave Flaubert	Bonnie Raitt
Stephan Foster	Frederic Remington
Jackie Gleason	Mark Rothco
Gluck	Jean-Paul Sartre
Dashiell Hammett	Ringo Starr
Lorenz Hart	John Steinbeck
Lillian Hellman	Elizabeth Taylor
Ernest Hemingway	Dylan Thomas
O. Henry	James Thurber
Dennis Hopper	Toulouse-Lautrec
Victor Hugo	Mark Twain
James Joyce	Maurice Utrillo
Frida Kahlo	Dick Van Dyke
Buster Keaton	Tennessee Williams
Jack Kerouac	Thomas Wolfe

entertainers, sports figures, fiction writers, artists and poets (29% to 60%) have higher rates of alcohol dependence or abuse than natural scientists, soldiers, social scientists, social activists and social figures (3 to 10%). . . . Progressively greater proportions of artistic types, compared to other types, succumb to alcoholism after age 20 and throughout much of the remainder of their lives. (1995, pp. 133–134)

These rates are considerably higher than the 7.1% rate of combined alcohol abuse and dependence of alcoholics in the United States based on an extensive survey by the National Institute on Alcohol Abuse and Alcoholism in 1992. Men (11%) greatly outnumber women (4.1%), and in contrast to eminent creators, rates of alcoholism declined with age rather than increased.

Higher rates of alcoholism among creative artists, especially writers, have been found in a number of other studies. One study found that 30% of the Iowa workshop for creative writers had a problem with alcoholism at some point in their lives. Another study found that female writers had an alcoholism rate of 20% relative to a control group rate of 5%. [*See* WRITING AND CREATIVITY.]

Higher rates of alcoholism in the creative arts could be encouraged by the nature of the work, which is often isolating and allows the individual to drink more easily. Alcoholism is found less frequently in scientific professions where personal vision is less important than producing objective data that can be replicated.

B. Families of Alcoholic Creative People

There appears to be a genetic component in alcoholism. Ludwig found 12.2% of the fathers and 2.4% of the mothers of eminent creative artists were alcoholic compared to 6.6% of the fathers and .5% of the mothers in other professions. Furthermore 10.6% in the creative arts had alcoholic siblings compared to 6.3% of others. Other studies found that 11% of the writers had at least one alcoholic parent compared to 7% of the total sample. Examples of creative people who came from alcoholic families include Charlie Chaplin, Tennessee Williams, Orson Welles, and Truman Capote.

In a study on painters, the only characteristic which differentiated excessive drinkers from moderate drinkers was having the same profession as their father. In one case, the son of a successful father exhibited anxiety over competition with the father. In another case, the son pursued painting to satisfy his father's unfulfilled ambition "at the cost of inner development and constant strain."

II. EFFECTS OF USE

A. Physical Effects

Small doses of alcohol may help stimulate some aspects of brain function but alcohol is otherwise a depressant. *Encyclopedia Britannica* states that as more alcohol is consumed, an individual becomes more depressed,

> going on to sedation, stupor and coma. The excitement phase exhibits the well-known signs of exhilaration, loss of socially expected restraints, loquaciousness, unexpected changes of mood, and occasionally uncontrolled emotional displays. This may result from an indirect effect of alcohol in suppressing the function of inhibitory brain centers rather than a direct stimulation of the manifest behavior. (Britannica Online)

Prolonged use of alcohol damages the health of many alcoholics. Consuming four drinks a day or more can cause high blood pressure, coronary heart disease and failure, and stroke. Prolonged alcohol use is also associated with brain damage and the development of neuropsychological disorders. Impairments may include deficits in short-term memory, disrupted cognitive and motor functioning, poor attention span, difficulties with problem-solving and learning new information, sexual dysfunction, and suppression of the immune system.

The lack of inhibition caused by drinking is directly linked to criminal behaviors, including physical violence and homicide. Legal problems as well as divorce also increase.

Alcoholism can cause death from cirrhosis of the liver and impaired motor ability relating in alcohol-related fatalities in automobile accidents, falls, and drowning. High levels of alcohol are found in 36% of suicides. [*See* SUICIDE.]

B. Effect of Use by Eminent Creators

Some eminent creative people believed alcohol was a vital component in their success. The most common use was to overcome fear and anxiety. Aristophanes, in a play written in 424 B.C., wryly commented on the benefits of alcohol: "When men drink, then they are rich and successful and win lawsuits and are happy and help their friends. Quickly, bring me a beaker of wine, so that I may wet my mind and say something clever." Dorothy Parker said, "Three highballs, and I think I'm Saint Francis of Assisi."

Other creative people drank to escape the difficulties of life. The sensitivity and awareness which made their work special also made them more prone to depression and a sense of isolation. In many cases, alcohol was used as a type of medication to dull the sharp edges of life. Tennessee Williams seemed to be speaking for himself when he had one of his characters in *Cat on a Hot Tin Roof* say, "Mendacity is a system that we live in. Liquor is one way out an' death's the other."

In some cases, creative professions may be the only work an alcoholic could do. The individual has the freedom to drink and work as a writer or painter. Utrillo, according to Sandborn, was slightly retarded. His family kept him supplied with wine and painting supplies.

A sense that alcohol somehow contributed to their creativity (perhaps used as a justification for their drinking) helped demolish the long-term productivity or shortened the lives of many eminent creative people. Younger creative people still have the physical resilience to drink heavily and get their work done, but as they age it becomes more difficult, which is not surprising considering the physical effects of alcohol.

Of course, alcohol can deter productivity even when it is not used while an individual is working. Albert Rothenberg defined three states of drinking for the writers he studied:

1. Early in their career, they only drink after work.
2. Drinking begins to occur during the day as the need for alcohol increases, which is the progression experienced by most alcoholics. In the case of writers, the loneliness of the job combined with the anxiety and uncertainty of the work can lead to a state of "irritability." Alcohol is used as a sedative which helps soothe frayed nerves.
3. The increased drinking results in a deterioration in the quality of the work.

Rothenberg cautioned that each case is individual and may be triggered by elements unconnected to writing such as genetics or family history. When the parent whom the writer lovingly and competitively identifies with is an alcoholic, then the dangers of alcoholism are particularly high. Examples include John Cheever and William Faulkner.

C. Experimental Research

Results of research using noneminent subjects indicates that the perception that alcohol influences creativity is greater than any real benefit to creativity that alcohol may give. The drinking of alcohol may exaggerate an individual's self-assessment of his or her work. One study found that low doses of alcohol did not affect the quality of creative work, but subjects who believed they had taken alcohol *thought* their work was better. In another study, subjects who *thought* they had taken alcohol produced more creative combinations of wildflowers even if they had a placebo. This suggests that just thinking one has drunk alcohol may loosen some people's inhibitions.

A few researchers have attempted to determine if alcohol facilitates creative writing under laboratory conditions. There are indications that alcohol significantly increases the number of words produced, confirming anecdotal accounts of writers who find alcohol an aid in producing work, but quantity does not necessarily equal quality.

One study measured the effect of alcohol on a control group, a placebo group, and an alcohol group during different phases of creativity. Moderate amounts of alcohol facilitated incubation and restitution in the college students, while harming the preparation, illumination, and verification stages. The researchers tied this in to self-reports of professional writers indicating they used alcohol primarily during the incubation and restitution stages of writing. They also concluded that the difficulty of creative writing leads to increased drinking. [*See* INCUBATION.]

Alcohol may reduce anxiety and tension for some writers, but there also appears to be a tendency for users to exaggerate the benefits, perhaps to justify its continued use. Because life circumstances are confounded with the propensity to use drugs, the causal relation of drugs to creativity remains uncertain. The fact that many creative people used alcohol moderately or heavily does not mean the alcohol *caused* creative solutions. None of these studies looked at how alcohol affects accomplished creative individuals under actual working conditions.

III. SUMMARY AND CONCLUSIONS

Numerous researchers have cited reasons why creative people would use alcohol. They include:

1. Opportunity. Writers, artists, and composers often work alone so they can drink more often without anybody knowing about it.
2. The difficulty of the work. Creative work is tough and uncertain, and the road to success is paved with disappointment and rejection. Creative artists suffer blocks at times. Alcohol may provide escape from the pain.
3. Stress. Success brings its own pressure. Creators often feel they must match or exceed their previous work. Simonton proposes alcohol use may provide the user with a self-handicap, a convenient excuse that justifies failure.
4. Social reasons. Many artists, writers, and musicians met in bars and restaurants where drinking alcohol was an accepted part of the ritual.
5. Depression. Alcohol is sometimes used as self-medication to ease depression even though in the long run it is a depressant.
6. Addiction. Some people simply cannot drink in moderation and eventually develop a dependency on alcohol. [*See* DRUGS AND CREATIVITY.]
7. Genetic predisposition. A much higher percentage of fathers, mothers, and siblings of eminent creative people were alcoholics.
8. As an aid. Some creative people have stated they felt alcohol helped their work, especially in overcoming anxiety during the initial sages of creation.

The number of variables involved make the relationship between alcohol and creativity a complex and intriguing area. Many questions remain unanswered. Research on alcohol and creative leaders in business, politics, and science needs to be done. Alcohol use peaked in 1980 and has been declining as awareness of the dangers of alcoholism and stricter drunk driving laws have been enforced. It will be interesting to see if the number of eminent alcoholic creators also declines.

While many creative people have claimed that alcohol helped them, the truth of this statement in objective terms has not been determined. Ludwig concluded 9% of his sample had helped their creativity by using alcohol; however, he cautioned that the perception alcohol helps creative work could be exaggerated by the properties of alcohol. He pointed to John Cheever, Eugene O'Neill, and Jackson Pollock as examples of creative people who gave up alcohol and then did some of their best work.

Heavy use of alcohol over a long period of time clearly damaged the careers of many eminent creative people. This can be seen by looking at the declining quality in the work of actors such as Richard Burton and John Barrymore and writers such as Truman Capote and Jack Kerouac. In addition, many alcoholic creative people such as Charlie Parker, Jack London, and Stephen Crane died from alcohol-related illness, accidents, or suicides. F. Scott Fitzgerald summed up the danger of drinking in his work and life: "First I take a drink. Then the drink takes a drink. Then the drink takes me."

Bibliography

Britannica Online. (1998). Alcohol; Physiological and psychological effects of alcohol: Intoxication: Effects on the brain.

Dufour, M. C., & Ingle, K. G. (1995, winter). Twenty-five years of alcohol epidemiology: trends, techniques, and transitions. *Alcohol Health & Research World, 19*(1), 77.

Gustafson, R., & Norlander, T. (1995). Effects of creative and noncreative work on the tendency to drink alcohol during the restitution phase of the creative process. *Journal of Creative Behavior, 29*(1), 25–35.

Lang, A., Verret, L. D., & Watt, C. (1994). Drinking and creativity: Objective and subjective effects. *Addictive Behaviors, 9,* 395–399.

Lapp, W. M., Collins, L., & Izzo, C. V. (1994). On the enhancement of creativity by alcohol: Pharmacology or expectation. *American Journal of Psychology, 107*(2), 173–195.

Ludwig, A. M. (1990). Alcohol input and creative output. *British Journal of Addiction, 85,* 953–963.

Ludwig, A. M. (1994). Mental illness and creative activity in female writers. *American Journal of Psychiatry, 151*(11), 1650.

Ludwig, A. M. (1995). *The price of greatness: Resolving the creativity and madness controversy.* New York: Guilford.

Roe, A. (1946). Alcohol and creative work. *Quarterly Journal of Studies on Alcohol, 2,* 415–467.

Rothenberg, A. R. (1990). Creativity, mental health and alcoholism. *Creativity Research Journal, 3,* 179–201.

Simonton, D. K. (1994). *Greatness: Who makes history and why.* New York: Guilford.

Wolfgan, L. (1997). Charting recent progress: Advances in alcohol research. *Alcohol Health & Research World, 21*(4), 277–287.

Altered and Transitional States

Stanley Krippner

Saybrook Graduate School

Altered States of Consciousness An "altered" conscious state can be defined as one that can be recognized by an individual (or group), or by an external observer of that individual (or group) as representing a major difference in behavior and experience from an ordinary baseline state of waking consciousness. One's altered state must be fairly stable over time, and involve changes in a number of the subsystems of consciousness. Both dreaming and nondreaming sleep qualify as discrete altered states.

Changes in Consciousness Changes in consciousness can be brought about by sexual, athletic, and recreational activity as well as by negative conditions like torture or trauma. Psychopathology provides other examples of changes in consciousness, for example, dissociative disorders, mood disorders, post-traumatic stress reactions, and psychotic episodes. Many drugs produce changes in consciousness; they may affect many subsystems of consciousness, but lack the stability to qualify as states of consciousness.

Consciousness The term "consciousness" derives from the Latin *conscire*, to know with, or to be cognizant of something. Consciousness in the ordinary waking state reflects the explicit knowledge of one's situation; it sometimes includes subjective awareness and intentionality, one's sense of personal existence, and one's participation in a shared plan.

Creative The term "creative" can be applied to any act, idea, or product that changes an existing domain, or that transforms an existing domain into a new one. A phenomenon is creative if it is novel and, in some manner, useful or appropriate for the situation in which it occurs.

States of Consciousness One's ordinary "baseline" state of waking consciousness can be compared and contrasted to "altered" states. Falling under this definition would be "involuntary possession states" and voluntary "mediumistic states of consciousness" where alleged entities gain control of an individual (and, sometimes, a group) for extended periods of time, bringing about profound changes in one's subsystems of consciousness.

Transitional States of Consciousness A "transitional" conscious state occurs between discrete states but lacks the stability of a discrete state. Typically, it lasts for a briefer period of time, and one may move in and out of the state during its duration. Hypnagogic states are transitional because they mark the shift between a baseline state (wakefulness) and a discrete altered state (sleep). Other examples include daydreaming and napping.

*This article explores the association between creative experience and behavior, and those aspects of waking human consciousness often referred to as **ALTERED AND TRANSITIONAL STATES.** All of these hypotheti-*

Copyright © 1999 by Academic Press
All rights of reproduction in any form reserved.

cal constructs (e.g., "creativity," and "consciousness") are social artifacts, and are viewed differently from culture to culture. As a result, several cross-cultural comparisons are made that demonstrate a wider variety of perspectives than those encountered by Westerners, whether they manifest creativity, study creativity, or simply appreciate creativity. Specific attention is given to changes in consciousness produced by the ingestion of psychedelic substances, by the practice of meditation, and by hypnotic induction. Changes in consciousness associated with hypnagogic states, hypnopompic states, and daydreaming are also considered.

I. CREATIVITY, CONSCIOUSNESS, AND CULTURE

The conception of human creativity varies from culture to culture; some societies reward original work that serves a social function, while other societies criticize behaviors and products that deviate from cultural norms. The terms in which people make sense of their world are social artifacts, products of historically situated interchanges among people. In the history of Western civilization, not all individuals have had equal opportunities for creative expression. For example, women's creativity was rarely valued or encouraged; they were given few occasions to develop the skills (e.g., critical thinking) or life circumstances (e.g., solitude) on which creative work often depends. [*See* CROSS-CULTURAL DIFFERENCES; WOMEN AND CREATIVITY.]

A. Historical Overview

The paintings in the Lascaux Caves of southern France date back at least 17,000 years; the prone figure depicted there is generally regarded as a shaman experiencing a changed state of consciousness, possibly as the result of ingesting a psychedelic substance. Because psychedelic (from the Greek words *psyche* and *deloun*, i.e., "mind-manifesting") substances helped many shamans enter the "spirit world," they became a technology for the production of mythic narratives, theatrical performances, chants, songs, dances, and other products that today are labeled creative. Traditional Siberian shamans still "journey" to the "spirit world"

with the aid of either or both psychedelic mushrooms and rhythmic drumming.

Initiates of the Eleusinian Mysteries in ancient Greece probably used a potion containing a psychedelic fungus to fathom what the poet Pindar called "the end of life and its god-sent beginning." India's Vedic hymns sing the praises of *soma*, an intoxicant that was "all-pervading, swift as thought"; it might have been a psychedelic mushroom.

In pre-Conquest Mesoamerica, there was no "art for art's sake"; art as a separate discipline and activity had not been socially constructed. Instead, the creativity of the natives who inhabited today's northern Central America and south-central Mexico put their talents to use in the service of their religious beliefs. Aztec poets and musicians rhapsodized about the "dream flowers" that took them to another world; artisans erected flower-laden poles to commemorate the feast of Xochipilli, the god of flowers, and portrayed Xochipilli in statuary bedecked with psychedelic plants. Wasson, writing in 1980, found similarities between the use of psychedelics in pre-Conquest Mexico and that in ancient Greece; mind-altering plants adorn both the vases of Attica and the architecture of Mitla.

B. Cross-Cultural Comparisons

Societies have constructed an assortment of terms to describe activities that resemble what Western psychologists refer to as creativity. The first hexagram (or *kuan*) of the Chinese "Book of Changes" (or *I Jing*) is *Ch'ien*, the "Creative Principle." This hexagram expresses both the creative action of the "Source of All" that causes "objects to flow into their respective form," and the "Superior Person" who interacts with these forms when the time is ripe. This Creative Principle functions when Superior Persons harmonize their way of life with the universal flow. The hexagrams were ritually derived by throwing sticks in a step-by-step manner that focused one's attention and enhanced one's associations to the resulting symbol and applications to daily life.

Most Oriental, African, and Native American traditions also use creative imagination to enrich and enhance everyday life; novel, original contributions were typically seen as gifts from deities or spirits who used humans as "channels." Yet in some of these societies an individual who produced something unprecedented (e.g., an unusual mask) was censured for breaking with tradition; talented craftspeople were valued but individuals with a flair for novelty were chastised. When the church's power was dominant, Western cultures tended to consider "channeling" as demonic; once medicine prevailed, such forms of experience were cast in psychopathological terms. By contrast, traditional Eastern cultures had intricate vocabularies that described the spiritual aspects of unusual changes in consciousness. Hindu and Buddhist texts are replete with discussions of attention, awareness, and their regulation.

Many tribal people go through the day in what Westerners would consider a well-organized hallucination, for the world they believe and live in bears very little resemblance to the lived experience of Westerners. In dreams and in waking visions, the Maya people once asked their deities to appear before them, thus remaining faithful to their shamanic tradition of visionary ecstasy that had bequeathed them a universe so intense it could overwhelm them at any moment. The pre-Conquest Mayan artists depicted an overlap between the world of everyday reality and the "spirit world," suggesting a baseline state of consciousness that was much more "dreamlike" than that of their European conquerors.

Freud's description of the conscious ego as the external boundary of an invisible matrix of volatile "psychic energies" that feeds and informs it resembles the shamanic energetic model of the human body embedded in a community and environmental matrix. However, from the shaman's perspective these "unconscious energies" were not blind, but keenly intelligent, originating in the earth itself rather than in the neurons of the brain.

II. CREATIVITY AND PSYCHEDELIC SUBSTANCES

Psychedelic substances and other drugs affect consciousness by modifying the process of synaptic transmission in the brain. Excitatory and inhibitory connections between neurons are carried out by transfer of special biochemicals called neurotransmitters across the synaptic gap between neurons. Drugs can affect synaptic transmission in a variety of ways, such as blocking the production or reception of a neurotransmitter or mocking a neurotransmitter, thus effectively increasing its activity level. The type of psychological effects that a drug has will depend upon which particular neurotransmitters it affects and how they are affected. In the case of psychedelics, the results seem to be a disruption of logical analysis and the automatic reality-checking functions of the brain, probably connected to the ability of these drugs to block serotonin transmission. In psychotherapy, psychedelics can produce a depatterning influence which breaks up the individual's habitual experiences of the world, tending to increase the individual's suggestibility and susceptibility to reprogramming. [*See* BRAIN BIOLOGY AND BRAIN FUNCTIONING.]

There have been several anecdotal accounts by creative individuals in Europe, Canada, and the United States who claim that their creative behavior has been positively affected by ingestion of psychedelics, including neurologist S. Weir Mitchell, psychologist Duncan Blewett, British writer Aldous Huxley, U.S. naval technician John Busby and the Canadian architect Kyo Izumi. [*See* DRUGS AND CREATIVITY.]

A. The "Model Psychosis" Assumption

Much of the initial research on creativity and psychedelics was based on the assumption that the drugs produced a psychosis. In 1955, a team of researchers administered LSD and mescaline to an artist, asking him to paint during his sessions. They concluded the pictures did not contain any new elements in the creative sense, but did reflect pathological manifestations observed in schizophrenia. Other research found that LSD users gave highly imaginative, although bizarre, responses to Rorschach inkblots. In summarizing his observations of LSD users in 1976, the psychoanalyst Silvano Arieti found the use of "primary process mechanisms" to be enhanced, but that the "secondary processing" required to put the imagery to creative use was impaired. These studies, and related research, conducted with both artists and nonartists, and with both laboratory subjects and "street users," identified many dysfunctional results of informal psychedelic drug usage but no conclusive data supporting the notion that psychedelics could produce a "model psychosis."

In 1988, T. E. Oxman and colleagues reported a content analysis of 66 autobiographical accounts of schizophrenia, psychedelic drug experience, and mystical experience, as well as 28 autobiographical accounts of personal experiences in ordinary consciousness. Finding that 84% of the samples could be categorized correctly on the basis of word frequencies, they concluded that there is a "clear dissimilarity" among changed states of consciousness, especially between psychosis and psychedelic drug states. This finding contradicts the "model psychosis" perspective and its assumptions about congruences between schizophrenia and experiences evoked by such drugs as LSD, mescaline, and psilocybin, which were termed "psychotomimetics" or "hallucinogens."

If this topic is approached from the perspective of aesthetics, creativity can be discussed as a discrete class of psychedelic phenomena. Because creativity (from the aesthetic perspective) does not pertain to the self but to a creative product (contemplated or actualized), it contrasts with the self-centered subjectivism of the "psychotomimetic" model. Creativity, of course, is only one of several classes of psychedelic phenomena, but one that can accelerate the incubation phase of the creative process. [*See* INCUBATION.]

B. Creativity Research with Unselected Subjects

A number of studies were conducted with unselected subjects, primarily college students, in the 1960s and 1970s in an attempt to determine the relationship between psychedelics and creative behavior. For example, the effects of LSD on creativity test scores was investigated as compared with a control group. The test battery was given before LSD ingestion, and alternative forms of the same tests were administered 2 hr after ingestion. It was observed that most of the comparisons on the creativity tests favored the LSD group. On the other hand, the LSD group did poorly on tests requiring visual attention.

In another study, one-third of subjects were administered a high dose of LSD, one-third a low dose, and one-third an amphetamine. A test battery was administered to each group prior to drug ingestion and again

at intervals of 2 weeks and 6 months after the third session. The low LSD and amphetamine groups obtained similar scores, but the high LSD group bought more musical records, spent more time in museums, and attended more musical events; neither group demonstrated higher scores on creativity tests. Another study dispensed psilocybin to volunteers, most of whom were able to complete a creativity test and a test for brain damage before the session, as well as 90 and 270 min after drug ingestion. A significant inverse relationship between the scores on the two tests was reported.

These and similar studies cannot be considered conclusive since they differed in many ways, for example, dosage, subjects, research setting, and research instruments. However, it appears that volunteers cannot expect their creative behavior to be enhanced as a result of their participation in an experiment with psychedelic substances.

C. Creativity Research with Selected Subjects

In the 1960s, LSD was administered to 50 well-known artists at the Max Planck Institute in Munich. The results varied but the artists concurred that the experience was of value and the work was placed on display in a Frankfurt gallery. In a study on the effects of mescaline and LSD on four U.S. graphic artists, a panel of art critics judged the paintings to have greater aesthetic value than the artists' usual work, noting that the lines were bolder and that the use of color was more vivid. A similar study giving LSD to American actors, artists, musicians, and writers resulted in judgments by a professor of art history that the LSD paintings received higher marks for imagination, especially in color, line, and texture, though the technique was judged to be poorer.

A study of professional workers in architecture, engineering, commercial art, furniture design, mathematics, and physics, showed that mescaline resulted in a statistically significant increase in creativity scores, with enhanced fluency of ideas, visualization, and field independence. Interview and questionnaire data suggested that about half the group had accomplished a great deal more during the mescaline session than would have characterized their ordinary workday. All subjects reported positive reactions to mescaline but a larger number of subjects were unable to concentrate on their projects because they were diverted by the experience itself.

D. Cross-Cultural Considerations

Before their contact with Europeans, native people did not view art as a separate enterprise. Artistic creativity was an integral part of such essential activities as the making of implements for food gathering and preparation, the fabrication of clothing and shelter, the construction of tools for healing and for warfare, and—perhaps most significantly—the execution of paraphernalia for the spiritual rituals that upheld cultural myths and imbued peoples' lives with meaning and direction.

The potent red mescal bean, *Sophora secundiflora,* has been found with the remains of the extinct bison and the tools and weapons of early North American hunters. Many of the chants and poems used in spiritual ceremonies make great demands on the practitioner; the Yakut shaman in Siberia has a poetic vocabulary of some 12,000 words for use in *Amanita muscaria* mushroom rites, as compared to 4000 in the ordinary language of the community. The Zuni rain priests of New Mexico have a special language with which they converse with spirit birds once they have ingested the mind-altering *Datura meteloides.*

The use of psychedelics is not a simple matter for native people; these substances are not taken trivially, for hedonistic purposes, for momentary pleasures, or for "cheap thrills." To maintain these standards, native groups require a precise amount of time for the preparation of psychedelic concoctions, and the mixture of ingredients must be precise. Even then, there may be an initial period of bodily discomfort, physical pain, or vomiting, followed by encounters with the malevolent entities who inhabit these realms.

Paradoxically, psychedelics foster creative behavior among native people by *reinforcing* the cultural myths and traditions. The *yage'*-ingesting Siona shamans of the Amazon do not experience random images; rather, their experience is an ordering of the induced visions into culturally meaningful symbols and experiences. On the other hand, psychedelics often stimulate creativity among specialists in industrialized societies by *deconditioning* them to their cultural traditions; in contrast to tribal shamans, their images are likely to tap into their personal rather than their social *imaginario.* Among indigenous people, psychedelics are used in a socially sanctioned ritual that gives free rein to the imagination in ways that it can access the socially constructed nuances of the natural and supernatural worlds. But for Westerners, users of psychedelics typically ingest psychedelics in a contracultural manner. This practice has its hazards, but has the potential of releasing one's imagination so that the imbiber can envision concepts and percepts outside of the socially constructed cultural mainstream.

III. CREATIVITY AND REVERIE

Discrete states of consciousness include sleep and ordinary wakefulness; the transitional states that connect them are worthy of attention in the study of creativity. The term "reverie" is defined in various ways but it is usually said to be "dreamlike" in that it is involuntary, fanciful, and imaginal, but does not occur during nighttime sleep.

A. Creativity and Hypnagogia and Hypnopompia

Investigators of intuition have reported an association with hypnagogic (from the Greek *hypnos,* or sleep, and *agogeus,* or conductor, i.e., leading into) reverie, the thoughts and images occurring during the onset of sleep. There is a similar association between intuition and hypnopompic (from the Greek *hypnos,* or sleep, and *pompe,* or procession, i.e., leading out of) reverie, which occurs as one awakens from sleep. These "twilight" states, referred to as hypnagogia and hypnopompia, resemble dreams in that both are marked by "primary process" thinking and contain visual, auditory, and/or kinesthetic imagery. However, material from these twilight states is not typically characterized by narration, as are dreams.

Hypnagogic imagery may render more obvious those images involved in scientific creative activity. Indeed, hypnagogic images seem to have been a critical factor in chemist Friedrich August Kekule von Stradonitz conceptualization of the structural formula of the benzene molecule.

Another episode of reverie resulted in an important development in mathematics. While still a teenager, in the late 1770s, Karl Gauss had an insight on how to construct a 17-sided polygon. This experience reportedly occurred during an afternoon hypnagogic reverie while he was resting in bed. By the time Gauss had reached the age of 21, he had initiated his theory of complex numbers.

Ludwig von Beethoven reported obtaining inspiration for a composition in 1821 while napping in his carriage en route to Vienna. Inspired by a hypnagogic episode, composer Richard Wagner went on to complete an entire opera, the first of his celebrated "Ring Cycle." William Blake claimed that images of spiritual beings started coming to him as a child and served as the basis for many of his later drawings. Sir Walter Scott wrote that "it was always when I first opened my eyes that the desired ideas thronged upon me." Thomas Edison often stretched out on his workshop couch; during these "half-waking" episodes, he claimed that creative images flooded his mind.

B. Creativity and Daydreaming

Autobiographies and biographies reveal a number of prominent individuals who seemed to utilize various types of daydreaming for creative purposes. Newton claimed to have solved many vexing problems in physics when his attention was waylaid by private musings. Debussy, the composer, used to gaze at the river Seine and the playful golden reflections of the sun to establish an atmosphere for his creativity. Brahms found that ideas for music came most effortlessly when he daydreamed. Cesar Franck, is said to have walked around with a dreamlike gaze while composing, seemingly unaware of his surroundings. The writer Schiller kept rotten apples in his desk drawer, claiming the aroma helped evoke creative reverie. John Dewey, the philosopher, observed that creative conceptions frequently occur when people "are relaxed to the point of reverie."

Jerome Singer and associates found evidence in both children and adults of frequent daydreaming among those whose written or dictated stories were rated by judges as the most original and creative. Daydreaming

as a child was less likely to be associated with psychotic episodes as an adult than the lack of daydreaming. Excessive daydreaming, of course, can promote a vicarious fantasy life, and hinder the implementation of realistic planning. Singer's team also reported that during passive, effortless indulgence of a wish in fantasy, eye movements were significantly lower than when subjects actively tried to suppress the fantasy or to speed up their thoughts. This essentially passive and uncritical condition is typical of some types of creativity. [*See* DREAMS AND CREATIVITY.]

C. Cross-Cultural Comparisons

The way a culture conceptualizes creativity automatically restricts it to some social practices and processes, and denies it to others. During the heyday of Maoist thought in China, creativity was a matter of teamwork and no individual artisan was allowed to sign a painting, claim authorship for an orchestral piece, or register credit for an invention—much less spend time in solitude entertaining daydreams. The composers of Indian ragas did not affix their names to their works, but this was for spiritual reasons, and in the Benin culture, the African deity Olokun can influence artists through dreams and reverie. There are any number of societies in which specialists are encouraged to put aside their rational problem-solving modes of thought in order for the divinities to work through them.

Reverie is a form of mental activity denigrated by action-oriented social groups immersed in the practicality of life. Often it is discouraged because it promotes a vicarious fantasy life that slows the implementation of realistic, socially approved behavior.

IV. CREATIVITY, MEDITATION, AND HYPNOSIS

Some researchers doubt that hypnosis is an altered state of consciousness. Much of this controversy depends upon how many subsystems of consciousness need to change for a condition to be dubbed an "altered state." The presence of psychophysiological markers identify dreaming and nondreaming sleep as altered states, even though sleeping subjects sometimes report dreams when their psychophysiology reveals no rapid eye movements, sexual excitation, or the loss of muscle tonus characterizing dream periods. There are psychophysiological markers for hypnagogia, hypnopompia, and napping, winning them the status of "states," albeit transitional ones.

In the case of meditation, a number of studies have identified psychophysiological markers, for example, reduced respiration rate and volume of air breathed, reduced oxygen consumption and carbon dioxide elimination, and reduced blood lactate. Heart rate and the skin's electrical conductance decreased. The skin's electrical conductance decreased; alpha brain waves (and sometimes theta brain waves) increased. All of this suggests reduced energy metabolism, reduced autonomic nervous system arousal, and reduced cortical energy metabolism, reduced autonomic nervous system arousal, and reduced cortical arousal. Additional research discovered that reduced arousal during meditation is due to its rest and relaxation aspects, rather than the specific meditation practice employed. However, it is probably more accurate to speak of "meditative states of consciousness" than to hypothesize a single "meditative state" because different practices may yield different phenomenological results. There are practices that emphasize rapid breathing and active movement rather than counting breaths, repeating phrases, or witnessing one's thoughts; it is likely that their psychophysiological correlates will differ and will diverge from the rest and relaxation markers currently identified.

A. Creativity and Hypnosis

The term "hypnosis" is often used to refer to a variety of structured, goal-oriented procedures in which it is claimed that the suggestibility and/or motivation of an individual or a group is enhanced by another person (or persons), by a mechanical device, by a conductive environment, or by oneself. These procedures attempt to blur, focus, and/or amplify attention and/or mentation (e.g., imagination and intention), leading to the accomplishment of specified behaviors or experiences. Considerable research data indicate that these behaviors and experiences reflect expectations and role enactments on the part of the "hypnotized" individuals or groups who attend (often with little awareness) not only to their own personal needs but to the interpersonal or situational cues that shape their responses.

Other research data emphasize the part that attention (whether it is diffuse, concentrated, or expansive) plays in hypnosis, enhancing the salience of the suggested task or experience. Both these bodies of hypnosis literature emphasize the interaction of several variables in hypnosis, suggesting that there are great individual differences in hypnotic responsiveness, and that—as a result—the subsystems of consciousness will be changed in a variety of ways. Seven features of hypnosis have been identified, many of which are linked to creativity: passivity, diffuse attention, fantasy production, reduction of reality testing, increased suggestibility, role playing, and (in some cases) posthypnotic amnesia.

Both hypnosis and creativity are fairly stable personality traits, as measured by several standardized tests. In addition, scores on hypnotizability tests correlate significantly with three interrelated constructs: absorption, imaginative involvement, and fantasy proneness. There is considerable evidence from the field of subliminal perception that the less aware a person is of a stimulus, the wider the network of associations primed by that stimulus. As a result one line of hypnosis research has been to recreate this "effortless" type of creativity in which subject and object merge, and absorption is heightened.

The construct of "imaginative involvement" is predictive of hypnotizability. High hypnotizables are more likely than low hypnotizables to report satisfying experiences in which they become engaged in fantasy while reading a book, listening to music, or participating in other activities that allow them to depart from their everyday reality.

Similarly, a study of "fantasy-prone" individuals who spent much of their time living in a world of imagery and imagination scored more highly than comparison groups on measures of hypnotizability, vividness of mental imagery, absorption, and creativity.

Another study compared high and low susceptibles on a battery of creativity tests. On eight out of nine tests, the high susceptibility group scored significantly better than the low group. In another series of experiments, high correlations were found between hypnotizability, creativity, and "effortless experiencing."

A summary of the research on hypnosis and creative phenomena showed that fantasy and absorptive experiences are concomitants of various changes in consciousness, including those due to hypnosis, they occur spontaneously in the context of a creative act, and they are often experienced by creative subjects who, as a group, seem more adept than their less creative peers at shifting cognitively from a higher to a lower level of psychic functioning—from a more active to a more passive condition. In addition, the ability to tolerate unusual experiences and become absorbed in a variety of experiences correlates highly with hypnotic susceptibility. But the relationship between hypnotizability and creativity test scores includes important individual differences; the personality characteristics that allow one person to be more susceptible to hypnosis than another coincide to some extent with those characteristics that make him or her more creative.

Because of the link between hypnosis and creativity, practitioners need to know with what facility a hypnotized subject can produce pseudomemories. Even the increase in memories later found to be veridical is often accompanied by an increase in memories found to be inaccurate. These pseudomemories attest to the subjects' creativity, but are often used inappropriately in psychotherapy.

B. Creativity and Meditation

The term "meditation" (from the Latin *meditatio*, or thinking over) is often used to refer to a variety of practices that are used to self-regulate one's attention. All meditative practices, "mindful" or "concentrative," "zen" or "transcendental," or "active" or "insight," attempt to bring the meditator into the "here and now," breaking through habitual patterns of behaving and experiencing.

The case for increased creativity during meditation rests on a practice's ability to assist the meditator to break through his or her socially ingrained patterns of perceiving and conceptualizing the world. If the linear, cause-and-effect way of thinking can be transcended, creativity may result. Creativity may be further enhanced by adopting a more circular way of thinking in which the focus is on relationships, possibilities, and recursive patterns rather than on linear causality and single-outcome events.

A summary of the research on meditation and creativity, concluded that the results are mixed. One group of researchers has found no relationship between cre-

ativity test scores and experience in meditation. Another group has reported significant increases in creativity scoring among practitioners of transcendental meditation (TM), and among zen meditators. One of the latter studies focused on students of zen koans, finding that they were able to eliminate prior interfering approaches to problem solving and enhance the unification of contradictory events. [*See* ZEN.]

Patricia Carrington has reported several cases of students whose grades have improved, whose emotions have stabilized, and whose artistic productions have flourished following their initiation of a meditation practice. At the same time, in a comparison of a group of teachers of TM with a group of nonmeditators; the former did no better than the latter on most measures, worse on a few measures, and better on one measure—an open-ended task requiring them to make up a story. It has been suggested that meditation may enhance the free flow of associations and open up new ideas for a meditator, but an abundance of meditation (probably the case with the group of teachers) may interfere with a person's logical problem-solving capacity.

Several TM teachers, citing research studies conducted in the 1980s, point out that students of meditation showed significant increases in scores on creativity tests, especially verbal originality and fluency of visual-spatial creativity. A meta-analysis of all existing studies of TM and "self-actualization" concluded that the magnitude of the effects was not due to expectation, motivation, or relaxation, but to TM practice itself.

C. Cross-Cultural Comparisons

Eastern and Western meditative practices have a long history; they have been viewed as spiritual exercises—means for attaining the special kind of awareness that can be arrived at in concert with other life practices. In contemporary industrialized societies, however, meditation tends to be goal-oriented toward practical goals. This type of meditator may not be tied into any belief system. The advantage is that he or she is free to use meditation outside of a spiritual context, combining it with other methods of self-improvement and medical or psychotherapeutic treatment. The disadvantage is that this meditator may not attain the peace of mind of the unitive "bliss" claimed by members of traditional schools of meditation. For the former, creativity is often a goal of meditation; for the latter, creativity is a by-product because meditation is not goal-oriented and is done for its own sake.

The history of hypnosis is more recent; in the middle of the 19th century, James Braid introduced the term "neuro-hypnotism" or "nervous sleep" (from the Greek *hypnosis,* or sleep). He later regretted his use of the term (hypnosis bears only a superficial resemblance to sleep) but it took the place of "mesmerism," "animal magnetism," and a number of other terms which were even less descriptive. It can be claimed that the roots of hypnosis reach back to tribal rites and the practices of shamans. Hypnotic-like procedures were used in the court of the Pharaoh Khufu in 3766 B.C.; priests in the healing temples of Asclepius induced their clients into "temple sleep," and the ancient Druids chanted over their clients until the desired effect was obtained. Herbs were used to enhance verbal suggestion by native healers in pre-Columbian Central and South America. However, it is incorrect to label these procedures "hypnosis" simply because they drew upon similar procedures, for example, suggestion, repetitive stimuli, and expectations of the client.

People, groups, and cultures are "creative" during those periods of time when they exhibit activities that are innovative for that specific group—that is, they yield concepts, items, or behaviors that address human needs (e.g., for survival, for enhanced work performance, for enjoyment, for aesthetic satisfaction, or for enriched quality of life) in ways considered valuable by a society. These novel concepts, objects, and behaviors (e.g., a scientific discovery, a mathematical theorem, a philosophical insight, an artistic masterpiece, a technological product, a military victory, or a diplomatic accomplishment) can be considered creative, although one social group might arrive at a different consensus than another group.

V. POSSIBLE MECHANISMS

Art involves the controlled structuring of a medium or a material to communicate as vividly as possible the artist's personal vision of experience. Art is one expression of creativity; as such, it communicates the artist's vision in such a way that disparities in that person's

knowledge are identified and addressed. If art resonates with a larger public, it has succeeded in filling some gaps in social knowledge or in resolving cultural contradictions. Scientific and technical creativity are other expressions of creativity; they also externalize the practitioner's inner world and hope that it will resonate with social needs. These individuals also attempt to supply missing information or material in a culture's legacy. The same can be said for creative individuals who work with ideas, with institutions, and with other people. But none of this labor is done in a vacuum; there are neurophysiological predispositions that interact with social and psychological variables in the development of a product, process, person, or press that is eventually deemed creative.

A. Neurophysiological Mechanisms

There are several perceptual mechanisms ordinarily driven by sensory input during one's baseline state of consciousness that are decoupled, totally or partially, from sensory input during many alterations in consciousness. A total decoupling takes place during dreaming while partial decouplings take place in hypnagogic or hypnopompic states, daydreaming, meditation, and some drug-induced or hypnosis-induced conditions. Transitions from such states represent a fertile ground for the development of creative ideas, because the perceptual mechanisms automatically linked to organizing the sensory inputs would occur automatically, occasionally constructing novel and useful images from fragments of internal neural noise and loosely guided consultations with memory. Contact with the linguistic system allows the abstract images and relationships to be translated into a communicable form. Spatial relationships are a powerful source of insight that can be analogically applied to invention and problem solving, especially tasks involving the relations, projections, symmetries, and transformations of objects in space.

There is a direct relationship between perceptual processes and creative thought. Implicit knowledge of visual relationships among objects, and the rules for transforming those relationships, may constitute the fundamental mental operations inherent in much of creative thought. Decoupling certain normally involuntary processes from their data source may allow those same mechanisms to operate as a primary generator of creative thought. This creative thought is not of the controlled variety but the product of involuntary mental operations that lead to spontaneous insight. The decoupling of normal sensory input during alternative states of consciousness should be viewed as distinct from restricting sensory input in a normal waking state of an individual in order to prevent interference with controlled manipulation of perceptual codes.

B. Psychosocial Mechanisms

In addition to studying the neurophysiological correlates of creativity and changes in consciousness, psychosocial variables demand consideration. The forms in which creative experiences are expressed cannot be separated from the person or the maker and the culture of which he or she is a part. Cross-cultural research has demonstrated that patterns of expectation within a particular culture have an *a priori* influence on creative experiences.

The effects of psychedelics upon creativity depend on more than their neurophysiological effects, which are produced by an interaction between pharmacological drug factors (type, dose), long-term psychosocial factors (culture, personality, attitudes, knowledge, beliefs, prior experience), immediate psychosocial factors (mood, expectations, group ambience), and situational factors (setting, instructions, implicit and explicit demands). For example, anthropologists who have observed effects of *ayahuasca* among indigenous people in the Amazon comment that its effects differ, sometimes strikingly, according to the environmental and ceremonial background against which it is taken, the ingredients that are used in its preparation, the amount of the drug imbibed, and the expectancy on the part of the intoxicants.

C. Research Perspectives

The formal study of creativity only dates back to Guilford's 1950 presidential address to the American Psychological Association in which he urged his colleagues to pursue this overlooked area and, later, proposed his structure-of-intellect model with its distinction between convergent and divergent (or lateral) thinking. The connection between changed states of

consciousness and divergent thinking was made, and investigations of the link between drugs, hypnosis, and creativity followed, soon to be followed by studies of additional altered and transitional states. Meanwhile, a number of investigators took a skeptical position regarding the importance of divergent thinking in creativity. A number of studies examining the performance of scientists on lateral thinking tests found that highly creative scientists did not use lateral thinking more often than less creative scientists on these tests.

1. Learning from the Past

A seminal research project was undertaken during the 1970s; R. K. Siegel conducted a systematic study of visual images produced by a variety of drugs. He was interested in several dimensions of these visual images, for example, color, movement, action, and such forms as spirals, trellises, tunnels, and webs. Siegel's subjects were trained to use an image classification system prior to the drug sessions. There were baseline and placebo sessions for comparative purposes.

In regard to reported images, the amphetamine (a stimulant) and phenobarbitol (a sedative) sessions did not differ from placebo sessions. However, the sessions with mescaline, LSD, psilocybin, and a synthetic compound based on active ingredients in marijuana produced similar images. In the psychedelic drug sessions, similar complex images did not appear until well after there was a shift to lattice tunnel forms; memory images emerged in the later stages of the appearance of complex imagery.

Noting that hypnagogic and hypnopompic images were accompanied by theta and low-frequency alpha brain waves, other research used biofeedback to teach subjects how to enter these states. There was an expected increase in the subjects' awareness of internal imagery and dream recall. What was unexpected was that most of their subjects reported an increase in "integrative experiences" and "feelings of well-being." These positive changes were amenable to intuition, insight, and creativity.

Several questions on research on hypnosis and creativity remain unanswered because of the absence of robust findings due to methodological differences in the studies, varied hypnotic responsiveness of the subjects, and the fact that creativity has been measured in disparate ways. Even when similar tests are used, they are administered differently, and the tests themselves admittedly assess a single instance or aspect of creativity. It may be that restrictions in awareness increase the priming of associative networks (outside of one's awareness) by reducing cognitive interference. As a result, new associations are made, giving rise to creative insights. Imagination or fantasy provides a continuous backdrop to mentation outside of awareness, and hypnosis may increase its accessibility.

Heart rate probably reflects shifts of attention from external to internal events, making it a potentially revealing way to assess the oscillation of attention from an external focus of concern toward the internal events they trigger, a process which is one aspect of creativity. A significant relationship has been reported between heartbeat rate variability and subjects' creativity scores. More creative persons tended to show higher cardiac variability.

The psychophysiological studies of zen meditators and yogic meditators revealed basic differences: the former group demonstrated "openness" to external stimuli but were not distracted by them; the latter demonstrated "detachment" from external stimuli. Neither group was distracted by the experimenters' clicks, gongs, or lights, but their brain wave recordings showed distinctly diverse patterns. In the light of this diversity, it is important that the type of meditation studied be identified in the assessment of research reports, as well as the length of time the subjects have been meditating. Further, it is common for meditation to blend into sleep during an experiment; hence, the images reported may be the result of hypnagogia and hypnopompia, and not meditation itself.

2. Planning for the Future

Future research might identify the extent to which individual differences in the recall of content from changes in consciousness might relate to instances of insightful creative thought, as well as to individual differences in attention and perceptual organization. Such data could provide a better grasp on the degree to which information processing in altered or transitional states actually constitutes a major source of creative productivity. Mental constructions occurring during an altered or transitional state can be useful only insofar as they are remembered, and insofar as they can be evaluated for application and worthwhileness. It may be that the degree to which decoupled automatic perceptual processes contribute to creative output has far more to do with facility in higher level cognitive processes such as memory storage, retrieval, search, and comparison than in individual differences in the perceptual organization processes themselves.

One common view of why individuals who manifest some of the streams of schizophrenic-like thought might be viewed as creative is that deficiencies in the normal involuntary perceptual organization processes lead to an increased likelihood of an atypical representation of a perceptual event. In other words, it may be the anomalous organization of sensory input coupled with sufficiently appropriate higher order processes to evaluate the potential value of a mental construction that lead to creative output. However, creativity that is attributable to looseness in perceptual organization in the presence of stimuli is very different from creativity that is attributable to perceptual organization processes decoupled from normal sensory inputs.

An increased frequency of transitions from transitional states of consciousness, as might be reasonably expected to occur in association with certain psychotic disorders, combined with unimpaired, or even superior, mechanisms of perceptual organization, thus represents a potential alternative route for contributing to creative thought by those individuals who possess dispositions toward cognitive disorders. Moreover, the relative weakness or looseness in organization processes and the ability to exploit involuntary organizational processes decoupled from sensory input may be distinct individual difference variables, both of which might relate to creativity in the general population.

In regard to the general population, "everyday creativity" is an overlooked phenomenon in a field which all too often emphasizes the exotic, the dramatic, and the spectacular. It is quite likely that creative work draws more upon the ordinary waking state with its intact subsystems of consciousness than upon altered and transitional states. Drugs can be ingested, meditation can be practiced, hypnosis can be utilized, and the contents of reverie can be recorded, but everyday behaviors and experiences can also provide inspiration for what later may become a novel approach to a long-delayed home repair, an improved golf stroke, a new recipe for a family dinner, a breakthrough in a troubled relationship, an ingenious logistical plan to divert restaurant leftovers to homeless people, a challenging educational technology, or any one of many other achievements. The need for creative approaches at all social levels has never been greater; their development and application need to reflect the concepts of "origin" and "to make," which so appropriately grounded the Latin word *creare*. [*See* EVERYDAY CREATIVITY.]

Bibliography

Battista, J. R. (1978). The science of consciousness. In K. S. Pope and J. L. Singer (Eds.), *The stream of consciousness: Scientific investigations into the flow of human experience* (pp. 55–90). New York: Plenum Press.

Csikszentmihalyi, M. (1996). *Creativity: Flow and the psychology of discovery and invention*. New York: Harper Collins.

Janinger, O., & Dobkin De Rios, M. (1989). LSD and creativity. *Journal of Psychoactive Drugs, 21,* 129–134.

Krippner, S. (1996). Cross-cultural perspectives on creative behavior and the use of psychedelics. In M. Winkelman & W. Andritzky (Eds.), *Yearbook of cross-cultural medicine and psychotherapy 1995: Sacred plants, consciousness, and healing* (pp. 91–107). Berlin: Verlag fur Wissenschaft und Bildung.

Krippner, S., & Dillard, J. (1988). *Dreamworking: How to use your dreams for creative problem-solving*. Buffalo, NY: Bearly.

Mavromatis, A. (1987). *Hypnagogia: The unique state of consciousness between wakefulness and sleep*. London: Routledge & Kegan Paul.

Murphy, M., & Donovan, S. (1988). *The physical and psychological effects of meditation*. Oakland, CA: Esalen Institute/ Dharma Enterprises.

Natsoulas, T. (1983). Concepts of consciousness. *Journal of Mind and Behavior, 4,* 13–59.

Rhue, J. W., Lynn, S. J., & Kirsch, I. (Eds.). (1993). *Handbook of clinical hypnosis* (pp. 691–717). Washington, DC: American Psychological Association.

Oxman, T. E., Rosenberg, S. D., Schnurr, P. P., Tucker, G. J., & Gala, G. (1988). The language of altered states. *Journal of Nervous and Mental Disease, 176,* 401–408.

Pekala, R. (1991). *Quantifying consciousness: An empirical approach*. New York: Plenum Press.

Shames, V. A., & Bowers, P. G. (1992). Hypnosis and creativity. In E. Fromm & M. R. Nash (Eds.), *Contemporary hypnosis research* (pp. 334–363). New York: Guilford.

Siegel, R. K. (1977). Hallucinations. *Scientific American, 237*(4), 132–140.

Singer, J. L. (1966). *Daydreaming*. New York: Random House.

Tart, C. T. (1975). *States of consciousness*. New York: Dutton.

Analogies

Michael D. Mumford

American Institutes for Research

Paige P. Porter

AON Consulting

Analogies A mapping of similarity or relationships between two or more phenomena.

Base A prior problem-solving experience used to understand a new problem.

Categories A concept or schema capturing an organized body of information about a class of objects.

Combination and Reorganization A process by which existing concepts are restructured to create the new understandings needed to solve novel problems.

Exemplar A member or illustration of a category.

Features General principles or properties that can be used to describe members of a category.

Mental Models A category or schema describing how a set of objects and variables operate as a causal system.

Metaphors Higher order features involving inferences about what a feature might represent.

Representations Cases abstracted from prior experiences to solve problems.

Target A new problem solved by using a base problem.

An analogy, in its simplest form, involves making a statement about the similarity, or relationships, linking two objects. The nature of ANALOGIES is aptly illustrated by the analogical reasoning problems we encounter on standardized tests; for example, "furnace is to house as engine is to car." Traditionally, analogical reasoning has not been seen as a key component of creative thought. With the growing awareness that creative thought depends on the combination and reorganization of extant knowledge structures, however, many scholars have come to believe that analogical reasoning may lay a foundation for creative thought across a wide range of endeavors. With this point in mind, we begin this article by examining the role of combination and reorganization in creative thought. Subsequently, we examine how analogical reasoning contributes to combination and reorganization, and how these reasoning skills are applied in "real-world" creative efforts.

I. COMBINATION AND REORGANIZATION

It is impossible for people to create new ideas out of the air. Thus, the basis for new ideas must be the

Copyright © 1999 by Academic Press
All rights of reproduction in any form reserved.

person's knowledge, experience, or expertise working with problems in a given domain. Certainly, the available evidence indicates that knowledge, particularly the complex, multifaceted, principle-based knowledge structures characteristic of experts, as opposed to novices, represent a necessary foundation for creative achievement.

While few would dispute the need for knowledge in creative work, this rather straightforward observation poses an important, perhaps fundamental, question that must be addressed in any attempt to account for creative thought: Exactly how do people use extant knowledge to create something new?

Over the years, this question has perplexed scholars, who have proposed a host of answers ranging from the notion of divergent thinking to the idea that creative thought might be based on remote associations. Certainly, many of these theories capture a grain of truth about certain aspects of the creative process. For example, divergent thinking may play a role in idea generation. By the same token, however, it is unclear how any of these mechanisms can give rise to the new concepts, or new understandings, that are the basis for creative thought. As a result, in recent years scholars have begun to focus on the combination and reorganization process as the key to creative thought. [*See* DIVERGENT THINKING.]

The assumption underlying the combination and reorganization model is that knowledge itself is not static. Instead, people create new knowledge by actively, consciously manipulating existing categories or concepts. When extant knowledge structures are combined, the new knowledge which results may allow people to identify new emergent features, properties, or principles. Along similar lines, by reorganizing the exemplars of a category, people may be able to reformulate knowledge in such a way as to identify new principles or relationships. In fact, studies of notables in the arts and sciences provide some support for this proposition. A classic example may be found in Gutenberg's development of the printing press, which was based on his observations of the wine press. Along similar lines, the computer has been used as an analogy by cognitive psychologists attempting to understand human cognition.

Recent efforts have tried to provide formal, experimental proof for this proposition. For example, one study developed a conceptual combination task where people were presented with mechanical parts and asked to combine these parts to create a useful new tool. The request to combine parts not only resulted in some creative new tools, but participants also identified new properties and new features which provided the basis for new ideas.

Another study asked people to solve a series of category combination or synthesis problems. People were presented with three standard categories (e.g., bicycle parts, sporting equipment, and sporting activities) defined in terms of four category exemplars (e.g., seat, tire, brakes, and wheel). They were then asked to combine these categories to create a new category that incorporated the relevant exemplars, provide a label for the new category, list additional exemplars of the new category, and list the major features of the new category. When judges were asked to rate the quality and originality of these three products, it was found that the quality and originality of these category combinations produced correlations between .40 and .50, with performance on two kinds of problem-solving tasks— one where people were asked to solve novel management and public policy problems, and one where people were asked to devise advertising campaigns for a new product, the 3D holographic television.

II. ANALOGIES

Taken as a whole, these studies, along with a number of other related investigations, have provided compelling evidence that combination and reorganization may represent the major process giving rise to the new ideas and new understandings that are the hallmark of creative thought. This conclusion, however noteworthy, poses a deeper, somewhat more subtle question. What cognitive operations allow people to combine and reorganize extant knowledge structures to create new ideas and new understandings? One plausible answer to this question may be found in recent work on analogical reasoning.

Studies of analogical reasoning have focused on how people use existing knowledge to draw inferences about new situations. In other words, a prior problem, the base problem, is used to draw inferences about a new problem, the target problem. Essentially, then, analogies promote the transfer of knowledge from prior experience to new situations through an assessment of the relevance of past experience to the target problem.

As a result, analogies depend on an initial assessment of similarity between the base and target problems. One way people appraise similarity between the base and the target is through overt similarity in the physical features of the problem. Both problems, for example, might involve stacking boxes. Indeed, the available evidence indicates that people use overt similarities to identify applicable analogies, particularly when they lack experience within a domain. As people acquire experience with exposure to multiple problems of a certain type, overt, physical congruence becomes a less powerful influence on similarity assessment. Instead, people begin to abstract principles, or features, that characterize the examples making up a concept, and they apply these features, along with prototypic exemplars, in assessing similarity.

Of course, identifying an analog from past experience is just the first step. People must use this experience to formulate a solution to the target problem. A number of models have been proposed to describe the mechanisms used to map relationships from the base problem to the target problem. Broadly speaking, these models assume a three-step process. First, people begin by identifying similar or related elements, or features, applying to both the base and target problems. Second, these linked elements are used to identify subsets of connections between the base and target. Third, these subsets of connected elements are used to construct an integrated explanatory structure that may be used to draw inferences and formulate a problem solution.

This general conception of analogies allows for many possible explanatory structures because analogies are constructed ad hoc, or "on the fly." Individuals might identify different subsets of connections and organize those subsets in different ways. Thus, one might ask how people consistently arrive at similar solutions to analogy problems. The emergence of consistent, coherent explanatory systems may be traced to the use of constraints. These constraints may involve preferred relational mappings (positive constraints) and/or implausible mappings (negative constraints). For example, "fear" would be related to "enemies," not "friends." Constraints are used to eliminate inconsistent or in-

appropriate connections, and identify appropriate connections, as people create explanatory systems. Some constraints may arise from the internal structure of the exemplars and principles involved in a problem. Other constraints, however, may be externally imposed by the goals, purpose, and solution requirements framing the problem situation.

This description of how people reshape past experience to create the explanatory systems used in solving analogies has a number of noteworthy implications. To begin with, analogical reasoning is an active, dynamic, conscious process where people seek coherent mappings which allow them to draw relational inferences. One implication of this statement is that processing load and the likely success of people's efforts will depend on the nature of the concepts involved, the relationships linking those concepts, and the clarity of relevant constraints. Another implication is that analogical reasoning will become more difficult as the base and target problems become more diverse, and fewer relationships among exemplars and features can be identified. Finally, with experience, and the accompanying increase in principle-based relationships, along with the imposition of multiple constraints, or structural requirements, it becomes easier for people to formulate viable relational structures.

Although analogical thought involves the active construction of coherent relational mappings, the nature of these mappings may be influenced by a host of other considerations. Clearly, the nature of these mappings will depend on the characteristics of the concepts, or categories, under consideration. Thus, available exemplars, particularly prototypic, or typical, exemplars, will have a strong influence on the nature of the resulting mapping. Along similar lines, salient, typical features used in organizing these prototypic exemplars may play a key role in analogical mappings, structuring constraints and imposing a host of given relational linkages.

In addition to the exemplars and features embedded in relevant concepts, the kind of relational mapping people construct will be influenced by the type of relationships being applied. One must remember that relational statements can be formulated using a number of different frameworks. For example, one can construct relational statements based on cause, purpose, time, common principles, and shared attributes, to mention only a few plausible frameworks for identifying relationships. These different types of relational frameworks will, in turn, influence the nature of the resulting relational mappings, and thus the kind of solutions people generate.

Along related lines, it should be recognized that relationships are organized in hierarchical networks. Thus, relational mappings can be constructed at different levels of abstraction. People may, as a result, use broader, more abstract principles to form relational mappings. In fact, metaphors represent a case in point, where the higher order implications of a category (e.g., birds) are used to identify relationships (e.g., birds fly, and flight represents freedom). These higher order, more abstract relational mappings may provide a particularly useful way of identifying viable relationships when people must work with diverse concepts. [*See* METAPHORS.]

III. ANALOGIES AND COMBINATION AND REORGANIZATION

Our foregoing observations suggest that analogical thinking, or the construction of new relational mappings, might represent the key mechanism underlying the generation of new understandings in combination and reorganization. A number of recent efforts have examined the feasibility of applying models of analogical thinking in understanding the combination and reorganization process. These studies have served not only to support the notion that analogical reasoning plays a role in combination and reorganization, they have also provided us with a new understanding of the combination and reorganization process.

One such study asked undergraduates to work on 12 category combination problems. People were asked to combine the three categories presented to create a new category. The instructions given to subjects varied so that people were asked to work through these problems in different ways. Depending on the condition, people were asked to identify typical or atypical features of the stimulus categories, identify common or noncommon features of the categories, and (to induce active elaboration) list or not list additional features of the new category they proposed. The resulting category labels and exemplars were rated for quality and originality by five judges.

In accordance with the notion that analogical thinking provides a foundation for successful combination and reorganization, it was found that these instructional manipulations contributed to the quality and originality of the products. Mapping shared atypical features, exerted the strongest effects on solution quality and originality. Apparently, successful combination and reorganization efforts call for active mapping of unusual features along with constraints that prohibit production of mundane solutions. However, the production of high-quality original products appeared to depend on subsequent elaboration, or exploration and refinement, of the resulting new ideas.

Not only do those findings point to the importance of analogical mechanisms in creative thought, they indicate that specific types of relational mappings contribute to creativity—more specifically, mappings that focus on shared atypical features while avoiding mundane commonalties. However, these effects hold only for relatively more similar categories, suggesting that different mechanisms may be involved when people are asked to combine highly diverse categories that have few, if any, concrete features in common.

When categories lack common features, successful combination and reorganization efforts may depend on use of metaphors, or higher order relationships, in mapping. A later study amended the instructions presented to undergraduates to encourage a search for metaphors (e.g., flight represents freedom) after identifying the more concrete features that might be used to describe category members (e.g., birds fly). It was found that instructions encouraging the use of metaphors indeed contributed to creative thought when people were asked to work with diverse categories. Thus, different types of relationships may be used in mapping, and the kind of relationships that prove most useful in constructing coherent relational systems will depend on the type of categories, or concepts, under consideration and their possible relationships.

Although these studies provide some compelling support for the importance of relational mapping in creative thought, they do not address what is, perhaps, the single most important outcome of these relational construction mechanisms. In constructing these new relational systems, new features or principles may emerge as exemplars, or category members, and are analyzed in new ways in a new system of relationships. These new features may, in turn, give rise to new ideas or new understandings.

In fact, some support for this proposition came from a study that asked people to combine a set of mechanical parts to create a new tool. They found that in combining these parts, new features emerged which provided a basis for generating new ideas about how these tools might be applied. Those effects, of course, are especially likely to occur when people actively search for coherences, attempt to account for anomalies in relevant exemplars, and try to identify features accounting for diverse exemplars and their interrelationships.

IV. APPLYING ANALOGIES

To this point, we have focused on the evidence indicating that relational mappings, at least certain types of relational mappings, can contribute to the generation of new understandings and new ideas in the combination and reorganization of extant knowledge structures. Although there appears to be some tangible support for the proposition, these experimental studies do not necessarily tell us a great deal about how relational mappings are applied in "real-world" creative efforts. Accordingly, in the following section we will consider some of what is known about how analogical mechanisms are applied in creative efforts.

Relatively few studies have examined how analogies are actually used in creative work. One notable exception, however, may be found in a study of productivity in microbiology laboratories. Using participant observation techniques, scientists were examined while applying analogical reasoning mechanisms to their research programs. Scientists were far more likely to apply near analogies, as opposed to more distant analogies, and the use of multiple, alternative near term analogies appeared to be related to scientific productivity.

These findings are noteworthy in part because they remind us of an important characteristic of analogies as they are applied in "real-world" creative efforts. More specifically, creative new ideas must be developed and applied within the context of given technologies, an existing zeitgeist, and available knowledge about the nature of the phenomenon at hand. As a result, near term, as opposed to more distant, analogies are more likely to provide a basis for generating the kind of workable new ideas that are required for effective, practical innovation. More distant analogies may prove less useful in generating workable new ideas. Nonetheless, these more distant, less direct analogies may still prove useful in highlighting key principles and issues or in defining the nature of the problem.

Those observations about the use of near analogies, as opposed to distant analogies, point to another issue of concern. More specifically, most significant creative efforts represent solutions to highly complex problems—problems that include a host of relationships, multiple restrictions, and a number of different types of knowledge. As a result, the construction of viable mappings and useful new relational systems will be an unusually demanding activity calling for substantial cognitive resources over long periods of time. Moreover, in grappling with multiple potential relationships, and a variety of sometimes contradictory constraints, one cannot expect that coherent solutions will appear immediately. Instead, multiple integrations of relational mappings will be built up over time, with these mappings, and their coherence, improving as a function of ongoing elaboration and extensions to related phenomena. This pattern of progressive refinement and extension seems to characterize creative efforts across the arts and sciences as witnessed by the efforts of both Darwin and Monet.

When considering those observations about the use of analogical mechanisms in creative work, one must bear in mind a notable proviso. Quite often, creative thought and the development of new ideas do not seem to involve this extended progressive refinement of initial relational mappings. Instead, ideas seem to emerge almost by magic without any real explanation for their development. In many cases, however, the generation of viable understandings resulting in workable innovations may not call for the construction of fundamentally new relational mappings. Instead, the accommodation, or incorporation, of new exemplars into existing structures may result in significant rearrangements of relationships, changes in constraints, and the emergence of new features or new principles. All of these changes in relational mappings may give rise to new ideas through the reorganization of existing relational structures. In fact, the available evidence indicates that the reorganization of extant relational maps may play a crucial role in creativity in fields ranging from design and engineering to business management. [*See* BUSINESS STRATEGY; DESIGN.]

In discussion of analogical mappings and their role in creative thought, psychologists tend to focus on the mechanisms giving rise to changes in these relational structures. Put more simply, we tend to focus on inferences about the target problem, forgetting the point that ultimately those inferences depend on the base problem used as a starting point. This comment is noteworthy because it suggests that creative efforts may depend as much on the cases, or mental models, initially used to understand the problem as attempts to construct coherent, new relational mappings. One example that tends to support this proposition may be found in the development of the telephone. Bell's success vis-à-vis Edison can be traced to the use of a more appropriate initial base model—the ear rather than the telegraph.

Of course, this example illustrates the potential importance of case-based reasoning, the use of available base solutions, as a tool for creative work. One point that immediately comes to the fore when examining studies of case-based reasoning is that creative thought is likely to benefit from the availability of a diverse body of cases applicable to the problem at hand. It is not enough, however, simply to have a number of cases available. Successful creative effort requires that cases be carefully selected for relevance to the problem. These cases, moreover, must be applied flexibly, being used as a tool for discovering relationships rather than as a tool that simply ensures the repetition of past experience.

The importance of the base problems, or cases, used to construct relational mappings has a number of subtle implications for creative efforts in the "real world." One implication pertains to the effects of context on people's creative efforts. Any case will, as a form of experience, be associated with a host of situational cues. These cues will, of course, vary in salience from time to time and setting to setting. As a result, at different times, people will tend to produce different ideas because changes in the situation will activate different clues. These changes in cues, in turn, bring to the fore different cases to be applied in mapping relationships. However, not all cues may be equally useful. For example, it has been shown that providing examples of prior unsuccessful decisions may make it virtually impossible for engineers to solve certain design problems.

Another implication of this observation pertains to a key characteristic of highly creative people. Typically, highly creative people not only have substantial expertise, they also have experience working in several related domains. This kind of background would, of course, provide a wider range of base cases for use in relational mapping. This more diverse set of base cases represents a source of alternative features as well as a set of alternative relationships and relational constraints. The availability of this material should, in turn, encourage generation of relational mappings based on shared atypical features. As noted earlier, use of this kind of material represents a particularly useful strategy when combining and reorganizing extant knowledge structures to generate new understandings and new ideas. [*See* DOMAINS OF CREATIVITY; EXPERTISE.]

V. CONCLUSIONS

The preceding discussion has, for the most part, focused on the role of analogical thinking, relational mapping, in the combination and reorganization process. The combination and reorganization process is ultimately the source of the new understandings that are the basis of creative thought. The relational mappings characteristic of analogical thinking provide the key mechanisms underlying the combination and reorganization process. By the same token, however, it should be recognized that creative thought involves a number of processes, such as problem construction, information encoding, and idea generation. Analogical thinking may also play an important role in the execution of some of these processes.

For example, the available evidence indicates that the identification of anomalous observations is of some importance during information encoding. Analogies, in particular broad mental models specifying expected relationships and relevant information, may serve as a framework for identifying these anomalies by establishing baseline, a priori expectations. Along similar lines, idea evaluation involves an assessment of workability, or viability, of potential ideas. Here, cases drawn from past experience can be used as a basis for projecting downstream consequences and assessing the likely outcomes, both good and bad, of pursuing a potential new idea. These, and a number of other applications of relational mappings, should be borne in mind in further studies intended to articulate the role of analogical thinking on people's creative efforts.

Although these issues warrant consideration in future work, the evidence accrued to date clearly indicates that analogical thinking is an essential requirement for successful combination and reorganization efforts. The evidence examined in this article indicates that relational mapping is necessary for the generation of new understandings in combination and reorganization. Moreover, in creating coherent new relational maps, new features and new structures may emerge that have far-ranging implications. In this regard, however, it is important to bear in mind a point made earlier. The kind of relational mappings that contribute to the creation of new knowledge structures (e.g., mapping shared atypical features) may not be identical to those called for in more routine analogical thinking. Thus, further work is needed examining the unique ways relational mappings are applied in generating new understandings.

Even bearing this caveat in mind, we believe that current work in analogical reasoning has much to say about creative thought and how we can go about improving people's creative thinking skills. One simple illustration may be found in feature mapping, a technique long used to stimulate creative thought in applied settings. Studies of analogical thinking, however, suggest a number of other, somewhat more novel approaches that might be used to enhance creative thought. One might, for example, encourage people to take into account atypical, or anomalous, exemplars as they try to create viable new relational mappings. Alternatively, one might encourage people to select a range of cases before starting work on problems, stressing the need to draw relationships from multiple cases. Thus current work on analogical thought suggests a host of promising new techniques that might be used to enhance creative thought.

Bibliography

Baughman, W. A., & Mumford, M. D. (1995). Process analytic models of creative capacities: Operations influencing the combination and reorganization process. *Creativity Research Journal, 8*(1), 37–62.

Carlson, W. B., & Gorman, M. E. (1992). A cognitive framework to understand technological creativity: Bell, Edison, and the telephone. In J. J. Weber & D. N. Perkins (Eds.), *Inventive minds: Creativity in technology* (pp. 48–79). New York: Oxford University Press.

Dunbar, F. (1995). How scientists really reason: Scientific reasoning in microbiological laboratories. In R. J. Sternberg & J. E. Davidson (Eds.), *The nature of insight* (pp. 316–345). Cambridge, MA: MIT Press.

Erickson, K. A., & Charness, W. (1984). Expert performance: Its structure and acquisition. *American Psychologist, 49,* 725–747.

Finke, R. A., Ward, T. B., & Smith, S. M. (1992). *Creative cognition: Theory, research and applications.* Cambridge, MA: MIT Press.

Gentner, D. (1989). The mechanisms of analogical learning. In S. Vosniadov & A. Ortney (Eds.), *Similarity and analogical reasoning* (pp. 199–241). London: Cambridge University Press.

Gentner, D., & Markham, A. B. (1997). Structure mapping in analogy and similarity. *American Psychologist, 52*(1), 45–56.

Holyoak, K. J., & Thagard, P. (1997). The analogical mind. *American Psychologist, 52*(1), 35–44.

Kolodner, J. (1993). *Case-based reasoning.* San Mateo, CA: Morgan Kaufman.

Architecture, Modern Western

Stephanie Z. Dudek

University of Montreal

Eclecticism Not following any one system, but selecting and using what are considered the best elements of all systems.

Functionalism Emphasis on purpose, practical utility, or adaptiveness; advocating the design of buildings and furnishings as a direct fulfillment of material requirements; architecture stripped of all ornamentation so that structure expresses the building's function and purpose.

Humanist Architecture Humanizes inanimate forms to emphasize the dignity and worth of the individual.

Mannerist The unrealistic treatment of space often in exaggerated postures, plastically rendered, with melodramatic effect.

Modernity Pertaining to or characteristic of contemporary styles that reject traditionally accepted or sanctioned forms and emphasize individual experimentation and sensibility; characterized by the progress of reason toward a social end; expresses the consciousness of an epoch that relates itself to the past in order to view itself as the result of the transition from the old to the new; modernity rebels against traditional doctrine.

Pluralism Stylistic variety; celebration of difference; otherness; irreducible heterogeneity.

Postmodernism Characterized by parody, nostalgia, pastiche, divergent signification, radical eclecticism, double-coding. The emphasis is purely on technique, pure scenography. Taste for disjunctions and collisions.

MODERN ARCHITECTURE, *as it manifested itself through what came to be called "The International Style," was officially launched by the Weimar School, later to be known as the Bauhaus School, under Walter Gropius (1883–1969) in 1919. It had a coherent ideology, a strong body of ideas about the discipline of architecture, a masterly grasp of a new design philosophy, and a clear statement of its social functions. "Form follows function" was its logo.*

The new design principles that the International Style championed can be reduced to four: (1) Emphasis on volume came to replace mass in building design, (2) reg-

Copyright © 1999 by Academic Press
All rights of reproduction in any form reserved.

ularity and not axial symmetry became the ordering device, (3) the visual focus was on surface articulation rather than decoration, and (4) arbitrary decoration was proscribed. The International Style had order in mind and led to a radical reform of the organization of the building industry.

Between 1920 and 1940 corporate capital and the International Style played a formative role in creating modern architecture. Large studios carried out the job of building, creating a new world adaptable to commercial exploitation. Modernism was dominant but pluralism, an arena where vested interests thrive, had established its supremacy. In this way the early commitment to progressive social change was subverted as the agenda moved to the creation of life style neighborhoods for the wealthy. The Postmodernists were haunted by the past and attempted to include past styles into modern buildings.

As the 20th century approaches its end, the complex, fragmentary nature of the building forms reflects the alienation of a sophisticated society. The users of the built forms are not sufficiently involved in the creation of their environment.

In Greek, the word "architect" stands for builder. *Webster's* dictionary definition of architecture is the art and science of building

At one time architecture meant building a shelter against the sun, wind, and rain. Survivors of the Ice Age sheltered in caves until they learned to build huts out of branches and the bones of mammoths. The first permanent settlements appeared circa 8000 B.C. as mud-brick villages in Asia Minor, but it was circa 3500 that cities began to appear with populations of several thousand. The ziggurat is the best known of the Sumerian building types. Its construction is reported as being extremely precise.

I. DEFINITIONS OF ARCHITECTURE

Vitruvius (Roman, 1st century A.D.) is said to have influenced every theorist of architecture since his time. He maintained that good architecture is always characterized by *firmitas* (structural soundness), *utilitas* (function), and *venustas* (delight). These aims, in one guise or another, have never been replaced.

Augustus Welby Pugin (1812–1852) believed that there should be no features about a building that are not necessary for convenience, connotation, or propriety. The smallest detail should serve a purpose, and construction itself should vary with the materials employed.

Batteux in 1747 and Pugin in 1841 clearly stated that architecture is not a spectacle but a service. It was understood that nothing ought to appear in a building which does not truthfully fulfill its function.

An architect must also ensure that the proposed building fits into and enhances the existing context and that it be a positive addition.

These ideals have continued on, but what distinguishes architecture in the 20th century is the new sense of space and the machine aesthetic. The 20th century has placed considerable emphasis on space as a positive architectural quality, thus giving it a new importance and interest. To Le Corbusier (French, 1887–1965), architecture was "the masterly, correct and magnificent play of masses seen in light." To Louis Kahn (American, 1901–1974), architecture was what nature could not make. (However, certain blind termites "build" soaring arches of mud, and the chambered nautilus "builds" a house of calcium carbonate around himself—architecture, then, may be also an instinctual art.)

For Mies Van der Rohe (1886–1969), architecture was the will of the epoch translated into spatial terms. It reveals a history of the "slow unfolding of form." The architect's goal was to make a satisfying shape. His own architecture was more concerned with getting the geometrical essences right than creating a well-functioning building.

Nicholas Pevsner (1902–1966), in *An Outline of European History,* maintained that the term "architecture" applies only to buildings with a view to aesthetic appeal. For him, architecture was a nonverbal form of communication, a mute record of the culture that produced it and a dialogue with the past. He added that the story of architecture is primarily a history of man shaping space.

The current definition of architecture is to see it as the science of building, a functional practice and a significant art.

Modernization has added few new basic building types to those that arose from the needs in Neolithic time because houses necessarily respond to the particular problems and concerns of climate, security, privacy, lighting, decoration, communication, and location. These have always been important factors and will always and by necessity affect architectural style.

Economic concerns recommend 90% utilitarian and 10% aesthetic allocation of economic resources to the building process, although in the case of monuments such as churches the prescription may be reversed. The methods and materials of construction are generally limited by the building codes of the territory. According to Adolf Loos (Austrian, 1870–1933), a notable figure in early 20th century architecture, only a small part of architecture belongs to art, namely, the tomb and the monument—and these are in fact the beginnings of the art of architecture.

According to Vincent Scully (American architectural historian), the radical difference between 20th century architecture and that of previous times began in the middle of the 18th century, marking the end of a humanist architecture and the beginnings of one concerned primarily with economic returns. The concern of early 20th century architects for progressive social change has been subordinated in the late 20th century to the clients' need to demonstrate wealth and political power.

II. GENERAL CONSIDERATIONS: ENVIRONMENT AND IDENTITY

If we begin with the premise that the body is the model according to which we construct our world, we see extensions of ourselves everywhere. The first technological revolutions, that is, tools and the wheel, extended our arms and legs (later we acquired wings); the telescope and microscope extended our eyes; the telephone and radio extended our ears; and most recently the electronic revolution extended the brain and vaulted us into outer space. The world is replete with objects that were fashioned in imitation of bodily functions. If we do not recognize them consciously, we nevertheless perceive them intuitively as outer parts of ourselves—our extended identity.

The house can be identified with the human body—windows for eyes, mouth for door, and rooms for private internal spaces. It has a front and a back. The decor within it reflects personal aspects of the self. The house can be beautiful or ugly, plain or decorated, slim

or bulky, tall or squat, open or defensive, warm or cold, etc. We tend to avoid shabby environments because they make us feel shabby; gaudy ones make us feel cheap. When people lived in the country, the body was extended into space, and the identity of the home was that much more important in order to keep people grounded.

III. GENERAL CONSIDERATIONS: SIGNIFICATION, OR WHAT DO BUILDINGS COMMUNICATE?

We are led to believe that well-built small buildings offer a sense of intimacy, place, home, ownership, and identity. On the other hand, large monuments offer a sense of grandeur but dwarf the human by their size and importance. While the first reaffirms our common humanity, the second allows us to recognize our innate capacity to transcend it. The splendor of the building materials—their beauty, sensuality, opulence, or brute force—may evoke a receptive or a discordant response. The ingenuity, virtuosity, daring, or disarticulation of the forms can be either stimulating or confusing.

IV. THE BEGINNINGS OF MODERN ARCHITECTURE

During the 19th century, the availability of structural cast iron resulted in its use in the construction of arched cast-iron bridges. Iron came into use also for buildings such as railway stations, clock towers, and train sheds. The culmination of cast-iron technology was Joseph Paxton's Crystal Palace (London, 1851), prefabricated in sections off-site. It became famous for its elegance and great size with a ground plan of 125×560 m and an elevation of 22 m. The use of wrought iron soon became common, and although the structural masterpieces of the industrial age were dazzling, they were almost empty of content (e.g., the Eiffel Tower). In the United States, traditional forms were discarded and new forms began to emerge reflecting the greater freedom of design provided by the use of a structural steel frame.

With the industrial revolution it had become clear that the modern age must project a style of its own.

In that sense, the simple, vernacular architecture of Charles Rennie MacIntosh (English, 1869–1928) was a clear reaction against 19th century Romanticism. It provided perhaps the first step toward a new approach in the manipulation of space.

The modern world, as it came to be known, began with World War I and its aftermath. Most of the West had industrialized and Russia had virtually moved from the past into the future. There was a belief among architects that the new materials and new techniques could bring new architectural solutions to cities, thus ending the squalor and the overcrowding that had characterized them. From 1917 to 1932 Russian artists and architects were free to experiment and art and architecture began to flourish. European Marxists looked to Russia for examples of new beginnings. The new beginnings, however, emerged at the Bauhaus in Weimar Germany.

The architects who have made spectacular contributions to the language of architecture in the first half of the 20th century are Alvar Alto, Reyner Banham, Le Corbusier, Buckminster Fuller, Walter Gropius, Philip Johnson, Louis Kahn, Ludwig Mies van der Rohe, Aldo Rossi, James Stirling, Louis Sullivan, Oswald Mattias Ungers, and Frank Lloyd Wright, to mention but a few. The architects of the last half of the century have faced quite different problems.

V. THE EMERGENCE OF THE INTERNATIONAL STYLE

Modern architecture, as it manifested itself through what came to be called the "International Style," was officially launched by the Weimar School, later to be known as the Bauhaus School, under Walter Gropius (1883–1969) in 1919. It had a coherent ideology, a strong body of ideas about the discipline of architecture, a masterly grasp of a new design philosophy, and a clear statement of its social functions. It was utopic, purist, idealist, and elitist. Its guiding principles were reason and logic. "Form follows function" was its logo. It had a brilliant group of spokesmen at the head— Walter Gropius and Mies Van der Rohe (1896–1969) in Germany, Jacobus Oud in the Netherlands, and Le Corbusier (1887–1966) in France. Philip Johnson (b. 1906) was responsible for its American evolution.

They were committed to the idealist tradition and were determined to offer a new vision of the social order. Modern architecture thus had both a physical locus and a center for the dissemination of ideas. Architecture was meant to crystallize the public realm, to foster long-term social goals, and to emphasize social meanings. It was political to the extent that architects were perceived to be an integral part of the public realm and should participate in decisions that state and government bodies arrive at, such as urban planning, the construction of public buildings, and the planning and construction of transportation systems.

Modern architecture had found both a clear conception of itself as a discipline and an image of its new role in society. If the International Style had done nothing more, it had already performed a great service by outlining a clear new image of the art of architecture.

The new design principles that the International Style championed can be reduced to four: (1) Emphasis on volume came to replace mass in building design. (2) Regularity and not axial symmetry became the ordering device. (3) The visual focus was on surface articulation rather than decoration. (4) Arbitrary decoration was proscribed. The goals and principles of the International Style were wedded to the first machine age aesthetic: the emphasis was on logic, technology, circulation, mechanical equipment, mechanical control, and above all mechanical structure. The design principles were logic and function; the social principle was that these design principles would lead to a new social order.

From the viewpoint of history at the end of the 20th century, it is clear that neither the clarity of its design principles, nor its functionalist and utopian philosophy, nor the rebellious temper of the times would have been enough to forge modern architecture into a truly International Style of building if technology and corporate capital had not been moving in the direction of mass production and had not been searching for more economical modes of construction and larger markets. New advances in engineering and in construction materials, the need for large-scale planning, and the constraining nature of machine age aesthetics (i.e., the geometry of the straight line and the right angle) dictated to a large extent the formal aesthetics of the International Style. However, the true catalyst for their use was the availability of capital.

In retrospect, it is clear that between 1920 and 1940 the International Style played a formative role in the evolution of all aspects of modern architecture. Specialized journals, publications, and conferences for the exchange of ideas brought concepts of modern architecture to a vast public. The International Congress of Modern Architecture (CIAM) was organized in 1928. CIAM discussed methods of construction that might be used in the organization of an entire city, and was instrumental in developing models for urban planning and administration. The Athens Charter, published in 1943 as a result of a meeting in 1933, established the predominant ideology of modern architecture.

The growth and expansion of the International Style into all the corners of the world is now ancient history. By the end of the 1950s the International Style had been universally appropriated and absorbed and was ready to be replaced by something new. Nevertheless, when Le Corbusier's Chapel of Ronchamps (1950–1955) was completed, his action was considered to be a sign of the "Crisis of Rationalism" and he was regarded as a traitor to the modern movement.

"Team 10," a group formed in 1956 to compete with CIAM, attacked functionalism. Calling for a new humanism, it directly challenged the CIAM old guard. As architectural critics and historians Manfredo Tafuri and Francesco Dal Co point out,

> The results of so much navigation in utopian waters remain limited to mere fragments which only marginally affect the global set-up. . . . A true and proper "architecture of bureaucracy" settled in everywhere, in Europe and America as well as in Asia. It was a matter of facilitating architectural designing for a vastly greater demand. . . . Symbols of efficiency, and a willingness to bow to the imperative of organization, the steel and glass sky scrapers speak of an inescapable collective destiny . . . glass phantasms populating the urban panorama from Boston to Tokyo and Johannesburg, from Montreal to Berlin and Stockholm.

The profession as a whole had been reorganized in order to reduce the time allotted to planning and building, as well as to achieve the typological standardization that an industrialized building industry demands. Not individual architects but large studios carried out their jobs according to assembly line standards. The common and easily assimilated language of the International Style had merely produced forms adaptable to commercial exploitation and the laws of the real estate market. It was clear that modernism was dominant in form but dead in spirit. Pluralism had established its supremacy.

VI. PLURALISM

Norman Foster defined pluralism as a "situation that grants a kind of equivalence; art of many sorts is made to seem more or less equal—equally (un)important." Art becomes an arena not of dialectical dialogue but of vested interests. This is even more true of the art of architecture in the latter part of the 20th century. The typical late 20th century artist-architect is "foot loose in time, culture and metaphor," with no concept of absolute criteria and values in response to the demand for creative as well as utilitarian products. In an anything-goes-society, both personal and collective identity are in jeopardy.

Many forces have contributed to the ascendance of pluralism in the field of architecture, including the fact that mass production and mass repetition, which were the once unmistakable foundations of modern architecture, have given way to more sophisticated modes of production leading to the emergence of a greater variety of personalized styles and products. By the 1950s the sense of security and order that the International Style had achieved as its "look," and which was already codified by the 1920s, had been totally undermined. The emerging new styles projected images of complexity, contradiction, and a virtuosity of dizzying proportions which could only threaten all previous identities and loyalties. Modern architecture and society had to face the fact that the utopian mission of the International Style had failed, that the rational, well-designed urban environment was not well organized and certainly not humane, and that it offered no sense of intimacy or well-being. The ideological force and moral convictions about the social good that had characterized the International Style as an identity-forming body had not been reflected in its constructions, and in its late period, the style had become preoccupied not with substance but with pure form as in the work of Peter Eisenman and Robert A. M. Stern, and in the late work of Mies Van der Rohe. By the 1950s, the sense of security and order that architecture is meant to project had become separated from function and from relevance to the world as lived. It had become clear that the machine aesthetic could not build a humane environment.

In rejecting modernism, the later 20th century architects rejected more than a style. They rejected the early commitment of modern architecture to a serious concern with progressive social change. By mid-century the social problems were alarming in the face of the collapse of housing programs, the waste of resources, and the worsening urban environment. However, the architects took refuge in stylistic exercises and tongue-in-cheek irony, rather than attempting to deal with the social tasks confronting society.

The values that had defined the modernist era—the desire to build a better world and the focus on purity, purpose, and the autonomy of the arts—had dissolved, and the formalist concerns with integrity and excellence were seen as delusions. The grounds given in the late 20th century for the rebellion against the International Style have been the style's agnosticism, neutrality, coldness, and lack of concern for the environment. Robert Venturi argued for complexity, contradiction, ambiguity, tension, and a messy vitality as the needed qualities of a more vital architecture. The 1960s and 1970s generation insisted on a return to symbolism, metaphor, and significance, wanting architecture to reach society at the level of common humanity. Architects young and old borrowed bits and pieces from the classical, baroque, mannerist, and rococo past, generally taken out of context and with no relevance to function. Historicist embellishment was expected to provide a sense of continuity and to repair and enlarge a much-impoverished self-image through the appropriation of forms of past grandeur.

When, as Charles Jencks (one of the most notable architectural historians and critics of the latter half of the century) pointed out, "the most talented architects are designing beautiful candle shops and boutiques for the sophisticated, and office buildings for soap and whiskey manufacturers . . . ," something must be wrong. . . . "If architecture concretizes the public realm and if that realm has lost its credibility because it is founded on a false idea of what allows men to govern themselves," then there can only be an identity crisis—a sense of dispersal, a fear of dissolution, and an apoca-lyptic vision such as has obsessed the literary and visual arts since the turn of the century.

VII. POSTMODERNISM

It was Jenks who coined the stylistic term "postmodernism" to cover pluralism as the principle of late 20th century architecture. Postmodernism has become as widely accepted a stylistic category for the architecture of the second half of the 20th century as the International Style is for the first half.

It was only in the 1970s that the historical limits of modernism, modernity, and modernization came into sharp focus. There was a growing sense that we do not need to complete the project of modernity which deals with the central issues of morality and freedom. Postmodernism integrated modernism and all its concerns with programmatic social change, but its agenda was different. It was preoccupied with stylistic exercises, historical references, language, and irony. The drift was to the right.

VIII. LATE MODERN VERSUS POSTMODERN

Late modernists took their theories to an extreme and developed a mannered modernism. Postmodernists differ to the extent that they codified their previous style and rejected the modernist theories.

Modernist style was characterized by anonymity. Late modernism differs by adding extreme articulation and extreme cellular multiplication to the design. Arata Isozaki and Herman Hertzberger are late modernists. Whereas the modernist aesthetic was purist, Hertzberger's aesthetic is impure and open to addition. However, the basic abstract style of concrete block, glass brick, and constructional expression remains.

A postmodernist style is less pure and more sensitive to the local area. Late modernists take technological imagery to an extreme whereas modernists never even attempted such feats. Jenks explains that the Pompidou Center in Paris falls into the late modern group because the expression of joints and structure is so obsessive and poetic that it dominates other concerns. Such structural acrobatics would have been condemned in the twenties. The competed structure is a reflection of the mecano-set image so popular in America. According to Jencks, the reference to historical models is a postmodern, not a late modern, feature, and in this building there is no evidence of a desire to comment on the context of Paris. In short, the Centre Pompidou is seen as a decorated toy box of technical tricks, painted in blues and reds. According to Jencks, the basic difference between late modern and postmodern styles is pragmatism versus idealism, and an abstract rather than conventional language of forms. It is obvious, however, that many architects would fall between the two stylistic modes.

Postmodernism's ironic temporality upsets the very reality of the cultural tradition. Postmodernism, however, tried to revisit culture by refusing to dismiss the challenge of the past. Postmodernism is, in fact, a haunting return to the past, to romance, and to authenticity.

For the postmodernist, the inclusion of past styles into modern buildings was expected to provide a sense of continuity and to enlarge a sense of self by extending the immediate concretized identity beyond its constrained contemporary margins. At the same time, postmodernism was a move toward popular culture. Modern architecture had not been able to guide social progress, to bring communal harmony, or to provide a progressive and humane environment. Modern buildings were seen as sterile, dumb boxes or cage constructions. The advent of the machine was no longer seen in a positive light. The younger generation attributed the ongoing world conflicts to technological overdevelopment and to corporate capital that had been pushing its acceleration with only the profit motive in mind.

With the disappearance of the idea of progress and the belief that architecture can make a difference, architects turned to competitive play. The style which is specific to postmodernism is identified as a sort of bricolage consisting of multiple quotations of elements taken from earlier styles and periods—an orgy of superstructures, fantasies, and novel ideas.

Although Jencks was among the first to use the term "postmodern" in architectural criticism, he also stressed that the modernist sensibility had not been entirely extinguished, and that much postmodernist work used modernism as a base to question, reinterpret, or invert.

Among many others, Michael Graves, Charles Moore, Arata Isozaki, Aldo Rossi, Philip Johnson, Hans Hollein, and Mario Botta can be described as postmodernists. Their architectural goals are to impress, to dazzle, and to call old ideas into question by transgressing old aesthetic visions and aims with, however, no higher social aim in mind. The new architecture flaunts its own absence of meaning, often showing a concern with decorative patterns. It purposefully tries to undermine customary space functions and limitations by building extremely flexible arrangements.

There was a continuing search for new solutions, particularly in the areas of skyscraper design. The major focus was on the organization of services and the uses of solar energy. The bottom of the building, which frequently opened as an atrium, began to receive greater attention (e.g., Citicorp Headquarters in Manhattan by Hugh Stubbins, 1978). Enrichment of skyscrapers became an important feature.

Both Philip Johnson's AT&T Building and the Humana Headquarters (Michael Graves) have been described as tragic monuments to an outmoded capitalism. From the point of view of style, the Humana Headquarters building has been described as contorted in order to gain more space. Further descriptions are that it is difficult to decide scale, difficult to identify the front doors, and difficult to understand what the skin is made of. At the same time, it has been recognized as a new step in the humanist tradition, and has achieved the status of belonging to the classical skyscraper type like those of Philip Johnson and Robert Stern. It is built in a monumental style which is accessible and free from cliché. According to Jencks it is the first step in a postmodern tradition in which art, ornament, and symbolism are happily combined.

The big lament at that time was that the work of Philip Johnson, Michael Graves, and many other postmodernists could be interpreted as evidence of architecture in retreat, commemorating an outdated, international capitalism.

IX. REFORM IN THE BUILDING INDUSTRY

It was only in the 1970s that the historical limits of modernity, modernism, and modernization came into sharp focus, and it led to the growing sense that it was not necessary to complete the project of modernity which deals with central issues of history, morality, and freedom. The International Style had order in mind. However, the modern movement led to a radical reform of the organization of the building industry, and to the production of goods that give a shape to the new technological universe connecting old concepts with new tasks.

A rich variety of museums emerged in the 1970s. The museums built in the 1970s reveal an interesting variety of approaches with a multivalence of meaning as the primary characteristic of this postmodernist phase. There was no genuine blueprint for a clear-cut style. Eclecticism was acknowledged as a desirable feature of the Western architectural world with no real attempt to go beyond it.

Alvar Aalto (1898–1976) believed that architecture may be seen as a kind of battleground for the quality of life of the man-in-the-street. His desire was to democratize his own production in order to bring it to a wider public.

X. PLASTIC ENVIRONMENTS AND PUBLIC SPACES

John Portman was determined to build a new kind of environment in which citizens would be drawn to participate. His first attempt was Peach Tree Center in the heart of downtown Atlanta. It consisted of tall shimmering glass mega buildings that contained a multitude of activities and attractive meeting places: a 73-story hotel containing 1074 rooms, a shopping mall, a conference center, bars, clubs, restaurants, and office space. It incorporated a glass skylighted multistory atrium landscaped with trees and waterfalls, and an art show space for overscale art works. Glass-enclosed elevators decorated with circus-like lighting added to the twinkling, kaleidoscopic atmosphere of activity and gaiety. The only drawback was that the complex was a gargantuan consumer of energy.

Such constructions have been labeled "plastic environments," but people have responded to them very positively. The concept reappeared in Embarcadero Center in San Francisco, in Place Bonaventure in Los Angeles, Renaissance Center in Detroit, and elsewhere. In spite of considerable criticism over the years for

having provided a "kitsch" environment, Portman was awarded the American Institute of Architects Medal in 1978.

Frank Gehry's Edgemar Center in Santa Monica California (1988) is another public mall plus theme park, with a museum, library, concert hall, and theater. Regarded as cities of consumption, such complexes are generally economically successful.

The conflation of the mall and the theme park in a wide range of building types (e.g., museum, library, concert hall, and theater) is one of the most interesting phenomena of the late 20th century. Museum building dates back to the Renaissance when building was for the rich. The mall offers easy museum access to the masses.

Since the 1980s, the most prestigious commissions have been for museums and cultural centers. And this is a global phenomenon in the design for public places.

One of the emerging problems of the century with which architects had to deal with was the growing density of the urban population. This resulted in revolutionary changes in building, one of which was the construction of "megastructures" of unprecedented grandeur. A megastructure is defined as a large frame in which all the functions of a city or part of a city are housed. Such structures have been made possible by present-day technology. They can be described as man-made features of the landscape.

XI. MEGASTRUCTURES

The first megastructures emerged in the 1910s, utilizing all the best formal inventions of the 20th century from "brut" concrete through tetrahedral space frames to round-cornered windows and transparent inflatable structures. They were proposed by architects themselves in their role as "comprehensive designers." However, the megastructure movement had a short lifetime before the concept was abandoned largely because megastructures left a great deal of freedom for the self-housing and self-determining inventions to the inhabitants. It proved to be a disastrous freedom and a responsibility to which the inhabitants of the megastructure could not respond. Thus, Pruitt-Igoe—built by the city of St. Louis, Missouri, in 1952–1955 (designer Minaro Yamasaki)—is one of the early megastructures which had to be destroyed due to the inability of the inhabitants to assume their responsibilities in taking care of it. What was lacking in the design concept was a reasoned and experienced view of how mass housing could be planned to involve the tenants' personal identification, concern, and sense of responsibility for maintenance and care.

To avoid the poor city planning which would result from capitalism gone wild, Regional Urban Design Assistance Teams (R/UDAT) were established by the American Institute of Architects (AIA). Their purpose was to counteract and to protest against the forces of big business, shrewd developers, and unintelligent government. The inhabitants of sites chosen for redevelopment would be asked for their reactions in time to forestall developments which were inimical to their interests.

Since the 1980s public participation has been strident and effective. It is now virtually impossible to build any public place without first polling public opinion. As a result many building project proposals have been revised or scrapped. A renewal of social idealism is evident in America and there is an increasing desire on the part of the public to take responsibility for the built environment.

XII. DECONSTRUCTIVE ARCHITECTURE

The most innovative and radical architects today have moved into the area of "deconstructive architecture." The term "deconstruction" was introduced by the French philosopher Jacques Derrida. The core of deconstruction is identified as the close reading of texts. To deconstruct a text is to draw out conflicting logics of sense and implication with the object of showing that the text never says exactly what it means or means what it says.

The late 20th century deconstructionist movement consists of a group of architects whose common goal is to move away from the rigidity and value structure of dialectic oppositions (e.g., structure vs. decoration, abstraction vs. figuration, or figure vs. ground). The goal of the deconstructivists is to explore the ground between and within these categories.

In 1988, Philip Johnson, the dean of the modern movement since the second decade of the century,

once more offered a crowning tribute to an architectural movement. The Deconstructive Architecture exhibition which he organized for the Museum of Modern Art in New York City in 1988 included the work of seven architects: Peter Eisenman, Bernard Tschumi, Frank Gehry, Daniel Liebeskind, Coop Himmmelbau, Zaha Hadid, and Rem Koolhaas. The basis for choosing these seven was in keeping with the definition of deconstructivism, which states that deconstructionists do not dismantle buildings but locate "inherent dilemmas within buildings."

With respect to deconstructionist architecture, Philip Johnson stated, "The changes that shook the eye of an old modernist like myself are the contrasts between the 'warped' image of deconstructive architecture and the 'pure' image of the old International Style."

Deconstructive work will involve references to the following:

1. Work that tends to juxtapose visual and textual elements, resulting in a critical interrogative exchange between them
2. The viewer/reader finds him or herself actively decoding the social constraints that are concealed within the work (i.e., in decoding what the concepts and their history not only state but hide as repression or dissimulation)
3. Deconstruction maintains the kind of double-edged relation to modernist themes and techniques that enables deconstructive analyses without reversing the concepts inherent in the built form

In short, the significance and sometimes the goal of this work can be restructured to reveal tactics and messages that are not evident on superficial viewing although they are obviously there. The deconstructive impulse is meant to disturb illusions about truth and about the complex politics that are responsible for building and thus for the crafting of a dangerous world. The serious attention to the realities of the architectural project is affirmative rather than negative. The application of deconstructive techniques to building and decoding architecture is riddled with problems—any of which stem from an inability to understand the language of form either by the architect or by the viewer. However, there is no set of codes and conventions to serve as the ultimate reference point for evaluating new work.

XIII. CRITIQUES OF POSTMODERNISM

Jenks defined postmodernism as "an interest in popular and local codes of communication, in historical memory, urban context, ornament, representation, metaphor, participation, the public realm, pluralism and eclecticism." The postmodern reaction was not only against everything that modern architecture had come to represent, but also it became clear that in rejecting modernism the postmodern architects had rejected its serious commitment to progressive social change, thus allowing capitalism to set the tone, guided primarily by market returns.

According to Frederick Jameson, the postmodernist, pluralist, schizophrenic period is a visible expression of "a new type of social life and a new economic order—what is euphemistically called modernization, post-industrial or consumer society, the society of the media or the spectacle, or multinational capitalism." As Jameson points out, the two significant features of this era are the transformation of reality into images and the fragmentation of time into a series of perpetual presents. They are both a function of the "penetration of advertising, television and the mass media generally to a hitherto unparalleled degree throughout society." Thus, contrary to the utopic and opposition stance of modernism and the founders of the International Style, postmodernism expresses the logic of consumer capitalism.

Architecture worked hand in hand with corporate capitalism to produce a built environment that despite the best will on earth had turned out to be alienating. In the first half of the century, it offered its consumers an alien and impoverished self-identity; in the second half of the century it reflected for its consumers the fragmentation, narcissism, and triviality fashioned for them by mass culture.

XIV. SUBVERSIVE MOVEMENTS

The late 20th century also saw the emergence of diverse architectural movements and groups that may be seen as socially subversive to the extent that their goals are meant to change society through architecture. There are at least five different groups that have called attention to this message by offering proposals as to how architecture may change society. However, only one group, Archigram, achieved any degree of relevance.

Archigram was established in 1964 in London with Peter Cook and Ron Herron among the members. Archigram wielded a great deal of influence and created the most vital high-tech group in the world. It was put on the map when Richard Rogers and Renzo Piano obtained the commission for the Centre Pompidou in an international competition. Rogers is also responsible for building Lloyds of London. The Lloyds Building has been described as one of the purest skyscrapers ever built.

By the mid-1970s the high-tech style had developed even further, and architects Leon Krier, Bernard Tschumi, and Rem Koolhaas were able to develop their own skills at the London school in order to continue their research at the Institute of Urban Studies in New York City (founded 1970). The strength of the New York institute lay in the exploration of alternatives to traditional ways of making architecture.

Rem Koolhaas is seen as a representative of noncommittal, abstract, and large-scale design. His influence lies in the novel appearance of his images. He is a member of Arquitectonica, a firm given to radical architectural projects.

Charles Jenks, the most trenchant critic of the situation of architecture at the end of the 20th century, stated,

> With the triumph of consumer society in the West and bureaucratic state capitalism in the East, our unfortunate modern architect was left without much uplifting content to symbolize. . . . There's not much the architect can do about it except protest as a citizen, and design dissenting buildings that express the complex situation. He can communicate the values which are missing. . . .

However, if we look at the kinds of communication which the postmodernist has attempted, this is precisely what he could not do. Without an internal locus (i.e., a moral universe to serve as a guide) the postmodern architect is buffeted about by the pluralist delusions of aesthetic contents borrowed from everywhere with little hope of any coherent program of his own.

It would be an error to settle for the standards set by postmodernism and its limitations. Architecture springs from impulses that must be described as ethical and cosmological, and if, in Western cultures, these impulses are currently squelched by the monetary values of the marketplace, other cultures are thriving and more than equal to the job of offering the virtues of commodity, firmness, and delight. For example, Third World countries demonstrate a resurgence of vigorous architecture offering forms "shaped by traditional cultural and religious patterns," to which Charles Corea, Balkrihsna Doshi (India), and Mario Botta (Swiss) find it easy to contribute. Common sense would suggest that architects need to be involved in the design and planning of a more humane modern environment.

XV. CONCLUSION

As the 20th century approaches its end, the complex, fragmentary nature of the building forms reflects the alienation of a sophisticated society. The users of the built forms are not involved, in any way, in the creation of their environment. They have no say about architectural issues that affect their lives, and they have not yet realized that a great deal of power lies in their hands.

There are serious social problems because buildings are not treated as needs but as commodities. They are not seen in relation to the needs of the entire society. The social history of architecture shows what is his-torically relevant, and what the pitfalls of irresponsible building are. In the industrialized world there are serious political concerns about the environment but little constructive action is envisaged. Among the problems are: (1) resource depletion, (2) pollution, and (3) scarring of the landscape. Architects cannot simply say these are not their problems. It is a fact that substandard environments distort lives, but the current market system offers no solutions.

Modern cities continue to be products of hypermobile capital and complex human migrations. The struggle for life space is serious. The history of planning is beginning but the domain of the political economy for the building and rebuilding of urban ensembles and the aggregation of physical structures has not yet sufficiently involved the profession of architecture in the search for solutions.

Bibliography

Betsky, A. (1990). *Violated perfection.* New York: Rizzoli.

Jencks, C. A. (1980). *Modern movements in architecture.* New York: Penguin.

Jencks, C. A. (1988). *Architecture today.* New York: Rizzoli.

Johnson, P., & Wigley, M. (1988). *Deconstructivist architecture.* New York: Museum of Modern Art.

Norris, C., & Benjamin, A. (1988). *What is deconstruction.* London: Academy Editions.

Papadakis, A., Cooke, C., & Benjamin, A. (1989). *Deconstruction.* New York: Rizzoli.

Riseboro, B. (1979). *The story of western architecture.* Cambridge, MA: MIT Press.

Roth, L. M. (1993). *Understanding architecture: Its elements, history and meaning.* New York: Harper Collins.

Tafuri, M., & Dal Co, F. (1986). *Modern architecture* (Vols. 1, 2). New York: Electa/Rizzoli.

Archival Investigation

Eugene I. Taylor

Harvard University and Saybrook Graduate School

I. Guiding Principles
II. Characteristics of the Investigator
III. Application to Creativity

Archival Investigation Both the science and the art of interpreting primary documents in the description, reconstruction, and corroboration of a subject, which in this case is creativity in all its varied forms.

Consensual Validation The most commonly used technique for assessing variables of creativity where a subject's responses to some task are submitted to a battery of raters who each are given the same general criteria for defining a specific trait and asked to rate the subject along a continuum. The subject's score would then be the average of the raters' responses.

Creativity A general trait of personality in which the person shows manifest ability to produce and develop original ideas; to devise new methods, construct hypotheses, offer novel explanations, and compose works of artistic merit, particularly originality in handling words and ideas related to artistic and scientific thought.

Experimental Psychology The experimental laboratory tradition in academic psychology that derives its origins from 19th century German experimental science, particularly emanating from the Leipzig laboratory of Wilhelm Wundt, first founded in 1879.

Hasselbach-Henderson Equation In the field of physical chemistry, the computation of many different variables at one time

in a single sample of blood; the historical precursor to the development of blood plasma.

Library Science The discipline concerned with transport, housing, indexing, cataloging, and preservation of books, pamphlets, letters, memorabilia, archival documents, and in some cases including film footage and art objects.

"Live Data" Numerical data collected on subjects that is still available for further analysis.

Logical Positivism A synonym for Viennese positivism. The positivist movement in Western science began in the 1820s with August Comte, who formulated a definition of the principles of scientific inquiry based on the rejection of metaphysics, meaning a description of causes outside the realm of the senses and the intellect.

Macrotheories of Personality Theories that attempt to encompass the total human personality in all its complexity, usually referring to theories of personality generated in the 1930s that stood opposed to the atomism of laboratory experiments with the white rat.

Normative Scholarship Traditional methods of scholarly research based on rational–empirical principles.

Personality The historical conception of the person in psychology, usually involving the study of both character and temperament.

Personology The multivariate study of personality at different levels of analysis first pioneered by Henry A. Murray at Harvard University beginning in the late 1920s.

Pregnant Anomaly A rich vein of information normally hidden from view.

Copyright © 1999 by Eugene I. Taylor
All rights of reproduction in any form reserved.

Qualitative Methods Research techniques in the social sciences, such as one-on-one interviews, that normally do not involve numerical quantification.

Trait A basic and enduring element of personality. In psychology, traits are usually thought of as derived from Temperament (an inherited tendency) or character (a learned predisposition that has been modified by the environment).

Viennese Positivism A movement in the philosophy of science in the 1920s originating in Vienna that followed the ideas of Ludwig Wittgenstein and posited the immediate conditions of an experiment as only that which could be perceived by the senses and rationally analyzed.

ARCHIVAL INVESTIGATION is both the science and the art of interpreting primary documents in the description, reconstruction, and corroboration of a subject, which in this case is creativity in all its varied forms. Its many aspects include discovery, identification, authentication, recovery, and transfer to appropriate archival repositories, followed by comparison with other related objects, documents, or collections, researching the background and significance of related subjects or biographies, and formal presentation to the disciplines and professions of original research based on such investigation.

Archival investigation is a science to the extent that it is the discovery and verification of concrete evidentiary material guided by a set of systematic rules of hypothesis formulation and testing, and an art to the extent that inference, deduction, and interpretation may require more than the normal amount of imaginative modeling of a situation in order to see through to the solution of a particular problem.

It is not library science in the formal sense of the word, which is involved more with transport, housing, indexing and cataloging, and preservation. Rather, it forms the basis of all forms of empirical scholarship that deal with the history and philosophy of a subject or that purport to use objectivity and analysis as the standard for evaluation. While it cleaves to the evidence as its primary foundation, it is inherently professorial and knowledge based, not artifact based, in that, within the Western academic tradition, the formal distinctions between the librarians and the faculty remain intact. The librarians are the conservators of the actual documents, while the professors remain the primary gateways to the scholarly interpretation and dissemination of the ideas.

I. GUIDING PRINCIPLES

Archival investigation follows the standard criteria of logical analysis of sensory data but expands somewhat on these possibilities. One must begin with minute observation. Examine completely the phenomenon under investigation, as the most insignificant detail may turn out to be the most important clue leading to further fruitful investigation. At the same time, if in an array of ordinary facts an unusual event presents itself, one does not hesitate to drop everything and follow that clue, as it often will lead to a pregnant anomaly, meaning a rich vein of information normally hidden from view. From an observation of the facts one constructs an array of hypotheses such that the most impossible are eliminated right away. What is left are only those that range from the most to the least probable, any of which may turn out to be the case.

II. CHARACTERISTICS OF THE INVESTIGATOR

Archival investigation is also carried on under a set of distinct guiding principles derived from the more creative end of the spectrum of normative scholarship. It requires more of a refined intuitive capacity and an optimistic, empathetically oriented human-centered approach than traditional methods of scholarly research based on rational-empirical principles alone. A traditional scholar will typically consult only finished collections that have been archived and indexed. The archival investigator may just as easily be a specialist in boxes marked "miscellaneous" and "unsorted"—one who is usually the first to sift through apparently irrelevant or indecipherable material and to extract out the most relevant and valuable documents. The traditional scholar usually works within the confines of the library where the archives are held, while the archival investigator is constantly prepared for invasion of unusual environments—the flooded sub-basement of an old record depository, armed with boots and flashlight; the dusty eaves of a family attic, wearing face mask and latex gloves; or the upper tiers of a barn where sealed trunks may have been stored.

The traditional scholar is often satisfied with the least amount of research which yields the single most emblematic fact of a subject area, while the archival investigator is interested in the widest possible variation of facts and hypotheses from which to make the best selection. One has to have the ability to see unusual or otherwise hidden analogies. One needs to have an increased tolerance for ambiguity. One needs highly developed skills of concentration, absorption, and selective perception in order to handle enormous amounts of miscellaneous material.

In addition to prior mastery of several fields, another necessary requirement is familiarity with relevant trades. One has to have thorough knowledge of used, secondhand, and antiquarian sources, not only regionally and nationally, but internationally, in addition to extensive knowledge of the content and history of a subject, as well as thorough knowledge of the location of previously cataloged collections.

Most importantly, for the archival investigator, observation must be both objective and empathetic, not merely objective alone—that is, one has to remain disengaged from the material and have one's own independent viewpoint, yet be able at any time to enter completely into the worldview of the person who created what is being observed and be able to reproduce that worldview as distinct from one's own. The standard of objectivity is higher than that in normative scholarship because the subjective factor is not restrained or denied; rather, it is accounted for as an alternative standard to the merely objective.

III. APPLICATION TO CREATIVITY

Archival investigation is a method of historical and philosophic scholarship that can be applied to understanding the process of creativity in a variety of different ways. Among them, creativity can be studied as a trait of personality. It can be defined operationally by qualitative methods used to study it; it can be ex-

plored by way of certain kinds of evidence, as in the evidence used to establish the sources of a person's creative capacities. It can also be applied to reconstruct the history of research on creativity. [*See* Definitions of Creativity.]

A. Creativity as a Trait of Personality

While all human beings have the capacity to be creative to one degree or another, the study of creativity as a trait of personality only began in the 1930s with the concomitant development of macrotheories of personality within the academic discipline of psychology. The scientific study of personality thus became the framework within which the scientific study of creativity could be carried on. One of the foremost examples of such macropersonality theories was the personology of Henry A. Murray at Harvard University. Murray was an M.D. and a biochemist by training who spent the majority of his career as a professor of psychology running the Harvard Psychological Clinic, a research facility established in the school of arts and sciences to study personality. Among other notable facts, he was B. F. Skinner's first psychology professor in 1929 and he gave Erik Erikson his first job in 1933.

Basing his conception of the person on a biological but person-centered model, Murray borrowed from experiments in physical chemistry he had conducted under L. J. Henderson in the early 1920s verifying the Hasselbach–Henderson equation, in which Murray was able to measure 17 different variables in a blood sample at one time (work which later led to the development of blood plasma). From this physiochemical model, Murray developed his theory of personology, the multivariate study of personality at different levels of analysis. This meant that a single individual was to be studied at many different levels of complexity and the results of this investigation evaluated by a team of researchers who had radically different kinds of expertise. Only in this way, Murray believed, could we arrive at an accurate picture that reflected the complexity of the whole person.

Murray's work is summarized in *Explorations in Personality,* which appeared in 1938, authored by 15 people. It was a case study of some four dozen Harvard undergraduates who had over a 10-year period become the most thoroughly tested subjects in the entire history of scientific psychology up to that time.

One of the key traits they measured was creative abilities. Creativity was considered a general trait of personality in which the person showed manifest ability to produce and develop original ideas, devise new methods, construct hypotheses, offer novel explanations, and compose works of artistic merit. As a psychological construct, it was introduced not to describe responses that were stereotypic, rigid, or banal, but rather ones that were novel, sensational, irresponsible, inconsistent, fickle, or odd. Insightful application to new conditions was called behavioral creativity. But the general term "creativity" was most especially employed to cover originality in handling words and ideas related to artistic and scientific thought.

A variety of tests of creativity were devised. The most commonly used technique for assessing variables of creativity was that of consensual validation. Here, a subject's responses to, say, a task of telling short stories, were submitted to a battery of raters who each had been given the same general criteria for defining a specific trait and were asked to rate the subject along a continuum. The subject's score would then be the average of the raters' responses. [*See* CONSENSUAL ASSESSMENT.]

While our most available source of information on these subjects has come from the published book by Murray and his colleagues, subjects' responses to all those measures are still available in the form of what is called "live data"; that is, all the data collected on creativity are still available for reanalysis and evaluation by interested researchers. The records of measures taken on Murray's subjects are kept at the Henry A. Murray Center for the Study of Lives at Radcliffe College in Cambridge, Massachusetts, and are available for examination by qualified individuals.

Murray himself wrote extensively on creativity as a normal dimension of personality development. In addition to his published articles on the subject, his correspondence, notes, and lectures can be found in the Henry A. Murray papers, currently on deposit in the permanent faculty collection at Pusey Library, the general archives of Harvard University.

The correlation of these collections constitutes an important archival definition of creativity as a trait of personality, particularly within the history of psychology.

B. Qualitative Methods in the Investigation of the Creative Process

Another application of archival investigation to creativity involves film footage preserving some of the more qualitative methods that have been used to study the phenomena. One such project was the Boston University Aesthetics Research Project, first launched by the late Sigmund Koch in the early 1970s, which employed in-depth subjective interaction between an interviewer steeped in the artist's work and the artist himself. The emphasis here was on the informed interviewer as an essence extractor superior to any intervening method of data collection when it came to drawing out the nuances of the creative process from the artist, *in vivo*. The idea was that the interview situation itself had to be carried off as a creative act if the true essence of creativity in the artist was to come through.

Koch had spent the majority of his career from the 1930s to the 1960s as an experimental psychologist studying motivation in the white rat. As a former student of the Viennese positivist Herbert Feigl, Koch was considered the foremost expert in the United States on the relation of logical positivism to experimental psychology.

Because of his reputation as a laboratory scientist, he was commissioned by the American Psychological Association in the early 1950s to undertake a massive reassessment of the field at midcentury. He brought 87 of the world's foremost psychologists together and had them write on their life work, comparing the ideal of a scientific psychology with the eventual outcome in their personal careers. The result, to everyone's complete surprise, was an extraordinarily low correlation between the principles of empirical science and how psychology as an alleged science was actually conducted. The experimental analysis of behavior had proved itself to be a complete failure.

While Koch's conclusions played a major role in ending a 30-year era where learning theorists held control of the academic discipline of psychology, his studies also had a profound effect on him personally. Unable to continue on as an experimentalist in light of such overwhelming proof of that endeavor as a failed scientific enterprise, he turned his attention full time to the study of artists and to the evaluation of the creative process, using qualitative rather than quantitative methods of investigation. He became the chief administrator for grants to artists through the Ford Foundation for two years before returning to academia to launch his project in cooperation with Boston University.

The project involved eight hours of in-depth qualitative interviews with 14 world-class artists in a variety of fields, from novelists, playwrights, and ballerinas to painters and poets. Among them were such figures as Saul Bellow and Toni Morrison. The eight hours of interviews were divided into three parts: biographical; issues of process and craft around major battles and important turning points in the artist's career; and the analysis of a single creative product from inception to finish. The final product was a series of tapes which Koch integrated into an acclaimed course on "Artists on Art" at Boston University in the last years of his life. He died in 1995 without publishing any major statement on the project.

Since then, the tapes have been archived at Boston University, but the original plan set forth by the Ford Foundation to produce copies, distribute them to a dozen centers around the United States, and to make transcripts of the interviews available was never completed. Koch's papers on the subject remain in a warehouse pending disbursement by the family. Eventually, his papers are to go to the Archives of the History of American Psychology at the University of Akron in Akron, Ohio.

C. Documents Leading to the Reinterpretation of the Creative Act

Archival investigation of creativity also involves the discovery and presentation of new evidence leading to the reinterpretation of established knowledge. A case in point is 19th century America's foremost landscape painter George Inness (1825–1893). Art historians have long attempted to place Inness within their framework of what is known, but he was not a Hudson River painter, an illuminist, nor an impressionist. Rather, the archival evidence, in Inness's own words, points to him as a Swedenborgian and transcendentalist painter—a fact completely unintelligible to art historians, for Swedenborgianism is a religion and there

are no identifiable transcendentalist painters, nor any such movement in American art history called "transcendental." The only thing he could be called was a Barbizon stylist, but he painted in America and not France when the Barbizon style was in vogue, although again, out of step with his times, the rage was for portraits, not landscapes.

On the other hand, Inness's relatives and students declared his work underived. Inness, himself, said that the true function of his art was to communicate that which was spiritual to the viewer, and we know that the great influence on his painting after 1863 was Inness's study of the works of the 18th century scientist and mystic Emanuel Swedenborg. Art historian Sally Promey has subsequently shown with reference to the archival evidence that Inness was a long-time member of the New York Swedenborgian churches and that Inness himself had contributed to the Swedenborgian literature by publishing his theory of color in light of the Swedenborgian doctrine of correspondences—that everything in nature is somewhere reflected in the life of the soul.

A study of the facts of Inness's biography in conjunction with this evidence further suggests that Inness got these ideas through William Page, a committed Swedenborgian and portraitist who was close to transcendentalist poets such as James Russell Lowell; that Page converted Inness to the doctrines of Swedenborg over a three-year period when the two of them taught painting at a former transcendentalist commune turned art colony in Rahway, New Jersey (where Emerson, Thoreau, Alcott, and others at one time had been frequent visitors); and that the New York social circle from which Inness drew many of his clients and patrons had strong links to both the Swedenborgians and the transcendentalists.

Perhaps the most important assessment to come from these facts, however, especially from a trio of Swedenborgian paintings Inness executed in 1867, was that Inness's most exquisite and refined pictures were not representations of outward nature, but rather interior landscapes depicting states of consciousness Inness himself was passing through in an inward journey toward spiritual self-realization. While Inness brought a high degree of expertise in painting, drawing, and color mixing to his art, the experience of creating a painting was discovered to be commensurate with his spiritual motive for painting. In other words, a dissociated form of concentration almost verging on trance would occur, allowing elements of the unconscious to express themselves through the artist's brush in both color and form. That his motives were more spiritual rather than merely aesthetic or moral guided his spontaneity toward higher rather than lower ends and assisted him, he said, in depicting "the reality of the unseen" in his pictures—meaning he was able to reveal what was truly spiritual but through the thoroughly natural means of the physical landscape.

In this example, Inness's paintings become the single, most important archival record of his personal inward journey. This shows us that, in the same way that every creative product has a history and a context that can be archivally reconstructed using books, papers, and memorabilia, a collection of art objects could be considered an archival repository, if treated as a cache of data from which to extract the elements of some larger picture—the history of an artist's career, the contribution of certain kinds of painting to the identification of a genre, or the identification of changing styles of painting over time. These are necessarily the questions raised by the art historian but they could just as easily be pursued by the discerning artist in search of inspiration or improvement of craft.

D. The History of Research on Creativity

Archival investigation can also be employed to reconstruct the history of how researchers have studied the phenomenon of creativity. Creativity was not directly known as a specific category of investigation in the late 19th century; it was rather most often subsumed under the more general rubric of literary or artistic genius. Geniuses have been definitely recognized throughout history, but closer scrutiny of their traits revealed a host of morbid elements. One idea prevailed in particular, that geniuses were not only different from the norm, but also exhibited traits similar to insanity. [See MAD GENIUS CONTROVERSY.]

The American philosopher-psychologist William James took up the study of geniuses in the 1860s when, as a young medical student, he had become a member of Darwin's inner circle of American support-

ers who first articulated the biological theory of natural selection. While everyone else in his immediate scientific community was preoccupied with the evolution of plants and animals, James was the first to take up the problem of consciousness in the context of the evolution of the species. We know this from recent archival discoveries of letters identifying James as author of some of the earliest but anonymous reviews of Darwin's ideas in the American literature of the 1860s.

While his work focused primarily on adaptation through conscious choices that humans make to alter their behavior of their environment, by the late 1880s, James also directed his attention to the mind of the creative genius. We know this from an examination of journal and magazine articles he wrote at the time on the subject of great men and women, great thoughts, and environments during a time when he was first constructing his psychology of individual differences. Geniuses are those who lead the way toward accomplishments the rest of us only dream about, and after they make them, the rest of us follow the new trail they opened because we now see what is humanly possible. They are the divine spark of humanity. And when we look into their thought processes, we see a ferment of ideas. We all make choices all the time, but while the rest of us usually limit ourselves to a small menu of possibilities, the genius is busy generating thousands of possibilities. Their choices are necessarily different because they are constantly brainstorming and then out of this welter drawing analogies that the rest of us never see.

Finally, James wrote about the problem of genius and insanity in his previously unpublished Lowell Lectures on "Exceptional Mental States," which he delivered in the fall of 1896. We know this from correlating 125 pages of James's handwritten lecture notes for the series with several hundred books from his personal library that contained annotations keyed to the lecture notes, which were recovered from Harvard's open stacks, where they had been deposited since 1921; we know it from reconstructing the history of Harvard's first three idiosyncratic library classification systems, instituted before the introduction of the more nationally standardized Dewey decimal system, which allowed us to retrieve books James had checked out of the library in preparation for the lectures, but then kept out for several years, extensively marked up, and then returned to the shelf where they had sat unopened until we pulled them from the shelves again 80 years later. We also know what James had to say about genius by correlating these materials with book reviews he had published on the subject during the same period.

From these archival materials, we see that James was trying to understand the creative genius in the context of the larger problem of how we conceptualize personality. Following the great Italian criminologist Caesar Lombroso, it was the prevailing opinion that "madness ferments in the dough of which great men are made." James was less certain that this was universally true. While there are certainly evil geniuses and creativity can always be employed to diabolical ends, many geniuses showed morbid and pathological traits, but at least they were not fatal. We should forgive them the one for their service to us by the others. He was also skeptical of the criteria by which someone made the biographical dictionaries, believing that sometimes the label of genius had been bestowed a little too blithely by public opinion upon some figures of history.

There were those all-important cases of the benign genius, however, which James said particularly in America were produced in abundant numbers—he mentioned such figures as John Greenleaf Whittier, Henry Wadsworth Longfellow, and Ralph Waldo Emerson. After presenting a succession of other cases, he was led from this to formulate the idea of a growth-oriented dimension to personality to which each one of us could strive and toward which the population appeared to be evolving. These were not traits outside ourselves, he said, but instead an integral but usually undeveloped part of the normal personality.

Thus, archival investigation, which is essentially a method of assessment based on primary sources, can fruitfully be applied to the study of creativity, which we normally might not think of as having such a historical and thematic dimension. At the same time, the examples presented here are only emblematic, as the field of application remains essentially unlimited.

Bibliography

Koch, S. (v.d.). Artists on art [Tape series of 14 different artists, each interviewed for eight hours]. Boston, MA: Boston University Creativity and the Arts Project, University Archives, Mugar Library, Boston University.

Murray, H. A., et al. (1938). *Explorations in personality*. New York: Oxford.

Murray, H. A. (v.d.). Unpublished papers on personology. Cambridge, MA: Henry A. Murray Research Center for the Study of Lives, Radcliffe College, Harvard University.

Taylor, E. I. (1997). The interior landscape: William James and George Inness on art from a Swedenborgian point of view. *Archives of American Art (Smithsonian Institution)*, *17*(1, 2), 2–10.

Winks, R. W. (Ed.). (1969). *The historian as detective: Essays on evidence*. New York: Harper & Row.

Art and Aesthetics

Stephanie Z. Dudek

University of Montreal

Bricoleur Making do with whatever comes to mind.
Camp Pretentious gesture, style, or form, especially when consciously contrived; displaying pretentiousness.
Collative Variables As per Berlyne, are complexity, novelty, surprise, and absurdity.
Concinnity Skillfully put together, well made.
Gnostic Pertaining to or having knowledge.
Heterogamous Having different origins, having unlike "genes."
Iconology Historical analysis and interpretive study of symbols or images and their contextual significance, study of icons, or symbolic representations.
Primordial Thinking Primitive, existing from the very beginning.
Saccade A rapid, jerky movement of the eye.
Schema Generalized diagram, plan, or scheme.
Semantic Meaningful, as in the meaning of a sentence.
Simulacra Unreal or superficial likeness, an image, or representation.

Syntactic Structural, as in the grammar of a sentence.
Veridical Truthful, corresponding to facts, actual.

*The present article offers a review of recent psychological theories and research on art, **AESTHETICS**, and perception. It is limited to literature in the visual fine arts.*

I. INTRODUCTION

Gustav Fechner's 1876 publication of his *Psychophysics* as a scientific study of aesthetics began at the point when art styles were still anchored in Renaissance thinking, although radical changes were already beginning to manifest themselves. The vision and practice of art had been seriously questioned by the romantic revolution at the end of the 18th century. The romantic focus on the individual as the source of artistic inspiration and style was rapidly undermining the Aristotelian system of aesthetics that had characterized Western art since the Renaissance. Impressionism was already on solid ground, despite fierce attacks by the Parisian critics. The criteria that had defined good art for two millennia, namely, beauty, order, proportion, unity, symmetry, and concinnity ("skillfully put together"), were seriously in question. Over the next 100

Copyright © 1999 by Academic Press
All rights of reproduction in any form reserved.

years they were to become virtually obsolete. The issues in the domain of aesthetics have changed radically since Fechner opened it up to psychology for research.

No research on aesthetics can be considered adequate without taking into consideration the aesthetic theories that have supplanted the traditional dogma established by Aristotle, and the problems that these new theories pose for psychological research on modern aesthetics.

Webster's 1989 *Encyclopedic Unabridged Dictionary of the English Language* defines aesthetics as a branch of philosophy dealing with such notions as the beautiful, the ugly, the sublime, and the comic as they are applicable to the fine arts. The goal of aesthetics is to establish the meaning and validity of critical judgments concerning works of art and the principles underlying or justifying such judgments. The derivation of "aesthetic" is from the Greek word *aisthetikos,* or "sensitive," which is to perceive. According to this definition we must conclude that aesthetics is nested in "sensitive perception" or "sensibility."

Aesthetics as a philosophical discipline attempts to arrive at a broad and encompassing view of all of the arts. It has evolved over two millennia as a branch of philosophy, but in addition to philosophers, 20th century artists and art critics have made sizable contributions to it. As a philosophical domain, aesthetics lends itself poorly to the types of quantification that characterize the social sciences. This presents serious problems for the field of cognitive science where Daniel Berlyne placed it as the study of aesthetic enjoyment and preferences. Redefined as "empirical aesthetics" it retains its philosophical foundations although now it includes attention to sampling procedures, research design, and statistical analysis of data. The concomitant hypotheses derive from psychologists, psychobiologists, philosophical aestheticians, information theorists, semioticians, and cognitive developmentalists.

For psychology, the most widely used instruments for studying artworks have been, and remain, scales of aesthetic preference, aesthetic response, and aesthetic judgment. The first two call for subjective reactions and are not related to the work of art as art; such responses cannot be categorized as either relevant or irrelevant to what art is. Perception was and is still considered as a key factor in creating a work as well as in eliciting responses to it. More recently, information

theory and modern theories of picture perception have sharpened the focus on the modalities by which the aesthetic response is achieved. Aesthetic judgment may require more complex responses such as identifying or classifying, analysis, interpretation, or evaluation. These are obviously more pertinent to the quality of the stimulus. Tests such as the Welsh Figure Preference Test or the Graves Design Judgment Test ask for preferences. The newly elaborated Aesthetic Judgment Test asks for judgments. As such it promises to provide a basis for explaining differences in aesthetic judgment.

Over the course of the 20th century, both art and the field of aesthetics have been completely revolutionized, and the relevance of aesthetics as traditionally conceived is no longer certain vis-à-vis contemporary art. Both philosophical and psychological aesthetics must be based on contemporary aesthetic experience, and since that experience is based on contemporary art, it is necessary to review briefly the position of the art of our time.

II. TRADITIONAL VERSUS MODERN THEORIES OF AESTHETICS

Aristotelian and Kantian theories of aesthetics laid great stress on the category of the transcendent object, that is, on a category of objects beyond the limits of possible experience and knowledge. The transcendent object is not responsive to linear or categorical analysis and is therefore not acceptable to modern experimental psychology. However, transcendent experience is accessible to the individual's private world and as such it can be and has been studied by phenomenological methodologies, including interviews, autobiographies, psychobiographies, and case studies.

The Greeks had no term for "artist" and no concept of the artist as conceived today. The artist was regarded as a craftsman or artisan, and the arts were assessed only in relation to the purpose for which they were made. Painting and poetry were "pleasure giving" arts creating simulacra of real things. The arts were regarded as handicrafts to serve purposes that were approved by society, and the criteria with which to judge such products were concreteness and craftsmanship. The artist's goal was to produce a representation of the ideal in the context of Plato's theory of ideas—to improve on and perfect nature by eliminating imperfections in order to arrive at an ideally beautiful figure according to the "idea" of the beautiful in the mind's eye. With this purpose in mind, Greek sculptors and Renaissance artists worked out the canons of proportion for the most perfect human figure. Plato envisioned education as a total environment and the arts were to play the key role in the education of the guardians and in the shaping of their environment. Overall, art had a social and educational function and its value was judged thereby. The national epics were "textbooks" and poetry was sung at all social gatherings, public and private, and at all the religious ceremonies recited under state auspices. It is evident that the most important goals of the arts in Ancient Greece were to mold fashions that would conform with the ideals of the state.

The Aristotelian criteria of good art, namely, beauty, symmetry, concinnity, determinate bounds, and above all order and unity in diversity, indicate that the desired response in the observer was to achieve a greater sense of inner equilibrium and balance. The viewer's aesthetic response was an acknowledgment of artistic success—art as spiritual ideal to emulate.

The concept of beauty as an intellectual idea came into prominence during the Renaissance, and it was not until the end of the 17th century that the notion of beauty as feeling and emotion rather than as idea began to emerge. In the 18th century, the concept of art as an object of beauty and value for purposes of sheer contemplation emerged, and it was not until the first half of the 20th century that the idea of art as a novel and original creation with autonomous criteria specific to art itself became established. This view emancipated the work of art from subjugation to all forms of instrumental purposes. Thus, by the mid-20th century the Greek and Renaissance ideals were no longer relevant, although the Freudian theory of sublimation by means of which libidinal and aggressive impulses are transformed into socially acceptable products bears some resemblance to the Greek aesthetic ideal of the "improvement of nature."

The success of the 20th century revolution in the arts was fully realized in the cubist, dadaist, constructivist, and surrealist movements in the first three decades of the 20th century. Further developments between the 1940s and the 1970s led to abstract expressionism and pop, op, minimal, and conceptual art. These are all expressions of a totally different spirit and a totally different concept of aesthetics than in any previous time. In the 1980s, with the demise of modernism and the ascendance of postmodernism, a pluralist philosophy has relegated aesthetics to a no-man's land. These postmodern movements have totally discarded the classical concepts of aesthetics as guiding directions in the creation and interpretation of art. Even the concept of unity in diversity has not been completely retained. The means by which the integrity of a created work is achieved are no longer relevant considerations, and often the artist deliberately works against such a possibility. Thus, the most relevant criterion for the evaluation of works of art—the new aesthetics—has at the end of the 20th century become significance, that is, the work's novelty and capacity to offer a new perception of reality.

A. Novelty as 20th Century Beacon

Neither the Greeks nor the Renaissance artists entertained a concept of novelty as an ultimate "good." Renaissance artists were content to use biblical and mythological themes as sources of inspiration, and in the first half of the 19th century this was still the most acceptable route. However, by the mid-19th century the impressionists were engaging the present, "immediate" moment, and tended to shy away from classical themes. Novelty quickly replaced beauty as the criterion of creative worth, and between WWl and WWII the dadaists and surrealists were particularly determined to burn all bridges behind them. The scientific explosion in knowledge had changed the 20th century mentality, resulting in a dynamic avidity for the new, the unexplored, and the challenging. Little feeling was left for the traditional or the spiritual. The mood was analytic and reductive. Ironically, at the same time, there was a need to turn to personal sources as the raw material of artistic creation as the surrealists did. This tendency continued throughout the 20th century (as is evident in conceptual art, body art, performance art, and happenings). A 20th century mode of art was defined as an intentional composition. One example of this type of work is Christo's "Valley Curtain," an enormous curtain of orange cloth spanning a valley. [*See* NOVELTY.]

B. Current Conceptualizations of Creativity

Defined as the raw material of the self, art emerges through the interaction of two levels of ideation: primary and secondary processes. A primary process gives the artist access to the self as raw material—to personal raw drives and desires, libido, and aggression. A secondary process is the transformative level. Colin Martindale identified primary process as essential to creation, changing, however, the terminology to "primordial thinking" in order to differentiate his theoretical position from that of Freud. Primordial thinking is free associative and undirected thought, thus increasing the probability of novel combinations. "Primordial thought" says nothing about its sources. The term "secondary process thought" describes conceptual thought and according to Martindale "cannot produce novel ideas." The final artistic product is therefore the result of unsolicited, urgently felt decisions made at the level of primary process and the intentional decisions made at the level of ongoing transformational activity by secondary processes. The primary ideation pumps in new drive material or, as primordial thought, contributes novel associations (in Martindale's terms). Thus, all aesthetic decisions with respect to perspective, chiaroscuro, color, smoothing, smudging, tearing, repainting, etc., are continually being made by the secondary process as the ongoing input of raw material keeps streaming in at the primordial level, directing the creative process. During the working process, the perceptual function provides the crucial contact between what the world will accept and the creator's personal strivings that need to be incorporated to effect a work of self-expression in symbolic form. The final emergent qualities of conscious thought attenuate tension and direct the execution of the work into a style that is either adapted to the social order or is transgressive. The choices are made by the artist according to a personal program, agenda, or disposition. Thus, whether art is transgressive or not will depend on whether constraints in the personality of the artist have steered him or her toward change and disruption or toward social compliance. The personality of the artist, his or her inner vision, fashions the style. In the 20th century, artists have felt impelled to create a "difference" and to create transgressive work in order to make an impact on the audience. The spirit of audacity and rebellion in art appears to characterize much of 20th century creative work.

C. Meaning in Art

How does "new art" come to have meaning and significance? Colin Radford suggested that meaning is achieved when the viewer identifies with the artist's intention. "Meaning may be derived from representation, but the nature of a work of art lies in the interpretation and presentation of the content." What comes between the work and the object it represents is "the technical skill and perceptual interpretation of the artist." As this author has pointed out, 20th century art found its expression through transgressive forms that blatantly rejected traditional concepts of content and Aristotelian criteria of composition, among which beauty had always been quintessential. However, although modern art went beyond and often against the meaning that is attached to publicly identifiable forms, it had every intention to communicate a specific message. And this is what differentiates art from an accident of nature. Radford stated that the artist "invents, imposes imaginings, re-organizes and generally utilizes the public form so that it may take on a multiplicity of meanings more or less within the framework of his initial intentions." In the 20th century the novelty and integrity of a work of art are its new "beauty." The experience of new work for itself alone opens the individual to new possibilities of questioning self, other, and society. If we look at art from this perspective the talk of "meaning" becomes irrelevant. Picasso's *Guernica* is an aesthetically significant painting in so far as it moves and disturbs the viewer, communicates an aspect of our pain, and speaks to the human condition. The viewer is invited to "read" it within the constraints of his own receptive capacity.

Semioticians like Jan Mukarovsky reject "the identification of a work of art with any subjective mental state . . . and reject any hedonist theory of aesthetics." This position has received very little acknowledgment in the research literature. Mukarovsky indicated that "it is the entire structure which functions as the signification of a work of art." The Prague School, of which Ladislaw Matejka and Irwin R. Titunik are spokesmen, is concerned with the autonomous existence and essential dynamism of artistic structure within the social system. To understand the evolution of art and its significance they feel one must see it in constant dialectical relationship with the evolution of other domains of culture. From their vantage point, laboratory aesthetics makes no sense.

III. 20th CENTURY VIEWS

A. Art as Feeling

Art defined as a significant symbolization and conceptualization of feeling in perceptible forms offers the viewer access to the most basic mode of artistic understanding. The immediate response is prior to understanding. Feeling must precede in order that the viewer arrive at some understanding of meaning in all areas of human perception. The importance of aesthetic experience has been underscored by stating that what is gained from it is a more basic yet richer form of knowledge than the knowledge typically "associated with scientific rationality." The first intuitions of "knowledge" are affective.

B. Art as Cognition

In contrast, cognitive theories of art naturally define the aesthetic response in cognitive terms, that is, as an inquiry into the "whole" in order to discover how the parts contribute to the force and integrity of the entire structure. Significance, in this respect, is something that impresses the viewer with its abstract rather than its empathic qualities. How does one evaluate a work presented by the musician John Cage entitled *4'33"* and consisting of silence?

Certainly it is a novel gesture but how does it qualify as art—that is, as an aesthetic object? For some, it would not qualify at all. As a form it is entirely empty and since it has no qualities we cannot perceive it, its darkness, its shape. Nor does it express any feeling; but the feeling that it provokes is to make the listener think about what music is and is not. In sum, Cage's *4'33"* does fall into the category of avant-garde art by its express intent to call into question what music is, to shock expectations, to change perceptions, and most important, to rethink our own definitions of art. How-

ever, it does not call out the aesthetic response. The preceding issues are crucial to an understanding and appreciation of modern art and aesthetics.

Martindale holds that a plausible theory of aesthetics will evolve from what we already know about cognition and the determinants of hedonic tone, that is, from continuing research in the fields of perception and cognition. Julian Hochberg, a consistent and productive researcher in this area, maintained that the perception of a visual scene involves an internal or canonical form through which to apprehend and assimilate pictures. Because of the existence of schemas, human beings tend to abstract semantic information—to assign denotative and connotative or expressive meanings to melodies, visual forms, literary work, etc. This suggests that the constraints imposed by canonical forms determine what is seen and how it is seen. Research in cognition has thrown considerable light on both the perceptual and the cognitive determinants of response to aesthetic stimuli.

C. Theories of Art—The Avant-Garde

To understand the philosophy underlying modern art and to understand modern aesthetics it is necessary to look at theories of avant-garde art. Changes in art theories since the middle of the 19th century have been rapid, radical, and disturbing. These changes, not always preceded by logically thought-out systems of belief, resulted in the overthrow of a 2,500-year-old value system and rendered classical aesthetics obsolete. The succeeding developments in 20th century art were unprecedented, with a progressive emergence of new modes of inspiration, execution, and presentation. The spearhead for these changes was the avant-garde, greatly assisted by the late 20th century's rapid developments in electronic media.

The avant-garde is by definition art that is ahead of its time and is shocking, disturbing, and therefore viewed as socially and aesthetically objectionable. Its specific aim is to undermine the existing order and to replace it by another. It attempts to do this by contradiction, challenge, confrontation, and self-assertion. The avant-garde first defines its distance from the establishment and tries with all its resources to make itself felt as a force aiming to redefine the limits of art. The new art continues to assert itself irrespective of the degree of success or opposition. The early impressionists, cubists, dadaists, surrealists, vorticists, and constructivists were all avant-garde artists whose art could not be evaluated by the standard aesthetic theory of their day.

The criteria for significance are difficult to establish. The novelty and abrasiveness of the avant-garde could never meet the standards of beauty that were the primary conditions of traditional aesthetics, but its own novelty made it readily recognizable as significant. Novelty is a contrast phenomenon, only visible when compared to other work. It cannot be appreciated if the work is seen by and for itself alone. The avant-garde artist consciously and deliberately creates the contrast effects.

Although novelty does not guarantee either quality or significance, it is clear that art cannot be significant unless it is new. Significance in turn depends on the relationship of art to reality. Significant art makes a change, a reorganization in human consciousness. The avant-garde was in conflict with traditional aesthetics from the moment of its conception because traditional aesthetics insists that a work of art exists outside of time, and that it communicates some value or message in symbolic form regardless of context. However, in order to be recognized as art, the avant-garde product must be seen in context; it is only novel and significant by virtue of the contrast it creates. Confrontation is not always its goal. Sometimes the goal may be to simply direct perception. [*See* CONVENTIONALITY.]

D. New Definitions of Art: The American Avant-Garde

The radical changes in aesthetic theory and in definitions and practice of art which occurred between 1860 and 1920 were products of European thinking. American interest in the avant-garde emerged with the Armory Show of 1913 held in New York. This show featured for the first time the work of Marcel Duchamp, and it had a powerful effect on American artists. American art, however, did not enter the international scene until the 1940s with Jackson Pollock's all-over drip paintings. Since that time American artists and American aesthetic theory have played a major role in influencing the evolution of modern art the world over. Much of the radical revisioning and artistic activity oc-

curred at the turn of the 1960s at a time when a large-scale revolution in social, sexual, and aesthetic values was taking place. The most radical contributors to aesthetic theory and to definitions of art at that time were Morse Peckham (philosopher), John Cage (musician), Merce Cunningham (dancer), Allan Kaprow (happenings), Jack Burnham (systems aesthetics), and the conceptualists (represented by Joseph Kossuth).

It is difficult to define art so as to accommodate the many current varieties of artwork—pictorial, verbal, literary, kinetic, cinematic, performance, and land art, to say nothing of social art. As a structure available to the collective consciousness, the work of art carries a relationship to the total context of social phenomena. It differs from the mundane, natural object by virtue of its intentional organization. This structure's essence is to be its own center, which has itself as the purpose of its creation. The perceiver is not called upon to adopt an emotional attitude but to understand it. However, unless the perceiver responds emotionally, he or she will not be able to understand the work of art as an aesthetic object reflecting the artist's attitude toward reality and his reconstruction of it. Accordingly, the art form reveals the essence of the lived human reality at a particular time and place. Its function, as such, is to point to the psychic realities (symptoms) as they are experienced by the perceiver's psyche. These will inevitably suggest directions that may be followed or avoided. As a coded message, it is an implicit disrupter of the status quo. A full response to it forces and extends the dimensions of mind and sensibility. At its deepest, art attains a symbolic sense of its own time for the artists and their societies, offering in this way some sense of transcendence over death.

Morse Peckham was among the avant-garde theorists who significantly expressed the temper of the times. *Rage for Chaos,* published in 1965, articulated his belief that art is not a search for, or expression of, order, as had been the thesis since Aristotle's time. On the contrary, as a perceptual configuration, modern art offers the opportunity to experience more disorder than any other human artifact. The experience is meant to produce disorientation so that the human being may learn to endure exposing him or herself to the tensions and problems of the real world. The artist's role is to violate rules. Modern art is meant to "break up orientations, to weaken and frustrate the tyrannous drive for order. Art is rehearsal for the orientation which makes innovation possible."

Post-World War II aesthetics were also greatly influenced by the musician John Cage, who is included in this survey because of his important influence on avant-garde thinking. Cage placed a great deal of value on purposeful violation of old aesthetic ideas, saying that "art, if you want a definition of it, is criminal action because it conforms to no rules." He presented an artwork entitled *4'33"* in which an eminent pianist sat silent for this period of time—and in this "silence" all the random and atonal ambient noises become the "music." Thus Cage imposed aesthetic value on things that ordinarily have none.

E. Conceptual Art

Conceptualism is the most important of the avant-garde movements to make a radical difference in the evolution of 20th century art and aesthetics. It came into being when Marcel Duchamp chose a ready-made bottle rack to serve as a work of art. He later offered a urinal to be exhibited in an art gallery. Duchamp's acts were conceptual: he deliberately chose objects that had no aesthetic qualities of any kind. These acts occurred in 1913, and although the impact of his gestures was immediately felt, "conceptual art" as such did not become a widespread movement until the 1960s. Duchamp's actions opened up the field of art to a multiplicity of gestures that have changed the nature of art—and also the concept of aesthetics.

In America, Joseph Kossuth produced a manifesto for conceptual art describing conceptualism as an inquiry into the foundations of the concept of art. "All art (after Duchamp) is conceptual (in nature) because art only exists conceptually." According to Kossuth, expressionist art was a mere "ejaculation" of no merit, comparable to visual muzak, and for him the change from appearance to conception was the beginning of modern art. Since the 1970s conceptualists have claimed that aesthetic considerations and art collectors are irrelevant to the condition of art. Art's ability to exist must depend on its not being entertainment. Kossuth maintained that if philosophy (and religion) is finished, it is possible that art's viability may be connected to its ability to exist as a pure, self-conscious endeavor, and that art may exist in the future as a kind of philosophy

by analogy. The idea was that conceptual art would eliminate the possibility of sales, thus making art a noncommercial commodity. However, this never became a reality.

By the 1970s Gregory Battcock maintained that there were no aesthetic criteria for judging conceptual works. The conceptual art framework should be judged by how effectively it changes cultural values, that is, for the ideas that it motivates. Aesthetic theories, as they modulate practice, become the fuel for social significance and a potential for change.

By insisting on a new language and a new content, avant-garde art attempts to recharge forms that have become invisible through familiarity and cliché. It does this by attempting to change consciousness through techniques of disorientation, purposeful violation of established codes, and exploding the art–life dichotomy.

For example, the following activities fall under the category of 20th century avant-garde art: On Kawara sent postcards from each site he visited, inscribing the date and time of writing; Michael Heizer bulldozed holes in the Nevada desert; *Running Fence* was built by Christo to run across 26 miles of northern California land to the ocean and he also wrapped a large section of the Australian coastline in cellophane; and John Cage performed his musical composition consisting of over four minutes of silence. Robert Smithson's *Spiral Jetty* was a 1500-ft.-long, 15-ft.-wide jetty made of mud, precipitated salt crystals, rocks, and water in Salt Lake, Utah. Joseph Beuys did a New York performance piece entitled, *I like America and America Likes Me,* in which he spent a week in a New York loft living with a live coyote. The public was invited to visit during Soho gallery hours. In all of these works, the finished product (when there is one) is often less important than the activity itself. For the most part, however, avant-garde art consists of objects recognizable as art—painting, sculpture, music, dance, or performance—but the aims are different from those of traditional art in ways that identify avant-garde art as instances of confrontation, challenge, and transformation.

IV. THE CHANGING SCENE

As products of the 1960s, minimalism and conceptualism were attempts to dematerialize the art object, hoping by this means to avoid commodity status and commercialization. Such artists manifested a disdain for what they considered to be self-indulgent, undisciplined emotionalism, that is, expressionist art. By the 1970s, a postmodern aesthetic began to emerge. According to Frederic Jameson, the reasons for this are (1) the ascendance of a postindustrial, multinational, multiconglomerate consumer capitalism, and (2) an increasingly powerful media society in which reality is steadily transformed into images where (3) time undergoes fragmentation into a series of perceptual presents in which relationships become characterized by deathlessness. The postmodern artist became a "bricoleur" in an age dominated by simulation and by an inundation of simulacra. A historical amnesia is the inevitable result, since new art loses its subversive charge by being immediately absorbed into popular culture. Whereas the surface of modern art was fragile, frequently manifesting what has been labeled as the pathology of texture, postmodern art has been described as a pastiche of stultifying, banal, popular images (e.g., graffiti, comic heroes, and "picture writing" lacking in subtlety and mystery). For example, TV soaps signal a realism in which they have absolutely no investment. In general, the style is camp, and the reference to life is mannerist and empty.

A. The Work of Art According to Theodor Adorno

Within the context of the many divergent views and theories of art over the century, T. W. Adorno provided what may be the most comprehensive and challenging analysis of the work of art. He was concerned with the relevance of aesthetics and the impact of art as a cultural phenomenon on society. His position differs significantly from that of traditional aesthetics. The subjective experience of art is itself meaningless, and

> in order to grasp the importance of art one has to zero in on the artistic object rather than on the fun of the art lover. The concept of aesthetic enjoyment was a bad compromise between the social essence of art and the critical tendencies inherent in it. In true art the pleasure component is not given free rein . . . and great art does not seek to produce pleasure as an immediate effect.

Many modern works simply left out the question of how good or bad they were. Their claim to excellence rests on their abstract opposition to the culture industry rather than on their content or the artist's ability to articulate this opposition. For Adorno, the central core of the artist's aesthetic is autonomy. Works of art can serve as standards against which life can be measured, and also as an acknowledgment or affirmation of what is being denied in the outside world. Art is meant to mock the system from which it springs—a system which glorifies the commodity. It also expresses currents of resistance to the very system that officially endorses it. Adorno maintained that if art were not autonomous it could not resist society. High art exists to acknowledge the needs and desires that are repressed by the institutions we live under, whereas the popular arts are heterogamous—they serve as commodities and are subject to the pressures of fashion and conformity (e.g., pop art is a commodity; it supports the status quo).

B. The Work of Art According to Arthur Danto

Arthur Danto attempted to identify what distinguishes a 20th century artwork from a mundane object, now that the borders between what once qualified as art and a mundane object, such as a Brillo box, have broken down. "Repleteness," a characteristic suggested by Nelson Goodman, is not a necessary or sufficient distinction in 20th century art. Danto explained that in order to evaluate a 20th century artwork, the object must fall under the structures of the art world and the evaluator must have some understanding of what these structures are; otherwise he or she cannot respond to it as art. Danto points out that what makes the difference between an artwork and a mere artifact is that the question of "What does it mean, what is it about?" can arise in the case of an artwork, even if it is not about anything, whereas the question is logically inexplicable in the case of a mere thing.

V. THE RESEARCH PSYCHOLOGIST'S VIEW OF ART

In an attempt to define the proper study of aesthetics for psychologists, Colin Martindale maintained that the proper study of aesthetics should be not the art object but the analysis of what constitutes an aesthetic response and how people process aesthetic information. The observer's aim is to achieve pleasure, or more accurately, to create for themselves the "potential aesthetic experience" contained within the artwork. Now the question arises, is the aesthetic response a good measure of this and how do we measure it? What is the relevance of affect and cognition in perceiving, interpreting, and appreciating a work of art?

With respect to the aesthetic response, Michael Polanyi and Harry Prosch maintained that there is a crucial difference between the beauty of ordinary life, such as a sunset or a beautiful woman, and the beauty of an aesthetic object. According to them, in creative work such as poetry and painting, imaginative effort is necessary in order to integrate parts to understand their meaning. In other words, an active intellect is required in the aesthetic experience of art.

According to modern theories of art today, the most relevant criterion for the evaluation of works of art is "significance," and that is based on novelty and capacity to offer a new perception of reality. Art theory and aesthetics now contend that art is good insofar as it can sustain aesthetic contemplation and has no other purpose than to be an object in its own right.

A. Experimental Research on Aesthetics

When Daniel Berlyne appeared on the scene in the 1960s, his main interests were in curiosity, exploratory behavior, and the search for novelty, but within a short time these interests led him into the experimental study of aesthetics. Berlyne presupposed a basically Darwinian, neutral, monistic theory about psychophysical relationships between mind, consciousness, and the brain. As a scientist Berlyne was looking for the biological basis of behavior—for variables that lead to arousal of the nervous system. Arousal has been identified as the psychophysiological energy dimension mediated by activity of the reticular system. Independent measures of arousal are the EEG, EKG, and EMG. Stated simply, Berlyne's psychobiological theory of aesthetics postulates that the hedonic tone of the stimulus is determined by its arousal potential. The latter is a function of three (and often four) variables

as follows: psychophysical (intensity, saturation, pitch, and brightness), logical (meaning or signal value), and collative (complexity, novelty, surprise, and absurdity) qualities. The fourth is contributed by nonfocal stimuli. Of the four, the collative variables are seen as contributing by far the largest share to arousal. Like Wilhelm Wundt, and Gustav Fechner before him, Berlyne found that arousal is most pleasant in the middle ranges of stimulation. He also incorporated information theory and therefore described a work of art as an assemblage of elements, that is, information. He was able to show that the pattern of the semantic and syntactic information contained in the artwork can be used to define style. He also made use of multidimensional scaling to obtain indices of stylistic similarity. Berlyne's importance to the field of aesthetics cannot be overestimated. However, he overlooked the reality of the organism as a dynamic and essential component in the response process to aesthetic stimuli.

Research on ambiguity, complexity, and preference for works of art has offered exemplary models of empirical research based on Berlyne's theory of arousal. Inquiries into collative variables have dealt specifically with response conflict and arousal generated by complex stimuli, such as cubist and nonrepresentational paintings, drawings by M. C. Escher, and complex checkerboard patterns chosen to generate high levels of uncertainty. Many of the studies were generally supportive of Berlyne's theories, but findings with respect to arousal went contrary to Berlyne's predictions. For example, ratings of interestingness and pleasantness increase with increasing complexity but decreasing levels of arousal. It is possible that interestingness and pleasantness depend on factors other than arousal, like, for example, social learning.

Berlyne rejuvenated a field that had fallen into virtual oblivion since Fechner's death. He gave it form, substance, and leadership. Aesthetics prospers as an active field of psychological research largely due to Berlyne's efforts. However, his approach combining information theory with behaviorism may not have been the most appropriate for a study of the effects of creative process. The behaviorist viewpoint excludes experience and subjective interpretation.

Berlyne's findings have come under increasing attack by Martindale and other researchers in the field of cognitive psychology. Martindale suspects that the arousal system may not be a necessary factor in explaining hedonic responses. Martindale pointed out that formal collative and psychophysical aspects of the work of art are the ones that people tend to ignore in their search for meaning. Martindale believes that the laws governing aesthetic pleasure are quite similar to the laws governing perception and cognitive processes.

In 1972, Hans and Shulamith Kreitler offered a homeostatic model of artistic perception, suggesting that the viewing of art results in a rise in tension followed by a reduction in tension. For Kreitler and Kreitler, pleasure is but one aspect of the response. They label their theory "cognitive orientation." Art gives the viewing subject an opportunity for cognitive self-extension.

One might add that it also gives the viewing public an opportunity to transcend the self through forms that continue to live on, allowing the carnal body to reflect its time, place, and spirit.

B. The Aesthetic Response

Although researchers have been evaluating the so-called aesthetic response by means of preference studies, virtually to the exclusion of everything else, there is no research on what exactly the aesthetic response might be in itself. Harold Osborne listed the following as characteristics of the aesthetic response while responding to an art work: (1) attention is focused, (2) the viewer does not conceptualize or think discursively, (3) the viewer does not analyze or dissect the stimulus into an assemblage of parts, (4) attention is arrested by the here and now, (5) there is no imaginative play or association, (6) there is a disinterested interest in the object as presented, (7) the absorbed viewer is said to be experiencing an enhanced reality as long as awareness is being expanded, and (8) the intense absorption may be described as an identification with the object.

Osborne suggested that it takes practice to be able to engage successfully in prolonged "disinterested" attention for as long as it is necessary to bring any masterpiece into full awareness. None of the researchers have paid any attention to this warning. Approaching the viewing of art from another position, Richard Wollheim suggests that great works of art have no exhaustive point, and deserve more thorough and intensive

study than is offered by the aesthetic response. With respect to the eight characteristics described by Osborne, there is no literature to indicate how many of these are normally present, nor how many should be present, and which ones are in fact crucial to establish the presence of an aesthetic state. Further, among Osborne's eight characteristics there is no reference to the experience of pleasure!

The major drawback to a serious study of art and aesthetics by psychologists has been the absence of a coherent philosophical position of what needs to be studied. Since psychologists have limited their aesthetic research study to the aesthetic response, it means that the study of art as art has been excluded. This makes sense if one focuses on psychology as a study of behavior (the subject's response), as Martindale has insisted. But the study is presumably of art and aesthetics, thus, the need to study art as art. This shortsightedness of study is not limited to psychology. University art and philosophy departments are in the same league. For this reason, questions dealing with the significance of art have been few. To the extent that questions dealing with the significance of art as art and concerns about its importance in a postmodern society have been investigated, it is artists and philosophers rather than psychologists who have done so. But, research by psychologists on cognition and perception as factors in the aesthetic experience has produced some interesting results.

C. Cognition versus Affect as Determinants of Aesthetic Response

The present status of the research on hedonic response does not allow us to determine conclusively whether a genuine aesthetic response of pleasure derives primarily from the formal qualities of the work of art or from an affective response to the stimulation. Wundt was of the opinion that affect comes first and carries the main weight, and R. B. Zajonc's work (to be discussed later) lends support to that position. Research findings are divided.

Martindale postulated that aesthetic pleasure is related to the net activation of a set of cognitive units. In other words, apprehension of a work of art will activate cognitive units in sensory, gnostic, semantic, and episodic analyzers. The pleasure engendered by the work will be a monotonic function of degree of activation. He underscores the fact that this cognitive model explains only disinterested pleasure. In cases where the arousal system becomes active, it will take over the determination of pleasure or displeasure. The activation of the cognitive unit depends on a whole complex of factors: how capable of activation the unit is, how strong the stimulus is, how much attention is paid to it, and to what extent lateral inhibition will subtract activation. Martindale maintains that stronger cognitive units code more prototypical and more frequently encountered stimuli. Whereas sensory and perceptual details are ignored or quickly forgotten, more abstract concepts are remembered. In other words, meanings or typicality are more important than psychophysical or collative variables in determining preference. The one exception may be the artists who by profession are trained to be more interested in formal issues and collative variables, that is, in the tricks of their trade.

D. Naive versus Experienced Viewers

In 1962, D. W. Gottschalk attempted to deal with the problem of what makes an aesthetic response different from mundane reality processing by comparing the reactions of naive and experienced subjects to a work of art. Subjects with a thorough knowledge of art (artists) explored the canvas in a very different way, focusing on structural features whereas the naive observer missed the interrelationship of parts, the subtle expressive features, and the material form and functions. The experienced viewers clearly showed a more sustained and critical evaluation, thus reflecting a different interaction with the object.

There is no reason to assume, however, that cognition was the dominant factor in releasing the pleasurable response, although it may have added to the pleasure by virtue of the challenge that synthetic activity presents. Ulrich Neisser, Wilhelm Wundt, and R. B. Zajonc have all clearly indicated that human thinking begins in an intimate association with emotions and feelings which is never lost. Moreover, almost all human activity serves not one but a multiplicity of motives at the same time. It would be difficult to imagine that an aesthetic response would not maintain this intimate contact with emotions in response to a freely chosen complex activity such as looking at art.

Aesthetic experiencing is clearly very complex, and both cognition and affect may be shown to interact in intricate ways. Such experiencing is colored by sources of information about art, by individual habits of information processing, by affect, by past experience, by personal values and prejudices associated with class status, by information about prototypical categories (such as structural properties, subject matter, and constantly evolving artistic forms), and by cognitive structures that provide bases for perceiving the object.

VI. COGNITIVE VERSUS PERCEPTUAL THEORIES OF AESTHETIC EXPERIENCE

Cognitive theories maintain that the perceiver brings together hypotheses, inferences, probabilistic weighting of cues, affective subtleties and associations in response to aesthetic stimuli. Perceptual theories assume that association is the primary mechanism of response. Schema theories (hypotheses, concepts, and categories) belong to the cognitive camp. They place emphasis on constructs as means of explaining the different responses to aesthetic objects. Schemata are essentially information-confirming procedures in which the individual checks a hypothesis aroused by central cognitive and motivational processes against information from the environment. Schemata are relatively stable mental structures.

Julian Hochberg, a veteran researcher in this area, has postulated that internalized mental structures are integral to the perception of pictures. His position is that features of the perceived object indicate what schema would be appropriate to the picture being viewed. The schema is determined by the viewer's prior aesthetic experience or training as well as by idiosyncratic characteristics. The schema gives the viewer a way of storing the results of peripheral inquiries and terminating them when the schema is sufficiently filled out for the task being pursued.

Response-oriented theorists such as James and Eleanor Gibson maintain that perception is the result of stimulus information coming to the organism and thus determining the perception of pictures. This theory assumes the invariance of the art object. The viewer's response is the result of sensory stimulation, which implies that the aesthetic response is not the construction of the viewer; therefore, all viewers should have a more or less similar response. While the perceptual theory may apply to the perception of pictures, this would not seem to hold for subtle works of art, which are by definition not invariant since no two people derive the same information from them.

In short, neither the schema nor the perception view of aesthetic experience is able to account for the interactive nature of human behavior in aesthetic experiencing. The more recent contributions are those of information processing. This position regards perception of artwork as inseparable from memory and the representation of information in memory. This makes the response infinitely more complex and unpredictable.

It is clear that attention to art is neither comprehensive nor common due to the fact that art works are complex and hence lead to sparse perceptual sampling. Moreover, values and experience will affect what is attended to in an artwork.

Studies have indicated that information, whether cognitive or affective, can be contacted without the subject's awareness of the item. It has been shown that mental structures have important influences upon the direction of current attention, that attention can be directed by a central decision or by peripheral events, and that either one can interact in aesthetic experiencing. It is possible to have conscious processing of information that is unattended at even the semantic level.

According to R. W. Neperud,

> The importance of stored information as a factor in directing human attention serves to support our view that the visual and verbal structures that an individual possesses are important constituents, along with the artwork, as to what will be perceived. . . . Thus the emotional bias of visual information may affect not only attention to that material, but also influence, independent of the subject's awareness, the direction of the central processing system.

In short, stimulus and stored information may interact to determine the interpretation of the stimulus, or art.

It is evident that an informational processing view must take attentive behavior into consideration, as this is unquestionably an essential dimension of aesthetics. Berlyne's work in the psychobiology of aesthetics was conclusive enough for Berlyne to sum up his position by stating that "there are ample grounds for believing that the variables to which information theory has drawn attention have a great deal to do with the motivational aspects of aesthetic form."

The weakness of Berlyne's position resides in the fact that motivation for him depends on the collative properties of the stimulus. The organism as a source of massive and complex input has been left out. A number of studies by other researchers have demonstrated a pervasive, affective, evaluative dimension underlying the individual's reactions to art irrespective of level of art experience. Zajonc has presented convincing evidence for the view that affect is present at all levels of information processing. In fact, one is led to believe that the emotional code might well be the third code to be added to the dual-code theory of information processing.

How individuals form and change prototypical categories is a crucial area for exploration in order to understand how they come to appreciate not only art but also their social world.

VII. AFFECT AS PRIMARY VARIABLE

Francois Molnar's extensive research led him to propose a science for visual art in which affect plays a crucial part. He made two assumptions as a result of reviewing the field of visual art research. (1) The aesthetic effect is an affective response, a reaction to a stimulus from the outside world, passing through sensory channels. (2) There are no works of art without sensory input. An affective response does not exclude the cognitive element. According to Molnar, the first stage of the aesthetic response begins at the retina with the retinal cells responding to the formal properties of the object. The retinal cells act as filters and as feature detectors. Technically, the individual does not know what he or she sees or even that seeing is occurring. What are recorded are differences in luminescence, lines, contours, and angles. This describes the processing of neural information. Molnar adds that sensory information is processed at the cortex only if it is accompanied by influences from subcortical areas. Meaning does not yet exist at the level where the aesthetic response begins. Aesthetic pleasure seems to be independent, at least at the start, of the cognitive system. The aesthetic effect begins at the level of the early sensorial information process. If a hidden structure of the work of art does exist it has to be looked for in the constituent elements of the image—in the features elaborated by various mechanisms during the early stage of vision. [*See* EMOTION/AFFECT.]

Molnar believed that one of the most efficient experimental methods to test this theory was to study eye movements because the primary sensory system and the motor system are closely linked. Molnar pointed out that visual exploration is carried out without awareness and the organism controls the direction of the gaze only in exceptional cases. Observation of eye movements can contain important information about the organization of the network. Molnar maintained that the eye does not necessarily seek out the region of semantically rich information. During a fixation, the observer is unaware of the momentary content of the vision. It is therefore not possible to talk about the primacy of cognition in exploration.

The research by cognitive psychologists focusing on cognition versus affect has centered on how individuals attend to, make sense of, and value particular visual phenomena. It has not attempted to look at qualities that define "art." The cognitive research can identify preferences for stimuli as well as the contextual variables that affect them. However, this adds little to our understanding of what makes a work of art the profound experience that it is, alive and palpitating to our senses through the centuries, revealing the predominating rhythm of its period.

VIII. THE PHILOSOPHER'S VIEW OF AESTHETICS

When contemporary philosophers and artists think about art they do not put the emphasis on hedonics. They have been concerned with the problems of art in a postmodern society where values no longer seem relevant, and they have worried about the veridicality of representation as experienced by the spectators.

The philosopher R. R. Wartofsky has expressed himself as follows:

> The radical epistemological conclusion is that there is no intrinsic, veridical, or 'correct' mode of representation that is not itself a product of the social and historical choices of norms of visual representations.

Truth in perception is bound to canons of the veridicality of representation; these, in turn, have a history and are rooted in our social practice and in our own activities of picturing and representing. Thus, it is we who create the very norms of veridicality by our pictorial practice. Such norms are not arbitrary, though they are conventional; they are not biological but historical.

Pictures are heuristic and didactic artifacts. They teach us to see; they guide our vision in such a way that the seen world becomes the "world scene." This position runs counter to positions taken by psychologists, for example, Hochberg and Molnar, who ground seeing in the biology of the eye.

Another important concern to philosophers as well as artists is how viewers interpret art. Sidney Finkelstein maintains that all scientific approaches to vision which reduce it to those properties that are shared by all viewers may be distorting the phenomenon they propose to be investigating. Accordingly, the individuation of seeing is irrevocable, and the artist in the process of creating in a highly idiosyncratic and dynamic way makes the individuating decisions. Moreover, it is not clear how and when such decisions and choices are made, but it appears they are made by the intentionality of the artist. This liberty is taken intentionally in the service of expressiveness, and the result is more effective than it would have been had the schema been "correctly" followed. This dynamic aspect of looking and seeing is equally applicable to the viewer. It has been shown that the "scan path" or repeated pattern of eye fixations is particular to a given individual. That is, sense and meaning will vary according to individuals and their histories—their mental "fixes" and the conditions of artistic representation. The modern visual culture is much more attuned to the way space "feels." But it is far from appreciating the many "translocal and transtemporal characteristics which give the work its unique distillation of a sense of being in the world." It has been noted that impressionistic paintings present a world of reveries and reminiscences. Form is a way of pointing to feelings, and space is filled with all sorts of motives—and the result is a richness of emergent awareness registered in the course of looking and seeing. Finkelstein underscores the fact that small differences in location and small variations in weight of rectangle, stroke, or color in relation to others give different meanings to forms in the visual field. "What is true of these paintings must also be true of vision itself, but in a larger and more labile sense. Experimental psychologists are not even aware of the need to be sensitive to such polyreferential qualities." Allan Pavio stated it is also important to focus our attention on those aspects that stress the influence of memory and its interactive nature in the perception and interpretation of what is seen, remembered, and interpreted. Knowledge of the biology of the eye will not provide the answers to such problems.

A. The Proper Study of Aesthetics

Richard Wollheim has given considerable thought to the significance of art and its nature as the proper study of aesthetics. For Wollheim it is categorically not the organism's response to it, as psychologists since Fechner have maintained. He regards aesthetic judgment as an artificial concept whose alliance with positivism and verificationism, as well as its commitment to the democracy of aesthetic pleasure, rules out not only the relevance but also the reality of art as art. Wollheim maintains that what brought art back into consequence was the publication of Nelson Goodman's *Languages of Art,* and it did so by bringing back meaning or content to art—thus meaning as the core of art.

Like Danto, Wollheim believes every work of art contains specific meanings. In *Painting as Art,* Wollheim presents an account of artistic meaning in four important propositions or principles. These are: (1) Each work of art has its own, its one and only, meaning. (2) This meaning is fixed by the fulfilled intentions of the artist, where intention is used broadly to refer to the desires, beliefs, emotions, fantasies, and wishes—conscious, preconscious, and unconscious—that cause the artist to make the work as he does. (3) The artist's intentions are fulfilled insofar as the work of art that they cause him to make causes in a suitably sensitive, suitably informed spectator the appropriate experiences. (4) The work of art that is the bearer of meaning thus fixed is identified in part by its history of production. The four principles can be restated as follows: (1) the principle of integrity; (2) the principle of intentionalism; (3) the principle of experience; and (4) the principle of historicity.

Of the four principles, the one which Wollheim feels may be the most difficult to accept is that of integrity,

namely, "one meaning and one right interpretation for each and every work of art." And yet, it is possible to see that the work which has a one and only meaning can be shot with ambiguity. It is possible to see that it may be layered, and that once these layers are excavated they could all fit together. It is even logical that for historical reasons meanings should be reformulated in order to keep them in touch with new realities. According to Wollheim, critics reject the first principle—that of integrity—as having staying power, but artists insist on it. Reformulating a principle does not mean changing its meaning. Wollheim's project for an account of meaning in art presents a challenge to deconstruction—which on principle is determined to call all meaning into question at the same time that it is searching for the truth in art. In the final analysis, Wollheim places meaning in the mental condition of the artist whose goal is to create an art that is able to communicate this fully and convincingly. What the spectator needs is sensitivity, not knowledge of the rules of the game. To support his position Wollheim states, "If artists over the centuries had not succeeded in putting across what they wished to convey, they would have turned to some other activity to transmit what they intended." Painting has survived as an art to give meaning to and claim intelligibility for its products.

The multidirectional efflorescence of 20th century art forms reflects the creative history of its feverish evolution—the mementos of its own hyperbolic time and place. As such they are indices of the bewildering complexity of society's evolution. No real understanding of the art of a century can take place without an appreciation of its current socially construed history, nor of the "psychology" which animates a particular time and place, nor of the "intimacy" of the symbols that describe its time. Psychologists, besides perceiving and cognizing, are expected to learn to read artistic symbols as the flesh, blood, and bones of a century exuding the essence of a people's joy, pain, and desperation in a time when nothing seemed impossible.

Bibliography

Adorno, T. W. (1984). *Aesthetic Theory.* New York: Praeger.
Arnheim, R. (1966). *Towards a psychology of art. Collected essays.* Berkeley: University of California Press.
Beardsley, M. C. (1958). *Aesthetics: Problems in the philosophy of criticism.* New York: Harcourt Brace.

Berlyne, D. E. (1974). *Studies in the new experimental aesthetics.* Washington, DC: Hemisphere.

Danto, A. C. (1981). *The transfiguration of the commonplace.* Cambridge, MA: Harvard University Press.

Dudek, S. Z. (1989). Written in blood. *Canadian Psychology, 30,* 105–115.

Gardner, H. (1985). *The arts and human development.* New York: Basic Books.

Holt, R. R. (1960). Cognitive controls and primary process. *Journal of Psychology Research, 4,* 1–18.

Martindale, C. (1990). *Clockwork muse: The predictability of artistic change.* New York: Basic Books.

Noy, P. (1968). A theory of art and aesthetics. *Personality Reviews, 55,* 623–645.

Wartofsky, M. W. (1979). Picturing and representing. In C. F. Nodine and D. F. Fisher (Eds.), *Perception and pictorial representation.* New York: Praeger.

Wollheim, R. (1991). The core of aesthetics. *Journal of Aesthetic Education, 25,* 37–45.

Art and Artists

Colin Martindale
University of Maine

I. Art
II. Artists

Art as an Open Concept The idea that art cannot be defined because all objects called art share no common set of features. Rather, they bear a family resemblance to each other.

Artist A creator such as a poet, painter, or composer who produces novel artifacts that are accepted as works of art.

Beauty An immediate sensation of disinterested pleasure.

Expressionism The idea that art consists of the expression of emotions.

Historical Definitions of Art Definitions of art that define something as art according to the historical conditions in which it was created.

Institutional Definition of Art Art is whatever an artist or the art world says is art.

Mimesis The definition of art as the imitation of real or conceivable objects; generally the imitation is assumed to be an improvement upon the objects represented.

Taste The facility to make reasonable aesthetic judgments.

ART has been defined in a number of ways. In this article, art is considered to include art in general: the visual arts, literature, music, etc. The definition of who is and who is not an ARTIST has varied considerably across time. In the broad sense of the term, Homer has always been considered to be an artist. However, the creator of a beautiful Greek vase or medieval icon was in his or her day considered a craftsman, but is now considered an artist. The traits of artists have been considered since the time of Plato. Only in the 20th century has the question received scientific attention.

I. ART

A. Definitions

Until the 19th century, there was not much controversy over the definition of art. Beginning with Plato and Aristotle, it was argued that art is based upon imitation of reality. For Plato, the objective world is an imitation of abstract ideals. Thus, art is an imitation of an imitation. Art, he held, should exhibit *kalos,* which can be translated as "truth," "beauty," or "good." Plato was critical of art because it elicits pleasures of a base rather than an intellectual nature. Philosophy rather than art is a surer route to *kalos.* The ancient Greeks viewed music as the most imitative of all the arts; it was held to imitate as well as induce various emotions. Plato would have banned most modes of music from his ideal Republic. All poetry, which was viewed as almost identical to music, would also have been banned.

Aristotle's definition of art was very similar to that of Plato, but his attitude toward art was positive rather

Encyclopedia of Creativity
VOLUME 1

115

Copyright © 1999 by Academic Press
All rights of reproduction in any form reserved.

than negative. Art was held to be imitation that induces pleasure. This induction of pleasure arises from the fact that detection of similarity brings about pleasure. For example, a metaphor or simile gives us pleasure because it calls to our attention a similarity that we had not previously noticed. Though art is mimetic, it is not supposed to be an exact imitation. Rather it should improve upon what it imitates. It must be unified and, in most cases, beautiful. For Aristotle, tragedy is the highest art form because it unifies the largest number of elements: plot, character, thought, diction, music, and spectacle. The plastic and pictorial arts are of a lower order in that they lack thought and music. Aristotle emphasized unity, as in his insistence of unity of time, place, and action in drama. However, his ranking of the arts based upon how many elements they bring together suggests that he believed that art must have both unity and variety.

Aristotle's definition of art was not really challenged until the 19th century. Argumentation concerned the definition of beauty rather than that of art. Expressionist definitions of art were introduced in the 19th century by Fichte, Shelling, Schopenhauer, and Nietzsche. Twentieth-century expressionist definitions were proposed by Tolstoy, Croce, and Collingwood. According to expressionist theories of art, art is the expression of an artist's emotion. In most versions, the goal of art is to elicit the same emotion in the audience. As Nietzsche remarked, previous theories of art focused on the audience. Expressionist theories focus upon the artist. This view of art was anticipated by Aristotle with his doctrine of catharsis. Tragedy induces mild emotions in the audience. In a homeopathic manner, this somehow purges the audience of stronger emotions of the same sort. Expressionist definitions of art need to be embedded in a more general theory. Otherwise, an artist's temper tantrum would qualify as a work of art. A bigger problem is that we generally cannot know the artist's emotional state when he or she created a work of art. Was a poet really sad when he or she wrote a sad poem? If not, then is the poem not a work of art? A worse problem is that many works of art do not seem to express any particular emotion. R. G. Collingwood argued that bad art fails to express emotion. However, if art is defined as the expression of emotion, this means that bad art is not art at all. Thus we would end in the absurd position of declaring that many great works of art are not really works of art. At worst, it would seem that expressive theories of art are prescriptive rather than descriptive. In the end, they come down to saying that a work of art *ought* to express an emotion. Expressive theorists, aside from their personal preferences, give no compelling reason for why this should be the case. At best, expressive theories give a partial definition of art: A lot of art works seem to express emotion, but a work of art does not necessarily have to express an emotion.

By the 1950s, so many things had been accepted as works of art that Morris Weitz argued that art is an open concept or what would today be called a fuzzy set. Wittgenstein argued that scientific categories are defined by a specific set of features, but this is not the case with natural categories. He used the concept of "game" to illustrate this. There is no feature that all things called games share. One might think that all games have a winning and losing side, but—unless one is a multiple personality—this is not true of solitaire. Perhaps all games are fun. Anyone who has ever played bridge with a fanatic who treats every hand as if it were the battle of Hastings knows this not to be the case. Rather, games share a family resemblance. They share some but not other features. Weitz argues that the same is the case for art. In her work on prototypicality, Eleonor Rosch showed that open concepts are fuzzy sets: items can belong to them to varying degrees. Further, people agree very well as to the degree to which an item belongs to a category—that is, as to its prototypicality. For example, everyone agrees that tables and chairs are highly typical items of furniture and that ashtrays and carpets are quite atypical items of furniture. In speaking of typical exemplars, we make categorical statements—for example, "A table is a piece of furniture." In speaking of atypical exemplars, we tend to use hedges—for example, "By some wild stretch of the imagination, one might call a telephone a piece of furniture." The same solution could work for art. Few people would disagree with the statement that "Rembrandt's paintings are art." We would be more likely to say that "in a certain vague sense, Duchamp's Fountain (a urinal) or Warhol's Brillo Box (a Brillo box bought in a grocery store) could perhaps be called art."

Given that all natural categories are fuzzy sets, Weitz's definition of art seems workable. However, it runs into problems as to individual differences as to the typicality of works of art. The person in the street is likely to say that Duchamp's Fountain or Warhol's

Brillo Box are not works of art at all. They would certainly say that recent exhibitions of completely blank canvases or happenings (e.g., an artist spending a week in an apartment with a coyote) are not art. However, such things have been presented as art and accepted as art by some. George Dickie defines art as anything that is presented and accepted by the art world as art. This definition works in that all works of art share the feature of being accepted by the art world as art. The art world is defined as those who produce art and those who consume or exhibit it—for example, buyers and museum curators. At first glance, this definition of art seems to work at least for the high arts. As Martindale has pointed out, the set of creators and consumers of contemporary poetry is essentially identical. They can define poetry in any way they want, as they exist in a closed system. If we consider the art world for classical music, the situation is quite different. Modern atonal composers may create whatever they want, but no one will listen to their compositions. In the case of visual arts, Dickie seems to think that the art world is more monolithic than it is. It is the case that the art world for visual arts is concentrated in New York City. It is also the case that many members of this small group will accept as art whatever the in-group says is art. However, the art world is not monolithic. Members of the American Society of Classical Realism, who adhere to the mimetic tradition, would reject blank canvases and happenings as art. The institutional definition of art fails, because different art worlds do not agree as to what is art and what is not art.

Theorists as diverse as Danto, Hegel, and Martindale argue that what is and what is not art is defined by historical circumstances having to do with what artists are trying to accomplish. Once the goal has been accomplished, art ends. The end of art has been proclaimed by Varari in the 16th century, Hegel in 1828, Delaroche in 1839 (due to the invention of photography), Spengler at the beginning of the 20th century, Danto in the late 20th century, and by Martindale at a date several hundred years in the future. [*See* HISTORY AND CREATIVITY.]

B. Beauty

Until the 20th century, it was assumed that except in certain special circumstances, art should be beautiful. What, then, is beauty? Until the 18th century, it was held that beauty is something inherent in an object. Plato and Aristotle more or less equated beauty with goodness. They held that both beauty and goodness are characterized by unity and proportion and that inner beauty of a moral or spiritual sense is better than mere surface beauty. St. Thomas Aquinas held that a beautiful object pleases us immediately and that beautiful objects are characterized by perfection, proportion or harmony, and brightness or clarity.

Eighteenth-century British philosophers such as Hume and Shaftesbury made the argument that beauty is a subjective sensation rather than a characteristic of objects in themselves. Read closely, though—they left beauty in the external object. Lord Shaftesbury first made the argument that the sensation of beauty is disinterested. That is, beauty cannot be felt if we look at an object with the desire of possessing it. However, this is unremarkable if beauty is a sense, as sensation must come before cognition or desire. For at least a brief moment, at least, beauty must be disinterested. Modern research by Hans J. Eysenck and others shows that preference for paintings is about the same if the painting is shown for 50 ms or for as long as a person wants to look at it. With an exposure duration of 50 ms, many people cannot even discern what they are being shown.

David Hume also argued that beauty is a subjective sensation, but granted that there must be something in the external object that provokes this sensation. Thus, Thomas Reid's common-sense critiques of Hume's skepticism were nothing to the point in this case, as Hume had already granted the point. Edmund Burke listed six things in an object that are likely to provoke the sensation of beauty: comparative smallness (large objects evoke a sense of the sublime rather than of beauty), smoothness, variety of parts, gradual variation as opposed to angularity, delicacy, and colors that are clear and fair but not too strong and never dingy or murky.

Francis Hutcheson was the first to define beauty explicitly in terms of uniformity and variety: If uniformity is equal, then beauty increases with variety. If variety is equal, then beauty increases with unity. Virtually everyone agrees with this—for example, Hegel, Fechner, and Eysenck. However in 1933, George Birkhoff made the argument that beauty is equal to order divided by complexity. Birkhoff provided exquisite measures of order and complexity for polygons, poetry, and other arts. However, his equation makes beauty a function of unity rather than of variety. Empirical research by Eysenck and others has shown that a much better measure of beauty is order multiplied by complexity. The philosopher Monroe Beardsley argued that beauty is function of order, complexity, and intensity. More recently, Thomas Kulka has made the argument that the relationship is multiplicative: beauty corresponds to order multiplied by complexity or variety by intensity. If any of these factors is zero, an object will thus not be beautiful. Given the variety of features that have been held to characterize beauty, Dugald Stewart held as early as the 18th century that beauty cannot be defined because it is what would today be called an open concept or fuzzy set.

In his *Critique of Judgment,* Immanual Kant made an important distinction between types of beauty. Pure beauty refers to a disinterested sensation of an object or action of absolutely no use. Examples would be the perception of dance or of a flower. Adherent beauty refers to appreciation of an object combined with awareness of the use to which it could be put. He argued that appreciation of human beauty can only be adherent. For example, a heterosexual male contemplating a nude female cannot appreciate her in a disinterested manner. He will almost immediately be aware also of the use to which she can be put (for example, child bearing). Modern research on hip–waist ratios and other factors causing judgments of female beauty supports this idea. In modern terms, Kant argued that with adherent beauty, we prefer the prototype or composite photograph and, as Plato argued, the ideal. Again, modern research supports his conjectures. As far as female beauty is concerned, the prototype and certain atypical exemplars are judged most beautiful. Composite photographs are generally more attractive than the faces composing them. However, extremely attractive people have atypical rather than prototypical faces.

C. Taste

People differ in their aesthetic judgments but not nearly as much as is commonly thought. In the 18th century, Edmund Burke pointed out that disagreements are often due to what we would today call restriction of range. He asks us to find a single person who would say that a goose is more beautiful than a swan or that a Friezland hen is more beautiful than a peacock. He then proposed an interesting thought experiment. Suppose that two observers are shown a beautiful marble-topped table. They will agree that it is beautiful. Now suppose that a very similar table is brought in. Our observers may now disagree as to which table is more beautiful, but this is due to small differences in opinion. Consider two visitors to a juried art exhibition. They may appear to disagree wildly, but the paintings have been preselected for their high quality. Had all paintings, no matter how bad, been exhibited, we would find a much higher degree of agreement.

Modern research has shown that people agree in their judgments of great art or of designs or of pieces of music or literature about as well as they agree about anything else (e.g., medical diagnosis, whether a scientific article should be accepted for publications, or the personality traits of their friends). In all of these cases, pair-wise agreement is around .20–.30, but if we compare how well two groups of people agree, we obtain reliability coefficients of around .80–.90 even for small groups. In general, experts on art agree somewhat more than do untrained people. There is also evidence for cross-cultural agreement both among experts and among naive subjects.

Still, it cannot be denied that people differ in what David Hume called their "delicacy of taste." There are certainly people who paint their house purple with orange trim and fill it with kitsch such as black velvet paintings and Hummel figurines. Others, with the same resources, live in what we would agree are more tasteful surroundings. David Hume argued that bad taste may be improved by practice or exposure but that people differ in their capacity for appreciating beauty. If one has never been exposed to classical music, he or she cannot be blamed for appreciating only popular music.

In the 20th century, a number of tests of aesthetic sensitivity, especially for music and the visual arts, have been devised. These generally consist of asking people to pick which of a pair of artistic stimuli is better. The pairs have been selected such that art experts almost uniformly agree that one member of the pair is better. When responses to such tests are factor analyzed, the first factor can usually be labeled "Taste" and the second "Simple versus Complex." The Taste factor has to do with a preference for stimuli that are more symmetrical, harmonious, etc. It is correlated with intelligence, social class, amount of exposure to art, and some personality variables. As for the second factor, introverts tend to prefer more simple stimuli, whereas extraverts tend to prefer more complex stimuli.

If the perception of beauty is immediate, factors such as intelligence and exposure to art must come into play. Popular music is extremely simple, whereas classical music is complex. The latter may not induce immediate pleasure in many people. It would require effort and cognition, which are inimical to an immediate perception of beauty. On the other hand, popular music may be too simple to induce a perception of beauty in those with better taste. In other words, people may differ in what is the optimal combination of unity and variety for them.

There are also social factors in taste. We are more or less told what we are supposed to like if we have good taste. For example, anyone who seriously claimed that the Spice Girls are better than Bach would be told unanimously by experts on music that he or she had bad taste. However, expert opinion is not historically stable. As far as preference for polygons goes, artists preferred simple ones in the 1930s, complex ones in the 1950s, and simple ones in the 1970s. To take a more extreme example, most art experts today would take a preference for Bouguereau over Monet as an index of bad taste. Just the reverse would have been the case 100 years ago. While he was president of the Royal Academy, Lord Leighton of Stretton would not allow exhibition of impressionist paintings. He would have taken a preference for Monet over Bouguereau as an index of horrible taste. [*See* ART AND AESTHETICS.]

II. ARTISTS

A. Definitions

Even though art is an open concept, it might seem that we can define who an artist is: An organism who produces or presents art. We must include presentation as well as production if we are willing to include found objects as art. We need to use the term "organism" rather than person if we are willing to define the

productions of chimpanzees and gorillas as art. The distinction between artist and craftsman is blurred. The latter term is usually used to describe someone who creates low art (e.g., cuckoo clocks or duck decoys) or utilitarian objects (e.g., pottery or furniture). Exactly which term to use becomes unclear when we are confronted with a craftsman of exquisite skill such as the art deco furniture maker Ruhlmann or an artist who produces low-cost copies of works of art. The distinction is also historically conditioned. When they were made, ancient Greek vases or medieval religious icons were produced by craftsmen, but today we would label these people as artists. The performing arts also present us with a definitional problem. Should actors, actresses, movie stars, motion picture producers and directors, and people who play in bands or orchestras be called artists, or should the term be reserved for the person who wrote the script? We begin to slip down a slope toward absurdity, as we will end up including lighting directors, stagehands, and chauffeurs as artists as well. One recalls Groucho Marx's comment that he would not want to be a member of a club that would accept someone like him. Probably few would object to calling an actress such as Sarah Bernhardt an artist, as she added so much to the script that was new or creative. However, we do not want to define whether or not one is an artist in terms of quality, because we would end up with contradictory statements such as "X is not a poet because he is a bad poet" (even though we just said that he is a poet). If we allow Sarah Bernhardt as an artist, then it would seem that we must allow all actors and actresses as artists no matter how bad they are.

It would seem, then, that "artist" is a fuzzy set just as are art and beauty. Rather than defining an artist in terms of the quality of his or her work, we can define an artist as to his or her typicality. The chauffeur who brought a movie star to the set certainly contributed to the motion picture, but his or her typicality as an artist is so low that we can round it off to zero. The movie star is probably a rather atypical artist as compared with, say, Shakespeare.

B. Characteristics

Theorists have commented on the characteristics of artists since the time of the ancient Greeks, but systematic research only began in the late 19th century. Until quite recently, comments have concerned different types of artists rather than artists in general. From Plato onward, poets have been considered the wildest or most inspired type of artist. Perhaps this is true, as no obvious training is needed to write poetry, and poets often begin to write great poetry at quite young ages. (As Joyce Kilmer pointed out, any fool can write a poem.) Plato argued that poets are inspired: they write fine things but do not understand them. If we look at the self-reports of poets and writers, they tend to agree. Blake said that he wrote his poem on Milton "from immediate dictation." T. S. Eliot claimed to have not the slightest idea what *The Wasteland* was about. Robert Graves argued that the muse is a real psychic entity: the poet is only a scribe who writes down what she dictates. On the other hand, it is clear that skill acquired from training is necessary in music, the visual arts, and architecture. If it stood, which it would not, no one would want to enter a building designed by an untrained architect guided solely by inspiration. Until the 19th century, no one would have taken seriously a painting done by someone without formal training in the techniques of painting. Another difference between artists that has been noted is that visual artists tend—with many exceptions—to be quite deficient in verbal and "left-hemisphere" skills. They tend not to be verbally fluent, and they tend to find geometry obvious but algebra incomprehensible.

No matter whether they are artists or scientists or mathematicians, creative people share a number of traits. For example, they love their "work," work almost constantly, and say that their ideas do not arise from logical problem solving. In 1999, Gregory Feist did a massive review of studies of artists (visual artists, writers, architects, and performing artists) versus nonartists and contrasted the findings of these studies with studies of scientists versus nonscientists. As compared with nonartists, the review found artists to be more extreme in six main areas:

1. Openness to experience, fantasy oriented, and imaginative
2. Impulsive and lacking in conscientiousness
3. Anxious, subject to affective disorders, and emotionally oversensitive
4. Driven and ambitious
5. Independent, nonconforming, and norm doubting
6. Hostile, aloof, unfriendly, and lacking in warmth

Scientists share some of these traits. However, as compared with scientists, artists are more anxious, rebellious, emotionally labile, and impulsive, and less socialized, conforming, and conscientious.

Bibliography

Davies, S. (1991). *Definitions of art.* Ithaca, NY: Cornell University Press.

Dickie, G. (1971). *Aesthetics: An introduction.* Indianapolis, IN: Bobbs-Merrill.

Feist, G. J. (1999). The influence of personality on artistic and scientific creativity. In R. J. Sternberg (Ed.), *Handbook of Creativity,* pp. 273–296. Cambridge: Cambridge University Press.

Kulka, T. (1996). *Kitsch and art.* University Park, PA: Pennsylvania State University Press.

Lindzey, G., & Aronson, E. (Eds.). (1969). *Handbook of social psychology* (Vol. 3). Reading, MA: Addison-Wesley.

Sternberg, R. J. (Ed.). (1999). *Handbook of creativity.* Cambridge: Cambridge University Press.

Articulation

Albert Rothenberg

Harvard University

Analogic Reasoning Drawing of inferences or conclusions based on likenesses and comparisons.

Catharsis Purging or discharge of unacceptable or unpleasant emotions.

Dialectical Reasoning Practice of weighing and reconciling juxtaposed or contradictory arguments for the purpose of arriving at the truth.

General Theory of Relativity Einstein's extension to gravitational principles of his earlier developed special theory of relativity. In the general theory, the laws of physics are the laws of geometry in four dimensions and these laws in turn are determined by the distribution of matter and energy in the universe. Postulates of the general theory have been upheld by measurements made during a solar eclipse and the theory has provided the basis for developments of nuclear technology and of the field of cosmology in the 20th century.

Hallucination A sense perception not based on objective reality.

Impressionism A theory or practice in painting, especially among French painters in the late 19th century, of depicting the natural appearances of objects by means of dabs or strokes of primary unmixed colors in order to simulate actual reflected light, and usually concerning the subject matter of outdoor scenes. Post-Impressionism contributed a new emphasis on geometrical structures in nature to this approach.

Inductive Reasoning The process of drawing out or making inferences or conclusions based on facts and observations.

Problem Solving Applying procedures for finding single or multiple solutions to unusual or complex problems or queries.

Semistructured Research Interviews Use of predetermined questions and categories for eliciting interview information relevant to specific preconstructed hypotheses. These questions and categories are not presented in a set sequence but according to the flow and logic of the interview interaction.

The process of creation in any field involves progression from emptiness or disarray to the development of tangible order. The primary operative factor for producing tangible order in created products is **ARTICULATION.** *Articulation consists of cognitive, affective, and motivational bringing together and separating at once. The term "articulation" derives from "joining, "joint," and "to join," and is a word and concept with a double sense. The articulation or joining of an element with another one produces both a coming together and a separation at the same time. This is demonstrated quite clearly in the common use of the word "articulate." A person*

Copyright © 1999 by Academic Press
All rights of reproduction in any form reserved.

described as "articulate" or as an "articulate speaker" is a person who is able to present ideas and words clearly and smoothly. Such a person articulates or joins his words and ideas by bringing them together and keeping them clearly distinct and separate at the same time. In this double sense, the articulation process operates within creative activity. The process involves a constant bringing together and separating, and separating and bringing together, throughout the entire course. This occurs in many different dimensions—conceptual, perceptual, volitional, affective, and physical. Articulation encompasses other types of creative processes. The Janusian process involves articulation of propositional ideas; the homospatial process involves the articulation of mental imagery. The overall articulation process operates throughout creative activity; it includes both processes and also follows after them, leading directly to a creative result.

I. THE ARTICULATION PROCESS

In producing a work of literature or art, as well as in developing a scientific theory, creative persons separate out critical aspects of the material they work with, and they bring or interconnect these separated elements together. For example, systematic assessment of successive manuscript drafts has determined that Eugene O'Neill used the process of articulation to develop the drama—with its classic metaphoric title—*The Iceman Cometh*. Conceived by O'Neill from the idea of Christ as an epiphanic bridegroom coming to the virgins (Matt. 25:5–6) and from an old bawdy joke about an adulterous iceman, the iceman cometh metaphor together with the dramatic substance simultaneously brought together and separated out elements of the sacred and the profane, salvation and icy death, sexuality and chastity, marriage and adultery, and other complex articulated factors.

II. ARTICULATION IN SCIENTIFIC CREATIVITY

Articulation is a constructive process and it differs from ordinary problem solving modes that use pre-dominantly stepwise types of reasoning such as analogic, inductive, and deductive. All of these types of reasoning may play a role at some point, but they do not account for the phenomena of making, presenting, and creating that directly result from articulation. In scientific fields, creative thinkers use ordinary problem solving modes, often at a high level of effectiveness, but make new discoveries and far-reaching formulations by separating out and bringing together key factors underlying controversy and confusion. From Einstein's own account of the development of the general theory of relativity, it has been determined that he separated and brought together, as an articulation, the physical facts and principles of motion and rest. This step resulted neither from inductive consideration of a series of empirical findings, nor from a direct deduction from theory, nor from consideration of an analogy. Such processes primarily set the stage for the particular articulating conceptualization and also operated later in the working out of the fully developed theory of general relativity. In a similar way, Niels Bohr's development of the theory of complementarity involved the separating out and bringing together of the conflicting elements of wave and particle theories of the behavior of light. [*See* PROBLEM SOLVING.]

III. THE CREATIVE FUNCTION OF ARTICULATION

Creativity consists of the production of, or the state of producing, entities that are *both* new and valuable. The creative function of articulation is to produce tangible entities that are new and separate from previously existing entities and, at the same time, are connected to their forebears. Creations always bear resemblance to preexisting natural entities and events, and they are also separate and sharply different in some way. Cezanne's revolutionary Post-Impressionist paintings, for instance, were radically different and separate but also bore resemblances and connections with the work of the Impressionists before him. With respect to the natural world, scientific creations are both separated out and joined to nature rather than being a submerged part of it. Hence, they are to some extent truly new, *ex nihilo*, free both of nature and of past events.

IV. ARTICULATION OF THE SELF AND THE OBJECT

In art especially, articulation functions to produce tangible created products and also has direct psychological functions for artists themselves. Together with articulating an artwork, creative artists struggle to articulate aspects of their selves and their inner worlds. The struggle to articulate on both aesthetic and psychological levels concomitantly produces effects that are important for the emotional appeal of art. These effects derive directly from the articulation of the self and the object, an articulation in which the creative person's both conscious and unconscious self are kept in constant separation and connection with the object or substance being formed. Because of this continual apposition and joining of self and object, there is ongoing interaction. The self and forming object interact to produce mutual modifications and transformations within both the creator and the work of art in progress. In this mode, which is the experiential process going on throughout the creation of an effective work of art, separation may at various points dominate over connection and vice versa, but both aspects are concomitantly present and are ultimately balanced in the final creation. [*See* SELF PROCESSES AND CREATIVITY.]

V. ARTICULATION IN THE ARTISTIC CREATIVE PROCESS

An example of this type of articulation in the world of visual art derives from Edvard Munch's creation of the artwork entitled in translation, *The Screech* or *Scream*. In his diary in 1892, translated and quoted by Reinhold Heller in his *Edvard Munch: The Scream*, Munch described the initial experience that inspired the creation as follows:

> I was walking along the road with two friends. The sun set. I felt a tinge of melancholy. Suddenly the sky became a bloody red.
>
> I stopped, leaned against the railing, dead tired, and I looked at the flaming clouds that hung like blood and a sword over the blue-black fjord and the city.
>
> My friends walked on. I stood there, trembling with fright. And I felt a loud, unending scream piercing nature. (p. 107)

Munch's visual hallucination of a bloody red sky provided the emotionally charged element or elements that he progressively articulated into a creation. Evidence from drawings and preliminary painting indicates that over a period of more than a year he separated and connected his self, as represented by a human subject viewing the sky, with nature.

In his first drawing right after the experience, Munch showed a solitary man far in the distance leaning in profile over a bridge and looking at the sky and a boat on a small lake. The self, represented by the leaning forward man, and the object were initially depicted as both separated and connected to some degree, but the self representation was at that point predominantly separate from the scene while looking at it, and being in the distance, the figure of the man was also quite separate from a viewer of the painting. In the next version, a painting, the still-profiled solitary man was portrayed by Munch as leaning in the front of the scene, producing more interaction and connection with the lake and with nature as well as a nearer, closer connection with the viewer. Introduced into the next two charcoal drawing versions was a round bowler hat on the man as he continued to look in profile at the lake. The rounded shape of the hat was gradually separated out and emphasized in the curved lines of both the sky and the man's body in Munch's final steps of development of the completed artwork.

Following this drawing, in a pen and ink sketch done the same year, he depicted the bowler-hatted man facing fully forward. This constituted the critical change of presenting the man side by side and connected with the depicted nature scene rather than turned in profile and observing predominantly in an onlooking and separate way. In the final version, first done as a lithograph and later as a painting, he drew the forward facing man with an oval open screaming mouth and with similarly shaped but differently oriented curves in both the red sky and the man's body. Through this front-facing juxtaposition and superimposition of the man's form and shape—the final representation of the artist's hallucinating self—with the shape and form of sky, Munch produced a fully articulated structure.

Munch carried out a process of separating and connecting the subject with nature. In several steps he separated the man or self from the background of sky and water and at the same time firmly connected the self to that surrounding natural world through the coordinate shapes of the arms, face, and body, thus articulating the feeling in his initial experience. He thereby produced a universal visual metaphor, a metaphor that provides much of the memorable aesthetic power of this painting. In verbal terms, the metaphor is described as "the scream of nature." [*See* METAPHORS.]

VI. ARTICULATION IN THE LITERARY CREATIVE PROCESS

Another example of the articulation process of self and object is the creation of a central metaphor in a poem by James Merrill entitled, "18 West 11th Street." The title consists of the street address of a brownstone house in Greenwich Village that Merrill lived in as a child. This house was much later during his adulthood accidentally blown up by a revolutionary group called the "Weather Underground" during a project of making bombs in the basement.

The central metaphor in the poem was, "A mastermind / Kept track above the mantel." In the long process of creation of this metaphor, Merrill made a final change from an immediately previous formulated phrase pertaining to a mirror, "A mental world kept track above the mantel," and in a semistructured research interview reported by Rothenberg, described the change verbatim as follows:

> Well, I just thought it [mastermind] was better than the "mental world" and it connected obviously with "saboteurs" [a theme in the poem]. I mean one imagines behind any plot there is a mind. And to make it the mirror! I suppose from the word "mental" it's not so far to get to "mind." But it seemed to me it was already there in a way, an embryo in the original phrase. But in a way obscured by the temptation of rhyme—mental and mantel. (1983, p. 63)

The "mastermind" mirror in the poem allows a passing through in imagination of both the poet's childhood images and the world of the Weather Under-

ground. The very first version of the metaphor that contained what he called the initial "embryo" of the final formulation was as follows: "I am running toward a further / Magic room. Jamb and lintel of scarred leaf / Tilt benevolently forward." There is no reference to a mantel but the idea of another world is suggested by Merrill's early construction of the phrase, "further magic room."

To create the metaphor as used in the poem, Merrill employed an articulation process of concomitantly bringing together and separating. He made more than 25 different versions of these lines. Each of these versions involved varying degrees of interaction and articulation between self and object. The final step consisted of focusing on the off-rhymed pair "mental" and "mantel." Separating out the idea of mind, and simultaneously bringing it together with another idea in the poem, the idea of "saboteurs," he articulated the word "mastermind" into the metaphor and into the poem.

On the basis of evidence from earlier work and a subsequent analysis of manuscript drafts and events, conducted with the poet himself in semistructured research interviews, the following process occurred. In the initial precursor of this metaphor, "Jamb and lintel of scarred leaf / Tilt benevolently forward," Merrill had referred to Christmas decorations and represented the scene as a Christmas setting in the living room. He then in several versions continued that idea and brought it together with the notion of an ideal room reflected in a mirror—an idea derived from Christmas wishes to live up to his ideal self. Next, he conceived of the idea of a mirror "leaning forward like a matriarch," in which he separated out another aspect of self, his internalized mother, and connected her—the matriarch—with the earlier idea of the benevolently tilted decorations. This idea was continued through other versions. Then, he superimposed together the words "lintel" (from "jamb and lintel") and "mantel" (from "ma" in matriarch), resulting in the formulation, "The lintel gleams / The magic world above the mantel." After 15 more variations representing continual articulation of self and object, he formulated, "A mastermind kept track above the mantel."

Through this concomitant bringing together and separating of self and object, this poet produced a metaphor that joined an aspect of the magic room idea of his childhood with the idea of the saboteurs of the

Weather Underground organization. Also, in a final stage, he had separated out the initial consonants of the off-rhymed words "mental" and "mantel" and connected them into another effective sound similarity: the combined alliteration and assonance of "mantel" and "mastermind." On another level, he had associated a mirror with his mother (the matriarch) and the mastermind idea related to what he described to the interviewer as her very high intelligence and domination. Therefore, in settling on the word "mastermind," he also articulated an underlying meaning of the original idea focusing on the mirror. This was, however, not a breakthrough of unconscious material but a gradual unearthing and shaping of what Merrill indicated was at one point "already there." The poet articulated the mastermind metaphor as an aesthetic unity and integration into the poem.

VII. ARTICULATION AS BIPHASIC

As also illustrated by the Munch and Merrill examples, the creative process is biphasic. There is an initial phase where emotionally laden stimuli, experiences, and concepts are taken in by a person intending to produce a creation. Analogous with the literal meaning of the term inspiration in breathing or respiration, the taken-in contents, like elements in inspired air, are modified and mentally interact both consciously and unconsciously. Not simply expired, as would be conceptualized by an incorrect older theory of the creative process as catharsis, the modified mental contents are articulated. Similar to inspired air in which vibrations and separations are produced by the voice apparatus and the brain to form words and language, the modified inspirations are articulated in a second phase.

Bibliography

Abler, W. H. (1992). Aesthetics and pragmatics in human ecological theory development and family therapy: Janusian, homospatial, articulation processes in theory and practice (Doctoral dissertation, Michigan State University). *Dissertation Abstracts International 53,* DA9302962.

Handler, L. (1996). Object relations: Self, object and the space in between. *Contemporary Psychology, 41,* 385.

Heller, R. (1973). *Edvard Munch: The Scream.* New York: Viking Press.

Merrill, J. (1972). 18 West 11th Street. In *Braving the elements.* New York: Atheneum.

Rothenberg, A. (1979). *The emerging goddess: The creative process in art, science and other fields.* Chicago: University of Chicago Press.

Rothenberg, A. (1983). Creativity, articulation, and psychotherapy. *Journal of the Academy of Psychoanalysis, 11,* 55.

Rothenberg, A. (1990). *Creativity and madness: New findings and old stereotypes.* Baltimore: Johns Hopkins University Press.

Rothenberg, A. (1994). Studies in the creative process: An empirical investigation. In J. M. Masling and R. R. Bornstein (Eds.), *Empirical perspectives on object relations theory.* Washington, DC: American Psychological Association Press.

Artificial Intelligence

Tony Proctor

Independent Lecturer, Writer, and Consultant, Lancashire, England

Case-Based Reasoning A type of expert system that uses previous cases having similar characteristics as a guide to problem solving.

Chaos Theory A modern development in mathematics and science which provides a framework for understanding irregular or erratic fluctuations in nature.

Expert System A computer program that acts like an expert consultant in prognosticating situations or diagnosing problems. It achieves this by referring to a large database of specific knowledge in a given area, and by using rules of supposition to draw conclusions.

Fuzzy Logic A logical reasoning system which uses multivalued (as opposed to binary) logic. While classical logic holds that everything can be expressed in binary terms—0 or 1, black or white, yes or no, etc.—fuzzy logic permits values between 0 and 1, shades of gray, and even partial membership in a set.

Natural Language Processing An implementation of AI which has as its purpose the interpretation and creation of meaningful human language expressions.

Neural Network A variety of information processing system whose architecture resembles the structure of biological neural systems. The neural network tries to simulate the way a brain and nervous system function by analyzing sensory inputs and calculating an outcome.

ARTIFICIAL INTELLIGENCE *is computer software that enables a computer (or robot) to carry on tasks we would consider intelligent if done by a person. It includes giving expert advice, understanding natural language, speaking intelligently and recognizing complex patterns. The three most important types of artificial intelligence at present are Expert Systems, Natural Language Programs, and Neural Networks.*

I. INTRODUCTION

This article concerns primarily how artificial intelligence (AI) can be used to help with problems and situations requiring creative input.

Anything that might aid the process of gaining creative insights is worth pursuing and evaluating for its usefulness and suitability. Artificial intelligence does appear to have something to offer, though not all its

Copyright © 1999 by Academic Press
All rights of reproduction in any form reserved.

artifacts are concerned with providing help of this kind. Moreover, AI is very much a developing discipline and its ability to make significant contributions to the domain of creativity or creative problem solving is very much tempered by the developmental progress that has been made in AI itself. There is, for example, a considerable difference between what is possible at some future date and what is practicable given the current state of knowledge and resources available. This is exemplified in particular in the case of expert systems and case-based reasoning, which have potential for application but are limited by our current ability to produce systems which can help with creative thinking and creative problem solving.

The term AI came into being in 1956, when a group of interested researchers met for an initial summer workshop. Those attending the event included Allen Newell, Herbert Simon, Marvin Minsky, Oliver Selfridge, and John McCarthy. Initially, researchers attempted to simulate the neural networks of the brain. The endeavors achieved only little success because of the lack of computer technology needed to undertake the immense calculations involved. In the late 1950s and early 1960s, however, Allen Newell, Herbert Simon, and J. C. Shaw developed their "logical theorist" computer program, and introduced symbolic processing. This meant that instead of building systems based on numbers, they attempted to build systems that manipulated symbols. Their approach has had considerable influence on the subsequent development of AI.

In 1968 Marvin Minsky defined AI as "the science of making machines do things that would require intelligence if done by man." As such one might describe AI as being one of mankind's most creative endeavors. The possibility of building a machine to replicate the human brain has intrigued people for hundreds of years. However, while AI may be defined as the ability of a machine to think for itself, it is debated among scientists and theorists whether computers will ever be able to think for themselves.

One famous test for intelligence has been the Turing Test. Proposed in the 1950s, it required a room with a human and an "artificially intelligent" machine to be linked to the outside by a terminal which could only convey text. An interrogator then had to distinguish between the human and the machine by asking a series of questions. If the interrogator could not tell the difference between the two, the machine was said to be considered intelligent. In November 1991 a number of machines were entered for the test; one called PC Therapist III won the prize for being the least distinguishable from the human controls. However, the Turing Test does have its limitations.

In 1980 John Searle published his well-known report on the "Chinese room." He proposed a room full of dictionaries and filing cabinets containing Chinese literature. A non-Chinese-speaking man was then shut in. Questions could be sent into the room on paper and after a while the non-Chinese-speaking man could produce an answer by looking through all the dictionaries and filing cabinets. This answer may be indistinguishable from one of a native Chinese speaker, yet the non-Chinese speaker may not understand anything of the question or answer. So from the outside it may seem as intelligent behavior, but inside it could not be classed as truly intelligent behavior. This is a major disadvantage of the Turing Test, as it does not give allowances for this situation. Without any adequate intelligence tests it is difficult to determine whether a machine is really intelligent.

II. OVERVIEW OF AI IMPLEMENTATIONS AND APPLICATIONS

There are two schools of thought on how to implement AI. One assumes that the aim is to develop intelligent machines by simulating the way the human brain is built. The other school favors creating complex computer software that simulates characteristics of human intelligence. The more popular implementation of AI are neural networks, chaos engineering, fuzzy logic, expert systems, and case-based reasoning. In addition to these the area of natural language processing has developed as an important aspect of AI. Natural language processing provides an intriguing area of research and development in its own right. Other areas of AI include speech recognition, vision, and machine learning.

It is useful to distinguish between tasks which involve synthesis and those which are analytic in nature. Artificial intelligence has been developed to help with both of these kinds of task. Synthesis involves such activities as planning, scheduling, design, tutoring, or learning and requires the computer to construct, as opposed to recognize, a solution. Analytic tasks, such as those performed by expert systems, rely on the recognition of solutions.

Artificial intelligence systems perform many tasks, ranging from medical diagnoses to mineral prospecting. Computers have also been programmed to display some degree of legal reasoning, speech understanding, vision interpretation, natural language processing, music creation, problem solving, planning, and learning. Most of these systems have proved valuable either as research vehicles or in specific, practical applications, but most of them are far from being perfected. [*See* COMPUTER PROGRAMS.]

III. NEURAL NETWORKS

A neural network is a variety of information processing systems whose architecture resembles the structure of biological neural systems. The neural network tries to simulate the way a brain and nervous system function by analyzing sensory inputs and calculating an outcome. A neural network is usually composed of simple decision-making elements called neurodes that are connected with variable weights and strengths. Memory is altered according to the pattern of the connection weights between the neurodes. The processing of information is carried out by changing and spreading the connection's weights among the network. Prior to use for problem solving a neural network must be trained what to do. It learns by naturally associating items it is taught and grouping them together. Additionally, it can retrieve stored information from incomplete or partially incorrect clues. Neural networks are able to generalize categories based on specifics of the contents.

Neural networks have been used in a wide range of applications, from the design of programs for guiding flight and battle patterns of military aircraft to predicting the prices of many stocks and bonds. The list of applications is expanding all the time and extends from biological and psychological uses to include uses as diverse as biomedical waveform classification, music composition, and prediction of the commodity futures market. Many if not all of these activities contain ele-

ments which might be classified as creative. In essence neural networks are able to detect patterns in whatever data are presented to them. This enables the user to comprehend the nature of the pattern and the factors that produce it. Armed with such information the user can then manipulate the factors influencing the pattern production to ascertain how the pattern can be changed. Effectively, the user is able to experiment with new ideas and simulate the outcomes of suing these ideas. Since trying out creative and innovative ideas usually carries some element of risk, the ability to test out ideas in a risk-free environment is appealing.

IV. FUZZY LOGIC

Creative thinking is often required to solve ill-formed or poorly formed problems. These are problems where there is a great deal of uncertainty and difficulty in making statements with complete precision. Fuzzy logic has a role to play helping us to get to grips with such problems. Fuzzy logic is multivalued (as opposed to binary) logic. While classical logic holds that everything can be expressed in binary terms—0 or 1, black or white, yes or no, etc.—fuzzy logic permits values between 0 and 1, shades of gray, and even partial membership in a set. Moreover, when the approximate reasoning of fuzzy logic is used with an expert system, logical inferences can be drawn from imprecise relationships.

Neural network technology can be used to produce a fuzzy logic system which does not provide precise answers and outcomes to every problem but which will give reasonably correct estimations. A fuzzy logic system attempts to categorize patterns according to other patterns which it has "learned" and makes use of this learning to suggest answers. This allows more fuzzy input to be used in the neural network and greatly decreases the learning time of such networks.

Fuzzy logic has many domestic applications. Home appliances are common applications and fuzzy logic is a part of the AI that helps to control such products as enhanced washing machines, vacuum cleaners, and air conditioners. some clothes washing machines automatically adjust for load size and dirtiness of the clothes. Some vacuum cleaners adjust their suction power according to the volume of dust and the nature of the floor. Fuzzy logic is also used to control passenger elevators, cameras, automobile subsystems, and smart weapons. Fuzzy logic seems to have potential for development as far as creative thinking is concerned. In conjunction with neural networks and expert systems, fuzzy logic offers a means of improving the power of such tools.

V. CHAOS ENGINEERING

Chaos theory, creative problem solving, and ill-defined problems are all interlinked. Chaos theory is a modern development in mathematics and science and provides a framework for understanding irregular or erratic fluctuations in nature. A chaotic system is one that shows "sensitivity to initial conditions." That is, any uncertainty in the initial state of the given system, no matter how small, will lead to rapidly growing errors in any effort to predict future behavior. In other words, the system is chaotic and its behavior can be predicted only if the initial conditions are known to an infinite degree of accuracy, which is impossible. Chaotic systems are found in many fields of science and engineering, and the study of their dynamics is of considerable interest. Chaos theory tries to make sense of the impossible and find order among seemingly random events. The theory came to life in 1963 at the Massachusetts Institute of Technology. Edward Lorenz, frustrated with weather predictions, noted that they were inaccurate because of the tiny variations in the data. Over time he noticed that these variations were magnified as time continued. His work went unnoticed until 1975 when James Yorke reported the findings to the American Mathematical Monthly publication. Yorke's work was the foundation of modern chaos theory. The theory is implemented by using mathematics to model complex natural phenomena.

Chaos engineering is an important area in AI, and applications for its use have been actively sought. It has already proven itself as a useful tool in financial investment problems in assessing market risk accurately. Chaos theory has proven to be useful in other applications as well. Once again, the focal point of interest in this implementation is the understanding of patterns in behavior. From the perspective of creativity the same

comments apply as those that were made with respect to neural networks and fuzzy logic. [*See* CHAOS THEORY IN CREATIVITY.]

VI. EXPERT SYSTEMS

An expert system is a computer program that acts like an expert consultant in prognosticating situations or diagnosing problems. It achieves this by referring to a large database of specific knowledge in a given area, and by using rules of supposition to draw conclusions. Nevertheless, for expert systems to operate well, certain prerequisites are required. Problems need to be clearly defined and be narrow in scope. Broadening the scope of a problem might not lead to a satisfactory outcome. For example, while an expert system may solve the narrowly defined problem of selecting the best means by which to deliver a promotional message for a specific marketing communications campaign, it might not be able to suggest the exact nature of the message. Thus while expert systems might be created to guide one through the process of creative problem solving, they might not help where ambiguous, subjective, or creative issues are at stake.

There should also be experts in the problem area who can express their knowledge as general guidelines for decision making or specific kinds of problem solving. Thus while a computer program can provide a framework for guiding people through the process of creative problem solving, it cannot necessarily provide the expert advice required for the solution of problems requiring creative insights and thus might not meet the exact requirements of expert systems.

Expert systems have proven effective in a number of problem domains and are primarily used as specialized problem solvers. The areas that this can cover include laws, chemistry, biology, engineering, manufacturing, aerospace, military operations, finance, banking, meteorology, and geology. Expert systems use knowledge instead of data to control the solution process. The technology has made its way into almost everywhere that human experts live. Expert systems have been applied in medical facilities, diagnosis of mechanical devices, planning scientific experiments, military operations, and teaching students specialized tasks.

Marketing-related systems have been developed to set marketing objectives and suggest strategy options, select creative advertising strategies, choose among alternative proposals for advertising copy, recommend promotion tactics, plan product portfolios, and screen new product concepts.

VII. CASE-BASED REASONING

Case-based reasoning has been proposed as a more psychologically plausible model of the reasoning used by an expert than the rule-based reasoning systems like expert systems. This type of system uses a different approach and cases to evaluate each input. Each case is matched to what a human expert would do in a specific situation. It is assumed that there are no right answers, but only those that were applied in other cases. To enable such a system to operate, a case library is set up and each decision or outcome is stored along with the case material. When offering an input question or problem to the system, it has to be entered in such a way that its features possess characteristics that are recognizable by the system and can be matched to a similar past problem and its solution, if such exists within the case library.

Expert system designers use case-based reasoning to capture expertise in domains where rules are ill-defined, incomplete, or inconsistent. Law is an example of a domain where case-based reasoning is applied. Layers and judges reason analogically with precedent cases; rule predicates are simply not sufficiently well-defined for them to infer correct decisions deductively. In fact, one "right answer" seldom exists to legal questions. Legal experts make competing arguments instead, pitting conflicting interpretations of cases and facts against each other.

Case-based reasoning is linked to analogical reasoning and hence seems to have the potential to be a suitable vehicle to assist in creative problem solving.

VIII. NATURAL LANGUAGE PROCESSING

This is an area where advancement is taking place but much still remains to be achieved. To say that natu-
ral language understanding has been achieved may be an overstatement, but considerable progress has been achieved towards this end. Natural language processing provides a useful interface with other types of AI software and this form of AI can also provide useful applications of its own right. Work on speech understanding, keyword assignment, information retrieval, message understanding, routing, and translation are the focus of research and development in this area. It has found extensive creative applications in the domain of text generation and particularly multimedia generation. The difficulty in this instance is extracting some kind of semantic meaning from a sentence. This is accomplished by parsing the sentence.

To date there has been a variety of natural language software developed and marketed. It has either been for amusement purposes or for serious application. The software developed for amusement purposes includes ELIZA and the PC Therapist. The more serious software includes the AI products ALVIN (which can answer virtually any question about DOS), the Q&A Intelligent Assistant, and AutoWriter, a unique program that can actually help one research and write a paper or business report. ELIZA was one of the earliest attempts by a researcher to produce a computer program which could converse with a user. It was created by Joseph Weizenbaum at MIT and seemed to mimic the responses of a Rogerian therapist. Students at MIT took this simple program very seriously, "conversing" with it for hours about their most intimate problems. ELIZA does not parse sentences, but instead only looks for keywords. The PC Therapist is much more sophisticated than ELIZA. It is an excellent example of true sentence parsing and machine learning. The PC Therapist stores everything that the user inputs into it in a knowledge base, which is made available during subsequent interactions and session. This enables conversational ability to improve. A conversation is a "one-time thing," as are most human conversations, and so the PC Therapist is programmed to never respond with these exact sentences again.

Q&A includes a database, a word processor, a report writer, and Q&A's built-in Intelligent Assistant. The Intelligent Assistant understands spoken English, and will prepare virtually any kind of report, or answer any question based on the data in the Q&A database.

ALVIN is a natural language query system that can answer virtually any question about DOS. AutoWriter is a unique program that will automate the research and much of the writing required for producing a paper, article, or report.

IX. LIMITATIONS OF AI IMPLEMENTATION AND APPLICATIONS

While there are some very good neural networks that perform their designed task well, there are others that perform poorly. Furthermore, these networks require massive amounts of computing resources. On the other hand, fuzzy logic has few shortcomings. Although some implementations are simple, these systems work quickly and accurately without expensive equipment. Fuzzy logic has enabled computers to calculate such terms as "large" or "several" that would not be possible without it. Chaos theory has potential for handling an infinite amount of variables. This gives it the ability to be a success in the financial world. Its high learning curve and its primitive nature, however, limits it to testing purposes at the present time. Finally, expert systems and cased-based reasoning systems provide an efficient, easy to use program that yields results. Designed correctly, they can be easily updated.

Other major limitations reflect the debate concerning whether machines can truly be considered intelligent. Key issues are the capability of machines to possess perception or to directly interact with the world at large and on apparent profound lack of common sense.

X. AI AND CREATIVITY

The debate as to whether a machine can think for itself has some bearing on the role that AI can play in the sphere of creativity. We can take the general debate a step further and ask the question of whether a computer can be creative or whether creativity is separable from the human mind. Computers clearly can be programmed to produce a credible, grammatically correct English sentence given a set of rules and a database of words. However, the ability to judge the creative value

of such a sentence, and if necessary to modify and improve its creative value, seems to demand an extensive base of experience and complex logic that is so far unique to human cognition. Given these limitations expert systems would seem to be most relevant to the notion of providing support for idea processing rather than its total automation. We might then ask whether expertise on creativity can be captured and effectively utilized within an interactive, user-controlled computer support system.

Arguably, people are intrinsically much more creative than even the best computer. Human experts can reorganize information and use it to synthesize new knowledge. An expert system, in contrast, is apt to behave in a somewhat uninspired, routine manner. Human experts handle unanticipated events by using imaginative and novel approaches to problem solving, including drawing analogies to situations in completely different problem domains. Programs have not had much success at doing this. All humans possess commonsense knowledge which represents a very broad spectrum of general knowledge about the world and how it functions. This commonsense knowledge is immense and represents a considerable challenge to program designers. On first thought it might seem that there does not appear to be any feasible way of programming it into a computer, though attempts have been made by the CYC project at MCC in Austin in this direction. It is commonsense knowledge which makes humans aware of what they do not know as well as what they do know. This essential difference allows the human to avoid wasting time searching for solutions that are impossible and to concentrate only on finding feasible solutions. A human would know, for example, that you cannot put a camel through the eye of a needle but a computer might search endlessly and in vain for a solution unless it was programmed initially to appreciate that this problem was an impossible one to solve. Finally, human experts can appreciate the overall aspects of a problem and conceptualize how it relates to the central issue. Expert systems, however, tend to focus on the problem itself and do not take account of issues which are relevant but separate from the problem.

Given our present knowledge about the processes used to develop and enhance creativity it might be concluded that there is no deep experience on the subject but that there are a number of useful methods and guidelines. A system that can guide the user in the application of such methods might not seem to be worthy of being referred to as an expert system—but this of course may be a matter of opinion.

Both experts and expert systems must possess a large repertoire of complex knowledge and be able to utilize and operationalize it within a problem situation. Expert systems should offer advice which can be acted upon and not merely prescriptions for how users can arrive at their own conclusions. Moreover, an expert system should also be able to explain its own reasoning as to how it reached its conclusions and advice to enable the user to assess the value of the advice proffered.

An expert system capable of acting as a creative consultant would have to be able to produce novel problem definitions and be able to respond to human reactions to these definitions with further meaningful comments, explanations, or modifications. The implication of this would be that such a system should possess an experience base as extensive as that of a highly experienced human adult. Moreover, a potentially useful knowledge base would not have to be limited to any particular domain since idea-generating methods themselves are premised on the notion that creativity requires the breaking down of overly constraining categories of knowledge and finding previously undefined associations.

While automation or expert systems seem to offer a basis of assisting the creative process, at the present time the nature of the creative process hinders the effective use of the pure forms of both these approaches. To give some idea of the potential problems involved, the CYC (from enCYClopedia) Project at MCC in Austin, a 10-year project, was begun in 1984 and aimed to enumerate tens of millions of commonsense facts that will ultimately "add up" to logical intelligence. The goal is a system that can understand and speak ordinary language, and detect violations of common sense as readily as humans can. The total number of "rules" required for this was subsequently revised upward by a factor of ten (to 20–40 million), and extended the time needed by another 10 years.

Case-based reasoning seems to offer one of the best short-term prospects for producing suitable vehicles to assist in creative problem solving. The database in this instance might contain documented problem solving case histories across many different domains. Such a database might be accessed in a way that it provides insights for problem solving through analogical reasoning.

Bibliography

ALVIN [Computer software]. Woodside, NY: Thinking Software.

AutoWriter [Computer software]. Woodside, NY: Thinking Software.

Barron, J. J. (1995, April). Putting fuzzy logic into focus. *Byte*, 111–118.

Butler, C. .& Caudill, M. (1990). *Naturally intelligent systems.* Cambridge, MA: MIT Press.

Colins, H. (1992, June 20). Will machines ever think?" *New Scientist.*

Crevier, D. (1993). *AI: The tumultuous history of the search for AI.* New York: Basic Books.

Ginsberg, M. L. (1993). *Essentials of AI.* Los Altos, CA: Kaufmann.

Luger, G., & Stubblefield, W. (1993). *AI: Structures and strategies for complex problem solving* (2nd ed.). Redwood City, CA: Benjamin–Cummings.

Minsky, M. (Ed.). (1968). *Semantic information processing.* Cambridge, MA: MIT Press.

Natural Language for Work, Q&A [Computer software]. Cupertino, CA: Symantec Corp.

Ono, T. (1993, April). Chaos is coming. *World Press Review*, 41.

Patterson, D. W. (1990). *Introduction to AI and expert systems.* Englewood Cliffs: Prentice Hall.

The PC Therapist [Computer program]. Woodside, NY: Thinking Software.

Riesbeck, C. K., & Schank, R. C. (1989). *Inside case-based reasoning.* Hillsdale, NJ: Erlbaum.

Schwartz, E. I. (1992, Nov. 2). Where neural networks are already at work. *Business Week*, 136–137.

Shapiro, S. C. (Ed.). (1992). *Encyclopedia of AI* (2nd ed.). New York: Wiley.

Associative Theory

Daniel Fasko, Jr.

Morehead State University

ASSOCIATIVE THEORY *is an explanation of the creative process. This article will present the associative theory to creativity, including research on approaches to assessing and analyzing this process. The chapter will conclude with implications for future research and practice.*

Associative Priming The effect of degree of association between a prime (first word) and target (second word), which results in quicker response times.

Associative Theory Creative thinking as the formation of "associative elements into new combinations which either meet specified requirements or are in some way useful" (Mednick, 1962, p. 221).

Brainstorming A technique to produce a "large *quantity* of ideas without regard to the *quality* of ideas" (Baer, 1997, p. 42).

Cognitive Overinclusiveness The tendency to consider a broad range of associations as possibly relevant to a problem, which allows for the production of creative ideas (Harrington, 1993).

Creativity A "process by which a symbolic domain [e.g., mathematics] in the culture is changed" (Csikszentmihalyi, 1996, p. 8).

Divergent Thinking The ability to "produce many ideas, . . . to produce unusual and original ideas, . . . and to take an idea and spin out elaborate variants of the idea. . . ." (Baer, 1997, p. 21).

Information Processing Refers to how people receive, store, and use information.

I. HISTORY OF ASSOCIATION AND CREATIVITY

Although Sarnoff Mednick's 1962 Associative Theory of creativity is studied most, Charles Spearman's model of creativity, postulated in 1931, is the precursor to those associative theories that followed. Spearman's model included three principles: (1) the Principle of Experience, (2) the Principle of Relations, and (3) the Principle of Correlates, which is most similar to Mednick's associative theory.

Mednick suggested that creative solutions to problems could be achieved through the three processes of serendipity, similarity, or mediation. According to Mednick, through serendipity "the requisite associative elements may be evoked contiguously by the contiguous [close proximity] environmental appearance [usually accidentally] of stimuli which elicit these associative elements" (e.g., the discovery of penicillin).

Copyright © 1999 by Academic Press
All rights of reproduction in any form reserved.

Similarity is where the "requisite associative elements may be evoked as a result of the similarity [on some dimension] of the associative elements or the similarity of the stimuli eliciting these associative elements" (e.g., the use of homonyms in writing). Lastly, mediation is the process whereby the "requisite associative elements may be evoked in contiguity through the mediation of common elements." An example would be using a vacuum cleaner to remove ceiling flies, the idea for which may come through an associative sequence of 'ceiling–floor–vacuum cleaner.' [*See* SERENDIPITY.]

The creative thinking process is defined by Mednick as "the forming of associative elements into new combinations which either meet specified requirements or are in some way useful. The more mutually remote the elements of the new combination, the more creative the process or solution." In addition, Mednick proposed that creativity was a function of an individual's "associative hierarchy." This hierarchy is the way in which individuals produce associations to problems.

Figure 1 depicts Mednick's concept of associative hierarchy. These slopes indicate that individuals with steep gradients tend to give common associations, but few uncommon associations to a word or problem. According to Mednick, those individuals with flat gradients initially give common associations, but then are more likely to make more uncommon or unique associations. Mednick predicted that a creative person would exhibit a flat hierarchy (slope) and that a less creative person would exhibit a steep hierarchy (slope).

Mednick suggested also that an individual who develops a large number of associations to a problem has a greater probability of developing a creative solution to the problem. In addition, he speculated that "previously learned or innately predisposed methods of approaching problems will influence the probability of a creative solution."

The alternative "bisociative" theory stipulates that creativity involves linking together previously unconnected frames of reference or associative contexts. No valid predictions related to creativity were produced from this interesting theory.

II. ASSESSING AND ANALYZING ASSOCIATIONS

To measure an individual's ability to make what Mednick referred to as remote associations, he developed the Remote Associates Test (RAT). The RAT consists of 30 sets of three independent words which share a mutual but remote association. In the test an individual must produce a fourth word which could be an associative link to the other words. An example would be the word "cheese" for the cluster of "rat, blue, cottage." An individual is allowed 40 minutes to complete the test, with the score being the total number correct. Mednick reported that the Spearman–Brown reliability of the RAT was .92 and .91 for samples of 289 undergraduate female and 215 undergraduate male students, respectively. He reported several studies that appeared to support his contention that highly creative individuals produced a greater number of less probable associates to a stimulus word. Thus, according to Mednick, an individual's creative potential could be measured with this test. Unfortunately, several studies that evaluated the criterion validity of the RAT indicated little support for this measure. Additionally, equivocal results were found for the suggestion of unusual associative skills in persons scoring high on the RAT. They also argued that the RAT does not tap the ability to find remote associates.

In an attempt to verify Mednick's associative theory of creativity, the creativity and associative strength of 30 undergraduate students was assessed by administer-

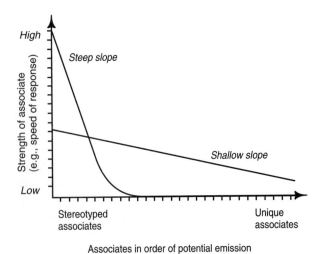

FIGURE 1 Hypothetical slopes of associative strength to a stimulus word.

ing the RAT and a paired-associate (PA) list, with half the 20 word pairs highly associated and half the other 20 word pairs weakly associated. It was hypothesized that highly creative individuals would show less variability than noncreative persons in their ability to learn items of "divergent" associative strengths. In addition, noncreative people would find the stronger associated pairs easier to learn than the weaker associated pairs. Results supported Mednick's theory that highly creative people have flat associative hierarchies and that less creative people have steep associative hierarchies. That is, high creative students showed less difference between item types than did low creative students. Thus, high creative people show less variability in their ability to learn and retrieve responses of high and low associative strength. Other studies, using alternative assessment instruments and materials have similarly shown that high creative students had a flatter response hierarchy than did low creative students.

High and low creative students also differ in the degree of response overlap. High creatives avoid repeating themselves more than do low creatives. Thus, these results suggest that Mednick's and others' interpretation of creativity as associative behavior should be revised to include the use of classes and class relations of conceptual structures in understanding the creative process.

Another word association test, the Kent–Rosanoff Word Association Test (KRWAT), has been used to study creativity. Responses here have been shown to be significantly correlated with creativity ratings for both engineering honor students and research scientists. There was an overall higher correlation between a domain-specific word list than of the general word list of the KRWAT. This further suggests needed revisions to Mednick's theory.

III. ENHANCING ASSOCIATIONS

Typically, the popular technique of "brainstorming" has been used to produce a large number of ideas or associations when one is involved in a task requiring creative thinking. Word association lists, such as Fisher's, which is a computerized dictionary of word associations developed in 1987, have also been used to produce creative thinking. Fisher's dictionary consists of 360 lists of associated words for specific topics, such as "crimson," "flamingo," "caboose," and "stoplight" for the word "red."

In a test to determine if Fisher's list would enhance creative productivity, subjects participated in a simulated work situation where they had to "think of cute or catchy phrases" to print under a picture on a t-shirt. Participants were assigned randomly to either an experimental group, who were given Fisher's association list to use, or a control group. All participants were paid and worked, on average, for a little over one hour. A second manipulation was conducted with the control group after the first session to determine if they would work longer and produce more ideas when given Fisher's list.

The group given Fisher's list worked at the task for a longer period of time than did the control group: 77.8 minutes versus 54.8 minutes, respectively. This represented a difference of 42% in time spent on task. In addition, the experimental group produced a larger number of ideas than did the control group: 87.4 ideas versus 63.7 ideas, respectively. Further, in the second manipulation, after being given the list, the control group worked an additional 51 minutes and produced 50 more ideas. Thus, it appears that even if one is fatigued on a task, one could work longer and produce more ideas with the Fisher list. In sum, the Fisher list increased productivity. However, these results do not suggest that the quality of ideas was improved. [*See* EN-HANCEMENT OF CREATIVITY.]

IV. DIFFERENT APPROACHES TO ASSOCIATIVE THEORY

Two competing approaches to Mednick's associative theory were presented by Hans Eysenck in 1960 and later by information processing theorists. For Eysenck creativity involves a nonrandom search-and-combine process seeking creative solutions to problems. Eysenck believed that the trait of "overinclusiveness" was central to creativity, and could be assessed by word association on divergent thinking tests. Cognitive overinclusiveness is the tendency to consider a broad range of associations as possibly relevant to a problem and which allows for the production of creative ideas. In a similar vein, divergent thinking is the ability to produce many ideas which may be unusual or are original. With regards to cognitive overinclusiveness, Eysenck suggested that it had a strong genetic influence and had an affinity with a personality factor he labeled "Psychoticism," which he believed predisposed people to behave creatively. [*See* DIVERGENT THINKING.]

There is substantial evidence in the literature supporting (1) the relationship between divergent thinking and creativity, and (2) the idea that creative thinking involves unusual associations or ideas. Thus, there appears to be a connection between the ability to generate associations, divergent thinking, and creativity. However, other cognitive abilities, besides cognitive overinclusiveness, may be important to creative thinking, (e.g., problem solving). Further, the production of unusual word associations and cognitive overinclusiveness may not be due to psychoticism. Moderately atypical associations have been found to be related to creativity, which contradicts Eysenck's theory that the production of unusual word associations, as demonstrated by psychotics, is related to creativity. There may also be other personality characteristics such as motivation, that may affect creative thinking. In sum, Eysenck's theory of creativity is intriguing, but empirical support is lacking, especially regarding the relationship between word associations, divergent thinking, and psychoticism.

Another approach to associative theory comes from the information processing perspective. Based on cognitive psychology research, an "associative priming" procedure (i.e., the effect of the degree of association between a prime and a target word) was hypothesized to be a more appropriate way to evaluate Mednick's theory. It was speculated that differences in the slope of the associative hierarchy should be mirrored in the slopes of the functions of the priming effects in terms of response facilitation to the degree of association between prime and target. According to the priming effect concept, there should be no differences in the slopes of the creative and uncreative groups, which contradicts Mednick's theory.

To test this, high and low creative students were identified, median age 16, with approximately an equal number of males and females, with the Thinking Creatively with Words (TCW) package. The first word (prime) is presented and then another (target) follows.

For each trial, the student was required to indicate whether the second word (target) was a word or nonword. Response times were taken on their decisions. Five lists of 40 word pairs were presented to the students with the 40 target words repeated in each list. Three of the lists included prime–target pairs with low, medium, and high associations. There was also an unrelated prime–target list and a neutral list, where each target word was paired with the word "blank."

The results indicated no interaction effect between creativity group and word association level, thereby contradicting Mednick's theory that the slopes of the associative hierarchies would differ for high and low creative people. These results, then, suggest that the associative hierarchies are similar for creative and uncreative people.

There was, however, a difference between the groups with regards to the degree of priming effects: primed responses of creative subjects were facilitated to a lesser degree than those of uncreative subjects. One persuasive explanation for this effect is that creative people have more links distributing activation from a given concept to other concepts. So, the more creative a person, the more associations she or he should be able to make. In explaining the finding that creative people exhibit smaller activation levels when responding to prime words, it has been hypothesized that in creative individuals concept nodes "fan out" to a greater number of associated nodes, and that activation to those nodes is then restricted within a given time period.

If, in fact, the "fan effect" is an automatic process, these results suggest further that the differences between the creative and uncreative groups can be accounted for by automatic processes. That is, they suggest that conscious strategies were not used.

V. CONCLUSIONS

So where do we go from here? Although others discussed the relationship of associations to creativity, it was Mednick's Associative Theory that set the stage for further experimentation and discussion. Mednick's predictions about associative hierarchies were supported by earlier research but subsequent research has suggested revisions and new thinking about this theory.

Interestingly, in his original study, Mednick even stated that "some of the positions which have been taken . . . are assumptions and not deductions. As more data are gathered some of these assumptions will assume the status of facts, some will be revised." The contributions of information processing theory to creativity opens the door to further studies of creativity, especially as it relates to assessing associative thought. This line of inquiry moves from the original stimulus–response investigations to a more cognitive explanation of associations and creativity.

In conclusion, associative theory is an intriguing attempt to explain creativity. Support for this theory comes from Mednick's and others' early research. There have been suggested revisions to the theory during the past 30 years. Some alternative approaches, such as Eysenck's and that coming from information processing theory, may continue to refine this theory. Granted there are other factors that influence creativity, but it was the associationists' theory which began efforts at linking this type of productivity to creative thinking.

Bibliography

Anderson, J. R. (1983). *The architecture of cognition.* Cambridge, MA: Harvard University Press.

Baer, J. (1997). *Creative teachers, creative students.* Boston: Allyn & Bacon.

Coney, J., & Serna, P. (1995). Creative thinking from an information processing perspective: A new approach to Mednick's theory of associative hierarchies. *Journal of Creative Behavior, 29,* 109–132.

Csikszentmihalyi, M. (1996). *Creativity: Flow and the psychology of discovery and invention.* New York: Harper Collins.

Eysenck, H. J. (1960). *The structure of human personality.* New York: Wiley.

Gilhooly, K. J. (1996). *Thinking: Directed, undirected, and creative* (3rd ed.). San Diego, CA: Academic Press.

Glover, J. A., Ronning, R. R., & Reynolds, C. R. (Eds.). (1989). *Handbook of creativity.* New York: Plenum.

Harrington, D. M. (1993). The problematic elevation of concepts to positions of preeminence. *Psychological Inquiry, 413,* 205–209.

Mednick, S. A. (1962). The associative basis of the creative process. *Psychological Review, 69,* 220–232.

Wallach, M. A., & Kogan, N. (1965). *Modes of thinking in young children.* New York: Holt, Rinehart, & Winston.

Attention

Glenn Toplyn

Mount Sinai School of Medicine

include those which focus on psychophysiological measures and on manipulation of arousal using stress and white noise. Further implications for a relationship between attention and creativity are suggested by studies of affect and creativity.

Arousal Generalized physiological activation, believed to be accompanied by diffuse stimulation to the cerebral cortex.

Associative Gradient The relative degree of conventionality versus unconventionality or novelty of associations in response to a problem.

Cue Utilization Attending to a range of environmental stimuli which can be used to aid problem solving.

Divergent Thinking The tendency to respond to problems with a diversity of ideas.

Ideational Fluency The capacity to generate a large number of associations with the consequence of more unique and novel ideas; a type of divergent thinking.

ATTENTION has been important to the study of the creative process and to understanding individual differences in creative potential. Associational theories of creativity have suggested that broad and diffuse attention is associated with indices of creative potential. The relationship between attention and creativity has been investigated in studies of cue utilization and arousal. Arousal studies

I. THEORETICAL CONSIDERATIONS

A long-standing hypothesis is that creativity is associated with broad and diffuse attention deployment. Individuals higher in creativity are hypothesized to include a wider and more diverse range of environmental stimuli in their field of awareness.

A theory of creativity associated with this hypothesis is called the associative basis of the creative process. This theory hypothesized that the thought process of creative individuals operated on a flat associative gradient. In general, associations are described as clustering along a gradient which differs in degree of conventionality versus unconventionality. That is, for any given problem there was likely to be associations which are common and frequently given and those which are novel and uncommon. Associations which are more conventional make up the preponderance of those given and can be visualized as forming a steep gradient, with many associations clustered closely together. On the other hand, associations which are more uncon-

Copyright © 1999 by Academic Press
All rights of reproduction in any form reserved.

ventional and less frequently given are called remote associations. Because they are fewer in number and vary in the degree to of uniqueness and originality they possess, they are considered to form a flat gradient. [*See* ASSOCIATIVE THEORY.]

Studies on creativity and attention have explored the question as to whether access to remote associations is related to broad and diffuse attention deployment. Two types of tests which are frequently used are the Remote Associates Test, or the RAT, and tests of divergent thinking, as exemplified by the ideational fluency tests. The tests differ in that for the RAT, there is one correct association for each test item. Divergent thinking, defined as the tendency to think of a diversity of ideas in response to problems, is measured by tests which tend to be open ended. For example, on ideational fluency tests subjects are given questions for which there are multiple associations and are asked to give as many associations as possible. Whereas the degree of remoteness is determined by the authors on the RAT, for fluency tests it is defined by its relative uniqueness within the test-taking sample. Studies of attention and creativity have used both types of tests. [*See* DIVERGENT THINKING.]

II. CUE UTILIZATION

Attention has been studied in relation to creativity through investigating the range of cue utilization among subjects who are also assessed on tests of creative potential. Attention is defined by the range of cues which are utilized in solving problems. The more incidental the cue in relation to the problem being focused on, the more the cue is on the periphery of the attentional field. A study testing high, medium, and low RAT scorers' utilization of incidental cues in a problem solving task, provided subjects with lists of words to memorize. While engaged in this task, another list of words were played over a speaker in the background. Following the memory task, the subjects were then asked to solve a list of anagrams. Solutions to some of the anagrams they were given had either been embedded in the memory list or were included in the list of words which were played in the background. High RAT scorers were found to solve more anagrams which had been cued. This was found for both types of cue presentation.

These results were criticized because the RAT was used. The study was replicated with a second measure, the Barron–Welsh Art Scale, a test of visual preference which has been associated with creative output. The results were not replicated for this test. The original study was also replicated using divergent thinking tests. A significant effect was found only for subjects who scored high on a nonverbal fluency task for anagrams cued by the memory list. The result was not found for the verbal fluency task for either task on the background presentation. Because the results were strongest with the RAT, but replication was only partial with divergent thinking tests, investigation of cue utilization as a test of attention and creativity has been inconclusive.

III. AROUSAL

A second approach to research on creativity has involved the study of arousal. Arousal is defined as a generalized level of physiological activation, thought to be accompanied by diffuse stimulation to the cerebral cortex and mediated by the ascending reticular activating system. Arousal has been described as being inversely related to attention deployment. As arousal increases, the range of cue utilization is reduced, so that only central and highly relevant cues are in the focus of attention. As arousal decreases, cues which are incidental, remote, and thus more on the periphery of attention become available.

The inverse relationship between arousal and attention has been applied to the relationship between attention and creativity. The hypothesis that lower arousal levels include broad and diffuse attention led to the hypothesis that lower arousal levels are associated with higher performance on tests of creative potential. This hypothesis has been investigated in different studies using psychophysiological recordings and through arousal manipulations using stress and noise.

A. Psychophysiological Measures

To test this, researchers looked at EEG results for subjects who had been assessed for creative potential using a composite of high scores on the RAT and the Alternate Uses Test. They assessed the percentage of time in basal alpha during resting states. Time in alpha represents the amount of time subjects exhibit slow alpha rhythms which are associated with states of relaxation, diffuse attention, and lower arousal levels. Less time in alpha, or alpha blocking, represents states of alert, focused attentiveness and higher levels of arousal. They found that the high-scoring group spent less time in alpha when idle, suggesting that during rest, they were at higher states of arousal.

In another study the same composite scoring system was used and skin potential amplitudes assessed during a habituation task. Skin potential is a measure of conductivity in the skin. Greater conductivity is associated with higher arousal. Subjects were tested for habituation to random presentations of 60 dB of white noise. Habituation was defined as the number of trials needed for subjects' skin potential to reduce in gamma amplitude to a negligible level of conductivity in response to the auditory stimulation. The more trials needed to reach habituation, the higher the arousal level. Results showed that the high-scoring group had higher skin amplitude and a longer number of trials to habituation as compared to the low-scoring group.

Both studies suggested higher, rather than lower, levels of arousal for the more creative subjects. However, the use of the composite scoring system as an index of creative potential is problematic. Other research on alpha percentages for subjects in resting states found no difference between high and low scorers on the Alternate Uses Test. It appears that the results from the divergent thinking test do not support the association of higher arousal with creativity.

Different results were obtained for the divergent thinking test when time in alpha was measured for subjects while they were taking the test. Subjects were tested on the Alternate Uses Test, the RAT, and the IPAT Culture Fair Test, a nonverbal measure of intelligence. Individual differences in performance on the Alternate Uses Test predicted differences in time in alpha while taking each of the tests. More time in alpha was found for high scorers, indicating lower levels of arousal, while low scorers exhibited more alpha blocking. This result was most pronounced when taking the Alternate Uses Test and was not found for high RAT scorers. High RAT scorers spent more time in alpha when taking the Alternate Uses Test than when taking the intelligence test.

These results suggest that individual differences on a divergent thinking test were associated with lower arousal levels. The difference with other studies is

that divergent thinking was reported independently and the physiological recording was taken during the test, as well as during other measures. Lower arousal, and by inference more diffuse attention, was associated with the activity of generating larger numbers of associations.

B. Stress

A different approach to investigating the arousal hypothesis has been to manipulate arousal levels and observe the effects on test performance. One way in which arousal levels have been manipulated to test the effect on creativity has been through the use of stress. Because stress should increase arousal levels and reduce the range of cue utilization, it has been hypothesized that stress should impair performance on tests of creative potential. Research has supported this hypothesis in studies on interpersonal stress. Subjects exhibited significantly more unique responses under low stress conditions than under higher stress conditions. The effect was more pronounced for males than females. However, a similar test of this hypothesis using the RAT was unable to replicate these results. The use of interpersonal behavior to induce stress has been criticized as being unreliable and difficult to replicate. There is too great a likelihood that different researchers will vary in how they behave with subjects among different studies.

One way this potential variability has been reduced has been through the use of a stressful film. Results showed a decrease in performance on the Consequences Test for subjects who saw the stressful film. For the RAT, results showed a marginal decrease, but a replication showed an increase.

Results from both studies indicate that stress decreased performance on divergent thinking tests. Both tests used measures which reflect a differential capacity for remote association. In one study the measure was of uncommon, unique ideas, and in the other of ideas which were conceptually "remote" as classified by independent judges. Effects of stress on RAT performance were inconclusive.

C. Noise

It has been mentioned that using interpersonal stress to induce arousal is open to variability. This is also true to a lesser extent for the stressful film because it induces arousal through creating dissonant cognition and affect in individuals who view the film. A type of arousal induction which further reduces the likelihood for individual variability is broadband white noise. This is because white noise is contentless. Noise induces arousal through increased auditory stimulation and is measured in decibels (dB).

As part of an investigation of stress and creativity, researchers looked at the effect of 75 dB on RAT performance. They found a marginal decrease in performance for subjects who took the test during noise as compared with both the high and the low interpersonal stress conditions. This effect was not replicated by others, however, suggesting caution in interpreting results.

A study investigating whether the effect of noise would be mediated by individual differences in ideational fluency hypothesized that there may be a differential response by high and low scorers to arousing properties of a test-taking condition. Subjects were classified as high or low in ideational fluency using two Wallach–Kogan measures, total number of ideas and number of unique ideas. Unique ideas were scored based on their occurring only once in the sample. Three noise levels of 60, 80, and 100 dB of noise were used to induce low, moderate, and high arousal while subjects were engaged in taking the fluency tests.

Results supported the hypothesis for the uniqueness measure. Subjects scoring high in unique ideas exhibited a curvilinear pattern to their responses, in which they scored highest for the moderate arousal induction of 80 dB of noise, while their scores were lower for the low (60 dB) and high (100 dB) arousal induction. Low unique responders did not show a significant difference between noise levels, although there was a marginal tendency for increasing their performance as the noise levels increased from low to high.

The finding was significant in suggesting that individual differences may mediate the relationship between creativity, arousal, and attention. The complexity of a task can be defined by the number of cues needed to fulfill the behavioral requirements of the task. For the ideational fluency tests used in this study, complexity can be defined as a function of the individual taking the test. This is because performance is better when more associations are produced and more cues are utilized. For high scorers, the test can be de-

fined as complex. For low scorers the test is simple, because fewer cues are utilized.

The difference in the complexity of the test for high and low scorers means different levels of arousal and attention deployment are optimal for the two groups when taking the test. This is because as task complexity increases, effective performance requires lower arousal levels to attend to wider range of cues. For high scorers, performance was highest under arousal of moderate intensity. The decrease in performance under high arousal can be attributed to a decrease in the range of available cues, while under the lower arousal level, an overabundance of cues may have reduced performance. For highly original subjects, attention needs to be of sufficient breadth to sample a wide range of cues, while at the same time being of sufficient strength to differentiate among cues of varying quality. For low scorers, originality increased as arousal increased. Because this group generated few associations, it is likely that they did not utilize a wide range of cues. Higher arousal and narrowed attention may have enhanced their capacity to focus more effectively on a constricted range of cues.

IV. AFFECT

In recent years, the role of affect has been investigated in relation to creativity. In general, different lines of evidence suggest affect is important to the creative process. The topic of attention is related because of data suggesting that affect enhances performance on tests of creative potential through enhancing access to a wider sampling of cues.

Research has compared the effects of a positive affect condition with a cued condition on a creative problem solving task. The task presents subjects with a box of tacks, a candle, and a book of matches. They are asked to attach the candle to a corkboard in such a way that it will not drip wax on the floor or table. Solving the task involves adopting multiple perspectives on the possible uses of the available materials to solve the problem. The transforming of cognitive set required to solve this task is an example of transformational thinking.

Affect was manipulated by showing subjects a comedy film prior to being presented with the problem solving task. This was compared with a separate condition in which the materials were displayed separately to cue alternate uses for each item. This display has been shown to facilitate performance on this task. A third condition presented subjects with a neutral film, while a fourth contained neither film nor cue.

Results showed that a higher number of subjects solved the task when shown the comedy film and when cued, as compared to the neutral conditions. There was no difference between the affect manipulation and the cued condition. It was concluded that the induction of positive affect allowed subjects to gain more access to cues regarding alternate uses for the available materials to solve the problem. Positive affect enhances access to material in memory, a consequence of which is a broadening of attention. As ideas become simultaneously available, attention becomes less focused and a wider range of cue utilization emerges.

Positive affect has also been found to enhance performance on RAT items of moderate difficulty. Both positive and negative types of affect enhanced performance on a divergent thinking test for total number of responses and negative affect enhanced original responses.

The role of negative affect is less clear. Studies on the effects of stress on creativity discussed earlier would suggest that negative affect decreases creativity. It has been hypothesized however that intensity of affect is more significant than whether the affect is positive or negative. Moderately intense states may be characterized by a controlled expression of affect which, whether positive or negative, may enhance access to material in memory and broaden attention deployment. At high intensity, such as in the stress studies, a reduction in cue utilization may occur and result in decreased creativity.

V. CONCLUSIONS

Research on the relationship between attention and creativity has offered qualified support for the hypothesis that broad and diffuse attention deployment is associated with higher levels of creativity. A problem with deriving conclusions from the data is that results from the RAT and divergent thinking tests have been inconsistent. The convergent properties of the single-solution format of the RAT differentiate it from divergent thinking tests, making it a less powerful index of creative potential.

The most direct evidence linking broad attention deployment with creativity consists of two findings: one, that high scorers on the Alternate Uses Test exhibited more time in alpha when their EEG measures were recorded while taking the test, and two, that individual differences on the uniqueness measure of the Wallach–Kogan tests mediated the effects of a noise-induced arousal manipulation. The first finding suggests that individuals higher in divergent thinking exhibit broad, diffuse attention and lower arousal as measured by physiological recordings while taking the test. In the second finding, the pattern of unique responses to a manipulation of arousal suggests that individual differences in originality are associated with different kinds of attention.

In the arousal manipulation, the pattern of results suggested that subjects high in originality experienced a benefit from a moderate, as compared to a low or high, arousal induction, while subjects low in originality showed marginal improvement as arousal increased to high levels. This pattern of response is consistent with broader attention and lower arousal for more, as compared to less original subjects because of the complexity of an ideational fluency test. The more complex a task, the lower arousal must be to attend to a sufficient range of cues. The complexity of the ideational fluency test increases as a function of the originality of the individual taking the test. Thus under high arousal and a constricted range of cue utilization, performance decreased for highly original subjects, but showed a marginal increase for subjects low in originality. Because the test is simpler for less original subjects, higher levels of arousal are more appropriate.

The benefit the more original subjects received under moderately arousing stimulation appears to have a parallel to research on affect and creativity. Results from different studies suggest that comedy or music can increase divergent thinking and creative problem solving, but stress can decrease divergent thinking and originality. This suggests that moderate intensity in affect, as with arousal, may enhance originality and divergent thinking.

It is possible to hypothesize that optimizing creativity includes an interaction of arousal and affect on attention. Arousal increases focus and discrimination in attention, while affect defocuses attention through increasing access to material in memory. Thus under moderately intense stimulation, the conditions may be present by which attention can be deployed to access a wide range of cues while at the same time retaining sufficient focus to discriminate among the quality of the available cues and discern those which mediate remote and original ideas. These conditions may be optimal for the kind of complex tasks, requiring diverse and original ideas, which lead to creative products.

Bibliography

Mednick, S. A. (1962). The associative basis of the creative process. *Psychological Review, 69,* 220–232.

Runco, M. A. (1991). *Divergent thinking.* Norwood, NJ: Ablex.

Russ, S. W. (1993). *Affect and creativity: The role of affect and play in the creative process.* Hillsdale, NJ: Erlbaum.

Toplyn, G., & MaGuire, W. (1991). The differential effect of noise on creative task performance. *Creativity Research Journal, 4,* 337–347.

Wallach, M. A., & Kogan, N. (1965). *Modes of thinking in young children.* New York: Holt, Rinehart, & Winston.

Attribution and Creativity

Joseph Kasof

University of California, Irvine

Consensus Generalization across actors; that is, the extent to which other actors behave similarly in a given situation.

Consistency Generalization across time; that is, the extent to which the actor behaves similarly in similar situations.

Dispositional A causal factor that is both relatively stable across time and internal to the actor.

Distinctiveness Generalization across situations; that is, the extent to which the actor behaves similarly in different situations.

Situational A causal factor that is external to the actor.

ATTRIBUTIONAL PROCESSES exert a powerful influence on the subjective reception of original products—whether a creation is evaluated positively or negatively, and how it is explained. This article presents an overview of attributional influences on the subjective reception of original products, focusing on how the evaluation and causal attribution of original products are influenced by covariation, perceptual salience, self-serving bias, status expectancy bias, in-group bias, and social loafing.

I. THE SOCIAL ECOLOGY OF CREATIVITY

Throughout history, creativity has been attributed primarily to the souls, genes, brains, personality traits, values, cognitive styles, special abilities, and other stable dispositions of "creative people" and "geniuses." Relatively seldom has creativity been attributed to situational causes. The tendency to attribute creative performance to dispositional causes has characterized not only laypeople, but scientists too. Traditionally, creativity research has been conducted primarily not by sociologists, economists, anthropologists, social psychologists, or environmental psychologists, but by personality psychologists and cognitive psychologists who searched for the distinctive attributes of "creative people" and "creative thought." Creativity was studied in a kind of intellectual vacuum, in nearly total disregard of the social and environmental context.

Recently, in contrast to the disposition-oriented focus of traditional creativity research, investigators have begun to examine contextual influences on creativity. These investigators, taking what may be termed a social-ecological perspective, have broadened their

Copyright © 1999 by Academic Press
All rights of reproduction in any form reserved.

focus to include not only the creative product and the creator but also certain elements of the situational context which influence the likelihood and degree of creativity. For example, Dean Keith Simonton has demonstrated that creativity is influenced by macrolevel and temporally distal phenomena such as political fragmentation and instability, civil disturbance, geographic marginality, and the availability of exemplars or models in prior generations, and Teresa Amabile has demonstrated that creative performance is affected by proximate situational variables such as social evaluation, surveillance, task constraint, and other elements of the work environment. Other researchers have demonstrated that the creation of original products may be influenced by such distal and ambient variables as organizational structure, social class, and occupation.

The attributional approach to creativity focuses on another fundamental aspect of the social ecology of creativity: the social reception of original products. Creativity researchers have defined the creative product as a product that satisfies two basic criteria: (1) the creative product must be unusually original, rare, novel, and statistically infrequent, and (2) it must be approved, accepted, valued, and considered "appropriate" or "good." By this definition, creativity is not a purely objective, fixed property inherent in the creative product; rather, in part it involves a subjective judgment that is conferred on the original product. The first criterion, which might be called the originality requirement, is objective; the second criterion, the evaluation requirement, is subjective. Another important element of the subjective reception of original products is that of causal attribution, which influences both the production and the evaluation of original products, as well as the assessment of creators. [*See* CREATIVE PRODUCTS; DEFINITIONS OF CREATIVITY.]

By focusing on the reception of original products, the attributional approach provides a theoretical framework for understanding a fundamental dimension of creativity that is beyond the scope of dispositional approaches and other social-ecological approaches to creativity. For example, dispositionally oriented creativity researchers have generally regarded variation in the evaluation of original products not as something to be explained, but as something to be systematically ignored. To this end, researchers have developed so-called "objective creativity tests" for which interrater reliability is nearly perfect and have used "blind" judges

to evaluate creations in ignorance of the creator's race, sex, physical attractiveness, nationality, and other "irrelevant" information that might significantly influence evaluation. Although this approach has important merits, in stripping the laboratory of such powerful influences, it reduces ecological validity, artificially inflates reliability, systematically obscures the subjective dimension of creativity, and overlooks some of the most powerful social determinants of creativity in the real world. The attributional approach, by contrast, regards the evaluation and the causal attribution of original products as dependent variables—as phenomena to be understood in their own right. Thus, a typical methodological strategy is to hold constant the creation and systematically vary extraneous factors such as the creator's presumed status or the creator's presumed membership in the judge's in-group versus out-group. It is thus possible to experimentally discover how the reception of original products is socially constructed.

The view that is emerging from these researches is that neither the original product nor the evaluations of that product arise in a social or environmental vacuum. Rather, each original act, and each evaluation of that act, is inextricably embedded in a webbed field of complex social and environmental influences. Ironically, the attributional approach itself provides a social-ecological explanation for why the attributional approach and other social-ecological influences have been so long ignored.

II. HOW PEOPLE EXPLAIN CREATIVITY

Theory and research on causal attribution have been concerned primarily with three major determinants of attribution: covariation principles, salience, and the self-serving bias. The human tendency to attribute creative behavior to dispositional rather than situational causes can be understood as a function of each of these three factors.

A. Creativity and Covariation

Harold Kelley's covariation theory helps to explain how people attribute creative behavior. Research supports Kelley's proposal that lower values for a behavior's consensus (generalization across actors) and distinctiveness (generalization across situations) lead to more internal attributions, while higher values for its consistency (generalization across time) lead to more stable attributions.

By definition, creative behavior is highly original, and hence very low in consensus. Thus, creative behavior is attributed very internally. Further, the more highly original a creative product is, the lower is its consensus value, and the more internal is the resulting attribution.

The inherently low consensus value of creative behavior leads to additional, more highly complex hypotheses which have been confirmed in experimental research. For example, the number of creative behaviors that are required before a creative disposition is inferred is lower than the number of noncreative behaviors that are required before a noncreative disposition is inferred. Similarly, the number of noncreative behaviors that are required before a previously ascribed creative disposition is disconfirmed is higher than the number of creative behaviors that are required before a previously ascribed noncreative disposition is disconfirmed. Moreover, the inference of traits from behavior is less influenced by situational factors for attributions of highly creative behavior than for attributions of less creative behavior.

The consensus variable also helps to explain exaggerations of the general tendency to attribute creative behavior dispositionally. According to the well-documented augmenting principle, when a factor that is thought to facilitate a certain behavior is present along with a factor that is thought to inhibit the behavior, greater causal weight is given to the facilitative factor. Thus creative behavior that is apparently performed under the handicap of adverse circumstance is attributed more internally than it would be otherwise. In one experiment, for example, researchers asked subjects to evaluate paintings that were attributed to artists described as having faced some physical or financial handicap or as not having faced such handicap. Subjects evaluated the paintings more positively when they were attributed to handicapped creators than to non-handicapped creators, and they more favorably assessed the future potential of artists when they were described as handicapped than when they apparently faced no handicap. In another experiment, collages that were created by adults and judged blindly to be more highly creative than those created by children were judged to be even more highly creative when they

were evaluated by judges who had been led to misattribute them to children. These double standards by which creations and creators are evaluated help to explain why levels of physical disability are high among persons considered to be highly creative and why precocious creativity varies directly with eminence.

Finally, consensus also explains deviations from the general tendency to attribute creative behavior dispositionally. When two or more scientists independently make the same theory, discovery, or invention at about the same time, the consensus value for the creation is higher than when it is made by only one scientist. Thus, such multiple creations are attributed less internally and more externally than are other creations; for example, multiple creations typically are attributed to situational causes such as cultural evolution or "the zeitgeist." Similarly, when a creation is the product of two or more collaborators, the consensus value for their creation is necessarily higher than it would be if the same creation were the product of only one creator. Thus, collaborative creations are attributed less dispositionally than are creations made by solo creators, and creators who are considered to be highly creative tend to be less collaborative.

Among Kelley's three information variables, consensus is the most vital in determining attributions of creative behavior because it is a necessary and central property of creative behavior, whereas distinctiveness and consistency are not. By its very nature, creative behavior must have low consensus value but need have no particular value on distinctiveness or consistency.

Nevertheless, when a creative product's distinctiveness value or consistency value is known, this information influences how the creation is attributed. For example, the domain in which a creative act is situated is one aspect of the situation that is relevant to the creative act's distinctiveness: The greater the number of domains in which an individual creates successfully, the lower is the distinctiveness value of any one of the individual's creative accomplishments, and hence the more internally the creative product is attributed. Hence, if two individuals achieve the same number of equally creative accomplishments, but one creator's accomplishments are distributed across a larger number of domains, that creator should be seen as the more creative of the two. Thus, "Renaissance men" such as Leonardo da Vinci are viewed as more highly creative than are other creators who have behaved just as creatively

but within a narrower spectrum of domains. [*See* DO-
MAINS OF CREATIVITY.]

Similarly, a creative product's consistency value can
influence how stable the attribution is. The more frequently an actor performs creatively in a given situation, the higher is the consistency value of the creative
act, and the more stable is the resulting attribution.
Consistently creative work is attributed to a creative
disposition such as enduring talent, whereas inconsistently creative work is attributed unstably to a mere
"one-hit wonder" or "flash in the pan" or to luck. The
consistency variable has been used to explain why eminence varies directly with both productivity and precocity across creators; why collaborative creations are
attributed more to the more consistently creative collaborator than to the less consistently creative collaborator; and why eminence is unusually high for successful creators whose death comes at an early age.

B. Creativity and Salience

A second major area of research on causal attribution has been concerned with perceptual salience.
One major finding is that people attribute greater causality to stimuli that are highly salient than to those
that are less salient. Salience is related fundamentally
to creativity attributions because creative behavior is
by definition unusually novel, and novel stimuli are
highly salient. Because creative behavior is highly salient, capturing attention to a high degree, creative behavior exacerbates the fundamental attribution error—
the tendency of observers to overestimate the impact of
dispositional causes of behavior and to underestimate
the impact of situational causes. Moreover, people who
are generally considered to be highly creative tend to
behave in a generally unconventional manner, resulting in heightened personal salience not only during the
act of creation but at many other times as well. This
heightened personal salience further exacerbates the
tendency of observers to attribute creative behavior to
the dispositions of creators, and to overlook important
situational influences.

Salience also helps to explain more highly specific
patterns of attribution. For example, consider how the
development and maintenance of stereotypes related
to creativity may be influenced by the illusory correlation effect, in which observers overestimate the covariance between unusual groups and unusual behav-

ior. This effect, which is thought to stem from the
intensified salience of combinations of individually salient stimuli, suggests that, all else being equal, people
should overestimate the prevalence of creative behavior among minority groups. Thus, for example, because the "mentally ill" are a numerical minority, and
a minority restricted to people who behave unusually,
co-occurrences of creativity and "mental illness" are
likely to be viewed as more highly correlated than they
actually are, thus contributing to an inflated stereotype
of the "mad genius." [*See* MAD GENIUS CONTROVERSY.]

Salience seems to affect how observers attribute collaborative creations. Because in such creations observers' attention is divided across multiple creators, observers should attribute collaborative creative products
less to the disposition of any one collaborator than if
the same product were created single-handedly. The
undivided attention received by lone creators may thus
help to explain why eminence varies inversely with the
percentage of creations coauthored; why eminent creators tend to be solitary, unsociable, and noncollabo-
rative; and why "wishing to be alone when creating
something new" is widely considered to be highly characteristic of "creative people."

For most collaborative creations, observers' attention
is not only divided across creators, it is divided unevenly across creators. For example, when a musical
group creates or performs a collaboratively written
composition, members differ in salience in ways that
may be wholly unrelated to their creative contribution.
"Lead singers," for instance, ordinarily are assigned to
that role because they are the group's best singer, not
because they are the group's most creative contributor
(indeed in some groups the lead singer creates little or
nothing creatively). Yet typically they capture an inor-
dinate share of the audience's attention: Observers' attention is drawn to the lead singer and away from other
members of the group by the focus of the spotlights,
the accentuation provided by directional microphones,
the contrast between figural vocal leads and background vocal and instrumental sounds, the semantic
nature of the sounds they produce, and so forth. Given
this uneven distribution of attention, observers should
tend to attribute the group's creations more dispositionally to the more salient collaborators. Thus, other
things being equal, lead singers generally should receive more undue credit for their group's compositions
than should the group's less salient collaborators.

Not only does salience "dispositionalize" attributions made by observers of creative behavior, it may have the same effect on successful creators' attributions of their own creative work. One reason for this is that the heightened attention which the creator receives from observers in turn heightens the creator's self-focused attention, thereby causing the self-salient creators to view themselves as being more highly causal. Cross-sectional studies have suggested that "creative people" are high in self-consciousness, and a recent longitudinal study found that the fame experienced by successful creators did indeed intensify the creators' self-focus, indicated by the use of self-referential words in the creators' lyrics and literary creations.

C. Creativity and Self-Serving Bias

Self-serving bias is a third major influence on causal attributions. The self-serving bias in attribution is the tendency to attribute desirable outcomes to stable, global causes within oneself and to attribute unwanted outcomes to unstable, specific causes in one's situation. Research has shown that this attributional bias is characteristic of clinically normal people. The creative product, by definition, is evaluated positively and hence is a desirable outcome for the creator. Thus, creators who have the usual self-serving attributional bias should be motivated to attribute their creative behavior to dispositional causes rather than situational or unstable causes. A variety of studies suggests that creators, both professional and lay, generally do attribute their creative behavior with a self-serving attributional bias. For example, both professional scientists and ordinary undergraduates are more likely to attribute their performance to their own dispositions when they believe that they have performed creatively than when they believe that they have performed less creatively. These and other studies suggest that creators generally are motivated to attribute their creative behavior dispositionally.

III. STATUS EXPECTANCY BIAS IN THE RECEPTION OF ORIGINAL PRODUCTS

Sociologists have found that when people work on a group task and are motivated to succeed, they utilize information about group members' status charac-teristics outside the group in assessing the members' contributions inside the group. Group members hold performance expectations of one another, expectations which are based partly on the group members' external status characteristics, and such performance expectations exert a prejudicial effect on the members' evaluations and attributions of one another's behavior. All else being equal, group members who have higher external status characteristics are granted more opportunities to contribute to the group, and the contributions they make are evaluated more positively than those made by group members whose external status characteristics are lower. These processes of status-based bias also influence evaluation in situations that do not involve co-action or collective tasks.

Status characteristics vary in the range of tasks to which their associated performance expectations refer. Specific status characteristics, such as one's ability to produce creative poetry, art, or science, evoke performance expectations and thereby bias judgments on a relatively narrow range of tasks. For example, poems are considered more creative and evaluated in a generally more positive light when the poet is believed to be a Pulitzer Prize winner or Nobel laureate in literature than when believed to be less distinguished; the expectation advantage conferred by honorific literary distinction is limited to tasks related to the domain of literature, and does not pertain to a wide variety of tasks in other domains.

In more than a dozen experiments, subjects were asked to evaluate original products allegedly made by creators whose apparent domain-specific status characteristics were manipulated. These experiments consistently demonstrate that the creator's domain-specific status characteristics significantly affect judges' evaluations of the original product.

In one experiment, for example, undergraduates were asked to evaluate various paintings that were attributed either to an artist entering a competition for the first time or to an artist who had received 10 distinguished awards and whose paintings had been exhibited at the Museum of Modern Art. Subjects evaluated the creativity, technical competence, and overall quality of the paintings as significantly greater when they were attributed to high-status artists than when they were attributed to lower-status artists.

Such findings from laboratory experiments correspond well with historical evidence on such phenomena as forgery and pseudonymous publication. Studies suggest that when a forger fools lay or expert judges into misattributing an original product to a creator whose domain-specific status characteristics are higher than those of the product's actual creator, judges evaluate the creation more positively than when they attribute it correctly to its maker. This, presumably, is the principal motive of forgers and helps to explain why "upward forgery," in which a low-status creator forges the signature of a higher-status creator, is far more common than "downward forgery," in which a high-status creator forges the signature of a lower-status creator. In the relatively infrequent cases in which an already high-status creator uses an obscure pseudonym and thereby fools judges into misattributing the creation "downward," judges' evaluations were less positive than when the high-status creator's true identity was known.

General status characteristics, such as gender, race, physical attractiveness, age, and socioeconomic status, evoke performance expectations that influence evaluations of performance on a relatively wide range of tasks. For example, research shows that physically attractive persons are stereotypically expected to be not only more highly creative than are physically unattractive people, but also superior on a wide variety of other tasks. Thus, in the absence of specific status characteristics that suggest a high level of creativity, judges should evaluate a creation more positively when they attribute it to a creator who has positive general status characteristics than when they attribute it to a creator who has negative general status characteristics. For example, essays should be considered more creative and evaluated in a generally more positive light when the author is identified as physically attractive than when the author is identified as physically unattractive.

Experimental research has generally found that judges' evaluations of original products are favorably biased by the physical attractiveness and socioeconomic status of the creator to whom they attribute the product. However, experiments into the effects of the creator's age, gender, and race or ethnicity have yielded very weak or inconsistent evidence of biased judgment, possibly due in part to flaws in experimental design.

In addition to studies into the effects of the creator's presumed status characteristics, several experiments have also demonstrated third-party status effects on the evaluation of original products. Judges are more likely to evaluate a creation positively when they believe that other judges approve of the creation; this explains the historical use of professional clappers, known as claquers, and the contemporary use of critical praise in the promotion of films and books and the use of taped applause and "laugh tracks" to enhance the evaluation of television programs. Moreover, judges' evaluations of original products are influenced more strongly by evaluations made by higher-status third parties than lower-status third parties. In one experiment, for example, judges evaluated literary passages more positively when the passages were accompanied by praise attributed to a high-status critic than by the identical praise attributed to a lower-status critic. Thus far, third-party status effects have been demonstrated only with domain-specific status characteristics; the possible influence of third parties' general status characteristics has not yet been investigated.

When judges have information about both specific and general status characteristics, performance expectations based on specific status characteristics that are believed to be relevant to the performance of a task override performance expectations based on general status characteristics that are not believed to be relevant to the task. Thus, a poem should be considered more creative and evaluated in a generally more positive light when it is attributed to a physically unattractive Nobel laureate in literature (low general, high specific status) than when it is attributed to a physically attractive but unaccomplished writer (high general, low specific status). Likewise, a poem should be evaluated more positively if it is accompanied by praise that is attributed to a literary critic who is physically unattractive but eminent than if the same praise is attributed to a literary critic who is physically attractive but unknown.

Aside from its impact on the evaluation of original products, the creator's status can also directly influence causal attributions of the creative product. The higher the creator's status characteristics, the more likely observers are to attribute a positively evaluated creation to internal, stable, global causes, such as "talent" or "genius." When a product is created collaboratively, or created simultaneously by creators acting independently of one another, observers are likely to attribute the creation more to the higher-status creator's dispositions than to the lower-status creator's dispositions. Consistent with this hypothesis, coauthored scientific publications are attributed more to the coauthor whose eminence is greatest.

Finally, various nonverbal and paralinguistic behaviors function as task cues, evoking performance expectations independent of specific and general status characteristics. Behaviors that express high task confidence are high task cues which evoke positive performance expectations, whereas behaviors that express low task confidence are low task cues, which evoke relatively negative performance expectations. Thus, creators whose behavior implies confidence enjoy an expectation advantage over creators whose behaviors makes them appear meek and uncertain. For example, creators can win greater approval for their ideas when they speak rapidly and without hesitations or hedges and while maintaining frequent eye contact than when they speak slowly, quietly, with frequent hesitations and hedges, while frequently averting their gaze, conceding the floor readily when interrupted, and otherwise behaving without confidence.

IV. IN-GROUP BIAS IN THE RECEPTION OF ORIGINAL PRODUCTS

The invention of the minimal group experiment by Henri Tajfel and his colleagues in 1971 provided a means by which mere membership in a group could be experimentally isolated from status, historical circumstance, competition for scarce rewards, and other known influences on in-group favoritism. In the minimal group experiment, subjects are randomly assigned into apparently meaningless or trivial social categories and then are asked to evaluate or reward anonymous others identified only by their membership in one's own or a different category. The groups are said to be "minimal" because mere membership in a category is extricated from all other variables: No social interaction occurs; tangible benefit is not possible; competition for scarce rewards is absent; and the basis of social categorization is explicitly random, meaningless, or trivial. The consistent result of hundreds of minimal group experiments is that subjects generally evaluate other members of their own category more positively than members of other categories. Evidently, mere cat-

egorization is sufficient to arouse favorable evaluation of the in-group over the out-group.

The most widely known explanation of in-group favoritism in the minimal group is Tajfel's social identity theory, which holds that the self-concept consists of two components: personal identity, which includes beliefs about one's individual characteristics, and social identity, which includes beliefs about others with whom one identifies, such as members of one's family, tribe, nation, or ethnic group. Overall self-esteem derives from the value one places on both one's personal and one's social identities. Research suggests that self-serving bias, in which self-esteem is maintained through favorably biased self-evaluation and which is common in clinically normal people, influences evaluation not only of the self but also of others with whom the self identifies. For example, in-group favoritism in the minimal group experiment varies directly with trait self-esteem and is increased by failure feedback among people high in trait self-esteem but not among people low in trait self-esteem.

Experimental research points to a pervasive in-group favoritism in the evaluation of original products. In one early experiment, for example, Harold Kelley assigned subjects to small groups and asked some subjects to leave the room while others noncompetitively created fables, housing developments, and toy constructions. All subjects then privately evaluated products created by their own and other groups. A significant bias favoring creations attributed to the in-group was found both among subjects who were present and among those who were absent during the group creation.

More recently, several fully minimal group experiments have uncovered in-group bias in the evaluation of original products. Noncompeting, noninteracting subjects showed in-group favoritism in assessing the creativity of painting titles attributed to members of the in-group versus out-group. In-group favoritism was found in evaluations of ideas allegedly generated in brainstorming groups, regardless of whether subjects had personally participated in the brainstorming task or merely observed. In this study, moreover, subjects high in trait self-esteem showed greater in-group favoritism than did subjects low in trait self-esteem.

The results of these and other laboratory experiments are consistent with those of nonexperimental studies that suggest widespread in-group favoritism in real-world judgments of original products. In a study of sex bias in book reviews, blind raters were asked to judge 180 book reviews written by professional psychologists and published in the journal *Contemporary Psychology*. Half the reviews were written by females and half by males, and the books under review were authored by males, females, or mixed-sex coauthors. Each review was judged for the degree of approval or disapproval expressed toward the book. Results indicated a significant interaction between author sex and reviewer sex: Own-sex evaluations were more positive than other-sex evaluations, and books by mixed-sex coauthors were approved to an intermediate degree.

Another examination of book reviews suggested a nationalistic bias. In a study comparing American, British, and West Indian reviews of novels by the Barbadian writer George Lamming, the West Indians' evaluations of the overall quality of Lamming's novels were found to be more favorable than those of the British or American reviewers.

Pervasive in-group bias in evaluating creations has also been found by the historiometric researcher Dean Keith Simonton, who has observed that an ethnocentric bias appears in who earns entries in standard reference works, and an analogue of this prejudice is conspicuous in all data having any historical depth. The former bias is expressed in the greater recognition given to compatriot creators than to foreign creators, and the latter bias, which Simonton calls "epochcentric," is expressed in favorable evaluation of creations made in one's own period and of past creations similar to those of own's own period. [*See* HISTORIOMETRY.]

In-group bias is also evoked by an original product's representation of the in-group and out-groups. All else being equal, creations that portray the in-group favorably are evaluated more positively than creations that portray the in-group negatively. For example, books, films, and jokes in which one group is depicted more favorably than another are evaluated less positively by members of the derogated group than by members of the flattered group. Research has found that people more favorably evaluate jokes that derogate an out-group than those that derogate their in-group, and this effect is exacerbated when the judge believes that the joke's creator is an out-group member.

Apart from its effect on evaluation, in-group bias also directly influences causal attribution of creative products. Research has documented a pervasive "group-serving attributional bias," wherein people tend to attribute positive outcomes to dispositional causes within the in-group and tend to attribute negative outcomes to causes external to the in-group. Thus, most people are more likely to misattribute out-group members' creative products to dispositional causes within the in-group than to misattribute in-group members' creative products to dispositional causes within an out-group. For example, in Nazi-era Germany, Nazis were more likely than Jews to misattribute Einstein's creative accomplishments to Aryan genes. Similarly, contemporary African-Americans are more likely than other Americans to misattribute to black Africans the creative works which historically have been attributed to ancient Greeks, a misattribution that self-described "Afrocentric" scholars have committed.

Although the categorical bases for some social identifications are fixed (e.g., gender, race, nationality), other social identities are quite mutable. Thus social identification is itself partly the product of biases that enhance or protect self-esteem. Social psychologists have documented a widespread tendency for individuals to identify with others who are successful; this self-serving tendency, known as "Basking in Reflected Glory," is heightened in individuals who have recently received unflattering self-relevant information, such as a low score on a purported test of creative ability. One manifestation of this bias is a tendency for individuals to identify more strongly with others who behave creatively, at least when the other's creative success does not outstrip one's own in a field that is high in self-definitional relevance. In two small-group experiments, for example, greater social identification was found between subjects who were randomly given positive feedback on an alleged creativity test than between subjects who were randomly given negative feedback on the test.

V. SOCIAL LOAFING IN THE RECEPTION OF ORIGINAL PRODUCTS

Social psychologists have discovered that, when co-acting with others on a task in which individual effort is not identifiable, individuals exert less effort on the task than when individuals act alone or when coactors' efforts are individually identifiable. This phenomenon, known as social loafing, has been documented in a wide variety of tasks, both physical and cognitive, including both the creation and the evaluation of original products.

Social loafing influences the reception of original products in several ways. First, the greater the degree of effort a judge spends in evaluating a product, the more polarized is the judge's evaluation; original products that are evaluated at least somewhat positively when only a small amount of effort is spent in judgment are, in general, evaluated more positively when a larger amount of effort is expended. Hence, social loafing in the evaluation of original products results in a shift toward evaluative neutrality.

Second, the amount of effort a judge spends in evaluating a product generally increases the degree to which the judge's evaluation is influenced by attributes of the creation and decreases the degree to which such judgments are influenced by extraneous factors, such as the creator's status characteristics or membership in the judge's in-group or out-groups. Hence, social loafing in the evaluation of original products increases the degree to which judges' evaluations are influenced by status expectancy bias, in-group favoritism, the attractiveness and connotations of the creator's name, and other biases based on normatively irrelevant information.

Third, the amount of effort a judge expends in considering the causes of an original product tends to cause the judge to attribute the product less dispositionally and more situationally. Hence, social loafing tends to "dispositionalize" judges' attributions of creative products, exacerbating the fundamental attribution error. This holds true not only for situations in which the creator saliently presents his or her own creation, but also for those situations in which a noncreating performer saliently presents a creation made by a nonperforming creator, for example, when a musician saliently performs a piece written by a composer who is long dead.

As an example of the preceding processes, consider the situation of a faculty recruitment committee given the task of evaluating many dozens of applicants for a faculty research position. In many such cases, committee members' judgments are pooled in a manner that eliminates or minimizes the salience of individual committee members' judgments. In such cases, especially given the burdensome nature of the task, committee members should be likely to loaf in evaluating the applicant researchers and in evaluating and attributing the applicants' research. Thus, judges should attribute the candidates' research more dispositionally than they otherwise would, and evaluations of the research and of the researchers should be more strongly influenced by status characteristics, such as the prestige of the letterhead on which the researchers have written their application letters, the prestige of the researchers' degree-granting institution, and the prestige of the journals in which the applicants' research was published; relatively little time will be spent reading the research that is being evaluated.

Social loafing in the evaluation of original products has been demonstrated in several experiments conducted by Richard Petty and his colleagues. In one experiment, the researchers asked subjects to evaluate an essay and a poem, and led the subjects to believe that they alone were responsible for the evaluation or that their responses would be pooled anonymously with those of other subjects evaluating the same essay and poem. Subjects who thought their evaluations would be pooled reported exerting less cognitive effort in their evaluations than did those who thought their evaluations were being made alone. On average, both the essay and the poem were evaluated positively by both groups of judges, and subjects who believed they were personally responsible evaluated the creations more positively than did subjects who believed their responses would be pooled.

In another experiment, Petty and his colleagues led subjects to believe that they alone would be evaluating an essay or that their evaluation of the essay would be pooled anonymously with those of other subjects, and each subject evaluated one of three essays concerned with the same theme: a "strong" essay that elicited predominantly positive evaluations in prior research, a "weak" essay that elicited predominantly negative evaluations in prior research, and a "very weak" essay that elicited even more strongly negative evaluations in prior research. Results showed that subjects who believed they alone were evaluating the creations judged the "strong essay" more positively and the "very weak essay" more negatively than did subjects who believed their responses would be pooled anonymously. (Evaluations of the "weak essay" were not affected by the experimental manipulation.)

It is important to note that social loafing does not occur to an equal degree in all situations in which coacting judges' contributions are not individually salient. Research has found that social loafing is greater when (a) judges' cultures are more highly individualistic rather than collectivistic, (b) the task is of little personal relevance for the judge, (c) the number of judges is greater, and (d) judges believe that their own efforts are not critically important for a successful outcome.

VI. CONCLUSIONS

The creation, evaluation, and causal attribution of original products are influenced by dispositional, external-nonsocial, microsocial, and macrosocial causes. For example, the creation of original products may be influenced not only by the creator's dispositions but also by noise in the creator's immediate surrounding, exposure to salient external contingencies, and ambient social forces within a culture, organization, and domain. Similarly, the evaluation of original products may be influenced by the judge's personality, in-group bias, national social mobility, and ambient social forces within a culture. Yet, for reasons that are explained by the attributional approach, both laypeople and creativity researchers have tended to attribute creativity predominantly to creators' dispositions and to ignore not only nondispositional influences on creators but also—indeed primarily—the audience factors that are so crucial in determining which messages are creative and which are not. Clearly, the reigning illusion of the independence of creativity from context is absurd, and the creator-centered, dispositionist agenda that has dominated creativity research since the field's inception can explain only a small fraction of the important determinants of creativity.

In contrast to the previous approaches to creativity, the attributional approach to creativity focuses on the social reception of original products. By examining the processes that influence the evaluation and causal attribution of original products, the attributional approach to creativity can discover what factors are responsible for historical, group, and individual variation in the social reception of original products.

Bibliography

Csikszentmihalyi, M. (1988). Society, culture, and person: A systems view of creativity. In R. J. Sternberg (Ed.), *The nature of creativity: Contemporary psychological perspectives.* Cambridge: Cambridge University Press.

Kasof, J. (1995). Explaining creativity: The attributional perspective. *Creativity Research Journal, 8,* 311–366.

Kasof, J. (1995). Clarification, refinement, and extension of the attributional approach to creativity. *Creativity Research Journal, 8,* 439–462.

Kasof, J. (1995). Social determinants of creativity: Status expectations and the evaluation of original products. *Advances in Group Processes, 12,* 167–220.

Taylor, G. (1996). *Cultural selection.* New York: Basic Books.

Autonomy and Independence

Gregory J. Feist

College of William & Mary

Attachment Style Consistent patterns of interaction between an infant or child and his or her primary caregiver that result in either secure or insecure emotional bonds.

Autonomy A tendency to move away from or to be relatively uninfluenced by others.

Creativity Thought or behavior that is assessed by others to be both original and useful.

Meta-analysis A review of the empirical literature that quantifies and averages results of all relevant studies to obtain an index of overall effect size.

Personality A person's unique behavioral tendencies that tend to remain relatively constant over time and across situations.

Personality traits have long been associated with creative behavior and one of the most consistent of these traits has been the tendency toward AUTONOMY. With a focus on its relation to creativity, this article will briefly review the empirical literature on the development of autonomous behavior and its related traits of introver- sion, internal locus of control, intrinsic motivation, self-confidence/arrogance, nonconformity/norm-doubting, and solitude, asociability, and antisociability.

I. INTRODUCTION

Creative people and the study of personality psychology share a fundamental commonality: the uniqueness of the individual. The essence of a creative person is the uniqueness of his or her ideas and behavior, whereas personality psychology is the study of individual differences (i.e., what makes people unique from one another). Therefore, it is only natural that personality psychologists would have turned their attention to a group of individuals whose most salient characteristic is their individuality and uniqueness, namely, creative people. [*See* PERSONALITY.]

Although interest and writings on the creative person reach back over a thousand years in Western culture (e.g., Plato and Aristotle), it has only been approximately 50 years since personality psychologists began their more systematic empirical investigations into the nature of the creative personality. Historically, some writers have argued that creativity and creative achievement are difficult to define and there is no consensus on their definition. Such a belief, however, is

Copyright © 1999 by Academic Press
All rights of reproduction in any form reserved.

not consistent with the modern era of creativity research. A vast majority of creativity researchers over the last 50 years have defined creativity the same way: originality/novelty and usefulness. Creative thought or behavior must be both novel and useful. It is easy to see why originality per se is not sufficient, because there would be no way to distinguish eccentric or schizophrenic thought from creative thought. Therefore, creative thought or behavior must also be useful or adaptive. Usefulness, however, is not meant in merely a pragmatic sense, for behavior or thought can be judged as useful on purely intellectual or aesthetic criteria. [*See* NOVELTY.]

The goal of this article is not to review all of the work on the creative personality, but rather only that subset that has focused on two key components of the personalities of creative individuals: autonomy and independence. One of the most distinguishing characteristics of creative people is their desire and preference to be somewhat removed from regular social contact—to spend time alone working on their craft, whether it be scientific discovery, writing a poem or novel, painting, or building a business. In other words, a unique trait of creative people is their disposition to be autonomous and independence of the influence of the group. The overarching behavioral principle of autonomy and its related personality traits is that it deals with one's relation with, and reaction to, other people; etymologically "autonomy" may mean self-governing, but psychologically self-governing is expressed by focusing attention inward and being independent from the influence of others. In other words, whether intentional or unintentional, autonomy involves a differentiation of self from other. Likewise, to be unique and original is to do things that others have not, whether it is flying solo across the Atlantic for the first time or working out the physics for the theory of relativity. This article will review those connections.

II. DEVELOPMENTAL ANTECEDENTS OF AUTONOMY AND INDEPENDENCE

What follows is a review of some of the evidence for a biological basis for a trait closely related to autonomy, namely, introversion. Introversion is a tendency to want to be alone and away from social stimulation, which is closely tied to the tendency toward autonomy.

A. Neuro- and Psychophysiology of Introversion and Creativity

One of the best known personality theorists and researchers of the second half of this century was Hans J. Eysenck. The essence of his theory is that there is a biological basis to the fundamental dimensions of personality, namely, extroversion, neuroticism, and psychoticism. This section will focus primarily on the extroversion–introversion dimension. One of the most robust findings in the literature on the biological basis of personality is that introverts and extroverts have different physiological reactions to a wide variety of stimulation. More specifically, introverts appear to have lower thresholds for arousal because they are much more reactive to stimulation. Both the central and autonomic nervous systems of introverts exhibit this greater reactivity. For example, especially when presented with moderately arousing stimuli, introverts tend to show greater cortical (EEG) reactivity, greater pupillary response, greater increases in heart rate, and greater skin conductance.

As will be discussed in more detail below, creative people tend to be more introverted than extraverted, although there are important qualifications to this trend. This being the case, one would expect creative people to have similar physiological reactivity as introverts (i.e., greater arousal). Colin Martindale and his colleagues have demonstrated just such a connection in a multitude of studies: creative individuals tend to have higher resting arousal levels. However, it must be pointed out that the relationship between physiology and introversion and creativity is by no means simple. In fact, piecing together all of the evidence suggests that the relationship is more curvilinear than linear, with task and level of stimulation moderating the relationship. In one of the few studies to directly examine EEG activity during creative problem solving, Colin Martindale and James Armstrong found that the resting cortical arousal levels of creative people were higher than less creative people, but during the inspiration stage of creative problem solving they were actually lower. Low cortical arousal, in turn, is associated with a widening of attentional focus, a correlate of creative problem solving. [*See* PROBLEM SOLVING.]

B. Birth Order

Beginning with Francis Galton in the latter part of the 19th century, researchers and theorists have argued that birth order has a definite impact on personality and personality development. Alfred Adler, for instance, afforded birth order a key position in his theory of personality and argued that firstborns are likely to have strong feelings of superiority and power among other things. More recently, Frank Sulloway has rejuvenated interest in birth order with a book entitled *Born to Rebel: Birth Order, Family Dynamics and Creative Lives.* In this book, Sulloway makes some rather strong assertions about the power of birth order to affect personality, in particular one's inclination toward accepting and conforming to convention and tradition or rejecting and rebelling against them. Some people, he argues, are inherently inclined to challenge, question, and reject social norms, and these people tend to be disproportionately later born.

Firstborn children are unique in that they are the only ones to experience a "dethroning" of their special relationship with their parents. Therefore, they tend to develop skills that aim at maintaining their privileged position and holding onto their power. Latter born children, on the other hand, have never experienced undivided attention from a parent, and hence have little interest in maintaining power. Indeed, they are likely to want to react against a firstborn's attempts at power and authority. Sulloway reviewed the literature on personality and birth order and reported that openness to new experiences (a willingness to try new things and ideas and to reject convention) is the personality trait most strongly related to birth order. Much of his book, in fact, is a demonstration of the impact of birth order on accepting or opposing new, revolutionary theories in science. Very consistently, laterborns are more likely to accept new and radical theories (such as Darwin's theory of evolution), and firstborns are more likely to resist and oppose radical theories. Sulloway, however, is not saying that firstborns are not creative, but rather that they are creative in a different way. Firstborns express their creativity within the status quo and through the intellect dimension (i.e., cultured, perceptive, curious) of openness. Laterborns, on the other hand express their creativity outside the status quo and through the nonconformist dimension (i.e., unconventional, daring, independent) or openness.

Indeed, other researchers who have studied creativity and birth order have found that firstborns were overrepresented among the highly creative. For example, in the early 1950s a classic study of creative scientists by Ann Roe found a disproportionate number of firstborns in her sample. Furthermore, Gregory Feist, in a sample of highly creative scientists, found a curvilinear effect, with both first- and lastborns being overrepresented. Perhaps the apparent contradiction between Sulloway and other researchers on birth order and creativity is just that. After all, Sulloway hardly discusses the birth order of highly creative people (indeed, creativity is not even in the subject index), but rather his focus is on people who are willing to accept or not the creative ideas of others. [*See* BIRTH ORDER.]

C. Parenting Style and Secure Attachment

One of the fundamental tenants of John Bowlby's attachment theory is that a responsive and accessible caregiver creates a secure base for the child, thereby laying the foundation for secure and confident exploration of the world by the child. Children who are secure and confident in exploring their world, in turn, are going to be more likely to ask questions, be assertive, persist at difficult tasks, do well in school, and find new and unusual solutions to problems (i.e., be creative). In short, security of attachment and parental facilitation of autonomy and independence are likely to lead to greater curiosity, confidence, achievement, and creativity in children. For instance, Richard Ared, Frederick Gove, and Alan Sroufe reported in 1979 that securely attached toddlers (18 month olds) were more curious and better able to cope with stress at age 4 and 5 than insecurely attached children. Similarly, in 1985 Ann Frodi, Lisa Bridges, and Wendy Grolnick reported that infants whose mothers encouraged autonomy were more task persistent and competent than were infants of controlling mothers. Finally, in the late 1980s, Laurence Steinberg and colleagues studied 120 families and found that parents who promoted autonomy and were accepting yet maintained control tended to have children who did well in school and were highly achieving. This is not to say that all creative people had warm and secure relationships with their parents. In fact, more often it is the opposite. As Arnold Ludwig has recently demonstrated, highly creative people, especially in art, are more likely to have come from either broken families (i.e., divorced) or have lost a parent to death before age 15.

III. AUTONOMY, CREATIVITY, AND THEIR RELATED PERSONALITY TRAITS

In many ways autonomy is a trait that clusters around other social dispositions: introversion, internal locus of control, intrinsic motivation, self-confidence/arrogance, nonconformity/norm-doubting, desire for solitude, and asocial and antisocial leanings. These traits are social because they each concern one's consistent and unique patterns of interacting with others.

A. Introversion

One of the more consistent findings from the personality literature of artists as well as scientists is that they tend to be rather introverted. For example, in a classic study concerning scientific creativity, Ann Roe in 1952 and 1953 reported that creative scientists were more achievement oriented and less affiliative than less creative scientists. This finding was followed up and replicated by people such as Bernice Eiduson, Jack Chambers, and Ravenna Helson. More recently, J. P. Rushton and his colleagues have reported that the more creative research-oriented psychologists were higher in independence and less extraverted than the more teaching-oriented psychologists.

B. Internal Locus of Control

Another personality trait that can be classified as a close relative to independence is having an internal locus of control. First proposed by Julian Rotter in the 1950s, locus of control concerns one's beliefs about who or what is the source of reinforcement for one's behavior. Without going into too much detail, there have been dozens of studies over the last 20 years examining the relationship between creativity and having an internal locus of control. Suffice it to say that the vast majority of these studies have shown that creative people are more likely to have an internal orientation than less creative people.

C. Intrinsic Motivation

Related to having an internal orientation, creative people also tend to be intrinsically motivated. The primary proponent of this view has been Teresa Amabile and her principle of intrinsic motivation. The essence of this principle is that people are more creative when they are motivated by intrinsic pleasures such as enjoyment, satisfaction, and challenge. The flip side to her argument is that when people are motivated by external factors such as evaluation, competition, reward, surveillance, and restricted choice, they tend to be less creative. In multiple studies, Amabile and her colleagues have found experimental support for the intrinsic motivation principle. Although much of the evidence for this comes from research on children, some has focused on adults. For instance, using students of English or creative writing, Amabile experimentally created intrinsic and extrinsic motivational states (by having participants complete a questionnaire based toward either the former or the latter motivational state). A control group also completed a neutral questionnaire. Immediately afterward, each participant was asked to write a short haiku-style poem. These poems were then rated by professional poets on their degree of creativity. As expected, the intrinsic and control groups wrote poems that were judged to be significantly more creative than the extrinsically motivated writers. Taken together, Amabile has demonstrated that reward and competition in education can inhibit creative performance. Such a conclusion has potentially serious ramifications for education, given the frequency with which evaluation, reward, and competition are used as motivators in the classroom. Perhaps such evaluation pressure is responsible for some of the test anxiety and underachievement of so many students. Based on Amabile's findings, perhaps educators should instead attempt to motivate students by creating intrinsically motivating conditions such as pleasure and interest.

Amabile's position, however, has not gone unchallenged. Mark Runco, for instance, has argued that some degree of negative affective state is important and maybe even essential in motivating a person toward creative achievement. After all, if someone were not dissatisfied with the current state of affairs, there would be no impetus to create something new and better. Moreover, Robert Eisenberger and his colleagues have found recently that, coupled with explicit instructions to be creative, certain rewards can actually increase rather than decrease creative performance in school children. To be fair, Amabile acknowledges that for creative people who are intrinsically motivated, extrinsic motivation may be a positive rather than a negative influence on their creative output. The safest conclusion then, is that extrinsic motivation in the absence of intrinsic motivation may undermine creative achievement. [See MOTIVATION/DRIVE.]

D. Self-Confidence and Arrogance

Another set of personality traits related to autonomy and which involve an internal locus are self-confidence and arrogance. People who are relatively independent of group influence are likely to have confidence in their ideas and abilities and may even develop a sense of superiority and arrogance toward others. In the highly competitive world of science, especially big science, where the most creative, productive, and influential continue to be rewarded with more and more of the resources, success is more likely for those who thrive in competitive environments, that is, for those who are dominant, arrogant, hostile, and self-confident. For example, Raymond Van Zelst and Willard Kerr collected personality self-descriptions on 514 technical and scientific personnel from a research foundation and a university. Holding age constant, they reported significant correlations between productivity and describing oneself as "argumentative," "assertive," and "self-confident." In one of the few studies to examine female scientists, Louise Bachtold and Emmy Werner administered the 16PF to 146 women scientists and found that they were significantly different from women in

general on 9 of the 16 scales, including dominance (Factor E) and self-confidence (Factor O).

E. Nonconformity and Norm-Doubting

A common notion of the creative person is that she or he is rebellious and often stubbornly nonconforming to social norms. Creative people are seen as "loners" or perhaps even "outcasts." The "lone-genius" myth may be as well entrenched as the "mad-genius" myth. In the 1960s, the social psychologist Soloman Asch conducted a series of studies that have now become classics in psychology. He was interested in the extent to which individuals would be influenced by group pressure even if they were fairly certain of their judgments. He devised a very simple study in which individual participants were unknowingly placed in a group of confederates, and had to publicly evaluate the length of a target line in comparison to three other lines, only one of which was clearly the same length as the target. The task was complicated by two things: first, the participant always was the last in the group to evaluate the line, and second, everyone reached consensus on the first few rounds and only after agreeing did the confederates start to give blatantly wrong answers. The object of the study was to see how frequently subjects would conform to group pressure and go along with obviously wrong evaluations. Surprisingly, 76% complied with group pressure at least once.

Social psychologists are primarily interested in the 76% who conformed to the power of the situation, whereas personality psychologists (especially those interested in creativity) are fascinated by the 24% who never conformed. Richard Crutchfield followed up Asch and investigated the personality traits of people who took part in a study similar to the one Asch developed. Most interestingly, highly creative people are more likely to be in the minority group that never conforms. Crutchfield explained this effect by arguing for the "intrinsic, task-involved motivation for creative thinking." As already mentioned, this line of thinking was later developed into the "intrinsic motivation principle" by Amabile. [See CONFORMITY.]

Rebellion against group influence is seen most clearly in artists. Artists, perhaps more than almost any other members of society, tend to question and rebel against established norms. Some may even argue that questioning, challenging, and pushing the limits of what is acceptable may be the defining traits of being an artist in modern society. The empirical literature on personality and artistic creativity supports the nonconforming, rebellious nature of artists. For instance, a classic study of architects by Wallace Hall and Donald MacKinnon found that the most creative had personalities that are conflicted, impulsive, nonconformist, rule-doubting, skeptical, independent, and not concerned with obligations or duties. More recently, studies using Cattell's 16PF have consistently reported that artists are low on Conformity (Factor G) and high on Radicalism (Factor Q_1) and Self-Sufficiency (Factor Q_2). [*See* CONVENTIONALITY.]

F. Solitude, Asociability, and Antisociability.

The high rates of norm-doubters among the highly creative suggests a willful and intentional desire to be alone and outside the influence of others. Anthony Storr wrote in his 1989 book, *Solitude,* that people in the late 20th century have wrongly come to view relationships as the only possible source of happiness to the neglect of one's intellectual and creative development. Moreover, creative and interpersonal skills are to some extent competing and even opposing forces. To be creative requires solitude—the capacity to be alone. As it is, many people are very much afraid of being alone and feel uncomfortable when confronted with themselves. Such is not the case with most creative people, who often have lives that not only provide much opportunity to be alone but actually require it. To quote Storr,

> Yet some of the people who have contributed most to the enrichment of human experience have contributed little to the welfare of human beings in particular. It can be argued that some of the great thinkers . . . were self-centered, alienated, or "narcissistic"; more preoccupied with what went on in their own minds than with the welfare of other people. (p. xiv)

Creative people also tend to be asocial and even antisocial, actively resisting cultural norms. As Gregory Feist recently found in a meta-analysis of the person-

ality and creativity literature, artists are especially distinguished by their low "socialization" scores on the major personality inventories. For instance, on the California Psychological Inventory (CPI) they were low on "responsibility," "socialization," "good impression," and "achievement via conformance"; on the 16PF they were low on "conformity" and high on "radicalism"; and on the Eysenck Personality Questionnaire (EPQ) they were high on "psychoticism," which consists of traits such as aloofness, impulsiveness, coldness, and antisocial tendencies. Research has also pointed toward a cluster of asocial and even antisocial personality dispositions associated with artistic creativity. In one of the earliest studies of its kind, John Drevdahl and Raymond Cattell examined the relationship between artistic creativity and personality in three samples of artists (writers, visual artists, and science fiction writers). All three groups were much lower than norms on the warmth scale. Similarly, in the 1970s Jacob Getzels and Mihaly Csikszentmihalyi investigated a sample of successful art students and found very low levels of warmth on the 16PF. Similarly, in 1993 Gregory Feist reported a structural equation model of scientific eminence in which the path between observer-rated hostility and eminence was direct and significant and the path between arrogant working style and eminence was indirect but significant. Finally, Hans Eysenck reported that traits such as aggression, aloofness, antisocial and egocentric behavior, and tough-mindedness tend to be higher in artists than nonartists.

IV. CONCLUSIONS

We have seen that a wide range of autonomy-oriented personality dispositions systematically covary with creative ability and creative achievement. We have seen that the desire to be alone and away from others may have a biological basis and that birth order and attachment are two important early influences on the development of autonomy and independence. In addition, we have seen that autonomy is a cluster of personality traits (introversion, internal locus of control, intrinsic motivation, self-confidence/arrogance, non-conformity/norm-doubting, solitude, and asocial or antisocial behavior), each of which is associated with creative performance.

Lest such conclusions be misinterpreted as arguing for the unimportance of social influence, it must be made clear that no one can ever be an "island unto oneself." We all live in a social world and survive in a social world. Others bring us into being and sustain us. We are because of others. Be this as it may, having the inclination, desire, and facility to remove oneself with some regularity from social contact and to be less influenced by the attitudes and values of others or groups of others seems to be related to solving problems in a unique and adaptive way, that is, creatively. But the relationship does not tell us anything directly about causality. Whether this tendency toward autonomy and independence is a cause of or an effect of creativity remains to be seen.

Bibliography

Amabile, T. (1996). *Creativity in context*. New York: Westview.

Eisenberger, R., & Selbst, M. (1994). Does reward increase or decrease creativity? *Journal of Personality & Social Psychology, 66,* 1116–1127.

Eysenck, H. J. (1995). *Genius: The natural history of creativity*. Cambridge, England: Cambridge University Press.

Feist, G. J. (1993). A structural model of scientific eminence. *Psychological Science, 4,* 167–177.

Feist, G. J. (1998). A meta-analysis of personality in scientific and artistic creativity. *Personality and Social Psychology Review, 2,* 290–309.

Sheldon, K. M. (1995). Creativity and self-determination in personality. *Creativity Research Journal, 8,* 25–36.

Storr, A. (1989). *Solitude*. New York: The Free Press.

Sulloway, F. (1997). *Born to rebel: Birth order, family dynamics, and creative lives*. New York: Pantheon.

Barriers to Creativity
and Creative Attitudes

Gary A. Davis
University of Wisconsin, Madison

Creative Attitudes Dispositions, temperaments, or orientations that influence one's way of feeling or acting in relation to creativity.

Creativity Consciousness Awareness and appreciation for creativity, creative innovations, and creative people.

Cultural Barriers Conformity pressures rooted in social influence, expectations, and social or institutional norms.

Emotional Barriers Aspects of personality or "emotional upset" that interfere with creative thinking; they may result from temporary problems (e.g., anger, fear, or hate) or more permanent sources of insecurity (e.g., anxiety, fear of failure, fear of criticism or rejection, or poor self-esteem).

Perceptual Barriers Habitual ways of seeing and comprehending that make it difficult to see new meanings, relationships, and ideas; perceptual set, mental set, or functional fixity.

Personality Distinctive individual qualities of a person, such as attitudes and ways of reacting, that reflect the person's essential character.

Self-Actualized Creativity A general form of creativeness, a lifestyle; it includes mental health and growth toward self-realization.

Special Talent Creativity High, perhaps recognized, creative productivity in a special area; it may or may not include mental health.

Two interacting concepts that influence both general and highly specialized types of creativity are removing or minimizing **BARRIERS TO CREATIVITY** *and fostering the growth of* **CREATIVE ATTITUDES.** *Barriers are blocks, internal or external, that either inhibit creative thinking and inspiration or else prevent innovative ideas from being accepted and implemented. Most barriers result from learning. They may originate with one's family, peers, community, or educational environment, or from others in the culture or business organizations. Creative attitudes are tied intimately to a creative personality. Creative attitudes include traits that predispose one to think creatively and be creatively productive. The contrast between creative and uncreative people lies more in barriers and uncreative attitudes than in differences in intelligence or thinking styles.*

The present discussion of barriers to creativity and attitudes that promote creativity is based on a broad

165

Copyright © 1999 by Academic Press
All rights of reproduction in any form reserved.

conception of creativity. As illustrated on the horizontal axis of Figure 1, a person may be low to high in general creativeness. One high in this trait takes a creative approach to most aspects of life. It is a way of living, growing, and perceiving one's world, as well as a way of thinking and solving problems. Such a person is mentally healthy and self-accepting, and grows toward self-realization. In the 1950s Abraham Maslow called this *self-actualized creativity.* As represented on the vertical axis of Figure 1, a person also may be low to high in recognized creative productivity, or what Maslow called *special-talent creativity.* By definition, a person high in this dimension has achieved recognition for socially judged creative achievement, for example, in art, science, or business. He or she may or may not be mentally healthy in the self-actualization sense.

The reason for noting this distinction, which acknowledges both a general creativeness and creative accomplishment in specific areas, is that several influential writers have argued recently that the word *creative* applies only when one's peers (or society) have judged one's work to be "creative." Further, the work must permanently alter the particular field. Such a definition restricts the word *creative* to only those who have achieved creative *eminence,* for example, Sigmund Freud, Pablo Picasso, T. S. Eliot, or Martha Graham. By exclusion, the remaining 99+% of everyone would be *not creative.* Vincent van Gogh, for example, would have been judged uncreative until later art critics agreed that his paintings were creative. For present purposes, a restrictive definition is inappropriate. The current more general and accepted definition acknowledges the obvious—that many, many people think and act creatively, some in just a few areas and some in all areas of their lives, and some achieve at least limited recognition. The broader definition also acknowledges the truism that everyone has an opportunity to live a more creative life and become a more fulfilled, creatively productive person.

I. BARRIERS TO CREATIVITY

The following five categories of barriers—learning and habit, rules and traditions, perceptual barriers, cultural barriers, and emotional barriers—will help distinguish blocks to creativity in different but overlapping categories. Some scholars argue that everyone is born creative, but early years of social pressures at home, at school, and in the community destroy lively imaginations and promote conformity.

II. LEARNING AND HABIT

The most obvious barrier to creative thinking and innovation simply is habit—our well-learned ways of thinking and responding. It begins early. We learn "correct" responses, routines, and patterns of behavior. We learn language habits and conceptual categories. We learn "the way things have always been done" and "the way things are supposed to be done." Over the years it becomes difficult to see and create new possibilities—to break away from or suppress our creativity-squelching habits.

When did you last try something truly new? An exotic restaurant? A new sport? A college course in an intriguing topic? Do old habits and expectations interfere with new ideas, activities, and possibilities?

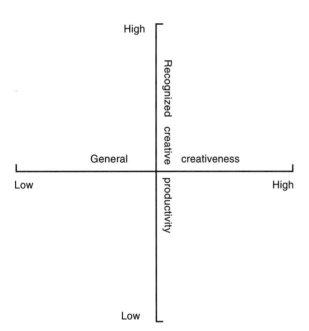

FIGURE 1 Two-dimensional illustration of personal creativeness. A person may be low to high in general creativeness, which is a lifestyle and a thinking style (Maslow's self-actualized creativity), and low to high in recognized creative achievement (Maslow's special-talent creativity).

Consider this puzzle: Remove six letters from ASIPXPLETLTERES. What word is left? (Answer at end of article.)

The ability to form habits and expectations is, of course, a necessary capability for humankind, one that directs our daily behavior. However, learning and habit are both a blessing and a curse.

III. RULES AND TRADITIONS

As with learning and habit, social groups—from one's family to educational, corporate, national, and international groups—could not function without the rules, regulations, policies, and traditions that guide personal, social, and institutional conduct. However, "guide" often means restrict, inhibit, or prohibit.

As an example of restrictive rules and traditions, in a 1995 article Don Ambrose criticized the inflexibility of school systems and other traditional organizations. He listed these traits of "dullard, brain-damaged bureaucracies inherited from the old industrial era": myopic and coercive leadership that treats employees as automatons; premature judgment; repressed creativity; anger, frustration, and resentment; inflexible conformity; reflexive ritual; inflexible attitudes; and being habit bound. Ambrose claimed that the absence of creative flexibility was due to top-heavy bureaucratic structures that put people into highly specialized roles, limiting employees' concerns to well-defined departmental work at a cost of large-scale visionary thought. Such employees have little reason to take risks beyond the confines of established procedures, particularly since mistakes are routinely punished.

In contrast, suggested Ambrose, "creatively intelligent post-industrial organizations" can improve creative thinking with visionary leadership; critical analysis and judgment; creative thinkers and creative teamwork; excitement, pride, and purpose; and flexibility, sensitivity, responsiveness, and dynamism. The issue is one of attitudes. A person can be inflexibly tied to rules, or can be creativity conscious—open, receptive, and encouraging of new ideas.

Van Gundy also described organizational barriers to creative innovation that are based in rules and traditions. One barrier is the status hierarchy. Lower-status persons are reluctant to suggest ideas to those in higher positions due to insecurity and fear of evaluation. If lower-status persons routinely are excluded from decision-making meetings, it is even less likely that their creative ideas will "trickle up." Also, if a new idea threatens to reduce status differences—such as giving every sales representative the title of "vice president"—the idea is certain to be resisted by persons at higher levels, such as current vice presidents. [*See* CORPORATE CULTURE.]

The formalization barrier refers to the degree to which following rules and procedures is enforced. If organization members clearly are expected to behave in prescribed ways, and innovation is not prescribed, few new ideas and proposals will appear. On the positive side, when an innovation is accepted, an efficient formal structure will expedite its implementation.

Procedural barriers include policies, procedures, and regulations (including unwritten ones) that slow or prevent creative innovation. Some examples include promoting administrators based on analytic skill, not on their creativity or ability to develop a creative atmosphere, and insisting on the slow, orderly advancement of an innovation early in its development, with excessive creativity-restricting control.

Rules and traditions keep the system working. However, like habit, such predetermined guides tend not to promote creativity.

IV. PERCEPTUAL BARRIERS

From a lifetime of learning we are accustomed to perceiving things in familiar ways, often making it difficult to see new meanings, relationships, and ideas. Psychologists refer to our predisposition to perceive things in certain ways as a perceptual set, a mental set, or functional fixedness. It is the reverse of flexible, innovative thinking. Perceptual sets are different for different people, rooted in our unique experiences, interests, biases, and values. Perceptual sets are tied to our tendency to make quick decisions and jump to conclusions, rather than flexibly see alternatives. [*See* FLEXIBILITY; INNOVATION.]

Perceptual barriers make us "kick ourselves" for not seeing a solution sooner. One classic demonstration showed that when a piece of string was needed to solve a problem, the string quickly would be perceived and used if it were dangling from a nail on the wall, but not if it were hanging a "No Smoking" sign, a mirror, or a calendar.

Perceptual blocks also prevent us from getting a complete and accurate picture of our world; the "real problem" or "truth" may be missed. For example, based on symptoms that seem familiar, a physician, auto mechanic, or computer expert may persist in misclassifying a problem and will recommend incorrect treatments. A school teacher who fixates on IQ scores will fail to perceive students who are highly creative, highly artistic, or gifted in a single area such as theater or computer programming. An instructor who successfully uses a particular teaching method for many years will not recognize another technique as being even more effective. Old habits interfere with new perceptions.

One creativity recommendation, "make the familiar strange," encourages us to see common objects and situations in new ways, to overcome too-familiar perceptual features, and to look for new and different ideas and perceptions. Much creativity involves a mental transformation—the perception of new meanings, combinations, and relationships that depend upon overcoming perceptual barriers.

V. CULTURAL BARRIERS

Cultural barriers amount to social influence, expectations, and conformity pressures which are based on social and institutional norms. Cultural blocks include habit and learning, rules and traditions, and more. They include conforming to the ways we think others expect us to behave and a fear of being different. The result is a loss of individuality and creativity.

Creativity leader Paul Torrance documented three developmental drops in creativity test scores. The first occurs when children enter kindergarten, an early time when conformity and regimentation suddenly become the rule. A larger decrease occurs in fourth grade, Torrance's infamous "fourth-grade slump." Both drops in creativity are social/cultural phenomena, not biological ones. Fortunately, due to increased creativity consciousness and efforts to teach creativity, the fourth-grade slump is disappearing. A third drop in creativity scores occurs in seventh grade as part of strong adolescent conformity. [*See* FOURTH GRADE SLUMP.]

Most dynamics of conformity pressures are not mysterious. It simply is uncomfortable to be different and to challenge accepted ways of thinking and behaving. We learn that it is good to be correct and bad to make mistakes. We learn that being wrong can elicit disapproval, criticism, or even sarcasm and ridicule. Being different or wrong raises fears of being judged foolish, incompetent, or stupid.

Expectations and conformity pressures also work in more subtle ways. The traditionally perceived role of females—overloaded with expectations and stereotypes—is a slow-changing difficulty that is yet to be overcome. There also are pressures to be practical and economical, which can discourage "idea people." We learn not to ask too many questions—although curiosity is a core characteristic of creativity. We learn that fantasy is a waste of time, that we should have faith in reason and logic, and that we should not "rock the boat." If cooperation is an accepted cultural or institutional goal, many people will temper their creative ideas in order to "fit in." [*See* WOMEN AND CREATIVITY.]

Van Gundy noted such subtle corporate cultural barriers as a reluctance to share ideas, a fear that innovation will change the uniqueness of the organization, a desire to protect the status quo, and the attitude that "creative types don't fit in."

Finally, the greatest cultural barrier is the culture itself. Western psychology traditionally ignores monumental cultural differences in creative attitudes and personality, creative productivity, creative opportunity, and general self-actualization. Think for a moment of the anticreative forces of tradition, conformity, and traditional roles of women in Spanish- and Arabic-speaking countries and many places in Asia, India, and Africa. [*See* CROSS-CULTURAL DIFFERENCES.]

VI. EMOTIONAL BARRIERS

Emotional barriers interfere with thinking by making us "freeze." You may wish to imagine a balance scale with "emotional upset" or "freezing" on one side and clear thinking on the other. As one side goes down, the other goes up. Some familiar emotional blocks are anger, fear, anxiety, hate, and even love. Some are temporary states, caused perhaps by problems with peers, parents, partners, or children, or by pressures and worries at school or work, financial stress, or poor health.

More permanent emotional blocks include chronic sources of insecurity and anxiety such as fear of failure, fear of being different, fear of criticism or ridicule, fear of rejection, fear of supervisors, timidity, or shaky self-esteem. [*See* EMOTION/AFFECT.]

While most emotional barriers interfere with the creation of ideas, some will block their adoption and implementation, for example, fear of taking risks and fear of uncertainty. Also, differences in needs and values may produce conflict and block the acceptance of an innovation.

While this article is not psychotherapy, one possible avenue for resolving emotional barriers is a two-step creative problem solving approach: First ask what the problem is, and then ask what we can do about it.

VII. RESOURCE BARRIERS

Resource barriers may seem a trivial form of barrier to creative thinking. However, they can and do stop creative productivity. As suggested by the name, resource barriers include shortages of people, money, time, supplies, and/or information that are needed for creative thinking or for the implementation of creative ideas. Conflicts are likely if resources are pirated from one department to develop an innovation in another. [*See* CREATIVE CLIMATE.]

VIII. STIMULATING CREATIVITY BY REMOVING MENTAL BARRIERS

Roger Von Oech's book, *A Whack on the Side of the Head,* addresses the problem of teaching creativity as a matter of removing 10 mental blocks—which sometimes requires a "whack on the side of the head." Space permits just a short review.

His first mental block is "The Right Answer," referring to the usual assumption that there is just one right answer. Rather, a creative person will look for the second, third, fourth, and so on right answers, which are likely to be more imaginative than the first. The second mental block is "That's Not Logical," which stems from our culturally rooted assumption that logical thinking is better than illogical thinking. With creativity, logical thinking often is best suited for an evaluative phase. A third mental block is "Follow the Rules," which means

thinking of things only as they presently are, not as they could be. Rule-inspecting and tradition-inspecting may be in order. "Be Practical" is the fourth mental block, which can interfere with the imaginative asking of that pivotal question, "What if . . . ?"

The fifth mental block is "Avoid Ambiguity." In fact, ambiguity is a subtle form of motivation that inspires imaginative thinking. Ambiguity also is an essential stage that occurs while we clarify a problem and consider possible solutions. Von Oech's sixth barrier is the assumption that "To Err Is Wrong." Innovation necessarily requires making mistakes and even failing, as Thomas Edison did quite regularly. Errors serve as stepping stones. Von Oech noted IBM founder Thomas J. Watson's quote, "The way to succeed is to double your failure rate." A seventh block is the notion that "Play Is Frivolous." In creative thinking, the wrongness here is obvious. Countless innovations and discoveries are born via playing with ideas.

Barrier number eight is "That's Not My Area." This rich block supplies an excuse for not even trying to solve a problem. Further, such a block prevents a thinker from looking to other fields for ideas and inspiration. "Don't Be Foolish," barrier nine, is a cultural barrier rooted in conformity pressures. "Fooling around" with ideas, like playing with possibilities, is a popular creative thinking occurrence. Finally, the tenth block is the self-squelcher, "I'm Not Creative." This one is a self-fulfilling prophecy—if you believe it, you will be right.

IX. IDEA SQUELCHERS

There are dozens of attitude-related idea squelchers which we use too often to stifle our own or others' creative thinking. As just a sample:

We've never done that before.
Are you nuts?
It's not in the budget.
It can't be done.
It's a waste of time.
It has limited possibilities.
Too academic.
This is the last try.
I'm telling you, it won't work.
You ask too many questions.
Don't step on any toes.

It won't work in our neighborhood.
We did all right without it.
Let's discuss it at some other time.
You've got to be kidding.
See? It didn't work!
You don't understand the problem.
Let's wait and see.
We can't do it under the regulations.
It'll mean more work.
Somebody would have suggested it before if it were any good.
No adolescent is going to tell me how to run this operation!

A good case could be made for the argument that all of us would be more creative were it not for external and internal barriers, blocks, and squelchers. Because of well-learned habits, an unsupportive or repressive environment, or our fears and insecurities, most people do not use their creative imaginations and abilities. *The challenge to anyone wishing to increase his or her personal creativeness is to understand, expect, and be ready to cope with barriers to creativity from the environment or from inside oneself.*

X. CREATIVE ATTITUDES

When we discuss creative attitudes we also are speaking of creative personalities. Decades of research with creative individuals, including persons who have and have not achieved creative eminence, focused on their attitudes and personalities, compared with con-

trols. As noted at the outset, *creativity* is most appropriately viewed as a way of living, thinking, and perceiving one's world. Creativity is rooted in one's attitudes and personality. This section will review recurrent patterns.

Over 200 adjectives and brief descriptions of creative attitudes and personality traits were sorted by the author into 15 intuitively defined categories of positive, socially desirable traits and 7 categories of negative, potentially troublesome traits. The "positive" versus "negative" judgments were subjective, as were some ambiguous decisions (for example, whether to place "adventurous" under "risk-taking" or "energetic"). The categories interrelate in the sense that all can be part of the stereotypical "creative personality." Of course, not all traits will apply to all creative persons; there simply are too many forms of creativity and creative people. Some traits even are contradictory, for example, "receptive to new ideas" versus "sarcastic." Finally, artistic/poetic creative people may be shy and withdrawn, not high in the energy, confidence, and humor that characterize the stereotyped creative person.

The categories of traits reflect the main, recurrent traits of creative people as found in the literature. The 15 categories of positive traits appear in Table I. The traits are mostly self-defining. However, we will comment briefly on each.

• *Aware of creativeness.* Most highly creative people are quite aware of their creativeness. They are in the habit of doing things creatively and they like being creative. Creativity consciousness is a common and important trait among creative people. *In improving our own creativity and in teaching creativity to others,*

TABLE I
Sample of Recurrent Attitudes and Traits of Creative People

1. *Aware of Creativeness*	
Creativity conscious	Values originality and creativity
2. *Original*	
Flexible in ideas and thought	Avoids perceptual sets
Challenges norms and assumptions	Sees things in new ways
Resourceful	Is a "what if?" person
Full of ideas	Imaginative
3. *Independent*	
Self-confident	Sets own rules
Individualistic	Dissatisfied with the status quo
Does not fear being different	Internally controlled, inner directed

TABLE I (Continued)

4. *Risk-taking*

Courageous

Not afraid to try something new

Willing to cope with failure

Does not mind consequences of being different

Rejects limits imposed by others

5. *Energetic*

Adventurous

High intrinsic motivation

Overactive, hyperactive

Enthusiastic

Driving absorption

Drive for accomplishment and recognition

Persistent, persevering

Sensation seeking

6. *Curious*

Experiments

Wide interests

Likes to hear others' ideas

Asks many questions

Open to the irrational

Seeks interesting situations

7. *Sense of humor*

Childlike freshness in thinking

Plays with ideas

Playful

Sharp-witted

8. *Attracted to complexity*

Attracted to the mysterious

Attracted to the asymmetrical

Attracted to ambiguity, incongruity

Attracted to novelty

Is a complex person

Tolerant of disorder

9. *Capacity for fantasy*

Animistic and magical thinking

Had imaginary playmates as a child

Mixes truth and fantasy/fiction

Believes in psychical phenomena and flying saucers

Theatrical interests

10. *Artistic*

Aesthetic interests

Sensitive to beauty

Enjoys art, music, creative dramatics

Good designer

11. *Open-minded*

Liberal

Receptive to new ideas

Open to new experiences and growth

Receptive to other viewpoints

12. *Needs alone time*

Internally preoccupied

Prefers to work alone

Introspective

Reflective

13. *Intuitive*

Perceptive

Sees relationships, implications

Good at problem finding

Observant

Uses all senses in observing

Heightened sensitivity to details, patterns

14. *Emotional*

Can express feelings, emotions

Sensitive

Moody

Has emotional highs and lows

Withdrawn

Needs attention, praise, support

15. *Ethical*

Altruistic

Idealistic

Empathic

Democratic minded

creativity consciousness is the number one trait to develop.

• *Originality.* The trait of *originality* is so basic that dictionaries often use the term interchangeably with *creativity*. Originality also may be considered a creative ability in the sense of one's capability for uniqueness and nonconformity in thought.

• *Independence, risk-taking.* These two traits interrelate closely, since a person cannot display high independence without the accompanying willingness to take a creative risk. The creative person must dare to differ, make changes, challenge traditions, make waves, and bend rules. Such independence and risk-taking expose the creative person to possible criticism and embarrassment, and the possibilities of failure or looking foolish. [*See* Autonomy and Independence.]

• *High energy.* A defining trait of creatively productive people is their extraordinarily high level of energy, which appears as enthusiasm, driving absorption, passionate interest, and an unwillingness to give up. Paul Torrance called it the *blazing drive.* Psychologist Calvin Taylor once quoted a scientist as claiming, with tongue in cheek, that the only way to stop a fellow scientist from working on a problem would be to shoot him. Frank Farley, past president of the American Psychological Association, frequently emphasized the *thrill-seeking* trait of creative people.

• *Thorough.* Of course, high risk-taking and energy are not enough. The committed creative person must finish the projects, preferably in an organized fashion.

• *Curiosity.* Along with originality and high energy, another classic trait is curiosity—a sometimes childlike sense of wonder and intrigue, a desire to understand one's world. He or she may have a history of taking things apart to see how they work and of exploring attics, libraries, and museums.

• *Humor.* Another frequent trait is a keen sense of humor. It relates to one's ability to take a childlike and playful approach to problems. Many discoveries, inventions, problem solutions, and artistic creations are the result of "fooling around" with ideas, playing with strange possibilities, or turning things upside down, backward, or inside out. A relevant quote is that "the creative adult is essentially a perpetual child—the tragedy is that most of us grow up" (Fabun, 1968, p. 5). Both Freud and Carl Rogers agreed that regression to a childlike state is an important feature of fantasy and creative thinking. [*See* Humor.]

• *Attraction to fantasy, complexity, and novelty.* The creative person's attraction to fantasy, complexity, and novelty may reflect the person's own complexity. A classic demonstration by Frank Barron and George Welsh showed that creative persons preferred smudgy, complex, asymmetrical drawings over simple and balanced ones. While novel ideas and innovations may excite creative people, others habitually may analyze defects and find fault. Tolerance for ambiguity, which relates intimately to complexity and novelty, is essential in the sense that—as we saw in Von Oech's fifth mental block—creative problem solving involves an ambiguous period in which the problem is clarified and solutions considered. One unique twist to the attraction to fantasy, complexity, and novelty is that creative people tend to be stronger believers in psychical phenomena and flying saucers, despite their generally higher intelligence level. [*See* Novelty.]

• *Artistic.* Artistic and aesthetic interests usually are keen. One explanation is simply that creative people are more likely to have been involved in, for example, music, dance, theater, art, or handicrafts. However, the trait extends to persons creative in science, business, and other traditionally nonart areas.

• *Open-minded.* A creative person, virtually by definition, must be receptive to new ideas and willing to look at problems from various points of view. Open-mindedness includes not fearing the new, different, or unknown and not making up one's mind in advance. The trait relates to Von Oech's creativity barriers of looking for just one right answer, being practical and logical, and avoiding ambiguity, frivolity, mistakes, and foolishness.

• *Needs for alone time.* The need to create demands time for thinking, reflection, solving problems, and creating. Creative children and adults often prefer to work alone, reflecting their creative independence.

• *Perceptive.* Perceptiveness and intuitiveness, whether in art or science areas, are common traits of creative people. There is greater sensitivity to details, patterns, implications, relationships, and "what should follow." Intuitive "mental leaps" are quicker. [*See* Perception and Creativity.]

• *Emotional.* The Dabrowski and Piechowski phenomenon of "emotional giftedness" or "overexcitability" usually happens in very high IQ gifted persons. The syndrome includes free play of imagination, vivid imagery, fantasy, paranormal thinking, metaphorical thought, inventions, and poetic and dramatic perceptions, as well as fast talking and extra high energy levels. The syndrome includes having emotional highs and lows, moodiness, and emotional sensitivity. [*See* OVEREXCITABILITIES.]

• *Ethical.* Another trait related to high mental ability and creativity, and one found in Terman's early studies of highly gifted children, is a tendency for ethical thinking and behavior—empathy, idealism, altruism, and simple helpfulness.

XI. NEGATIVE TRAITS OF CREATIVITY

A discussion of creative attitudes and personality would be incomplete without acknowledging traits and dispositions that disturb supervisors, parents, teachers,

and peers. Table II lists negative, sometimes upsetting characteristics of creative individuals that surfaced in the search for creative traits mentioned earlier. The traits may stem from a creative student's independence, unconventionality, persistence, and perhaps curiosity and humor. The items were placed into the seven categories of *egotistical, impulsive, argumentative, immature, absentminded, neurotic,* and *hyperactive.* Many are likely to cause personal or social adjustment problems.

XII. CREATIVITY, PSYCHOSES, NEUROSES, AND SOCIOPATHY

Another aspect of the creative personality that cannot be ignored is the tendency for a small proportion of creatively productive persons to be slightly mentally disturbed, and even to have mentally ill relatives. For

TABLE II
Recurrent "Negative" Traits

1. *Egotistical*	
Intolerant	Snobbish
Self-centered	Claims the rest of the parade is out of step
2. *Impulsive*	
Acts without planning	Capricious
Careless	Disorganized with unimportant matters
Impatient	Tactless
Irresponsible	
3. *Argumentative*	
Cynical	Defiant
Rebellious	Sarcastic
Uncooperative	Stubborn
Little regard for rules, conventions, mores, law, authority	Autocratic
4. *Immature*	
Childish	Silly
Sloppy	
5. *Absentminded*	
Forgetful	Careless
Mind wanders	Watches windows
6. *Neurotic*	
Aloof	Mildly sociopathic
Temperamental	Unable to control emotions
Low frustration tolerance	Uncommunicative
7. *Hyperactive*	
Overactive, physically and mentally	

example, in their 1950s study of the creative personality at the University of California at Berkeley, Frank Barron and Donald MacKinnon found a tendency for high-level creative people, such as creative women mathematicians, to be rebellious, undependable, irresponsible, and inconsiderate, and to have fluctuating moods. Barron and MacKinnon's creative writers scored in the top 15 percentile on *Minnesota Multiphasic Personality Inventory* measures of psychopathology: *hypochondriasis, depression, hysteria* (anxiety, uncontrolled behavior), *psychopathic deviation, paranoia, psychasthenia* (fears, phobias), *schizophrenia,* and *hypomania.* However, strong *ego strength* scores indicated they could better deal with their troubles. Psychologically, said Barron, they were both sicker and healthier than the average person.

In a 1988 study of historically eminent persons, Herbert Walberg concluded that about a fourth to a third showed definite introversion or neuroses. Also in 1988 Solomon and Winslow reported that a sample of business entrepreneurs showed mild sociopathy and/or were social deviates. A 1995 study of male and female eminent persons by Walker, Koestner, and Hum indicated that the creative achievers were rated significantly higher than average on impulsivity, depression, and general neuroticism. Richards turned the usual procedure around, finding that a sample of manic-depressives were rated higher in creativity than were controls.

Concluded Barron, "mad as a hatter" is high praise when applied to creative people. The relationship continues to be an intriguing one. [*See* MAD GENIUS CONTROVERSY.]

XIII. CONCLUSIONS: ATTITUDES THAT OVERCOME BARRIERS

We have seen that blocks and barriers—learning and habit, rules and traditions, and perceptual, cultural, and emotional barriers—will interfere with creative thinking and innovation. Again, a common argument is that we all are born creative, but early years of socialization and education create habit- and tradition-based barriers to imaginative thinking and innovation. We have also seen that all creative people show a relatively recurrent syndrome of creative attitudes and personality traits—awareness of creativity, originality, independence, energy and motivation, risk-taking, curiosity, humor, attraction to complexity and fantasy, artistic interests, open-mindedness, and perceptiveness.

Of course, creative attitudes and personalities plus overcoming personal and environmental barriers do not present a total picture of the creative person. For example, other important factors discussed in this encyclopedia are intelligence and thinking styles, innate creative abilities related to the specific medium (e.g., art and mathematics), training, an existing body of knowledge, plus such matters as opportunity and chance. Nonetheless, an awareness of necessary creative attitudes and personality traits and a readiness to deal with environmental and personal barriers are central to creative development and productivity.

As to the puzzle in Section II, try removing S-I-X L-E-T-T-E-R-S.

Bibliography

Adams, J. L. (1986). *Conceptual blockbusting: A guide to better ideas* (3rd ed.). Reading, MA: Addison-Wesley.

Davis, G. A. (1998). *Creativity is forever* (4th ed.). Dubuque, IA: Kendall/Hunt.

Fabun, D. (1968). *You and creativity.* New York: Macmillan.

Parnes, S. J. (1981). *Magic of your mind.* Buffalo, NY: Bearly Limited.

Van Gundy, A. B. (1987). Organizational creativity and innovation. In S. G. Isaksen (Ed.), *Frontiers of creativity research* (pp. 358–379). Buffalo, NY: Bearly Limited.

Von Oech, R. (1983). *A whack on the side of the head.* New York: Warner Communications.

Behavioral Approaches to Creativity

Robert Epstein and Gaynell Laptosky

United States International University

Contingency of Reinforcement The relationship between behavior, its consequences, and its antecedents.

Generalization The spread of effect from one stimulus to another.

Generativity Theory A formal theory of the creative process that suggests that new behavior is the result of an orderly competition among previously established behaviors.

Modeling Demonstrating a behavior to someone you want to engage in that behavior.

Operant Behavior Behavior that is modifiable by its consequences.

Prompt A verbal or physical signal to engage in a particular behavior.

Reinforcement The delivery of a reinforcer.

Reinforcer A consequence of behavior that strengthens that behavior.

Self-Management The use of behavior modification techniques to change one's own behavior.

Stimulus Equivalence The spontaneous emergence of a perceived relationship between stimuli.

A **BEHAVIORAL APPROACH** to creativity focuses on the relationship between an individual's behavior and events in and properties of the individual's environment. This approach employs techniques such as reinforcement, prompting, modeling, and environmental manipulation to enhance creativity. It differs from cognitive approaches in its avoidance of mentalistic language and construct-based models.

I. BACKGROUND

Behavioral psychology has its origins in the work of Ivan Pavlov (1849–1936), Edward L. Thorndike (1874–1949), John B. Watson (1878–1958), Clark L. Hull (1884–1952), B. F. Skinner (1904–1990), and others. The modern discipline is dominated by Skinner's work, which focuses on *operant behavior*—behavior that is modifiable by its consequences. Behavioral psychologists have typically studied the observable behavior of both animals and people as well as techniques for strengthening or weakening behavior.

Generally speaking, creativity has been of little concern to researchers and practitioners working in the behavioral tradition. Skinner himself wrote about it rarely and never conducted research on creativity per se. As both inventor and author, Skinner would probably be

Copyright © 1999 by Academic Press
All rights of reproduction in any form reserved.

considered a highly creative person, but as a scientist he seemed unconcerned with the processes that might account for his creativity. In his later writings, such as *The Technology of Teaching,* published in 1968, and various essays he wrote for students, he offered advice about how to promote creativity, but his advice was informal and was based on neither research nor theory.

Behavioral psychologists have avoided studying creativity for three reasons: First, the concept of creativity suggests that people initiate action, whereas Skinner and other early behaviorists believed that all behavior is determined by a person's genetic endowment and environmental history with no real initiative taking place. Second, behavioral psychologists have generally preferred to work from the simple to the complex, basing their terms and concepts on animal studies rather than borrowing terms from the vernacular. Consequently, terms like *creativity* (along with *intelligence, love, humor,* and so on) are viewed with suspicion. Third, behavioral psychology tends to be practical and goal directed, focusing on methods for modifying existing behavior in specified ways rather than on allowing behavior to vary unpredictably.

Nevertheless, beginning in the late 1960s, a few behavioral psychologists began to apply behavioral methods and concepts to the study of creativity. Especially notable are a series of studies by Elizabeth Goetz and her colleagues, which showed that reinforcement could be used to promote creativity in preschool children. By 1985, research studies by Goetz and others prompted a critical review by Andrew S. Winston and Joanne E. Baker of 20 "behavior analytic studies of creativity." The review concluded that behavioral techniques appear to increase creative responding, but it also noted a number of difficulties: possible confounds between instructions and reinforcement contingencies, failure to assess the value or usefulness of creative products, and little or no follow-up to determine whether creativity persisted after training.

Another behavioral model of creativity was proposed by D. H. Wells in 1986. Wells adopted a widely used definition of creativity, namely that it refers to behavior that is both novel and useful, and suggested that one's creative ability is determined by a lifetime of reinforcement and punishment of such behavior. Thus, according to Wells, creativity can be encouraged by the con-sistent reinforcement of behavior that is both novel and useful. [*See* NOVELTY.]

Finally, studies by Robert Epstein beginning in the late 1970s led to the development of Generativity Theory, a formal theory of creative behavior that can predict creative performances moment to moment in time in laboratory settings in both animals and humans. According to Generativity Theory, creative behavior is the result of interconnections among previously established behaviors, and research has shown that the process of interconnection is orderly and predictable. Generativity research has led in recent years to new techniques for training creativity and to assessment tools for measuring competencies related to creative performance. [*See* GENERATIVITY THEORY.]

Although behavioral psychologists have made some headway in the study of creativity, the behavioral perspective is not without its critics. Robert J. Sternberg, Paul G. Muscari, and others have expressed concerns that a scientific analysis of creativity might trivialize or depersonalize the concept. Sternberg cites studies by Janet Metcalfe, which suggest that insightful problem solving is qualitatively different from other types of problem solving, as evidence that creativity cannot yet be understood in rigorous terms. Others, such as Peter Trower, fault behavioral psychology for ignoring both cognitive and volitional aspects of behavior. But the most substantive controversy about the behavioral approach to creativity has focused on an empirical issue: Can reinforcement be used to enhance creativity, or might it actually be detrimental to creativity?

II. REINFORCEMENT AS A TOOL FOR PROMOTING CREATIVITY

In 1969 Karen Pryor and colleagues discovered that a porpoise that was receiving food for displaying a new behavior at a daily animal show began spontaneously emitting complex and unusual behaviors. Many of these behaviors had never been seen before in this or in any other porpoise at the park. With a second porpoise novel behaviors were reinforced with food in daily training sessions. By the 16th session the porpoise began emitting multiple new behaviors during each session. In the final sessions (31 and 32) the animal immediately produced a new behavior at the onset of the session and never replicated an old behavior. Moreover, both porpoises showed increased tendencies to display unusual behavior in response to everyday situations.

Elizabeth Goetz, Donald Baer, and their colleagues carried out a number of studies showing that reinforcement can be used to promote creativity in preschool children. In 1971 Goetz and Baer used block constructions as a medium for the observation of the development of new behavior. A baseline level of creativity was established for each of three 4-year-old girls by scoring the number of forms contained in her block constructions. Following this the girls received verbal praise, sometimes containing a description of what was of interest in their constructions, for each new block form that appeared during the course of a session. This was followed by sessions in which the children received praise each time a block form was repeated. Finally, the children were again praised for the production of new block construction forms. Block constructions were scored for form diversity (the number of different forms produced per session) and new forms (the number of forms per session that had not been produced in any previous session). Goetz and Baer found that form diversity scores were greater when the children were praised each time a different form appeared and less when the children were not praised or when praise was given for replicating previous forms. New forms emerged almost exclusively during sessions in which the children were praised. The children also spent longer periods of time at the block-building task when they were praised.

In 1972 Elizabeth Goetz and Mary Salmonson sought to determine whether descriptive praise is more effective than general praise in promoting creativity in children. Creativity was assessed by scoring the easel paintings of three preschool girls for form diversity and new forms. A list of 25 different objectively defined forms was used for scoring. The authors found that the greatest increases in form diversity occurred when the girls received descriptive praise rather than general praise. A later study showed that form diversity could be maintained for at least ten weeks after praise was discontinued.

A 1977 report by Goetz and colleagues explored whether reinforcing creative behavior in one activity would increase creativity in other activities. In the first of two studies, two subjects—a 5-year-old boy and a 3-year-old girl—received descriptive praise for producing new and diverse forms in easel paintings. The experiment consisted of a baseline-treatment–reversal-treatment design. Painting sessions were followed, either immediately or on the next day, by block-building sessions. No praise was given for form diversity or new forms produced during block building. In general, both form diversity and new forms increased in painting in response to praise. A pattern of increases in form diversity in block constructions appeared, which paralleled the increases produced by praise in paintings, but the increases were much less pronounced in the block-building task than in the painting task. Form diversity in both tasks dropped during the reversal phase of the experiment. New forms did not appear in the block constructions. In other words, there appeared to be some generalization of form diversity but not of new forms.

In the second study, three male preschool children received tokens (redeemable for a toy at the end of the session) and descriptive praise for producing form diversity and new forms in felt-tip-pen drawings. One of the three boys also received tokens and praise for form diversity and new forms produced in Lego constructions. All drawing sessions were followed by painting sessions. Form diversity and new forms were tracked for all of these activities. All of the children displayed an increase in form diversity in their felt-tip-pen drawings as a result of reinforcement. Two of the three children also displayed some subsequent increases in form diversity in their paintings. These two children displayed maintenance of this of diversity in their paintings and drawings at a 2-month follow-up. No generalization of form diversity was observed from the drawing to the building tasks. The child who had received diversity training in Lego construction did not generalize this behavior to block building. In other words, for two of three boys, creative tendencies generalized to a similar activity but not to a dissimilar one. A study of tool use in preschool children found a similar generalization pattern.

In all of the studies mentioned thus far, praise was given every time the subject displayed a behavior that was targeted for increase—a high labor-intensive training regimen. In subsequent research Goetz found that relatively low rates of reinforcement can promote creative behavior, which suggests that the creativity of children that occurs during free play in classroom settings may result from low rates of reinforcement of creative behavior.

Goetz summarized the results of these and other reinforcement studies in 1982 and offered seven tentative conclusions: (a) Various types of contingent praise can be used to reinforce novel behavior. (b) Generalization of creative behavior occurs in some instances. (c) Minimal amounts of reinforcement can be used to increase novel behavior. (d) Verbal prompts can be combined with reinforcement to promote creative behavior. (e) Creativity is limited by neither materials nor time. (f) Maintenance of creative behavior can occur following training. (g) Creativity can be coded for the purpose of training and research.

Reinforcement has also been studied as a means to promote creativity in the use of language. A variety of studies have shown that originality and creativity in writing can be improved using behavioral techniques. Writing becomes more creative when certain aspects of writing—such as the use of action verbs—are reinforced. Unfortunately, in many of the studies reinforcement is often combined with instructions or modeling, which makes it difficult to isolate the effect of reinforcement alone.

The effect of modeling and reinforcement on the creation of generative sentences was studied in two experiments conducted by George T. Endo and Howard N. Sloane, Jr., in 1982. In the first study four children were presented with nouns with which they were to fabricate sentences. An adult then made statements to the children in which nonhuman nouns were personified, such as "Glasses are afraid of stones." The models received general praise and tokens for their statements. Following each modeled statement, the children were given the opportunity to make a different sentence with the same noun. If the children were able to do so they received praise and tokens. In a second modeling session, nonpersonified sentences were modeled and reinforced. During the first and second sessions of modeling, probes were conducted in which models made incorrect sentences and the children were given the opportunity to correct them. Personification, which was absent in the children's sentences at baseline, developed and increased quickly in response to modeling and reinforcement.

In a second experiment, children were given nouns different than those used by the models, and the models presented five sentences to the children before the children composed their own sentences. No personified sentences were made by the children at baseline, but personification quickly developed and increased in response to modeling and reinforcement. In this experiment generalization to new words occurred. In both experiments personification decreased to levels approaching baseline when nonpersonified sentences were presented to the children.

In another study, published in 1973, third graders wrote short compositions in response to slide-projected pictures. Compositions were scored for the number of different parts of speech employed, and independent judges rated the compositions for creativity. Praise and free time were used to reinforce increases in the frequency of word usage. Word-usage scores remained fairly stable during baseline but increased in response to reinforcement, and when the use of action verbs was reinforced, compositions were judged to be highly creative.

A different type of study was conducted with eight fourth and fifth graders by John Glover and A. L. Gary in 1976. Creativity was defined in terms of four dimensions of behavior: *fluency* (the number of ideas produced), *flexibility* (the variety of ideas produced), *elaboration* (the expansion of ideas produced), and *originality* (the statistical uncommonness of the ideas produced). Subjects were taught these criteria and given early recess and snacks for meeting these criteria in lists they generated to describe different possible uses for an item. Following instruction and reinforcement, these criteria were met substantially more than during a baseline period. Scores on the Torrance Test of Creative Thinking also increased significantly as a result of the instruction and reinforcement.

In a related study by John A. Campbell and Jerry Willis, instruction and reinforcement were combined in a multiple-baseline design to increase fluency, flexibility, and elaboration in the written compositions of 32 fifth graders. Following a baseline period, elaboration of ideas was reinforced with tokens and praise in ten daily writing sessions. In ten subsequent sessions, elaboration and flexibility were reinforced, and in the final ten sessions, elaboration, flexibility, and fluency were reinforced. Children's scores in the three areas improved in response to specific reinforcement requirements; in other words, when only elaboration was reinforced, flexibility and fluency did not increase. Scores on the Torrance Test of Creative Thinking also improved.

Reinforcement was also shown to increase the creativity of lists of applications of psychological concepts made by 31 high school students. The students were required to write one paper per week on a topic related to psychology. The last section of each paper consisted of a list of all the different ways the psychological concept could be applied. During baseline (the first three papers) all of the students received feedback that their applications lists were "good." At the end of the third week the scoring criteria for creativity were explained and the students were told that they would receive extra credit for creative responding. As a result, students' scores in the four areas being measured (fluency, flexibility, elaboration, and originality) increased. Scores on the Torrance Thinking Creatively with Words Test also increased.

The writing of college students can also become more creative in response to reinforcement and instruction. This was demonstrated in a study by John Glover in which 14 undergraduates were taught the four behavioral dimensions of creativity and awarded class points for applying these principles to making lists of unusual ways to use randomly selected items and to solve everyday problems. Class papers were rated for creativity, and the Torrance Test of Thinking Creatively with Words was administered at the onset and conclusion of the study, as well as 11 months after the study ended. Fluency, flexibility, and originality increased in response to instructions and reinforcement. What's more, scores on the Torrance Test increased significantly from pre- to post-treatment conditions, and this increase was maintained in the follow-up test. The experimental group's scores were also significantly higher at posttest than the scores of a control group.

Reinforcement has also been used to promote creativity in the business world. For example, a 1991 study by Julie M. Smith and her colleagues increased the number of innovations made by employees of a public utility company. The company had been relying on a suggestion box to collect ideas from employees, but this method had a poor yield—an average of only 38 ideas per year had been collected over the previous 10 years. A system was introduced in which cash rewards were given for clearly defined types of suggestions. A rating system was devised to assess the potential benefit of each suggestion, and cash awards were made accordingly. In the first 9 months after this new program was instituted, 65 employees submitted a total of 89 suggestions, 12 of which were implemented.

A very different line of research suggests that reinforcement may be detrimental to creativity—and even, perhaps, to performance in general. Studies conducted in the 1970s showed that people who have been rewarded for engaging in an activity engage in that activity less often following reinforcement than they did before reinforcement—a phenomenon called the overjustification effect. A 1977 review of the relevant literature suggested also that reinforcement produces behavior that is repetitive and uncreative and that reward can interfere with people's problem-solving abilities. In a 1979 study and subsequent research, Teresa Amabile showed that reinforcement and "external evaluation" can interfere with artistic creativity. People who have been rewarded for behaving in certain ways can become dependent on that reward, performing poorly when reward is unavailable.

A meta-analysis of studies purporting to show various detrimental effects of reward, published by Robert Eisenberger and Judy Cameron in 1996, concluded that reward has negative effects under limited conditions that are easy to avoid. Negative effects typically attributed to reinforcement are actually produced by certain reinforcement *procedures,* not by reinforcement in the broad sense. For example, shifting from high-reinforcement to low-reinforcement conditions is easily detected and ultimately leads to low rates of responding in the low-reinforcement situation. Reinforcing specific properties of behavior—a certain type of brush stroke, for example—results in the repetition of those properties. Presenting too many reinforcers—a phenomenon called "satiation"—lowers the effectiveness of reinforcement. Using a large, salient reward that's present during a learning session is distracting, as anyone knows who has tried to train a dog while holding a piece of steak.

Generally speaking, reinforcement seems to interfere with creativity only it is used inappropriately. For example, in a 1988 study by B. A. Hennessey and Teresa Amabile, children completed a painting task before constructing collages. Those children who were praised for their paintings—*irrespective of the quality of their work*—made subsequent collages that were less creative than those produced by children who were not praised for painting. It is not surprising that when trivial properties of behavior are reinforced, trivial behavior results, but it is also clear that reinforcement can be used to encourage novel and useful behavior—the behavior most people call creative. [*See* MOTIVATION/DRIVE.]

III. OTHER BEHAVIORAL METHODS FOR PROMOTING CREATIVITY

Reinforcement is often supplemented with other behavior-change methods, such as modeling and instruction. The latter two methods, along with various sorts of environmental manipulation, component-skills training, self-management training, goal setting, and problem-solving training, have been shown to foster creativity in a variety of settings.

Many authors who do not adopt behavioral methods or terminology per se have long recommended various changes in the physical and social environment—sometimes called climate or culture changes—to foster creativity. For example, in a 1987 article about boosting creativity in the workplace, Bruce G. Whiting suggested methods like "allowing people room" (reducing the level of supervision), "using diverse groups" (providing diverse social stimuli), and "information exchange" (giving people materials that describe activities in other parts of the organization). Others speak of creating a "nurturing" environment (one in which negative feedback is minimized), providing "socioemotional support" (praise and other positive feedback for creative behavior), providing "task support" (stimulating work materials), and providing "incentives" (rewards for creative behavior). Many of these suggestions are vague, unfortunately, and their effectiveness may be unsupported by data. [*See* CONDITIONS AND SETTINGS/ENVIRONMENT.]

A Turkish study published in 1993 proposed that creativity in children can be stifled by cultural demands for discipline and conformity. One hundred ninety-two children in the third and fourth grades were

rated using the Torrance Test of Creative Thinking and the Teacher Perception Scale (a measure of divergent thought and classroom nonconformity developed for this study), and, indeed, a significant correlation was found between creativity and nonconformity. Because this is a correlational study, however, it does not necessarily demonstrate that experience or the current environment stifles creativity. It may simply be the case that nonconformists are creative. [*See* CONFORMITY.]

Expectation by teachers or supervisors is another environmental factor that has been said to influence creativity. For example, Robert Rosenthal and colleagues found that when teachers were told that randomly selected children would make significant increases in creativity during the upcoming school year, those children showed significant gains in creativity as assessed by scores assigned to their drawings by a panel of eight professional artists. The teachers were observed to interact more often and in a slightly more *negative* manner with the children identified as having creative potential, but the precise nature of the interaction was not specified.

Component skills training is another method sometimes used by behavioral psychologists to promote creativity. Kent Johnson and T. V. Layng have described programs in which component skills—for example, basic arithmetic skills—are learned to "fluency," which means that the behavior must be swift and must be recur quickly after periods of disuse. Fluency in components of a complex repertoire results in the emergence the complete repertoire without the need for additional training. For example, fluency in arithmetic skills gave rise almost immediately to the ability to solve real-world story problems—novel behavior of the sort some would call creative. Learning-disabled children taught using this method advance on the average at the rate of 2 to 3 school years per year of instruction, and adults initially performing at the eighth-grade level gain almost 2 years on the average per 20 hours of instruction. Other studies have also shown that teaching component behaviors can be helpful in getting behavioral repertoires to generalize to new settings.

Self-management training—the deliberate use of behavioral technique for changing one's own behavior—can also foster creativity. John Glover has outlined a nine-step model for modifying one's own behavior in which the goal is to emit behavior that is especially fluent, flexible, elaborate, and original. Glover recommends keeping records of behavior, setting goals, arranging consequences, and other self-management techniques. A 1989 study by Dennis Duchon has shown that goal setting alone can boost ideational creativity.

Self-management training has also been shown to promote problem-solving skills. In a study of two developmentally disabled adults employed at a community work site, the subjects were trained to use a four-step self-instructional method to solve problems and to reward themselves for doing so. Their ability to solve novel work-related problems independently increased dramatically as a result of training, and this ability was maintained over a 6-month follow-up period.

A 1989 study by Ellen Langer and her colleagues examined the effect of instructions on creativity with fourth graders, high school students, and college undergraduates. When information was presented in less-than-absolute terms, learners were more likely to use that information in creative ways. A statement like "a meta-poem uses rhyming words" produced writing that was less creative than that produced by a statement like "a meta-poem *could* use rhyming words." Apparently instructions that set boundaries on behavior—even by implication—can stifle creativity.

In a related study, instructions given to three groups of normal adults trying to solve a conceptual problem were varied. Group 1 was warned about various emotional and conceptual blocks to problem solving at the onset of the 30-minute session. Group 2 received similar instructions at the beginning of the session and also halfway through the session, and Group 3 received similar instructions every 5 minutes during the session. On the average, subjects in the second group performed far better than subjects in the other two groups, which suggests that instructions can assist in problem solving as long as the instructions are not excessive.

Other studies have suggested that prompts and modeling can increase the number of creative behaviors children emit.

Some behavioral psychologists teach problem-solving strategies in order to enhance an individual's ability to generate and test novel solutions to novel problems; because such behavior is both novel and useful, it satisfies a common definition of creativity. According to one report, the major components of this type of training include: (a) problem identification, (b) goal defini-

tion, (c) generation of alternatives, (d) comparison of consequences, and (e) selection of the best solution. Eight adolescent boys who had been diagnosed with conduct disorder showed improved problem-solving ability when taught these skills. Three of the boys were able to apply their new skills to problem social situations outside the training setting.

IV. MEASURING CREATIVE BEHAVIOR

Behavioral psychologists concerned with creativity tend to focus on creative behavior per se rather than on creative ability or creativity as a personality trait. Under what conditions does such behavior occur, how can such behavior be defined, and how can we detect and measure such behavior? These are the basic questions.

Unfortunately, there is no consensus among behavioral psychologists (or, for that matter, among other professionals) about how to define and measure creative behavior. The problem stems from the fact that the language of creativity is part of the vernacular; it is imprecise and employed inconsistently. Typically, behavior or the product of behavior is judged to be creative only if it has value for some community, and this makes the language of creativity especially capricious. For example, a painting considered creative by one community—say, the squiggly lines of Jackson Pollock—would be considered trash by another, and, to make matters worse, these judgments change over time.

Howard Sloane and his colleagues have suggested that it is neither the behavior nor the product of behavior that leads to the judgment of creativity. Rather, we call behavior "creative" when behavior is controlled by nonobvious multiple stimuli—in other words, when it is difficult to discern all of the controlling sources of the behavior. Arguing against this view is the fact that people often label highly unusual products creative (for example, the moveable art of Alexander Calder or Einstein's theory of relativity) based on properties of the products alone. Moreover, virtually all behavior is controlled by multiple, nonobvious stimuli, yet very little behavior is considered creative.

To simulate the judgment of the community, researchers often rely on independent judges, supervisors, teachers, or colleagues to determine whether behavior or its products are creative. In the Rosenthal study mentioned above, for example, eight professional artists—two musicians, two writers, a graphic artist, a dancer, a photographer, and a singer—scored children's drawings for creativity. But Goetz rejected the use of judges as unscientific and subjective. In her research, she typically predefined categories of novel forms she expected to find (in block building, painting, and collage making) and then tabulated occurrences in each of the categories. The judgment of judges, said Goetz, is "fickle" and "idiosyncratic." The studies by Glover and his colleagues also tended to use relatively objective measures of creativity (e.g., word counts indicating fluency, flexibility, elaboration, and originality) rather than relying on the subjective judgments of independent judges.

In the organizational setting, creativity is sometimes measured by counts of suggestions placed in suggestion boxes, number of patents applied for or issued, or number of publications. An ambitious study published in 1960 by William Buel sought to validate a behavioral rating scale of individual creativity at an oil company. Buel had supervisors give behavioral descriptions of their most and least creative employees. A selection of these statements was compiled into an assessment checklist, which was then use to rate other employees. Other supervisors, in turn, rated the creativity of those employees. Statistical analyses of the scores and rankings led to the selection of items that seemed to predict creativity best. Only modest correlations were found, however, between test scores and various objective measures of creativity, such as patent submissions.

V. GENERATIVE ASPECTS OF BEHAVIOR

Behaviorism, a philosophical doctrine developed by John B. Watson, B. F. Skinner, and others, suggested that people lack an inner, initiating self or agent. An organism, said Skinner, is simply a locus through which its genes and experience act to produce behavior. An organism is not responsible for its actions, and, although it may behave in novel ways, in no sense could it be said to *initiate* action, creative or noncreative.

Two things can be said about this viewpoint. First, although behaviorism helped drive behavioral research in the first half of the 20th century, most researchers who study behavior today do so without any guidance from behaviorism. Behavior is a legitimate subject matter for science, and it is possible to study behavior without being constrained by any particular philosophical doctrine. Second, whether an initiating agent exists or not, it is clear that virtually all behavior is *generative,* meaning that behavior continuously varies in novel ways. Sometimes the variations are trivial, and sometimes they are significant—so significant that the community calls them "creative."

In recent years researchers have looked at several generative aspects of behavior. Stimulated by a paper published by Murray Sidman in 1971, scores of studies have now been performed that examine a phenomenon called "stimulus equivalence": When someone is taught the relationship between Stimulus A and Stimulus B (e.g., the written word *cat* and a picture of a cat) and is also taught the relationship between Stimulus B and Stimulus C (e.g., a picture of a cat and an arbitrary symbol), a relationship between A and C may emerge spontaneously (e.g., the person may now be able to pair the word *cat* with the symbol). Equivalence relations of various sorts have been identified and studied. Because these relations are not specifically instructed or reinforced, their appearance is considered to be generative. Equivalence relations have been shown to emerge in animal behavior, but they are particularly common in human language.

A report published in 1993 extended the concept of stimulus equivalence to sequences of as many as five stimuli. In experiments with college students and children, a computer touch screen was used to teach subjects to select five symbols in a particular sequence (e.g., A1-A2-A3-A4-A5). When the sequence was mastered, test trials showed that many subjects also had learned the relationship between both adjacent (e.g., A2-A3) and non-adjacent (e.g., A1-A3) pairs of symbols. Even more striking, when subjects were taught two different sequences (e.g., A1-A2-A3-A4-A5 and B1-B2-B3-B4-B5), some subjects also learned the relationship between ordered pairs in different sequences (e.g., A1-B3 and B2-A4).

Organisms also have a tendency to manipulate objects in creative sequences. Both human and animal infants engage in combinatory play, behavior that seems essential to the emergence of tool use and other creative behaviors. A 1993 report by G. C. Westergaard describes combinatory play in baboons as young as 2 months of age. When given simple objects (a ball, a rod, and a bowl), three out of four of the baboon infants observed spent more than half of each 15-minute session picking up the objects in pairs and touching them against each other in various ways. By the time the infants were six-months old, they were able to use one or more of the objects as tools. In a 1945 investigation of problem solving, six young chimpanzees that had never had the opportunity to handle sticks could not use sticks to retrieve objects beyond their reach. When sticks were placed in their cages, however, each chimp handled the sticks spontaneously. After just three days of stick play, each of the chimps was able to solve a variety of novel problems. These and related studies on problem solving and tool use suggest the existence of two generative behavioral processes: combinatorial play and spontaneous problem solving.

Problem-solving behavior is necessarily both novel and useful, at least to the organism. Because a particular problem-solving performance may not be useful to the community (for example, when a child first climbs on an object to extend his or her reach), the community might not label the behavior creative, but the distinction is trivial. In any case, a century of research on problem solving in both animals and people, beginning with the work of Edward Thorndike, has revealed a variety of determinants of this important category of generative behavior. [*See* PROBLEM SOLVING.]

Behavioral theories of problem solving have typically characterized it as an interconnection or integration of previously established behaviors. For example, in 1955 Irving Maltzman proposed a behavioristic theory of problem solving inspired by the work of Clark Hull. According to Maltzman, problem solving was the result of "combinations and recombinations" of "habit strengths" (the strength of the relationship between a stimulus and a response). Hull himself proposed a similar theory in 1935, but neither Hull's nor Maltzman's approach allowed specific predictions to be made. A formal, predictive theory of creativity and problem solving, called Generativity Theory, was proposed by Epstein in the mid-1980s. As in earlier theories, Generativity Theory suggests that new behavior emerges from the interconnection of old behaviors; however,

this approach uses equations and computer-modeling techniques to predict novel performances in the laboratory continuously in time, and it has also been used to engineer novel performances in both animals and people.

VI. CONCLUSIONS

Behavioral psychology, the branch of psychology that focuses on behavior rather than cognition, has shed light on several aspects of the creative process, both from a practical perspective and a theoretical perspective. On the practical side, behavioral psychologists have shown that a variety of techniques can spur creativity, including reinforcement, instructions, modeling, self-management training, environmental manipulation, component-skills training, generalization training, goal setting, and problem-solving training. On the theoretical side, behavioral psychologists have developed both informal and formal models of the creative process, most of which view creativity as the result of an interconnection or integration of previously established behaviors.

Bibliography

Eisenberger, R., & Cameron, J. (1996). Detrimental effects of reward: Reality or myth? *American Psychologist, 51*(11), 1153–1166.

Epstein, R. (1996). *Cognition, creativity, and behavior: Selected essays.* Westport, CT: Praeger.

Goetz, E. M. (1989). The teaching of creativity to preschool children: The behavior analysis approach. In J. A. Glover, R. R. Ronning, & C. R. Reynolds (Eds.), *Handbook of creativity* (pp. 411–428). New York: Plenum Press.

Glover, J. A. (1980). *Become a more creative person.* Englewood Cliffs, NJ: Prentice-Hall.

Johnson, K. R., & Layng, T. V. J. (1992). Breaking the structuralist barrier: Literacy and numeracy with fluency. *American Psychologist, 47*(11), 1475–1490.

Skinner, B. F. (1968). *The technology of teaching.* New York: Appleton-Century-Crofts.

Smith, J. M., Kaminski, B. J., & Wylie, R. G. (1990). May I make a suggestion? Corporate support for innovation. *Journal of Organizational Behavior Management, 11*(2), 125–146.

Winston, A. S., & Baker, J. E. (1985). Behavior analytic studies of creativity: A critical review. *The Behavior Analyst, 8*(2), 191–205.

Alexander Graham Bell

1847–1922
Inventor of the telephone

Michael E. Gorman

University of Virginia, Charlottesville

ALEXANDER GRAHAM BELL was an inventor best known for the telephone. He was also an accomplished teacher of the deaf who married one of his pupils, Mabel Hubbard. Bell started on his invention career at the age of 11, with a device to remove the husks from wheat. But his major accomplishments were as a telegraph inventor. Initially, he focused on a new form of multiple telegraph, but by 1875 he was working on a device that would produce both speech and musical signals, which he patented in 1876. He spent most of the next decade defending this patent in court; it became the basis for the Bell Telephone Corporation, whose stock made Bell a millionaire. He worked on a variety of other inventions after the telephone, including airplanes, speedboats, phonograph records, and kites, but never again made a breakthrough to equal the telephone. Bell continued to play an active role in teaching the deaf, and also became president of the National Geographic Society and a regent of the Smithsonian.

I. BACKGROUND

Bell was born in Edinburgh, Scotland, in 1847. His grandfather was a teacher of elocution and his father had continued in this business, developing a form of visible speech. Bell and his brothers were trained in

A portrait of Alexander Graham Bell taken in later life (American Telephone & Telegraph Co.).

Copyright © 1999 by Academic Press
All rights of reproduction in any form reserved.

this visible speech and gave demonstrations in which their father would write down a sound made by a member of the audience, and the Bell brothers would enter the room and reproduce it. Bell's father also encouraged the brothers to build a model of the human vocal chords. From his family, Bell acquired expertise in speech and audition. In 1866, he became interested in Helmholtz's apparatus for reproducing vowel sounds electromechanically. Bell came to believe that this device could transmit vowel sounds electronically, a creative error that spurred him to think about using tuning forks to send multiple, distinct tones over the same wire, creating a harmonic multiple telegraph.

Unfortunately, Bell's brother, Alexander Melville, died of tuberculosis in 1870. In order to preserve the health of their remaining son, the Bell family moved to Canada that same year. Bell eventually became Professor of Elocution at Boston University in 1873. He continued to experiment with multiple telegraphy, and in 1874 became aware that at least one other inventor was doing very similar work: Elisha Gray. These two inventors each thought the other was stealing his ideas, because their telegraph devices were based on the idea of sending multiple tones over the same wire.

II. THE TELEPHONE

In 1875, Gardiner Hubbard and Thomas Sanders provided funding for an assistant, Tom Watson. On June 2, 1875, while Bell and Watson were trying to transmit multiple distinct tones over a single wire, one of the steel reeds got stuck and when Watson plucked it to free it, Bell heard clearly in the other room a composite tone. He instantly saw that this single reed could be used to transmit speech. This act of serendipity was made possible by Bell's unique background and experience; he alone saw the potential in what for most inventors would have been an annoying error. Bell had Watson construct the first telephone that night. Unfortunately, it did not work very well, but Bell was convinced he had the principle on which speech and telegraphic transmission would be based, and he began to write a patent. The application was filed by Gardiner Hubbard on February 14, 1876.

On the same day, a few hours later, Elisha Gray showed up at the patent office with a caveat for a speaking telegraph. (An inventor could file a caveat to signal his intention to complete an invention and file a formal patent at a future date.) Bell's patent focused on the form of current one would have to use to transmit speech; Gray's caveat focused on a transmitter that used liquid as a medium of variable resistance. Bell's mental model for his device was the human ear; Gray's was a string telephone. The patent and the caveat were thrown into interference, but based on the fact that his patent came in earlier, Bell was awarded a patent on March 7th, 1876.

He did not succeed in transmitting speech until a few days later, and to do it, he used a device that bore a superficial resemblance to Gray's liquid transmitter. This has led to speculation that Bell somehow stole the telephone idea from Gray. Bell did learn from an examiner that his interference with Gray concerned the use of liquid as a resistance medium, and that may have encouraged Bell to do more experimenting with liquids. In the end, he returned to devices that used a heavy metal diaphragm to induce or alter a fluctuating current in an electromagnet without any intervening resistance medium. It was left for other inventors like Thomas Edison to perfect a superior form of transmitter based on the use of carbon as a resistance medium.

Bell spent much of the succeeding decade in court, defending his patent for the fledgling Bell Corporation. He married the daughter of his principal backer, Gardiner Hubbard, on July 11, 1876. She had been one of his deaf pupils. The stock the couple held in the growing Bell Corporation made them both wealthy, even after Bell retired from the company in 1879.

III. OTHER INVENTIONS

Bell continued to invent for the rest of his life, although he never scored another success on a level with the telephone. He sought to repeat his earlier success with a device called the photophone, in which light was translated into electricity. He hired another assistant and replicated the kind of intense experimenting that led to the telephone, even experiencing a moment of joy similar to the first transmission of speech. In the former case, Bell uttered the famous words,

"Watson, come here, I want you"; in the latter, Bell's new assistant Tainter sent Bell a message to come to a window and wave his hat, and Bell reported doing so with vigor. Bell hoped the photophone would surpass Edison's carbon transmitter: it required no wires, and could be said to anticipate fiber optics. However, the ease with which a beam of light could be interrupted consigned this device to obscurity, even though Bell thought of it as his greatest invention.

When he was awarded the prestigious Volta Prize in 1880 for his invention of the telephone, Bell invested the money in a laboratory to continue the photophone work. But he wanted a project that would pay, and he saw an opportunity to leapfrog his rival Edison, whose phonograph was still a prototype poorly suited to commercial use—much like Bell's early telephones. It was Bell's assistants who developed and patented an improved method for engraving phonograph recordings in 1886; Bell had become increasingly distant from the actual research. Bell put his share of profits from the successful invention into a trust fund for research on the deaf.

When James A. Garfield was shot, Bell tried to develop a device that would detect the bullet, but it failed because the bullet was too deep. However, his telephonic bullet probe was used by others in the days before x-rays and even after, when x-rays were inconclusive. Bell also invented a crude form of iron lung.

In the 1890s he experimented with flying machines, trying an analogy to his earlier telephone work. If a heavy metal diaphragm was, paradoxically, the most sensitive membrane for a telephone, why not experiment with heavy flying machines? Bell initially teamed up with Samuel Langley, secretary of the Smithsonian. Langley flew a model, but failed with a full-sized airplane. Bell's own interest in flight turned to kites, and his wife Mabel helped him find another Watson: Casey Baldwin. Out of this collaboration came an idea ahead of its time: using tetrahedral supports in construction, Bell founded an Aerial Experiment Association that included himself, Baldwin, and Glenn Curtiss. Bell was one of the independent discoverers of the idea of using ailerons and his group built and flew several successful planes before breaking up.

By now, Bell had settled at Beinn Breagh, an estate he purchased in Canada. Bell and Baldwin also worked on hydrofoils, translating Bell's principle of heavy diaphragm for the telephone and heavier-than-air flying machine into heavier-than-water speedboats. The work was briefly suspended during World War I, because Bell did not want to pursue research with naval implications in a neutral country, but was renewed when the United States entered the war. Bell's final hydrofoil design set a world record in 1919, but by then, the Navy no longer had any interest. Bell also conducted experiments in an effort to breed multinippled sheep.

IV. TEACHER AND MENTOR

Bell was not only an inventor. He continued his important work in teaching the deaf, and he also encouraged creative intellectual work by others. He took over as president of the National Geographic Society during a time when the Society was flagging and hired Gilbert Grosvenor, an energetic young editor who realized Bell's vision for a more popular, accessible magazine and a membership in the thousands. Bell also served as regent of the Smithsonian and used his own money to provide resources for geniuses like Charles Peirce. Bell was a collaborator in his own work and encouraged others in theirs—even competitors like the Wright brothers, whose success he greeted with enthusiasm. Bell died at his beloved Beinn Breagh on August 2nd, 1922, with Mabel holding his hand.

Bibliography

Bruce, R. V. (1973). *Bell: Alexander Graham Bell and the conquest of solitude.* Boston: Little, Brown.

Gorman, M. E., Mehalik, M. M., Carlson, W. B., & Oblon, M. (1993). Alexander Graham Bell, Elisha Gray and the speaking telegraph: A cognitive comparison. *History of Technology, 15,* 1–56.

Birth Order

Frank J. Sulloway
University of California, Berkeley

Birth Order The sequence by which children are born into a family. The most important birth-order positions are eldest, middle, and youngest. As a rule, birth-order differences in personality arise as a result of how children are raised (functional birth order, or rearing order) rather than the sequence in which they are born.

Five Factor Model of Personality A model based on the analysis of psychological questionnaires and natural language. Derived from factor analysis, this model posits the existence of five basic personality dimensions (conscientiousness, agreeableness, openness to experience, extraversion, and neuroticism—also known as "the Big Five").

Parental Investment The nurturing that parents give to offspring, which can be emotional as well as physical. In Darwinian theory, parents are expected to invest diffferentially in offspring based on criteria such as age, sex, birth order, and cues of phenotypic quality. Parents make these discriminations in an effort to maximize their reproductive fitness—that is, the number and quality of offspring they successfully rear.

*By influencing the strategies that siblings develop in competition for parental favor, **BIRTH ORDER** fosters differences in personality that in turn correlate with differences in creative achievement. The nature of the relationship between birth order and creativity has long been controversial owing to the failure of researchers to specify exactly what kinds of creativity they have in mind. Firstborns and laterborns do not appear to differ in overall levels of creativity, but they do differ in the ways by which they attain creative distinction.*

I. BIRTH ORDER AND EVOLUTIONARY PSYCHOLOGY

In order to understand the association between birth order and creativity, it is first useful to review the relationship between birth order and personality, which owes itself to biological as well as environmental influences. Because there are no genes for being a firstborn or a laterborn, birth-order effects represent one of the best demonstrations of the power of the environment. Nevertheless, birth order interacts with other influences on human behavior, including genetic predispositions, that are known to be under biological control. Biological influences on personality may be separated into ultimate and proximate causes. Ultimate causes

Copyright © 1999 by Academic Press
All rights of reproduction in any form reserved.

are those that are attributable to evolution by natural selection. By contrast, proximate causes encompass those physiological influences operating during the lifetime of the organism. Proximate causes also include environmental influences, which typically interact with genetic and physiological processes.

Viewed in these terms, sibling rivalry provides an ultimate cause of some aspects of personality development. Darwin's theory of natural selection offers an explanation for this part of the story, because it tells us that siblings are biologically driven to compete for parental favor. On average, siblings share half of their genes. In the early 1960s, William Hamilton recognized that natural selection acts to maximize what he termed "inclusive fitness." This form of Darwinian fitness is defined as an individual's own reproductive success, together with his contribution to the reproductive success of close relatives, discounted according to their coefficient of relatedness. Based on Hamilton's theory, siblings are expected to compete for scarce resources whenever the benefits of doing so are greater than twice the costs. In general, an offspring's idea of fairness is to keep two-thirds of any scarce resource for him- or herself and give only one-third to a sibling. Competition for parental investment is the main cause of sibling rivalry.

By itself, competition among siblings does not lead to birth-order differences in personality. But birth order provides a powerful proximate (and environmental) source of sibling strategies. These tactical differences arise because birth order is correlated with differences in age, size, power, and status within the family. These physical and social disparities cause siblings to experience family relationships in dissimilar ways and to pursue differing ways of optimizing their parents' investment in their welfare.

Competition for parental love and favor has been an important driving force in human evolution, just as have parental decisions about how to invest in their offspring. Before 1800, half of all children did not survive childhood, and even minor differences in parental favor would have increased a child's chances of reaching adulthood. Children who lived long enough to become the eldest in a family were often a better Darwinian bet for their parents, because they had survived the perilous years of life and were more likely than their younger brothers and sisters to reach the age of repro-duction and to pass on their parents' genes. In every society surveyed by anthropologists, eldest children are accorded higher status. For example, many traditional societies condone infanticide, especially when a child is deformed or when a slightly older infant is still breast-feeding, but no society condones the killing of the older of two siblings.

Parental investment strategies tend to be variable because birth order is only one of many relevant factors in these decisions. Besides taking into account the relative quality of their offspring, parents may invest differently in children based on such factors as the parents' age and the resources available to them. Primogeniture has generally been practiced by affluent parents in agrarian societies, where wealth is tied to land; but this inheritance system is much less common in mercantile societies where wealth can be acquired rapidly through entrepreneurship. Under these conditions, parents tend to hedge their bets by investing equally in all of their offspring.

Even if parents do not favor one child over another, sibling rivalry influences the dynamics of family life because competition serves to limit favoritism. Such competition typically involves the cultivation of family niches that correspond to differences in birth order. That families provide offspring with a series of niches is a conclusion supported by research in behavioral genetics. One of the most remarkable findings in psychology during the last two decades is the discovery that brothers and sisters raised together are almost as different in their personalities as people who grow up in separate families. Based on studies of twins raised together and apart, behavioral geneticists have concluded that only about 5% of the variance in individual personality traits is attributable to the shared environment—that is, growing up in the same family—whereas 35% can be assigned to the nonshared environment. About 40% of the overall variance is believed to be genetic, and the remaining 20% is attributable to errors of measurement. These findings have begun to reshape the understanding of personality development by suggesting that the family is not a single environment, but rather a collection of microenvironments or "niches." The main reason why the shared family environment does not have a greater impact on personality is that very little of the family experience is actually shared. For example, brothers and sisters are at different ages when they experience the same events, and siblings often interpret shared experiences differently. Two particularly important and systematic sources of nonshared experiences are gender and birth order.

II. BIRTH ORDER AND PERSONALITY

Psychologists have investigated the consequences of birth order ever since Charles Darwin's cousin Francis Galton reported, in 1874, that eldest sons were overrepresented as members of the Royal Society. After breaking away from Sigmund Freud in 1910 to found a variant school of psychoanalysis, Alfred Adler highlighted social influences on personality, including birth order. A secondborn, Adler regarded firstborns as "power-hungry conservatives." He characterized middleborns as competitive, and youngest children as spoiled and lazy.

During the half-century since Adler's speculations, psychologists have conducted more than 2,000 studies on the subject. This literature has often been faulted, and critics have rightly argued that the findings conflict and that most studies are inadequately controlled for social class, sibship size, and other background influences that correlate with birth order and can lead to false conclusions. The reality of these reported differences is nevertheless supported by meta-analysis—a technique for aggregating findings from different studies in order to increase statistical power and reliability. Considering those well-designed studies that adjust for social class or sibship size, meta-analysis reveals consistent birth-order differences for many personality traits. These findings may be summarized in terms of the Five Factor Model of personality.

Controlled studies generally report that firstborns are more *conscientious* than laterborns, a difference that is exemplified by their being more responsible, ambitious, organized, and academically successful. Laterborns appear to be more *agreeable* than firstborns, in the sense of being more tender-minded, accommodating, and altruistic. Laterborns are also more *open to experience,* as expressed by their being more adventurous and unconventional. Differences by birth order are more restricted for the two remaining dimensions of

the Five Factor Model. Firstborns appear to be more *neurotic* than laterborns, in the sense of being temperamental and anxious about their status. In addition, firstborns are more *extraverted* than laterborns, in the sense of being assertive and dominant, whereas laterborns are more extraverted in the sense of being sociable and fun-loving. Dominance and sociability are substantially different personality traits, even though they are classified together within the Five Factor Model. Firstborns tend to have higher IQs than laterborns, but this difference is small, especially after being controlled for differences in family size. On average, IQ falls one point with each increase in birth rank within the family. (Proponents of the Five Factor Model consider IQ to be a sixth factor, largely independent of personality.)

The personality differences that I have just reviewed are generally consistent with a Darwinian framework, albeit with an emphasis on adaptation through learning. Unlike the propensity to compete with one's siblings, which is an ultimate cause of sibling conflicts, personality is a product of innumerable proximate causes that spur individuals to adapt themselves to the surrounding world. Firstborns often seek the favor of their parents by acting as a surrogate parent toward their younger siblings. As a result, firstborns tend to be parent-identified, conscientious, and respectful of authority. Laterborns cannot baby-sit themselves, so they look for an unoccupied family niche, in part by cultivating latent talents that can be discovered only through experimentation. For this reason, they are often more exploratory and open to experience. Another reason for the divergent personalities of siblings is the different strategies they employ in their relations with one another. These strategies involve behaviors that are typical of mammalian dominance hierarchies. Because firstborns are bigger, they are more likely to employ physical aggression and intimidation, and in general they are more likely to boss and dominate their younger brothers and sisters. Laterborns tend to use low-power strategies, such as whining, pleading, cajoling, humor, social intelligence, and, whenever expedient, appealing to parents for help. Two or more laterborns may also join in coalitions against the firstborn.

A Darwinian approach also leads to specific predictions about middle children, who lack the advantages of being either first or last. When resources are scarce, parents are expected to invest preferentially in first-borns because they are the first to reproduce. Older parents are expected to invest preferentially in last-borns because these offspring are the most vulnerable to disease and, after parents have ceased reproducing, are the last children they will ever have. As Catherine Salmon and Martin Daly have shown, middle children often respond to their Darwinian handicap by becoming peer oriented and independent of the family. Compared with firstborns and lastborns, middle children are less closely identified with the family, less likely to turn to their parents for help in an emergency, and less likely to report having been loved during childhood. Compared with their siblings, middle children typically live farther away from their parents. In addition, they are the least likely sibling group to visit, and to encourage their own children to visit, close kin. Consistent with their greater allegiance to the peer group, middle children also are the most inclined to diplomacy and cooperation, strategies that may reflect their proclivity for mediating disputes between their siblings. Martin Luther King, Jr., the middle of three children, got his start as a champion of nonviolent reform by trying to prevent his younger brother from teasing their older sister.

Only children represent a controlled experiment in birth-order research. Because they experience no sibling rivalry, they are not driven to occupy a specific family niche. Like other firstborns, they are generally ambitious and conform to parental authority, because these attributes are valued by parents. Contrary to psychological folklore, only children do not appear to be more neurotic or less sociable than other children.

There is often a greater difference between a firstborn and a secondborn child, or between a secondborn and a thirdborn, than there is between the firstborn and the thirdborn. The reason is that sibling competition promotes mutual differentiation in order to minimize direct conflicts, and children who are farther apart in age have less need to compete. This process of sibling differentiation, which is sometimes called de-identification, extends to relationships with parents. When a firstborn identifies more strongly with one parent, the secondborn is likely to identify more strongly with the other parent.

Some of these contrasts are striking. Voltaire, the third of three children, had an acrimonious relation-ship with his elder brother Armand, who became a follower of the Jansenists, a fanatical Catholic sect. Voltaire was particularly repelled by Armand's belief in the need to forgo life's pleasures in order to win God's grace. As a leader of the French Enlightenment, Voltaire was especially noted for his relentless attacks on the Catholic Church. He chose literature as a profession partly to spite his brother, whom he had repeatedly bested in impromptu poetry contests devised by his family.

A different example of sibling contrasts involves the consumer rights advocate Ralph Nader and his three older siblings. In early adolescence, the Nader children took a globe of the world, divided it into four equal portions, and assigned one part to each child. Thereafter, each specialized in the history, culture, and languages of his or her own quarter of the globe. By minimizing direct competition, the Naders were also cooperatively pooling their resources as a family unit, collectively enabling them to learn more about the world. As Darwin recognized in the *Origin of Species* (1859), diversification is an effective way to reduce competition while also realizing the benefits stemming from the division of labor.

A. Direct Sibling Comparisons

Birth-order differences in personality vary in magnitude and sometimes even in direction, depending on how they are measured. When assessed by self-report questionnaires, birth-order effects are typically modest and nonsignificant. Yet systematic differences by birth order are generally found when parents rate their own offspring or when siblings compare themselves with one another. In a recent study by Frank Sulloway, 660 business leaders were surveyed. In self-reported ratings, firstborn CEOs did not differ significantly from laterborns on 10 of the 11 personality traits included in the survey. After providing these self-assessments, respondents were asked to compare themselves with their siblings, using the same 11 personality scales. A comparative method of assessment possesses several advantages over more customary methods of self-report. In particular, direct comparison anchors the scales. Additionally, comparative judgments among siblings eliminate any confounding effects associated with differences between families. Using such comparisons, 8 of the 11 traits included in the survey elicited significant differences by birth order. Relative to their older siblings, laterborn business leaders were more tender-minded, cooperative, flexible, submissive, empathetic, liberal, unconventional, and even-tempered. Overall, comparative ratings resulted in birth-order differences that were 5 times as large as those previously obtained without using direct comparisons.

A follow-up study involving 6,053 individuals aged 8 to 95 (mean age = 36.8, *SD* = 17.1) has yielded similar results for a broad array of personality traits. Subjects rated themselves on nine-step bipolar scales using adjective pairs that were chosen to represent the 30 facets of the NEO PI-R, a comprehensive personality inventory based on the Five Factor Model. Firstborns were asked to rate both themselves and their next younger sibling, whereas laterborns were asked to rate themselves and their next older sibling. Based on direct sibling comparisons, 23 of the 30 bipolar adjective pairs yielded significant differences, and 26 of the 30 adjective pairs produced correlations in the expected direction. As anticipated, firstborns were judged to be more conscientious than their younger siblings, whereas laterborns were judged as being more agreeable and open to experience. For neuroticism, a dimension for which birth-order differences were expected to be mixed, firstborns were predicted to be more anxious and quicker to anger—expectations that were both confirmed. Laterborns were predicted to be more depressed, vulnerable, self-conscious, and impulsive, but only the last two predictions were confirmed. As anticipated, results for extraversion were also mixed. Laterborns were more affectionate, fun-loving, and inclined to seek excitement. Firstborns were more energetic and dominant.

Controlling for age, sex, sibship size, and social class, the partial correlation between birth order and a scale score of predicted differences was .20, with birth order accounting for 4.1% of the variance. Two other family background variables—sibship size and social class—account for less than 0.1% of the variance in this scale score of predicted differences, as also does age. By comparison, sex explains 2.1% of the variance. (Laterborn personality traits resemble those observed in females.) Controlled for the linear effect of birth order on the scale score, there was also a significant quadratic trend: middle children scored higher than last-

borns on some personality scales, particularly those related to agreeableness (Table I).

Measured in terms of an overall scale score that reflects predictions about birth order, age and sex account for substantially less variance in personality scores than does birth order. It is important to note, however, that age and sex explain considerably more about personality as a whole than they do about birth-order-related traits. Sex differences in my study account for 8.3% of the variance in dimension scores for the Big Five, and age explains another 2.6% of the variance. In accounting for 4.1% of the variance in these same dimension scores, birth order is substantially more influential than age, but less so than sex. Still, on two dimensions of the Five Factor Model (conscientiousness and extraversion), birth order has greater influence than either age or sex.

One should bear in mind that birth order is only a proxy for the real causes that lie behind sibling differences in personality, namely, disparities in age, size, status, and power within the family system. Not all firstborns adopt the role of a surrogate parent toward younger siblings, and some firstborns are less bossy than others. Individual differences in physical size, temperament, and opportunities for surrogate parenting help to explain why some individuals deviate from the patterns of personality that are generally expected by birth order. In the study summarized in Table I, individuals were asked to what extent, during childhood, they acted as a surrogate parent toward their siblings, and also to what extent they bossed their siblings around. High scores for surrogate parenting behavior and bossiness reflect typical firstborn behaviors and are strongly correlated with birth order (*r* = −.56 for the composite measure). This indicator of family niches also accounts for 10.5% of the variance in personality scores, making it considerably better at predicting personality than any other variable in the study. The predictive success of this variable lies in large part in its ability to account for exceptions to predictions based on birth order. For example, laterborns (often eldest daughters) sometimes report having done substantial surrogate parenting with respect to their younger siblings. These individuals also tend to describe themselves as having firstborn personality traits.

Other studies using the NEO Personality Inventory and comparable instruments have generally yielded

TABLE I

Birth-Order Effects in Scale Scores for the Big Five Personality Dimensions Based on Direct Sibling Comparisons

Personality dimension[a]	Partial correlation with birth order[b]	N	p <
Conscientiousness	−.18	4,507	.0001
• Firstborns are more *deliberate, dutiful, effective, energetic,*[a] *hardworking, organized, self-disciplined,* and *under control*[a]			
Agreeableness	.10	4,510	.0001
• Laterborns are more *acquiescent,* cooperative, *easygoing,*[a] *modest,* straightforward, *unassertive/submissive,*[a] tender-minded, and *trusting*			
Openness to experience	.08	4,484	.0001
• Laterborns are more aesthetically inclined, *prone to fantasy, attentive to inner feelings, untraditional, attracted by novelty,* and *drawn to ideas*[c]			
Extraversion	.14	4,404	.0001
• Laterborns are more *affectionate, excitement-seeking, fun-loving,* and gregarious			
Neuroticism	−.04	4,278	.001
• Firstborns are more *anxious,* as well as more prone to depression and feelings of vulnerability	−.04	4,278	.001
• Laterborns are more *self-conscious*	.05	3,548	.005
Scale score for personality differences, as predicted[d]	.20	4,177	.0001

[a]Each of the 30 bipolar adjective pairs, representing the 30 facets of the NEO PI-R, is classified under the Big Five dimension on which it has its highest factor loading. Four of the 30 adjective pairs have their highest loading on a personality dimension other than the one for which they were selected. "Assertive (dominant)/unassertive (submissive)" has its highest loading on Agreeableness (−.54) rather than Extraversion (.32). Similarly, "quick to anger/easygoing" has its highest loading on Agreeableness (−.55) rather than Neuroticism (.47). "Impulsive/under control" has its highest loading on Conscientiousness (−.59) rather than Neuroticism (.24). "Energetic/leisurely" has its highest loading on Conscientiousness (.47) rather than Extraversion (.28).

[b]A positive partial correlation denotes a higher score for laterborns. For each bipolar trait, a sibling difference score was calculated using z-scores and then used to compute each scale score in terms of *predicted* differences. Italicized traits exhibit significant birth-order differences. (All statistical tests are two tailed.) All partial correlations are controlled for age, sex, sibship size, and social class. All dimension scale scores except Neuroticism exhibit a significant quadratic effect, controlled for the linear trend, indicating a higher score for middleborns. For one dimension (Agreeableness), the quadratic trend is larger than the linear trend. Excluded from these statistical results are 548 only children, 71 twins, 112 subjects reporting an age gap of more than 9 years between themselves and the sibling they also rated, 86 subjects whose biological and functional birth orders do not coincide, and 726 subjects who did not provide information on one of more of the dependent or independent variables.

[c]Being "drawn to ideas" was predicted to be a firstborn trait.

[d]Some respondents made ratings on fewer than 30 bipolar adjective pairs. In these cases, scale scores have been computed from the observed data.

null results, although most of these studies have possessed only moderate statistical power and none have employed the method of direct sibling comparison. Based on similar discrepancies between self-report ratings, which often yield meager results, and significant differences as judged by family members, some researchers have argued that birth-order effects are parent specific and do not hold up outside the family.

When assessed meta-analytically, however, studies involving nonfamily members exhibit significantly more findings of a confirmatory nature than are expected by chance. Confirmatory findings are also especially likely to occur whenever studies involve real-life behavior. In addition, if birth-order effects are specific only to childhood (and the family milieu), one might expect these differences to diminish with age. In the study reviewed in Table I, birth-order effects do decrease modestly with age for conscientiousness, but they increase modestly for agreeableness. Overall, there is not a significant diminution in the scale score for predicted birth-order effects by age.

The method of direct sibling comparison does not prove that birth-order differences in personality exist outside the family milieu. Direct sibling comparisons may also be susceptible to "contrast effects," whereby small but real differences between siblings are magnified, exaggerating the variance explained by birth order. However, when the scores in Table I for direct sibling comparisons are transformed into binary outcomes (i.e., being higher or lower than a sibling on each trait), birth-order effects are only slightly reduced. Another possibility is that these comparative measures reflect shared stereotypes about personality, rather than true differences. In an effort to determine whether birth-order differences are recognized by people other than siblings, study participants were asked to rate their spouses. Significant birth-order differences emerged in the expected direction, although the mean effect size for the Big Five personality dimensions is somewhat smaller than for direct sibling comparisons. Controlling for age, sex, sibship size, and social class, the partial correlation among spouses between birth order and a scale score for predicted personality differences is .12, which accounts for 1.4% of the variance ($N = 822$).

An analysis of the scores for individual traits reveals that spouses are detecting the same birth-order differences that they reveal when they compare themselves with a sibling. A convenient way of demonstrating this point is to compare the effect sizes for birth order, on a trait-by-trait basis, with the effect sizes for the same traits as judged by spouses. These two sets of effect sizes are substantially correlated ($r = .61$, $N = 30$ traits, $p < .001$). In other words, those traits that are strongly associated with birth order in sibling relationships are the *same* traits that are strongly associated

with birth order in married couples. Relative to firstborn spouses, for example, laterborn spouses are perceived to be less conscientious, but more agreeable, extraverted, and open to experience. A similar pattern in birth-order effects is found among college students who rated both a sibling and a roommate ($r = .72$, $N = 30$ traits, $p < .001$; for roommates, the partial correlation between birth order and a scale score for predicted personality traits is .16, $N = 165$, $p < .05$). Thus birth-order differences are not restricted to family members or the family milieu, as some psychologists have claimed. Rather, these differences tend to manifest themselves in intimate living situations.

III. GENDER, AGE SPACING, AND OTHER MODERATING INFLUENCES

Birth order is only one influence among many that contribute to the development of personality. Accordingly, there are exceptions to any generalization on this topic. The largest source of exceptions are those arising from genetic differences, which collectively explain about 40% of the variance in individual traits. Additionally, as children grow up and spend more time outside the family, they are increasingly influenced by peer groups and by life experience more generally. Some of these extrafamilial influences may nevertheless reflect differences that already exist between siblings.

There is growing evidence that some birth-order differences in personality are influenced biologically by the prenatal environment. Among males (but not among females), laterborns are more likely to become homosexuals. Unlike other behavioral effects associated with birth order, the operative factor is number of older brothers rather than relative birth rank from eldest to youngest child. In other words, a lastborn male who is the eldest of his sex is no more likely to become a homosexual than is a firstborn. These findings can be explained by assuming that a small proportion of mothers develop antibodies to one of the male-specific minor histocompatibility antigens. It has been hypothesized that such immunological responses prevent subsequent male fetuses from being fully transformed from female to male.

These findings about male homosexuality suggest that other aspects of personality—specifically, those involving gender-related traits such as tender-mindedness—might also be influenced by the prenatal environment. If such biological effects exist, they appear to be very small in normal populations. For example, meta-analysis of the birth-order literature reveals no significant difference in the frequency of birth-order effects by sex, including for behaviors specifically related to agreeableness and extraversion, which include many gender-related traits. In the study reviewed in Table I, birth-order effects were just as substantial among women as among men. For males, moreover, number of elder brothers had no relationship with gender-related traits, with birth order being controlled. In short, the link between number of elder brothers and gender-related traits appears to reflect a developmental outcome of nonpsychological origin that is confined to male homosexuals.

Gender also contributes to personality, doing so in ways that parallel the influence of birth order on some personality dimensions—particularly extraversion and agreeableness. These similarities arise because birth order and gender have comparable effects on the strategies siblings use as they jockey for position within the family. Partly for genetic reasons and partly because of socialization, females tend to be less aggressive than males, just as laterborns tend to be less aggressive than firstborns. Gender also modifies the forms taken by aggression. Firstborn males are more physically aggressive than laterborn males, whereas firstborn females are more verbally aggressive. In addition, males and firstborns tend to be more assertive and tough-minded, whereas females and laterborns tend to be more affectionate, tender-minded, and cooperative. Women tend to be conscientious, whereas laterborns do not, so these behavioral parallels do not apply across the board.

Birth-order effects are modified by age gaps as well as by the sex of siblings. The influence of birth order is muted when the age gap is so small that the relationship between siblings is nearly equal, and also when the age gap is so large that they do not compete for the attention of their parents. When middle children have a large age gap between themselves and their next older sibling, but a small gap between themselves and their next younger sibling, they are more similar to firstborns in their personality.

Although laterborns tend to be more socially liberal, as well as more adventurous and unconventional than their older siblings, there are exceptions to these generalizations that are attributable to other aspects of family dynamics. Firstborn children of socially liberal parents tend to become liberals themselves because they generally conform to parental values. A laterborn child of liberal parents may become a conservative just to be different. Furthermore, firstborns sometimes become social or political radicals because they are in conflict with their parents instead of identifying with them. Mao Zedong, the eldest of four children, was radicalized by conflict with his father, a cruel and tyrannical man who mistreated his wife, his children, and the workers on his farm. Mao once said that there were two political parties in his family, and that he was the leader of the opposition. In general, laterborns are likely to rebel even if they do not have Attila the Hun for a father or the Wicked Witch of the West for a mother. They have elder siblings to induce them to identify with the underdog.

The consequences of birth order are often strongly dependent on the behavioral context, which is one of the most important moderators of human behavior. In different situations, the same person may behave quite differently, and the relevance of birth order likewise varies with the situation. For example, a firstborn may act in a dominant manner toward a younger sibling or a spouse, congenially toward peers, and in a subordinate manner toward authority figures—a behavioral style that constitutes a "pecking order personality."

Social categories such as age, gender, and socioeconomic status entail standards of behavior that can influence personality. In connection with the study summarized in Table I, respondents assessed the personality of a close friend ($N = 1,002$). Significant birth-order differences emerged, but they did so in interaction with other variables. Upper-class respondents, as well as older respondents, saw their best friends as exhibiting the traits generally expected by birth order. In contrast, college students—especially those from lower-class backgrounds—did not perceive these same birth-order differences. For example, college students did not describe their firstborn friends as being particularly conscientious or conventional, whereas older respondents did.

These seemingly contradictory results are best understood in terms of the attributes that are important for success within each socioeconomic class, and during different stages of life. College-age students, especially from lower-class backgrounds, are likely to prefer friends who are sociable and who know how to have a good time. Because firstborns are more socially assertive and inclined toward leadership roles than are laterborns, they respond to these behavioral norms by projecting a gregarious and outgoing "persona." When people graduate from college, take a job, and marry, they assume new life roles and greater responsibility. Within such older populations, birth-order effects in personality increasingly conform to the expected pattern. Firstborns, who tend to be more conforming than laterborns, are especially affected by such life transitions. Compared with other individuals, firstborns are significantly more variable in terms of how their personalities are perceived across the social categories of age, class, and marital status. The more responsibility and status firstborns have acquired—for example, by getting married—the more they are judged by their friends as manifesting a typical firstborn personality.

These findings make sense from the perspective of evolutionary psychology, which is also a form of social psychology. The personality traits that are typically associated with birth order develop in the service of competition for scarce resources, principally parental investment. Adolescent individuals do not generally command scarce resources, so their behavioral priorities tend to be different from those of adults. A firstborn who aspires to social approval may be dutiful at home (especially during childhood), agreeable and gregarious during adolescence, and competitive and self-disciplined as an adult member of the workforce. The expression of personality traits related to birth order is likely to be sensitive to these transitions in the life course. In short, birth-order differences are not parent specific, but they are often situation specific. Research on birth order and creativity strongly reinforces this important conclusion.

IV. BIRTH ORDER, OPENNESS TO EXPERIENCE, AND CREATIVITY

As Robert R. McCrae has demonstrated, the various facets of openness to experience can be divided into two contrasting groups. One group reflects "intellect"

and is typified by adjective labels such as *intelligent, perceptive, curious, creative,* and *cultured.* The second group is defined by adjective labels that are closely associated with "nonconformist" thinking, including *daring, unconventional, original, independent,* and *liberal.* Not surprisingly, the "intellect" component of openness is more strongly correlated with IQ and years of education than is the second, or "nonconformist," component. Because firstborns tend to have higher IQs than laterborns, and because firstborns also tend to excel at acadmeic pursuits, they are expected to express their creativity most strongly via openness in intellect. By contrast, laterborns are expected to express their creativity in ways that exemplify the nonconformist bent of their personalities. [*See* INTELLIGENCE.]

Much of the existing research on birth order and creativity is marred by two shortcomings. First, investigators have generally failed to distinguish sufficiently between differing types of creativity; second, researchers have not usually studied creativity in real-life terms. In their monumental review of the birth-order literature from 1940 to 1980, Cécile Ernst and Jules Angst summarized the results of 28 relevant studies. Eleven of these studies, which included such measures as the need for autonomy and the frequency of unusual word associations, showed no differences by birth order. The other 17 studies produced significant findings, but these results were largely contradictory. For example, 3 studies indicated that firstborns were more likely to prefer complex polygons (interpreted as a sign of greater creativity), whereas another 5 studies showed that laterborns preferred complex polygons. Even if these 8 studies of visual preference had yielded consistent results, it may be questioned whether a partiality for gazing at complex polygons is diagnostic of creative achievement in real life. After all, a preference for parsimony and simplicity, not complexity, lies at the heart of modern science.

Research on divergent thinking is another area where birth-order findings have tended to conflict. Inasmuch as divergent thinking correlates substantially with IQ (a firstborn trait) as well as with unconventional thinking (a laterborn trait), this construct conflates these two different forms of intellectual ability. In fields such as literature, architecture, invention, and science, studies of creative achievement are generally limited by a failure to consider the nature of the creative act. It should come as no surprise that research in these various intellectual domains has generally yielded inconsistent results. [*See* DIVERGENT THINKING.]

Some of the most compelling evidence for birth-order differences in creativity comes from intellectual and social history, especially in areas where the nature of the creative act is sufficiently public to be classified by experts in terms of differing forms of openness to experience. Considerable research indicates that later-borns are more inclined than firstborns to change their views during times of radical political, social, or scientific change. This is because radical revolutions tap the nonconformist component of openness. During the Protestant Reformation, laterborns gave their lives to serve rebellion and firstborns to preserve orthodoxy. Laterborns were proportionately nine times more likely than firstborns to suffer martyrdom in support of the Reformed faith. In countries that turned Protestant, such as Henry VIII's England, firstborns were five times more likely than laterborns to become martyrs by refusing to abandon Catholicism. (These statistics are corrected for the greater number of laterborns in the population.)

The responses of scientists to radical conceptual transformations show similar differences. The Copernican revolution challenged church doctrine by asserting that the earth rotates around the sun. During the first half-century of this debate, laterborns were five times more likely than firstborns to endorse this heretical view. Nicholas Copernicus himself was the youngest of four children. George Joachim Rheticus, the young colleague whose zealous efforts finally prodded the 70-year-old Copernicus into publishing his unorthodox theory, was also a lastborn. In Darwin's own era, younger siblings were 10 times more likely than elder siblings to become evolutionists. Darwin himself was the fifth of six children, as was Alfred Russel Wallace, codiscoverer of the theory of natural selection (Figure 1).

During other notable revolutions in science, including those led by Bacon, Descartes, Newton, Lavoisier, and Einstein, laterborns have been 2 to 10 times more likely than firstborns to endorse the new point of view. This trend holds true even when the initiators of revolutions, such as Newton and Einstein, happen to be firstborns. Laterborns are more likely to endorse radical revolutions even after their scientific stance

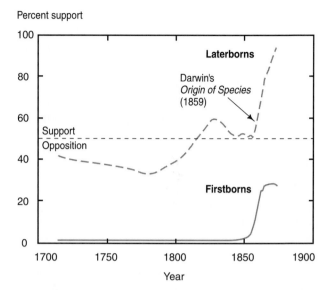

FIGURE 1   The reception of evolutionary theory from 1700 to 1875 by birth order ($N = 448$). During the long period of debate preceding publication of Darwin's *Origin of Species* (1859), individual laterborns were 9.7 times more likely than individual firstborns to endorse evolution. These group differences are corrected for the greater frequency of laterborns in the population. (From Sulloway, 1996, p. 33.)

has been controlled for social attitudes (which are themselves a good predictor of the acceptance of such events). Accordingly, birth-order effects cannot be reduced to attitudinal differences, although birth order does influence social attitudes, which in turn influence openness to radical innovations.

A. Social Desirability Effects

Birth order exerts substantially more influence on behavior during radical revolutions than it does on self-reported personality traits, including those directly related to openness to experience. Radical revolutions typically constitute struggles over who controls valuable resources. It should come as no surprise that revolutionary challenges to the status quo provide a better test of personality differences (including those associated with birth order) than do self-report questionnaire data. In the study whose results are summarized in Table I, firstborns claimed to be significantly more open to experience than their own younger siblings ($d = .16$, equivalent to a correlation of .08). But laterborns claimed to be even more open to experience than their own older siblings ($d = .33$, equivalent to a correlation of .16 *in the opposite direction*). The significant net difference between these two correlations strongly suggests that laterborns are more open to experience than are firstborns, despite firstborns' claims to the contrary. That the judgments of firstborns were generally incorrect about this aspect of their personalities is corroborated by their responses to an open-ended question. Subjects were asked, "What would your friends consider to be the two or three most unconventional or rebellious things, if any, that you have done during your life?" In answering this question, the number of words that respondents wrote down was significantly correlated with their total score for openness to experience. Relative to firstborns, laterborns tended to produce longer responses and to list a higher proportion of truly unconventional behaviors, as assessed by independent judges.

Other findings from this study reinforce the conclusion that social desirability influences self-reported judgments about personality. For example, older respondents believed that they were just as open to experience as younger respondents ($r = .00$). Yet these same respondents claimed that their siblings and friends were significantly *less* open to experience with age (mean-weighted $r = -.14$). Both answers cannot be correct, and real-life evidence helps to arbitrate this issue. During radical revolutions, age is a reliable predictor of responses to change. As I have documented in a study of 121 major controversies in science and social thought, older individuals generally oppose radical changes (mean-weighted $r = -.21$, $N = 4,505$). In my questionnaire study, people appear to have correctly recognized in others what they failed to acknowledge in themselves, namely, a reduction in open-mindedness with age.

When we consider the fact that social desirability biases can produce correlational discrepancies as large as .3, and that most birth-order effects are about one-third this magnitude, it becomes more clear why self-report data might tend to underestimate birth-order differences. On every dimension of the Big Five, social desirability effects dwarf those associated with birth order. Unfortunately, we cannot assume that such social desirability biases cancel themselves out with the use of direct sibling comparisons, because research has

consistently shown that firstborns are more likely than laterborns to conform to social expectations. Because the degree to which self-ratings are embellished in a favorable direction is probably different for firstborns and laterborns, it is difficult to know what is the true influence of birth order for any particular personality trait. For these reasons, real-life behavior remains the best test of the magnitude of birth-order differences in personality.

Age and birth order are only two of many significant predictors of individual responses to radical change. Being socially liberal is another substantial predictor. So is parent–offspring conflict, which disrupts birth-order effects among firstborns and makes them into "honorary laterborns" in terms of openness to experience. Multivariate models that include these and other predictors of openness to radical innovation are significantly more powerful than predictions based on single variables. In general, people who are the most likely to endorse radical changes are also more likely than average to *initiate* such changes. Hence a willingness to endorse heterodox viewpoints is a necessary, but by no means a sufficient, condition for intellectual discovery.

These findings do not mean that young people, laterborns, and social liberals have a monopoly on scientific creativity or truth. For example, laterborns run the risk of accepting new and radical viewpoints too quickly, just as firstborns run the risk of resisting certain kinds of necessary changes. Laterborns were nine times more likely than firstborns to support Franz Joseph Gall's false theory of phrenology—the notion that character can be read by tracing bumps on the head. Firstborns correctly rejected this theory as pseudoscientific. (They also disdained phrenology because of its materialistic implications.)

During everyday "normal" science, firstborns have a small but consistent advantage over laterborns. They are more successful academically and are more likely to become scientists in the first place. In addition, firstborns tend to win more Nobel prizes, which are generally awarded for creative puzzle solving (openness in the sense of "intellect") rather than for revolutionary innovations (openness in the sense of "nonconformity"). Einstein revolutionized physics with his theories of special and general relativity. The Nobel Prize committee was wary of these theories and honored him instead for his discovery of the photoelectric effect.

Owing to publication of the *Origin of Species,* Charles Darwin lost a knighthood that he had previously been slated to receive. A good indicator of a radical scientific revolution is the widespread opprobrium, not the accolades, that initially befall the instigators.

When scientific innovations involve ideologically conservative implications—as occurred, for example, with vitalistic doctrines during the 17th and 18th centuries—firstborns possess an even greater intellectual advantage over laterborns than they do during "normal" science. Historically, firstborns have repeatedly championed new theories that bolstered God's role in the Creation. Assessed jointly in terms of birth order and the ideological implications of innovations, four classes of innovation are possible, but only two have ever been documented. For example, laterborns have generally led radical revolutions, such as Copernicanism and Darwinism, that strongly challenged social and religious authority. Firstborns have generally backed innovations, such as eugenics and spiritualism, that also appealed strongly to religious and political conservatives. By contrast, there has never been an instance of a firstborn-backed radical revolution; nor has there ever been a case of a conservative revolution that was advocated by laterborns and opposed by firstborns. In sum, the relevance of birth order to scientific innovation is strongly dependent on the nature of the innovation (Figure 2). [*See* INNOVATION.]

V. BIRTH ORDER AND ACHIEVEMENT

Controlled for social class and sibship size, firstborns are overrepresented as scientists. Among laterborn scientists, middle children are particularly underrepresented, as they are among eminent individuals. These findings accord with the evidence that firstborns are more conscientious than laterborns, and that parents, especially under conditions of limited resources, tend to invest preferentially in firstborns and lastborns.

On closer examination, evidence from the history of science indicates that firstborns and laterborns tend to achieve eminence in dissimilar ways. Firstborns have generally excelled in the physical sciences, where intellectual problems tend to be more clearly defined than

in the life sciences. By contrast, laterborns have gravitated toward the biological and social sciences, where success often depends on knowing what the most important problems really are. The scientific achievements of laterborns have been facilitated by their tendency to pursue multiple research interests, a strategy that has been particularly fruitful within the life sciences where unsolved problems often transcend disciplinary boundaries. Charles Darwin distinguished himself in geographic exploration, geology, zoology, botany, ethology, and psychology. His knowledge of these diverse disciplines was crucial to his ability to develop his theory of evolution by natural selection. [*See* DARWIN, CHARLES; EMINENCE.]

Laterborns often achieve distinction in those walks of life that allow expression of their tender-minded qualities. For instance, laterborns are overrepresented among winners of the Nobel prize in literature and peace. Among participants in the abolition and Black Rights movements—who were mostly laterborns—middle children were the most likely group to employ nonviolent methods of persuasion. By contrast, firstborns and lastborns advocated militant strategies. During the French Revolution, firstborns such as Maximilien Robespierre rose to power within the National Convention by supporting the Reign of Terror. Younger siblings (particularly middleborns such as Georges Jacques Danton) opposed these extreme political measures and were ultimately responsible for the overthrow of Robespierre's Montagnard (and largely firstborn) political party.

The relationship between birth order and creative achievement has not yet been studied with sufficient rigor for many intellectual domains, including music, art, literature, and business. When undertaking such future studies, researchers should bear in mind the differing kinds of openness to experience and their potentially distinct relationships with birth order. Studies also need to be controlled for other covariates—especially sibship size, social class, parent–offspring conflict, and social attitudes—that are required either for methodological reasons or because these variables moderate the influence of birth order. Ordinal position is only a proxy for differences in family niches (such as acting as a surrogate parent), and these proximate–causal mechanisms of personality development need to

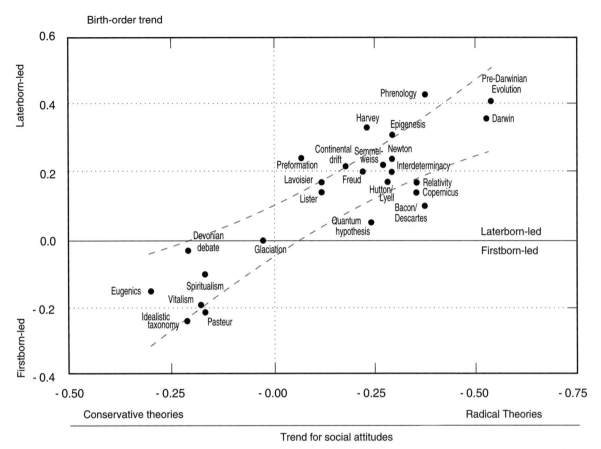

FIGURE 2 Birth-order effects in science, as they relate to the religious and political implications of 28 different innovations. The vertical axis depicts the correlation of birth order with support for scientific innovation ($N = 2,013$). All events above the horizontal line (0.0) were endorsed by laterborns and opposed by firstborns, whereas all events below the line reflect greater support by firstborns. The horizontal axis indicates the correlation of social attitudes with support for each innovation. Events to the left of the vertical line (0.00) were endorsed by social conservatives and rejected by social liberals. Events to the right of the same line reflect support by social liberals and opposition by conservatives. Determinations of social attitudes involve more than 19,000 ratings made by expert historians, who judged the religious and political attitudes of participants in these 28 debates. The dashed lines indicate the 99% confidence limits for the regression line. This analysis establishes a simple generalization: *The more socially radical the innovation, the more it was supported by laterborns and opposed by firstborns.* Missing from the history of science are two classes of potential events. There are no radical revolutions that are backed primarily by firstborns, just as there are no conservative theories that are backed primarily by laterborns. (From Sulloway, 1996, p. 332.)

be investigated in greater detail. Finally, the nature of the behavioral situation is often a powerful moderating variable. In radical revolutions, birth-order effects tend to fade over time, as new and initially controversial ideas become more widely accepted. In addition, some new ideas are more controversial than others and tend to elicit correspondingly larger birth-order effects. National differences sometimes mediate these effects.

Given their allegiance to Descartes' rival theory of celestial mechanics, French physicists—especially firstborns—manifested strong opposition to Isaac Newton's theory of universal gravitation. British scientists, including firstborns, welcomed Newton's ideas. Ultimately, the relationship between birth order and creativity needs to be approached in meta-analytic terms that include explicit roles for the nature of the innovation, as well as the social and intellectual contexts in which such innovations arise.

VI. CONCLUSION

Birth order provides one important source of personality differences, which in turn underlie differences in creative achievement. Disparities in birth order cause siblings to experience the family environment in dissimilar ways. In addition, birth order introduces the need for differing strategies in dealing with sibling rivals as part of the universal quest for parental favor. This is a Darwinian story, albeit with a predominantly environmental twist. Siblings appear to be hardwired to compete for parental favor, but the particular strategies they adopt within their own family are determined by the specific niche in which they have grown up. As children become older and leave the family, they modify their behavioral strategies—both competitive and cooperative—as they adapt themselves to new life roles. The enduring imprint of childhood learning, and its manifestations in adult personality, is nevertheless discernible in those abilities that come to us most naturally and that owe themselves to prior niche partitioning within the family. Through its context-sensitive relationship with birth order, creative achievement represents a case in point. Evidence from intellectual and social history highlights the conclusion that firstborns and laterborns do not differ in overall levels of creativity. Rather, brothers and sisters are preadapted to solving disparate kinds of problems, which they generally tackle using differing kinds of creative strategies.

Acknowledgments

For advice in connection with some of the research on which this article is based, I thank Paul T. Costa, Jr., Jerome Kagan, and Robert R. McCrae. I also thank two anonymous referees for their comments on an earlier draft of this article. This article was partially prepared while the author was Fritz Redlich Fellow at the Center for Advanced Study in the Behavioral Sciences. I am grateful for financial assistance furnished by the Center's Foundations Fund for Research in Psychiatry and by the National Science Foundation (Grant SBR-9022192).

Bibliography

Blanchard, R. (1997). Birth order and sibling sex ratio in homosexual versus heterosexual males and females. *Annual Review of Sex Research, 8,* 27–67.

Ernst, C., & Angst, J. (1983). *Birth order: Its influence on personality.* Berlin/New York: Springer-Verlag.

McCrae, R. R. (1994). Openness to experience: Expanding the boundaries of Factor V. *European Journal of Personality, 8,* 251–272.

Salmon, C. A., & Daly, M. (1998). Birth order and familial sentiment: Middleborns are different. *Evolution and Human Behavior, 19,* 299–312.

Somit, A., Arwine, A., & Peterson, S. A. (1996). *Birth order and political behavior.* Lanham, MD: University Press of America.

Sulloway, F. J. (1996). *Born to rebel: Birth order, family dynamics, and creative lives.* New York: Pantheon/Vintage.

Sulloway, F. J. (in press). Birth order, sibling competition, and human behavior. In Paul S. Davies and Harmon R. Holcomb III (Eds.), *The evolution of minds: Psychological and philosophical perspectives.* Dordrecht/Boston: Kluwer Academic Publishers.

Zajonc, R. B., & Mullally, P. R. (1997). Birth order: Reconciling conflicting effects. *American Psychologist, 52,* 685–699.

Brain Biology and Brain Functioning

Norbert Jaušovec

University of Maribor

Alpha Rhythm Regular (7–14 Hz) wave pattern in EEG found in most people when relaxed with eyes closed.

Chaos Theory The study of unstable aperiodic behavior in nonlinear deterministic dynamical systems. Elements in such a system have nonlinear influences on each other.

Column Hypothetical unit of cortical organization representing vertically organized intracortical connectivity.

Dichotic Listening Procedure of simultaneously presenting different auditory input to each ear.

Electroencephalogram (EEG) A method for recording the electrical activity of the brain.

Event-Related Potential (ERP) Complex EEG waveform that is related in time to a specific sensory event, divided into different components that are related to cerebral processing (for example, P300).

Hemisphericity The organization of functions primarily on one side (left or right hemisphere) of the brain.

Neocortex Newest layer of the brain; has four to six layers of cells.

*This article will give an overview of findings describing the relationship between creativity, special talents, intelligence, in relation to **BRAIN BIOLOGY AND FUNCTIONING**. The structure of the neocortex will be outlined, as well as the methods used to investigate neocortical activity related to cognitive processes. The neural structure of the neocortex will be described, with special emphasis on columns of various size and corticocortical interactions. A further outline will be provided of the subdivision of the neocortex in relation to the most prominent sulci and gyri of each hemisphere and their relation to physiological and psychological functions. A description will be given of the techniques and methods used to measure brain functioning, like electroencephalography, magnetic resonance imaging, and positron emission tomography. An overview of studies investigating the relationship between creativity, special talents, intelligence, and brain functioning will be presented. Some classical studies relating hemisphericity and creativity will be summarized, as well as some newer findings proposing that an enhanced development of the right cerebral hemisphere may be associated with extreme intellectual giftedness. Further, some recent and ongoing studies relating the lower mental activity of gifted and creative individuals during problem solving to the nonuse of many brain areas not required for the problem at hand will be introduced. The research findings will be discussed in the light of different creativity theories.*

Copyright © 1999 by Academic Press
All rights of reproduction in any form reserved.

I. NEOCORTICAL STRUCTURE

Humans encounter what is "out there" by means of a few million fragile never fibers. These fragile fibers are also responsible for all actions and creations performed by humans "out there." The human brain develops in phylogeny by the successive addition of more parts which empower humans for more complex behavior. Thus the brain stem, limbic system, and neocortex form three distinct levels which metaphorically correspond to three creatures: alligator, horse, and man.

The neocortex composes most of the forebrain by volume, with an area of up to 2500–3000 cm^2 and a thickness of only 1.5 to 3.0 mm. It seems that the neocortex is a device for the most widespread diffusion and mixing of signals. Therefore some authors have made the analogy between cortical functioning and the density of social gathering in a mob, or with the collective interactions of waves and individual particles in hot plasma systems. This interconnectivity in the neocortex is made possible by cortical neurons—pyramidal cells and interneurons. Nearly every pyramidal cell sends an axon into the white matter, and most of these reenter the cortex at some distant location in the same hemisphere (corticocortical fibers) or opposite hemisphere (commissural fibers). In addition, multiple branches of the axon provide input to regions within a 3-mm radius. The average number of synapses per cortical neuron is about 10^4. Neocortical neurons are arranged in overlapping modular columns of different sizes. An example of such a unit is the corticocortical column with a 2- to 3-mm thickness and a diameter of about 0.3 mm. There are about 2×10^6 corticocortical columns. It has been speculated that each module projects to perhaps 10 to 100 other modules and receives input from the same number. An even smaller arrangement of about 110 neurons—the minicolumn with a diameter of about 0.02—0.05 mm—has also been proposed as a basic functional unit of the neocortex. Still another processing unit, the macrocolumn—with a diameter of 0.5 to 3 mm—has been identified in the neocortex.

The next step up in the neural hierarchy may be loosely defined in terms of numbers and types of cells at various cortical depths (cytoarchitectonic level). At the beginning of the 20th century Brodman subdivided each hemisphere into approximately 50 regions. The linear scale associated with a Brodman area is about 5 cm and contains 10^8 neurons. This scale is close to the spatial resolution obtained with high-resolution electroencephalogram (EEG) scalp recordings.

The next higher scale is based on the wrinkled surface of the neocortex consisting of clefts and ridges. A deep cleft is called a fissure, and a sulcus if it is shallower. A ridge is called a gyrus. Ten major subdivisions of the neocortex are based on the major sulci and gyri. These are the frontal, precentral, parietal, occipital, and temporal lobes of each hemisphere. The linear scale associated with a lobe is approximately 17 cm. Finally the last level represents both hemispheres with a linear scale of 40 cm.

To illustrate the immense complexity of the neocortex, one could imagine that if the neocortical state were to be defined by the distribution of binary states of each unit, then on the level of 10 major lobes there are 1024 possible states (2^{10}). On the scale of Brodman areas there are 10^{32} states. This number corresponds to large grains of sand that could be packed into the earth. The next level, the macrocolumn, comes up with the unimaginable number of 10^{3162} states. For comparison, the number of electrons that could be packed into the volume of the known universe is approximately 10^{120}.

II. NEOCORTICAL ORGANIZATION

Most neuroscientists have no difficulty accepting the idea that certain functions are related to certain structures in the brain. However, some would agree that only physiological functions, not psychological ones, are structure bound.

The most prominent and visible division is on the level of both hemispheres. Significant anatomical asymmetry in a large series of human brains has been described. Even greater interest has been devoted to the functional differences between both hemispheres. One could speak of a left-brain, right-brain mania which was provoked by some laboratory findings of limited generality. In the sixties, the Nobel laureate Roger Sperry and his colleagues demonstrated that split brain patients had a unique behavioral syndrome. "Split brains" were epileptic patients with a complete section of the corpus callosum which was done in order to prevent the spread of the seizure to the opposite hemisphere. The phenomenon observed in these patients was that when the left hemisphere had access to information it could communicate this information by talking about it. By contrast, the right hemisphere had good recognition abilities but was unable to speak. In a typical experiment performed by researchers the respondent was asked to look directly at a dot in the center of his visual field. Then a picture of a cup was flashed briefly to the right of the dot (left hemisphere). The respondent reported that he saw a cup. Next time, a picture of a spoon was flashed to the left of the dot (right hemisphere). This time the respondent replied that he saw nothing. When asked to reach under the screen with his left hand (right hemisphere), and to select, by touch only, the object he had just seen, he selected a spoon.

The asymmetry was also found in the intact brain. For that purpose dichotic listening tasks were performed. In the procedure pairs of stimuli were presented simultaneously to the right and left ear of subjects (say, "three" and "four"), who were then asked to recall as many of the digits as possible. Dichotic listening tasks revealed left ear advantages (right hemisphere) for melodies and environmental sounds, and right ear advantages for digits, words, nonsense syllables, and Morse code. Similar findings were reported using EEG and lateral eye-movement measures. The idea behind lateral eye-movement measurement is that reflective questions engaging the left hemisphere (verbal processing questions) would yield right lateral eye movements, while questions engaging the right hemisphere (spatial processing questions) would result in left lateral eye movements. The data on cerebral lateralization are summarized in Table I. These basic data have generated the idea that the hemispheres represent two distinct modes of cognitive processing. Some of these interpretations have strayed a long way from the original data. An overview of the speculations and hypothesized functions of the right and left hemispheres is presented in Table II.

On the next lower scale, that of the 10 lobes, most is known about the occipital lobes. Their main function is vision. Separate anatomical regions within the occipital lobe are involved in the perception of form, movement, and color. The parietal lobe can be divided into three functional zones. The somatosensory func-

TABLE I

Summary of Data on Cerebral Lateralization in Right-Handed People

Left hemisphere	Right hemisphere
Letters, words	Complex geometric patterns, faces
Language-related sounds (digits, words, nonsense syllables)	Environmental sounds, melodies, musical chords, emotional sounds and human melodies, complex pitch perception
Morse code, difficult rhythms	Tactile recognition, Braille
Complex voluntary movement	Movements in spatial patterns
Verbal Memory	Nonverbal memory
Speech, reading, writing, arithmetic	Geometry, sense of direction, mental rotation of shapes

TABLE II

Summary of Speculations and Hypotheses on Cerebral Lateralization in Right-Handed People

Left hemisphere	Right hemisphere
Systematic and controlled	Playful and loose
Inhibited in responding emotionally	Responds with emotions, feelings
Dependent upon words for meaning	Interprets body language
Produces logical ideas	Produces humorous ideas
Objective processing of information	Subjective processing of information
Serious, systematic in solving problems	Playful in solving problems
Receptive, abstract thinking	Self-acting, concrete thinking
Dislikes improvising, not psychic	Like improvising, highly psychic
Little use of metaphors and analogies	High use of metaphors and analogies
Deals with one problem at a time, sequentially	Deals simultaneously with several problems at the same time
Critical and analytical in reading	Creative, synthesizing, association in reading
Logical in solving problems	Intuitive in solving problems
Grasps certain, established truths	Grasps uncertain truths

tion is located in the most anterior zone. The superior parietal region is devoted to the visual guidance of the hands, limbs, head, and eyes. The inferior parietal region is involved in spatial cognition. The temporal lobes participate in the analysis of auditory and visual information that allow for the processing of speech and the recognition of form. The medial temporal cortex is also important for long-term memory. The frontal cortex can be divided into three areas: the motor and premotor cortex, responsible for making and selecting movements, and the prefrontal cortex that controls cognitive processes. The frontal lobe has been associated with many cognitive functions which are close to the general factor of intelligence, fluid intelligence, metacognition, thus monitoring and controlling the cognitive process, and divergent thinking.

III. ELECTROPHYSIOLOGY AND NEUROIMAGING

A simple method for recording the electrical activity of the brain is electroencephalography. To record an EEG a small metal disk is attached to the scalp to detect the electrical activity of neurons in the underlying brain area. This activity is then amplified and displayed on an oscilloscope, computer, or chart recorder. The main issues currently confronting EEG researchers are the choice of the number and placement of electrodes and the choice of parameters used to describe EEG recording. Most often 16 to 20 electrodes are used. These are placed according to the Ten–Twenty Electrode Placement System (Figure 1). However, some newer sophisticated imaging systems are capable of simultaneously recording up to 256 channels.

EEG measurement requires collection of a huge amount of data which are unusable in raw form. Therefore they are subjected to data reduction methods. Most often a Fast Fourier Transformation (FFT) is performed on artifact-free chunks of data to derive estimates of absolute power values, or relative percentage power values in different frequency bands (delta, 0.5 to 4.5 Hz; theta, 4.6 to 7.5 Hz; alpha, 7.6 to 14.0 Hz; beta-1, 14.1 to 28.0 Hz; and beta-2, 28-1 to 50 Hz). The majority of analyses focus on measures in the alpha band (7.5–13 Hz). Evidence indicates that alpha power is inversely related to mental effort. A second

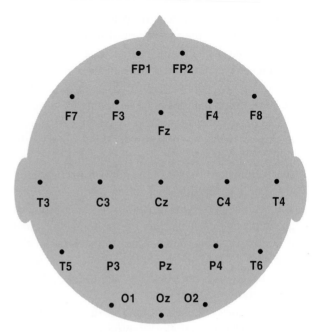

FIGURE 1 Ten–Twenty Electrode Placement System of the International Federation.

measure (e.g., the Lyapunov exponent λ_1, correlation dimension D2, or Kolmogorov entropy K2) introduced recently is used to indicate deterministic chaos. Chaotic dynamics differ from periodic and quasi-periodic systems in being sensitive to initial conditions, and therefore unpredictable over extended time periods. Even if two stats are only infinitesimally different, after a short time this difference will become very large. On the other hand, chaos is different from random processes in that it is fully deterministic and has a structure. Recent progress in nonlinear dynamics has provided algorithms for quantifying chaos using experimental time series. An example of such a time series could be the ongoing neural mass activity as recorded through the EEG. Research has shown that "less chaotic patterns" are associated with deep sleep or pathology, intermediate values are found during the awake (eyes closed) state, and the highest values are associated with mental activity. The relationship between EEG power measures and measures obtained by nonlinear analysis is still unclear.

Yet another measure using a similar recording technique to the ongoing EEG is average evoked potentials (AEPs), also called event-related potentials (ERPs).

ERPs consist of a brief change in EEG signal in response to a sensory stimulus. The changes are small and hard to see in the background of EEG activity. Therefore sensory stimuli are given repeatedly and the brain activity is averaged. Major interest was devoted to the so-called late components in ERPs that occur 100 ms after the stimulus.

The main problem related to EEG recording is artifacts caused by movements (e.g., eye-blink artifacts). Despite these difficulties the EEG has several advantages. It is still the only method that allows real time observation of brain activity. Further it is totally noninvasive and inexpensive to apply.

The newer technologies, positron emission tomography (PET) and magnetic resonance imaging (MRI), will probably have an immense impact on our understanding of the biological basis of intelligence and creativity. PET takes advantage of the unique characteristic of positron-emitting radiotopes. During the uptake period given by the half-life of the isotope (a few minutes to 30 min) the subject works on a task given by the experimenter. then the subject is placed in a ring of sensors that measure the by-products of the decay of the radioactive isotopes. The idea is that areas of the brain that are active will use more glucose, and hence become more radioactive than less active brain areas. The data are accumulated for the entire brain by sections or slices.

MRI produces a picture of any structure showing differences in tissue density. It is based on the principle that hydrogen atoms behave like spinning bar magnets in the presence of a magnetic field. When radio waves are beamed across the atoms, they emit detectable radio waves that are characteristic of their density and their chemical environment. MRI can be used to assess changes in blood oxygenation, which is a functional MRI (fMRI). The latest major development in imaging is the magnetoencephalogram (MEG) that measures tiny magnetic fields in the brain. An advantage of MEG is that it can locate the source of activity; thus it can record activity in the sulci.

IV. BRAIN AND INTELLIGENCE

Almost two centuries ago gross anatomical features of the brain were thought to be related to personality traits such as wit, causality, self-esteem, and many others. The idea was that the shape of the skull—bumps and depressions—indicated the size of the underlying brain area, and in that way pointed to a more or less developed trait. These bumps were measured using a method called cranioscopy.

Today, methods used to measure brain activity and ability have become much more accurate and sophisticated. Yet, knowing about the immense controversies in psychology concerning IQ, giftedness, and creativity, and similar debates in neuroscience on the use of the EEG and other techniques, one can imagine how difficult it is to give a more definite answer to the question, are the differences in ability related to brain differences?

Most of the studies that tried to relate brain size and intelligence reported rather low correlations of about 0.35. similar findings were reported when comparing IQ results of war veterans before and after injury. Even the most serious damages to the brain resulted in a decline of only 10 IQ points. Based on these findings one could conclude that intelligence does not have much to do with our brain.

More informative are EEG measures. The main finding of this research was that verbal intelligence was related to the 13-Hz EEG activity in most of the 16 brain areas (ten–twenty electrode placement), and was the strongest in the central areas in the premotor cortex and lowest in the occipital areas. It was further established that low beta activity was related to the capacity of numerical functioning and that left occipital activity was related to performance IQ. Much less decisive is the interpretation of these findings. As the 13-Hz EEG is an alpha band frequency associated with wakeful relaxed states of the brain, one could conclude that a highly activated brain is not necessarily the most intelligent.

Most of the research done with ERPs demonstrated a negative correlation (-0.15 to -0.9) between so-called late components (P300) and intelligence. The negative correlations mean that persons with longer latencies have lower IQs. An interesting finding is also that the length of the ERP wave positively correlates with intelligence ($r = 0.80$). Yet another similar measure is the number of zero-crossings of an ERP wave (how many times the wave crosses the x-axes). It was found that a mean IQ of 105 corresponded to

2.9 zero-crossings, a mean IQ of 107 corresponded to 3.5 zero-crossings, and a mean IQ of 110 corresponded to 3.9 zero-crossings.

Even though all these findings point to a relationship between the electrical activity of the brain and intelligence, they allow only for speculation about the structure of intelligence. Do shorter latencies mean faster processing by more intelligent persons? Are longer ERP waves the characteristic of more complex and elaborated thinking processes by persons with a high IQ? [*See* INTELLIGENCE.]

V. CREATIVITY, GIFTEDNESS, AND BRAIN FUNCTIONING

Researchers investigating the relationship between creativity and brain function were most attracted by hemisphericity. From a theoretical viewpoint, this is a reasonable inference. Several authors recognized the importance of conceiving two or more opposites for the creative process. Various names were suggested to describe this process of combining opposing entities: (1) The Janusian process is the simultaneous conceptualization of opposite or antithetical ideas. The term derives from the qualities of the Roman god Janus. This god had faces that looked in diametrically opposite directions simultaneously. (2) Bisociation describes the creative process as an act of combining unrelated structures, separate ideas, facts, and frames of perception within a single brain, and (3) hemispheric bisociation is the synthesis of two different neurological planes. Therefore, two hemispheres representing two distinct modes of cognitive processing were the ideal neurological explanation of creativity. [*See* JANUSIAN PROCESS.]

Still another characteristic in the creative process, the phases of incubation and illumination—where attention to the problem is defocused and solutions to problems spontaneously appear—gave rise to speculations that creativity is related to the nonspeaking right hemisphere. Further support for such ideas could be found in psychoanalytic explanations of creativity. For Freud, creativity is an expression of repressed personal experiences inherent in our personal unconscious. By contrast, Jung understood creativity as a product of archetypes which are the heart of our collective unconscious. [*See* INCUBATION.]

Two concepts relating creativity to hemisphericity were proposed. First, creativity was mainly seen as a right hemispheric process, or second, as an alternation between left- and right-hemisphere modes of processing. It was suggested that in the first phase there is little or no interhemispheric communication. Thus, both hemispheres can independently develop their own processes. The second phase consists of a more intense communication between the two hemispheres. In that period, imagery generated in the right hemisphere can be realized through the left hemisphere.

Moderate research support was found for the relationship between hemisphericity and creativity. It was found that the relationship between creativity and right hemispheric activation as determined by EEG was not a general one. A difference between more and less creative respondents was found during creative production but not during basal recordings or during a reading task. The major shortcoming of these early studies is a methodological one. In many studies, recording sites were restricted to temporal and parietal regions, and seldom more than four electrodes were used. [*See* SPLIT BRAINS: INTERHEMISPHERIC EXCHANGE IN CREATIVITY.]

Evidence for greater involvement of the right hemisphere in creative thinking was also obtained using eye gaze and inventories to determine hemisphericity. On the other hand, examining the performance of more and less creative individuals on dichotic listening tasks revealed that the more creative individuals displayed a left hemisphere advantage.

Recently the idea of a right hemisphere advantage in highly gifted individuals has gained new theoretical support. Giftedness is seen as a kind of "left hemisphere pathology." This speculation is supported by several research findings and opinions. Some neurologists have explained individual differences in intelligence by the negative environmental influence on our brain. Others have been attracted by similarities displayed by exceptional individuals in domains like music, mathematics, and chess. There are three characteristics that relate gifted chess players like Fischer and Capablanca, composers like Mozart and Rossini, and mathematicians like Gauss. First, all of them had profound, original insights as preadolescents; second, all three domains of chess, music, and mathematics are dominated by males; and third, all three domains involve highly nonverbal capacities. [*See* GIFTEDNESS AND CREATIVITY.]

The hormonal theory could explain some of the characteristics displayed by gifted individuals. According to this theory the presence of intrauterine testosterone produced by the developing male fetus slows the development of the left hemisphere, which leads to compensatory enhanced development of the right hemisphere. In females no such compensatory process is necessary. A series of experiments established a link between extreme intellectual precocity and left-handedness, immune disorders, and myopia, each of which may be considered by-products of advantaged right-hemispheric development. These findings could be only partly replicated using EEG technology. In resting conditions, the left hemisphere of the mathematically gifted individuals—and not the right as expected—was more active. During mental activity on a nonverbal task, a significant reduction of alpha power over the right hemisphere among the mathematically gifted students was established, while no such alpha suppression was found among the group of average individuals. On the verbal task no significant difference in alpha suppression between the two groups of individuals was found. However, several other EEG studies indicated no significant differences in hemispheric activity between gifted and average students. Similar findings were also reported using neuroimaging techniques like PET and fMRI.

Recently, researchers have described negative associations between brain activity under cognitive load and intelligence, giftedness, or special talent. Also pointing in this direction are the findings of a positive correlation between IQ and the 13-Hz EEG (alpha wave indicative of a relaxed mental state), mentioned earlier, and EEG recordings of chess players prior to their games indicating higher alpha activity. These findings were more systematically investigated in a series of PET studies. It was found that during problem solving, high-IQ subjects had lower overall metabolic rates than subjects with a low IQ. These findings suggest that high-IQ subjects did not have to work as hard at solving problems as did low-IQ subjects. Similar findings using the EEG were also reported. The main finding was that during problem solving gifted and more intelligent students exhibited a higher alpha power than did average students. It was further found that gifted

individuals, in comparison with average ones, showed lower entropy (a measure of low deterministic chaos), indicating less complex neural mass activity when solving tasks involving arithmetic operations and deductive reasoning.

The results reported, even though different neuropsychological techniques and measures were used, suggest that intellectually competent individuals during problem solving were less mentally active than individuals with average intellectual abilities. However, the interpretation of these results given by researchers differed markedly.

Some authors have suggested an efficiency hypothesis to explain the results from the PET studies. It was suggested that intelligence is not a function of how hard the brain works but rather of how efficiently it works. This efficiency may derive from the nonuse of many brain areas irrelevant for good task performance as well as the more focused use of specific task-relevant areas. Research has further shown that the characteristic of gifted boys was a finely tuned capacity for activating, or inhibiting, the very brain regions that play, or do not play, specialized roles in the performance of a specific task. During word processing gifted individuals activated frontal regions, whereas those of average ability activated temporal regions. On the other hand, during mathematical reasoning a higher activation of the temporal lobes was observed in mathematically gifted males, but not in females.

A second explanation for the observed differences in mental activation between individuals of average and high IQ could lie in the ability of good problem solvers to better structure the problem space, and in their ability to bring order into their thoughts and operations. It seems reasonable that high-IQ persons reduce the complexity of their mental schema by making it more abstract. Therefore, when involved in problem solving, able individuals showed higher alpha power (lower mental effort) than average individuals. However, no empirical evidence was found that could confirm this hypothesis. In an EEG study, gifted and average individuals memorized lists of words and pictures that either allowed, or did not allow, for classification into more abstract categories. For both types of lists, gifted individuals displayed higher alpha power than average ones.

Still another explanation for the difference in mental

activity between gifted and average individuals when involved in problem solving could be the speed of mental processing. Hence, what would be crucial for the reported differences would be not how efficiently the brain works, but how rapidly it operates. This speculation is supported by research into individual differences using the cognitive-correlates method. The findings could be summarized as indicating that individuals with higher levels of verbal ability are faster at retrieving more abstract categories from long-term memory. Research using EEG technology did not support the speed hypothesis. Gifted individuals, in comparison with average ones, displayed less mental activity (their alpha power as compared to the resting condition of eyes open showed a lower decrease in magnitude, as well as lower entropy measures). The differences were more pronounced with complex tasks involving short-term memory, proportional thinking, and arithmetic operations than with basic tasks involving processing speed.

The conclusion drawn from this finding is that processing speed is not the main reason for the displayed differences in mental activity. It seems that the efficiency hypothesis far better describes the results obtained. This efficiency may derive from the more focused use of specific, task-relevant areas of gifted students. Support for this conclusion can be drawn from the fact that the greatest differences in alpha power were observed over the frontal areas, which are mainly related to problem solving and general intelligence. The fact that differences in alpha power were most pronounced for the tasks involving short-term memory could be indicative of a more efficient memory use by gifted individuals.

Pointers in this direction are being given by expert–novice comparisons of the role of domain-specific knowledge in problem solving proficiency in a number of domains. Experts differed from novices not only in the amount of knowledge they possessed, but also in the organization and accessibility of that knowledge. Further support for the efficiency hypothesis could be implied from the fact that gifted individuals, while solving the different tasks, used processes which displayed a similar complexity of neural mass activity; by contrast, average individuals displayed a greater diversity in the complexity of neural mass activity. The differences were extremely pronounced over the right hemisphere. Recent findings have shown that giftedness is related to strategy flexibility, which means that intellectually competent individuals changed their solution approach in relation to the problem type. However, the problems used in the study did not greatly differ. All of them could be classified as well defined, having one correct solution. Hence, there was no need for the strategy change displayed by the average individuals. [*See* EXPERTISE.]

Less clear-cut is the comparison of EEG measures between gifted and average individuals during resting conditions (e.g., eyes closed or eyes open). Nonlinear dynamical analysis of multichannel EEGs showed that during resting conditions subjects with high IQs demonstrated higher dimensional complexity in the EEG pattern than subjects with low IQs. Higher dimensional complexity is usually explained as indicative of a more complex pattern of brain activity. Some other EEG studies using Kolmogorov entropy, another measure of low deterministic chaos, and average amplitudes of alpha power showed no significant differences between gifted and average individuals.

VI. DIFFERENCES BETWEEN CREATIVITY AND INTELLIGENCE RELATED TO BRAIN FUNCTIONING

A major issue for a better understanding of ability is what kind of processes people use when they solve different types of problems. There exist numerous psychological studies on processes involved in problem solving using different approaches and methods, and even different names for similar or equal psychological phenomena. For instance, the trait-factorial theory discussed the difference between creativity and intelligence, while, on the other hand, the information-processing theory spoke of processes involved in solving well-defined and ill-defined problems.

A powerful strategy for finding the right paths in the problem space of well-defined problems is means–end analysis. Means–end analysis is the main process which humans use when they solve problems. This process is determined by two key features: difference reduction and subgoaling. Difference reduction is the tendency to select operators that produce states more similar to the goal state. The interim states in this reduction process are subgoals. Some authors have argued that even in dealing with ill-defined problems, solvers use heuristics not unlike those that they use for well-defined problems, such as subgoaling. The generalization that can be drawn is that creative problem solving is only a special case of the general problem solving strategy of means–end analysis. A contrary assumption, namely, that creative problem solving has a broader field of application than means–end analysis—which is a useful strategy only with problems that have a known solution—has been suggested by other researchers. [*See* PROBLEM SOLVING.]

A recent series of studies used activation parameters like heart rate (HR) and blood pressure (BP) to establish the differences between the thinking processes involved in solving closed and creative problems. The idea behind these parameters (HR and BP) is that the typical reaction to sensory rejection or mental work is tachycardia; in contrast, sensory intake tasks are associated with decreased heart rate. The results obtained in these studies showed a continuous increase in HR during the respondents' solution of well-defined problems, and a sudden increase in HR when respondents solved the insight problems. These results suggest a more incremental solution approach to well-defined problems and a more sudden solution, described as illumination, to insight problems. Subjects' HR during the solution of creative and divergent production problems—which are also classified as ill-defined problems—was less regular and was interrupted by several decreases/increases in HR, which could indicate the strategy of hypothesis testing.

These findings could be replicated in a recent study using EEG methodology. In this study the solution process was divided into several subprocesses, which could be broadly classified as processes involved in the solution of the problem and those involved in preparing and planning the solution of the problem. An EEG was recorded while students solved the different phases. It was found that ill-defined problems seemed to be more demanding in the preparation phase than were closed problems. More mental effort is needed to understand and plan the solution of ill-defined problems. This seems quite reasonable, since the characteristic of ill-defined problems is a vague and ill-defined goal state with a complex problem space. Thus, before one can start solving this kind of problem the essence

of the problem must be selected, and then the goal or goals must be defined. On the other hand, for well-defined problems no such preparation is needed.

A second finding was that during the solution of the well-defined problem the respondents displayed less alpha power (higher mental activity) than during the different solution phases (solution, information selection, and analogous solution) of the ill-defined problem. The interpretation of this finding in relation to supposed cognitive processes involved in the solution of well-defined problems lies in finding a solution path through the well-structured problem space. It can be hypothesized that this process, because of the number of elements which must be controlled in the working memory, is more demanding than the testing of different hypotheses. Another explanation could be that the characteristic of creative solutions is that they emerge in relaxed mental states. The results of both studies suggest that different processes are involved in solving well- and ill-defined problems.

VII. FACTS AND SPECULATIONS

This overview of the relationship between the brain and ability has raised many questions—some of which may never receive an ultimate answer. Still, the examinations reported have also provided data important for a better understanding of intelligence and creativity. To pinpoint just some of them, the hypothesis that gifted individuals use only brain areas relevant for the task at hand could suggest that intelligence is related to "less chaotic" and more "simple" ways of thinking. But is this also true for creativity? Evidence from some research suggests that at least in the first stages of creative production more complex thinking patterns are found; however, the solution process following these early stages is characterized by lower mental activity. [*See* BRAIN AND THE CREATIVE ACT.]

On the other hand, it is too early to argue that biological evidence supports one theory of ability or another. For instance, the modular theory of mind would favor an intelligence theory of several types of intelligence that exist as independent categories; by contrast, the idea that the neocortex is a device for the most widespread diffusion and mixing of signals would be in favor of the general intelligence factor.

Researchers investigating individual differences in ability are frequently disappointed by the fact that there are considerable differences at the behavioral level (e.g., the creative output of an artist or novelist compared with the writing and drawing of average people), whereas differences observed and measured in the cognitive processes or brain functioning are often trivial. This could be explained by the fact that ability is a complex system of independent parts. Thus, no single biological measure will account for a large portion of the variance in ability. Another explanation could be provided by chaos theory, in which small reasons can provoke tremendous consequences. [*See* CHAOS THEORY IN CREATIVITY.]

Bibliography

Detterman, D. K. (1994). Intelligence and the brain. In P. A. Vernon (Ed.), *The neuropsychology of individual differences* (pp. 35–57). London: Academic Press.

Eysenck, F. (1995). *Genius: The natural history of creativity.* Cambridge: Cambridge University Press.

Gazzaniga, M. S. (1985). *The social brain.* New York: Basic Books.

Giannitrapani, D. (1985). *The electrophysiology of intellectual functions.* Basel: Karger.

Jaušovec, N. (1994). *Flexible thinking: An explanation for individual differences in ability.* Cresskill, NJ: Hampton Press.

Kolb, B., & Whishaw, I. Q. (1996). *Fundamentals of human neuropsychology.* New York: Freeman.

Kunzendorf, R., & Sheikh, A. (1990). *Psychophysiology of mental imagery: Theory, research, and application.* Amityville, NY: Baywood.

Brain and the Creative Act

Karl H. Pribram

Stanford University and Radford University

CA3 An easily distinguishable layer of cells, one of three that make up the hippocampal cortex.

Episodic Process that refers to episodes in one's own experience.

fMRI A technique of imaging body organs and tissues based on resonance with atomic nuclear oscillations.

Isomorphism Of the same shape.

Semantic Meanings that refer to objects and occurrences that can be pointed to.

Sinusoidal Wave A regular, unchanging waveform.

Synaptodendritic A connection web formed by the junctions among nerve cells.

As noted by Arthur Koestler, the pattern underlying the **CREATIVE ACT** *is the "perceiving of a situation or an idea in two self-consistent but habitually incompatible frames of reference. The event in which the two [frames] intersect, is made to vibrate simultaneously on two different wavelengths, as it were. [The event] is not merely linked to one associative context, but is 'bisociated' with two."*

I. INTRODUCTION

Creativity has several dimensions, only one of which will be discussed in this essay: the creative act that precipitates the creative process. As has been pointed out repeatedly, creativity is made up of 1% inspiration and 99% perspiration. Nor is reinventing the wheel a truly creative act. Part of the perspiration consists of preparing—pruning overgrowth by taking inventory of what has already been accomplished—before setting out to invent.

Koestler's poetic description of the creative act is intuitively appealing, but the job of science is to show "how" a process works. Psychological science devolves on showing how our experience comes about, and part of this demonstration centers on discovering (uncovering) the concomitant physiological processes that take place within the experiencing person.

Observations made in the clinic of persons who have sustained injuries to their brain have shown that these injuries can dramatically change the person's experience. The changes are verbally reported by the patients, and verbal tests can be devised to explore the extent and

Copyright © 1999 by Academic Press
All rights of reproduction in any form reserved.

depth of the changes. Also, the changes are often expressed in nonverbal behavior and can be explored in the laboratory by carefully producing similar brain injuries in nonhuman subjects (for instance, in monkeys) and extensively studying the behavior of these subjects. Further, the anatomical connections and the electrical activity of the parts of the brain that were injured in the patients can be studied in the nonhuman subjects.

The current article will review highlights and insights of research on the hippocampal system (including e.g., the adjacent entorhinal, perirhinal, and cingulate cortices). The hippocampal system deals with recombinant processing of experience, or what Arthur Koestler called bisociation.

II. THE HIPPOCAMPAL SYSTEM

Much work has been done on the "loss of memory" with H.M., a patient whose hippocampus was removed as treatment for epilepsy and with patients with similar brain damage. Several important findings have emerged from these studies. First, under certain conditions, using probes such as parts of nonsense "words" that had to be recognized as having been encountered before, research showed that postoperative experience appears to be stored but is not ordinarily accessible to retrieval. Second, skills can be readily learned and remain accessible. Third, repeated experience that consistently refers to objects and occurrences can become stored and retrieved.

This last finding was dramatically confirmed in monkey experiments in which animals with their hippocampal system removed perfectly remembered, without rehearsal, for two years a problem they had been taught. Thus, the simple view that the hippocampal system is necessary for memory storage, which is so often found in writings about this system, is no more tenable than the view that it is the seat of emotions.

III. THE TYPES OF REMEMBERING

Independent of these brain-related studies, Endel Tulving, on the basis of studies with human subjects, was able to divide memory processing, remembering, into three fundamental classes: semantic, skill, and episodic. Semantic processing deals with reference to—

the meanings of—identifiable objects and occurrences (access to a stored dictionary). The processing of skills devolves on being able to successfully manipulate one's environment. Episodic processing is the ability to more or less accurately remember episodes of events that have personal meaning and relevance.

This classification is tailor-made for correlation with the findings on subjects with brain damage. Studies on monkeys and humans had shown that carefully made removals of portions of the posterior convexity of the brain cortex, the sensory-specific "association" cortex, impairs referential processing. (The term "semantic" is ordinarily restricted to referential language abilities which are deficient in monkeys.) The role of the cortical areas surrounding the central fissure of the cortex in processing skills is well documented, and the findings on subjects with damage to the hippocampal system already described indicate that this system is involved in episodic processing.

Recent findings on children born with hippocampal damage have shown that skills and semantic processing can develop without impairment despite a totally defective episodic processing ability. (This independence of development is also true of the skill vs. semantic processing systems.) Of course, this does not mean that the three processing systems do not ordinarily interact. In fact, their interaction lies at the root of creativity.

Before detailing a model of creative interaction, we need to understand more fully what episodic memory processing entails. In the experiments with monkeys, the tasks on which subjects with hippocampal system damage are impaired are composed of ever-changing trials. Nonetheless there are recurrent regularities that make it possible to solve the tasks. For instance, reward may be dependent on always choosing a cue that had been seen just previously, or conversely choosing a cue different from the previously presented sample. A sample is not necessary, however. The task may involve going to a location other than the one that had been rewarded on a previous trial. To solve such tasks the monkey has to develop strategies such as "win–stay" or "win–shift."

The development of strategies (as opposed to tactics, which entail the development of skills) entails the use of what have been called cognitive maps. The results of animal research on the behavioral functions of the hippocampal system can thus be understood in terms of its role in the development of strategies utilizing cognitive maps. The maps form the context within which skills are carried out and within which referential (semantic) meaning becomes relevant to a more encompassing scenario.

For humans, this strategic context is composed of episodes, components that, together with other episodes, form a scenario or personal narrative. Though the hippocampal system is essential to the utilization of episodes, their construction involves other brain systems such as those centered on the amygdala, whose activity is essential to marking the beginning and end of an episode, and the anterior frontal cortex, which determines the occasions, and relationships among occasions, where and when utilization becomes effective.

IV. A MODEL OF THE NEUROPHYSIOLOGY OF CREATIVITY

So far, I have reviewed evidence regarding the development of a single strategy, the mapping of a single cognitive context within which experience is experienced and behavior is deployed. But what of creativity, the bisociation of contexts by an experienced event?

An ensemble of comprehensive contexts can become stabilized under conditions in which probabilities play a minor role. These conditions provide simple recurrent regularities, as, for example, those that often characterize physiological states such as hunger and thirst. In these instances the stabilities define steady (homeostatic) states at equilibrium. When, however, probabilities play a significant role, stabilities occur far from equilibrium. Such stabilities are subject to destabilizing influences. When stabilities far from equilibrium become perturbed, they provide the ground for creative innovation.

Research with monkeys has shown that probabilistic strategies fail to be undertaken in instrumental conditioning situations after removal of the anterior frontal cortex (and in classical conditioning situations after removal of the amygdala system). When these systems are intact, probabilistic strategies are the rule; as noted, stabilities far from equilibrium are vulnerable to perturbation. This vulnerability was shown to have the advantage that when the parameters of the conditioning situation change, the monkeys with intact brains readily adjust their behavior to the change whereas the monkeys who had been subjected to the brain resections were stuck in their behavior patterns and thus failed to adjust to the new circumstances.

Appendix C of Karl Pibram's *Brain and Perception* develops a mathematical definition of context. Two types of context are distinguished: local and comprehensive. Local contexts constitute reference frames for objects and occurrences. Comprehensive contexts are those that provide the boundaries to an experienced episode. It is these contexts that are involved in bisociation. Their development is necessary for experiences to become familiar and/or innovative. A mathematical geometry—a mathematical map—describing comprehensive contexts is presented in terms of vector spaces (vectors are lines that have length and direction).

Neurophysiologically the vectors represent the amplitude and phase of oscillations of electrochemical polarizations in the synaptodendritic processing web of the hippocampal cortex. The length of the vector indicates the amplitude of oscillation, and its direction the phase—the coherence with respect to other oscillations. The evidence on which this model is based and the manner of its operation are presented in the appendix to this article.

Appendix F of *Brain and Perception* demonstrates an additional value that accrues to probabilistic strategies. When the comprehensive contexts that map individual strategies become perturbed, the critical vectors that specify each context are no longer aligned within the map but come to point along many independent directions. Neurophysiologically, this is indicated by desynchronization of hippocampal electrochemical activity. Desynchronization allows novel associations to occur in which several independent contexts can be associated on the basis of the amount of alignment of their vectors, that is, of the alignment of phases of electrochemical oscillations. Again, the evidence on which this model is based and the manner of its operation are described in the Appendix.

V. THE ACT OF CREATION

In humans, perturbation is produced when different comprehensive contexts become equiprobable. The buildup during the telling of jokes prior to the punch line, the enhancement of suspense in a play or narrative, and the frustration accompanying an unsolved problem all provide such an increase.

In science, the creative act often employs the use of metaphor, analogy, and model building. Such activity was called "abduction" by Charles Sanders Peirce, who contrasted it with induction and deduction. In fact, Peirce indicates that abduction consists of the inspiration that produces the creative act. He relegates induction and deduction to perspiration: induction consists of preparatory activity while deduction brings the creative act to consummation. The search for the neurophysiological "how" of creativity has tracked Peirce's insights: The holographic metaphor has given rise to parallel distributed processing (PDP) models that inductively summarize current data. A critical point of issue has arisen deductively: Is the model to remain solely probabilistic or is a holographic-like process actually involved? The Appendix details this issue. [*See* ANALOGIES; ENSEMBLE OF METAPHOR; METAPHORS.]

VI. APPENDIX

The model of creativity (innovation) developed in *Brain and Perception* and in subsequent essays proposes that sensory input is relayed to the hippocampal–parahippocampal system and simultaneously to the sensory-specific "association" systems of the neocortical isocortex. When a match exists between the patterns elicited in hippocampal and neocortical systems, the input is considered "familiar" and the matching activity ceases. When, on the other hand, a mismatch exists, the input is considered "novel" and the matching operation continues interactively until the neocortical pattern has been modified sufficiently to produce a match. J. L. McClelland, in collaboration with D. E. Rummelhart and Bruce MacNaughten, has developed a simulation of this matching process using parallel distributed processing programming architectures. This simulation relies on statistical (that is, probabilistic) relations among neuronal firing patterns and does not directly entail the relations among phases of oscillatory activity within the synaptodendritic processing web of hippocampal layers. I propose in the following exchange that *both* the probabilistic and a holographic-

like phase encoding are involved, and that the phase encoding takes place as a synaptodendritic microprocess while the probabilistic process is macroscopic, involving internal hippocampal circuitry.

The argument runs as follows: McClelland presents a precise model of how hippocampal intervention—which is present whenever a stimulus is novel to the organism—can lead to dysfunction (catastrophic interference) as well as to creative innovation. However, McClelland also shows how a hippocampal input to the cortex can, at other times, lead to learning. According to McClelland, nonlimbic learning is slow and is produced "via interleaved presentation on a representative sample of an entire domain of knowledge."

Learning can also occur in the absence of the hippocampal formation. Could this be due to a difference in brain organization between rodent and primate, such as the massive increase in the area of the frontal cortex? Animals with more complex nervous systems actually learned more slowly than animals with simpler nervous systems but that the range of what can be learned increases with an increase in brain complexity. McClelland's model shows precisely how an increase in the complexity of the brain can accomplish this enhanced range.

As an addition to the overall model presented by McClelland, there are elaborations of its neurological underpinnings that can fill out the particulars of the "how."

McClelland and colleague's model directly matches hippocampal activity with the activity of the cortical convexity (as would be expected of a comparator). On the input side such a model is plausible. However, their model also demands such a comparator process on the output side. This is implausible in view of results obtained by Paul MacLean and Karl Pribram when mapping cortical connectivity by strychnine neuronography. While they were able to readily show multiple inputs to the hippocampal formation, they were totally unable to activate *any* isocortical region by stimulating the hippocampal cortex. The finding was so striking that MacLean developed the theme of a schizophysiology of cortical function.

On the other hand outputs from the hippocampal system are plentiful to the amygdala, to the nucleus accumbens septi, and to other subcortical structures via the fornix. Confirmation of the difference between input (encoding) and output (decoding) operations involving the hippocampal formation has recently come from studies in humans using *f*MRI. Encoding into memory was found to activate the parahippocampal cortex (including the entorhinal and perirhinal cortex, which receives input from the remainder of the isocortex), whereas decoding (retrieval) was found to activate the subiculum, which provides the major *subcortical* output of the hippocampal region via the fornix.

The subcortical nuclei do not have the laminar structure of the cortex and so are poor candidates for the type of point to point match we might ordinarily conceive. On the other hand, a match could readily be achieved if the comparison would involve a stage during which processing entailed a distributed stage. Such a stage is present in McClelland's model and when a holographic memory is used to store and retrieve information. It is the evidence that a distributed store is, in fact, built up in the hippocampal formation during learning that makes this sort of model plausible. Philip Landfield and John O'Keefe have developed this sort of model.

Both McClelland and Pribram agree on the distributed nature of the hippocampal process. However, McLelland states his argument in probabilistic terms, while Pribram states his holographically. McClelland has the advantage that the intervention of anterior frontal processing (probably by way of the cingulate cortex) can readily alter the probability structure envisioned by McClelland. At the circuit level of processing Pribram supports his model.

Nonetheless, at the level of processing at the level of the synaptodendritic web, the level that *generates* oscillations such as the theta rhythms, holographic-like interference patterns—that is, phase encoding—is possible. In support of such a possibility, a researcher at the University of Southern California (personal communication) had the following experience: From microelectrode data, he had modeled in hardware, using parallel distributed architecture, the processes going on in CA1 and CA3. He then tried to connect the two processors and ran into an incredible mass of wires, where tracing connections proved all but impossible. As a result he gave up this approach and substituted an optical system to make the connections. Now there is a small box labeled "hologram" that makes the connections almost instantaneously. What needs to be done now is to test whether indeed phase encoding exists in the hippocampal cortex.

Bibliography

Isaacson, R. L., & Pribram, K. H. (Eds.). (1986). *The hippocampus, volumes III and IV.* New York: Plenum.

Koestler, A. (1964). *The act of creation.* New York: Macmillan.

Pribram, K. H. (Ed.). (1994). *Origins: Brain & self organization.* Hillsdale, NJ: Erlbaum.

Pribram, K. H. (1971). *Languages of the brain: Experimental paradoxes and principlesin neuropsychology.* Englewood Cliffs, NJ: Prentice-Hall; Monterey, CA: Brooks/Cole (1977); New York: Brandon House (1982). [Translations in Russian, Japanese, Italian, and Spanish.]

Pribram, K. H. (1991). *Brain and perception: Holonomy and structure in figural processing.* Hillsdale, NJ: Erlbaum.

Pribram, K. H. (Ed.). (1998). *Appalachian Conference: Vol. 5. Brain and values.* Mahwah, NJ: Erlbaum.

Pribram, K. H., & King, J. S. (Eds.). (1996). *Learning as self-organization.* Hillsdale, NJ: Erlbaum.

Brainstorming

Tudor Rickards

Manchester Business School

Brainstorming In informal usage, any process in which a team deliberately engages in the generation of ideas. More formally, an individual or group process of idea generation following structural guidelines for weakening intrapersonal and interpersonal barriers to the generation of new and useful ideas.

Electronic Brainstorming (EB) Brainstorming conducted within some electronic support system through which intrapersonal and interpersonal idea generation processes are mediated.

Heuristics Generally taken to mean discovery processes. Here the term "practitioner heuristics" refers to the largely undefined processes through which practitioners acquire rules of thumb regarding the selecting and enacting of a specific brainstorming variant.

Interactive Group Brainstorming Brainstorming in groups whose members interact during brainstorming to enrich ideas.

Nominal Group Brainstorming (NGB) Brainstorming within which the participants do not interact, but generate their ideas in isolation.

BRAINSTORMING, *when used without further qualification, may refer to a wide range of different approaches intended to generate ideas more effectively than through unstructured efforts. The technique may involve individual or team efforts, and may be mediated by trained facilitators, electronic support systems, training, or combinations of these and other factors. Practical evidence shows that in most circumstances electronic support systems enhance idea generation, and interactive groups are less productive than the combined outputs of individuals (so-called nominal group modes). However, there may be some preference among users for less-effective over more-effective modes. There is no clear theoretical model indicating which mode is most effective for a given set of circumstances. However, in practice this potential difficulty can be sidestepped through the use of a cocktail of techniques.*

I. ORIGINS

The principles behind brainstorming can be traced back to Eastern religious ceremonies in which participants were instructed to speak spontaneously and with an emptying of the mind of critical thoughts. Its modern applications are widely associated with the work of Alex Osborn, a partner in the advertising agency Batten, Barton, Durstine, and Osborn. His earliest work

Copyright © 1999 by Academic Press
All rights of reproduction in any form reserved.

emerged as America applied itself to the challenges of entering the second world war.

Osborn considered that the majority of members of the U.S. workforce was being denied a voice. He believed that status pressures and insensitive behaviors inevitably reduced the contributions of all but a few dominant participants in meetings. He began to experiment with a meeting structure to neutralize the blocks and free up the idea generation processes. Osborn had no concern for formal definitions, content to repeat a dictionary definition which in effect described brainstorming as a conference technique by which a group attempts to find a solution for a specific problem by amassing all the ideas spontaneously contributed by its members.

Osborn's ideas provoked scorn from academic and practical business critics. One author in the 1950s called the whole business "cerebral popcorn." Nevertheless, brainstorming gained increasing attention, not least through Osborn's indefatigable efforts as publicist. Over a period of decades he documented accounts of many successful practical outcomes of brainstorming sessions. In 1954, he founded the Creative Education Foundation (CEF) in Buffalo, which developed into an influential focus for research into his broader ideas for stimulating ideas in the interests of societal ideals. In time the CEF became associated with training in, and the practice of, creative problem solving (CPS), particularly with the Parnes–Osborn model, which incorporated and extended the principles of brainstorming. The model is named after Osborn and his protégé, Sid Parnes, who together helped organize a series of conferences first in Buffalo, and subsequently in many other locations around the world.

In practitioner accounts the term may refer to:

1. Any efforts at idea generation, generally within a small team of brainstormers
2. The divergent, idea generation part of a more general search for new and valuable ideas
3. The divergent stages within the Parnes–Osborn creative problem-solving model such as generating new ways of viewing the problem ("problem finding"), or new ideas or new approaches for progressing ideas into actions ("acceptance finding")

II. OSBORN'S PRINCIPLES

Osborn's approach is based on two interrelated concepts, the principle of deferment of judgment and the principle of extended search. Deferral of judgment refers to an individual's effort at self-expression without censorship of his or her own thoughts, and without criticism of those ideas expressed by others. The second principle seeks to stretch the participants beyond the first, and more automatic or routine, ideas to arrive at ideas that have a greater level of originality and at the same time relevance.

These principles are actualized in the context of a brainstorming meeting or session sometimes restricted out of necessity or choice to a few minutes, or extended to several hours. The session is given its structure through a moderator or facilitator who seeks to keep the participants following four operating guidelines: (1) criticism is ruled out, (2) freewheeling is welcomed, (3) hitchhike (improve) on ideas, and (4) go for quantity.

If the two principles and four guidelines are consciously acknowledged and followed, a meeting may unequivocally be regarded as close to Osborn's concept of group brainstorming.

The further the meeting departs from the overt adherence to the rules, the greater the likelihood of ambiguity about its relationship with that original format. For example, an *ad hoc* group may be formed without training or inclination to collaborate. In this case, even if the principles and rules are proposed by a team leader, it is unlikely that they are followed in practice. Conversely, the procedures designed to support the deferral of judgment may be innovations that modify or replace Osborn's rules. Here the process may become known as another idea generation or creative problem-solving technique, although it may arguably be understood and studied as a version of brainstorming.

III. BRAINSTORMING AND CREATIVITY

Brainstorming has been closely associated with the creative problem-solving movement, where it is widely acknowledged as one of the best-known creative problem-solving techniques. The validation of such claims is not a straightforward matter, in part because of uncertainties surrounding the characterization of the creative process. At least four possibilities can be considered. [*See* PROBLEM SOLVING.]

A. Brainstorming Enhances the Generation of Creative Breakthroughs

Despite extensive documented evidence, there is no well-documented evidence that brainstorming procedures have been implicated in the generation of substantial creative breakthroughs. On this kind of criterion, the link between creativity and brainstorming must be considered a tenuous one.

B. Brainstorming Is Associated with Statistically Rare Outputs of Meetings

An association can be made between creativity and the statistical rarity of ideas from a creativity session. This is a weaker criterion than in the preceding section. Osborn cites many real-life illustrations of unusual ideas, some of which were effectively implemented. Other supporters of the technique have made similar claims. However, a comprehensive review of techniques for stimulating creativity, little substantiated evidence was found that brainstorming produced more statistically rare ideas than did more conventional meetings.

C. Brainstorming Leads to a Creative Climate

The principles and structuring associated with brainstorming produces a creative climate. This may directly or indirectly support creativity. Practitioners of brainstorming describe how a successful session produces an enhanced sense of "flow," associated with a creative climate. Self-report inventories suggest that Osborn-type interactive brainstorming may be enjoyed more by participants than are noninteractive mode brainstorming. There is some evidence that brainstorming supports the attainment of such a creative mood within a group. Here the assessment relies on self-reports of the creative process, and may be regarded as an inter-

subjective or interpretational treatment. [*See* CREATIVE CLIMATE.]

D. Brainstorming Is a Component within the Development of Creative Potential

The most studied approach has been the Parnes–Osborn CPS system, in which the brainstorming procedures are an essential component for developing a capacity at divergent ideation. The most comprehensive studies have been made at the University of Georgia, at the Torrance Center, over a period of many years. Later reviews offer general support to the conclusions from the Torrance studies. In summary, educational programs based on such CPS methods are associated with enhanced performance subsequently, as measured by tests of divergent skills. The results have been criticized because links with real-world creative achievements have been less clearly demonstrated. [*See* DIVERGENT THINKING.]

IV. THE NOMINAL–INTERACTIVE MODES DEBATE

In the 1950s and 1960s, a major research issue concerned the relative merits of nominal group brainstorming (NGB) and interactive group brainstorming (IGB). The research has suffered from serious differences of viewpoint and interpretation of empirical results. Historically, these can be regarded as attempts in the 1950s to refute Osborn's claims for interactive brainstorming, that then became conflated with debate on the relative merits of NGB modes over IGB modes of the technique.

A. The Erroneous Downgrading of Brainstorming

Osborn had consistently supported his claim for brainstorming by documenting quantitative evidence of superior idea generation outputs through use of the technique. Such a view could be simply tested by studying the relative merits of a brainstorming team against individuals engaged on the same task and provided with the same set of procedural instructions.

Evidence of this nature indicated that such individuals had outperformed the brainstorming group. This result heralded many other studies extending the range of other experimental conditions. The results were consistent for absolute number of ideas generated.

The evidence regarding the quality of ideas generated was far less clear. This is partly a consequence of difficulties in establishing satisfactory criteria for quality of ideas. Quality of ideas assessed as novelty and relevance turns out to be dependent on experimental contingencies. Sometimes researchers found in favor of the nominal group conditions, and less frequently in favor of interactive brainstorming. Overwhelmingly, however, if tested, the control groups left to deal with the challenge without brainstorming treatments were worse or nonsignificantly better than groups in brainstorming mode. [*See* NOVELTY.]

The empirical results showed that the interactive group condition never outperformed the nominal group version. This result was particularly clear-cut, across a range of conditions, for absolute number of ideas generated.

The confusion, however, lay in the interpretation of the results. What had been demonstrated conclusively was that under laboratory conditions, NGB was more productive in absolute numbers of ideas generated than was IGB. Osborn's colleagues pointed out in vain that NGB and IGB were no more than variants of brainstorming, and that the results actually confirmed that both variants were more productive in quantity of ideas than were control groups not engaged in brainstorming. This point has tended to be unremarked, and in less careful texts, the assumption is often stated or implied that brainstorming is an ineffective means of generating ideas.

B. The Superiority of Nominal Group Brainstorming

Some researchers looked for explanations of the superiority of NGB over IGB. It has been argued that real-life conditions might demand interaction among participants—to share information, for example. Studies showed that the established superiority of NGB was reduced, and sometimes eliminated, according to the type of problem being examined.

Under laboratory conditions, the absolute number of ideas generated within a period of time under NGB conditions have almost always exceeded those from IGB conditions, and have rarely failed to match or exceed them in quality, a more difficult characteristic to assess in an unambiguous and satisfactory fashion. In real-life conditions, the problems may require idea sharing and trust building, believed to require more interpersonal interactions. In making statements about the superiority of NGB over IGB, such qualifications should be kept in mind.

V. FIELD STUDIES

A. Selection of Techniques: Cultural Preferences

Following the lead of Osborn, most reports of industrial uses of brainstorming in North America have favored interactive variants that are versions of Osborn or Parnes–Osborn procedures. However, this preference may be partially explained in terms of culture. As is shown in Table I, such interactive approaches are favored in North America and in some Anglo-Saxon cultures. Other cultures, notably in northern Europe and Japan, have shown a preference for noninteractive approaches. [*See* CROSS-CULTURAL DIFFERENCES.]

B. Selection of Techniques: Practitioner Heuristics

One important research question concerns the matching of creativity-spurring techniques with various specific features encountered in practical situations. There is still a great deal of work to be done to provide satisfactory answers to the problem of technique selection. The difficulty arises because the most experienced practitioners tend to rely on a few favored techniques, applied to a limited range of problems. In time each practitioner builds up a set of rules of thumb or heuristics which are brought into play in the selection of a technique variant under a given set of conditions. These rules of thumb have some use in offering the less-experienced practitioner a shortcut to developing her own set of heuristics. A set of heuristics illustrating factors influencing the practitioner's selection of brainstorming is shown in Table II. Heuristics indicat-

TABLE I

Cultural Preferences for Brainstorming Modes in Industrial Applications

Interactive modes	Nominal group modes
• Parnes–Osborn CPS system (N. America) Sequences of divergent and convergent stages. IGB principles hold for the divergent stages. A typical version comprised the stages ⟨O⟩ ⟨F⟩ ⟨P⟩ ⟨I⟩ ⟨S⟩ ⟨A⟩ (objectives, facts, problem defining, ideation, solution seeking, and acceptance seeking).	• Metaplan (Germany, Scandinavia) Ideas are written on cards, one per card. Facilitation helps structure the material generated. The cards are assembled on large sheets of paper for classification and exploration purposes.
• Synectics (N. America) Training and facilitation help shape constructive team dynamics; novel ideas are sought through special processes, especially involving metaphors.	• Round-robin brainstorming (Germany) Ideas are written and exchanged sequentially to stimulate further ideas and extensions to existing ideas.
• MPIA System (UK) Modified version of Parnes–Osborn model for applications within industrial projects: ⟨M⟩ ⟨P⟩ ⟨I⟩ ⟨A⟩ (mess mapping, perspectives, ideas, and actions)	• KJ technique (Japan) Ideas on cards, and then patterns sought using intuitive powers of participant(s)
• Brain calming (India) Facilitated process to produce a meditative state prior to developing shared images and ideas	• NM technique (Japan) A kind of visual brainstorming in which images rather than words are developed

ing conditions which seem to be less favorable for brainstorming are summarized in Table III. [*See* HEURISTICS.]

C. Selection of Techniques: The Cocktail Approach

Surprisingly few studies have attempted to study industrial groups trained in creative problem-solving techniques tackling realistic problems in order to establish which techniques are effective in which kinds of circumstances. Research evidence supports and refines the heuristics developed by experienced brainstorming practitioners. The situation may call for the development of marginal extensions to current thinking, or call for more revolutionary breakthroughs. The participants may also have biases favoring marginal extension ideas or breakthrough ideas. They may also be trained or untrained, committed or distant from the problem, and with wide or narrow ranges of professional disciplines.

The cocktail approach recognizes that several techniques may be appropriate, each with some advantages and disadvantages. For example, nominal group approaches may generate more ideas in unit time, inter-

active approaches may be more supportive of the Osborn principles of hitchhiking or idea improvement, and of shared acceptance and ownership of ideas generated. The cocktail approach would involve the use of both interactive and nominal group variants.

The cocktail approach may be preplanned, or it may arise as a result of unplanned circumstances that cropped up during the brainstorming. For example, the experienced facilitator is sensitive to the level of speculation within an idea-seeking group. The ingredients available for her to mix a cocktail of techniques would include variants that increase the levels of speculation of ideas for a group producing ideas with little evidence of imagination. Conversely, the facilitator may wish to cool down a group that has become overheated. The ingredients, and some recipes for mixing them into a techniques cocktail, are shown in Table IV.

D. Key Findings from Practitioner and Research ("Field") Studies

The least contentious conclusion to be drawn from practitioner and field research studies is that a great deal of work is still required in order for us to understand

TABLE II

Problems Suited to Brainstorming, Illustrating Its Industrial Applications

General context	Features believed to favor brainstorming	Specific examples of topics successfully brainstormed
Concepts for new products, markets, and applications	Large numbers of ideas required from a range of people with different knowledge and experiences to increase search rationality	New uses for superadsorbent cellulose; new markets for noise detectors
Quality teams and suggestion schemes	Incremental improvements emerging based on tacit knowledge and power to act	Reduced defective products from a production line
Public planning events	Chance for all stakeholders to share in planning ideas	Stakeholders explore means of improving neighborhood security
Strategic planning	Helps prevent a team from targeting too narrow a focus, and from indulging in habitual responses	Strategic options open to an international corporation for managing its dealer network
Event management	Complex topic likely to require cross-fertilization of ideas ("hitchhiking")	Preparing for the unexpected surprises in an international athletics meeting
Business process reengineering studies	To fit within the more structured components where new ideas are required on targeted improvement areas	Simplifying the work flow through a factory manufacturing fine chemicals

TABLE III

Problems Less Suited to Brainstorming

General context	Features[a]	Specific examples
Problems with one or a small number of "correct answers"	The total search set does not need to be brainstormed	Who should win our *Sales Person of the Year* award? Should we form a joint venture with Ninjaworld, Inc.?
Extremely diffuse and complex situations[b]	No clear criteria for evaluating ideas produced	How to be number 1 in environmental friendliness; how to decide what to decide
Problems requiring a vocabulary of a highly specialized kind	Outsiders unable to contribute, so that expert assumptions are difficult to challenge	How to reduce the steps in the synthesis of alpha-bromo pheromones using the ethanol process
Problems requiring the compliance of people who cannot be involved in the idea generation or evaluation processes	More difficult to find collaborative or win–win ideas	How to persuade the government to drop product liability legislation
Decision-making focus	Skills at convergence more important than skills at divergence	Where should we locate our research laboratories?

[a]These features believed to hinder brainstorming are illustrative and not mutually exclusive for a specific problem type.

[b]These problems can be prestructured using the more complex systems incorporating brainstorming (e.g., see Table I for details of Parnes–Osborn and MPIA approaches).

TABLE IV
The Ingredients Available for Mixing into a Techniques Cocktail

Conditions	Possible ingredient introduced
The group has difficulty escaping from the kinds of mundane ideas expected in any discussion meeting	The facilitator invites the group to suggest "wouldn't it be wonderful" ideas, or the facilitator selects a more visual and nonverbal approach such as a metaphor to escape temporarily from the bounds of reality
The group postpones judgment enthusiastically and seems unable to connect fantasies back to real-world possibilities	The facilitator finds a way to refocus the group toward a better fantasy–reality balance; a switch to nominal group work "to tame down one of your favorite crazy ideas" may be tried
The group has a strong bias to incremental ideas, yet the situation requires a few breakthrough ideas	The facilitator introduces variants with decreasing levels of structure, beginning with reversals, "let's turn this idea upside down," leading to "try linking your idea to whatever comes out of this fortune cookie"

the practical scope and limitations of brainstorming as a technique for stimulating the creative ideas of individuals, and more specifically of idea-seeking groups.

Simplified versions of reality in controlled conditions have tended to favor nominal group versions. Yet the choice under practical conditions may be influenced by a range of other factors or contingencies. The cocktail principle sidesteps some of the unknowns in technique selection, but we have few well-grounded research principles on which to build a more satisfactory set of practical rules of thumb or heuristics.

VI. ELECTRONIC BRAINSTORMING

Since 1987, a substantial body of empirical data has emerged which has redirected attention to the possible mechanisms of electronic brainstorming processes. In some contrast with earlier studies, which originated in the psychological and educational domains, the work has originated in the literature of information science, diffusing into other fields, notably that of cognitive psychology and management science. Citation evidence shown in Table V suggests that interest in electronic brainstorming is growing. However, the citations of electronic brainstorming that mention creativity are declining in numbers over a period in which citations for creativity are showing a modest increase in numbers.

A. Similarities with the 1960s Studies

The growth in interest in electronic brainstorming in the 1990s reflects interest in the general issue of elec-

TABLE V
Creativity and Brainstorming Citations[a] since the Emergence of Electronic Brainstorming Studies (1987)

Period	Creativity citations	Brainstorming citations	Electronic brainstorming citations[b]	Brainstorming and creativity citations[c]
1987–1991	1,802	245	20	65
1992–1997[d]	2,469	309	44	50

[a] AB Inform database of 1,000 managerial and social scientific periodicals.
[b] Estimated by identifying citations including the terms "brainstorming" and "electronic." Marginally more citations were identified using the terms "brainstorming" and "computer" or "computers."
[c] Estimated by identifying citations including the terms "brainstorming" and "creativity."
[d] Estimated to November 1996.

tronic support systems for managerial functions. The intensity of effort indicates a surge of interest with similarities to the nominal–interactive debate of the 1960s. Both groups of workers have attended to the issue of technique superiority. Both found quantity of ideas generated to be the simplest reliable surrogate measure of performance, and acknowledged the difficulties in assessing creativity directly. It has proved a persistent methodological difficulty even to arrive at a widely accepted means of assessing the quality of brainstorming performance from examination of the ideas generated. Both sides agreed that when the operational conditions were carefully matched, nominal group methods generally generated more ideas in unit time than interactive group methods. This finding has been reached through studies that in the main have been conducted under controlled ("laboratory") conditions, with classical and unrealistic ideational tasks (e.g., consequences of an extra thumb, or new uses for a common object). In each era there has been a tendency among researchers and reviewers to infer from the undisputed evidence that nominal groups generation a greater quantity of ideas—that nominal groups are superior to interactive methods. As a consequence of this inferential leap, the persistent preference in some cultures for the interactive brainstorming mode is regarded as a regrettable departure from rationality.

B. Advances Made through Studies of Electronic Brainstorming

Studies of electronic modes of brainstorming have fueled interest in a research topic that was beginning to run out of steam. If Buffalo was the focal point of the earlier surge of interest, the annual *Hawaii International Conference on Systems Sciences* (HICSS) has arguably provided the dominant networking location of systems studies of electronic brainstorming since its founding meeting in 1967. HICSS has attracted the leading researchers in the new field, and its annual conference reports provide notice of the latest developments well in advance of publications in the scholarly journals.

In the 1990s, an important theme was that of establishing the performance capabilities of electronic brainstorming modes. The nominal versus IGB debate was revived as a spin-off of this preoccupation. By the late 1990s, the theme had been broadened to explore a wider range of issues arising from the mediation of individual and group behaviors by electronic sup-

TABLE VI
Issues Highlighted through Electronic Brainstorming (EB) Studies

Issue	Key features	Notes
Anonymity	Enhances EB (and NGB) by overcoming evaluation apprehension	Need for anonymity runs counter to the openness characterizing creative teamwork
Process satisfaction	EB mostly found more enjoyable than non-EB modes; some groups report lower levels of satisfaction for EB over non-EB modes	A "dislike of efficiency at expense of individual freedom" explanation has been proposed; this would also apply to IGB preferences over NGB modes
Blocking mechanisms studied	Production blocking; evaluation apprehension; social loafing (or free riding); motivational factors	More research required; both motivational and cognitive factors seem likely to play a part in explanatory models
Other factors requiring further study	Group size effects; group attitudes and involvement; training effects (group and facilitator); facilitation effects; task features and structuring; geographic features (proximal or distributed membership)	The available evidence suggests there are considerable interaction effects, making predictions of outcomes of specific sessions difficult; this in turn indicates benefits from experimentation using cocktail approaches

port systems. The unresolved issues are summarized in Table VI.

VII. CONCLUSIONS

After 50 years of applications, brainstorming continues to occupy a niche in the activities of practitioners and social-scientific researchers interested in structured approaches for stimulating creativity. There is no shortage of practitioner-oriented advice on brainstorming. The practical evidence is that the application of Osborn's rules leads to behavioral and ideational gains over outputs of conventional individual and group work. However, the application of these rules in nominal groups is even more efficient, and electronic versions may be yet more efficient in idea generation outputs.

Yet, efficiency may not be everything. Participants may prefer less-efficient, interactive modes. From a practical point of view the cocktail approach to design that includes various nominal and interactive techniques seems promising. Indeed, the Parnes–Osborn creative problem-solving model can be regarded as a framework for developing appropriate cocktails of techniques. Each of its stages provides a divergent phase in which brainstorming variants may be applied.

Does brainstorming offer convincing claims as a means of purposefully stimulating creativity? Such a question can only be indirectly answered by empirical means, in the absence of universally agreed upon operational and theoretical definitions of creativity. Some practitioners, particularly those interested in electronic support systems, may regard the matter of creativity as a side issue. The more pragmatic issue is whether brainstorming, or some cocktail of techniques, provides the users with a preferred means of idea generation, in individual or group applications.

Regardless of its contributions to our knowledge of creativity stimulation, brainstorming seems likely to play a role as a means of investigating the processes of idea generation at individual and group levels.

Bibliography

Anson, R., Bostrom, B., & Wynne, B. (1995). An experiment assessing group support, system and facilitator effects on meeting outcomes. *Management Science, 41*(2), 189–208.

Couger, J. D. (1995). *Creative problem solving and opportunity finding.* Danvers, MA: Boyd & Fraser.

Goodman, M. (1995). *Creative management.* London: Prentice Hall.

Parnes, S. J. (Ed.). (1993). *Sourcebook for creative problem-solving.* Buffalo, NY: Creative Education Foundation Press.

Rickards, T., & De Cock, C. (1994, Nov.). Creativity in MS/OR: Training for creativity—Findings in a European context. *Interfaces,* 59–73.

Stein, M. I. (1975). *Stimulating creativity: Vol. 2. Group procedures.* New York: Academic Press.

The Brontë Sisters

Charlotte Brontë (Currer Bell) 1816–1855

Emily Brontë (Ellis Bell) 1820–1849

Anne Brontë (Acton Bell) 1818–1848

Poets and novelists

Charlotte Brontë: *Juvenilia, Jane Eyre, Shirley, Villette,*
and *Collected Poems*
Emily Brontë: *Collected Poems* and *Wuthering Heights*
Anne Brontë: *Collected Poems, Agnes Grey,* and
The Tenant of Wildfell Hall

Joyce VanTassel-Baska

College of William and Mary

THE BRONTË SISTERS, taken as a collective, constitute the leading English novelists of the 19th century. The three sisters and their brother, Branwell, grew up in the small Yorkshire town of Haworth, children of the local curate. From very young ages, all exhibited a precocity for writing and drawing that was fueled by their mutual interest and need. Although writing in relative obscurity for a major portion of their brief lives, nevertheless, all three sisters had a major impact on the English novel and therefore on world literature. Charlotte's character of Jane Eyre *constitutes the earliest example of the independent woman in literature—resourceful, introverted, and clear in her standards and values regardless of external influences. Charlotte's portrayal of women as independent personalities was manifested through a forceful personal narrative style that*

Portrait of Charlotte Brontë. Used with permission from CORBIS/ Historical Picture Archive.

Copyright © 1999 by Academic Press
All rights of reproduction in any form reserved.

Portrait of Emily Brontë. Used with permission from CORBIS/Historical Picture Archive.

established her as one of the most brilliant novelists of her time. She is compared favorably with Thackeray and Dickens, and the only female writers from that period who rivaled her were Eliot, Austen, and her own sister Emily. Emily's Wuthering Heights *provides a brilliant depiction of human passion played off against the wilds of nature and the inevitability of fate. Her juxtaposition of the locale of the moors, so deeply known to her, with the hatred and revenge instincts of her characters provides an intensity rarely found in fiction of any era. Her style of first person narration, outside of a traditional time sequence, also presages more modern techniques. Anne's work, beside Charlotte's and Emily's, appears rather bland, yet her quiet piety seeps through in the use of prose and revealing language in both her novels. Choosing the vocation of governess and the setting of the moors, she combines two of her sister's novelistic devices yet emerges with her own original style in both* Agnes Grey *and* Tenant of Wildfell Hall. *While more muted than her sisters' works, Anne's contributions have been assessed as being major in their own way, and thus fulfilled her strong desire to do some good in the world before she left it, as noted by Chitham's 1991 biography of her.*

I. THE EARLY LIFE

The Brontë sisters in childhood shared solitude and seclusion, intelligent companionship, and intense family affection that also manifested itself in a love of animals. Struck early by family tragedy in losing a mother before Charlotte was six, and two older sisters shortly thereafter, the remaining children turned inward and to each other for survival and comfort. Tutored by their scholarly father from early ages and surrounded by stimulating books and magazines, the Brontë children lived in a created world. They reveled in a mysterious supernatural force fueled by the engravings of John Martin, the plays of Shakespeare, the writings of Byron and Sir Walter Scott, and the naturalistic setting of the Yorkshire moors. The Brontë children shared an important perspective on the power of creation. They created the imaginary worlds of Gondal and Angria, using Patrick Brontë's gift to Branwell of toy wooden soldiers as the stimulus for imaginative story development. The children created a language for the soldiers, a cartography of their landscape, and whole plays that gave the soldiers life. These intensely romantic influences in childhood affected the Brontës throughout their lives, always seeking for and finding excitement in the ordinary. Charlotte, Anne, Emily, and Branwell were all precocious and voracious readers from an early age as well as young practicing artists, pursuing assiduous copying of drawings that interested them, especially Bewick's woodcuts of British birds. The Brontë children also were well versed in history and the politics of the day, appropriating leading British figures for their plays and debating the motivations of such figures. Charlotte at age 14 drew up her list of life's works, an impressive 22 volumes, and exhibited a strong knowledge of literary form. Not only did the early reading, drawing, writing, and family discussions serve to stimulate the Brontës' imagination, it also provided intensive practice in literary and artistic traditions.

II. THE TAPESTRY OF WORK AND LIFE

The Brontës have attracted substantial scholarship about their lives and works. They have been the subject of multiple biographical studies, and have left substantial personal writings to be analyzed by scholars. They were also prolific in their published manuscripts, leaving enough work to trace the development of form, style, and content. In the case of Charlotte Brontë, even her juvenilia, the 22 little books she wrote in collaboration with her siblings, constitutes a separate area of study, still being deciphered by scholars.

The Brontës are an excellent example of writers not formally shaped by educational institutions. Modern writers can learn their craft through school and college programs, special seminars and workshops, and formal mentors, but none of these opportunities were available to the Brontës, who led sheltered lives mostly in the context of family. Social context and the historical period in which they lived also may have limited their talent development based on issues of gender and, with the Brontës, class as well.

Like other women of their respective historical periods, the Brontës lived with their birth family or at least nearby. The Brontës never lived anywhere else but Haworth during their entire lives except for one year in Brussels for Charlotte and less time for Emily.

Family provided the basis for friendships, education, and financial and social support. As a result, each writer was geographically grounded as well, accounting for the strong use of "place" in their work. Pollard cites Charlotte from her letters of a bleak Haworth: "No other landscape than a monotonous street — of woodlands, a grey church tower, rising from the center of a churchyard so filled with graves that the raxes weed and coarse grass scarce had room to shoot up between the monuments" (1988, p. 84).

The intellectual quality brought to bear in their work is consonant with the internal influences seen in other studies of creative people. Committed to a vision of an ideal, they worked on a statement of meaning. For the Brontës, the ideal conveyed a sense of justice for their female characters. Underlying all of their work was the curiosity to explore new forms and meanings and the concomitant persistence to work hard and alone, absorbing themselves in writing for long periods of time.

Overexcitability, an extreme desire to engage the personality in certain types of experiences, in intellectual, emotional, and artistic dimensions of their lives, was very apparent from an early age. The Brontës were described as high-strung, fascinated by ideas, and in-

Portrait of Anne Brontë. Used with permission from CORBIS/Historical Picture Archive.

terested in the artistic domain all their lives. A nervousness, possibly of genetic origin, strongly affected both Branwell and Charlotte. While both were outgoing and exuberant, they were prone to overstimulation. Branwell is said to have had a nervous breakdown while away at school, therefore accounting for his father keeping him closer to home. His overwrought tendencies tinged with romanticism led to his ultimate humiliation and demise at the hands of his tutee's mother, whom he adored and who would reveal his weakness toward her; Branwell's boyhood was viewed as self-indulgent, in manhood leading him to an addictive lifestyle culminating in an early death in 1848.

For the Brontë children, the act of creating stories and sharing them with each other built a closeknit partnership of the imagination wherein each child became a character and wrote from that perspective over a period of 16 years, according to Spark's 1993 review of essays. It was, however, the quality of emotional sensitivity that fueled their work, and transmitted that feeling into art. And clearly for each of them, real talent and insight were present in their ways of expressing meaning in written form.

According to Alexander's 1991 work on the analysis of the Brontë juvenilia, this juvenilia is the best record we have of the development of writing genius. More importantly, this early work was the basis for all of Brontës' adult work. The particular gift that allowed them to survive as leading writers of the Victorian period lies in their intensity of expression, and their ability to describe with powerful detail the settings, feelings, and the natural world that their characters inhabit. These qualities originated in childhood as a game of Gothic-type motifs for the Brontës to amuse and confound each other.

Great poetry and great art served as major influences on the Brontës' aesthetic sensitivity and creative bent. All of the Brontës painted and used visual art as an adjunct to their writing. Each worked diligently at illustration, exhibiting substantial powers of conceptualization though limited skill in execution. Gaskell notes in her biography of Charlotte, and later Emily, that the sisters were particularly interested in painting and the works of great artists as growing children. For example, Charlotte drew up a list of painters whose works she wished to see by age 13. Moreover, the painstaking reproductions of all three sisters helped to develop important skills of observation and analysis needed to become great novelists. They were especially fond of John Martin's engravings of lost cities of the ancient world, for they awakened in the Brontës a feeling for imagery corresponding to their appreciation of Byron's poetry.

The central motivating theme for all of the Brontës' works is a sense of justice for that which is morally and ethically right. She and her siblings had richer imaginations, greater drive, and more intellectual energy than other Victorians of the time, setting them apart from peers. The Brontës were also highly conscious of the role that writing played in their lives, stating that work was a wonderful companion. Through the assertiveness of Charlotte, all three women's work was published under the male pseudonyms of Currer, Ellis, and Acton Bell, only later to be revealed as written by women living in a remote area of the country.

For their time, the Brontës could also be considered feminist writers, especially Charlotte. From her early juvenilia to her mature novels, her female characters are vividly portrayed. In fact, all of the Brontë sisters' novels were considered too raw at first publication because of their passionate intensity and portrayal of women rebelling against the social norms of the times. The Brontës' continual quest for the real behind the conventional in female characters marks them as the most important fictional writers of their time on the plight of women, as noted by the recent biographies of the sisters by Frasier and Barker.

Charlotte Brontë in particular strove to overcome her sheltered experience in the act of writing by contemplating feelings or experiences related by other people until she was able to understand and describe them in writing. In a letter to a publisher, included in Gaskell's 1992 biography, she noted,

> Is not the real experience of each individual very limited? And, if a writer dwells upon that solely or principally, is he not in danger of repeating himself, and also becoming an egotist? Then too imagination is a strong, restless faculty which claims to be heard and exercised. (p. 184)

The Brontë sisters possessed a mental initiative that allowed them to compensate for and overcome limited experiences in the world.

III. RELATIONSHIP TO CREATIVITY

Evidence for the development of their creativity focuses on several variables, cited in VanTassel-Baska's 1998 chapter on creativity, all of which the Brontë sisters exhibited deeply. Informally, the Brontës developed the facilitating processes necessary to create original products in a given domain, such as fluency, a flair for novelty, insight and intuition, use of imagery, and an ability to use metacognitive strategies effectively. Their early childhood preoccupations clearly enhanced these process skills and honed them to high levels for use in adulthood. Their internal factors of creativity include intelligence; such personality variables as openness, intensity, and nonconformity; psychoticism; and mental energy. The Brontës all possessed these qualities and exhibited them in life as well as in their work. Their external factors of creativity include the powerful role of educational variables, strong family values that support the work, and the social-cultural context. While not all of these were favorable to the Brontës, by sheer perseverance their creativity prevailed over limitations in education and social environment. The role of the family was a strong positive influence on the development of the Brontës as artists. Not only was their father a strong intellectual and moral force in their lives, but they were each other's influences as supporters and critics of their evolving writing talents.

Personal catalysts for the Brontës that spurred them to creative heights appeared to include the adversity of coping with early deaths in the family of two sisters and a mother, the isolation of Haworth and the parsonage, their individualistic natures, and the natural setting of the Yorkshire moors.

Using life material as subject matter for character models and lived experience in the natural world, the Brontës evolved a unique form of communication for their period and in the process lived a creative life of the mind.

Bibliography

Alexander, C. (1993). That kingdom of gloom: Charlotte Bronte, the Annals and the Gothic. *Ninteenth Century Literature, 47*(4), 409–436.

Barker, J. (1994). *The Brontes.* New York: St. Martin's Press.

Chitham, E. (1991). *The life of Anne Bronte.* Cambridge, MA: Basil Blackwell.

Fraser, R. (1988). *The Brontes: Charlotte Bronte and her family.* New York: Fawcett Columbine.

Gardner, J. (1992). *The Brontes at Haworth, a life in letters, diaries, and writings.* London: Collins and Brown.

Gaskell, E. (1992). *The life of Charlotte Bronte.* London: Dent.

Piirto, J. (1992). *Understanding those who create.* Columbus, OH: Ohio Psychology Press.

Pollard, A. (1988). *The landscape of the Brontes.* London: Michael Joseph.

Spark, M. (1993). *The essence of the Brontes: A compilation with essays.* London: Peter Owens.

VanTassel-Baska, J. (1995). A study of the life themes in Charlotte Bronte and Virginia Woolf. *Roeper Review, 18*(1), 14–19.

VanTassel-Baska, J. (1998). *Excellence in educating the gifted* (3rd ed.). Denver: Love.

Business Strategy

Cameron M. Ford

University of Central Florida

Competitive Advantage An attractive position relative to competitors within the structure of a specific industry domain.

Creative Strategic Actions Discrete strategic activities that are judged to be differentiated (novel) and legitimate (valuable) by stakeholders representing particular strategic domains.

Developmental Change Influenced by the natural progression of an entity through a path-dependent sequence of states or stages.

Differentiation The process of creating novel product or service attributes that are valued by stakeholders.

Evolutionary/Revolutionary Change Influenced by selection and retention processes in the task environment that determine the viability of specific variations.

Intentional Change Influenced by goal formulation and decision processes that lead to the purposeful enactment of variations.

Routines Programmed or habitual responses to recurring situations (work procedures, regulations, decision rules, behavioral norms, habits, etc.)

Stakeholders People who can significantly affect or are significantly affected by the actions of an individual, group, or organization.

BUSINESS STRATEGY *is a broad term that encompasses the various processes, actions, and outcomes, internal and external to a firm, that determine business success. As an academic and practical discipline, business strategy considers processes underlying strategic decision making, the development and deployment of organizational resources and capabilities, the positioning of specific products or services in competitive markets, and attributes of business environments that influence a firm's success.*

I. OVERVIEW

A number of diverse analytical frameworks have been developed during the past 40 years to help business managers address the immensely complex task of conceiving, implementing, and monitoring an organization's strategy. The eclectic intellectual roots that underlie these frameworks have, unfortunately, produced considerable fragmentation and confusion among both academics and strategic managers. Academics have

Copyright © 1999 by Academic Press
All rights of reproduction in any form reserved.

developed valuable depictions of certain aspects of business strategy. Each of these unique insights has helped identify certain factors or conditions that can contribute to a firm's success. However, narrow and overstated theoretical positions have prevented researchers and practitioners from developing a holistic understanding of the dynamic processes that lead to sustainable competitive advantage.

One potential focal point for proposing a more integrated view of strategy may be creativity. Regardless of one's leanings with respect to available conceptions of business strategy, one issue on which all agree is the importance of differentiation as a key to long-term profitability and survival. Although the connection is seldom emphasized in the strategy literature, the concept of differentiation goes hand in hand with concepts such as novelty and creativity. Put simply, differentiation implies novelty within a particular strategic domain, and novelty is the most salient attribute of creativity. Therefore, one could argue that creativity serves as the basis for product or service differentiation. [*See* NOVELTY.]

This argument should be an easy sell to most managers. In fact, there seems to be growing consensus that creativity is becoming more important in strategic settings. Strategic domains are increasingly characterized by hypercompetition (rapidly escalating competition and strategic maneuvering), greater demands from consumers, and more emphasis on innovation. Companies must be able to rapidly develop and deploy creative products and services just to stay competitive.

In 1996 Barnett and Hansen captured the essence of this 21st-century plight by employing the metaphor of the Red Queen from Lewis Carroll's *Through the Looking Glass*. In the book, Alice notices that she appears to be stationary even though she is running a race. The Red Queen's response is that Alice must be from a slow world, because in a fast world one must run just to stay still. Applied to strategic domains, the metaphor describes how strategic actors rapidly introduce new products or services that increase the level of competition faced by rivals. Rivals are forced to respond in kind, thus increasing the competitive pressure on the first organization. This firm must retaliate by introducing new creations, and the cycle continues. Environmental factors such as information technologies and globalization have accelerated the pace and complexity of these competitive processes. These processes have elevated the importance of fostering creativity to one that should haunt all strategic managers. Where creativity may once have been a key to success, it now seems to be a prerequisite to survival. Given this, one would think that strategists interested in producing novel and valuable solutions would rush to adopt the contributions presented by the creativity literature. Similarly, creativity researchers could hardly find a better domain than business strategy to demonstrate the utility of their ideas. Yet neither discipline has sought out the other.

The purpose of this article is to suggest ways in which current views of creativity can enrich the study and practice of business strategy. Cameron Ford's 1996 theory describing creativity within complex, pluralistic business settings will be used to guide the description of three sequentially related change processes affected by creative strategic action: intentional change introduced by strategic actors, evolutionary and revolutionary change in strategic domains, and developmental change reflected in organizational learning processes. Ford's theory describes how intentional actions influence, and are influenced by, evolutionary change processes in social contexts. It proposes that three interrelated subsystems, namely actors (the sole source of creative variations), fields (defined as stakeholders who populate and effect the structure of a domain), and domains (defined as rules, language, customary practices, etc. that characterize a recognized area of action) together contribute to the occurrence and definition of a creative act. Fields and domains represent the social context that determines the consequences of actors' behavior. Actors serve as the sole source of variations (i.e., novel actions). The stakeholders who constitute a field and personify a domain serve to select among novel variations, retaining those deemed to be valuable elaborations of the domain and rejecting the others. The elaborated domain provokes learning and developmental change, which alter actors' patterns of thought and action. Based on their interpretations and capabilities, actors make decisions regarding subsequent behaviors within the domain, and so on. These events continue in an ongoing, evolutionary cycle of variation, selection, and retention processes. Describing the relationships among intentional, evolutionary/revolutionary, and developmental change processes may provide the basis for a more integrated understanding of creative business strategy.

II. CREATIVE STRATEGIC ACTION AS THE BASIS FOR INTENTIONAL CHANGE

Michael Porter, the leading industrial and organizational economist in the strategy field, developed an insightful critique of popular conceptions of business strategy. In his view, the basic unit of competitive advantage is the discrete activity. Porter argued that

A firm is a collection of discrete, but interrelated economic activities such as products being assembled, salespeople making sales visits, and orders being processed. A firm's strategy defines its configuration of activities and how they interrelate. Competitive advantage results from a firm's ability to perform the required activities at a collectively lower cost than rivals, or perform some activities in unique ways that create buyer value and hence allow the firm to command a premium price.

Porter further argued that the most important gap in our understanding of effective business strategy concerns the dynamic processes through which individual behaviors (i.e., discrete activities) produce competitive advantage. Current models of strategy are fairly effective at describing a firm's success at a given point in time (a cross-sectional, static analysis). However, our understanding of the intentional change processes that allow firms to *arrive* at an attractive competitive position (a dynamic, longitudinal process) is less well developed. Porter argued that we need to understand how strategic decision makers create sustained patterns of creative activity that enhance customer value (e.g., an innovative product or service), reduce expenses associated with a given activity (e.g., process innovations), or link previously unrelated activities (e.g., designing products to be easier to manufacture and service; using information technology to transmit orders between producers and retailers).

A theory of individual creative action embedded within an organization's strategic milieu may help explain how individuals' creative behaviors can be chan-

neled over time to produce advantageous competitive positions. As Porter noted, "the essence of strategy is choice." Ford's creativity theory can be usefully employed to address this challenge because it clearly frames creative behavior as a personal choice. He describes individual and contextual features that influence individual's choices between adopting routine solutions and enacting creative solutions in business settings. This theory clearly delineates two distinct management challenges associated with promoting creativity in organizations. The first is to create a context that promotes the desirability of pursuing creative behaviors. The second is to simultaneously reduce the salience and attractiveness of organizational routines. Only when creative options become relatively more attractive than routine options is it subjectively rational for individuals to choose the creative path. When a firm's management successfully creates these two conditions, its organization is likely to realize the pattern of creative discrete activities necessary to sustain an attractive competitive position.

There is a long history of studying intentional choice (and change) in the strategy discipline. This perspective emphasizes decision making and the development of elaborate goal hierarchies as the key processes through which strategic managers govern behavior throughout a firm. This strategic choice perspective focuses managers' attention on the goal of improving the fit between current environmental demands and firm capabilities. Strategic managers are agents responsible for employing vigilant, systematic and rational decision-making processes.

Unfortunately, strategic actors typically fall short of this ideal. Empirical research reveals that they are vulnerable to a variety of decision-making biases and cognitive limitations that influence the quality and creativity of their choices. Overall, this research demonstrates that strategic actors are not too different from the rest of us. Their choices are usually solution driven—multiple alternatives are rarely considered. Routine solutions with a track record of success are generally preferred because their outcomes are more certain and realized more quickly than creative alternatives. Furthermore, decision makers are slow to see changes in strategic environments, so their faith in the efficacy of tried-and-true alternatives tends to outlive its usefulness. Because of these prevalent patterns in strategic managers' choices, business organizations typically enact strategies that exploit current skills and, therefore, encourage adherence to previously successful routines. This makes a firm vulnerable to competitive pressures caused by creative competitors.

How can an organization encourage managers to consider a broad range of potential solutions, experiment, and take prudent risks? Put differently, how can managers articulate their strategy so that it simultaneously promotes creativity and constrains routines? In 1998, Frank Barrett provided some interesting insights by suggesting an analogy between jazz improvisation and business strategy. He describes a jazz piece as a special type of coordinating device that has minimal structures (i.e., chords and a melody) that allow maximum flexibility (i.e., improvisation). The song structure acts as an unquestioned (i.e., taken for granted) limitation that facilitates and constrains players' activities. This structure allows each player to know what the other players are doing so that there is a continuous sense of cohesion and coordination as action proceeds. Perhaps counter-intuitively, this structure frees players to entertain creative variations (improvisations) in their work. Players can elaborate on chords and scales in ways that suggest alternative paths. They cannot, however, ignore the contextual rules of the song.

In a similar vein, one can think of a business's strategy as a theme that simultaneously constrains and empowers organizational actors. Organizational actors can act in a coordinated fashion around the central goals and value premises of the organization. Simultaneously, when circumstances arise that temporarily shift an individual's role from supporting player to featured performer, the individual can feel free to improvise with novel ways of enhancing stakeholder value. There are important constraints on utilizing business strategy as a foundation for individual improvisation. It is obviously critical to have talented players who are willing to work together as the team. This suggests that human resource management practices (recruiting, selecting, training, appraising, rewarding, etc.) must effectively identify and develop the talents and motivations of individual players. Furthermore, a corporation's culture must reinforce and amplify the company's strategic intent before a firm can realize a high level of creative initiative. [See CORPORATE CULTURE.]

For individual players to enact a firm's strategy at the level of discrete activities, the strategy must have several characteristics. First, it must clearly communicate the firm's ultimate strategic intent, or terminal goal. This statement typically evokes domain domination or competitor conquest as a firm's overarching purpose. This clear statement of intention provides structure, like a song, that can align individuals' choices. It is also important for these intentions to be lofty, but broad. Low aspirations allow players to rely on tired, routine phrases. But high aspirations (e.g., to be recognized as a leading contributor to a domain), coupled with fear of being overtaken by competitors, create a sense of competitive urgency that requires individuals to embrace continual learning, risk taking, and innovation. Armed with a clear understanding of the rules of the game and a sense of competitive urgency created by high aspiration levels, individuals simply need guidance on the best means to achieve the firm's ends. Highly innovative firms often make the relationship between creative activities and strategic success explicit in their mission statements. For example, 3M is famous for its stated objective that 25% of its revenues every year must come from new products. A clear, urgent, procreativity strategy dramatically reduces the equivocation inherent in the choice between routine and creative behavioral options. Such a statement does two things. It inspires individuals to invest effort into creative alternatives that can induce intentional strategic change. But just as important, it creates an environment in which those who adhere to routines are subject to scorn and ridicule, like a jazz musician who relies on stock phrases.

To summarize, creative discrete activities are a major source of strategic differentiation and sustainable competitive advantage. Individual actors are more likely to choose creative over routine acts when the strategy of their firm clearly states the ultimate goals of the firm, creates high aspirations, and explicitly identifies creative activities as the means for achieving the firm's goals. As stated previously, it is important that an organization's culture, administrative systems, human resource management practices, and technology reinforce and amplify the articulated strategy.

However, identifying goals and empowering decision makers to introduce creative variations to a business's strategic domain does not ensure firm success. As Michael Porter stated in 1991, "Firm profitability can be decomposed into an industry effect and a positioning effect. Some firm successes come almost wholly from the industry in which they compete; most of their rivals are successful too!" Therefore, in addition to understanding intentional strategic change as a source of variations, it is also important to examine evolutionary and revolutionary change processes that reflect selection and retention processes in particular competitive domains.

III. EVOLUTIONARY AND REVOLUTIONARY CHANGE IN STRATEGIC ENVIRONMENTS

Evolutionary perspectives on strategy describe how strategic domains influence, and are influenced by, intentional actions. This perspective seeks to describe changes that occur over time in industrial domains and how domain characteristics influence the viability of strategic variations. Some researchers argue that organizations are relatively powerless in the face of evolving environments and must adapt themselves to the sweeping forces of industry evolution if they are to survive. In this view, strategic managers must conform to the changing requirements of their respective industries. Others suggest that individual firms can introduce variations that change the evolutionary path of an industry, effectively rewriting the rules of competition to favor the innovating firm. Whether a firm seeks to adapt or to influence the selection criteria of a particular strategic domain, strategic managers must be intimately familiar with the selection processes that affect their businesses.

The most important domain for strategic managers to consider is the consumer market. As discussed previously, achieving competitive advantage requires a firm to differentiate its offerings from those of competitors. Differentiation can result from intrinsic product or service characteristics (e.g., creative design features, high quality) or from relatively low prices for a given product or service (resulting from maintaining low operating expenses). The concept of differentiation is specifically bound to the judgments of consumers (stakeholders) representing a particular industry or market domain. The key attributes consumers use to evaluate the value of a variation (i.e., a product or service) are price, image, design, quality, and support. Based on their evaluations of these attributes, consumers will either select or reject specific market entries.

Thus, a firm can focus its creative energies on adding value in a variety of ways. Consumer recognition of low prices, impactful advertising, novel product attributes, unusual reliability, or adroit service could all add value and serve as a source of potential competitive advantage. Highly successful firms often focus on developing a reputation with respect to a primary attribute. For example, Wal-Mart is known primarily for low prices, Honda for high quality, and Rubbermaid for innovative designs.

Industries are typically characterized by long periods of incremental, evolutionary change. In such environments, firms must work to stay close to their customers. Strategic managers must understand the evolutionary trajectories of their markets and play their hand accordingly. However, there is a danger associated with waiting for customers to tell you what they want. Industries are occasionally transformed, or even destroyed, by the introduction of highly creative strategic variations. This often occurs when firms develop new ways of providing value that consumers have never considered. Countless products and services have created or redefined consumer preferences (overnight shipping, CD players, home improvement superstores, etc.). Introducing highly novel variations is incredibly risky. However, these variations can create revolutionary discontinuities that rewrite the rules of a domain. This process invariably favors creative actors and cripples inflexible incumbents.

However, undertaking discrete activities that create differentiation in consumer markets is a necessary, but not sufficient, condition for business success. Selection processes are also dependent on adhering to standards of legitimate (i.e., value adding) behavior upheld in a variety of strategically relevant domains. For example, government regulators may forbid the introduction of certain variations, or banks may not be willing to provide financing for creative proposals. This second strategic challenge emphasizes the need for businesses to be viewed as legitimate actors by a broad range of constituencies. It is beyond the scope of this article to provide an in-depth description of the selection processes enacted by the variety of stakeholders facing modern, global corporations. However, Table I lists some of the prominent domains with their respective stakeholders that commonly affect the selection or rejection of strategic initiatives. The table also provides speculations about the primary selection processes or criteria

TABLE I
Common Strategic Stakeholders and Their Primary Selection Criteria

Domains	Stakeholders	Primary interest
Markets	Consumers	Differentiation • Price • Design • Quality • Image • Support
Industry	Suppliers, competitors	Legitimacy achieved by conforming to industry practices
Technology sector	Consumers, competitors	Differentiation that conforms to the parameters of a dominant design
Financial sector	Banks, investors	Legitimacy based on an appropriate balance between variation risk and expected financial returns
Government sector	Government agencies, regulatory agencies	Legitimacy based on conforming to legal and regulatory requirements
Sociocultural sector	Community groups, activist groups	Legitimacy based on contributing to local interests or political causes
Human resource sector	Employees, unions, universities	Differentiation based on image/reputation and legitimacy based on adopting leading employment practices

employed by stakeholders in each of the listed domains. Navigating a creative strategic initiative through the complex mosaic of contrasting and competing preferences upheld by different stakeholders is an immensely complex challenge.

The extent to which a specific industry, with its respective range of stakeholders, is receptive to novel propositions is influenced by the evolutionary development of that industry. At the inception of a market domain, variations are introduced at a furious pace by firms hoping to conquer the market. However, most variations fail in emergent markets (i.e., they are not selected). The range of organizational offerings and practices narrows with time. As a market gradually becomes more established, stakeholders become better able to develop expectations of legitimate or acceptable behavior. Industries at this stage of evolution probably support a higher survival rate for creative variations (of course, the range of variations is restricted by the major tenets associated with the industry's dominant design). Once an industry stabilizes into a more mature market, stakeholder preferences and expectations may become particularly ridged. In these settings creative proposals may be seen as unreliable, untrustworthy, and unnec-

essarily risky. For example, electric cars have made little impact on the mature automotive industry because of restrictive government regulations, oil industry resistance, utility company shortcomings, incompatible technological standards, and lukewarm consumer interest.

So, in addition to focusing internally on the challenges associated with spurring purposeful creativity, strategic managers must look externally to the evolutionary dynamics in their environment. This challenge requires managers to learn how to play by the rules of many different task domains. It also suggests that managers consider creative ways of altering domain characteristics so that they might favor their firm's strategic competencies.

IV. DEVELOPMENTAL CHANGE THROUGH ORGANIZATIONAL LEARNING

A final strategic challenge returns the manager's attention to activities within the firm. In addition to the firm-level intentional and domain-level evolutionary/

revolutionary change processes discussed thus far, it is also essential to emphasize the importance of developmental change at the firm level. These processes support an organization's ability to create and sustain a pattern of creative discrete activities.

Probably the most relevant developmental processes for strategic managers to understand are those related to organizational learning. Organizational learning describes a path-dependent process through which individual actors accumulate, communicate, institutionalize, and utilize their knowledge to make sense of incoming information. Organizational learning results when actors analyze their strategic domains and utilize that information to modify current routines and practices. Continuously experimenting with new behaviors (e.g., creative endeavors) tends to broaden individuals' behavioral repertoires, thereby promoting organizational flexibility. This can help firms to initiate and adapt to both evolutionary and revolutionary change. Perhaps more important, continuous learning improves the odds that a firm can be an industry vanguard that shapes the selection rules of an industry. Alternatively, firms that promote adherence to inferior procedures and routines will learn little from their experiences. This retards a firm's development and limits its strategic flexibility. It is unlikely that these firms will be able to sustain the pattern of creative discrete activities necessary for sustainable competitive advantage; change within their strategic domains will simply pass them by. Such firms are at great risk in the face of rapid or discontinuous change.

Organizational learning also develops the ability of organizational actors to recognize the value of new information, assimilate it, and utilize it to productive ends. This ability makes it possible for smart firms to recognize subtle changes in the environment and better understand the implications of those changes to the firm. Organizations that lack this capacity will be slow to notice evolutionary changes in the domain and are likely to be ambushed by revolutionary change. Knowledgeable firms are better able to accurately evaluate selection processes that affect the viability of creative alternatives. These improved assessment skills reduce the risk associated with introducing strategic variations.

A critical point related to this developmental change process is that once a firm has fallen behind its competi-

tors in terms of its collective knowledge, it is unlikely to ever catch up. The reason for this is that knowledgeable individuals and organizations will glean more information from new experiences than a relative neophyte will. Given a common set of experiences, knowledgeable leaders will continue to expand their advantage over less knowledgeable competitors. This is why knowledge is often described as the only real source of sustainable competitive advantage. These processes are particularly important in knowledge-intensive domains such as telecommunications, pharmaceuticals, or software development. Often, the only way for laggard competitors to overtake their creative competitors is by instigating revolutionary change. This may level the playing field again. The odds of succeeding in revolutionary endeavors are slim, however. As a result, firms with limited intellectual resources are likely to fail in time.

V. SUMMARY: THREE CHALLENGES ASSOCIATED WITH MANAGING STRATEGIC CHANGE

Business strategy is better thought of as a journey fraught with unexpected twists, turns, and pitfalls rather than as a static position on a strategic map. This journey involves several different dynamic change processes. Strategic managers can seek to induce intentional change through the introduction of new products, services, processes, or organizational relationships. Managers must also be aware of the evolutionary trajectory of relevant domains that affect their intended strategies, and be prepared to adapt to discontinuities associated with domain revolutions. Finally, top management must invest in the intellectual resources that promote positive developmental change.

Each change process suggests a distinct management challenge. One challenge is to promote intentional change. This requires top management to articulate a clear, urgent, pro-innovation strategy. Managers must also spread their "religion" by developing cultural and administrative systems that reinforce and preserve the clarity of their strategic message. Most importantly, strategic managers must continually reinforce high aspirations. This tends to make adhering to routines relatively less attractive when compared to experimenting with creative variations. Strategic leaders need to stress the importance of deliberately exploring the limits of their firms' capabilities and embracing errors as a source of learning. Barrett quoted Keith Jarrett, a veteran jazz musician, who described the tension between seeking the comfort of playing stock phrases and pushing oneself to higher levels: "The music is struggle. And what most leaders are the victim of is the freedom not to struggle. And then that's the end of it. Forget it!" In the context of strategic management, Jarrett's message bluntly warns that once organizational actors believe they have reached their aspirations, they are unlikely to move beyond their stable routines. Constantly pushing the boundaries of organizational and personal aspirations is probably the most important motivational challenge facing strategic managers.

Evolutionary and revolutionary change obviously cannot be managed in the same way as intentional change. Strategic managers, nevertheless, can play a critical role in the way strategic domains are interpreted and enacted. Strategic managers must determine how the selection processes of various domains are likely to affect a firm's activities. They must also select strategic domains within which to compete. The most fundamental question in corporate strategy is, "What business should we be in?" Mergers and acquisitions permit quick entry into desirable settings, and divestitures allow firms to flee when domains look bleak. The most promising strategic management technique with respect to gauging and influencing environmental change is cooperative stakeholder management. Strategic managers need to assess the extent to which various stakeholder groups contribute to a firm's level of environmental uncertainty. This analysis should lead to a prioritization of the strategic importance of different stakeholders. For those stakeholders that are deemed highly influential, strategic partnering tactics may be employed. These tactics can improve the creativity of a firm's strategy in three ways. Strategic partners may be an important source of creative ideas. For example, firms often enter joint R&D efforts with competitors or invite customers to work on product design teams. Partnering can also improve a firm's understanding of the selection criteria employed within a particular strategic domain. For example, serving on community boards or committees can help individuals understand local interests and concerns. Finally, cooperative tactics can be used to influence the selection processes in a strategic domain. For example, including labor leaders on boards of directors or creating other joint management/employee committees may make organized labor more receptive to creative management proposals. These tactics can positively contribute to intentional creativity as well as a firm's ability to influence the evolution of stakeholder preferences.

Developmental change requires strategic managers to invest in intellectual resources and develop flexible administrative systems. Successfully meeting this challenge provides a firm with a broad repertoire of strategic options that can be quickly deployed to meet new challenges. Top managers must create a culture that encourages individuals to undertake creative actions as a means of improving their understanding of ambiguous strategic environments. Widespread experimentation throughout an organization will produce diverse information, knowledge, and capabilities that can support multiple perspectives and creative approaches. When lessons are distributed via information technologies, cross-functional teams, and so on, creative insights and enhanced capabilities are likely to result. It also does not hurt to hire talented individuals and to invest in various forms of more traditional employee training.

By recognizing and embracing the challenges associated with intentional, evolutionary/revolutionary, and developmental change, managers can enhance their odds of achieving the holy grail of business strategy: sustainable competitive advantage. However, *all* of these challenges must be addressed. Failing to attend to one will weaken a firm's ability to respond to the other two. Also, these challenges are not battles to be won, but unending journeys to be traveled. Creative strategic management can allow a firm to choose its own path.

Bibliography

Barnett, W. P., & Hansen, M. T. (1996). The red queen in organizational evolution. *Strategic Management Journal, 17*, 139–157.

Barrett, F. J. (1998). Creativity and improvisation in jazz and organizations: Implications for organizational learning. *Organization Science, 9*, 605–622.

Ford, C. M. (1996). A theory of individual creative action in multiple social domains. *Academy of Management Review, 21,* 1112–1142.

Harrison, J., & St. John, C. (1996). Managing and partnering with external stakeholders. *Academy of Management Executive, 10,* 46–60.

Hitt, M. A., Keats, W., & DeMarie, S. M. (1998). Navigating in the new competitive landscape: Building strategic flexibility and competitive advantage in the 21st century. *Academy of Management Executive, 12,* 22–42.

Mintzberg, H. (1988). Generic strategies: Toward a comprehensive framework. *Advances in Strategic Management* (Vol. 5, pp. 1–67). Greenwich, CT: JAI Press.

Porter, M. E. (1991). Towards a dynamic theory of strategy. *Strategic Management Journal, 12,* 95–117.

Lewis Carroll
(AKA Charles Lutwidge Dodgson)

1832–1898

Writer

Author of *Alice in Wonderland* and *Through the Looking Glass*

Delmont Morrison

University of California, San Francisco

CHARLES DODGSON was a mathematician and logician who taught at Oxford University, England, from 1851 to 1892. Under the name of Dodgson he wrote on mathematics and symbolic logic. He met Alice Liddell when she was 4 years old. On July 4, 1863, while on a rowing outing on the Isis river with Alice and her sisters he told the story of a little girl who went down a rabbit hole and had many adventures. Alice was 10 years old and Charles was 30. As a gift to Alice, Charles wrote and illustrated the story for her. In 1865, under the name Lewis Carroll, he published it as Alice's Adventures in Wonderland. *Although Charles had been a frequent visitor to the home, three years after the boat outing Mrs. Liddell did not allow him to have social contact with her daughter again. The first book on Alice was a popular success and made Lewis Carroll famous. Six years later he wrote* Through the Looking Glass *and his fame as a fantasy writer for children was secure. Lewis Carroll's works are classics of nonsense, parody, and satire, and have contributed to popular awareness such characters as Humpty Dumpty and the Mad Hatter. Charles Dodgson is considered a pioneer in early photography. Although he took many pictures, including*

Lewis Carroll—Self portrait.

Copyright © 1999 by Academic Press
All rights of reproduction in any form reserved.

famous people such as Lord Tennyson, he is best known for his portraits of little girls. In the final part of his life Charles Dodgson turned his attention and talent to books on logic. His final book, Symbolic Logic I and II, *completed around 1894–1898, is considered by some authorities as a significant contribution to the study of logic at that time. He was finishing the second part of this book when he died of pneumonia at the age of 66.*

I. EARLY YEARS

Charles Dodgson came from a family with strong ecclesiastical traditions. His father was a clergyman. His great-great-grandfather and great-grandfather were both clergymen and the latter had been a Bishop. The family was pious and took life seriously. However, Charles, the eldest son, showed early signs of irreverent humor. During his first 11 years the family lived in relative isolation. His playmates were his sisters. There were two sisters before Charles, and five girls and two boys afterward. Perhaps reflecting some family stress, seven of the children, including Charles, *stammered.* Charles began writing family magazines when he was 13 and published a short humorous story when he was 23. His early writings show the same parody and humor found in his adult works, and some, such as poems in the family magazine *Mismatch,* appear in his later writings such as *Jabberwocky.* Although he appears to have been happy at home at age 14 he entered public school at Rugby. This experience was a very unhappy one for Charles and contributed to his general aversion to young boys that continued throughout his lifetime. In contrast to other people's positive memories of him as a boy, Charles always viewed himself at that age in very negative terms. While at Rugby he maintained close ties to his brothers and sisters and wrote material for them that later appeared in *Alice in Wonderland* and *Through the Looking Glass.*

II. OXFORD

Charles demonstrated considerable skill in mathematics and in 1851 he entered Christ Church, Oxford, as a student. He spent the rest of his life there. In keeping with the family tradition he entered Oxford with the plan to be ordained. However, his diary entries indicate considerable ambivalence regarding the matter. He was ordained a Deacon but finally in 1862 he made the official decision to not take the priestly orders.

As faculty at Oxford he had difficulty as a teacher probably due in part to his stammer. His diary entries indicate his interest in theater and he published parodies in various magazines under the name of Lewis Carroll. During his early years at Oxford he also developed an interest in photography that he maintained for 25 years. At the time photography had been in existence for 17 years and Charles was 24 years old. He was a pioneer in this new field and he published articles and stories about the subject. Charles had public exhibitions of his photographs and he was invited to write a review of the 1860 London Photographic Society exhibition.

III. PHOTOGRAPHY AND ALICE

In 1855 Henry George Liddell became the Dean of Christ Church Oxford. He arrived with his wife, a son, Harry the eldest, and three daughters, Lorena, Alice, and Edith. Soon after the Liddells arrived, Charles met the children and was soon photographing them. He became a frequent visitor to the Liddell's home, apparently to see the children for there is little indication that he developed a friendship with either parent. His contact with the girls was frequent but his relationship with Alice grew over the years. His photographs of her, such as Alice as a young beggar, indicate his complex feelings for her. It was on an outing with the three sisters that he first told the story of Alice's adventures underground. During that same year something happened because he fell out of the good graces of Mrs. Liddell. Three years later he seldom saw Alice again. Although he now had no contact with her he wrote *Through the Looking Glass,* which is the further adventures of Alice. For lack of documentation, the reasons for the disruption of his relationship with Alice are not well established. However, there is some evidence that Charles was interested in eventually marrying her.

The two stories inspired by Alice are at one level descriptions of growing up in a dream world inhabited by characters who are animals and humans who are unpredictable. In her encounters Alice reflects common

Portrait of Alice Pleasance Liddell.

ment or the theater. He had a bag of gifts and objects for magic tricks to gain an initial contact and he frequently gave a copy of his books on Alice as a gift. His many letters to little girls during this time are full of the nonsense found in his books, but frequently are vaguely concealed love letters full of sexual flirtations. He seldom entertained an adolescent girl or a mature woman. There is little to indicate that he had sexual contact with any female. He found young boys repulsive and never had a relationship with one. Photography allowed Charles to hold the idealized image of his girl friends permanently and at one time he had a list of 107 little girls who were photographed or to be photographed. Suddenly in July of 1880, what had been a long standing passion in his life was given up. With little explanation in either his diaries or his letters at the time, Charles took no more pictures.

IV. PARALLEL THOUGHT

One of the most interesting aspects of Charles Dodgson's personality is how he managed and generally succeeded publicly, if not internally, in keeping the imaginative side of his personality, which appealed to his little girl friends, separated from his more linear, logician side. Although the use of a pseudonym in published writings was not uncommon in the Victorian Period, in Charles's case it would seem that Dodgson and Carroll genuinely reflected aspects of one personality that functioned in two different affective styles: the evocative images in the Alice stories and the dry formulas of symbolic logic.

As a student at Rugby and Oxford, Charles demonstrated outstanding scholarship and talent in mathematics, classical humanities, and divinity. However, as a teacher in his chosen field of mathematics and logic it would appear that he was less than inspiring to his students and he gained little satisfaction from it. There are also indications that he found giving sermons a burden. The liveliness of his thought expressed in his fantasies for children was not expressed in his lectures and sermons. Perhaps his lifelong problem with stuttering accounts for some of this.

His early years at Oxford are noteworthy for his publications of nonsense and parody rather than logic. For example, after becoming secured in 1851 as a life

sense in an illogical and often frightening context. The jokes are always based on faulty syllogisms. Whatever the reason for his failure in his relationship with Alice, Charles Dodgson spent a great deal of his time after this entertaining little girls and photographing them. The photographs of the girls were often in various costumes that he provided, but frequently the photographs were of nude little girls. Most of the nude photographs have been destroyed, and there were many of them, but four have survived. That these were images of childhood innocence and purity is difficult to support, especially the reclining nude of Evelyn Maud Hatch.

His affection for little girls was captured in photography and Charles spent a great deal of his time in meeting them during vacations at the seashore, some friend's house, or on the train. He always obtained consent from the parents and took great delight in entertaining these prepubescent friends at his apart-

member at Oxford, his major works beside the two Alice stories are *Phantasmagoria and Other Poems, The Hunting of the Snark,* and *Sylvie and Bruno.* The first two continue the exploration of fantasy found in the stories of Alice while *Sylvie and Bruno,* published at the time he was ending his career at Oxford, is a mix of fantasy and moral tale. Whereas the other children in *Sylvie and Bruno* are presented in ideal terms and generally not burdened with the more common childlike emotions, one boy, Uggug, is a hideous fat boy whose major function in the book is to be unpleasant. The book itself was a failure and is structurally unsuccessful in the attempt to combine a fairy tale with a moral message regarding the importance of Christian love. The story, combined with Charles's diaries and letters, is consistent in establishing the negative image that he had of young boys. Passages from the book indicate that when Uggug looks at Sylvie in a sexual way he becomes even more animal-like than usual.

At the time he was writing *Sylvie and Bruno,* Charles published several mathematical works under his own name. He had been teaching mathematics for 22 years. Three years later, in 1879, he published under his own name *Euclid and His Modern Rivals.* The years 1880–1881 appear to be important for Charles because he gave up his photography and lecturing. His letters and diaries from this time reflect a return to his long-lasting interest in word games and logic. For approximately the last 12 years of his life there is little original work on fantasy and Charles turned his attention to the problems of logic. He would not answer mail addressed to Lewis Carroll. There is considerable evidence that Charles found logic as a source of joy and order with the significant feature that it will "give cleanness to your thoughts and see your way through a puzzle," to quote from the preface to one of his works on logic. The result of his efforts at this time was *A Game of Logic,* which was written for the general reader, and his more ambitious project, *Symbolic Logic, Part I.* Charles thought that *A Game of Logic* was written in such a style to appeal to children whereas *Symbolic Logic* addressed advanced logical concerns regarding paradoxes. *Symbolic Logic* went through four printings in his lifetime. He was writing *Symbolic Logic, Part II* when he died, and a manuscript of that book has been recently found. Although none of his contemporaries thought that his contributions to logic were exceptional, recent evaluations by such authorities as Bertrand Russell indicate that he was an original thinker who advanced logic beyond its Aristotelian limits to the methods of modern thought.

V. CONCLUSION

As a boy Charles Dodgson demonstrated a talent in mathematics and a joy in word games, puzzles, and nonsense. Up until age five his only playmates were four younger sisters. He saw himself as an undesirable boy and although he demonstrated more than a usual amount of affection for prepubescent girls, he disliked boys that age and avoided their company. Charles Dodgson–Lewis Carroll was characterized by a unique synthesis between fantasy and logical thought in a personality where concepts of self were rigidly separated and unavailable to conscious exploration. As Lewis Carroll, Charles attempted to establish affectionate relationships with very young girls in an effort to express the more affect-laden images of his thought. In his creation of images growing up in the Alice stories he combined fantasy and logic as they had never been combined before. Interrelated with his affection for the real Alice Liddell and romantic images of that ideal was his lifelong passion for photography. Combining his interest in science and technology, as well as allowing him a socially acceptable avenue for his erotic wish to possess prepubescent girls, photography gave Charles Dodgson a great deal of aesthetic and erotic pleasure. His creative efforts in his stories for children, really little girls, and his photographs of little girls are instructive examples of the contribution of conflict to creativity. These two passions, love of little girls and photography, dominated his early life. As he grew older he returned to the study of mathematics and symbolic logic. He pursued these with passion and took pleasure and comfort in the order and rules of that mode of thought. However, the unique creativity of his thought found expression in the irrational and illogical stories he wrote for an imagined little girl who was to never return his love.

Bibliography

Carroll, L. (1936). *The complete works of Lewis Carroll.* New York: Modern Library.

Carroll, L. (1953). *The diaries of Lewis Carroll* (R. L. Green, Ed.). London: Gassell and Company.

Carroll, L. (1979). *The letters of Lewis Carroll* (M. N. Cohen, Ed.). New York: Oxford University Press.

Cohen, M. (1996). *Lewis Carroll: A biography.* New York: Knopf.

Phillips, R. (1972). *Aspects of Alice.* London: Gollancz.

Morrison, D., & Morrison, S. L. (1991). The voyeur and his muse: Lewis Carroll and "Alice." *Imagination, Cognition and Personality, 10*(3), 213–229.

Paul Cézanne

1839–1906
Painter

Pavel Machotka

University of California, Santa Cruz

CÉZANNE is a painter of timeless accomplishment, radical innovation, and inestimable importance for the art of the 20th century. Paradoxically, the work by which he influenced those who followed was very different from the painting he had intended to do as a young man. His initial aims were to represent events, mostly imaginary and highly emotional; his achievements, however, were paintings that were based on close observation of visual reality, complex yet resolved, and revealing a simultaneous interest in the structure of things and the richness of perception. This change seemed more a matter of internal development than of external constraints, and was due to a change in the importance of perception, rather than imagination, as the starting point of his work.

I. CHILDHOOD AND ADOLESCENCE

To understand how Cézanne created, ideally we should emphasize in equal measure the era in which his early ideas were formed, the teachers and contemporaries who influenced him, and the early experiences which determined his character. We should also look at the makeup of his adult personality, the material support available to him, the conditions under which

he worked, and the specific talents that gave his work its form and quality. Alas, no account of a painter is

Paul Cézanne: Self-portrait before a pink background, c. 1875. Used with permission from Erich Lessing/Art Resource, NY.

Copyright © 1999 by Academic Press
All rights of reproduction in any form reserved.

that complete, and no interpretation of creativity that firm; in Cézanne's case, although there is much information on his adult life and the context in which he developed and worked, the record of his childhood is incomplete. And talent, of course, is always difficult to analyze.

Nevertheless, we do know something about his childhood and considerably more about his adolescence. Born in 1839 in Aix-en-Provence, France, as the first of three children of Louis-Auguste Cézanne—a self-made man who rose from hatter to banker by dint of honest, hard work—and Anne-Elizabeth Aubert, who later became Louis-Auguste's wife, he held his father's character and practical attainments in awe but resembled his mother in temperament: lively, and possibly nervous and depressive. He received an excellent education in the public schools of Aix, and at the age of 13 formed a close friendship with an equally sensitive and intelligent young man who later became the novelist Emile Zola.

We must note right away that his temperament was not suited for what was expected of him, that is, to follow in his father's footsteps—even with the refinement of law training—and we would be right to suspect that his attitude toward his father was a mixture of admiration and rebellion. Both aspects of the attitude ultimately bear on his work. During his adolescence, however, the friendship with Zola (and a third companion, Baille) was formative, and crucial emotionally and aesthetically. Rewald, on whom all the biographical information here is based, writes,

> The three friends found themselves closely drawn together by a number of unusual interests and ambitions, and at school they came to be known as the "inseparables." They took longs walks together over the countryside around Aix, and passed the time fishing, swimming, and reading verses by Homer and Virgil. . . . Artistic questions particularly absorbed them and they discussed everything that was on their minds, persuading each other that they had a great and extraordinary destiny. Zola wrote poetry which he read to his friends, and they in turn wrote verses. Zola found Cézanne's more poetical than his and encouraged him to continue his efforts. (Rewald, 1976, p. 76)

The friends in fact also wrote three-act comedies in rhyme, and pretended to hunt; but according to Zola's later notes, "The hunt always ended in the shade of a tree, the three of us lying on our backs with our noses in the air, talking freely of our loves. And our loves, at that time, were above all, the poets."

Even such a brief reconstruction of the adolescent years says much about the conditions of Cézanne's future work. There is the love of the beautiful countryside, the capacity for intense friendship, the apartness from the crowd—and the intellectualized handling of adolescent concerns—the capacity for intense artistic work, and of course the dawning decision to dedicate oneself to art. What Zola and Cézanne understood by art, and by its purpose, was not yet divided into the visual and verbal. Art served to express the emotional concerns already evident to them: love, romance, disappointment, remorse, guilt, and even death.

They resolved that if they succeeded in becoming artists, these would be their subjects. Real love would be postponed for now; it would be achieved only through becoming an artist. One is reminded of Freud's comment on the role of wishes in creating art: the artist creates because his unfulfilled wishes drive him, and later, when he has succeeded in expressing them in an artistic way, reality may grant them. As a description of Cézanne's and Zola's initial motives—of their direct sublimation of personal concerns into artistic ones—this is quite apt; but we shall see that motives change as artists grow, and that Cézanne grew into a different artist than he had foreseen.

II. ATTEMPTING TO MAKE A DECISION

When Cézanne was 19, Zola left for Paris to become an artist, and the two friends expected to join him after taking their exams. Cézanne in fact took three years to get away (Baille never did), and the hesitations of those three years, and the correspondence he kept up with Zola, help us reconstruct his psychodynamics. Zola tried to bolster Cézanne's self-confidence and kept encouraging him to come to Paris. Cézanne instead studied for his baccalaureate exams, and to satisfy his father entered law school. This failed to interest him; increasingly he dreamed of painting, and enrolled in the free drawing academy of Aix, where he at least studied from plaster casts and the living model. He also became acquainted with the work—some of it landscape work—of Provence's painters. Eventually his father came to understand that painting was what Cézanne most wanted to do, gave him a monthly stipend, and went with him to Paris to help set him up. It should be noted that Cézanne, fearing his father's reaction, never confronted him openly, and that without the latter's unstated understanding and ultimately lifelong material support, would never have become a painter.

In the intervening correspondence Cézanne often gave vent to his robust poetic talent and inadvertently preserved for us a record of his inner conflicts. Writing spontaneously, in addition to the chatty news, he might begin or end with a poem. In one poem, Hannibal feels guilty before his father for having stayed up and caroused instead of defending his country; in another, a young man lost in the woods is about to be rescued by a beautiful woman who bares her breast to him, only to turn into a skeleton as he attempts to kiss her. Pleasure seemed always alloyed with pain, guilt, or even death. Cézanne began his artistic career, then, with more than the usual anxiety about love and a more than usual fear of his father; he also went to Paris with some training in art and acquaintance with Provençal painters, and the conception of art as predominantly narrative.

He was also easily discouraged; he returned home after five months and resigned himself to working in his father's bank. This, too, made him utterly unhappy, and a year later he was back in Paris. He returned to the studio where, without instruction, he could work from the model. There he met some of the young painters who, 12 years later, would exhibit together and receive the nickname "Impressionists." Monet and Renoir, nearly the same age, would eventually become his friends, and Pissarro, 10 years older, would become friend, supporter, and admirer—not a trivial feat in the early years—and later embody and communicate a devotion to landscape painting when they came to paint side by side.

III. EARLY DEVELOPMENT AS A PAINTER

For the first 10 years or so of his painterly career Cézanne's subject were mostly narrative but his style varied considerably. The narrative pictures were quite unlike his mature work: religious scenes alternating with sexual ones, to be replaced with an orgiastic banquet, a lugubrious picnic scene, an autopsy, or a murder. The mood might be straightforwardly narrative or ironic; within the composition there might be a bald man looking on, resembling the Cézanne of the time (see *Pastorale,* Figure 1). Many paintings, though not all, are dark in tonality, and equally many depend on an interplay of slashing diagonals for their organization. In some respects his subjects appeared to continue the concerns he had shared with Zola when they were 16, but they also served to illustrate stories, fables, and myths; the two purposes were closely joined.

What is remarkable about the early paintings are two qualities. One is their uncommon verve—their utter frankness and originality. No painter of his time painted anything so risky and occasionally so blatant, or so free of the constraints of previous painting authority. The other is the evidence they give—when one sees the originals, rather than reproductions—of a search for a self-consistent style. Over 10 years the style changed radically, sometimes abruptly, but within each painting it remained consistent. Even in the face of the apparently turbulent subjects, which seemed closely connected with the tenor of the fantasies Cézanne had written out in his poetry, he seems to have been able to exert some degree of painterly control.

Nevertheless—and we reach the crux of the psychodynamic question regarding the evolution of his style and his ultimate discovery of a mode of working that was as satisfactory as it was successful—his most successful paintings were done from observation. Portraits (*Louis-Auguste Cézanne, père de l'artiste, lisant L'événement* of 1866, *Achille Emperaire* of 1867–1868) and still lives (*La pendule noire* of 1867–1869) can be counted as the masterpieces of this first decade, and several landscapes are calm and well realized. What they have in common is a mode of working—they are no longer based in imagination—and a fully realized form: a well-balanced composition free from excessive tensions.

IV. PISSARRO AND THE OBSERVATION OF NATURE

Clearly Cézanne's best painting would depend on harnessing his powerful temperament by observation.

FIGURE 1 Cézanne, *Pastorale*, ca. 1870. Musée d'Orsay, Paris. Used with permission from Erich Lessing/Art Resource, N.Y.

We do not know to what degree he was aware of this; we can say at least that in his old age he was quoted by a young friend (Gasquet) as saying that his only method afterward was "hatred of the imaginary." We can assume that he would have been confirmed in this development by painting in Pissarro's vicinity, between 1872 and 1874, sometimes side by side in the open air. Pissarro taught and exemplified a patient observation of nature, and Cézanne even began to record the effects of light—in the manner of the colleagues who would hold their first exhibit in 1874 and receive their nickname from Monet's painting, *Impression, Sunrise*. We

may conclude that not only would Cézanne be supported by Pissarro in valuing observation over fantasy, but that he would see the expressive possibilities of landscape.

In the years to follow he would give up the effects of light but continue to observe attentively. A certain conservatism (which could be observed much later in his political views), shown in his admiration for the art of the museums, made him turn away from his colleagues' flocculent innovations and return to portraying the solidity of things. Paradoxically, this conservative bent created his most radical innovations.

It must also be added that Cézanne never gave up painting from imagination altogether; although by the mid-1870s he no longer painted scenes of sexuality and violence, he did replace them with bather compositions, male or female. He remained deeply attached to this subject, and in fact by the end of his life painted almost as many bathers as landscapes; they were followed by still lives and portraits. With some exceptions, the bathers, too, are held in somewhat less esteem than the later work done from observation, and thoughtful critics have asked themselves why. Fry presumed that Cézanne, unlike, for example, Titian, simply did not have the capacity to summon up a serviceable image of the human body. But we may suppose as well that his imagination was constrained by the anxiety which it evoked, and in this connection we may remind ourselves of the evidence of his early poetry, in which impulse so easily arouses guilt or evokes punishment.

For Cézanne, then, creating came to rely on a broader kind of sublimation: in part the sexual and aggressive impulses were turned toward the more gentle sight of nudes bathing—in part the sheer vigor of his energies was directed toward passionate observation. (That he became deeply attached to observing is shown in part by comparisons of his landscape paintings with the views that served as their motifs. The correspondence is surprisingly close—Machotka's book shows a large number of them in color—and indicates attentive observation as well as an ability to capture his perceptions in a unified and self-consistent manner; see Figures 2 and 3.) One may also say that Cézanne's successful creating meant finding a "conflict-free" sphere in which to work, that is, to work in the pleasurable sphere of observation rather than the ambivalent one of expressing fantasy.

V. MATURE STYLES

The concepts of need (as in the need to express fantasy or the need for fame) and defense (whatever one does to avoid anxiety brought on by needs) are necessary for understanding a painter's psychodynamics, but they are not sufficient. One must also note certain aesthetic purposes, which are fully conscious and less reducible to personal organization. In Cézanne's case

FIGURE 2 Photograph of site in Figure 3 (Machotka, 1996).

there is certainly a search for a consistent style—a style that would be adequate to his subject matter, to the needs of his compositions, and to his perceptions. One must mention all three purposes, because it is perhaps for meeting them all so well, for the sense, as Fry (1989, pp. 83–84) puts it, that "the smallest product of his hand arouses the impression of being a revelation of the highest importance," that he is known, admired, and indeed revered.

During the first 15 years of his career as a painter, Cézanne's search for style was serious and often successful, but neither linear nor smoothly progressive. Toward the end of the decade of the 1870s, however, it culminated in a new method of laying down touches of paint in parallel to create a surface at once lively and controlled, one in which every part of the canvas responded in some manner to every other part. At its inception, the method seemed useful for controlling the vividness of his imaginative subject matter, but by 1879–1880 he came to use it in still lives and landscapes, above all to order his perceptions of the motif's complexities. He was justly proud of his achievement and somewhat unreasonably protective of it, and he resented Gauguin for adopting it for his own painting in 1881. Because short touches laid in parallel also

FIGURE 3 Cézanne, *L'Eglise de Montigny-sur-Loing,* 1904–1905; BF #970 Gallery XVII. © The Barnes Foundation. Merion, Pennsylvania. Reproduced with permission. All rights reserved.

formed a group with an upper and lower boundary at right angles to each touch, the method would help him align vague surfaces with other, much clearer ones. As Machotka shows, in landscapes it might serve both to order a chaotic expanse of foliage and to align it with one or another major structural line such as a tree trunk or bridge support. His paintings took on a character of unusual unity—a unity achieved not through repetition but through thoughtful opposition and internal resonance.

We must remind ourselves that neither the conscious purposes nor the particular talents by which they are realized can be accounted for by psychological means—or indeed by any other means. The one is a mysterious consequence of thinking and feeling, and the other an apparent given, sharpened through experience. Cézanne's achievements cannot be understood through his personality alone, no matter how much his personality, and its development, help us understand his early interests and later renunciations.

The parallel touch—this cornerstone of his mature work—was further transformed in the mid-1890s into a system of smaller patches of color. They were sharply bounded on top, and depending on how they were needed in the composition, they would either overlap those above them, producing a receding surface, or move both in front of some and behind others, indicating a more disorderly surface such as foliage. In them, the parallel touch was suppressed, though detectable; it was the patches themselves that became the structural unit.

These remarks should not be read as suggesting that Cézanne worked by formula, and even less that the formula might be learned. On the contrary, the parallel touches no less than the later patches were used flexibly for a variety of purposes and variously for different subjects—indeed, they were needed neither in the still lives nor in the portraits—and what they have in common is the sense they give us of revealing a rich and attentive perception of the objects they help portray.

The patches were the invention of a man of about 55 who was yet to paint his greatest work. It is one of the unanalyzable mysteries of the course of life that some artists—Titian and Cézanne among painters, and Verdi and Janáček among composers—should find not only a new style but a new inventiveness and productivity at a time when their physical energies might be thought to diminish. One can think of no common thread binding these artists, save for the obvious emancipation from their former work and willingness to search for new forms.

VI. CÉZANNE'S ACHIEVEMENTS

Cézanne's turn from imagination to perception was a precondition of his best work, not the achievement itself. Seen externally, his work encouraged young painters who followed—in 1907, within a year of his death—to create their own systems of parallel touches and patches to analyze the surfaces of objects and recombine them in new ways to produce new objects. From this way of seeing Cézanne's work, Cubism, the first revolutionary movement in painting of the 20th century, was born. If the Cubists misinterpreted Cézanne—by forgetting the function of color in creating form, for example—they nevertheless produced extraordinary achievements of their own.

Seen internally, and apart from their effect on later painting, his achievements may be illustrated, though hardly encompassed, by looking again at Figures 2 and 3. *L'Eglise de Montigny-sur-Loing* was painted in 1904–1905, about two years before his death, and shows a perfectly satisfying view of a northern French town's Romanesque church. Yet how much grander the painting is, even in its unfinished state, than the photograph. Cézanne has both accepted the view as he saw it and transformed it nearly imperceptibly: he has noted all the hard, flat surfaces—in relation to each other—and given us an indication of their local color, but he has also brought the receding diagonals—the edges of the various roofs—close to the horizontal. This has the effect of making the scene appear as just flatter enough than it is to keep it close to the physical plane of the canvas, thereby reminding us that the painting is as much a physical object as it is a representation, and ultimately making the church and buildings appear more stable, even monumental.

Parenthetically, the patches he used here are not the ones previously described; here they are mere notations, strung out horizontally, and serve as a kind of shorthand to indicate what might later be elaborated more formally. But the unfinished state of the painting is neither unusual nor troubling. As with other unfinished canvases, because Cézanne has firmly placed the objects in relation to each other, and given us at least a hint of their color harmony, he has said in some ways all that needs saying: the painting has its full structure already, and if we should wish to fill in the blanks, we could, but there seems no need to.

While such comparisons may help us see his achievements, they are not necessary. Fry's sense of "revelation of the highest importance" in Cézanne's paintings, although not put as felicitously by others, is widely shared. We may see it in a sense of the "rightness" and permanence of the objects he portrayed, and in the richness, tension, and ultimate resolution of his way of seeing them. His compositions are complex, but they are also richly resonant internally, their parts calling attention to each other, their oppositions resolved, and their details placed into a more encompassing order. In them one sees both the interconnections between things and, in Cézanne's phrase (quoted by Gowing), the "logic of organized sensations" by which the painting process is governed.

Bibliography

Freud, S. (1968). *A general introduction to psychoanalysis* (J. Riviere, Trans.). New York: Liveright. (Original work published in 1920)

Fry, R. (1989). *Cézanne, a study of his development.* Chicago: University of Chicago Press. (Original work published in 1927)

Gowing, L. (1977). *The logic of organized sensations. Cézanne: The late work.* New York: The Museum of Modern Art.

Lewis, M. T. (1989). *Cézanne's early imagery.* Berkeley: University of California Press.

Machotka, P. (1996). *Cézanne: Landscape into art.* New Haven: Yale University Press.

Pemberton, C. (Trans.). (1991). *Joachim Gasquet's Cézanne.* London: Thames and Hudson.

Rewald, J. (1976). *Cézanne, letters.* New York: Hacker.

Rewald, J. (1986). *Cézanne.* New York: Abrams.

Chaos Theory and Creativity

David Schuldberg

The University of Montana

Attractor A region in the space describing the behaviors of a system toward which the system will tend to go and where it will tend to stay. *Strange attractors* characterize chaotic behavior and consist of confined trajectories that describe a system that is never in the same state and moving in the same direction twice.

Bifurcation A system's transformation from one type of system into another, for example, from a system with periodic motion to a system in chaos. This is to be distinguished from a *catastrophe,* which refers to a seemingly discontinuous change in one system.

Chaos A class of dynamic behavior of deterministic systems characterized by sensitive dependence on initial conditions, diverging but constrained trajectories that imply unpredictability, and complex organization or structure. *Complexity* is sometimes used as a synonym for chaos.

Dissipative Systems Systems, such as living systems, that are using up energy.

Fractal A pattern characterized by possessing similar structure at different magnifications, more roughly described as self-similarity at different scales; strange and other complex attractors generally have fractal microscopic structures.

Nonlinearity A term describing a relationship between two variables or a causal relationship between components of a system that is *not* strictly proportional and thus cannot be represented as a straight-line graph on ordinary graph paper.

State Space A space containing representations of the possible conditions or locations of a system. "Phase space" is sometimes used as a synonym for state space, but a location in phase space describes not only the current state of the system but also where it is moving next.

Systems Theory Theory describing the behavior of composite entities composed of changing, interacting, and interconnected parts whose functioning emerges from the mutual influences of the parts.

CHAOS THEORY, *more technically called nonlinear dynamical systems (NLDS) theory, is an exciting, rapidly developing area of mathematical theory with increasing application in the physical, biological, and social sciences. Nonlinear dynamical systems have great metaphorical appeal; this article outlines areas where they may help elucidate creativity, an elusive, sometimes near-magical phenomenon that has defied simple psychological explanations. Nonlinear dynamical systems theory is supplying useful models for understanding many aspects of human behavior. Chaotic or near-chaotic systems*

Copyright © 1999 by Academic Press
All rights of reproduction in any form reserved.

can demonstrate surprising flexibility and adaptability. Despite old-fashioned connotations of the word "chaos," these systems demonstrate order, complexity, and self-organization. Relatively simple, mechanistic, completely deterministic systems can be capable of surprising, discontinuous, and seemingly unpredictable change. While the tone of this article is generally speculative, it is hoped that the predictions and suggestions made here will bear fruit in deeper understandings of creativity as the metaphorical connections it describes are made more rigorous.

I. POTENTIAL CONTRIBUTIONS OF CHAOS THEORY TO THE STUDY OF CREATIVITY

Nonlinear dynamical systems theory has had such recent popularity that some workers refrain from using the word "chaos" because its usage has become so loose as to be meaningless. However, the theory is finding rigorous application to a variety of human processes, including cognition, motor behavior, learning, development, attitude formation, affect, social processes, psychopathology, and perception. The field is changing rapidly as new phenomena are explored using dynamic models and new methods of data analysis; these approaches appear useful at both neuronal and higher levels of conceptualization. So far the application of dynamical systems ideas to psychology has been piecemeal, without systematic understanding of the relationship between new models and familiar theories and notations. This article describes connections between new theory and well-known problems in creativity.

II. DEFINITION OF NONLINEAR DYNAMICAL SYSTEMS

NLDS theory describes the behavior of systems that, first of all, change with time; this is the meaning of the word "dynamic," which refers to the action of forces producing motion. In addition, the theory describes systems where at least some of the relationships among the system's components are nonlinear. In contrast, much work in mathematics and the sciences has historically focused on linear systems, where change in one part results in directly proportional change in an-

other part of the system, and where the relationship between change in variable A and change in variable B can be represented graphically by a straight line.

Linear systems have many desirable properties and are often amenable to analytic mathematical solutions that describe or predict their behavior over time. Research in psychology has focused on linear models, and, despite the importance of longitudinal work, has also emphasized cross-sectional or short-term relationships among variables. For example, the correlation coefficient tests fit to a straight-line relationship between variables, often measured at a single time.

Figure 1 depicts a simple linear dynamical system. It is composed of a block resting on a frictionless surface, attached to a solid wall by a "linear" spring whose restoring force is proportional to how far it is pulled or pushed. If the block is pulled and released, it oscillates back and forth in a smooth, identically repeating pattern, easily modeled and predictable with one simple equation.

In contrast, NLDS theory studies situations where the relationship between a change in variable A and a change in variable B is represented by some curve other than a straight line. Such nonlinear relationships are undoubtedly the rule in nature, with linearity representing a useful simplification or special case. For example, a discontinuous or all or none response, such as reaching the threshold for a neuron's firing, is a nonlinear one.

The behavior over time of systems that contain nonlinearities is often complex and interesting; it can become progressively more difficult to predict with the passage of time, even in the absence of technically defined chaos. Nonlinear systems are difficult to solve mathematically, and this is one reason that they have been avoided in many areas of science. However, this complexity also lends them much of their current ap-

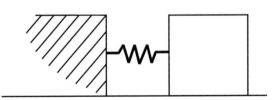

FIGURE 1   A simple linear dynamical system.

peal. They promise ecologically valid explanations of complicated real-world processes and appear particularly relevant to problems that have historically eluded explanation. One reason for the current onrush of interest in these systems is that computer technology has made it possible to model and display the behavior of complicated systems without solving them mathematically.

A. Characteristics of Nonlinear Dynamical Systems

NLDS models are applicable to psychological phenomena for several reasons. They allow deterministic causal models to be compatible with observations of complicated, often unpredictable manifest behavior that is sometimes discontinuous, suddenly changing, unexpected, or surprising. The behavior of deterministic systems can appear disorderly, noisy, and random. Yet, despite their resistance to prediction, such systems also have surprising order and organization. For example, the seemingly random development of snowflakes observes very strict symmetry and results in uniquely beautiful physical objects that possess similar properties. Some of the features described here, such as the absence of a simple analytic mathematical solution for a system's behavior, are not necessarily associated with chaos; others, such as strange attractors, specifically characterize chaotic systems.

1. Change with Time

By definition, dynamical systems involve temporal processes. All human activity, of course, also changes with time. Psychological and social systems exist in a temporal context; this is apparent in responses to the environment and in novel, self-initiated action. Longitudinal development across the life cycle is also dynamic. Problems arise from the fact that most psychological research relies on short-term observations of long-term phenomena.

2. Systems and Open Systems Properties

Systems are wholes composed of multiple interconnected parts; interconnection can be defined according to rules and regulative processes. The cybernetic models of communication, control, and automation developed in the 1940s and 1950s contain many of the features of more recent theory, but they tended to emphasize linear effects, to be limited to relatively simple causal loops, to suppose that accurate information is transmitted throughout a system, to stress unidirectional rather than reciprocal causation, and to focus on stability, homeostasis, and regulation rather than apparently less orderly behavior.

Opponent-process models, which refer to such opposing activities as excitation and inhibition in neural circuits, and dialectical models, describing the synthesis of conflicting ideas, have historically been popular in psychology and biology. These models, which are amenable to explanation by multiple interacting, possibly hierarchical processes, are enriched by the addition of the simple but complexifying properties of nonlinear coupling; attention to potential nonlinearity in such old models opens new vistas.

Many existing models suppose closed systems, viewed as self-contained and isolated from other systems and the external environment. In contrast, open systems are embedded in, and exchange inputs and outputs with, the surroundings. Bodies are open systems; there are transfers of energy and information to the physical and social environment. Bodies are also dissipative systems, constantly using energy, and this has important implications for the complexity of human behavior.

B. The Behavior of Nonlinear Dynamical Systems

NLDS are capable of many different sorts of behavior, regular as well as chaotic. Some of the following characteristics apply specifically to chaos and complexity.

1. Unpredictability and Sensitive Dependence on Initial Conditions

Some systems—for example, the linear device in Figure 1—are easily predicted. However, the complex behavior of other systems can make simple mathematical solutions difficult. There are two issues here. One concerns difficulty in reducing the motion of a system to a simple predictive equation. This is the case for many nonlinear systems, chaotic or not.

The second issue involves the fact that at times nonlinear systems enter regimes of chaotic behavior. A defining characteristic of chaotic systems is sensitive dependence on initial conditions. Very small differences in such a system's starting state can result in very large differences in its later behavior. The same is true for small perturbations introduced from the outside. Visualizing a system as following a path or trajectory over time, this means that paths through points that are very close together will diverge radically later on, something that has major implications for observations and predictions. Unless the position and motion of the system are observed exactly, one cannot know accurately where it will be later. Less-than-perfect observation of a chaotic system results in predictions that are increasingly inaccurate with time. This is sometimes discussed as compounding of error.

While such unpredictability is superficially similar to what is described by the Heisenberg uncertainty principle, the Heisenberg principal operates only at very small, subatomic scales. In contrast, our uncertainty about future states of a macroscopic chaotic system does not originate with minute quantum effects. Rather, the unpredictability of chaos is fully compatible with completely Newtonian physics; it occurs only because it is very difficult, due to measurement error and imprecision of observations, to specify exactly where a system is and where it is going at a particular moment. If we did know these facts exactly, we could predict where even a chaotic system would be in the future. This form of unpredictability distinguishes the chaos of deterministic systems both from quantum uncertainty and from the randomness of genuinely stochastic, nondeterministic systems.

What we colloquially call a "random" event may be completely determined, yet still unpredictable. Galton's famous peg-board generates the normal probability curve from marbles falling through an array of pegs. For all intents and purposes the marbles' paths are governed entirely by the completely mechanistic and deterministic causal laws of Newtonian physics as they wobble through air currents and spin and bounce off pegs. Yet, the trajectory of any given ball is difficult to predict due to its dependence on initial conditions and sensitivity to the effects of uncontrolled variables. Phenomena that are taken as prototypically random—the unpredictability of any marble's behavior and the neat, repeatable distribution of many balls in a bell curve—emerge from completely deterministic, nonquantum events.

This has interesting implications for human behavior. Social scientists generally study the mind with deterministic models, yet are puzzled by failures at prediction and control, especially in policy, social research, and intervention. Moreover, in contemplating their own lives, many believe in free will; for example, that they defy prediction by others, are capable of spontaneous action, and sometimes elude even *self-*control. NLDS theory defines deterministic models that also encompass unpredictability and can help solve some of human science's methodological and philosophical problems.

Difficulties in prediction and control are simply properties inherent in real life; however, cross-sectional causal and locally linear psychological models are likely to be at least partially correct. The fact that psychological models have overemphasized linear relationships is a flaw that, in principle, is relatively easily corrected. A larger problem is that many small, simple causal systems are likely to be involved in such interesting psychological phenomena as creative cognition, and these subprocesses are coupled in ways that are presently unknown and unstudied.

2. Intractability

A good deal of ongoing human behavior is intractable, and not only in the sense of eluding self-control and defying intervention. Certain classes of problem are notoriously difficult and apparently insoluble; the creativity question is one of these. It is likely that dynamical systems approaches will help with tackling such difficult theoretical and practical problems. It is even useful to search for places where older models and methods have failed, to let frustration be our guide and note dynamics researcher and cardiologist Ary Goldberger's reference to problems "whose only apparent unifying theme was their 'resistance' to traditional models" (Goldberger & West, 1987, p. 195).

3. Catastrophic Change and Bifurcation

Another characteristic of dynamical systems is the possibility of sudden qualitative changes in behavior. Such radical shifts are called catastrophes. Examples of seemingly discontinuous psychological change are the "falling off the wagon" of an alcoholic, insight into a difficult problem, and "aha" experiences in psychotherapy. Such processes have been modeled by catastrophe theory, a field that saw a surge of popularity in the social sciences in the 1970s. Catastrophe theory and NLDS theory have substantial overlap.

In addition to manifesting catastrophic state changes, a system can also change into a qualitatively different one, something termed bifurcation. For example, a system may change from periodic to chaotic behavior as the values of its parameters are changed.

4. *Apparent Regularity without Identical Repetition*

Periodic regularity, repetition, and cyclic and contained temporal processes characterize the stable oscillations or dynamic equilibria traditionally explained in classical dynamics. Greater irregularity in oscillating systems has been attributed to random noise, error in measurement, and extraneous variables. While error and noise are important concepts, it is now worthwhile to ask whether seemingly noisy fluctuation might indicate that a process is a candidate for explanation using nonlinear dynamics.

With NLDS interest extends to include bounded but irregular fluctuations and unstable equilibria. Much of human behavior appears to be oscillating and generally bounded, but only approximately regular and also capable of astonishing us. New research on normal and disordered biological rhythms has suggested that both overregulation and underregulation are sometimes maladaptive. Even the relatively bounded behavior of the well-functioning organism is sometimes adaptively chaotic, allowing organisms to change, self-organize, restructure, develop, mature, and senesce.

5. *Chaotic Behavior and Complexity*

Not all NLDS are in chaos, but the possibility of chaos is one of the interesting features of this class of systems. Because chaotic phenomena are ever-changing, never going through the same state with the same velocity (speed and direction) precisely twice, these systems can be capable of constant originality and innovation. Chaotic systems are characterized by so-called strange attractors, regions containing bounded but ever-changing (never-crossing) trajectories in phase space.

A system's phase refers both to the location of the system's elements at a given time and to where they are heading next. Phase space diagrams help to clarify the change, structure, and repetition of complex, time-dependent phenomena.

6. *Types of Attractors*

An attractor defines a region in phase space where a system will tend to go and tend to stay. A fixed-point attractor represents a single unique place where a changing system will tend to go. If friction is added to the system in Figure 1, the block will eventually stop moving, a situation represented by a fixed-point attractor consisting of a single position and no movement. A second type of attractor is a periodic or limit-cycle attractor. An example describes the motion of the pendulum of a grandfather clock. As long as the clock is kept wound, even if something bumps into the pendulum it will return to the same regular swing. Such attractors characterize many systems of classical dynamics.

In contrast, chaotic systems have strange attractors, a delightful term that refers to patterns in phase space that never repeat. Although a system orbiting a strange attractor may be in the same location at different times, it is never going in precisely the same direction or at the same speed through the same place; its trajectories in phase space do not cross. This corresponds to the unpredictability of systems in chaos; very close but not precisely identical paths diverge and may lead to vastly different outcomes later. The beauty of strange attractors is that they include elements of both order and disorder, divergence and convergence. Motion around them is bounded but never repeating. This represents an antithesis to stasis and repetition; a system orbiting a strange attractor is constantly engaged in novel behavior.

7. *Dissipative Systems and the Edge of Chaos*

The "edge of chaos" refers to a condition of systems that have not settled into motion around a strange attractor or the fractal-like order characteristic of chaos. This represents the edge of order, like the point between water's freezing and melting just prior to the orderly formation of a snowflake. A related concept refers to "dissipative" systems that are using up energy, also termed far-from-equilibrium systems by Prigogene, Stengers, and others. A dissipative system is illustrated by a person who is falling and running forward, constantly off-balance. Walking is indeed similar to such a state of falling forward; stopping demonstrates that halting really does feel like catching one's fall and does not result in a state of stillness. Even standing still is pregnant with novel possibilities.

8. Scaling, Symmetry, and Self-Similarity: Fractal Phenomena

Strange attractors can also demonstrate very interesting microscopic structures, including now-familiar fractal patterns with properties of self-similarity across different temporal or spatial scales. The idea that behavior shows similar patterning over different temporal scales is related to the concept of "style" and Wittgenstein's notion of family resemblance concepts.

Observations of similarity across scale are common in clinical psychology in describing phenomena that occur in miniature in the recapitulation of old interpersonal patterns, a form of personal self-similarity. Freud noted both mastery-oriented and self-defeating forms of repetition, using the terms "working through" and "repetition compulsion" to describe healthy and unhealthy forms of similar phenomena. One way to describe this difference is by contrasting periodic and strange attractors.

Self-similarity (rather than self-identicalness) also provides a useful definition of the consistency of personality, which can be viewed more formally as a group of psychosocial systems properties. Individuality can be conceptualized as a person's complexity, the depth and detail that emerge when someone is known by others. Consistency occurs across different time scales and does not imply that people always do the same thing, even in very similar situations. Viewing personality styles as strange attractors with fractal properties encompasses self-contradiction, an important part of the human soul and the material of much art; this reconciles both cross-situational differences in behavior and within-subject inconsistency with personal "identity."

Fractal phenomena are also observed in temporal patterns such as the dripping of a faucet. These fractals and attractors suggest the usefulness of moving from a purely linear view of time to a combination of linear and cyclic pictures. From this perspective, regular and seemingly periodic eras of human life appear as attractor regions that we enter, cycle around, and leave.

While orbiting occurs, life appears to encompass repetitive and nearly symmetrical beginnings and endings, narrative-like episodes. Then the story changes, as our lives depart for new regions.

9. Self-Organization

Some authors, notably Stuart Kauffman, have emphasized chaotic systems' self-organizing structures, including properties of symmetry and self-similarity. They argue that this represents a special sort of systems-level order, "order for free," that occurs even though dissipative systems are using up energy. These visions of order and organization indicate how the idea of progress may be reclaimed in the face of entropy. Thus, creation may represent a dissipative process that leads to the self-organization of artistic products.

C. Nonlinearity Can Make Even Simple Systems Complex

Relatively simple biological and psychosocial systems, if they include nonlinear causal relationships, are capable of complex and chaotic behavior. Thus, the unpredictability, intractability, sudden changes, and robust adaptiveness of psychological processes can become comprehensible, even rational, and potentially amenable to deterministic models. (It is important to note that this nonlinearity does not refer to relationships between inputs and outputs of whole systems, but rather to nonlinear linkages among the internal components of a system.)

As mentioned, nonlinearities are widely appreciated in the social sciences but also commonly ignored, and there are many well-known curvilinear relationships in psychology. The Yerkes–Dodson curve, usually presented as an inverted-U function of the relationship between physiological arousal and performance, is a widely known example. In addition, systems that include time delay are more complicated than systems involving immediate response.

Figure 2 illustrates a nonlinear system composed of two simple systems from Figure 1, coupled together by a nonlinear "hard" spring in the middle, one whose restoring force is represented by a function of the form $F = k_1 x + k_2 x^3$. With certain parameters this system can exhibit chaotic behavior; it can serve as an analogue for two coupled self-regulating systems.

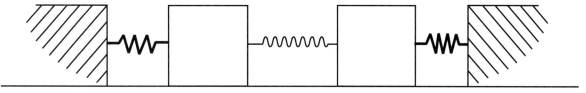

FIGURE 2 A nonlinear dynamical system consisting of two systems from Figure 1 coupled in the middle with a nonlinear spring.

III. APPLICATIONS OF NONLINEAR DYNAMICAL SYSTEMS THEORY TO THE CREATIVE PROCESS AND PRODUCT

The remainder of this article explores how concepts from NLDS theory are applicable to some core problems in creativity research.

A. Nonlinear Dynamical Systems in Creativity and the Arts

1. Temporal Changes

Creative products emerge through dynamic processes. The invention of something new unfolds over time, although a flash of insight may seem instantaneous. Creative activities have been described as comprising successive stages of generativity and consolidation, incubation and elaboration. "Regression" and the association of ideas also unfold in time. Creative work changes over a person's life span as work's meaning and valence are modified with changing cultural contexts and the creator's stage of life. Genres, styles, and movements emerge historically and are pushed along by generations of participants.

Researchers including Colin Martindale, Dean Keith Simonton, and Sidney and Ethel Blatt have studied such changes over historical time periods. However, while it is common to speak of the process of creating something new and thus to invoke dynamic and temporal phenomena, creativity researchers often take a static trait approach rather than a dynamic transactional one, for example investigating divergent thinking as an individual difference variable instead of studying the process of divergence in solving a problem. [*See* DIVERGENT THINKING.]

2. Systems and Open Systems in Creativity

a. The Creative Process
The creative individual responds to and works on fluctuating problems and is embedded in a social and cultural milieu, even if he or she works in isolation. These observations define creativity as a systems phenomenon. The creator, the artistic medium, and the problem to be found or solved; economic factors, the wider culture, and technology; other individuals, including muses, caretakers, critics, competitors, cronies, colleagues, groupies, grant managers, audiences, and patrons, can all play roles in the process.

The fact that work occurs in historical and cultural surroundings means that creativity is also an *open*-systems phenomenon; the creator is not completely self-contained. Creative endeavors involve adaptation to events in the environment, and creative behavior must be context-adaptive and context-sensitive. This adaptiveness defines the possibility of communication, reciprocal feedback loops connecting creator and public. Behavioral dialogue is a feature of successful artistic work, where a piece of art "speaks" to the audience; the viewer or listener is taken by the hand and helped to see, understand, and change, willingly or unwillingly. This is related to the communicability of a work and may define the difference between "true art" and "psychotic art." True art is not completely autistic, although it may remain mute during the artist's lifetime. This suggests an interpersonal but possibly asynchronous view of creative production.

Creative activity can also require perceptual connection to the social or natural worlds. There is feedback between the perceiver and the perceived, and the creative individual is modified as well as attempting to mold the world as materials—to accommodate as well as assimilate. Several definitions of creative activity include the term "adaptive," including Guilford's "adaptive flexibility" factor and adaptive regression in the service of the ego. The word "adaptive" can mean useful, but it also implies that creative activity is connected to reality.

The creative process also includes self-stimulation and internal feedback. Tobi Zausner notes that art appears to involve "autocatalysis" as the artist responds to the work itself as well as to feedback from the environment. This is related to Maturana and others' "autopoiesis," the self-creating property of living systems.

b. Systems Properties of Creative Products
Creative products result from the interaction of multiple coupled adaptive processes directed at interlocking problems. Two or more factors influencing one activity, such as simultaneously linked problem-solving strategies, produce dialectical dynamic tension in a system. Given nonlinear coupling, a combination of relatively simple processes has the potential of leading to complex behavior patterns, deep and textured forms of life.

An example of simple systems yielding interesting and "intelligent" behavior comes from new approaches to robot navigation employing multiple processes with relatively simple, sometimes hierarchical, rules instead of relying on complete mental maps of the robot's world. This represents a conceptual shift from systems based on intensive computation and complicated internal representations to the use of simpler perception–action schemes—from "top–down" executive functioning to "bottom–up" distributed processing with partially autonomous and coupled processes. A robot with rules such as "avoid obstacles," "follow walls," and "find doors" can navigate smoothly and quickly without any internal map of the surroundings. This approach is similar to the Santa Fe Institute "Swarm" project's modeling of the collective behavior of abstract agents.

Similarly, a creative product can emerge from solutions to many small and unrelated technical problems, not necessarily requiring a grand design imposed from the top. The suggestion has been made by the evolutionary biologist W. D. Hamilton and others that modular systems with different agendas and purposes may have evolved separately, accounting in part for the robust but sometimes contradictory nature of the heuristics and goals that guide organisms' lives.

Dialectical and opponent processes are components of many extant psychological models that are readily extended to models composed of interacting subsystems. For example, Frederick Abraham cites Howard Gardner's model of creativity using three coupled processes involving the individual, the discipline, and the judgmental society. Any such coupled push–pull model represents a useful place for theorists and researchers to consider NLDS approaches to potentially creative behavior. Both art and science sometimes involve the recognition and resolution of contradiction and opposition; the reconciliation of opposites can be framed in terms of coupled and competing subsystems.

B. Characteristics of the Creative Process and Product

1. Unpredictability and Sensitivity to Initial Conditions
The unpredictability of creative work can be rephrased by saying that the creative process is not analytic in the mathematical sense; creative trajectories do not reduce to simple equations, and insight emerges from heuristics rather than algorithms that guarantee solution. It is possible to provide guidelines and specify procedures to assist in creative brainstorming but not to write a cookbook for generating creative ideas themselves. Indeed, if we found such a cookbook, we might not want to call the results creative.

This is not to say that creative work cannot be modeled or implemented using deterministic processes; however, these must be recognized as dynamic iterative activities whose results generally cannot be predicted in advance. Creative thought, as all human behavior, can emerge from mechanistic processes and still be utterly surprising, again due to the fact that even nearby states of a complex system can diverge, sometimes radically, with time.

2. The Creativity Question as Intractable
This article has discussed two forms of intractability, both applicable to problems in creativity. First, facilitating creativity is difficult; it may even be paradoxical to push for a creative solution. Second, the *study* of creativity has tantalized theorists and researchers. In-

deed, one hint that the puzzle of creative thought might be amenable to NLDS models comes from this very difficulty in characterizing the structure and essence of creative activity.

3. Catastrophic Change and Bifurcating Systems

The phenomena of creativity exhibit both near-regularity and sometimes wild or catastrophic sudden fluctuations. An example of near-periodic creative activity is the innovation that takes place within periods of normal science. In contrast, there may be qualitative leaps in ideas and artifacts in cases of insight and inspiration, illumination experiences, when breaking old genres or styles, and during scientific revolutions.

Bifurcation refers to the transformation of one system into a different type of system, for example, from one characterized by periodic attractors to one in chaos. Zausner refers to creativity as a process by which subsystems bifurcate into a new order. The area of transition between a system on the edge of chaos and a new chaotic system may be especially important to understanding the creative process.

Chaotic phenomena can also settle into stable attractor regions. The transitions from inspiration, through consolidation, and then to working out a single creative solution may correspond to bifurcations into systems with different sorts of attractors.

4. Near-Periodicity in Creativity

Creative activity can require repeated jousts at the same problem. Psychoanalytic ego psychologists have described play as repetition aimed at mastery, and many workers have commented on creative activity's playful and restitutive aspects in adults and on the inventiveness of children's play. In adults, playfulness is part of the regressed quality observed in some creative work.

Play or art may each solve a psychological problem posed for them, or they may represent mere neurotic-like repetition without working through. In dynamic terms the question is whether work on a difficult problem is periodic, repetitive, or ultimately nonproductive and stuck, or whether some novel creation will eventually emerge. As already noted these distinctions can be expressed with reference to different types of attractors. [*See* PLAY.]

5. Chaos, Complexity, and Creativity

A number of theorists discuss how systems in or near chaos may be capable of creative behavior, and several characteristics of chaos are relevant to creative processes and products. For example, Zausner again notes how the artistic process is very sensitive to stimuli and speaks of the role of the "inconsequential" in art, described as unpredictable but not random. Relevant to the contrast between top–down versus low-level distributed processing introduced earlier, she also addresses the question, "Doesn't the artist have a plan for the painting?", describing how a work of art is more of an emergent phenomenon than a planned progression toward a goal visualized in advance. Frederick Abraham has spoken of creativity as "self-organizational bifurcations," observing that chaos and instability facilitate creativity. The late poet laureate Howard Nemerov spoke metaphorically of chaos as the primordial order before creation.

Theorists Ben Goertzel, Ronald A. Finke, and others are developing concepts of chaotic logic and chaotic cognition. Theorist and clinician Michael Butz also describes the relationship between creativity and chaos, referring to psychic swings and oscillations that are not strictly speaking periodic, with structure emerging from this chaotic behavior. Psychologist Phyllis Perna speaks of cycles of disorganization and reorganization; inspiration may be a chaotic state, with elaboration representing an attractor region where the creative process settles in. The creative process must avoid stasis, stagnation, and premature closure, all possible forms of capture by fixed-point or limit-cycle attractors. Systems that exhibit chaotic behavior may possess healthy flexibility, adaptability, readiness for change, and openness to new information. To quote the neurologist Walter Freeman, "Chaos provides the system with a deterministic 'I don't know' state within which new activity patterns can be generated. . . ." (Skarda & Freeman, 1987, p. 171), and he also discusses how perception of a novel stimulus may correspond to a chaotic system's settling into a more stable attractor.

6. Attractors in Art

Preceding sections have suggested a central role for attractors in explaining creative cognition. This section will elaborate their usefulness for describing the creative product and for defining genres or styles.

The vicissitudes of the creative process can be modeled as sets of trajectories in some phase space—variations in the position and direction of the behavior of multiple problem-solving heuristics. When a trajectory is within the region of a particular attractor, work remains within a genre, style, school, theoretical orientation, or set of conventions; style is an attractor in a region of phase space. The production and variation of themes and motifs within a single work can be described in similar ways. Allan Combs has observed that, in general, states of consciousness can be viewed as attractors.

Temporal patterning can also be understood in this way with reference to attractors. This allows discussion of rhythmic phenomena (such as cycles of fashion, the rediscovery of old ideas in science and mathematics, and recapitulations of thematic material within a single work), the entrainment and synchronizing of different systems (for example, the progressive adherence to a particular scientific theory or artistic school, or the contained progression of normal science), and the emergence of a new paradigm when radical new ideas seem to be in the air (evidenced in simultaneous but independent scientific discoveries). The sequence of individual creative episodes may also be cast in phase space terminology.

7. Creativity and Dissipative Systems: The Edge of Chaos

Ruth Richards and others are now exploring the importance of edge of chaos phenomena to creativity. Frederick Abraham notes the possible adaptive significance of structures than can operate at this edge. There is a good deal of speculation about optimum cognitive sets or facilitative environments for endeavors such as brainstorming. These conditions may be ones that maintain a system somewhere between stasis (or periodic, repetitive, well-regulated behavior) and a chaotic state, associated with Csikszentmihalyi's "flow" and analogous to the condition between solid and liquid just prior to crystallization. The edge of chaos may also shed light on so-called "transitional" or "liminal" phenomena, terms that refer to experiences that lie in frontiers between psychological states or cultures and are important in play, creativity, and psychotherapeutic change. [*See* BRAINSTORMING.]

Edge of chaos phenomena are observed in dissipative systems. Zausner views the artistic product as manifesting order, while the process of creativity is dissipative, with the uniqueness of a work of art coming from a coalescing of dissipative structures. She also comments on the potential for disorder in this process, with a fine line between "breakthrough and breakdown"; creativity and psychopathology may be very close together. In a similar vein, Aldous Huxley wrote about how the mescaline experience was poised between "heaven" and "hell" (consider these as two attractors), and David Schuldberg speaks of both "giddiness and horror" in the creative process. [*See* MAD GENIUS CONTROVERSY.]

8. Symmetry and Fractal Properties in Creativity

Some fractals depict the self-similar patterning of nonrepetitive but organized chaotic trajectories around strange attractors. Zausner notes that periods of creativity also appear to be self-similar, with alternations of episodes of inventiveness and reflectivity. In addition, works of art are unique; the result of the creative process is unpredictable but not disordered. She comments on the self-similarity of a single artist's style, related to descriptions of genre, style, and personality. An artist's works bear family resemblances to each other; these family resemblances reflect the dynamics of their parentage.

Fractal structures also have important aesthetic qualities. For one thing, they are similar (although commonly not identical) at different magnifications. To a connoisseur of beaches a string of California beaches is recognizable, as well as distinguishable from Cape Cod beaches, at many scales: in an aerial photograph, when viewed from a headland, while walking along a beach, and even from the perspective of lying prone contemplating the tiny fringes of a tidepool. Miniatures have an important relationship to art and other creative endeavors; a symbol, a statistical model, and a mathematical notation all can be considered miniatures. Levi-Strauss states that "all miniatures seem to have an intrinsic aesthetic quality" (1966, p.23), precisely because they are small and complete. Similarly Ruth Richards has commented that people find fractal patterns beautiful and are drawn to phenomena, such as waterfalls and beaches, that instantiate them.

Another issue concerns the ambivalent relationship

between symmetry and creativity: There is a tension between symmetry's sometimes inherent beauty and the contrasting importance of asymmetry and cognitive complexity. The items on the Barron–Welsh Art scale preferred by more creative groups tend to be figures that are asymmetrical and complex. Creativity involves both symmetry and symmetry breaking, and the nonidentical self-similarity of some fractals provides a metaphor for reconciling these ideas.

9. The Creative Process as Self-Organization

Creativity involves processes of self-organization, related to Maturana and Varella's "autopoietic" organization of structures that are "continually self-producing." Works of art, new scientific theories, and novel solutions to engineering problems can be viewed as emergent structures, possibly consequences of coupled processes of problem solving as already described. Emergence provides a way of conceptualizing the new information produced in the history of culture.

C. Nonlinearity and Creativity

Creative products, no matter how complex, can be viewed as artifacts that emerge from relatively simple and comprehensible psychological and sociological processes, but only if these simple systems involve dialectical or opponent processes, or coupling, and nonlinearity. Some nonlinear relationships in psychology have already been discussed. Richards and others have proposed and demonstrated an "inverted-U" relationship between creativity and psychopathological characteristics. More basically, adaptiveness, health, and well-being do not generally proceed in simple linear fashion from the application of positive behaviors or virtues. More is not always better, nor is a happy medium. Thresholds, floor and ceiling effects, dose–response functions that level off, double-edged personality characteristics, and interactions between two or more causal variables can all introduce nonlinear dynamics into a psychological system. Simonton, David Harrington, and others have commented on various nonlinear relationships in creative processes.

The simple nonlinearly coupled model in Figure 2 can be applied to creative processes. This can be demonstrated by defining its horizontal axis as ranging from "intrapsychic-focus" at the left to "environmental focus" toward the right. The motions of the blocks then trace oscillating paths of incubation and possible access to primary process at the left of the figure, alternating with editing, dissemination, performance, and receiving critical feedback in regions to the right. Strange attractors in the phase portraits of the blocks' motions would indicate that this system was producing constrained novelty; the system could also settle into stable or repetitive, less creative states.

IV. SPECIFIC PHENOMENA IN THE CREATIVE PROCESS

A. Intuition

In *Being There* neuroscientist Andy Clark describes an approach to cognition emphasizing environmentally engaged heuristics and modular low-level problem solving, rather than top–down executive-dominated processes. Similar dynamic processes may be involved in induction and insight. Mandell and Salk, describing how rational thought might arise out of intuitive processes, discuss how the fact that "structure arises autonomously from the superficially random motions of complex cooperative systems suggests that 'intuitive' statistical field properties may be the source of more linear 'reason'" (1984, p. 311). In this view humans' apparent rationality arises from intuition, not vice versa! [*See* INTUITION.]

B. Brainstorming, Improvisation, and Juxtaposition

Processes of recombination and going beyond the information given are used in brainstorming techniques aimed at facilitating induction. A crucial question concerns the role of improvisation, a term commonly applied both to inventiveness and to kinds of performance. How does improvisation occur? [*See* IMPROVISATION.]

Juxtaposition, superimposition, and accretion can provide routes to new ideas. A related concept is Albert Rothenberg's "homeospatial" thinking. These are combinatory forms of the "blind variation" discussed by D. T. Campbell in his account of creative and other cognition. Juxtaposition and recombination of unlike elements, sliding various unrelated concepts past each other, examining match and mismatch for interesting features, noting how mismatches can create conceptual connections, and discarding unproductive correspondences (part of Campbell's "selective retention") can result in creative products. Richards discusses the importance of the experience and reconciliation of contradictory moods.

Superimpositions are temporary and indeterminate, and they may display a playful attitude toward more "rational" methods of combination. A similar phenomenon occurs in "contaminations" of concepts on the Rorschach inkblot test. Ralph Hoffman has put forward a memory overload model of contamination using a neural net simulation. Similar noun–noun combinations are important in the creative verbalizations of children.

Juxtaposition is related to techniques of non-hierarchical combination in artistic forms such as collage and assemblage; this process does not strive for superordinate categories or an implicit top–down organization, and combinations can initially be force fit together. Bricollage, the handyman's method of improvisational problem solving usually directed at a repair, represents a combination of top–down and bottom–up processing. In bricollage the worker has an end in mind—to repair a broken object or solve a problem at hand. The process utilizes planning, but it uses heuristics and does not allow textbook solutions such as those found in a service manual, where factory-specified parts are required. Both materials and tools may be used in ways for which they were not intended. To quote Thomas Alva Edison, "To invent, you need a good imagination and a pile of junk." Creative bricollage is also related to nonnarrative expositional forms, where elements and moods are laid one upon the other and a story does not follow a standard progressive form.

C. Temporal Changes in the Cultural Milieu

A related topic concerns the cultural spread of ideas and the diffusion of innovation and acquisition of expert performance, as well as progressions of grasping a new idea or paradigm, beginning to utilize it, and making it ones own. There are dialectical processes of acceptance and rejection, accommodation and assimilation, and we can view creativity as resulting from tension between adaptive and conservative processes. Such activities, also, are coupled according to rules that define (probably nonlinear) dynamical systems.

Martindale and Simonton discuss variations over time in new ideas, tastes, aesthetic values, and movements. Martindale has noted that fashion tends to follow a pattern of incremental changes; when a change has gone too far, a trend reverses. Thus, men's ties become wider; the fashion then changes and they get progressively narrower, until the sequence again reverses. Such oscillation can be modeled from the perspectives of both classical and nonlinear dynamics. However, this may well represent motion around chaotic rather than periodic attractors because in such cases history does not precisely repeat itself. A style, even a nostalgic one, never returns exactly. For example, the irony and distance of "retro" fashion imply that bell-bottoms in 1996 were not quite the same as the bell-bottoms of 1969; if the trajectory of a 1990's sixties revival is traversing a strange attractor, 1990's retro will also be followed by something recognizably not-quite-seventies.

D. Evolutionary Epistemology and Emergent Order: Creative Cognition

Evolutionary epistemology studies how new ideas and new knowledge emerge analogously to the evolution of biological structures through Darwinian natural selection. Chaos theory has found applications in evolutionary theory, and a fruitful line of inquiry involves pursuing how processes of mutation, selection, and adaptation can be applied to creative cognition. Specifically, the way that creative cognition "channelizes" into particular paths (in the evolutionary biologist C. H. Waddington's image) implies emergent order and can be conceptualized with basins of attraction in "fitness landscapes." Attempts have been made to model such attractive processes using neural networks and other techniques, for example, in simulating schizophrenic cognition; this approach is applicable to problems in insight. Particularly relevant is the experimental work of the social psychologist Robin Vallacher analyzing the temporal formation of attitudes as attractors.

V. CONCLUSION

A. Further Steps in a Dynamical Systems Program for Creativity

Creativity theorists will want to consider how dynamical models can illuminate the phenomena of originality. Psychological models that contain a term for time, include potential nonlinearity, or refer to dialectical processes all represent places where these new models and techniques may be applicable. Systems whose behavior shows bounded but nonidentical repetition, change, and sometimes qualitative jumps also deserve a new look. The referents of many psychosocial phenomena relevant to creativity involve dynamic processes. For example, how might regression in the service of the ego unfold over time? What is the temporal patterning of a "remote associate" on Mednick's test? What is the trajectory of a career in creativity or leadership? What is the phenomenology of the transition between periods of incubation and elaboration? Further specification of the qualitative dynamics of these processes will point to new and testable models.

B. A Preoperational View of the Dynamics of Improvisation

This article will conclude with an argument for a relationship between creativity and relatively simpler forms of cognition, akin to Piaget's conception of preoperational thought. The juxtapositions and recombinations previously mentioned are similar to the strategies of classification used by the preoperational child who employs one-dimensional schemes to classify objects that can really only be exhaustively sorted with a two-way or more complicated scheme. For the child different classificatory dimensions cannot consistently be held in mind at the same time; systems of classifying fluctuate and compete.

In the case of a creative adult, nonexhaustive classification strategies represent heuristics and not science—practical wisdom and not theory. (See Ruth Richards' Bibliography entry for another post-Piagetian view of creative thought.) In most important senses real objects do vary on too many attribute dimensions to be categorized exhaustively, even by mature and wise adults. While we may look down on the dimension-reducing strategies of the child or "simple" adult, when we make sense of our own lives, our attempts at planning, steering, and rational control are limited and historically conditioned. Our vision with regard to our selves and our epoch is myopic; Henry Murray noted what a person "cannot tell" about his or her own life. There are also limits to how abstractions can clarify our lives, and the way we think about ourselves is noncomprehensive. Living through everyday language employs very incomplete views of the world.

How, then, do we manage to be as successful as we are? It is because, while we use simple processes, we use many of them in parallel. We employ multiple coupled heuristics and do the best we can. People's dynamic tools for understanding are not limited in any avoidable sense. The rules of thumb of everyday cognition are limited only in the sense that they do not live up to grandiose, totalizing dreams of perfect scientific understanding and control. Real life necessarily involves bottom–up processing and improvisation in real time and requires everyday creativity, for better or worse.

Because we operate according to multiple heuristics, our thoughts and actions are not generally reversible, in contrast to the schemas of formal operational thought. Tobi Zausner speaks of the irreversibility of the process of painting, a feature that situates art outside of formal operations and in the realm of dissipative systems, the domain of heuristics. However, when chaos is involved, the product of even simple systems can be complex.

This discussion is connected to Wittgenstein's analyses of the limits of language. In everyday use language does not have too much trouble living with big ideas, as long as we refrain from philosophizing or psychologizing. We *inhabit* big ideas and necessarily grapple with existential concerns; the fact that life's rules of thumb are not algorithms that guarantee solution puts limits on social science and denies a truly comprehensive view of life or the ethics of living well. However, this does not limit what may be *possible* in everyday life and in everyday creativity; limits of understanding are not the same as those circumscribing what is possible.

Preoperational cognitive processes and the properties of NLDS are superimposed in our use of everyday language and practical wisdom. Everyday life is deterministic yet unpredictable, very complicated but also organized, self-similar and recognizable from day to day, and sometimes strikingly beautiful. We live creatively and improvise in the moment, yet lack the unattainably huge computational power to form a lasting, stable big picture and to steer steadily toward a single life goal. Operating only by benchmarks and approximations, our apparent mental stability is really a falling forward—a far-from-equilibrium condition, dissipative, and always unstable. We *must* improvise.

Creativity in art, science, and other endeavors is related to the aesthetic qualities of everyday life. Although not reducible to algorithms guaranteeing solution, everyday life has striking beauty and some order, amidst its constant flux. To live every day requires backing away from enlightenment ideas of progress and perfection and embracing the rough-hewn beauty of our real world.

Bibliography

Abraham, F. D., Abraham, R. H., & Shaw, C. D. (1990). *A visual introduction to dynamical systems theory for psychology.* Santa Cruz, CA: Aerial Press. [Now published by Dakota Press.]

Goldberger, A. L., & West, B. J. (1987). Applications of nonlinear dynamics to cardiology. *Annals of the New York Academy of Sciences, 504,* 195–213.

Guastello, S. J. (1995). *Chaos, catastrophe, and human affairs: Applications of nonlinear dynamics to work, organizations, and social evolution.* Mahwah, NJ: Erlbaum.

Kauffman, S. (1992). *The origins of order: Self-organization and selection in evolution.* Oxford: Oxford University Press.

Kelso, J. A. S. (1995). *Dynamic patterns: The self-organization of brain and behavior.* Cambridge, MA: MIT Press.

Levine, R. L. & Fitzgerald, H. E. (Eds.). (1992). *Analysis of dynamic psychological systems, Vol. 1. Basic approaches to general systems, dynamic systems, and cybernetics.* New York: Plenum.

Levi-Strauss, C. (1966). *The savage Mind.* Chicago: The University of Chicago Press.

Lewin, R. (1992). *Complexity: Life at the edge of chaos.* New York: Macmillan.

Mandell, A. J., & Salk, J. (1984). Developmental fusion of intuition and reason: A metabiological ontogeny. In D. Offer & M. Sabshin (Eds.), *Normality and the life cycle: A critical integration,* pp. 302–314. New York: Basic.

Masterpasqua, F., & Perna, P. A. (1997). *The psychological meaning of chaos: Translating theory into practice.* Washington, DC: American Psychological Association.

Prigogene, I., & Stengers, I. (1984). *Order out of chaos.* New York: Bantam.

Richards, R. (1996). Beyond Piaget: Accepting divergent, chaotic, and creative thought. In M. A. Runco (Ed.), *Creativity from childhood through adulthood: The developmental issues (New directions for child development,* No. 72, pp. 67–86). San Francisco: Jossey-Bass.

Runco, M. A., & Richards, R. (Eds.) (1996). *Eminent creativity, everyday creativity, and health.* Norwood, NJ: Ablex.

Skarda, C. A., & Freeman. W. J. (1987). How brains make chaos in order to make sense of the world. *Behavioral and Brain Sciences, 10,* 161–195.

Sulis, W., & Combs, A. (1996). *Nonlinear dynamics in human behavior.* Singapore: World Scientific. [Especially chapters on creativity by Kahn, Zausner, and F. Abraham.]

Cognitive Style and Creativity

Øyvind Martinsen

University of Bergen

Geir Kaufmann

*Norwegian School of
Management*

Cognition The process of perceiving, recording, storing, organizing, and using information.
Cognitive Strategies Systematic methods people use to process information and solve problems.
Cognitive Style Consistent individual differences in the ways people experience, perceive, organize, and process information.
Validity Correspondence between what test scores purport to measure and what they actually measure.

COGNITIVE STYLE can be defined as the manner or way of processing information. In this article we will present an overview of research on cognitive styles and focus on both findings and problems associated with this construct and its relation to creativity. Because of the amount of research and the limited space here, we will summarize only the major theories and findings within this area.

I. THE CONSTRUCT OF COGNITIVE STYLE

As a construct, cognition has a wide scope and includes perception, memory, language, learning, thinking, problem solving, and creativity. Over the years style researchers have identified several types of individual differences in several such aspects of human information processing, and many of these types of individual differences have been defined as stylistic constructs. Cognitive style has been defined in general terms as consistent individual differences in the ways people experience, organize, and process information. Operational definitions of cognitive style have focused on a person's typical mode of cognition as reflected in, for example, his or her main dispositions in perception, the organization of information in memory, the preference for different kinds of general problem solving strategies, the speed and accuracy of decision making under uncertainty, the preference for types of problem solving, or the profile of intellectual dispositions. Because of the various uses of the style construct in different areas of psychological research, it has been necessary to make further distinctions between cognitive styles, learning styles, defensive styles, and other uses of the style construct such as expressive styles and response styles.

Copyright © 1999 by Academic Press
All rights of reproduction in any form reserved.

While theoretical and operational definitions such as the preceding ones may appear relatively simple, it must be emphasized that the construct of cognitive style has been associated with several problems during its research history. These problems have been related to measurement issues and theoretical issues, but problems have also been evident in inconsistent findings across tasks and across samples. Such problems impact on the validity of the construct. The more important problems can be grouped into five major issues.

First, most style researchers have made a distinction between cognitive styles and cognitive abilities or intelligence. While cognitive styles are defined as describing how or in what way we process information, cognitive abilities are defined as how *well* we process information. Cognitive abilities describe how much, how well, or how accurate we process visual, semantic, or numerical stimuli, while cognitive styles describe functional dispositions toward processing information in certain ways like, for example, the types of general strategies we tend to use when working on problem solving tasks, the types of problems we prefer to work on, or whether we primarily perceive wholes or parts of a problem solving or learning task. Lack of, or low, correlation between style and ability is commonly seen as a necessary condition for a style construct to be valid. Not all the postulated style constructs have, however, been found to be uncorrelated with measures of intelligence. [*See* INTELLIGENCE; PROBLEM SOLVING.]

A second issue is that the psychological basis for many style constructs can be seen as an accumulated personality impact on cognitive processes. This means that our profile of, for example, motivational dispositions, openness, and anxiety may make us become disposed toward using certain modes of information processing unless the task demands in the situation "force" us into other modes of processing. Consequently, cognitive styles can be described as being placed at the intersection between personality and cognition. An implication of this is that cognitive styles should be more strongly related to various personality constructs than to intelligence, and that style should be seen as a disposition more than as a situational preference. Not all researchers have specified such relations between style and personality in their theories.

A third issue is related to a distinction between task-specific strategies and higher-order strategies, some-

times called metastrategies, where styles should be more strongly associated with the latter than the former. A task-specific strategy can be seen as, for example, a relatively specific procedure that can be used to solve a particular class of problem solving tasks. A number of researchers have seen cognitive style as more strongly associated with those higher-order strategies that are executed in planning, monitoring, and selection of task-specific strategies. An implication of this is that styles should be more consistent across tasks and over time than task-specific cognitive strategies. This issue has, however, received relatively little attention in practical research on cognitive styles.

A fourth issue is that style constructs have commonly been defined as being bipolar. This means that one end of a style continuum should be associated with certain characteristics, while the other end is associated with other, often opposite, characteristics. Those in between the extreme scorers are seen as being more flexible or mixed in their dispositions. However, the hypothesis of bipolarity has rarely been examined. To investigate this issue demands that each pole is operationalized separately and that scores on both poles are correlated with each other. Bipolarity can be inferred to the extent that there is a relatively strong, negative correlation between the two pole operationalizations. Associated with the bipolarity issue is also the hypothesis that both poles of stylistic constructs should be value free. In practice one pole of most style constructs has tended to be more valued than the other.

The fifth issue is that cognitive style theories should be related to more general theories of cognition and eventually also to theories of personality in a broader perspective. This would imply that styles should be defined in a way that makes their operationalization meaningful in a perspective extant to the style construct itself. This has not always been the case for style theories, and several theories have been formulated based on more loosely defined ideas.

While these and other issues are important for future research on cognitive styles, they are also important as a framework for evaluating the validity of previous research on cognitive styles. If a cognitive style construct has low validity, it will not advance our understanding of creativity.

Despite controversies and disagreements, cognitive style has been a popular construct in psychological and educational research. Since the early 1950s several thousands of studies on style constructs have been published in journals and in edited and authored books. A number of these have touched on the relationship between cognitive styles and creativity. Moreover, several theories have been postulated over these years and cognitive style has indeed been looked upon as a promising construct. The main reason for this is that it has been seen to hold potential to represent some of the missing pieces of the puzzle from the classic experimental research on human cognition, where individual differences generally have been perceived as irrelevant, or as a "nuisance" in terms of error variance. The construct of cognitive style has been used to describe how individuals process information in different ways and to show that the inclusion of data on individual differences adds to our knowledge about human cognition beyond classical experimental research and beyond variables associated with academic intelligence. As regards the relations between cognitive styles, creativity, and problem solving, an important question has been to investigate if people solve problems or create novel and useful solutions in predictively different ways.

II. THEORIES OF COGNITIVE STYLES AND THEIR RELATIONSHIP TO CREATIVITY

A. Cognitive Controls

Work on cognitive controls began in 1953. The point of departure was psychodynamic theory. A cognitive control was seen as a hypothetical construct in the sense of a delay mechanism that directs the expression of needs in socially and situation-specific acceptable ways. Seven different controls were theoretically specified and operationalized: tolerance for unrealistic experiences, conceptual differentiation, constricted–flexible control, leveling-sharpening, scanning, contrast reactivity, and field articulation. These several control constructs were originally measured experimentally, while other measurement methods were developed later for some of them. Cognitive styles were defined as patterns of controls identified through the statistical technique called cluster analysis.

As regards the validity of the cognitive control theory, several criticisms have been put forward. It has been argued, among other things, that various controls did not appear consistent through different studies, and that correlations with different criteria were seldom significant. There have been theoretical inconsistencies associated with cognitive control research, and it has been argued that cognitive controls to a large extent were value directional and unipolar. Related to creativity, the relation between cognitive controls and creativity was investigated in a sample of gifted children. The study did not yield consistent results as regards the relation to creativity. Still, it was possible to isolate three styles (clusters) in this sample, which may imply that there are differences in the stylistic dispositions of gifted students beyond the level of ability. Still, the preceding criticism leads to the conclusion of not sufficient support of the validity of stylistic constructs associated with cognitive controls. Consequently, the relation to creativity is uncertain.

B. Field Dependence–Independence

In 1954 research was initiated on field dependence and independence as a stylistic construct. This construct was defined as a process variable, representing the degree of autonomous functioning in assimilating information from the self and field. On the basis of several later theoretical and empirical developments, field dependence–independence was defined as a bipolar construct, where field-independent subjects were seen as being better at cognitive restructuring, while field-dependent subjects were seen as being more socially adept because they were more sensitive toward external referents. Moreover, field-dependent and -independent subjects could be fixed (those who appeared not to have any capacity for the properties associated with their opposite style), or they could be mobile (those who appeared to be more flexible between the two types of styles). Thus, some people were seen as more flexible than others with respect to their stylistic dispositions. These stylistic properties were measured with two different tests. One was the Rod and Frame Test, where the task involved ignoring a visual or postural context to locate a true vertical. The other was the Embedded Figures Test, where the task involved locating a previously seen simple figure in a new figure where the simple figure had been embedded by a more complex design.

The theory of field dependence–independence was very popular and generated a substantial number of studies until around 1980 when the interest in the construct declined. During the eighties several researchers criticized this theory for the frequently found high correlations with measures of spatial intelligence. Based on such findings it became uncertain whether field dependence–independence was a measure of style or ability.

As regards the relationship between field dependence–independence and creativity, results from several studies have supported that field-independents are more creative than field-dependents. It has been argued that mobile subjects would be more creative because of their ability to be flexible between the two stylistic modes. While this work seems interesting from a creativity perspective, it is nevertheless necessary to interpret these results and ideas cautiously given the present conceptual status of the theory of field dependence–independence. Several attempts to reformulate this theory indicate that research on field dependence–independence will continue in spite of previous disappointments.

C. Reflectivity–Impulsivity

This cognitive style dimension describes differences in decision speed under conditions of uncertainty. Its primary measure was the Matching Familiar Figures Test, where individual differences in speed and accuracy of decision making (conceptual tempo) under uncertainty was measured. Time to make decisions and errors in the accuracy of decisions were combined to categorize children as impulsives or reflectives, or more precisely as fast-responding/high-error, fast-responding/low-error, slow-responding/low-error, or slow-responding/high-error types.

Previous reviews of this theory show, on the whole, positive conclusions for reflectivity–impulsivity as a style construct. The overall conclusions from these reviews show that reflectivity–impulsivity are moderately stable and generalizable across similar tasks. Task performance for reflectives and impulsives is dependent on task demands. Thus, reflectivity–impulsivity

may describe a bipolar construct where each pole has at least some positive value, although being impulsive has been found to be associated with lower intelligence and lower motivation than reflectives in other studies.

The study of creativity and reflectivity–impulsivity has provided mixed results. For example no significant differences were found among conceptual tempo groups on a series of common creativity and problem solving tasks. Fast/accurate and slow/inaccurate subjects had greater originality scores than slow/accurate and fast/inaccurate subjects. Relationships have been found between reflectivity–impulsivity and some facets of musical creativity, and reflective subjects scored higher than impulsive subjects on Torrance Tests of Creativity. Although no clear pattern in these findings has emerged, where significant relationships have been obtained, reflectives have had higher scores.

D. Adaption–Innovation

While the already discussed theories of cognitive style were not developed with direct relevance to creativity, the style theory set forward by Michael Kirton in 1976 has made a special contribution to the study of creativity at the conceptual level. In this theory Adaptors and Innovators (A-I) are seen as describing two qualitatively different and consistent individual approaches, manifest in preferences for different types of problem solving, creativity, and decision making. Kirton makes a distinction between style and level of creativity. As regards the level of creativity this is defined through a comparison of people's creative ideas or products. As regards the style of creativity, adaptive creativity is directed toward improvements within an existing framework, while innovative creativity is directed toward some basic change of the existing framework surrounding a particular state of affairs. However, individuals are not seen as being fixed at either end of the A-I continuum and when individuals depart from the behavior associated with their preferred style this has been called coping behavior. It is argued that the adaptive–innovative continuum should be unrelated to the level of creative performance.

In several studies, it has been demonstrated that the Kirton Adaptor–Innovator inventory (KAI) does not in general correlate with measures of intelligence. On the other hand, a relatively strong relationship has been shown between several personality traits and the KAI, in particular between KAI scores and the sensation seeking trait. This means that Innovators tend to have a higher need for stimulation and excitement than Adaptors. Based on these style–intelligence–personality correlations, basic requirements for a theory of cognitive style seems to be fulfilled.

As regards creativity, Kirton's research shows that KAI scores are uncorrelated with various measures of divergent thinking. This has been taken as support for the idea that there are different types of creativity along the adaptive–innovative dimension that are independent of level of creativity. Generally speaking, however, zero correlations as such do not support the hypothesis that there are different types of creativity; they only support an idea of unrelatedness. Moreover, some studies indicate that Innovators have higher scores on at least some measures of creativity. On the other hand, it was found that Adaptors perceived creative products in their workplace as more logical, useful, and adequate than Innovators, while Innovators perceived creative products as more original and transformational than Adaptors. These findings were interpreted to support Kirton's theory that there are different types of creativity. However, self-reports on both style and creativity evaluations do not necessarily support this idea. Indeed, to investigate the style–level issue further, experimental studies are necessary where the style–level hypothesis is subject to more rigorous tests. In such experimental studies the type of task may be an experimental condition, and performance can be studied through style by task, and eventually through style by creative ability by type of task interactions. A study of group problem solving is more promising in this regard, but still not satisfactory as a true test of the hypothesis of different types of creativity for adaptors and innovators.

Although Kirton's theory is interesting and may aspire to become set breaking within the area of creativity research, the bulk of research on the theory is correlational or factor analytic. This implies that some of this research may lack the necessary control to make causal inferences. This is a limitation when it comes to testing the main hypothesis in the adaption–innovation theory. Further efforts should thus be made to dem-

onstrate experimentally that Adaptors and Innovators indeed utilize qualitatively different strategies that are uncontaminated by level of creativity, and that these strategies have different implications for the direction of effort in creativity, problem solving, and decision making. Kirton's idea of a distinction between the style and the level of creativity is interesting, but the support for this idea is so far not sufficient to warrant such a conclusion.

E. Assimilation–Exploration

The theory of Assimilator–Explorer (A-E) cognitive styles has been proposed by Geir Kaufmann and Øyvind Martinsen. In a quasi-experimental study of individual differences in problem solving strategies on a water-level task, some subjects were observed to spontaneously vary their solution strategies without any prompting by task requirements or instructions. These subjects were labeled Explorers. Those who followed the prespecified algorithm throughout were labeled Assimilators. Thus, the assimilation–exploration theory of cognitive styles (A-E styles) describes individual differences in dispositions toward using problem solving strategies.

Kaufmann's theory on assimilation–exploration is based on cognitive schema theory with special reference to Piaget's core concepts of assimilation and accommodation. Assimilators are seen as more rule-bound in problem solving behavior, and as having a disposition toward interpreting new events in terms of existing knowledge. Accommodators change schema more easily when precipitated by the task requirements. In an expansion of Piagetian theory, Explorers are seen as having the strongest disposition toward novelty seeking, which manifests itself in a search for new types of solutions and new ways of solving problems without any external pressure to do so. The A-E styles are seen to be rooted in a biologically based preference for stimulus variability versus stimulus stability. The finding that individual differences in this style distinction predict performance in highly unfamiliar tasks was cross culturally replicated. While the theory of A-E styles shares similarities with Kirton's A-I theory, the most important difference between the two theoretical approaches is that Kaufmann sets the style distinction within the context of problem solving in general, rather than within the more specific domain of creativity. Moreover, the A-E theory has been formulated as an expansion of a theory in cognitive psychology while the A-I theory has been formulated based on observations of change processes in organizations.

In a validation study, Explorers had higher scores on motivation and absorption (openness), while the style distinction between Assimilators and Explorers was uncorrelated with general intelligence. There were also significant differences in the mean scores for students in different types of educational settings, with art students having the highest scores (more explorative). A significant correlation was also found between the A-E styles and scores on the Wallach and Wing creative activities checklist (Explorers having higher creativity scores), but only a weak, yet still significant, correlation with measures of verbal and figural fluency. Taken together, the correspondence between the A-E theory and the pattern of empirical findings is consistent with the requirements in basic definitions of cognitive style.

Other studies have sought to validate the more specific nature of the A-E styles. The most important hypothesis has been that Assimilators need task-relevant experience to use their preferred mode of processing efficiently, while Explorers are more efficient when they can explore the task environment without being too strongly influenced by internal or external rules or directives to find the solution. Research findings support these ideas. In another study, it was found that Explorers and Assimilators reacted differently from the same instruction to utilize certain problem solving strategies on creative problem solving tasks. This finding was interpreted as experimental validation of the idea that people with different stylistic dispositions normally utilize qualitatively different problem solving strategies.

In Martinsen's expansion of the A-E theory, it has been argued that the A-E styles can be seen as a central indicator of task-specific competence, but that this task-specific competence not always will lead to superior performance. Other conditions would contribute to impair or facilitate performance beyond the degree of compatibility between stylistic dispositions and task demands. In this regard interactive effects between stylistic disposition, degree of task-relevant experience, the type of task, and the salience of motivation arousing conditions together would influence performance.

The general idea in this theory was that the complexity of the task will determine the optimal level of motivation for the task, while the A-E styles along with other conditions would determine the total strength of aroused motivation. The idea of overmotivation indicated that some tasks are optimally solved with a high level of motivation while other tasks are optimally solved under conditions of low motivation (complex tasks like many creativity tasks).

Supporting these ideas, the A-E styles were found to interact with the motive to achieve success. Explorers performed well under conditions of low achievement motivation while Assimilators performed well under conditions of high achievement motivation on creative problem solving tasks. In another experiment, the previous findings of interactions between A-E styles, experience, and motivation were integrated in a study where both the task structure and the level of achievement motivation were manipulated experimentally. The pattern of findings from this study could be interpreted as overmotivation effects for Assimilators and Explorers on structured and unstructured tasks, respectively. More recent studies have shown related interactions on the Remote Associates Test and on insight problems when the strength of achievement motivation has been measured or the perception of task-specific competence has been manipulated experimentally. Finally, a similar pattern of interaction was found but under a different experimental paradigm where positive mood was compared with a control condition. Based on this line of research it seems supported that stylistic dispositions are dominant in "normal" settings, while increased motivation or positive affect are forces that heavily influence our stylistically based use of problem solving strategies.

Thus, although it can be expected that Explorers have higher creativity scores overall, this relationship seems to be strongly moderated as a function of the strength of motivation, mood influences, perceived competence for the task, level and quality of past experience, and the level of optimal motivation for the task. Within this theoretical framework, the theory of A-E styles has shed new light on the classic controversy between the Gestalt and the Behaviorist psychologists on the function of experience in insight. Additionally, the theory of the A-E styles may shed new light on the relation between motivation and creative problem solving and on the relation between positive mood and creative problem solving. Consequently, this theory may have fruitful implications in several areas of research beyond its "home-base" in problem solving. Validation of findings against a broader range of measures of creativity must, however, be done in future research before such a conclusion can be fully supported. Also, more recently developed measurement procedures where Assimilation and Exploration are measured with independent subscales must be further validated. In the general perspective, we believe that an experimental, interactionist approach is particularly useful in cognitive style research. Only through such analyses may we unveil the answer to the question of whether people with different stylistic dispositions indeed utilize different approaches that yield the kind of incremental validity in predicting performance that is premised in the very concept of a distinction in cognitive styles.

F. Intellectual Styles

In 1988 Robert Sternberg put forward the most complex style theory to date. The theory is linked to the constructs of adaptation, selection, and shaping, which are part of his theory of intelligence. It should be noted that Sternberg's conception of intelligence is broad and that he has made a distinction between capacities for self-government and the way in which the individual executes mental self-government. He argues, like other style researchers, that measures of capacity and style should be unrelated at a general level, while styles can be related to more local domains of capacities. Moreover, the function of intelligence is metaphorically linked to the function of government, couched in the concept of mental self-government, which includes an assumption that people govern themselves in the same way as societies do. Self-government has several aspects and the intellectual styles are posited to have similar aspects: function, form, level, scope, uses, and leaning.

The number of stylistic constructs varies slightly in different versions of the theory. However, in Sternberg's latest version, "uses" are not included. The three major functions are the legislative (creation), executive (implementation), and judicial (evaluation) styles. Four major forms of government are the monarchic (preference for one goal at the time), hierarchic (prefers mul-

tiple goals ordered in a hierarchy), oligarchic (prefers multiple goals where each is equally important), and anarchic (avoids rules and systems). Two basic levels of government are the global (preference for general problems demanding abstract thought) and the local (prefers tasks that require detail and precision). Two domains in the scope of government are the internal (preference for tasks that allows people to work alone) and the external (prefers tasks that allows working together with others). Two leanings are the conservative (preference for the familiar and traditional) and the liberal (preference for going beyond existing rules and regulations).

Sternberg's theory shares similarities with other theories of cognitive styles: styles are placed at the interface between personality and cognition, styles express the manner of cognition, and styles should be uncorrelated with intellective capacity. Sternberg's theory, much like Kaufmann's previous theory, has also been developed within a theory of intellectual functioning, which may simplify both the operationalization and the evaluation of the stylistic dispositions compared with other style theories. However, cognitive styles have normally been defined as bipolar constructs while intellectual styles are defined as a number of unipolar constructs that together create a stylistic profile. Thus, the bipolarity assumption that is common in most theories of cognitive styles is relinquished in the theory of intellectual styles. This implies that stylistic profiles can be measured in a normative way, where combinations of stylistic scores can be combined in different ways. This is a new and interesting perspective in style research.

Sternberg has reported insignificant correlations between the 13 previously described stylistic dispositions and measures of IQ and grade point average (GPA) scores. The judicial, global, and liberal styles correlated significantly with SAT Math scores but not with SAT Verbal scores. However, correlations between several styles and grades were reported where the direction and magnitude of the correlations were dependent on the type of subjects and education the students were taking. This is a finding that supports the idea that styles describe competencies in local domains. A number of correlations were also found between the various thinking styles and other style measures, as well as with the Myers Briggs Type Indicator, which measures personality types based on Jung's ideas. The 13 thinking styles could be reduced to five latent variables through factor analysis. Taken together these findings generally support basic validity for a style theory.

As regards the relation to creativity, Sternberg included styles in his investment theory and found negative relationships between creativity and the executive, conservative, and monarchic styles. These styles describe a preference for rule-following behavior, and a combined score of these styles was significantly and negatively correlated with an overall measure of creativity. The other stylistic constructs did not correlate significantly with the measures of creativity and it was unexpected that the legislative style was not correlated with the measures of creativity. Thus, the relation between the various thinking styles and creativity needs replication, but also extensions to shed further light on how the various styles eventually relate to various facets of creativity at the procedural level. Thus, future experimental studies are necessary to shed further light on these problems.

While other style theories perhaps can be criticized for being too limited in their scope, Sternberg's theory can be questioned for the high number of stylistic dispositions that have been included in the theory. The principle of parsimony (simplicity within the boundaries of validity) and future factor analytic and regression analytic studies may eventually suggest reducing the number of thinking styles. Beyond this question related to the number of styles, the theory is interesting because of its comprehensive scope.

G. Other Approaches

There are several other interesting theories of style that have, or may turn out to have, implications for how people create. In one such theory, stylistic constructs, or propensities, has been suggested to be related to five phases in the process of reflective thought. These propensities have been described as the tendency to recognize a problem (problem recognition), the number of hypotheses enumerated before any evidence is considered and the tendency to consider habitual hypotheses as opposed to new ones (enumeration of possibilities), the tendency to search for confirming versus disconfirming evidence (reasoning), responsiveness to evidence as opposed to prior beliefs (revision), and stringency of the criterion for stopping

the whole process (evaluation). No data have been reported, but the theory warrants further scrutiny, particularly with respect to its relevance for creativity.

In a related perspective, a theory has been proposed of problem solving styles that are argued to be related to the creative process. This theory argues that there are two main stylistic dimensions, one describing two different ways of acquiring knowledge, and the other relating to two different ways of using knowledge. The two different ways of getting knowledge are through experiencing and ideation, and the two different ways of using knowledge are through thinking and evaluation. Various combinations of these stylistic attributes yield different typological interpretations, and these are labeled Generator, Conceptualizer, Optimizer, and Implementor. Additional and more elaborate profile interpretations are also suggested. The measurement of these stylistic dispositions seems to be partially ipsative. Such measurement procedures are primarily intended to measure the relative strength of dispositions within an individual, and comparisons across individuals should generally not be done based on such measurement procedures. Moreover, the interpretation of several statistical analyses based on ipsative data can be problematic, and ipsative scores are generally more expedient for individual counseling purposes rather than normative research purposes. Thus, this theory has its main strength as a counseling tool, and has limited value for the study of the style–creativity relationship in a normative perspective.

There are several other theories of cognitive styles that could have been mentioned here. However, these theories have not brought sufficient novelty into this field of research, they have not been studied specifically in a creativity perspective, they are more closely associated with ability or personality, or they are outdated.

III. DISCUSSION AND FUTURE DIRECTIONS

Although cognitive styles indeed have important functions in creative information processing, it seems obvious that cognitive style alone is not sufficient to "explain" creativity satisfactorily. This is also evident in several theories of creativity and related processes where cognitive styles have been included together with various personality traits, motives, abilities, experience, and social and training factors. In most of these theories, set-challenging or novelty seeking versus set-accepting and rule following thought have been emphasized as important for creativity.

Even in the present context of many cognitive style theories, the several findings of associations between cognitive styles and creativity, and the several theories of creativity that include cognitive styles, we may still point to some important limitations. In this regard there seems to be three major areas that may be improved in future research. The first concerns the validity of cognitive style constructs, the second concerns the design of studies on cognitive styles and creativity, and the third concerns the perspectives on style–creativity research.

First, the validity of several cognitive constructs must be further investigated. Through the history of style research, close links have been found between intelligence and styles, and between various measures of styles and personality. Further work is necessary to investigate whether cognitive styles represent a unique construct, or whether it boils down to stylistic expressions of ability and personality constructs. The older theories, like field dependence–independence, must be developed in line with newer theories to further validate the uniqueness of this construct. On the other hand, the more recent theories of adaption–innovation, assimilation–exploration, and thinking styles stand in need of sharper examination on the merit of their discriminant validity against personality constructs.

Second, the research designs that are most frequently applied in stylistic research on creativity seem to be nonexperimental or correlational. This limits our understanding of the results and our possibilities of making causal inferences about style–creativity relations. If we are to investigate the possibility that cognitive styles, for example, describe different ways to be creative, it is indeed necessary to apply aptitude–treatment interaction studies to shed light on such issues. In research designs like this, individual differences in cognitive styles are combined with experimental manipulations of task contents, work conditions, or other situation conditions, with the inclusion of necessary controls for alternative interpretations in terms of abilities and personality factors. Such research designs have been rare during the history of style research.

Third, it seems necessary to investigate further the relationship between cognitive styles and creativity based on different conceptions of creativity. Presently we have at least three different perspectives on creativity that are important for stylistic research. One of these perspectives is a micro or ipsative perspective, where an individual's creativity is based on a comparison between the degree of novelty in a product or idea and that in the same person's previous products or ideas. This is an individual perspective where everyone can be seen as creative. A second perspective is a macro or normative perspective where a person's creativity is compared with other persons' creativity from an objective perspective. This is the invention or innovation perspective where only a few people are creative. The third perspective is a component perspective, which can be integrated with either of the two preceding micro and macro perspectives. Here, the stylistic influence on various subcomponents of creativity (like insight, analogical reasoning, remote associations, ideational productivity, convergent thinking, and so on) can be studied. Style researchers need to be more aware of the several conceptual and operational distinctions that can be made in creativity research and to adjust their research designs accordingly. Thus, the criteria and designs in style–creativity research must be specified based on a priori theoretical and/or operational definitions of creativity or creativity relevant processes.

Based on this overview of current research on individual differences in cognitive styles, the hypothesis that cognitive styles do indeed have a function in creativity seems to draw considerable support. Still, all the present theories need to be developed further in order to yield more precise information on the relations between style and creativity. Meeting this requirement also depends on the further progress in creativity research, where the criterion problem is multifaceted and difficult to solve.

Bibliography

Goldstein, K. M., & Blackman, S. (1978). *Cognitive style.* New York: Wiley.

Kaufmann, G. (1995). A theory of cognitive strategy preferences in problem solving. In G. Kaufmann, K. H. Teigen, & T. Helstrup (Eds.), *Problem solving and cognitive processes. Essays in honor of Kjell Raaheim* (pp. 45–76). Bergen: Fagbokforlaget.

Kirton, M. J. (Ed.). (1989). *Adaptors and innovators. Styles of creativity and problem solving.* London: Routledge.

Kogan, N. (1983). Stylistic variation in childhood and adolescence: Creativity, metaphor and cognitive styles. In J. H Flavell & E. M. Markman (Eds.), *Handbook of child psychology: Vol. 3. Cognitive development* (pp. 630–706). New York: Wiley.

Martinsen, Ø. (1995). Insights with style. In G. Kaufmann, K. H. Teigen, & T. Helstrup (Eds.), *Problem solving and cognitive processes. Essays in honor of Kjell Raaheim* (pp. 77–117). Bergen: Fagbokforlaget.

Martinsen, Ø. (1997). Cognitive styles and their implications for creativity. *High Ability Studies, 8,* 135–158.

Messick, S. (1987). Structural relationships across cognition, personality and style. In R. E. Snow & M. J. Farr (Eds.), *Aptitude, learning and instruction: Vol. 3. Conative and affective process analysis* (pp. 35–77). Hillsdale, NJ: LEA.

Messick, S. (1994). The matter of style: Manifestations of personality in cognition, learning, and teaching. *Educational Psychologist, 29,* 121–136.

Sternberg, R. J., & Grigorenko, E. L. (1997). Are cognitive styles still in style? *American Psychologist, 52,* 700–712.

Sternberg, R. J. (1997). *Thinking styles.* Cambridge: Cambridge University Press.

Collaboration and Competition

Jock Abra
University of Calgary

Gordon Abra
University of Arizona

Bisociation The process of bringing together several previously unrelated ideas to achieve a novel, creative combination.

Collaboration A situation in which several individuals work together as a team to achieve creative ends.

Collective Art Group activities such as singing and dancing, the one type of creative activity that for Erich Fromm satisfies the need for intimacy in a satisfactory way.

Compensation Making up for one's perceived inadequacy in one area by a greater drive for success in another.

Competition This occurs when several participants in a situation are interdependent, in that the movement of one toward a goal that all are seeking decreases the chances that the others will also reach it.

Cooperation This occurs in such situations of interdependence, when the movement of one participant toward that common goal increases the chances that the others will also reach it.

Intimacy Also known as encounter or relatedness, it is the experience of gaining contact with other people, not only physically/sexually, but psychologically.

Intrinsic Motivation This occurs when an activity such as creating is an end in itself and done for sheer enjoyment, as opposed to extrinsic motivation, when creating is a means to another end, such as material rewards.

Priority Disputes Episodes, most common in the sciences, in which several people independently accomplish the same achievement and a controversy ensues over who did it first, for example, Newton versus Leibnitz over the invention of calculus.

*Cooperation, **COLLABORATION**, occurs when several participants in a situation are interdependent, in that the movement of any one of them toward a goal they all seek increases chances the others will also reach it. **COMPETITION**, however, occurs when movement of any one toward that goal decreases chances of success for the others. Creativity usually implies an individual activity and most studies have addressed it as such, but in many respects it involves and is greatly influenced by other people and an individual's relationships to them. This article discusses some of these factors. One main concern will be the motivation for creative work, because this probably in good part reflects desires for a certain type of relationship, either for one of cooperation that results from intimacy and equality with others, or for one of competition that aims for power and superiority over them. Much of the discussion will focus on collaborations, exemplified by such immortal teams as Gilbert and Sullivan or Watson and Crick, wherein several persons work together to realize a great achievement. Such situ-*

Copyright © 1999 by Academic Press
All rights of reproduction in any form reserved.

ations reveal many social factors that operate more subtly, if at all, in private activities such as writing poetry.

I. AVAILABLE EVIDENCE

Liberal use will be made of anecdotal evidence and introspective reports from eminent creators, so the reasons for including such relatively informal sources should be made clear at the outset. The rigorous empirical evidence from controlled, laboratory studies that modern psychology prefers offers advantages of reliability and quantification, but it also has weaknesses, notably that it stems from contrived circumstances whose relevance to realistic ones may be tenuous. This is certainly true of most studies of collaboration. For example, one of the first attempts to assist creativity, Osborn's brainstorming technique, involved groups working together, but this and most other such studies involved a group of virtual strangers coming together for a relatively brief duration. Many real-life collaborations, on the other hand, are highly intimate interactions spanning months or years so that, as in any long-term relationship, personal traits and temperaments take on major importance. Such cases also differ in that successes and failures may be highly visible, and reputations, egos, and a great deal of money may be at stake. [*See* BRAINSTORMING.]

In a similar vein, there are many controlled studies of groups solving problems, but doing this, or concocting an invention such as the proverbial better mouse trap that meets a clearly defined problem of technology, is a quite different matter from situations involving genuine creativity, such as making a film. A problem holds out the prospect of a certifiably right answer that fulfills specific criteria, so that when that answer is found, its appropriateness is apparent and generally agreed upon. However, in many creative pursuits, especially in the arts, solutions are evaluated by arbitrary value judgments—no poem or film is "correct" beyond question—first by the creators themselves and later by others such as critics and the general public, and as history repeatedly shows, opinions will probably differ. Therefore creators can never be sure how a solution will be received, which introduces a host of complicating factors, notably intense anxiety about its reception. Genuine creativity, therefore, demands a willingness to risk public opposition and ridicule.

The subjects used in most lab studies provide a final limitation. If, as is the case here, the matter of interest is great achievement such as the work realized by the Mozarts, George Eliots, and Einsteins that by consensus has eventually been accepted as great, it is questionable that findings from more general populations such as university undergraduates can be applied indiscriminantly to such elite ones. Most of those subjects, even if they have scored highly on a purported test of creative ability, have not yet verified by deeds that they are capable of achievements of this magnitude, and most never will. For all these reasons, most available empirical evidence is of doubtful relevance to understanding the matters of concern here, and in any event, even if the foregoing problems are not sufficient reason for downplaying such evidence, the point is academic. Studies of group processes in situations involving genuine creativity are few, so one has little choice but to fall back on informal evidence, with a view to generating suggestive hypotheses that may then be subjected to more rigorous evaluation. Various theories of creativity that stem from diverse traditions such as psychoanalysis, existential philosophy, and cognitive and behaviorist psychology will also be exploited for the same purposes. Kurt Lewin suggested that nothing is so practical as a good theory, and certainly theories can be extremely helpful when the aim is speculation.

II. THE PREDOMINANCE OF COLLABORATION

It is striking that collaboration has been so rarely studied, since it is nowadays so common. Indeed, in a sense almost every act of creativity involves it. For one thing, previous work in and the traditions of a field always influence even the most innovative work, if only as something to react against. Isaac Newton, a reclusive lone wolf if there ever was one, nonetheless admitted in a rare moment of humility that if he had seen further than others, it was because he had stood on the shoulders of giants. In a similar vein, even those involved in solitary pursuits trade ideas and mutual criticisms of their work; witness such intimate partnerships as writers Lillian Hellman and Dashiell Hammett, or artists Jasper Johns and Robert Rauschenberg. But the main reason collaboration is almost inevitable is that, apart from a few exceptions such as poet Emily Dickinson or writer Franz Kafka, most creators want to communicate with an audience of some kind and this relationship is in a real sense a collaborative one. Jean-Paul Sartre, for example, saw reading as a creative activity. Since writers cannot detach themselves from their own books so as to experience them as someone else would, they must have readers to complete this missing element, for without it a work does not truly exist. A writer therefore needs a gift from those readers of their freedoms, which allows the latter to interpret the book however they see fit—to think about it without the writer compromising that freedom by imposing any particular viewpoint. In short, writer and reader become equal partners.

Still and all, there are some creative activities in which collaboration is particularly manifest to the point of being in practice inevitable. The dancer is a choreographer's instrument of expression, equivalent to a painter's canvas, so although a few choreographers create dances for themselves, most prefer to use someone else and few works could come into being at all without interactions of some sort. Likewise in modern science, no one person can have all the expertise that most major projects demand. The Manhattan Project that fostered the atomic bomb was among other things a mammoth exercise in teamwork, as are typical modern laboratories with their plethora of graduate students, postdoctoral fellows, technicians, and test tube washers. A supposed head, then, as often as not serves as a kind of orchestra conductor whose main job is to keep these various components working together productively by providing not only creative ideas, but whatever else is necessary to sustain activity, so such people need the abilities of administrators, diplomats, and psychologists. Similarly, live theater and film involve not only writers, but directors, designers, performers, and countless others bearing such tantalizing titles as Key Grip or Best Boy, whose unique contributions each affect the final product. Indeed, filmmaking success nowadays depends as much as anything on the creativity (if such it be) of special effects experts. In any event, directors of major films have as much in common with generals commanding armies as with poets concocting verses.

III. TYPES OF COLLABORATIVE RELATIONSHIPS

The foregoing implies that collaboration can take many forms, and a few of these will now be described, for these differences probably affect the psychological and sociological factors that are in operation. First, collaborations may be fixed, or open-ended. In the first, epitomized by a company putting on a play, members come together for a specific project and upon its completion go their separate ways. They therefore know going in that any feelings of team or togetherness must be temporary. On the other hand, chamber music or jazz groups presumably stay together so long as satisfaction and productivity thrive. As well, collaborator interactions may be intimate or remote, ranging from constant face-to-face discussions of the sort Watson and Crick conducted as they sought the structure of the DNA molecule, to people who design sets or lighting for actors they never meet but whose success their work greatly affects.

Collaboration may also be homogeneous or heterogeneous. In the first instance, exemplified by groups of dancers or actors, each participant performs roughly the same service, but not in the second. Which implies another difference that may be as important as any in determining the properties of collaborative relationships: whether they are horizontal or hierarchical. In the first, more democratic case, participants carry roughly equal weight in decision making and therefore responsibility, while in the second, some opinions have priority, with extreme instances becoming virtual tyrannies.

Concerning the horizontal type, several heads may in truth be better than one when all share a common vision and they can feed off one another; thus composer Leonard Bernstein observed that collaboration can get to the point where you are not sure who wrote what. At its best, then, such an arrangement realizes Gestalt psychology's tenet of the whole being greater than the sum of its parts. Another noted composer, Richard Rodgers, described the landmark musical *Oklahoma!* as a work created by many that gave the impression of having been created by one, and Gilbert and Sullivan, who when working separately produced nothing but mediocrities, together forged masterpieces. Such situations therefore also exemplify Skinner's notion that successful relationships feature reciprocity, an "I'll scratch your back if you scratch mine" arrangement in which participants each deliver rewards to partner(s) when the latter act suitably, and receive in kind from them. Hierarchical relationships, however, imply differences in power and dominance. Collaborators often possess not shared but contrasting visions and in such cases dictatorship must replace democracy or only vapid compromises that please no one will result. The theater has been described as a collective art in which the strongest participant rules, that is, the one who because of his or her track record or box-office clout has the so-called "muscle." Thus even among the all-star assembly that devised the musical *West Side Story*—Bernstein, Sondheim, Laurents, etc.—director/choreographer Jerome Robbins had the final say.

These variations in the form of collaboration have implications for the relationships among those involved. First, in horizontal situations, assigning credit for achievements becomes problematic, especially when fame and/or fortune follow, since it has been found that people generally overestimate their own contributions to group projects. The order of names on publications may be a special bone of contention. In the social sciences, first authorship usually implies the person who has been the foremost contributor and, since gaining peer respect and recognition are major incentives for scientists, billing can become as contentious an issue as in films. Similarly, the animosities simmering among the team seeking a treatment for diabetes boiled over when Nobel Prizes loomed, since members vehemently disagreed about those who deserved it. Hierarchical situations present a different source of potential conflict. Regardless of their position in the hierarchical pecking order, individuals tend to view, and describe, those equal with or above them as collaborators. They are seen as working together toward a common goal, the project is described as "ours," and each person's contribution is seen as substantial. However, those having higher status or influence refer to their relationship with those beneath as not collaborative but "consulting." They regard the latters' input as peripheral, and tend to downgrade their contributions, viewing the project not as ours, but "mine."

Finally, one heterogeneous relationship, that of creators with critics, those tastemakers whose judgments seminally determine creators' ultimate success, is in-

triguing precisely because participants disagree about whether it is horizontal or hierarchical. Most critics see it as a collaboration between equal colleagues who are working together to improve the initial work. Their contribution, they feel, is to act as mediators to, and educators of, the general lay audience. Their main task is to clarify and interpret that work to assist its reception, whereas they view judging its success as far less important, something they must do simply because audiences and employers demand it. However, to creators, because their work involves huge investments of ego and self—in a real sense creative work resembles removing your clothes in public—those judgments are all that matter. To disrobe and have an onlooker observe, "You are really ugly," does not exactly make one's day! Many creators see critics, therefore, not as partners but as powerhungry exploiters whose superior position makes them immune to counterattack, if not as parasites who feed off the labors of others for their own selfish purposes. Hence the differing reactions when those judgments are negative. Stereotypic critics are honestly if naively bewildered by the creator's anger; after all, they were only trying to help.

Jean-Paul Sartre's compelling, too-little-noted description of relationships offers much for understanding the hierarchical type in particular. In his view, existential philosophy's fundamental tenet is that "existence precedes essence." Thrown into existence without a predetermined nature, or essence, we have complete psychological freedom to choose our actions and it is these choices that create our essence—who we are for the moment. Thus what we do determines who we are and the latter constantly changes unpredictably, since each new act may well negate it. However, a key event in creating essence occurs when we interact with someone else and come under their gaze. For Sartre, Hell is Other People, because these confrontations inevitably breed power struggles as antagonists try to retain their freedom to create themselves while imposing on that Other whatever properties, and hence essence, they choose for them. Both can no more retain the final power of choice than can the earth and sun both center the solar system, so egalitarian relationships are romantic fictions.

Joseph Mazo's study of the New York City Ballet implies that such organizations exemplify Sartre's scenario. Hierarchical dictatorships, they resemble nothing so much as the military, with the footsoldiers being the dancers over whom choreographers/directors (in this case, arguably the greatest in classical ballet, George Balanchine) rule regarding not only artistic and professional but personal matters, such as whether to have families. Dancers routinely describe themselves as physical masochists because in their most stressful art, pain is a constant companion which they must endure and perhaps almost perversely enjoy. Might they be psychological masochists as well? Moreover, many renowned choreographers have been described as control freaks who need to feel power. Which may explain a seeming paradox: despite the inherently social nature of their work, many are also described as loners. Why avoid the company of others? Perhaps because only in this way can one have complete control to do, and become, whatever one wishes. Compromise is always necessary when other people are involved.

Spoto's study of Alfred Hitchcock describes hierarchical relationships within the film world and suggests the image Hitchcock's TV program promoted of a droll, lovable Englishman apparently hid insatiable needs for power (in this case, Spoto speculates, stemming from feelings of inferiority due to a working-class background and a constant struggle against obesity). For one thing, every technical and performance detail was worked out beforehand to forestall possible accidents that would threaten his sense of control. His films, therefore, were already complete in his mind, so that actually shooting them seemed to him a bore (on occasion, he fell asleep on the set). It is suggestive, then, that so many of his films feature victims of circumstance, in the wrong place at the wrong time. This need for control also made him a card-carrying compulsive as regards neatness, and a player of sometimes unforgivably cruel practical jokes (humiliating others proves your power over them). It affected his relationships both with his collaborators, who were told exactly what he wanted and given little credit, and with the audience, whom he described as a passive instrument on whom he could play whatever notes he pleased, with their reactions, whether laughter or fear, virtually guaranteed. It may also explain his fondness for the suspense genre. When people are unsure about what will happen next, and terrified about the possibilities, they are at your mercy.

It is another recurring event, however, that especially recalls Sartre. If masochists gain power by submitting, so can a sadist's insatiable drive for power result in a seeming winner who loses. Hitchcock was constantly prone to infatuations with the glacial blonds, epitomized by Grace Kelly, who starred in many of his films, and as he aged, his attempts to control not only their on-screen but off-screen lives, such as their clothing and hair styles, became ever more blatant. (In a textbook example of art imitating life, in *Vertigo* James Stewart literally remakes Kim Novak into the image of his great love whom he believes has committed suicide). These attempts reached their zenith with one Tippi Hedron, a Hitchcock discovery (she had never acted before) whom he starred in *The Birds*. He controlled every aspect of her performance and demeanor—as someone said, he was doing *Vertigo* with Tippi Hedron—but again infatuation took over, this time leading him to proposition her overtly. When he was firmly rejected, he experienced the subjugation that is the Sartrian sadist's inevitable fate.

IV. MOTIVES FOR CREATIVE WORK: COMPETITION AND COOPERATION

The hierarchical–horizontal distinction leads to another concern. Creativity presents no shortage of riddles, but none more puzzling than the reasons people indulge in it at all, because at least when viewed from a purely rational or utilitarian angle, it makes little sense. Prospects of material reward, especially in the arts, are far fewer than for public apathy or ridicule, and creative work also results in constant dissatisfaction, frustration, and anxiety. If the apparent negatives far outweigh the positives, such as brief moments of euphoria, why go to the trouble? Yet for understanding and promoting creativity, this may be as important a question as any, because one quality that virtually all great achievers have in common is enormous drive and single-minded determination.

How collaboration might affect motivation is difficult to decide. On the one hand, that participants have someone else to whom they must answer may be helpful, if self-discipline lags and one cannot get down to work. Being part of a team also counteracts the loneliness that solitary work can foster—playwright Moss Hart preferred to collaborate for precisely this reason—and may lessen the fear of ridicule from others, especially for truly innovative work, since individuals are more willing to go against group norms when others do so as well. Like misery, nonconformity seems to love company. On the other hand, one likely reason to create is to release a vague but haunting mental image in an external expression that captures it effectively. If several minds hold different images, the result may be a compromise that satisfies no one. As another possible impediment to effectiveness, highly cohesive groups may breed groupthink, wherein members are reluctant to voice valid objections to a seeming consensus, which may explain why groups as compared to individuals in problem solving display a reduction in the number and quality of ideas. Perhaps it is easier to march to a different drummer when walking alone than when in a parade. (Which in turn calls into question the purported benefits of practices such as brainstorming. Still, some authorities suggest that working alone facilitates only the initial generation of ideas, whereas groups excel in evaluating and refining those ideas.) [*See* GROUP CREATIVITY.]

To return to motivation, Amabile has shown that when one believes that one's work will later be evaluated by others, its creativity suffers, presumably because extrinsic motivation, that is, creating as a means to another end (in this case impressing someone else), replaces the more productive intrinsic kind, wherein it is an end in itself. Therefore collaboration might also be detrimental because such evaluation by partners, of not only finished products but rough drafts or vague hunches, is constant and by no means always kind. Choreographers endure grimaces of displeasure or boredom that some dancers are all too skilled at emitting when the virtues of a suggested movement are not immediately apparent, and when the young Stephen Sondheim submitted a lyric to his collaborator on the musical *Do I Hear a Waltz,* Richard Rodgers evaluated it before the entire cast with the encouraging comment, "This is SHIT!" Still, it is noteworthy that Sondheim's later productivity hardly suffered, so Amabile's findings may apply only to the children and neophytes who have constituted her main subject populations. For practicing professionals, evaluation, whether from collaborators, critics, or audiences, is a constant prospect, so those who cannot produce their best work in such circumstances will not survive for long.

In any event, some other probable motives for crea-

tivity involve our needs for relationships. It is often pointed out that these social needs are far more important to humans than to other animals, so it is reasonable to suspect that this most characteristically human of activities (no animal has contrived anything remotely comparable to *War and Peace* or the *Jupiter Symphony*) reflects uniquely human needs as well. People can relate to one another in either a cooperative or competitive manner and we will now consider how these desires may impel not only collaborations (of the horizontal and hierarchical kind, respectively) but creative work of all kinds. [*See* MOTIVATION/DRIVE.]

A. Cooperation

Even Sartre, that unrivaled advocate of power struggles, saw the writer–reader partnership as being one between equals, and many creators view their works as symbolic gifts to the public, gifts that share an essential part of themselves. But horizontal collaborations on the face of it provide cooperative situations nonpareil, when they become exercises in teamwork. Dancer–choreographer relationships can vary enormously in this respect, but many involve mutual give and take, with each suggesting possibilities, and final choices being those that both find satisfactory. Likewise, directors Sidney Lumet and Harold Prince report that they must have a sense of family to work effectively, and Franco Zefferelli abandoned several projects that did not give him feelings of love.

That said, the most effective form of cooperation in collaborative relationships probably differs from more personal situations. In the latter, liking among participants, and presumably therefore prospects of their relationship succeeding, increases with their similarity, especially in basic attitudes and values. However, many less than likable people have been effective collaborators. The irascible Richard Rodgers teamed successfully with both Lorenz Hart and Oscar Hammerstein II, men of radically different work habits and personality. Similarly, Gilbert and Sullivan lay at opposite ends of every personality dimension, Gilbert being a dictatorial, abrasive egocentric, and Sullivan a gentle "nice guy," ever anxious to please. Friendship was therefore out of the question from the start, and they rarely met, preferring to conduct their interactions at arms length via intermediaries. Yet the results speak for themselves. In this regard, analogies with sports help clarify many of creativity's phenomena, and teams have special relevance to collaboration, because again several individuals must work together toward a common goal, in this case, winning. But too much togetherness among team members off the field, it seems, not only does not necessarily help but may hinder success. It is commonality of purpose, a shared drive to excel, that is important. A number of successful teams, such as the Oakland A's and New York Yankees baseball dynasties of the 1970s, had members who could barely put up with one another on a personal level. Thus that supposed necessity for success, team spirit, may result from, rather than cause, winning, because when losses mount, team spirit usually suffers. [*See* TEAMS.]

By the same token, too much similarity among collaborators may actually be counterproductive. One common view of creative thinking, captured by Arthur Koestler's notion of bisociation, is that several ideas, each perhaps familiar in themselves, are brought together to achieve a novel combination, for example, when Darwin provided a plausible account for an ancient concept, evolution, by incorporating the mechanism of natural selection. But the probability of achieving original, worthwhile combinations increases with the number of diverse ideas available, and partners of one mind would provide fewer of these than when they have different expertises and outlooks. In the same vein, Adam Smith asserted that a division of labor, wherein each person contributes a special, differing expertise to a problem, enhances productivity (and also, Durkheim added, feelings of solidarity and group). In short, in the collaborative as opposed to personal sphere, partner diversity may offer more prospects for success.

Another personal quality that successful collaborators may need is suggested by Howard Gardner's views. Abilities in various activities such as music, mathematics, and language are supposedly independent, so creativity is not wide-ranging but specific to a field and one is talented *for something*. It is immediately apparent that most of us are better at some things than others and that someone supremely capable at one thing may be hopeless at another, but the notable point is that one of the seven abilities Gardner identifies is for interpersonal relations, so special talent here may be another requirement for collaborators. That said, creative people in every field tend to be introverted, with some such as Newton and Emily Dickinson being virtual re-

cluses, and the people skills of even such able collaborators as choreographers Jerome Robbins and Antony Tudor, to say nothing of the aforementioned Richard Rodgers and Hitchcock, were notoriously lacking. Which suggests again that the interpersonal elements required for success may differ from those needed in other kinds of relationships. One likely attribute is a thick skin to handle the criticism and disagreements that invariably arise, because in relations among collaborators as opposed to friends or lovers, the quality of the final product is more important than how one feels while interacting.

But if partner diversity is preferable, how can this be reconciled with that cliché explanation for successful collaborations, "a meeting of minds?" Does this not suggest that partners must also be on the same wavelength? Our guess is that there must be common ground regarding fundamental matters such as the ultimate goals and directions. Both Watson and Crick saw the structure of DNA as a worthwhile problem and model building as a promising way to tackle it, and Rodgers and Hammerstein felt an immediate commonality about the form and future direction of musical theater. It is about superficial matters of detail that differences can be fertile, for what is more stimulating to thought and discovery than a good argument? However, we cannot argue productively with someone who rejects our most dearly held suppositions. Discussions now become merely frustrating, and soon angry silences take over. Alternatively, others whom we suspect do not share those suppositions cause most of us to opt for politeness over candor to avoid unpleasantness, and as Crick pointed out, politeness is the enemy of effective collaboration, which requires candor, even rudeness. Either way, communication founders, at which point a collaboration is dead in the water, because if various ideas are to be combined, each must be brought into the open.

At a theoretical level, both Erich Fromm and Rollo May have linked cooperative motives to creativity via the human desire for intimacy, the experience of contacting others not only physically, as in sex, but psychologically. However, they appear to part company thereafter. For May, creativity is the means par excellence for satisfying this desire. Fromm did see collective art, group activities such as singing and dancing, as an effective means to this end, but otherwise creative work seemed to him a less satisfactory solution because it lacks the direct contact with another person that only the act of love can provide. This view, that such work represents a kind of compensation for inadequate intimacy, has much to recommend it. It is notable how few great lives have featured intimacy; such isolates as Newton and Franz Kafka are only extremes of a general pattern. As always, there are exceptions. The Roberts, Schumann and Browning, experienced immortal love affairs, and Tolstoy enjoyed both a childhood filled with love and later, at least during the years when he produced his greatest literary works, a seemingly idyllic marriage (his wife virtually collaborated in the writing of *War and Peace*). However, these are exceptions, and Fromm's account gains more credibility if the intimacy need is broadened to include a need to be loved, because its frustration could instill that apparent motive for so much work, the desire for recognition. More generally, van Gogh's letters to his brother Theo reveal his intense need to not only give but to receive affection. Sadly, this supreme social misfit had a genius not only for art but for turning others off, so his every attempt at a relationship led to eventual rejection. Did this instill the frenetic drive to paint that characterized his final years?

Alternatively, some people may voluntarily choose creativity over genuine intimacy. Loving another person is risky. One is vulnerable—to losing independence and self, but above all the loved person, be it through rejection or bereavement. Creativity involves considerable risks as well, notably of failure, but perhaps these pale in comparison to those of genuine love. Is it more devastating to be told by critics and audience that you have come up short, or to have someone who has become the very center of your life maintain that "we can still be friends"? As well, creativity offers greater possibilities for control. Given enough persistence, a product can be revised into a reasonable approximation of that ideal in the mind, but significant others must be taken as given, warts and all, and as the truism has it, trying to change them into what one wants is both futile and harmful (although most people in relationships have a go at it nevertheless). Director/choreographer Bob Fosse's life, as his autobiographical film *All That Jazz* shows, featured a dizzying series of extramarital dalliances, but he and his psychiatrist agreed that he was terrified by deep emotional involvements. Fosse's observation is therefore suggestive that he was always frightened when beginning a project,

until he gained a sense of its direction, whereupon he felt in control. Evidently it was the anticipation of this that kept him coming back for more.

B. Competition

Turning to this other form of relationship, Alfie Kohn has asserted that competition is a scourge of modern North American life that can and should be eliminated (and that his work earned the American Psychological Association's "Excellence in Media" award suggests that many social scientists agree). There can be no doubt about its many evils: the rat race of capitalist economies that reduces so many to neurosis, and the damage to children's sports such as Little League baseball when winning becomes overemphasized, to say nothing of the ultimate abomination, war itself. Nonetheless, we take issue with Kohn's recommendations as being both impossible to realize and undesirable, because competition also has positive results. In particular, according to the tenets of evolution, ongoing creativity characterizes nature and that creativity relies on competitive mechanisms, natural selection and survival of the fittest. Therefore, there is every reason to suspect that the human variety might do so as well, given its many similarities to nature's version that Skinner pointed out.

Kohn describes several popular beliefs about competition and then tries to demolish each, but only two are relevant here. The first such myth is that competition is inevitable, being a part of human nature bred into our genes. In fact, Kohn claims, we learn to be competitive through the great teacher, experience, and the tendency can therefore be eliminated by eradicating conditions that promote it. Thus he takes a clear stand on that most pervasive issue, nature versus nurture. Unfortunately, psychologists have learned to their sorrow that the issue's importance is equaled by the difficulty of obtaining conclusive answers. In most cases, strong arguments can be made on both sides, and this is certainly the case for competition, aggressiveness, and the like. Kohn's stance is problematic not because he opts for nurture, for there is compelling evidence to support such a position—for example, there are nonviolent societies that feature minimal competition, so it does seem possible to eliminate it—but because he dismisses nature as if the matter had been settled, when in fact as usual the jury is still out. Those uncompetitive societies no doubt involve different genetic pools, so any "competitive genes," if such there be, may have been bred out or never instilled.

However, our main response is that whether competition stems from nature or nurture becomes academic if in practice it is inevitable, and, as evolution in nature shows, this must be so whenever the supply of a commodity exceeds demand for it, which is precisely the situation in most fields wherein creativity occurs. As a result, those involved must be at least able to endure competition or be trampled underfoot, and someone who is driven by and thrives on it would have a distinct advantage. In the arts, competition is a fact of life. Admittedly, there are those who have disagreed, notably pianist Glenn Gould. For Gould, the arts enhance civilization because they lift it above jungle law and survival of the fittest, so for them to involve competition is contradictory. He therefore deplored that rite of passage through which so many Canadian youngsters have passed, the local Music Festival wherein scores of them compete for victory.

Still and all, there can be no doubt that there are far more talented artists than the traffic will bear, so poets must compete for publication, painters for gallery showings—the list is endless. Similarly for performing artists. The musical *A Chorus Line* poignantly dramatized auditions for Broadway shows, otherwise known as "cattle calls," wherein several hundred vie for the few jobs available, and since nowadays only a very few instrumental musicians can have international performing and recording careers, the main way to attract notice is to do well in a major competition such as the van Cliburn. Certainly such situations are distressing, for even those eliminated early are talented and deserving, but what are the alternatives?

Scientists too must compete, for the limited funds available (many forms of science cannot be done without hefty largesse from public or corporate purses), for that absolute requisite for the modern researcher, frequent publication (rejection rates of reputable journals exceed 80%), and for that preeminent incentive, peer respect and reputation. According to James Watson's *The Double Helix,* he and Crick sought DNA's molecular structure because that ultimate accolade, the Nobel Prize, surely awaited those who found the answer. To Watson, the situation resembled a race against others also in the hunt, since only the victors could garner this greatest of spoils (although Crick denied that Watson's

scenario applied to himself). Idealists may assert that everyone can come first if we accept anything and everything as equally worthy; thus Carl Rogers refused to judge whether devising a meat sauce showed more or less creativity than formulating a theory of relativity. However, this practice too seems to us both impossible and undesirable. People cannot avoid making value judgments and expressing preferences—it is truly said that "everyone's a critic"—and if the wheat is not separated from the chaff, works of quality will be buried beneath masses of mediocrity. As nature reminds us, selection and therefore competition is necessary if superior possibilities are to emerge.

Several theoretical accounts sound these competitive themes. We have seen how Sartre stressed such motives, and so did another representative of the existential tradition, Albert Camus. As he sees it, life provides no certain answers to the fundamental questions everyone asks, such as what it means, yet we desperately want such answers. Life will inevitably end, yet we long to live forever. Placing us in a situation that must deny us these satisfactions represents the absurd, and it and the Being that perpetrated it, God, are the sworn enemies of the metaphysical rebel. For Camus, creators exemplify such people. In concocting products that part company with the absurdity God provided, they tacitly suggest how it could be bettered—van Gogh described life as one of God's first drafts that did not turn out well—and if their products achieve immortality, they symbolically defeat death. Thus it is anger against God and death and the desire to defeat them that energizes creative work; indicatively, poet Dylan Thomas exhorted his dying father not to go gently into that good night, but rage, rage against it.

The second belief Kohn disputes, that competition is productive because it fosters such things as creativity, is one that Watson himself, due to his reading of the DNA episode, strongly promoted. Kohn however disagrees and again there is evidence to support him, notably Johnson and Johnson's many studies in which subjects placed in cooperative situations, wherein they work together toward a common goal, consistently outperform those in competitive ones. However, just as great athletes like Mohammed Ali need worthy opponents like Joe Frazier to achieve their full potential, in other bailiwicks, alternatives that seem unacceptable may stimulate us to clarify those we prefer instead, just as we can only understand a concept such as black by placing it against its opposite. Philosophers Nietzsche and Kant were driven by desires to answer Darwin and Hume, respectively, and Gestalt psychology began as a revolt against Wundt's structuralism, as did the Humanistic movement against the dominant psychologies of the day, psychoanalysis and behaviorism.

So too in the arts. The romantic movement that affected every 19th century European form, by emphasizing individual over collective concerns and feeling over reason or empirical evidence, openly reacted against the Enlightenment, as did the modern dance movement pioneered by Isadora Duncan and Martha Graham against everything for which classical ballet stood. Moreover, as satire reveals, most humor at base targets some antagonist or scapegoat. Finally, consider "priority disputes," those surprisingly common, sometimes extremely nasty episodes in which several people independently realize the same achievement and then clash over who thought of it first (famous examples include Newton versus Leibnitz over calculus and Darwin versus Wallace over evolution). If motives were truly selfless and purposes cooperative, no one should care so long as the discovery is made, but in reality less admirable but more human motives, notably of ego, predominate. People do care. Very much. Indeed, many renowned scientists have possessed strongly combative streaks, one example par excellence again being Isaac Newton. Episodes of enmity were by no means limited to the calculus affair but arose repeatedly, encompassing the amazing array of fields in which he was expert. In fact Anthony Storr attributed his obsessive drive to solve nature's puzzles to an intense need to gain a sense of control over it that only perfect clarity could provide. Supposedly, this need stemmed from his having been abandoned in infancy by his mother. The resulting insecurity left him feeling trapped in a situation over which he had no control.

In this regard, it is well to remember what transpires when societies purportedly succeed in minimizing competition. Margaret Mead compared the cultures of Samoa, which stressed cooperation and togetherness, and Bali, wherein ruthless competition and antagonism reigned. Not surprisingly, mental health and happiness were more prevalent in the first case, but indicatively, Bali was far more productive in a creative sense, suggesting that competition, and the insecurities and unhappiness that oftentimes result, may be the price that

must be paid. Hierarchical collaborations, with their blatant power and dominance relationships, make the same point. That supposed simulation of the military, the New York City Ballet, also gave rise to a stream of Balanchine masterpieces, such as *Agon* and *Concerto Barocco.* Do these sublime ends justify the means? It is a moot point. On the other hand, those uncompetitive societies also devalued concrete achievement and so accomplished little in the way of it. Which suggests that to eliminate competition, people hereabouts would have to adopt the same attitude and this we are loathe to do. A familiar novel portrays a culture in which competition and achievement have gone by the boards. It is called *Brave New World* and we would not wish to live in such a one.

Kohn contends that motivation need not decrease when cooperation replaces competition. Athletes, for example, if trained from infancy in the former, should enjoy games far more and become quite as proficient. We remain skeptical. Experience with not only adults but youngsters indicates that for many, when winning is not the aim, enjoyment and interest soon decline. Admittedly, most participants, certainly amateurs, garner their greatest satisfactions not from winning but from feeling that they have done their best. However, although there is no logical reason why this should be so, *psycho*logically most of us, unless we are *trying* to win, do not put out the extra bit of effort that allows us to do our best and thus gain that ultimate reward. In other words, rather than doing our best in order to win, we must be trying to win in order to do our best. To some, the reducio ad absurdum of the need for victory gone mad is immortal football coach Vince Lombardi's aphorism, "Winning isn't everything, it's the only thing." Yet he was also heard to say, "Winning isn't everything, trying to win is." Precisely.

What of Johnson and Johnson's many demonstrations that cooperative situations surpass competitive ones in enhancing creativity? These studies run afoul of problems raised earlier; due to the tasks and subject populations used, the findings may not generalize to real-life great achievement, and this problem is compounded here because purely cooperative or competitive situations untrammeled by their opposite are set against each other. However, in practice far more often than not both mechanisms occur together as part and parcel of the same situation, so they are as inextricably linked as yin and yang. Sports again help clarify the point. Teammates working toward a common goal nonetheless compete for playing time and starting assignments, and on the other hand, most athletes feel camaraderie not only with teammates but with opponents; witness the postgame revelry with them that is such an integral part of the rugby tradition. So too in other fields. Dancers in companies compete for roles and collaborators in the sciences must decide who receives first authorship in publications and hence the lion's share of the credit (the disciples of equality have not, to our knowledge, found a way for everyone to be listed first), and yet both artists and scientists develop friendships and feelings of group with others who also compete for available rewards. Moreover, Johnson and Johnson, when they speak of the constructive results of disagreements within cooperative situations, tacitly recognize that the two mechanisms are inescapably linked.

Otto Rank made the same point theoretically. Creative work supposedly stems from two desires, (a) for individuation, to express one's unique self and independence from others, which implies competitiveness, and (b) for identification, to share universal human experiences, which enhances togetherness. The two motives wax and wane, and different forms of art result depending on which is dominant, but the key point here is that all art supposedly involves aspects of both, with the greatest art (for Rank, the art of ancient Greece) being that which achieves a balanced integration. As poet Earle Birney put it, listeners hear both a poet's individual, separate identity, and the human cry that is his certificate of humanity.

Another point vis-à-vis competition on which Kohn takes a stand is the familiar notion of competing with oneself. Does this not exemplify competition's productive aspects? For Kohn, however, such a mechanism, even if it occurs, does not constitute genuine competition because it lacks the element of either/or — of victor and vanquished — and he dismisses it as being not worthy of serious consideration. This position too is unsatisfactory. Many people invoke the mechanism and regard it as introspectively valid, which suggests that they believe that they can and do compete with themselves, and that this stimulates many activities, including creativity.

Several theoretical accounts imply a similar mechanism. Adler maintained that creativity stems from compensation. Those who feel inferior in some way supposedly try to make up for it by an increased drive for success elsewhere; thus the philosopher Kierkegaard's outspoken assertiveness may have reflected compensation for his sickly physique and hunchback, and the poet Byron's arrogant independence his acute sensitivity about his clubfoot. As another variation, Nietzsche and later Maslow argued that the ultimate satisfaction comes from becoming the best person one potentially can be. However, this is difficult. It demands hard work, and a part of us prefers the ease of underachievement, making what Nietzsche called "self-overcoming" of those slothful tendencies mandatory. Bandura's perspective is also helpful. In any activity, each person sets internal standards of the performance they expect of themselves, for example, a student aiming for a "B" in a course. Reaching one's standard indicates success and is rewarded with feelings of pride and self-satisfaction, whereas coming up short results in guilt and shame, so the same achievement may represent success to one person and failure to another if they possess different standards (and those who achieve great things tend to be perfectionists). When one tries to match standards set by oneself, is this not competing with yourself?

Bibliography

Abra, J. C. (1997). *The motives for creative work: An inquiry.* Cresskill, NH: Hampton Press.

Bliss, M. (1982). *The discovery of insulin.* Toronto: McLelland & Stewart.

Kohn, A. (1986). *No contest: The case against competition.* Boston: Houghton Mifflin.

Mazo, J. (1974). *Dance is a contact sport.* New York: Da Capo Press.

Pearson, H. (1950). *Gilbert and Sullivan.* Markham, Ontario: Penguin.

Sartre, J. P. (1965). *What is literature?* New York: Harper & Row.

Spoto, D. (1983). *The dark side of genius: The life of Alfred Hitchcock.* New York: Ballentine Books.

Watson, J. D. (1968). *The double helix.* New York: New American Library.

Westfall, R. S. (1980). *Never at rest: A biography of Isaac Newton.* New York: Cambridge University Press.

Componential Models

Todd I. Lubart

Université René Descartes

Compensation An interdependency between components through which a low level of one component can be offset by a high level of another component.

Component An element that determines or is involved in a phenomenon (such as creativity).

Confluence Approach A theoretical perspective in which several components must converge to yield creative behavior.

Interaction An interdependency between two or more components through which the effect of one component is modified by the presence of others.

Model A schematic representation of a phenomenon.

Profile The pattern describing an individual's level on several components.

Resources Abilities, skills, traits, and/or dispositions that are useful for creativity; often used as a synonym for components.

System A macro-level description of a set of closely related components.

COMPONENTIAL MODELS *are attempts to specify the set of abilities, skills, traits, dispositions, and/or pro-* *cesses that are involved in creative behavior. Models vary on the nature of the components for creativity as well as the way that the components work together and interact with each other. Advantages of componential models include their capacity to capture the complexity of creativity and to account for diverse aspects of creativity, such as its partial domain specificity. Some disadvantages of these models are their reduced parsimony and the difficulty involved in testing these models. Componential models can be extended to group and organizational levels of creativity. Componential models have implications for measuring creative potential and enhancing creativity.*

I. ALTERNATE CONCEPTIONS OF THE COMPONENTS FOR CREATIVITY

A. Three-Component Model

Teresa Amabile, in 1983, proposed one of the first detailed componential models of creativity in her work on a social psychology of creativity. This model was updated in Amabile's 1996 book, *Creativity in Context*. In this model, there are three components for creativity: task motivation, domain-relevant skills, and creativity-relevant processes.

Task motivation involves an individual's reasons for

Copyright © 1999 by Academic Press
All rights of reproduction in any form reserved.

engaging in a task and the person's attitude toward the task to be accomplished. Intrinsic motivation, considered important for creativity, arises from inherent qualities of a task, such as the challenge that the task offers. Extrinsic motivation, arising from sources exterior to the task (such as a reward for task completion), tends to have a negative influence on creativity. However, extrinsic motivators may have a positive effect on creativity in certain circumstances (e.g., when a high level of intrinsic motivation is present). The social environment influences the level of task motivation. For example, work recognized socially as important may enhance intrinsic motivation whereas competition with co-workers may undermine intrinsic motivation. [*See* MOTIVATION/DRIVE.]

Domain-relevant skills include knowledge, technical skills, and special talents relevant to the task domain. For example, domain-relevant skills for creativity in science may be factual knowledge about a problematic phenomenon, technical skills for laboratory procedures, and a special talent for mental imagery. Creativity-relevant processes include a cognitive style that facilitates coping with complexity and breaking one's mental set during problem solving, the use of heuristics for generating novel ideas (e.g., trying a counterintuitive idea when stuck on a problem), and a work style characterized in part by persistence and sustained attention to a task. [*See* COGNITIVE STYLE AND CREATIVITY; HEURISTICS.]

The creativity-relevant processes are considered to apply to all tasks for which creativity is sought, whereas the domain-relevant skills and task motivation components show greater task specificity. These three components are considered as necessary and sufficient for creative work. An individual's level on the three components determines that person's creative performance on a task. If one component is absent (e.g., no domain skills) then creativity will not be possible.

Amabile's componential model also specifies how the three components enter into the creative process. The creative process has several phases that do not necessarily occur in a fixed sequence; these phases are (a) problem or task identification, (b) preparation (gathering relevant information), (c) response generation (seeking and producing potential responses), and (d) response validation and communication (testing the possible response). The outcome of this process may be a successful product, a failure, or some progress toward one's goal which leads to a return to one or more phases in the process. Each component is proposed to be especially influential for creativity during certain phases of the work on a task and not others. Intrinsic task motivation is particularly important for problem identification and the initiation of work on a problem. Intrinsic task motivation also plays an important role in the response generation phase such as through the effort expended to generate and explore possible responses. Certain types of extrinsic task motivation can be beneficial for the preparation and response validation–communication phases because these phases may involve substantial work but do not focus on producing novel ideas. Domain-relevant skills play a key role in the preparation and response validation–communication phases. Creativity-relevant processes are important for the response generation phase. Task motivation can be affected by the outcome of the creative process (e.g., motivation may increase if there is some progress toward a goal). Task motivation can also lead to the acquisition of domain-relevant skills and promote set-breaking tendencies, which are part of the creativity-relevant processes component.

B. Investment Approach: A Confluence of Six Resources

Robert Sternberg and Todd Lubart proposed an investment approach to creativity in a 1991 article and their 1995 book, *Defying the Crowd*. The investment approach builds, in part, on Amabile's work as well as several other proposals. According to this perspective, creativity requires a confluence of six distinct but interrelated resources. A creative person is one who possesses the necessary resources and employs these resources to "buy low" (pursue ideas that are new or out of favor but have potential), and after developing these ideas, to "sell high" (presenting the production publicly, at the right moment for the production to be appreciated). These resources for creativity are specific aspects of intelligence, knowledge, cognitive styles, personality, motivation, and environmental context. Three intellectual abilities important for creativity are the synthetic ability to define and represent problems in new ways, the analytic ability to recognize which ideas are worth pursuing, and the practical ability to "sell" one's work to others—to persuade them of the value of the new work. The combination of these abilities is also important (e.g., one must have new ideas and be able to transmit them effectively to other people). With regard to knowledge, some knowledge is necessary to make a contribution to a field but too much knowledge can result in an entrenched perspective (seeing a problem in terms of old schemas). For thinking styles, a preference for thinking in novel ways of one's own choosing and a preference for working with the "big picture" rather than the details are considered important for creativity. Creativity-relevant personality attributes include perseverance, willingness to take risks, willingness to tolerate ambiguity, openness to new experiences, and individuality. The motivation for creativity may be either intrinsic or extrinsic as long as the motivator energizes a person to work and allows the person to keep his or her attention focused on the task. Finally, the environment is considered a resource for creativity because it can provide physical or social stimulation to help generate ideas and to nurture these ideas. The environment additionally evaluates creativity through social judgment. [*See* CONDITIONS AND SETTINGS/ENVIRONMENT; PERSONALITY.]

With regard to the confluence of resources, Sternberg and Lubart propose that creativity involves more than a simple sum of an individual's level on each of the components for creativity. First, there may be thresholds for some components (e.g., knowledge) below which creativity is not possible, regardless of an individual's level on the other components. Second, partial compensation may occur between the components in which a strength in one component (e.g., motivation) may counteract a weakness in another component (e.g., knowledge). Third, although each component contributes in its own way to creativity, a component is always acting in the presence of other components and this coaction can lead to interactive effects. For example, high levels in both intelligence and motivation could multiplicatively enhance creativity.

A person's set of resources, called his or her portfolio, yields a latent potential for creativity which is partially domain specific. When a person invests his or her resources in a task, then creative behavior can result. The

level of creative performance depends on both the individual's resources and the requirements of the task which is undertaken.

C. The Interactionist Approach

A third approach to creativity that may be considered componential is Richard Woodman and Lyle Schoenfeldt's interactionist model. In this model, creative behavior results from a complex interaction between a person and a situation. The model is composed of three main components: antecedent conditions, characteristics of the person, and characteristics of the situation. Antecedent conditions refer to preexisting circumstances that influence the current state of a person, a situation, and their interaction. Some examples are biographical variables such as family socioeconomic status or previous experiences in a particular situation. Person-centered characteristics include cognitive abilities and styles (e.g., divergent thinking or field independence/dependence), personality traits (e.g., dogmatism), and organismic variables (e.g., attitudes, values, and motivations). Situation-related characteristics include social influences (e.g., role models, rewards, and social evaluation) and contextual influences (e.g., physical environment, organizational climate, and culture).

D. Systems Approach

Systems approaches can also be considered componential in a broad sense of the term. Mihalyi Csikszentmihalyi together with David Feldman and Howard Gardner have taken a systems approach to creativity. The individual, a first system, draws on information in a domain and transforms or extends it via cognitive processes, personality traits, and motivation. The field, a second system, consists of people who control or influence a domain, evaluate, and select new ideas (e.g., art critics and gallery owners). The domain, a third system, consists of a culturally defined body of knowledge which incorporates creative products and can be transmitted from one person to another. Individuals are influenced by both the field and the domain systems and can induce changes in these systems. In an alternative proposal, Howard Gruber and his colleagues have developed the evolving-systems approach. In this approach, an individual's knowledge, purpose (set of goals), and affect (e.g., joy or frustration) develop over time and interact to amplify deviations that a person encounters during a task, which in turn can lead to creative productions.

E. Cognitive-Components Approach

This set of models focuses on the cognitive abilities and processes involved in creative thinking. Of all the componential models of creativity, these cognitive models are closest in their conception to the well-known componential models of intelligence proposed by Robert Sternberg and other authors. Historically, J. P. Guilford's work on creativity during the 1950s to 1970s can be viewed as an early cognitive componential approach to creativity. Guilford highlighted the relevance of certain abilities for creativity, such as sensitivity to problems, divergent thinking, and evaluation skills, and proposed how these abilities enter into the problem solving process in his Structure of Intellect Problem Solving Model.

More recently, Michael Mumford and his colleagues have specified a set of cognitive components that participate in the process of creating new ideas. These components include problem construction, information encoding, category search to access information, specification of best fitting categories, combination and reorganization of category information, idea evaluation, implementation, and monitoring. Ronald Finke, Thomas Ward, and Steven Smith in their geneplore model posit generative and exploratory phases of the creative process. The generative phase of creative thinking involves the construction of loosely formulated ideas called preinventive structures. Generative componential processes include knowledge retrieval, idea association, synthesis, transformation, and analogical transfer. The exploratory phase of creative thinking refers to the examination, elaboration, and testing of the preinventive structures. Exploratory componential processes include interpretation of preinventive structures, hypothesis testing, and searching for limitations. The geneplore model proposes that there is a cyclic movement between the generative and the exploratory phases. Finally, Mark Runco and Ivonne Chand have proposed a two-tier componential

model. The primary components are problem finding skills, ideation skills, and evaluation skills. Secondary components, which influence the primary components, are knowledge and motivation.

II. STRENGTHS AND WEAKNESSES OF COMPONENTIAL MODELS

One of the strengths of componential models is their capacity to integrate cohesively many findings about the nature of creativity. By varying one or more parameters in these general models, one can account for diverse manifestations of creativity. For example, several studies have found that creative behavior is partially domain specific. In other words, there is some consistency across tasks but a person may be creative in one domain of activity and not another. Componential models can account for this pattern because some components for creativity are posited to be domain or task specific, such as knowledge, whereas other components are more generally applicable across domains, such as the ability to synthesize information. Furthermore, a person's profile across several components may fit more or less closely the requirements of a given task, and this leads to variations in the level of creative performance across domains. Componential models can, additionally, account for the wide range of individual differences in creative behavior—from very low levels to eminent levels of creativity. Individuals with very low levels of creativity may have either low levels on each of the components for creativity or a very low level on one of the components such that compensation between the components is impossible. Eminent creators have nearly optimal levels (for a given task domain) on all of the components for creativity. The positively skewed distribution of creativity with very few highly creative people can be explained by a componential model because the probability of having an optimal level on each component needed for creativity is small. Furthermore, if the components combine multiplicatively, then high levels on several components will yield an extremely high level of creativity.

Certain weaknesses of componential models can also be noted. For example, because componential models specify numerous components and interactions between these components, they have been criticized for lacking parsimony. Additionally, componential models are difficult to test. A complete test of a componential model requires that all of the components are measured for each person (as well as measuring the creative behavior of the person). The contribution of each component and the interactions of the components can then be studied. Only a few studies of this type have been conducted. A final weakness of componential models is their lack of specification. For certain models, the nature of the components is well specified but the optimal levels of each component and the interactions between components are less clear. Obviously, future work can address these criticisms.

III. EXTENSIONS OF COMPONENTIAL MODELS

Componential models tend to focus on creativity at the individual level of analysis. In other words, these models seek to specify the components that will account for individual differences in creativity. However, the logic of componential models can be applied to creativity at the group or organizational level. For example, Teresa Amabile has proposed an extension of her componential model to the organizational level. Part of the model for organizational creativity consists of the componential model for individual creativity, which also describes creativity in small groups. In addition to the three individual-level components (intrinsic motivation, task-relevant skills, and creative thinking processes), there are parallel components at the organizational level of activity. There is the organization's motivation to innovate (including the value placed on innovation and desire to innovate), the organization's resources in the task domain (e.g., human, material, and financial), and the organization's skills in the management of innovation. These organizational components influence both the creativity of individuals (and small groups) and the creative process of the organization as a whole. For example, the organizational motivation to innovate influences the individual's or small group's intrinsic motivation to do a task and the organization's statement of its mission or project agenda.

Similarly, Richard Woodman and his colleagues have extended the interactionist model. For creativity at the group level, important components are the creative behavior of individuals, the interactive combination of individuals in the group (e.g., group composition), group characteristics (e.g., norms, size, and cohesiveness), group processes (e.g., work methods), and contextual influences (e.g., organizational characteristics and task characteristics). Organizational creativity, in turn, is the product of the creative behavior of several groups with additional contextual influences that operate specifically on the organization as a whole.

IV. IMPLICATIONS OF COMPONENTIAL MODELS

A. Measuring Creative Potential

Based on the tenets of componential models, potentially creative individuals can be identified by measuring each component necessary for creativity. An individual can be described as having a componential profile which will be more or less an ideal for creativity. The ideal profile for creativity is hypothesized to differ to some extent for each specific task and for each domain of work (e.g., visual art, literature, or science). The identification of potentially creative people involves a comparison between an individual's profile over the set of components for creativity and the profile of components needed for creativity in a particular task.

If creativity tests are used to evaluate creative potential, the extent to which these tests assess all of the components needed for creativity must be analyzed. Several of the available creativity tests emphasize certain cognitive components of creativity, such as divergent thinking. However, the evaluation of creative potential based on only one or a few cognitive components would be partial and imprecise. According to some componential models, an assessment battery for creative potential should include measures of intellectual abilities, task-relevant knowledge, cognitive styles, task motivation, and specific personality traits. [*See* DIVERGENT THINKING; APPENDIX II: TESTS OF CREATIVITY.]

B. Enhancing Creativity

One way to enhance creativity is by training the components needed for creative behavior. Most creativity training programs or techniques focus on certain cognitive components. A complete training program would seek to enhance all components involved in creativity (cognitive and noncognitive). Additionally, creativity training can be tailored to each person after determining which components are not at their optimal level for the individual.

Another way to enhance creativity through a componential approach is to train people how to use best the componential resources that they have. People can learn to use certain components during one phase of a task and other components during a later phase of a task. In some cases, creative performance can also be enhanced by matching people with tasks in order to maximize the fit between a person's componential profile and the components that a task requires. A final implication of componential models for enhancing creativity is that a particular creativity training program may have differential effects because people start with different componential profiles and because the components may interact with each other. Thus, enhancing one component (e.g., acquiring domain-relevant knowledge) may in turn affect another component (e.g., risk taking or motivation). [See ENHANCEMENT OF CREATIVITY; TEACHING CREATIVITY.]

Bibliography

Amabile, T. M. (1988). A model of creativity and innovation in organizations. *Research in Organizational Behavior, 10,* 123–167.

Amabile, T. M. (1996). *Creativity in context.* Boulder, CO: Westview.

Conti, R., Coon, H., & Amabile, T. M. (1996). Evidence to support the componential model of creativity: Secondary analyses of three studies. *Creativity Research Journal, 9*(4), 385–389.

Csikszentmihalyi, M. (1988). Society, culture, and person: A systems view of creativity. In R. J. Sternberg (Ed.), *The nature of creativity: Contemporary psychological perspectives* (pp. 325–339). New York: Cambridge University Press.

Feldman, D. H., Csikszentmihalyi, M., & Gardner, H. (1994). *Changing the world: A framework for the study of creativity.* Westport, CT: Praeger.

Finke, R. A., Ward, T. B., & Smith, S. S. (1992). *Creative cognition: Theory, research, and applications.* Cambridge, MA: MIT Press.

Gruber, H. E. (1989). The evolving systems approach to creative work. In D. B. Wallace & H. E. Gruber (Eds.), *Creative people at work: Twelve cognitive case studies* (pp. 3–24). New York: Oxford University Press.

Lubart, T. I., & Sternberg, R. J. (1995). An investment approach to creativity: Theory and data. In S. M. Smith, T. B. Ward, & R. A. Finke (Eds.), *The creative cognition approach* (pp. 271–302). Cambridge, MA: MIT Press.

Mumford, M. D., Mobley, M. I., Uhlman, C. E., Reiter-Palmon, R., & Doares, L. M. (1991). Process analytic models of creative capacities. *Creativity Research Journal, 4*(2), 91–122.

Runco, M. A., & Chand, I. (1995). Cognition and creativity. *Educational Psychology Review, 7*(3), 243–267.

Sternberg, R. J., & Lubart, T. I. (1991). An investment theory of creativity and its development. *Human Development, 34,* 1–32.

Sternberg, R. J., & Lubart, T. I. (1995). *Defying the crowd: Cultivating creativity in a culture of conformity.* New York: Free Press.

Woodman, R. W., Sawyer, J. E., & Griffin, R. W. (1993). Toward a theory of organizational creativity. *Academy of Management Review, 18*(2), 293–321.

Woodman, R. W., & Schoenfeldt, L. F. (1990). An interactionist model of creative behavior. *Journal of Creative Behavior, 24*(4), 279–291.

Computer Programs

Tony Proctor

Independent Lecturer, Writer, and Consultant, Lancashire, England

Groupware Computer software which can be simultaneously accessed by more than one individual making use of networked computers.

Idea Processor A computer program which assists the process of ideation.

Mindmap A graphic technique which facilitates recording thoughts and associations through a connected nodal structure.

Outliner A program which allows the user to enter written text in a random or unstructured fashion and facilitates the reordering and restructuring of the entries in a more meaningful way.

Task Management Package A computer program which facilitates the planning and costing of project management.

COMPUTER-ENHANCED CREATIVITY SOFTWARE *can be categorized in five ways: (1) creative problem solving programs, (2) outlining and presentation programs, (3) thesaurus programs, (4) incubation programs, and (5) groupware programs. One can also distinguish between programs that are designed for individual use and programs that are designed for use with groups. Other types of programs—spreadsheets, simulation packages, databases, and business games—can also be applied in a manner that assists the creative thinking and problem solving processes.*

I. HISTORY

Computer-aided creative thinking and problem solving mechanisms began to appear in the late 1970s. The methods employed had a theoretical basis in the work of Rogers, Maslow, and Kelly. In 1954 both C. Rogers and A. Maslow supported the view that self-discovery might improve creativity, while G. A. Kelly argued that the loosening of constructs led to the gaining of creative insights.

In 1979 Rokeach assembled a computer program which enabled individuals to examine their own value systems. This work showed the potential effects that a computer program could have for clarifying the user's own knowledge. Another program, Planet, designed by M. L. Shaw, helped the user to uncover the themes and variations in his or her own individual problems. A

Copyright © 1999 by Academic Press
All rights of reproduction in any form reserved.

central component of the program was the Repertory Grid discussed by Kelly, and it is this which helped comprehension of the classifications people construct around their experiences and, if required, to reconstruct views on a problem. A later program, Cope (now marketed as Decision Explorer) was devised by Colin Eden in 1985 and was designed to help map the relationship between ideas connecting interrelated sets of problems.

The 1980s saw a growth in interest in the development of computer programs to aid creative thinking and creative problem solving. Brainstorm was typical of a number of programs designed to help people be more organized in their thinking. Essentially, it was an idea processor working rather like a word processor and a database combined. It allowed the user to type in ideas or the outline of a plan or schedule as it came to mind. One could then subsequently reorganize the ideas or points under any number of headings or subheadings so that the structure of the document and one's thinking were both more meaningfully organized. These latter kind of programs were simpler mechanisms than previous ones and provided no structuring mechanisms other than those the users wished to develop for themselves.

All of the preceding programs assisted in making the users more aware of their own cognitive models—that is, how ideas and concepts are related to one another in the mind of the users. None of the programs, however, facilitated the destructuring of the user's thinking in order to provide a basis for creative thought. The fact that people understand how their thoughts are organized is not always a sufficient condition to encourage the generation of insights. In 1955 Kelly argued that it was first necessary to go through the process of destructuring existing thought patterns before one could hope to gain any insights into a problem situation.

Some of the programs developed in the 1980s attempted to introduce mechanisms that would help people to destructure their thinking and reorganize their thoughts. Brainstormer was based upon the "morphological method" and divided a problem along major dimensions or themes. These were then subdivided further, thereby creating a hierarchy. The subdivisions of the major themes were then listed along the dimensions of a box and all possible combinations were generated. Brian was another such program. It presented a structured approach to creative problem solving and facilitated three-dimensional morphological analysis. Morphy combined the morphological approach with randomly generated words to act as suggestions for descriptors or attributes to be listed under the problem dimensions identified by the user. The use of random words in the latter led to the consideration of attributes which might not normally be considered and thence to the revelation of unusual insights into a problem. Morphy grew out of work conducted by its creator with an earlier program, Brain, which was developed in 1985. The latter made extensive use of random word generation and the production of semimeaningful statements as stimuli to thought.

Yet another line of development was reflected in the Idea Generator in 1985. The program encouraged the user to employ a fairly wide range of analogical reasoning methods. These included asking the user to relate to similar situations to the problem, thinking up metaphors for the situation, and developing other perspectives. The program also included sections which helped people focus on goals and on the reverse of goals. In addition there was a section which helped the user evaluate ideas.

Several of these early programs attempted to take people through a number of stages of creative problem solving (e.g., Brain and the Idea Generator) while others made specific use of the computer's ability to randomize events (Morphy) or help in recording and restructuring ideas (e.g., Brainstorm). Some of the programs facilitated more than one of these features.

II. STRUCTURED APPROACH TO CREATIVE PROBLEM SOLVING IN COMPUTER PROGRAMS

In 1988, Van Gundy proffered a practical guide to creative problem solving. Six stages were suggested: (1) objective finding, (2) fact finding, (3) problem finding, (4) idea finding, (5) solution finding, and (6) acceptance finding. Objective finding is intended to narrow down the focus for problem solving efforts. The divergent portion of objective finding begins with a search for concerns, challenges, and opportunities that need to be tackled. Convergence is then used to select the most important objective area. Fact finding involves gathering all the information relevant to the problem. Problem finding involves gradual development of the broadest possible statement of the problem. By beginning with the original fuzzy statement of the problem and progressing toward a broad statement, a large number of options can be examined. It concludes with the selection of the most promising statement. Idea finding makes use of different techniques to produce insights into a problem. Solution finding employs various methods to evaluate ideas that have been produced at the previous stage. Acceptance finding is concerned with developing and evaluating ways to implement a final solution. Because the solution selected from the previous stage is still regarded as tentative, the objective of this stage is to ensure that it will be accepted by other persons involved. Van Gundy's phases provide a framework within which to develop and use creative problem solving aids and hence to form a potential theoretical framework against which an integrated idea processing support system can be constructed.

To be of assistance, the computer-assisted techniques should have the following features:

1. Facilitate movement through any or all of the stages of creative problem solving, that is, problem definition, idea generation, idea evaluation, etc.
2. Provide mechanisms which stimulate thought
3. Provide a structuring framework within which to define problems, generate ideas, or evaluate ideas
4. Facilitate or improve the use of conventional creative problem solving aids

III. TYPES OF PROGRAMS

Today, there is a whole variety of computer software which can be used to assist creative problem solving. This ranges from purpose-built software to general purpose software which can be used to stimulate creative thinking. In addition, some software is useful for the individual working alone while other software is of benefit to groups of individuals working on a problem or project together (see Figure 1).

There are various ways of classifying creativity programs. These may be summarized under the following headings.

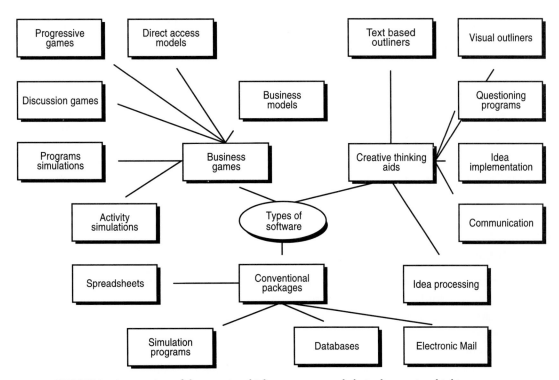

FIGURE 1 An overview of the ways in which computers can help in the creative thinking process.

A. Text-Based Outliners

Modern word-processing packages usually have an outliner mode built in. They are designed to help structure one's thoughts when preparing reports, articles, or other literary endeavors. Brainstorm was a forerunner of such features.

B. Visual Outliners

Several programs attempt to automate the process of drawing graphical outlines, mind maps, and concept maps. These programs are useful for presentations and publication. There have been a number of good mind mapping programs produced commercially. A good example is Inspiration, and others include Info Map Lite, Mindman, and Idea Tree.

Inspiration helps one to generate insights, produce concepts in diagrammatic form, and create outlines. In the diagram view one can make free-form visuals, diagrams, and presentation graphics, while the integrated outline view allows one to expand ideas into outlines and written documents. Inspiration facilitates mind mapping. A mind map develops like a web created by a spider, gradually growing larger and larger and in a fashion where all the information is interconnected and interrelated. The structure which emerges encourages one to build on ideas by recording everything added and keeping everything easily legible. A mind map is created as a series of interconnected boxes. Starting with one box, one types in associations and then creates more boxes that branch out from the first. If ideas from that branch dry up or something else occurs to one as one is generating insights, one can click on another box and start a new branch. One can move, duplicate, and delete thoughts at will and when one has finished it is possible to save, export, or print mind maps.

C. Questioning Programs

Several programs take input from the user and then use sets of questions, keywords, or exercises to provoke new ideas. IdeaFisher and MindLink both make use of this approach.

IdeaFisher helps one to create mental associations starting from the input of a word or concept. Idea-Fisher includes a feature called the Qbank which provides several lists of questions to point one in the right direction if one does not know how to proceed in a project. It is also possible to construct one's own lists of questions and these can be stored in the program for use on a future occasion. IdeaFisher is built around a database called the IdeaBank, which contains more than 60,000 words organized by major categories (such as Actions, Animals, Colors, The Senses, Emotions, and Places) and topical categories (groups of related concepts such as "achievement," "success," and "failure," or "adolescence" and "stereotypes of teenagers"). All of the entries in the IdeaBank are cross-referenced by concept and association. One can use free association, moving from one word or phrase to the next. IdeaFisher automatically records findings on the Idea Notepad and the contents of this can be exported as a text file. The program permits one to generate new ideas based on combinations of words. One types in two words, and IdeaFisher creates a list of people, animals, verbs, adjectives, and phrases that are all associated with that word combination in some way or other.

MindLink Problem Solver integrates idea generation and problem solving by combining a collection of creative thinking tools and techniques into a flexible, learn-while-using problem solving program. The program includes a relational database for storage and retrieval of ideas. This allows users to create a database of ideas that can be retrieved for use on future problems (using keywords and text searches). MindLink Problem Solver is divided into six modules. Any module can be accessed by clicking on its icon located in the opening window. Modules are ordered in a logical fashion, moving from the easiest to harder to use but more powerful modules. These are named, respectively, Gym, Idea Generation, Guided Problem Solving, Problem Solving, Evaluate and Refine, and the relational database (Thought Warehouse). The program provides a structured approach to creative thinking. A problem or challenge is typed in, and the program presents questions and exercises that help one examine the problem from different angles. One can save responses to MindLink's questions as a text file for use in other applications.

D. Idea Processing

There are many different idea processors. The Axon Idea Processor offers a visual workbench with a range of tools to record, process, and manipulate ideas. It is a sketchpad for visualizing and organizing ideas and its user interface is especially designed to support the thinking processes. Unlike a word processor, which is designed for text formatting, it handles the upstream idea processing, whereas a word processor handles the downstream formatting.

The Idea Generator Plus boosts creative thinking and planning skills by dividing the problem solving process into three logical parts.

1. "Problem Statement" helps users define their problems and related objectives and give their brainstorming session a tight focus.

2. "Idea Generation" allows users to choose from seven thought-provoking techniques to create many new ideas and solutions. For example, one technique is to consider other perspectives. Another is to think of metaphors for the situation. And a third technique is to reverse your goals (to discover what to avoid!).

3. "Evaluation" enables users to find their best ideas, by ranking ideas against objectives and considering long- and short-term costs and benefits. Reports list the new ideas, numerically ranked, for further consideration and analysis.

The Creative Decision Support System (designed by the author) is structured around a variation on the ideas of the creative problem solving process as previously outlined by Van Gundy. In this case, however, a seven-stage process has been adopted: (1) problem identification, (2) fact finding, (3) problem definition, (4) idea generation, (5) refining ideas, (6) evaluation, and (7) implementation. The package runs under Microsoft Windows 95 and possesses all the usual save, load, cut, paste, and print facilities. In addition, under the Utilities menu there is a drag and drop facility which allows the user to view any text file or run any program that the user has on the system.

E. Idea Implementation

Once one has a good idea, it needs to be implemented. Depending on the size and scope of the project, one could use a project management package (e.g., Time Line), a task management package, or perhaps just a to-do list manager.

F. Communication (and the Internet)

Worldwide communication, including the Internet, is a good way to bring people together for sharing ideas. Various Internet access providers, for example, Compuserve, offer facilities for bringing people together in a virtual meeting room and facilitating the generation of ideas and discussion. Meeting room technology transforms the way people meet, improving the performance of people and the organization. It can be used for brainstorming, problem solving, team building, strategic planning, and interactive learning.

G. Group Creative Problem Solving Aids

Networked personal computers permit the use of software which can assemble and amalgamate the ideas of different individuals working together on a problem. For example, a team of problem solvers can use such an application to evaluate and rank ideas which have either been generated in a group brainstorming session or are the result of individual efforts collated on the network. This sort of software is time-saving and permits equality of opportunity to input ideas to all members of a group. It also makes it easier to gain a consensus of opinion.

Experience indicates that the merging of different perspectives and views is a productive way of obtaining new insights into intractable problems. GroupSystems, developed at the University of Arizona in cooperation with IBM and other manufacturers, is built around idea generation, idea organization, idea evaluation, and issue exploration. The idea generation phase incorporates an electronic brainstorming tool which is used to record anonymous comments from group members. Traditional brainstorming, Delphi, and nominal group methods are used to promote independent idea generation.

Other products aiming to achieve the same kind of goal include Team Focus, also developed at the University of Arizona, and VisionQuest, developed by Collaborative Technologies Corporation. TeamFocus facilitates "electronic meetings" on a "decision network." Team members can work from any location provided they have suitable computer hardware. [*See* TEAMS.]

Aspects is a simultaneous conference software program. It enables users of networked machines or modem-linked machines to view graphic or text documents in a real time environment. Users can of course be in different rooms in different buildings and can make changes to documents at any time. In this way a consensus of opinion about the subject under scrutiny can be achieved. An added feature is that users can communicate with each other without interrupting the ongoing work. The software facilitates creative problem solving techniques.

OptionFinder is another package which can be used by a group. It is readily available in the United Kingdom and is designed to provoke thought and explore the different opinions held by the people who use it. The system consists of a public screen and a single personal computer loaded with the software. The system is portable and is used to facilitate voting on issues identified by a facilitator. Voting is anonymous but comment is not. Voting analysis is displayed in a graphical format, either on an x–y grid or as a bar chart on the public screen. This analysis of opinion enhances evaluation and feedback. It clarifies whether there is consensus of opinion or whether there is disagreement. Confirmation of conflicting beliefs can induce thought-provoking exchanges and new ideas.

IV. CONVENTIONAL SOFTWARE

A. Spreadsheets

Spreadsheets facilitate creative problem solving. Simple or complex mathematical models can be constructed with the aid of a spreadsheet and subjected to a sensitivity analysis. This is both a powerful and a simple way of encouraging creative thinking. It encourages people to try out ideas in a risk-free environment and provides a ready-made tool for doing so. M. Jackson has provided ample illustrations of the use of spreadsheets for this purpose. Her illustrations cover many aspects of business, including database management, statistical analysis, survey data, analysis of relationships, sales forecasting, financial planning, cost estimation, budgeting, decision modeling, sensitivity analysis, and simulation.

B. Simulation Packages

Simulation packages such as Micro-Saint and Dynametrics can be used to enable complex processes in organizations to be modeled. Based upon sampling real data, simulations of activities can be carried out on a microcomputer. It might be difficult, expensive, or even dangerous to experiment in the real world with such activities but on the computer these problems are removed. As in the case of the spreadsheet, people are encouraged to try out their ideas in a risk-free environment.

C. Databases

A firm's internal records can be scanned to help solve customers' problems. In addition, external databases can be searched for information which has an influence on pending organizational decisions. It is also possible to use databases to search for new product ideas, as suggested by J. Bar.

D. Electronic Mail Systems

The use of an electronic mail system for creative problem solving purposes illustrates how a general purpose computer installation can aid the creative thinking process. It facilitates the informal exchange of ideas. Moreover, from using electronic mail systems in this way a new kind of software called "groupware" has evolved. Groupware is the name given to computer software that enables remote users to swap ideas and other information. Several software houses offer groupware packages, and among those available is Lotus Notes.

V. BUSINESS SIMULATORS

Business games were designed as aids to management development and training. They provide a vehicle by which principles and practice can be learned and experienced. Yet the business game also contains something which is vitally important in the management situation but which is seldom found in practice: it allows the individuals to take risks and make mistakes—to play out hunches and follow up wild ideas. Business games by their very nature encourage creative thinking and ideas by helping people to overcome some of the well-known barriers to creativity such as the pressure to conform and the fear of looking foolish.

Business simulators offer the opportunity for individuals to test out ideas and take risks in a safe environment. They can be made to provide positive feedback when satisfactory decisions or suggestions are made by the user or when creative and sensible suggestions are made. Conversely, negative reinforcers can be employed when rash or uncreative actions or suggestions are made.

Bibliography

Elgood, C. (1990). *Using management games.* Aldershot: Gower.

Jackson, M. (1988). *Advanced spreadsheet modeling with Lotus 123.* Chichester: Wiley.

Proctor, T. (1985). BRAIN: The computer program which brainstorms. *Simulation and Games,* Dec.

Van Gundy, A. B. (1992). *Idea power.* New York: American Management Association.

Concepts of Creativity: A History*†

John Dacey

Boston College

Associationism The proposition that the mind consists entirely of ideas (words, images, formulas, etc.), each of which is associated with other ideas. Thinking, therefore, is simply a process of moving from one idea to another by way of a chain of associations.

Bicameral Mind The concept, popularized by Julian James, that the mind is composed of two chambers, one in which de-

sirable innovations are inspired by the gods, and a second chamber in which more mundane thoughts are produced by the person.

Biopsychosocial Theory The belief that all human acts are born of a complex interaction of biological, psychological, and social forces.

Cerebral Localization The principle that each of the various human abilities is located in the lobes, which are sections of the brain.

Fundamentalism A movement or point of view characterized by rigid adherence to fundamental or basic principles.

Gestalt German for "mental patterns or forms." Gestalts have complex relationships, and are more than merely "associated" with each other. As mental patterns, they form ideas that are grater than the sum of the parts.

Humanism The belief that humans have the ability to solve problems through their own mental efforts, without having to rely on inspiration from the gods or from God.

Muse A spiritual intermediary for the gods. A person who felt a creative impulse would invoke the appropriate muse for assistance.

Original Genius As opposed to mere talent, this refers to the ability to create fundamentally new and highly valuable ideas and products.

Paganism The religious belief that many gods play roles in human behavior.

Plenum A space which is totally filled up with objects, such that none may move unless they all move. An example would be the ball bearing ring which supports the fluid motion of wheels.

*Adapted with permission from *Understanding Creativity: The Interplay of Biological, Psychological, and Social Factors* by John Dacey & Kathleen Lennon. San Francisco: Jossey-Bass, 1998.

†It must be noted that there are two ways in which this chapter is limited historically. First, it is Eurocentrically oriented. This is so because of the difficulty encountered in finding non-Eurocentric writings on the topic. Second, it ends at the turn of the 20th century. This is so because a number of other chapters in this encyclopedia report most adequately on this period.

"Introduction," "Glossary," "Summary," and "Conclusions" Copyright © 1999 by Academic Press. All rights of reproduction in any form reserved.

WHAT IS CREATIVITY and how does it work? Answers to these two questions have ranged as far as creative thought itself often does. In one sense, the story is simple. From earliest times until the Renaissance, it was widely believed that all desirable innovations were inspired by the gods or by God (depending on the creator's religious orientation). During the Renaissance, this view began to give way to the idea that creativity is a matter of genetic inheritance. In the beginning of this century, the debate turned to an argument over the relative contributions of nature versus nurture. In recent decades, there has been growing acceptance of biopsychosocial theory, that is, the belief that all creative acts are born of a complex interaction of biological, psychological, and social forces. How these changes in the popular conception of creativity emerged, however, is far from simple and not without controversy. Prior to the 19th century, very little was written about the nature of creative thinking. Although there had been extensive theorizing about other human capacities, conjecture about the origins of creative productivity had been impeded by the belief that it was too obscure, too multifaceted, and too ethereal to allow for intellectual analysis of its process. The first effective scholarly inquiry was undertaken only a little over a century ago. Research on the creative process was deterred not so much by ignorance as by the conviction that the nature of innovative thinking was already understood: it was thought that it came as a gift from above.

I. THE BICAMERAL MIND

The earliest explanation, one that is largely inferred from the writings of Homer and the authors of the Bible, was that the mind is composed of two quite separate chambers (this concept is unrelated to the current knowledge that the brain is composed of two hemispheres). The first scholarly treatise to document this view was written by psychologist Julian Jaynes. He coined the term "bicameral mind" as a label for this phenomenon. Throughout early human history, Jaynes posits, people uniformly believed the chamber of the mind in which new thoughts occur was controlled by the gods. Thus they thought that all creative ideas come from the gods, usually through the mediation of a muse, a sort of intermediary for the gods. A person who felt a creative impulse would invoke the appropri-

ate muse for assistance: Calliope for epic and heroic poetry; Clio for history; Erato for love poetry; Euterpe for music and lyric poetry; Melpomene for tragedy; Polyhymnia for songs or hymns to the gods; Terpsichore for dance; Thalia for comedy; and Urania for astronomy. A major function of the mind, then, was as a receptacle for supernatural innovations. It was believed that the gods projected their ideas from Mount Olympus by inspiring (literally, "breathing into") this first chamber.

Belief in this origin of creative thought was deeply held, as can be observed in this quotation from the epic Greek bard, Hesiod. He describes what some muses said to him one day:

> "Listen, you country bumpkin, you swag-bellied yahoo, we know how to tell many lies that pass for the truth, and we know, when we wish, to tell the truth itself." So spoke Zeus' daughters, masters of wordcraft, and from a laurel in full bloom they plucked a branch, and gave it to me as a staff, and breathed into me divine song, that I might spread fame of past and future, and commanded me to hymn the race of the deathless gods, but always begin and end my song with them. (Cited in Boorstin, 1992, p. 34.)

The purpose of the second chamber of the mind was to express inspiration through the more ordinary mechanisms of speech and writing. It was considered to be the public representative of the first chamber. The second chamber also was used to express such mundane thoughts as "I am hungry."

The bicameral process is exemplified in the tales of Homer, in which the characters are able to accomplish great acts, but only as directed by the gods. In their most important achievements, Homer's heroes did as they were inspired to do, carrying out the strategies given them. This was no passive act, however. They could choose not to follow the inspiration given them and some did. Thus when they effectively followed the instructions of a god in battle, they were credited with great bravery, but not with the idea for the act. When they wrote a beautiful poem or play, they were admired for having produced it, but mainly because they had been chosen for the honor.

Many early thinkers, Plato and Aristotle among them, believed that the "creativity" chamber also housed madness when the spirit of the Muse was present. Hans

Eysenck cites Plutarch's description of Archimedes, the great geometrician:

> . . . how, continually bewitched by some familiar siren dwelling within him, he forgot his food and neglected the care of his body, and how, when he was dragged by force, as often happened, to the place for bathing and anointing, he would draw geometrical figures in the oil with which his body was anointed, being overcome by great pleasure and in truth inspired of the Muse. (1995, p. 126)

This "madness" was not the same as insanity, however. As Eysenck points out, "in Latin there is no linguistic distinction between *madness* and *inspiration. Mania* and *furor* are terms that cover many different non-rational states like anger, passion, inspiration and insanity" (1995, p. 130).

Perhaps the first to challenge the concept of the bicameral mind was the philosopher Aristotle in the fourth century B.C.E. Although he agreed with his predecessors that inspiration involved madness, he suspected that great insights begin as the result of a person's own thoughts, through a process which has become known as associationism. This view proposes that the mind consists entirely of ideas (words, images, formulas, etc.), each of which is associated with other ideas. Thinking, therefore, is simply a process of moving from one idea to another by way of a chain of associations. Aristotle suggested that mental associations are formed between events and objects that occur in the same place, that occur at the same time, that are similar, or that are opposites.

For example, the associationist view might speculate that the prehistoric builder who thought of moving huge blocks of temple stones by repeatedly placing wooden rollers in front of the stones got the idea from remembering playing with toy blocks and sticks as a child. The situations may be different, but the method of transportation is similar. Another example would be an imaginative chef's ability to create a delicious new dish by combining ingredients called for in a previously used recipe, but in a different way. At any rate, for some reason Aristotle did not pursue this insight, and belief in the bicameral mind lived on for several more centuries.

Jaynes states that by the end of the medieval period, speech, writing, and other mental operations grew more complex. As a result, it was recognized that thought could actually originate within a person's mind, and the notion of the bicameral mind eventually broke down. In its place came self-awareness, which led to insight into the human potential to create. As this became more clear, there was an inevitable questioning of vast areas of "knowledge." After many divergencies, the recognition that humans can take responsibility for what is known and invented provided the opportunity for the development of scientific methodology itself.

For this monumental achievement to occur, however, other innovations were required. So many of these innovations come to us from the Greeks in the three centuries before the acendency of the Roman Empire, and so few from the medieval Europeans. Both cultures accepted the concept of the bicameral mind, so why was there so great a disparity between the durability of the creative products of the pagan Greeks and the fundamentalist medieval Europeans? It appears that although both groups shared the conscious concept of creativity (the "gift from above" view), the *unconscious concepts* held by the two cultures were quite different. In this difference lies the answer.

II. PAGANISM VERSUS FUNDAMENTALIST RELIGION: THE GREEKS

During the so-called "Golden Age" (500 to 200 B.C.E.), the Greeks invented most of our Western literary and political forms, developed many innovations in the arts, and shaped the disciplines of history, medicine, mathematics, and philosophy. Only portions of their written output still exists, perhaps about a fifth. Not a single one of their public buildings and only a few of their statues remain standing. And yet it is their oratories, plays, and histories that are still found worth reading in the world's colleges and universities, and their buildings and sculpture that are emulated more than any other. Historian Daniel Boorstin compares them to other civilizations:

> Inquiry for its own sake, merely to know more, philosophy on the Greek model, had no place in [a world view such as the Confucian, Incan, Buddhist, or Christian] tradition. Greek philosophers, beginning with Thales, were men of speculative temperament. What

was the world made of? What are the elements and processes by which the world is transformed? Greek philosophy and science were born together, of the passion to know. (1992, p. 46)

To what may we attribute this flourishing of passionate imagination? An insightful hypothesis has been put forth by historian Moses Hadas. He suggests that the Greeks were prolifically creative because they were free of many of the cognitive restraints that afflicted other major civilizations. It is true that they were economically secure and had ample assistance in their daily lives from their slave system but, Hadas argues, their main asset was the absence in their lives of the religious beliefs that fettered most other societies. They believed their ideas were inspired by the gods, but by gods who existed in proliferation and who cared little about the lives of humans. Although they were concerned about displeasing their gods, the Greeks saw no reason to think that self-expression would distress them. After all, the more beautiful or original their creative product, the more likely was it to have been given them by their pleasure-loving gods.

In making this case, Hadas compares classical Greece and its pagan beliefs to medieval Europe and its fundamentalist Christian orientation. He argues that it was not so much the restrictive teachings of early Christianity or the "otherworldliness" of the religion that caused inhibition of creative thought throughout the medieval period (the end of the 4th through the 12th centuries), but its claim to exclusive validity. In its struggle to gain acceptance and then dominance, early Christianity was harsh in its rejection of deviant ideas, which were considered heretical. Beginning with the execution of Arias and continuing through the use of several forms of inquisition, the Church dealt harshly with the progenitors of such thinking.

The polytheistic Greek religion, on the other hand, allowed the individual to exercise choice among various classes of deities. The scope of individual autonomy was infinite, and the Greeks were of the belief that the actions of the gods were unpredictable—they could never assume to know what the gods thought or felt.

Hadas buttressed his case for a sharp distinction between the attitudes of Greek paganism and the Christian religion by pointing out what Greek paganism did *not* have:

- Churches
- Family allegiance to one point of view (members of Greek families were free to choose any god to worship, or none at all)
- Strong prejudices against older or newer beliefs
- Dogma
- Sacred books revealed by a spiritual being, detailing that dogma
- Priests
- Claims to infallibility
- Epic religious stories (e.g., the Garden of Eden and the escape from Egypt)
- A clear concept of sin
- True villains (because many religious views were simultaneously acceptable, persons whose views were diametrically opposed still could respect each other—there were no heretics)

Perhaps the clearest view of the Greek ideal can be seen in their emulation of heroes, as compared to Christian attitudes toward saints. A Greek hero was "any deceased person worthy of a cult, that is, of receiving offerings of flowers or wine on his special anniversary" (1965, p. 201). The offerings were not meant to appease him or her, but to serve the people. For example, Hadas points out, "we eat cherry pies and chocolate hatchets [on George Washington's birthday] to serve ourselves, not our first president" (1965, p. 201). The main distinction, he argues, is that "a man approaches sainthood to the degree that he *suppresses* the impulses of ordinary humanity and assimilates himself to a pattern outside humanity. A man becomes a hero to the degree that he emphasizes his human attributes" (1965, p. 201). Hence Greek pagans were encouraged to perceive excellence as a more readily attainable goal than were medieval Christians.

The single "sacred source" the Greeks did have was the poetry of Homer. This was the one source of information that all Greek children learned, and its code was therefore accepted with as little question as we accept the facts of the multiplication table. There, it appears, is the explanation for the relentless Greek drive for excellence in all aspects of their lives, and for the quality of their production in the arts and crafts. A person composed music or wrote poetry not merely for self-expression or profit, but as an entry in the national contest for the approbation of society. The main objective was honor. Even the potters who fashioned the cheapest household bowls took pains to sign their work. When the vases were artfully crafted, both potter and painter signed the bottom. All Greeks knew who designed the Parthenon, but the builders of the great Christian cathedrals remain anonymous. Cathedral architects chose not to put their names on their work because the work was for the greater honor and glory of God, so it would be prideful and disrespectful to display authorship.

From Homer through the Epicureans, we can see that significant and persistent value placed on the self-sufficient individuals. To quote Hadas,

> The Homeric warrior [knew that] what was decreed for him by a power outside himself he could not alter and need not bother to understand; he was definitely the captain of his soul, but made no pretense of being master of his fate. So the hero of tragedy knew that he must behave well as a man; the disasters that might befall him had no relationship with his own excellence. (1965, p. 208)

Because the gods played so small a role in their daily existence, the Greeks were free to do whatever they wished, so long as it was honorable. The breathing of life into a Greek person's creative process may have been influenced by a heavenly source, yet the credit went to the individual responsible for the creation. Hence the fabulous 300-year-long cornucopia of creativity that was the Golden Age.

III. PAGANISM VERSUS FUNDAMENTALIST RELIGION: THE MEDIEVAL EUROPEANS

A squelching of free thought begins in the late Hellenistic period as paganistic Romans come to accept the claims of their all-powerful emperors to have become gods themselves. Under them, Rome became famous for its "universal" codes of behavior, which covered one's duty to the state. On the other hand, the Romans were not so different from the Greeks in their attitudes toward religious imperatives. It was not until the rise of Christianity, with its fervent devotees, that we see a strict code of behavior enforced by powers in this world who were exclusively backed by the Power of the next.

This extensive change in philosophy was accompanied by, and probably abetted by, another sweeping event. Barbarian tribes began attacking the Roman Empire from several sides in the fifth century and systematically ravaged huge territories. This onslaught eventually destroyed faith in the Roman religion and prepared the ground for a new one.

The most notable group of invaders, the Vandals, deeply penetrated the Empire and nearly destroyed Rome. The Vandals were a Teutonic tribe that governed their North African kingdom from 439 to 534. Other tribes, such as the Huns, Vikings, and Visigoths, also invaded and pillaged large tracts of the Empire. While in the process of rampaging the lands, and especially the cities they wished to conquer, they destroyed any books or other written materials they could find. They had a savage disregard for intellectual or spiritual enlightenment, being interested only in the spoils of battle and the domination of their victims.

An exception to this was Alaric, who together with his horde of Goths smashed through the gates of Rome at midnight, August 24, 410. He prevented his men from putting the torch to everything, saying that while he wished to destroy the Roman Empire, he had no desire to harm the many Christians who then inhabited the city. Soon a few treasured works hidden in the city were spirited off to Moslem strongholds. Throughout the medieval period other precious tomes were rescued by an unlikely source: the reclusive Christian monks based on secluded islands off the Irish west coast. They secretly made it their business to locate the hidden writing not only of Christians but, amazingly, of the pagan thinkers as well. Not only did the monks preserve these works, but they painstakingly and artistically handcopied the writings in an attempt to perpetuate these obscure pockets of intellectuality. The efforts of these monks must be considered a critical contribution to human creativity, for although the marauders were frequently successful in ravaging the lands, they were never able to destroy the words that would so stimulate thinkers in centuries to come.

The work of these monks is an example of how the Dark Ages were not totally devoid of creative achievements. The famous *Book of Kells,* produced by the monks over many years, is an exemplar of the level of their creativity. Another such example is the work early in the fifth century of Saint Augustine, Bishop of Hippo. In his brilliant treatise, *The City of God,* written between 413 and 426, he argued that Plato and the Greeks were wrong in their belief that life is a series of repetitious cycles. He offered the life of Christ and the subsequent new view of humanity offered by Christianity as an argument against that position. He was probably one of the first to discredit the idea that all creative ideas come straight from God, devout though he was. In fact he was awed by the creative powers of his fellows, although he could not resist chastising them for the purposes to which such gifts were often put:

> . . . man's invention has brought forth so many and such rare sciences and arts (partly necessary, partly voluntary) that the excellency of his capacity makes the rare goodness of his creation apparent, even when he goes about things that are either superfluous or pernicious, and shows from what an excellent gift he has those inventions and practices of his.
>
> What millions of inventions has he against others, and for himself in poisons, arms engines, stratagems, and such like? (cited in Boorstin, 1992, p. 51)

Further evidence of medieval creativity was the work of the Roman Boethius, who served as counselor to Theodoric, King of the Visigoths. This ingenious scholar single-handedly produced the *quadrivium,* which offered explanations of the four "mathematical" disciplines: arithmetic, music, geometry, and astronomy. Together with the *trivium* (grammar, rhetoric, and logic) later assembled by others, they formed the basic curriculum for the handful of scholars who struggled to keep knowledge alive during the Middle Ages.

Such contributions notwithstanding, the situation in the Western world in the fifth century was rather grim, as Christopher Dawson so succinctly described it. He disagrees with Hadas' position that fundamentalism was the major cause of the lack of creative output, however, After all, he argues, the Moslems were as rigidly fundamentalist as the Christians and yet the Moslems made many creative contributions. Rather, he ascribes the superiority in creative output of the Greek and Moslem cultures over the medieval Christian culture as the result of the Christians having been reduced to a simple agrarian culture by the invasions of numerous outsiders. It may well have been the case that the tight grip of the Church on the minds of the population was welcomed as a consoling relief from the fear of vandalism and starvation alike. In fact, as is so often the case at the macrosocial level, establishing causation is a perilous pursuit. For example, it could well have been that the fundamentalist posture of the medieval Church and the low level of creative output in medieval times were both the result of the destabilized political and economic environments brought about by the widespread vandalism. As Dawson states,

> But while there is no reason to suppose that the Dark Ages were dark [solely] because they were religious, it is none the less difficult to exaggerate their darkness, both as regards scientific knowledge and the completeness of the break between the science of antiquity and the science of modern times. Here the traditional view is justified, and it only becomes false when this judgment is extended from the early to the late Middle Ages so as to make the scientific development of Western Europe begin with the Renaissance. In reality the recovery of Greek science and the restoration of the contact with the main tradition of Greek thought was one of the most striking achievements of medieval culture. And it is even more than this: it is the turning point in the history of Western civilization, for it marks the passing of the age-long supremacy of oriental and eastern Mediterranean culture and the beginning of the intellectual leadership of the West. It is, in fact, a far more important and original achievement than anything that the Renaissance itself accomplished. For the Renaissance scholars, in spite of their originality, were carrying on a tradition that had never been entirely lost: the tradition of humanism and classical scholarship that was founded on Cicero and Quintillian. But the rediscovery of Greek thought by the medieval scholars was a new fact in the history of the west: it was the conquest of the new world. (1954, pp. 246–247)

IV. THE RENAISSANCE AND THE BEGINNINGS OF HUMANISM

Dark as the medieval period was, nothing that happened during its 800 years could compete with the catastrophe of the Black Plague, which, by the time it ended around 1350, had decimated fully one-third of the population in the West. As a result, however, new emphasis on the individual took place and with it came a loosening of reflexive obedience to clerical rule. Because workers had become so scarce, they found they were in a much stronger bargaining position with the feudal hierarchy as well. This change brought about a shakeup of the entire social structure, and with it a widespread challenge to the belief system of the previous millennium.

For example, artisans began to win acclaim and patronage for themselves. This is similar to the attitude of the ancient Greeks who took pride in all their creations, from the most minimal to the most spectacular. Painters again signed their artwork, abandoning pious humility for personal pride in their craft. Guilds were formed to foster the growth of individual crafts and skilled trades. The principal source of patronage was no longer the Church, but rather wealthy princes and merchants whose pride in artful possessions was no longer considered a sin. The emphasis in the work of the poets, painters, and philosophers was still on the glory of God, but as reflected in the countless joys of *human* existence.

Also at this time we see widening criticism of what has been considered the acme of Church power, the inquisition. This tribunal, with its witch hunt for heretics and its infamously murderous "auto-de-fe" ("prove your love of God by admitting your guilt"!) had exerted a chilling influence over independent thought for many years. As it lost its power, the Holy Roman Empire declined in importance and the papacy was weakened by schism. Among the major causes of this breakdown were the executions by fire of such popular Church critics as Jan Hus and Girolamo Savonarola, and the publication of the 95 theses of Martin Luther, which began the Protestant Reformation. There was a reformation of the Church itself at this time, but it came too late to stave off the winds of change. Simultaneously, the national monarchies increased in strength and prestige. At the beginning of the 1400s, the population of Europe was better off financially than at any time since before the fall of Rome.

Now we see the inauguration of humanistic philosophy, the belief that we ourselves are responsible for much of what happens to us. This view was not generally anti-monotheistic, but rather co-monotheistic. The resurgence of creative production on so grand a scale was inspiring, and piqued the curiosity of those who wished to understand the complexities of minds that were capable of such accomplishments.

The term "renaissance" originally referred to the revival of values and artistic styles of the classical age. By the 1500s, the word had acquired a broader meaning: it was becoming known as one of the great ages of human cultural development, a distinct period signaling the dawn of the modern era. Essentially, a breakdown occurred in the rigid social order that had so dominated societies in Europe, manifesting itself in cultural and intellectual advances. The style of the Renaissance music, literature, and arts is quite distinctive, and ultimately this intellectual and spiritual revolution sparked a drive in the people to release themselves from the medieval traditions. The historian Nicolas Berdyaev describes the period this way:

> In the creative upsurge of the Renaissance there occurred such a powerful clash between pagan and Christian elements in human nature as had never occurred before. In this lies the significance of the Renaissance for the world and for eternity. It revealed the activity of the pagan nature of man in creativeness, and at the same time the activity of his Christian nature. (1954, p. 116)

The Christian ideas had been accepted for a long time, but the pagan ideas were rapidly being reintroduced. This came about through the influx of scholars from the Moslem countries, and by the circulation of the magnificent books, produced and kept safe over the centuries by the Irish monks. Spurred by these "new" old ideas, the best minds experienced a sense of freedom encouraging an inquiry into everything, even the most cherished of beliefs. From this resurgence sprang the scientific, artistic, philosophical, and political revolutions that came to be referred to as the "Age of Enlightenment."

V. THE AGE OF ENLIGHTENMENT AND A FLOURISHING HUMANISM

By the beginning of the 18th century, the spate of knowledge born of the work of such giants as Copernicus, Galileo, Hobbes, Locke, and Newton solidified belief in the scientific process. Faith in the ability of humans to solve problems through their own mental efforts (known as humanism) grew rapidly. Spiritual works such as the Bible waned in their authority, and were viewed with impunity by some scholars as literary efforts rather than as the word of God. The rights of individuals to come to their own conclusions began to gain acceptability.

In 1767, the first major inquiry into the creative process took place. William Duff was one of the first to write about the qualities of original genius (as distinguished from talent, which is productive but breaks no new ground), and his insights were strikingly similar to more modern attempts to unravel the mysteries of the creative mind. What set Duff apart as an important figure in the study of creativity is that he was the first to suspect the biopsychosocial nature of the process.

Duff was principally interested in determining the cognitive traits that were responsible for the variance he observed in the accomplishments of people. He was not only concerned with hereditary influences, but also with the times in which his subjects lived. As we shall see, it would be quite some time before others would agree that social influences play a role in creativity.

The main qualities that Duff considered fundamental to genius were imagination, judgment, and taste. Any one of these three characteristics alone would not result in the caliber of genius of Shakespeare; rather he thought the combination of the three ingredients to be essential. He argued that imagination contributed the most, in that the mind not only reflects on its own functions, but also organizes its ideas into new associations and combinations of an infinite variety. Duff felt that all discoveries and inventions in science and art were the result of imagination. Judgment, he asserted, is that ability that evaluates ideas or options, and acts as a counterbalance to the influences of imagination. Taste supplements judgment, providing a sense of aesthetic quality to the cold evaluative nature of judgment.

The publication of Duff's work was one of several events that set the stage for scientific research on human thought, which would late prove essential to the demystification of the creative act. Here is a brief list of major Enlightenment milestones that helped break the path:

- The spread of social and philosophical opposition to church and state authority

- The institution of the British Royal Society, the first research organization
- A plethora of developments in the natural sciences
- Separation of the idea of creativity from more ordinary notions of genius (as in, "He has a genius for poetry")
- The doctrine of individualism
- Three enormously influential books: Francis Bacon's *Advancement of Learning,* Adam Smith's *The Wealth of Nations,* and Thomas Malthus' *Essay on Population*

Robert Albert and Mark Runco have summed up the contributions of this period to a new concept of creativity:

> Tedious and tangential as they were at times, nevertheless, the debates through the 18th century eventually came to four important acceptable distinctions, which were to become the bedrock of our present-day ideas about creativity: 1. Genius was divorced from the supernatural; 2. Genius, although exceptional, was a potential for every individual; 3. Talent and genius were to be distinguished from each other; 4. Their potential and exercise depend on the political atmosphere at the time (this last distinction would not be recognized for many years, however). (1997, p. 26)

VI. THE DEBATE OVER ASSOCIATIONIST AND GESTALT VIEWS

Throughout the 19th century, a major shift in the conception of the creative act occurred. With the renunciation of divine inspiration as the sole cause of creativity came a transmigration to what may be the opposite extreme: great men are great because they have inherited a serendipitous combination of genes from their forebears, which produce a mind of intensely find acuity (decades would pass before the recognition of women of genius). This assumption grew as medical science produced evidence of heritability of physical traits. Moreover, this concept seemed to jibe with the recognition that high-level mental ability runs in families.

For a while, a debate raged over just how specific inherited traits might be. Jean Lamarck believed that learned traits could be passed on genetically. Charles Darwin demonstrated that he was wrong, confirming that genetic change occurs not as the result of practicality but through random mutation, over eons of time.

So what explanation did 19th century science offer as to how geniuses formulate their brilliant ideas? A subordinate question was, does a genius search for knowledge elementally (from parts or elements of a problem to the whole) or holistically (from a sense of the whole of the problem to its parts)? Two scientific camps were formed. They have become known as the associationist (a branch of behaviorism) and the Gestalt positions. From this seemingly academic debate came one of the greatest advances in our understanding of the creative act itself.

Research on the history of creativity often cites Sir Francis Galton as having conducted the first scientific research on the nature of genius. He was the second great associationist, after Aristotle, and was highly respected in 19th-century England as a multifaceted scientist. He was a eugenicist, meteorologist, evolutionist, geographer, anthropologist, and statistician, and he probably should be credited as the world's first cognitive psychologist. Building on his friend Charles Darwin's groundbreaking insights of evolution, natural selection (survival of the fittest), general diversity, and adaptation, he made inestimable contributions to our thinking about creativity.

One of his most interesting experiments was his attempt to measure the workings of his own mind. The descriptions of his findings have been insightfully analyzed by Crovitz in his book, *Galton's Walk* (1970). The walk referred to is one taken by Galton down London's Pall Mall, during which he meticulously recorded every thought that crossed his mind. His goal was to

> show how the whole of these associated ideas, though they are for the most part exceedingly fleeting and obscure, and barely cross the threshold of our consciousness, may be seized, dragged into daylight, and recorded. I shall then treat the records of some experiments statistically, and shall make out what I can of them. (Galton, 1879, p. 148)

He was awestricken by his tabulations:

> The general impression they left upon me is like that which many of us have experienced when the base-

ment of our house happens to be under thorough sanitary repairs, and we realize for the first time the complex systems of drains and gas- and water-pipes, flues, and so forth, upon which our comfort depends, but which are usually hidden out of sight, and of whose existence, so long as they acted well, we had never troubled ourselves. (Galton, 1879, p. 149).

His most important conclusion:

> The actors on my mental stage were indeed very numerous, but by no means as numerous as I had imagined. They now seemed to be something like the actors in theatres where large processions are represented, who march off one side of the stage, and going round by the back, come again at the other. (Galton, 1879, p. 162)

At first glance, this conclusion may not seem earthshaking, but Galton had actually discovered two principles which have had enormous impact on our thinking about thinking. The first is his notion of "recurrence." This holds that the conscious mind is like a plenum. A plenum is a space which is totally filled up with objects. An example would be the ball bearing ring which supports the fluid motion of wheels. Little balls fill two concentric rings and roll around in the hub of the wheel, making the wheel spin much more freely than it would otherwise. Each ball can only move by taking the place of the ball in front of it. There is no place else to go. The only possible movement is cyclical movement.

Galton argued that this is what happens in the conscious mind. It is always, at any one point in time, filled up, and thoughts can only follow each other around. He found this positive, because otherwise, he believed, conscious thought would be random and would have no order. Orderliness is essential to logical thought.

However, if this were the only way the mind could process information, there could be no new thoughts, and therefore no creativity. The second and more important discovery Galton made was that new input can come into this plenum from another part of the mind. The source of this input is the unconscious, the "basement" of the mind. And most important of all, the unconscious can be made conscious through association of thoughts. Thus was discovered the critical notion of "free association." The concept was certainly revolutionary: "ideas in the conscious mind are linked to those in the unconscious mind by threads of similarity" (1879, p. 162). At the turn of the century, Sigmund Freud and his associates would bring this notion to fruition.

Of particular note in Galton's research is his use of statistical analyses in the study of individual differences among geniuses. The modern statistical principles of correlation and regression evolved from Galton's findings, gleaned from biographical sources for his subjects in various fields and their families. This methodology was incorporated into the studies of other researchers who pursued the study of creativity at the onset of the 20th century and the years to follow.

Galton was convinced that mental capacities are inherited. He believed that these capacities follow certain laws of transmission that can be determined by observation. He examined the hereditary nature of mental abilities in subjects recognized by society as "geniuses" in an attempt to show that genius is an inherited trait in the same manner that physical features are inherited. In Galton's view, geniuses possess natural ability in terms of intellect and disposition that leads to this reputation, urged on by some internal stimulus that strives to overcome any obstacles.

This definition originated with Galton. Historian Jacques Barzun describes several iterations in the meaning of genius:

> In ancient and medieval times, a genius or a demon was a person's guardian spirit, giving good or evil advice on daily affairs. Then genius came to mean a knack of doing a particular thing—a gifted person was said to "have a genius" for calculation or public speaking. It gradually acquired a more honorific sense. By the 1750s genius was defined by the poet Edward Young as "the power of accomplishing great things without the means generally reputed necessary to that end." This notion fitted Shakespeare's case, for he was thought lacking in discipline, learning and art. He had a wild, untutored genius.
>
> In the next generation came the subtle shift from "having" genius to "being" a genius, with no limitation such as Young included in his praise. A genius was now a fully conscious, competent and original "creator," and only two classes of artists were recognized:

the geniuses and the nongeniuses, the second group being dismissed as "talents." Unable to create, they followed the path blazed by the geniuses. (1964, p. 147)

For Galton, then, genius resides in persons who are the beneficiaries of exceptional inheritance, especially of brain cells. He refused to believe that early experience or the immediate environment played much of a role in the creative act.

Opposed to Galton and his associates was the other group of theorists, known collectively as Gestalt psychologists They argued that creativity is a much more complicated process than merely associating ideas in new and different ways. They believed the whole of any idea always amounts to more than merely the sum of its parts, and referred to associationism as "brick-and-mortar" psychology. Gestalt psychology started with the work of von Ehrenfels, also in the latter half of the 19th century. It was founded originally on the concept of "innate ideas," that is, thoughts that originate entirely in the conscious or unconscious mind, and do not depend on the senses for their existence. Max Wertheimer, an early 20th century Gestaltist, argued that associationists dissect the thinking process, assume that the process is an aggregate, but actually offer a picture that is stripped of life.

The Gestalt position held that creative thinking is the formation and alteration of "Gestalts," which is German for "mental patterns or forms." The elements of Gestalts have complex relationships, and are far more than merely "associated" with each other. Great paintings are made up of elements, all of which are interrelated such that the whole is greater than the sum of the parts.

Wertheimer stated, for example, that creative musicians do not write notes on a paper in hopes of achieving new associations. Rather, they conceive of a half-formed idea of the finished piece of music and then work backward to complete the idea. They develop an overview of the entire structure and then rearrange its parts. Creative solutions are often obtained by seeing an existing Gestalt in a new way. This can happen when we change the position from which we view a scene or problem, or when the personal needs that affect perception change.

Imagine that coming back to work after lunch, a person notices the display window of a clothing store.

Brightly colored apparel stands out in the foreground. The pastel curtains behind are not so prominent. This individual does not notice at all that the window dresser has left part of a sandwich on the floor. However, suppose he looks at that store window when he is on his way to lunch. The sandwich will leap into the foreground, and he will hardly notice the clothing.

Gestaltists argued that getting a new point of view on the whole of a problem, rather than rearranging its parts, is more likely to produce creativity. Why is a new point of view so hard to achieve? Many impediments exist. First of all, most people do not like problems, because problems are stressful. Distressed thinkers usually react to problems with rigidity.

As is often the case in scientific inquiry, the disagreements between the advocates of the associationist and Gestalt positions still produce wonderful new insights into the process even today. In many ways, the current field of cognitive psychology represents an amalgam of these two positions. Coexisting with the struggle to understand the workings of genius was the zealous effort to reveal the workings of the brain itself. This endeavor also contributed to a new, more scientific understanding of the creative act.

VII. NINETEENTH CENTURY BIOLOGY OF THE BRAIN

It should be no surprise that our knowledge of the way the human brain works is quite recent in the history of medical research. Less than 200 years ago, no one was sure that the various areas of the brain had isolable functions. The first person to suggest this was a German anatomist, Franz Gall, who did so early in the 19th century. His research led him to believe that speech is located in the frontal lobes, those sections of each hemisphere located toward the front of the head.

This is the doctrine of cerebral localization. Unfortunately, most scientists dismissed his report because he included in it the argument that the shape of the skull reflects the person's personality traits, and so it would be possible to study those traits by examining bumps on the head. This idea became known as "phrenology," and has long since been discredited.

Although most doctors branded Gall a quack, he did have some followers. The French professor of medicine

Jean Bouillard offered a large sum of money to anyone who could produce a patient with damage to the frontal lobes who had no loss of speech. The knowledge of the landscape of the brain was so primitive in those times, however, that for some years the question remained unresolved.

In 1861, the stalemate ended dramatically. A young French surgeon, Paul Broca, learned of cerebral localization at the meeting of the Society of Anthropology and was reminded of a patient of his who had long suffered from speech impairment and some right-side paralysis. Two days after the meeting, the man died. Broca quickly got permission to autopsy his brain, and found what he was looking for: a region of tissue damage (a lesion) on his left front lobe. Some months later a similar situation occurred to another patient with the same results. Broca brought this patient's brain with him to the next Society meeting, and created a furor. Many were impressed, but those who dismissed localization accused him of lying.

Interestingly, while everyone noted that in both cases the lesions were frontal, no one seemed to see the *left-side* link. Only after eight more autopsies did Broca publicly announce this finding. The notion that the left side of the brain could more powerfully direct mental processes in some persons, and the right side in others, was put forth even later. It came about mostly because it was learned that equal amounts of lesion do not have equal amounts of disruption. By 1868, John Hughlings Jackson, the eminent British neurologist, was guessing that one side may "lead" the other. Increasingly, there was evidence that the interactions between halves are complex, and different in different people. It was learned that areas involved in speaking are not the same as areas given to understanding the speech of others. The discovery of "apraxia," the inability to perform physical functions such as combing one's hair, led to many new hypotheses.

Eventually, it was accepted that most people are right-handed because their left brains are dominant. It was concluded that the right brain had few important functions, serving mainly as a backup to the more powerful left. In the 19th century biological battles, we see the dim beginnings of the debates over how interactions of the two hemispheres across the corpus callosum contribute to creative thinking. The general position of those students of genius and of brain biology was that genetic inheritance ruled creative ability. The first scholarly questioning of this position came at the turn of the century from the man some have called the first true psychologist, William James. [*See* SPLIT BRAINS: INTERHEMISPHERIC EXCHANGE IN CREATIVITY.]

VIII. NATURE *AND* NURTURE

William James was the first scientist to make a case for the interaction of the environment with genetic inheritance. As James put it, "The only difference between a muddle-head and a genius is that between extracting wrong characters and right ones. In other words, a muddle-headed person is a genius *spoiled in the making*" (1880, p. 442). Thus James argued that environment is a more powerful influence than genetic inheritance in determining ability. Whereas Galton claimed that the frequency of creative ability within certain well-known families was due to genetics, James believed that the conditions of one's upbringing, such as the philosophy of the parents, were more important than genes. In his time he was virtually alone in putting forth this idea.

With Galton and Freud, James was a leader in thinking that the ability to get in touch with one's unconscious ideas is vital to giving birth to originality. This is how he described the process:

> Most people probably fall several times a day onto a fit of something like this: the eyes are fixed on vacancy, the sounds of the world melt into confused unity, the attention is dispersed so that the whole body is felt, as it were, at once, and the foreground of consciousness is filled, if by anything, by a sort of solemn surrender to the empty passing of time. In the dim background of our mind we know meanwhile what we ought to be doing: getting up, dressing ourselves, answering the person who has spoken to us, trying to make the next step in our reasoning. But somehow we cannot start; the *pensée de derrieux la tête* [literally, "thoughts of the back of the head"] fails to pierce the shell of lethargy that wraps our state about. Every moment we expect the spell to break, for we know no reason why it should continue. But it does continue, pulse after pulse, and we float with it, until—also without reason that we can discover—an energy is given, some-

thing—we know not what—enables us to gather ourselves together, we wink our eyes, we shake our heads, the background-ideas become effective, and the wheels of life go round again. (1880, p. 447)

James clearly recognized the importance to creativity of "thoughts of the back of the mind," but he did not pursue it. If he had, he might have added the third piece to the modern concept of creativity, the psychological element. The progenitor of this element would be Sigmund Freud.

IX. SIGMUND FREUD AND THE PSYCHOLOGICAL VIEW

The chief proponent of the view that creative ability is a personality trait that tends to become fixed by experiences that take place in the first five years of life was Sigmund Freud. In general, he and his early psychoanalytic followers saw creativity as the result of overcoming some traumatic experience, usually one that had happened in childhood.

Often such an experience is buried in the unconscious. Although hidden from conscious awareness, this material could nevertheless have a powerful impact on a person's behavior. In his 1895 book with Josif Breuer, *Studies on Hysteria,* Freud discussed his discovery that the contents of the unconscious could be revealed by suggesting certain key words to patients (as well as by hypnosis). The contents of their unconscious would come forward through their seemingly random associations to those words. These contents were then dealt with by allowing conscious and unconscious ideas to mingle into an innovative resolution of the trauma. The creative act was seen as transforming an unhealthy psychic state into a healthy one.

Freud characterized the unconscious mind as having a weak concept of time and space, and as being largely involved with images rather than words. He saw the unconscious as being limited to a more primitive language that is likely to take place in dreams and in so-called "Freudian slips." He also was adamant that creativity almost always stems from original ideas, often first produced in symbolic form, in this nebulous world of the unconscious mind.

Freud's explanation of the creative process depended

heavily on his ideas about defense mechanisms, which are unconscious attempts to prevent awareness of unpleasant or unacceptable ideas. The literature describes almost 50 different kinds. Because defense mechanisms prevent an accurate perception of the world, and because they use up psychic energy, they usually interfere with creative productivity. There are, however, a few mechanisms that occasionally can lead to creative insights. Briefly defined, they are:

- Compensation. Attempting to make up for an unconsciously perceived inadequacy by excelling at something else (e.g., if unable to be a superior athlete, become a sports writer).
- Regression. Reverting to behaviors that were previously successful when current behavior is unsuccessful (e.g., when becoming frustrated with a problem, act childishly silly about it).
- Displacement. When afraid to express your feelings toward one person (e.g., anger at boss), expressing them to someone less powerful (e.g., yell at son).
- Compartmentalization. Having two mutually incompatible beliefs at the same time (e.g., "I am above average in my schoolwork," and "Most of the kids are a lot smarter than me").
- Sublimation. When unable to fulfill one's sex drives, making up for it by being creative in some artistic way (e.g., become a great violinist).

Freud firmly believed that people are most motivated to be creative when they cannot directly fulfill their sexual needs. Hence he believed that sublimation was the primary cause of creativity. The link between unconscious sexual needs and creativity began in the early years of life. Although many people do not think of children as having sexual needs, Freud argued that at the age of four, it is typical for children to develop a physical desire for the parent of the opposite sex. Since this need is virtually never met, sublimation sets in, and the first vestiges of a fertile imagination are born. He traced many specific artistic works to the artist's sublimation. For example, he suggested that Leonardo da Vinci's many paintings of the Madonna resulted from a sublimated longing for sexual fulfillment with a mother figure, having lost his own mother early in his life. As he put it,

Should we not look for the first traces of imaginative activity as early as in childhood? The child's best-loved and most intense occupation is with his play or games. Might we not say that every child at play behaves like a creative writer, in that he creates a world of his own or, rather, rearranges the things of his world in a new way that pleases him? (1917/1957, p. 21)

Some of his followers disagreed with his emphasis on sublimation, ascribing other defense mechanisms as the source of creative thought. For example, Ernst Kris argued that only people who are able to "regress in the service of their egos" into a more childlike mental space are likely to be creatively productive. Thus for Kris, regression was the most productive defense mechanism.

In the writings of James and Freud, we see the beginnings of a biopsychosocial model of creativity. In their time, the debate about the roles of "nature versus nurture" raged, and continued to do so for several decades. However, in their writings we can see early recognition of the tripartite view that all aspects of human development involve biological, psychological, and social elements. Despite an enormous surge in research on the topic since the middle of this century, however, the fruition of the concepts they pioneered has been seen only recently. We are seeing more and more explorations of the creative act using the biopsychosocial model to guide theory and research, and as a result, we are seeing more complex, but also more satisfying, answers to the many questions bred by the study of creativity.

X. SUMMARY

In conclusion, there have been three distinct stages in the history of the concept of creativity. From prehistory until well into the medieval period, it was generally considered to be a mysterious, supernatural process—a gift from the gods or from God, depending on the religion of the culture (e.g., Greek, Hindu, Egyptian, or Incan versus Moslem, Jewish, or Christian). As the Renaissance led to humanism, the concept of inherited genius took over. Gradually, psychological and contextual influences received more recognition.

New conceptualizations have proliferated in this century: the cognitive theories of Wallas, Terman, Kohler, Piaget, and Wertheimer; the personality theories of

Freud, Jung, Adler, Rank, Rogers, MacKinnon, Barron, Roe, Helson, and Maslow; and the research on the brain of Penfield and Sperry are only some of the most highly regarded early work. Where are we headed? The biopsychosocial model, which seeks to "stand on the shoulders of giants" by combining the three essential elements into new explanations, is in the ascendancy. The other articles in this encyclopedia are filled with ideas about the recent past, the present, and the future of thinking about creativity. It will be fascinating to see whether these efforts will prove as productive as those of the brilliant foreparents of creativity theory.

Bibliography

Albert, R. S. (1992). *Genius & eminence.* New York: Pergamon.

Albert, R. S., & Runco, M. A. (1999). A history of research on creativity. In R. Sternberg (Ed.), *Handbook of creativity.* Cambridge: Cambridge University Press.

Barzun, J. (1964). *Science: The glorious achievement.* New York: Basic Books.

Boorstin, D. (1992). *The creators.* New York: Random House.

Dacey, J., & Lennon, K. (1998). *Understanding creativity: The interplay of biological, psychological, and social factors.* San Francisco: Jossey-Bass.

Dawson, C. (1954). *Medieval essays.* New York: Image Books.

Eysenck, H. J. (1995). *Genius: The natural history of creativity.* Cambridge: Cambridge University Press.

Feldmen, D., Csikszentmihalyi, M., & Gardner, H. (1994). *Changing the world: A framework for the study of creativity.* Westport, CT: Praeger.

Hadas, M. (1965). The Greek paradigm of self control. In R. Klausner (Ed.), *The quest for self control.* New York: Free Press.

Simonton, D. K. (1994). *Greatness: Who makes history and why.* New York: Guilford.

Sternberg, R. (In press). Darwinian versus Lamarckian mechanisms in the formation and evolution of creative cognition. *The Journal of Creative Behavior.*

Terman, L. M. (1959). *Genetic studies of genius* (Vol. 5). Stanford, CA: Stanford University Press.

Conditions and Settings/Environment

David M. Harrington

University of California, Santa Cruz

Audience Any persons other than the original creator who come in contact with a novel act or product. All acts of social creativity must involve an audience.

Creative Audiences Audiences which use the novel acts and products of others as seeds for their own creative activities.

Creative Ecosystem The entire system from which creative activity emerges, including three basic elements, the centrally involved creative person(s), the creative project, and the creative environment, as well as the functional relationships which connect them.

Creative Environment The physical, social, and cultural environment in which creative activity occurs. Creative environments may involve nested environments, for example, a research laboratory nested within a research institute, nested within a university, nested within a particular state or nation, nested within a particular time in history. A creative environment is one of three basic elements in a creative ecosystem.

Creative Seeds The initial "seeds" around which creative interests and activities first develop. Seeds may consist of problems or projects presented or discovered. Seeds may also consist of new ideas, perspectives, images, sounds, objects, materials, processes, or tools which elicit the curiosity and attention of creatively inclined people and which eventually evoke creative activity. Seeds are sometimes experienced as emerging from the self in the form of powerful images, mysterious phrases, haunting feelings, or dream fragments from which creative activity evolves.

Data Smog A term, perhaps coined by Shenk, referring to the overwhelming and conceptually suffocating mass of information and data available in the contemporary world, especially on the worldwide web. Data smog is due in large part to the absence of gatekeepers.

Ecological Perspective A view of human creativity which metaphorically draws from concepts found useful in the study and description of biological ecosystems. The ecological perspective emphasizes the dependence of creative people and creative projects upon the physical, social, and cultural resources within their creative ecosystems and upon the arrangements, relationships, and interdependencies which connect creative people to those resources, to one another, and

Copyright © 1999 by Academic Press
All rights of reproduction in any form reserved.

to people able to drive and create value from their creative actions.

Feedforward   Information about the general properties of highly valued creative work which is provided before creative work is undertaken. Contemporary poets, for example, might learn or be told that good poetry is usually concise and might use this knowledge to help them guide their own work.

Gatekeepers   People whose roles in a creative ecosystem give them the power to decide whether or not particular creative acts or products are placed into channels of transmission or creative outlets by which they can become visible to relevant audiences. In the literary world, for example, editors, publishers, and owners of bookstores function as gatekeepers.

Geography of Creativity   A phrase calling attention to the fact that many forms of creativity are unevenly distributed around the world due in large part to variations in cultural values and economic wealth.

Niche Audiences   Relatively small audiences with specialized interests, tastes, and backgrounds. Many important forms of social creativity are of direct interest only to niche audiences.

Nourishing and Informative Audiences   Audiences which foster creativity by directing resources, money, recognition, feedback and appreciation back to creative people whose work they have found valuable.

Person–Environment Fit   Refers to the fact that no single environment best suits all creative people and that the degree of good "fit" between creative people and their working environments can influence creative productivity.

Private Creativity   An act of creativity which is of direct value only to the person(s) who initiated it. Products of private creativity are typically viewed only by their creators. A poem read only by the poet is an act of private creativity. (Distinguished from acts of social creativity which involve an audience which may derive or create value from the original act or product.)

Process-Entailed Needs   Needs generated by a creative project which must be met if the project is to be completed successfully. (Somewhat analogous to the "biochemical demands" which biological processes and organisms place upon the ecosystems in which they live or die.) For example, the creation of a mathematical proof will require mathematical knowledge, imagination, and time on the part of people involved in constructing the proof.

Responsive Audiences   Audiences which derive or create value from the novel acts or products in which they come in contact, thereby completing the fundamental cycle of social creativity.

Social Creativity   An act of creativity which is of direct value to someone other than the person who initiated it. Writing a poem that is read and appreciated by someone other than the poet is an act of social creativity. Acts of social creativity always involve an audience.

Talent Scouts and Agents   Anyone in a creative ecosystem who formally or informally helps identify or promote creatively talented people or their work with the conscious intention of doing so.

Zones of Concentration and Absorption   Times and places where people can become deeply absorbed in their creative work and where they can achieve levels of concentration not achievable in other settings.

This is an article about CONDITIONS that tend to foster or inhibit complex acts of social creativity. Acts of social creativity involve the production of novel ideas, images, products, processes, or performances which become directly valuable to people other than those who initially produced them. Writing a novel which is read and appreciated by others is an act of social creativity. Writing a poem which is read only by the poet is not. Though some of the conditions described in this article may enhance private creativity and relatively simple acts of social creativity, the focus here will be upon factors that foster complex acts of social creativity. This article presents the view that most instances of complex social creativity depend upon physical, social, and cultural resources available within the worlds in which they are carried out and upon a variety of arrangements, relationships, and interdependencies which connect creative people to those resources, to one another, and to the people who derive and create value from their creative actions. Because life processes in biological ecosystems also depend upon functional relationships and mutual interdependencies which connect organisms to one another and to the various resources and processes within their ecosystems, some of the concepts useful in understanding biological ecosystems may be helpful if applied metaphorically to the study and understanding of creative environments. Consider, for example, the following ecological concepts and their apparent relevance to creative environments and creative people.

I. AN ECOLOGICAL VIEW OF CREATIVE ENVIRONMENTS

A. The Importance of Person–Environment Fit, Environmental Modification, and Personal Mobility

Biologists often note that an organism's chances of survival are more a matter of good fit between the organism and its ecosystem than a matter of some inherent and transcendent property of the organism or of a particular environment. In fact, environmental properties that promote the development of some organisms often threaten the existence of others. So it is in the world of human creativity, where no single environment best suits all creative people or all creative projects. For example, some creative people thrive in competitive situations, whereas others function more creatively in collaborative and cooperative ones. Obviously, the motivational needs of both types of people cannot be met in exactly the same setting. Ecosystems which provide one type of setting and not the other will systematically impair the creative productivity of those ill suited to the ecosystem's motivational "style." But ecosystems complex enough to provide both types of settings may be able to reap the benefits of their co-operative *and* competitive creators. (The value of diverse niches generalizes to issues beyond motivational style, of course.)

Biologists also describe several methods by which complex organisms modify their habitats and by which mobile organisms migrate to environments better suited to their needs. Creative people engage in analogous behaviors when they shape their environments to better serve their creative impulses or migrate to environments particularly well suited to their creative needs.

In summary, then, it seems plausible that human ecosystems large and complex enough to contain a variety of niches and which also enable people to construct or seek out microenvironments well suited to their creative needs and styles should tend to support higher levels of creativity than ecosystems which do not.

1. Very Good Environments Are Neither Necessary nor Sufficient for Creativity

Though creative people often attempt to seek or construct environments that support their creative activities, it is important to understand that very good environments are neither necessary nor sufficient for creativity to occur. Acts of creativity sometimes emerge from very difficult or even hostile conditions, thereby revealing that good environments are not always necessary. The fact that creative efforts often fail in highly supportive environments (sometimes simply because the projects are too hard or because luck is bad) shows

that very good environments do not guarantee the success of creative endeavors.

2. Good Environments Are Generally Helpful

Though very good environments are neither necessary nor sufficient for creativity to occur, it seems very plausible that good environments are generally helpful in the sense that they typically increase the likelihood that creative activities will be undertaken and completed successfully. Establishing supportive environments may be analogous to eating well, exercising, and not smoking: while these practices do not guarantee desired outcomes, they generally improve the odds.

B. Creative People, Projects, and Environments Place "Demands" on One Another

A second set of ecological concepts relevant to creativity revolve around the fact that organisms and life processes place biochemical demands upon the ecosystems in which they function. If ecosystems can meet those demands, the organisms and processes making them will generally survive, but if ecosystems cannot, the organisms or processes making them will fall. Biologists use the term "carrying capacity" to refer to an ecosystem's ability to support certain levels of biochemical processes and living organisms. An ecosystem's carrying capacity is thought to be a function of the biochemical demands imposed by various biological processes and organisms on the one hand, and the resources and functional relationships within the ecosystem which help meet those demands on the other. Roughly speaking, biochemical demands and ecosystem resources must balance one another if a biological ecosystem is to remain healthy.

A metaphorical translation of the ecological concept of biochemical demand into psychological concepts such as "needs," "motives," or "expectations" may help us think about the creative health and creative carrying capacities of human ecosystems. It may be useful to view creative people, creative projects, and creative ecosystems as placing "demands" or expectations upon one another which must be met if creativity is to flourish.

In the first place, creative people typically place "demands" upon their creative projects by expecting them to satisfy and fulfill them in various ways. Projects which fail to provide adequate satisfactions are apt to be abandoned and avoided.

Creative people frequently place demands upon the environments in which they work by expecting certain levels of freedom and support for their creative activities and by tending to abandon environments which do not provide that freedom and support.

Creative projects also generate a variety of process-entailed needs which must be satisfied by the people who undertake them, by the ecosystems in which they are undertaken, or, more typically, by some combination of the two. For instance, a particular project may require knowledge and skills which must either be supplied by the creative people initially involved in the project, by the surrounding environment, or by a combination of both. Similarly, an especially challenging project may require either considerable courage on the part of the individuals directly involved in it, considerable encouragement on the part of the surrounding social system, or both. In general, if a creative project's needs are met by those who undertake it or by the surrounding environment, the project will succeed, but if those needs are not met, the project will fail.

The social components of ecosystems also sometimes place "demands" upon creative people and their projects. For example, social systems frequently expect the creative projects and creative people for which they have supplied resources to "pay for themselves" by somehow enriching those social systems. Private patrons, funding agencies, corporate headquarters, and other providers of resources tend to support people and projects which provide good returns on investment and tend to withhold or withdraw support from people and projects which do not.

Creativity tends to flourish in ecosystems where the reciprocal interdependencies connecting creative people, projects, and environments are well satisfied whereas creativity tends to falter and wither over time in ecosystems where they are not.

C. Important Caveat

Any contemporary effort to summarize what is known about environmental influences on creativity must deal with the fact that the empirical literature on creative environments is fragmentary, often anecdotal, and generally far less systematic and trustworthy than psychologists are accustomed to dealing with. As a consequence, attempts to offer comprehensive accounts of creative environments must necessarily engage in speculations which go far beyond the available information. With that understood, let us now consider some of the ways in which environmental factors either appear to serve the needs of creative people and their projects or ways in which they would presumably do so, given the ecological and theoretical perspective proposed here.

II. A NEARBY SOCIAL SYSTEM (OR AT LEAST AN ADVOCATE) THAT VALUES THE RELEVANT FORM OF CREATIVITY

Social systems often exert substantial control and influence over many of the resources, social arrangements, and rewards which help support creative activity. The values which social systems place upon novelty and change in particular spheres of activity strongly influence the forms and levels of creativity which take place within those social systems. In general, any given form of creativity tends to occur more frequently and readily if the surrounding social system values creativity of that form than if it does not. For example, technological innovation and artistic creativity tend to occur more frequently in social systems that value those forms of creativity than in social systems that do not.

Complex social systems, including modern societies, large organizations, and even heterogeneous families, often contain a variety of subsystems which differ in their attitudes toward particular forms of creativity. As a consequence, creatively active people often find that their endeavors are valued and supported by relatively small social systems residing within larger social systems which may be indifferent or even hostile to their efforts.

If unable to locate existing social systems which value their creative endeavors and help support them, creative people sometimes create and mobilize their own groups of creative collaborators and supporters. The early French impressionists, for example, were a relatively small group of creative people who joined forces and pooled resources in order to pursue creative goals which were often resisted by the dominant social system. Similar functions were provided by certain after-work computer clubs in the early days of Silicon Valley where young computer pioneers sparked and sustained one another's creative activities long before the economic potential of small computers had been widely recognized. These small supportive groups, so often crucial especially in the early stages of creative efforts, can take a variety of forms, including informal affiliations within large organizations, circles of creative friends, groups organized specifically to provide common support for particular types of creative activities (such as writers' groups), "creative cliques" within schools, and creative partners.

In some cases, creative people are able to obtain support for their work by locating or creating new audiences for their products and by obtaining support from those newly acquired audiences and from the progressively widening social system which these new audiences often draw into the process of support. The creative expansion of Silicon Valley was hastened by such a process as new audiences for Silicon Valley's novel products provided the resources necessary to produce ever new objects, ideas, and processes which then fed Silicon Valley's further and continuing development.

In other cases, creative people locate or are located by individuals who function as advocates of their work and who provide them with or help them acquire needed resources. Such advocates sometimes take the form of parents (especially in the case of younger creators), friends, and mentors. In the business world these advocates are sometimes known as "idea champions" or "product champions." In artistic worlds, influential critics sometimes play these advocacy roles.

If creative people are unable to locate small social systems, audiences, or advocates to support their creative activities, and if they are unable, uninterested, or unwilling to construct such small social systems, they will typically need to meet all of their project's needs themselves by drawing upon their own resources, skills, and personal strengths and by supplementing them by appropriating additional resources and supports from the indifferent or resistant social worlds in which they work. Such individual efforts are often far more draining than socially supported work. As a consequence, it seems likely that creatively talented people functioning without social support are generally less productive than those whose social worlds (or microworlds) value and support their creative endeavors.

How is it that supportive social systems actually foster the types of creativity which they value? Exactly what functions do they provide? And, for that matter, what functions can creative people sometimes provide for themselves if their social worlds do not help provide them? It is to these questions that we next turn.

III. A RICH MOTIVATIONAL MILIEU

People are motivated to undertake creative activities by a wide range of pleasures and satisfactions, some of which flow directly and immediately from those activities and some of which depend upon positive reactions from the social world. Creativity is thus most apt to occur in settings where people have opportunities to discover and experience the immediate process pleasures associated with creative activities and where creative work is apt to elicit rewarding social responses. Six methods to establish supportive motivational milieus are indicated in the following list. [*See* MOTIVATION/DRIVE.]

1. Satisfy potentially more urgent basic needs and motives (e.g., food and shelter) so that time and energy are freed for other creative activities

2. Provide children with opportunities to sample and experience a wide variety of creative activities to allow discovery of the activities which they especially enjoy

3. Provide free choice in the selection of creative projects and roles so as to maximize the experience of direct process pleasures

4. Provide classic social rewards, including public recognition, approval, honor, appreciation, opportunities for competitive success, economic rewards, power, and pathways to socially valued and economically viable adult roles

5. Provide rewards of particular relevance to creative people, especially the power to select future creative projects, the freedom to pursue those projects in their own ways, and the resources to do so

6. Support the development of personal belief systems regarding the transcendent importance of creative activities (often a personal characteristic of many

who are creatively productive throughout their adult lives)

IV. DEVELOPMENT OF PERSONALITY CHARACTERISTICS AND STRENGTHS NEEDED FOR CREATIVE ACTIVITY

Personality psychologists have identified a number of personal qualitites which tend to characterize creatively effective people and which probably help them function creatively. These qualities include active curiosity, broad interests, tolerance of ambiguity, self-confidence within one's field of creative activity, a powerful sense of agency and self-efficacy, independence of thought and judgment, imaginative and intellectual power, a capacity for hard and self-disciplined work, a self-narrative that portrays the self as a creatively productive person, and a philosophical commitment to and belief in the importance of one's chosen creative activity. Families, communities, organizations, or societies which foster the development of these personal qualities should thereby tend to foster higher levels of creativity among their members than social systems which do not. [*See* PERSONALITY.]

V. DEVELOPMENT OF SKILLS AND KNOWLEDGE

Creativity requires skills and knowledge. Therefore social systems (ranging from families to societies) which educate and train all of their children, including those born into poverty, discrimination, or other unpromising circumstances, generally increase the likelihood that those children will possess the skills and knowledge they need to function creatively as adults. Social systems which do not do so run the risk of failing to benefit from the creative potentials which lie unidentified and undeveloped within their own youth. The case of Isaac Newton nicely illustrates the fact that great potential can emerge from seemingly inauspicious circumstances. Newton's biological father was unable to sign his own name and his biological mother exhibited no outward signs of exceptional intellectual capacity. Yet, by any reasonable standard, Isaac New-

ton possessed extraordinary intellectual capacities for creative work. Fortunately, Newton happened to be raised in a place and at a time where the talents of a clever schoolboy from a modest background could be noticed and where such a child could go on to receive an education at the finest university in the land. [*See* KNOWLEDGE.]

VI. PROVIDING GOOD PROBLEMS AND GOOD CREATIVE SEEDS

Creative episodes often begin when creatively inclined people come in contact with or generate what may be thought of as good creative seeds. Creative seeds sometimes appear in the form of problems or projects. The challenges of writing an end-of-millennium novel, helping to find a cure for AIDS, or trying to compose a complex piece of music are examples of potentially creative problems or projects. In school and work settings, problems and projects are sometimes explicitly presented as possible tasks from which people are encouraged to choose. In other settings, such projects simply exist in the social milieu as tasks which people are free to undertake or ignore as they choose.

Creative seeds also appear in the form of new ideas, perspectives, images, sounds, objects, materials, processes, or tools which creatively inclined people encounter in the outside world and are intrigued by. It should be noted that many creatively active people move through the world sensitized to input which might prove useful to their various creative endeavors. Writers and visual artists, for example, often report noticing conversations, people, sounds, settings, images, or colors which they either immediately recognize as helpful to a currently active project or which they view as a good enough "seed" to record in a notebook for further exploration and possible germination.

Environments which contain unusually good problems, projects, or seeds are often described by creative people as "stimulating," "inspiring," and "exciting" as compared to environments which contain fewer good seeds and which are therefore often described as "uninspiring," "dull," or "sterile." It seems very likely that such frequently noted environmental differences do affect creativity.

A. Assistance in Identifying Good Seeds and Good Problems

Creative ecosystems are often enhanced by the presence of individuals who have a particularly keen sense for good problems, fertile seeds, or appropriate projects and who are able and willing to direct others toward them. This attention-directing function is often provided by colleagues, supervisors, patrons, or teachers. Particularly productive research laboratories, for example, often contain scientists who are notably effective at identifying and formulating good research problems. Similarly, teachers at almost any level of instruction who are renowned for their capacity to foster creativity in their students often turn out to be highly skilled in their ability to present open-ended problems, questions, prompts, and assignments to their students which are particularly evocative and well suited to their students' skills, interests, and backgrounds.

B. The Propagation of Seeds across Cultural and Disciplinary Boundaries

Some scholars have suggested that creativity tends to flourish in those times and places where cultures come in contact with one another. Indeed, many creative ecosystems appear to have benefitted from the fact that they have existed near cultural crossroads, have contained somewhat permeable cultural boundaries, or have included people from a variety of different cultural backgrounds who have brought with them creative seeds in the form of ideas, images, knowledge, tools, experiences, perspectives, metaphor systems, and new conceptual frameworks. A similar form of cross-fertilization also frequently occurs when the boundaries of academic disciplines or professional "guilds" are first crossed and the perspectives, ideas, tools, and images of one field become creative seeds in another.

C. Ecosystems which Reseed Themselves

Some ecosystems are renowned for the fact that they are able to continually reseed themselves over a long period of time by generating a prolific flow of good seeds and good problems for themselves. Silicon Valley is an excellent example of such a self-seeding ecosystem in which new ideas and products generated within the ecosystem immediately become seeds for subsequent cycles of creativity within the system.

More generally, one's own creative works and those of others often function as particularly effective seeds. Artists, for example, are often stimulated by their own works and those of other artists. Scientists routinely find food for thought in their own research and in the work of other scientists. Creative business people frequently build upon their own previous work and are often especially adept at improving upon the innovative business products and practices of others. By virtue of this fundamental mechanism, creativity tends to be a self-perpetuating process at both the individual and the social level.

D. Summary

In summary, the creative potential of an ecosystem is often substantially enhanced by the presence of unusually good problems or projects, an unusually rich assortment of good creative seeds, and people who direct attention toward them. Whether people actually do anything with those problems, projects, and seeds, however, is a separate issue and one to which we next turn our attention. [*See* CREATIVE CLIMATE.]

VII. FOSTERING INITIAL ENGAGEMENT

I have never started a poem yet whose end I knew.

Robert Frost

Of course, I don't go into the studio with the idea of 'saying' something—that's ludicrous. What I do is face the blank canvas, which is terrifying. Finally I put a few arbitrary marks on it that start me on some sort of dialogue. I need a dialogue to get going.

Richard Diebenkorn

One does not wait for inspiration. If you keep working, it comes.

Alexander Calder

People must often engage the materials of their creative projects, especially complex ones, long before they know how they will reach their goals, often well before the goals themselves are particularly clear, and sometimes, as we see in Diebenkorn's and Calder's remarks, before a single spark of inspiration has been struck. Pens must be put to paper, brushes to canvas, hands to clay, fingers to musical instruments, and minds to daunting tasks if creativity is to have a chance at all. Unless and until this crucial step is taken, all the supportive motivational milieus and good creative seeds in the world will come to absolutely nothing.

Creative ecosystems often encourage initial engagement by establishing some of the following conditions.

1. Providing a sense of justifiable hope. Creative activity is more apt to be initiated under conditions of justifiable hope than under a sense of hopelessness or helplessness. Justifiable hope involves a sense of personal agency and self-efficacy as well as a sense that one's social system is apt to persist long enough to make attempts at social creativity worth the effort. Confidence in one's own powers probably comes largely from two sources: prior success with similar tasks and expressions of encouragement from credible sources. Confidence that one's social system will persist long enough to make social creativity possible is heavily dependent upon the social realities of the time.

2. Triggering initial engagement by assigning or inviting projects with deadlines attached. Though assignments and creative invitations associated with deadlines may fail to produce work on the desired date, they frequently succeed in hastening creative engagement and sometimes succeed in triggering creative activity that might not otherwise have been initiated.

3. Providing respected creative roles. Many acts of creativity are initiated by people attempting to fulfill the expectations of professional roles they have chosen to play. The availability and attractiveness of such roles in the social environment thus can foster creative activity.

4. Establishing an experimental, risk-taking, "hands-on" attitude. Creative ecosystems which encourage risk-taking, experimental, and "hands-on" attitudes often give people the social permission needed to plunge into creative activities. Less creative environ-

ments, by contrast, often inhibit initial engagement by discouraging risk-taking, by punishing failure, and by conveying a "don't get your hands dirty" attitude to those who might otherwise be tempted to risk creative engagement.

5. Certain solitary forms of creative activity can be very isolating. Some people therefore find it easier to initiate and sustain solitary creative activities when they are conscious of others at work nearby. Hence, for example, the establishment in some locations of "writers' rooms" and the use by some writers of public libraries as places in which it is possible to work without a disturbing sense of social isolation. The proximity of others involved in their own creative work may also foster initial engagement by helping people view their creative work as normative and therefore a perfectly sensible activity to undertake. Some people also describe being stimulated to creative action by a contagious "creative energy" experienced when working in close proximity to other creatively active people. And for some, awareness of creative peers at work nearby creates an energizing sense of competition which helps them initiate their own work. Not surprisingly, of course, many creative people experience proximity to people engaged in their own creative work as so distracting that it reduces their willingness or ability to undertake their own work. The fact that people vary widely in their reactions to this salient feature of working environments is another vivid illustration of the general phenomenon that circumstances which may foster creativity in one person may inhibit it in another. Once again, it seems reasonable to suppose that ecosystems which provide environmental variety with regard to this feature should tend to foster higher levels of creativity than those which do not. [See Autonomy and Independence.]

6. Easy access to resources. Creative ecosystems and many creative people also foster initial engagement by making possible rapid and easy access to the work spaces and materials needed when inspiration strikes or when it needs to be kindled. The construction of studios, workshops, laboratories, and writing rooms in close proximity to places of residence reflects this desire to minimize delay between the urge to engage the materials of one's creative work and the ability to do so.

VIII. AVAILABILITY AND MASTERY OF TOOLS, PHYSICAL RESOURCES, AND SPACE

Once engaged with a creative project, and sometimes in order to become engaged, creative people often need access to various crucial resources, including time, information, space, physical materials, tools, instruments, equipment, collaborators, advisors, assistants, and zones of concentration and absorption.

A. Tools and Equipment

Some tools and pieces of equipment are essential for certain types of creativity to occur. Filmmakers, for example, must have access to cameras and film; oil painters need paint, brushes, canvas, and a place to paint; AIDS researchers must have access to sophisticated laboratory equipment; and so on. Environments which do not contain the tools necessary for particular forms of creative activity simply cannot support them.

B. Adequate Space

Tools and physical resources are of little use unless people have the space in which to use them effectively. The lack of adequate space can strangle or deform some forms of creative activity almost as effectively as can the lack of time.

C. Resource Scarcity, Specialized Training, and the Geography of Creativity

Creative fields and projects differ in the physical and spatial resources they require, in the scarcity and expense of those resources, and in the amount of specialized training necessary to use them. For example, the process of conducting experimental research in high-energy physics requires access to scarce and extremely expensive pieces of equipment as well as expensive training in their use. Because some creative resources are extremely expensive, the wealth of nations sometimes determines whether certain forms of creative activity do or do not occur within their boundaries. Disparities in the distribution of expensive equipment needed for certain creative activities also leads to the migration of scientific talent and energy from one country to another and even from one region of a country to another in what has come to be known as "brain drain" and "brain gain." From a global perspective, economic wealth is a powerful factor influencing levels of certain forms of resource-intensive creativity.

D. Forms of Ascribed Status also Influence Access to and Mastery of Needed Tools and Resources

Access to the resources and training needed for many resource-intensive forms of creativity is often influenced by gender, ethnicity, and economic status within nations. Children of white, upper middle class parents in the United States, for example, generally have greater access to the paints and canvases, musical instruments, workshops, desktop computers, special lessons, and rooms of their own that foster certain forms of creative activity than do children of poverty-stricken barrios or ghettos. Social systems which exercise social and educational discrimination restricting access to and mastery of creative tools on the basis of factors unrelated to a person's potential ability to use them should tend to have lower creative carrying capacities than social systems which provide more open access to those tools and training.

IX. ACCESS TO INFORMATION AND NEW PERSPECTIVES

Some forms of creativity feed on information and new perspectives much as biological processes feed on energy and nutrients. It is therefore common to see creative people reading widely, listening to one another's music, watching one another's plays or films, exploring galleries and museums, attending conferences, traveling the world, and, more recently, searching the world-wide web for information and perspectives relevant to their creative endeavors. It is also common to see creative people exchanging ideas in face to face contact with one another, especially over food or drinks. It is noteworthy that many accounts of unusually creative environments emphasize the importance of settings in which ideas are shared and explored in the convivial safety created by eating and drinking together. The presumed importance of information exchange in scientific settings has been noted frequently by sociologists of science and has also generated a small research literature concerning the impact of architectural arrangements on information flow. Opportunities for easy information exchange are also typically viewed as axiomatic by those attempting to construct scientific environments from scratch.

In summary, ecosystems which provide good access to and transmission of new information and new perspectives should tend to support higher levels of creativity than ecosystems which do not.

X. AVAILABILITY AND EFFECTIVE ORCHESTRATION OF GOOD COLLEAGUES AND ASSISTANTS

Many creative projects require more knowledge, skills, imagination, energy, motivation, and personal strengths than any one person can provide. As a consequence, creative colleagues and assistants are often required. The need for creative collaborators and assistants who can be assembled quickly and easily into working teams often becomes a social and economic force leading people who are involved in similar or related forms of creative activity to congregate near one another in what eventually become vibrant centers of creative activity. At various points in history, for example, certain large cities (e.g., Paris, Vienna, New York City, and Los Angeles) have become important centers of creativity due to in part to their having become targets of a selective creative migration. Selective migration also frequently produces critical creative masses in settings such as artistic or literary communities, business organizations, research institutions, and universities. [*See* COLLABORATION AND COMPETITION.]

A. Effective Orchestration of Colleagues and Assistants

Not surprisingly, individually creative people do not always work well together. Intragroup incompatibilities and conflicts, lack of trust, distaste for collaborative

work, and poor leadership sometimes produce groups in which the creative whole is substantially less than the sum of the creative parts. The effective functioning of creative groups is generally enhanced by the presence of compatible and complementary individuals, an effective group leader, and a surrounding social system that supports collaborative activity.

B. Appointment and Acceptance of an "Aesthetic Arbiter"

In many fields, creative success is as much a matter of taste and judgment as it is a matter of generating new ideas. Groups are notoriously poor at exercising good taste consistently over time. This problem seems especially acute in collaborative forms of artistic creativity, and less serious in cases of collaborative scientific or technical creativity, possibly because the latter fields are usually guided by more stable, consensual, and explicit criteria than are many artistic fields. There is interesting anecdotal evidence suggesting that collaborative musical, theatrical, and dance groups tend to function more creatively when they are able to explicitly or implicitly appoint an "aesthetic arbiter" who is given the responsibility and power to make the final aesthetic judgments relevant to a particular creative project. In cases involving groups which have collaborated for long periods of time and through many projects, a shared aesthetic sensibility sometimes emerges which is sufficiently well understood and embraced by all members of the group—a more "democratic" process may prevail. [*See* GROUP CREATIVITY.]

C. Social Support for and Resistance to Visibly Collaborative Creativity

The effective functioning of potentially creative groups is also influenced by the attitudes of the social systems in which they are embedded regarding collaborative, as opposed to individual, creative work. Social systems vary widely in how they view collaborative creativity. In the contemporary western world of high art, for example, collaborative visual art is typically viewed less positively than art produced by one individual. In earlier historical periods, however, the use of assistants in the production of fine art was widely accepted.

In other spheres of creative activity, by contrast, collaborative work is valued as highly or even more highly than individual creativity. In many research and development units residing within business organizations, for example, scientists and engineers who can collaborate creatively with others are viewed as more valuable than those who cannot.

It seems likely that ecosystems which value, reward, and support both individual *and* collaborative creativity will tend to sustain higher levels of creativity than those which do not.

XI. TIME

For many creative people, time is the most precious of all resources, without which creative work is simply impossible. Creative people often want to spend as much time as possible on their projects and to exert as much control as possible over the configurations of time they can devote to their creative work.

Control over configurations of time· is important for several reasons. Whereas some creative people can work effectively in many short blocks of time, other people need relatively long periods of time in which to work. Furthermore, while some projects can be advanced in many short work periods, others require long segments of time for progress to be made. In addition, some people have very strong preferences for time of day (and sometimes even time of week or year) in which they can do their best creative work. For example, some work best early in the morning, some late at night, and so on. And finally, creative people often want the freedom to plunge quickly into creative work in response to suddenly emerging ideas or to a strong sense that conditions are "right" for creative work to occur. For all of these reasons, creative people want as much control as possible over the configurations of work time available to them. It therefore seems reasonable to suppose that ecosystems which grant such control should tend to have greater creative carrying capacities than those which do not.

 The issue of how much total time people are able to devote to their creative activities is, of course, influenced by individual motives, values, and personal circumstances on the one hand, and social factors on the other. Social systems certainly influence the total time devoted to creative activities by exercising some control over the amount of time needed to sustain life, competing social obligations, potential distractions, and the reward structures which influence the degree to which it is sensible to spend time on particular types of creative work.

People whose daily lives are primarily spent sustaining basic survival typically have very little time to devote to other creative endeavors. Ecosystems which help people satisfy their basic needs with minimal expenditures of time should therefore be expected to support higher levels and wider ranges of creativity than less supportive ecosystems. From an historical and global perspective, such differences undoubtedly account for very large percentages of the variance in time devoted to the forms of activity considered "creative" by contemporary scholars working from the luxurious perspective of highly industrialized societies.

Social systems can also facilitate creativity by removing competing obligations. In family settings this might be achieved by one partner assuring another that she or he can ignore domestic responsibilities for a period of time during which total creative absorption is fully legitimized and supported. In managed research settings this might involve a research supervisor announcing that a particular project is to take immediate priority over all others. In certain retreats for artists, musicians, and writers, relief from competing social obligations and even from the need to prepare one's food or care for one's living space is typically provided. (The fact that some creative people prefer the diversions and stimulation of daily life to the protected sanctuary of such retreats again reminds us to avoid a one-size-fits-all approach to creative environments.)

Social systems sometimes encourage creativity by removing salient and highly attractive alternatives to creative endeavor. For example, parents sometimes limit their children's television-viewing hours to encourage more creative activities.

In general, though not perfectly, a social systems's reward structure for various forms of creative and noncreative activities reflects that social system's values. In many ways these social values influence individuals' decisions about how and where to spend their time. For example, if families can be more easily supported and social approval more easily garnered in a particular society by creating computer technology than by writing haiku poetry, more time and energy will tend to be devoted to the former than the latter activity in that society. As noted at the outset of this article, therefore, any particular form of creativity will tend to occur more frequently if the surrounding social system values creativity of that form than if it does not.

XII. ZONES OF CONCENTRATION AND ABSORPTION

I find it is very important to work intensively for long hours when I am beginning to see solutions to a problem. At such times atavistic competencies seem to come welling up. You are handling so many variables at a barely conscious level that you can't afford to be interrupted. If you are, it may take a year to cover the same ground you could cover otherwise in sixty hours.

Edwin Land, inventor of the Polaroid camera

As creative people have long understood, and as we see illustrated in the preceding account, creative episodes often involve the evocation and orchestration of multiple strands of marginally conscious thought and feeling which are often difficult to evoke and which are very easily disrupted by interruptions and distractions. Creative people have for centuries sought and constructed zones of concentration and absorption in which they can evoke, sustain, and keep these delicate filaments in play and in which they can avoid the interruptions and distractions which threaten them. In general, ecosystems which provide such zones of concentration and absorption or which facilitate their construction should be expected to support higher levels of creative activity than those which do not.

A. Places of Intense Collaborative Interaction Are Sometimes Most Helpful

People working on inherently collaborative creative activities often construct or seek zones of concentration and absorption very different from those which support more solitary activities. People involved in collaborative work sometimes report that such efforts are most productive when the individual members of the creative team are able to easily shuttle back and forth between places of intense face-to-face collaboration and places which support solitary concentration.

B. Respect for and Accommodation of Individual Differences Regarding Zones of Concentration and Absorption

The conditions which constitute an effective zone of concentration and absorption for one person may not constitute such a zone for another. Ecosystems which respect and accommodate such individual differences presumably sustain higher levels and a greater variety of creativity than those which do not. Whether or not particular environments accommodate these differences sometimes depends upon whether their "managers" (e.g., administrators, supervisors, teachers, or parents) view such accommodations as wise investments in creative talent or as needless "pampering." In some cases, ecosystems and the creative individuals within them simply cannot afford to make such accommodations or to construct idiosyncratically supportive microenvironments. Again, economic wealth can play an influential role in these matters.

C. Patience with Nonconscious Processes and the Need for Zones of Concentration

In large ways and small, those who interact with creative people can express respect for and patience with the nonconscious processes underlying creativity, with the difficulties involved in keeping multiple strands of thought in mind, and with the resulting need for zones of concentration and absorption. People who are involved in extremely cognitive forms of creativity are often experienced by those around them as forgetful and distracted, for they do in fact periodically slip into their private zones of concentration, sometimes in the midst of social interactions and activity. Amused patience with such private retreats is probably more helpful than is angry and uncomprehending irritation.

XIII. FOSTERING SUSTAINED ENGAGEMENT

On the occasion of receiving the Nobel Prize for physics, Max Planck remarked,

Looking back . . . over the long and labyrinthine path which finally led to the discovery [of quantum theory],

I am vividly reminded of Goethe's saying that men will always be making mistakes as long as they are striving after something. During such a long and difficult struggle the researcher might be tempted again and again to abandon his efforts as vain and fruitless . . . The steadfast pursuance of one aim and purpose is indispensable to the researcher and that aim will always light his way, even though sometimes it may be dimmed by initial failures.

Albert Einstein has also described the misgivings and failures of confidence often associated with creative work:

These were errors in thinking which caused me two years of hard work before at last, in 1915, I recognized them as such. . . . The final results appear almost simple; any intelligent undergraduate can understand them without much trouble. But the years of searching in the dark for a truth that one feels, but cannot express; the intense desire and the alternations of confidence and misgiving, until one breaks through to clarity and understanding, are only known to him who has himself experienced them.

Creative scientists are not alone in describing their work as involving periods of guided trial and error. The writer Aldous Huxley, for example, once described his own writing process as follows:

All my thoughts are second thoughts. . . . I work away a chapter at a time, finding my way as I go. I know very dimly when I start what's going to happen. I just have a very general idea, and the thing develops as I write. Sometimes—it's happened to me more than once—I will write a great deal, then find it just doesn't work, and have to throw the whole thing away. I like to have a chapter finished before I begin on the next one. But I'm never entirely certain what's going to happen in the next chapter until I've worked it out. Things come to me in driblets, and when the driblets come I have to work hard to make them into something coherent.

In addition to being dependent upon the elusive nonconscious processes described in the previous section, creative people involved in long, complex projects frequently find themselves having to rely upon the inherently unpredictable vagaries of exploration, ex-

perimentation, and barely guided trial and error as they work at or slightly beyond the edges of their zones of competence. The unpredictability and fragility of these processes often stir feelings of confusion, frustration, anxiety, misgivings, and self-doubt such as those reflected in the remarks of Planck and Einstein.

Unless these potentially process-terminating feelings are avoided or neutralized, creative projects may be truncated or abandoned prematurely. Creative ecosystems help resist these potentially process-terminating feelings and forces in several ways, some of which merit special mention.

A. Direct Assistance Sometimes Needed

The special challenges of the middle phases of complex projects often place more demands on creative people than they can meet alone. People involved in collaborative work turn naturally to colleagues and assistants for help at such times. People involved in comparatively solitary creative activities, however, may need to step out of their solitude to ask others for assistance. Because some people have chosen solitary creative activity precisely because it permits them to work alone, it may be necessary for the surrounding social system to actively offer help to solitary creators during these very difficult phases of their work.

B. Continued Access to Resources Is Often Essential

Continued access to key resources sometimes becomes problematic when projects take longer than originally planned, when they begin moving in unanticipated directions, or when the creators themselves begin showing signs of confusion or self-doubt. Ecosystems which can tolerate these ambiguities and uncertainties will generally be able to support to successful completion many creative projects which would be terminated prematurely in less accommodating ecosystems.

C. Encouraging Motivational Milieus Can Be Especially Important at These Times

Supportive and encouraging motivational milieus often become particularly important when the frustrations, uncertainties, and misgivings of especially complex projects loom larger than the pleasures flowing directly from the activity. Creators often report being sustained during such periods by beliefs that their creative activities are honorable activities which may advance valued human enterprises, benefit other people, or bring meaningful rewards to themselves. Such beliefs are influenced by the realities and ideologies of the surrounding social system and may be enhanced by knowledge that a potentially receptive audience is eagerly awaiting the work in progress.

D. Explicit Encouragement Almost Always Helpful

Despite the popular myth that creative people are too independent and self-sufficient to need or benefit from personal encouragement, much anecdotal evidence suggests otherwise. Creatively effective people have often described the positive impact which words of encouragement and understanding from credible sources have had upon their creative work, particularly at times of unusual creative challenge and stress.

XIV. FOSTERING TENTATIVE COMPLETION

Interestingly enough, some of the same forces and processes which make it difficult for people to stay engaged with their creative projects can also make it difficult for them to stop.

A. Rewards That Outweigh the Safety and Pleasure of Perfecting and Perseverating

In some cases, ecosystems fail to provide rewards for completing projects which outweigh the intrinsic pleasures and safety of continuing to work on projects indefinitely. After all, if creative activity is intrinsically satisfying, and if continuing to tinker with and "perfect" a project is safer than facing the risk of criticism when it is completed and presented to the world, motivational inducements may be needed to bring creative activity to a halt.

B. Good Feedforward

Creative people often resist completing their projects out of concern that their final work does not yet meet their own standards or those by which they believe they will be evaluated. Such concerns are a natural consequence of the inherently fuzzy criteria sometimes applied to creative acts and products. These uncertainties can sometimes be reduced by providing good "feedforward" in the form of information about desirable qualities of creative products that is provided before creative activity is undertaken. Though creative people are always guided by their own tastes and sensibilities, good feedforward can help them take into account the values and tastes of relevant audiences if they wish to do so. Good feedforward can also function as a counterweight to the solipsistic tendencies which sometimes engulf people during solitary creative work. Young people are often provided feedforward in classrooms, studios, museums, galleries, theaters, laboratories, workshops, or other settings where high-quality creative products or acts are visible and, in some cases, discussed. It is almost certainly much easier to provide good exemplars and useful feedforward in fields where the qualities of excellent work are relatively stable and where broad consensus regarding those qualities exists, such as in contemporary science, than in fields such as contemporary high art in the western world, where such stability and consensus are lacking.

C. Good Feedback and Normative Opportunities for Modifying and Revising

Good feedback on work in progress can also help people complete their projects, especially if normative opportunities exist to modify work in response to such feedback. In some settings the process of revision and modification is encouraged and viewed as an entirely natural part of the creative process. In other settings (or in the eyes of some creative people), the need to revise is viewed as evidence of an embarrassing creative inadequacy. In general, ecosystems which provide good feedback and which provide normative and socially approved opportunities for revision should help people bring their creative projects to tentative conclusion.

Useful feedback also occurs more quickly and naturally in some fields than in others. Computer programmers, for example, are often able to receive ongoing and automatic feedback as to whether their new code works by simply testing it. Inventors can often receive immediate feedback about whether their new products work by simply trying to use them. In other fields, such as many of the arts, however, feedback is much slower and requires the involvement of other people whose judgments may be unreliable. People working in fields where feedback is rapid, automatic, and not dependent upon others' judgments appear to have some important advantages over individuals working in creative fields where feedback is slower, less automatic, and more dependent upon the imperfectly reliable judgments of others.

D. Norms for Completing Projects

Environments in which clear norms have been established for completing creative projects should be expected to generate higher levels of creative productivity than environments in which it is normative and perhaps even socially desirable to have projects forever "in progress."

E. Means of Combating Perfectionism

Some creatively talented people are seriously handicapped by excessive perfectionism which manifests itself as endless efforts to perfect final products before showing them to others. Ecosystems which contain wise mentors, sensitive colleagues, or psychotherapists able to help people control their perfectionistic tendencies probably enhance creativity by so doing. In addition, ecosystems which emphasize the fact that a "good enough" product is usually better than no creative product at all probably tend to promote higher levels of creativity than those which emphasize the criteria of ideal creative products without acknowledging the range of acceptability around those ideals.

F. Deadlines, Again

And finally, where rewards, good feedforward, timely feedback, opportunities for revisions, norms for completing projects, wise counsel, and good therapy fail, deadlines may succeed. Creative ecosystems frequently help people overcome procrastinating and perseverating tendencies by providing realistic deadlines in the form of dates for the openings of plays, exhibitions, performances, films, conferences, and so forth. (Incidentally, deadlines often provide perfectionists with acceptable excuses for producing less than perfect work.) When employed sensitively, deadlines can promote creative closure on projects that might otherwise never be completed.

XV. TRANSMISSION OF COMPLETED PROJECTS TO RESPONSIVE, NOURISHING, AND SOMETIMES CREATIVE AUDIENCES

A picture lives its life like a living creature, undergoing the changes that daily life imposes upon us. That is natural, since a picture lives only through him who looks at it.

Pablo Picasso

Much as the acts or products of organisms in biological ecosystems have direct value only to those organisms whose metabolic processes can assimilate and make use of them (e.g., the nectar of a particular type of flower may be of direct value to some but not all insects), so it is frequently in the world of social creativity where many novel acts and products are of direct value only to those people whose interests, backgrounds, training, skills, knowledge, and imaginations permit them to derive value from them. Acts of social creativity therefore frequently depend upon the existence of audiences capable of deriving and creating value from the novel acts or products made visible to them and upon the existence of means by which novel acts and products are transmitted to such audiences. (The term "audience" refers to anyone other than the original creator(s) who comes in contact with any given novel act or product.) Audiences can foster social creativity in at least three ways.

A. Responsive Audiences

Responsive audiences derive or create value from the novel acts or products in which they come in contact, thereby completing the fundamental cycle of social creativity. Some instances and forms of social creativity place greater demands upon audiences than do others. The ability to read, coupled with an average attention span and a modest level of imagination, may be all that is required to derive and construct value from a typical novel, for example, whereas an exceptional background in mathematics, unusual patience, and an extraordinary attention span may be necessary to derive and construct value from a new mathematical proof. The preparing and cultivating of audiences capable of deriving or constructing value from new work is an important function of creative ecosystems which foster social creativity.

B. Nourishing and Informative Audiences

Members of nourishing and informative audiences foster creativity by directing resources, money, recognition, feedback, and appreciation back to creative people whose work they have found valuable, thereby facilitating and, in some cases, slightly guiding their continued creative endeavors. In many cases, the presence or absence of a nourishing audience can make the difference between the shriveling and abandonment of a line of creative work or its elaboration and expansion.

C. Creative Audiences

Members of a creative audience enhance the creative vitality of their ecosystems by using the products of others as seeds for their own creative activities. Creative audiences, even more than responsive audiences, typically require special experiences and training to serve this crucial function. Ecosystems which provide such experiences and training foster their own long-term creative health in doing so.

D. Transmission Channels, Talent Scouts, Agents, Gatekeepers, and Creative Outlets

In order for creative products to find their natural audiences and in order for audiences to find the new ideas, acts, and products from which they are apt to derive value, creative people and their natural audiences must be connected by good transmission channels. The flow of creative products into and through these channels is often influenced by people who function as formal and informal "talent scouts," "agents," and "gatekeepers" and whose activities therefore affect the creative health of their ecosystems.

1. Important Audiences, Agents, Talent Scouts, and Gatekeepers in the Local Zone

Friends, peers, parents, and teachers often constitute important audiences, agents, and talent scouts in what may be thought of as the "local zone." These members of the local zone can identify and encourage creatively talented people, supply them with resources and opportunities to pursue their creative activities, and promote their talents and work to more influential people in the local or extended zone who might be of even greater assistance. The presence of people effectively fulfilling these roles in the local zone can sometimes make the difference between whether creative talents and efforts do or do not become known to a wider audience.

2. Audiences, Talent Scouts, Agents and Gatekeepers in the Extended Zone

The number and quality of talent scouts, agents, and gatekeepers (e.g., editors, reviewers, publishers, gallery owners, producers, and those who control access to performance venues) in the extended zone become crucial determinants of whether creative products and their natural audiences ever find one another. The personal tastes, imaginativeness, and proactive efforts of those who play these roles can influence the well-being of creative ecosystems in powerful ways.

3. Channels and Outlets for Creative Work

The number and variety of transmission channels and outlets for creative work can also affect an ecosystem's creative vitality. In assessing an ecosystem's creative health it is therefore important to determine, for example, whether there are enough galleries, theaters, performance spaces, publishers, magazines, professional journals, conferences, bookstores, trade shows, television channels, independent movie studios, and other creative channels and outlets to connect creative people and their products with the audiences apt to derive or create value from them. It is also important to assess the degree to which those channels, venues, and outlets are accessible to all creatively active people who wish to make use of them and to all members of their natural or potential audiences.

E. Transmission Channels, Gatekeepers, Creative Outlets, Audiences, and the Nourishment of Creativity in an Increasingly Interconnected World

Issues having to do with transmission channels, gatekeepers, and creative outlets are currently being widely discussed by people concerned with the health of many contemporary creative ecosystems. The massive consolidations occurring in the worlds of mass communication, entertainment, and publishing in the United States, for example, have raised grave concerns about the future ability of creative people and their sometimes small niche audiences to connect with, cultivate, and nourish one another.

At the same time, more optimistic prognosticators believe that opportunities presented by technological advances such as the worldwide web may help specialized creators and their "niche" audiences find and nourish one another more effectively than ever before. Those less optimistic, however, fear that control of these initially "open" technologies will become consolidated in the hands of a relatively few gatekeepers whose concerns with mass audiences will result in neglected niche audiences and the creators who serve and are served by them.

The opportunities created by the worldwide web have raised another interesting question about the role of gatekeepers in creative ecosystems. Some observers believe that this astonishing communication system will provide the means by which new information, ideas, and images can flow freely and uncensored from creators to audiences around the globe precisely because there are essentially no gatekeepers controlling the flow of material through this vast network. Recently, however, many users of the worldwide web have begun expressing serious concern about the proliferation of material which, because of its unedited,

unverified, and enormously widely varying quality, threatens to engulf users of the system in a form of "data smog" that overwhelms the senses and the mind. The problem of data smog exists in large part, of course, precisely because there are almost no gatekeepers imposing quality control on the material moving across this network.

The eventual impact of these issues on creative ecosystems which are increasingly embedded within a densely interconnected global communication system remains unresolved.

XVI. CONCLUSIONS

In the end, of course, whether complex acts of social creativity do or do not occur depends absolutely upon whether talented and creatively inclined individuals commit themselves to the uncertainties and pleasures so often associated with creative projects, whether they avail themselves of the resources and support within their ecosystems, whether they remain engaged with their projects long enough for imagination to do its work, and, in many cases, whether they happen to be the beneficiaries of reasonably good luck. As this article has also tried to make clear, however, creative ecosystems and environments can often appreciably influence the likelihood that particular projects will be undertaken by particular people, that needed resources and support will be available, and that creative projects will be completed successfully and made visible to audiences able to derive value from them and to nourish their creators.

Bibliography

Arieti, S. (1976). *Creativity. The magic synthesis.* New York: Basic Books.

Bennis, W. (1997). *Organizing genius. The secrets of creative collaboration.* Reading, MA: Addison-Wesley.

Beveridge, W. I. B. (1957). *The art of scientific investigation.* New York: Vintage Books.

Gardner, H. (1993). *Creating minds.* New York: Basic Books.

Harrington, D. M. (1990). The ecology of human creativity: A psychological perspective. In M. A. Runco & R. S. Albert (Eds.), *Theories of creativity* (pp. 143–169). Newbury Park, CA: Sage Publications.

Huxley, A., Wickes, G., & Frazer, G. (1963). In Van Wyck Brooks (Ed.), *Writers at work: The Paris Review interviews.* New York: The Viking Press.

Lasswell, H. D. (1959). The social setting of creativity. In H. H. Anderson (Ed.), *Creativity and its cultivation* (pp. 203–221). New York: Harper & Bros.

Planck, M. (1933). *Where is science going?* London: Allen & Unwin.

Stein, M. I. (1953). Creativity and culture. *Journal of Personality, 36,* 311–322.

Wiener, N. (1993). *Invention. The care and feeding of ideas.* Cambridge, MA: The MIT Press.

Conformity

Kennon M. Sheldon

University of Missouri-Columbia

Acceptance Conformity that involves both acting and believing in accord with social pressure.

Compliance Conformity that involves publicly acting in accord with social pressure while privately disagreeing.

Ego-Involved Motivation In which action is prompted by an ulterior desire for social approval or a positive self-image.

Informational Social Influence Conformity that results from accepting evidence about reality provided by other people.

Interpersonal Climate The sense of pressure versus freedom promoted when authority figures are controlling versus autonomy-supportive.

Normative Social Influence Conformity based on a person's desire to fulfill others' expectations, often to gain acceptance.

Reactance A motive to protect or restore one's sense of freedom in the face of normative influences.

Task-Involved Motivation In which action is prompted by an intrinsic interest in the task itself.

CONFORMITY and creativity "don't mix." More technically, a large body of research documents the negative effects of conformist pressures (broadly defined) upon creative achievement. This research has investigated (a) situational factors which promote conformity and thus negatively influence momentary creativity, (b) personality traits or styles which promote conformity and thus negatively influence sustained or lifetime creativity, and (c) developmental processes by which people overcome conformist tendencies on their way to becoming creative. I will consider each of these areas in turn, after first defining conformity and then considering some general reasons why conformity and creativity are often at odds.

I. DEFINING CONFORMITY

According to *Webster's New World Dictionary*, conformity is "action in accordance with customs, rules, prevailing opinion, etc.; conventional behavior." As this definition implies, people may be powerfully influenced by social forces. Social influence can be informational or normative. Informational influence leads individuals to alter their behavior to accord with new knowledge obtained from others, whereas normative influence leads individuals to alter their behavior to accord with the conventional beliefs or practices of others. Informational social influence can aid the creative process, by enhancing a person's perception. For example, thoughtful criticisms of an artist's work

Copyright © 1999 by Academic Press
All rights of reproduction in any form reserved.

from other members of a workshop may help to sharpen the artist's vision. In contrast normative social influence often works against creativity, in part by producing inaccurate perception. For example, Asch's classic studies in the 1950s showed that participants will agree with an incorrect group consensus regarding the length of presented line segments, ignoring the clear evidence of their own senses. Because it has received the most attention I will focus on normative conformity, and its potentially negative effects on creativity. [*See* CONVENTIONALITY.]

Another important distinction in the conformity literature is whether or not conformists actually believe the normative opinions that they espouse. Some individuals may be sufficiently lacking in self-confidence that they endorse a group's incorrect opinion both inwardly and outwardly. This form of conformity is termed acceptance. Research has made it clear that individuals who do this are unlikely to be creative. Other individuals may toe the party line in order to avoid making waves, while still maintaining a private, countervailing opinion. This form of conformity is termed compliance. The potential for individual creativity is more likely to be maintained in the compliance case, although by withholding their true thoughts from others, such "expedient" conformers risk missing important feedback and information.

With more careful analysis the neat distinction between private acceptance and mere public compliance blurs. In most cases, normative influences concern more than simple perceptual judgments that have clear correct answers (e.g., the Asch line-length experiments). Group-level normative forces are most likely to play a role in the case of complex, many-sided issues, which have tangled ethical and doctrinal implications. Because of the ambiguity of many normatively informed issues, individuals may "mistakenly" accept a prevailing opinion without realizing that it does not accord with their own prior inclinations or creative interests. Also, individuals may come to unwittingly accept a normative attitude that they originally merely complied with, because of self-perceptual or dissonance-reduction processes. In either case a danger is that over time people may lose, or fail to develop, the ability to discern their own values and interests. The inimical effects of such an occurrence will be discussed.

A final definitional issue concerns that of reactance.

Those faced with strong normative pressure have a third option besides public compliance and private acceptance: they can resist, putting up a struggle against group norms. Although such counterconformity can serve many useful functions, one danger is that the potential creator may become distracted by rebelliousness for its own sake. In other words, those who make a point of going against group opinion may, ultimately, be just as controlled by group processes and forces as those who passively go along with group opinion.

II. WHY CREATIVITY AND CONFORMITY "DON'T MIX"

Most commentators agree that there are powerful conflicts between creativity-related and conformity-related motives. Behavioral conformity typically involves a desire to be approved of by others, along with a corresponding fear of being rejected or ostracized by others. This desire is deeply rooted: given the importance of maintaining cohesive functioning within the small groups in which our ancestors lived, there is good reason to believe that evolutionary pressures selected for a strong motive to be approved of by "the group." People's fears of being rejected by social groups if they do not conform are often justified—many experiments have demonstrated that those who persistently flout normative opinion are punished by, and finally excluded from, the groups of which they are a part. Interestingly, such results suggest that humans, besides having a built-in motive to seek approval by groups, also have a built-in motive to "stifle" those who challenge the status quo of their social groups. This tendency to resist others' *non*conformity is also likely to be antithetical to creative accomplishment, insofar as it prevents individuals from thinking about the new ideas or possibilities suggested by others.

In an influential early (1962) chapter, Richard Crutchfield described conformist motivation as ego-involved. Conformists are strongly focused on how they are perceived by other group members, and their primary goal is to protect or enhance their self-image and self-esteem. In contrast, creative performance tends to require strong task involvement—that is, an exclusive focus on the problem at hand, in combination with a desire to get to the bottom of things no matter where the search leads. Unfortunately, the "search" may often lead in directions which contradict or upset established beliefs, practices, or bureaucracies. In order to develop and market their new ideas individuals must often be willing to diverge strongly from group norms and accepted behavior, risking alienation and potentially drawing the group's wrath. Thus, one way in which conformist pressures may inhibit creativity is by reducing a person's willingness to follow through with a new idea or course of action. This may occur to the extent that a person's task-involved motivation is overwhelmed by his or her approval motivation. [*See* MOTIVATION/DRIVE.]

A second potential negative effect of conformist pressures, already alluded to, is that they may cause people to lose touch with their own perceptions and thought processes. Creative activity depends on individuals' ability to access, and engage in open dialogue with, their own experience. Very often the first glimmerings of a new idea or approach are subtle and evanescent, at the "fringes" of consciousness. To the extent that individuals rely on others for guidance on how to think and behave, they may lose the ability to recognize and grasp such glimmerings within themselves. For example, one important first step in the creative process involves explicitly recognizing that there is a problem to be solved. Group mentalities are notoriously resistant to such recognition (e.g., when Kennedy's "group-thinking" advisors did not perceive the obvious flaws in the Bay of Pigs plan). Those who are overinvested in group approval may fail to notice their own nagging doubts or reservations regarding a course of action, or fail to recognize the seeds of a promising new idea when it occurs to them.

Thus far in this article, the negative effects of conformity upon creativity have come about because group minds tend to resist or discourage innovation. However, it is also possible for negative effects to occur even when groups openly *welcome* creativity. For example, art professors may encourage students to compose works which are unusual and original, and students may receive many kinds of social rewards for succeeding in this aim. However, a large literature indicates that cognitive functioning can be impaired to the extent that people become explicitly oriented toward such extrinsic rewards. Specifically, reward- or approval-oriented motivation has been associated with

less cognitive flexibility, more shallow processing of new information, less integration of new information with preexisting knowledge, and less creativity in general. These decrements occur in part because thoughts of reward may intrude into actors' minds, distracting them and dividing their attention. In contrast those who can remain intrinsically or task-motivated are more likely to maintain access to their own deeper cognitive resources, and thus are more likely to be creative.

To summarize, excessive concern for group norms and opinions is likely to inhibit a host of motivational, cognitive, and self-regulatory processes essential to innovation. Such concerns may reduce the quantity of one's motivation to pursue an innovative line of thinking, as when one fears rejection by the group, or such concerns may detract from the quality of one's efforts, when they involve excessive focus on receiving anticipated social rewards or avoiding anticipated punishments. It is worth noting at this juncture, however, that social groups need not *necessarily* pull for conformity. Some research suggests that group processes can even enhance individual creativity (such as group brainstorming techniques, or corporate climates which intentionally focus on change and encourage unconditional respect for each group-member's creative efforts). However, ego-involved motivations easily emerge even in the most egalitarian of social contexts, perhaps explaining why group contexts have a negative effect upon creativity on the whole.

III. CONFORMIST FORCES WITHIN SITUATIONS

Research on the contextual determinants of creativity has focused on the impact of authority figures upon creative performance. In 1995, Sternberg and Lubart noted a variety of perplexities in this literature. For example, some research suggests that creativity is enhanced when authorities set limits, explicitly structure the task, set up competitions, spell out criteria for evaluation, and render judgment upon individuals' performances. However, other research indicates that external constraints, competition, and evaluation pressure all *detract* from creativity. Sternberg and Lubart suggest that these contradictory research findings are in part due to differences in the difficulty of the creative tasks employed in different studies, differences in subjects' prior experience with the tasks, or differences in subjects' initial arousal levels.

In addition to these possibilities, an important general factor determining when external constraints are detrimental may be the interpersonal climate in which they are administered. The theories of Amabile, Deci, and Ryan suggest that whenever constraints are viewed as controlling, they will tend to reduce task motivation and hence creativity. Presumably this is because a controlling authority's demeanor induces reactance or approval motives, or leads individuals to become overly focused on extrinsic rewards or punishments. As already noted, any of these foci can drain away cognitive and self-regulatory resources. In contrast, if evaluations and constraints can be delivered in a noncontrolling, informative way, helping to better define the task while still supporting personal autonomy, an optimal context for intrinsic motivation and creativity may result. [*See* CREATIVE CLIMATE.]

Much research, conducted in both educational and work environments, is consistent with this conclusion. For example, teachers who conduct classes informally, welcome unorthodox views, allow students to choose what to investigate, and treat students as individuals are most likely to produce creative students. Similarly, "open" classrooms, in which students are allowed considerable flexibility and individualized effort is encouraged, tend to produce more creative students than do traditional classrooms which rely on drill, large group instruction, and carefully prepared curricula, and which emphasize exams and grading. Paralleling these findings, Amabile has identified manager characteristics conducive to creativity. Managers who set challenging goals and then grant employees substantial freedom and control over their work, who are not overly strict and can evaluate work nonthreateningly, and who encourage new ideas are most likely to engender creative performance in their subordinates. In contrast, organizations in which there is defensiveness, a lack of freedom, and an unwillingness to risk change do not function as creatively; in such contexts, conformity and rigidity are likely to "rule the day."

Normative forces work not only at the level of the group, classroom, or organization. Increasing attention is being given to cultural differences in conformity and the effects of such differences upon the creativity of citizens within various cultures. For example, recent research has examined aspects of Japanese, Turkish, Senegalese, Sudanese, and Israeli culture which may predispose citizens of those societies towards unthinking obedience and conventionality. Much will be heard in the future from this promising area of research. [*See* CROSS-CULTURAL DIFFERENCES.]

IV. CONFORMIST FORCES IMPORTED INTO PERSONALITY

Besides studying social contexts which increase conformity and thus detract from creativity, researchers have also studied personality traits and styles related to conformity. In other words, conformity can be an enduring state of mind, not just a product of momentary situational influences. Such personality styles may develop when a child's efforts at independent self-expression are repeatedly punished or discouraged by parents or peers, or when love and affection are given only when the child conforms to rigid rules and regulations. This treatment may create an abiding insecurity and anxiousness regarding the approval of others, crippling the growing person's ability to be creative (although some have argued that early experiences of alienation can catalyze the formation of powerful creative personalities). Sulloway's 1996 work indicates that birth order may also influence the acquisition of conformist traits. First-borns, being more naturally aligned with parents, are more likely to uphold the status quo. Although they tend to become high career achievers, they do so through relatively low-risk ventures and tend to resist important innovations in their fields. In contrast later-borns, having less power and receiving less attention, may be "born to rebel" against the familial status quo. Later, they may be more likely to make innovative contributions to their fields, and quicker to recognize and support legitimate paradigm shifts within their fields. [*See* BIRTH ORDER; PERSONALITY.]

Little research has directly studied the relation of conformist traits to creativity. Instead, research has focused on the opposite pole, personal autonomy, considered one of the "core characteristics" of the creative personality. Autonomy refers to the preference for regulating oneself, instead of being regulated or controlled by social forces. Related personality traits include Independence of Judgment, Self-Directedness and Self-Determination, Self-Sufficiency, Self-Assertiveness, and Individuation. Such traits have been repeatedly shown to predict both momentary and lifetime creativity. This is because those high on these dimensions tend to (a) show less suggestibility and less need for the approval of others; (b) more courage and persistence in the face of criticism and pressure from others, and more willingness to express dissenting opinions; (c) more ability to maintain their task-involved or intrinsic motivation, and less susceptibility to ego-involved or performance motivation; and (d) more ability to maintain contact with and behave on the basis of enduring personal feelings and attitudes, rather than responding in a chameleon-like manner to momentary contingencies and norms. Although most of these findings are correlational, some experimental work has been conducted. For example, Crutchfield and his associates demonstrated in the late 1950s that those high in autonomy-related traits are much less likely to conform to the (incorrect) group opinion in the Asch line-length paradigm, compared to those low in such traits. [*See* AUTONOMY AND INDEPENDENCE.]

One way of explaining the autonomy–creative relationship is to posit that autonomous individuals are more inclined to perceive potentially controlling social environments primarily in informational terms. This could give them at least two extra resources in their creative efforts. First, because they are not heavily dependent upon others' approval, autonomous persons may be better able to take what is useful from the comments and opinions of their peers, while rejecting and discarding that which is not useful. That is, their autonomy may "inoculate" them against the danger of losing touch with their own perceptions as they make contact with others' ideas. Second, the ability to perceive potentially controlling events in informational terms is likely to help individuals to maintain their intrinsic or task-focused motivation, and thus maintain full access to cognitive resources. Individuals do in fact differ in the ability to shrug off potentially coercive input. For example, Deci and Ryan report that women are more likely to interpret ambiguous social feedback as controlling, detracting from their intrinsic motivation and perhaps creativity.

Another way of understanding the relationship between personal autonomy and creativity is in terms of an "evolving systems" model. Gruber's psychobiographical studies reveal that important new themes and realizations tend to emerge slowly within the work of notable innovators, rather than occurring in moments of sudden insight. For example, although the first inklings of the theory of evolution appear in Charles Darwin's notebooks early on, the model matured slowly and required much of Darwin's life span to be worked out fully. This indicates that lifelong persistence and dedication to self-posed and self-defined problems may be crucial for the development of extraordinary creativity. Such long-term task-involved motivation is unlikely to be manifested in those who are easily swayed by popular opinions of the moment, and who take the cue for their work from current fads and trends. [*See* EVOLVING SYSTEMS APPROACH.]

A related perspective concerns the progression of an organismic integration process, occurring in a deeper way or at a faster rate within notable creators. Sheldon proposed an "attunement" hypothesis, in which autonomous persons are in better touch with the inner organizational tendencies that are inherent in developing life. Although such integrative tendencies are natural, they are also fragile, and may be forestalled to the extent that the person cannot detect his or her own authentic reactions amidst the din of social influence. Creative accomplishment may thus be viewed as a mere side effect of a more general integration process, which occurs automatically to the extent that people are fully "in touch" with themselves. This understanding of creativity is similar to that advocated by Maslow and Rogers, with their concepts of self-actualizing or fully functioning persons.

V. CREATIVE PERSONALITY DEVELOPMENT AS THE OVERCOMING OF CONFORMIST TENDENCIES

As suggested by the preceding, a number of theories posit that exceptional creativity occurs only after would-be creators have succeeded in psychologically differentiating themselves "from the crowd." Most prominent among these is the psychodynamic model of Otto Rank, published in 1932. Rank proposed three *types* or *stages* of personality: a conformist, adapted type who takes his cues from those around him; a conflicted type, who has broken free of norms, but is confused and unhappy; and a creative type, who has gone through both of the latter stages to emerge with a powerful creative voice of her own.

A substantial body of research supports Rank's conception. For example, MacKinnon used the typological model to characterize the three groups of architects examined in the well-known IPAR studies. The nationally renowned creative architects in this sample were a good fit to Rank's "creative" prototype; the less renowned associates of these architects fit the "conflicted" prototype; and a control group of ordinary architects well fit the adapted or "conformist" prototype. Consistent with Rank's developmental assumptions, notable innovators often report an early sensitivity to controlling influences, which results in early rebellion against the status quo. For example, Hammer, in his extensive 1984 study of adolescent artists, found that the most gifted among them were experiencing profound conflict and emotional turmoil, and were also engaged in a retreat from their peers. These efforts at detachment were motivated by an attempt to "resist the corroding effects of overconformity." Similarly, Getzels and Jacksons' studies of highly creative and highly intelligent youths in the early 1960s showed that creative youths were more mocking of conventional aspirations and beliefs, and were much less popular with their teachers, despite the fact that their level of academic achievement was no less than the high-IQ group.

Creative individuals may begin to resist conventional thinking at a relatively early age, in response to particular developmental crises or environments. For example, in 1966 Torrance identified a "fourth grade slump" in creativity, driven by children's increasing sensitivity to peer opinion at this age. A young child's ability to stand up to such early conformist pressures may represent a significant developmental achievement, and may serve as an important predictor of later creative achievement by that person. To be creative, one must sometimes "defy the crowd"; perhaps the sooner this occurs, the better. As noted, however, those seduced into pursuing nonconformity for its own sake, rather than as a way of gaining the freedom to work, may yet be slaves to group opinion. [*See* Fourth Grade Slump.]

Bibliography

Amabile, T. (1996). *Creativity in context.* Boulder, CO: Westview Press.

Crutchfield, R. (1962). Conformity and creative thinking. In H. Gruber, G. Terrell, & M. Wertheimer (Eds.), *Contemporary approaches to creative thinking.* New York: Atherton Press.

MacKinnon, D. (1965). Personality and the realization of creative potential. *American Psychologist, 20,* 273–281.

Sheldon, K. (1995). Creativity and self-determination in personality. *Creativity Research Journal, 8,* 25–36.

Sternberg, R., & Lubart, T. (1995). *Defying the crowd.* New York: The Free Press.

Sulloway, F. (1996). *Born to rebel: Birth order, family dynamics, and creative lives.* New York: Pantheon Books.

Consensual Assessment

Beth A. Hennessey

Wellesley College

Teresa M. Amabile

Harvard University

Conceptual Definition of Creativity A product is considered creative to the extent that it is both a novel and an appropriate, useful, correct, or valuable response to an open-ended task.

Construct Validity The strength of the link between the term used to refer to a particular phenomenon or construct (e.g., "creativity") and the actual features of the behavior or outcome being measured (e.g., "degree of novelty" or "degree of appropriateness").

Convergent Validity A means of establishing a test's validity by demonstrating the degree of relationship between a variety of measures of the same construct.

Ecological Validity The generalizability of an experimental result to a relevant real-world population, setting, or situation.

Operational Definition of Creativity A product or response is considered creative to the extent that appropriate observers independently agree that it is creative. Appropriate observers are those familiar with the domain in which the product was created or the response articulated.

Reliability The reliability of a measure involves its consistency. In the case of the Consensual Assessment Technique, reliability is measured in terms of the degree of agreement among raters as to a product's level of creativity, technical goodness, or aesthetic appeal compared to other products in the same domain.

Validity The validity of a test or procedure refers to whether it is measuring what it is purported to measure.

CONSENSUAL ASSESSMENT *is a technique used for the assessment of creativity and other aspects of products, relying on the independent subjective judgments of individuals familiar with the domain in which the products were made. Creativity is a concept that is difficult to define and even more difficult to measure. The majority of creativity researchers and theoreticians believe that the key to understanding this phenomenon lies in the study of individual difference variables and the unique constellation of traits that make up the creative person. Others focus their attention on the creative process. A third group has chosen to concentrate on the fruits of that process—the creative product. But how are we to decide whether one product is more creative than another? Is it appropriate for such creativity criteria to be laid out by the researcher? Or perhaps the creators themselves should have the final say? The Consensual Assessment Technique (CAT) for assessing creativity is based on the assumption that a group of independent expert raters, persons who have not had the opportunity to confer with one another and who have not been*

Copyright © 1999 by Academic Press
All rights of reproduction in any form reserved.

trained by the researcher, are best able to make such judgments. Over 20 years of research have clearly established that product creativity can be reliably and validly assessed based upon the consensus of experts. Although creativity in a product may be difficult to characterize in terms of specific features, it is something that people can recognize and agree upon when they see it.

I. THE UNIQUE ASSESSMENT CONCERNS OF CREATIVITY RESEARCHERS

Most empirical investigations of creativity have employed some form of paper-and-pencil creativity test as their primary dependent measure. A variety of personality check lists, developed by Gough, Torrance, Cattell, and others, have often been used to identify highly creative persons. However, by far the most popular creativity indices have focused on behavioral factors. These behavioral assessments typically include a series of scales similar in administration and form to traditional intelligence tests. In fact, many of the items that Guilford originally developed to target the divergent thinking component in his structure-of-intellect theory have served as the prototypes for these creativity tests. Perhaps the most widely used creativity assessments of this type are the Torrance Tests of Creative Thinking (TTCT, also known as the Minnesota Tests of Creative Thinking). This series of tests elicits oral, written, and drawn (non-verbal) responses which are scored in terms of four criteria: (1) fluency, the production of large numbers of ideas; (2) flexibility, the production of a wide variety of ideas; (3) elaboration, the development or filling out of ideas; and (4) originality, the use of ideas that are statistically infrequent.

What does it mean when someone scores high (or low) on these creativity tests? Should high scorers be considered "creative persons"? There is evidence that some creativity tests do accurately tap one or more creative abilities or predispositions. However, it is unlikely that a single test could be developed that would capture the full range of creative abilities. Moreover, a variety of social and environmental factors have been found to influence test results. A number of studies have revealed that scores can be improved simply by

telling subjects that creative responses will be valued. Testing environments can also influence test outcomes, and many investigations have shown variability in creativity test scores under different testing conditions and time constraints. [*See* CONDITIONS AND SETTINGS/ ENVIRONMENT.]

Even if these contextual and situational factors could be controlled for, the construct validity of many of these tests has been questioned, as has the convergent validity of different test procedures considered together. This validity issue is especially problematic given that many of the leading creativity tests have been validated against one another. A final concern is that although the scoring procedures utilized in many of the creativity tests are purported to be objective, performance is often rated according to criteria based upon the test constructor's own, intuitive notion of what is creative. [*See* APPENDIX II: TESTS OF CREATIVITY.]

II. EARLY APPLICATIONS OF CONSENSUAL ASSESSMENT

Mindful of these and other difficulties inherent in the creativity testing process, a small but ever-growing number of researchers have chosen to follow a very different path. It is this group's conviction that creativity judgments can ultimately only be subjective. Rather than attempting to objectify the creativity measurement process, these investigators rely on the consensual assessment of persons or products. Although used much less frequently than creativity tests, this subjective assessment process has a long history. As early as 1870, Galton was relying on biographical dictionaries to select outstanding literary men and scientists—a technique that depended on the subjective assessment of both Galton and those who had compiled the dictionaries. Castle also used biographical dictionaries to construct an initial sample of subjects for a study of highly accomplished men and women, and Cox drew her pool of geniuses for a personality study from Cattell's list of the 1,000 most eminent individuals in history. More recently, Simonton, in a study of sociocultural influences on creativity, developed a measure of creativity based on frequency of citation in histories, anthologies, and biographical dictionaries.

Other investigations have relied on the judgments of a select group of experts to assess the creativity of particular individuals. For example, an expert-nomination procedure was carried out by MacKinnon and his colleagues for a series of studies in the 1960s at the Institute for Personality Assessment and Research in Berkeley, California. In order to gather their subjects, these researchers asked the dean and four colleagues at the College of Architecture at the University of California to list and rate the 40 most creative architects in the United States. Similarly, Helson and Crutchfield gathered mathematicians' nominations for the most highly creative women in their field; and Barron requested that three professors of English and one editor of a literary review suggest names of creative writers.

Shifting their focus away from the creativity of persons, some researchers have asked raters to make assessments of the creativity of particular *products*. In the majority of investigations of this type, the researcher has either presented judges with his own definition of creativity for them to apply or has trained them beforehand to agree with one another. While such methodologies may successfully avoid many of the problems inherent in paper-and-pencil creativity tests, the fact that judges have been carefully instructed in the rating process calls into question both the claim of judge-based subjectivity and the meaning of interjudge reliability. Rather than impose specific definitions of creativity or related dimensions, researchers would more closely approach consensual assessment by allowing judges to make their own, independent product assessments.

In 1976, Getzels and Csikszentmihalyi did just this when they requested that four different groups of judges (two experts and two nonexperts) use their own individual criteria when rating subjects' drawings on originality, craftsmanship, and overall aesthetic value. Sobel and Rothenberg also utilized this subjective assessment technique when they asked their raters, two accomplished artists, to judge sketches on originality, value, and overall creative potential guided only by their own subjective definitions of these dimensions.

Investigations such as the ones described above managed to overcome much of the criticism levied against the earliest applications of consensual assessment to product creativity, yet a variety of difficulties

still remained. First, many of the procedures being utilized failed to differentiate between the creativity of products and other related constructs such as technical correctness or aesthetic appeal. Further, most researchers utilizing consensual assessment procedures were dong so without the benefit of clear operational definitions. Nearly all contemporary definitions of creativity are conceptual rather than operational. They were never intended to be translated into actual assessment criteria. Either investigators failed to explicitly state the definition of creativity guiding their research or they presented conceptual definitions that did not adequately reflect the rating procedures they had chosen to utilize.

III. CREATIVITY RESEARCH WITHIN A SOCIAL-PSYCHOLOGICAL CONTEXT

The consensual assessment of creativity was formalized and systematized by Amabile's work in the social psychology of creativity, beginning in the late 1970s. The goal of Amabile's research program was to examine the effects of various social and environmental variables on creative performance. In a wide range of studies, it has been found that certain social constraints dampen creativity. For example, expected reward and expected evaluation both have undermining effects.

Amabile's original research paradigm compared the creativity of two groups of products—products produced by subjects performing under some extrinsic constraint versus products produced by subjects in the absence of such constraints. When this program of investigation was begun over 20 years ago, it was found that existing creativity measurement tools, including available consensual assessment methodologies, could not meet the unique research requirements of investigators interested in the social psychology of creativity. The majority of available assessment techniques resembled personality or IQ tests in that they viewed creativity as an enduring personality trait. Aside from the methodological limitations of these tests, previously described, the tests were unsuitable because of the purpose for which they had been designed. Whether they requested that a picture be completed, unusual uses for a brick be generated, adjectives describing the self be selected, or remote associations be discovered, most paper-and-pencil measures had been specifically constructed to maximize individual differences. They had been constructed to do exactly what social psychologists try to avoid.

Researchers taking a social-psychological approach most often seek to control for and, as much as possible, eliminate within-group variability in their dependent measures in order that these measures might detect more global between-group differences produced by experimental manipulations of social and/or environmental factors. In such studies, individual differences constitute the error variance. What are needed are measures that deemphasize subject differences—measures, in other words, that do not depend heavily upon the level of individual subjects' skills or the range of their experience.

Clearly, none of the available measures of creativity could serve these particular research requirements. The pioneering peer nomination procedures utilized by researchers like MacKinnon were inadequate for the particular needs of social psychologists, as were the consensual assessment procedures developed by Getzels and Csikszentmihalyi. Techniques resulting in global assessments of an individual as creative on the basis of a lifetime of work are, like the paper-and-pencil measures, constructed to detect relatively permanent personality characteristics and are inappropriate for the study of more unstable environmental and situational influences. Even those assessment procedures that have judges rate single products were likely to be too sensitive to large and stable individual differences in performance. In most previous subjective assessment methodologies, the task presented to subjects has drawn upon special talents or experience-related skills. What were needed were measures that deemphasized such individual differences between subjects.

Amabile's first step was to solve the criterion problem in creativity research with the adoption of two complementary definitions of creativity: an underlying conceptual definition that can be used in building a theoretical formulation of the creative process and an operational definition that is readily applicable to empirical research. The Consensual Assessment Technique (CAT) is grounded in just such an operational definition of creativity: a product or response is creative to the extent that appropriate observers agree it is

creative. Appropriate observers are those familiar with the domain in which the product was created or the response articulated.

Importantly, this consensual definition is based on the creative product rather than the creative process. Not only has a clear articulation of the creative process yet to be developed but, more importantly, any identification of a thought process as "creative" must finally depend upon the fruit of that process—a product or response. In most respects, this emphasis on product is not new. The majority of creativity assessment techniques, in fact, require that subjects produce something—a list of ideas, a series of pictures, or the like. What does set this methodology apart from the rest is that rather than responding to a series of predetermined items or questions, subjects are required to produce an actual product such as a poem, a collage, or a story. Perhaps the most important feature of this consensual definition is its reliance on subjective criteria. In this way, it overcomes the difficulty of attempting to specify ultimate objective criteria for identifying products as creative. Indeed it may be impossible to articulate such ultimate criteria. Just as the judgment of attitude statements as more or less favorable or the identification of individuals as more or less "physically attractive" depends on social context, so too does the judgment of creativity. Certainly there must be particular characteristics of attitude statements or persons or products that observers systematically look to in rating them on scales of favorability or physical attractiveness or creativity, but in the end the choice of these characteristics is a subjective one. [*See* CREATIVE PRODUCTS.]

As do most researchers in the field, Amabile also uses a conceptual definition of creativity to guide her work: A product or idea is creative to the extent that it is a novel and appropriate response to a heuristic (open-ended) task. Again, it is important to point out that this approach is not very different from a number of others that have come before it. Despite the implicit emphasis on the person in creativity assessment, most explicit definitions have used the creative product as the distinguishing sign of creativity. Indeed, the criteria of product novelty and appropriateness have long been seen as the hallmarks of creativity by a number of theorists.

The CAT attempts to capture the essential characteristics of the conceptual definition of creativity. First, subjects are presented with tasks that leave room for considerable flexibility and novelty of response. Second, these are tasks for which the range of appropriate responses has been clearly identified in subjects' instructions. Finally, the experimental activities employed are all heuristic in nature—judges are only asked to make ratings of open-ended tasks.

In employing the assessment technique, researchers must be careful not to impose this conceptual definitional framework upon their judges. Rather than being forced to comply with the investigator's own (possibly erroneous) views, judges should be guided by their individual subjective conceptions about creativity. There are several reasons to believe, however, that the conceptual definition underlying the ratings made by judges is not very different from the conceptual definition presented earlier. First, there exists a wealth of data that demonstrate that judges' ratings of product creativity are highly positively correlated with their assessments of product novelty. In addition, as already noted, each creativity task administered according to CAT specifications has been specifically designed so as to define the range of appropriate responses. The task parameters presented to subjects almost necessitate that their responses stay within certain boundaries. And when these boundaries are transgressed to any significant degree (e.g., a haiku to be written about winter instead discusses spring), judges' assessments of product creativity tend to be negatively affected.

IV. REFINING THE CONSENSUAL ASSESSMENT TECHNIQUE

The CAT rests on two important assumptions. The first assumption is that it is possible to obtain reliable judgments of product creativity, given an appropriate group of judges. In other words, although creativity in a product may be difficult to characterize in terms of specific features, it is something that people can recognize when they see it. Furthermore, people familiar with such products can agree with one another on this perception. A second assumption is that there are degrees of creativity, that observers can say, at an acceptable level of agreement, that some products are more or less creative than others.

Since it is desirable for social-psychological research

that there not be large individual differences in baseline performance on the target experimental task, the CAT as it is typically used requires that the creativity task not depend heavily upon specialized skills, such as drawing or verbal facility, that some individuals will have undoubtedly developed more fully than others. (More recent applications of the technique in subject populations with higher degrees of expertise, such as artists or poets, have utilized tasks more dependent upon skill.) In addition, the task should be open-ended enough to permit considerable flexibility and allow for novelty in responses. In addition, of course, the task must be one that leads to some clearly observable response. In this way, the creativity assessment procedure is similar to real-world assessments of creativity—where appropriate judges, experts in such widely disparate domains as the visual arts and the sciences, make ratings of products in their domain according to their own, subjective criteria.

A. Procedural Requirements

Researchers deciding to utilize this consensual assessment procedure must make certain that a number of requirements are met. First, the judges should all have had some experience with the domain in question, although the level of experience for all judges need not be identical. When the CAT was first developed, the term "expert" was used to describe an appropriate body of raters. Over the years, however, extensive work with this methodology has brought about a tempering of this view. Basically, the method requires that all those rating products be familiar enough with the domain to have developed, over a period of time, some implicit criteria for creativity, technical goodness, and so on. When asked to rate the creativity of paper collages, both children and adults from a variety of backgrounds have produced highly reliable assessments. When dealing with a more specialized and esoteric field, such as physics or computer programming, however, the range of "experts" (i.e., appropriate observers) would certainly have to be considerably narrower. In either case, it is the judges' familiarity with the domain that is important, not the fact that they, themselves, may have produced work rated as highly creative.

A second requirement is that the judges must make

their assessments independently. They are not trained by the experimenter to agree with one another, are given no specific criteria for judging creativity, and are not allowed to confer in their assessments.

Third, judges should be instructed to rate the products relative to one another, rather than rating them against some absolute standards they might hold for drawing, sculpture, poetry, and so on. This is important because, for most studies, the levels of creativity produced by the "ordinary" subjects who participate will be very low in comparison with the greatest works ever produced in that domain.

Fourth, each judge should view the products in a different random order. If all judgments are made in the same order by all raters, high levels of agreement might reflect methodological artifacts.

Finally, if this technique is to be used to evaluate performance on a task to which it has not been applied in the past, judges should be asked to rate the products on other dimensions in addition to creativity. Minimally, they should make ratings of technical aspects of the work, and if appropriate, its aesthetic appeal as well. These additional assessments make it possible to examine the degree of relatedness or independence of these dimensions in subjective judgments of the products in question.

Once the judgments are obtained, ratings on each dimension should be analyzed for interjudge reliability. In addition, if several subjective dimensions of judgment have been obtained, these should be entered into a factor analysis to determine the degree of independence (discriminant validity) between creativity and the other dimensions investigated. Finally, if the products lend themselves to a straightforward identification of specific objective features, these features may be assessed and correlated with creativity judgments.

B. Reliability

Given the consensual definition of creativity, the most important criterion for the results of this assessment procedure is that the product ratings be reliable. In order to compute reliability, researchers originally utilizing the CAT relied upon the Spearman–Brown prediction formula, which is based on the number of judges (n) and the mean interjudge correlation (r):

$$\text{reliability} = \frac{nr}{1 + (n-1)r}.$$

This technique yields results highly similar to the Cronbach coefficient alpha as calculated by the "reliability" procedure in SPSS (Statistical Package for the Social Sciences). In the interest of simplicity, in recent years researchers employing the CAT have relied upon the SPSS calculation as their measure of interrater agreement. Finally, if researchers desire that judges be considered a random effect rather than a fixed effect, they may use the intraclass correlation to assess reliability. In practice, the result obtained by this method is often similar to that obtained by the Spearman–Brown and coefficient alpha methods. In most instances, a reliability figure of .70 or higher can be considered evidence of an acceptable level of agreement between judges. Once such a level is reached, it is then appropriate to compute a sum (or an average) across all ratings given to each product. These sums (or averages) then constitute the unit of analysis for further computations.

By definition, interjudge reliability in this method is equivalent to construct validity: If appropriate judges independently agree that a given product is highly creative, then it can and must be accepted as such. In addition, it should be possible to separate subjective judgments of product creativity from judgments of technical goodness and aesthetic appeal. Within some domains, it may be difficult to obtain ratings of product creativity that are not highly positively correlated with judges' assessments of product technical goodness or aesthetic appeal. Yet it is essential to demonstrate that it is at least possible to separate these dimensions; otherwise the discriminant validity of the measure would be in doubt. In other words, judges might be rating a product as "creative" merely because they like it or believe that it is technically well done.

C. Supporting Data

Numerous studies over the past 20 years have demonstrated that the CAT does, in fact, yield reliable measurements appropriate for social-psychological studies of creativity. The product most frequently produced by subjects and rated by judges has been the paper collage. Participants in these investigations are presented with a piece of cardboard, glue, and a variety of colored pieces of paper of different shapes and sizes. In order to broadly control for content and detail, they are often instructed to make a design that "makes them feel silly," and they are given approximately 15 minutes to engage in the task. In the majority of instances, professional artists and/or graduate students in the studio arts have served as the "expert" judges. In those investigations employing elementary or preschool students as subjects, classroom art teachers familiar with the work of children have also been recruited. For collage ratings, 8–10 judges have typically been employed. Without exception, raters have yielded highly reliable assessments of collage creativity (Table I).

Equally important as interrater reliability is the requirement that judges' assessments of certain additional product dimensions not correlate highly with their ratings of creativity. Here, too, the results have been encouraging. In keeping with most theorists' conceptions of creativity, ratings of novelty and originality have typically been highly related to ratings of creativity, while ratings of various aspects of collage technical goodness have not usually been significantly correlated with creativity assessments. As an example, Table II presents data on 22 collages made by elementary school subjects and rated by seven artist judges.

Finally, the requirement that individual difference

TABLE I
Creativity Reliability Data on Collages

Subjects	Judges	Reliability
80 children	11 artists	.80
60 undergraduate women	14 artists	.75
58 children	12 elementary school teachers	.70
41 children	15 artists	.79
40 undergraduates	12 artists	.77
87 undergraduates	8 artists and art students	.78
151 undergraduates	10 artists	.80
50 children	5 adults familiar with children's art	.82
118 children	5 art teachers	.72

Note. All studies were conducted by members of Amabile's Research Group at Brandeis University. Reliabilities are coefficient alpha.

TABLE II
Correlations between Dimensions of Judgment for Artist Judges

Dimension	Correlation with creativity	Correlation with technical goodness
Dimensions correlated significantly with creativity		
Creativity	—	.13
Novel use of materials	.81[a]	.04
Novel idea	.90[a]	.19
Liking	.72[a]	.31
Variation in shapes	.62[b]	.06
Symmetry	−.59[b]	.27
Detail	.54[b]	.19
Complexity	.76[a]	−.02
Dimensions correlated significantly with technical goodness		
Technical goodness	.13	—
Planning	−.04	.80[a]
Organization	−.13	.82[a]
Neatness	−.26	.72[a]
Balance	−.24	.64[b]
Pleasing placement of shapes	.32	.60[b]
Pleasing use of color	.25	.47[c]
Representationalism	−.18	.54[b]
Expression	−.05	.52[c]
Dimensions correlated significantly with both		
Aesthetic appeal	.43[c]	.59[b]
Display	.56[b]	.56[b]
Effort evident	.64[b]	.55[b]

Note. All data taken from Amabile (1982). Correlations with no superscripts are not significant.
[a] $p < .001$.
[b] $p < .01$.
[c] $p < .05$.

variables, such as subject age, not be predictive of creativity on the collage task has also been met. Among the numerous studies involving children as subjects, it is unusual to find any systematic relationship between assessments of collage creativity and artist age. Gender differences in creativity of response are even more rare—with only a single study indicating that girls scored higher on collage creativity than boys.

Although the collage measure has had the greatest amount of use, researchers have also employed a wide variety of other creativity tasks in their investigations using the CAT. In an attempt to assess the impact of social constraints on verbal creativity, they have, for example, asked adults to complete five-line "American haiku" poems. In an effort to reduce product variability and make the judging task somewhat more manageable, subjects are typically provided with the first line of the poem they are to write. In one study, this technique was successfully adapted for use with young children. Sitting in front of a computer screen, subjects were prompted in a question and answer interactive format to enter one-, two-, or three-word lines. Other measures of verbal creativity that have also proven useful involve completing sentences; writing essays, descriptive paragraphs, and free-form poems; coming up with captions for cartoons; and telling a story to accompany an open-ended picture book without words. This storytelling task has been used successfully with children as young as first grade. Subjects look through the book with the experimenter and then are asked to tell a story by saying "one thing" about each page.

Each of these verbal tasks has also yielded highly reliable creativity assessments. Whether they are poets rating haikus, elementary school teachers rating children's stories, or graduate students rating cartoon captions, judges show consistently high interrater agreement.

In addition to measuring artistic and verbal performance, researchers have also used tasks designed to investigate what might be called creative problem solving. One assessment procedure taps spatial-mathematical creativity in children and calls for the construction of a geometric design on a computer screen. Another activity requires that young subjects fill in the outline of a geometric shape with colored pieces of felt. Problem-solving tasks involving adult subjects include the construction of computer programs, building structures from ordinary materials, generating survival ideas or ideas for high-tech products, and coming up with business solutions. Although none of these techniques has been used to the same extent as collage making or many of the verbal creativity tasks, it is encouraging that judges have rated products produced by children and adults with high levels of reliability.

Clearly, the CAT has wide-range application. It has been successfully employed with both children and adult subjects and allows for the assessment of creativity in a number of different domains. In recent years, subject populations have been expanded beyond undergraduates and elementary school children, demonstrating that the work of professional artists, professional art students, computer programming students, student poets, and employees of a high-tech company can also be reliably assessed by the CAT. For these reasons, an ever-growing number of researchers have come to rely on this assessment technique.

V. TAKING A CLOSER LOOK

What exactly are judges doing when they rate the creativity of these products? Although they are not provided with a definition of creativity, they consistently and reliably identify a quality in a wide variety of products that is most often distinct (as demonstrated by correlational and factor analyses) from both technical execution and aesthetic appeal. On what are these creativity assessments based? Do judges somehow make implicit assumptions about the products' creators or their creative processes? Recently, Hennessey conducted a series of four studies with these questions in mind.

The first of these investigations was designed to determine whether raters employing the CAT are able to reliably assess the creativity of the *process* that went into producing a product. Undergraduate students were asked to rate colored geometric line designs that had been created on a computer. Subjects in the Product Condition sat in front of the computer and rated each design for creativity, technical goodness, and likableness. Subjects in the Process Condition were shown not only the final product but also the steps that went into producing that product. It was their task to make ratings of creativity, technical goodness, and likableness for the procedures that resulted in the creation of the designs. Reliability was high and results suggested that raters have no more difficulty making assessments of process than they do finished products. Furthermore, there appears to be a strong and positive relationship between the ratings of process and product for the dimensions of both creativity and technical goodness.

In the second study, undergraduate students, none

of whom had been involved in the initial study, served as judges. The same geometric designs were employed, and all procedures and instructions were identical to those utilized previously, except that each of the judges made both process and product assessments. Reliability was again acceptable, and judges appeared to have no more difficulty rating process than they did products. Data analyses took two distinct approaches. First, as in the initial investigation, a sum over all ratings was computed for each of the designs assessed, and correlations were performed. Once again, assessments of product and process were closely related. Because the same raters had, in this instance, made ratings of both process and product creativity, it was also possible to take a within-subjects approach and compute process–product correlations *separately* for each rater. These within-rater analyses revealed that, for creativity, approximately half of the judges showed a significant positive relationship between product judgments and process judgments.

Taken together, the results of the two investigations reveal that untrained observers can recognize and agree upon not only the creativity, technical goodness, and aesthetic appeal of computer designs but also the creativity, technical goodness, and aesthetic appeal of the processes that went into producing those designs. Furthermore, correlational analyses performed both across and within judges demonstrate that these subjective assessments of process creativity tend to be strongly and positively related to a variety of other product and process dimensions.

A third study was later designed to explore whether these same results would obtain when more "real-world" products—namely, drawings produced by an eminent artist—were assessed. Undergraduate students again served as judges in this experiment, and "products" to be rated consisted of videotaped segments of the processes that went into completing four Picasso drawings and stills of those drawings taken from the movie, *The Mystery of Picasso.* Experimental procedures and data analyses paralleled those employed in the second study. Reliability was again acceptable for creativity and technical goodness ratings made in both the process and the product conditions, and analyses revealed that correlations between ratings of process and ratings of product were of approxi-

mately the same magnitude as those obtained in the two previous investigations.

While these findings are most useful for demonstrating the utility and validity of the CAT, they tell us only very little about what judges are actually doing when they make their ratings. Are they, for example, considering only the final product? Or do they also take into account other factors—factors such as information about the circumstances in which a product was produced or characteristics of the creator? In investigations employing the CAT, judges are typically given very little information about the persons who have made the products they are to rate. Most often, they are instructed in the assessment process and are told simply that the materials they will be viewing were produced, for example, by university undergraduates, or preschoolers, or graphic art students. Implicit in this procedure is the assumption that creativity is a unitary construct independent of factors such as age or experience of the creator.

This premise that knowledge about a creator's age will not significantly affect raters' judgments has been subject to very little empirical testing, but at least one group of theorists have asked whether measures of product creativity derived from one cohort can validly be applied to another—whether the same creativity criteria can be used for products produced by children and adults. Smith and Carlsson, for example, consider preschoolers' attempts at creative activity as more or less premature or accidental and conclude that not until the age of 10 or 11 years do we enter the first stage of "true creativity." Wolf and Larson echo these sentiments, and others, including Elkind, have observed that it may be the child's inability to incorporate all of the "facts" and his inability to change in light of new facts that helps account for the apparent creative character of his work. In other words, children's responses may be viewed by adults as creative by virtue of what they omit rather than what they include.

The last in the series of investigations conducted by Hennessey was intended as a preliminary exploration of the impact of artist age information on judges' creativity assessments. Two sets of collages were collected—one from elementary school children and the other from college students. University undergraduates who had been told which products had been produced by children and which had been produced by adults then rated the collages' creativity according to CAT guidelines. Acceptable levels of reliability were reached and these ratings were used to identify products, produced by both adults and children, that had been judged with the greatest consistency. Five children's and five adults' collages were then selected to represent each of the following categories: high creativity, moderate creativity, and low creativity.

During the main experimental session, one group of undergraduates, none of whom had participated in previous experimental sessions, were asked to judge these collages after receiving accurate information about the age of the artists. A second group was asked to rate the same collages after receiving false information as to the age of the artists. Children's products were identified as having been produced by adults, and adults' products were labeled as children's. Finally, a third group of undergraduates were asked to judge the collages without being given any information as to the age of the artists.

Reliabilities were highly acceptable for all three of the judgment conditions. An examination of the ratings indicated that age information did, in fact, have a significant effect. The highest creativity ratings were given to adults' collages which had been falsely labeled as children's products. The lowest creativity ratings were given by judges who had received no age information to collages that had been produced by children. Overall, it was found that those raters receiving age information about the artists, whether accurate or reversed, gave products higher ratings of creativity than did raters for whom no age information was available. Within age information groups, no significant differences emerged between judges' creativity ratings of children's and adults' collages.

Six of the 33 judges polled reported that they had considered artists' ages when making their product assessments. Two other respondents mentioned "fighting" against the tendency to take artist age into consideration. As a final tally, 15 of the 33 judges held the expectation that adults should be more creative than children. Two judges expected that children should show greater creativity than adults, and one respondent felt that it was entirely inappropriate to compare products made by children and adults, as each age group is "creative in its own way." Judges did not hold

higher expectations for one age group over another, nor did they employ separate creativity criteria for products they believed had been produced by children and adults. Contrary to expectation, it was the mere availability of age information and not the specific adult or child label that affected raters' judgments. Whether raters were given an accurate or a reversed age label, they judged children's collages to be higher in creativity than did raters given no age information. This finding suggests that creativity theorists and researchers wishing to employ the CAT must be certain to note whether age information has been made available, either purposefully or unintentionally, to judges. Similarly, careful assessments should be conducted to determine whether raters have made any age inferences on their own.

Clearly, the availability of age information about an artist can significantly influence subjective ratings of products. Another related issue is whether individuals can make reliable ratings of the creativity of their own work. In studies where subjects were unfamiliar with the creativity task presented to them, self-assessments of creativity were found to be generally uncorrelated with ratings made by others. However, in situations where subjects had had some experience with the target task, there has often emerged a moderate correlation between self-assessments of product creativity and the mean ratings made by others. This finding is particularly impressive given the fact that individuals judging their own work were asked to make their assessments relative to products they had produced in the past, while the judges with whom their assessments were being compared made their ratings relative to products produced by the other subjects in the study, or relative to only a small selection of the subject's prior work.

While a few investigators have found self-assessments to be a useful research tool, there does exist some research evidence which cautions that there may be important differences between intrapersonal and interpersonal judgments. For example, while artists' self-ratings have been found to correlate with judges' ratings, the artists have also tended to rate themselves higher in creativity than did judges. As some have argued, just because individuals have proven capable of producing art, does not mean that they will be reliable or accurate when judging it.

A variety of papers have carefully explored these and other issues concerning the question of who should be considered an "appropriate" judge. In one study, parents and teachers were found to be equally accurate at recognizing the creativity of children's ideas. But other investigators found that young children's judgments about art were considerably different from those offered by older children. Runco and his colleagues asked college students to produce three three-dimensional artworks which were then rated by the subjects themselves, a group of their peers, and three professional artists. Analyses revealed that the student subjects saw significant differences in the creativity of their own three art projects. Similar differences also were reflected in the peer ratings of the artwork. The assessments made by the professional artists, however, failed to reflect significant differences in creativity between products. These results point to the fact that, at least when the artistic creativity of nonprofessionals is being considered, it may be important to take into account differences in ability between subjects and judges. It would seem that the question of judge expertise becomes most important as the level of subjects' expertise increases. In other words, judges should be closely familiar with works in the target domain at least at the level of those being produced by the subjects.

VI. SOME RECENT CONSIDERATIONS

Over the years, the CAT has come to serve as an invaluable tool for a number of creativity researchers. This methodology has now been extended to a variety of tasks in a variety of domains, and the diversity of subject populations being studied is also constantly growing. In addition to examining the creativity of "novices" from undergraduate student and elementary school populations, the CAT has now been successfully applied to products produced by professional artists, professional art students, computer programming students, student poets, and employees of a high-tech corporation.

Also expanded is the CAT's applicability to a variety of research designs. In the beginning, this method had been utilized only in studies that yielded one product per subject. But lately, researchers have begun to explore the utilization of the CAT methodology in repeated-measures designs. Phillips, Amabile, and Collins recently designed an investigation to explore possible differences in creativity between professional artists' commissioned works and their noncommissioned (self-initiated) projects. Expert-artist judges were presented with products made by each of several artists and were asked to rate each work relative to the other works produced by that same individual. Because it is unlikely that the works of any one artist will differ dramatically among themselves, it was not surprising that this task proved considerably more challenging for judges than the more usual prospect of rating individual pieces from different artists relative to one another. Yet despite the difficulties, acceptable levels of reliability were reached and the CAT proved useful for within-subjects as well as between-subjects creativity assessment.

Perhaps most exciting of all have been recent efforts to apply the CAT in situations of individual-difference assessment. In its original incarnation, the CAT was presented as most useful in social-psychological studies of creativity. The argument was made that if tasks applied to the CAT were as free as possible from reliance on special domain skills, then variability due to individual difference would be minimized and the possibility of detecting global, social-environmental effects would be greatly increased. While Amabile and her colleagues still believe this to be the case, they have since broadened their view.

In a number of recent studies, the CAT has proven extremely useful as an individual-difference measure. In two investigations, for example, artists' portfolios were rated (as a whole) relative to one another. Not only were independent judges able to make these relative creativity judgments with a high degree of reliability, but the mean creativity ratings correlated significantly with other individual-difference measures in each of the two studies. In addition, judges have been able to reliably rate collections of children's works (short poems) relative to one another, and even in studies where only one product is produced per subject, significant correlations have been found between judge-rated creativity and certain individual-difference measures. Finally, when CAT creativity measures from different products produced by the same subjects in different studies are correlated, there is a considerable degree of consistency.

It would seem, then, that the CAT can be applied both in social-psychological studies of the effects of environmental variables on creativity and in situations calling for individual creativity assessment. It must be cautioned, however, that the CAT has only proven useful in identifying differences between the creative performances of individuals *in a certain type of task* in a *particular domain* at *particular points in time*. It would be inappropriate to gather product creativity scores as a means of assessing a person's overall degree of creativity (a concept that many would argue is inappropriate in itself).

Clearly, the CAT has been a great boon to many creativity researchers. It has broad application, is theory driven, and can be adapted to suit a wide variety of research situations. Despite these advantages, however, it should not be considered an ultimate and universally useful means of creativity assessment. Indeed, the CAT has some specific limitations. First, if time concerns are paramount, this method is decidedly impractical. Choosing an appropriate task as well as an appropriate body of judges can be extremely time consuming, as can the assessment of products and the necessary statistical data analyses.

In addition, it may be difficult to apply this measurement procedure to products that are at the frontiers of a particular domain of endeavor. Consider, for example, revolutionary theories in science or revolutionary works of art. It would be difficult to use this method to assess the creativity of such products because it is precisely their revolutionary nature that makes it difficult for people, even so-called experts in their field, to agree on the level of creativity evident. This problem could be considered within the context of the "familiarity" criterion proposed earlier. These products are so different that no one is sufficiently familiar with the domain to serve as an "appropriate" judge.

A related issue involves the fact that the reliability— and hence the validity— of judgments obtained by this method is necessarily limited by historical time and place. It is doubtful that a group of Italian Renaissance painters would agree with a group of contemporary American artists in their judgments of any given group of paintings from any era. Importantly, these limitations are not peculiar to the CAT. Rather, they are shared by all existing creativity assessment methodologies. Paper-and-pencil measures and personality inven-

tories are also historically and culturally bound. They, too, are formulated according to prevailing notions about what is novel and what is appropriate, which invariably change over time.

In spite of these limitations, the CAT has, we believe, many important and unique strengths. In addition to being highly reliable, it adds ecological validity to the measurement of creativity. Using materials that allow for considerable flexibility in response, subjects actually create something that "real-world" creators might make. Subjective judgments of these products are then obtained from appropriate observers. Not only does the creativity task itself mimic real-world performance, but the assessment technique parallels real-world evaluations of creative work. Perhaps most importantly, the existence of a unique subjective construct called "creativity" has been demonstrated. Although judges are not provided with a definition of creativity, being instead asked to use their own subjective definitions, they consistently and reliably identify a quality in a wide variety of products that is distinct from technical execution and often from aesthetic appeal as well.

Although the CAT is considerably more time consuming than the majority of standard creativity tests, its greatest strength rests in the flexibility it affords to creativity researchers:

1. The CAT can be used to obtain reliable assessments of the relative creativity (technical goodness, aesthetic appeal, etc.) of products made by a variety of individuals.

2. In situations where several examples of each individual's work are available, the CAT is also useful for gathering data on the relative creativity (technical goodness, aesthetic appeal, etc.) of several of the same person's products. And, in fact, in these same instances, the CAT is equally useful as an individual-difference measure of creative performance on particular tasks in particular domains for a given time period.

3. Finally, the CAT can be expanded to new domains and new tasks that are quite different from those originally envisioned.

In mimicking the way in which creativity is judged every day in the arts, the sciences, and the professions, the Consensual Assessment Technique can bring creativity from the realm of the mysterious and the mystical, where it has lived for centuries, to the realm of the understood and the accessible.

Bibliography

Amabile, T. M. (1982). Children's artistic creativity: Detrimental effects of competition in a field setting. *Personality and Social Psychology Bulletin, 8,* 573–578.

Amabile, T. M. (1996). *Creativity in context.* Boulder, CO: Westview.

Isaksen, S. G. (Ed.). (1987). *Frontiers of creativity research: Beyond the basics.* Buffalo, NY: Bearly Limited.

Isaksen, S. G., Murdock, M. C., Firestien, R. L., & Treffinger, D. J. (Eds.). (1993). *Understanding and recognizing creativity: The emergence of a discipline.* Norwood, NJ: Ablex.

Sternberg, R. (Ed.). (1988). *The nature of creativity.* New York: Cambridge University Press.

Consistency of Creativity across the Life Span

Robert R. McCrae

National Institute on Aging, National Institutes of Health

Correlation A quantitative measure of the degree to which two variables increase or decrease together, ranging from -1.0 (exactly opposite trends) to $+1.0$ (exactly similar trends).

Cross-Sectional A study design in which younger and older individuals are assessed on a single occasion.

Divergent Thinking The ability to generate multiple possible solutions to a problem.

Longitudinal A study design in which the same scales or tests are repeatedly given to the same individuals over a period of time.

Openness to Experience A broad personality trait marked by an appreciation of novelty and variety and a high tolerance of ambiguity.

Creative individuals are characterized by distinctive cognitive abilities (divergent thinking) and personality traits (Openness to Experience). Studies of adult development have shown that individual differences in both abilities and personality are highly stable, and that some mental abilities decline with age. Together, these findings help explain **CONSISTENCIES IN CREATIVITY** *as well as the decline in creative productions with age.*

I. THE PSYCHOLOGICAL BASIS OF CREATIVITY

Creativity can be seen as an extraordinary gift possessed only by a tiny elite of men and women whose inventions, discoveries, and artistic creations have made them famous. Alternatively, it can be seen as an attribute that all people possess in varying degrees, expressed perhaps in a witty remark or in the artful way one lays out the rows of a vegetable garden. It is this garden variety of creativity that psychologists have most frequently studied, generally with the tacit assumption that what is learned about the psychology of everyday creativity will also apply to works of genius. Researchers interested in explaining individual differences in creativity have usually focused either on special talents and cognitive abilities or on attitudes, motives, and other aspects of personality. Life span developmental psychologists, in turn, have studied the consistency of intelligence and personality for decades, and their findings shed light on the consistency of creativity across the life span. [*See* EVERYDAY CREATIVITY.]

A. Cognitive Abilities and Divergent Thinking

Although no single definition of creativity is universally accepted, most conceptions argue that creativity involves the production of novel solutions to problems. (It is easier to see the relevance of this definition to scientific creativity than to artistic creativity, but many have argued that writing a symphony or painting a picture is essentially a matter of solving artistic problems.) The capacity to solve problems is, of course, one of the hallmarks of intelligence, and high intelligence is frequently found to be a correlate of creativity. However, many highly intelligent people are not creative; they learn rapidly and can solve problems by using standard methods, but they rarely devise new ways of solving problems. [*See* INTELLIGENCE; NOVELTY.]

A number of researchers have proposed that a certain level of intelligence is necessary but not sufficient for creative problem solving. Others have argued that a particular form of intelligence, divergent thinking, is the key. Divergent thinking is the ability to generate many different possibilities for solving a problem. It is assessed by tests of fluency, flexibility, and originality; for example, respondents might be asked to name as many objects as they can that fall in a certain category (say, "objects with sharp edges") or to imagine the consequences of an event or circumstance ("What would happen if people had eyes in the back of their heads?"). People who generate many answers to these kinds of questions, especially if their answers are unusual, are deemed high in divergent thinking ability. Divergent thinking is related to general intelligence, but it is a better predictor of creative achievements than are other forms of intelligence such as memory or reasoning ability. [*See* DIVERGENT THINKING.]

B. Personality Traits

Creative people are distinguished not only by their talents and abilities, but also by their characteristic attitudes, motives, and dispositions. In their review, Barron and Harrington noted that creative individuals have frequently been characterized by their broad interests, independence of judgment, and toleration of ambiguity. People from several different fields who were judged to be notably creative described themselves on an adjective checklist as inventive, reflective, unconventional, and individualistic, whereas those who were judged uncreative described themselves as conservative, cautious, and conventional. [*See* PERSONALITY.]

All these traits are themselves interrelated and help to define one of the five basic dimensions of personality, Openness to Experience. Highly open people have a vivid imagination, aesthetic sensitivity, a rich emotional life, a strong need for variety, broad intellectual interests, and liberal values. This constellation of traits is found in young and old, in men and women, and in cultures from the Philippines to Finland. Individual differences in Openness appear to be a basic part of human nature, and studies of twins suggest that the disposition is substantially influenced by genetic factors.

There are several lines of evidence to support the view that creativity is especially related to Openness. Case studies of highly creative individuals such as the poet and essayist Diane Ackerman and the philosopher, novelist, and composer Jean-Jacques Rousseau document extremely high levels of Openness. In volunteer samples, measures of Openness are correlated with scales designed to assess creative personality. Further, Openness as assessed by self-reports and by peer and spouse ratings has been shown to be related to measures of divergent thinking. Finally, the association of Openness with creativity makes theoretical sense: Open people seek out new experience, prefer complexity, and have a style of consciousness that easily makes new associations between remote ideas. These characteristics would motivate and facilitate creative thinking.

Contemporary models of personality structure suggest that Openness is one of five basic factors, the others being Neuroticism, Extraversion, Agreeableness, and Conscientiousness. Although they may be relevant in particular fields—Extraversion might be needed by a creative salesman—most evidence suggests that these other factors are not systematically and strongly related to creativity in general. Despite stereotypes, creative people as a group are not plagued by anxiety and depression, are not social isolates, and are not misanthropic or undisciplined. Individual artists may fit that description—Rousseau certainly did—but it is not accurate in general.

At least two competing theories of personality and creativity point to traits other than Openness as important factors. Reflecting the widely held belief that genius is akin to madness, Hans Eysenck has argued that creative individuals are characterized by a dimension he calls Psychoticism, which also characterizes individuals prone to antisocial behavior and severe mental illness. Empirical evidence in support of this theory is mixed; some studies find correlations between psychoticism and measures of creativity, whereas others do not. Further, interpretation of the evidence is complicated by the fact that Eysenck's Psychoticism scale has been widely criticized as a measure of proneness to psychosis. Instead, it seems to reflect low Agreeableness and low Conscientiousness, characteristics not usually associated with creativity.

A second alternate theory has been offered by Michael Kirton, who argues that there are different ways of being creative that he calls adaption and innovation. Innovators (who are high in Openness) generate many ideas that go beyond traditional solutions to problems; adaptors (who are high in Conscientiousness) pursue solutions systematically within a conventional framework. If, like Kirton, we equate creativity with problem solving, then this is a reasonable position, because conscientious people certainly do solve problems. If, like most other writers, we regard solutions as creative only when they are novel and original, then only innovators would be considered creative. [*See* ADAPTATION AND CREATIVITY; INNOVATION.]

Kirton also makes an important distinction between creative style and creative level. An innovative, open individual may generate many possible solutions to a problem, but whether they are insightful and ingenious or bizarre and silly depends on the creative level of the individual, which may reflect experience, knowledge, and cognitive ability. In general, it seems likely that truly creative accomplishments will most often come from people who are intelligent, open to experience, and prepared by education and training.

II. LESSONS FROM LIFE SPAN DEVELOPMENTAL PSYCHOLOGY

A. Mean Level Changes in Abilities and Personality

Defining creativity within the context of familiar dimensions of cognition and personality allows us to draw on the large research literature on life span development in these areas that has been accumulated over the past 20 years. Much of that research has been concerned with charting the developmental curves—

changes with age in the average or typical levels—of cognitive and personality variables. Both cross-sectional studies that compare younger and older individuals and longitudinal studies that trace the same individuals over time are useful here. [*See* DEVELOPMENTAL STAGES.]

Empirical studies were essential, because preconceptions and speculative theories about the aging process were substantially in error. In the area of cognition, there was a widespread presumption that all mental abilities declined with age, especially advanced age. Thinking on adult personality was dominated by elaborate theories of developmental stages and crises. Erik Erikson's model of eight stages of psychosocial development is still included in most introductory psychology textbooks. In the 1970s, newer theories arose in which transitional periods like the midlife crisis were prominent. All these theories suggested that personality changes in major ways throughout adulthood, and the careers of artists like Whitman and Gauguin were often cited as examples of the dramatic ways in which lives could change.

But research using large samples and longitudinal designs presents a strikingly different picture. Studies of cognitive performance typically show changes in the average level of performance that vary with the particular cognitive ability involved. Vocabulary tests, which reflect accumulated learning or crystallized intelligence, are very stable, showing only a tiny decline in men and women over age 65. Tests of reasoning ability, spatial ability, and visual memory (forms of fluid intelligence) show much more pronounced changes with age, with accelerating losses in the oldest groups. [*See* AGING.]

In 1987, McCrae, Costa, and Arenberg reported on a large-scale study of divergent thinking in adult men aged 17 to 101. Their battery of tests included four measures of fluency (the ability to generate many appropriate exemplars of a category) and scores for obvious and remote consequences of hypothetical situations. Figure 1 shows the average age trends for these six measures. Except for remote consequences, which declines linearly, all the measures show a curvilinear pattern, tending to increase slightly from 20 to 40 before declining thereafter.

In the area of personality, large-scale empirical studies failed to find support for stage or crisis theories.

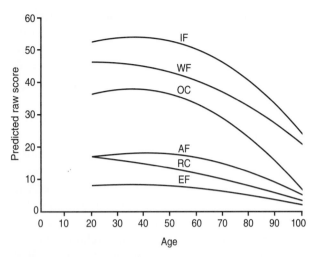

FIGURE 1 Curves representing divergent thinking test scores from age 20 to age 100. AF, Associational Fluency; EF, Expressional Fluency; IF, Ideational Fluency; WF, Word Fluency; OC, Obvious Consequences; RC, Remote Consequences. Adapted from McCrae, Costa, & Arenberg, 1987, *Psychology and Aging, 2,* 130–137.

Some people do have periods of crisis, but they are not clustered around any single age. There was little evidence that any kind of change occurred in discrete stages, and results from longitudinal studies that had begun tracking the same individuals years earlier showed something even more surprising: In contrast to the declines found in cognitive abilities, there was very little change of any kind in personality traits after age 30. People did not become withdrawn or depressed or rigid with advancing age, except for the small proportion who developed disorders like Alzheimer's disease. Instead, the predominant trend was stability. In one study, 205 men were retested after 24 years on a measure of Thoughtfulness, a scale related to Openness (and divergent thinking). Instead of a decline, there was a statistically significant increase in Thoughtfulness— although it was trivial in magnitude. For all practical purposes, this personality trait was unchanged over a quarter century.

There are changes in personality in adulthood, but by and large they occur in the early years, from age 18 to age 30. Cross-cultural studies have shown the same developmental trends in the United States, Germany, Portugal, Italy, Croatia, and South Korea: Between late adolescence and middle adulthood Openness declines.

It appears that individuals are most open to experience when they are just entering adult life, and after a moderate decline, they remain at their characteristic level of Openness for the remainder of their lives.

B. Stability of Individual Differences

Stability of mean level implies only that, on average, people neither increase nor decrease. However, individuals might change dramatically, as long as the increases of some balance the decreases of others. In order to know how well rank order is maintained, longitudinal designs are necessary in which the same people are retested after an interval of years.

It has been known for some time that there is considerable stability of individual differences in intelligence. High school grades are excellent predictors of college grades, and formal longitudinal studies of adults show extremely high retest correlations (around .90) for measures of IQ over intervals as long as 20 years.

A subset of the men who took divergent thinking tests in the study by McCrae and colleagues were tested again six years later. Retest correlations for the six tests ranged from .61 to .81; stability for the sum of the six tests was .87.

Until several longitudinal studies reported very similar results, most psychologists had assumed that personality would show far less stability of individual differences. Life experiences, changes in physical health, retirement, and widowhood would surely have profound impacts on personality traits, they argued. But study after study found instead that personality traits seemed to transcend all these environmental influences. Those people who had initially scored highest on measures of Neuroticism or Extraversion were also among the highest scorers when retested 10 or 20 years later. Measures of Openness to Experience had only infrequently been included in longitudinal studies, so evidence on its stability is more recent. In a 1988 study, Costa and McCrae reported six-year retest correlations of their measure of Openness based on both self-reports and spouse ratings. For younger (25 to 56) and older (57 to 84) men and women, these stability coefficients ranged from .73 to .87—values close to the upper limit of perfect stability. Studies by other investigators using scales related to Openness have also shown high levels of stability over intervals of up to 30 years. People who are curious, sensitive, and imaginative at age 30 are also likely to be curious, sensitive, and imaginative at age 80; those who are dogmatic, narrow, and habit-bound in old age were probably already dogmatic, narrow, and habit-bound in youth.

C. Creativity in Childhood

This article focuses on the adult portion of the life span, in part because there is controversy about whether creativity can be meaningfully assessed in children. Studies of eminent scientists and artists rarely include children because (aside from a few prodigies) children do not have the accumulated knowledge and experience to make substantial creative contributions. However, children certainly differ in openness and intelligence, and thus they are likely also to differ at least in the potential for creativity.

There is some evidence that very young children (around age 5) are more unconventional in their thinking than older children (age 10)—perhaps because young children simply have not yet learned how to think conventionally. Of perhaps greater interest are the results of longitudinal studies that have shown at least some evidence of stability of individual differences. Russ, Robins, and Christiano administered tests of divergent thinking abilities to first and second graders and readministered them four years later. They reported retest correlations from .30 to .46—certainly better than chance, but much lower than the retest correlations seen in adults over a longer interval. Similar correlations have been reported for personality variables in children; in general, it seems that personality and creative abilities are not yet clearly formed in young children. One consequence is that children who seem to lack creativity may yet develop it by the time they are adults.

III. CONSISTENCY OF ARTISTIC AND SCIENTIFIC CREATIVITY

The personal experience of great artists often suggests that creativity is extremely unpredictable. On some occasions inspiration seems endless, with a torrent of ideas, images, or melodies. On other occasions there is no inspiration at all; the dreaded writer's block

can last for months or years. But viewed from a larger perspective, a much more consistent picture is seen. Shakespeare, Beethoven, and Michaelangelo consistently, if not invariably, produced masterpieces of an order that most other artists consistently fail to attain. Formal studies of the lives and work of creative scientists and artists have reached clear conclusions on the basis of the long-term patterns of creative production.

To the extent that real creative achievement is truly related to factors of ability and personality, it should be possible to anticipate the results of these studies. Because individual differences in both intelligence and personality are highly stable, we would expect that differences in creativity would be stable—and this is precisely what a number of studies have shown. Those men and women who are outstanding in their fields in their early careers are most often the same ones who will be outstanding in their later careers. Indeed, stable individual differences in creativity are so pronounced that a small percentage of field leaders account for most of the significant work in most fields. The 19th century produced scores of composers, but the enduring classics are almost all from the pens of Schubert, Chopin, and a dozen others. It was the consistency of their achievement that made them immortal.

Different predictions about the developmental curve of creative production would be made on the basis of studies of abilities and personality. The divergent thinking data in Figure 1 suggest that creativity should rise in the early career and gradually decline with age. By contrast, the developmental trends of Openness suggest that individuals will be most creative in late adolescence, and show a constant level of creative achievement after age 30.

When a tally of productions—scholarly papers, published compositions, poems, or canvases—is used as the measure of creative achievement, Simonton has shown that the data do resemble those in Figure 1. Despite their extreme Openness, adolescents apparently have not yet mastered their subject well enough to make many meaningful contributions. Training and experience are needed to channel their creative potential into creative productions. And despite their unflagging interest in novelty and variety, older individuals do show some loss of creative power. Declines in health may account for this in part, but the continuing decline in divergent thinking ability and other forms of fluid intelligence is also probably a factor. Einstein and Tolstoy at age 70 were probably still far more creative than the average person, but less than they once had been. [*See* PRODUCTIVITY AND AGE.]

The fact that the consistency of creative achievement can be predicted from the consistency of cognitive and personality traits provides indirect evidence that divergent thinking and openness in fact underlie creativity. More direct evidence is provided by longitudinal studies of individuals. Ravenna Helson followed the careers of Mills College graduates from 1957 on. At age 21 the women completed three measures of creative potential; at age 43 they were described by expert raters; and at age 52 their lifetime career achievements were judged for creative production. Women who scored high on creative potential at age 21 were described by raters at age 43 by phrases like "has a wide range of interests" and "tends to be non-conforming"; those who scored low on creative potential were described by "favors conservative values" and "uncomfortable with uncertainty and complexity." Further, creative potential scores at age 21 were substantially correlated with creative career production at age 52. Self-reports of traits related to Openness to Experience at age 21 predict real creative achievement 30 years later. This is remarkable evidence of the intimate and enduring relations between personality and creativity.

Yet there is something odd about the claim that there is great consistency in creativity—where is the novelty and originality in a life of consistency? The answer, of course, is that it is novelty itself that is consistent. A novelist—say Horatio Alger—who writes the same story over and over may sell many books, but is not likely to be judged by history as a great artist. The truly great always find something new. Beethoven went through distinctive early, middle, and late periods, and Picasso made abrupt shifts in his style at several points in his career. Indeed, creative geniuses may shift from one discipline to another altogether. Rabindranath Tagore, the national poet of India, began as a writer, became an educator, and at age 67 turned his attention to drawing:

> Formerly my mind used to hear the voice of the sky and the music of the wind; words used to come to it out of the air. Now it has its eyes open to the world of forms and the crowds of lines. . . . They reveal themselves to me in ever-new gestures; there is no end to their mystery. (Chakravarty, 1961, p. 43)

Thus does an enduring fascination with the world fuel the creative mind.

Bibliography

Chakravarty, A. (1961). *A Tagore reader.* Boston: Beacon Press.

Helson, R. (In press). A longitudinal study of creative personality in women. *Creativity Research Journal.*

Kirton, M. (Ed.). (1989). *Adaptors and innovators: Styles of creativity and problem solving.* New York: Routledge.

McCrae, R. R. (1987). Creativity, divergent thinking, and Openness to Experience. *Journal of Personality and Social Psychology, 52,* 1258–1265.

McCrae, R. R., & Costa, P. T., Jr. (1990). *Personality in adulthood.* New York: Guilford Press.

Runco, M. A., & Charles, R. E. (1998). Developmental trends in creative potential and creative performance. In M. A. Runco (Ed.), *Handbook of creativity* (pp. 113–150). Cresskill, NJ: Hampton Press.

Simonton, D. K. (1997). Creative productivity: A predictive and explanatory model of career trajectories and landmarks. *Psychological Review, 104,* 66–89.

Contrarianism

Mark A. Runco

California State University, Fullerton

Contrarianism Intentionally doing what other people are not doing. Adapted from economics, it is now a popular tactic for ensuring originality in many other creative endeavors.

Creativity Original and useful or appropriate behavior, solutions, or insights. The usefulness criterion implies that contrarianism is not sufficient for creativity; contrarianism only guarantees originality.

Dark Side of Creativity Original and operational solutions and inventions used in immoral ways. One result of contrarianism that is not directed toward creativity but is instead directed toward unconventionality.

Misplaced Investments Occurs when a contrarian tactic is used, but used to the extent that the person is not investing enough time and energy into the topic or problem itself. Time invested into being different is often time away from good focused work, and focused work is frequently necessary for creative insight.

Oppositional Thinking Proclivity toward unconventional behavior. It leads persons to do what others are not, but it is often not a conscious decision and is therefore not strategic nor related to intentional creativity.

Postconventional Contrarianism The recognition of rules and conventions, but making decisions for one's self. Exercising discretion before acting in a contrarian fashion. It may also be viewed as discretionary originality.

Originality is a critical aspect of creativity, and a contrarian tactic has a high probability of leading to an original idea or behavior. This article explores the pros and cons of the contrarian tactic. It appears that CONTRARIANISM can be useful some of the time, but that it is far from sufficient. It does not guarantee creativity and may lead the potential creator astray.

I. INTRODUCTION

Mickey Mouse was created by Walt Disney in the late 1920s. Mickey was a result of some collaboration; Disney worked with his brother Roy and Ub Iwerks. Disney could no longer use his "star performer," Oswald the Lucky Rabbit, because his old distributor held the rights. Disney needed a new star, and Mickey was conceived.

Why a mouse? As a matter of fact Walt apparently wanted a cat. He discussed this with Roy and Ub, and they decided on a mouse. That decision was implicitly contrarian. Disney and his collaborators wanted to do what no one else was doing. One cat was already

Copyright © 1999 by Academic Press
All rights of reproduction in any form reserved.

widely known (Krazy Kat) and a second feline would be unoriginal. They decided on a mouse to be unique.

Interestingly, the original suggestion was to call Mickey "Mortimer," but Walt's wife Lily decided that Mickey was more appropriate. Although Disney's biographer did not describe the history of Mickey Mouse in terms of group dynamics or strategic thinking, what went on can be described in terms of certain group dynamics and certain strategies, Walt being very contrarian, and Lily making sure that the new mouse would have a name which would sound right to the general public. "Mickey Mouse" has a nice ring to it, and like other creative names, labels, and titles, it is fitting in some aesthetic sense. This is true of all creative insights and ideas, not just names, labels, and titles, Creative work is original, but it is more than just original. It is original and fitting.

II. RATIONALE
FOR CONTRARIANISM

The rationale for contrarianism is as follows: Originality is a critical aspect of creativity, and a contrarian tactic has a high probability of leading to an original idea or behavior. It is a very practical tactic because people can think about what others are doing to judge their thinking or behavior. If you ask them to "be original," they may have some difficulty. There is no criterion with which they can actually judge their originality. But if you tell them to "do what others are not doing," they have something concrete to think about and to use in their judgments.

It is easy to be taken in by this strategy—to be convinced of its value. There are several reasons for this:

First, as just noted, it is operational and practical. It gives individuals something they can use when judging their ideas or behavior.

Second, novel behaviors and actions are salient. For this reason the contrarian results of the tactic are easy to see.

Third, it is an easy tactic to explain to others. Teachers, for example, can easily describe this tactic to their charges. A number of empirical projects have demonstrated how easily original thinking can be enhanced with some simple instructions.

Fourth, there are many cases supporting the use of this tactic. The next section of this article reviews example cases. The pros and cons of the contrarian tactics are then explicated.

III. CREATIVE PERSONS WHO HAVE USED CONTRARIAN STRATEGIES

Many famous creative persons have used a contrarianism tactic, in addition to Walt Disney.

Gandhi was a contrarian, especially in his methods of passive resistance. These were fitting, given his beliefs and objectives, and original. He found a way to both resist (which is in itself contrarian, at least vis-à-vis the British) and remain a passivist.

James Watson, who shared the Nobel prize for his work on the structure of DNA, was contrarian. He collaborated with Francis Crick, but the competition with Linus Pauling was fierce. Sometimes competition requires contrarianism in that you do not want others to do what you are doing—or at least not until you have finished or established yourself. [*See* COLLABORATION AND COMPETITION.]

In the medical research field, Heimlich (who developed the Heimlich maneuver) was long known as a maverick and nonconformist. Most recently he proposed curing patients with AIDS by giving them malaria. The *Los Angeles Times* claimed that "this is not the first time the 74-year-old Heimlich's headstrong approach to medicine has shocked, even outraged the Establishment." Heimlich was quoted as saying, "I don't do ordinary things. I don't follow all the rules if there's a better, faster way to do it" (Oct. 30, 1994, p. A30).

The *Los Angeles Times* also published an article, "Renegades Reinvent the Bicycle." Apparently the mountain bike—a modification of what *Britannica* called "the most efficient means yet devised to convert human energy into propulsion"—"came out of nowhere, a product of counterculture—invented by hippies, no less, a ragtag of pot-smokers and Haight-Ashbury drifters who barely got through high school" Note the term "counterculture"—a group of contrarians.

A final example from the *Los Angeles Times* should be given. I am referring to rock 'n' roll. In a 1998 *Times* book review rock is called "a disagreement with established power—a refutation of authority's influence" (April 15, 1998, p. E6).

Nor is rock 'n' roll the only rebellious kind of music. Duke Ellington was, for instance, quite the contrarian. Arnold Ludwig, author of *The Price of Greatness,* explained how

> this response style can play an important role in creativity . . . illustrated, for example, in the compositions of Duke Ellington. Knowingly or not, Ellington exploited traditional musical rules as inspiration for his jazz. If he learned that he was not supposed to use parallel fifths, he immediately would find a way to do so; if told that major sevenths must always rise, he would write a tune in which the line descended from the major seventh; and if the tritone was forbidden, he would find the earliest opportunity to use it and, to emphasize the point, would let it stand alone and exposed. (1996, pp. 7–8)

The comment, "knowingly or not," is critical because by definition tactics and strategies are intentional. Unintentional contrarianism may best be viewed as "oppositional thinking," which Ludwig defined as "the almost automatic tendency to adopt a contrary or opposite response" (1996, pp. 7–8).

Ludwig gave Freud as a second example. Certainly Freud's work was original, and yet it fit with his observations and with certain lines of medical theory. Freud was oppositional, and perhaps contrarian, in his efforts to do original work and in his nonconformity.

In the arts, Picasso described cubism as follows: "We were trying to move in a direction opposite to Impressionism." This is pure contrarianism, especially in the direction—namely, opposite to impressionism. It is not just a reaction to others, and not just different, but *opposite.*

Stephanie Dudek argued that the dadaists and surrealists were "particularly determined to burn all bridges behind them." In this light, contrarianism breaks with traditions. That implies that the avant-garde is inherently contrarian. As Dudek put it, avant-garde is

> by definition art that is ahead of its time, that is shocking, disturbing, and therefore viewed as socially objectionable. Its specific aim is to undermine the existing order and to replace it by another. It attempts

to do this by contradiction, challenge, confrontation, and self-assertion. (in press)

Turning from the visual arts, consider Bruce Lee. He developed his own system of martial arts—Jeet Kune Do—but had to fight the established schools (no pun intended) because they did not want to teach any such techniques outside of Asia.

Howard Gruber described how the famed developmental psychologist Jean Piaget used several specific strategies in his work. First, he suggested that Piaget always thought with a pencil in his hand. This is a simple but useful tactic, given how fleeting creative insights can be. Second, Piaget read outside his own field. Third, he did not read inside his own field. And last, he always had a target or "whipping boy."

B. F. Skinner also suggested that scientists read outside their own field. This is a kind of contrarianism. Focusing on what goes on outside one's own field, and thus avoiding one's own field, is even more contrarian.

Dr. Seuss (Theodor Seuss Geisel), a prolific author of children's literature, broke rules on every page of every book. He made up his own words, used many an ungrammatical sentence, and defied the laws of physics in the actions of his characters. Gertrude Stein and e. e. cummings also come to mind; they too broke certain literary traditions.

Although instructive, these cases—Disney, Gandhi, Heimlich, Ellington, Freud, Picasso, Piaget, and Skinner—are famous creators. Generalizations from them are therefore questionable.

IV. CONTRARIANISM IN THE SERVICE OF CREATIVITY

Two distinctions should be emphasized. First is the distinction between contrarianism and oppositional thinking. The former is intentional and the latter an unintentional tendency toward nonconformity and unconventionality. Similarly critical is the distinction between contrarianism that is intentionally used for the sake of creativity, and that which is used merely to ensure originality and salience.

Contrarianism does not guarantee creativity; it can have other results or be directed to other objectives, including originality. But originality does not endure creativity; it is necessary but not sufficient. It follows that contrarianism for the sake of originality may lead only to deviance and not to creativity.

Salience is a possibility because contrarianism does lead to originality—the contrarian is different and unique—but this can just attract attention. Original behaviors and actions are salient. They grab our attention. Creativity, on the other hand, probably is much more likely when the intention is toward creativity. This is "contrarianism in the service of creativity." When that is the case, there will be some fit, some appropriateness, as well as originality. Recall here that creativity requires both originality and appropriateness. Contrarianism only contributes to the former and can inhibit the latter.

Even for contrarianism in the service of creativity there are potential problems. First is what has been called "misplaced investments." This occurs when the creator uses a contrarian tactic, but does so to the extent that he or she is not investing enough time and energy into the topic or problem itself. Time invested into being different is often time away from good focused work.

A second potential problem is that contrarianism can lead the individual to break rules that should not be broken. It may be that the creator is reinforced for contrarianism because it leads to creative insights, but then fails to exercise discretion and applies the same tactic in areas where some conventionality should be respected. If contrarianism leads the individual to break the important rules that keep society running smoothly, we have yet another example of what Robert McLaren called the "dark side of creativity." [*See* DARK SIDE OF CREATIVITY.]

V. CREATIVITY AS POSTCONVENTIONAL CONTRARIANISM

One useful way to think of contrarianism is as postconventional creativity. This term is used in developmental theories. They typically cover three stages of development: preconventional, conventional, and postconventional. A child in the first stage is unaware of rules, norms, and conventions, and in fact does not recognize the value of rules. His or her games are ever-changing; there are no stable rules to keep them moving toward an objective. Moral judgments at this age are based on rewards and punishments rather than a sense of right and wrong. The child is, however, often quite creative in art and expression. Ask a group of preschoolers to draw pretty trees and you will get mostly trees without green leaves. They pick their colors based on preference rather than convention.

Not so individuals in the conventional stage. They are well aware of rules—and in fact hold to very literal interpretations of them. They see the value of conventions for fitting in, but sometimes put a bit too much effort into doing just that. The result is a tendency away from anything unconventional and original. Conventional individuals respond to peer pressure and hate bending rules. This explains the fourth grade slump, when many children become noticeably less original in their ideation. Conventionality also leads them to a literal use of language, and it certainly is apparent in their games (playing by the rules) and their art. Children in this stage are likely to draw trees with green leaves. [*See* CONVENTIONALITY.]

The third stage is postconventional. Here the individual is aware of rules, norms, and conventions, and typically abides by all. He or she does, however, make decisions for him- or herself. Conventions are taken into account, but so is the immediate context. If asked to draw "what trees look like," leaves may very well be green, but if asked to draw what trees should or could look like, the leaves may be rainbow colors or whatever color is the individual's favorite.

This same capacity to recognize conventions but think for oneself is exactly what was meant earlier by exercising discretion. With that kind of discretion, contrarianism will be used appropriately, for creativity.

Bibliography

Ludwig, A. M. (1996). *The price of greatness: Resolving the creativity and madness controversy.* New York: Guilford Press.

Rubenson, D. L. (1991). On creativity, economics, and baseball. *Creativity Research Journal, 4,* 205–209.

Rubenson, D. L., & Runco, M. A. (1992). The psychoeconomic approach to creativity. *New Ideas in Psychology, 10,* 131–147.

Rubenson, D. L., & Runco, M. A. (1995). The psychoeconomic view of creative work in groups and organizations. *Creativity and Innovation Management, 4,* 232–241.

Runco, M. A. (1991). On economic theories of creativity [Comment]. *Creativity Research Journal, 4,* 198–200.

Runco, M. A. (1995). Insight for creativity, expression for impact. *Creativity Research Journal, 8,* 377–390.

Runco, M. A. (unpublished manuscript). Dare to be a radical—But don't be a damn fool: Intentional deviance vs. contrarianism in the service of creativity.

Sternberg, R. J., & Lubart, T. (1991). Short selling investment theories of creativity? A reply to Runco. *Creativity Research Journal, 4.*

Watson, J. D. (1968). *The double helix.* New York: New American Library.

Conventionality

David A. Pariser

Concordia University Montreal

Artistry as a Cycle of Schema and Corrections Gombrich's hypothesis, first put forward in *Art and Illusion,* that historical changes in visual representation—and changes in visual representation in the lifetime of some artists—are governed by a feedback process requiring acquisition of a rote graphic formula (a schema), and then a series of "corrections" to that schema, which moves the representation in the direction of greater optical accuracy. The process of schema and corrections as employed by Gombrich seeks to explain the development of realistic and illusionistic representational styles in the course of Western art history.

Artistry as the Quest for Equivalent Statements in a Medium This is the Gestalt counterpart to the notion of schema and corrections. Arnheim, in *Art and Visual Perception,* proposed that the organization and development of visual representations is based on the artist's quest for those structures and forms in a given medium that function as equivalents for the chosen referent. This means that visual representations are never arbitrary tokens. It also means that making a visual representation is never a quest for verisimilitude, but is always a search for a representational form that exploits the special characteristics of the chosen medium and that embodies the dynamic qualities of the referent. From the Gestalt point of view, a style such as naturalism rather than being the highest pinnacle of artistic achievement is just one of many equally effective representational systems.

Artists as Problem Finders The notion that one of the most distinctive traits of all artists is their unquenchable drive to find new problems to solve. It is this quest for problems rather than solutions that motivates creative people like artists and musicians. The term was coined by Getzels and Csikszentmihalyi in their 1976 study of artists titled *The Creative Vision.*

Conventionality At the macro level, the quality of being governed by custom, folkway, or socially sanctioned prescription. At the micro level, the arbitrary assignment of meaning to an image or representation solely on the basis of agreement between artist and audience.

Perspective A geometrically based system of representation that purports to give the viewer of a drawing or painting the same visual information about a real world scene as he or she would receive if standing in front of the scene itself. The question of whether or not perspectival rendering is an arbitrary conventional system or is an optically based natural system of representation has been hotly contested by many students of perception, among them Arnheim, Goodman, and Gombrich. For an excellent discussion of the relationship of perspective, iconography, and perception one should consult Kubovy's 1988 book titled *The Psychology of Perspective and Renaissance Art.*

Copyright © 1999 by Academic Press
All rights of reproduction in any form reserved.

*This article considers five questions that relate to **CONVENTIONALITY**: (a) What sorts of conventional limits have diverse cultures and epochs established for artists? (b) What role does conventionality play in the way in which audiences approach an artwork? (c) What role does conventionality play in the micro processes of visual representation and art historical change? (d) What in the visual arts is not conventional? When does the unconventional or preconventional become conventional? (e) What is the relationship of conventionality to the creation of a successful artwork?*

I. DEFINING CONVENTIONALITY: OF RABBIS AND CADENZAS

With solemn affection a Rabbi touches the hem of her prayer shawl to the scrolls of the Torah; an exuberant crowd at a baseball game chants and claps in unison; a pianist launches into her own contribution to a sonata—the cadenza; with meticulous care, a student produces a rote copy of a landscape painted centuries earlier by a revered Chinese master; a taxonomist gives a newly discovered fossil a Latin name. These illustrations are all instances of behavior shaped by custom. No matter how varied in purpose and setting, each act is shaped by cultural history, authority, or social precedent. What all these diverse acts have in common is their conventionality.

What then is a convention? According to the 1994 *Roget's Thesaurus,* it is broadly defined as "custom, use, usage, standard usage, standard behavior" and further on "established way, . . . time-honored practice, tradition, standing custom, folkway . . . prescription." *Conventionality* is therefore the quality of being governed by custom, folkway, or prescription. But how far does this get us in understanding the role that conventions play in the arts?

In his 1968 book, *Languages of Art,* Nelson Goodman showed how ambiguous the term can be by pointing out two ways in which it can be used. Witness the contrast, he said, between "very conventional" (as in "very ordinary") and "highly conventional" or "highly conventionalized" (as in "very artificial"). Used in the first sense then, Norman Rockwell, and the authors of Harlequin Romances, TV sit-coms, and soap operas, can all be characterized as conventional artists. Used in the other sense, rarified artistic performances and products such as Baroque music, Noh theater, Restoration drama, and pre-Raphaelite paintings are also conventional. Here the term suggests that works so characterized are part of an exotic or over-refined artistic system such that only the most elite audience members can appreciate them. So Goodman's comment alerts us to two of the contradictory ways in which the term can be used.

II. CONVENTIONALITY AT THE MACRO AND MICRO LEVELS

One way to eliminate some of the confusion associated with the term conventionality is to use it in reference to the set of formal and thematic limits prescribed by social groups for artists. This covers the meaning of the term at the level of the arts as a social practice. I refer to this as the macro level. But on other occasions, the term is introduced into a discussion of the artistic process as it unfolds at the personal level. At this micro level, social injunctions and prohibitions are less pertinent. What we consider at this level is the semiotic process itself: By what means does a mark, a blob, a movement come to stand for something else—real or imaginary? It is at the micro level that the term is far more contested.

Theoreticians have very different explanations for how artists—or anyone making representations in a medium—actually establish a correspondence between the symbol and the thing for which it stands. For Goodman, the key mechanism for representation is the arbitrary assignment of referential meaning. The artist operates by arbitrary fiat. For others, the mechanism of representation is the artist's discovery of equivalent statements in a medium. The artist's choice of symbolic equivalences is not arbitrary, but is in fact governed by the artist's sensitivity to the formal correspondences that exist between visual symbols and the things that they stand for.

A. Macro-Level Considerations: Social Controls on Representation— What Conventional Limits Do Diverse Cultures and Historical Epochs Establish for Artists?

Conventionality at the macro level is just one part of the scaffolding within which artists construct solutions to problems they have chosen. Part of this scaffold consists of an artist's strong sense for the physical qualities of the medium: Clay will only assume certain forms and support a certain weight, ink splatters, stone breaks, paint bleeds and runs, an improperly tuned instrument makes odd noises, the human body can only bend in certain ways, a flat surface can never achieve full plasticity (except for a holographic image), and so on. The physical characteristics of the chosen medium are one set of constraints that all artists must deal with, and each culture makes its own conventional demands on the artist to demonstrate physical and technical mastery.

Skilled handling, or mastery, (variously defined) is an expectation that permeates artistic practice across the world and throughout history. Yet there have also been artists and cultures who appreciated the special character of a work produced when one forgets orthodox ideas about technique. For instance, in the film *Painters Painting* the American abstract expressionist de Kooning revealed his pleasure upon discovering that painting with an uncontrollable floppy long-handled brush yields exciting effects and new visual ideas. Nearly 300 years earlier, the Chinese artist Tao-chi investigated a similarly out-of-control process in the random and artless conjunction of ink and paper in his proto-abstract expressionist explorations called "Ten Thousand Ugly Ink Dots." Tao-chi, like de Kooning, was obviously stimulated by the unforeseen effects that result from handling a medium with less than the usual control. Tao-chi was deliberately following what was, even at that time, something of a convention in Chinese art; the exploration of spontaneity. De Kooning, with a typically Western sense of bravado, may have had the impression that he was among a vanguard of artists who dared to lay down the conventional crutch of technical skill, but as we can see, he was not the first to delight in turning his back on notions of material skill.

Social prohibitions and imperatives provide the basis for clearly articulated macro-level conventions. For example, in many cultures, there are strict prohibitions covering the representation of sacred subject matter. Certain branches of Islam and Judaism still forbid the representation of the human figure because people are reputedly made in the Divine image. This sort of prohibition nearly came to pass in the Christian world as well. The Second Church Council of Nicea of 787 A.D. came close to banning all representational devotional images on religious grounds, but did not do so. Artists whose subject matter touches on religious themes must keep the concerns of the faithful in mind—or violate them at great personal risk. Joyce certainly won no applause from the Vatican for his unorthodox use of church rituals in *Ulysses*. A more recent example is the well-known plight of Rushdie whose novelistic description of the Prophet Mohammed brought down an execution order on the author's head.

Many cultures have regulated the portrayal of the human form. The Hellenic Greeks, for example, sought to portray physical perfection and did so through representations of the idealized human body. Statues of perfectly formed nude figures were accepted as part of any public vista. But the cultural heirs of the Greeks, the repressed Victorians, were so uneasy with any reference to the human body that even the legs of tables had to be modestly covered.

There are even social expectations governing the physical state of art objects. According to the noted anthropologist Clifford Geertz, in some African societies wooden sculptures of important members of the community are usually left to decay so that their declining physical state exemplifies the declining importance of the memorialized statesman. Some Western monuments have the opposite aim. Made of durable marble and bronze, they are intended to preserve memories in pristine form by thwarting the corrosive powers of time.

Books of artistic instruction provide another reference guide to cultural expectations. For example, the widely known Chinese *Mustard Seed Garden* book is a valuable source of information about the basic conventions of Chinese brush painting. This book illustrates the precise strokes, sequences, shapes, and forms that make up the backbone of classical Chinese painting. Similar books of formulas can also be found in the history of Western art. Present-day amateurs pick up how-to-draw books and watch television shows that feature step-by-step drawing instruction. During the 19th century in the United States, large numbers of children and adolescents learned to draw by copying from standardized images.

Most cultures provide an environment filled with conventional imagery for their members. Of course, children are encouraged to acquire such imagery. In fact, those who study artistically gifted children, all agree that one of the identifying features of visually gifted children is their ability to quickly pick up the conventional images that surround them. Such children learn to draw what they see in popular images and from life with noteworthy ease. For example, where comic book and cartoon pictures are available, gifted children are prone to pick up this style with greater ease than their peers. The easy acquisition of the visual conventions associated with a culture may indicate that a child is "at promise" for becoming a visual artist, perhaps in the same way that a child with a good musical ear has the potential for becoming a musician.

Sometimes artists take a hand in changing socially imposed conventions. Modernist artists who celebrate freedom and the impulsive act have on occasion published manifestos that redefine their field of activity. In France, there were the anti-academic "salons for the rejected" where the Fauves and Impressionists first showed their work. In Quebec, leading artists presented an impassioned renunciation of the oppression of the Church and the Academy in favor of Modernism. The "Refus Global" published in 1948 was signed by artists who set forth a new social compact that was to govern the future of the avant garde. In China, at the close of the Cultural Revolution, many artists took personal risks in order to display works that affronted what was then a politically imposed set of artistic protocols.

As we can see from the cases just mentioned, cultures the world over reserve the right to identify and constrain the artistic activity of adults and children alike. Artists must acknowledge conventions—either in the observance or in the breach—but they cannot act completely independently of the social understandings that hem them in. Some artists only feel authentic if their work violates accepted folkways, customs, and the canons of artistic decorum. Just as most artists are constrained by conventions on the macro level audience members are equally constrained, for *they* must decode an artwork in relation to conventional expectations.

B. Macro-Level Considerations: Social Controls on Responding to Representations—Conventional Limits for Audience Response

The annals of polar exploration provide a striking example of how artistic conventions influence the be-

havior of the audience. During the winter of 1912, a handful of men from the Scott expedition waited for the return of the doomed south polar party. Six men occupied a cramped shelter on the shore of the Antarctic ocean. They faced starvation, frostbite, filth, and an unceasing wind. But almost as daunting as these physical torments were the psychological strains of living crammed together for months on end. These were three officers and three enlisted men. The scant living space was divided between the two groups. David Young, Canadian playwright, noted a modicum of privacy was achieved by establishing an imaginary wall between the officers and the enlisted men. Everyone behaved as though neither sound nor light could pass through the barrier. The arrangement mutually agreed to by all, effectively put limits on friction between the ranks.

The explorers had borrowed a device from the theater known as the "fourth wall," the conventional barrier that separates the audience from the performance. This fourth wall has two key features in common with the way all other artistic conventions function: (a) A convention is always the result of a mutual agreement between artist and audience and (b) knowledge of conventions guides audience members in attending to some aspects of the work and ignoring others. In this instance the marooned explorers agreed to be blind and deaf to a selected part of their environment. They agreed to "frame" a space and erase what it contained.

Thus, artistic conventions sometimes channel the response of the audience. When watching a film we generally know what to attend to and what to ignore: In Hollywood films from the 1950s and 1960s, the scenes that appear under the opening credits can generally be ignored. We know that we are not expected to attend to the action in the background too carefully except to pick up on the general mood and locale. Likewise, when reading, the numbers on the pages of a novel can almost always be ignored because we know they do not contribute to the narrative. Except when otherwise alerted, we can safely ignore the smell or weight of a painting. Thoroughly acquainted with the conventions that govern reading novels, looking at paintings, and watching films, we know which dimensions of the work are important and which are not. This sort of knowledge is conventional.

Conventions also assist the audience in interpreting specialized imagery and specialized sorts of cultural or historical information. For example, when a knowledgeable viewer looks at a devotional picture, the objects that are depicted in association with certain figures (the lion of St. Mark, the Keys of St. Peter) help the viewer to identify the various saints, because these objects are habitually associated with the various saints. Similar sorts of conventional associations are used in films: At the close of *Blade Runner,* the dying android who has just spared the hero's life unclenches his own mechanical fist and releases a white dove. If we are familiar with religious iconography we can identify the bird as a symbol of the android's soul. (Like Pinocchio, the android has been transformed by his good deed, from an automaton into a "real live boy"). Audience familiarity with Christian iconography and the plots of children's stories makes possible a coherent interpretation of the event.

In a movie it is the customary use of cutting, framing, and sound that tells the knowledgeable audience the difference between an interruption in the temporal flow (flashback or flash-forward) or an interruption in spatial setting (e.g. meanwhile, back at the ranch . . .). Standard intonations and locutions in an oral story let us know when the tale starts and when it is coming to an end.

At the macro level then, conventions establish the socially agreed-upon devices that mark the artist's intentions for the benefit of the audience. Like the men of the Scott expedition, audiences know that they should attend to certain things in the work and to ignore others. But does this mean that any and all conventions (macro and micro) are simply arbitrary devices cooked up at a committee meeting? This question is best answered when we consider one of the most basic artistic acts—visual representation.

C. Micro-Level Considerations: The Debate on How Symbols Denote Their Referents—What Is the Role of Arbitrariness–Conventionality in the Use of Visual Symbols?

There are several schools of thought on this matter but two basic positions can be identified. Some propose that visual representation is an exercise governed almost exclusively by conventions because images depend on inculcation for their capacity to represent. In Goodman's notorious locution, "Almost any picture may represent almost anything; that is, given picture and object, there is usually a system of representation . . . under which the picture represents the object." Goodman proposed that all visual representations relate to the things that they stand for, in almost the same way that words stand for things. No one would claim that there is any compelling connection between the sound or look of the word *cat* and the animal itself. The word is simply a linguistic tag that a given speech community has agreed to use. Goodman's surprising claim is that images, even very realistic ones, refer to their referents by virtue of the same sort of consensus as spoken language. Images convey information by virtue of the agreements that exist between artist and audience. In other words, all images convey information *on an arbitrary basis.*

Rudolf Arnheim did not agree: The process of visual representation is certainly the result of an understanding between audience and artist; however, this understanding is not an arbitrary exercise of power or persuasion but is based on the structural similarities that artists discover for themselves and that audiences recognize. Take as an example young children's use of circles to stand for the face or the human body. Extreme conventionalists such as Goodman might argue that this frequently occurring symbol in children's drawings is an ad hoc schema imposed by the culture and learned by the child. Arnheim claimed that the child uses the circle for two reasons: (a) It is the simplest spontaneous form and one of the first that the child can control, and (b) the circle and the face share a nonarbitrary structural similarity, namely they are both closed organic forms. It is on the basis of this common property, not on the basis of social convention, that the young child assigns the meaning "face" to the circular form. It is also on the basis of this common property that audience members understand what the child has in mind. No "conventional" understanding is required. So the child's use of a circle as a face is, for Arnheim, an example of a representation that is constructed by finding an "equivalent statement in the medium." Ernst Gombrich took a stand similar to Goodman's "arbitrary" position and used it to explain the changes we observe in the history of Western art. If all representations are arbitrary signs, then the history of art can be understood as just a series of changes in received ways of making images. This is a major part of Gombrich's approach.

D. Micro-Level Considerations: The Debate on How Symbols Denote Their Referents—Conventionality and Historical Change in Western Art

Gombrich claimed that typical changes in Western art since the Egyptians are due to a shift in emphasis from showing that which is timeless, complete, and conceptual to showing that which is visually transitory and conceptually idiosyncratic. In other words, there has been shift from conceptual to illusionistic imagery. Gombrich proposed that the ultimate goal of Western art is to create the illusion of vision itself. Gombrich's hypothesis is that over the centuries artists produced work in accordance with what he calls the law of "schema and corrections" and that through the operation of this law, Western artists began to edge closer and closer to visual verisimilitude. Gombrich believed that visual artists when working from nature, rely initially on the visual "schemata" provided by artistic tradition and custom. These they put down on the drawing surface, regardless of what they see before them. Once the conventional form is drawn, then the step of "corrections" can take place. The observant artist begins to match the rote graphic formula to perceptual impressions of the world "out there." The mechanism behind the changes in Western art is, according to Gombrich, the process of "schema and corrections" or, in another of his formulations, "making always comes from matching."

Three examples nicely illustrate Gombrich's case for the dominance of visual conventions. He referred to two Renaissance prints of a beached whale. One Italian woodcut shows a whale that washed ashore at Ancona in 1601. The artist claimed that he made the drawing on the beach. Yet, according to Gombrich, this print is identical to a Dutch engraving made in 1598 of another hapless whale. It seems that the Italian printmaker borrowed the image lock stock and barrel and simply changed the label. Gombrich made a second observation about the Dutch print: The whale's flipper, because of its proximity to the eye, has been drawn as an external ear. This obvious mistake (whales have no external ears) is due, said Gombrich, to the power of the conventional formula for the human face. The same confusion of flipper with ear is found in the later Italian print. This artist, said Gombrich, like all other artists, owes much more to pictures that he has seen than to the study of nature. Gombrich offered a similar demonstration of the way in which artists depend on familiar formulas when he traced the long history of rhinoceros drawings and prints. Gombrich showed that even those artists who claimed to have drawn the bulky animal "from life" always had the 1515 Durer woodcut of that animal in their mind's eye. We are showing a 1766 engraving of an African rhino, supposedly made from life, that bears unmistakable traces of the original Durer woodcut. Another example of the artist's dependency on visual conventions is that of Chiang Yee, who toured England's Lake District in the 1930s and produced paintings of local scenes in the idiom of classical Chinese landscape. Gombrich showed that the artist picked out those aspects of the landscape for which he had the corresponding formulas—clouds, mists, distant hills—while other "more Western" elements were overlooked. Artists, said Gombrich, do not paint what they can see—they see what they can paint. In other words, the conventions for representation govern vision.

In spite of the persuasive examples that Gombrich introduced, Arnheim developed a critique of Gombrich. For if an image rendered is always based on a convention recalled, one has to ask, where did the *first* traditional image come from? Equally puzzling is the question of how the artist can ever see clearly enough to note the difference between the conventional schema for a thing and the thing itself. How does the artist take the vital step of "corrections" if vision as well as representation is governed by visual conventions?

Visual schemata, noted Arnheim, cannot dominate perception or representation for the logical reasons given earlier. But his argument goes well beyond this. He takes it as axiomatic that creating effective images is always based on finding structural correspondences between referent and image—as, for example, in the case of the child who represents a face as a circle. As any referent always possesses a defining structure, it is the presence of this underlying structure in the image that determines the satisfactory organization of the representation, be the medium verbal, visual, or plastic.

Arnheim took particular exception to Gombrich's notion that change in the visual arts is impelled by the quest for visual illusion. For Arnheim, representation worthy of the name can never be explained as a quest for the simple imitation of external forms. Poet Seamus Heaney in his 1995 Nobel acceptance speech made just this point about the "truth" of poetry. He cited the American poet Archibald MacLeish, "'Poetry should be equal to / not true.'" With this quote Heaney underlines the fact that in poetry as in all art, the quest is not for verisimilitude, but for a statement that evokes the referent through equivalence. And this is the crux of Arnheim's objection to Gombrich's claim that the history of visual art is guided by the quest for the truthful rendering of optical impressions rather than the discovery of convincing but equivalent statements in a medium.

In his critique of Gombrich, Arnheim stated, "The artist is rarely concerned with making things look real. He wants them to come alive. Is this a quest for illusion?" He summed up his argument thus, "[I]f conventional devices make a picture readable, they are also known to deaden it." And the psychology of representation is presumably the story of how things "come alive." Arnheim has also discussed the history of artists' attempts at representing a horse in motion. Up until the point where the photographer Muybridge had made time-lapse photographs of a galloping horse, the disposition of the animal's legs was a matter of conjecture. Artists hit upon a series of conventional poses to suggest the running animal. Arnheim observed that "The conventional attitude of the galloping horse with outstretched legs, as seen in Gericault's Derby at Epsom . . . was used in Mycenaean, Persian and Chinese art, and reappeared in Europe in the British color prints of the late eighteenth century." Muybridge's photographs proved incontestably that a running horse never stretched back and front legs away from the body at the same time. The photographs proved that artists' renderings going back to antiquity were naturalistically incorrect. Yet, many 19th- and 20th-century artists continued to show running horses in the classic carnival horse attitude because "the maximum spread of the legs translates the intensity of the physical motion into pictorial dynamics." This is a clear instance when the rules of "making and matching" do not apply.

The example also illustrates what Arnheim meant by an image possessing life. The two-dimensional image of the horse with legs outspread suggests speed and energy much more effectively than an equally flat but more photographic image showing the horse with its legs naturally arranged. The reason is that the factually

correct image of the horse running makes a closed two-dimensional form on the surface of the page. This form is static, whereas the antique version is more dynamic—a better translation onto a two-dimensional surface of what is happening on the race track. So here we have a visual convention that endures for two reasons: (a) the weight of tradition and authority are behind it, and (b) because the convention effectively embodies in a two-dimensional medium the vitality of the real thing.

So ultimately, for Arnheim, the distinction that matters is not between conventional and unconventional representations but between those representations that are dead and those that are alive—in exactly the way that the time-honored image of the moving horse is more vital than an "accurate" high speed photograph. Readers with a precise frame of mind may object to the way that the term *vital* is used in this context and bemusedly inquire as to just what sort of "life" we have in mind here. There is no litmus test for artistic vitality, but it is certain that the more vital representations are those made by artists who know at least as much about the medium itself as they do about what is represented. Granted that artistic vitality is hard to pin down, but one thing is sure—this sort of vitality has nothing to do with "realism" or accuracy of representation. No person who has ever looked at images, watched films, listened to music, or read books will deny that in some cases there is the experience of what Jerome Bruner calls effective surprise, that is, the shock with which a work speaks to the viewer. What should be plain from the example of the racehorse picture is that the fact that a work of art is conventional or unconventional, realistic or unrealistic is irrelevant to the effect that it can have on its audience.

III. WHEN IS A CONVENTION NOT A CONVENTION? CHILDREN'S GRAPHICS AND MODERNIST ART

One of the requirements for any satisfactory definition is that we are told not only what the thing in question is, but also what it is not. Conventionality takes in a lot of territory. So what aspects of the visual arts are nonconventional? Something is not a convention if it is not subject to the control of social agreements. For example, color names are conventional, but the physical phenomena to which the names refer are not conventions—those vibrations on the visible spectrum exist independent of the way that humanity segregates them. So in this example the physical phenomena are aconventional, but the names assigned to them are conventional. (As it turns out there is a systematic relationship between the number of identified colors in a given language and discrete parts of the visible spectrum. So we know now that even the color names that we use and the sequence in which color names appear are not totally conventional.) Other visual phenomena are also nonconventional. For example, as the Gestalt psychologists have demonstrated, the way that we automatically segregate the visual field into objects and into figure and ground is not subject to convention. It is preconventional.

One needs to keep in mind that unconventionality of the sort associated with the avant-garde artists like Picasso or others who enjoy shocking their publics is simply a reaction to conventions that eventually becomes conventional in its own right. In many cases, the revolutionary art of today becomes the orthodoxy of tomorrow. Thus, the true opposite of conventionality is found in work by naif artists, the mentally handicapped, and young children. For here we see features of symbolization that emerge without any sense of social understanding or any sort of social contract. This sort of work can fairly be called aconventional, and this is the true opposite of conventional work. The most common example of such work is found in the drawings and paintings of young children, for they are still in the process of acquiring adult conventions.

Because children the world over make similar marks on surfaces and use one object for representing another, these activities can be called preconventional or aconventional. There is no doubt that children from the earliest ages on look at images made by adults and by other children in their environment, but it is not until late childhood that they begin to master the conventions of their cultural environment. What is striking is that even when children attempt to copy adult images, their preconventional control of graphic representation limits their responses in a predictable way. In much the same way, a young child imitates adult speech with errors in syntax that reflect the developmental immaturity of the child's language production skills.

The phenomenon of children's preconventional attempts at visual representation is interesting in two respects. First, when children copy from adult work, as they frequently do, we can see the child's struggle to adapt preconventional imagery to conventional adult requirements. Second, and most confusing, in the late 19th and 20th centuries, Western artists reclaimed the preconventional forms of children's early graphic exploration and turned them into adult artistic conventions. The direct result of this deliberate importation of children's motifs and artistic practices into adult art is that it is now possible to confuse an adult artists work with that of a child—something unheard of in earlier centuries.

A. A Child Copies Adult Imagery

Two striking images by a 6-year-old girl show how a child can employ preconventional forms and organization while imitating conventional imagery. Consider the two drawings in Figures 2 and 4. These are by a 6-year-old girl, who studied and then drew the man and woman that appear on a Japanese Noren cloth that hung in her room (figures 1 and 3). The child is of Japanese descent but she was raised in Quebec and spent time drawing typical cartoon and television images. The results of her study of the Noren cloth demonstrate that although she has the limited graphic resources typical for her age (her drawings do not suggest volume or light), she is still able to create faces that have expressions similar to those on the cloth. She has succeeded in rendering the tilt of the woman's head, her coy look, and the man's aggressive facial mask.

What we have here is a translation from a conventional adult idiom to a child's preconventional graphic vocabulary. As with any good translation, we appreciate the excellence with which an equivalent message emanates from both versions. But we can distinguish between the adult representational conventions, such as the use of line to suggest planes turning in space and the accurate rendering of ornament and expression. In the child's drawing we recognize universal elements found in all children's drawings: simple outlines, self-contained circles, and irregular closed forms. In the adult image the man and woman are presented at dramatic angles; the child's rendering adheres to a vertical-horizontal axis—except for the eyes of the woman, which have been drawn on a diagonal. These two

FIGURE 1 Copy of female figure on Noren cloth curtain as drawn by a 5-year-old girl with a magic marker and crayons.

FIGURE 2 Female figure on Noren cloth curtain.

FIGURE 3 Male figure on Noren cloth curtain.

FIGURE 4 Copy of male figure on Noren cloth curtain as drawn by a 5-year-old girl with a magic marker and crayons.

drawings by the 6-year-old show the process whereby a child, using preconventional graphic strategies, begins her struggle to achieve the conventional models presented to her in her environment. The theme of the two protagonists, male and female, and their expressions are captured in the child's visual language, but some aspects of the child's use of the drawing medium are still preconventional.

B. Appropriating the Preconventional Imagery of Childhood

What of the adult artists who used children's preconventional images and turned them into conventional pictures? Children, unlike artists, do not make images that intentionally flout adult conventions; they make images in ignorance of these conventions. Certain modernist and post-modern artists have studied and appropriated these typical children's approach to drawing. Thus, the preconventional imagery that is typical of almost all children in their kindergarten and early elementary years becomes conventionalized in the work of notable painters such as Picasso, Klee, Arp, Miro, Dubuffet, and the Dutch group Kobra. The use of space and form typically encountered in the paintings and drawings of young children become conventional approaches when found in the work of adult artists.

As a case in point, it has been widely observed that at an early stage in their graphic apprenticeship, children make drawings in which vertically oriented objects such as houses and cars are always drawn at right angles to the edges of the page—or to base lines—regardless if that edge is itself vertical or horizontal. Thus one commonly finds drawings of cities by young children from all over the world in which buildings are oriented at right angles to several edges of the page. As a result, the buildings do not stand parallel to each other but appear to be lying down on either side of the street. Children make these sorts of drawings as a result of the logic of visual thinking—not as a result of some sort of visual convention absorbed from other images or because the children wish to show a bird's-eye view. Klee appreciated the integrity and logic of the child's aconventional approach, and he borrowed this spatial arrangement for his own work. Thus, in his 1924 painting *Botanical Theatre,* Klee showed a childlike plan view of a garden. Many plants are oriented to the

edges of the page, in exactly the same way that children orient their figures to edges and baselines. By borrowing a "naturally occurring" system of visual organization, Klee invented a new modernist convention. In this way, what was preconventional in the child's picture becomes conventionalized in Klee's picture. Of course, the audience needs to know what reasons lie behind Klee's choices. These can be found in his essays on art.

IV. CONCLUSION: THE IRRELEVANCE OF CONVENTIONALITY TO ARTISTIC SUCCESS

At the macro level, conventions identify the socially determined ranges within which the artist is permitted to operate without negative sanctions. Social understandings determine the material and thematic limits for the artist. By the same token, conventions at the macro level provide useful limits and reference points for audience members when they interpret an artwork. An audience member familiar with certain artistic conventions will know what to look for, will note the omission of certain expected elements, or will note the significant intrusion of unexpected elements. Conventions establish the sort of creative decorum by which artists are supposed to abide, and they provide audience members with the necessary key expectations with which to approach an artwork.

But at the micro level, the notion of conventionality as an explanation for the way that symbols function is less straightforward. As we have seen, Goodman and Gombrich agreed that the very act of representation itself—the symbolizing process whereby one thing comes to stand for another—is based mostly on consensus and tradition. Unlike Goodman, Gombrich is convinced that perspectival rendering is not an arbitrary symbolic code. Goodman's tough-minded stance is that once there is mutual agreement between artist and audience, issues like the natural affinity between symbol and referent, or the excellence with which the symbol equates to its referent, are philosophical red herrings. According to Goodman, from the simplest act of visual representation to the most sophisticated, the artist is simply conforming to social fiat or proposing a new and arbitrary connection. But Arnheim would observe that even in the case of such an arbitrary action, one must still explain the fact that artist and audience find ways of making a correspondence between the representation and the referent. It is this process of finding links between representation and referent that is simply not addressed by Goodman's conventionalist model.

The question that Goodman did not answer, and that Arnheim attempts to answer is, "What governs our choice of the features in the graphic symbol to match with features in the referent?" There are limits to the persuasive power of a purely social process in determining that from now on *x* will stand for *y*.

Arnheim contended that if all symbolic representations are just a matter of convention, then one ignores the very thing about artistic representations that is the source of their greatest fascination and power—namely, the fact that some representations work better than others. Noted art critic Robert Hughes put it this way:

> It is in the nature of human beings to discriminate. We make choices and judgments every day. These choices are part of real experience. They are influenced by others, of course, but they are not fundamentally the result of a passive reaction to authority. And we know that one of the realest experiences in cultural life is that of inequality between books and musical performances and paintings and other works of art. Some things do strike us as better than others—more articulate more radiant with consciousness. We may have difficulty saying why, but the experience remains.

It is uncontroversial to assert that at the macro level conventions are the socially created platform on which all artists labor. But the proposition that at the micro level all artistic representation is limited to an exercise in conventional production and conventional representation is far more contentious for it sheds no light on two remarkable facts: One is that symbolic representation is possible in the first place and the other is that we know from our own experience that certain instances of representation are far richer and more vital than others and that such noteworthy instances have nothing to do with the presence or absence of artistic conventions.

Bibliography

Arnheim, R. (1966). Art history and the partial god. In *Towards a psychology of art* (pp. 151–161). Berkeley and Los Angeles: University of California Press.

Arnheim, R. (1976). *Art and visual perception: A psychology of the creative eye*. Berkeley, CA: University of California Press.

Geertz, C. (1976). Art as a cultural system. *Modern Language Notes, 9,* 94–120.

Getzels, J., & Csikszentmihalyi, M. (1976). *The creative vision*. New York: Wiley.

Golomb, C. (1992). *The child's creation of a pictorial world*. Berkeley, CA: University of California Press.

Gombrich, E. (1960). *Art and illusion*. Princeton, NJ: Princeton University Press.

Goodman, N. (1968). *Languages of art: An approach to a theory of symbols*. Indianapolis, IN: Bobbs-Merrill.

Kubovy, M. (1988). *The psychology of perception and Renaissance art*. Cambridge, England: University of Cambridge Press.

Pariser, D. (1984). Two methods of teaching drawing skills. In R. MacGregor (Ed.), *Readings in Canadian art education* (pp. 143–158). Vancouver, BC: Wedge Publications.

Willats, J. (1997). *Art and representation*. Princeton, NJ: Princeton University Press.

Winner, E. (1996). *Gifted children: Myths and realities*. New York: Basic Books.

Corporate Culture

Cameron M. Ford

University of Central Florida

I. Overview
II. Creative Action in Social Domains
III. Normative Affects of Corporate Culture
IV. Shared Meanings That Spur Creative Action
V. Summary: Collective Creativity

Creative Actions Behaviors or outcomes that are judged to be novel and valuable within a particular domain.

Routines Programmed or habitual responses to recurring situations (work procedures, regulations, decision rules, behavioral norms, habits, etc.).

Schema Cognitive structures that represent the common features of repeated experiences.

Sensemaking The process through which individuals utilize their schemas to interpret information and develop an understanding of a particular situation.

Stakeholders People who can significantly affect or are significantly affected by the actions of an individual, group, or organization.

CORPORATE CULTURE (also referred to herein as culture) can be defined as a pattern of shared meanings (concepts, beliefs, expectations, values, etc.) that evoke normative thought and behavior from organizational actors. The shared meanings that constitute a corporation's culture can vary on three dimensions: content, in-tensity, and degree of integration. Content refers to the specific ideas encompassed by a culture (views of competitors, standards for ethical behavior, attitudes toward customers, etc.). Intensity refers to the expected consequences associated with conforming to or violating shared understandings. Intense norms carry significant benefits for those who conform and present harsh consequences to nonconformists. Finally, the degree of integration refers to the extent to which meanings are shared throughout an organization. Intense meanings whose content is well integrated tend to be highly influential and may effectively describe the general character of a corporate culture.

I. OVERVIEW

The concept of corporate culture has long been a focal point for attributions about organizational processes and outcomes. Consequently, it is frequently mentioned as a potent contributor to creative action. But just as often corporate culture is portrayed as a significant obstacle to creative endeavors. These opposing depictions suggest that the relationship between corporate culture and creativity may present an organization's management with a paradox between the respective benefits of aligning collective behavior and empowering individual creativity. Conformity to cor-

Copyright © 1999 by Academic Press
All rights of reproduction in any form reserved.

porate values and goals can direct the collective energies of employees toward realizing desired organizational outcomes. Especially in companies that compete on the basis of high-reliability services (e.g., Federal Express) or high-quality products, adherence to established work processes and controls is a principle source of competitive advantage. On the other hand, individual creativity allows companies to resolve novel problems and develop new market offerings and technologies. This is especially important in the long term because creative individual actions contribute to organizational learning and competitive differentiation, the heart and soul of sustained organizational vitality. Ultimately, business success requires capitalizing on the benefits associated with both routine and creative actions. The problem that arises, however, is that during specific episodes of behavior, individuals must choose between routine and creative behaviors. [*See* CONFORMITY; NOVELTY.]

Corporate culture has been noted as a primary organization-level factor that influences this choice. Corporate cultures impose mental and behavioral routines on organizational actors. Through the process of socialization, new employees gradually learn the language, symbols, and other shared meanings characteristic of a culture. To remain a member in good standing, employees are expected to adhere to the most cherished cultural routines (work processes, business models, decision methodologies, etc.). Especially in organizational settings, powerful normative processes create a context in which thought and behavior often becomes routine driven. Therefore, organizational settings often become unreceptive to creativity because of the development of potent and diverse normative influences.

Consequently, the paradox between aligning with others and introducing creative variations looks rather one sided to most employees. Given the choice between time-tested routines that produce relatively certain, near-term consequences and creative alternatives that are typically disruptive, uncertain, and prone to failure, most individuals opt for the safe haven of culturally sanctioned routines. Framed this way, it is hardly surprising that corporations have trouble harnessing employees' creative potential.

However, shared meanings held by organization members have the potential to reframe this paradox in a manner that makes creative options attractive to a broader range of employees. This article reviews several issues that contribute to a broad understanding of the complex relationships between corporate culture and creative action. The article first reviews the major tenets of a systems' view of creativity as a conceptual backdrop for describing how culture affects creativity (and vice versa). Next, different dimensions of culture are described as a means of depicting why mature organizations with strong cultures usually lose their ability to evoke creative contributions from their members. This gloomy depiction nevertheless allows room for suggesting specific shared meanings capable of easing the tensions associated with individuals' choices regarding routine and creative actions. Therefore, the article concludes by describing a configuration of shared meanings that promote the viability of creative actions without sacrificing the potency of focused collective effort.

II. CREATIVE ACTION IN SOCIAL DOMAINS

Culture can act as both a facilitator and a constraint to creative individual action, and creative individual action can alter shared interpretations underlying a corporation's culture. To understand how, it is useful to employ an evolutionary model of how creative actions in social contexts develop. The systems view of creativity seeks to describe the social processes through which specific actions come to be defined as creative. It proposes that three interrelated subsystems, the person, the field (defined as those people who populate and effect the structure of a domain), and the domain (defined as the rules, language, customary practices, and so on of a recognized area of action) together contribute to the occurrence of a creative act. Fields and domains represent the social context that influences individuals' actions. The person serves as the sole source of variations (i.e., novel actions). The people who comprise the field and personify the domain serve to select among novel variations, retaining those deemed to be valuable elaborations of the domain and rejecting the others. The elaborated domain then guides individuals' interpretations of legitimate and illegitimate behavior. Based on these interpretations, individuals make decisions regarding subsequent behaviors within the domain, and so on. These events continue in an ongoing, evolutionary cycle of variation, selection, and retention processes. [*See* SYSTEMS APPROACH.]

The boundaries of the systems view of creativity were expanded by Cameron Ford, who noted that evolutionary change models developed in organizational theory, business strategy, and innovation research, employ identical concepts to describe processes that lead to conformity. Juxtaposing evolutionary models of creativity and conformity highlights the tension inherent in the choice between these two types of behavior. Exacerbating the problem for organizational actors is the fact that they are usually simultaneously accountable to a variety of stakeholders representing different domains of thought and action. For example, most employees face demands from their supervisor, their work group peers, their organization, their profession, customers, and so on. Thus, creative acts in organizational settings rarely rise or fall based on the preferences of one group of stakeholders or the rules of a single domain of action. Creative acts must typically withstand the scrutiny of stakeholders representing multiple domains of action each with their own sensibilities regarding the desirability of particular creative acts. The upshot of Ford's theory is that influencing creativity in organizations (where normative processes are powerful, pervasive, and arise from a variety of sources) involves two conceptually independent management challenges: facilitating creativity and constraining routines.

Stanley Harris has offered a metaphor to describe corporate culture that is useful for understanding how individuals navigate the complex mosaic of demands presented by diverse stakeholders. He suggested that individuals develop schemas reflecting different stakeholders and their respective domains (a management schema, a finance schema, a customer schema, a peer schema, etc.). When making sense of their circumstances and making decisions about their behavior, individuals engage in "mental dialogues" with prototypical stakeholders from relevant domains (e.g., "I wonder what my peers would say about this idea?"). Harris summarized his schema-based view of culture by arguing that individuals "choose to behave in response to . . . contrived mental dialogues between themselves and other contextually relevant (past or present, real or imagined) individuals or groups." These mental dia-

logues influence the goals, expectations, and emotions that guide individuals' efforts to please important stakeholder interests. Harris's mental dialogue metaphor is a useful way to link the shared meanings (schema) that comprise corporate culture to individual behavior. Put simply, shared meanings encourage shared responses to organizational events.

Viewing an organization as a constellation of stakeholder groups is especially helpful for understanding how corporate culture impacts individuals' choices regarding creative action. Recent research on corporate cultures has moved beyond simplistic depictions of culture as a monolithic set of interpretations shared by all organizational members. Consistent with the theoretical foundations described earlier, new proposals have explored the implications of viewing organizations as more fragmented collections of meanings—some broadly shared, some locally shared, some not shared at all. This research better captures the rich and complex influence corporate culture has on individuals' preferences for routine and creative behavior. The next section describes general characteristics of organizational cultures. It also explains why "strong" corporate cultures typically lead organization members to adopt routine solutions to organizational problems.

III. NORMATIVE AFFECTS OF CORPORATE CULTURE

As defined previously, corporate culture can be thought of as shared interpretations held by an organization's members. Deeply held meanings provide employees with a set of organizational certainties that can be taken for granted on a day-to-day basis. The shared interpretations that characterize a corporate culture helps direct and coordinate collective effort. Viewing culture as an aggregation of individuals' interpretations (i.e., schemas) can enrich our understanding of culture's impact on creative action. For example, the particular meanings, or content, upheld by different cultures can vary. Action in one firm may be guided by a belief in the importance of creativity, whereas employees in another firm focus their attention on reducing costs. The impact of shared meanings depends on the intensity of employees' beliefs in those meanings. Intensely held meanings exert a strong influence on individual behavior by creating potent expectations regarding positive or negative consequences associated with different behavioral options (e.g., "If I do A, then B will happen; if I do X, then Y will happen"). Finally, corporate cultures can vary in the extent to which interpretations are shared among organizational actors. This has been described as a culture's degree of integration. The following sections describe each of these dimensions in greater detail.

A. Culture Content

This dimension refers simply to the specific ideas that comprise a corporation's culture. In one organization employees may believe that they work in a competitive industry that demands high levels of customer service. Members of another organization may focus their attention on complying with government regulations. Similarly, corporate leadership may be held in high regard in one firm but may be widely viewed as exploiting and untrustworthy in another. The content of a corporate culture is reflected in the specific beliefs, expectations, and values ingrained in employees' schemas. Socialization processes utilize rites of passage, rituals, symbols, and native language to produce common understandings regarding ideas that are central to a culture. Corporate leaders, especially organizational founders, play a very important role in establishing the central themes that over time become accepted as "the way things are done around here." Shared meanings can also be generated through discussions with coworkers thereby creating meanings shared at the group level. Organizational systems, particularly appraisal and reward systems, can also have a powerful influence on shared interpretations. Exposure to shared experiences is the basis of socialization processes that communicate "appropriate" culture content to organizational newcomers.

The primary creativity-related problem associated with culture content is that the viability of specific ideas shared in an organization tends to fade over time. Business models that once led to industrial domination inevitably become outdated. For example, IBM's strongly held belief in the primacy of mainframe computers was born out of the company's overwhelming dominance of that industry segment. However, this same belief blinded IBM from seeing the potential of personal computers. Despite its immense resources, IBM has never been able to overcome the smaller firms that have come to dominate the PC market (Compaq, Dell, Gateway, etc.). Industry leaders seldom recognize or participate in major innovations (e.g., typewriters to computers, harvested ice to refrigerated ice), because established firms with high profits are almost always risk averse. In stable and effective organizations, efforts focus on incremental improvements of existing concepts. There is little incentive to introduce creative variations because they are disruptive, unpredictable, and risky. In short, success creates a shared mind-set of "If it ain't broke, don't fix it."

Current structures, processes, and incentives overwhelmingly favor adhering to established organizational routines. As a result, successful firms typically fall into "competency traps" in which continued investments in skills that led to past success make a firm increasingly vulnerable to obsolescence. Organization members (i.e., field members or stakeholders) who populate these corporate domains also become heavily invested in organizationally sanctioned patterns of thought and action. Therefore, creative proposals that are (by definition) at odds with the corporate domain's norms face enormous obstacles. Individuals working in cultures characterized by time-tested, widely respected business models can easily imagine the dialogue(s) that radically new ideas are likely to evoke. These negative expectations usually quell individuals' desires to promote creative solutions. In sum, prolonged success tends to narrow the range of ideas that qualify as legitimate culture content. This helps explain the indisputable fact that mature organizations seldom lead, or successfully participate in, major waves of industrial change.

B. Intensity

This aspect of corporate culture refers to the expected consequences associated with conforming to or violating shared understandings. Intense meanings carry significant benefits for those who conform and present harsh consequences to nonconformists. Intensity captures the extent to which particular meanings create positive or negative expectations for individuals contemplating a particular course of action. When a culture's content creates intense expectations among organizational actors, it is likely to have a major influence on individuals' motivation and behavior. When shared interpretations do not have clear motivational consequences, their ability to direct and energize employee behavior is diminished.

As an example, imagine a company in which top management professes a new interest in high-quality work but does not back up this statement with changes in work processes, reward systems, training programs, and so on. In circumstances such as these, organizational actors are likely to hold a shared understanding of top management's desires. Yet one would expect little change in behavior because following management's initiative offers no clear benefits, and ignoring management's call presents no obvious costs. Alternatively, when corporate leaders back up their rhetoric with reward systems, budget allocations, and so forth, employees quickly learn that deviating from shared understandings carries dire consequences. In short, intensely held culture content engenders strong expectations regarding consequences associated with conformist and deviant behaviors. As a result, intense meanings are more likely to influence organizational behavior than motivationally neutral beliefs.

C. Degree of Integration

The third dimension on which corporate cultures vary is their degree of integration. Cultures can be described on a continuum between being highly integrated or fragmented. A highly integrated, or unitary, culture values consensus among organization members, consistency among cultural manifestations, and low levels of ambiguity. These characteristics simplify organization members' schemas and resultant sensemaking processes. This model of unitary culture is equivalent to the strong culture model that continues to dominate laypersons' conceptions of corporate culture. Unfortunately, routine patterns of thought and action promoted by strong culture often have a devastating impact on an organization's creative output.

This monolithic view of corporate culture is usually an oversimplification. Few cultures are fully integrated. More commonly there is a less integrated view of corporate culture in which shared meanings are held primarily at the subunit level. These are called differentiated cultures. The processes that produce differentiated cultures are fairly straightforward. Shared interpretations arise from shared experiences with organizational systems and processes. To the extent that organizational actors' experiences are differentiated systematically—by departmental affiliation, for example—a corporation's culture is likely to become differentiated. Even though some meanings may be shared at the organizational level, in a differentiated culture intensely held meanings exist primarily at the group or departmental level.

In a differentiated culture, inconsistencies among cultural manifestations are common. For example, employees in an R&D unit may share an intense belief in the value of creativity. Meanwhile, manufacturing employees in the same company may focus on adhering to quality control standards that leave little room for variations. Obviously, strongly held subunit perspectives can create conflict and ambiguity at the corporate level. However, in a differentiated culture this ambiguity is interpreted in such a way that it does not intrude on the clarity of a subunit's culture.

Fragment cultures are those in which few shared interpretations exist. In this case, one could argue that the corporation lacks a culture (based on our definition of culture as shared meanings). Organizational actors must focus on making sense of the ambiguity in their unstructured environment. Fragmentation is an unstable state, however. Sensemaking processes should eventually produce meanings that are shared at some level of the organization.

Linking cultural integration to creative action brings us back to the paradox between the benefits of aligning collective effort and empowering individual creativity. On the one hand, shared goals, values, and language facilitate focused effort, open communication, and trust, all of which typically facilitate creativity. On the other hand, shared interpretations induce routine patterns of thought and action that can render creative action illegitimate. This paradox highlights the tension between creativity and legitimacy that is so central to understanding creativity in organizational settings. This trade-off is analogous to the development of shared understandings, or paradigms, in scientific disciplines/domains. Less integrated paradigms tend to have higher levels of variation but suffer from a relative lack of legitimacy. Highly integrated paradigms enjoy the benefits of high legitimacy but are characterized by less intellectual variation.

Research on industrial innovation provides further insight to the relationship between cultural integration and creative action. Industries, like scientific paradigms, begin as ill-specified domains and evolve into well-structured, clearly understood domains. Early in an industry's evolution entrepreneurial firms compete on the basis of new product development. The success of these firms depends on their ability to create new products or services to satisfy customer needs. However, once a dominant design emerges that standardizes product attributes, the "QWERTY" typewriter keyboard, the VHS video format, etc.) firm success depends more on process innovations that improve efficiency and lower prices. A dominant design is analogous in some respects to an intellectual paradigm that becomes unquestioned by stakeholders in the domain. Industry participants, or stakeholders, develop shared understandings that lead to standardized products and methods that define the character of businesses within the industry. Inevitably, actors outside of the industry create new ways of providing value to consumers that deviate from the industry's conventional wisdom, thus making the industry obsolete.

This discussion of corporate culture attributes should lead the reader to conclude that intense, unitary cultures usually produce conformity to business routines that have been successful in the past. This is functional until a creative variation is introduced that leads to shifts in stakeholder preferences and domain characteristics. Unfortunately, established firms usually have difficulty, despite their immense resources, adapting to changes in competitive domains. Even though strong corporate cultures typically have a negative long-term influence on an individual's creative ability and motivation, one can envision exceptions to this rule. Next we will examine a configuration of shared meanings that may resolve the paradox described earlier between aligning collective action and empowering creative action.

IV. SHARED MEANINGS THAT SPUR CREATIVE ACTION

The prior discussion offers few rays of hope for those who wish to develop a creative culture. One must understand that the normative forces of corporate culture can be quite formidable and that organizations usually err by unwittingly encouraging high degrees of mental and behavioral conformity. Nevertheless, a specific configuration of shared meanings is likely to encourage collective creativity. These meanings act in concert to communicate an intense shared understanding of the legitimacy and necessity of creative actions. The meanings described next are interrelated and mutually reinforcing. If any one of them is absent, individuals are likely to retreat to the presumed safety of well-understood organizational routines. Corporations that are viewed as long-term innovators and industry leaders (e.g., Southwest Airlines, Rubbermaid, Coca-Cola, 3M, Home Depot, General Electric) hold these ideas as core ideals that drive the continual evolution of their respective businesses.

A. Strategic Vision

Creativity in organizational settings is different from more aesthetically oriented domains because there are commonly accepted, legitimate ways of justifying the value of particular business solutions. So, unlike the arts where value cannot be objectively defined, a restricted range of widely employed metrics typically defines value in business. For individuals to link their novel ideas to the generation of business value, they must have a sophisticated understanding of the outcomes desired by a corporation's leadership. This meaning is usually described as a strategic vision. A unitary and intense understanding of an organization's purpose makes it easier for individuals to assess the value added of novel proposals. This shared understanding of purpose provides individuals with a framework and language for articulating the business case underlying novel proposals. This process can facilitate the adoption of creative solutions.

Perhaps ironically, having a culture that is intensely integrated regarding appropriate ends makes it easier to empower individuals to be creative regarding means. Thus, a culture with a shared vision overcomes the paradox between alignment and empowerment by aligning individuals toward specific goals while empowering them to employ means of their own creation.

B. Empowerment

Innovative firms (i.e., those with a track record of creative action) universally preach the virtues of empowerment-oriented management—and they practice what they preach. They employ rhetoric and resources to guide the development of intellectual resources in their firms. Empowered employees are characterized by self-confidence, intrinsic motivation, and skill. These are all traits associated with creative individual action in organizational settings. Once employees are endowed with these characteristics (through training, development programs, challenging assignments, etc.), they are expected to produce an economic return by exercising discretion and creativity on their jobs. Whereas a shared vision demands an integrated understanding of corporate goals, a belief in empowerment allows fragmentation around means toward accomplishing these goals. Corporations often try to communicate this lesson during their socialization process by presenting stories of creative corporate heroes who fought through red tape and bureaucracy (i.e., organizational routines) to enact creative solutions that furthered the corporations ends. The lack of agreement regarding appropriate routines characteristic of an empowerment-oriented culture implies that the role of corporate leadership is to set goals, provide resources, and get out of the way.

Overall, a shared belief in empowerment creates a supportive, equitable environment where people feel safe exploring the value of new ideas. It also promotes a focus on results that allows individuals more room to create new paths toward corporate goals.

C. Competitive Paranoia

A shared meaning that reinforces and adds intensity to a corporation's vision is a shared belief that rival companies pose significant threats to continued success (and, by implication, continued employment). Corporations whose employees share an intense, highly integrated respect of their competition are unlikely to rest on their laurels. A healthy fear of rivals (real or imagined) helps successful firms fight off complacency engendered by long periods of success. Highly effective corporate leaders are often masters of creating this shared belief. Andy Groves, the founder of computer chip manufacturer Intel, crystallized the central importance of this shared meaning when he titled his most recent book *Only the Paranoid Survive*.

Recent empirical research in the business strategy field suggests that firms who compete with strong rivals are more creative and healthy than firms in monopoly positions. Research on strategic evolution also demonstrates that corporate innovation is spurred by the necessity of keeping up with skillful rivals. These findings closely mirror the proposals offered by a systems view of creativity. As rival firms introduce variations that elaborate an industrial domain, other firms in the industry must respond in kind or drop out. This process leads to fast-paced industrial change and high levels of corporate creativity. When it comes to creativity, it seems that corporations play up (or down) to their level of competition. [*See* BUSINESS STRATEGY.]

A shared understanding of threats posed by competitors promotes discomfort with the status quo and continually raises aspiration levels. Periodically raising the bar reminds individuals that there is always room for improvement and that success is often harder to sustain than to achieve. These meanings reduce the attractiveness of routine options. They also encourage individuals to consider new avenues of achieving the shared corporate vision. However, a threatening external strategic domain must be juxtaposed against supportive internal domains before individuals are likely to present creative proposals. Creating a shared understanding that the organization is supportive, but the strategic environment is threatening promotes a "We are all in this together" feeling. This makes it relatively easy for individuals to imagine positive mental dialogues with other organizational insiders. Thus, individuals can feel less threatened by dynamics associated with creative action and organizational change.

D. Proactive Change

As implied by the previous discussion, a common vision held by empowered employees who recognize potent threats to their continued success are more likely to embrace creativity and change. Furthermore, empowered employees are likely to be more capable and intrinsically motivated with respect to creative action.

However, relying exclusively on external threats to instigate episodes of organizational change limits a firm to reacting to events rather than taking more proactive measures. Reactive, event-driven change is the normal mode of managing change in most companies. This is an erratic strategy that places a corporation in the position of playing by someone else's rules. Although a shared understanding of external threats promotes a general appreciation for creativity, risk taking, and teamwork, it does not provide the discipline necessary to sustain creative productivity.

Innovative companies believe that creative action and change should be time, rather than event, driven. These firms utilize specific rules to create the discipline necessary to undertake proactive change. For example, 3M requires 30% of its revenues to come from new products every year. Thus, 3M employees hold a shared urgency to introduce new products regardless of what their competitors have done recently.

Proactive change requires an intensely held, integrated understanding of the strategic vision. It also requires confident, empowered employees with the personal and organizational resources necessary to live up to the challenge. The pace of change is dictated by the general evolutionary trajectory of the industries (domains) within which a firm competes. This trajectory is determined in large part by the actions of competitors. However, proactively introducing variations into industrial domains can wrest control from competitors and shape the rules of competition to favor the competencies of an innovating firm. Another highly charismatic corporate leader, GE's CEO Jack Welsh, articulated this benefit of time-paced, proactive change by warning strategists to "Control your destiny or someone else will."

V. SUMMARY: COLLECTIVE CREATIVITY

Returning to the paradox between the respective benefits of aligning collective effort and empowering individual creativity, one can see that this paradox can only be resolved through the development and maintenance of a fragile set of shared meanings. The configuration of meanings I have described here create coherence out of the multiple, conflicting task domains that confront organizational actors. As mentioned earlier, organizational settings require individuals to navigate creative proposals through a diverse gauntlet of stakeholders with different preferences and degrees of influence. Negative expectations related to this daunting task are typically sufficient to induce individuals

to choose a safe routine over a treacherous creative option. In the creative culture I have described here, relevant stakeholders within the organization would be expected to give supportive responses to a contrived mental discussion of creative solutions. Perhaps more important, mental dialogues extolling the virtues of previously successful routines could be expected to produce criticism. A culture that evokes these kinds of mental dialogues makes creative options relatively more attractive in relation to routine options. Influencing the relative attractiveness of these two behavioral options is the key to influencing creativity in organizational settings. The culture described here gives creative actions a fighting chance of being preferred over the tried-and-true actions of the past.

Ultimately, top management is responsible for creating, articulating, and reinforcing these shared meanings. Furthermore, organizational systems that have an impact these meanings must be aligned with top management rhetoric. For example, reward and appraisal systems must focus on the merit and creativity of individuals' performances. Information technologies that allow individuals to leverage and share their intellectual resources must be provided. Articulating and institutionalizing a creative culture is a formidable challenge that has been mastered by only a few. The accomplishments of these few stand testament to the fact that sustained success does not inevitably lead to failure. However, one should not underestimate the magnitude of the challenge. Corporate leaders must consistently communicate the importance of these ideas and take actions that reinforce their words.

Bibliography

Csikszentmihalyi, M. (1988). Society, culture, and person: A systems view of creativity. In R. J. Sternberg (Ed.), *The nature of creativity: Contemporary psychological perspectives* (325–339). New York: Cambridge University Press.

Ford, C. M. (1996). A theory of individual creative action in multiple social domains. *Academy of Management Review, 21,* 1112–1142.

Harris, S. G. (1994). Organizational culture and individual sensemaking. *Organization Science, 5,* 309–321.

Martin, J. (1992). *Culture in organizations.* New York: Oxford University Press.

O'Reilly, C. (1989). Corporations, culture, and commitment:

Motivation and social control in organizations. *California Management Review, 31,* 9–25.

Shapira, Z. (1995). *Risk taking: A managerial perspective.* New York: Russel Sage Foundation.

Simonton, D. K. (1988). Creativity, leadership, and chance. In R. J. Sternberg (Ed.), *The nature of creativity: Contemporary psychological perspectives* (325–339). New York: Cambridge University Press.

Utterback, J. M. (1994). *Mastering the dynamics of innovation.* Boston: Harvard Business School Press.

Counseling

David K. Carson

University of Wyoming

Convergent Thinking Convergent thinking (CT) is characterized by reasoning that brings together relevant information and arrives at a firm conclusion based on this information—often through the recognition and expression of preestablished or externally dictated criteria. It tends to be analytical and focuses on reaching a correct solution to a problem or issue.

Creative Process The act of creating, usually involving several stages or phases, that includes various dimensions of creative thinking and emotional expression or involvement. In counseling this process is dynamic and interactional.

Divergent Thinking Divergent thinking (DT) is characterized by thought processes that radiate outward and explore new ideas that are generated from the original notion. It often entails achievement of conclusions open to individual interpretation through the synthesizing or integration of pieces of information originally thought to be unrelated or even antithetical. DT is a central feature of creativity.

Elaboration The ability to develop, embellish, or complete an idea or concept.

Flexibility The ability to produce a large variety of ideas.

Fluency The ability to produce a large number of ideas.

Intuition The ability to attain direct knowledge or insight without rational thought and inference. While intuition is often thought to be a characteristic of highly creative individuals, such is not always the case.

Originality The ability to produce ideas that are novel, unusual, unconventional, or not obvious. Originality is believed to be the centerpiece of creativity.

Resistance to Premature Closure Resistance of an individual to leap to conclusions prematurely without considering the available information. The creative person is able to stay open and delay closure long enough to make the mental assent that makes possible original ideas.

In a narrow sense **COUNSELING** *is a process that involves the use of psychological methods in giving professional guidance and assistance to individuals, couples, families, or groups. From a broader perspective, counseling involves the use of interpersonal interactions, including but not limited to those between therapist and client(s), to identify, process, and resolve relational, cognitive, emotional, cultural, and/or spiritual issues that hinder client development or growth. There are many*

Copyright © 1999 by Academic Press
All rights of reproduction in any form reserved.

counseling theories, each espousing its own philosophical and theoretical biases in pursuit of these goals. This article will explore how creativity and counseling are interrelated, on both a conceptual and a practical level.

I. POSSIBLE LINKS BETWEEN CREATIVITY AND COUNSELING

Providing a meaningful discussion of the relationship between creativity and counseling is an onerous task, given the abstract nature and seemingly countless definitions of these constructs that have appeared in both the classical and contemporary literature. While a host of modern counseling techniques have claimed to be efficient, effective, and some even "creative," the majority of these approaches provide little evidence that they are helpful to clients longitudinally. Moreover, for many individuals, couples, and families, change appears to be a slow and painful process. Thus, "quick fixes," results, or "products" may be nonnormative in both creative and psychotherapeutic endeavors. In addition, notions of creativity have generally been scarce in the counseling theory literature. Yet, creativity appears to be more intimately interwoven with the counseling process than perhaps many clinicians or researchers have realized.

Abilities such as originality, flexibility, resistance to premature closure, and other aspects of divergent thinking are often associated with healthy functioning. In addition, therapeutic approaches that promote good mental health often parallel activities or behaviors which enhance creativity, with similar desired outcomes or "products." These may include: (a) increased personal growth, awareness, and self-confidence; (b) improved problem-solving abilities (e.g., via the generating of multiple ways to look at a phenomenon or approach a situation); (c) enhanced human relationships; (d) a strong but balanced internal locus of control and responsibility; and (e) the giving up of traditional patterns of living and acquisition of new perceptions and roles. Traditionally, counseling has been less often defined as a process of creation than of helping, education, personal development, and repair. However, D. H. Frey, in 1975, noted that "in the broadest sense, counseling is actually a creative enterprise within which client and counselor combine their resources to generate a new plan, develop a different outlook, formulate alternative behaviors, begin a new life" (p. 23). According to Frey, there are many times in counseling when therapists cannot rely on technical skill alone (or the latest gimmicks) but with inventiveness and creativity have to turn within themselves and inspire their clients to follow suit for solutions to problems. Getting "stuck" in the counseling process may often reflect a lack of or need for creativity more than anything else.

Clients then are coproducers of both the processes and the products of counseling—many of which call for creative thought and action. In 1989, P. P. Heppner and colleagues discussed the two major areas of counseling in which creativity occurs. These include understanding a client's problem and facilitating client change. These investigators suggested that, since counseling has been said to involve both scientific and artistic elements, "creativity within counseling can be the link between the predictable and the mysterious in human interaction, the known and the unknown" (p. 272).

II. CREATIVITY AND DIVERGENT THINKING

Creativity, like any human behavior, occurs in a complex historical and interpersonal context that includes reciprocal interactions of people, cultural domains, and social institutions. It generally refers to activities or products that are truly original and break new ground. E. T. Dowd, in 1989, indicated that creative endeavors generally result in "strikingly new formulations that are not derived from what preceded them and in that sense represent a discontinuity" (p. 233). There is debate over whether creativity must involve the production of something or can simply take the form of pure mental activity/ability even if it is not "used" or manifested to others. However, the scientific study of creativity becomes difficult if there is no creative product to measure or behavior to observe. On the other hand, if creative thinking is not apparent to others, does this mean that it does not exist or serves no purpose? Not necessarily. A person may cognize in a highly creative manner long before a creative product or change in behavior is exhibited.

A central feature of creativity is divergent thinking (DT). According to E. Paul Torrance, divergent thinking involves four main components—all of which can be assessed in individuals through both verbal and figural methods. These include *fluency, flexibility, originality,* and *elaboration.* These modes of thinking appear to precede or at least accompany corresponding modes of behavior; thus, it is not surprising that divergent thinking is generally associated with good mental health. These characteristics appear to be associated with the client's ability to master his or her environment *and* the counselor's skill at his or her craft.

Divergent thinking tends to be tentative and exploratory, and is oriented to the development of possibilities rather than data, to speculation rather than conclusions. Other characteristics of DT include a tolerance for ambiguity and inconsistency, the ability to hold contradictory ideas simultaneously in one's mind, and the ability to incorporate and modify new ideas. Dowd describes DT as the ability to maintain flexible constructs and avoid a premature "hardening of the categories" or "immaculate perception." Convergent thinking, on the other hand, is characterized by reasoning that brings together the relevant data and arrives at a firm conclusion based on these data. It tends to be deductive rather than inductive. Thus, divergent thinking can be thought of as more intuitive and less data-based (or data-bound) than convergent thinking.

Frey suggests that therapeutic innovators are constantly able to focus on the interplay of convergent and divergent thinking, alternately "busting out" by combining what was before uncombinable and then carefully evaluating these combinations for the best ideas and approaches with their clients. Moreover, personal or relational difficulties of clients often seem to be augmented by an imbalance in convergent and divergent thinking (e.g., a deficiency in DT and overuse of convergent thinking). Thus, some clients become paralyzed in their own paradigms. For example, they may focus excessively on the "problem," the person making them miserable, and/or their own repeated failed attempts to resolve a difficulty or feel better, rather than being able to imagine alternatives or try out new behaviors or methods of problem solving. For many clients in counseling, increasing their divergent thinking and feeling can be an important first step toward positive change. [See DIVERGENT THINKING.]

III. BLOCKS TO CREATIVITY, PERSONAL GROWTH, AND PROBLEM SOLVING

It may be that some of the same blocks to creativity are those that hinder problem-solving skills, personal growth, and fulfillment. These include fear of failure; preoccupation with order and tradition; resource myopia (i.e., failure to recognize one's own strengths and those of others); overcertainty (i.e., persistence in behavior that is no longer effective—dogmatism or inflexibility); a reluctance to exert influence (desire not to appear pushy or a "don't rock the boat" attitude); a fear of play (overseriousness and desire not to appear foolish) and lack of humor or appreciation of humor; fear of letting imagination roam; and a squelching of "What if?" thinking and fantasizing. Other blocks to both personal growth and creativity can include a tendency toward analysis to the preclusion of synthesis, movement toward premature closure, a preoccupation with private worries and insecurities, or environmental restraints (e.g., at home, school, or work). For example, premature closure may involve stereotyping individuals or groups based on insufficient knowledge of or experience with them, or drawing conclusions and making decisions before all facts or options have been carefully considered. The implication of these blocks to counseling seems obvious. If the counselor does not detect or respond to these inhibitors in the context of therapy, the process of change and growth is likely to suffer. Moreover, creative approaches can help both counselor and clients produce more creative outcomes in decision making, planning, goal setting, and problem solving. These include futuration (examining a situation from a futuristic point of view); imagery and visioning; suspending judgment, recognizing and exercising multiple options and choices; and learning to integrate thought and emotion (i.e., balancing intellectual and emotional intelligence).

IV. CREATIVITY IN SOME PROMINENT THEORIES OF COUNSELING

Some prominent and enduring counseling theories have acknowledged the centrality of creativity, especially with regard to the counseling process and the nature of change. For instance, according to Freud, creativity is the main ingredient in the positive defense mechanism of sublimation. From an Adlerian perspective, the counselor encourages innovative responses from clients, with creative expression being an indicator of growth. In accordance with humanistic and existential theories (e.g., Rollo May), the readjustment of personality tensions has been equated with creativity, in that the process of change involves risks and creative acts. Gestalt theorists view creativity (e.g., trying out new behaviors that may seem strange or unconventional) as a means toward integration and change. From some cognitive psychology perspectives, enhancement of divergent thinking or new visual images is often a prerequisite to behavioral change and emotional relief. Finally, from some linguistic/communications perspectives, the "language of change" essential to psychotherapy may involve the creative use of metaphors, stories, parables, fairy tales, and other methods that, according to Gladding, "can open up a whole new world to clients and offer them choices and ways of looking at the world that they would not otherwise discover" (1995, p. 4).

V. CREATIVITY AND GRADUATE TRAINING IN COUNSELING

While graduate training in counseling and therapeutic expertise has its legitimate role and often forms the basis of creative and successful interventions, it is Frey's view that many counselor education programs have made it difficult for trainees to accept themselves as innovators and creators, perhaps because they are taught to apply the ideas of presumed "experts" and do not feel they have the right to create ideas and their own unique interventions themselves. Yet, perhaps more than ever in today's world of unprecedented flux and change, the counseling process requires inventiveness and informed, responsible creative effort (i.e., not just something because it is new, intriguing, or recently popular). Creativity is also essential in counseling because of the complexity and multiplicity of presenting problems encountered, and in many cases the necessity of using short-term solution-focused therapy due to recent restrictions posed by managed care in countries such as the United States. Facilitating creativity

in counselor trainees does not have to be done at the expense of the more traditional educational objectives, but can coexist with the rigor and demonstrable competence required by counselor educators and supervisors.

There are various aspects of creativity—all of which can be viewed as an integral part of the counseling enterprise. These include: (1) the creative environment (the climate, situation, or place in which creativity comes about); (2) the creative product; (3) the creative process; and (4) the creative person.

VI. THE CREATIVE ENVIRONMENT AND COUNSELING

The creative environment is not one that simply allows for spontaniety and free expression of client(s) or therapist but one where creativity is facilitated through intense, invigorating stimulation and interaction. Counselors provide these kinds of environments in part through unconditional acceptance of and regard for clients as unique individuals, encouraging clients to feel safe in being themelves and respected regardless of their presenting problems, being genuine and real, and perhaps by providing a comfortable and aesthetically pleasing physical setting in which to work. Clients, too, are partially responsible for establishing a creative environment through their willingness to self-transpose, learn, and grow. Sometimes changing the environment, either in the context of therapy or in the clients living, employment, or educational situation, may free up creative energy. For example, working with children and adolescents in milieus other than one's office (e.g., the park or basketball court) may not only help counselor and client build a greater rapport, but also release creative potential. Freeing creative energy in children and adults may also involve making some basic changes in the client's eating, sleeping, leisure, and/or exercise patterns. [*See* CREATIVE CLIMATE.]

VII. THE CREATIVE PROCESS AND COUNSELING

There are several stages or phases a person goes through in the creative process. These include: (a) preparation (acquiring skills and background information, resources, and sensing and defining a problem); (b) concentration (focusing intensely on the problem to the exclusion of other demands—a trial and error phase that includes false starts and frustration); (c) incubation (withdrawing from the problem; sorting, integrating, clarifying at an unconscious level, and relaxation and solitude); (d) ideation (generation of ideas that are not judged or evaluated); (e) illumination (an "Aha!" stage, often sudden and involving the emergence of an image, idea, or perspective that suggests a solution or direction for further work); and (f) verification, elaboration, and production (testing out the new idea, and evaluating, developing, implementing, and convincing others of the worth of the idea). These stages may parallel the processes of therapeutic change. In counseling, for example, "preparation" entails the building of a safe and secure therapeutic environment (analogous to the establishment of the creative environment discussed earlier). Concentration becomes a key component of the assessment phase, and incubation, the problem exploration phase. Gradually then, old ideas or behaviors are "reframed" so that clients can develop new ways of looking at things, see alternatives, and feel more empowered to make a change in their lives (ideation and illumination). Reframing thus involves a combination or transformation of information, often in unique or novel ways, that is used to elucidate or resolve a client's problem by extending the client's experiential world in some manner. New ideas and behaviors are then practiced or "tested out" in real-life situations (evaluation). Finally, verification/production can be seen in a changed lifestyle over time (the "creative product" in counseling).

Just as in counseling, these stages of creative process are not necessarily linear and distinct but often follow a pattern of spiral reincorporation. Moreover, what often appears as client "resistance" in counseling may actually be a failure on the part of therapist, client, or both to find a creative solution to the impasses that are common in many helping situations. There are also both content and process variables affecting counselor creative processes. Process variables include counselor knowledge bases, self-efficacy, mental and emotional well-being, ability to remain open to new information, receptiveness to one's own experiences in therapy (e.g., dealing with countertransference issues), and effort and involvement. Sometimes counselors may try

too hard, become overinvolved with clients, get too concerned about their own "performance," or miss important information because of narrowly focused attention. Creative insight may be most likely to occur during periods of relaxed tension when solutions are not forced. From this perspective, counseling becomes one of the most productive settings to study creativity within the context of interpersonal relationships. In addition, in 1980 H. P. Cole and D. Sarnoff suggested that "the modeling of creativity by the counselor may well have transfer effects beyond those consciously perceived by the client" (p. 144). With regard to the creative product, then, one important goal of the counseling process might be the increased creative ability of the person(s) being counseled.

The creative process in counseling may also include the use of a variety of cognitive operations on the part of the counselor in bringing about therapeutic change, and in some cases the therapeutic enhancement of these capacities in clients. Present in many effective approaches to counseling is the facilitation of deferred judgment in the face of strong feelings and perceptions on the part of the client, and the initiation of processes that lead to divergent thoughts and emotions. As Cole and Sarnoff have indicated, "divergent production and deferred judgment are means to insure large numbers of diverse responses increasing the likelihood of finding a problem's 'good solution'" (p. 145). However, therapists might exhibit or employ creative abilities that include but extend beyond divergent thinking, such as intuition and ability to state "hunches"; a capacity to recognize connections and patterns; resistance to premature closure in one's thinking; ability to abstract; ability to integrate and synthesize information; and metaphorical logic and communication. For example, therapists who do frequent checking and hypothesizing with clients (e.g., "It seems to me what might be happening is. . . ," or, "I wonder if she might be feeling. . .") often seem to facilitate the process of change, regardless of whether their stated hunches are accurate.

VIII. THE CREATIVE PERSON AND COUNSELING

With regard to the creative person, creativity experts assert that creativity is probably not a general "trait," but that people are more or less creative in specific areas or domains. Teresa Amabile suggests that creativity is best conceptualized not as a personality trait or a general ability but as a behavior resulting from particular constellations of personal characteristics, cognitive abilities, and social environments. While not all highly creative individuals possess each of these qualities and abilities, commonly observed characteristics are listed in Table 1.

In 1975, Rollo May suggested that many of the same characteristics and capacities that have been used to describe highly creative individuals are also those which typify effective counselors and psychothera-

TABLE I
Common Characteristics of Highly Creative People

Unconventionality (free spirit; unorthodox); openness to both "inner" and "outer" experiences; taking advantage of chance/ alertness to opportunity; ability to accomplish things that go beyond the logical; expectations of follow through; empathy and superawareness of the needs of others; charisma; a sense of the future; flexible and skilled decision making; independent style/tendency to set one's own agenda; sensitivity; hard working/persistent; copes well with novelty; finds order in chaos; asks "Why?"; often prefers nonverbal communication; aesthetic taste and imagination (e.g., appreciation of art, music, culture); a preference for complexity and yet appreciation of simplicity; keen attention; motive and the courage to create; relative absence of repression and suppression; often a theme of remembered unhappiness in childhood; considerable amount of psychic turbulence (usually only in eminently creative people, but not usually manifested as psychiatric disorder); a tendency toward introversion; tolerance of ambiguity; willingness to surmount obstacles; taking advantage of chance; willingness to grow and change; high intrinsic motivation; a desire for recognition; emotional expressiveness; ability to transform from the figural to the verbal and then verbally express; questions social norms, truisms, and assumptions; extends or break boundaries; willingness to take a stand; keen evaluative abilities (e.g., can accurately evaluate the shortcomings of one's own work); humor and an appreciation of various types of humor; colorfulness and richness of imagery; fantasy proneness; unusual visualization/internal visualization; generally a strong internal locus of control; autonomy; independence of judgment; self-confidence; openness to new ideas and experiences; a wide range of interests, curiosity, and enthusiasm; vivid imagination and a sense of wonderment; playfulness.

pists. To a large extent, the processes of counseling and of creativity require similar integrative abilities (e.g., holding seemingly contradictory information simultaneously in one's mind, or remaining open and ready to various information retrival processes, including inner sensations, images, symbols, dreams, hunches, and fantasies). Creative therapists are also more likely to risk failure, show courage, and combine sensitivity, open-mindedness, and divergent thinking with more traditional "scientific" behaviors and modes of cognizing that include rigorousness, convergence, impartiality, objectivity, and tough-mindedness. Further, experienced clinicians know that therapeutic change often occurs on multiple levels, including cognitive, emotional, behavioral, interpersonal, and intuitive. Insight, experience, and personal and professional maturity should not be underestimated with regard to their role in creative counseling. Hence, as Frey indicates, passion and reason are more integrated in creative counselors, "leading them to achieve a larger and more comprehensive perspective that transcends imposed dichotomies and thus links divergent elements that might not otherwise be united" (p. 25).

IX. CREATIVE TECHNIQUES AND COUNSELING

Creative approaches to counseling allow clients to communicate their thoughts and feelings spontaneously in a caring and nonthreatening environment. The use of techniques that allow clients to create and express themselves in nonverbal ways are often less threatening, and can help clients gain an understanding of their strengths as well as their weaknesses and conflicts. For example, journaling, art, drama, play, or music therapy can help clients become aware of and express feelings and unconscious material (e.g., due to traumatic experiences) in ways that allow them time before taking ownership of these thoughts and feelings. Further, creative "products" can provide a permanent, tangible record of progress throughout the course of therapy. [*See* CREATIVE PRODUCTS.]

Creativity in counseling involves a complex interaction of counselor training and qualities, client personalities and presenting problems, structural and systemic considerations (especially in group and family counseling), and the circumstances in which counseling is taking place. For example, a highly creative and well-trained therapist whose personality mixes well with that of a particular teenager and her parents in family therapy may still be met with a great deal of resistance from parents who find it difficult to remove their child from the "identified patient" role and face the reality of serious difficulties in their marriage. That is, marital dynamics which have become unhealthily homeostatic and where parent denial is high may make it difficult for the therapist to assist the struggling teenager and move the family forward. One could argue that creative solutions to problems are more likely to occur under certain, more "ideal" conditions (e.g., therapist and clients like each other, clients are bright, problems that do not seem insurmountable, etc.). If, for example, the parents just described are creative thinkers, change may be more probable even if they are somewhat resistant to change. On the other hand, conditions in counseling are rarely ideal, and creativity in both therapist and client(s) might be best manifested in a context where conditions are far from optimal and problems are numerous.

In terms of the counselor and creativity, creative interventions require that counselors devote time and energy to being flexible, spontaneous, and sometimes provocative. For example, in his 1995 article, S. T. Gladding wrote that enactment "is a creative procedure for making the covert overt and informing clients of possibilities they either failed to recognize or were afraid to try previously" (p. 8). The circumstances, however, have to be right for a given intervention to be successful. As Gladding (p. 9) notes, "one way of setting up circumstances so therapeutic creativity is possible is to make therapeutic sessions more similar to play than to work. By doing so, clients are attracted to participating in activities the counselor may suggest because therapeutic directives are seen as non-threatening and even fun." This is not to diminish clients' pain or the struggle required in many cases for change, but to simply suggest that successful therapy may involve a combination of "play" and hard work, and that creativity at some level may be a requirement for successful intervention. Therapists who work regularly with children and/or families may find this especially true. Furthermore, it is easy for clients and sometimes therapists to become more problem oriented than solution oriented, and to focus on clients' limitations rather than areas of resiliency, that is, to concentrate more on resolving clients' difficulties than building on strengths, opportunities, and possibilities. On the other hand, "dramatic" or "fun" interventions associated with creativity are probably a relatively small part of therapy in most cases, especially with adults. Working hard on changing one's perspectives through the exercise of divergent thinking abilities, or newly directed trial and error behavior, may be as creative in the long run as attempts at radical breakthroughs via fast and unconventional methods.

Finally, Gladding goes on to discuss a number of "specific creative exercises in counseling" the reader may find interesting and helpful that are included under the general categories of music, visual arts, and writing. Other creative techniques have been highlighted in a 1994 article by M. J. Heppner and colleagues. These include guided imagery, idea journals, 1-min free writes, genograms, early recollections, collage and other art mediums, analysis of hero and heroines, timeline analyses, and life mapping.

X. SUMMARY AND CONCLUSIONS

While there are many advantages of using creativity in counseling, Gladding suggests that the most vital role of creativity in people-helping might be that it instills hope within clients that their lives can be better. Frey adds to this notion:

> The redefinition of counseling as an exercise in creativity allows us to draw on more resources in our struggle to help our clients, including such resources as intuition and our own ingenuity. We can be more sure of ourselves and our ability to provide help because we can more fully enter the relationship. We can be there as total persons, bringing our rationality as well as our intuition. This is a reasonably obvious conclusion: If we grow in our inventiveness, so too should our counseling become more bold and innovative (p. 27)

Creative counseling often extends beyond the 50-min session. Counselors might engage clients in therapeutic activities outside the office or elicit the participation of others in the life of the client or family. It is also important to point out that increased creativity in clients or use of creative insight or techniques in therapy does not automatically result in therapeutic change. The volitional/motivational aspects of counseling remain perhaps the most perplexing, and it is in this domain that creativity can play a strategic role. There is little doubt, however, that creativity in counseling is correlated, at least to some degree, with counselor experience and expertise. Creative-minded counselors are also better able to see connections between counseling theories and methods, as well as past and present experiences and needs of clients, and integrate this understanding with the present counseling environment, dynamics, and practices. They may also be more sensitive to the contextual and systemic factors involved in the genesis and maintenance of clients' difficulties, and their capacities/opportunities for change. P. P. Heppner and colleagues (1989 p. 278) summed things up poignantly:

> It is our hunch that more experienced, highly skilled, and creative therapists have well-differentiated roadmaps of the counseling process for different types of clients, and that they can process information more quickly, accurately, and in nonlinear ways. Their successful experiences may in turn bolster their therapeutic confidence, which in turn allows them greater tolerance for risk taking and ambiguity. Most likely, these counselors can also discriminate between relevant and less relevant information and, subsequently,

may have more time to concentrate on finding the missing piece or to combine information in unique and helpful ways.

Bibliography

Barron, F. (1988). Putting creativity to work. In R. J. Sternberg (Ed.), *The nature of creativity: Contemporary psychological perspectives* (pp. 76–98). New York: Cambridge University Press.

Benjamin, L. (1984). Creativity and counseling. *Highlights: An ERIC/CAPS Fact Sheet* (ED 260 369). Ann Arbor, MI: School of Education, University of Michigan.

Cole, H. P., & Sarnoff, D. (1980). Creativity and counseling. *Personnel and Guidance Journal.* 59(3), 140–146.

Dowd, E. T. (1989). The self and creativity: Several constructs in search of a theory. In J. A. Glover, R. R. Ronning, and C. R. Reynolds (Eds.), *Handbook of creativity* (pp. 233–242). New York: Plenum.

Frey, D. H. (1975). The anatomy of an idea: Creativity in counseling. *Personnel and Guidance Journal,* 54(1), 23–27.

Gladding, S. T. (1995). Creativity in counseling. *Counseling and Human Development,* 28(1), 1–12.

Heppner, P. P., Fitzgerald, K., & Jones, C. A. (1989). Examining counselors' creative processes in counseling. In J. A. Glover, R. R. Ronning, & C. R. Reynolds (Eds.), *Handbook of creativity* (pp. 271–280). New York: Plenum.

Heppner, M. J., O'Brien, K. M., Hinkelman, J. M., & Humphrey, C. F. (1994). Shifting the paradigm: The use of creativity in career counseling. *Journal of Career Development,* 21(2), 77–86.

May, R. (1975). *The courage to create.* New York: Bantam.

Witmer, J. M. (1985). *Pathways to personal growth.* Munci, IN: Accelerated Development.

Creative Climate

Göran Ekvall

University of Lund and FA Institute, Sweden

Corporate Culture Deep-rooted belief and value systems that influence all facets of an organization's construction and functioning, such as goals, strategies, structuring, policies, routines, and facilities, which in turn influence the organization's climate.

Innovation A creative idea that has been applied.

Leadership Style The way a leader, formal or informal, influences co-workers.

Organizational Climate Recurrent patterns of behavior, attitudes, and feelings that characterize life in an organization.

Psychological Climate The individual's perception of the organizational climate.

An organizational phenomenon that has gained increasing attention by researchers in many disciplines, is the **CREATIVE CLIMATE.** *Environmental influences on creativity have attracted researchers of different disciplines. Both child psychologists and historiographers have studied the childhood circumstances of creative people. Educational researchers have taken interest in the way the school system and its ideologies, structures, and pedagogics affect the creative motivations and development of pupils. Historians and cultural geographers have been engaged in describing historical periods and geographical regions where creativity in arts, literature, and science has flourished. Organizational researchers have studied the factors that stimulate or block creativity and innovations in companies and public service organizations. This last field of research has by far been the most extensive since the early 1970s, probably due to an accelerating demand on organizations for adaptations and innovations.*

I. THE CLIMATE METAPHOR

The climate concept, when applied to social settings, is a metaphor transferred from meteorology. This metaphor is very much used in western cultures, in conversations and in media, to describe qualities of the social environment. It obviously possesses communication value. There is someting in the analogy between weather conditions in a region and features of social contexts that facilitates characterizations and discussions. Experiences of social life can be referred to contrasting weather conditions such as warm and cold,

Copyright © 1999 by Academic Press
All rights of reproduction in any form reserved.

windy and calm, rainy and sunny, and foggy and clear, thereby giving the climate concept its symbolic meaning in the social context.

Social and behavioral scientists studying organizations have adopted the climate metaphor as a theoretical construct for understanding, explaining, and describing organizational processes and their effects. In a famous leadership experiment of the late 1930s, the term "social climate" was used to denominate the different sociopsychological conditions created by experimentally introduced leadership styles. Since the 1950s the number of studies on organizational climate reported in scientific journals of different languages has been impressive. The intense interest in the subject shown by researchers is mirrored in a series of extensive reviews of theory and research in the field of organizational climate during the last three decades.

There seems to be agreement among researchers to view organizational climate as a molar concept that stands for phenomena belonging to the organization and not to its "molecules," that is, individuals and jobs. Climate is thus an attribute of the organization, something existing inside the organization as a social-psychological reality. However, the consensus is not total about the content of that reality. Many researchers confine the climate concept to behaviors, attitudes, and feelings that characterize the life in the organization, that is, are common and tend to appear with most members of the organization, more or less, when similar situations arise. Other researchers have enlarged the concept domain to include more formal principles and practices, such as reward systems, promotion strategies, or leadership—factors that in the more confined model are conceived as determinants of the climate.

Still others have the climate concept invade the corporate culture domain by including dominating values and beliefs in the climate construct. This approach consequently makes it difficult to separate the two concepts, which may lead to theoretical as well as empirical and practical complications, because these two kinds of phenomena are on different levels of accessibility for study and for interventions and play different roles in the organizational drama. B. E. Ashfort has suggested that even though culture and climate are connected, the difference is real and meaningful. The culture consists of deep-rooted, partly preconscious beliefs and assumptions which exert influence on the climate through values and norms. Culture lies behind and influences. Climate is a derivative of culture. Climate is nearer the observable reality than culture.

Organizational climate as a molar concept, separate from other organizational constructs, is composed of recurrent patterns of behavior, attitudes, and feelings. These patterns are on the surface of the life in the organization, are more easy to observe than the culture elements of basic values and belief systems and, yet are usually not easy to change, at least not in the short term.

Climate so defined tends to be local and varied, in some cases considerably, between departments and workgroups, even if structural and cultural elements of the larger organization apply. That might be the reason why the term "organizational climate" sometimes is exchanged for "workplace climate" or "workclimate." The cause of the climate variation between subunits of the organization to occur, in spite of obvious similarities in, say, tasks, work routines, formal regulations, technology, premises, competencies of the staff, and general mission goals, is to be found in the local leadership, both formal, executed by the manager, and informal, exerted by one or more subordinates with leadership drives and comptencies. In most cases there are enough degrees of freedom for local leaders to influence the climate substantially by their leadership styles and their skills at utilizing the free space granted them and eventually extending it. Staff members who do not act as informal leaders but more as individual troublemakers can have a destructive impact on the climate, especially in small units and where the leadership has insufficient capability to handle such persons and the relations problems they cause.

Organizational climate has been studied with different methodological approaches: the researcher interviewing members of the organization, questionnaires handed out or mailed to all members or samples thereof, systematic behavior observations during short periods, or the researcher working in the organization and making observations according to ethnological research strategies. Questionnaires are most common. The individual member is requested to inform how he or she perceives the climate in different aspects by marking multiple-choice items of the rating-scale type. The ratings made by all respondents are aggregated to be the organization's score. The items are phrased in a descriptive way, not in an evaluative manner. The respondent is presented statements about behaviors, attitudes, and feelings and has to rate to what degree these are prevalent in the organization. This approach is different from questionnaires measuring attitudes and job satisfaction, where the individual and his or her personal reactions and evaluations are the object of the study. Here the organization is the object, and the climate is a property of that object, which is studied by way of the organization members' perceptions and descriptions.

In the context of organizational processes, climate plays the part of an intervening variable (Figure 1) which affects the results of the operations of the organization. The climate has this modifying power because it influences organizational processes such as problem solving, decision making, communications, coordination, controlling, and psychological processes of learning, creating, motivation, and commitment. The organization has resources of different kinds—people, money, machines, etc.—which are used in its processes and operations. These operations bring out effects of many kinds and on different levels of abstraction; high or low quality of products or services; radically new products or only small improvements in the old ones; high or low well-being among employees; and commercial profit or loss. Climate exerts a strong influence on these outcomes. But the effects in turn influence both resources and climate. The causal picture becomes complicated. Good or bad circular movements are in action.

Organizational climate arises in the confrontation

between individuals and the organizational situation. Routines, rules, procedures, strategies, policies, and physical environment are all such factors in the organizational situation which evoke reactions in the people involved. It is these reactions in the form of behavior, feelings, and attitudes that constitute the climate. But we also have to count the people themselves as part of the organizational situation. Individual A is a factor in B's environment, and vice versa. Thus the interaction between organization members is an important part of the climate.

An exhaustive model of the etiology of organizational climate would have to be extremely complex. Many different kinds of variables affect climate. Moreover, the relations between some of these variables can also exert an influence on climate; for example, an equivalent degree of decentralization can generate quite different climates in two organizations if the age composition of the workforces is not the same. In an all-embracing model, the role of the individuals—as articulators, creators, and describers of the climate—must be clarified. The effect of external factors such as technology, markets, ownership conditions, assets, and so on must also be taken into account as modifying influences on the relations between other variables and climate. And not least, both strategic and personal leadership must be directly included in the model.

The relation among the basic values and beliefs of the corporate culture on the one hand, and climate on the other, should also be subjected to theoretical elucidation and empirical study.

II. THE FOURTH "P" OF CREATIVE STUDIES

In 1961 Mel Rhodes found 40 definitions of creativity. He clustered these into four groups: person-centered, process-centered, product-centered, and press-centered, which then became the renowned P's of creativity. "Press" represents significant determinants of behavior in the environment, a term emanating from the personality theory of Henry Murray. Later, authors in the creativity domain have let this "P" mean "place" in a broad sense, including social and psychological aspects, which in Murray's press concept are in focus. [*See* FOUR P'S OF CREATIVITY.]

The "press" studies can be divided into three groups:

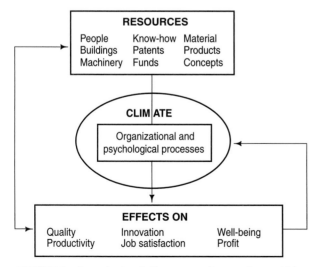

FIGURE 1 Organizational climate as an intervening variable.

those concerning the childhood of the geniuses, those concerning regions and epochs where and when creativity has bloomed, and those concerning organizations. The climate concept has mainly been applied in the last group of studies; in fact the social climate concept has come to be understood as organizational climate. This article is for these reasons focused on the organizational climate.

III. THE CLIMATE OF THE INNOVATIVE ORGANIZATION

The innovative organization is an organization that has the capacity to adapt to survival-decisive changes in its business environment by the development of products, services, processes, systems, structures, policies, etc. Such adaptations require climates that stimulate creative behavior. The picture of the creative social climate that has emerged from some large research programs in the USA and Europe is next sketched.

Employees in this type of an organization experience their jobs as challenging and meaningful. Most identify themselves with the activities and goals of the organization. They see that their own needs for stimulation and improvement can be met within the framework of the company's operations and objectives. Therefore they are eager to see the company succeed and they strive to promote this by considering improvements and new potential solutions.

New ideas result from the meeting and confrontation of various experiences, knowledge domains, viewpoints, values, and recognized yet specifically distinct ideas. Consequently, much debate goes on in the innovative organization. There is a constant exchange of ideas. A variety of thoughts and ideas are tossed up in the air. Ideas travel through the organization by means of many natural informal contacts, ideally meeting other ideas. In other words, the organization consists of a wealth of ideas and in this sense is creative. Creativity is a prerequisite for innovation. The intense generation of ideas and debate creates a liveliness which the employees find stimulating, increasing their perception of work as a challenge.

If debate is to be an ongoing process, it must take place in an atmosphere of openness and trust. Each idea

presented is met with respect and considered without bias. The ridiculing of suggestions and ironic and cynical comments do not exist. As a result, people dare to toss even vague intuitions and half-baked ideas into discussions. This gives them quick feedback, helping and stimulating the thinking process, while at the same time fueling the thoughts of others. The support of ideas is always present. It is a psychological sense of security and a joy in discussing ideas constructively which prevail, the equivalent of which is not found in bureaucratic organizations where people watch out for the errors and mistakes of others. Frictions and oppositions in the innovative organization are maintained on a cognitive level, and all efforts are made to keep them from becoming personal. Major battles about solutions and objectives are not uncommon, but the debates do not cross the line to become wars between people. Frictions are accepted and encouraged because they are recognized as important generators of ideas.

However, should the friction show a tendency to become personal and destructive, this is taken care of and resolved at an early phase. Personal antagonism which turns into hate paralyzes the creative thought process, and therefore does not belong in the innovative organization. Energy channeled into aggression is of no benefit to the organization, nor is it healthy for any of the parties involved.

Organizations characterized by control and restraint become boring and tense. The result is listlessness and people slow down, protecting themselves from boredom by dragging themselves through the workday in a state of semisomnolence. This attitude does not foster new ideas of initiative. However, it is known that creative ideas are often born in an atmosphere of playfulness and that humor shares certain qualities with other creative products. Consequently, a free, relaxed exchange of ideas and an atmosphere where humor is common are characteristic of innovative organizations. Innovation starts with new ideas, and these occur easily in a playful atmosphere, where the critic/censor found within each person is forced into the background. [*See* HUMOR; INNOVATION; PLAY.]

Creativity and innovation require an extensive and richly nuanced influx of information. The innovative organization receives much input from the surroundings, and an abundant flow of thoughts and information between different divisions and functions is also found.

People have great freedom to search for information and take the initiative to bring about change. This freedom of mobility to contact others and search for information and support wherever it may be available is important in all phases of the innovation process. When people can cross boundaries freely, discovery of problems and opportunities for improvements rise substantially, counteracting the blindness caused by complacency and overfamiliarity. Projects can be more realistically formulated and designed when consideration can be given to individual experiences and viewpoints. During the implementation phase, freedom and the exchange of information serve multiple essential functions: there is greater opportunity to avoid resistance, since it is possible to sense criticism and deal with it earlier, and there is more effective distribution of news through the company. Looking for contacts and information and taking the initiative to implement change are thus permitted and natural for the individual employee in the innovative organization.

Innovative activity implies uncertainty about the outcome. This is the major factor which distinguishes it from routine operations. Innovation involves risk. Consequently a risk-taking mentality is found in innovative organizations. People are eager to take the initiative in an experimental spirit. But risk-taking applies to operations, not the individuals themselves. Individuals dare to focus on change because a failure does not have to be synonymous with personal catastrophe. Mistakes are punished in a bureaucratic atmosphere, so people avoid taking the initiative and risking failure. In the innovative organization there is greater allowance for mistakes. Uncertainty caused by innovative activities becomes tolerable, and even stimulating, because of the presence of personal security combined with trust in co-workers and managers. Tolerance for uncertainty, experimentation and the readiness to make decisions on the fly and capture the moment are perhaps the most distinctive features of the innovative climate.

IV. CREATIVE CLIMATE AND ORGANIZATIONAL OUTCOME

The validity of the organizational climate concept as a modifier of creative outcomes in organizations has been studied along two lines: the effects on individuals' creative behaviors and the effects on the creative achievements of organizations and groups.

As innovations in products, services, and processes are readily observable and important criteria for the success of organizations, and as innovations have their origin in creative acts, the innovativeness of the organization has been a cardinal criteriom against which to test the external validity of the creative climate concept and measurement tools. The research design has been to identify innovative and noninnovative organizations and then obtain measures of the climate (usually by questionnaires) and compare these two groups of organizations in respect to climate. A variant of the design is to compare organizations known for radical innovations with organizations characterized by incremental innovations.

A different design, applied in some studies, is to ask a sample of respondents who have wide working-life experiences to rate both the most innovative and the least innovative organizations they have worked with. The aggregated scores for the two kinds are treated as climate patterns, typical of innovative and noninnovative, stagnated organizations.

The accumulated body of research on climate and organizational creativity undoubtly indicates that the climate makes a difference. The question of exactly how strong the influence of climate can be has not, however, been answered by these kinds of research designs, because there are forces in both directions in operation, as the model in Figure 1 predicts; the climate influences outcomes but these in turn affect the climate. Field experiments are needed to analyze the complicated causal relationships. Unfortunately the few studies reported where the climate has been improved by organizational development programs and innovative achievements measured have at the same time changed several other parameters besides climate, which blurs the picture. And even if more rigorous field experiments could be designed, definitive answers would not be obtained. The causal circular processes could not be stopped for a study; the improved creative climate brings increased innovative achievements, which makes the climate still more creatively stimulating, which improves the innovations, etc. It would not be possible to know where and when in the circular process the influence of climate on outcomes peaks and the influence of outcomes on climate starts. We obviously have to be contented with the conviction that the climate plays a role in the creative-innovative achievements of the organization since we cannot be sure how great or intricate this role is in the innovation dramas, generally or in specific scenarios.

V. CREATIVE CLIMATE AND THE INDIVIDUAL

The individual member of the organization perceives its climate and can describe it, either with words or by putting marks on a rating scale. The single individual's perception of the climate is often referred to as "psychological climate." Studies focusing on the individual instead of the organization draw samples with respondents belonging to different organizations. The research question is how the individual's perception of the climate in his or her organization influences job satisfaction, motivation, well-being, etc. When this kind of research has been done with creative reactions as the outcome variable, the respondent is requested first to describe the climate and after that to indicate how supportive or blocking this climate is to his or her creativity.

One example is a study carried out by S. G. Isaksen and colleagues in 1995. The respondents, 1,844 employees from different types of organizations, described the climate in their work environments by a questionnaire and then rated how the work environment stimulated their "personal creativity." The results were clear-cut; the more challenge, freedom, support, trust, prestige-free discussions, humor, and risk-taking the individual perceived in the immediate social work environment, the higher he or she rated the possibilities to personally act creatively.

This kind of study has a different target than the organization-oriented study. Where the latter is centered on the effects part of the model in Figure 1—the innovative outcomes of the organization—the individual design is centered on the middle, processes part: individual creative acts, influenced by climate. The aim is to find which climate aspects have stimulating effects on the organization members' possibilities and motivations to be creative at the workplace and which aspects are hampering creative actions. Studies with this strategy and design have produced knowledge in ac-

cordance with the results of the organization-oriented research, which is no surprise as innovations have their origins in individual creative acts.

VI. DETERMINANTS OF THE CREATIVE CLIMATE

The social climate of an organization arises as the members of the organization meet with and respond to organizational principles, structures, procedures, traditions, systems, norms, and other kinds of realities in their daily work and presence in the organization. These organizational parameters thus influence the behaviors, attitudes, and feelings that constitute the climate. They are the antecedents of the climate.

The research on the creative organizational climate is still far from conclusive etiological knowledge, that is, which the most determining factors are, how they interact, how they might be modified by organization external circumstances, etc. There are, however, some concepts on which the research reports, experiences, and statements presented in the management of innovation literature converge. These concepts or domains of organizational conditions are

- Goals and strategies of the business
- Leadership styles, that is, the way the managers influence their subordinates
- Organizational structure dimensions, including the management and control systems
- Personnel policy, especially concerning recruitment and rewarding
- Resources of different kinds
- Workload.

A. Goals and Strategies

It makes a difference on the climate if the organization uses what has been named a "positional" strategy or an innovative strategy to reach its goals, that is, if the main strategic intention is to pave the way for the already existing and established products or services or if the dominant strategy is to continuously present new products or considerable improvements and adaptations of the old. When goal clarifications and strategic directions expressed by the top management in documents, such as annual reports, letters of policy, and mission statements, include messages of innovation targets, this brings stronger impetus to the members of the organization to behave creatively than when only market shares, productivity, and quality are called attention to as clue figures. If innovation is stressed in matters of strategy, people feel more free to think different, to put forward new ideas, to take time for reflection, and to try things out even when the odds are against them. If, on the contrary, efficiency and short-run profits are all that matter, people become preoccupied with speed and routines, and lose the motivation to perform creative acts. The innovative strategy promotes the development of the creative climate that it needs. The "positional" strategy brings forth the climate that is suitable for its goal.

B. Leadership Styles

A manager's leadership style is the way he or she influences the subordinates to contribute to the goal attainment of the organization. The research on the manager's role in the shaping of the climate of the organization unit he or she is responsible for has clearly indicated direct leadership as an important determining factor. The common variance for the manager's leadership behavior style and the climate, as perceived and described by the subordinates, varies between 30 and 60% in different studies. These figures do not of course tell the exact story of the degree of the manager's influence, because there might sometimes be forces in the opposite direction—when the climate acts upon the manager, who adapts his or her leadership behavior to the prevailing climate structure. However, observations from case studies where managers have moved to new departments and in a short time come to change the climate there radically—constructively or destructively—indicate that the results of the correlation studies mainly expose the manager's influence.

What characterizes the leadership behavior of the manager who has been successful in generating a situation, where people utilize their creative drives and talents (a creative climate)? Is he or she a highly creative person becoming a model for the subordinates to imitate? Not necessarily. Is he or she an idea generator who sprays suggestions over the environment? No, that type of behavior is not creative leadership and it is not leadership in any sense. It has been shown in several studies to bring stress, frustration, and passivity into the situation. A creative person in a leadership position is not the same as a creative leader. The latter is a leader who makes the subordinates behave creatively.

The leadership behavior that encourages a creative climate is strongly oriented toward change and toward people and relations, but is not controlling or rules-oriented. These kinds of leaders have plans and ideas which they share with their subordinates and ask them for contributions in solving problems. They are sensitive to new ideas and supportive of them. They encourage debates and contradictory views but try to settle personal, emotional conflicts. They allow risk-taking and accept failures. They avoid being controlling and bureaucratic, and they tend to defend the territory against formalistic attacks coming from administrative quarters. This kind of leadership has much in common with the "transformal" leadership described in modern leadership theory. [*See* LEADERSHIP.]

C. Structure

In organization theory the formal aspects of an organization are usually referred to as structure. Some structure variables have been shown to consistently covary with dimensions of the creative climate—positively or negatively—and can therefore be assumed to be important determinants of that kind of climate. The structure variables most distinct in this respect are Centralization, Formalization, Order and Plainness, Goal Clarity, and Heterogeneity.

- Centralization has been operationally defined by questions about top management control, one-way communications, and narrow delegation.
- Formalization has been defined as a strict, comprehensive, and imperative system of written rules, intricate decision procedures, and communications tied to the channels mapped out by the organization chart.
- Order and Plainness, as operationally defined, describes clear roles, requirements, instructions, responsibilities, schedules, and plans.
- Goal Clarity has been covered by questions about the existence of clear goals for the organization as a whole and for subunits.

• Heterogeneity has been defined as variety in terms of lines of trades, products and services, professions, and competencies. "Manifoldness" and "complexity" are other names used in some studies for this structure variable.

The results of the different studies converge. Centralization shows negative relations to dimensions of the creative climate. Strongly centralized decision systems thus are associated with climates that restrict creativity and innovation, an outcome of the studies that should not be a surprise to anybody familiar with the literature on innovation.

Formalization has similar relations to the creative climate as Centralization according to the results: negative correlations with the climate dimensions. The strongest negative correlation appears, as could be expected, with Freedom. This too, as in the case with Centralization, accords with established knowledge of the hampering effects of rigid bureaucracy on creativity. This could not be otherwise, as the object of bureaucratic principles is to achieve stability and standardization, and to avoid flexibility and change.

With the more supporting and less constraining aspects or shapes of bureaucracy, here named Order and Plainness, the research results point in the opposite direction. This structure dimension has consistently shown positive correlations with the creative climate, and it has had negative correlations with Formalization. These two structure variables should be conceived as two qualitatively different sides of bureaucracy: one (Formalization) characterized by intricate and imperative rules, routines, and systems, generating formalistic, safe-playing attitudes and behaviors, which is the antipole to the creative climate, and the other (Order and Plainness) implying plans, coordination, clear roles and responsibilities, information routines, feedback systems, and fair and consequent personnel policy, all promoting psychological security and trust in the organization and its management. The security and trust make people feel free to express views and ideas and stimulate them to problem-solving activities aimed to improving the competetive situation of the organization. There are, however, indications of complications in the positve picture of Order and Plainness as a force promoting a creative climate. A creativity inside restrictions is promoted but not a more radical and

boundary-breaking creativity. The positive correlation pattern for Order and the creative climate tends to plane down at higher levels of Order and Plainness for some dimensions of the creative climate, most clearly for freedom and risk-taking.

Goal Clarity shows positive relations to the creative climate in most of the studies. But results in some studies cast doubt on the generally favorable effects of Goal Clarity on creative climate and the innovativeness of the organization—results that consist of zero-correlations between Goal Clarity and risk-taking and some highly innovative organizations with creative climates but with low Goal Clarity as perceived and rated by the employees. One inference could be that these organizations might be still more innovative if they had clearer goals. Another inference, perhaps more daring, would be that the unclear goals were contributing to the climate that made radical innovation possible and allowed freedom for divergent experimentation and generated debates about goals and strategies. It is a well-known phenomenon that ambiguity is not threatening to highly creative people. On the contrary they become stimulated by it—they see possibilities in an unclear situation. But it is also known that people with above-average creative potentials, but with less self-confidence than highly creative people, often need frames and goal direction in order to realize their latent creativity.

The heterogeneous organization with its variety of products, processes, and competencies has higher potential for producing creative mental connections than the more uniform organization where all members work in the same domain and have similar training and experiences. The heterogeneity can, according to research results having bearing upon the issue, lay ground for fruitful debates and idea encounters, which are important aspects of the creative climate, provided that other structural and management principles do not prevent communications across boundaries.

D. Personnel Policy

Principles and practices of recruitment and selection of personnel and of rewarding achievements of different kinds of course have effects on the climate. It is the members of the organization who carry and manifest the climate, and they are at the same time environmental factors in relation to each other. The climate is shaped in the interaction between the members and between the members and the organizational conditions. Characteristics of the people—their psychological traits, drives, motivations, ambitions, etc.—constitute the potentials and the limits for the development of the climate. For that reason, recruitment, selection, and rewarding principles are important determinants of the climate.

An organization that in its search for employees stresses psychological traits such as adaptability, sociability, agreeableness, cautionsness, ambition, and conscientiousness, but which is avoiding the curious, original, inquiring, open-minded persons, prepares the ground for a less creatively stimulating climate than the organization that opens the door for the change-minded personalities. To let people with creative attitudes and problem-solving styles enter the workforce must, however, be more than a recruitment practice, if the creative climate and innovative outcomes shall be realized. Creative ideas and innovative achievements must be demanded by management, and be paid attention to and rewarded; otherwise the recruited highly creative persons tend to quit and the less creative tend to be extremely adaptive, that is, passive and manifesting instrumental attitudes to the work. If, on the other hand, change initiatives are welcomed, realized, and rewarded, all members of the organization, the more as well as the less creative, become spurred to contribute with ideas.

E. Resources

The resources of an organization are of many different kinds, both hardware and software, that is, both material things such as buildings and computers, and propellants such as capital and the knowledge, competencies, and motivations of its employees. The climate influences how the resources are utilized and how efficient the investments in resources are being transformed into effects (Figure 1).

Resources are not only the basics of the organization, the utilization of which the climate influences, they also influence the climate by way of their adequacy, in qualitative and quantitative terms, with regard to the organization's tasks, targets, and demands. The influences are, however, not consistent, especially not con-

cerning the creative aspects of the climate. A lack of resources of some kind may restrict the possibilities to try out new ideas and to take risks, and thus also dampen the motivation to behave creativily. On the other hand, a lack may stimulate creative problem solving in order to compensate for the lack. It depends on the circumstances which effects a specified lack of resources will have on the climate; for example, how crucial and central to the operations the resource is or how it is understood and accepted by the people in the organization.

F. Workload

Research on workload, the quantity of work required, and the creative climate has revealed complicated relations. In some studies the correlations have been positive, and in others negative. High workload may either support or counteract the development of a creative climate. The inconsistency of results can be explained with reference to stress theory and by the fact that the work settings and the kind of employees studied have varied between the research projects. Stress theory makes two distinctions which are relevant here, one between "overstimulation" and "understimulation," and the other between "positive stress" and "negative stress." When there is high workload, a situation where the employees experience overstimulation can arise. When there is low workload, the employees may experience understimulation. Positive stress comes when people feel that they can manage the situation and meet the requirements even if these are high. Positive feelings of challenge, autonomy, achievement, competence, and self-esteem accompany this experience. Negative stress results when people experience that they have lost control—that they are victims of forces they cannot manage. Anxiety and depressive feelings follow.

Negative stress can result both with overstimulation caused by high workload and with understimulation caused by low workload. Feelings, attitudes, and reactions associated with negative stress are ingredients of the noncreative climate. This is one of the reasons why the research on workload and the creative climate has shown inconsistent results. Another is that only a high workload, implying achievement demands, and not a low one can bring positive stress, and the creative climate is characterized by high challenges and motivation, which are feelings and drives included in the mental state of positive stress.

High workloads thus can bring both positive and negative stress and consequently either a creativity-supporting climate or a suppressing one. The crucial issue is at what point the workload tips over from being stimulating, experienced as challenging demands, to being a blocking "overload." This point varies between situations, depending on individual and intergroup differences, which is a third cause of the inconsistent research results concerning workload and the creative climate.

VII. CREATIVE CLIMATE AND ORGANIZATIONAL DEVELOPMENT

Management practice makes use of three strategies, connected with the P's of creativity, Person, Process, and Place, in order to raise the level of creativity in the organization in terms of more creative outcomes, that is, the product "P." The Person approach is to recruit into the organization people with creative records. The Process approach is to train the staff in creative thinking and problem-solving methods. The Place approach is to start organizational development programs aimed at changing the internal environment in a more creatively and innovatively stimulating direction.

Since an organizational setting that promotes (or at least accepts) creative and innovative actions is a prerequisite of recrutiment and training efforts to be successful, the development approaches in many cases must start with the internal environment, that is, the Place approach. Recruiting highly creative persons to an organization whose climate, structures, practices, values, leadership styles, etc., are markedly conservative and bureaucratic is almost foredoomed to failure. The creatives usually give up after a period of fruitless warfare and quit. The odds for training in creative problem solving in a conservative organization are just as bad. The learned methods tend to be forgotten when the trainees are back in the organization, because the routines, practices, and structures do not allow new ways of tackling problems.

A change process aimed at raising the creative and

innovative competence of the organization should start with a look at the internal environment. If it is mature and ready to harbor creative people and utilize creative ways of solving problems, recruitment and training strategies can be applied, but if this is not the case the process must start with an organizational development program.

The organizational climate has proved to be a serviceable platform from which to start such programs. The climate is a manifestation of the total dynamics of the organization—a melting pot of all energies operating in the organization. A picture of this climate is like a kind of general diagnosis of the "mental state" of the organization. With this overall diagnosis as a basis, targeted studies and change interventions can start, guided by the indications from the climate. The prospects to hit the most crucial spots are good by applying such an approach. It is quite natural that the most clearly creative aspects of the climate carry the diagnostic power in regard to change processes.

Bibliography

Amabile, T. M. (1983). *The social psychology of creativity.* New York: Springer-Verlag.

Ashforth, B. E. (1985). Climate formation: Issues and extensions. *Academy of Management Review, 10*(4), 837–847.

Burnside, R. M., Amabile, T. M., & Gryskiewicz, S. S. (1988). Assessing organizational climates for creativity and innovation: Methodological review of large company audits. In Y. Ijiri & R. L. Kuhn (Eds.), *New directions in creative and innovative management: Bridging theory and practice* (pp. 169–186). Cambridge, MA: Ballinger.

Ekvall, G. (1987). The climate metaphor in organization theory. In B. M. Bass & P. J. D. Drenth (Eds.), *Advances in organizational psycholoy.* London: SAGE.

Ekvall, G. (1996). Organizational climate for creativity and innovation. *European Journal of Work and Organizational Psychology, 5*(1), 105–123.

Isaksen, S. G., Winsemius, A. C., & Lauer, K. J. (1995). A test of the validity of the climate for creativity questionnaire. *CPU-report.* Buffalo, NY: The Creative Problem Solving Group.

Turnipseed, D. (1994). The relationship between the social environment of organizations and the climate for innovation and creativity. *Creativity and Innovation Management, 3,* 184–195.

Van Gundy, A. (1987). Organizational creativity and innovation. In S. G. Isaksen (Ed.), *Frontiers of creativity research.* Buffalo, NY: Bearly Limited.

Creative Products

Karen O'Quin

SUNY College at Buffalo

Susan P. Besemer

SUNY College at Fredonia

Consensual Assessment Teresa M. Amabile's term indicating that a product or response is creative to the extent that appropriate observers independently agree that it is creative.

Domain A specific discipline, such as art, business, education, or science.

Elaboration and Synthesis Susan P. Besemer's term (sometimes called "Style") for whether a product is well crafted or elegant, or referring to how the solution is implemented or worked out.

Novelty The newness of a product; the extent to which it is original or statistically infrequent.

Resolution A product's value or usefulness, or the extent to which it solves a problem.

It seems logical that creative people and creative processes can only be identified via prior identification of their products, broadly defined to include nontangible outcomes such as ideas. This article will present a brief history of theory and research on creative productivity, address measurement issues across different disciplines, *and consider the effects of culture and society upon evaluation of* **CREATIVE PRODUCTS.**

I. INTRODUCTION

The root of the English word "create" lies in the Latin *creare*, "to make" or "to produce." Creation implies production, so the term "creative product" almost seems redundant. In this article, the term "product" is used in a liberal sense to mean expressed ideas as well as observable outcomes (such as a poem, dance, essay, cake, computer program, or machine tool). The product, broadly defined, seems synonymous with creativity.

Despite its importance, however, the product almost seems to be an afterthought in the history of the study of creativity. Most of the theory and research in creativity has focused on the study of the creative person and, to a lesser extent, the creative process. Such a focus has largely eclipsed the study of the very thing that allows us to determine whether a person or process is creative: the product.

A. Criteria of Creativity in Products

The common wisdom in the field of creativity studies is that there are two major components that combine to mark creativity in products. The first of these

Copyright © 1999 by Academic Press
All rights of reproduction in any form reserved.

two elements is novelty, originality, or a demonstration of newness in the product. There can be no definition of creativity in products which does not include novelty, although novelty needs to be considered relative to a given population of products (e.g., products of children should be judged relative to those of other children). It seems impossible to imagine a truly creative product that has no elements of newness. [*See* NOVELTY.]

The second major component that is commonly thought to be important to creativity is the product's value or usefulness, or the extent to which it solves a problem. Without this second criterion as a necessary component of creativity in products, bizarre outcomes such as the "word salad" (senseless phrases which are often highly novel) sometimes produced by those with schizophrenia would be considered creative.

In addition to these two widely recognized criteria which define creative products, it has been argued that there is at least one more component. When products are marginally new, or the value that they add is only incremental to the existing standards of a field, they are not usually termed "creative" unless something in the *way* that they are made, presented, finished, or implemented adds to the overall product concept. This third component, sometimes called the product's style, elegance, or aesthetic quality, is often missing in the usual definition of creativity in products.

B. Evaluation Is Inevitable

It is an inevitable fact that creative products are evaluated, either explicitly or implicitly. Evaluation is important in education, because students' works of art, writing, and science are evaluated as evidence of skill and learned behaviors, as well as of aptitude. In business, new product ideas are routinely screened to pick those with the most promise for development and introduction to the market. Works of art, and of the performing arts, are subjected to art criticism, music criticism, and published reviews.

In 1989, P. E. Vernon summarized what was believed to be the consensus definition of creativity as a person's capacity to produce ideas, inventions, artistic objects, insights, restructurings, and products which are evaluated by experts as being of high scientific, aesthetic, social, or technological value. Several elements

of this definition, particularly evaluation, will be revisited in the present article.

II. HISTORY AND MEASUREMENT

The formal psychological study of creativity probably began in earnest in 1950 when the then President of the American Psychological Association, J. P. Guilford, stated the need for a rigorous consideration of the subject in the journal *American Psychologist*. He outlined his understanding of creativity, defined the known intellectual ground, and called for scholarly investigation into the concept. His focus was the creative person, although he briefly addressed creative behavior in terms of the production of ideas. Guilford's Structure of Intellect (SOI) model, in which he described convergent and divergent thinking, greatly influenced creativity studies over the next two decades, particularly its emphasis on creativity as a personality trait. [*See* PERSONALITY.]

In the 1950s and 1960s, occasional gatherings of young creativity researchers were held at mountain resorts in Utah, where the basic concepts and issues for research were deliberated. The transcripts of these "Utah Conferences" reveal that the criteria that should be used to evaluate creative production were often debated. Researchers of the time frequently did not differentiate between the criteria for judging creativity in persons with criteria for judging creativity in products.

The psychologist Carl Rogers attended a similar conference held at Ohio State University. The conference inspired him to include a chapter on creativity theory in his 1961 book, *On Becoming a Person*. Despite his "person" approach, he said,

> In the first place, . . . there must be something observable, some product of creation. Though my fantasies may be extremely novel, they cannot usefully be defined as creative unless they eventuate in some observable product—unless they are symbolized in words, or written in a poem, or translated into a work of art, or fashioned into an invention. (p. 349)

Also in 1961, Mel Rhodes described the four strands of creativity as being the person, the process, the environment (or "press"), and the product. These categories, which Rhodes called "the four P's," have served an organizing function for research in creativity since the 1960s. It is interesting to note that Rhodes stated flatly that objective investigation into the nature of the creative process could proceed in only one direction: from product to person and then to process and to press. However, very little research in creative studies has started with the product. [*See* FOUR P'S OF CREATIVITY.]

In 1968, Donald W. MacKinnon asked, "what are creative products, and by what qualities are they identified?" (p. 435). MacKinnon identified five criteria for creativity in products: the product's originality, its adaptiveness (its ability to solve a problem), its elegance and other aesthetic qualities, its transcendence (the ability to transform or transcend reality), and its "realization" (the product's development and elaboration, evaluation, and communication to others). It seems likely that he expected this topic would soon be thoroughly explored, and he pointed the way to such scholarship by his own research on architects identified as especially creative by their peers. In 1975, MacKinnon ventured to guess that the explicit determination of the qualities that identify creative products had been largely neglected because we implicitly know—or think we know—a creative product when we see it.

Some scholars, in fact, seemed to be pessimistic about whether the qualities that identify creativity in products will ever be developed. It has been argued that objective ultimate criteria for identifying products as creative may never be articulated.

Other theorists had no such qualms. In 1980, Larry Briskman argued forcefully for a product-oriented approach to scientific and artistic creativity. He firmly stated that it was impossible to identify creative people or creative processes independently of the creative product and our evaluation of it. He said that creative people and creative processes can only be identified via prior identification of their scientific or artistic products. Briskman contended that we cannot even *describe*, let alone understand or explain, the creative process without reference to the products that are its outcome. In fact, he argued for the "priority of the product." Briskman also noted how, during the creative process, an artist or scientist constantly interacts with his or her product as it comes to fruition.

Teresa M. Amabile has employed a product-oriented operational definition of creativity in numerous studies. She and her colleagues use a "consensual assessment" definition of creativity, that is, a product or response is creative to the extent that appropriate observers independently agree that it is creative. In her studies, product evaluations are usually made by expert judges; the goal of such evaluations is most often to observe changes in the level of creativity caused by variations in the social treatments of the participant groups. [*See* CONSENSUAL ASSESSMENT.]

Susan Besemer and her colleagues have carried out the most comprehensive work in the study of characteristics of creative products. In 1981, she and Donald Treffinger completed an in-depth analysis of the literature of creativity and evaluation in many creative endeavors. Their purpose was to locate and synthesize the criteria that had been used to judge creativity in products. They reviewed more than 90 sources in the creativity literature, and the literature of invention and patents, education, business, and the arts.

More than 125 criteria were identified, and drawn into a taxonomy that allowed for meaningful discussion across disciplines. That taxonomy, the Creative Product Analysis Matrix, has three dimensions, or three distinct categories under which the criteria of creativity fall. These categories are Novelty, the elements of newness in the product; Resolution, how well the product fills the need or works to resolve the problem for which the product was created; and Elaboration and Synthesis (sometimes called "Style"), which considers how the solution is implemented or worked out. Although none of the criteria were original, as they had all been previously published, the construction of a three-dimensional model for identifying creative products was a new approach to the field.

Susan Besemer and her colleague Karen O'Quin later completed several additional studies taking the broader approach recommended by MacKinnon. Their research focused clearly on the products themselves. It did not attempt to judge the creativity of a person through evaluating his or her product, nor did it attempt to deduce the process through the product. It simply looked objectively at products to identify their characteristics. Table I presents the most recent version of Besemer's three-dimensional model of creative product analysis, which has been refined and changed through

TABLE I

**Besemer's 1997 Dimensions and Facets
of Creative Products**

Novelty dimension	Resolution dimension	Elaboration and Synthesis dimension
Surprising	Logical	Organic
Original	Useful	Well-crafted
	Valuable	Elegant
	Understandable	

Note. These dimensions are measured with the Creative Product Semantic Scale. Each facet contains 4 or 5 items answered in a 7-point semantic differential format. For example, one item from the "original" facet follows: (original) 1–2–3–4–5–6–7 (conventional). An item from the "elegant" facet follows: (coarse) 1–2–3–4–5–6–7 (elegant).

several empirical studies using a wide variety of creative products.

A. Measurement

In 1994, Hans Eysenck reviewed the literature on the measurement of creativity as a trait, noting Spearman's early attempts to measure fluency, or the number of ideas produced by an individual. Spearman's work then became integrated with Guilford's concept of divergent thinking that emerged in the 1950s. Note that fluency involves the production of ideas (which might be considered miniproducts); measures of fluency often simply count the number of ideas produced. Sometimes, the ideas are judged for originality, but rarely for any of the other criteria that might be applied to creative products.

A number of researchers have used measures of creativity which indirectly relate to products, some have measured creativity with global judgments of products, and some have devised domain-specific measures. However, few studies have attempted to develop general criteria that can be applied to creative products across many disciplines.

1. Measures Relating Indirectly to Products

A number of measures that have been used by creativity researchers over the years can be seen as indirect measures of product creation: peer and teacher nominations, measures of eminence, and self-reported creative activities and achievements.

a. Peer and Teacher Nomination
Peer nomination is a common measure of creativity. With this technique, experts in a particular domain are asked to nominate especially creative members of their fields. Presumably, knowledgeable peers of a scientist, architect, poet, or artist who identify a target person as being creative must to some extent be considering the quality and/or quantity of that person's work.

Similarly, teacher nomination is often used to measure creativity of children. If a teacher can indeed make judgments of a child's creativity independently of judgments of intelligence or likability, the teacher must be considering (at least to some extent) the child's work in arriving at the judgment.

There is some disagreement in the literature about how well judgments of product can be intellectually separated from judgments of the person. Attributions and evaluations of original products can be biased by the evaluator's perceptions of the creator. Despite such issues, however, there is undoubtedly considerable influence of productivity on peer and teacher nominations of people as being creative.

b. Measures of Eminence
Another indirect approach to measuring creative production is to study eminent people. Donald W. MacKinnon was one of the pioneers of such an approach in his 1962 study of 40 of the most creative architects in the United States. He used peer nomination to identify them, but eminence has been measured in other ways. For example, in 1994, Colin Martindale noted that prices for artists' paintings have been measured over time; prices of works by a particular artist tend to fluctuate wildly for several generations after the artist's death, then settle down to some "proper" place. Another interesting measure of eminence is the amount of space devoted to works by various composers by the Boston Symphony Orchestra over time. [*See* EMINENCE.]

Starting in the 1970s, Dean Simonton has conducted an impressive research program examining eminent people in several fields such as music and science, usually by analyzing published historical and biographical data. For example, he measured the amount of space devoted to philosophers and composers in different reference works. In some cases, Simonton directly studied the products of eminent people; for example, he analyzed the melodic originality of composers by measuring the note-to-note transitional improbability (surprisingness) in their works. Michael D. Mumford and Sigrid B. Gustafson have suggested that creativity be defined as the production of novel, socially valued products, a definition that essentially restricts creativity to those people with outstanding occupational achievements.

c. Self-Reported Creative Activities and Achievements Several researchers have used lists of achievements in science, art, literature, and music to assess creativity. Typically, respondents indicate whether they have won awards in science fairs, have exhibited or performed works of art, have had poems, stories or articles published, have had roles or leads in plays, etc. In general, the total creativity score is simply the number of activities checked or listed. Clearly, creative productivity is being measured, although there is often no indication of the extent to which respondents are being truthful in their self-reports.

2. Global Judgments

Some researchers have felt that it is not absolutely necessary to define creativity in general, nor to define it in products. In the creative studies literature, identifying creative products is often a step intended ultimately to assist in the identification of creative persons, so the definition (or the criterion) is not as important as the identification itself. In the "real world," a global judgment of the creativity of one or more products is often made by a panel of expert judges. This judgment may be part of the process of selecting children for programs for the gifted and talented, or for special awards. In some cases, such judgments are made by the assessment of a portfolio of work, but sometimes one single product is judged. For example, high school students who enter the annual Westinghouse Science Talent Search are evaluated primarily on the basis of an original research paper.

A similar global evaluation is often used in business to select new product ideas to develop for production. For example, one study found that senior managers said screening of new product ideas usually was an informal process; in less than 2% of the screening decisions did evaluators use a formal checklist questionnaire or scoring model to rate project ideas. Global evaluations are also frequently used in the art field.

Perhaps the world's most influential researcher using global assessments of creativity in products is Teresa M. Amabile. In numerous studies, she and her colleagues have used expert judges to evaluate creative products. The technique is fairly simple. Participants are asked to create something on the spot (such as a collage, story, or poem), which is then rated by experts for creativity. This measurement technique, called consensual assessment, assumes that experts over the course of years have developed their own implicit criteria within their own domains by which they evaluate creative products. Amabile sees no advantage in specifying criteria to be used by the judges in making their evaluations. The interjudge reliabilities of the creativity assessments has typically been high enough that even if the criteria have not been made explicit, the judges must have been exercising implicit criteria which their experience and discipline-related expertise had internalized.

One drawback to the consensual assessment technique is that creativity scores can be compared only within a particular sample; no norms can be established for comparisons with products from other samples. However, for many research and educational uses, within-group comparisons are enough.

A second issue of concern with such a technique is that in at least two of Amabile's studies, judges' ratings of creativity have been highly correlated (as high as .94) with their liking for the products. Such high correlations with likability suggest that global judgments of creativity may be clouded by preference. However, even with these drawbacks, the judgments of products made consensually by experts are likely to be more stable and more valid measures of creativity than regular divergent thinking creativity tests.

3. Specifying Criteria to Evaluate Creative Products

There is no question that indirect and global measures advance the field in general, but they do not address the issue raised by MacKinnon early on. What are the attributes by which creativity in products can be determined?

Creative product analysis asks the question, "How do you know it's creative?" and attempts to answer the question by looking at the characteristics and qualities of the product which mark its creativity. This question has been asked in domains such as art, engineering, chemistry, new product development, and education.

a. Specific Domains Attempts have been made to develop judging instruments specific to different domains. In the education field, there have been several important efforts. For instance the Detroit Public Schools' Creative Products Scales are designed to measure performance in five areas: art, music, creative writing, performing arts, and dance. Within the five areas are 11 scales, each reflecting the distinctive characteristics of the particular area.

In another example, the Student Product Assessment Form contains 15 items that ask judges to rate both individual aspects of the product (such as appropriateness of resources, originality, logic, sequence, and transition) and to make global assessments of the overall excellence of the product. For the nine individual ratings, judges are provided with a summary statement and examples of high-quality work to help them establish clear criteria for judgment. Several studies, most with gifted children, have found good reliability and encouraging evidence for validity of this measure. Researchers have similarly attempted to specify criteria for evaluating art works, and evaluating products from the business world.

b. General Criteria An early attempt to specify general criteria was made in 1975 by Irving A. Taylor. He described a scale of product attributes for creativity assessment. In the Creative Product Inventory, he suggested seven criteria for product evaluation: generation, reformulation, originality, relevancy, hedonics, complexity, and condensation.

The most thorough of the few attempts to develop a general measure for recognizing creative products has been made by Susan Besemer and Karen O'Quin. In 1989, they developed an instrument called the Creative Product Semantic Scale (CPSS). It contained 55 items organized into subscales meant to measure three major dimensions of creative products: Novelty, Resolution, and Elaboration and Synthesis (Style). Recently, Susan Besemer has revised and reorganized the subscales, as indicated in Table I. This recent research has also yielded support for the three-dimensional nature of the CPSS.

Few people disagree with the importance of the Novelty dimension, but some facets of Resolution have raised eyebrows. It is sometimes said that art products are not "useful." However, the history of art is full of examples of art that has been useful for religious, ritual, patriotic, or even propaganda purposes. One can also consider the psychological usefulness of art, both to the creator, and to the viewer who may be stimulated by the work of art in several ways, from simple enjoyment to more complex cognitive effort. Another problem associated with Resolution is the concept of "valuable"; does it mean valuable monetarily or conceptually? In empirical testing, valuable has been a highly reliable facet, indicating good agreement about the value of a stimulus product. Elaboration and Synthesis has been questioned because some people feel that such aspects of products are subjective, ambiguous, and difficult to agree upon. However, empirical testing has shown a high degree of reliability in these judgments.

Over the years, the CPSS has been extensively tested, by both Besemer and O'Quin, and by others who had a need for a structured approach for considering product creativity. Scholars in such fields as computer-assisted design, textile design, business, education, and management information systems have found the instrument useful in their studies.

III. CHALLENGING CONCEPTUAL ISSUES

Four important conceptual issues have played central roles in the theory and research on creativity in products. First, what are the defining characteristics used to evaluate creativity in products? Second, what effects might evaluation have on potentially creative performance? Third, to what extent are the criteria used to evaluate products different across domains (the many diverse settings in which creative products are found)? Fourth, what are the effects of culture upon evaluations of creativity? Each of these questions is more complex than it appears on the surface.

A. The "Criterion Problem"

Throughout the literature, a critical central issue emerged, termed "the criterion problem": what are the criteria by which creativity should be measured? A closely related question is whether tests commonly used to measure creativity in a person (such as tests of divergent thinking) actually predict creative production. This problem encapsulates an essential operational definition for the field, because the research questions of empirical studies are based on issues of definitions. The criterion problem is one that is still to some extent unsettled.

B. The Effects of Evaluation

The fact that the things that people make are so frequently subject to the judgment of others can have important effects on the creator. Evaluation may either encourage or inhibit the maker's best efforts. Although it must be acknowledged that products will be judged, the manner in which they are judged can be very important to the future efforts of artists, inventors, and others who are bringing new works into being. Much too often, the products created are judged in a quick, superficial way, without the kind of objective analysis which could benefit their creators and the field at large.

Hasty evaluation can affect creativity in schools, business, and the world of art. This problem can be seen in schools, where the standard exists that a student's creation must be a bit different, but not too dissimilar from others in the same category. Businesses get stuck, sometimes, in the same paradox. While looking for that critical "creative spark," there is a substantial pressure to select new product ideas which are product line extensions rather than the riskier, but potentially more profitable, truly novel product ideas. Note the frequency of movie sequels!

Although it may seem that the arts would be more accepting of shocking novelty, art is always judged within the framework of criteria for technical expertise that reinforces the standards of the culture and the day. David N. Perkins has stated that in the arts, slowing down the process and agreeing on some general principles would encourage shared standards of quality, while not glossing over the potentially valuable novelty which can emerge unexpectedly in the experimentation of the creative process. He called it "constructing a common aesthetic reality." Perkins suggested that with effort and practice, common perceptions and evaluations of works of art could be achieved.

Another aspect of the issue of evaluation is the question of whether or not untrained judges can make informed and valuable judgments. It seems likely that whether an expert judge is needed depends upon both the age of the creator and the domain in which the creativity takes place. When judging a child's science fair project, one needs to know something about the scientific method, but it is not necessary to be an expert in the particular domain of the project. If one is judging the creativity of a mathematical theory, then one must be an expert in mathematical theory. The more "cutting edge" a product is in a specific domain, the more likely an expert judge will be required.

A current emphasis in research is on identifying the characteristics that creative products share, perhaps in varying proportion. It is important to separate the concept of the work's subsequent evaluation from its creation, alternating the generative and focusing phases of thought. This change in point of view is informed by the research of Teresa M. Amabile. Her work has shown the negative effect that believing one's efforts would be evaluated could have on learning, as well as the beneficial effect that creative activity has in softening the awareness of upcoming evaluation.

C. More Universal Criteria?

A third challenging issue in the study of creativity in products is an often implicit assumption that the discoveries about product characteristics in one discipline are unique to that field. There are so many different fields of creative production, including the arts, sciences, business, and education, that practitioners in each of these fields assume that their worlds are unique and need special ways of evaluation that are exclusively theirs. This assumption encourages the development of specialized judging instruments that may limit the ability to make valid comparisons across disciplines.

It is true that all areas where judgments about creativity are being made have their own unique, often technical, criteria or standards of quality. However, at a slightly higher level of abstraction, it is possible to deduce similar schemes for analyzing and discussing the products of differing disciplines. Making comparisons at this level allows different types of products to be compared, facilitating the general development of more widely applicable standards of judgment. The idea that there can be domain-specific criteria does not rule out the possibility that there can also be more universal criteria applicable to products in many domains.

D. Effects of Culture

Social institutions, creative ideologies, economic support for creators, patronage, outlets for creative products, and societal values may all affect creativity, as can one's social environment (including power, independence, and communication). Simon Schaffer has asserted that the status of famous scientists is not a simple consequence of unique individual merit, but is socially ascribed. Some influential social group has to value an idea if it is to be recognized, preserved, and communicated. In science, the evaluation often involves the explicit identification of the idea as "a discovery," and myths often arise about the suddenness with which it happened. Historically, there are often other similar ideas which would have merited the name "discovery" but that did not receive it. Thus, Schaffer argued that a scientific discovery is identified as such not intrinsically, but largely extrinsically, in terms of what relevant people think about it.

Some people have suggested that because standards of evaluation are not absolute, researchers may as well abandon any attempts to specify criteria for creative production. We disagree. Although the varying effects of societal and cultural standards make the task more difficult, the notion that evaluation of some sort takes place is universal.

A product must be socially approved at some level in order to be creative. One important question is, "Approved by whom?" Can a product be judged by its own creator as being creative without being judged as creative by the wider world? That certainly happens. A bright child's creative product may not be judged as creative by humankind, but many such products are proudly displayed by parents in their homes, taped to the doors of refrigerators. On the other hand, some works of classical composers such as Mozart, Beethoven, and Pachelbel are widely acclaimed both by experts and laypersons, and have been used in advertising campaigns for popular commercial products.

The "worth" of evaluations of creativity depend to some extent upon the quality and expertise of the eval-

uators. The more people who independently recognize a given product's creativity, and the higher the levels of expertise of the judges, the more lasting the judgment is likely to be. The creator, although probably not as objective as other evaluators, often has his or her own sense of judgment about whether a particular product is more or less creative than some other product that he or she has done.

Another important question is, "Judged in comparison to what?" Clearly, the products of children should be judged in comparison to those of other children of similar age, although the works of the rare child genius like Mozart may obviate this necessity. However, even among adults, novices in a domain are typically judged differently than masters of the craft. The issue of subjectivity is inescapable. Judgments about creativity must always be made in context, and made relative to the set that is being judged. Attempts at quantifying creativity are based on trying to make the evaluation more thoughtful, less hasty, and less subjective, but some level of subjectivity will remain.

Using multiple judges for important decisions can help reduce subjectivity, but judges are embedded in their societies, cultures, and time periods. Expert judges who apply internalized criteria can alleviate some problems by assuming a common standard of technical quality, but experts often perpetuate the status quo. Using a validated judging instrument can allow even naive judges to make informed judgments.

IV. INVENTIONS AND INNOVATIONS

The purpose of the present article is not to examine the fairly extensive literature on invention and innovation. Much of this literature focuses less on the product itself and more on the marketing issues that are likely to affect the success of the product. [*See* INNOVATION; INVENTION.]

V. LOOKING TO THE FUTURE

The need for returning to MacKinnon's questions about creative products becomes clear when focusing on creative persons and creative processes. It is obvious that even extremely creative individuals vary on the creativity shown in any particular work. Some products may be more or less creative because the makers were working in a new or a well-learned domain, were more or less successful that day at expressing their creativity, or had more or fewer restrictions on their work at the time. Makers may have been feeling well or ill during the time that they worked on the product, or they may or may not have been affected by certain environmental factors. Because of the variance in the creativity of any particular product, it seems risky to expect a product, made only as a result of an unexpected "assignment" on a creativity test, to be representative of a maker's usual level of creativity.

Likewise, few would expect a creative person to be equally creative in all domains of his or her life. Some exercise their creativity mathematically, some artistically, and some in business, for example. Creativity tests that pose a creative task are more valid for those whose creativity is manifested in the domain that is being tested. For example, to do poorly in the creativity shown in an art task does not mean that one's mathematical creativity has been adequately assessed.

Another caution exists because of what we know about the process of creativity. Creativity may take place as a result of divergent thinking and the development of several options before the completion of the task. Creativity tests that demand that the first and only product of the exercise be judged for its creativity do not benefit from this awareness. The instruction, "Do this task now, and Be Creative!" can be intimidating to people who prefer to take their time and adopt a more experimental approach. Again the work produced may not be representative of the maker's usual creativity. A portfolio approach to assessment of creativity, in which a person's *best* works are evaluated, seems much more promising. [*See* APPENDIX II: TESTS OF CREATIVITY.]

Several researchers have found the Creative Product Analysis Matrix and the CPSS useful in their own studies. Although the efforts of Susan Besemer and her colleagues are an important step in the right direction, it is not expected that a perfect measure to assess creative products has been developed. In the meantime, there is more work to be done. Researchers must be persuaded of the importance of "product" measures of creativity, whether indirect, global, or facet based. A

number of incremental steps can be taken to advance the field. One of these steps is development of norms for broad categories of products using the CPSS or other measures. With a sufficient body of literature, researchers will know general ranges to expect for products of children, college students, experts in a field, etc.

Next, the whole issue of evaluation needs increased attention. Researchers have begun to be more aware of the effects of society and culture. Undoubtedly, evaluations of creative products are affected by judges' expectations, time period, cultural background, etc. Absolute standards of creativity do not exist.

A recurring issue concerns whether "lay" judges and experts can agree on product evaluations. Some authors have suggested that judgments are more likely to converge with regard to "mainstream" products, but less likely to be similar regarding extremely innovative products in particular domains. Others have argued that the judgments of professionals or experts are best. It is also possible that professionals, although capable of producing creative products, might be unreliable or inaccurate when judging them, perhaps because they rely on high-level, esoteric, or idiosyncratic standards.

Finally, in order for the field to advance, we need to develop a common language to facilitate communication across different domains. Seeing the similarities in creative products of scientists, artists, dancers, chefs, schoolchildren, and entrepreneurs will help us to know the true meaning of "creativity."

Bibliography

Amabile, T. M. (1983). *The social psychology of creativity.* New York: Springer-Verlag.

Besemer, S. P., & O'Quin, K. (1993). Assessing creative products: Progress and potentials. In S. G. Isaksen, M. C. Murdock, R. L. Firestien, & D. J. Treffinger (Eds.), *Nurturing and developing creativity: The emergence of a discipline* (Proceedings of the 1990 International Conference on Creativity Research, pp. 331–349). Norwood, NJ: Ablex.

Briskman, L. (1980). Creative product and creative process in science and art. *Inquiry, 23,* 83–106.

Csikszentmihalyi, M. (1988). Society, culture, and person: A systems view of creativity. In R. J. Sternberg (Ed.), *The nature of creativity: Contemporary psychological perspectives.* New York: Cambridge University Press.

MacKinnon, D. W. (1968). Creativity: Psychological aspects. In

D. L. Sills (Ed.), *International Encyclopedia of the Social Sciences, Vol. 3.* New York: Macmillan.

Perkins, D. N. (1979). Evaluative response to art. In C. J. Nodine & D. J. Fisher (Eds.), *Perception and pictorial representation.* New York: Praeger.

Rhodes, M. (1961). An analysis of creativity. *Phi Delta Kappan, 42,* 305–310.

Rogers, C. (1961). *On becoming a person.* Boston: Houghton-Mifflin.

Schaffer, S. (1994). Making up discovery. In M. A. Boden (Ed.), *Dimensions of creativity.* Cambridge, MA: Bradford.

Taylor, I. A., & Getzels, J. W. (Eds.). (1975). *Perspectives in creativity.* Chicago: Aldine.

Creativity in the Future

Bonnie Cramond

The University of Georgia

Future Problem Solving A program designed to teach students to solve world problems of the future through a six-step process of identifying challenges, selecting an underlying problem, producing solution ideas, selecting criteria, applying criteria, and developing an action plan.

Fuzzy A problematic situation that is presented to students from which they must choose a central problem for solution.

Trend analysis A way of studying the future by examining current trends to predict the direction and intensity of changes in the future.

CREATIVITY IN THE FUTURE *is a prediction influenced by trends and current knowledge of forces that will likely impact both adaptive and expressive creativity in the near future.*

I. NEED AND PROBABILITY FOR CREATIVITY IN THE FUTURE

"In a time of drastic change, it is the learners who inherit the future. The learned find themselves equipped to live only in a world that no longer exists" (Hoffer, 1973, p. 22).

A. Problem Solving

Using trend analysis, we can predict that in the future the world will continue to become increasingly complex with problems requiring novel and elegant solutions. Geopolitical restructuring will continue to break down former nations like the Soviet Union, Yugoslavia, and Czechoslovakia into smaller national units while other small countries will unite for greater economic power, as with the European Economic Conference. Natural resources such as oil, gas, and forests will continue to diminish faster than they can be replaced. Population growth will continue to outstrip food production, and climatic changes will disrupt agricultural production. Established methods of addressing problems will no longer be viable, and the

Copyright © 1999 by Academic Press
All rights of reproduction in any form reserved.

necessity of finding and defining potential problems before they erupt will be more critical. Survival of the species will require adaptation to changing conditions through creativity. According to E. Paul Torrance, "when a person has no learned or practiced solution to a problem, some degree of creativity is required" (1988, p. 57).

B. Expressive Creativity

In addition to problems, the complex and crowded world will increasingly bring more stress to people. One proven method of stress reduction is through expressive arts. Thus, there is good reason to believe that creative expression will increase as a means of adapting to the future. New technologies enable people to express themselves in a wider variety of ways and provide a wider potential audience for the arts. For example, what television did for writers, producers, entertainers, advertisers, etc., in the 1950s and 1960s, the Internet and the World Wide Web provided for creative expression in the 1990s. Now, a writer or artist need not find a willing publisher or gallery in order to have the work widely available to individuals around the world. Perhaps this is why futurists are predicting a 21st century renaissance of the arts. The extension of existing technology and the creation of new technologies will provide opportunities for some and create limits for others. Changes in the medium affect not only the product, but the process and artist as well as the art patrons. In the future, the arts may no longer be considered the sole province of the financially elite, but become increasingly available to the technologically elite.

II. SOCIAL IMPACT

A. Acceptance of Multicultural Expressions

As the world becomes smaller and more interconnected, people are becoming more accustomed to art forms from other cultures. van Gogh's incorporation of Japanese components in his art, like the Beatles' use of a sitar in their rock compositions, are examples of early uses of exotic elements combined with the familiar to create new forms. As world travel increases, satellites bring images from around the world into our homes, and usage of the Internet expands at an astounding rate, various cultural expressions become more accessible and familiar. This should bring increasing amalgamation of art forms in the near future, and a greater subsequent search for the exotic and novel.

B. Tolerance for a Broader Range of Deviance from the Norm

Increased exposure to various expressions should also bring increased tolerance for diversity. For example, television viewers of the 1990s saw characters from different ethnic groups, age groups, geographical regions, religious beliefs, and sexual orientations in similar human conditions. We need not like or agree with others' expressions to be familiar with and tolerant of them. Whether increased tolerance will make it easier for creative individuals, who are often very deviant from the norm, to find acceptance or will make it harder for them to rebel against the norm remains to be seen. However, in this age of knowledge explosion, the creator has become as visible as the creation. Perhaps this is what led one of the first celebrity artists, Andy Warhol, to predict that in the future everyone would have 15 minutes of fame. The fame and wealth of a Bill Gates, Helen Hunt, or Stephen King may be as motivating to some aspiring creators as it is disheartening to others.

III. EDUCATIONAL CHANGES

A. The Knowledge Explosion and Technology

As anyone who has searched the Internet for the answer to a simple question is well aware, knowledge explosion is not an overstatement as a description of the availability of information today. The amount and interconnectedness of information is expanding so rapidly that it is changing not only what we teach, but how we teach it. The sheer amount of information demands that there be a shift from content to process emphasis in schools. Important process training will increasingly include skills to acquire, store, and transmit information. In 1970, Slade wrote that children of the future will have to master the two new information systems: *data in motion,* the computer, and *image in motion,* communication systems such as film, video, and satellite communications. But, it will not be enough to simply retrieve and disseminate information. In order for our children to be contributors to the future, they will need to have the skills to help them evaluate the preponderance of information available and synthesize it in meaningful ways.

B. Future Problem Solving

In 1974 E. Paul Torrance created the Future Problem Solving Program (FPS) specifically to teach students to address the problems of their future creatively. Students practice and train on "fuzzy" situations that are based on projected problems of the future such as prisons in space, famine, international terrorism, and the like. Students brainstorm the many possible problems inherent in the fuzzy, select and write one problem statement, and then do research on the topic to gain as much information as possible. They then brainstorm many possible solutions, select and apply criteria to choose the best solution, and devise a plan for selling the solution to the key individuals involved in decision making. Students work in groups vying with other groups to choose the best solution, thus learning skills of both cooperation and competition. Other components of the program have groups of students applying the process to solve real problems in their communities or writing fictional scenarios about the solutions to problems of the future. [*See* COLLABORATION AND COMPETITION; GROUP CREATIVITY; PROBLEM SOLVING.]

IV. PREDICTION

In 1981, R. Buckminster Fuller reflected on his childhood at the turn of the last century. He recalled that as people tried to predict the future in the new century, they could not begin to conceive of automobiles, electrons, travel to the moon, or even air wars as reality. Only about 1% of the world was literate, and fewer still thought of humanity in world terms. We, too, are poised on the brink of change with the coming new millennium and cannot presume that we are more precognitive about what lies ahead than were our predecessors. However, one prediction that was true then will undoubtedly be true again: successful adaptation to world change and the continued civilization of our world depends on creative endeavors. [*See* ADAPTATION AND CREATIVITY.]

Bibliography

Fuller, R. B. (1981). *Critical path.* New York: St. Martin's Press.

Hoffer, E. (1973). *Reflections on the human condition.* New York: Harper & Row.

Slade, M. (1970). *Language of change: Moving images of man.* Toronto: Holt, Rhinehart, & Winston of Canada.

Torrance, E. P. (1988). Creativity as manifest in testing. In R. J. Sternberg (Ed.), *The nature of creativity* (pp. 43–75). New York: Cambridge.

Torrance, J. P., Torrance, E. P., & Crabbe, A. B. (1981). *Handbook for training future problem solving teams.* Cedar Rapids, IA: Future Problem Solving Program, Coe College.

Creativity in the Moral Domain

Mary Lee Grisanti and Howard E. Gruber

Teachers College, Columbia University

Creative Altruism The active, innovative expression of altruistic feeling and principle.

Evolution of Belief Systems Belief systems are developmental, and undergo change over the lifespan; evolution of belief systems refers to the global and systematic basis for an individual's or group's beliefs.

Extraordinary Moral Responsibility Exceptional perception and acceptance of moral challenge—as opposed to moral creativity which describes an innovative response to such a challenge.

Moralities System of values which guide individual and social freedom.

Moral Reasoning The ability to analyze a situation in terms of relative rightness and wrongness.

Utopian Thinking As a dynamic process, utopianism can be a feature of creativity. All creators give themselves license to imagine their work in perfect conditions—whether that be a frictionless engine or an exquisitely receptive audience. In

particular, social utopianism as a process can be key to the creative approach to social problems.

In dreams begin responsibilities. . . .

W. B. Yeats

MORAL CREATIVITY *is creativity for a moral purpose. Thus, it is an aspect of many other acts of creativity, but on its own is a creativity of action—creativity whose end product is the better life of human beings. It is social and collaborative, yet may entail a personal inner transformation which is capable of impelling an ordinary man, woman, or even child to extraordinary action, for example, risking his or her own life to save the lives of others. Many of the things we ought to do come to us with their meanings and their demands upon us clear and ready-made. And often enough, we do what we ought—because we can. A stable civilized society would not be possible if that were not largely the case. Rationally, the concept of "ought" is applicable only when a person is the potential source of a possible event. It does not make sense to say that a person ought to do something if he cannot do it. But when we cannot— when a moral imperative is present but the problem is so overwhelming as to challenge a person's ability to*

Copyright © 1999 by Academic Press
All rights of reproduction in any form reserved.

address it—creativity becomes necessary. Not everyone takes up the challenge. Those who do often have special skills, powerful motives, and courage beyond the ordinary. But sometimes they are simply ordinary people presented with extraordinary moral opportunities. In the course of facing terrible, seemingly intractable problems, they innovate. They go where no one has gone before, and change the road ahead for everyone around them. Moral creativity can be seen in the extraordinary legacies of great moral leaders, but is also within the reach of all us.

I. CREATIVITY IN THE MORAL DOMAIN

This most human use of talent shares many features associated with creativity, as it has been explored through various cognitive approaches. Yet, relatively little has been done to examine the relation of creative thought to the values and intentions of the creators, and to chart the course between innovation and responsibility. This lack of integration is a special problem in understanding creativity in the moral domain.

Any examination of the link between morality and creative thought must also call into question the very idea of science as value-free fact, since it entails the fusion of values with behavior. It forces us to simultaneously confront and embrace paradoxes of experience—to balance dream with duty. As a subject of scientific inquiry, moral creativity is in some ways new and not precisely defined. Yet moral creativity is an ancient idea, one with deep roots in the arts and aesthetics as well as education.

II. THE BREAK WITH TRADITION

Plato answered the question, "can virtue be taught?" by giving this educational duty to poets. He believed that the stories we tell young people are singularly important in developing an adult human being capable of living out a fully human destiny—intellectually, politically, and morally. From this source, the idea of education as an *ars moralis* (moral art) evolved, influencing educators, the educated, and by extension, artists. The guiding idea was that education and the arts each in

its own way awakened the individual to life's possibilities within the framework of enduring moral choices. This idea continues to influence educators in our time. Dewey wrote explicitly of the kinship between education and art, believing that the moral imagination was as much the educator's responsibility as the artist's. The philosopher Maxine Greene has also explored the kinship of art, and its speculative creativity, with education, and its ethical goals: the balance of what *might* be with what *ought* to be. But as the understanding of human understanding moved from philosophers to psychologists, the characteristics of scientific research often seem to separate creativity from morality to better discern each at work.

Creativity and the development of moral reasoning have been prominent subjects of post–World War II psychological research, each viewed in its own way as instrumental to the building of a technological society. Yet, their study has been largely unconnected.

Creativity research has been particularly fruitful in yielding new understandings of the complexity of human capacities. Case study methodology has helped bring to light the magnificent variety in human capacities and motivations. Howard Gardner's theory of multiple intelligences specifically delineates a domain of ability in interpersonal relationships. If we use this framework, moral creativity could be understood as a function of talent in interpersonal relationships (at its zenith, leadership) combined with moral purposefulness. Gardner's work includes a case study of Gandhi, who is emblematic of moral creativity at work. [*See* MULTIPLE INTELLIGENCES.]

But case studies of creative leadership are only occasionally studies of moral creativity, and even Gandhi raises difficult questions regarding, for example, the equality of women. It is all too apparent that great creativity, in leadership, as in other activities, is as liable to self-serving ends as to altruistic ones. It may be equally useful to link moral creativity to opportunity, essentially locating it in a sociopolitical space as well as in the individual.

III. THE DEVELOPMENT OF MORAL CREATIVITY

Every society has some set of moral expectations, a code of conduct that is supposed to remain inviolate regardless of the vicissitudes of social existence. We tend to look at these codes as ideals, or eternal "oughts" as opposed to presently possible "cans." This logical relation between "ought" and "can" was discussed at length by Fritz Heider in his seminal work, *The Psychology of Interpersonal Relations*. But Heider does not take up the question of moral creativity.

It should be obvious that creative exploration of both the desirable and the possible, and especially the zone in which they overlap, is appropriate in order to decide one's responsibilities. But before we can do something, we must understand what needs to be done. By this logic, an individual's moral potential is dependent on his or her ability to recognize the rules of his or her society and to reason out a relation to these rules in context. This has led to a tendency to treat the development of moral reasoning as if it would account for the whole of human moral behavior. The development of moral reasoning, however, is a necessary but insufficient cause for moral creativity—for the simple reason that even a child knows that those who reason best do not always reason fairly or kindly or for the good of anyone else. Although we may understand the most moral solution to a dilemma, we may be unable to rise to the challenge of acting upon that knowledge.

Moral creativity exceeds the mere understanding of a moral problem; it requires a sustained effort that changes as it is challenged. In this sense, moral creativity is developmental. Ann Colby and William Damon examined the lives of a number of moral exemplars looking for developmental patterns and found three such patterns: maintenance of moral commitment over long periods of time in the face of hardship, constant recreation of situations which stimulate and enlarge the exemplar's moral concerns, and interpersonal interactions which subject the exemplar's ideas to tests of challenge and criticism. These patterns have much in common with the development of both creativity and morality.

While moral creativity may develop over the lifespan, it may occur spontaneously when an individual is presented with an unprecedented moral opportunity. When one is on the verge of moving from experience to action, one encounters a set of choices. Sometimes these choices are only implicit or unconscious—and it takes conflict or other means to make the choice psychologically available. Only then does potential

moral action become a choice, and a human being free to choose. In the literature of moral exemplars—for example, rescuers in the Holocaust—one frequently hears the words, "I had no choice. It was just something I had to do." But the fact is that such behavior is rare. It involves risks which most people will never take. There is a dimension of resistance and voluntary agency—whether psychological or political or otherwise—which characterizes moral creativity. It is in this sense that Paolo Freire's work examines education as a developmental process of moral creativity: a dialectical process which stimulates inner transformation from social perspectives, the goal of which is freedom and dignity.

Moral creativity today relies on the contemporary understanding of morality as an astonishingly rich and varied domain, seen not as a fixed code but as a way of thinking which can accommodate other ways. It is not relative, but holistic. An act of moral creativity may transgress conventional boundaries; it shares with creativity the power of innovation to change the moral landscape as we know it.

IV. MORE THAN ONE MORAL SYSTEM

The modern scientific study of moral thought can be said to have begun with Piaget's celebrated work, *The Moral Judgment of the Child* (1932). Piaget was well acquainted with Freudian theory. One of its main tenets was the idea that morality is imposed upon the child by parental pressures and constraints; the child is thought of as uncivilized, requiring to be tamed if he or she is to live in society. Piaget's very different view takes issue with Freud, offering instead a developmental-rationalist view of the growing child, as against Freud's instinctualist-animalist conception. The child has a capacity for moral judgment, which may emerge without instruction, like the capacity to understand the principle of conservation—that water poured from a tall, narrow container into a short, wide one retains the same quantity.

The name most associated with the study of moral reasoning in our time is that of Lawrence Kohlberg. Like Piaget, Kohlberg focused on children's moral judgment and on the development of moral thought from childhood to adolescence. As empirical scientists, both used similar techniques: present the child with an anecdote that contains a moral dilemma, and then interview the child as to his or her thinking about how to cope with the problem. (Piaget also studied children's games to explore the relation between the normative and the ethical.) Kohlberg did much to elaborate and codify the rationalist-cognitivist-developmental views of morality that he shared with Piaget, positing a developmental trajectory that moves in steps of increasing perspective-taking from egocentric and authoritarian motives for morality to altruism and universal principles like justice and the sanctity of life. Kohlberg eventually went beyond Piaget in proposing two later stages of mature moral development.

This identification of morality with renunciation of all self-interest ultimately goes too far. Stages 5 and 6 of Kohlberg's moral development scale describe a morality in which individuals are able to take an extreme opposite perspective, and finally, an entirely universalized perspective. So few individuals achieved this end of the spectrum that researchers stopped testing for it in the usual course of their work. Historians may question whether those acting on the broadest, most universalized ideas of justice might not sometimes perpetuate the most pervasive harm.

It is widely agreed that the Piaget–Kohlberg tradition made justice the central concern. Moreover, justice was defined as the defense of the individual's rights. The famous dilemma of Hans, whose wife needs expensive medicine or she will die, is seen as a challenge to property rights, since advanced placement on the test is achieved if the child says that in such circumstances it may be morally permissible to steal. Critics of Kohlberg point out that individual rights, central to the very structure of the problem, vary with the kinds of lives individuals actually live in society. Those with less property—or fewer choices—may be oriented to very different values. Kohlberg's most significant critic, Carol Gilligan, challenged the preoccupation with autonomy and equality as male, and emphasized an alternative moral outlook based on attachment and care, which was more characteristically female. Justice and caring have come to be seen as balancing the scale of moral behavior, both necessary but neither sufficient.

Other moral orientations have emerged. Donald Campbell, following Solomon Asch, describes a truth morality. This only seems to conflict with more relativistic notions; after all, every individual's or group's psychological sense of truth may indeed function as the highest good to which a moral framework can be oriented. Rachel Carson advocated planetary morality, an extension of the codes governing human relationships to our relations with all species and the environment.

Of late, an evolutionary model of psychology has come into fashion, the principal moral value being not altruism but Darwinian species survival. In this scheme, mothers protect their offspring to give the greatest reproductive opportunity to their own genes, and may kill their offspring when one too ill unbalances the resources necessary for the many. Some of E. O. Wilson's work may offer intriguing theoretical insights into what might be a biological basis for morality. But this position can become reductionist in the extreme—leading to the claim that all human functions are subordinate to what sociobiologist Richard Dawkins has called "the selfish gene." Such an abstract conception may indeed be the inheritor of Kohlberg's ultimate stages of morality—morality so abstract as to be unfeeling. Kohlberg's theories have been productively challenged, revised, and reinvented by others who have shown that we cannot morally dispense with another's understanding of morality, and that the most functional account of morality is the most inclusive.

V. THE ETHICS OF CARE

In 1982, 50 years after Piaget's work on moral judgment, Carol Gilligan brought out her seminal work *In a Different Voice: Psychological Theory and Women's Development*. A critical idea that emerged from her work was that concern for the other is the primary moral compass point among women, as opposed to concern for fairness and equality among men. While others later demonstrated that both women and men are able to use both justice and caring orientations, Gilligan's main points stand: first, that there are multiple routes to moral judgment, and, second, that emotion is critical to the connection between moral judgment and moral action. This perspective has transformed our thinking about morality. Kohlberg's cohorts were entirely composed of white, middle-class males; no longer could testing done on any one group—particularly the dominant one—presume to speak for human nature.

More than a system of morality based on a different imperative, Gilligan's work has emerged as the basis for an understanding of morality founded on the psychological primacy of relationship. As we construct ourselves out of many different images of others, we construct morality in relation to others. If this orientation poses unanswerable questions as to the nature of the "highest good," it also offers perforce a basis for creativity. Relationships call on us to create moral frames, which nurture their best possibilities. Thus creativity and qualities of humanness—character, love, and integrity—ideally develop together. This conception has affinities with developmental schemata like Erikson's, in which the changing life tasks of the maturing human being evoke wisdom and an enlightened participation in community. However, moral creativity resists accommodation to any stage theory. Examples such as Mathieu Froment-Savoie, a gifted 11-year-old boy who marshaled his imagination to fight cancer, attest to the unpredictable leaps that moral creativity can take in the lifespan. Froment-Savoie was a world-class cellist, a protégé of Yoyo Ma, when he was stricken with cancer. Forced to give up the cello, he wrote his autobiography, which is a creative object lesson in how to cope with pain and death with courage and honesty. Oskar Schindler is noted for his late and unprecedented telescoping of moral development. Lawrence Blum has written a recent and compelling analysis of Schindler's motives for rescuing over a thousand Jews from the Nazis. Blum asserts that Schindler could not have been so effectively and imaginatively moral if he had not first been so prodigiously amoral.

If morality is viewed as a systematic orientation, most of these systems have some features to recommend them. However, all fail if they neglect or exclude the others. Rather than engaging in an all-or-nothing debate on the relative merits of different moralities, the best solution may be to consider them as different facets of a complex whole.

VI. THE AESTHETIC DIMENSION

Creativity has an aesthetic dimension—a preference or concern for unity, wholeness, and elegance. It is integrative, recombining and linking ideas across conventional boundaries. When this aesthetic feel is ex-amined in conjunction with morality, an entire tradition emerges of the artist as moral agent in society. In this sense, much art has been and continues to be created with moral intentions and spiritual aspirations. In this century, artists such as those of the Bauhaus movement have been in the social and political avant-garde, calling attention to moral problems of their time. It is not possible in a short article to do more than skim the surface of this tradition.

The relation of the arts to moral creativity deserves examination. There are a number of ways in which artistic creativity could be important to moral creativity. For instance, the ability of artists to function on more than one level of reality is an asset in imagining a better world while avoiding the ethereality of much utopian thinking. In addition, art speaks through feeling and there can be no such thing as an unfeeling morality— that would be fascism.

The old idea of education as a moral art raises new possibilities for nurturing moral sensitivity while empowering creativity. Technology will increasingly demand that we be more fluent in visual and other metaphorical systems. The arts stand to play a more important role in education. If the link between the aesthetic and ethical is not neglected, this may become a form of moral education that breeds moral creativity. This has been as yet little explored, but the increasing presence of artists in schools and community projects might generate original perspectives and pedagogies which use the power of self-expression to link the resources of art and conscience.

VII. EXTRAORDINARY MORAL RESPONSIBILITY

In 1983, prompted by the vision of society in crisis, Howard E. Gruber and Helen Haste brought together at Yale an eminent group of researchers in cognition and development in a conference on Research Needs in the Study of Extraordinary Responsibility sponsored by the Social Science Research Council. Its purpose was to ignite research into the kind of creativity humanity needs to survive in the postnuclear, post-Holocaust age. Many of the most interesting efforts to link creativity to responsibility have come out of ideas propagated by participants in this conference. Gruber's description of extraordinary moral responsibility encapsulates what moral creativity might mean.

> In summary, a person who displays extraordinary responsibility has high levels of moral reasoning, concern for issues of great import, strong moral passion and courage, and a propensity to translate thought and feeling into effective action. This is a person who takes moral initiatives, rather than only responding to situations that are thrust upon her or him. (Gruber, 1985)

In looking at moral creativity as active and evolving, an attitude toward an undertaking, the concept of extraordinary moral responsibility is akin to Gruber's approach to other creative work, and gives insight into how creativity in one area can be harnessed to moral purposefulness. A special issue of the *Creativity Research Journal* (in 1993) dedicated to moral creativity is one example of the growth of interest in this area.

Howard Gardner, Mihaly Csikszentmihalyi, and William Damon have recently joined in work they call "Humane Creativity," which calls upon those with the greatest gifts of talent and success to take greater care and responsibility for how their gifts are used. It is a short but decisive step from this responsibility to the active, creative assault on humanity's most overwhelming problems.

A short step, and a leap of faith. Both creativity and morality share a subtext of the ability to believe in something different and better—a kind of faith. Faith and spirituality have emerged as subjects of recent psychological research. Optimism, hope, courage, and altruism—attributes of moral character—are increasingly studied for therapeutic and educational insight. Such insight could spark innovation and creativity in the ways we currently approach many seemingly hopeless human problems.

In speaking about moral creativity it is particularly important to stress that just as there is a creativity of everyday life, there is a moral creativity of everyday life. There are always opportunities for individuals to innovate compassionately in their daily routine.

The real and present threats to our fragile planet and species increase the urgency of moral restraint and moral purposefulness. As a single idea, moral creativity bridges the abyss between lonely genius and social responsibility—between moral reasoning and moral action.

Bibliography

Colby, A., & Damon, W. (1992). *Some do care. Contemporary lives of moral commitment.* New York: Free Press.

Dawkins, R. (1976). *The selfish gene.* Oxford: Oxford University Press.

Gilligan, C. (1982). *In a different voice.* Cambridge: Harvard University Press.

Gruber, H. E. (1989). Creativity and human survival. In D. Wallace & H. E. Gruber (Eds.), *Creative people at work.* New York: Oxford University Press.

Gruber, H. E. (1993). Ought implies can. *Creativity Research Journal, 6*(1,2).

Kohlberg, L. (1971). Stages of moral development as a basis for moral education. In C. M. Beck, B. S. Crittenden, & E. V. Sullivan (Eds.), *Moral education: Interdisciplinary approaches.* New York: Newman Press.

Noddings, N. (1984). *Caring. A feminist approach to ethics and moral education.* Berkeley: University of California Press.

Siler, T. (1998). *Think like a genius.* New York: Bantam Books.

Creatology

István Magyari-Beck

Budapest University of Economic Sciences

Creative Process Any kind of problem solving on any level of a culture or civilization which contributes to the elimination of crises situations.

Creative Product The result of the creative process which helps with the survival of social entities on different levels of a culture and/or civilization.

Creativity as an Ability All sorts of capacities on any level of a culture and/or civilization which make possible successful creative processes.

Creatology A term coined for a new cross-disciplinary science of creativity, emphasizing the fact that creativity cannot be reduced to psychological phenomena.

Creatology Matrix A frame of reference for ordering the main subtopics of the creativity question. The creatology matrix can also serve both as the registration of the results of investigations into creativity and as a general project for further research.

CREATOLOGY is a term for a new cross-disciplinary science of creativity. This article gives a summary of the creatological way of thinking.

I. THE GENERAL CONCEPT OF CREATOLOGY

A. What Is Creativity?

Creativity as an English word originally meant a special ability of an individual to create something new, useful, and valuable which is or will be accepted by the members of a certain culture and/or civilization, be it regional or organizational. However, after a considerable period of scientific development related to creativity, today the experts of this field mean by this term a large domain of factors and results connected with the aforementioned ability at different levels of human society. Thus, the word creativity has already lost its previous, merely linguistic meaning and has gradually acquired a position of a new scientific term which should be defined in a new and much larger way within its own scientific frame of reference. [*See* DEFINITIONS OF CREATIVITY.]

B. The Main Tasks of Creativity Scholars

One of the most important tasks of creativity scholars is to introduce and build a large but detailed frame of reference for the collection of data and theories of creativity. In this way, it is possible to prevent an "entropy" of facts and ideas about creativity. It is exactly this task that creatology intends to solve.

Copyright © 1999 by Academic Press
All rights of reproduction in any form reserved.

C. Support of a New Discipline of Creativity from the Field

Outstanding scholars and organizers working in the field of creativity realized the necessity of compiling a new science of creativity. Creativity is cross-disciplinary in nature and of interest to an international community of psychologists, sociologists, historians, managers, economists, artists, educators, and many other specialists. This state of affairs raises the problem of identity for the members of the community in question. Without an encompassing term for entitling this domain and the community of scholars working in this domain, it will be impossible both to solve the identity problem and to organize and finance the field in question as an integral whole. The proposal for this encompassing term is "Creatology."

II. THE CREATOLOGY MATRIX

A. The General Creatology Matrix

The heart of this discipline is the so-called creatology matrix (Table I). This matrix has three terms on its top line, namely, Ability, Process, and Product. These terms also define three columns of the matrix. All the matrix's columns are subdivided horizontally according to the levels at which both Ability, Process, and Products can and have to be investigated. These levels are as follows (from the top to the basics): Cultures, Organizations, Groups, and Persons. Thus, the creatology matrix has 12 squares, pointing at the most crucial questions of the studies in creativity, defined in the already mentioned large way, namely, creative societies; creative organizations; creative teams; creative people;

creative processes at the levels of society, organization, team, and person; creative products of a culture; organizational innovation; the special features of creative results generated by teams; and subjective creation.

B. The Detailed Creatology Matrix

All the squares of the creatology matrix can be subdivided. Here, that subdivision will be presented as this matrix was developed originally. This subdivision reflects the usual way sciences and disciplines are working on their subject matter. At first, any topic or subtopic can be studied in a verbal, qualitative manner. Verbal, qualitative theories are, as a rule, the first results of investigations into all kinds of reality. The next steps in the course of investigations can be either the quantification of data by measuring them, and thus the forming of mathematical models in the domain, or the introduction of a normative approach, which in turn introduces the application of the knowledge already obtained in the field. It is possible to apply both qualitative and quantitative knowledge. It means that the descriptive and normative approaches are as general as the qualitative and quantitative methods. As a result, all the squares of the creatology matrix can have four subsquares: that of qualitative descriptive studies of creativity, that of quantitative descriptive studies of creativity, that of qualitative normative application of the knowledge obtained about creativity, and that of quantitative normative application of the knowledge obtained about creativity. This last approach is in fact also the very general definition of "engineering." However, in the domain of creativity it would be too early to speak of the theories and practices of engineering. Except for some of the main 12 squares of the creatol-

---

TABLE I
Creatology Matrix

Levels	Stages		
	Ability	*Process*	*Product*
Culture	1.1. Creative culture	1.2. History	1.3. Creative product
Organization	2.1. Humanist organization	2.2. The process of innovation	2.3. Innovation
Group	3.1. Team	3.2. Creative techniques	3.3. Complex products
Person	4.1. Creativity as an ability of individual personality	4.2. Problem solving	4.3. Subjective creation

ogy matrix, the subsquares of quantitative normative approaches are for the time being empty. There can be other ways of subdividing the creatology matrix's squares. Moreover, it is not necessary to subdivide all the squares in the same way. Different squares can be subdivided differently. The creatology matrix will then be a flexible matrix.

C. The Starting Point and Directions of Studying Creativity on the Basis of the Creatology Matrix

In this section the problems ordered and raised by this matrix will be discussed. It is advisable to start the study of creativity at the top level of the creatology matrix. The reason for this proposal comes from the lessons of the history of sciences and disciplines: in the realm of very successful natural sciences as, for example, physics and biology, the search for regularities began on the macro level of planets, plants, and animals. The thorough analysis of these entities was only the second step of inquiry. Second, it is also advisable to start the study of creativity with investigations into the right column of products (Table I). The reason for this comes from the lessons of epistemology: the description of visible, consequently well-identifiable outcomes should be the first phase in any type of research, and should be followed by their explanation(s). Turning to the creatology matrix, the research strategy to be followed would begin by investigations into the upper right corner of the matrix and continue in the left and downward direction, approaching the lowest left corner. That is, the measuring of creativity as an ability of individual personality should be based on the studies pursued first in every other square the creatology matrix contains.

III. CREATIVE PRODUCTS

A. Creative Products at the Level of Cultures

1. Creative Products and the Survival of Cultures and/or Civilizations

The two trends just mentioned in Section II.C emphasize the research of creative products at the level of cultures. These creative products serve the survival of the culture and/or civilization in question. It is comparatively easy to observe a kind of historical competition between cultures and/or civilizations. In the long run, those cultures and civilizations that flourish produce more creative products, solving the basic problems of their existence. Some cultures and civilizations weak in creativity try to get the upperhand over other ones using weapons as the ultima ratio regum instead of peaceful means of creativity. However, these societies can usually be successful—if they are successful at all—only in the short term. One example was the war between the Spanish military superpower and the small but highly creative Holland in the 16th and 17th centuries when Holland won. [*See* CREATIVE PRODUCTS.]

2. Simple Results and Creative Products

From the point of view of creatology, there is a remarkable difference between the mere results of arts, sciences, and so on, on the one hand, and the creative products in the same domains on the other. Namely, creative products should meet all the requirements of morality characteristic of those cultures or civilizations for which those products have been created. This thesis introduces the "relativism of creative products" into their theory: what is creative for a certain culture or civilization may not be acceptable for another culture or civilization. Likewise, what is creative for a certain period of a culture and/or civilization may be absolutely rejected in another period in the same culture.

3. Measuring Creative Products in Science: Scientometrics and Creatometrics

More than three decades ago, a new discipline of scientometrics was elaborated. Scientometrics proposed to measure the quality of any results of scientific inquiry by counting the publications and quotations of an author. The representatives of scientometrics supposed that the editorial boards of outstanding international journals and fellow researchers are able to faultlessly evaluate new scientific results. Thus, the only task of a specialist in scientometrics remains to be the counting of the aforementioned indicators: publications and quotations. Unfortunately, the history of sciences does not prove this hypothesis. Most of the really great breakthroughs in the arts and sciences were at first rejected by their contemporary experts and only later accepted, usually by new generations. Consequently, creatologists cannot avoid a direct participation in the process of evaluation of the results of arts, sciences, technology, and so on. Because of these critical considerations it would be advisable to formulate a new subdiscipline of creatometrics for the evaluation of creative products in any domain, including science, so as to replace the not-so-successful directions of thinking rooted in traditional scientometrics.

B. Innovations and Creative Products

Creative products at the level of organizations are called innovations. Creatology classifies at least three sorts of innovations: decline, fashions, and progress. Some innovations can lead to a decline in the civilization. Others can change the situation without deteriorating or developing the conditions. These latter innovations are examples of different fashions. Finally, there are innovations promoting progress. This sort of innovation can be identified as a creative product. Survival and progress do not contradict each other. It is a widely accepted philosophical truth that without progress there cannot be whatever survival of whatever living entity. There were a number of examples of devastating innovations during the decades of socialism in Central and Eastern Europe and Asia.

C. Creative Products at the Group Level

A creative product generated by teams is a situational phenomenon. If a question is such a difficult one that no single person can answer it alone, then forming a team can result in desirable answers to the same question. No other constant characterization of a creative product achieved by teams could be found in the research conducted by the present author.

D. Subjective and Objective Creations

1. From the Subjective Creation to the Objective One

A creative product ripens from the subjective creation to the objective one by the way of its gradual acceptance. This ripening may be a long process. [*See* CONSENSUAL ASSESSMENT.]

2. From Learning to the Objective Creation

There is no necessity for an objective creation to be first a subjective one. A great number of discoveries and inventions are made in one culture and later adapted by other cultures.

3. The Logical Relationship between Subjective and Objective Creations

The set of subjective creations and the set of objective creations can be illustrated by two Venn diagrams partially intersecting each other. The three main subsets of creations are: (a) subjective creations which are not (or are not yet) objective creations, (b) subjective creations which are simultaneously objective creations, and (c) objective creations which have never previously been subjective creations.

E. Creative Products and the Survival of Social Entities

It is possible to demonstrate that creative products make possible the survival of social entities at all levels of society. Creative products save a culture vis-á-vis the challenges of another culture. The United States of America would be unthinkable without the works of William James and John Dewey who founded the pragmatical view by which North America has reached its identity as a culture highly independent of its European roots. Progressive innovations save a firm vis-à-vis the challenges of another firm on the market. Subjective creations save a personality vis-á-vis the challenges of another person or life condition. The only exception to this rule is the creative product reached by a creative team which puts an end to the functioning of this team which came into existence or was organized for—and only for—the solution of that problem. However, there are also many examples of durable teams. The so-called famous Copenhagen Circle which emerged around the personality of the great physicist Niels Bohr before the Second World War was such a durable team, because its members raised new problems to be solved after solving the previously raised ones.

IV. CREATIVE PROCESS

A. History as a Creative Process

1. *Crisis and Beyond*

Creative process at the level of cultures is the elimination of crises, after which—as a rule—new crises appear. This process is called "history." A crisis is defined in creatology as a system of problems launching an attack on the existence of a social entity: at this level, on culture. Many examples of this rule can be found, in economies. The economic policy of the New Deal, introduced by President Franklin D. Roosevelt in the United States, showed that a market economy can improve and maintain the living standards of people in a better way than how economies are improved and maintained in socialist countries. The New Deal thus solved the crisis of market economy vis-á-vis the leftist attack before World War Two.

2. *Creative Process: Stabilization and Destabilization*

There are two sides of crisis elimination. The first one is restoration of social equilibrium. The second one is the overturning of social equilibrium. Overturning calls for new creations. The two main attitudes of people, as far as the creative process is concerned, can be explained on this basis. Some people prefer to pay attention to the first side of the creative process. They are prone to regard the creative process as a kind of social "stabilizer." Other groups of people prefer to pay attention to the second side of the creative process. They are prone to regard the creative process as a kind of social "destabilizer." The support or rejection of the creative process by the members of a culture depends on the value they attribute to social stability, on one hand, and lack of social stability on the other hand.

3. *Sources of Crises*

A crisis can appear and grow from inside and/or from outside of a society. When crises have their sources within a society, that society is likely creative. If crises are the results of interventions from outside, be they military, economic, informational, and so on, then the society is typically less creative. There is no such thing as an absolutely noncreative society.

4. *A Competition between the Number of Solutions and the Number of Problems Created by These Solutions and Their Outcomes*

Hungarian philosopher and graphic artist, Lajos Szabó formulated an attractive maxim to express how solutions of problems raise further problems. He said, "Any problem can be solved at the expense of creating three new ones." The essence of this maxim is that creativity not only builds but can also destroy the culture in which it is flourishing. If the number of problems grows faster than the number of solutions, a culture will collapse.

B. Creative Processes in Organizations

1. *A Formal Flow of Information*

From the creatological point of view, there exist two main conceptions regarding organizational creative processes. One such conception outlined creative processes in organizations as interactions of formally arranged subdivisions. These subdivisions have the following functions: research, development, implementation, production, and sales. Originally, these five functions were put in the form of a one-way line, called a chain of innovation. The linear form of the line did not allow for any feedback mechanism, in the absence of which no one could evaluate innovation. The establishment of the circle of innovation process allowed for sales—to inform the research phase about the success or failure of an innovation. Both the linear and circular forms of innovation suffered from a fault. Namely, both are hierarchies: a chain is a severe hierarchy, whereas a circle is a soft hierarchy. And as research in experimental and social psychology have shown us, complex problems can only be solved in an antiauthoritarian, democratic climate of homogeneous nets of information. Accordingly, the five functions and their organizational departments have been reorganized in theory to make up a so-called total graph, where every function and its department is connected with every other function informationally. The advantages of such a configuration are self-evident: every function and its department can reach every other function and its department directly without using mediators. The time necessary for reaching the same results in this pattern can naturally be much shorter than in the cases of chains or circles.

2. An Informal Flow of Information

To fully utilize a total graph, sociometrical considerations should be introduced to improve the relationships among the departmental members. Sharing a common goal can help all members work together in a more cohesive manner.

3. The Psychological Bias in the Theory of Organizational Creative Processes

There is another conception of organizational creative processes as merely psychological phenomena, having nothing to do with the formal arrangement of organizations. This does not take into consideration the contextual character of creativity, where personality is only a part of the situation, and hence is unacceptable in the creatological point of view.

4. The Psychological Bias in the Practice of Organizational Creative Processes

If a firm offers a sabbatical for employees, so as to give them an opportunity to discover and/or invent something new, valuable, and useful, then it follows that the firm does not regard itself as a place of excellent conditions for either discovering or inventing valuable things. However, as far as research institutes and universities are concerned, they have been established exactly for giving the best conditions for creative work to scholars, scientists, and professors. This is why it is surprising that these organizations are largely utilizing sabbaticals.

C. The Creative Process in Teams

1. The Dominance of Normative Approaches in the Investigations into Group Creative Processes

A great number of creative techniques have been invented and developed, to make better use of one's brainpower. The queen among these techniques is the CPS: (Creative Problem Solving) technique invented by Alex Osborn and Sidney Parnes and developed by the Center for Studies in Creativity in New York.

2. CPS as a Special and Unique Creative Technology

CPS has absorbed most creative techniques worth mentioning—for example, brainstorming, the method of forced relationships, and convergent techniques—and thus has become more than a simple technique: it has become a "creative technology." But from the point of view of scientific and practical aspirations it would be premature for the CPS technique to lay claim on being an encompassing method for the future. Note that using a descriptor in front of the abbreviation "CPS" narrows the overgeneralized meaning of "CPS," to a more specialized technique suitable for unique and valuable features.

3. The Question of Paradigmatic Backgrounds

The sequences of widening and limiting the alternatives of possible advancements six times (mess finding, data finding, problem finding, idea finding, solution finding, and acceptance finding) reflects a variety generation and variety reduction principle. This can be regarded as one of the most special and prominent western cultural paradigms. Variety generation and variety reduction is a model of thinking about domains. This way of reasoning can be found behind Hegelian philosophy, Darwinian biology, Smithian economics, Kuhnian epistemology, and many other western achievements beyond CPS. Thus, CPS is—again from the creatological point of view—a real creation, as it helps with the survival of western culture in a relatively new area of research, namely, creativity.

D. Creative Problem Solving by an Individual Personality

1. European and American Starting Points in the Studies of Creativity

In the next square of the creatology matrix, the subject matter is the creative problem solving of an individual personality. Different European schools that worked on the topic of creative processes of individual personalities were not able to find a common denominator and form a synthesis. For the time being, the only logical way of arranging the wide variety of theories and experimental results obtained by European scholars seems to be the historical one.

2. Creative Problem Solving versus Idea Generation by Individual Personalities

The gap between European and American studies resulted in a concept of the creative process of an individual personality as being mere idea generation. However, creatology returns to the original conception that all kinds of problem solving is creative activity. From the point of view of creatology there is no such thing as routine problem solving, and there is no such thing as creative problem solving that is different from problem solving in general. Any problem solving is creative at least in a subjective sense. Now, what about idea generation? Is it somehow different from problem solving or is it basically the same activity? A creatological way of thinking accepts the Freudian subconscious, and accepts with it the problems hidden from the personality in that subconscious. The greatest idea generators may be the persons whose subconscious is full of problems. A suppressed problem generates a lot of ideas on the one hand, but on the other, it cannot give clues for the evaluation of ideas from its own point of view because of the suppression the givens and the goals of that problem suffers from. The ideas of such a person come and go without finding their places as solutions. A personality is also a process of problem solving, be in conscious or subconscious. An optimal form of this kind of life was described by Mihály Csíkszentmihályi, who coined the term "flow" to give an expression to the optimal life experience. [*See* Personality.]

3. The Principle of Situativeness

The principle of situativeness is important for creatology. Many experiments on problem solving behavior have neglected the content factors which presumably also determine human reasoning. The main concern of experimenters had been formal operations used by the participants, yet the same intellectual effort resulted in different outcomes if applied to different topics. As an example, let us imagine that we have two different societies. In one of them, people are engaged in difficult but unimportant tasks of self-administration. In another society, people are engaged in similarly difficult but meaningful—artistic, scientific, practical,

and so on—tasks which have to do with the maintenance of their culture. Which of these cultures has more chances for survival in the historical competition among cultures? In all likelihood, that one making use of human capital is better: that is, where people are working on meaningful tasks, putting aside tasks of self-administration. If any society is a product of its members then it is reasonable to come up with a new term of a "user-friendly society," meaning that kind of society where people need not work on worthless problems. This idea can serve as an introduction to the next square of the creatology matrix dealing with the notion of a creative society.

V. CREATIVITY AS AN ABILITY

A. Creative Culture

1. A Scientific Project of Comparative Studies in Creative Cultures

To identify the extent to which a society is creative, the number of creative results should be established, be those results artistic, scientific, technical-technological, and so on, by their nature. It is necessary to eliminate the differences in the size of different cultures' populations. This elimination has to be done by the division of the quantity of creative results by the number of a culture's population. To begin with, the creative minimum should be established for all of the possible types and sorts of creation, and only those pieces of art, literature, technical inventions, and so on have to be counted which either reach this minimum standard or are above it.

2. A Classification of Cultures from the Point of View of Their Creativeness

Two different kinds of pieces of information are available after the comparative research proposed is completed. One of them discloses those directions in which different cultures are "talented." Great Britain has become famous for its technical and organizational civilization. Hungary has a great poetry. Certain cultures have reached great achievements in almost all of the branches of spiritual and practical life. France and Germany are two such cultures. Although France has been greater in the realm of fine arts—painting—Germany has given better results in philosophy. Italy has been a leading culture in all branches of art and music, but—apart from the period of the Renaissance—has not had as deep insights into the natural sciences as Great Britain, France, and Germany.

3. The Forces of Social Creativity as an Ability of Cultures

The "engine" of social creativity is the state of crises. A society on the margin of existence and nonexistence, but which is able to escape collapse is creative. Its creativeness is proportional to the danger which threatens its existence, but which is repeatedly eliminated by the creative problem solving activity.

B. Creative Organizations

1. Bureaucratic Organizations

Three types of organizations deserve the most attention from a creatologist. These are bureaucratic, organic, and humanist organizations. A bureaucratic organization is an organization where everything is settled and arranged by strict organizational rules. If an individual, irregular event appears in such an organization a bureaucrat immediately creates a rule to eliminate that event as an irregular and individual one. Since creativity as a product, process, and/or ability is always appearing as an individual, new, and irregular event, a bureaucratic organization by no means can be creative, or it can present only a minimum of creativity.

2. Organic Organizations

An organic organization follows the model of living organisms in that it tries to adapt itself to the environment. An organic organization allows responsibility by more than one employee for the same outcome, and widely allows teamwork and discussion among members of the organization. Given that the main value in an organic organization is its adaptability to outer requirements, this type of organization is much more creative than a bureaucratic one.

3. Humanist Organizations

Both bureaucratic and organic organizations regulate organizational events from the outside, which means that the members of these organizations have rules imposed on them. The ideal type of creative organization differs from bureaucratic and organic organizations by the visible freedom of its members and a conscientious staff. This is also a humanist organization organized by and through the employees' minds. Employees have the freedom to freely contribute and an inner and clear conscience and commitment, which prevents the replacement of freedom by anarchy.

C. Creative Teams

A creative team is a small working group of people established for the solving of individual complex problems. A small group is a group where the members can communicate with each other directly, and without the risk that the direct communication will divide the group into parts. Direct communication intensifies the process of solution finding. Complex problems are the problems which cannot be solved by any one individual alone. Teams are usually the temporary gatherings of specialists having no predetermined hierarchical role structure. Creative teams can be very much evaluated and appreciated by the creatological way of thinking because they are the examples of ancient preformal and, thus, also prebureaucratic forms of social units in which no institutional obstacles hinder the free flow of creative contemplations. [*See* TEAMS.]

D. Creative Personality

The creatological concept of creative personality contributed to the psychological theory of creativity as an ability. A creative personality identifies himself or herself with the basic cultural paradigms of that culture for which he or she creates. For creatologists the set of formal mental operations a creative personality can use to create new, valuable, and useful things is only a secondary consequence of the person's interests in basic cultural paradigms and their application. If somebody is interested in certain achievements he or she will train himself or herself to do his or her job. This view is very close to new conceptions indicating that real-world problem finding is more predictive of creative accomplishments than other measurements. Creativity manifests itself first and foremost in the process of solving real-life problems.

Bibliography

Coleman, S. E. (1993). *A qualitative analysis of the 1991 International Creativity Working Research Meeting.* Buffalo, NY: Center for Studies in Creativity, State University of New York.

Csíkszentmihályi, M. (1990). *Flow, the psychology of optimal experience.* New York: Harper & Row.

Isaksen, S. G., Murdock, M. C., Firestien, R. L., & Treffinger, D. J. (Eds.). (1993). *Understanding and recognizing creativity: The emergence of a discipline.* Norwood, NJ: Ablex.

Isaksen, S. G., Murdock, M. C., Firestien, R. L., & Treffinger, D. J. (Eds.). (1993). *Nurturing and developing creativity: The emergence of a discipline.* Norwood, NJ: Ablex.

Magyari-Beck, I. (1984). Notes on the concepts of "innovation" and "creative product." *Science of Science, 2,* 159–169.

Magyari-Beck, I. (1990). An introduction to the framework of creatology. *The Journal of Creative Behavior, 3,* 151–160.

Magyari-Beck, I. (1997). Should the studies in creativity be a serious scholarly enterprise? A continuation of a friendly discussion with Teresa Amabile and Scott G. Isaksen. *Creativity and Innovation Management, 1,* 60–64.

Okuda, S. M., Runco, M. A., & Berger, D. E. (1991). Creativity and the finding and solving of real-world problems. *Journal of Psychoeducational Assessment, 9,* 45–53.

Rickards, T. (1988). *Creativity at work.* Oxon, UK: Gower.

Crime and Creativity

Richard Brower

Wagner College

Actus Reus An illegal act.

Anomie The weakening of social norms. When anomie exists in a society, a person has few guidelines for socially appropriate behavior.

Beccaria, Cesare An 18th century Italian philosopher who argued that crime could be controlled by punishments only severe enough to counterbalance the pleasure obtained from them; creator of the idea that the punishment should fit the crime.

Consensus View of Crime The belief that the majority of citizens in a society share common ideals and work toward a common good and that crimes are outlawed because they conflict with the rules of the majority and are harmful to society.

Diminished Capacity Mental impairment less severe than insanity.

General Intent The intent to commit the actus reus.

Labeling Theory Society's response to crime defines some people as criminals.

Legal Insanity The inability to distinguish between right and wrong.

Local Legal Culture The attitudes, values, and expectations toward law and legal practice in specific communities.

Paradigm Term popularized by Thomas Kuhn. A paradigm is a collective, socially shared schema and serves to explain phenomena until replaced by a better paradigm.

Pendulum Swing The alternating emphasis on crime control and due process in the history of criminal justice.

Recidivist Repeat offender.

Zeitgeist The tone of the times.

CRIME can be defined as an act or omission violating the law of a community, state, or government and punishable under the law. Attitudes toward crime and its punishment vary widely from epoch to epoch and across cultures. An act considered punishable as a crime in one culture and at a particular point in time might be perceived as praiseworthy in other contexts. Over the years, a number of eminently creative people have been branded criminals, and many have been jailed, including Cervantes, Bertrand Russell, Galileo, Oscar Wilde, O. Henry, Herman Melville, Henry David Thoreau, and Gandhi.

I. TYPES OF CRIMINALITY

Crimes committed by creative individuals can be seen as two general types, (1) creative acts or creative products that are seen as criminal, or (2) lifestyles that are seen by society as criminal. Examples of the first

Copyright © 1999 by Academic Press
All rights of reproduction in any form reserved.

type would include Galileo, Egon Schiele, O. Henry, and Lenny Bruce; these are individuals who were jailed because their product, theory, or performance was considered criminal by society. The second type consists of individuals who are singled out as criminals because of their lifestyle; this would include Oscar Wilde, Cervantes, O. Henry, and Herman Melville. All were jailed because of activities and behaviors not directly related to their creative production. Oscar Wilde, for example, was jailed in Victorian England for homosexuality and O. Henry was jailed for unpaid debts.

The main crimes that are perceived as threatening to the existence of the state have been constant over the years. They are: (1) treason (levying war against the government), (2) sedition (stirring up treason or rebellion), and (3) crimes against public decency (illicit sexual conduct, gambling, unpaid financial debts, and drug offenses).

The metaphor of a wedding cake has often been used for the criminal justice process. A wedding cake is narrow at the top and gets progressively wider toward the bottom. The wedding cake model of criminal justice divides cases into different tiers: (1) a few celebrated cases in the top tier, (2) a greater number of "real crimes" in the second tier, (3) most ordinary felonies in the third tier, and (4) the vast numbers of misdemeanors in the fourth tier. By far, the greatest number of cases fall in this last category.

II. CREATIVITY, CONFORMITY, AND REBELLION

There is a central problem for the creative mind, which is an essential tension between creativity and conformity. Conformity is doing things as others do and have done; on the other hand, creativity is doing things in a novel way as well as breaking out of established patterns. As a result of this break, the creator is frequently seen by society as a rebel, a deviant, and a gadfly. Creativity and deviance are in many ways synonymous. The creator must rebel against, contradict, and negate established ways of thinking. New ideas commonly are met with societal repression. It takes time for culture to accommodate to the unfamiliar. For these reasons, Galileo, Martin Luther King, Jr., Henry David Thoreau, and others have spent time in jail. The

creator is often faced with a society that finds his or her production offensive, monstrous, or crazy. The school of painters known as impressionists were considered mad and their art decadent by many critics when it was first promulgated in the mid-1800s. The American poet Walt Whitman was considered an oddball and madman by many critics when his "Leaves of Grass" was first published. [*See* Conformity; Conventionality; Novelty.]

Henry David Thoreau, Martin Luther King, Jr., Thomas More, Socrates, Galileo, Jesus Christ, and Joan of Arc are all historical figures whose names evoke awe and strong emotions. They have been immortalized in books, movies, and television programs, and some (Jesus Christ, Martin Luther King, Jr.) have official holidays in the United States dedicated to them. One thing they have in common is they were all placed in jail by their cultures for their unorthodox, nonconformist views. Some of these individuals—Socrates, Joan of Arc, Thomas More, and Jesus Christ—were put to death by society. The views of these people were seen by conventional standards to be so dangerous that elimination of the individual was the only way to keep the rebellious thoughts from spreading. There are many other cases of individuals being persecuted for their nonconventional views. Victor Hugo, perhaps France's greatest writer and creator of *Les Miserables* and *The Hunchback of Notre Dame,* was forced to leave his homeland and go into self-exile to avoid being arrested by the French government because of his written attacks on that institution. Emile Zola, in response to writing *J'Accuse,* fled his homeland.

III. EXEMPLARY CASES

Leni Riefenstahl was born on August 22, 1902. She is considered by some to be a war criminal and by others a film genius. Early on, she was a ballet dancer, painter, and actress; she was athletic and attractive. In 1932 she directed her first film and drew the attention of Adolf Hitler. Following his accession to power, he chose her to film a Nazi party rally. Riefenstahl used 36 cameramen and assistants to chronicle the rally in perhaps the most notorious documentary ever filmed, *Triumph of the Will* (1935). The film is a masterwork of montage, editing, camera angle, and chiaroscuro. After

World War II, she was imprisoned by the French for taking an active part in the Nazi propaganda machine and spent almost four years in various prisons and detention camps. She always contended she was merely a filmmaker and had no intentions to support the Nazis. She later tried in vain to resurrect her career, failing several times to actualize filming projects in Africa and elsewhere, and worked instead as a still photographer for European magazines.

The French painter Gustave Courbet (1819–1877) was jailed due to his involvement as both an artist and an art administrator. Courbet served as chairman of the Art Commission under the short-lived commune; he was accused of having dismantled the Colonne Vendome and was imprisoned at Sainte-Pelagie, where he painted some fine still lifes. *The Stonebreakers* (1850) and *Burial at Ornans* (1851) were criticized as being "distasteful."

Edward Dmytryk (1908–present), a Canadian-born film director, made several socially oriented films in Hollywood in the 1940s. His fellow director Sam Wood appeared before the House Committee on Un-American Activities in the 1950s, during the great "red scare" and blacklisting of perceived communists at the time, and gave Dmytryk's name as a possible communist sympathizer. Refusing to appear before the committee, Dmytryk was fired by RKO film studios and went to England to make movies there, unfettered by the severe limitations imposed in Hollywood by both the government and the studio executives. Forced to return to the United States to renew his passport, he was arrested and jailed for six months. Later, he recanted and himself named names before the committee, and subsequently resumed making films in Hollywood.

In 1922 Gandhi (1869–1948) was given a six-year jail sentence, of which he served two years, for his nonviolent practice of mass civil disobedience. He was jailed for launching a civil disobedience movement that was pivotal in undermining the British political hold in India. His calling came to him late. In early adulthood, he went through a crisis in which he was a lawyer at his father's urgings. His efforts at law were disastrous; during one case before the bar, he reports in his autobiography that he got so tongue-tied that when he went to speak, nothing came out but a few incoherent stammerings. Gandhi's doctrine of "passive resistance"

was based on an idea he got from the American writer Henry David Thoreau.

Gandhi reports in his autobiography he had a succession of early experiences that shaped his vision of passive resistance. It was not, though, simply a matter of experiencing certain events, but rather Gandhi mentally operated on his experiences in such a way that it gave form and meaning to his philosophy and his actions.

One of the most famous demonstrations of civil disobedience of all time was the Salt March of 1930, in which Gandhi demanded the abolition of the state tax on the sale of salt. The salt tax, he felt, was especially unethical and immoral since it had its greatest impact on the poorest of the Indian people. In pursuit of its abolishment, Gandhi organized a 165-mile walk to the sea so that people could procure their own salt. This demonstration brought a lot of empathetic international attention to Gandhi's cause and proved an enormous embarrassment to the British government. Subsequently, Gandhi and some of his followers, including Nehru, were jailed.

Emma Goldman (1869–1940) was an American anarchist, editor, and lecturer who devoted her adult life to social causes. She was born to Jewish parents in Kovno, Lithuania, and early demonstrated a rebellious spirit. At 16 years of age, she went to America with her sister, and they settled at Rochester, New York. In 1889 she moved to New York City to join anarchist causes. In 1893 she was jailed for nine months on a charge of inciting to riot after telling a crowd of unemployed workers to steal food and other things if they were in need. In 1906 she founded *Mother Earth,* an anarchist publication which she edited until its suppression in 1917. She was jailed again in New York in 1916 after giving a public speech favoring birth control. When World War I began, Goldman opposed entry into the war, and was again jailed and sentenced to two years. When she completed her jail sentence, she was stripped of her U.S. citizenship and deported to Russia. In Russia, she continued her anarchistic expressions and fled that country, fearful of social oppression and imprisonment. In 1931 she published her autobiography, *Living My Life.* While living and working in Toronto, she died from a stroke at age 70.

In Tahiti, in 1891, the artist Paul Gauguin (1848–1903) was jailed for writing a letter criticizing the local government officials. He was seen as a gadfly by the officials. Gauguin liked women. He set out to find one in Tahiti. At a neighboring village he was offered the hand of a young native named Tehura who was barely in her teens. Gauguin was immediately attracted to her and she to him, and it was decided there would be a week's trial marriage to ensure that the partners were free of disease and willing to freely extend the relationship. After a week, she agreed to remain permanently, and, with Tehura by his side serving as a model, the artist was inspired to work hard and executed many works of his nude wife, including the famous, *The Spirit of the Dead Is Watching.*

Nicolaus Copernicus (1473–1543), the noted Polish astronomer, became a canon in 1497, but did not take holy orders. He spent several years studying and lecturing throughout Europe before settling in Prussia in 1505. His great work, *De Revolutionibus,* outlines his theory that the earth revolves around the sun and was published in the last year of his life. For this reason, it is quite likely that he avoided societal repression, which is not the case for Galileo. Galileo (1564–1642) was placed under house arrest during the last eight years of his life for extending Copernicus's idea that the earth was not the center of the universe. Galileo had a history of confrontation as well as being an independent thinker. As a child he was an annoyance to his teachers; he questioned and contradicted at every turn. His father wanted him to be a physician but the youthful Galileo chose science. As a scientist, he entered Pisa University as a student in 1581. At 19 years of age he observed a swinging lamp in the cathedral at Pisa which led him to investigate the properties of a swinging pendulum. When only 25, he taught math at the University of Pisa. After three years he was forced to resign, in trouble due to his original ideas and forceful expressions. In 1592 he became professor of mathematics at Padua, where he made a telescope and his observations led to a number of discoveries that marked a scientific revolution in astronomy. Galileo discovered the satellites of Jupiter, supporting the planetary theory of Copernicus. In 1592, he moved to Florence as mathematician to the Duke of Tuscany. He observed sun spots and the existence of Saturn. From 1613 to 1615 he was confronted by the Holy Office of the Church and warned not to teach his neo-Copernican doctrine. In 1632, Galileo promulgated his great work,

The Dialogue of Two Systems of the World, and the controversy of planetary motion was reopened. Summoned to Rome by the Church, he recanted and was placed under house arrest in Florence. He spent his remaining years there, becoming blind in 1637 and dying in 1642.

IV. THE ZEITGEIST AND THE INDIVIDUAL

Creativity by its very nature involves nonconformity and a departure from old, traditional ideas. There are mechanisms of society—roles, paradigms, habits, accepted ways of doing things—that resist change. However, a zeitgeist—the entire philosophical and spiritual temperament of a culture—can vary as to the receptivity to new ideas. Einstein, for example, overturned Newtonian physics and was a hero; Galileo, on the other hand, overturned the then-conventional view that the earth was the center of the universe and was condemned, detained, and forced to recant.

Certainly, many creators were immediately recognized by their contemporaries, such as William Shakespeare, Charles Dickens, Albert Einstein, and Walt Disney. On the other hand, some creators encountered enormous resistance to their ideas, such as Courbet, Egon Schiele, Walt Whitman, Charles Darwin, and Semmelweis. In the case of Semmelweis, it might be said that today's rebellion can become tomorrow's conformity, In 1847, Inaz Semmelweis (1818–1865), a Hungarian physician, got the idea that patients were contracting puerperal fever due to the preexamination procedure of the doctors. The disease, he reasoned, was being carried to the patients on the hands of the medical staff, and he devised a procedure in which the hospital personnel washed their hands immediately before the examination with a solution of chlorinated lime. Unfortunately, his ideas were not well received. He embarked on a crusade to have his procedure accepted, and in a great part due to the public ridicule and resistance that his idea received he had a mental breakdown and was assigned to an asylum in 1865. Some time later, Pasteur followed up with Semmelweis's discovery, and, partly because people were more willing to accept the idea and partly because Pasteur was a better salesperson than Semmelweis, the notion of washing hands in chlorinated lime before medical examinations found wide acceptance.

How the perceptions of zeitgeists vary regarding deviance can be seen by comparing Lewis Carroll (1832–1898) and Egon Schiele (1890–1918). Both men used nude, underaged girls as models; Carroll photographed them and Schiele painted them. However, Schiele was jailed for lewdness and Carroll was not. Carroll's zeitgeist was 19th century and pre-Freudian; people did not see sexual implications in his conduct. Schiele's zeitgeist, on the other hand, was 20th century and post-Freudian; there was a heightened sensitivity to the sexuality of children and a changed attitude about a child as a sexual cathexis for an adult. Whether a given act is perceived as deviant, and leads to societal repression, depends in part on the nature of the act within the societal framework or zeitgeist, and in part on what society does about it. There is another issue to consider. Even when an individual is persecuted by society, often there is a fence that divides supporters from detractors. Freud and Darwin, for example, were condemned by the religious community but staunchly supported by some members of the scientific community to which they belonged. A further dichotomy can be made. For some individuals, part of their total work might be accepted while another part is rejected; the sculptor Epstein provides an example of this type of division.

One of the most repressive zeitgeists to be found historically is the society headed by the Nazis in Germany in the 1930s and 1940s. Many works of art, including paintings and musical compositions, were banned. The Nazi government sponsored art shows that displayed "decadent" art (the artist/teacher Paul Klee was included). Many famous people, including Albert Einstein and the composer Richard Strauss, fled Germany to avoid persecution. In fact, German scientists who fled Germany played a pivotal role in developing military technology that helped win World War II for the United States and its allies.

V. CRIME, CREATIVITY, AND PARADIGMS

Thomas Kuhn introduced the idea of a paradigm shift. Paradigms are patterned knowledge bases that are culturally shared to explain and give meaning to phenomena. Kuhn suggested that societies have paradigms to explain experiences. A paradigm will exist, according to Kuhn, until a better one comes along. In pre-Copernican days, for example, people believed that the earth was the center of the universe. Copernicus and Galileo suggested a different paradigm in which the earth circled the sun. The new paradigm was not warmly received by everyone, since it contradicted cherished beliefs. Extending Kuhn's idea of paradigm, I introduce a distinction between "hard" paradigms and "loose" paradigms. A hard paradigm is one in which cherished beliefs are protected and maintained for a number of reasons, including emotional, philosophical, and personal. On the other hand, a "loose" paradigm has gaps, questions, and omissions for which people beg for answers; it welcomes a new perspective. Galileo stepped into and confronted a "hard" paradigm; people who supported the prevailing zeitgeist that existed prior to Galileo's theory were not interested nor motivated to seek or explore new explanations. Galileo was imprisoned. Einstein introduced his theory of relativity to a zeitgeist that welcomed a fresh, novel, organized theory that explained the currently unexplainable. Einstein was a hero in the United States. He is a cultural icon. His face can be seen on t-shirts as well as innumerable posters. [*See* PARADIGM SHIFTS.]

VI. THE PSYCHOLOGY OF REBELLION

By rebellion, the individual both affirms his own uniqueness and establishes a principled connection with all of humanity. It is, for example, an appropriate and normal part of a child's development to rebel. There are at least two important phases of developmental rebellion that all or most people negotiate: (1) the "terrible twos" and (2) adolescence. Around two years of age, it is normal for the child to say "no" to a host of demands from its caregivers. This negativism allows the child the opportunity to test the waters of autonomy. Adolescence, in addition, is notorious as a period of rebellion, and quite likely is a crucial epoch for the adolescent to establish an identity separate from the identities of others. Negativism as affirmation is part of the normal development of the self.

Creativity commonly involves two struggles: the struggle to have one's ideas accepted and the intra-psychic struggle for order. Creativity is an inner struggle to rebel against chaos, apathy, and death. All rebellion, ultimately, is a rebellion of the self.

We all have daily instances where deviance not only confirms our identities but also is an antidote for alienation in the face of oppression and impersonal conformity. Some individuals, however, for example, Gandhi and Galileo, go considerably beyond a daily, commonplace nonconformity.

It seems self-evident that there are times when conformity is a good and useful thing. For example, it is important for automobile drivers to conform to the rules of driving, otherwise there would be total chaos on our roads; individualized patterns of driving would be very dangerous, and it would be impossible to predict what any given driver would do. On the other hand, the conformity of blindly sending people to their deaths by execution during Hitler's regime was a bad type of conformity.

Probably the single most prevailing symptom of ineffective rebellion is the individual's unwillingness to understand or pay the price of the rebellion. Effective rebels are fully aware of the consequences of their decisions and actions. Benedict Arnold presents an example of ineffective rebellion. In 1777 Congress passed over him and appointed five generals for the army. He was upset about this injustice, and General George Washington wrote that he intended to correct the unfair decision. In spite of Washington's support, Arnold was not promoted. Later, in 1778, he was promoted to a command in Philadelphia, but soon became involved in arguments with the local authorities, and was court-martialed. The court-martial decided that he be reprimanded by his commander, who was Washington. Washington reluctantly executed the request, and assured Arnold that he had his support. In 1780, Arnold was given a command at West Point, and apparently his bitterness resulted in his immediate plotting to surrender West Point to the British. The rest is history.

The plot was uncovered, the British gave him refuge, and his name became associated forever with backstabbing treachery. He died in obscurity, despised by both Americans and British alike, his name forever linked with heinous deception.

The philosopher Kalhil Gibran has said that "tolerance is strength." Societies need not only to recognize their creative individuals but additionally need to afford a supportive climate that allows for a variety of perspectives. A social tapestry that is composed of a narrow, dichotomous range of values—for example, Nazi Germany—is aesthetically, emotionally, and philosophically empty, and lacks the internal integrity and energy for its own survival. Variety is strength, as Darwin well knew.

It is not only a need to change that which currently exists but especially a love of life that motivates the creator to seek change. Love and the will to transform that which is loved are interconnected aspects of the creative process. Paul Klee noted that the creative life is one that finds delight in the presence of the seemingly most mundane events. Extraordinary creativity commonly requires extraordinary courage to pursue a vision in the face of criticism, oppression, and the recoil of the emotional investment society has to continue what is, even though what is may no longer work or is not justifiable for ethical and moral reasons.

Bibliography

Brower, R. (1994). *Paths of eminence*. New York: Whittier.

Gruber, H. E. (1989a). The evolving systems approach to creative work. In D. B. Wallace & H. E. Gruber (Eds.), *Creative people at work*. New York: Oxford University Press.

Gruber, H. E. (1989b). Creativity and human survival. In D. B. Wallace & H. E. Gruber (Eds.), *Creative people at work*. New York: Oxford University Press.

Henri, R. (1923). *The art spirit*. Philadelphia: Lippincott.

Walker, S. (1993). *Taming the system*. New York: Oxford.

Walker, S. (1994). *Sense and nonsense about crime and drugs*. Belmont, CA: Wadsworth.

Critical Thinking

Mark A. Runco

California State University, Fullerton

Convergent Thinking Whereas divergent thinking allows the individual to find numerous and original ideas, convergent thinking allows the individual to find the one correct or conventional idea.

Learning Advantages of Creativity The idea that a creative thinker can adapt well and, if interested in the subject matter, will use his or her skills and do well in school.

Valuation This process is selective rather than divergent, but not critical, nor evaluative. The focus of valuation can be originality. When it is, ideas are selected not because they are correct or conventional, but because they are original.

Creative thinking is typically characterized as free, flexible, open, and divergent. Most contemporary models of the creative process do, however, acknowledge the role of very different (e.g., critical and convergent) processes. This article reviews the role played by convergent and **CRITICAL THINKING** *in creative problem solving. It examines various kinds of critical and convergent processes (e.g., evaluative and valuative), compares their value in the educational setting and in brainstorming, and briefly reviews the research showing connections between critical and creative processes.*

I. BACKGROUND

A pendulum metaphor can often describe what happens in the sciences. Psychology in the United States, for example, was once behavioristic; only observable behavior was seriously considered appropriate for "scientific" studies. The pendulum began swinging back in the 1950s and especially the 1960s, and covert processes and subjective subjects have since often been studied. Cognitive psychology is represented at every large university, and most small ones.

The pendulum metaphor can also describe what has happened within the studies of creativity. In fact, the initial position was that the IQ was at first highly respected but then widely criticized. Creativity became a more attractive option as IQ tests became more questionable. There were of course other factors contributing to the attractiveness of creativity as a subject matter. Sputnik, for instance, suggested that the United States was falling behind technologically in the late 1950s—and perhaps also falling behind educationally as well.

Copyright © 1999 by Academic Press
All rights of reproduction in any form reserved.

Within the young field of creative studies, divergent thinking was once widely embraced. Tests of divergent thinking offered an alternative to tests of the IQ, and the tests elicited ideas that were often clearly original. The divergent thinking model made a good deal of sense and was theoretically sound. The pendulum started to swing, however, when the limitations of these tests were uncovered. At first, performances on divergent thinking tests were taken as indicators of actual creativity. This is an exaggeration; they measure ideational skills, including originality, but not creativity per se. As one researcher described the problem, divergent thinking tests, designed to predict creative performances, were misinterpreted as criteria rather than predictors.

Divergent thinking tests provide originality scores, and originality is critical for creativity. Divergent thinking tests do not provide creativity scores. Nor does a score from a divergent thinking test—even a high score—guarantee creative performance in the natural environment. Much more is needed to predict actual creative performance. Although this was difficult to see when the enthusiasm for divergent thinking was at its peak, now it is clear that creative work often requires critical and convergent thinking as well as divergent thinking. [*See* DIVERGENT THINKING.]

II. VARIETIES OF CRITICAL THINKING

Critical thinking can take many forms. For this reason there are diverse theories of the relationship between critical thinking and creative processes.

The most literal kind of critical thinking is literally critical: it is analytical and of special value when problems or errors need to be identified. In the edited volume, *Critical Creative Processes,* Michael Mumford and colleagues recently suggested that a naturalistic tradition is apparent in the social sciences, and it posits that

> ideas must be carefully evaluated to establish their merits and potential flaws. This tradition is alive and well in the critical-thinking literature. Investigators in this area stress the need to evaluate ideas and arguments in terms of their strengths and weaknesses and in light of our biases as human beings. . . . In this

sense, critical thinking represents the antithesis of creative thought. In fact, it is commonly assumed that critical thinking may inhibit creative thought, contributing to the production of useful, new ideas only in the later stages of the creative process, where we must evaluate the merits of a new idea.

Indeed, one way to conceptualize the relationship of critical and convergent thought with divergent thought requires a sequence or stage model. These are quite common. Usually the assumption is that creative thinking requires that a person first generate options using divergent thinking skills and then select the best idea or ideas from that set of options using critical thinking skills.

The selection of the best, correct, or conventional idea or answer involves convergent thinking. Convergent processes move from data, clues, or parts of the problem to a specific idea. They are distinct from divergent processes in that usually convergent processes lead to one idea, rather than a large number, and in that they focus on correct or conventional rather than original ideas. Convergent thinking may differ from more literal critical thinking because it does not connote criticism. Both critical thinking and convergent thinking can inhibit creative thought, but as the stage models predict, some time one or both may be necessary for creative thought.

III. EDUCATIONAL ADVANTAGES OF CRITICAL THINKING

There are at least three reasons why critical and convergent thinking have an advantage over divergent thinking in educational settings. One is that work in groups can require conformity. Everyone in the group may need to work on the same information, which implies a convergence. Additionally, convergent thinking tasks have correct answers, and thus they can be scored in an objective fashion. This makes grading easier and accountability is ensured. A third reason is that it is easier to think critically—critical thinking may be the preferred mode of thought, at least in the United States. The individual expends less effort when evaluating ideas that others have generated than when generating the ideas for him- or herself.

To the degree that criticism inhibits divergent thinking, it poses problems for enhancing the creativity of students. What is needed is recognition that convergent thinking works with divergent thinking, and that both are necessary.

IV. CRITICAL PROCESSES IN BRAINSTORMING

Brainstorming is a common group problem solving technique. Its assumptions parallel those of the stage theories mentioned above. In particular, brainstorming assumes that critical thinking can and should be postponed. Just as was the case in the stage models, brainstorming assumes that an evaluation stage is best as the final stage of creative problem solving. Creative thinking is protected from evaluation until all ideas have been put on the table. Participants are asked to generate as many ideas as they can, regardless of the quality of the ideas, and to postpone criticism. The assumption is that critical processes can be kept distinct from divergent processes. [*See* BRAINSTORMING.]

This is not reasonable. First, it may not be possible to keep the two separate, and further it may not even be desirable to do so. In fact, it may be that evaluations should be practiced beforehand and then utilized during brainstorming.

It is likely that there is some recursion among the stages of the creative process. Ideas may be generated early on, but they are probably evaluated as they are formed and as they rise to consciousness. Without some evaluation, at least on the personal level, ideas would be randomly generated.

Recursion among stages would allow the individual to evaluate ideas, and then attempt to implement or verify them, and perhaps go back and generate more ideas. Recursion allows interaction among stages of the process and makes the stage model more realistic.

V. VALUATION VERSUS EVALUATION

There is a kind of evaluation that is distinct from convergent and critical processes. It can also be distinguished from divergent processes, but those divergent processes probably benefit when they utilize these special skills. They are selective rather than divergent, but not critical and not evaluative. They are instead "valuative." The focus of valuation can be originality. When it is, ideas are selected not because they are correct or conventional, but instead because they are original. Instead of focusing on what is wrong with the options, valuation allows the individual to focus on what is useful in ideas, even if those ideas are varied and unusual.

VI. RESEARCH ON VALUATION AND CREATIVITY

There are different definitions and conceptions of critical thinking, and various definitions of creative thinking. The range of relationships that may exist between critical and creative processes is, however, even larger than this may suggest. This is because any one definition of either critical or creative thinking may be operationalized in several ways. Hence, even if the focus is on critical processes, defined as analytical and critical in a literal sense, there are still several assessment options. And each may suggest somewhat different relationships with creative thinking.

Tests of traditional intelligence typically emphasize convergent thinking. When scores from these tests are correlated with various indexes of creative thinking, a threshold may be suggested. This threshold indicates that a minimal level of traditional intelligence is necessary for creative ideation. Above that threshold the individual may or may not be creative. This is because intelligence, though necessary, is not sufficient for creative ideation. Below the threshold everyone is relatively uncreative. They lack basic information processing skills. [*See* INTELLIGENCE.]

A second line of work suggests that creative thinking supports critical thinking. A few educational theorists have, for instance, written about the "learning advantages of creativity." The idea is that a creative thinker can adapt well and, if interested in the subject matter, will use his or her skills and do well in school.

The claim that valuative processes are distinct from critical and creative processes was supported in recent empirical work. This line of research is the most compatible with the notion of critical and creative processes working together.

VII. CONCLUSIONS

It may be best to conceptualize critical processes along a continuum. Convergent processes may be the most general label, with evaluative and valuative processes distinct from one another but both subsumed under convergent thinking. The recognition of valuative processes which appreciate originality makes the recursion among stages that much easier. It also makes the stage model less reductionistic and thus more realistic.

Bibliography

Runco, M. A. (Ed.). (In press). *Critical creative processes.* Cresskill, NJ: Hampton Press.

Cross-Cultural Differences

M. K. Raina

National Council of Educational Research and Training, New Delhi, India

Apollonian and Dionysian Values The Apollonian genius represents the principle of composure and the Dionysian genius represents the principle of storm.

Brahma, Vishnu, and Mahaeswara Siva, also known as Mahesh or Mahaeswara, one of the major gods of the later Hindu Pantheon, forms with Brahma (the highest self, creator of the universe) and Vishnu (personal god of love and mercy) the great triad of Hindu deities. Siva is the lord of the dance, *Nataraja* "dance-king," who executes the cosmic dances that typify the ordered movement of the universe.

Brahminic Values Values followed by members of the highest order of caste.

Contricipation A term coined by Morris I. Stein that relates to appreciation and support of the creativity of others. Everyone contributes to or appreciates the creative process; *contributors* and *appreciators* need each other.

Creativogenic Society A term coined by Silvano Arieti that refers to a society based on fair and just laws, providing the best possible psychological, sociocultural, and economic conditions for all citizens. Arieti has listed nine factors that make a society creativogenic.

Sahrdaya "Sharing the heart"; one who through education and sensibility is a proper connoisseur of creativity; the critical audience.

Tao In its operation, Tao is characterized by *wu-wei* (literally, "no action"), which really means taking no unnatural action. It means spontaneity, noninterference, letting things take their own course. Those who follow this natural way will abide with the one, the eternal, and the whole and will achieve a life of peace, harmony, and enlightenment.

Creativity can be conceptualized as a process of perceiving new relationships and new challenges, coping with changing situations, and expressing one's unique per-

Copyright © 1999 by Academic Press
All rights of reproduction in any form reserved.

ceptions and responses whether through the symbolism of art, through meaningful and appropriate social action, or through widening the knowledge base so that answers to individual and societal problems can become available. **CROSS-CULTURAL** *creativity is found in any or all of these human endeavors. It makes its solid contribution to the maturity, delight, and well-being of man. Underlying this process is a deep concern on the part of the creative individual as to how to interact with his or her environment—natural, cultural, and sociopolitical.*

I. INTRODUCTION

Creativity, it is maintained, is an original transaction between an organism and its environment, and for most human beings the environment is the culture providing the matrix and the content for creativity; indeed, it is the context of all creative behavior. Culture fosters creativity to the extent that it provides an individual with the opportunity to experience the many facets of creativity and define appropriate outlets for creative expression. Adopting the interactionist position, May, in 1959, argued against localizing creativity as a subjective phenomenon and studying it in terms simply of what goes in a person, because it is a process interrelating the person and the person's world.

There exists a cultural and national dimension to both the concept and the phenomenon of creativeness that affect creative process and its end result. In 1975 Getzels highlighted the fact that over and above the biological, psychological, societal, and group contexts of behavior is a cultural context composed of characteristic values. He elaborated:

> Yet clearly there are patterns of values that distinguish one people from another, or the same people in one era or another. For example, different cultures have been said to reflect *Apollonian* or *Dionysian* values. Distinctions have been made between peoples or periods dominated by a pattern of values composed of "the work-success ethic," "future-time orientation," "individualism," and "Puritan morality," or a pattern of values composed of "an ethic of sociability," "present-time orientation," "togetherness," and "moral relativism" . . . What are the pervasive philosophies of life in different cultures at different periods that influence the magni-

tude and character of the creative work that will be undertaken? What kinds of values contribute to what kinds of creativity in what types of individuals in what places during what historic periods? If the fullest possible answer to questions of this order are to be found, the study of creativity will have to become more cross-cultural (less time-bound and less place-bound) than it has.

Though formidable conceptual problems hamper analysis of the impact of culture on creative expression, the understanding and study of cultures in relation to this important human functioning has its own right for research. However, most of the creativity research has not resulted in the enlargement of our vision of creativity beyond the ethnocentric confines. The greatest amount of attention has been given to creativity studies in "developed, achieving societies" and most of the research has been nation-oriented rather than international, resulting in the neglect of cross-cultural research. A survey in 1974 by Raina and Raina showed that only 0.58% of literature is devoted to cross-cultural explorations, marked by radical exclusion of the study of creativity in other cultures. During past decade or so, not many cross-cultural studies were reported in the *Journal of Creative Behavior, Creativity Research Journal,* or *Journal of Cross-Cultural Psychology.* Because most of the creativity research has been pursued within narrow ethnocentric boundaries, following the framework of Western ontology of the mind, not many have studied seriously how various civilizations and philosophies have defined and approached creativity. Only a few have strived to transcend this limitation when they have attempted to be enlightened and inspired by views and concepts other than the Western ones. Of course, some scholars are seriously committed to transcending the limitations of any one culture. However, such attempts are rare and relatively unpopular. Plenty of cross-cultural research is needed before we will have an adequate or very complex understanding of the role of educational, social, and political factors in facilitating or inhibiting creative potential. In 1959 Mead, as a result of her studies, pointed to "the light that cross-cultural studies can throw on the problems of creativity" besides providing, to some extent, foundations for theory development. In fact, Mar'i in 1976 attempted to draw the attention of researchers to the need of a cross-cultural theory of creativity and presented some possible categories that may guide research in this area. The conclusion was that a complete theory of creativity will ultimately be as much a theory of environments as of persons, but perspectives for such a theory will emerge only when we are sensitive to the unlimitedness of environments in various indigenous and other national cultures. Creativity research pursued and organized within this framework will be characterized by a phenomenon that Raina, in 1996, called the "Torrance phenomenon," which symbolizes genuine attempts to study and understand creativity and its functioning in one's own culture and subcultures and, more important, in other national cultures and subcultures, which, in turn, shall possibly crystallize, enrich, extend, and expand the nature and concept of creativity. This phenomenon stresses moving from exclusivism and intolerance, to inclusiveness and tolerance, to studying different cultures and minds.

II. PHILOSOPHICAL TRADITIONS, CULTURAL FORCES, AND CREATIVITY

Each culture evolves over history its own view of human nature, growth, potential, and limitations, and there may be as many views and realizations of human potential as there are discrete societies in the world. It is these deep-seated ideas and ideals that form the mind, which may be understood in their fullest significance.

Being a global issue, the idea of creativeness has been considered as universal, a deeply rooted and central concept in both the Occident and the Orient. However, some important differences have been noticed in underlying goals, which reflect a more basic cultural difference generally recognized between East and West. Creativity in the Occident would be more product-centered, whereas in the Orient, a product-centered creativity is often less valued than what might be called as a process-centered creativity. In the process-centered creativity, the person's aim is to be fully awake and alive, the ultimate goal being personal enlightenment.

The unique contributions of Oriental psychological processes to the creative process have been defined as to their past sources, present contributions, and future potentialities. Making comparisons with the Western orientation, what characterizes the East is the subjectifying attitude, the West, the objectifying one. Whereas Eastern cognition is believed to be interested in consciousness itself, Western cognition is interested in the objects of consciousness. The distinct Eastern view of creativity is reflected in the description of the creative artist found in Maduro's 1976 anthropological field study of traditional painters in India. Recently, *Taoistic cognition, Taoistic objectivity,* and *Taoistic creativity* has been psychologically reinterpreted making use of the original verses from one of the Chinese treatise, which does not explicitly offer any psychology of creativity but provides metaphors for creators to develop their own psychology of creativity. Taoistic creativity involves incubation, synthetic thinking, and the unification through the opposites. Lao Tzu's Taoism is mainly related to artistic creativity; it has influence on mental health and scientific creativity also. The *Chinese view* of *cosmic creation* has been described as an ongoing process, developing and unfolding. The Oriental concept of creativity stresses themes of development and progress toward the realization of the universe. In contrast, *Judaic* and *Greek views* of *cosmic creation* involves an abrupt production of the universe by an uncreated being who brings order to the formless void. As noted by Lubart in 1990, the modern Western concept of creativity does stem from this origin, then the perceived spontaneity of creativity and the locus of creativity in the individual logically belong together.

Analyses of the Western theory of creativity from the point of view of Indian philosophical tradition has brought into focus the varying intellectual traditions from which stem notions of creativeness. To some, Indian culture provides few scientific and mathematical models of creativeness that stand evidence for a theory, whereas in the West scientific method becomes synonymous with problem solving. Thus, the emphasis on science in the West associates creativity with inventiveness and the religious tradition in India with spiritual realization. The creative process is considered to be spiritual, objective, synthetic, and conforming. Creative performance terminates in worship. Further, analysis indicates that the Hindu mind views the creative process as a means of suggesting or recreating a vision, however fleeting, of a divine truth and regards art as a means of experiencing a state of bliss akin to the absolute state of *ananda* or *jivanmukti* (release in life). The image of dancing Siva, Nataraja, is the supreme symbol of all aspects of life as much as dance itself, which represents the synthesis of all aspects of creative activity. Evidence for a process model congruent with the oriental definition of creativity comes from a study of Indian painters who described a four-stage model based on an ancient Indian text. Emerging from the reports of Hindu artists in the Nathdwara community, this process description shows some similarity to the Western view. However, the emotional, personal, and intrapsychic elements that are present in the Oriental definition of creativity also dominate the Oriental view of the creative process.

Some worthwhile attempts have also been made in some countries to describe the creative process in native metaphors that are derived from cultures' creation myths. For example, the creative process is described as the continuity of Brahma, Vishnu, and Mahaeswara working in tandem creating, maintaining, and destroying to re-create. From the Indian perspective, *Vak*—a word that has multiple and interrelated meanings, primarily indicating "activity," "knowledge," and the "power of speech itself" conceived in the form of layers, the inmost being, cosmogenic energy itself, the wellspring of existence, of reality—forms the essence of creative energy.

A comparison and contrast of the theories of creativity in the East and the West, with a view to discover which approach leads more directly to creativity, has resulted in examining the conventional wisdom that the Eastern methods or views tend to be more intuitive, whereas Western approaches tend to be more logical. Although the differences in the two approaches were confirmed, some similarities were also found. Most important, comparing the two approaches confirmed that both methods can be seen as fitting into a single overall pattern. Some parallels and differences are also described by comparing Mahesh Yogi, Plato, and Jung.

Most of these contributions, though valuable and based on distinct conceptualizations emanating from different cultural traditions, are limited in their explanation and in pointing out what is basic to a particular conceptualization as it relates to creativity and its process. One realizes immense difficulty in dealing with these issues, particularly when they concern an infinite variety of philosophical concepts, methods, and attitudes that make up the philosophical tradition in certain cultures. It is therefore essential that cultures be understood correctly and profoundly—an understanding that must include a deep knowledge of all fundamental aspects of the mind and major aspects of the life of a people.

III. CREATIVITY AND CULTURAL DIFFERENCES

At least from the time of Aristotle, E. Paul Torrance wrote in 1997, it had been assumed that creative achievement is influenced by culture. The saying that "What is honored in a culture will be cultivated there" is attributed to Aristotle. Not many specific insights or research findings about these relationships existed. Accordingly, Torrance a pioneer in cross-cultural creativity research, has believed that comparative studies of creativity in children show a promise in pointing the way to the creation of conditions that will produce healthier, more creative people.

The universality of creativity is really amazing—the fact is reflected in a bibliography, extending across 20 different countries, which indicates that almost every country in the world is concerned about stimulating and developing the creativity of its children. However, creativity across cultures can take various shapes and forms; for instance, some societies can vary in their degree of receptivity toward original ideas in proportion to their level of cultural development. Analyses have shown that in different societies, particularly the traditional or indigenous sociocultural systems, a very uncommon creative idea or person is less encouraged. Original ideas, processes, and products can be accepted and promoted more easily when they are placed within the framework of the values of the sociocultural system. Thus, ideas that emphasize more skills of verbal expression and more collective spirit, like modification and improvement, will be encouraged more than radical or uncommon ideas. Thus, in some indigenous cultures, creativity can also take the form of modification and adaptation—the trend that has been observed by investigators in some other similar sociocultural context. Mead, in her discussion of innovation in traditional cultures, found that Samoan people were only allowed to change the details of their dance, not the basic form of it. In other words, the culture allows them to add details, not to invent. Given the dominance of *Brahminic values* in the Indian tradition, activity and intervention in the real world have low status in the Indian society. They are frequently associated in the mind of the Indian with the non-Brahminic lifestyles and little cultures of society. On the other hand, intellection, particularly speculating and metaphysical explorations, are considered liberating and nonpolluting. It is therefore not surprising that one of the distinctive characteristics of the creative Indians is their disproportionate and unexpectedly high performance on measures of verbal creativity. Analyses of research has indicated that the kind of creativity Indian society nurtures is closely related to the cultural definitions of the high and the low, the legitimate and the nonlegitimate, and the pure and the impure.

One should therefore be cautious in approaching the issue of culture as it relates to creativity, particularly in those cultures that are traditional and multicultural, because vast differences can exist in the ways in which creativity is manifested and perceived. Even within a particular society, varying cultural definitions of divergence and social sanctions may be available to the divergent in the society. For example, in a society where the traditional concepts of the high and the low intersect status and class differences, that which is divergence in one sector or stratum need not be so in another. Thus, although the Brahminic concepts of creativity and divergence are dominant in India, they are not the only ones current in the society.

Different cultures tend to foster their own distinctive intellectual styles, which, in turn, presumably influence the form that creative expression will take. Drawing on anthropological materials from different primitive cultures, Mead studied relationships between the forms provided by a culture and the creativity of the individuals within the culture, on which statements of regularities may be based. Studies of styles of thinking and learning, examined in two cultural contexts, have suggested a reexamination of Western reverence for logic and intellect over intuition and creativity. [*See* INTUITION.]

IV. MEASURED CREATIVITY: CROSS-CULTURAL VARIATION

Some of those who have approached creativity psychometrically, though within the framework of person-

environment interactions, have used various instruments to measure creativity in different cultural settings, of course, with different objectives. The openendedness of the test tasks and the universality of the stimuli have made some creativity tests, in this case the Torrance tests, readily adaptable to different cultures and subcultures. The test tasks, it is claimed, bring out cultural differences, and a test task that would not elicit cultural differences would not be very useful in comparative studies. As such, Torrance tests are widely used in cross-cultural studies of creativity, however, to some it is difficult to determine whether creativity as embodied in the Torrance tests is congruent with the actual definitions of creativity in the cultures studied. Some hold the view that in applying a complete Western perspective to assess creativity in a traditional or indigenous context, there is a serious problem in seeing this context as an impediment to creativity. Studies that have made comparisons between and within cultures using psychometric procedures are described in the following sections. [*See* APPENDIX II: TESTS OF CREATIVITY.]

V. CONTINUITY AND DISCONTINUITY IN CREATIVE THINKING: A CROSS-CULTURAL PERSPECTIVE

In some cultures a rather severe discontinuity in creative functioning and development has been noted in children at about ages 9 and 10 (fourth and fifth grades). In some, development is relatively continuous. In others, there is little growth during the elementary school years. In most, however, there are discontinuities. There are a number of indications that these discontinuities occur within a culture whenever children in that culture are confronted with new stresses and demands. Investigations of the universality of the slump in creative development at the fourth-grade level were made cross-sectionally in each of the following cultures: India, Norway, Germany, Western Samoa, Australia, mainstream U.S. culture, and the segregated African American culture. Later, other data were collected to explore specific issues from the following cultures: France; Greece; Mexico; and the Chinese, British, Malay, and Tamil cultures in Singapore. It was thought that data thus derived would help resolve the issue as to whether the fourth-grade slump in creative development is culture bound or natural and inevitable. [*See* FOURTH GRADE SLUMP.]

These studies yielded many insights regarding creativity and culture. Almost all of the children in the cultures did experience a slump in creative thinking ability but at different times. Children in the U.S. mainstream culture showed this discontinuity earliest, but children in Germany and India did not experience a discontinuity until the fifth grade for verbal and in the sixth grade for figural. Children in the other cultures experienced very little discontinuity but neither did they show much growth. In Western Samoa, the children in the native schools followed this same pattern, but those in schools operated by the Mormon missions with teachers trained in the United States showed the same discontinuity but at a later time than in the United States. Apparently, children in the mission school took on characteristics of the U.S. culture. Whether British and American influences have been strongest, the discontinuities are clearest, where the native cultures and language predominates, the continuities are clearest. In India, children in Sikh and other native culture schools showed continuity in development, whereas the fourth-grade slump was apparent in mission schools and in private schools, both reflecting strong British influences. In the first three grades, children in the latter schools functioned at a higher level than those in native culture schools but showed little or no growth.

In contrast to the preceding study, some studies are available that indicate no discontinuity in a few cultures outside the United States. Two studies are noteworthy. Studying 1165 third- through sixth-grade children drawn from six state and six Steiner schools in England, Scotland, and Germany examined by age, grade level, sex, and within country and cross-culturally, it was found that (a) children of upper grade levels scored higher on all of the creativity variables, with few exceptions, than children of the lower grades; only on a few of the figural tasks were significant discontinuities, evidenced by the fact that (b) older children obtained higher creativity scores than their younger peers, with few exceptions. Few significant decrements in creative development were noted in either school system, in another study, as a result of an analysis of cross-cultural data. It is a matter of debate whether the culture in these school systems was continuous, but one can attribute discontinuity in the U.S.-dominant culture to the process of ego development, rearing, and peer expectations. However, such a phenomenon may not exist in a continuous culture like India where the process of ego development takes place according to a model that differs sharply from the normative model of Western psychology, and continuity in India case reflects a continuity of emotional and social environment. The pattern of age-associated increases are reported to be the same cross-culturally in another study using a cross-cultural replication strategy with Chinese residents of Hong Kong; adolescents scored significantly higher than preadolescents on all the three auditory divergent thinking stimuli used.

VI. COMPARATIVE STUDIES OF CREATIVE ACHIEVEMENT AND MOTIVATION

To judge the influence of cultural factors on creativity, besides Torrance many investigators have made use of data from creative thinking test performance and personality measures of creativity.

Analyses of the data showed a differential level of functioning of various cultural groups on the figural and verbal measures of fluency, flexibility, originality, and elaboration. The cultures considered to be more highly developed stand separately from the so-called underdeveloped cultures. Even on measures of creative personality, in line with a cultural definition of divergence, differences have been noticed. Differences have been explained as follows: In the more developed cultures, complexity and elaboration are required for satisfactory adjustment. In the less developed countries, such complexity of thinking might be maladaptive. Something simpler is frequently more effective in these cultures. Comparing students in Japan and the United States who entered college in 1975, American students performed significantly higher on measures of verbal creativity. However, Japanese students exceeded their American counterparts in elaboration. In another study, American students exceeded their Japanese counterparts only in figural fluency, whereas the Japanese students predominated in flexibility, originality, elaboration, resistance to premature closure, breaking or extending boundaries, unusual visual perspective, humor, feeling and emotion, fantasy, and movement. Torrance maintained that the American students responded impulsively and logically to the task and produced a large number of responses with low levels of creative strength, whereas their Japanese counterparts responded reflectively and intuitively and produced a smaller number of responses characterized by higher levels of creative strength. The differences in performance and perceptions can be explained on the basis of values and traditions of respective cultures. Such influences as traditionality-modernity and level of modernization are forwarded as plausible reasons for differences.

Torrance also derived two indexes that he believed would be related to the level of creativity of children being educated in each culture. One of these indexes was based on the diversity of the occupational aspirations expressed by the subjects, as this would reflect the opportunity they had for the expression of their creativity. The other index was based on teachers' responses to the ideal pupil checklist, which required teachers to rate the extent to which they encouraged or discouraged each of 60 characteristics that had been found to be related to creativity. Data were available on cultures mentioned earlier. The 11 cultures and subcultures were ranked on the creativity of the subjects and each of the predictor indexes. Rank order correlations showed almost perfect correlation. The only slight deviations were Western Australia and the Singapore cultures. The Australian children perceived limited occupational opportunity in creative occupations. The Australian teachers were also a little harsh in discouraging creative characteristics. The Tamil and Chinese subcultures in Singapore were also harsh in discouraging creative characteristics.

VII. SEX DIFFERENCES IN CROSS-CULTURAL PERSPECTIVE

Sex differences in levels of creativity have been reported to be influenced by culture. Boys in the Western Samoan and Mexican cultures have excelled girls in figural creativity. Further examination revealed that in Mexican culture only males are permitted to paint the pottery, the chief product of the area. In Western Samoa males are the official artists of the culture. In India males excelled females in verbal creativity. A study has indicated that girls scores were lower than the boys both in the United States and in Indian societies,

whereas sex differences in creativity were greatest in India. The smaller sex difference in the United States sample is interpreted as reflecting the greatest freedom and individuality permitted in American girls. It was concluded that individual creativity is likely to increase as societies move toward a less restrictive normative code. Another study revealed more differences between Mexican men and women on causal and creative thinking. Sex and cultural differences were also found in a study of creativity of children in India, Afghanistan, Iraq, and Lebanon. Impact of culture on expression of creativity is reflected in the finding that ideas described by girls were generally in the area of arts, crafts, and communication, whereas boys dealt primarily with mechanical arts and agriculture.

Generally, African, Arab, and Islamic social and cultural elements seem to affect the behavior of individuals and groups differently. These elements reinforce more freedom and independence for males and less for females. Also it seems that other specific factors can affect the differences between males and females in psychological functioning, particularly creativity. Among these factors are the level of modernization, the level of education, and the degree of authoritarianism.

Psychological research relating to sex differences in creativity lacks agreement, though in most of the studies in traditional cultures and societies males have scored better than females. Various social and cultural explanations have been forwarded for this trend. Each society tries to establish a congruence between the skills it values and the strata it honors. In a society that values the masculine over the feminine, the abstract over the concrete and the manual over the nonmanual, perhaps one can expect sex differences to emerge.

VIII. CULTURES DEFINE CREATIVITY OUTLETS: DIFFERENCES ARE NOT DEFICITS

Torrance tests are claimed to ensure disadvantaged children a fair chance to demonstrate their creative potential. These tests have been used in various researches in which comparisons in terms of either race, or socioeconomic status, or both, have been made. Most racial comparisons have involved blacks and whites drawn from the same geographic areas or from a variety of geographic areas. In Wisconsin, no statistically significant differences between blacks and whites on any of the Torrance measures was noticed. Similarly, no differences were found in Florida between the two groups. In a rural Georgia town, study has shown that the whites excelled blacks on the verbal measures, but there were no differences on figural measures. In fact, black students excelled on elaboration. Torrance's study in middle Georgia showed that black children excelled their white disadvantaged counterparts on figural measures. Similar results were obtained in the metropolitan Atlanta area. Under the very informal and free atmosphere of the creativity workshop and in individual testing situations, the verbal creative thinking performance of black children reached a level commensurate with advantaged children under similar conditions. In the case of Aboriginal and disadvantaged European children living in Australia, no significant differences between the two ethnic groups on tests of divergent thinking were found. Such results led Torrance to observe that the disadvantaged too have creative positives of their own, which may be attributed to the availability of various kinds of resources and to what is rewarded and encouraged.

IX. THE CULTURAL LEVERS: THE REWARDING AND PUNISHING FORMS

The emergence of creative persons (as we know them) may presuppose a certain view of the individual on the part of the culture and of the individuals themselves. Analyses of the studies regarding the cross-cultural patterning of human relations indicates that cultures perceive and evaluate differently various kinds of behaviors, personality characteristics, and the mental functioning of the young and the adults alike. It implies that thought and creativity are conditioned by sociocultural structure. From this follows the common belief that one of the most powerful ways in which a culture encourages or discourages creative behavior is the way by which teachers and parents encourage or discourage, reward or punish certain personality characteristics as they develop in children or the behaviors that manifest those characteristics.

Using Ideal Pupil Checklist with teaches and other educators from five rather distinct cultural groups

(United States, Germany, India, Greece, Philippines), it was concluded that all five cultures may be unduly punishing the good guesser, the child who is courageous in his or her convictions, the emotionally sensitive individual, the intuitive thinker, the individual who regresses occasionally and plays or acts childlike, the visionary individual, and the person who is willing to accept something on mere say-so without evidence. On the other hand, all of them may be giving unduly great rewards for being courteous, doing work on time, being obedient, being popular and well liked, and being willing to accept the judgment of authorities.

Numerous studies have examined cultural and subcultural differences in the perceptions of teachers and parents concerning creative children in various countries. Most of the studies suggest that the cultures studied deemphasized people's self-acting nature and emphasized the receptive nature. However, one notices many cultural variations. Torrance felt that most highly industrialized countries tended to show a closer agreement with the perception of experts on creative personality than less developed countries. The mothers from the countries showed more agreement among themselves than with the experts.

A few studies have determined shift, if any, in the values favorable or unfavorable to the development of the creative personality as a result of social and cultural change. Initial results, as noted earlier, in all the countries indicated that classroom teachers and parents held values inconsistent with enhancing students' creative growth. During the ensuing years, studies have found that the creative values of parents and teachers have not changed much since the studies conducted by Torrance in the United States. A study of the behaviors prized by both the elementary and junior high school groups and also the adults indicated that rather than qualities that make for creativity, values expressed in the Puritan ethic are more closely perceived—that is, determination in applying energy to getting work on time and remembering well what is supposed to be done. Another study on social and cultural changes in creativity indicated a high degree of association between the perceptions of 1961 and 1977 teachers; similar results were obtained comparing 1961 and 1990 teachers, suggesting that not much change has taken place in the perceptions as a result of change in times.

In the Australian setting, the issue of the generalizibility of the Torrance's study was further investigated in Western Australia. In the ideal child research area, study of the elementary and secondary schoolteachers showed that in the 1980s teachers agreed more with the creativity experts on the personal characteristics that should be encouraged in children. However, the amount of agreement, though similar to a sample of U.S. teachers, is still low.

The impact of a given culture cannot remain as constant, noted Ludwig in 1992. Many other factors need to be taken into account. A holohistorical (cross-historical) study of the causes of creative florescences in particular periods of time in certain countries has shown that the more politically fragmented a civilization, the higher its creativity level. Studies are also available that indicate that creativity tends to thrive more during civil disturbance and ideological diversity than during times of political cohesiveness, tranquility, and uniformity, the more traditional, monolithic, stable, and homogeneous the culture, the less tolerance for innovation and change. [*See* POLITICAL SCIENCE AND CREATIVITY.]

Studying alternate centuries during the 2300 years of Indian civilization, making for 12 sample periods and replicating Naroll's 1971 study, a regional study of Indian sociopolitical variables and creativity, using regional histories of India including several non-English sources and cross-lagged correlational techniques to test quasi-experimentally the causal links between important variables, showed that for India, loose federation of states had little to do with the formation or development of high creativity, but after the pattern or style of India was established, sociopolitical structures continued to stimulate creativity. The study has, however, generated many further possibilities.

Through cross-cultural and transhistorical surveys, Simonton's 1975 and 1980 studies identified many factors that explain the emergence of creativity in various periods in history. A certain degree of affluence in a society and physical proximity to one or more larger cultural centers are other conditions that have often been linked to creativity. To the extent that a culture embodies or maintains these political, economic, and geographical conditions, that culture should be more conducive to creativity. Arieti in 1976 proposed the concept of *creativogenic culture,* which makes available

to an individual creative elements that are perceived or accepted as such if similar characteristics exist within the individual. A creativogenic society offers the individual the possibility of becoming great, but it does not make the occurrence of greatness automatic. Arieti proposed nine conditions present in a creativogenic society that will facilitate greatness. Whether some cultures possess these conditions more than others over the course of history, and how these cultures support these traits, are topics that deserve further research, suggested Lubart.

X. ATTITUDES TOWARD DIVERGENCY: CROSS-CULTURAL ANALYSES OF IMAGINATIVE STORIES

Each society differs in its attitude about uniqueness and divergence, something that is very crucial in creativity in any culture. Very early in his research, Torrance wondered about how cultures differed in their attitude regarding being different or exceptional in any important way. He and his associates choose imaginative writing as the vehicle through which they examined this issue. Children from a variety of cultures were asked to write stories about animals or people with some divergent characteristics, revealing in fantasy material their perceptions about divergent behavior and how their culture deals with such behavior. Children from the United States predominantly wanted to cure the character of the divergency—stop the monkey from flying, get the lion to roar, have the boy to give up his dream of being a nurse, and so on. This reflects the society's tremendous concern about exceptional children and their education. The French children, on the other hand, wrote stories about how their characters enjoyed their divergency. This too, can be recognized as the stereotype of French culture—or perhaps, it is more than a stereotype. Both of these dominant themes are in contrast to the dominant theme of the Greek stories. The Greek children wanted to understand the divergency. They were not concerned about curing their character of the divergency or enjoying it. Interestingly, a study showed that Delhi children more frequently perceived positive values of the divergency to the divergent subject. In this context, Nandy and

Kakar observed in 1980 that the kind of creativity that helps one to actualize theoretical and aesthetic values is generally highly individualistic and assumes some extent of interpersonal withdrawal and a certain asocial lonely self-exploration, in turn historically valued by the Indian society as intrinsically superior to other forms of knowledge.

Studies have also been concerned with the effects of what might be called a national personality type on children's responses to open-ended stories. Using Anderson Incomplete Stories each depicting a conflict between a child and the child's teacher, parent, neighbor, or peer, data were gathered from more than 10,000 children in the fourth and seventh grades from eight countries: England, Finland, the United States, Sweden, Norway, Mexico, Brazil, and Germany. Large and significant differences, consistent with the hypotheses about the impact of culture on creativity, were found.

XI. IMAGES OF THE FUTURE AND CHARACTERISTICS OF GIFTED CHILDREN AROUND THE WORLD

In conceptualizing the practical abilities lying within the realm of the future reaches of creative potential, Torrance has pleaded that another important practical ability that seems to lie within the realm of the further reaches of creative potential is a sense of the future—having a strong, rich, and accurate image of the future. Accordingly, Torrance pioneered an international study of the image of the future, based on the scenario-writing contest, of the gifted and talented around the world. He received support from colleagues in the following countries: Australia, Bahrain, Brazil, Canada, Kuwait, New Zealand, the Philippines, Republic of South Africa, Taiwan, the United Kingdom, and the United States.

A significant aspect of the study was the attention given to the influence of national cultures on the future images of gifted and talented children, the extent to which the scenario writers see themselves as future inventors and scientific discoverers/developers. Scenarios from all around the world about the threat that gifted children see to their tomorrow—nuclear warfare, nuclear waste, cosmic radiation, environmental pollution, underground cities, threats to the family,

and the like—are available. Torrance and associates have linked these concerns to creativity, human development, and the messages the children of the world are trying to communicate. [*See* CREATIVITY IN THE FUTURE.]

XII. CREATIVITY AND THE MENTORING PROCESS: CROSS-CULTURAL PRACTICES

Mentoring as it has occurred and evolved over a period of time in different cultures is deeply embedded in the history of a culture. Each culture has had to find a way whereby its youth can be guided and protected until their creative potential can be realized. Almost always wherever independence and creativity occur and persist, there is some other individual or agent who plays the role of a mentor. The person may be called guru, sponsor, patron, tutor, sensei, or something else, depending on the culture and time in history. The information about the process of mentoring as it exists in various cultures and societies, and the way it aids creativity in the United States, in India, in the Arab culture in Spain, and in many other countries, is available with the Georgia Studies of Creative Behavior in the United Studies.

XIII. NURTURING CREATIVITY

The procedures and materials currently available for the direct teaching of creative thinking are plentiful and varied. While considering issues about nurturing creativity, it is important to realize that there is a wide range of sociopsychological and educational variables that might influence creativity. The list of variables may include both global environmental features as well as more narrowly defined social factors. A study of the arts education for young children in China and the United States in the context of creativity and skill development showed that if there is too great a leaning in the direction of untrammeled creativity—the American risk—the child may end up without skills and thus be able to communicate only with him- or herself. On the other hand, if there is unrelieved focus on skill development—the Chinese danger—the child may end up unable to depart from the models that he or she has absorbed.

Unfortunately, there is a paucity of empirical research and inquiry on the cross-cultural implications of creativity training that practitioners can read to help them plan and deliver more effective cross-cultural creative problem solving training. Some initial attempts have been made to understand the impact of culture on creativity training. However, the issues surrounding cross-cultural creative problem solving had been well defined or explained. Therefore, an initial attempt was made to identify possible issues for further exploration and study, and it was found that basic guidelines and techniques of creative problem solving work cross-culturally. [*See* PROBLEM SOLVING.]

Another procedure, which helps in teaching and practicing creative negotiation skills based on the sociodramatic model developed by Torrance and associates, has the potential of becoming a useful tool. Torrance found it to be a powerful tool in learning and psychotherapy throughout the United States and in India, South Africa, Japan, Australia, and Brazil.

To aid creativity, the study of Zen using cybernetics and information theory has been advocated. Zen, considered as an abductive technique, may unify Eastern and Western abductive techniques. This is perhaps indicative of future trends in the study of the development of creativity.

Thinking about creativity in certain cultures does not focus attention solely on problems of the creative individual, as we commonly do in our discussions of the creative process, but goes beyond it and shows equal concern for issues that relate to what has been called *contricipation* or what in India is called as *sahrdaya*. No longer a unit, *sahrdaya* is a part of creative continuity that has the imagination and culture to be able to enjoy aesthetically and provide joy and enthusiasm to the creator. Thus he or she is a crucial component in nurturing creativity according to Indian cultural tradition.

XIV. CONCLUSION

That all human cultures, even the most rudimentary, in accordance with their own logos, have developed a variety of models of mental processing and of how the mind works and creates makes us recognize the legitimacy of relative realities and pluralistic worldviews and decenters our metatheoretic orientation. It permits us to question our concept and understanding of creativity, which remains skewed because it is based on studies of societies that are largely homogeneous and uniform and have almost exclusively focused on the individual and have marginalized the role of culture. Our perspective will be enlarged when we become sensitive to the unlimitedness of environments and also of minds and models in various societies. Western psychological concepts and theories, which are the products of a particular set of sociohistorical conditions, may not be universal. It is therefore important that different cultures and subcultures be studied not only to gain insight into creative functioning but to better understand the character of scientific and psychological inquiry itself. Only in this way will there be any genuine interchange among the cultures, any increase in understanding that takes full account of the other form within the individual's cultural framework, which can be brought into sharper focus by comparing it with the representational worlds of individuals belonging to other cultures. We will begin to approach authoritative answers only after we have carried out careful ethnographic studies in different settings and understood the assumptions and values that permeate those settings. Much can be learned from the ethnographies of cultural anthropologists. The risk of imposing an alien ontology and an alien epistemology will not be productive; instead indigenous ways of looking at creativity in specific sociocultural perspectives in terms of culturally provided categories may be justified. Active alternatives like hermeneutic and phenomenological approaches have a potential within creativity research that has scarcely been explored.

In the psychological study of creativity, as an alternative to what has been called the methodological battle cry of prediction, and control, which serves as the criterion for evaluating our practices, we might see the legitimacy of psychology as variously dedicated, for example, to articulating multiple perspectives, fostering appreciation of others, building relations among people, furthering people's sense of well-being, or generating a self-reflective consciousness, noted Misra and Gergen in 1993. The fact that anyone undertaking cross-cultural research should have a sense of balance and empathy acquires added significance in studies on cross-cultural differences in creativity. Acquiring empathic sensitivity to other cultures requires immersing oneself in that culture's worldview in order to observe in oneself the effect of such an immersion. This will have a strong overall liberalizing effect in understanding and appreciating cultural differences in creativity. There is an inherent message in the observation that suggests that methodological issues are never purely and simply methodological.

Bibliography

Arieti, S. (1976). *Creativity: The magic synthesis*. New York: Basic Books.

Getzels, J. W. (1975). Creativity: Prospect and issues. In I. Taylor & J. W. Getzels (Eds.), *Perspectives in creativity*. Chicago: Aldine.

Lubart, T. I. (1990). Creativity and cross-cultural variation. *International Journal of Psychology, 25,* 39–59.

Ludwig, A. M. (1992). Culture and creativity. *American Journal of Psychotherapy, 46,* 454–469.

Maduro, R. (1976). *Artistic creativity in a Brahmin painter community* (Research Monograph No. 14). University of California, Berkeley, Centre for South and Southeast Asia Studies.

Mar'i, S. K. (1976). Toward a cross-cultural theory of creativity. *Journal of Creative Behavior 10,* 108–116.

May, R. (1959). The nature of creativity. In H. H. Anderson (Ed.), *Creativity and its cultivation*. New York: Harper.

Mead, M. (1959). Creativity in cross-cultural perspective. In H. H. Anderson (Ed.), *Creativity and its cultivation*. New York: Harper.

Misra, G., & Gergen, K. J. (1993). Beyond scientific colonialism: A reply to Poortinga and Triandis. *International Journal of Psychology, 28,* 251–254.

Nandy, A., & Kakar, S. (1980). Culture and personality. In U. Pareek (Ed.), *Survey of research in psychology*. Bombay: Popular Prakashan.

Naroll, R., Benjamin, E. C., Fohl, F. K., Fried, M. J., Hildreth, R. E., & Schaefer, J. M. (1971). Creativity: A cross-historical pilot survey. *Journal of Cross-Cultural Psychology, 2,* 181–188.

Raina, M. K. (1996). The Torrance phenomenon: Extended Creative Search for Lord Vishwakarma. *Creativity and Innovation Management, 5,* 149–168.

Raina, M. K., & Raina, U. (1974). Creativity research in cross-cultural perspective. *Indian Educational Review, 9,* 140–167.

Simonton, D. K. (1975). Sociocultural content of individual creativity: A transhistorical time-series analysis. *Journal of Personality and Social Psychology, 32,* 1119–1133.

Simonton, D. K. (1980). Thematic fame, melodic originality, and musical zeitgeist: A biographical and transhistorical content analysis. *Journal of Personality and Social Psychology, 38,* 972-983.

Torrance, E. P. (1998). Reflections on emerging insights on the educational psychology of creativity. In J. Houtz (Ed.), *The educational psychology of creativity*. Cresskill, NJ: Hampton Press.

Marie Sklodowska Curie

1867–1934
Physicist

Awarded Nobel Prizes for Physics and Chemistry

Becky J. Thurston

University of Hawaii, Hilo

MARIE SKLODOWSKA CURIE was one of the first woman scientists to win worldwide fame and one of the great scientists of this century. She had degrees in mathematics and physics. Winner of two Nobel prizes, she performed pioneering studies with radium and polonium and contributed profoundly to the understanding of radioactivity.

Perhaps the most eminent of all women scientists, Marie Sklodowska Curie is notable for her many firsts. She was first to use the term "radioactivity" for this phenomenon. In 1903, she became the first woman to win a Nobel Prize for Physics. She was also the first female lecturer and professor at the Sorbonne University in Paris (1906). In 1911, she won an unprecedented second Nobel prize (this time in chemistry) for her discovery and isolation of pure radium and radium components. She was the first mother–Nobel Prize Laureate of a daughter–Nobel Prize Laureate; her oldest daughter, Irene Joliot-Curie, also won a Nobel Prize for Chemistry (1935). She received 19 degrees, 15 gold medals, and many other honors. In 1995 Marie Curie's ashes were enshrined in the Pantheon in Paris; she was the first woman to receive this honor for her own achievements.

Marie Curie. (Copyright Wide World Photo.)

Copyright © 1999 by Academic Press
All rights of reproduction in any form reserved.

I. BACKGROUND

Marie Sklodowska was born in 1867 in Poland, the fifth and youngest child of Bronsilawa Boguska, a pianist, singer, and teacher, and Wladyslaw Sklodowski, a professor of mathematics and physics. Descendants of Catholic landowners, her parents were intellectuals whose opportunities were restricted by the Russian domination of Poland. At age 10, Marie was left motherless. Her father took boarders into his home; Marie helped with housework and became a governess for six years so that her sister Bronie might study in Paris and become a medical doctor. In 1891 Marie also went to Paris and after several years of spartan living and intense study she received a *licence,* or master's degrees, in physics and mathematics at the Sorbonne.

Marie was married to Pierre Curie, also a physicist, in a civil ceremony in 1895, followed by a honeymoon which was a three-week bicycle tour. Living near poverty they gave up social contacts and recreation for their dedication to research. Marie's first scientific work was on the magnetic properties of tempered steel (1893). Then, learning of Becquerel's discovery, she selected the radiation from uranium for her doctor's thesis. After observing that uranium ore (pitchblende) was several times more radioactive than uranium, the Curies came to believe that the ore contained a new element or elements more active than uranium.

Working under miserable conditions in a shed, the Curies carried out the chemical concentration of some 100 kg of uranium ore supplied by the Austrian government to obtain a specimen from which spectroscopic identification was made of a new element which they called "polonium." Marie later discovered a second element in pitchblende, which she named "radium." By 1902, she had isolated .1 g of pure radium salt and had determined the atomic mass of radium as 225 (226 is now accepted). In 1903, Marie, her husband, and Henri Becquerel received the Nobel prize in physics for their work on radioactivity. It was not until 1910 that she finally obtained 1 g of the pure radium metal. The Curies also determined that the beta rays emitted by radium were negatively charged particles (electrons).

The birth of her two daughters, Irene and Eve, in 1897 and 1904 did not interrupt Marie's intensive scientific work. She was appointed lecturer in physics at the *École Normale Supérieure* for girls in Sèvres and introduced there a method of teaching based on experimental demonstrations. In 1904, Marie was finally named as Pierre's assistant at the *Faculté des Sciences* where she had long worked without pay.

Confident of medical and industrial applications, a French industrialist constructed a factory near Paris for the extraction of radium from pitchblende. The Curies took out no patents and claimed no royalties, thereby renouncing a fortune. The sudden death of Pierre Curie in a road accident in 1906 was a bitter blow to Marie Curie, but it was also a decisive turning point in her career. Marie's life became even more devoted to continuing her research and raising her daughters.

In 1906, the physics chair created for Pierre was bestowed on Marie and for the first time a woman taught at the Sorbonne. As had Pierre, Marie declined the recognition of the *Légion d'Honneur,* asking only for the means to work. Albert Einstein once said of her that "Marie Curie is, of all celebrated beings, the one whom fame has not corrupted." Five years after her husband's death, Marie received the 1911 Nobel prize, in recognition of her work in isolating radium in its pure metallic form and developing the first international standard for measuring the substance. She was nominated for the French Academy of Sciences that year, but was rejected by one vote after a slanderous campaign was waged against Marie by a competitor. Marie's supporters and co-workers were shocked by this defeat but she made no comment on her rejection.

In 1910, Marie worked with the Radiology Congress in Brussels to establish official standards for radium needed in therapy and research. The Congress defined the "curie" as the unit of radioactivity. During World War I, Marie, with the aid of private gifts, equipped ambulances (which she could drive) with portable x-ray equipment; she became head of radiological services for the Red Cross. Her wartime experience led her to write the book, *La Radiologie et la Guerre.*

In 1914 Marie Curie helped found the Radium Institute in Paris, and was the Institute's first director. Through the Radium Institute, the Curie Foundation, and her membership in the Academy of Medicine, Marie Curie pursued goals such as "curie therapy" and the establishment of safety standards for workers. Marie Curie has been honored more than any other scientist on the postage stamps of many nations; many picture the benefits of x-ray diagnosis, the use of radium in the treatment of cancer, and the gift of 1 g of radium to Madame Curie by grateful women of America.

Madame Curie's health declined partly due to the lethal effects of her prolonged exposure to nuclear radiations. She had cataract operations, and suffered from lesions on her fingers and from leukemia. She died in a sanatorium in the French Alps in 1934. After her death the Radium Institute was renamed the Curie Institute in her honor.

II. CREATIVITY AND EMINENCE

For decades, scholars have studied creativity by examining eminent individuals and those factors that appear to influence or be related to creativity. Marie Curie demonstrated many of the personality characteristics common to eminent individuals and she experienced many of the environmental and social factors frequently encountered by eminent individuals.

III. PERSONAL CHARACTERISTICS AND CREATIVITY

Scholars do not know whether personal qualities can be a direct cause of creativity, but it does seem clear that they are intimately involved in the process. Marie Curie demonstrated the following personality characteristics common to eminent individuals: propensity to persevere, intellectual competence, academic propensity, risk taking, force of character, and independence.

Marie Curie's perseverance, intellectual competence, and academic propensity are unquestioned. She spent six years as a governess so that her older sister Bronie might study in Paris and become a medical doctor, knowing that when Bronie obtained her licence, Marie would have the opportunity to attend university. Marie spent four years of spartan living and intense study so that she could receive a master's degree in physics and a year later, a master's degree in mathematics.

From childhood, Marie was remarkable for her prodigious memory, and at the age of 16 she won a gold medal on completion of her secondary education at the Russian lycee. Her intellectual competence and academic propensity were also evident in her later academic accomplishments. Among those taking the *licence es sciences* exam Marie ranked first, and among those taking the *licence es mathematiques* exam she ranked second.

Marie Curie was not afraid to take risks and her forceful character led her to a level of independence unusual for her time. In France during this period, women, especially gifted women, were scorned. The Belle Epoque writer Octave Mirbeau wrote during this period that a woman "is not good for anything but love and motherhood. Some women, rare exceptions, have been able to give, either in art or literature, the illusion that they are creative. But they are either abnormal or simple reflections of men." When studying in Paris, Marie lived alone for almost three years. It was a life which, as she wrote later in *Autobiographical Notes,* gave her a sense of liberty and independence.

Later, Marie showed incredible strength of character when she foresaw the immense labor necessary in attempting to chemically concentrate uranium in order to study radium. Knowing the small means to accomplish this task at her disposal, she plunged into the adventure wholeheartedly.

IV. ENVIRONMENTAL INFLUENCES

Marie Curie was influenced by many of the environmental and social factors common to eminent individuals: she came from a culturally and intellectually advantaged family; she had the presence of many adults other than her parents; she was exposed to eminent adults during her formative years; and she experienced an early parental death.

Marie's family came from the peculiarly Polish form of landed gentry known as *szlachta,* nobles who in previous centuries had fought for the republic but who valued their independent authority and participated with equal voice in the parliament of the land. During Marie's time, both sides of her family had been reduced to the position of minor *szlachta.* Though very poor, the family, like many of the intelligentsia, viewed education as a powerful weapon, an unlimited resource which could fundamentally change and ennoble society. Many members of Marie's family were teachers and the overall welfare of the children was primary. "My father," Marie's brother remembers, "was concerned about our health, our physical development, our studies and even our free time, for which he tried to provide us with ideas and games." In the Sklodowski household, play was learning and learning was play. Although women were excluded from university in Poland, Marie and her sisters grew up assuming higher education was their right.

While growing up, Marie and her siblings had the presence of many adult role models, especially female role models. Marie Curie could look to her own family for examples of female independence. There had been her mother, the forceful headmistress, and there was Uncle Zdzislaw's wife, Marie Rogowska, the tall blonde who founded factories and ran the family estates, defying the rules of dress and decorum along the way. But the most pertinent example may well have been Aunt Wanda Sklodowska, "the most educated of all" the women, according to Marie's brother; she had attended university in Geneva and developed a "literary career."

Later, Marie may have been influenced by another remarkable woman, Jadwiga Szczsinska-Dawidowa. Dawidowa, responding to the yearnings of young Polish women for higher education, began to organize a clandestine academy for women. Marie was apparently involved in the secret academy almost from its inception.

Along with these adult role models, Marie was exposed to eminent adults during the formative years of her career. While at the Sorbonne in Paris she followed the lectures of Paul Appel, Gabriel Lippmann, and Edmond Bouty. There she became acquainted with other physicists who were well known—Jean Perrin, Charles Maurain, and Aimé Cotton.

Research suggests that the experience of an early death of a parent and/or an older sibling is not necessarily an impediment to the achievement of creative achievement and eminence. Such an event can be an opportunity and a challenge to healthy ego development. At age 7 Marie experienced the death of her cherished oldest sister Zofia from typhus, and that of her beloved mother at age 10 from tuberculosis. It may have been these premature deaths that in Marie evoked the agnosticism that would later bolster her faith in science.

Bibliography

Albert, R. A. (1983). *Genius and eminence.* New York: Pergamon Press.

Curie, E. (1937). *Madame Curie.* New York: Doubleday.

Quinn, S. (1995). *Marie Curie.* New York: Simon & Schuster.

Dance and Creativity

Judith B. Alter

University of California, Los Angeles

Choreographers The people who select or invent the movements (including postures, gestures, and steps) the dancers should do, determine how to perform those movements (their timing and rhythms, energy level, accents, and emotional interpretation), and decide where the dancers will move (directions and levels that make patterns in space) in the performance space during the dance. Choreographers are the primary creators of dances.

Dance A sequence of selected, practiced, and aesthetically organized bodily movements (organized most often in rhythmic patterns) performed for a special purpose (for religious ritual, for social interaction, or for art/entertainment) and accompanied by sounds or music. Often, though not always, dancers wear special costumes for the dance performance, which is held in a selected and hallowed location suitable for dance.

Improvisation Moving in a free manner to find or invent new movements, patterns, and phrases to go beyond familiar movement vocabulary. It is comparable to spontaneously inventing melodies in jazz music or playing around with clay before deciding to sculpt a specific figure.

Vocabulary of Dance Movements Found in particular training techniques and performance styles, this vocabulary is a selected collection of postures, gestures, and steps with their accompanying patterns in space, use of levels, recognizable rhythms, and choices of energy expenditure.

*Human beings have combined **DANCE AND CREATIVITY** as far back in history as there are records of any kind. Cave paintings from the late Stone Age found in Europe, Russia, and Africa show what appear to be dancing human figures with hunted and valued animals. Dance is difficult to define and in some cultures it may not even be identified or named as a separate activity or entity by its participants. Its social, ritual, and art/ entertainment functions in human societies are complex and overlap. This article will consider dance creativity, its creators, their creative processes, and their most innovative types of work.*

I. INTRODUCTION

A dance is an entity, a physical activity in which one or more people participate. Dance is also an academic field with a body of knowledge. Dance scholars employ various methods of analysis: historical, anthropological, kinesiological, critical, compositional, theatrical, technical, and so forth. Dance, as an autonomous field of study in universities and colleges, separated from the

Copyright © 1999 by Academic Press
All rights of reproduction in any form reserved.

academic fields of music or theater in the middle of the 20th century. One consequence of this recent scholarly development is the relative lack of studied documentation. Theater, music, folklore, and even law archives contain information about dance for scholars to study; and because of this recent scholarly attention to dance a dearth of reliable and translated information exists in the areas of historical, ethnological, theatrical, and critical study about Asian and African dance.

To engage in the activity of dance, the participants, usually called *dancers,* perform *dances,* which are composed or choreographed by choreographers. They make their dances for art/entertainment, ritual, or social purposes; sometimes these purposes are combined and involve other "art" activities and artifacts such as music, spoken text, and designed objects. Dancing plays a part in social activities such as recreation and courtship and in other cultural art/entertainment activities such as drama, opera, musical theater, and, in this century, film, and video performances. Though this article emphasizes the historical innovations in art/entertainment and social dance in Europe and the United States, how innovation occurs in traditional dance activities in other areas in the world is also explored.

II. DANCERS: THE CREATORS AND RECREATORS

The initial creative work in dance is done by choreographers. These artists, whose medium is movement, make dances to express their artistic ideas. Their creative process, like that of other artists, is initiated by many stimuli: a movement phrase or sequence; a commission to choreograph a work or works for an opera, musical, or film; a piece of music or art; an emotional or conceptual idea; or, as Mary Wigman described, a serendipitous handclap expressing an immediate feeling of joy. Their creative processes proceed like that of other creative people: sometimes the dance evolves quickly and at times slowly; they work and rework their dances, stop work on one piece to complete another dance, and adjust the dance for different performers and different occasions or stage spaces.

Dancers who perform these dances also utilize their creative capability, because they literally recreate them in their performances. Hence the title of performing artist is given to great dancers as well as musicians and actors. Although these performers do not originate the works they perform, the greatest dancers recreate them at a level of interpretative excellence that is often called artistry.

In psychological studies of the creative capacity of dancers or potential of dance students, researchers have found that, like other creative individuals, dancers and dance students are above average in intelligence. Dance students are significantly more positive, flexible, achieving, and dominating than average college students. Dancers and dance students also have wide interests and are often competent in one or more arts other than dance. They give a significantly high number of human movement responses on the Rorschach test; this gives indirect evidence of their kinesthetic preferences and sensitivities. This preference for movement or movement satisfaction is indicated on other measures, either standardized such as the dynamism scale on the Barron-Welsh Revised Art Scale or on individually devised tests. Dancers and choreographers most commonly combine their kinesthetic intelligence with either their visual/spatial or musical intelligences. [*See* MULTIPLE INTELLIGENCES.]

Historians offer some evidence that high levels of kinesthetic intelligence, like the other intelligences, runs in families, and like circus performers, children of dancers often become dancers. In studies by Alter of contemporary dancers, often those dancers who remain in the field the longest and become choreographers have parents with unfulfilled cultural goals— that is, if given the opportunity the parents would have participated in a performing art. As children, these parents even specifically wanted to dance but were unable to, although they may have participated in sports or some other nonart physical activity such as hiking or climbing and often remain active or involved as spectators in these activities.

Evidence in biographies and autobiographies illustrates that beyond kinesthetic, musical, and visual intelligence, choreographers demonstrate high levels of verbal, interpersonal, and intrapersonal intelligences. They need a combination of effective verbal and interpersonal skills to communicate with company members (as a teacher, director, adviser), business agents, set and costume designers, musicians, and backers when directing a performing company. Gifted choreographers also demonstrate acute self-knowledge and intra-personal intelligence when finding, clarifying, building, and realizing the concepts on which they base their choreographies. These concepts may stem from emotional, visual, musical, historical, abstract, or a combination of stimuli.

Choreographers also utilize their logical/mathematical intelligence when organizing, arranging, and re-arranging movement sequences and the dancers who perform these sequences in time and space. The timing of these movements in relation to the music or sound accompaniment also requires choreographers and dancers alike to employ this ability with intense concentration. Dance scholar Vera Maletic observed that all the intelligences identified by educational psychologist Howard Gardner were also described by dance critic Edwin Denby 40 years earlier. The observations of Maletic and Denby, that outstanding dancers integrate all their intelligences, apply to the choreographers most widely recognized for their creative contributions to dance.

Little is known about the choreographers of the ritual, folk, and social dances, which most of the world's peoples perform at some time in their lives. Like folk crafts, these dance creations are mostly unsigned; for these communal dances, the creator, arranger, or developer is unknown. But, like any other dance work, a master dance maker choreographed the dance. Dance historians surmise that for ritual dances, such as processions and other group ceremonies, the religious leader also led and arranged the dances. Musicians who composed the music or the poets whose words were sung as hymns may also have organized the bodily action for which the hymn was written. E. Louis Backman demonstrated that hymns of the 7th, 8th, and 9th centuries were dance-songs. They gave the parishioners instructions about what they should be doing with their bodies during the hymn in the same way that the American folk (dance) song "Skip to my Lou" gives instructions, such as "lost my partner" or "find another."

Folklore scholars such as Lewis Spence have traced folk dances to their "pagan" ritual origins. People in village communities and ethnic churches in urban centers continue to perform these dances at weddings and other group occasions. Although the community dancers do not know who originated the dances they enjoy,

some participants may know who innovated changes or invented the new variations that they perform. This awareness of acknowledged dance leaders further contributes to scholars' assertions that folk dances are composed by talented dancers and not by the "folk."

Social dance historians have traced dances such as the waltz, polka, and rhumba to their folk and ritual origins. In some instances, scholars have also identified the occasions when particular dance masters have adapted these kinds of social recreational dances for formal theatrical presentation. During the 14th, 15th, and 16th centuries, dance masters in Italian, French, and Spanish courts adapted peasant (folk) dances for royal entertainments. Names such as Guglielmo Ebreo (William the Jew) (b. before 1440) and Antonio Cornazano (1431–c. 1500) are associated with these court dances (although they did not create them but only arranged them, an adaptive creative process in itself). These dance masters wrote treatises, which have been translated and published, enabling contemporary dance scholars and dancers to recreate these dances in a manner similar to the way early music scholars are reconstructing music written during the early Renaissance in Europe.

III. THE CREATIVE PROCESSES OF DANCE

Much is known about contemporary processes for creating dances; these methods may, perhaps, be extrapolated to past practices. This article emphasizes current methods choreographers or company members describe. Twentieth-century dance critic and theorist John Martin (1893–1985) identified three elements for any art form including dance: the instrument (training the body), the form (composing the dance), and the medium (performing it for an audience). The following discussion of the creative processes for dance describes the creative properties of each of these elements.

A. Training the Body

Dancers in art/entertainment dance attend classes to train their bodies to perform the dances that choreographers *set* on them; they informally call these technique classes. Most dancers do not regard this part of their training as creative because the origin of these techniques remains hidden. These techniques can be compared to the scales and chord sequences that a pianist practices at the beginning of a training session. Like practicing the piano, what dancers do in these technique classes are often short, isolated sections of movement phrases from dances that they must master with natural ease to perform them well. Because few teachers explain that these traditional classroom techniques were once created by choreographers to train their dancers to dance their dances, few students realize that the separate movements they practice in several directions around the body (such as to the front, sides, diagonals, and back) on different levels (such as on the ground, standing, and in the air), and moving through space in many directions originally came from dances that a choreographer invented. The process in which the choreographer engages to analyze and systemize the movements in their dances into a cohesive technique sequence is one of the hidden creative achievements of the activity and the field of dance. Although these systems of technique are described by their generic names such as ballet, modern, jazz, and tap, specific systems are often associated with their choreographer-originators or developers—for example, Cecchetti and Vaganova in ballet, Graham, Limon, and Hawkins in modern dance, and Luigi, Cole, and Giordano in jazz.

Ballet technique is the most commonly known theater dance technique; dancers in many countries in Europe, North and South America, Russia, and Asia study and perform it. The positions, steps, and gestures all have French names, which are used wherever it is taught. The formal system of ballet technique began in the early 1700s in the French court, but simple forms of the steps and movement sequences came directly from the peasant social dances that court dance masters from earlier centuries taught to their royal students. Great ballet dancers, teachers, and choreographers have developed the virtuosic range, enlarged the vocabulary, and formalized the structure of ballet technique since then. In its characteristic body position, the spine is held firmly vertical and the legs, knees, and feet remain outwardly rotated from the hip socket, commonly called *turnout*. Ballet's aesthetic goals of decorous symmetry, harmony, and balance are similar to those of the other arts of Baroque Era in which it developed. Traditionally the dancer always faces front while moving forward, backward, sideways, and on the diagonals. Because the first ballets were court entertainments for royalty, the theater convention of never turning the back to the (king) audience comes from the rules of dramatic and opera productions in which those early ballets were staged.

When folk and ritual dances are still part of social or ceremonial life of the originating community, the training techniques are usually not systematically organized in classes; people learn to dance these dances by dancing them. As children they start by following entire simple and highly repetitive dances. Thus beginning dancers master the vocabulary of movements little by little in the context of an entire dance in its social or ritual setting. When the dances are transplanted to other locations and occasions, dance leaders often establish training schools, which may be named after their original location such as China or Scotland or after their dance master teachers rather than choreographers. In both their original and transplanted locations, teachers in these schools emphasize the need to continue and pass on their ancient and often ritual tradition. The creative process for ritual and folk dance, therefore, occurs in an acknowledged yet more subtle manner than in art/entertainment dance. The master teachers accomplish gradual innovation in the techniques of these dances through their own performed interpretations and when they teach and coach their students.

These training methods of dance technique for art/entertainment, ritual, and social dance can be compared to different approaches to the teaching of reading: separate words and short phrases or entire sentences. In both styles of technique training, students usually imitate their teachers and repeat these techniques many times for many years until they become automatic. Though several systems of dance notation exist, unlike music students, few dance students learn how to read and write these notations in the context of their technique training.

In all these dance training systems, over years or centuries, a recognizable *vocabulary of dance movements* emerged. In ritual and social as well as the traditional forms of art/entertainment dance, such as European ballet or South Indian Bharata Natyam, a collection of postures, gestures, and steps with their accompanying directions in space, use of levels, characteristic rhythms, and choices of energy expenditure make up these vocabularies. Choreographers arrange and re-arrange these movements and instruct performers in the correct execution of these step sequences. These identifiable movement vocabularies are distinguishable by their unique characteristics the way personal and cultural music styles are.

In the early 20th century in Europe and the United States, artists in most arts rejected the technical and related aesthetic traditions of the past and began to discover new techniques and motivations to create their art products. Similarly, dance innovators rejected the limitations of the ballet aesthetic and technical movement vocabulary as the basis of theater dance and established the contemporary expectation for modern dancers to invent a new technique vocabulary along with their new dances. The abstracted emotional content of each dance provided the impetus for finding new movement instead of using the practiced vocabulary of training technique. In these new modern dance techniques, none of the previous ballet limitations applied. Dancers fell to and rolled on the floor; contracted and twisted the parts of the spine; used asymmetric and "ugly" shapes; used movement patterns with irregular rhythms and dissonant effects; performed in bare feet wearing simple, even neutral, costumes; and used music or sound scores with just percussion instruments written for the dance after it was completed. Participants in early modern dance experienced firsthand the creative process of their body training techniques.

B. Choreographing the Dance

Improvisation is one of the primary creative processes that choreographers use to discover new movements for their dances. Though more common among modern dance choreographers, some ballet and jazz dance composers use improvisation as part of their choreographic method. Tap dancer composers invent primarily by improvising. Dance innovators have invented many methods of improvising. In the late 1960s and 1970s some performers, called post-modern dancers, performed these improvisations themselves the way that jazz musicians use improvisation as their performance. [See IMPROVISATION.]

Dance innovators have invented a wide variety of improvisation techniques. Isadora Duncan (1878–1927),

widely credited as the major originator of what became known as modern dance, imitated the rhythmic wave patterns found in nature such as the wind, water, electricity, sound. She called this natural movement. Great classical music written by composers such as Chopin, Gluck, Wagner, Beethoven provided another stimulus for her original dance movement. Audience members began to describe her dances as interpretative because she used these great pieces of music as inspiration for her works. Another major source of inspiration on which she improvised was deeply felt emotions such as love, grief, and courage. Her many followers used these sources as well.

Ruth St. Denis (1877–1968), another early modern dance innovator, used pictures of Middle Eastern and Asian dancers and then the stylized versions of the dances themselves as sources for a new theatrical dance form. She and Ted Shawn (1891–1972) her partner and codirector of their company also worked out what they called music visualization, which coordinated movement more directly to the accompanying music than did Isadora Duncan. This choreographic method resembled the work of Swiss music educator Emile Jaques-Dalcroze (1865–1950), whose movement system and method of teaching rhythmic sensitivity to musicians contributed to early modern dance in Europe and especially to the work of Rudolf Laban (1879–1958), Mary Wigman (1886–1973), and British choreographer Marie Rambert (1888–1982).

The students of these modern pioneers, as dance historians call Duncan, St. Denis and Shawn, Laban, and Wigman, went on to devise their own methods of improvisation to find new movements for their choreography. These early modern dance choreographers emphasized the expression of genuine and universal feelings and many responded to the political, economic, and social issues of their countries and the world. To do this, for instance, students studying with Mary Wigman in Germany in the 1930s and 1940s would, like Duncan, improvise on emotional themes, such as hate, pain, anguish, devotion, longing, patience, or determination. Students of Laban might improvise on movements used in their work, such as hammering, lifting, sewing, weaving, or everyday gestures such as greetings, beckoning, refusing, or arguing.

As modern dance choreographers experimented with finding natural movement, they evolved guidelines to help students discover new movements from which they would make their own dances. An example will illustrate these general guidelines. To compose a dance about greeting, students might improvise with a simple wave hello. To vary this everyday gesture, one can enlarge the wave, make it very small, do it slowly or very quickly, wave reaching high in the air, even jumping, or along the ground, behind the back, or over the shoulder. The wave hello can be executed with varying emotional intensities: lazily, eagerly, with irritation or affection, shyly or abruptly, in a silly or sad way. The same variations can be done with other parts of the body, not just with the arm and hand. These variations on one gesture can be done traveling or in place—sitting, standing, walking, running, turning, sliding; they can be done using varied rhythms and tempos, in different directions, and so on. The principles of movement improvisation are comparable to those used by musicians and artists to vary and develop melodies and designs.

These modern dance choreographers evolved a craft for improvisation to facilitate the creative process of finding expressive and new movements for their dances. They also introduced these creative processes of improvisation and dance composition to the training of dance students and company members. Evidently, formal study of dance composition was not part of a professional dance student's training until the advent of modern dance in the 20th century.

The treatise *The Art of Making Dances* (1959) by Doris Humphrey (1895–1958) makes a major contribution to the understanding of how choreographers guide their creative process. Humphrey was a member of the Denishawn dance company until 1929 when she and Charles Weidman (1901–1975) left to begin their own company. Few choreographers before her had produced a book that gives such detailed insight into the craft of choreographing and, thus, allows readers to grasp the rigor and discipline of the creative process of dance making at the time, the mid-20th century, when modern dancers had developed their work to a recognized level of excellence.

Humphrey's guidelines for making dances resemble the composition methods used in other mid-20th century arts. The appropriate choice of dance theme, she explained, must be unique to the medium of movement. Dances evoke emotion by resonating with the kinesthetic sense of audience members and thus can reach the depths of experience of human beings. To craft this theme into a dance, Humphrey identified the essential components: variations of the movement theme such as varying a melodic line; phrasing of movement sequences; dynamics, including accents and the high point or denouement of the entire dance; rhythm—breath, emotional, and musical; psychological and physical motivation; everyday gestures enlarged into dance movement; symmetry and asymmetry of bodily design; space usage on stage and spatial relationships of one or more bodies to each other and to the stage space. These guidelines also applied to groups. She concluded her analysis of dance craft with suggestions for sound, music, and verbal accompaniment as well as sets, props, and choreographic forms such as ABA (A, first theme; B, second theme), rondo, chorus-verse, and free form. She derived her ideas from her own experience of making dances as well as from her understanding of how good visual and musical art works, even theater productions, are composed.

The guidelines, called expressionistic, set down by Humphrey were the ones younger modern dance choreographers rebelled against. Choreographers such as Merce Cunningham (b. 1919), influenced by his musician colleague John Cage (1912–1992), used chance methods of finding movements that were meant to express no emotion. Cunningham quoted Marshal McLuhan, "the medium is the message," to explain his choreographic intent. Another rebellious choreographer, Alwin Nikolais (1912–1993) had his company members improvise in time, space, and energy to find neutral movements and costumed his dancers in abstract shapes. Both choreographers believed that movement is expressive the way abstract painting is and need not deliberately convey emotional or symbolic meaning.

In 1963 British ballerina, teacher, and director Peggy Van Praagh (1910–1990) and critic and historian Peter Brinson (1923–1995) wrote *The Choreographic Art: An Outline of its Principles and Craft* to describe the creative processes of constructing a ballet. In their book the authors consider some of the same topics about which Humphrey wrote, such as theme and the relation of the dance to the music and design aspects of the production. The contents of Van Praagh and Brinson's book show the formal and motivational differences between modern dance and ballet.

A ballet, Van Praagh and Brinson explained, is constructed by at least four cooperating artists one of whom may be its author: the poet or writer, composer, set and costume designer, and the choreographer. Any of these artists may devise the theme, be it narrative, mood, or abstract, and outline the scenario of its development. The choreographer then works with his or her trained dancers, the plastic material of ballet. The "limitless (movement) possibilities are limited in practice by the dancers' training, the choreographer's training and the needs of design, gravity and rhythm" (p. 197). He or she can utilize the conventional ballet movement vocabulary or invent new steps to accomplish the main task of composing the solo; duets, called *pas de deux* (steps of two); group dances; and dramatic climaxes (*pas d'action*). Choreographers in the many countries where ballet companies work apply variations of these basics because their ballet heritages can be traced to the original Italian-French school of ballet. Even the Russian tradition, which integrated into ballet its own folk movements, energy, and aesthetic, came from the Italian-French school.

Traditional folk and contemporary social (ballroom) dances provide a continuing source of movement for ballet and modern dance choreographers. They use folk and social dance steps, styles, energy, or all features to enrich their art/entertainment dances. Like ballet, the art/entertainment form of jazz dance started as folk and social dance.

Over its 400 year history in the United States, jazz gradually developed as a theater form with its own movement vocabulary, choreographic guidelines, and performance styles. The uniqueness of jazz dance parallels jazz music: it is highly rhythmic, syncopated, improvisational, and overtly emotional. West Africans who came to North America as slaves contributed the basic features of jazz dance: isolated body parts moving rhythmically and percussively, a bent-forward body posture with the action exploding from the hips, animal imitation, and a satiric attitude toward any subject matter. Its earliest theater form was tap dance. When "talking" motion pictures began, movie producers asked the tap dancers to add more upper body movement to their dancing because the microphones placed on the floor to record the tap sound also picked up extraneous noises behind the camera not meant to be heard. Dancer/choreographers like Fred Astaire and

Gene Kelly added movements from ballroom dance; Jack Cole and Matt Maddox added movement from modern dance and East Indian forms; Katherine Dunham integrated Cuban, Brazilian, and Haitian movements; Bob Fosse and Gower Champion used variations of popular jazz social dances like the black bottom, the jitterbug, and the frug; and Jerome Robbins combined ballet precision with Latin ballroom dances like the cha-cha and mambo.

The choreographic method for jazz recommended by the few authors who have written about it resembles the method used by ballet choreographers: find a suitable theme, select appropriate music, and work with standard and invented jazz movement vocabulary to express the movement ideas. Jazz dance choreographers have often made major contributions to Broadway musicals some, like Bob Fosse, Gower Champion, and Jerome Robbins, have directed or codirected them using their choreographic creative ability to organize the dynamic action of the entire show, not just the dances interwoven into the story line.

All the authors of the books or articles on choreographic method recommend their guidelines not as prescriptions to follow rigidly but as a base on which to make variations and departures. They all agree that dances need unity, variety, contrast, surprise elements, and dynamic interest. They must be kinesthetically interesting and express movement ideas that cannot be expressed in any other means or medium.

In the 20th century, folk dances were more likely to have a choreographer or arranger's name associated with them than in previous centuries. Whether these dances are "signed" or not, they have a remarkably recognizable form the world over. The human activities of song making, story telling, picture drawing, play acting, and dance composing are found in every culture, and all children are capable of making, performing and recognizing these aesthetic forms. In the folk dance forms around the world, people are organized in circles, lines, couples, trios and quartets, or combinations or variations of these. Like the folk music and songs that frequently accompany them, the movement sequences are often in verse/chorus, theme, and variations or repeated sequences, which speed up or slow down, shorten or lengthen in regular countable units. The dances have themes and names that convey their origins and functions: in work (harvesting, fishing, horseback riding), in courtship (flirtation, displays of skill and strength, capture), or in celebrations of events (weddings, baptisms, namings, or victories). In each culture the variety ranges from dances easy enough for children and elders to perform to virtuosic ones used by special groups to show off their skills. The choreographic achievement made by the often anonymous dance masters who composed these dances is remarkable and evidently long lasting though only recently have dance ethnologists such as Joan Kealiinohomoku, Elsie Ivancich Dunin, and Adrienne Kaeppler been studying the life span of these kinds of dances.

Some social dances, like the waltz and polka, began as folk dances and have become part of urban popular recreational dance practice. In the beginning of this century, ballroom dance instructors Vernon and Irene Castle popularized among their upper- and middle-class clientele dances like the back bottom and jitterbug done by African Americans and poor white Southerners in speakeasies and jook joints. These dances are not attributed to any choreographer. Social dance historians dispute the exact location and origin of many of them. In the middle of the 20th century, dances seen on the television program *The American Bandstand* became very popular at high school and college proms and other social occasions such as weddings or coming-of-age celebrations where people dance. Social dance teachers composed some of these dances to music on single 45 rpm records to increase sales. Dance makers themselves began making new dances to compete with other popular ones. Dance scholar Gretchen Schneider discovered similar practices were occurring among competing ballroom dance teachers in Chicago in the late 19th century. Although people in many parts of the world do not dance in couples, Schneider suggested that where social dancing in couples is a courtship pastime, such competitive practices may have gone on for a long time. Social dance choreographers or arrangers in Europe and the United States have applied their creative capacities to this dance attraction for centuries.

C. Performing the Dance

In 1956 outstanding modern dance performer Pauline Koner (b. 1912) began to teach the art and craft of performing and, thus, challenged the idea that superb performers are born and not made. She derived the principles by analyzing her own practice and that of other great dance performers. By teaching these essentials of performance to students of dance, theater, and opera, she successfully improved their performing abilities.

The primary elements of dance performance, for Koner, include emotion, motivation, focus, dynamics, and movement texture; these essentials are the art elements. The focus of the mind, Koner stressed, is as important as gravity is to the body. Although she identified six categories of focus—inner, directional, area, magnetic, body, and dramatic—their central feature is concentration, utter and complete from the beginning of the performance to the end. In coaching students on how to focus she advises, "Never feel you are *doing*, always feel you are *being*. With all senses alert, seek out your deepest feelings—make the immediacy of each moment come alive." (p. 19).

Like music, the dynamic elements of a dance performance consist of nuance, color, and contrast applied to movement in time, energy, and spatial range. Whereas dynamics and focus enhance the color and contrast of movement, the elements of movement texture center on how movement is performed. The most important of these is weight. It is the element that the early modern dancers contributed to concert dance and contrasted to the essential lightness of ballet. To move limbs, Koner asserted, push through the density of space and yield to the pull of gravity. To communicate this awareness dancers must modulate their energy. Each of the other elements Koner considered in her discussion of movement texture also vary energy: accent; suspension; rebound; movement overtones of isolations; flutters, tremors, shivers; and, finally, stillness.

Koner called the last section of *Elements of Performance* "Secondary Elements: The Craft." As important as the primary elements (the inner person), the secondary elements relate to the outer person: stage and hand props, fabric, costume, and stage decorum (such as bows, entrances, and exits). All the instructions center around focus and concentration from the moment the dance begins until the curtain closes at the end. The skillful and sensitive application of the primary and secondary elements in a performance requires performers to integrate their intelligences with their technical and creative capabilities. Koner's analysis of the rich and complex nature of performance backs up the results of both psychological studies and art critics' evaluation of performing-artistic excellence. Highly talented performing artists literally re-create choreographers' works in their own unique manner, which is recognized by audience members and critics.

IV. HISTORICAL OVERVIEW OF SELECTED INNOVATIONS IN DANCE

Dance historians trace innovation by analyzing the interaction among the three elements just described. Training the body in new ways creates fresh choreographic possibilities, which in turn require dancers to increase their performance capabilities. Other factors, such as changes in the shoe, the costume, the stage space, the audience, and the location, stimulate innovations, as do the social, political, economic, and artistic climate in which the artistic activity occurs. Though the following overview of innovations centers on Western dance it provides examples of the nature of creative changes that occur in the histories of dance in other parts of the world.

Dance innovations among the ancient peoples in the Egypt and the Middle East are difficult to ascertain because of the kind of records available to historians. Art conventions limited how Egyptian people were represented: the upper classes were shown only in profile, and thus the dance movements that they were executing may be distorted. The limited visual and hieroglyphic evidence shows that dance functioned primarily as ritual: the pharaoh was the religious leader and led the courtiers and his subjects in religious ceremonies. Dance served more than a ritual function. Records show that court entertainers performed dances that included acrobatic movements and professional women dancers entertained the people at the edge of the large crowds gathered for royal funerals. [*See* INNOVATION.]

As it did in Egypt, ritual dance played an important part in the lives of the peoples in the ancient Middle East. Because of strictures against making graven images of human beings among the ancient Jews, historians only know from verbal descriptions when and why these people danced: in religious processions and encircling the altar; for celebrations of victories, weddings, first fruits, and harvests; for supplication; and for nonreligious occasions such as funerals. Many of the psalms in the Bible are dance songs. Stone relief carvings and written descriptions of other Middle Eastern peoples such as the Hittites and Babylonians give evidence of dance being similarly integrated into their ritual practices. Dance also played a part in courtship among the ancient Jews. As part of the new year celebration, unmarried women, all dressed in white, danced for eligible men to watch and choose a bride from among them.

This discussion thus far has not identified any specific innovative dance practices. That does not mean they did not occur, but only that dance historians have insufficient evidence on which to draw conclusions. The information does serve as a baseline for understanding some of the innovations in dance practices that followed.

More evidence exists about the various kinds ritual dances and dancers in ancient Greece than for ancient Egypt and the Middle East. Much of it is gleaned from the writings of philosophers Plato and Aristotle, the Roman satirist Lucian, and from numerous artifacts showing dancer/actors in a wide variety of dance positions. Like Egyptian art this pictorial evidence is also mediated through the Greek art conventions. T. B. L. Webster used carbon dating of pottery to catalog the increased range of movement depicted on these artifacts. Many kinds of ritual dances are pictured, including animal imitation, harvest, and other nature festivals such as wine pressing.

The famous Greek plays from the Golden Age of Athens during the 4th century B.C., limited though they are in number, provide primary-source verbal evidence of dance practice at that time. The primary change was the decreased role played by dance compared to its predominance in the dramatic dithyramb ceremonies, which were thought to be the source of the tragedies. The actors' roles became more important and fewer dancers made up the choruses. Dithyrambs had 50 dancers, whereas the choruses had 24, then 18, and eventually 8 to 12 members. Like the actors in these plays, the dancer-chorus members spoke and sang while they danced and gestured to convey their emotional responses to the action. Dancer/actors in the comedies and satyr plays, if the pictorial evidence is accurate, played bawdy characters with slapstick, action. The detail available about the dances for tragedies, comedies, and satyr plays includes their names: emmeleia, kordax, and sikinnis, respectively.

The innovations for dance in ancient Greece appear to be in the specialization of roles—into actor, dancer, and musician from just dancer—among the amateur players who performed in the annual ritual play competitions. Change also occurred in the settings themselves. The first identified locations for these ritual dance ceremonies were the round and flat grain threshing floors, the orchestra. During the Golden Age of Athens, official theaters were built to enlarge the space for the performers and audience members with the round flat surface remaining in front of the raised stage. The increased distance over which the voice and movements needed to be projected required changes in performance style for the dancers and actors. In the state-supported ritual theater performances, male amateurs played all the parts. They wore masks, which hid megaphone-like mouthpieces to help project the words of their characters to the large audiences. Masks also protected their personal identities. When the Greek empire was in decline, professional mime troops of slaves or freemen roamed the countryside performing satiric and politically radical skits. These troops may have included women.

The development of mime—postures, gestures, and actions with clear and literal meanings—was the primary innovation in dance made by players in the ancient Roman empire. Though today the words *pantomime* and *mime* are used interchangeably, *mime* was the term used for acting (sometimes in bawdy plays), whereas *pantomime* referred specifically to silent acting. Christian authors refer to pantomiming and dancing as *saltatio,* thus the expressive use of the body separate from speaking began to emerge as a recognized activity. In the public arena the Romans copied and developed the ancient Greek theatrical forms and methods. Eventually these combined with indigenous amateur-mimed witty and bawdy songs sung at weddings, called Fescennine and Atellan fables, satiric and politically irreverent performances about small-town life from the area of Campagna. This melding of satiric songs and stories eventually developed into what became known as commedia dell'arte. Improvisational traveling companies performing commedia dell'arte were the source of the first professional women dance specialists when ballet was no longer an activity for amateurs in the courts of aristocrats.

During the Middle Ages and Renaissance, social dances (or folk dances, which are often old social dances from specific countries) for courtship and community celebrations continued to be popular as recreation when people gathered at fairs and for religious occasions. During the winter months these dances provided recreation and entertainment indoors where space allowed. Modified and dignified versions of these social dances were the source of ballet, as described earlier.

After the fall of Rome the integrated performing arts of dance, music, and theater evolved both in the Christian church and among the people in the various emerging countries in Europe. The separation and specialization of the activities and roles developed gradually. Social dances were so popular that the leaders in the Christian church, beginning in the 7th century, forbade dancing on church grounds and in cemeteries if it led to fornication; otherwise even the Church fathers, themselves, danced on regular occasions in their ceremonies and special holiday celebrations. They danced, sang, and acted in dramatized renditions of Bible stories and saints lives. As the centuries passed and these religious performances were staged outside the church, professional theater guilds took over. These performances helped the church leaders communicate with their increasingly diverse congregations. A major innovation was their theatricalization of the mass. By appealing to the aesthetic sensitivity of their congregants with kinesthetic, auditory, and visual stimuli the Christian leaders utilized colorful practices similar to the so-called pagan religious ones they sought to supersede.

The next major innovation in dance performance developed in the context of court spectacles held by the newly emerging royal political leaders in countries in Europe. They imitated the church's increasingly elaborate and formal dramatic presentations, called *Laudi* in the 13th century, *Divozione* in the 14th century, and *Sacra Rapprasentazione* in the 15th century. The most notable imitator was Lorenzo de Medici, Lorenzo the Magnificent, of Florence in his famous *Trionfi* of the late 1400s. These costumed parades with verse, song, and some dance celebrated the life and mythology of ancient Rome, newly discovered by archeologists and uncovered in restored manuscripts found in church libraries.

Other aristocratic families in Italy, Spain, Portugal, and France also staged outdoor spectacles to celebrate victories, royal weddings, the reception of celebrities, anniversaries. The overall purpose for the decorated carts, elaborately costumed participants, songs, verses, and dances was to display the power, wealth, and influence of their sponsor. The Roman and Greek mythological figures and symbols were used as thinly veiled propaganda. Until 1581 no literary or formal theme united the parts.

Catherine de Medici married Henri duc d'Orleans who in 1547 became Henri the Second of France. When she moved to France from Italy, Catherine brought along a company of commedia dell'arte players, along with the set and costume designers, and hired an Italian dancing master who had come to France in 1555, Baldassare de Belgiojoso (15??– c. 1587) (who changed his name to Balthasar de Beaujoyeulx). All had experience mounting the Medici *Trionfi*. Though Catherine staged several court spectacles before 1581, *Le Ballet Comique de la Reine Louise* choreographed by Beaujoyeulx was the first to have a central organizing theme. Beaujoyeulx integrated the best elements from earlier forms of court entertainments: tournaments, masquerades, and pastorals.

The music, verse, and dance in *Le Ballet Comique de la Reine Louise* were composed to harmonize according to the practice of measured verse. Musicians and poets in the music Academy of St. Cecilia, founded in 1570 by Jean Antoine de Baif (b. 1532), were trying to blend verse, music, and song in the manner they thought the ancient Greeks had achieved. This ideal unity among the arts became the goal of dance reformers for several hundred years.

The dances in these court spectacles were the popular court social dances with names such as Pavanne, Basse dance, Galliard, Tordion, Volta, Courante, Gavotte, and Branle. Classical music lovers will recognize these names because recordings of early music contain the accompaniment to these dances. In these spectacles, which often included an elaborate banquet, the dances were interspersed among the sequence of songs, recited verse, and orchestral interludes. The dances were performed in geometric designs and did little to carry forward the action of the story. The dancers wore the clothing of the court, which included heavy wigs and many layered and tightly bodiced finery. The audience was seated above the dancers in balconies on three sides of the ballroom floor where the performance was staged. From this vantage point audience members could see the dance designs most clearly. To change this early form of dance performance into the

virtuosic specialty of today, innovations in the costume, shoe, and stage space were necessary.

In the second half of the 1600s during the reign of Louis the XIV, several changes occurred. With Molière (1622–1673) as playwright and Lully (1632–1687) as musician, court entertainment moved onto a proscenium arch stage. Molière integrated the action and humor of commedia dell'arte into his plays, while Lully and the dance master Beauchamps (1631–1719) created dance movements that conveyed expressive content of the plot using pantomimic gesture. Lully also established a department of dance in the Royal Academy of Music, which became known as the Paris Opera where the famous ballet school and company worked. The ballets were usually performed at the end of the first and the beginning of the third acts of operas. When in 1672 Lully took over as director of the academy, he completed the transition of ballet and opera to professional status.

Beauchamps is credited for having codified the turnout, the basic five positions of the feet, and systematizing the teaching of ballet. He introduced female dancers into the company and even evolved a notation system for recording dance. In 1700 his system was published by Roaul Auger Feuillet (c. 1650–1709).

Even with technique and dance content changing, the court costume with wig and mask prevented dancers from becoming very expressive. These innovations were made by dancers in England, where the rules of the French Academy did not limit subject matter to classical themes and the time span of the story to 24 hours. In his ballet *The Loves of Mars and Venus* (1717), dancer, theorist, and choreographer John Weaver (1673–1760) tried to convey the action of the story with only movement and not depend on spoken word or song. In 1734 a young dancer trained in a commedia dell'arte company, Marie Salle (1707–1756) choreographed *Pygmalion*, where she wore a simple costume rather than the usual corset, petticoats, and pannier and let down her own hair instead of wearing a wig.

These costume and movement style changes took almost another hundred years to become standard practice on European stages. Three reformer choreographers are credited with fostering what became known as ballet d'action: Jean-Baptiste de Hesse (1705–1779), Franz Anton Hilverding (1710–1768), and Jean George Noverre (1727–1810). In their teaching, choreography, and Noverre in his *Letters on Dancing and Ballets* (1760) as well, they espoused the integration of mime, steps, and postures all to convey the content and real human emotions of the dance narrative without text. They also urged simplified costumes, elimination of the masks, and the coordination of the music with the narrative and set design.

Choreographers and dancers helped gradually to implement some of the goals of ballet d'action. They modified the costume by shortening the skirts, using lighter fabrics, and replacing the heeled shoe with a sandal or flat-heeled slipper. Wigs and masks were finally eliminated, and dancers no longer sang or recited poetry. New literary and poetic themes in the ballet stories gave dancers opportunities to demonstrate increased technical virtuosity and dramatic expressivity. Audiences for the opera where ballet companies were housed grew to include middle-class patrons. To satisfy this widening audience and to add local color, choreographers included variations of popular social dances, such as the mazurka, waltz, polka, and tarantella.

In the first half of the 1800s, the romantic period in art, literature, and music stimulated the greatest changes in ballet, changes that gave it the characteristics with which today's audiences are familiar. Themes centering around mystical characters, mysterious events, and distant lands required dancers to simulate flying and floating. At first dancers were lifted by wires, but when too many accidents occurred, the women dancers stiffened the toes of their ballet slippers and eventually developed the pointe shoe. The fantasy creatures in the stories wore the dress of the restoration, the bouffant skirt made of layers of tulle known as a tutu. Gaslight in theaters and on stages, for the first time, allowed a darkened house and many variations of stage lighting not available before. Credit for these changes goes to many designers, poets, choreographers, and dancers from all over Europe, too many to name here. The romantic revolution began with heightened expressivity, which in turn stimulated technical innovation. This innovation led to greater virtuosity, which essentially took over especially as the political changes that created democracies all over Europe enabled more people to attend theater performances previously unavailable to them.

Political changes in Russia at the end of the 1800s and at the beginning of the 1900s gave impetus to major changes in ballet. Beginning of the 1700s, famous European dancers and choreographers had retired in Russia to help create and sustain the czar's ballet company at the Maryinsky Theatre in St. Petersburg and later in Moscow. In Russia, like in the United States, Britain, Spain, and Germany, foreign choreographers and dancers, mostly French and Italian born, were featured in ballet until the 20th century. The Russian revolution in dance occurred because an impresario, Serge Diaghilev (1872–1929), had the insight and persuasive powers to compel gifted and experimental choreographers, outstanding dancers such as Tamara Karsavina (1885–1978), innovative composers such as Igor Stravinsky (1882–1971); and avant-garde painters and designers such as Leon Baskt (1866–1924) and Pablo Picasso (1881–1973) to work together to invent new ballets with nontraditional ballet technique, unusual themes, exceptional music, and exotic costumes. For the first time, evidently, Diaghilev enabled audiences to attend entire evenings of just dance performance; dance was separate from opera. His work with his Ballet Russe from 1909 to 1929 achieved the goals that Noverre had articulated almost 150 years before. The names of his choreographers still resonate with dance audiences: Michael Fokine (1880–1942), Vaslav Nijinsky (1889–1950), Leonide Massine (1895–1979), Bronislava Nijinska (1891–1972), Serge Lifar (1905–1986), and George Balanchine (1904–1983), as do some of the most famous dances they choreographed.

After Diaghilev's death in 1929, the Russians from Ballet Russe spread all over the world to perform, teach, and choreograph. This is the same time when modern dancers, such as Martha Graham, Doris Humphrey, Rudolf Laban, and others named earlier, were establishing their own dance companies; evolving new dance vocabularies, choreographic methods, costume and set designs, sound accompaniment; and reaching new audiences who supported professional dance that satisfied contemporary aesthetic needs.

During the second half of the 20th century, dance companies from countries around the world began touring with performance versions of their ritual, folk, or social dances. Choreographers from many countries, such as the Philippines, Mexico, India, Russia, Basque country, the Caribbean Islands, and Africa, selected and arranged their dances to please foreign audiences. Recently, performers dancing Argentinean tangos have toured. Whereas the arrangers are credited with organizing and directing these companies, the region of origin and reason for the dance were noted in the programs. In these performances of traditional ritual and social dance, the creative product of that particular culture took precedence over the individual and probably unknown creator. The joy of dancing for courtship and play has sufficient meaning to the dancers and audience members; the creative act of making those dances is either taken for granted or forgotten.

The processes of training, choreographing, and performing dance require the creative capabilities of dance teachers, choreographers, and dancers in the activity of dance, no matter for what purpose it is being performed: art/entertainment, social, or ritual. Innovations range from major choreographic breakthroughs to minor technical developments in training or performing. Though they evolve more quickly and overtly in some cultures and historical periods than in others, these creative changes in dance practices occur in all societies.

Bibliography

Alter, J. B. (1984). Creativity profile of university and conservatory dance students. *Journal of Personality Assessment, 48,* 153-158.

Alter, J. B. (1991). Dance-based dance theory: From borrowed models to dance-based experience. New York: Peter Lang.

Au, S. (1988). Ballet and modern dance. London: Thames and Hudson.

Buckman, P. (1978). Let's dance: Social, ballroom and folk dancing. New York: Paddington Press.

Clarke, M., & Crisp, C. (1992). Ballet: An illustrated history. London: Hamish Hamilton.

Cohen, S. J. (Ed.). (1998). International encyclopedia of dance. Oxford: Oxford University Press.

Koner, P. (1993). Elements of performance: A guide for performers in dance, theatre and opera. London: Harwood Academic Publishers.

Stearns, M., & Stearns, J. (1968). Jazz dance: The story of American vernacular dance. New York: Macmillan.

Van Praagh, P. & Brinson, P. (1963). The choreographic art: An outline of its principles and craft. London: A&C Black.

Wallace, C. M., McDonagh, D., Drunesedow, J. I., Libin, L. & Old, C. (1986). Dance: A very social history. New York: The Metropolitan Museum of Art, Rizzoli.

Wigman, M. (1931). Composition in pure movement. *Modern Music, 8,* 20–22.

Dark Side of Creativity

Robert B. McLaren

California State University, Fullerton

Anthropogenic Originating in human activity; revealing the specific and original influence of human behavior, as on the environment.

Bête Noire Literally a "black beast" (French); a specter or bugbear; any object of hate or fear.

Daemonic In classical Greek mythology, a supernatural intelligence often, but not always, malevolent. A genius.

Ex Nihilo "Out of nothing" (Latin); a concept of the original creation of the universe solely by the will of God. Plato scornfully asserted that artists and other "creative" people actually do not create anything, but merely manipulate the material of the already existing world. Augustine concurred, stating that God alone can call forth something out of nothing.

Hoi Polloi "The many" (Greek); often used in a derogatory sense of the common herd, the masses, or even "the great unwashed."

Ontology The study of the *ontos,* or the nature of being (Greek). The essential question is, what does it mean for a thing or person to "be" as opposed to to not being? At the personal level a related question is, what kind of creature am I, and is my existence derived from some ground of being? For ex-

ample, am I rooted in soulless matter or perhaps in the being of a Creator?

Polis City, or "the body politic" (Greek), from which we also derive such words as police, policy, and polite; anything to do with the people in a governmental region.

Teleology The study of final causes (Greek); the ends toward which things develop in order to fulfill themselves; for example, the *telos,* or intended purpose, of the acorn is to become an oak tree—treeness is the "cause" or purpose of the acorn's existence.

_{Creativity clearly has its **DARK SIDE,** but the problem lies not alone in the fields of endeavor where it is enlisted (art, science, technology, etc.), but within the creative impulse itself, its narcissistic temptations, and our ways of responding to its urging. There is something of irony in the fact that, amid almost universal enthusiasm for the idea of creativity, we hear echoes of unease when it is discovered that our creative efforts, whether in the arts, sciences, technology, or social strategies, are often placed in the service of coercive, prurient, and even lethal pursuits. This is not to overlook such positive components of creativity as its tranformational capacity, or the employment of divergent thinking and intentionality which promise highly beneficial fruits. Indeed these are applied to the fullest in such endeavors as will be discussed here. But if we are to be honest in our quest to}

Copyright © 1999 by Academic Press
All rights of reproduction in any form reserved.

understand creativity we must acknowledge that it has its dark side, arising from something deep within the same human nature that promotes it. Art has been employed to celebrate faith, beauty, nobility, and love. But artistic innovation was also exercised by the ancient Assyrians to decorate their homes with the peeled and painted skins of their fallen enemies, and by the Nazis to fashion lampshades of the skins of holocaust victims. The entertainment enterprise historically engaged the finest playwrites and performers of Greece, but also the bloody spectacles of the Coliseum of Rome; and it has included a wide array from inspiring oratorios to sheer pornography. The creative impulse also led to the hideously clever torture devices of the Spanish Inquisition, the sweatshops and mines of the Industrial Revolution, and the gas furnaces of Auschwitz. Through the ingenuity of nuclear technology, one man, a president or dictator, can press a single button to set in motion weapons of global annihilation.

I. THE CREATIVE IMPULSE

Rooted in a yearning to make things better than they are, creativity should be distinguished from the mere manipulation of familiar objects for the sake of novelty. The need to make a more efficient tool, a better weapon, or an improved mode of transportation or communication is, in popular parlance, "the mother of invention." Innovation, according to Jean Piaget, is a necessary component of the process of transformation, itself a form of interpreting the objective world "to make sense of it," and improve on it. [*See* INNOVATION; NOVELTY.]

Creativity emerges from a longing for unrealized perfection in its absolute sense. It carries with it a dissatisfaction with things as they are, and a zeal to reform them—to "ennoble" or even to emancipate them from the fetters of conditions that now prevail, or to bring the actual world into conformity with the ideal world.

The attempt to portray an experience of perfection whether in paint, words, or music always falls short. Yet the artist feels compelled to try. Hence the creation of portraits which eliminate imperfections and highlight features which come closest to what the artist (or subject) deems perfection. Dissatisfaction with such prettification (and thus falsification) of reality is echoed

in the oft-quoted "paint my picture truly like me . . . pimples, warts, and everything" of Oliver Cromwell. The poet Keats despaired of the capacity of words to convey the truth and beauty he sought to capture, and lamented, "the brave music of a *distant* drum!" (Italics his, to express the inaccessibility of the ideal.) Herein too lies the moral precariousness of aestheticism: the temptation to substitute make-believe for reality, and then not merely "settling" for the results (but in the manner of Pygmalion, falling in love with it).

In our proclivity for linking creativity with inspiration and divine principles, we ignore its close affinity with hubris, the sin of pride. One of history's earliest legends has to do with the creation of the Tower of Babel, where every artifice was employed to devise a tower so magnificent that it could reach the very portals of Heaven. Humankind would thereby be able to climb to the gates of Paradise and claim its blessings without moral deserving. According to the story, their punishment was to have their language confused and "to be scattered abroad across the face of the earth." Pride and conceit underlay their misuse of the gift of creativity, and this ultimately led to humankind's mutual estrangement. From that point on, all human inventions, from the chariot wheel to atomic fission, seem to bear the stigma of the Babel experience. Hence the lament in Ecclesiastes, "God made men upright, but they have sought out many inventions," and the Psalmist's echo, "They became unclean in their acts, and played the harlot with their inventions."

It has been in the service of religion that creativity has often been seen at its most seductive and problematic. Temples and cathedrals, with their golden altars and lavish furnishings, have often been erected at great cost to the general population, whose need for food, housing, and the basics of survival was sacrificed. It has been argued, perhaps with some justification, that without these many synagogues and churches the call of the prophets for justice, and of Christ for compassion for the poor and destitute, would not have been heard. But it can also be pointed out that elaborate services of worship, if lacking these socially beneficial actions, become merely aesthetic exercises in self-indulgence.

The daemonic aspect of creativity, however, lies at a deeper level. In classical Greece, the creative individual was seldom exalted (except for the temporary hero of the Olympic games), but was held to be a part of the whole polis. Artists through the Middle Ages almost never signed their work. The Renaissance changed the focus of attention and of responsibility to the creative individual himself. The spotlight of fame was turned onto the Great Masters, who engaged in rivalries of intense nature. Hero worship and "star" status encouraged the notion that the genius could afford to be irresponsible because of being uniquely different, above the crowd, and superior to the hoi polloi. Not only is ethics devalued in the veneration of the genius, but the spiritual life, including moral discipline and grace, is also rejected. It is not just incidental that one of the first targets of 20th century dictators has been religion, the worship of a god whose moral and spiritual requirements call all persons, including dictators and their enterprises, to account. The creative dynamic is substituted for religion as well as for morality. "Productivity becomes in itself the meaning and principle of life." Karl Marx insisted, "man is free only if he owes his existence to himself," so religion and God are reduced to irrelevance. And to be sure, the more we live among our artificial structures and machinery, the more strongly grows the impression that we are self-sufficient. The more creative we think ourselves to be, the more we confound ourselves with the Creator, and the postulate of autonomy becomes unconditional. Absolute freedom for the creative individual is mandated at all costs, to be guaranteed by constitutions and safeguarded by the courts.

The history of our century, which Winston Churchill called "this hideous epoch in which we dwell," may force a reexamination of such confidence. Borne in on a wave of unprecedented optimism, largely because of the vast accumulation of 19th century inventions, the 20th century was first lauded by the poet Algernon Swinburn: "Glory to man in the highest, / For man is the master of things." Yet, as Larry Rassmussen reminds us, "no other century comes close for sheer deadliness. Perhaps as many as 187,000,000 people have died as the result of warfare in this century, the equivalent of one-tenth of the total world population when the century began." Add to these deaths those brought on by poverty, disease, self-poisonings through tobacco and alcohol, and the rampant rise of homicides due to the proliferation of technologically improved guns and other weapons, and T. S. Eliot's epitaph for

our generation is poignantly appropriate: "Miserable cities of designing men, / Lost in the mazes of your own ingenuity."

More fully to understand our dilemma, we need to see how it is reflected in specific areas of human endeavor.

II. THE ARTS

From the earliest human records it has been evident that the aesthetic impulse has evoked some of the most ennobling of creative efforts. From cave paintings and primitive sculptures, to the pyramids of Egypt, the Parthenon of Greece, the cathedrals of Europe, and on to the most imaginative of modern creations, the arts have provided the medium for expressing what humankind has hoped represents our species at its best. There is no claim that such people were "creators" in any divine sense, inasmuch as they did not create anything *de novo,* and certainly nothing *ex nihilo* as was attributed to God. The most they could accomplish was to arrange objects and sounds in pleasing fashion, and for this they have sometimes been awarded lasting appreciation.

To be sure, many would affirm that no literal representation of nature can qualify as art. It has already been noted that in a period of outstanding painting and sculpture in classical Greece, Plato expressed disdain for those who rearranged or imitated the factual world. But the issue with Plato was not simply that such imitators of nature were engaged in deceiving the senses, but that their work was a threat to the integrity of mind and spirit. The enjoyment they yield, he writes, "excite irrational pleasures," whereas art must always have rationality as its goal. He applies this specifically to music, insisting that tunes and melodies conceived in abstraction from the moral temper is music with its soul gone, and therefore "intolerable and blasphemous."

Plato's insistence that art must serve "the moral temper" carried over into the world of medieval Christendom, where artists were employed to symbolize hidden truths of the faith, and were largely controlled by ecclesiastical mandate to carve or paint according to specifications. The Virgin Mary was almost always clothed in blue, and her halo had to be of a specific diameter relative to her head (and Joseph's and other saints' halos were scaled down proportionately). The works were almost never signed by the artist. But with the Renaissance, "the beauty of holiness" became virtually "the holiness of beauty." Works of art were no longer just symbols or reminders of the holy things, they were themselves objects of veneration. Michelangelo not only signed his works, he carved his name on the strap that crossed Mary's breast in the larger-than-life *Pieta,* where no one could miss it.

Rembrandt turned from flattering portraiture, the highest form of commercial art in his day, to pursue lonely and financially hazardous experiments in biblical illustration. Johann Sebastian Bach, who dedicated nearly all his vast musical output "solely to the Glory of God," was asked how faith in God and man can be communicated in art. He replied,

> In the architecture of my music, I want to demonstrate to the world the architecture of a new and beautiful social commomwealth: each instrument in counterpoint, and as many contrapuntal parts as there are instruments. Each voluntarily imposing on itself the limits of its individual freedom for the well-being of the community; an enlightened freedom. The harmony of the stars in the heavens, the yearning of brotherhood in the heart of man.

By the age of the Enlightenment, however, such sentiments were passé, and during the 18th and 19th centuries the focus of Solger, Shelling, Schliermacher, and Nietzsche narrowed the function of art to expressions of reason and aspirations to individual freedom. Nietzsche in particular rejected any notion that the arts should serve to accomplish anything except to express the artist's will. His "art for art's sake" decried all outwardly imposed restrictions, and especially moral purpose: "The struggle against purpose in art is always the struggle against its being subordinated to morality."

The principle dangers in creativity within the arts then, are that the productions become a substitute for reality, or that they become rivals to faith, or that they lead nowhere except to the aggrandizement of the isolated artist and his will. In the first instance they serve as a narcotic, lulling our senses so that we no longer deal with the world as it is. Nietzsche, in fact, declared, "we have art in order that we may not perish through

the truth." But there is much in the real world that cries out for correction: the truths about poverty, hunger, domestic violence, crime, warfare—the list is endless. If art serves only to distract us with make-believe, it falsifies reality and becomes, at the very least, antisocial. Far from giving us a beatific vision, it ends in a negation of life and becomes a draught of sedative.

In the second case, where art substitutes for religious faith, it not only erects a new form of idolatry but also cuts the nerve of moral effort. It makes no demands on us as faith does: demands for integrity, brotherhood, and concern for the well-being of others. It makes of us mere spectators of life, a phenomenon which can be witnessed in churches no less than in theaters. Worshippers may become wrapped in the aesthetics of the service, but drop away from being enlisted in outreach to the poor (supplying food, the building of shelters, hospitals, etc.) if the organ is poorly played, or the seat cushions are uncomfortable. Tolstoy related a story of a woman who loved the theater, where she would weep copious tears for the characters on stage, while her coachman froze to death waiting for her outside the theater. She was merely annoyed at the inconvenience.

Third, where nothing matters but the individual will of the artist, the creative spirit is reduced to hedonism, frequently leading to isolation from those who do not share that self-centered expression, and at worst may become imperious. Goethe refused to become involved in a project for much needed social reform because, as he said, "Ich denke an meine ruhe" ("I must think of my tranquility"). The artist may enjoy having people around, but only insofar as they yield the adulation the artist feels is due. Such a one wants to enjoy them, but seldom to serve them. Thus Ayn Rand declared, "I swear by my life—and my love of it—that I will never live for the sake of another." If sufficient popularity and wealth can be gained, the artist may set a trend against which other artists hesitate to inveigh, so whether in painting, music, literature, architecture, or the dance, the power of a few proclaimed "geniuses" threatens to become autocratic and tyrannical.

Where creativity in the arts leads to such consequences, there is nothing to prevent its use for garnering profits from the most trivial to the most destructive ends. One has only to note how often the arts have been employed to advertise products which are known to be useless, unsafe, or, as in the case of cigarettes, potentially deadly. Where humane values are flaunted by the media in favor of the "bottom line," where anti-Semitism or anti-religious or ethnic themes are promoted for political gain, the polis suffers. [*See* ADVERTISING.]

Perhaps the most influential venue for creative expression among the arts is the most recent, the joining of film and television. This medium swallows up more than a quarter of the waking hours of both adults and children. With its enormous potential for good or ill, its reach into the minds of the viewers exceeds that of religious and political institutions, and may exceed that of our education system. The dark side of this powerful form of creativity? Its overall impact, as attested by countless studies, has been to strain our sense of values, and contribute to the increase in violence and vulgarity in our everyday lives. Prime-time schedules are largely made up of mindless sitcoms and action drama laced with violence. News programs pursue murders and rapes. Further, the influence is exported, so that violent gangs in Mexico, South American and European countries use Los Angeles style names, graffiti, tatoos, and weapons, all copied from U.S.A.-made films and television. [*See* TELEVISION AND CREATIVITY.]

III. SCIENCE

Can science per se have a dark side? Among the problems that darken the scientific enterprise are the presuppositions that practitioners bring to their research, and which influence their conclusions. Aristotle is widely respected as one of the greatest minds of our species, who advanced the cause of early science both through his extensive observations and cataloging of data, and his identifying of logical fallacies which get in the way of logical, deductively achieved conclusions. But Aristotle intruded certain assumptions about the nature of reality, and the way things and events move toward preset fulfillment: a teleological concept. Further, he assumed God had set these patterns in motion, and on this basis rejected the atomic theory of Democritus as fundamentally atheistic (an atheism later championed by Lucretius). What the early Church Fathers failed to realize was that in adapting the pre-Christian Aristotle's assumptions to medieval science, they were importing a theology which viewed the uni-

verse as a virtual emanation of God. Nature itself was divine, impregnated with "final causes," thus inadvertently but effectively substituting nature for God. Fortunately, within the church there were also men like Roger Bacon and Rene Descartes, devoutly religious but opposing Aristotle's imminent deity with the biblical concept of God as transcending the created world. In this, they laid the groundwork for modern science, by insisting that science (and therefore scientists) must be free from deductive presuppositions, and become inductive, working from empirical observation and controlled experiment.

It was another assumption of scientists as 18th century rationalism emerged that the universe is rationally constructed. The belief in an orderly, regular, and logically designed cosmos, and the belief that this orderliness is intelligible to the human mind precisely because we have been created in God's own image, was clearly derived from Judeo-Christian and Islamic theology. With the rationalist movement, the orderliness of nature eventually became transmuted into a mechanistic, self-sustaining system where God appeared no longer needed as a causal explanation. If deity is an irrelevance, then perhaps other concerns attendant upon theology could also be dismissed; this supposition led to the premise of "the moral neutrality of science," as well as to the diminution of the moral authority of institutional religion.

Moral neutrality appeared, at first blush a welcome antidote to much of the squabbling that tainted religious administrations during and immediately after the Renaissance, and which had put at risk many involved in scientific pursuits. With the exhilarating advances made in 19th and early 20th century science and technology, the concept of social and ethical disinterestedness was all the more appealing.

Then came the first atomic bomb, killing a hundred thousand people in Hiroshima, and another comparable population shortly thereafter in Nagasaki. Warfare has always been a grim reminder of mankind's persistent inhumanity in employing evermore sophisticated means of destruction. But this was different. It raised for the first time the very real prospect of civilization's capacity for self-annihilation. Robert Oppenheimer's lament, "science has known sin, and that is a knowledge we dare not lose," coming from the man perhaps most responsible for that bomb, continues to haunt scientists and ordinary citizens after half a century. Had creativity gone amok? British physicist C. P. Snow echoed Oppenheimer's distress: "I don't believe any scientist of serious feeling can accept [moral neutrality], letting the conscience rust." Yet realistically one must acknowledge that it is scientists, as well as politicians, military personnel, and indeed society as a whole, not science per se, who must carry the burden of responsibility. Albert Einstein expressed it well: "Science can only ascertain what is, but not what should be, and outside of its domain judgements of all kinds remain necessary." We may recognize an interdisciplinary invitation in Einstein's further comment that "all religions, arts and sciences are branches of the same tree." Value-sustaining enterprises among these may inform the work of the scientific research community by stimulating more creative dialogue and interaction with the public who will benefit from or suffer the consequences of their work. [See SCIENCE.]

IV. TECHNOLOGY, BUSINESS, AND POLITICS

At first consideration, it may seem parsimonious to place such seemingly unrelated and specialized areas of endeavor in juxtaposition. But the reason becomes clearer when we consider how in a market economy they become so mutually dependent as to be symbiotic. Perhaps two current examples will suffice at this point.

The weapons industry, the product of impressive technological advances over the centuries, has drawn upon the inventive resources of great numbers of creative people. The international arms trade has become the very substance of economic survival for many countries, requiring the cooperation of both business and politics. Virtually all nations factor it into the economy. In 1994, American firms were responsible for 72% of all arms sales to third world countries, and to one or both sides of 45 out of 50 ethnic and territorial wars being waged. In 1997, we saw the successful urging by Congress for $7 billion more in weaponry than the Pentagon deemed either necessary or prudent for our own defense program. At the civilian level, the public outcry for gun control in the face of rising numbers of tragedies has met with iron resistance by industry, business, and political factions. Laws adopted

in California in 1989, and by the federal government 5 years later to ban assault rifles and pistols, have been effectively circumvented by the very creative (not to say guileful) manufacturers of "copycat" guns whose trade names are technically not covered by the laws. It is estimated that there are now three times as many such weapons in circulaton as before the laws were enacted, and the death toll, particularly among children and other innocent bystanders, increases.

Again, it may be noted that scientific research in 1954 revealed that ammonia in cigarettes boosts nicotine's impact 100-fold. Now it is alleged before the courts that at that time the tobacco industry employed the technology to utilize ammonia in the manufacture of cigarettes, they were fully aware of the heightened addictive properties of their product, but hired attorneys to carry out plans to defraud the public. Artists both graphic and musical, as well as the media, were employed to make cigarettes more appealing through advertising in print and on the airways. Creativity was certainly in evidence at every level, and now that the lawsuits are before the courts, scientists, technicians, industrial magnates, and politicians are all drawn into the debate. Meanwhile the death toll among cigarette users, who may have become addicted and unable to break the habit, has mounted to the tens of thousands annually.

Examples of creativity's dark side in technology and related fields across the centuries also reveal that science has almost always undergirded technology. To be sure, Ancient Romans, constantly engaged in such technical achievements as aqueducts, vaulted domes, improved road construction, and indoor plumbing, and yet were incurious people when it came to science. Their spur was, more often economic, political, and military. But this may have been a partial reason for Rome's downfall: without scientific underpinnings, their technology could only advance so far, and was inadequate against the sheer mass of barbarian invasions. Without education in science, their successors had no understanding of what they inherited or captured, and either destroyed it or let it deteriorate in neglect. Parenthetically, it should be noted that this is a concern of modern educators, as test scores fall among our American public school students in mathematics and the sciences in international competition.

The "Age of Cathedrals" that came at the end the

Dark Ages was still largely the product of trial and error, rather than a knowledge of geometry, or the physics of stress, coefficiency of friction, expansion, etc. As for cosmology, the medieval world lagged far behind the Greeks of a thousand years earlier.

It was not until the Renaissance that Western culture began to recover some semblance of scientific technology (though it should be noted that in the Muslim world, the sciences of mathematics, astronomy, and medicine experienced remarkable advances ahead of Christendom). It was the Industrial Revolution that brought about the most dramatic renewal, but also revealed the distorted visage of creativity in the realms of technology—in its interplay with business and politics.

The Industrial Revolution began in 18th century England, marking the shift from an agrarian economy with handcrafted products to one of machine-dominated industry. When goods could be manufactured en masse instead of piecemeal, family life was the first serious victim. Husbands and fathers, unable to stay near home where the family had previously shared much of the labor, would walk or ride carts to the nearest cities where they worked in crowded, unsanitary conditions 12 to 14 hours daily.

It was soon discovered that women and children could be hired more cheaply, so with no child-labor laws to protect children, whole families moved to the cities to join the labor force. Thousands of men were replaced and, humiliated by being unemployed, turned to crime and drink. "Worse still," wrote one historian, "mothers and fathers in some cases lived on the killing labor of their children" just to eat and stay alive. It was not unusual for children of both sexes 4 and 5 years of age, with an iron chain fastened to a belt between their legs, to haul tubs of coal up subterranean roads as many as 16 hours a day. Countless numbers died in the mines.

In addition, the compacted populations overtaxed the sewage systems in the cities. In most locations these "systems" were composed of nothing more than a drainage ditch down the center of the streets awaiting the next rain to carry the filth to the nearest river. One physician of the time, John Snow, described in detail a series of cholera outbreaks in London and Paris in 1849. Charles Dickens raged against the number of public hangings of desparate men who broke machinery in factories to protest the way machines displaced

people (which "sabotage" Parliament decreed a capital offense). The collaboration of technology, business, and politics appeared to be one of mutual support against the very workers who kept the system going.

Considering these conditions, to which must be added the transporting of millions of slaves from Africa to the Middle East, Europe, and America, it may be that certain social movements sometimes characterized as "revolutionary" were inevitable. These were in part a reaction against the Industrial Revolution, and against the entrenched powers of business and government. They included *Naturphilosophie,* and the Reign of Terror in France; the diatribes of Karl Marx in Germany and England; the Civil War in America; and the Russian, Chinese, and Cuban revolutions in the 20th century. The creativity which made the Industrial Revolution possible fostered unprecedented dissension, conflict, and bloodshed.

There were also positive enterprises, such as the abolitionist and labor movements of the 19th century, and the civil rights movement of the 20th. And it must not be forgotten that the era which extended from roughly 1750 to World War I was a period of equally unprecedented creative advances in the sciences—inventions from the telegraph and steam engine to photography, electric lights, and powered flight. The conquest of many diseases through the researches of Edward Jenner (best remembered for his vaccination against smallpox), Louis Pasteur (immunization against typhoid and diphtheria), Sir Humphry Davies (anaesthetics and antiseptics), Ignaz Semmelweis (reducing deaths from puerperal fever), and others represented the first real progress in medicine since ancient times. There is no doubt that life was both enriched and extended for millions of people through innovations in agriculture and the chemical industries, not to mention civil engineering and communications.

Euphoria over these achievements tends to distract us from certain harsh realities. When our century began, technology was not yet capable of altering whole life systems on our planet. As our century comes to its close that capability is at hand. Growing populations were not yet threatening to overbalance earth's ability to sustain us in terms of food, water, and breathable air; today that prospect is at the top of the agenda of numerous international organizations. We reject for ourselves the destructive reputation of the ancient

Vandals who sacked Rome, but in our zeal to "be creative" on behalf of our own comfort, aesthetic well-being, and personal longevity, we have plundered our planet. Forty million acres of trees are lost annually because of unrestrained logging and burning. More than half the planet's sea and river life is depleted through overfishing. Fifty thousand plant and animal species become extinct each year. Toxic emissions continue to rise and diminish the protecting ozone layer, threatening to raise global temperature as much as 6 degrees in the next century with such consequences as coastal flooding and forced population relocation.

In the name of creativity, we are squandering our own life-support system, and thereby endangering our children's and their children's capacity to live. A United Nations-sponsored summit was held in 1992 in Rio de Janeiro to discuss these issues, but very little has occurred to reverse the trends despite rhetorical promises among politicians and business leaders. We in the industrialized nations have available to us more scientific knowledge about the human impact on the ecosystem, and more capacity to respond in terms of policy decisions and technical implementation, than any previous generation. The question is whether we will be as creative in our solutions as we have been in creating the problems to be solved. Helen Caldicott, founder of Physicians for Social Responsibility, warns that if present practices of despoiling earth's resources continue, the planet itself may have no more than 10 years to reach a "point of no return," beyond which belated efforts to restore it will be too late.

V. THE ENVIRONMENTAL CONUNDRUM

It is quite clear that humans belong to the same earth-bound community of living beings as all other species. We are surely the strangest of all creatures, not only in our vastly more complex cerebral development, but in the fact that despite being puny by physical comparison with many other species, we have come to dominate the entire ecosystem. Hardly any aspect of the earth remains unaltered by us, from agricultural transformation of land masses, to increased carbon dioxide and evermore lethal toxic gases released into the atmosphere, to the uses and abuses of both fresh and salt water bodies, and driving to extinction about one quarter of all bird species. Further, our military arsenals now include the very real potential for the annihilation of all life, including our own, making us more like a cancer on the planet than a benign species.

Our most serious question concerns the "why" of the matter. If earth is our home, and we are an integral part of the fabric of its life-forms, how is it we have treated it as an object apart from ourselves to be exploited and despoiled? Few other higher animals will foul their own nests. Seldom do conflicts within a given species like wolves, lions, or bears become deadly; nowhere among the higher orders is there concerted warfare against the settlements of other members, yet historian Edward Gibbon observed that our recorded history is "little more than the register of the crimes, follies and misfortunes of mankind."

Paradoxically, this reality emerges precisely because we are a creative species. All organisms modify their environments to some degree, but only humans do it by intent and design. Our creativity has produced some radically altered states of affairs. Consider, for example, the modern increase in carbon dioxide. The combustion of fossil fuel, a product of our very creative employment of natural resources for improving human living conditions, spews over 5 billion metric tons of CO_2 into the atmosphere every year. This has caused a measurable contamination of the atmosphere globally and is the most important contributor to the growing greenhouse effect on the climate. Global warming causes more rapid evaporation of surface moisture, and hence more droughts in some areas, more rainfall in others, more lost crops, and more storms and floods. If current trends persist, global warming will raise sea levels as much as 3 ft., posing risks in both expense and fatalities to hundreds of millions of coastal dwellers (nearly 60% of Americans live in coastal regions), and to the existence of some island states.

Human ingenuity has also altered the global "fixity" of nitrogen, by way of manufactured fertilizers and fossil fuel combustion. Fixity is of course essential for life, in that nitrogen can only be utilized by organisms when bonded with carbon, hydrogen, or oxygen. Biochemists, writing for the journal *Science* (July 25, 1997), estimate that natural processes, apart from human intervention, account for 90 to 130 million metric tons of fixed nitrogen annually on land, and possibly an equal amount in the marine system. The problems with anthropogenic domination of the ecosystem appear when a doubling of natural concentrations of nitrous oxide (a greenhouse gas) is noted; there is a two-thirds increase in ammonia emissions globally, and acid rain and photochemical smog are seriously on the increase throughout the world. Further, both air quality and climate are adversely affected by oxidized sulfur gases. Many synthetic chemicals, such as organo-chlorine compounds like polychlorinated biphenyls, persist for decades in the environment, causing devastation of birds and other wildlife.

Clear-cutting of forests has not only reduced vast timber resources and habitats, but has led to severe erosions, the runoff of which has clogged streams and rivers, killing whole species of fish. Meanwhile, the Florida Everglades have been so violated by the sugar industry's overuse, fertilizer runoff by farming, flood control, and urban sprawl that it will require an estimated $5 billion to reclaim it.

VI. SOME UNCONVENTIONAL CONCLUSIONS

Civilizations grow and thrive by the power and strategies of human creativity. Individuals within the culture may be creative, but a civilization proper requires that their ideas be adopted by the society so that, for example, written communication becomes standardized; an economic structure is set up which supports trade and fosters political controls; urban life provides stability, governed by leaders who articulate the norms of societal comportment; and, perhaps most importantly, room is made for diverse, heterogeneous cultural traditions. Within such structures the arts and sciences, technology, business, and political activities are fostered by the most creative citizens.

The dark side of scientific and technological creativity is in the quest for a radical autonomy apart from the constraints of social responsibility. To be sure, the "disinterested pursuit of knowledge" is critical to basic research. But "disinterested" means free from prejudice; it does not imply indifference. When Nazi scientists of Hitler's Third Reich placed their knowledge and skills without reservation at the disposal of the fascist state, ready to torture and annihilate millions of fellow hu-

man beings, they abdicated their essential obligation to the human race. The concept of being one's "brother's keeper" is a metaphysical one, but one which is disavowed at grave peril to the human enterprise, and indeed to planetary survival.

Prior to the meeting of the Parliament of the World's Religions in Chicago, 1993, a document was prepared with the title *Toward a Global Ethic,* and signed by 145 delegates from virtually every major religious tradition on earth. It affirmed that the world is in agony, and condemned the abuses of our creative powers and of earth's ecosystems, as well as the poverty, injustice, and warfare that attend these. The document affirmed humankind's interdependence, and called upon all of us to seek, among other things, creative ways to fulfill our obligation to respect and foster human dignity, individual rights, and the search for truth in freedom. Far from a collection of normative cliches, it challenged the more than 6,800 delegates and 30,000 attendees to the highest possible standards of creativity on behalf of the world's populations. Similar documents are issuing from the United Nations, and from a host of organizations representing the realms of the arts, business, the environment, law, the sciences, technology, etc. Aware of the downside of so many of our ventures in this century, ours might almost be called an Age of Exhortations. Perhaps this is a necessary stage. When Pandora's box was emptied of all its negatives, the one positive element remaining was hope.

Bibliography

Barrett, W. (1978). *The illusion of technique.* New York: Anchor Press/Doubleday.

Bergson, H. (1946). *The creative mind.* New York: Philosophical Library.

Gardner, H. (1982). *Art, mind and brain.* New York: Basic Books.

Ghiselin, B. (1984). *The creative process.* Berkeley, CA: University of California Press.

Rassmussen, L. L. (1997). *Earth community, earth ethics.* New York: Orbis Books.

Rosenthal, J. H. (1995). *Ethics and international affairs.* Washington, DC: Georgetown University Press.

Runco, M. A. (1990). *Theories of creativity.* Newberry Park: Sage.

Stackhouse, M., McCann, D. P., Roels, S. J., & Williams, P. N. (Eds.). (1995). *On moral business.* Grand Rapids, MI: Eerdmans.

Taylor, C., & Barron, F. (1975). *Scientific creativity.* New York: Huntington.

Charles Robert Darwin

1809–1882

Naturalist

Author of *On the Origin of Species* and *Descent of Man*

Robert T. Keegan

Pace University

Charles Darwin.

CHARLES DARWIN was an English naturalist who proposed the theory of natural selection to explain the evolution of life on earth. Darwin constructed this theory in a series of notebooks that he kept during the 2 years following the nearly 5-year circumnavigation of the globe aboard H.M.S. Beagle. Although he had his basic insight into the mechanism of natural selection in 1838, 20 years passed before his theory of evolution was made public. In 1859, Darwin published On the Origin of Species. *Though Darwin did not explicitly state in Origin that humans had evolved in the same manner as all life on earth, the implication was clear. This aspect of the book sparked lively debate in scientific, cultural, and religious circles as it challenged traditional views on the nature of humanity. In 1871, Darwin explicitly discussed his views on human evolution in* Descent of Man, *further fueling the controversy. In addition to the pivotal role Darwin played in the establishment of evolutionary theory, he also made substantial contributions to the fields of geology, zoology, psychology, botany, ecology, and other related fields in natural history. More than a century after his death, Darwin's ideas remain central to the biological and social sciences and continue to energize debates about human nature in cultural and religious contexts.*

Copyright © 1999 by Academic Press
All rights of reproduction in any form reserved.

Charles Darwin was born on February 12, 1809, in Shrewsbury, England, the fifth of six children. Charles' paternal grandfather was Erasmus Darwin, a highly regarded physician, a poet, a proponent of evolution, and a founder of the Birmingham Lunar Society, which brought together some of the most original thinkers in science and technology of the time. Charles' maternal grandfather was Josiah Wedgwood, a successful entrepreneur and innovator in ceramics technology, and a member of the Lunar Society. Charles' father, Robert Waring Darwin, was a well-respected physician in the Shrewsbury area and his mother, Susannah Wedgwood, was an intelligent woman and a knowledgeable pigeon fancier. Charles was baptized in the Anglican faith despite the tradition of free-thinking agnosticism in the Darwin line and Unitarianism in the Wedgwood line.

I. CHILDHOOD AND EARLY ADOLESCENCE: DISCOVERING THE WONDERS OF NATURAL HISTORY

The life of Charles Darwin supports a concept of creativity in which hard work plays the central role, not some special type of thinking such as divergent or primary process thinking. Interests that arose as hobbies in childhood and adolescence were gradually extended and refined to become the work of science in adulthood. As Howard Gruber has written, Darwin is best understood as an evolving system. Darwin had to organize and reorganize his knowledge, his purposes, and his emotions in such a manner as to enable him to carry on work over a long period of time. This period of long work was necessary for Darwin to construct a new point of view about nature, which was his great accomplishment.

Darwin was not a child prodigy. He seems to have been a typical boy of his age, well placed by geography, social fashions, and social standing to acquire an interest in the natural world of plants, fish, birds, insects, and rocks. As a young boy, Charles' education took place at home. At age 8 he was sent to a day school.

Charles' mother died when he was 8 years old. This loss has been used by psychoanalytically oriented writers to explain Charles' creativity. They propose that Charles was motivated to search for order in nature the rest of his life in response to this abrupt change in the domestic order. While no doubt a tragic event, Charles' everyday routine may not have significantly changed as a result of his mother's death. Through a combination of conventions of Charles' social class and Susannah's frequent illnesses, Charles had relatively little direct contact with his mother. Upon her death, Charles' three older sisters took charge of running the household and caring for the three younger children. Stability was also underpinned by staff members and a nanny named Nancy who were part of the household staff for years before and after Susannah's death.

Charles' father, a gentle man, became rigid, depressed, and overbearing at times following his wife's death. Though a certain measure of tension existed in their relationship until Charles established himself in adulthood, Charles greatly loved and admired his father.

Charles' formal education continued in 1818 at the Shrewsbury School. The education at this school was classical—study of Greek and Latin, some ancient geography and history, Shakespeare, and an emphasis on memorization, making up verses, and recitation. In his *Autobiography* Charles wrote of this school, "The school as a means of education to me was simply a blank." This statement is typical of Charles' attitude toward learning in the classroom throughout his years of schooling. Outside the classroom Charles showed zeal in pursuing his hobbies. He became an avid collector of minerals and insects, an enthusiastic birdwatcher and hunter of birds, and an accomplished horseman. During this time, Charles also gained an appreciation for experimental science. With brother Erasmus in a homemade laboratory, the two conducted chemical experiments. This activity earned him the nickname "Gas" at school.

At age 16, Charles went to Edinburgh University where he joined his brother in the study of medicine. Charles largely dismissed the value of his classes at Edinburgh, although a course he took with Professor Robert Jameson taught him skills in how to collect, preserve, and transport specimens and provided him with field experience in geology. Charles also had access to the very fine natural history collection at the museum in Edinburgh and the university library.

Charles spent 2 years in Edinburgh. During the first year, his brother Erasmus was with him. In the first year, Charles witnessed two operations, in the years before general anesthesia, one of which was on a child. He left the operating room before they were completed and wrote in his *Autobiography* that "the two cases fairly haunted me for many a long year." Neither Darwin brother was genuinely interested in medicine, but they plumbed the library for books on natural history and walked together to the Firth of Forth, an estuary that was rich with invertebrate fauna. After Erasmus left in March of 1826, Charles continued to walk these beaches, collect specimens, and record them in a pocket diary. He made the acquaintance of other students who had an interest in natural history and met Dr. Robert Grant, a zoologist who would become very influential during Charles' second year at Edinburgh. Charles began taking taxidermy lessons from a freed slave, John Edmonstone, during this period, and had almost daily contact with him for a period of 2 months. John likely spoke to Charles of his life as a slave in South America and his travels with his master through the South American rain forest, and must have sowed the seeds for Charles' later desire to travel to exotic places in pursuit of natural history.

II. LATE ADOLESCENCE: A TURNING POINT

Upon his return to Edinburgh in November 1826 without Erasmus to rely on for companionship, Darwin sought the company of other students who shared his interests. Charles immediately joined the Plinian Society, a club for students and faculty interested in natural history. Darwin began accompanying the zoologist Dr. Robert Grant on walks to the Firth of Forth. Charles even went out on trawlers to collect live specimens of marine invertebrates for Dr. Grant, becoming, in effect, a research assistant. Grant became Charles' first important mentor outside the family.

The Plinian Society was the forum for two formative events in Charles' life that second year in Edinburgh. In March 1827 a student named William Browne presented a paper supporting a thoroughly materialistic view of consciousness and mind as nothing more than the physiological activity of the brain; no spiritual agency needed to be invoked to explain mental phenomena. The minutes of Browne's talk were stricken from the record. This censorship of a materialist view

of life alerted Darwin to the dangers of proposing a materialistic explanation of nature.

At that same meeting, 18-year-old Charles made his first public presentation of discoveries he had made in natural history—that the eggs of one marine invertebrate were capable of locomotion and that the black globules contained in old oyster shells were, in fact, leech eggs. Charles had done the private work of collecting, observing, and analyzing his specimens, and he had reviewed scholarly publications to make sure no one else had made these discoveries. With this presentation, he was for the first time making his work public, a prerequisite for a life in science.

Edinburgh provided an environment that nurtured Charles' real interests in his later teenage years. The importance of the person–environment fit in the later teen years remains an underexamined question in the literature on creative thinking. Cases such as Charles Darwin in Edinburgh and Albert Einstein at Aarau suggest that it is a matter of great importance for the individual in the later teenage years to find an environment in which one can independently pursue one's own interests in accordance with one's own style of learning, supported by knowledgeable adults.

Taking stock of Charles as an evolving system as he left Edinburgh, his sense of purpose for a life in science had undergone significant transformation in his 2 years there, as evidenced by his presentation at the Plinian Society. His affect had changed as his love of nature and his love of science coalesced. His knowledge of natural history had been greatly expanded, especially as a result of his interaction with Dr. Grant. He left Edinburgh a very different person from when he first arrived there.

In the summer of 1827, Charles and his father agreed that medicine would not be Charles' career. Instead, Charles would attend Christ's College at Cambridge University in order to prepare for a career as a clergyman in the Anglican church. Religious zeal was not the motivation on either Darwin's part. For Robert Darwin, this career path held the prospect of providing respectability and a steady income for his son. For Charles, it held the prospect of a lifestyle he could enjoy. As a country parson he would have ample time for hunting, fishing, and collecting.

Darwin went to Cambridge in January 1828. There, he reconstructed a number of the circumstances that he had found helpful in the pursuit of his real interests in Edinburgh. Creativity requires the construction of a milieu in which sustained learning and work can proceed, and Charles was a good craftsman in this regard. Edinburgh had provided the natural environment and the personal support to engage in the serious study of marine invertebrates, in the form of the Firth of Forth and Dr. Robert Grant. Cambridge provided the natural environment and personal support to engage in the serious study of entomology, in the form of the Cambridge fens and the Reverend John Stevens Henslow, professor of mineralogy and later botany. Darwin formed a very close relationship with the young professor. Beetle collecting became a passion during Charles' years at Cambridge. As he had employed trawlermen working in the Firth of Forth to collect marine invertebrates, he employed bargemen to collect beetles in the wetlands surrounding Cambridge. Charles continued this pattern of enlisting the help of others in his researches in natural history throughout his lifetime.

Having successfully completed his final exams, Darwin accompanied the Cambridge geologist Adam Sedgwick on a short geological expedition through North Wales, a trip arranged by Henslow. Henslow believed that Charles would greatly benefit from doing field work with Sedgwick. Returning home from Wales at the end of August 1831, Charles read a letter from Henslow informing him that the captain of H.M.S. *Beagle*, Robert FitzRoy, was seeking a well-bred man to serve as a companion and naturalist on a voyage to survey the southern coasts of South America and Tierra del Fuego and then circumnavigate the globe. The voyage was expected to take 2 years and Charles would not receive a salary. Despite his father's initial objection, on December 27, 1831, Charles sailed from Plymouth, England, on a voyage that would last almost 5 years.

III. THE VOYAGE OF THE *BEAGLE*: FIRST THEORY

The voyage of the *Beagle* should be viewed as both a remarkable personal journey for Charles Darwin and as one more journey in a tradition now known as the "voyages of discovery." These sailing expeditions were carried out for military, commercial, and scientific purposes, and include the fabled voyages of Captain

Cook, the mutiny on the *Bounty,* the efforts to discover whether there was a great southern continent (Antarctica), and the search for a northwest passage from the Atlantic to Pacific through Canada. There was an established role for a naturalist on these journeys.

Darwin was now on his own. Mentors such as Robert Grant and John Henslow had played an important role in the formation of Darwin's views on nature. Deprived of easy and frequent contact with these men, Darwin adopted a new mentor, the geologist Charles Lyell. Darwin would not meet and become personal friends with Lyell until after the *Beagle* voyage, so this mentorship took place not through direct contact but through Lyell's comprehensive, three-volume, roughly 1400-page *Principles of Geology* in which the uniformitarian view of geology was explained. The crux of this point of view was that the geological forces at work in the present, at their current intensities, were the same as those that acted in the past. Lyell rejected the popular notion that great and unique cataclysms in the past could account for the present geological features of the earth. The "gradualism" in this theory—that great changes could occur through a series of small changes that continued and accumulated over long periods of time—had a profound effect on Darwin.

Darwin's letters during the voyage reveal the rapid effect that Lyell's views had on him. The power of the *Beagle* voyage on the formation of Darwin's view of nature stems from the co-occurrence of his absorbing a new point of view at the same time the raw material of nature was being directly experienced. For example, following a devastating earthquake in Chile, Charles assessed the amount of land elevation that had taken place. He found it to be several feet. Darwin saw this effect as supporting Lyell's idea that mountain ranges could be formed by gradual but continual uplift of the land on the order of inches and feet.

After spending over three and a half years in and around the southern portion of South America, the *Beagle* arrived in the Galapagos Islands. While Charles was there, he had no great insight into evolution, but his experiences in these islands would later inform his thinking on this issue. It was during the three and a half weeks sailing from Tahiti to New Zealand that Charles made his first major creative contribution to science: a theory of coral reef formation. Gruber keenly noted in 1981 that this theory "bears a striking *formal* resemblance to his later work on organic evolution" (p. 101). It was a thoroughly gradualist theory, based in Lyell's own theory of coral reefs, but it was an improvement on Lyell's theory. Charles was able to explain different *types* of coral formations (fringing reefs, atolls, and islands) as structures representing different *phases* of a single gradual process of formation. The *gradual* accumulation of very small changes, the deposition of coral skeletons, over extremely long time periods created something significant in nature that had not previously existed.

IV. THE FRUITFUL USE OF ANALOGY: CONCEIVING OF NATURAL SELECTION

The 2-year period following the return of the *Beagle* to England in October of 1836 marked a time of intense and productive work for Charles. By March of 1837 he was convinced that evolution had occurred and provided the best explanation for why there were different species in the natural world. This belief in evolution preceded his understanding of how it might occur and put him at odds with the great majority of scientists at the time, including Charles Lyell.

In July of 1837, Darwin opened the first notebook in what would become a series of notebooks devoted to thinking through a theory of evolution. These notebooks provide one of the best records of creative thinking in process. They show Darwin's assembling of a huge amount of information in natural history, mixing his personal observations with those of others who wrote in this field, comparing his ideas with the largely discarded views of the earlier French evolutionist Jean Baptiste Lamarck, coming to perceive the problem of explaining how species change as uniquely his own problem to solve, and eventually sketching out a series of theories of evolution only to discard them as too deeply flawed. Some of these notebooks were especially devoted to exploring issues that Darwin knew were potentially explosive, issues such as extending the theory of evolution to human beings, thereby accounting for human intellect, existence, and morality through a natural and thoroughly materialistic mechanism without invoking the concept of a Divine origin.

Within this 2-year period, Darwin also presented a paper on how topsoil was created through the action of earthworms eating, digesting, and then excreting castings of fine particles of organic material at the openings of their burrows. The analogy with the coral reef theory is clear—so-called "lowly" organisms could build large and significant features of the surface of the earth through the accumulation of tiny changes over immense periods of time.

An entry in one of the notebooks of this period, the one known as the C notebook, raises an important question for those who wish to understand creativity: What role does metacognition play in creative thinking? For Charles Darwin, the answer is that it played a significant role. In thinking about human evolution, Darwin wrote on page 74 of this notebook, "The believing that monkey would breed (if mankind destroyed) some intellectual being though not MAN,—is as difficult to understand as Lyell's doctrine of slow movements." Here is explicit recognition of the analogy between the uniformitarian view of geology and Darwin's emerging theory of evolution—new things can be created through the slow accumulation of small changes. He then goes on to write on page 75, "This multiplication of little means & bringing the mind to grapple with great effect produced is a most laborious & painful effort of the mind." Darwin recognized the value of this gradualism as a strategy for problem solving. He had already used it productively in explaining the formation of coral reefs and topsoil, but he implies in this quotation that others may have difficulty in accepting this approach to explaining the natural world. (See Barrett et al. entry in Bibliography for quoted material in this paragraph, p. 263.)

The culmination of this 2-year period of intense work came on September 28, 1838, when Darwin, writing in the D notebook, had his great insight into the mechanism of natural selection. The context for this insight was Darwin's reading of Thomas Robert Malthus' *Essay of Population*. This essay led Darwin to realize that the tendency toward overpopulation in human population that Malthus clearly outlined must also apply to the rest of nature, and that competition and struggle for scarce resources was the *inevitable* result of this situation. Combined with his understanding of hereditary principles that the traits of parents are likely to be passed to offspring and his crucial move to accept that variation was ubiquitous in nature *without* understanding or having to explain the mechanism that produced this variation (he attributed variation to "chance," a word indicating his inability to explain the source of variation, not a belief that it was a truly random process), Darwin put it all together. Organisms which by chance had a variation that was adaptive, that is, one that helped in the struggle for scarce resources, would survive and pass this trait to offspring. Over enormous periods of time, the accumulation of these new adaptive traits would result in an organism so different from its ancestor that it would constitute a new species.

It is characteristic of Darwin's style of thought that in the same passage in which this crucial insight occurs, he uses a metaphor to capture the essence of the idea. He compares nature to "a force like a hundred thousand wedges," some wedges forcing their way into the economy of nature and some wedges being forced out. This metaphor highlights the idea of struggle and extinction. Other metaphors Darwin used at other times include the "tree" image to capture the branching structure of nature and the "entangled bank" metaphor to emphasize the fullness and diversity of nature. Use of metaphor was an important part of Darwin's creativity.

For the next 20 years, Darwin refrained from making his theory public. Much has been written on this delay. Stomach maladies plagued him throughout his lifetime following the voyage of the *Beagle*. Explanations of Darwin's illness and delay have ranged from psychosomatic causes stemming from fear of the reaction his theory would provoke, to hyperventilation syndrome, to a tropical disorder he picked up while on the *Beagle* voyage, to the felt need to do more work on the theory to solve problems remaining with it and to inoculate it from the criticism it would almost certainly engender. In this 20-year period, Darwin worked assiduously for 8 years to understand and explain variation in just one group of marine invertebrates, barnacles. He also had major insights into how natural selection could work at the level of the group instead of just at the level of the individual, and how natural selection would lead to the multiplication of species (Darwin's principle of divergence) since a local environment can support more life-forms if organisms divide resources rather than compete for the same resources.

Darwin's long public silence on his theory of evolution came to an end in 1858 when he was set into motion by a letter he received from a young naturalist working in the Malay Archipelago, Alfred Russel Wallace. In addition to this common experience of archipelagos, Wallace also had read Malthus. In this communication Wallace outlined a theory of evolution so similar to the one Darwin had worked out over the preceding 20 years that it stunned Darwin. Darwin recognized that he could not simply go ahead and publish his own views after receipt of this letter, but a clever solution was worked out by two friends who knew Darwin's ideas on evolution, Joseph Hooker and Charles Lyell. Darwin had formed a friendship with Hooker in 1843 and had enlisted his help in gathering information on botanical subjects. The solution consisted of having portions of an essay on natural selection Darwin had written in 1844 and part of a letter Darwin had written to American botanist Asa Gray of Harvard in 1857 explaining his views on evolution read in addition to Wallace's paper at the July 1, 1858, meeting of the Linnean Society by the society's secretary.

At the time Darwin received Wallace's letter, he had completed 10 chapters in a work known as *Natural Selection,* a manuscript of over a quarter of a million words and estimated to be a bit over half completed from what Darwin intended. In light of the absence of any significant reaction to the joint presentation of his and Wallace's views at the Linnaean Society, Darwin saw a need and an opportunity to further explain his views. He set to writing an "abstract" of *Natural Selection* and the result was the approximately 500-page *Origin of Species,* one of the most important publications in the history of science and the work that reveals Darwin as a creative thinker of the first rank.

V. AFTER *ORIGIN:* CONCLUDING A CREATIVE LIFE

The publication of *Origin* when Darwin was age 50 was the signal achievement of his career. However, Darwin continued to produce important and innovative scientific books and papers, a striking example of sustained creative output throughout a full adult life. Over the final two decades of his life, Darwin's most creative work occurred in botany, guided by the principle of natural selection. He wrote books and papers describing remarkable structures and behaviors in plants and brought a genuinely ecological approach to his analyses by focusing on insect–plant interactions. In addition to these botanical works, he published important books on variation in domesticated animals and plants and human evolution, and in the year before his death, a book length treatment of a subject he addressed over 40 years earlier, how earthworms form topsoil, reaffirming the gradualism that had worked so well for him over his lifetime. Charles Darwin died on April 19, 1882, and was laid to rest 1 week later in Westminster Abbey amid the graves of other great creators in British arts and sciences.

Bibliography

Barlow, N. (Ed.). (1958). *The autobiography of Charles Darwin.* New York: Norton.

Barrett, P. H., Gautrey, P. J., Herbert, S., Kohn, D., & Smith, S. (Eds. and Transcribers). (1987). *Charles Darwin's notebooks, 1836–1844: Geology, transmutation of species, metaphysical enquiries.* Ithaca, NY: Cornell University Press.

Darwin, C. (1859). *The origin of species by means of natural selection, or the preservation of favoured races in the struggle for life.* London: John Murray.

Darwin, C. (1872). *The descent of man, and selection in relation to sex.* London: John Murray.

Darwin, C. (1821–1862/1985–1997). *The correspondence of Charles Darwin* (F. Burkhardt et al., Eds.) (Vols. 1–10). Cambridge: Cambridge University Press.

Desmond, A., & Moore, J. (1991). *Darwin: The life of a tormented evolutionist.* New York: Warner Books.

Gruber, H. E. (1981). *Darwin on man: A psychological study of scientific creativity* (2nd ed.). Chicago: University of Chicago Press. [Originally published in 1974 together with *Darwin's early and unpublished notebooks,* transcribed and annotated by P. H. Barrett. New York: Dutton.]

Gruber, H. E. (1985). Going the limit: Toward the construction of Darwin's theory (1832–1839). In D. Kohn (Ed.), *The Darwinian heritage* (pp. 9–34). Princeton, NJ: Princeton University Press.

Keegan, R. T. (1989). How Charles Darwin became a psychologist. In D. B. Wallace & H. E. Gruber (Eds.), *Creative people at work: Twelve cognitive case studies* (pp. 107–125). New York: Oxford University Press.

Kohn, D. (Ed.). (1985). *The Darwinian heritage.* Princeton, NJ: Princeton University Press.

Leonardo da Vinci

1452–1519

Painter, sculptor, architect, and engineer

Painted the *Mona Lisa*

Leonard Shlain

University of California Medical School, San Francisco

*History is replete with geniuses. Their contributions to the advancement of knowledge and enhancement of the arts has greatly embellished the human adventure. There is, however, a division of genius. Those individuals who have contributed to the field of science have not made a comparable contribution to the field of art and vice versa. Only one individual—**LEONARDO DA VINCI**—in the entire historical record has been able to bridge the two fields of art and science and make Nobel-prize quality contributions to both. An examination of the unique way that Leonardo's brain was wired holds the clue to his genius.*

I. INTRODUCTION

History is replete with remarkable men and women, but only once in the historical record has there appeared an individual who has no peer: such a one was Leonardo da Vinci. The quintessential Renaissance man, Leonardo made his mark as a theorist, an engineer, an artist, and a scientist. While there have been many famous thinkers, engineers, inventors, artists, and scientists whose work could be compared to Leonardo's, what makes Leonardo unique is that one would

Leonardo da Vinci, self-portrait. Used with permission from Alinari/Art Resource, NY.

Copyright © 1999 by Academic Press
All rights of reproduction in any form reserved.

be hard pressed to find another thinker, engineer, inventor, artist, or scientist who also made significant contributions to the other fields mentioned. In terms of sheer creative intensity across the spectrum of human endeavor, Leonardo has no equal.

II. HISTORICAL BIOGRAPHY

Born in 1452, Leonardo was the illegitimate child of an illiterate peasant woman and a Florentine lawyer. He was initially raised by his mother; then, before the age of five, he was separated from his mother and brought into the household of his father, a man of means who apparently did not care much for the young Leonardo.

Leonardo had few friends during childhood and developed a highly sensitive, dreamy nature. Like many creative people he enjoyed his solitude.

As young man, Leonardo had a penchant for exotic practical jokes. Using a connecting tube, he once attached some bellows to the shriveled dried intestines of a bull and placed the guts in one room while he stood with the bellows in another. When people arrived in the room they barely noticed the prunelike coils, but were soon discomfited and then stupefied as a huge balloon suddenly started to fill the available space, crowding them against the opposite wall.

Leonardo's fecund imagination poured forth a constant stream of discoveries, gadgets, engineering marvels, and farsighted contrivances. He invented the helicopter, parachute, submarine, turn screw, and tank. Leonardo was extremely visual and expressed his ideas primarily through drawings. He made many contributions to science, both in theory and in application, but paradoxically he is principally studied in art history classes.

He believed in pure mathematics as the highest expression of the human mind and stated, "There is no certainty where one can neither apply any of the mathematical sciences nor any of those which are based upon mathematical sciences." The subject of motion intrigued him and he made significant contributions to the field of mechanics. Leonardo's compelling studies of the muscular movements of men and horses, exemplified in his cartoons from his *Battle of Anghiari,* are the most detailed anatomical descriptions of men and animals in motion that have ever been produced. He published a book that still remains the definitive study of equine anatomy. His interest in the principles of movement carried him deep into the field of anatomy so that his contributions changed forever the way future students of this subject would be taught. The first modern medical textbook, Andreas Vesalius's *De humani corporis fabrica,* published in 1543, owes an enormous debt to Leonardo's earlier anatomical studies.

Leonardo also attempted to understand the concept of inertia and came astonishingly close to the central clue that allowed Isaac Newton to elaborate his laws of motion two centuries later. Leonardo wrote, "All movement tends to maintenance, or rather all moved bodies continue to move as long as the impression of the force of their motors (original impetus) remains in them." (Wallace, 1966, p. 12) The principle of inertia was called the Principle of Leonardo until Newton published his *Principia.*

Leonardo, the artist, analyzed the visual world with a scientist's eye. In a sampling of his precepts one finds,

> When you have to draw from nature, stand three times as far away as the size of the object that you are drawing. . . . Every opaque object that is devoid of color partakes of the color of that which is opposite to it, as happens with a white wall. . . . The shadows cast by trees on which the sun is shining are as dark as that of the center of the tree. . . . The sun will appear greater in moving water or when the surface is broken into waves than it does in still water. (Wallace, 1966, p. 175)

Leonardo was a pioneer in the study of light, and he revealed revolutionary insights about its nature. Leonardo understood that images were reversed upon the retina. He is generally credited with the invention of the camera obscura, upon which the principle of modern photography rests. He studied optical illusions and his explanations for them still apply today. He sketched an instrument to record the intensity of light that differed little from the one developed by Benjamin Thompson, an American, three centuries later. Leonardo was also fascinated by shadows and worked out the geometrical details of the umbra and penumbra that are still in use by present-day astronomers. He was familiar with eyeglasses and suggested in the 15th century the possibility of contact lenses. He investigated the phenomenon of the iridescence of peacock feathers and oil on water. He was the first person in the historical record to make the all-important surmise that light traveled through space and time. Extrapolating from water waves and sound waves he wrote,

> Just as a stone thrown into water becomes the center and cause of various circles, sound spreads in circles in the air. Thus every body placed in the luminous air spreads out in circles and fills the surrounding space with finite likenesses of itself and appears all in all and all in every part.

Leonardo, the most visual of scientists, waxed poetic when describing the sense of sight by which we perceive light:

> The eye, which is the window of the soul, is the chief organ whereby the understanding can have the most complete and magnificent view of the infinite works of nature.
>
> Now do you not see that the eye embraces the beauty of the whole world? . . . It counsels and corrects all the arts of mankind. . . . It is the prince of mathematics, and the sciences founded on it are absolutely certain. It has measured the distances and sizes of the stars; it has discovered the elements and their location. . . . It has given birth to architecture and to perspective and the divine art of painting.
>
> Oh, excellent thing, superior to all others created by God! What praises can do justice to your nobility? What peoples, what tongues will fully describe your function? The eye is the window of the human body through which it feels its way and enjoys the beauty of the world. Owing to the eye *the soul is content to stay in its bodily prison, for without it such bodily prison is torture.*
>
> O marvelous, O stupendous necessity, thou with supreme reason compellest all effects to be the direct result of their causes; and by a supreme and irrevocable law every natural action obeys thee by the shortest process possible. Who would believe that so small a space could contain all the images of the universe. . . . (Argüelles, 1975, p. 22)

His most enduring contributions to our knowledge of light were not written in words, however, but rather they can be seen in his paintings. Leonardo was able to coax out of brush and paint a rare quality of light. No artist before or since has achieved the mysterious opalescence of the distant atmosphere. His ineffable vistas of faraway mountains, the wordless interplay of ethereal light upon a woman's smile, and the rippling fasciculations of a horse in motion, all are bathed in a light that at once is representative of the visual world and at the same time contains a sfumato that gives his works an almost otherworldly quality.

Leonardo's technical innovations and scientific discoveries are insufficiently acknowledged by science historians because Leonardo was so ahead of his time. His imagination so far outstripped the technology of the 15th century that many of his most brilliant inventions and theories could not even be tested.

Leonardo was also interested in the nature of abstract designs. In his *Treatise on Painting* (not published until 1651), he spoke of a method "of quickening the spirit of invention." He advised artists,

> You should look at certain walls stained with damp, or at stones of uneven colour. If you have to invent some backgrounds you will be able to see in these the likeness of divine landscapes, adorned with mountains, ruins, rocks, woods, great plains, hills and valleys in great variety; and expressions of faces and clothes and an infinity of things which you will be able to reduce to their complete and proper forms. In such walls the same thing happens as in the sound of bells, in whose stroke you may find every named word which you can imagine. (Gombrich, 1956, p. 188)

Leonardo's interest in images without things led him to be the first European artist to draw a landscape. In so doing, he took the important step away from concrete and symbolic representation toward abstraction. Pure landscapes were utterly unimaginable to Greek, Roman, or Christian artists because they did not include the usual hierarchy of man-made things or people; instead they are the beginning of a recognition of patterns rather than objects. His interest in abstract pattern intensified until Leonardo became preoccupied with pure geometrical designs. His notebooks are filled with pictures that have no identifiable image. Later in Leonardo's life, he composed many drawings for his *Eruption of the Deluge* (1514), that second coming of the flood that would purify the sins of humankind with water. In these drawings, the complex shapes of massive walls of falling water achieve a level of art-without-an-image that anticipated by 400 years the abstract works of Wassily Kandinsky, Kazimir Malevich, and Piet Mondrian.

Although Leonardo never published a single book, his writings were extensive. The scattered and disarranged pages of notes he left behind have been indexed somewhat haphazardly over the ensuing centuries, resulting in the *Codex Atlanticus,* which contains 1222 pages bundled together, evidently not in the order Leonardo wrote them. In these pages are some of the astonishing revelations of the Renaissance's most incisive mind. In one line Leonardo states with conviction, "The sun does not move," thereby anticipating both Copernicus and Galileo. The many pages of notes include an astonishing array of drawings of aerial maps, swirling water, plants, grand irrigation schemes, anatomical studies, and the ever-present profiles of faces of every physiognomic variation.

III. RIVALRY WITH MICHAELANGELO

Like most historical geniuses, Leonardo had to contend with a rival artist, Michelangelo, who also excelled at engineering but cannot compare to Leonardo in the scientific endeavors. The living presence of an artist who could challenge Leonardo led to an inevitable confrontation.

According to the Renaissance art historian Vasari, Leonardo and Michelangelo disliked each other intensely. Leonardo, who enjoyed wearing the latest fashions, had frequently made belittling comments about the coarse and peasant-like appearance Michelangelo presented in his sculptor's working clothes and his ever-present pale patina of marble dust. Leonardo's remarks made their way back to Michelangelo and they did not endear the painter to him. When Michelangelo learned that the Duke of Sforza, the ruler of Milan, had commissioned Leonardo to cast an equestrian statue, he sneered contemptuously, believing that the dilettante painter could never complete such a project.

Leonardo, of course, was up to the task. There had been many man-on-a-horse monuments and Leonardo was determined to create something the likes of which the world had never seen. He set out to create an object

not only of great beauty, but also the largest, most daring equestrian statue ever conceived.

When Leonardo finished making a model in plaster, it was so magnificent the townspeople urged him to place it outside in the piazza for all to behold in the sunshine. Meanwhile the artist busied himself with the engineering details of the proposed casting and informed his patron, Sforza, he would need 200,000 pounds of bronze. Sforza dutifully began to accumulate such a large quantity of the expensive metal, but not without a nagging doubt about the wisdom of commissioning such a large and expensive statue. Shortly thereafter Sforza found himself pressed by the armies of the French at his gate. He directed the bronze he had put aside for Leonardo's statue to be cast into cannons instead. Depressed, Leonardo departed for Florence.

The horse suffered the fate of the martyrdom of St. Sebastian. When the French mercenaries forced the gates, they were confronted by a piazza deserted save for a towering clay horse, which must have appeared to them as a Trojan horse in reverse. In the victory celebration that followed, drunken soldiers began shooting arrows at the vulnerable *cavello,* and continued to do so into the night. In the morning, the arrows were removed and the mortally wounded horse was exposed to the elements. Rainwater seeped into the arrow tracks, and within a few months the erosive effect caused the horse to disintegrate.

One day soon after in Florence, Leonardo passed a group of young men in the piazza who were discussing Dante's *Inferno.* They asked Leonardo for his interpretation just as Michelangelo, who was also living in Florence, deep in thought, rounded the corner. Michelangelo was known to have studied Dante zealously. Leonardo, in a gentlemanly fashion, said, "Here is Michelangelo; let us ask him as he will know." Michelangelo, however, misunderstood and thought Leonardo was making fun of him. Michelangelo exploded:

> Explain them yourselves! You made a design for a horse to be cast in bronze, and, unable to cast it, you have in your shame abandoned it. And to think that those Milanese capons believed you! (Wallace, 1966, p. 76)

Leonardo flushed deeply but made no reply, turned on his heels, and strode away. These two titans never spoke to each other again, but Leonardo, as best we know, never again spoke or wrote ill of Michelangelo.

IV. PARADOX OF HIS PERSONALITY

Leonardo had a penchant for secrecy and loved to decode and write in cryptograms, and he enjoyed trying to decipher occult messages from the past. In Leonardo's voluminous writings, personal statements are curiously absent. Upon learning of his father's death, for example, Leonardo made the following dispassionate entry in his journal:

On the ninth of July 1504, Wednesday at seven o'clock, died Sen Piero da Vinci, notary at the palace of the Podesta, my father, at seven o'clock. He was 80 years old, left ten sons and two daughters. (Wallace, 1966, p. 11)

Despite his personal reserve, Leonardo was the exemplary Renaissance man. By reputation, he was gentle and generous, and he was an accomplished musician and a pleasant, witty conversationalist. Leonardo developed a philosophy akin to St. Francis of Assisi's early in his life. He had a reverence for all living things and frequently bought caged birds just so he could set them free. He became a vegetarian because he did not believe one should ever kill a living creature.

It is a paradox that Leonardo, who was reputed to be unable to harm a fly, nevertheless expended considerable amounts of his genius designing engines of war. In the course of his career, he invented some of the most gruesome devices to grind and rend the flesh of enemy soldiers. Without the faintest moral compunction, he solicited employment from the infamous Cesare Borgia and left his post as Borgia's military engineer only when he discovered that a fellow worker of his, also in Borgia's employ, had been strangled to death for some unknown reason by their mutual patron.

V. HOW LEONARDO WAS UNIQUE

To highlight the fact that Leonardo stands alone, imagine that in every year of human history a Nobel prize committee had granted an award for the outstanding artistic achievement as well as for the most meritorious scientific one. To be fair, let us broaden the scope of the word "scientist" to include everyone who ever pondered the nature of "nature," including Pythagoras, Plato, St. Augustine, Aquinas, Kant, Dalton, Darwin, and Freud.

Despite the numerous artistic titans and the many giants of science, the fact that leaps out of the historical record is how rarely anyone would have ever qualified for *both* awards. While there have been artists who dabbled in science and scientists who displayed an artistic bent, there is almost no one who was able to make an outstanding contribution to both fields. Brunelleschi and Alberti would certainly be nominated. In the realm of art, Michelangelo, Voltaire, Goethe, and Wagner spring to mind, but their scientific contributions would not be considered Nobel prize material. Correspondingly, not a single artistic creation of Nobel prize caliber has ever issued forth from any of the men or women who applied their talents primarily to solve the problems posed by science.

How odd that in all of recorded civilization only one person could lay clear-cut claims to both prizes. It speaks to the sharp divisions in our culture between art and science that we have produced only this one indisputable exemplar of the total integration of creativity's dual aspects at such high levels. The existence of even this one individual, however, points the way to the possibility and the importance of healing the artificial rift between these two sides. Somehow Leonardo merged the processes of seeing and thinking, and the profusion of images and insights that emerged from that cross-fertilization was cornucopian.

VI. LEFT BRAIN–RIGHT BRAIN SPLIT

To better understand this amazing Italian's creativity, we must take a short excursion and examine how the human brain processes information. All vertebrates from fish onward have a bilobed brain, that is, a right hemisphere and a left hemisphere. In all animals with this configuration, each side of the brain performs in a mirror image fashion the same tasks as its opposite side. Only humans have sharply diverged from this arrangement. While each side of the human brain is similar in appearance to each other and resembles the configuration of other animals, each lobe of a human's brain performs functionally different tasks. This specialization is called hemispheric lateralization. (Some other higher mammals and birds exhibit brain lateralization but none approach the extent to which this feature is present in humans.)

The evolutionary reason for this arrangement is nature's decision to dedicate one hemisphere primarily for language. This then became the left hemisphere in right-handed people. Slightly over 90% of the population is right handed and 90% of their language centers reside in their left hemisphere. (The arrangement is not so lopsided in women, homosexual men, and left-handed people of both sexes.) The other hemisphere, the right side, then became the primary location for functions that used to reside in both lobes, but because of space requirements now had to be squeezed into the right lobe. Since language is processed one word at a time, one sentence at a time, and one paragraph at a time, the left hemisphere functions primarily in time. All of the other human abilities and concepts that are time dependent, such as arithmetic, causality, determinism, logic, and rationality, require a well-developed linear sequential time sense.

The left hemisphere controls the act of willing through its agent the right hand, which carries out the commands of this hemisphere. The right hand is the agent of action and aggression. In battle or the hunt, the right hand swings the club or sword, throws the spear, and pulls the trigger. It is the right hand that hammers the nail while the left one steadies the nail. As such it is more dominant than the left hand. The four cardinal abilities of the left hemisphere are language, numeracy, abstract thinking, and doing.

All the human abilities that depend on holism and simultaneity, such as the recognition of spatial relationships, were crowded into the remaining right hemisphere. Pattern recognition, identifying faces, manipulating three-dimensional objects in space, appreciating a 70-piece orchestra, or deciphering inner emotional states through a person's expressions or gestures fall under the purview of the right brain. The left hand, controlled by the right brain, is often the one that cradles a baby, carries what the right hand has gathered, and wards off blows. Its function is more protective and nurturing. The four cardinal features of the right hemisphere are perceiving patterns, recognizing faces, synthesizing music, and creating the existential state of being.

Immanuel Kant proposed that human beings have two innate dimensions built into their brains which they use to construct their perception of reality. Kant imagined these two parameters as time and space. In many ways, the hemispheric lateralization scheme recently elucidated by neuroscientists seems to confirm Kant's speculation. The right hemisphere is predominantly a spatial hemisphere. Driving, dancing, skiing, and seeing the relationships of the parts to the whole are better handled by this hemisphere. On the left, every function that takes place there is time dependent. One could almost say that the left hemisphere is a new sense organ designed by evolution to perceive time. It differs from our other conventional sense organs in that it does not have an opening to the outside world through skin or skull.

Because the loss of speech results in a catastrophic effect on human communication, the left hemisphere has been commonly referred to as the "dominant" hemisphere and the right hemisphere is called the "nondominant" one. Researchers have identified the right hemisphere as the side best suited to process novel information; the left side is better at organizing and retrieving information that has already been learned. One could say that creativity is more a right-brained function than a left one.

While not scientifically proven, it is also fair to say that the right hemisphere has those attributes that are commonly associated with the feminine and the left has those that are traditionally thought of as being masculine. Intuition, holism, synthesis, simultaneity, and emotions have been traits we usually associate with the feminine. Linearity, sequence, reductionism, analysis, and duality are concepts traditionally associated with the masculine. In a similar duality, science is traditionally associated with the left hemisphere and the masculine, and art is traditionally associated with the right hemisphere and the feminine.

This background discussion of right–left brain dichotomies is necessary to understand the unique creativity of Leonardo. To integrate so seamlessly the two hemispheric functions, Leonardo must have been born with some very peculiar wiring in his brain. We know several startling things about his mental faculties, the most striking of which was that he was ambidextrous and could write with equal facility forward and backward (mirror writing). Some of these features are found in people with dyslexia, a gender cognitive syndrome (affecting boys over girls 9:1) in which the letters "b" and "d," and "p" and "q" are frequently transposed. Many neuroscientists theorize that dyslexia may be due to a failure of brain dominance. In the dyslexic child, both hemispheres have nearly equal responsibility for the generation and understanding of speech, written language, and hand dominance, instead of the conventional arrangement in which hand preference and the preponderance of speech centers lie in the dominant lobe. Although today dyslexia is generally considered a learning disability, it did not hinder Leonardo. Perhaps his near equilibrium between his lobes allowed him to range back and forth between two different mental processes, one rooted in space and the other in time. In this way he achieved a depth of understanding about this world that has rarely, if ever, been equaled.

The equality of Leonardo's hemispheres enabled this dual man to perceive space and time differently from any artist or scientist before him. Spatially, Leonardo elevated the artistic practice of sfumato to its apogee. It was his vision of deep space and the way atmospheric conditions changed distant light that revealed the subtleties of depth to all viewers of his art. This feature of reality had gone unnoticed by previous artists.

In the most famous painting in the world, his *Mona Lisa,* Leonardo imbued this obscure young woman with an eternal aura of mystery. A significant part of her inscrutable countenance lies just at the edges of the viewer's perception, for on either side of her head Leonardo created different distant landscapes that do not coincide: One is painted in a perspective that makes it closer than the other. While few people are consciously aware of this slight difference in the third dimension of depth, it is not unperceived by the viewer's eye, and this paradox of space heightens the enigmatic quality of the *Mona Lisa*'s smile.

Leonardo's ability to perceive time was also *sui generis.* He observed and recorded in his drawings the complex sequence of pigeons' wings fluttering in flight, as well as the patterns made by fast-flowing water. It was not until time-lapse photography was invented

300 years after he worked that anyone else could slow down these visual blurs, and then the studies photographers made confirmed what Leonardo had seen. He alone, among all the world's artists, was able to see time in slow motion, and in the case of his flowing water drawings he was able to transfix time so that it stopped. He worked out a bird's wing's sequence of flight and the still frame pattern of rivulets capturing the motionless complex whorls and eddies. Perhaps the nondominance of his hemispheres allowed Leonardo to envision time as an "all-at-once" phenomenon, rather than perceive it in the conventional "one-at-a-time" sequence.

Further evidence that Leonardo's time sense was different from other people's is his reputation for procrastination. In one case, Leonardo set an all-time record for time elapsed between accepting a commission and delivering the finished painting—23 years! In another, Pope Leo X commissioned Leonardo to paint any subject he wished. Absorbed as always in technical matters, Leonardo started to compound a special varnish for the finish of the unpainted picture. The pope, checking on the progress of his commission, threw up his hands in disgust and exploded, "This man will never accomplish anything! He thinks about finishing the work before he even starts it!" If Leonardo did not envision time as a linear sequence running from beginning to end, perhaps for him the end was the same as the beginning. Aware of his unusual ability to see time all-at-once, he once remarked, "We know well that sight, through rapid observation, discovers in one glance an infinity of forms; nonetheless, it can only take in one thing at a time." (Wallace, 196, p. 12)

In ancient mythology the wisest figures were hermaphrodites. For example, Tiresias, the hermaphroditic blind seer in many Greek dramas, was the one character who could see the clearest. On the continuum of masculine to feminine, homosexuality falls somewhere in the middle. If the left hemisphere represents the masculine in both men and women, and the right hemisphere represents the feminine in both men and women, then someone who had a near equilibrium between the two cortical sides would likely be homosexual. Besides his ambidexterity, Leonard's homosexuality was well recorded. In his case, considering his genius and ability to see into the future, perhaps it would be more appropriate to think of Leonardo's balanced brain as the factor that made him one of history's nonfictional hermaphrodites.

Although he lived more than 400 years ago, the achievements of Leonardo continue to fascinate a populace that still operates primarily out of either one or the other side of the psyche. In *The Innocent Eye,* Roger Shattuck reports that for a stretch of 50 years—from 1869 to 1919—a time characterized by a burst of artistic and scientific creativity in the West, there was an average of one full-length book per year published on the subject of Leonardo—more than about any other individual. This literary outpouring came from such diverse authors as Bernard Berenson, Jakob Burckhardt, Sigmund Freud, and Paul Valéry, to mention but a few. The number of books still being published about the life and work of this phenomenal artist/scientist suggests that his combination of artistic humanism and scientific curiosity attests to the public's continuing awe of Leonardo.

If Leonardo could integrate the two halves of his divided psyche, then how might the rest of us learn to do so? Perhaps the left hemisphere, the language lobe, has been given too much weight in Western culture. Perhaps dependence on left brained thinking and a denigration of right hemispheric thinking prevents us from being more creative. Clearly, Leonardo's brain differed from the ordinary in that he had a more balanced outlook. The following analogy will help to illustrate why the full integration of the attributes from each hemisphere will enhance a new way to see and think, which in turn is the essence of creativity.

VII. NATURE OF INTEGRATED PAIRED SENSE OF SIGHT AND HEARING

One of the most compelling features of our sensory apparatus occurs as the result of the quirk of overlapping fields. When a paired sense such as vision or hearing appreciates the same perception from two slightly different positions in space, something unique emerges. For instance, since both our eyes face forward, we see essentially the same picture with each eye at any given moment, but because the distance between the skeletal orbits of the two eyeballs is minimal, each retina registers its impression from a slightly offset point of view.

When we view an object with one eye, we perceive only two vectors of space: perpendicular height and horizontal length. However, when we open our second eye, we provide our brain with information from a slightly different angle. Somewhere within the matrix of the visual cortex, the brain overlaps the information from these two angles to create, almost magically, the third dimension of depth.

Our brains operate in the same sort of way with our hearing. Each of our ears listens to the same sounds; however, each takes in auditory information from a different point in space. Again, this distance between our ears, though small, is enough to create a third dimension of sound that we perceive as depth. Everyone knows this who has listened to music through a pair of stereophonic earphones and heard the sound as if it emanated from a point directly above the head. This occurs even though the listener *knows* that the sound from each speaker is entering each ear on the head's opposite sides.

We can also discover a new dimension when we attempt to understand art and science in terms of each other. Our language certainly recognizes this, which is why, when we say a person is "well rounded," or that he "has depth," we commonly mean he can see the world through the different lenses of art and science and, by integrating these perspectives, arrive at a deeper understanding of reality. These colloquial expressions indicate that, unconsciously, we realize that someone who has the ability to knit together two basically different hemispheric points of view is richer for it. We refer to them in words evocative of depth—"multifaceted" or "multidimensional." The right and left hemispheres offer overlapping viewpoints of the same thing. Using both hemispheres allows us to see it in the full glory of three dimensions and understand its existence in an extended "now." The synthesis will produce a heightened awareness and appreciation of the world we live in, two preconditions for creativity. Meister Eckhardt, the medieval mystic, wrote,

"When is a man in mere understanding?" I answer, "When he sees one thing separate from another." And when is a man above mere understanding? That I can tell you: "When a man sees All in all, then a man stands beyond mere understanding." (Leshan, 1966, p. 70)

VIII. CONCLUSION

Using both brush and pen, Leonardo changed the way we see the world, and this subtle shift in mind-set prepared people to be receptive to the changes in perception that were destined to bring forth the modern world. This extraordinary individual was arguably the most creative individual in history. He created the sobriquet "Renaissance man" because of the outstanding contributions he made not to just one field but across a spectrum of fields, beginning with art at one end and science at the other.

Bibliography

Argüelles, J. (1975). *The Transformative Vision*. Boulder, CO: Shambhala.

Berenson, B. (1896). *The Florentine painters of the Renaissance*. London: Putnam's Sons.

Clark, K. (1939). *Leonardo da Vinci*. New York: Viking.

Freud, S. (1947). *Leonardo da Vinci: A study in psychosexuality*. New York: Random House.

Gombrich, E. (1956). *Art and Illusion*. Princeton, NJ: Princeton University Press.

Leshan, L. (1966). *The Medium, The Mystic, and the Physicist*. New York: Viking.

Möller, E. (n.d.) *Leonardo da Vinci: An Artabras book*. New York: Reynal and Morrow.

Vallentin, A. (1938). *Leonardo da Vinci: The tragic pursuit of perfection*. New York: Grosset & Dunlap.

Vasari. (1550). *Lives of the painters* (1st ed.). Florence.

Wallace, R. (1966). *The World of Leonardo*. New York: Times Books.

Definitions of Creativity

Arthur J. Cropley

University of Hamburg

Creativity Paradox The simultaneous coexistence in creativity of psychological elements that seem logically to be mutually contradictory.

Divergent Thinking A kind of thinking that concentrates on producing a large number of original or unexpected ideas (contrast with "convergent" thinking).

Effective Novelty The decisive property of ideas, behaviors, or products that involve genuine creativity.

Intelligence Threshold An IQ score beyond which creativity is thought to become independent of intelligence.

Phases of Creativity Stages in the process of producing a creative product.

Pseudocreativity Behavior that is stereotypically thought to indicate creativity, although it does not (contrast with "genuine" creativity).

Secondary Creativity Creativity involving novel application of the already known (contrast with "primary creativity" that involves a genuine breakthrough).

Serendipity The act of discovering something genuinely valuable by accident.

Sociocultural Validation The acceptance by the social environment that a product is creative.

Sublime Creativity Creativity leading to great works, major discoveries, etc. (contrast with "ordinary" or "everyday" creativity).

*Although the modern **DEFINITION OF CREATIVITY** has moved away from aesthetics and discovery to an emphasis on meeting competition, the idea of novelty is central (although not necessarily sufficient). Also necessary are relevance and effectiveness, as well as ethicality. Novelty is understood in different ways, and this leads to a distinction between creativity in the sublime and in the everyday sense. Although both creativity and intelligence require knowledge and effort, they can be distinguished from each other, and much the same can be said about creativity and problem solving. Creativity can also be defined as a social phenomenon that is facilitated by some social factors, and inhibited by others. One important social setting is the place of work, where an interaction between the person and the environment affects the process of innovation. Focusing on the individual person, creativity is defined as an aspect of thinking, as a personality constellation, and as an interaction between thinking, personal properties, and motivation. This interaction involves a number of paradoxes, in that apparently contradictory elements have to coexist for creativity to emerge.*

Copyright © 1999 by Academic Press
All rights of reproduction in any form reserved.

I. THE CHANGING UNDERSTANDING OF CREATIVITY

Interest in creativity is not confined to modern times. To take one example from the ancient world, Plato discussed society's need for creative people in his *Ion,* and suggested ways of fostering their development. Over the centuries painters, sculptors, poets, writers, and other workers in the creative arts have frequently discussed creativity, one theory widely accepted in the 19th century being that it was closely aligned to madness. In more recent times, researchers prior to and shortly after the Second World War looked at creativity in mathematics and the natural sciences, as well as in professions such as architecture. In these discussions, creativity had strong aesthetic connotations, and was largely seen as a medium for beautifying the environment, a form of self-expression and communication, or a way of understanding, opening up or coping with the previously unknown. [*See* CONCEPTS OF CREATIVITY: A HISTORY.]

Immediately after the "Sputnik shock" of the late 1950s, emphasis in the USA shifted to physical sciences and engineering, and creativity began to be seen as a way of keeping up with the competition (especially with the Soviet Union in the "space race"). In more recent years, discussions of creativity have become prominent in business, again with an overwhelming emphasis on meeting competition, this time for markets and market shares. Research in this domain focused at first on invention of new products and production processes, for instance, through studies of patent holders. More recently there has been considerable emphasis on creative management, especially creative leadership, innovation, and the management of innovation, with research focusing on productivity, effectiveness, and the like.

Most recently, discussions have been broadened again. Creativity has been seen as the only uniquely "human" characteristic, defining an area where, for instance, microelectronics cannot go. In this view, creative thinking is a bastion of human dignity in an age where machines, especially computers, seem to be taking over routine skilled activities and everyday thinking. An extension of this point of view is to see creativity as an element of mental health: Through its perceived connection with flexibility, openness, cour-

age, and the like, which are themselves seen as both prerequisites for and results of a healthy personality, creativity is thought to foster positive adjustment to life. In educational settings, creativity is seen as a special approach to learning that involves both "creative" teaching and "creative" learning strategies. These strategies facilitate learning and are simultaneously a result of appropriate teaching and learning. [*See* ARTIFICIAL INTELLIGENCE; EDUCATION.]

II. BASIC THEORETICAL ISSUES

A. Is It Enough Simply to Be Different?

Shortly after the Second World War researchers in aesthetics concluded that the only constant factor in virtually all discussions of creativity is *novelty.* Novelty was later defined in a more psychological way as the achieving of "surprise" in the beholder. Subsequent discussions made the important point that surprisingness alone is not a sufficient condition for creativity. It is possible to speak of "pseudocreativity," which is novel only in the sense of nonconformity, lack of discipline, blind rejection of what already exists, and simply letting oneself go. These properties may be observed in many genuinely creative people, and thus confused with creativity, but they are not actually part of it. It is also possible to distinguish what can be called "quasicreativity." This has many of the elements of genuine creativity—such as a high level of fantasy—but the connection with reality is tenuous. An example would be the "creativity" of daydreams. [*See* ART AND AESTHETICS; CONFORMITY; NOVELTY.]

Genuine creativity requires a further element over and above mere novelty: A product or response must be relevant to the issue at stake and must offer some kind of genuine solution, that is, it must be effective. Otherwise every farfetched, outrageous, or preposterous idea or every astonishing act of nonconformity would, by virtue of being surprising, be creative. Thus, creativity is nowadays widely defined as *the production of relevant and effective novelty.* What is meant by "effective" may differ between, let us say, fine art and business. In the former case, criteria such as aesthetic pleasingness play an important role, while in the latter perhaps increased profit or avoidance of layoffs, or even simply survival of a company. These two aspects of effectiveness need not contradict each other, although they are often seen as mutually exclusive; for instance, it is possible for a book to be commercially successful and at the same time be written in elegant, even beautiful language.

The term "creativity" has highly positive connotations. It is difficult to think of the effective and relevant novelty of new weapons of mass destruction as creative, even though they might contain all the necessary elements previously discussed. Indeed, revolutionary new ideas can have dramatic consequences for life, human and otherwise, that are not necessarily of a benign kind but which may be conceivably malignant. Thus, in addition to being effective and relevant, creativity has an ethical element. Nowadays this aspect has become particularly urgent in science (see, for instance, discussions of cloning human beings), business, commerce and manufacturing, and engineering, where the need for environmental responsibility is increasingly being stressed.

B. Is a Unified Definition of Creativity Possible?

In recent writings, a number of authors have argued that creativity can only be defined in particular areas such as fine arts or science. In these discussions, the nature of the product is often emphasized. Some researchers emphasize concrete products, such as a work of art, a machine or a design, a production process, or a solution method. Others emphasize more abstract products such as new ways of thinking about an area or the production of new ways of symbolizing it. [*See* CREATIVE PRODUCTS.]

The role of a physical product is particularly obvious in fine art or the performing arts (where specific works or performances are judged by specialized critics as well as interested members of the public); science (where peer judgment is of great importance); engineering, architecture, and the like (where creative work usually leads to concrete products that are sometimes the source of public and professional controversy); or in business, where a concrete product is the usual result of creativity. In some branches of science, for example, in mathematics or philosophy, novel ideas or

symbol systems may well be the usual result of creativity. In this chapter novel "products" will be understood in both senses: physical products on the one hand, and new ways of symbolizing an area on the other. The two kinds of product are possible in all fields of creativity, and both may be identifiable in more or less all creative achievements, concrete objects being more prominent or dominant in some situations, and symbol systems in others.

There is no doubt that in specific fields, possession of relevant specialized knowledge (for instance, in science), the ability to use special tools (e.g., sculpture), mastery of instruments (e.g., music) or skill in specific techniques (e.g., creative writing) are important. In fact, knowledge, special skills, techniques, and similar factors play a role in all fields of creativity. The relative importance of particular factors is greater in some domains than in others—knowledge is perhaps more important in science, and technique in music, to take two examples. The specific contents of these elements also vary according to the particular field or activity in question: the specific knowledge required in designing and building bridges may not be very relevant for creative research in, let us say, botany, but both require a knowledge base. Both mathematical creativity and creative writing require mastery of a set of abstract symbols for representing ideas, although the two symbol systems may be quite different. Thus, there is specificity in creativity, but a general approach is also possible. [*See* KNOWLEDGE.]

C. Can Everybody Be Creative?

Creativity obviously involves something new and different. However, this raises the question for whom a product, process, or idea should be new: for all of human history, for the society or the era of the creator, or for the creator alone? Requiring that products be new in all human history would mean that a person would not be regarded as creative if someone else somewhere else had had the same idea at some time or other, even though the first person knew nothing of this. On the other hand, defining creativity in terms of the point of view of the person in question only would mean that total ignorance would guarantee creativity, since every idea would be new for someone who knew nothing!

A related problem is that of creativity in children.

It is commonplace to speak of childrens' creativity, even if the term is applied to rudimentary applications of fantasy such as crude drawings, simple and highly stereotyped stories, or everyday pretend games (see the earlier reference to quasicreativity). In looking at this issue, three phases of creativity have been described by researchers: the preconventional phase (up to the ages of between 6 and 8 years), the conventional phase (from ages 6 to 8 years to about 10 to 12 years), and the postconventional phase (from about 12 years of age and extending into adulthood). Preconventional creativity displays spontaneity and emotional involvement, and may lead to aesthetically pleasing products, but it is environmentally cued, because it is dominated by perception (especially visual) of the immediate concrete environment. Conventional creativity involves thinking, but becomes increasingly rulebound and therefore stilted, as critical and evaluative skills develop. The crucial element in postconventional creativity is that the individual takes account of external constraints and conventional values, but is able to produce novelty despite this.

The difference between the preconventional phase and the postconventional can be stated rather baldly by saying that, in the main, children less than about 10 years old produce novelty as a result of being ignorant of the constraints of the external world, whereas people in the postconventional phase are familiar with these constraints, but are able to transcend them. For some writers this means that children cannot be creative. However, other authors argue that what is missing in the novelty production of children is the regulatory element of self-evaluation. Their productions may be novel, spontaneous, uninhibited, and even aesthetically pleasing, but they usually lack accuracy and adaptation to the constraints of reality, or what might be called "control."

The word "creativity" is also used in everyday language to refer to the works of people like Michelangelo, Einstein, or Shakespeare. In other words, "creativity" has at least two meanings. The first of these is production of products that are novel in the sense that they have only recently come into existence, regardless of relevance and effectiveness—such as is almost always the case with a child's drawing on what was until a few minutes before a blank piece of paper. This form of creativity can be contrasted with production of great works that are novel in the sense that they are widely hailed as enlarging human perspectives in some way not previously seen in all history. The latter involves "sublime" creativity, and the former "ordinary" creativity.

Even in the case of sublime creativity it is possible to distinguish between two ways of producing effective surprise: by means of new applications of existing principles or by development of new principles. Some writers have contrasted "secondary" creativity (a different application of the already known) and "primary" creativity (development of new principles). Other authors have distinguished between "minor" creativity (extending the known) and "major" creativity (going beyond the known). The highest form of creativity, which may lead to a "revolution" in an area, requires introducing a new "paradigm."

A more differentiated approach in this connection is the distinction among "levels" of creativity: "Expressive spontaneity" requires only the free production of ideas, without regard to their effectiveness or relevance. Expressive spontaneity has a role in some creativity training procedures such as brainstorming, and may well be helpful in the production of novelty, but may often lead to pseudo- or quasicreativity and is not sufficient by itself for sublime creativity. "Technical creativity" requires unusually high levels of technical skill, for instance, with words, paints, a musical instrument, or other tools. Obviously extremely important in some creative activities (such as painting or playing music), technical skill is not sufficient as a universal definition of creativity. "Inventive creativity" involves applying the already known in new ways, "innovative creativity" requires expanding known principles, and "emergent creativity" encompasses the development of new principles. Although some children produce "sublime" creativity, this is not the general rule. However, many children show expressive spontaneity, despite a lack of knowledge of a field or absence of skill with tools or special techniques. In this sense such children can be said to display creativity, but only at a humble level.

The distinction among levels and kinds of creativity can also be applied to discussions of creativity in adults. About 25 years ago the idea of creativity in the person who will never achieve anything creative was introduced into the discussion. More recently, there has been a considerable amount of research on "everyday" creativity. Although they may not produce innovative or emergent creativity, a high proportion of adults engage in the production of (at least for them) new ideas or products, for instance, in the course of "creative" hobbies. Thus, it is possible, in the sense of everyday creativity, to speak of creativity as a widely distributed characteristic seen in large numbers of people, although to a greater or lesser degree in different people. [*See* EVERYDAY CREATIVITY.]

D. Can Creativity Occur by Chance?

Although early studies of creativity supported the view that it frequently results from sudden bursts of inspiration, opinion is divided among contemporary researchers. In relevant case studies, many acknowledged creators have described the way in which their "inventive," "innovative," or "emergent" creativity appeared without effort on their part. The mathematician Poincaré, for instance, reported that he received his novel equations in a dream, while A. E. Houseman described how the lines of his poems simply appeared in his head. Mozart reported that he never revised his work, but wrote down complete music that occurred to him in its final form. This has encouraged the idea that creativity and hard work are irreconcilable, and has led to conclusions such as that simply relaxing or letting ideas flow will lead to creativity. However, interpreters of Poincaré's memoirs fail to mention that he had been working on his problem for many years and that he possessed a vast amount of relevant knowledge accumulated by hard work. Houseman's descriptions of his effortless production of poetry go on to recount how after the first free flow of six or eight lines the next one or two took hours to emerge, and Mozart's account is inconsistent with the fact that corrected early versions of his music have been found.

In fact, a number of researchers have confirmed the role of systematic hard work in creativity. In general, an "apprenticeship" of 10–15 years seems to be necessary for acquiring the necessary fund of knowledge and skills, even in the case of famous youthful prodigies such as Mozart, who, it is true, produced creative music in his teens, but started his interaction with music

by playing at the age of four! It seems to be appropriate to adopt an adapted version of Edison's saying, replacing his word "genius" with "creativity": "Creativity is 1% inspiration, 99% perspiration!"

A related question is whether creativity can result from chance or luck. There are many examples of apparently lucky combinations of events that led to acknowledged creative solutions: for instance, Pasteur, Fleming, Roentgen, Becquerel, Edison himself, Galvani, and Nobel all described chance events that led to breakthroughs. Just what is meant by chance can be divided into four sets of circumstances: blind chance (the individual creator plays no role except that of being there at the relevant moment); serendipity (a person active in a field hits upon something novel and effective without actually looking for it); the luck of the diligent (a hardworking person eventually stumbles onto something); and self-induced luck (special qualifications of a person—such as knowledge, close attention to detail, or a willingness to work long hours— create the circumstances for a lucky breakthrough). Case studies suggest that genuinely creative results require a combination of all four kinds of luck, which raises the question of whether it is a matter of luck at all! [*See* SERENDIPITY.]

E. What Is the Role of Knowledge in Creativity?

Some writers have argued that creativity need not require effort or specialized knowledge. However, the importance of knowledge of the field for achieving effective surprise is now widely accepted. Land, the inventor of the Polaroid camera, rejected the idea of sudden inspiration or chance discoveries in explaining his own achievement of effective novelty. He argued that he had had a purpose—the invention of a camera that developed its own pictures on the spot—and that all the necessary knowledge already existed. His achievement was to assemble this knowledge and work his way through it to the almost inevitable result, the polaroid camera.

Without questioning the importance of familiarity with a field, recent research has looked at the problem that, although working successfully in a field over a long period of time (i.e., becoming an expert) can provide a knowledge base that can be manipulated to yield effective novelty, it can also produce a kind of tunnel vision that narrows thinking and restricts it to the conventional. In the absence of appropriate personal properties such as "openness to the spark of inspiration," flexibility, or courage to try the new, great expertise can inhibit the production of novelty. In order to achieve effective surprise, experts need to be capable of seeing the contents of their field in a fresh light. Creative experts often show a freshness and openness that is more typical of beginners; this has been referred to as the "novice effect." I once attended a lecture by the then 70-year-old Nobel Prize winner Hans Selye, who apologized for being in plaster from his toes to his hip—he had fallen out of a tree a few days before after he saw something that seemed odd and interesting in the tree and climbed it in order to have a better look! [See EXPERTISE.]

F. What Is the Relationship of Creativity to Intelligence?

Conventional intelligence is heavily dependent on recognizing, recalling, and reapplying, and requires among other things substantial knowledge of facts, effective acquisition of new facts, rapid access to the contents of memory, accuracy in finding the best answer to factual questions, and logical application of the already known. Creativity, on the other hand, requires production of novelty, that is, departure from the facts, finding new ways, inventing answers, and seeing unexpected solutions. The initial position adopted in the 1950s and 1960s by psychologists was that creativity and intelligence are thus separate, more or less competing or even mutually exclusive dimensions of intellect. However, later theory has emphasized that the two overlap or interact. Some writers have referred to this interaction as involving "true" intellectual giftedness, with neither intelligence alone nor creativity leading to the production of effective novelty. In studies of achievement at school or university level, for instance, it has been shown that, by and large, those students are most successful who display both creativity and intelligence. Recent research on practical creativity has shown that engineers rated as "creative" displayed a combination of characteristics. One conceptualization of the interaction was to see creativity as a way of ap-

plying intelligence or of organizing ideas, the difference between the two being that they are thinking styles or tactics. [See COGNITIVE STYLE AND CREATIVITY.]

An early conceptualization of the way creativity and intelligence interact was the threshold model, according to which a minimum level of intelligence is necessary before creativity is possible. A slight extension is the idea that as intelligence approaches this threshold (corresponding to an IQ of perhaps 130) from below, the possibility of creativity rises (i.e., creativity and IQ are positively correlated below the threshold). When intelligence lies above the threshold, increases in intelligence have no consequences for creativity (i.e., IQ and creativity are uncorrelated once intelligence is high enough). This view has been expanded somewhat by the idea of a "one way" relationship between creativity and intelligence. Intelligence determines the upper limits of a person's ability to obtain and store information, without actually being itself part of creativity. The degree of creativity depends upon the amount of divergency displayed in the processing of the information made available by intelligence. An approach even more clearly oriented toward information processing is the idea that intelligence involves channel capacity, with creativity being the result of flexible and versatile handling of information delivered by the channel, and lack of creativity resulting from conventional use of this information. [See INTELLIGENCE.]

One approach has involved identifying six "facets" of creativity: knowledge, insight, intrinsic motivation, the courage of one's convictions, special personal factors such as flexibility and willingness to take risks, and relevance. These facets overlap partially with facets of intelligence. Knowledge is closely linked with it and is indispensable for a high IQ. Insight involves particularly effective selection of information and may be favorable for high intelligence, but is probably not absolutely necessary to obtain a high IQ. Intrinsic motivation is favorable for the acquisition of knowledge, but it is possible to operate rapidly, accurately, and logically without it. Flexibility and risk taking may even detract from performance on an intelligence test. Summing up, it can be said that creativity and intelligence are neither identical nor completely different, but are interacting aspects of intellectual ability. The achieving of effective surprise, especially in practical settings, requires both. It is important to bear in mind, however, that creativity is not merely a matter of cognitive processes such as knowing, thinking, recognizing remembering, or puzzling out, but that it also involves factors such as motivation, personal properties, and feelings (see also Section IV).

G. What Is the Relationship of Creativity to Problem Solving?

The term "problem solving" has a special meaning in current research and theory, especially in psychology, and has its own research tradition separate from creativity research. It is often discussed in cognitive terms or as a special form of information processing. In conventional problem solving research the person solving the problem knows that it exists and understands the nature of the problem, intends to solve it, possesses special knowledge, some or all of which is required to solve the problem, and knows what form the solution will take. Creativity researchers, however, distinguish between problem solving and creative problem solving. The latter is required when one or more of the elements just mentioned (knowledge of the problem, of the means of solution, and of the nature of the solution) is missing. In other words, creativity can be involved in problem solving but is not always necessary, while not all problem solutions are creative.

One way of showing the role of creativity in problem solving is to divide problems according to (a) their degree of definition; (b) the degree of familiarity of the means for solving them; and (c) the clarity of the criteria for recognizing solutions. Clearly defined problems that are solvable by means of standard techniques and for which there are obvious and well-known criteria identifying the solution constitute "routine" problems. They can often be solved without the help of creativity, although when existing knowledge is applied in settings where it has previously been treated as irrelevant, a certain "technical" or "inventive" creativity occurs. Nonetheless, creativity is not absolutely necessary, and is probably not usual. By contrast, some ill-defined problems require, in the first instance, becoming aware that there is a problem at all and finding a way of defining it; second, working out techniques for solving the problem; and third, development of criteria for recognizing a solution. Such "complex" or "intractable" problems demand a high level of creativity.

Early in the present century a German chemist was engaged in research on how to kill bacteria with poisonous chemical substances. Each evening he prepared cultures on petri dishes and allowed them to grow overnight on a layer of nutrient. Each day he exposed the cultures to various toxic chemicals, but without any success in killing them. One morning he entered his lab to find all the cultures dead. After microscopic examination of the dead cultures he discovered that they were contaminated by mold spores. He concluded that these spores were killing the bacteria and making his research impossible. After a careful search he discovered a patch of mold on the wall of his lab and was delighted to be able to report in a communication in a chemistry journal that he had destroyed the mold and could now grow bacteria successfully. He also reported that, unfortunately, he could find no way of poisoning them! Neither the chemist himself nor, apparently, anyone who read his report realized that he had discovered penicillin. All that was necessary was for a reader to have recognized that the solution had been achieved (the bacteria were dead) and to have redefined the solution as getting the mold to grow again, and a Nobel Prize would have been there for the taking.

The chemist was confronted by a routine problem. His clear definition of what he wanted to achieve, how to go about achieving it, and what would constitute a solution actually inhibited recognition of the "real" solution. This suggests that routine problems may inhibit the production of novelty (see also earlier discussions of high expertise and creativity). It is also conceivable that the reverse could occur: Creativity could inhibit the solving of routine problems, for instance, by making them fuzzy and thus blocking the emergence of a simple solution. In the case of intractable problems, on the other hand, creativity may be necessary: Creativity researchers speak of "problem awareness," "problem recognition" and the process of "problem finding" or "problem definition," which they see as major elements of creativity. It is possible to distinguish between seeing problems that are already evident in the present organization of available information and are obvious to any qualified observer, discovering hidden problems as a result of an intensive analysis of a situation, and inventing problems that are only apparent after the available information has been reorganized according to novel principles. A number of researchers see the finding of "good" problems as the vital step in creativity.

The question also arises as to whether creativity always involves solving problems. If "product" is understood broadly enough, effective novelty could be argued always to lead to a product, even if this is in the form of an idea or the act of transferring a procedure to an unfamiliar setting. It is also possible to define "problem" very broadly, for instance the problem of communicating a poet's sense of awe to readers or the problem of capturing the beauty of a sunset on canvas. Using such broad definitions, it could be argued that creativity always involves a product that solves a problem. However, conventional problem solving research in psychology understands "problem" and "solution" in a much more concrete way. [*See* PROBLEM SOLVING.]

III. CREATIVITY AS A SOCIAL PHENOMENON

A. The Social Rules

Creativity requires doing things differently from the way they are usually done, or even defying the norms of society, what some writers have called "contrarianism" (although they were writing about giftedness in general, and not specifically creativity). In a certain sense, creative people defy the rules, even those who do not call attention to themselves through antisocial behavior. Thus, creativity can be seen as a "failure" to conform to the norms of society. [*See* CONTRARIANISM.]

In principle, all people are capable of a wide range of responses to life situations, but in the process of growing up they learn that most of these are forbidden, and usually restrict their responses to a narrow range of socially tolerated behaviors. This has the advantage that life becomes predictable, since it is more or less known what can be expected in everyday situations, but the disadvantage is that unusual, unexpected reactions are discouraged and become rare. There are even rules about which opinions are correct, indeed about the right way of thinking and the contents of correct thought. Societies are prepared to tolerate the breaking of the rules to a certain degree, which rules can be broken, or how large a deviation is accepted varying from society to society and from time to time, as well as according to the age, social position, occupation, and other characteristics of the individual doing the rule breaking. For instance, the North American society would tolerate deviations from the norms for behavior at a wedding by a 21-year-old art student that would not be tolerated from the local bank manager. In general, there are rules about breaking the rules. People publicly acclaimed as creative break these rules, but succeed in staying within acceptable limits. If they do not, they are likely to be regarded as eccentric, immoral, mentally disturbed, or criminal rather than creative, with the possibility of being criticized, shunned, or even locked away.

Research indicates that some people may function as facilitators of creativity by energizing, activating, or releasing it in others, without necessarily producing effective novelty themselves. Such creativity facilitators can be humble and unsung people, such as a grade school teacher. In mature workers, such as scientists, working in a team may provide contact with facilitators. An important function of such people is to offer creative individuals a safe space where they can break the rules without sanctions, as well as to offer them a positive perspective on themselves, for instance the view that their ideas are not crazy but creative. This recognition can help to foster the courage to deviate from what everyone else is doing by, among other things, offering an opportunity to test the limits of the acceptable without risk or feelings of guilt. The groups of which a person is a member—either intimate groups such as the family, more public groups such as playmates or friends, or more or less formally defined groups such as experts/critics, colleagues, or employers—can also foster creativity by offering a social environment marked by recognition and encouragement (or, of course, hinder or block it by withholding such positive feedback). Some researchers regard exposure to a congenial environment as the crucial factor in the emergence of creativity. [*See* CREATIVE CLIMATE; CONDITIONS AND SETTINGS/ENVIRONMENT.]

B. Sociocultural Validation

Science, art, and indeed all fields of creativity are themselves subsystems—aesthetic/professional and social—to which the points just raised can also be applied. A creative product must not only be novel, but must also be communicated to other people and, most important in the present context, be accepted or at least tolerated by them. This acceptance involves "sociocultural validation" of a product, without which it is not creative in the aesthetic/professional sense. Without sociocultural validation it is not possible to speak of "creativity," but only of the "production of variability." Some theorists have argued that "creativity" is not really a property of products or processes at all, but that it is a category of judgment in the minds of observers, often acknowledged experts or specialists. In some areas the rules for applying the label "creative" are well established, with the result that there is a high level of agreement not only among judges, but also between experts and ordinary members of the public. In other areas, however, there is less agreement, with the result that there are often controversies, for instance, over the quality of a painting, a book, or a piece of music. This approach not only places great emphasis on communication, but it also emphasizes the final step in the emergence of a creative product: the phase of validation by the surrounding society.

The sociocultural validation of products does not occur in an economic/political vacuum. It is striking that research has shown that there is a relationship between the economic/political situation of a society and the contents of the relevant and effective novelty created in that society: After an economic depression, there may be a burst of, let us say, literary creativity, after a successful war (if any war is ever "successful") creativity in the performing arts, after an unsuccessful war creativity in business and industry, and so on.

C. The Organizational Environment

In business and industry, the emphasis is frequently on innovation rather than creativity. The difference is that innovation requires not only creating novelty, but also putting it into concrete practice in a particular setting. Thus, in a certain sense, creativity can be seen as a prerequisite for innovation or as encompassing a stage or phase of innovation. Several definitional problems are easy to solve in the framework of innovation, for instance, the question for whom novelty should be surprising, relevant, and effective, or the issue of chance: Innovation requires the deliberate introduction of ideas, products, production, or marketing processes, and the like that are novel for a work group or an organization into which they are introduced. Effectiveness is also, at least in theory, easy to judge: production rises, sales improve, costs sink, absenteeism or staff turnover falls, or accidents in the workplace occur less frequently, to give some concrete examples. [*See* BUSINESS STRATEGY.]

Innovation can also be seen as a process having two phases. In the initial ideational phase, ideas emerge that are new for the setting in which they occur. These ideas can be novel in an absolute sense (i.e., involving "innovative" or "emergent" creativity), but they need not be. For instance, a manager could make suggestions based on standard practice at a former place of work, but which are novel in the new workplace. Applying the already known in a new setting constitutes a creative act ("inventive creativity"), but only involves "minor" or "secondary" creativity. After this ideational phase comes the behavioral phase, in which the novel idea is put into practice. Creativity can occur without the behavioral phase, but this phase is essential for innovation. [*See* INNOVATION.]

Of great importance in innovation is the fact that novel ideas have to be inserted into an existing context (a business, production process, management team, etc.). The "context" is usually referred to in the relevant research literature as the organization. The process of insertion seems to occur in steps or phases, described in, for instance, the five-phase model involving "agenda setting" (the problem is defined and possible solutions considered), "matching" (the suitability of possible solutions is considered), "redefining/restructuring" (the innovation is adapted to the specific situation of the organization or the organization adapts itself), "clarifying" (the organization grasps what the innovation is all about), and "routinizing" (the innovation becomes part of the daily life of the organization).

Researchers have described aspects of the organization that facilitate or block innovative behavior, and these bear a strong similarity to the properties of the "congenial environment" described by creativity researchers. Among these factors are freedom to make decisions, support from colleagues with whom one directly works, and facilitating attitudes or other factors (e.g., leadership style) of superiors. Inhibiting factors include negative aspects of the organizational climate, negative attitudes and leadership style of superiors, and inhibiting structures of command. In the case of the individual person, innovation often demands acquisition of new skills on the one hand, and cognitive reorganization on the other (changes in thinking strategies, in the organization of knowledge, or in ways of evaluating work activities). These can lead to a conflict of values with a resultant uncertainty or anxiety, and may have consequences for the self-concept. As a result, personal characteristics of the individual such as openness for the new, willingness to take risks, and flexibility interact with the characteristics of the organization to facilitate or inhibit innovation and to moderate its psychological consequences.

IV. THE PSYCHOLOGICAL BASIS OF CREATIVITY

Researchers in the 1960s established the three P's approach in psychological research on creativity. It involves (a) novel *products* such as objects, machines, works of art, ideas, solutions to problems, industrial or production processes, and the like; (b) psychological *processes* such as fantasizing, diverging from the customary, or inventing that lead to novel products; or (c) *personal properties* of the person that permit or even promote the production of novelty, including openness for the new and a self-concept as an innovator. This latter dimension can be expanded to include (d) *motivation,* such as willingness to take risks and a drive to find new approaches. [*See* FOUR P'S OF CREATIVITY.]

Although products are of great interest to artists and business people, they present serious problems for a psychological discussion. Artistic products are often the subject of great controversy, with serious differences of opinion about their degree of novelty and especially their effectiveness: criteria vary from beholder to beholder (for instance, art, literature, or theater critics) and from epoch to epoch. The perceived creativity of paintings has been shown by researchers to vary according to the audience's beliefs about the identity of the painter or the amount of time they believed was expended on completing the work. The psychological discussion has, as a result, concentrated on the process, person, and social environment.

A. Thinking Processes

The decisive event in modern psychological analyses of creativity was the acceptance speech in 1950 of the new president of the American Psychological Association, J. P. Guilford. In a nutshell, he complained that existing concepts of intelligence visualized it as the finding of single correct answers to circumscribed problems. By contrast, he argued that intellectual power could also be applied to the finding of substantial numbers of new, original, and unexpected answers, quite possibly to loosely defined problems. He referred to this process as a special kind of thinking, which he labeled "divergent." Guilford's original paper had the title "Creativity," and the equating of creativity with divergent thinking quickly established itself, especially after the Sputnik shock already mentioned. [*See* DIVERGENT THINKING.]

Other researchers have also concentrated on thinking processes as the basis for creativity. A well-known popular scientific approach emphasized "lateral" thinking. Other concepts are "janusian" thinking (named after the Roman god Janus, who could look backward and forward at the same time), "homospatial" thinking (ideas from different domains are brought together in the same space), "biphasic" thinking (the first phase being an uninhibited combinations of ideas, which are then organized and sorted out in the second phase, for instance, according to social acceptability), and "tertiary" thinking (in the psychoanalytic sense, primary process and secondary process thinking are combined). [*See* HOMOSPATIAL PROCESS; JANUSIAN PROCESS.]

Associational theories emphasize the process of linking ideas. The theory of "remote associates" is based on the observation that in the course of their experiences, people learn a number of responses to a particular stimulus. Some of the stimulus–response associations occur frequently, and others seldom. As a result, people learn a hierarchy of associations. Pairings that occurred frequently in the past stand high in the hierarchy and have a higher probablity of being chosen when the stimulus occurs again than associations which occurred infrequently in the past. These less-likely associations are "remote" and the person who makes them produces unusual or unexpected ideas. A similar approach is seen in the theory of "bisociation," which assumes that ideas occur in "matrices" or fields. Normally, ideas from the same field are combined in a process of association. However, some people combine ideas from separate matrices in a process of bisociation, which, by virtue of the fact that the ideas are not normally found together, means that the combination is surprising. [*See* ASSOCIATIVE THEORY.]

B. Personality

A number of writers have emphasized the importance of personality in creativity, some even arguing that creativity may have little to do with cognitive processes at all, and may be the result of a special personality constellation. Reviews of the relevant research typically list characteristics such as flexibility, sensitiveness, autonomy and ego strength. Recent analyses of earlier research, however, suggest that the relationship between creativity and personality is by no means simple and straightforward. It is not possible to identify a certain kind of personality profile that is typical of the creative, regardless of their field, and that also distinguishes the creative from the noncreative. A recent study emphasized the importance of a "complex" personality that combines, among others, sensitivity with toughness or high intelligence with naivité. Striking in the discussion of this point is that the personality characteristics regarded as important for creativity sometimes seem to be contradictory: for instance, the creative personality seems to be simultaneously stereotypically "masculine" (autonomy, self-confidence, toughness) and yet stereotypically "feminine" (sensitive, intuitive, responsible). According to one study, creativity requires possession of a "paradoxical" personality characterized by seven polarities: openness combined with a drive to close incomplete gestalts; acceptance of fantasy combined with maintenance of a strong sense of reality; critical and destructive attitudes together with constructive problem solving; cool neutrality combined with passionate engagement; self-centeredness coexisting with altruism; self-criticism and self-doubt together with self-confidence; and tension and concentration side by side with relaxedness. [*See* PERSONALITY.]

C. Motivation

The creation of novelty requires not only appropriate thinking and personality, but also the desire or at least the readiness to diverge, take risks, defy conventional opinion, or expose oneself to the possibility of being wrong: in other words, appropriate motivation. A position that is widely accepted in recent writing is that creativity is based on intrinsic motivation, the wish to carry out an activity for the sake of the activity itself, and not in the hope of obtaining external rewards. This latter form of motivation (seeking of external rewards) is referred to as "extrinsic." Extrinsic motivation may inhibit creativity or even be fatal to it. It is extremely seductive, and once people have been exposed to it they are in danger of shaping their behavior, and even their thinking, into forms that lead to external rewards, such as personal recognition by peers, colleagues or superiors, praise, promotion, or fame. [*See* MOTIVATION/ DRIVE.]

According to the "triad" model, there are five classes of creativity motive: instrumental motives, playful motives, intrinsic motives, control motives, and expressive motives. In contrast to the emphasis on intrinsic motivation, this approach argues that creativity can be a means to an end; for example, a person might write a book in the hope of making money. Motives interact or change with time. To take an example, a person might begin to write novels in order to earn money—instrumental or extrinsic motivation—but might become aware in the course of writing of the feeling of having an important message that must be expressed regardless of the consequences (expressive or intrinsic motivation). At a particular time a creative person may be dominated by extrinsic, at another by intrinsic motivation. Such "individual structures of motivation" are capable of changing with time, so that a given person might at one point be more extrinsically motivated, and at another more intrinsically. The idea of a dynamically changing structure of creativity motivation is supported by the "evolving systems" approach, according to which a creative product emerges as the result of a long process of development of knowledge, emotions and feelings, and goals. [*See* EVOLVING SYSTEMS APPROACH.]

D. Creativity and Madness

The idea that there is a connection between creativity and madness is one of the oldest issues in modern psychology, and was already a subject of empirical investigation a good 100 years ago. Contemporary research has adopted two approaches, either studying acknowledged creative people to see if they are more frequently mentally disturbed than chance would predict, or working with people already regarded as mentally ill or at least "eccentric" in order to see if they show more creativity than the general population. Studies in Britain, where being eccentric is accepted without great stigma, have shown that many eccentrics hold patents, some of them several. At a more theoretical level, it has been shown that there are some similarities in schizophrenic and creative thinking (i.e., cognitive similarities), schizophrenics making, for instance, more remote associations and thinking more divergently. However, schizophrenic thinking does not favor production of effective novelty, despite its divergent nature. Schizophrenics are frightened by their own unusual ideation, whereas creative people are positively motivated by it. [*See* ECCENTRICITY; MAD GENIUS CONTROVERSY; SCHIZOPHRENIA.]

It has also been shown that mood disturbances are much more common among acknowledged creative people than in the general public. However, the connection between mood disturbance and creativity does not seem to involve a direct causal relationship. Instead, both mood disturbance and creativity seem to be related to emotional lability and greater sensitivity to external stimuli or internal mood fluctuations, thus producing an apparent causal relationship. Mood states such as manic disorders could also reduce fear of embarrassing oneself or promote self-confidence, once again creating an erroneous impression that the manic disorder causes the creativity. Generally, the position of clinically oriented researchers on creativity is that it requires a high level of mental health, or even that creativity promotes mental health. [*See* MOOD.]

V. THE PSYCHOLOGICAL PARADOX OF CREATIVITY

The "classical" description of the emergence of creative products is the phase model, which was first introduced into creativity research about 75 years ago. In early research four phases or stages were distinguished: In the first, referred to as the phase of *information,* a person becomes thoroughly familiar with a content area. In the *incubation* phase the person "churns" through the information obtained in the previous phase until a solution appears; this marks the phase of *illumination.* The solution may seem to the person in question suddenly to have appeared from nowhere, because its emergence into consciousness may come all at

once, thus creating the subjective feeling of creativity without perspiration. This would explain why some creative people overlook the phases of information and incubation in describing their own creativity. Finally comes the phase of *verification,* in which the person tests the solution thrown up in the phases of incubation and illumination.

There is disagreement among more recent theorists and researchers about whether incubation processes are chaotic and more or less random, with a solution popping up out of the seething cauldron of ideas and being recognized or not according to the ability of the person in question to recognize that a solution is at hand or the openness of this person for new solutions, or whether incubation follows strict rules, for instance, running through all logical possibilities until an answer is found. Recently, it has been recognized that the latter would involve vast numbers of "empty trials," and would be extremely inefficient. Some writers have argued that the process must be shortened either by means of intuition, a sensing that certain approaches offer more promise than others, or via metacognitive processes (for instance, rules showing how to recognize that some lines of attack are dead ends, criteria for evaluating the usefulness of what has been achieved to date, or strategies for generating promising new approaches). [*See* INTUITION; METACOGNITION.]

Empirical studies of the process of creation in people actually engaged in producing something new, as well as retrospective studies in which acknowledged creators described how they obtained new ideas, have cast doubt on the validity of the phase model. Nonetheless, it offers a helpful way of disentangling a number of issues in the definition of creativity. For this reason, it will be retained here as an aid to the present theoretical discussion.

Figure 1 shows an expanded phase model incorporating the additional phases of *communication* and *validation.* The figure goes beyond a depiction of the phases of creativity to show how different psychological factors (see Section IV) are of particular importance in the emergence of a creative product in different phases of the production process. In each phase (see left-hand column), core psychological processes (second column) are applied to the results of the previous phase (third column), to produce the material for the next phase. The psychological processes are made possible or at least

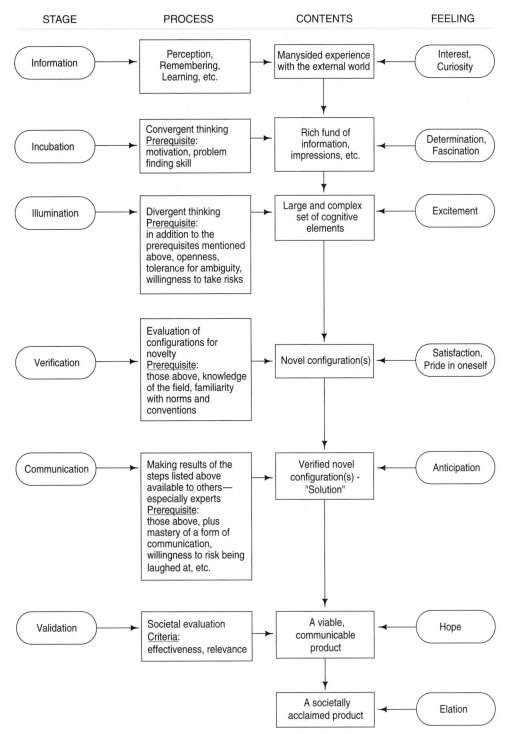

STAGE   PROCESS   CONTENTS   FEELING

FIGURE 1   The psychological elements involved in achieving a creative product. This figure is reprinted from M. Runco (Ed.) (1997). *Handbook of Creativity, Vol. 1* (p. 100). Hampton Press, Cresskill, NJ, with permission.

facilitated by factors such as motivation, openness for the new, or willingness to take risks. The total process is accompanied in its various phases by feelings such as fascination, pride, or satisfaction.

Figure 1 depicts a successful process of creation which culminates in a socially validated product. In practice, the process can be broken off earlier, for instance, when evaluation of the product to date indicates that it is a failure. The creative process can also start part way through, for instance, when a person returns to an earlier novel configuration to verify it. It can also function as a kind of spiral; for example, new information could make it possible to verify a novel configuration that had earlier been rejected.

An expanded phase model is helpful in sorting out one aspect of creativity that has already been touched upon without being made explicit: the definition of creativity involves reconciling apparently mutually contradictory positions—defining creativity involves a number of "paradoxes." Among these are the following: (a) creativity involves difference from the everyday, but is found in everybody; (b) novelty, the single essential element in creativity, is necessary but not sufficient to define it; (c) creativity is not the same as intelligence, but it is also not completely different; (d) creative production requires deep knowledge, but freedom from its constraints; (e) creativity implies bringing something new into existence, but can be studied without reference to products; (f) creativity requires deviating from social norms, but doing this in a way that the society can tolerate; (g) creativity requires combining contradictory personality characteristics; and (h) opposite kinds of motivation can lead to creativity. The phase model suggests that the paradoxical combinations occur in different phases of the process of production of novelty: for instance, convergent thinking might dominate in the phase of preparation, divergent thinking in that of illumination, modesty in the phase of verification, and self-confidence during communication. Thus, the paradox of creativity may not be the problem it appears to be.

Bibliography

Amabile, T. M. (1996). *Creativity in context.* Boulder, CO: Westview Press.

Csikszentmihalyi, M. (1996). *Creativity: Flow and the psychology of discovery and invention.* New York: Harper Collins.

Gardner, H. (1995). *Leading minds: An anatomy of leadership.* New York: Basic Books.

Eysenck, H. J. (1995). *Genius: The natural history of creativity.* New York: Cambridge University Press.

Glover, J. A., Ronning, R. R., & Reynolds, C. R. (1989). *Handbook of creativity.* New York: Plenum Press.

Runco, M. A. (Ed.). (1991). *Theories of creativity.* Newbury Park, CA: Sage.

Simonton, D. K. (1994). *Greatness: Who makes history and why.* New York: Guilford.

Sternberg, R. J., & Lubart, T. I. (1995). *Defying the crowd: Cultivating creativity in a culture of conformity.* New York: Free Press.

Design

Gabriela Goldschmidt

Technion, Israel Institute of Technology

*The world we live in is full of artifacts; to make these artifacts they must first be designed. In modern times, **DESIGN** is a professional activity that is practiced by designers in a variety of design fields such as architecture, engineering, or industrial design. Creative design is held in great esteem, but we still know little about design cognition and the cognitive abilities and strategies that contribute to creative design thinking.*

Computer Aided Design (CAD) Technique involving the use of special computer applications to assist designers, primarily in drafting and otherwise representing and modeling design information, designed objects, and other artifacts.

Design Cognition Cognitive aspects of design thinking and the study of these aspects. Research in design cognition is aimed at learning how designers think.

Human Factors Physiological and behavioral characteristics of humans that determine what they can do, physically and mentally, with reasonable ease, convenience and safety.

Orthogonal Projections A drafting system that is attributed to Raphael, one of Italy's great Renaissance artists and architects. The system allows the specification of any object or space through three kinds of projections: view, plan, and cross section.

Vernacular and Indigenous Design Design that is typical to a region or place; employs common, conventional, and typical forms and materials, and shies away from nontraditional features. Design that develops naturally, using local resources, and in response to basic needs.

I. INTRODUCTION

According to Herbert Simon, "Everyone designs who devises courses of action aimed at changing existing situations into preferred ones." As far as material artifacts are concerned, we may elaborate: To design is to plan for the making of something new. Designing entails generating, transforming, and refining descriptions and specifications of different aspects of a still nonexistent artifact and making representations of it that enable communication and examination of the ideas involved, which ultimately enables the production or construction of the artifact. We concentrate on the design of tangible artifacts, which is practiced in the traditional design professions: architecture, the art of designing buildings, deals primarily with space that

Copyright © 1999 by Academic Press
All rights of reproduction in any form reserved.

is enclosed by the material elements of buildings. Architecture is considered, if not the mother of all arts, definitely the mother of all design domains. Several engineering domains include design components and, most prominent, are the younger vocations of industrial design, which grew out of product design, graphic design, fashion design, and several others. The term *design* is also used in the context of nontangible constructs, such as social design. In this and similar cases, the term that should be used is *planning*. Planning is defined by *Webster's Third International Dictionary* as "the establishing of goals, policies, and procedures for a social or economic unit" and it should be distinguished from design.

Design has always been closely associated with creativity because new artifacts are often expected to be innovative and original—two hallmarks of creative products. Therefore, designers are expected to be creative persons who exercise creative processes. The making of artifacts is readily associated with technology, and their appearance is naturally related to the visual arts. Design is therefore seen as a merge between the two, with a possible dominance of either an artistic tendency or a technological bent. But more often than not, both the appearance and the function of designed artifacts are expected to meet standards of excellence based on state-of-the-art technologies as well as artistic norms. Designers are seen as synthesizers whose craft is to respond to the various design requirements in an integrative and holistic way. The capacity for synthesis is, by wide agreement, a quality of the creative designer. It is more difficult to specify the attributes of the design process, and it is particularly challenging to designate what makes it more or less creative. After briefly outlining the history of design and its practice in the modern era, our discussion of design will relate to design products, to designers, and finally to practice—the process of designing.

II. HISTORY

Builders and tool makers have designed artifacts since the dawn of prehistoric times. Design was an inseparable part of all material production of ancient cultures, but it did not exist in its own right until it ceased to be an automatic by-product of the making of artifacts. This takes us to the twilight of the Middle Ages, during which there were arts and artists, and crafts and craftsmen; often the boundary between them was not very sharp. Design was carried out by exceptionally gifted craftsmen and artists. Buildings, for example, were designed by their chief masons, and most of the design was carried out in situ as construction progressed. Design first emerged as an independent activity during the Renaissance. The design of buildings began to be entrusted to specialists, before and apart from their construction. This development coincides with an important invention: the drawing system known as orthogonal projections, attributed to the painter and architect Raphael, who lived in Italy in the 15th century. Orthogonal projections made it possible to represent accurately and fully all components and elements of physical entities. The system, known today as technical drafting, enables the preparation of complete sets of production, assembly, or construction specifications by parties that are independent in time and location from construction or production. In that sense design resembles musical composition: a standard notation system using notes and other graphic symbols makes it possible to write music, thus separating composition from performance. Design was, nevertheless, still closely associated with the arts and with crafts, and Leonardo da Vinci, symbol of the Renaissance, was a painter as well as a designer of both buildings and machines. [*See* DA VINCI, LEONARDO.]

The technological and social developments associated with the Industrial Revolution naturally led to division of labor and later to specialization, including in design. Design, believed by many to be an offspring of architecture, had to be increasingly concerned with routines of industrial production, which were very different from methods used in architecture. The design of machines required different expertise than that useful in the design of buildings, and both had little to do with the styling of textiles, for example. Eventually even the various aspects of the design of a single entity began to require more qualifications than could be expected in one domain: thus for example, architecture became separate from structural engineering, although they are closely interrelated in the design of the same structure. Structural engineering, like most engineering domains, is more analytic than synthetic today, and therefore its affinity to design is limited. However, engineering still incorporates design, and this is particularly true for mechanical engineering, although other domains such as structural, electric, and chemical engineering, for example, also involve design. The most important development of the late 19th and early 20th century was the emergence of product and then industrial design as a major independent discipline. Many industrial designers were trained as architects and practiced in both fields, but industrial design definitely grew to possess its own identity as a profession. A growing middle class became, along with industry itself, the new market for designed artifacts—consumer goods as well as tools, machinery, and other implements.

In Europe, the turn of the century was dominated by the Arts and Crafts Movement, which stressed the need to overcome machine-induced standardization and anonymity through the use of decorative arts. This was an era of inventions and development of new materials, which opened many new design options. Yet often there was a discrepancy between new materials and old forms that were preferred by Arts and Crafts designers, resulting in products whose design did not take full advantage of the new potentialities. Thus cultural factors did not always match technological capabilities. But in the early 20th century, the very same features of standardization, perfection and functional bareness that frustrated Arts and Crafts designers began to capture the imagination of artists, architects, and designers who identified in them a potential for a new machine esthetic. The newly born Modern Movement no longer saw industrial production as opposing arts or crafts but rather as its ally. The precursor of the Modern Movement, the German Werkbund that was founded in 1907, also marked a move of design leadership from England to continental Europe. In 1919 the German architect Walter Gropius founded the Bauhaus, an avant-garde school of art, crafts, and design, to which architecture was later added. The Bauhaus attracted some of the most distinguished artists of the time and had become a haven of experimentation and innovation in all design fields. It had a strong and lasting influence on designers, design educators, and theorists that extended well beyond its native Germany and prevailed long after the school was closed by the Nazis in 1933. The Bauhaus was unique in promoting close cooperation between the various design fields and activities; its famous basic design course, which all students took during their first year of studies, is to this day a cornerstone of many design and architecture curricula the world over. There were intensive ties between Bauhaus artists and designers and their peers elsewhere in Europe, notably in The Netherlands (the "De Stijl," Dutch for "The Style," movement) and Russia (the Constructivist Movement). Many Bauhaus teachers moved to the United States when the school closed, thereby forging a link between European and American design.

The Bauhaus stressed functionality above all other design criteria, and functional merits were also expected to be visibly noticeable in designed artifacts. With this creed the Bauhaus adhered to the dictum "Form Follows Function." The functional designs that Bauhaus teachers and students undertook were expected to be sophisticated both technologically and aesthetically; they were to be original and innovative, and they were to synthesize art, crafts, and technology in a unique combination. New materials were exploited, new production techniques used, and the wise interaction between color and good form replaced any need for ornament or decoration. Chairs designed in the Bauhaus by Marcel Breuer and Ludwig Mies van der Rohe, for instance, were the first to use tubular steel for the frame, while the seating and back surfaces were made of traditional leather or cane. Figure 1 shows one of Breuer's early steel chairs. The search for synthesis made the Bauhaus into a huge laboratory in which much creativity was invested in experimental work. Photography and motion pictures were first combined with painting, sculpture, and architectural design to produce such new results that new names had to be invented for them, such as collage, relief-construction, and photomontage. Because of its revolutionary character, the Bauhaus developed a strong communal cultural identity that gave rise not only to individual creativity but also to group creativity and to creative design education, which many design schools tried to emulate in later years with, alas, limited success.

In the second half of the 20th century, design has been recognized as an important element of economic development, because it is a decisive factor in the image and marketing potential of most manufactured goods. Creative design is therefore held in great esteem

FIGURE 1   *Wassily.* This lounge chair designed by Marcel Breuer in 1925 was the first piece of furniture to use tubular steel. It was named after Breuer's Bauhaus colleague, the painter Wassily Kandinsky. Photograph courtesy of Knoll, New York.

and no effort is spared to develop tools that are intended to promote and support design creativity. Design education is institutionalized, with emphases on technological excellence, aesthetic appeal, cultural significance, ecological soundness, and good management of production and marketing. Of special importance are human factors that deal with user friendliness and safety of use, both mentally and physically. Creative design must still cater, by way of synthesis, to all design criteria together in a unified, elegant, and original solution.

III. DESIGN PRODUCTS

The products of physical design are artifacts such as machines, buildings, clothes, advertisement posters, furniture but also printed circuits or an anesthesia system for a hospital operating room. Good, solid design products are practical and fulfill users' needs. They may be typical in the sense that they are improved descendants of a common prototype. By contrast, creative products are usually nontypical; they have no family resemblance to a prototype and the further away they are from a pedigree, the more novel and innovative

we must assume they are. Products that achieve the highest acclaim and praise—and which are seen as most creative—are original, possibly surprising, even at the cost of practicality and superior performance. [*See* CREATIVE PRODUCTS.]

The tension between a creativity imperative, which hinges primarily on a visible overriding design idea on the one hand, and performance requirements based on needs and resources on the other hand, is very strong in all design domains. An example of a design product that received the highest possible acclaim for its creativity, and the worst critical appraisal conceivable for its performance, is the well-known Sydney Opera House designed by Jorn Utzon, which is illustrated in Figure 2. Utzon's proposal for the opera building won the first prize in an international design competition in 1957, where it overshadowed more than 200 other competition entries. The prize was awarded because the judges were struck by the unusually creative design. It won against all odds: Utzon's entry was liable for disqualification under four out of six disqualification clauses of the competition regulations. In addition, it was also not clear at that time whether a structural solution could be found for the ambitious shells

FIGURE 2   Sidney Opera House by Jorn Utzon, 1957–1973. (a) Sketch by Jorn Utzon. Reproduced with permission. (b) The finished building. Photograph courtesy of Terry Purcell.

that adorned the building like huge sails; the absence of a solution (which was reached only years later) could have jeopardized the construction of the building. The erection of the building was a lengthy and problematic process. It was completed only in 1973 and it cost much more than was originally estimated. There is consensus that as an opera house, its performance is rather poor. Nevertheless, within a few years it had become one of the most famous buildings in the world, a symbol of Sydney and indeed, of Australia. The Danish architect Utzon, who was a persona non grata in Australia for many years following the scandalous cost and the incredible problems associated with the building, was finally invited to Sydney as a guest of honor because of this creative tour de force.

Quality and creativity in design, then, are by no means synonymous. A list of criteria for excellence was compiled in 1992 by Dana Cuff, who studied architectural practice. The list, based on architects' stances and opinions, makes no reference to creativity or to innovation. Rather, it stresses a balance between goals and constraints, and it highlights the social aspects of the process of design in which designers operate in teams, along with clients, consultants, and other concerned parties. When assessing teamwork, creativity as a criterion for successful design appears to lose some of its edge, as compared to the criteria by which the work of individual designers is evaluated. In fact, we can distinguish between two design cultures: one that deals primarily with everyday needs and everyday things that are made to meet those needs. The products in question are often designed "unselfconsciously," to use the terminology of Christopher Alexander. By that we mean that products come into being through a lengthy evolutionary process in which many individuals contribute to the shaping of practical, ceremonial, or decorative artifacts that are transformed over time, using readily available resources and techniques, until they best serve the purpose for which they were created. Such designs are user oriented: they prevail because of their responsiveness to user needs. Creativity is of little concern and so is the designer, who often does not exist as an individual. Accordingly, a famous exhibition (and a book) of what was termed "non-pedigreed architecture" that was mounted at the Museum of Modern Art in New York in 1964 was called by its curator, Bernard Rudofsky, "Architecture Without Architects."

In a historic dimension, we may talk about vernacular or indigenous design to best describe this kind of conventional design, which is intimately related to local conditions and to shared values of a community.

Design products, whether "unselfconscious" or, on the contrary, "selfconscious," are well rooted in the particular cultures in which they were created. The common denominator of design features in a given culture is style, and little connoisseurship is required to determine which style an artifact belongs to. In our times, rapid cultural changes have caused equally fast shifts in style that succeed one another very rapidly. Today's styles are less local and more universal, but they are short lived. In this reality the individual designer is placed at the center of attention. Thus, for example, we have ordinary chairs and we have an Eames Chair, named after its designer Charles Eames. Likewise we may have an Ettore Sottsass typewriter or even a Philippe Starck toothbrush, all named after their designers. These products have not necessarily been proven to be of a superior quality to others of the same category, and their claim to fame rests solely on the alleged creative touch of their designers. In a consumer society such as we live in today, however, there is a great demand for designer objects, which have become status symbols. Consumers, who pay considerable amounts of money for signature items, appear to feel that some of the creative traits of these artifacts are transmitted to them by proxy through ownership of these objects, thereby contributing to their own self-esteem and social standing.

Truly creative products are often revolutionary. They may not reach commercial success until quite some time after their first appearance and sometimes only after they have been somewhat modified and popularized at the hands of a subsequent designer or manufacturer. An example is the development of modern desk lamps, or task lights. The most successful and influential such lamp created in the 20th century is the Luxo lamp, an adjustable-arm, cantilever task light designed in Norway by Jac Jacobsen in 1937. Luxo lamps and their imitations are to this day the most popular desk lamps the world over. But the first Luxo lamp was derived from the British Anglepoise, designed by George Carwardine in 1934. Carwardine worked with a spring manufacturer and his design makes very clever use of springs to give the lamp unprecedented flexibility in its

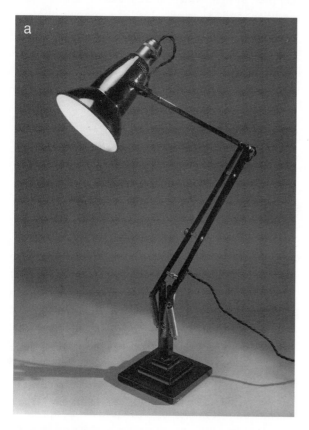

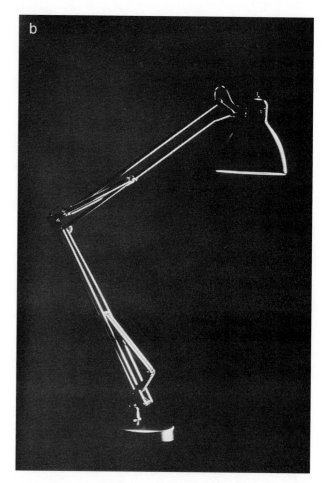

FIGURE 3   Desk lamps. (a) *Anglepoise* by George Carwardine, 1934. © Science & Society Picture Library, Science Museum, London. Reproduced with permission. (b) *Luxo Model L-1* by Jac Jacobsen, 1937. Photograph courtesy of Luxo Italiana.

ability to move the light to wherever it is needed, while the stable basis stays motionless. Carwardine is the ingenious designer of a classic product, but the later Luxo design by Jacobsen became the most popular and successful product of its kind. Figure 3 shows the classic Anglepoise and the popular Luxo that followed suit. Design classics are exhibited in museums and their reproductions are sold as collectors' items.

IV. DESIGNERS

Whereas all humans engage in design on various occasions, professional designers are specialists who have received a formal design education. For the most part, the professional practice of design (in several dis-

ciplines) is a licensed activity, controlled by legislation. On the basis of their inclinations and skills, designers are usually assigned to the concept formation or the later production phases of design development. Concept formation is more readily associated with creativity than is production. In the United States, many architectural firms have design and production divisions. Architects in a design division enjoy a higher professional status, which stems from an appreciation of an elevated measure of creativity that they presumably manifest in their work. Other design fields have similar status structures.

The judged creativity of a designer often hinges on how he or she is seen (by peers, mostly) as form giver. Not much has been published on designers' creativity in any design field. An exception is a comprehensive study on personality correlates of creative American architects, conducted by D. W. MacKinnon and his associates in the 1960s.

MacKinnon compared a group of 40 very creative male architects with two groups of less creative architects and with other professionals. The participants were selected on the basis of expert and peer creativity rates and on the number and length of publications by and about them and their work in the professional literature. Compared to other professionals, the creative architects scored well above average in tests measuring concept mastery and in a general information survey. They reached the highest scores in the Gottschaldt Figure Test, in which subjects are required to isolate and identify simple geometric figures that are embedded or hidden in larger, more complex figures. They showed a remarkably high preference for complex, asymmetrical, and dynamic figures, as opposed to simple and symmetrical ones. In these tests their scores fell shortly below those of artists, who scored highest, and were higher by approximately 33% than those of research scientists and "ordinary" architects. When checked for the profile of their values, these architects emerged as holding aesthetic and theoretical values in high esteem, placing lower importance on economic and social values, and subscribing to average and just below average political and religious values, respectively. Creative architects showed a tendency to be perceptive, as against judgmental types, meaning that they are open to new experiences and awareness without rushing to conclusions about things. Of the two kinds of perception tested, sense and intuitive perception, creative architects manifested themselves as belonging to the latter category. Intuitive perceivers concentrate on possibilities of things perceived, whereas sense perceivers center their attention on things as they are. In the general populations there are 25% of intuitive perceivers; the rate for creative architects is 100%, whereas their "ordinary" and creative but not very creative colleagues number 59% and 84%, respectively.

As far as their personalities are concerned, creative architects exhibit an uneven profile of personality structure. For example, they tend to be introverts, but at the same time they have social skills and they prefer to exercise control over others and be in positions of authority. They value independence, they are self-assertive, and they are nonsubmissive to authority, to the point of rebelling against it, if their views clash with those of authority. We may also add that MacKinnon, whose creative architects were all males, found among them a high measure of femininity. When the study was conducted, there were few female architects or architectural students in the United States. This has changed and toward the end of the 20th century we find a large and rising number of female students in architectural schools, reaching 65% in some cases.

MacKinnon's study refers to architects only, and we do not have similar data for other designers. We can assume that architects are placed approximately in the middle of a spectrum that has more artistically inclined designers such as graphic designers at one extreme and mechanical designers, who are presumably more scientifically oriented, at the other. Artistic creativity has been seen as involving more synthetic thinking, as opposed to scientific creativity, which according to that view requires more analytic thinking. However, recent studies show that this is not necessarily the case, and that the differences in modes of thinking are smaller than had been believed for the two types of creativity: This enables us to see technical inventions and artistic innovations as being of a kind. We may therefore postulate that the personality correlates of creative architects are more or less typical of other designers as well. It is quite possible that any differences that might be found could easily reflect style differentials more accurately than variations related to particular design domains.

V. THE DESIGN PROCESS

In today's world, most designers are associated with private design firms or consultancies, large or small. A work of design is usually commissioned: A designer (or design firm) is invited to submit a design proposal by a client, who could be the owner of a property in the case of architecture, or by an industrial or commercial enterprise that is interested in a new product. At other times commissions are awarded following a design competition. In rare cases are works of design self-initiated by designers, who then look for an investor. Design commissions normally take the form of a contract between the designer and the client. Upon initiating the process of design, a document called a *program* or *brief* is produced, which describes the purpose and objectives of the design, its scope, and other requirements, constraints, and aspirations. Programs and briefs vary significantly in contents, extent, and level of detail.

A. Design Methods

Whatever the institutional context, the actual design process normally starts with the development of a preliminary proposal by an individual designer who is charged with this task. This initial phase is considered the locus and crucible of creativity, as one first translates into form the various fragmented pieces of information one holds: images of similar entities, abstract ideas, technical data, ideals of beauty, forecasts of performance, appeal to users, and so on. The creative phase of the design process had for a long time been seen by many as mysterious and unexplainable, similar to the process of creating works of art. Designers referred to it as "magic." This irrational approach has undergone change since the advent of cognitive science in the 1960s, which coincided with a massive shift in paradigms regarding the design process within the design professions and particularly in architecture. Architects felt that traditional modes of designing were no longer adequate and that the magnitude and complexities of many tasks required more effective design methods than the ones that were habitually employed. It is in this climate that the Design Methods Movement (this unofficial name was coined long after the movement was born) was launched. Its members aspired to advance prescriptive models of the design process based on their visions of the optimal design process, which were speculative for the most part. For example, several models that were proposed in the 1960s described a linear design process, going through iterative phases of analysis, synthesis, and evaluation. The model that R. D. Watts adopted from M. D. Mesarovic is shown in Figure 4. Budding computational techniques were enlisted for assistance; they were used to achieve three types of objectives: (a) computer aided design (CAD) was used for drafting. (b) Optimization techniques, which were developed in the framework of operations research, were implemented. The relevance for design lay in problem decomposition and partitioning, which enabled the representation of interrelated

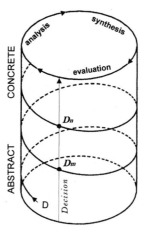

FIGURE 4 Iterative sequences of analysis, synthesis, and evaluation in a linear design process, as modeled by Mesarovic in 1964 and adopted by Watts in 1966. D = Design. D_m = State of design decisions at time m in the process. D_n = State of design decisions at time n in the process, one iterative cycle further in the linear process.

subproblems and therefore design subgoals. In architecture, space allocation programs were written to help break down space requirements into manageable units. These programs grouped together spaces (rooms) that were functionally related to each other so as to generate an efficient layout in terms of proximity of spaces. In large building complexes that include hundreds or even thousands of spaces, this is a major design concern. (c) Somewhat later, Data Bases were compiled to serve as memory aids.

The Design Methods Movement did not succeed in revolutionizing the design profession or in turning it into a science, as some hoped. Critics claim that in fact the imposed methods stifled the creativity of those who tried to use them. Instead, all design domains realized that unless a better understanding of design thinking was gained, it would be hard to develop tools that could assist the process of designing and improve on its results, at least in the decisive initial phase. This realization gave birth to research on design cognition, in which a quest for, and into, creativity plays a major role. Nevertheless, new design methods continue to be developed; many of them capitalize on computational possibilities. These second- and third-generation methods are not prescriptive and are seen as design support tools. In addition to a variety of advanced CAD tools, they also include methods that build on precedents and exemplars that are deposited in the computer's memory, together with analytic tools that render them relevant for the design problem in question.

B. Design Cognition Research

The young domain of design cognition (or design thinking) research is interdisciplinary, with researchers coming from all design fields as well as from cognitive psychology and computer science. The basic question they ask is: What makes a design process effective or productive, to use the terminology of Gestalt psychology. At the base of investigations of the design process is its definition as a problem-solving process, in the widest sense possible. There is considerable agreement among researchers that for the most part design problems belong to the category of ill-structured (or ill-defined or wicked) problems, as opposed to well-structured (or well-defined) problems. Ill-structured problems are vague at the outset, have no clearly specified goals, and have no algorithms that determine steps to be taken toward a solution. Ill-structured problem solving therefore necessitates a search that may lead to more than one solution—sometimes quite a number of acceptable solutions. Successful ill-structured problem solving is creative by definition, and design is seen as a paramount example of such problem solving. [*See* PROBLEM SOLVING.]

From a cognitive point of view, the search at the front edge of the process of designing is difficult to study because the manner in which the search is conducted appears to be chaotic and disorderly. Most researchers accept one or another version of the notion of a *problem space* within which the design search takes place. The major question asked by researchers concerns the rules that govern activity in the problem space. Instead of prescribing design methods, this line of research is interested in revealing prevailing cognitive design strategies and in modeling design reasoning. It is believed that if we knew more about how designers reason and what strategies they use in generating, testing, and selecting design solutions, we could come closer to an understanding of the attributes that contribute to design creativity. Following in the footsteps of similar quests in other fields, students of design thinking are therefore working to develop descriptive models of the design process or specific aspects of it.

A major research methodology in this endeavor is *protocol analysis*, which utilizes on line records (verbalizations, graphic output) of think-aloud design exercises. Despite its limitations, this method allows researchers to come close to what actually goes on in the designer's mind. The episodes recorded in protocols serve as rich data that reflect cognitive activity more directly than post-factum descriptions of such activity, even by the designers themselves, and it enables the development of descriptive, as opposed to prescriptive, models of the design process. By coding individual design moves or operations into which protocols are parsed (short segments of verbalizations), using a variety of category schemes (such as problem domain or designer's actions), it is possible to follow the development of the contents and structure of design activity very closely. Figure 5 reprints an analysis based on a protocol, made in 1994 by Terry Purcell and colleagues. It depicts the progression of a 2-hour design session in terms of the designer's moves, coded into analysis, synthesis, and evaluation. This on-line study reveals that almost throughout the design session, these activities are undertaken in parallel. As demonstrated by this study, the process of designing is different from, and much more complex than, a process dominated by discrete activity sequences, as speculated by Watts 30 years earlier (Figure 4).

Because we can also count coded design moves or other phenomena, it is possible to correlate them with properties of the resultant designs, which are assessed independently. This gives us a suitable tool for the exploration of design creativity. Other research methodologies include, among others, direct observations and computational simulations. The latter are carried out as artificial intelligence projects. Advances in neurocognitive sciences are likely to lead to improved research methodologies of cognitive activities in the future.

C. Visual Thinking in Design

An important aspect of design cognition that existing research methodologies, including protocol analysis, have difficulties dealing with is the fact that so much of design activity is based on visual thinking. Some of the

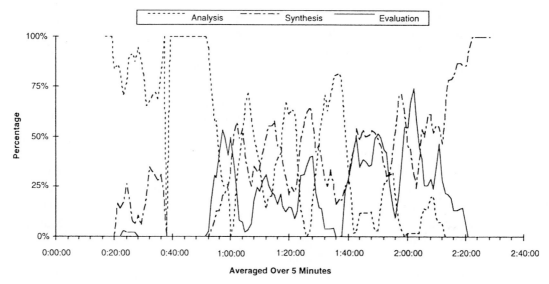

FIGURE 5 Parallel activities of analysis, synthesis, and evaluation in a design process, as plotted by Purcell, Gero, Edwards, and McNeill in a protocol analysis study in 1995. The axes indicate 5-minute time intervals in the process and the percentage of time spent in each activity. From *Analysing design activity.* N. Cross, H. Christiaans, & K. Dorst, eds. © John Wiley & Sons Ltd. Reproduced with permission.

most effective design strategies are related to visual representations. They include the use of similes, such as metaphor and analogy, and more generally heavy reliance on interaction with visual displays, both external and internal, in the form of imagery. Research indicates that success in the use of these strategies appears to be positively correlated with the rated creativity of design products.

The publication of Rudolf Arnheim's *Visual Thinking* in 1969 marked a shift toward the appreciation of non-verbal cognition and intelligence. However, whereas instances of visual thinking are amply reported and illustrated, research on the central role played by visual cognition in problem solving remains rather anecdotal in the literature. Imaging techniques used in neuro-science for the purpose of mapping the brain have contributed to the comprehension of the pictorial nature of visual imagery, but not to the explication of modes in which it is utilized in creative problem solving such as designing. A series of experiments carried out by Ronald Finke and associates have demonstrated the power of imagery to assist in inventive creation. Using imagery, subjects combined given shapes into practical objects. Many of these imagery-induced invented objects scored high in the creativity assessments they were subjected to. Interestingly, most subjects reported

that they first played with the given shapes, trying to combine them in different ways until an attractive composition was formed; only then did they look for a function that the imaged configuration could fulfill. This imagistic process bears great resemblance to the process experienced by designers at an early phase of preliminary design. Although design is always carried out with a goal in mind, the goal is often sufficiently vague (as is the case in ill-structured problem-solving instances) to allow several search directions. Trial and error, utilizing random shapes, is therefore a common design heuristic. In fact, we know that play and the deferment of commitment to a solution are characteristic of creative designing (and of ill-structured problem solving in general). [*See* HEURISTICS; IMAGERY.]

Inner representation in imagery, important as it may be, is not the sole mode of representation utilized in creative problem solving: external representation is equally useful. In addition to passively using information inferred from visual sources, problem solvers frequently use paper and pencil to make representations in the course of complex problem solving. In the case of designing, these representations usually take the form of drawings of all kinds. Finished drawings are made for the purpose of communicating design ideas to others and, in terms of the creative process, they are of little interest. Much more interesting are diagrams and rapidly hand-drawn sketches that are made at the front edge of the process, while ideas are still tentative and designs are partial and conditional. Diagrams are rather abstract—they depict relationships among elements and components of the designed entity, and they are made by designers in practically all design disciplines. Sketches are more concrete and often figurative in their depiction of candidate shapes and forms in an emerging design; see, for example, Figure 2(a). Sketches are made in abundance by architects, product and graphic designers, fashion designers, and others who design tangible artifacts.

Findings on the creative potency of imagery inspired subsequent research that set out to examine whether creativity in problem solving is augmented by the use of sketching, as compared to the use of imagery alone. Some studies found that sketching provided no advantage over imagery in reaching creative solutions. These results, however, refer to unskilled sketchers only. Subsequent research, which compared skilled sketchers to unskilled ones, showed that skilled sketchers (design students) reached significantly higher creativity rates for their synthesized inventive objects than their unskilled peers (psychology students). These results are in agreement with results obtained in other investigations that show that breakthroughs and creative leaps in the design process are often achieved while designers are actively engaged in sketching. Most researchers agree that sketching is more than a memory aid whose purpose it is to record externally images that are generated internally. Rather, inner representation in imagery and external representation in the form of sketching collaborate in an interactive process that allows entities like design objects, which do not yet exist and have never been perceived, to be conceived and brought gradually to completion through sequences of transformation and refinement.

The process of designing has been described by Donald Schön as a dialogue that the designer conducts with his or her materials, and it has been argued by other students of the design process that the design sketch "amplifies the mind's eye." These descriptions are particularly appropriate for the feedback loop that is created during sketching, as single sketches or entire series of sketches "talk back" to the designer who creates them. A sketch's "backtalk" provides more information than was invested in its making, as random relationships on a sheet of paper (or on a computer screen) suggest new possibilities that the designer is invited to discover and make use of.

We thus affirm that cognitive strategies, especially those that hinge on visual cognition, are the key to a better understanding of design in general and design creativity in particular.

Bibliography

Alexander, C. (1964). *Notes on the synthesis of form.* Cambridge, MA: Harvard University Press.

Cross, N., Christiaans, H., & Dorst, K. (Eds.). (1996). *Analysing design activity.* Chichester, England: John Wiley & Sons.

Gero, J. S., & Maher, M. L. (Eds.). (1993). *Modeling creativity and knowledge-based design.* Hillsdale, NJ: Erlbaum.

Lawson, B. (1997). *How designers think.* (3rd ed.). Oxford: Architectural Press.

MacKinnon, D. W. (1970). The personality correlates of creativity: A study of American architects. In P. E. Vernon (Ed.), *Creativity* (pp. 289–311). Harmondsworth, England: Penguin Books.

Margolin, V., & Buchanan, R. (Eds.). (1995). *The idea of design.* Cambridge, MA: MIT Press.

Norman, D. A. (1988). *The psychology of everyday things.* New York: Basic Books.

Papanek, V. (1985). *Design for the real world.* (2nd ed.). Chicago: Academy Chicago Publishers.

Petroski, H. (1992). *The evolution of useful things.* New York: Alfred Knopf.

Row, P. (1987). *Design thinking.* Cambridge, MA: MIT Press.

Developmental Trends in Creative Abilities and Potentials

Mark A. Runco

California State University, Fullerton

Assimilation The process by which information is altered to fit into existing cognitive structures. In behavioral terms it reflects the construction of personal interpretations of experience.

Conventionality Behaviors that fit with norms, expectations, rules, and conventions.

Fourth Grade Slump The drop in original thinking and behavior that occurs for many children at about age 9.

Problem Finding Occurs before a problem can be solved. Operationally, it may involve the identification of a problem or the definition of an ambiguous situation into a workable problem.

Strategic Creativity Actions or processes used intentionally to increase the likelihood of original insight or creative behavior.

There are two general perspectives on human development. One emphasizes continuities; it holds that development is smooth, gradual, and consistent. The other perspective emphasizes stages or discontinuities. In this view children in different stages think in idiosyncratic ways. The thinking characteristic of one stage of development is supposedly qualitatively different from that of the other stages. Such idiosyncratic thinking tendencies would of course influence everything children do, including their problem solving and more generally their reacting in original and creative ways to particular experiences. Not surprisingly, there are also two general perspectives on DEVELOPMENT and creativity. One holds that children are incapable of creative work. This difference between children and adults assumes a major developmental discontinuity. The other perspective suggests that children are creative—perhaps even more creative than adults. This possibility can be explained from both continuity and discontinuity perspectives.

I. DEVELOPMENT AS EXPERIENCE

Continuity theories of development assume that the more experience an individual has, the more mature and capable he or she will be. Experience supplies knowledge, or information, and once obtained that information can be put to use. Since experience is obtained in a gradual fashion, a little bit each day, so too is the increase in one's maturity gradually developed. This increased experience may directly influence creative potential. This is, after all, the crux of "expertise," and famous creative works are often produced by experts. [See Expertise.]

Copyright © 1999 by Academic Press
All rights of reproduction in any form reserved.

There is, however, also a possibility that experience may lead an individual to make certain assumptions which in turn preclude original thinking. Experience may lead individuals to think that one method is best, and they can easily come to rely on that method, thus becoming inflexible and rigid in their thinking because of their expertise. In this light children's lack of experience may keep them from performing creatively (if they lack important information), but it may also keep them from making unoriginal assumptions. They may be more open-minded than someone who has more experience.

In discontinuity theories experience contributes to development, but developmental progress is constrained, at least within stages. Thus if a child is in what is called the "conventional stage," he or she is sensitive to conventions, norms, and peer pressure. New information and experience may be useful to the child, but it cannot take him or her to a new stage of development until the child in question is of an age where he or she is ready to make the move. The four most commonly recognized stages of cognitive development are "sensorimotor," "preoperational," "concrete operational," and "formal operational." An alternative conception better applies to moral reasoning, artwork, language, and originality in children and adolescents. This alternative describes "preconventional," "conventional," and "postconventional" stages. Children in the middle stage are likely to be very literal in their use of language (and thus avoid creative metaphors and the like); they are likely to prefer realistic, perhaps representational, art (and thus stop making art that is wild and unconstrained); and they are unlikely to give truly original ideas (perhaps falling into the quite common "fourth grade slump"). [*See* FOURTH GRADE SLUMP.]

The four more common stages are suggestive of the kinds of information the individual may be capable of accommodating. The sensorimotor child, for example, only grasps information from immediate sensory or motoric experience. The preoperational child develops the ability to deal with symbolic information, but he or she is not yet very logical in the conventional sense until the stage of concrete operations. At that point the individual has the potential to be very logical, although he or she is still limited in the kind of information that can be used. As the name of the stage implies, at this point the individual is only capable of dealing logically with concrete information. Only in formal operations can the individual deal logically with hypothetical and highly abstract information.

A fifth stage of development—the postformal stage—has also been proposed, but it has received much less attention and confirmation than the other four. It would be an important stage because one manifestation of it is a kind of "problem finding" whereby the individual recognizes that problems can be redefined to be workable. This kind of activity is an important part of many creative achievements. [*See* PROBLEM FINDING.]

What is most important here is that the stages are qualitatively different, and the differences are manifested in what information individuals can use in their thinking. Clearly there are implications from this for parents and educators. Simply put, children in different stages require different kinds of experiences. They require experiences that communicate different kinds of information, information that is appropriate to their stage and cognitive tendencies.

Stages are also implied by the various descriptions of developmental trends in creativity. The fourth grade slump implies that development can be characterized by a U-shaped function. Other functions, including a J and an inverted J, have also been reported. The ages of the slumps and peaks vary, depending on the measures used to estimate creativity.

Slumps and peaks have also been found throughout adulthood. In certain areas (e.g., mathematics), the peak is in the 20s. In other domains (especially those dependent on large knowledge bases), peaks are much later. In some of the arts there are even peaks in the 80s and 90s, especially if the artist initiates the "old age style." [*See* OLD AGE STYLE; PRODUCTIVITY AND AGE.]

Given the variety of measures used and the lack of replication used in research in this area, most trends are at this point merely suggestive, or at best descriptive, of certain groups. The evidence for individual differences suggests that slumps in creativity are not inevitable. Creative performances no doubt reflect both nature and nurture. While certain abilities or aptitudes may be expressions of the degree that biological potentials are fulfilled, similarly, slumps may occur as an individual's reaction to his or her environment and experience.

II. DEVELOPMENTAL DIFFERENCES IN COGNITIVE PROCESSES

Importantly, the cognitive mechanisms used when processing information may not change all that much in the various stages of development. These mechanisms are thought to involve a kind of assimilation of information and a kind of accommodation of that information. As noted above, the information that can be accommodated differs at different ages, but this is because experience is always interpreted in the light of the individual's existing cognitive structures—his or her current understanding of the world—and not because the mechanism or processes differ.

Children may seem to be uncreative because they have particular responses to their experiences. Indeed, one reason children are occasionally described as uncreative is because they may not express their insights. Even if they create some new insight, it may be a personal accomplishment and not one that they express. They are not, in this sense, productive. The expressive and productive components of creativity can be separated from the creative components, however, which means that children can in fact be creative even if they do not have anything to show for it. This may be clearest in their pretending and imaginary play, and in their tendency to lose themselves in the play, even if there is no end objective of that play activity. It is also apparent in children's new understandings of their experiences. Those new understandings are probably useful (at least for the child him- or herself) and original (again, at least for the child him- or herself), and that means they are creative. Creativity is typically defined in terms of originality and usefulness. Each of these may be defined in relative terms; what is original to a child may not be original to an adult. Yet the process used by the child to find or construct that new insight is probably the same process that is used by a mature expert. The difference is in the expression and in the product. Children can then think creatively even if they are not productive. [*See* DEFINITIONS OF CREATIVITY; INSIGHT; PLAY.]

Another difference between the creativity of children and adults involves intentions. Children's creativity may be unintentional, at least some of the time. Their originality may appear to be accidental, as is the case when a child says something that seems insightful or funny to adults but was simply an effort on the child's part to find the words to capture an idea. In this view children may often do something creative just because they do not know any better. Because they do not know the conventional way to say something ("children say the darndest things") or the conventional way to react to something, they may make up their own description or reaction. Does this lack of intentions imply that the result is any less original and appealing? Is it uncreative because it was not planned? This question has been debated a great deal lately, but it is clear that if accidental insights are deemed uncreative, many serendipitous discoveries (e.g., penicillin) will also need to be reevaluated. [*See* SERENDIPITY.]

Once again this same issue can be turned to the advantage of children. Perhaps children are unintentionally creative in part because they are so spontaneous. That spontaneity has many benefits. It precludes the rigidity and inflexibility mentioned above, for example, and it probably ensures a kind of mindful awareness of one's experience. Improvisation of all kinds is creative and necessarily spontaneous. [*See* IMPROVISATION.]

III. STRATEGIES, FLEXIBILITY, AND ASSUMPTIONS

Children can be strategically creative. The empirical research for this shows how well they react to "explicit instructions" designed to communicate strategies. Most children, gifted and nongifted alike, respond well and use the strategies to find original ideas. This of course has clear implications for education. It also implies that children's creativity can be intentional, for strategies are by definition intentionally used.

The position that children can be *more* creative than adults was suggested when inflexibility was tied to expertise. Children lack expertise (and may even lack certain basic kinds of information) and this may ensure that they are *not* inflexible. Children also avoid making assumptions that adults often make. Assumptions, like conventions, are often very useful, but they can lead to routine and uncreative behavior. Because they lack experiences children have not yet developed those assumptions. They may try to fly and only conclude that they cannot leave the ground after they try again and again, running up and down a sidewalk, flapping their arms like wings. Adults will not even try to fly; they assume it cannot be done. Of course in this instance they are correct—humans need airplanes and jets—but the point is that assumptions can keep an adult from even considering certain options. [*See* FLEXIBILITY.]

Assumptions can be tied to the information children lack because they are constructed as the individual learns more and more about the world. Many things come to be taken for granted. This can be beneficial because it makes information processing more efficient. We do not always need to examine all details of every experience but instead can focus on novelty and make assumptions about (and not even bother with or devote cognitive resources to) things we have experienced again and again. There is a cost, however, because assumptions lead to routine behavior, and that is never original. Children do not have the experience to develop the same assumptions, and they thus avoid these routines. In this way they may find original ideas more easily than adults, at least some of the time. The same tendency can give a novice in a field an advantage. The insights of Piaget, Freud, and Darwin have been attributed to their abilities to take a new perspective within one field, and that may have resulted from their studying one field and then moving into a new one. Some contemporary scientists explicitly recommend this kind of movement, from topic to topic or even field to field, as a means for maintaining the novice's original perspective. [*See* DARWIN, CHARLES ROBERT; FREUD, SIGMUND; PIAGET, JEAN.]

IV. POTENTIAL VERSUS ACTUAL PERFORMANCE

Consider also the idea that individuals sometimes have the potential to be creative but do not take advantage of it because they are constrained by cultural convention and taboo. This is yet another way of saying that experience can inhibit original thought by narrowing the options considered. Surely conventions must be learned, and many of them contribute to the smooth flow of social interaction. But it is difficult, if not impossible, to be original in a conventional way.

This is the point of many creativity techniques which focus on the "conceptual blocks" that keep a person from seeing a problem, tack, or solution clearly. Those blocks, be they cultural, social, intellectual, or perceptual, may depend on experience. Once again, if the child lacks that experience, he or she will not have the same blocks. [*See* BARRIERS TO CREATIVITY AND CREATIVE ATTITUDES.]

There is a time to be conventional and a time to be unconventional. Truly creative work occurs when unconventional thinking and behavior is appropriate—when it is only disruptive in a manner than gets people to reevaluate their experience. The point is that originality alone is sufficient for creative work. Creative contributions are original, but they are also timely. They fit in; they solve a problem. Creativity requires a kind of discretion. Surely we do not want children who are original all of the time. Instead, parents and educators need to ensure that children do not lose their capacity to be spontaneous and flexible. Many children do seem to lose this capacity; many experience a "fourth grade slump" at about age 9. At that age they are very sensitive to conventions: They react to peer pressure more than any other time; their art becomes highly representational and realistic; and they stick to the rules in their games rather than making them up as they go along.

The trick is to encourage children's originality while allowing them to learn important conventions. In that way they will use their discretion and know when to exercise their originality and when not to. They will be strategically creative.

Bibliography

Dudek, S. Z. (1974). Creativity in young children: Attitude or ability? *Journal of Creative Behavior, 8,* 282–292.

Rosenblatt, E., & Winner, E. (1988). The art of children's drawings. *Journal of Aesthetic Education, 22,* 3–15.

Runco, M. A. (1996). Creativity from childhood through adulthood: The developmental issues. *New Directions for Child Development.* San Francisco: Jossey-Bass.

Runco, M. A., & Charles, R. (1997). Developmental trends in creative potential and creative performance. In M. A. Runco (Ed.), *Creativity research handbook.* Cresskill, NJ: Hampton Press.

Deviance

Jonathan A. Plucker

Indiana University

Mark A. Runco

California State University, Fullerton

Contrarianism Behavior that is intentionally different or opposite from what others are doing.

Deviance Different from what is typical; differing from the norm.

Eccentricism Tendency toward unusual and sometimes outlandish behavior that may contribute to original thinking or may result from it.

Open-Mindedness Tendency to consider all options and tolerate or even appreciate different perspectives.

Psychosis Disorder characterized by a loss of contact with reality.

Tolerance Seeing the value in behaviors or ideas even though they are deviant.

*The word **DEVIANCE** may elicit various negative images. Indeed, there may be a general tendency to think of a deviant as someone who is suffering psychopathological distress, or someone who is a danger both to individuals and to society in general. There is another perspective which views deviance statistically, as a departure from the mean or another measure of central tendency. Most dictionaries contain definitions involving departure from societal norms. Taken collectively, these implicit theories and formal definitions imply that deviance entails a departure from prevailing cultural, political, physical, behavioral, emotional, and psychological norms. Someone who dresses in black on a hot sunny day, someone who scores very high or very low on a test relative to his or her peers, or someone who eats all of their food through a straw are all examples of behavior that would be considered deviant. Deviance is necessary for societal and cultural evolution. In the Darwinian model, deviance provides the variation from which adaptive ideas and behaviors are selected. Conversely, research in social psychology suggests that a lack of deviance within a group usually results in poor decision making and problem solving.*

I. RELEVANT ASPECTS OF CREATIVITY

Research on the personality correlates of creative behavior imply a profile of creators that is in many ways similar to the above-mentioned deviance definition: unconventional behavior, avoids entrenched ways of thinking, dissatisfied with the status quo, sets own rules, takes risks, rejects limits imposed by others, is

Copyright © 1999 by Academic Press
All rights of reproduction in any form reserved.

willing to try new things, is open to new experiences and growth, and is receptive to new ideas. Indeed, the idea of originality assumes unusualness, uniqueness, or novelty, each of which requires some sort of deviance. Something or someone is unusual in comparison to something else. Typically that thing or person is different from a collection or group rather than a single instance. That group represents the norm. You cannot be like the norm and yet unusual, unless you are unusual in one particular way but fit the norm in all others. Similarly, you cannot be original unless you are unlike the norm. Deviance is, then, assumed by unusualness, uniqueness, originality, and novelty—and at least one of these is required for creativity. Originality, for example, is probably the most widely recognized aspect of creativity. It is necessary, though not sufficient.

The *Scales for Rating the Behavioral Characteristics of Superior Students* is often used by teachers to identify students' creativity. It includes the following descriptions of students' behavior: often offers unusual responses, is uninhibited in expressions of opinion, is sometimes radical in disagreement, is more open to the irrational in himself, is nonconforming, accepts disorder, and does not fear being different. [*See* APPENDIX II: TESTS OF CREATIVITY.]

While people generally value creativity, both research and conventional wisdom suggest that creative individuals and the creative process test norms, question authority, and push limits. They explore and often seek out deviance, suggesting that the distinction between creativity and deviance is often blurred and difficult to identify. Given the common connotations of the concept of deviance, it might be worthwhile to recognize the value of deviance. Popular use of the adjective "creative" in phrases such as "creative accounting" and "creative financing" quite frequently implies unethical and negative behavior. Creative work can be deviant—and yet not unethical.

II. ISSUES AND IMPLICATIONS

Given both the negative connotations of deviance and the possible importance of deviance to creativity, an analysis of the comorbidity of creativity with different types of deviance is necessary. In this section, the relationships between creativity and open-mindedness, psychosis, contrarianism, eccentricism, crime, and drug use and abuse are explored.

A. Open-Mindedness

Creativity is often defined as a complex construct or a syndrome, the idea being that more than one trait and ability is involved. This is pertinent in that autonomy, nonconformity, or even deviance may interact with a person's open-mindedness, a fairly common personality trait of creative individuals. Perhaps creative people, because of their open-mindedness (willingness to consider other ideas and concepts), are more accepting of the deviance of other individuals.

There is very likely a functional connection between open-mindedness and deviance within the individual: Individuals may consider what are unconventional and even deviant thoughts and behaviors because of their open-mindedness. This is a critical notion in several ways. Not only does it help explain the relationship between deviance and creativity; it also suggests that open-mindedness by one person may ensure that they will be tolerant and perhaps even appreciative of the creativity and apparent deviance of other persons.

Because open individuals may be more accepting of other deviant individuals, we might expect a kind of Matthew effect, found in other areas of creativity research, where those with something (in this case the right combination of open-mindedness and originality) will obtain and generate even more of it. Perhaps parents who have those traits will model and value them, and thereby raise children who also have them. The tolerance supplied by the traits may subsequently generate increased creativity in others who are raised in the same environment. [*See* MATTHEW EFFECTS.]

This may also lead to an increased distance between creative and uncreative persons. This may explain why there are certain expectations for creative persons, such as the stereotypes commonly held about artists and other unambiguously creative individuals and their eccentricities.

B. Psychosis

Hans Eysenck suggested that both the capacity for creativity and the tendency toward mental disorder resulted from the same underlying process. He suggested that the commonality might be "overinclusive thinking," which occurs when an individual fails to distinguish between things which are dissimilar. The assumption is that thinking is often conceptual; we recognize some things (e.g., dogs, cats, and other animals) as similar, and other things (e.g., animal, vegetable, and mineral) as dissimilar. Overinclusive thinking occurs when something that does not belong in one category or concept is included in it. At the extreme, this leads directly to psychotic ideation. The psychotic individual is viewed as out of touch with reality—a deviant, at least in thinking, and often in manifest action. Other times overinclusive thinking can allow the individual to find unusual but useful connections among ideas. In this way it can lead to creative thinking.

Overinclusive thinking may run in families. This would explain why creative persons often have relatives who suffer from some sort of disorder. Those suffering from the disorder are psychotic, while those not suffering may be creative—and both are overinclusive. This line of work has yet to be independently confirmed.

C. Contrarianism

Creative thinking is often more intentional than the section above might imply. Sometimes it is a result of tactics or strategies. One tactic is the contrarian one. Here the individual ensures that his or her actions are original by intentionally doing what others are not doing. The economic metaphor is "buying low while others are selling high." This tactic often works well because it does indeed ensure originality, and as noted above, originality is the most commonly recognized facet of the creativity complex. There is however the caveat that contrarianism can be used in a manner that is contrary to creative achievement, and contrarian behavior is not necessarily creative. It will, however, likely appear as deviance, and for the same reason it ensures originality. A contrarian tries to find the margin, tries to be an outlier, and is therefore trying to be in some sense a deviant. [*See* CONTRARIANISM.]

D. Eccentricity

Eccentricity is a type of deviance that is often mistakenly associated with psychosis. While schizophrenia and other mental disorders usually lead to dysfunction, eccentrics tend to function well (albeit in ways that appear strange to most people). In both cases, the concept of freedom—to think and behave as one wishes—is present, but the exercise of personal freedom is less dysfunctional in the eccentric. [*See* ECCENTRICITY.]

Studies of eccentrics tend to report that highly gifted individuals exhibit signs of eccentricity, and eccentrics are often creative. The relationship between eccentricity and creativity is hypothesized to hinge on the fact that individuals exhibiting both tendencies are individualistic and apt to go against established norms for behavior. Perhaps the most notable example of eccentric creativity is Albert Einstein, whose behavior was often described as erratic or eccentric (e.g., wearing slippers or pajamas to formal events). [*See* EINSTEIN, ALBERT.]

It has been suggested that eccentricity is a predominantly Western phenomenon. This follows from the emphasis on rugged individualism and privacy rights in the Western world. Since most studies of eccentrics have focused solely on the United States, England, and other Western European and North American countries, little evidence is available to evaluate this hypothesis.

E. Crime

Throughout history, many creative individuals have spent time in jail. This is not surprising, because creativity is often perceived as a form of deviant behavior which can frighten people and threaten established societal norms.

At the extreme are creative persons whose entire lifestyles and value systems reflected their originality, whose general behavior patterns expressed the same, and who clearly did not fit well into society. It may be that some of these individuals were deviant in thought, allowing them to produce creative works, but led them to break society's laws. Just as is the case with the relationship between health and creativity, we cannot be certain of the direction of effect: Whatever underlies deviance may contribute to creativity, allowing the individual to think in an unconventional fashion, or creative thinking may demonstrate to the individual the value of bending or breaking rules. The creator may be increasingly reinforced for the bending or breaking of rules in a manner that suggests what the operant psychologists call shaping, and if reinforced, the disregard for rules will increase in frequency. It may generalize to all norms and rules, including laws. Thus the joy of creative work may lead to more general deviant behavior, or a deviant proclivity may provide original insights. It may of course be bidirectional as well.

A subtle distinction can be made between creators who were jailed because their creative activities were perceived to be threatening (e.g., Socrates, Thomas More, and Galileo) and those who saw a stint in jail as furthering their creative endeavors (e.g., Thoreau, Gandhi, and Martin Luther King, Jr.).

Russell Eisenman has, however, investigated the creativity of prisoners and found little evidence that convicted criminals are more creative than noncriminals. To the contrary, Eisenman believes that prisoners are generally less creative than nonprisoners, although creative prisoners do exist. [*See* CRIME AND CREATIVITY.]

F. Drug Use and Abuse

At first glance, considerable evidence linking drug use and creativity appears to exist. Many eminently creative individuals, including Ernest Hemingway, Edgar Allan Poe, Tennessee Williams, Jackson Pollock, John Belushi, and Eric Clapton, abuse or abused alcohol or other drugs. Potential explanations for the apparent relationship include creative individuals' penchant for risk-taking, the disinhibitive effect of alcohol and other drugs on creativity, and the role of drugs in easing the stresses of the creative life.

But a deeper look at the issue raises serious questions about the relationship between drugs and creativity. First, while the deviancy necessary for drug use and creativity is often mentioned as a reason for suspecting a relationship, it is worth noting that the use of many drugs, especially nicotine and alcohol, is quite common and thus not dramatically deviant. Second, much of the evidence supporting the presence of a positive effect for drug use on creativity is anecdotal in nature; indeed, empirical research generally does not support a strong, positive, causal relationship between creativity and drug use. To the contrary, long-term use of alcohol, marijuana, and other drugs appears to have a negative effect on creativity. Even in studies which partially confirm disinhibiting effects, other factors appear to hinder the degree to which individuals capitalize on the production of disinhibited ideas.

However, this is not to say that creativity does not lead to drug use. Creative success often leads to the amassing of financial resources that increase the ability to obtain drugs, and people may turn to drugs to alleviate the many stressors associated with creative activity. A relatively new hypothesis is that people who consider themselves to be creative may experience pressures to conform to societal expectations for creative individuals' behavior. For example, a writer may react to stereotypical depictions of the "alcoholic writer"—stereotypes held by society and the other writers in his or her peer group—by using alcohol more frequently. [*See* ALCOHOL AND CREATIVITY; DRUGS AND CREATIVITY.]

III. CONCLUSION

Consider the anecdotes surrounding the lives of creative individuals such as Einstein, Poe, Kafka, Martha Graham, and others mentioned in this article. Their deviant behavior was frequently considered outlandish or dangerous and threatened to overshadow their creativity. Their deviance was often such that only the most sympathetic friends and family members could tolerate it. Steven Spielberg's mother has observed that if she had known the typical means for dealing with her son's frequently bizarre behavior, the arts would have lost a major creative talent. Instead, she simply tolerated her son's deviant behavior and encouraged his creativity.

We each need to accept the role of deviance for both creative work or individuals and for societal progress. It should be accepted because we need to tolerate it—or we will lose it, and thereby lose an opportunity to enhance creative work and societal progress. Indeed, regardless of the ambiguity of research on creativity and deviance, most researchers voice the same basic conclusion: tolerance for creative ability.

More specifically, what is needed is (a) increased tolerance for seemingly deviant behaviors and (b) discretion about when to be deviant and tolerant and when not to be deviant and tolerant. Clearly, both can be taken to an inappropriate extreme. What is needed is an appropriate balance, namely, ethnically and creatively deviant behavior.

Bibliography

Aronson, E. (1994). *The social animal* (7th ed.). New York: W. H. Freeman.

Barron, F. (1963). *Creativity and psychological health: Origins of personal vitality and creative freedom.* New York: Van Nostrand.

Gardner. H. (1993). *Creating minds: An anatomy of creativity seen through the lives of Freud, Einstein, Picasso, Stravinsky, Eliot, Graham, and Gandhi.* New York: Basic Books.

Gould, S. J. (1996). *Full house: The spread of excellence from Plato to Darwin.* New York: Harmony Books.

Grant, V. W. (1968). *Great abnormals: The pathological genius of Kafka, van Gogh, Strindberg and Poe.* New York: Hawthorn Books.

Rothenberg, A. (1990). *Creativity and madness: New findings and old stereotypes.* Baltimore, MD: The Johns Hopkins Univ. Press.

Runco, M. A. (Ed.). (1996). Creativity from childhood through adulthood: the developmental issues. *New Directions for Child Development, 72.*

Ward, C. (1991). *Influences: Voices of creative dissent.* Bideford, Devon, UK: Green Books.

Weeks, D., & James, J. (1995). *Eccentrics: A study of sanity and strangeness.* New York: Villard.

Dialectical Thinking: Implications for Creative Thinking

Bernice Yan and Patricia Arlin

University of British Columbia, Canada

Creativity A multifaceted term often including concepts of novelty, innovation, and effectiveness.

Dialectic In philosophy, the term has been used to refer to different concepts including form of reasoning, logic dealing with contradictory aspects of knowledge, and a related family of worldviews.

Dialectical Thinking A specific form of postformal reasoning that involves the coordination or integration of contradictory views or frames of reference.

Equilibration A fundamental principle of development described in Piaget's theory of cognitive development through which qualitative change potentially takes place.

Nonabsolute/Relativistic (N/R) Thinking A form of higher-order thinking that is operationally defined as multiple-frame operations on ill-defined problems and is associated with a nonabsolute worldview. It is considered a commonality underlying some of the most representative models of postformal reasoning.

Postformal Reasoning A form of higher-order thinking that employs a kind of logic that is different from that of formal (abstract logical) reasoning.

Problem Finding A specific form of postformal reasoning that involves the raising of generic questions from ill-defined problem situations. It is also a concept used to designate the fifth or postformal stage in cognitive development.

DIALECTICAL THINKING is in and of itself a creative process. To recognize its creative aspect, one has to appreciate the very nature of dialectical thinking.

I. ORIGINS AND MEANINGS OF *DIALECTIC*

The term *dialectic* (*dialektikos* in Greek) means dialogue or conversation, which can be interpreted as communication within the self or between the self and others. The concept of dialectic has a long philosophical tradition dating back to the ancient Greek philosophers Zeno of Elea (who, according to Aristotle, was the inventor of dialectic), Socrates, Plato, and Aristotle. Ancient dialectic concerned the art of conversation or debate and its use as a method of inquiry for the purpose of generating knowledge or seeking truth through reasoning. Dialectic has thus become a topic of epistemology, a branch of philosophy which concerns the nature of knowledge of reality.

Over time the concept of dialectic has evolved and

Copyright © 1999 by Academic Press
All rights of reproduction in any form reserved.

extended to include a family of dialectical worldviews regarding the nature of reality. Modern dialectic probably originates in some of the philosophical ideas of the Renaissance and culminates in the philosophical writings of the 19th century, particularly those of Hegel on dialectic idealism. Hegel's theory represents an integrative and elaborate view of the logic of dialectic. According to Hegel, the essence of dialectic is contradiction, which is inherent in everything and which is the source of change. The logic of dialectic (which Hegel called the objective or absolute mind) is equivalent to some kind of natural law of the universe. Externally it governs the development of world history, and internally it governs the rational process. The above processes are so because the rational process is part of the developing universe. Thus for Hegel, the external (objective) and the internal (subjective) processes of dialectic are unified into a dialectical whole. Marx's dialectic materialism was derived from Hegel's theory but the emphasis was shifted from idealism to materialism and dialectical analysis was applied to the economic–political domain.

As mentioned earlier, the concept of dialectic has changed over time such that the term *dialectic* has spawned very diverse connotations and has been used in many different contexts. Therefore, no simple account can do justice to such a recondite philosophical system. In the present context, *dialectical thinking* refers to a form of reasoning associated with the logic of dialectic. Dialectical thinking is regarded as a form of higher-order thinking, specifically postformal reasoning, for which creativity is necessary. However, before we examine dialectical thinking as a specific form of reasoning, it is necessary that we understand the salient features of a dialectical worldview.

II. SALIENT FEATURES OF A DIALECTICAL WORLDVIEW

Dialectical thinking is often associated with the familiar three-step formula—Thesis-antithesis-synthesis. However, this three-step formula as a form or structure of reasoning must be understood within the context of a comprehensive dialectical epistemology (worldview). In their discussion of a dialectical worldview, most re-

searchers in developmental psychology (including Basseches, Bidell, Reese, Tolman, and Riegel) would at least include the following salient features.

A. Part-Whole Relationship

In any dynamic system, the relationships among parts and between parts and the whole are viewed as interconnected, interdependent, and interactive. Moreover, the whole at one level of existence could be a part of another whole at another level of existence. Thus, in Hegelian terms, a thing has no being of its own but only in something else. This concept of part-whole would serve as a basis for understanding the nonabsolute or relativistic nature of existence in a dialectical worldview.

B. Change

Change is considered inherent and inevitable when reality is viewed as being dynamic as opposed to static. As a dynamic system is in a state of constant flux, the balance within the system has to be adjusted constantly. When the balance is upset, the system is said to be in a state of disequilibrium; and when balance restored, the system in a state of equilibrium. However, both states are transient and alternating. Thus any state of existence is impermanent. Therefore, change is self-perpetuating.

C. Qualitative Transformation

Development can be regarded as a change with direction or purpose as distinguished from a change without any direction or purpose. Development in a dialectical sense occurs through qualitative transformation of a system. In the course of development, a system becomes more and more comprehensive, coherent, and efficient. That is, a system is not only just becoming quantitatively more complex but also qualitatively more advanced because the complexity of change is of such magnitude that a qualitative transformation occurs as a result of the development. Thus development can be construed as progress, which evolves through qualitatively different stages and is potentially nonteleological (without a fixed end point).

D. Contradiction-Resolution

The concept that contradiction is inherent in everything implies that inherently, everything or every issue has an opposing tendency. The nature of the relationship between the opponents is said to be contradictory (e.g., good versus bad, living versus nonliving, and have versus have-not). Contradictions or conflicts arising within any system are considered sources of disequilibrium. The contradictions need to be resolved for the system to restore equilibrium. The state of equilibrium is transient nevertheless, because as new contradictions arise, the system enters another phase of disequilibrium. And as it strives to resolve the ever-emerging contradictions, the system itself becomes more and more comprehensive, coherent, and efficient, thus perpetuating its own existence. In brief, contradiction-resolution is the major principle through which the development of a system occurs.

E. Thesis–Antithesis–Synthesis

The three-step formula (thesis–antithesis–synthesis) represents the form or structure of reasoning associated with dialectical thinking. A thesis refers to the statement and an antithesis refers to the counterstatement in a dialectical analysis; and both constitute the contradictory aspect of an argument. The synthesis refers to the resolution that is achieved through the coordination or integration of the contradictory parts into a dialectical whole. As the whole is viewed as greater than the sum of its constitutive parts, a qualitative change would have to occur. A synthesis would in turn become a new thesis, and the cycle would repeat itself endlessly in a dialectical analysis. The three-step formula can be regarded as the core feature of dialectical thinking embedded in the context of a dialectical worldview.

III. DIALECTICAL PERSPECTIVE IN DEVELOPMENTAL PSYCHOLOGY

The dialectical perspective has an enormous influence on the formulation of theories in different disciplines including developmental psychology. The dialectical perspective has been employed explicitly or

implicitly by some researchers to explain the different aspects of cognitive development (the development of reasoning). Examples range from Vygotsky in the 1920s to Basseches in the 1980s. Vygotsky held cognitive development to be a product of the dialectical interaction between the self (internal) and the environment (external). In his view, the role of cultural context is stressed throughout the course of development. Piaget, Vygotsky's contemporary, construed cognitive development as the coordination between change (growth) and stability (the lack of growth) of internal cognitive structures, with equilibration of cognitive structures as the goal of development. He proposed formal (abstract logical) reasoning as the fourth and final stage of cognitive development. Contrary to Piaget's proposal, Riegel in 1973 emphasized the role of disequilibrium (contradiction and change) in the course of cognitive development. He also argued that "primitive" dialectic is in fact used by people at different developmental stages, but that it is the conscious and systematic use of dialectical thinking that marks the final stage of cognitive development. Arlin in 1974 proposed a possible fifth stage or postformal stage of cognitive development and suggested problem finding as a model of postformal reasoning in that the cognitive process of problem finding in essence involves the creative use of dialectical thinking because it involves the abilities (a) to question the existing state of affairs (thesis); (b) to identify contradictions (antitheses); and (c) to invent new ways of reformulating old problems (syntheses). Basseches in 1980 translated the general concept of dialectical thinking into specific moves of thoughts, and his research provided empirical evidence in support of dialectical thinking as an instance of higher-order cognitive development. [*See* DEVELOPMENTAL STAGES.]

IV. DIALECTICAL THINKING AS A SPECIFIC FORM OF POSTFORMAL REASONING

A. Basseches's Model of Dialectical Reasoning

Basseches's model represents an interpretation of dialectical thinking in terms of cognitive processes. In

1980 Basseches operationally defined dialectical thinking with 24 dialectical schemata or "moves of thought," which are organized into four major categories: (a) motion-oriented schemata (emphasizing change), (b) form-oriented schemata (emphasizing wholeness), (c) relationship-oriented schemata (emphasizing constitutive relationship), and (d) metaformal schemata (emphasizing integration of all of the preceding categories). According to Basseches, it is the category of metaformal schemata that represents dialectical thinking in its mature form. The salient features of metaformal schemata include the following:

- Location of contradictions or sources of disequilibrium
- Resolution of contradiction
- Operation on open self-transforming systems
- Identification of qualitative change within a system
- Comparison and contrast among systems
- Coordination of multiple systems

B. Formal versus Postformal Reasoning

The contrast between formal and postformal reasoning provide a framework for the understanding of the creative nature of dialectical thinking, a specific form of postformal reasoning.

In Piaget's theory of cognitive development, which espouses equilibration as the goal of development, formal reasoning is considered the final equilibrium. The major characteristic of formal reasoning is the ability to engage in abstract logical thinking, which includes the features of hypothetic-deductive reasoning, of thinking in terms of propositions, and of making logical inferences. Generally speaking, formal reasoning operates on well-defined problems that can be represented by closed systems. For well-defined problems, all the information necessary to produce a solution is given or can be derived from what is given. In this case, it is possible to produce one or a few solutions and creativity is not required in the process.

In contrast to formal reasoning, postformal reasoning refers to the cognitive stage developed beyond formal reasoning. Since the 1970s, a multitude of models of postformal reasoning has been proposed to challenge Piaget's conception of formal reasoning being the end point of cognitive development and to account for the complexity and creativity involved in higher-order thinking that is beyond the framework of formal reasoning. Some of the most representative models include problem finding (Arlin), dialectical reasoning (Basseches), relativistic operations (Sinnott), and reflective judgment (King and Kitchener). In 1984 Kramer suggested three common features shared among postformal models: (a) nonabsolute/relativistic thinking, (b) contradiction, and (c) integration (the last two being characteristics of dialectical reasoning). Yan and Arlin in their 1995 study provided strong empirical evidence in support of nonabsolute/relativistic (N/R) thinking as a common factor underlying these postformal models and suggested that the transition from formal to postformal reasoning involves a paradigm shift from closed to open system thinking. Nonabsolute/relativistic (N/R) thinking as a general form of postformal reasoning is operationally defined as "multiple-frame operations on ill-defined problems." And dialectical thinking as a specific form of postformal reasoning can be defined as integration of contradictory frames in the context of an open system.

The creative aspect of postformal reasoning in general lies in the fact that this kind of reasoning operates on ill-defined problems, which can be represented by self-constructed as well as open systems. For ill-defined problems, the information given is not complete. The person engaged in solving an ill-defined problem would need to generate information beyond that which is given or known and to define and evaluate the problem from multiple perspectives. This kind of problem solving is very similar to the real-life problems one encounters for which it is not possible to expect any absolute or objective solution. In this light, postformal reasoning would necessarily imply uncertainty, indeterminacy, and subjectivity and is, therefore, fundamentally creative at its core.

V. IMPLICATIONS OF DIALECTICAL THINKING FOR CREATIVITY

A. Self-Perpetuating Renewal and Advancement in a Dialectical Process

The ways to define the term *creativity* are as creative as the meaning of the term itself. All in all, at least three concepts are considered vital in the definition of creativity: (a) novelty, (b) innovation, and (c) effectiveness (or usefulness). Based on these three concepts, an argument can be made that the overall process of dialectical thinking is in and of itself a creative process. One reason is that the three-step formula of dialectic (thesis–antithesis–synthesis) is designed like a feedback loop that would repeat itself endlessly. In this dialectical process, there is a constant opposition between creative change and the natural tendency to seek stability. This constant opposition creates a discomfort zone from which new and better ways of representing reality continually emerge. The overall process of dialectical thinking is, therefore, in essence a process of self-perpetuating renewal and of self-perpetuating advancement. Thus the essence of a dialectical process is compatible with the vital concepts (novelty, innovation, and effectiveness) in the definition of creativity.

Some of the highest forms of creative thinking appear to be dialectical in nature. They often involve processes such as combining and recombining ideas, searching for complementarity, and coordinating multiple perspectives. Arlin in 1990 also noted that being dissatisfied with the status quo, seeking new ways to formulate old problems, and noticing discrepancies unnoticed before are elements of intuition linked to creative processes that are dialectical in nature. In fact, each of these processes of creative thinking can be regarded as part and parcel of problem finding, a concept originally used in the definition of a fifth/postformal stage in cognitive development. According to Arlin's model, problem finding involves (a) questioning the existing state of affairs (thesis), (b) identifying contradictions such as discrepancies and anomalies (antitheses), and (c) inventing new ways to reformulate old problems (syntheses). In this light, the process of problem finding could be used to illustrate a creative use of dialectical thinking and the functions of dialectical creativity.

B. The Double Functions of Dialectical Creativity

The creative mechanism is built into the form or structure of the three-step formula of dialectical thinking as illustrated next.

1. *Thesis:* In establishing a thesis, one is required to formulate a concept for analysis (e.g., light is particle-like.).

2. *Antithesis:* In producing a contradictory view of the thesis, one is in fact generating an alternative concept that is in conflict with or in opposition to the original concept (e.g., light is wavelike).

3. *Synthesis:* To integrate the contradictory concepts into a dialectical whole, one would have to construct a whole new concept that is neither p nor q alone (e.g., Bohr's principle of complementarity).

In a dialectical process, the double functions of creativity are exercised. The positive function of creativity generates and constructs new concepts one after another. The negative function of creativity destroys preconceptions, displaces concepts, and breaks mental sets that would block imagination. Concurrent to the process of affirming new concepts, old concepts are being negated. For example, the concept of light as particles (thesis) is negated by the concept of light as waves (antithesis). Then the concept of complementarity (synthesis) negates both of these concepts. Eventually, the principle of complementarity (now a new thesis) might have to be replaced by a new theory (antithesis). This process refers to the notion of "negation of negation" in a dialectical process. Thus each of the double functions (positive and negative) is equally important to a creative thinking process.

C. Unleashing the Limit of Imagination in a Dialectical Worldview

When the process of dialectic is put in the context of a dialectical worldview, the creative nature of dialectical thinking would be magnified. From a dialectical perspective, every "thing" is inherently contradictory with no limitation to the number of contradictions for each thing. In fact, each thing, as a part of a whole and also the whole of many parts, has multiple properties. As the thing interacts with a broader milieu, the number of properties multiplies and the nature of the properties changes. As one property has inherently one set of contradictions, one thing with multiple properties would have multiple sets of contradictions and, therefore, multiple corresponding resolutions. In this light, the development of a creative process in a dialectical sense is not only nonteleological (without a fixed end point) but is also potentially multidirectional (with multiple pathways and possibilities).

A dialectical worldview can be represented as an open dynamic system that emphasizes change and the nonabsolute nature of existence. Such a view allows for the recognition of the plurality and plasticity of things and, therefore, unleashes the limit of imagination.

VI. CONCLUSION

Dialectical thinking as a specific form of postformal reasoning is creative in its very nature, because it provides the form or structure of thinking that facilitates a creative thinking process as well as provides a worldview that supports such a process. Many creative thinking processes, including problem finding, complementarity thinking, and multiple-perspective taking, are, in fact, developmental and fundamentally dialectical in nature with reference to the basic form of dialectical thinking. However, dialectical thinking as a tool cannot operate in a vacuum. That is, appropriate content knowledge and imagination are necessary to feed the creative process of dialectical thinking.

Dialectical thinking addresses the very core of cre-ative thinking. As implied in the axiom of dialectic that "everything is inherently contradictory," there are always different ways of looking at everything. Therefore, everything can potentially be opened up for imagination, and everything can potentially be subjected to creative change.

Bibliography

Arlin, P. K. (1975). Cognitive development in adulthood: A fifth stage? *Developmental Psychology, 11,* 602–606.

Arlin, P. K. (1990). Wisdom: The art of problem finding. In R. J. Sternberg (Ed.), *Wisdom: Its nature, origins, and development.* New York: Cambridge University Press.

Benack, S., Basseches, M., & Swan, T. (1989). Dialectical thinking and adult creativity. In J. A. Glover, R. R. Ronning, & C. R. Reynolds (Eds.), *Handbook of creativity.* New York: Plenum Press.

Hegel, G. W. F. (1910/1967). *Phenomenology of mind.* New York: Harper and Row.

Reese, H. W. (1982). A comment on the meanings of "dialectics." *Human Development, 25,* 423–429.

Riegel, K. F. (1979). *Foundations of dialectical psychology.* New York: Academic Press.

Tolman, C. (1983). Further comments on the meaning of "dialectic." *Human Development, 26,* 320–324.

Yan, B., & Arlin, P. (1995). Nonabsolute/relativistic (N/R) thinking: A common factor underlying models of postformal reasoning? *Journal of Adult Development, 2*(4), 223–240.

Isak Dinesen

1885–1962

Author

Wrote *Out of Africa, Seven Gothic Tales, Winter's Tales, Last Tales, Shadows on the Grass, Ehrengard, Anecdotes of Destiny, The Angelic Avengers, Carnival, Letters from Africa: 1914–1931, On Modern Marriage and Other Observations.*

Shirley Linden Morrison

College of Notre Dame, Belmont, California

ISAK DINESEN was a Danish writer who married Baron Bror von Blixen, moved to Africa and established a coffee farm in Kenya from 1914 to 1931. Her experiences with the African people enabled her to write Out of Africa, *required reading for U.S. Peace Corps members working in Africa. It was the loss of her coffee farm that led to her writing when she returned to Denmark. She wrote in English; her first book,* Seven Gothic Tales, *became an immediate success in the United States. She worked in the genre of the tale and in nonfiction narrative. Internationally admired by other authors and poets, she was a literary force both in the United States and in Denmark. When Ernest Hemingway accepted the Nobel Prize for literature, he cited Isak Dinesen as a writer who also deserved it.*

Isak Dinesen. (Copyright Rungstedlund Foundation.)

I. BACKGROUND

Isak Dinesen, Karen von Blixen, was born in Denmark on April 17, 1885, as Karen Christentze Dinesen (Tanne). Her parents were Wilhelm Dinesen (1845–

Copyright © 1999 by Academic Press
All rights of reproduction in any form reserved.

1895) and Ingeborg Westerholz (1856–1939). There were four other Dinesen children: Inger (Ea), born in 1883; Ellen (Elle), born in 1886; Thomas, born in 1892; and Anders, born in 1894.

In Denmark, Dinesen and her sisters were privately educated, which meant that they were expected to marry and were not prepared to earn a living. Later they attended the Ecole Benet, where Dinesen showed a talent for drawing. Dinesen's family history formulates a basis for her creativity and the subsequent relationships in her life.

Karen Dinesen was the second-born child. The first-born daughter, Inger, was smothered by the Westerholz females, and the father, Wilhelm, had been excluded. Overwhelmed by this enormous female presence, Wilhelm promised himself that the next child would be his. Karen Dinesen was the only one of the five siblings who became extremely close to her father.

Wilhelm told her stories of his life. He had gone to America as a young man; it was a romantic pilgrimage from Quebec to Chicago to the wilderness around Oshkosh, Wisconsin, where he bought a cabin and renamed it Frydenlund. He lived there alone for months, during which time he hunted and he baked his own bread. He loved the Indians and saw them as romantic figures, powerful and wise.

Dinesen spoke of her father's total acceptance of and love for her as a small child. She adored him and did not want to share her intimacy with him with anyone. She took pride in being her father's girl, not "theirs," her term for the Westerholz women. Wilhelm confided in her, treated her like an adult, and shared confidences with her, especially when he was troubled. That is why she was devastated at the age of 10 when her father committed suicide in 1895.

In Wilhelm's suicide note to his wife, Ingeborg, he wrote that the two other girls would fend for themselves, "but my heart aches for little Tanne." He did not mention his two sons, Thomas (age 3) and Anders (age 1). Karen (Tanne) Dinesen felt an enormous guilt that somehow she was powerless to dissuade Wilhelm from his ultimate fate: He hanged himself from the rafters of his apartment.

Thomas believed that his father had been suffering from syphilis. Ironically, when he shared this revelation with Karen Dinesen, years later, she herself was suffering from syphilis. "My father's destiny," she said,

Isak Dinesen (Karen Blixen) at 30 years of age taken outside of Karen House in Kenya. (Copyright Rungstedlund Foundation.)

"has, curiously enough, to a great extent, been repeated in my own."

Dinesen grieved for her father, even into adolescence. She thought "constantly" about her father and felt his absence from her life as an intolerable tragedy. At the age of 15, in the following letter, she makes a passionate plea to him:

My dear and beloved friend, my wise and gentle brother:

If you had been on earth still, I should have come to you and you would have taught me to love and to approach thine [sic] light, but you are gone away to high worlds, I know not where you dwell, spirit that I love. But do not leave me alone, if your spirit dwells still sometimes on earth, where you loved and suffered, let it dwell within me, who love you. And give me only once a token that you live and are the same, and that my spirit could reach thine, and if you give it me, I shall follow your footsteps and be your disciple, today and always. Perhaps I shall be it in all cases, but you know, my brother, how hard it is to be alone, be with me, and give me your bless [sic] dear beloved brother, my master, and teacher, my dearest friend.

It is significant that this letter was written in English, a foreign language to Dinesen, but a foreign language can provide distance and thus protect one's emotions. It can also ensure privacy.

This letter is also a remarkable example of Dinesen's romantic ideation of her father. She literally attempts to merge her identity with Wilhelm, to become him in order to possess his characteristics. His wisdom, his power shall be hers. She will not feel so vulnerable; she will not be alone. Her choice of words to address Wilhelm reveals her feelings toward him: "dear beloved brother, my master and teacher, dearest friend, wise and gentle brother." Theirs was a relationship that transcended father and daughter in an intimate and interdependent way, for Dinesen becomes both *personas*. That sense of union extended into her later life. When her marriage and her farm were both foundering, she wrote to her mother:

> If I can make something of myself again, and can look at life calmly and clearly one day—then it is Father who has done it for me. It is his blood and his mind that will bring me through it. Often I get the feeling that he is beside me, helping me, many times by saying: "Don't give a damn about it."

Dinesen's idealization of her father and her subsequent romantic ideation of him pervaded her life. It was the first link to a series of romantic ideations and losses that also led to her creativity as a writer.

The second significant male in Dinesen's life was Bror von Blixen (1886–1946). Though he became Dinesen's husband, it was his twin brother, Hans, with whom she fell madly in love at age 24. Hans, who raced horses and airplanes, rejected her, and Bror was not interested in her either until he realized that she was passionately in love with Hans. Then he assiduously courted her.

Hans's rejection was very difficult for Dinesen. Her maxim was that the final word as to what one is worth lies with the opposite sex. So it was Bror whom Dinesen accepted as her husband after his third proposal. Her family fought the engagement; her friends questioned her integrity in marrying the twin of the man whom she really loved. All of this made her more te-

nacious in her decision to marry Bror, to leave Denmark, and to begin their coffee farm in 1914.

It was Bror von Blixen who taught her how to shoot. He took her on safari with him, and she loved it—even the skinning of the lion down to his "elegant bones." It was von Blixen who gave her syphilis, a fact long hidden in her earlier biographies. Dinesen returned to Denmark for medical treatment in 1915, and by 1916 the disease was under control and she was noninfectious. Von Blixen never hid the fact that he slept with native women, and syphilis was almost epidemic among the Masai women.

In Africa it was Bror, not Hans, who became a romantic legend, immortalized as Robert Wilson in Hemingway's "The Short Happy Life of Francis Macomber," and worshiped for his enormous courage and spirit by Beryl Markham in *West with the Night*. He became the standard by which hunters were measured. Dinesen loved this aspect of von Blixen, and she loved being the "Baroness."

Though Dinesen tolerated von Blixen's affairs and entertained a few of her own, she did not want the divorce. Von Blixen left the house in 1919 and divorced her in 1922. It was in 1918 that Dinesen met Denys Finch-Hatton. Finch-Hatton, too, was a superb hunter who frequently went on safari with von Blixen (von Blixen would laughingly introduce Finch-Hatton as "my friend and my wife's lover"). A year after the divorce, Finch-Hatton moved his things to the farm.

Denys Finch-Hatton (1887–1931) was the great romance of Dinesen's life. Adored by everyone at Eton, enormously successful at Oxford, worshiped in Africa, his charm, wit, and intellect were tremendously admired. Like Wilhelm and like Bror, Finch-Hatton came and went frequently; he, too, was restless. In 8 years of living on the same farm, he and Dinesen actually spent only 2 years and 2 months together. The constant separation heightened their passion: a blatant definition of romantic love. They never dealt with reality, and Dinesen catered to his every wish. He enriched her life with music and poetry; he gave her a new perspective of Africa from his small plane. Good food, fine wines, stimulating conversation—these were the things they shared.

Midway in their relationship, Dinesen (age 41) thought she was pregnant. She cabled Finch-Hatton, using the code name Daniel for the child. Finch-Hatton replied, "Strongly urge you to cancel Daniel's visit." A second cable read, "Do as you like about Daniel as I should welcome him if I could offer partnership but this is impossible." Given her age and medical history, Dinesen probably had a miscarriage: Daniel was never born. This was a reality she could not ignore. Nor was the loss of her farm in 1931. Never economically viable, the coffee farm finally folded. Again, Finch-Hatton refused to help her. There was no offer of marriage, no arrangement for her economic security. She returned to Denmark, to her mother's house at Rungstedlund. The couple later quarreled, and he took back his ring. It was Beryl Markham whom Finch-Hatton invited to accompany him to Voi, his final and fatal flight in his gypsy moth. At first she accepted, then refused because her flight instructor, Tom Black, had a "bad feeling" about her going. It was a fatal crash that claimed Finch-Hatton's life in 1931.

Ironically, it was only in Finch-Hatton's death that Dinesen finally possessed him. She picked his gravesite which they had once chosen, and presided at his funeral; she acted as the significant woman in his life, changing the stories of their last moments together. But this romantic ideation was not enough. Dinesen attempted suicide, slashing her wrists in a friend's house before she left Africa. She also left a suicide note, which has since vanished from the von Blixen archives. Though she lost a lot of blood, her attempt served as a catharsis from her excruciating pain. It is not insignificant that Dinesen attempted to replicate her father's demise.

Wilhelm was the idealized male model whom Dinesen repeatedly sought. Her choices of von Blixen and Finch-Hatton reflected her narcissistic needs. She projected onto these men what she felt she wanted, needed, to be complete. What she desired from both men was an intimacy, a commitment that even her father had not given her. Had she transcended her narcissistic needs, she might have observed that neither of the two men possessed nor desired a capacity for intimacy or commitment. They had much in common: their physical prowess as hunters, their courage, their independence from convention, their need for adventure and solitude, and their reluctance for commitment in relationships.

The two men were blatant in their words and actions. Dinesen saw and responded to what she wished

to see. Von Blixen was uncultivated and rough beside Finch-Hatton, but she fought the divorce because she felt vulnerable, abandoned. With Finch-Hatton, the scenario was repeated. Things went well until she needed him. The possession, the control that she desperately sought, always evaded her—until later in Denmark where she met Thorkild Bjørnvig.

Dinesen returned to Denmark to live with her mother at Rungstedlund and began writing *Seven Gothic Tales*. Published in 1934, it was a huge success both in the United States and in England. In 1938 *Out of Africa,* an account of her life on her coffee farm in Kenya and her experiences with the native Africans, marked Isak Dinesen as a modern classical writer. She explained why she chose Isak Dinesen as her pen name. Dinesen was her family name and a connection with her father, Wilhelm. Isak means "laughter" in Hebrew, and like the biblical Sarah, who miraculously bore Isaac past her prime, Dinesen now bore her literary creations past her own prime. She had found laughter, she said, and she continued writing: *Winter's Tales* was published in 1942 and *The Angelic Avengers* followed in 1946.

In 1949, Thorkild Bjørnvig, a young Danish poet, entered Dinesen's life when she was 64 years old, living in Denmark, and experiencing "a period of great starkness in her life." The more a "productive dimension" eluded her in her own writing, the more she considered turning Bjørnvig into a poet. "Imperfect and incomplete alone, together they would be a unity." Once more Dinesen was engaged in romantic ideation, searching for the male to bring her to perfection. They formed a pact, a mystical union, a vow of eternal love. Bjørnvig would justify her efforts by becoming a first-class poet by bringing glory to them both.

Dinesen began by trying to make Bjørnvig "a man of the world"—like her father, Wilhelm, or Finch-Hatton. This relationship lasted for 4 years (until 1953). Though Bjørnvig had a wife and son, Dinesen repeatedly claimed him: he lived in her house for months at a time. She dominated him, played God with his life, caressed and bullied him simultaneously, and spoke of leaving Rungstedlund (her family estate) to him if he would live with her. When Bjørnvig fell in love with a young woman, Dinesen felt betrayed, both as a woman and as his "god." When the affair ended, Bjørnvig returned to his wife and attempted to break the pact with Dinesen. The following is an excerpt from the pact:

> You shall belong to no one and to nothing, to no party, to no majority, to no minority, to no society except in that it serves me at my altar. You shall not belong to your parents, nor to your wife nor children, nor to your brothers and sisters, nor to them who speak your language, nor those who speak any other—and best of all to thine own self. You shall belong only to me in this world.

Dinesen signed this document and gave it to Thorkild Bjørnvig. It took time. In one of their last meetings, on a walk, they encountered a snake lying in the sun. It did not move as they approached it. How each construed the snake as a symbol defines their relationship. Dinesen saw it as a good omen, something to protect them both from good and evil. Bjørnvig saw it as an indication of Dinesen's satanic power over him. He wrote his final good-bye to her, and she accepted it. But she did not completely relinquish her control over him. She used him in her fiction.

Like most writers, Dinesen exploited her experiences and transformed them into her tales. In "The Dreamers" from *Seven Gothic Tales* she creates Pellegrina Leoni, a great opera diva who allegedly died in a theater fire in Milan 13 years before the story begins. Though she recovered from the burns, Pellegrina lost her voice and would never sing again. She insisted on a burial service, and the world believed her to be buried in a little cemetery in Milan. She had attempted suicide and now felt that Pellegrina was indeed dead. "I will not be one person again . . . I will be always many persons from now. Never again will I have my heart and my whole life bound up with one woman, to suffer so much."

Pellegrina admonished her Jewish friend, Marcus, "Be many people." And she does precisely that: She becomes Ollala who inhabits an Italian brothel; she is also Madame Lola, a milliner by day and a revolutionist by night; she is also a religious martyr named Madame Rosalba. Three men fall in love with each female character whom they have met, and when they tell each other their stories, they all define "their woman" as the possessor of a deep, white scar from her left ear to her collarbone who is followed by a very wealthy, elderly

Jew. When each man tries to possess her, or force her into a fixed identity, she disappears.

Pellegrina's rejection of self, of identity, evolves from her excruciating pain: the loss of the beautiful voice that defined her. Knowing who she is and who she was, she consciously assumes a myriad of identities. In becoming all of these women, she is none of them. She has traded the myth of Pellegrina for a series of mythic women, none of whom really exists; she is spiritually dead.

When Pellegrina is discovered by her three former lovers, she throws herself from a precipice and loses consciousness. When she awakens, she is Pellegrina, the opera diva, and she attempts to finish the aria of *Don Giovanni* that she was singing the night of the fire. She has returned to herself.

Dinesen admitted that Pellegrina represented herself; that the loss of the diva's voice by fire symbolized the loss of her farm. It is likely that this loss extended to Finch-Hatton, to her broken marriage, and even to Wilhelm. Her loss was inextricably bound to these men to whom she looked for her own identity. The romantic ideation in her life evolved into her fiction. It became a powerful source for her creativity.

Later, Pellegrina Leoni becomes the focal point for Dinesen's relationship with Thorkild Bjørnvig, the young Danish poet. Dinesen admitted that his violent rejection of her possessiveness formed the basis of her story "Echoes" in *Last Tales*. The theme again deals with romantic ideation, with the possession of the qualities of the idealized romantic figure. Pellegrina no longer has a voice, but she has a young pupil, Emanuele, who sings like an angel. Pellegrina wants total control of and adulation from him. When she first hears him sing, she is convinced it is the voice of the young Pellegrina Leoni.

> She felt her own lungs drawing breath in his body and his tongue in her own mouth . . . she made him talk and made his eyes meet hers, and she sensed, as she had often done before, the power of her beauty and her mind over a young male being, her heart cried out in triumph: "I have got my talons in him. He will not escape me."

And later, "In three years we two will be one, and you will be my lover, Emanuele." Pellegrina's possession will be complete when she also sexually rules Emanuele. He will become *her* voice, the manifestation of her talent, her creativity, her genius. But Emanuele finally fights for his freedom, his identity. When Pellegrina pricks his finger with a needle, takes three drops of blood on her handkerchief, and sucks them, he believes she is a witch or a vampire and he flees. When she pursues him, he hits her with a large stone, drawing blood from her head. It is only his violent action that enables him to free himself from her possession.

Pellegrina needs Emanuele to be whole, to be vital. First, she idealizes him, and then she needs to possess him. There is also an inherent narcissism here, because Pellegrina does not think or care about Emanuele as a person, but as an extension of herself.

Thus the theme of romantic ideation permeates the life as well as the writing of Karen von Blixen, whom the literary world knew as Isak Dinesen. Although the men in her life whom she wished to possess finally eluded her—her father, Wilhelm; her husband, Bror von Blixen; her lover, Denys Finch-Hatton, and the young poet, Thorkild Bjørnvig—she possessed a portion of all of them in her writing as she sought out the idealized male figure as a way to make herself complete.

In 1955, Dinesen's spinal nerves were severed in surgery; 6 months later she experienced extensive surgery for a stomach ulcer. As a result she was virtually an invalid and never regained her health, but she continued to write: *Last Tales,* 1957; *Anecdotes of Destiny,* 1958; *Shadows on the Grass,* 1960 (a return to Africa and the native Africans). She was appointed an honorary member of the American Academy and was one of the founders of the Danish Academy. *Letters from Africa (1914–1931)* was published posthumously in 1978.

On September 7, 1962, Dinesen died peacefully in her sleep at Rungstedlund; she was 77. She was buried at the foot of Ewald's Hill (named for a poet) on her family estate.

Bibliography

Dinesen, I. (1981). *Letters from Africa: 1914–1931.* Chicago: Universtiy of Chicago Press.

Hannah, D. (1971). *"Isak Dinesen" and Karen Blixen: The mask and the reality.* New York: Random House.

Langbaum, R. (1964). *The gayety of vision.* New York: Random House.

Lasson, F. & Svendsen, C. (1970). *The life and destiny of Isak Dinesen.* New York: Random House.

Migel, P. (1967). *Titania.* New York: Random House.

Thurman, J. (1982). *Isak Dinesen: The life of a storyteller.* New York: St. Martin's Press.

Discovery

Robert Root-Bernstein

Michigan State University

Aesthetics The set of criteria used to decide what is worth investigating and to compare the relative values of discoveries and inventions.

Anomaly An observation that is reproducible but that challenges current theory by refusing to fit within its explanatory framework.

Hypothesis A provisional explanation of phenomena devised with the intention of testing its adequacy.

Illumination A sudden insight following a long period of fruitless problem-solving effort, resulting in a previously unimaginable solution to a puzzle.

Invention The creation of something novel by intention (as opposed to serendipity—see below).

Serendipity Searching for one thing and finding another either as a result of error, unexpected observation, or unpredicted results.

Theory A broadly explanatory, mature hypothesis that has been repeatedly challenged by skeptical testing, the predictions of which continue to be validated without yielding contradictory results or significant anomalies.

DISCOVERY can generally be defined as the finding of something unexpected that yields, in Jerome Bruner's phrase, an "effective surprise." That is, discoveries change not only the extent of what is known but also how we think about it. Discoveries, in short, cause us to rethink and restructure knowledge and the actions we derive from it.

I. DEFINITIONS OF DISCOVERY

Scholars have offered many definitions of discovery, each of which captures a different facet of the subject. For Nobel laureate Albert Szent-Gyorgyi, "Discovery is seeing what everyone else has seen and thinking what no one else has thought." Even in the discovery of new phenomena, there is always a concomitant intellectual or theoretical leap. At least a dozen people saw the fogging of photographic plates by radioactive materials before William Roentgen recognized the puzzle that this phenomenon represented. The result was the discovery of X rays. More than two dozen bacteriologists saw antagonisms between microbes before Alexander

Copyright © 1999 by Academic Press
All rights of reproduction in any form reserved.

Fleming thought to explore their antibiotic applications and gave us penicillin. Even the discovery of a new species of plant or animal is only interesting or important in the context of broader issues of pharmacology, taxonomy, evolution, or ecology. Martin Harwit has therefore noted that "the distinction between mere detection and actual recognition of a new phenomenon is therefore crucial. We may now be detecting many phenomena that we do not recognize."

To discover something requires understanding the meaning of what is found or invented within a broader context of human knowledge. The more profound the discovery, the more data or phenomena it connects, the broader its applications and the more diverse its meanings. Nothing has been discovered if its meaning is not understood.

Discoveries also link observations, ideas, or theories not only in new but often in previously unsuspected ways. At its most extreme, discovery can be almost Janus-like: the melding of two opposing faces or concepts into one body. This is Albert Rothenberg's view. It was thought during the 1920s, for example, that either Darwinian evolution or Mendelian genetics had to be wrong because Mendel's laws assumed conservation of genes, whereas evolution required constant sources of genetic novelty. The conflict was resolved when T. H. Morgan and H. J. Muller discovered mechanisms of genetic mutation. *Either-or* became *and*. Rothenberg's view also captures the essence of discovery as the linking of apparently unconnected concepts such as electricity, magnetism, and motion in the work of J. C. Maxwell or of comparative anatomy, paleontology, geology, geography, and animal breeding in the work of Darwin. Prior to the work of these scientists, these fields had developed without regard for one another.

An equally broadly applicable analogy has been provided by Arthur Koestler who suggested that discoveries have the same basic structure as jokes. Jokes often employ structures in which the listener is led to expect one outcome and is surprised to find that the punch line provides a very different resolution. Indeed, many scientists have commented that the greatest discoveries are often met with the same sort of surprised laughter elicited by a good joke. Sometimes the laughter is born of surprise, sometimes of disbelief, sometimes of ridicule. [*See* HUMOR.]

One critical issue on which debate persists is whether discovery is a process or an act. Is the discovery, as Koestler would have it, made at the exact time one has the surprise, or is the preparation that sets the discoverer's mind-set for the surprise also an integral part of the process, as Henri Poincaré has argued. Is discovery synonymous with inspiration (the sudden illumination that has given rise to the popular image of a lightbulb going off in one's head) or the 99% perspiration that Thomas Edison insisted was necessary to make the inspiration occur and pay off. This article assumes that discovery is, indeed, a process in which inspiration plays only a small role.

The basic model of the process of discovery has a series of interlinked steps. A problem is recognized; its nature is defined, relevant information is gathered, hypotheses concerning possible solutions are invented, tests of the hypotheses are devised, and a comparison between the results of the tests and the various hypotheses is made; more often than not, the cycle is begun again as new, unforeseen problems are recognized. Sometimes, however, the predictions made by one of the hypotheses appear to match the outcome of its tests. Then the investigator must verify the insight, communicate the results, convince colleagues of the legitimacy of the result, and generally show that what has been discovered allows new sorts of things to be studied or outstanding problems resolved in a novel and useful manner.

One of the most critical aspects of any discovery is that it changes the way scientists think about and therefore do science. This change can be theoretical, experimental, or even institutional. More and more investigators are recognizing that part of this process involves social forces that determine the latest fads and therefore that aesthetic considerations, such as how the discovery fits into current fashions, may speed or delay acceptance and recognition of the discovery. Thus, the process of discovery is complex, involving philosophical, empirical, theoretical, aesthetic, and social elements. The surprise of insight that some investigators identify with discovery is but one temporally distinct phase of this complex process.

II. WHO DISCOVERS

Every discovery to date has been made by a person. In the age of computers, this is not a trivial statement. So far, several computer programs have generated novel proofs of previous conjectures made by human beings, but no computer has yet generated a new and useful problem, hypothesis, or conjecture, let alone observation. As Poincaré once said, logic proves, it does not invent. Thus far, his statement has proven to be true. Whether computers will be able to be programmed to have imagination in the future will stand as one of the greatest challenges of artificial intelligence. [*See* ARTIFICAL INTELLIGENCE; IMAGINATION.]

Given that people have made all known discoveries up to the present time, one must ask what characterizes discoverers. It is clear that the ability to make discoveries is just as asymmetrically distributed in the general population as is, say, musical or artistic talent. Whereas nearly everyone can learn to do an experiment or play an instrument, very few have the talent of an Einstein or a Mozart. The difficulty is that recognizing this talent is not a trivial problem. Einstein's potential was certainly overlooked well into his adult years. A few eminent scientists have, however, displayed the same sort of precocity as Mozart. William Bragg, who won the Nobel Prize at the age of 22, is one example. [*See* TALENT AND CREATIVITY.]

Notably, studies of precocity among scientists, as determined by high standing in science talent search competitions for high school students, show that precocious teenagers have no higher probability of staying in science as a career than do other students planning science careers. Although some national winners have gone on to win Nobel Prizes, the majority have not even remained within science. Intelligence tests, standardized tests such as achievement tests, tests of divergent thinking, and psychological profiles have also failed to identify any significant predictors of who will succeed in science. A significant number of eminent scientists have moved into science careers only during or after college, in fact, so that their talents were at best late blooming. [*See* DIVERGENT THINKING; APPENDIX II: TESTS OF CREATIVITY.]

The factors that do seem to correlate significantly with the ability to make discoveries are of quite unexpected sorts. One is training with a previously successful discoverer. Nearly all Nobel Prize winners have studied with a previous laureate at some time during their schooling or early careers. Whether such training conveys certain tricks of the trade, creates personal networks of power that help to facilitate the acceptance of discoveries, or both, is not clear from current

studies. In any event, there are clearly established lineages of eminent scientists that can be traced for many generations.

Another personal correlate for success as a discoverer is hobbies, or intensive leisure time activities. Those scientists whose work is recognized as being the most important for their science (as measured by honors, total citations to their papers, or the number of individual high-impact papers they publish) tend to engage intensively in hobbies such as painting, music, writing poetry, sculpture, professional-level chess, or other endeavors that require significant time and energy to master. These discoverers are often highly talented in their avocations, so that a significant proportion of Nobel laureates report that they have faced difficult career decisions between science, one of the arts, and sometimes the law or business as well. A few, such as Desmond Morris, who is a professional painter as well as ethologist, and Aleksandr Borodin, whose musical compositions are better known than his chemistry, have even managed to carry on joint careers.

Mitchell Wilson, a physicist, inventor, novelist, and historian of technology, noted that the reason hobbies may correlate with scientific success is that the discoverer needs not only expert knowledge, but a poet's affinity for words and their meanings, the artist's ability to observe and think graphically and dynamically, and the musician's appreciation for complex patterns and the finesse of playing instruments—in this case scientific ones as well as musical ones. A breadth of skills therefore hones the scientist's talents for discovering.

Nonscientific talents may also hone the discoverer's thinking skills. A direct correlation has been found between the ability of eminent scientists to think in three dimensions and their participation in the arts. Musical ability also seems to improve visualization as well as kinesthetic sensibility. Similarly, verbal skills are highly associated with verbal hobbies such as poetry. The ability to think in three dimensions, dynamically, to use kinesthetic thinking skills, and to utilize an unusually broad range of nonverbal forms of thinking, is in turn highly correlated with the importance and number of discoveries a scientist makes. As Max Planck, who received a Nobel Prize in physics, once commented, "the creative scientist needs an *artistic* imagination."

Age is also certainly related to the probability of making discoveries. Young scientists are more likely to make discoveries than older ones and the earlier that a scientist has the opportunity to do independent research, and the earlier he or she publishes, the greater his or her probability of long-term recognition. The probability distribution of making a discovery varies by specific discipline, however. The probability peaks at around 25 years of age for mathematicians, 30 for physicists, 35 for chemists, and in the early forties for biologists. As with all statistical distributions, there are, in this case, many important, exceptions. Some mathematicians have made their first major discovery in their sixties, and some biologists have done their best work in their late teens. [*See* DISTRIBUTION OF CREATIVITY.]

What is perhaps more interesting about age and the probability of discovery is that there are two very different groups among discoverers themselves. The dominant group consists of people who make a single important discovery during their lifetimes—a Jonas Salk with his polio vaccine or Watson with the structure of DNA (deoxyribonucleic acid). These people tend to stay within the field of their expertise. The minority group consists of individuals who make multiple, major discoveries often spanning their entire careers. These people tend to change fields often and are characterized by having made three or more major discoveries by their mid-forties. Such people tend to state explicitly that they use field changing, or what has been called the novice effect, purposefully to stimulate new ideas. Linus Pauling, who worked on chemical bonding, protein structure, DNA, hemophilia, vitamin C, and many other scientific problems, is typical. Such field changers state that they are invigorated by having to grapple with new problems and to master new scientific tools, while they also bring to the new field their experience and knowledge of the ones they have explored previously. Insights, they say, often result from this melding of previously separate knowledge and practices. [*See* INSIGHT.]

Although the most successful discoverers tend to be productive, productivity cannot be used as a measure of either discovery or the potential to discover. There is no statistical significance between the number of papers produced by one-time discoverers and multiple discoverers. Indeed, there is no correlation between productivity and discovery at all. Gregor Mendel produced a mere seven papers and revolutionized science by inventing the basic principles of genetics. Banting

gave the world insulin and a lifetime total of fewer than three dozen papers and earned himself a Nobel Prize. James Watson's total scientific output consists of fewer than 50 scientific papers, and yet he too revolutionized science with his discovery of the structure of DNA, the molecule containing the genetic code.

Some discoverers are, on the other hand, prolific. Pauling produced many hundreds of papers, as have most of his Nobel-winning colleagues, and Thomas Edison produced 1093 patents, still a record for an individual inventor. Edison, however, never discovered any new principles or devised any theorems that contributed to science, whereas another great inventor, Michael Faraday, not only invented electrical motors and generators but also provided the intellectual basis for the science of electromagnetism. He, in other words, not only created new things but explored and explicated their meaning. He thereby raised his work from mere invention to the plane of real discovery. Thus, simply being prolific does not necessarily lead to discoveries. Indeed, some of the most prolific scientists are also the most obscure. John Edward Gray, a 19th-century botanist whose work is largely forgotten, produced 883 papers. Similarly, the most prolific author in current computer sciences, with more than a thousand papers, has not, according to his colleagues, ever written one worth reading and most of his papers have never been cited by anyone in the computer literature, including himself. Clearly, the quality of the discoveries or inventions made by an individual are, in the long run, of much greater consequence than the quantity.

It is also worth noting that a significant number of discoveries have been made by amateurs. Amateur astronomers have been responsible for the first sightings of the planet Pluto and of many of the comets that have been named. Amateur geologists are a constant source of new finds for paleontologists and are responsible for the discoveries of some of the most outstanding dinosaur remains found in recent years. Dedicated investigators such as farmer Wilson Bentley, known to posterity as "the snowflake man," have provided some of the best data and many of the key concepts in meteorology. Also it is worth remembering that Charles Darwin, Jane Goodall, Dian Fossey, and many other eminent biologists have also been amateurs. What makes a discoverer is not necessarily formal training but the acquisition of expertise by dint of simple hard work and hard thinking. [*See* EXPERTISE.]

Indeed, in the fields of ignorance, there are no experts; for if the experts had the answers, then persistent unsolved problems would not exist. Discoverers, no matter what their educational background, are therefore always pioneers.

III. HOW DISCOVERIES ARE MADE

Discoveries come about in as many ways as there are discoverers. Some general strategies seem to work more often than others, however. Peter Medawar, a Nobel laureate in biology, has admonished students that if they want to make an important discovery, they must choose a big, important problem. G. P. Thomson, a Nobelist in physics, noted that there is no correlation between the difficulty and the importance of a problem. The big ones can be just as easy to solve as the little ones. Neils Bohr, another physics laureate, suggested that the best problems can be found by focusing on paradoxes—the places where theories and observations are noncongruent or contradictory and thus of the sort Rothenberg described. Physicist and historian of science Thomas Kuhn noted that revolutions in science always follow the recognition of outstanding anomalies to the assumptions underlying a field. Pauling, in turn, argued that the key to success is to "have lots of ideas and throw away the bad ones." Almost everyone agrees that the greatest discoverers have great courage when it comes to speculating and inventing. Thus, the greatest discoverers are also universally characterized as having made some of the biggest scientific blunders on record. Einstein, for example, announced at least three times in his life that he had invented a unified field theory to explain all of physics. He was demonstrably wrong each time. The lesson is that to succeed in science, you must dare; and to dare, you must be willing to fail.

Error itself is a frequent source of discoveries. "Man errs, so long as he is striving," said Goethe. Indeed, every discoverer of note has made errors from Newton and Vesalius to Einstein, Crick, and Watson. What distinguishes the discoverer from the forgotten scientist is that the discoverer recognizes in his own errors the seeds of new possibilities. As Magendie, the founder of

modern physiology, often said when an experiment gave a result different from that he predicted, "I was mistaken, but it is much more interesting than if I had succeeded. . . . A new phenomenon, so much the more important as it is so little expected." Similarly, J. J. Thomson was fond of saying that "though a theory might be Bohemian, it might be the parent of very respectable facts." What counts in science is the dialectical process of self-correction that constantly pits theory and experiment against one another. In fact, if one follows Sir Karl Popper's philosophy of science, then error is the only true method of science, because Popper maintains that theories can only be disproven, but never verified. The best scientists are therefore often those who actually search for errors. [*See* DIALECTICAL THINKING: IMPLICATIONS FOR CREATIVE THINKING.]

Error is, of course, only one of many strategies employed by successful discoverers. Some discoveries have resulted from scientists taking infinite pains with the minute details of systems they are studying. The discovery of the element argon resulted from the observation by Lord Rayleigh that nitrogen prepared from the air is heavier volume for volume than that prepared from chemical compounds. This observation suggested that something must be contaminating the aerial nitrogen. This contaminant turned out to be argon.

Another common strategy is to extrapolate. As soon as Rayleigh announced the discovery of argon, William Ramsay predicted that an entire column of previously unsuspected inert gases must be present in the periodic table of elements, and he proceeded to isolate them. Rayleigh and Ramsay both won Nobel Prizes for their work.

Other scientists have played mental games with current scientific dogmas, turning them on their heads, contradicting basic premises, or simply wondering "what if" some principle that everyone considered to be unquestionable were not. Curare, which kills by paralysis, for example, has been turned into a useful drug by harnessing its paralytic effects for surgical procedures in which complete cessation of movement is necessary on the part of the patient. A deadly poison thus gives life. Analogies, metaphors, and even the re-creation of ancient historical experiments have all been touted as additional aids to discovery. [*See* ANALOGIES; METAPHORS.]

In conjunction with various strategies of research,

many scientists and inventors have also discussed the mental tools that they have used to make their discoveries. Their descriptions are generally similar and quite surprising. To begin with, very few scientists use either mathematics or verbal languages to do their thinking. Einstein, in fact, stated explicitly (in what may amount to an overstatement) that, "No scientist thinks in equations." He then went on to explain that in his case, he did his problem solving by using "certain signs and more or less clear images which can be 'voluntarily' reproduced and combined . . . as well as muscular feelings." Einstein also noted that the use of words and equations came only when the images and feelings had become well enough developed that they needed to be formally tested and communicated. Cyril Stanley Smith, a metallurgist, also noted that "The stage of discovery was entirely sensual and mathematics was only necessary to be able to communicate with other people." Notably, both the use of visual images, kinesthetic feelings, and other nonverbal forms of thinking, as well as the secondary nature of words and mathematics, have also been reported by a very large number of other eminent scientists and inventors including Richard Feynman, Nichola Tesla, Charles Kettering, Stanislaw Ulam, Santiago Ramon y Cajal, Joshua Lederberg, Jonas Salk, and Barbara McClintock. [*See* IMAGERY.]

McClintock, whose work in genetics earned her a Nobel Prize, is also remembered for explicitly speaking about her "feeling for the organism." Far from attempting to be objective about her work, she studied each individual plant until she knew it so intimately that she empathized completely with it. She even found that she could do this with chromosomal preparations, imagining herself down among the genes. "The important thing," she said, "was that you forget yourself." Indeed, Jonas Salk reported that his best ideas about how to fight polio came from "imagining myself to be a virus." Physicists have reported "becoming" photons, electrons, and black holes. Ethologists such as Jane Goodall, Dian Fossey, and Desmond Morris, who study animal behavior, say that their best ideas have come from empathizing so completely with the animals that they can imagine being one themselves. Thus, Joshua Lederburg, another Nobel laureate, proclaimed that every scientist "needs the ability to strip to the essential attributes some actor in a process, the ability to imagine oneself *inside* a biological situation; I literally had to be able to think, for example, 'What would it be like if I were one of the chemical pieces of a bacterial chromosome?'"

This nonverbal, nonmathematical nature of creative thought creates some interesting conundrums for understanding the nature of discovery. What is Stan Ulam talking about when he claims to "calculate, not by numbers and symbols, but by almost tactile feelings combined with reasoning"? To what was Richard Feynman referring when he talked about solving quantum physics problems using "acoustical images"? How do objective and verifiable results come from a process of thinking that has been described as entirely sensual, empathic, and subjective? Here, physicist-novelist C. P. Snow may hold the key:

> If we could follow the process of scientific thought through many minds, as it actually happens and not as it is conventionally expressed after the event, we should see every conceivable variety of mental texture. . . . There are exactly as many ways of approaching the scientific world as there are individuals in science. It is only because the results are expressed in the same language, are subject to the same control, that science seems more uniform, than, say, original literature. In effect, in the end, it *is* more uniform.

Unless we recognize the idiosyncratic and nonlogical nature of thinking itself, and the immense constraints that logical systems of communication place on how we express our insights, we cannot make progress on this thorny problem. There is clearly a process of translation between individual and the scientific collective that is as essential to success as having the insight itself.

IV. WHEN DISCOVERIES ARE MADE

The temporal patterns of discovery, and especially when individuals are most likely to have their insights, are perhaps the least-studied aspect of the discovery process, but some interesting phenomena have been noted. The influence of age and changing fields was noted earlier. People tend to make discoveries within 5 to 10 years of entering a field, and they tend to have only one major insight per field they enter. Thus changing fields tends to restart the discovery clock, as it were.

Equally important to understanding discovery is that insights seem to occur more often when scientists are *not* directly working on a problem than when they are. Thus, several studies have shown that only about a third of scientific problems are solved by a direct, brute-force approach. An equal number are solved when scientists give up on the original problem and begin working on a related problem. The remaining third of the problems get solved during leisure-time activities, which range from going on vacation to taking a shower to dreaming the answer in one's sleep. Some investigators, such as Linus Pauling, have even gone so far as to claim to be able to program their minds to make use of this leisure time. Pauling said that when he worked on a problem that he could not solve directly, he would turn to something else during his work hours and think very hard about the unsolved problem every night before he went to sleep. After a few weeks, he would forget to think about the problem before he slept, and then, within a few days, almost inevitably, he would wake with a plausible answer. Other scientists, such as Poincaré and August Kekule, the discoverer of the structure of benzene, have reported using similar techniques of purposeful meditation or relaxation to stimulate ideas. [*See* DREAMS AND CREATIVITY.]

This phenomenon of nonconscious problem solving raises interesting questions for understanding the nature of discovery. As Poincaré noted, it is almost as if the conscious mind, employing the rules of logic, can prevent insights from occurring. In fact, the nature of many discoveries is such that they do break the rules of logic as they are understood at the time, or posit the existence of phenomena that are unknown and so beyond the knowledge of reason. [*See* ALTERED AND TRANSITIONAL STATES.]

One other temporal pattern also characterizes the nature of discovery. Discoveries as a whole tend to occur during times of economic growth and cultural mixing. The Scientific Revolution, for example, occurred during a period of prosperity associated with the Renaissance and this historical period is also characterized by many voyages of discovery that led to trade—both economic and intellectual—between cultures as diverse as the Europeans, Arabs, Chinese, and Native Americans. Other major periods of innovation in the sciences, such as the Industrial Revolution and the post-Sputnik era, are also associated with such economic and cultural prosperity.

V. WHAT IS DISCOVERED

Much of the literature on discovery assumes that what is discovered is a solution to a problem. Thus, one popular book about discovery is actually titled *The Search for Solutions*. In fact, discovery is better characterized as a quest for questions. The problem must be discovered before the search for its solution begins. Indeed, as noted earlier, one of the most fruitful strategies for discovering is to find anomalies and paradoxes that reveal the limitations of current theory and practice.

The greatest scientists have often, therefore, excelled at discovering new problems. As Camille Jordan wrote in praise of fellow mathematician Henri Poincaré, "He solved problems which before him nobody would have even dared to pose." Indeed, it is a truism in science that properly defining a problem gets an investigator more than halfway to its solution. Thus, Einstein once wrote:

> The formulation of a problem is often more essential than its solution, which may be merely a matter of mathematical or experimental skill. To raise new questions, new possibilities, to regard old problems from a new angle, requires creative imagination and works real advance in science.

Being able to perceive problems where no one else sees them is therefore one of the most important skills a discoverer can cultivate.

Different types of problems lead to different types of discoveries. If we ask "what is energy or velocity, or what species is this," the problem involves one of definition and will require invention of a concept or taxonomy. If we ask what governs the manner in which weights fall or why species are distributed as they are through space and time, then we are dealing with problems of explanation, and these require the development of a theory. To test the adequacy of a theory or definition, one will need data, and one therefore has a problem of experimentation or observation. In some cases, the experiment or observation cannot be made using existing techniques. Human eyes cannot see ultraviolet light or objects smaller than a cell. Such problems require the invention of new techniques or instruments for observation and analysis. This conjunction between problem type and the nature of what is discovered or invented may seem obvious, but experience shows that many theoreticians act as if they believe that all problems can be solved by inventing or enlarging a theory, whereas many experimentalists approach every problem as one that can be solved by gathering more data. Much time is wasted in science as a result.

Problems, of course, are only one of many things that can be discovered and one need not invent a problem to solve it. Outstanding problems are often as widely disseminated and discussed by scientists as are great experiments and theories. James Watson and Francis Crick, for example, tackled the well-defined problem of how genetic information is encoded and transmitted by living organisms. They neither discovered the problem nor the fact that DNA carries genetic information. They did, however, make the very remarkable discovery of how the structure of DNA itself carries information and is adapted to replicating itself. This structure was quite unexpected.

Watson and Crick's discovery was made possible by other types of discoveries. W. H. and W. L. Bragg had previously invented the technique of X-ray crystallography by which the structure of DNA was analyzed; Linus Pauling had developed sophisticated physicochemical modeling methods that Watson and Crick could apply to DNA; and so forth. In addition, Watson and Crick's discovery led to other discoveries. All of modern genetic engineering is based on the manipulation of DNA sequences and the enzymes that control DNA in cells—not one wit of which was foreseen even at the time of Watson and Crick's work (ca. 1950). Thus, it is correct to say that every discovery builds on other discoveries and makes new ones possible. This is what Isaac Newton meant when he said, "If I have seen further than other men it is because I have stood on the shoulders of giants." The structure of discovery is a very complex and tightly woven tapestry of ideas, observations, techniques, explanations, and inventions.

Mention of invention raises the important issue of distinguishing between it and discovery. In general, scientists usually argue that inventions are made with intention, whereas discoveries occur serendipitously.

Had Galileo known that there were mountains on the moon, he could not have discovered them. Had Columbus known of the Americas, he could not have discovered them. On the other hand, Galileo could not have discovered the telescope. That required intention. Morse could not have discovered the telegraph nor Fulton the steam-driven boat nor the Wright brothers powered flight by accident. These had to be planned. This is not to say that in carrying out plans to build an invention, one will not stumble across unforeseen principles or phenomena of nature and thereby make a discovery. Nor is it to say that discoverers are not also inventors. More often than not, a discovery can only be made because of a technological invention or can be interpreted only in light of a theory that is invented in response to what is discovered. Thus, invention and discovery are integrally entwined and both can be the results of the investigative process. [*See* INVENTION.]

VI. WHERE DISCOVERIES ARE MADE

Interestingly, there appears to be a geography of discovery, and its form is full of surprises. One might expect discoveries to cluster in the major centers of science at any given historical period because these centers are where the most prominent scientists are to be found. For various reasons indicated earlier, including the inverse correlation between age and discovery and the generally conservative tendencies of most major institutions, the most interesting science is usually done in peripheral institutions.

Before proceeding further with this point, it is first important to distinguish between what Thomas Kuhn has characterized as normal and revolutionary science. Kuhn defined normal science as having a well-articulated paradigm, or set of problem-solving techniques, that can be described in textbooks and classrooms and implemented in laboratories. In essence, normal science focuses on areas of science in which a major advance has opened up a well-defined set of problems that can be addressed with a fair assurance of success. Revolutionary science, on the other hand, overtly challenges the assumptions of existing problem-solving modes. It undermines textbooks, makes standard classes irrelevant or outmoded, and creates new methods of working and training.

In addition to Kuhn's normal and revolutionary science, historians of science have generally begun to recognize yet a third category of science as well: new sciences. There was, for example, no science of physical chemistry until the late 19th-century when a number of scientists began to realize that the techniques of physics could be applied to chemistry, thereby revealing many new phemonena that were unpredicted and unprecedented. Physiology, immunology, biophysics, and ethology are other examples of new sciences that emerged during the past century carving out new scientific territories without attacking existing sets of theories, practitioners, institutions, or textbooks.

Each of these three types of science has its own geographical distribution. Normal science does indeed tend toward the established centers of science. This is because these centers have the resources and funding to attract recognized discoverers. Funding, in turn, is dependent on granting agencies or patrons being able to identify fields in which progress is most likely. Such fields are those in which the major discoveries have already been made. The major scientific institutions at any given historical time are usually engaged in what might be characterized as developmental, rather than breakthrough, science. Thus, if one looks at where Nobel laureates end their careers, they often end up at Harvard, Stanford, MIT, Cambridge, Oxford, Paris, Berlin, and so on.

Breakthrough or revolutionary science tends toward the geographical peripheries of the scientific collective at any given time. Innovators tend to be people who go their own way rather then follow the crowd. They pay the price of having to work in third-rate conditions with inadequate funding and resources. But as one scientist said, one makes a choice between the "shackles of the palace or the freedom of the shack." Thus, if one looks at where Nobel laureates train as undergraduates and obtain their first employment, it is most often at institutions that have no particular claim to prestige. In some cases, experts at major institutions actually force innovators out. William Shockley, one of the inventors of the transistor, for example, refused to allow the group of men who invented the integrated circuit, or "chip," to stay in his laboratory, considering their work irrelevant and unlikely to succeed. They were forced to create a small company to continue their work. Many small computer innovators and biotechnology companies have begun under similarly discouraging circumstances, when large companies have refused to sanc-

tion work that ran counter to their established research directions.

New sciences also tend to emerge on the geographical peripheries of science. This phenomenon is related to breakthrough or revolutionary science—except that no field exists previously to revolutionize. Notably, only two sets of institutions tend to take up new scientific fields: major institutions that purposefully restructure existing departments to create a new one to embody the new science and its discoveries, and, more frequently, new institutions. Discoveries, in other words, tend to flourish where new opportunities for personal and institutional growth are available.

VII. WHY DISCOVERIES ARE MADE

What motivates scientists to make discoveries? The basic drives seem to be control, curiosity, necessity, serendipity, or aesthetics. Often several of these drives are at work simultaneously. [*See* Motivation/Drive.]

Einstein commented that one of the primary reasons he became a scientist was to avoid the daily hassles of life. Many studies of the psychology of scientists and engineers suggest that they have a need for control. Creating theories or performing experiments provides that control. Control, in turn, yields power, because understanding nature allows human beings to manipulate nature's laws. Thus, discovery provides a means for individuals to obtain power over nature and their own circumstances.

Necessity can also be a motive for discovery. "Necessity is the mother of invention" is a well-known saying, no less true for its triteness. It is certain that many scientists, such as Louis Pasteur and Jonas Salk, have tackled questions of the cause of diseases precisely because of the threat these diseases posed to human beings.

At least half of all discoveries occur serendipitously, however. A careful distinction must be made here between serendipity and chance or accident. Chance or accident denote total lack of control of the process leading to discovery. No discovery has ever been made by chance or accident, despite many articles and books on these topics. When the laboratory notebooks detailing discoveries are examined, they inevitably reveal that all discoveries begin with some goal in mind. Those discoveries that are often said to have occurred by chance or accident, in every case, turn out to have been made while looking for something else. Finding one thing while searching for something else is the definition of serendipity. The term originated in a story by Horace Walpole called the "Princes of Serendip," which concerned the adventures of the princes as they went in search of various treasures and were continuously, and fruitfully, sidetracked by more interesting adventures. Thus, Fleming, for example, discovered the antibiotic enzyme lysozyme in his mucus and tears when trying to isolate a virus that causes colds. Intention set up the experiments; serendipity yielded the surprising discovery. [*See* SERENDIPITY.]

Perhaps the most unexpected and yet common motivation for discovery is aesthetic. A very large number of scientists are drawn to science in the first place by the beauty of the experimental preparations they examine in the microscope or the sublimity of the intellectual constructs that we call theories. Santiago Ramon y Cajal, who won a Nobel Prize for his work in neuroanatomy, often waxed eloquent over the magnificent scenes that the architecture of the brain afforded, whereas Max Planck said forthrightly that he was drawn to physics by the beauty of the laws of thermodynamics. In some cases, the desire to recreate literal physical beauty has even led to discoveries. For example, C. T. R. Wilson became so enamoured of the coronas and glories that he observed when climbing in the Scottish hills that he decided to recreate them in his physics laboratory. His success not only allowed him to make these beautiful optical phenomena at will, but the resulting cloud chambers also allowed subatomic particles to be observed for the first time and earned Wilson a Nobel Prize. Similarly, it appears that Fleming's habit of making "paintings" in petri dishes using a "palette" of colored microorganisms provided the basic techniques and observations that led to his discovery of penicillin.

VIII. DISCOVERY OUTSIDE OF THE SCIENCES

It is important to ask whether discovery within the sciences is the same as discovery in other fields of endeavor such as geography or even the arts. The answer depends largely on whether one looks primarily at the *products* of the discovery process or at the *process* itself. The literature comparing science with the humanities and arts is clearly split as to whether nonsciences make discoveries or progress in ways similar to the sciences. It is generally accurate to say that all those authors who compare the products of the sciences with those of other disciplines find that science alone makes progressive discoveries, whereas those who compare the processes by which people in different disciplines work claim that people in all fields make discoveries.

Similarities may also hide differences, however. Even within science itself, there are very different ways of making discoveries. Geology and paleontology present cases of sciences in which it is rarely possible to make what most scientists would characterize as predictions. In general, predictions are defined as constituting the description of events or phenomena before they have happened. Geology and paleontology, however, deal largely with things that have already happened. Thus, philosophers characterize the description of as yet undiscovered artifacts or physical objects by those in historical fields as properly being called *postdictions* or *retrodictions*. Each discipline, in other words, may require a different set of logical and physical tools in order to make discoveries, and the nature of these discoveries may differ quite markedly even when they proceed from the same basic process of investigation.

The distinction between prediction and retrodiction is critical for analyzing whether fields such as history and philosophy can make discoveries. It must be obvious that they cannot discover new things that have never existed before. But it must be equally obvious that they have the same ability as geology to unearth things that have previously existed and been forgotten and to provide a general understanding of the processes that guide the past and our understanding of it.

Artists and musicians can also be said to make discoveries and inventions comparable to scientists. Artists, for example, have discovered perspective, anamorphosis (the process of mapping an image onto a nonflat surface), optical illusions, the techniques necessary for casting sculptures (which usually anticipated existing engineering capabilities), techniques for displaying motion (including motion pictures), and even the process of pixelization that underlies all modern computer and CD-ROM visual technologies. Musicians have similarly invented harmony, counterpoint, twelve-tone and other "natural" scales, and many other aural phenomena we take for granted. There is no reason, as artist–inventor–neurobiologist Todd Siler has commented, that these sorts of discoveries should be valued any less than those within the realm of science. Each is an intellectual addition to the panoply of human understanding.

Equally to the point is the undeniable fact that a large number of *scientific* discoveries have been made by professionals in the fine arts, most of whom had little or no formal scientific or engineering training. Here are a few examples. The concept of camouflage, both as a biological principle explaining animal adaptation and as a military technology, was discovered by portrait painter Abbott Thayer at the end of the 19th century. The principle of geodesy was discovered by architect-inventor Buckminster Fuller and applied to making geodesic domes long before it was applied by scientists to understanding the structures of spherical viruses or for synthesizing C60 carbon compounds now known as fullerenes. The equally basic physical principle of tensegrity was worked out by Fuller and fellow artist Kenneth Snelson, who used it to make sculptures. Tensegrity is now thought to underlie the structures of cells and is being applied to the building of stable platforms for use in space. And musician-inventor George Antheil collaborated with actress Hedy Lamarr to invent the concept of frequency hopping, in which a message is encoded in constantly varying frequencies to protect it from detection or interference from enemy sources. Frequency hopping is the basis for protecting a great deal of military communications at present.

These examples demonstrate that there is no fundamental difference between the thinking of the scientist, the artist, the composer, and the writer, or their work could never overlap so significantly. Thus, there is no reason to believe that discovery is the preserve of sciences or engineering alone. Unfortunately, too little research has yet been done comparing the thought processes of scientists, artists, writers, and others. Such comparisons would undoubtedly bear interesting fruit. For example, historian of technology Thomas Hughes has noted that "the invention of machines, devices and processes by metaphorical thinking is similar to verbal creation, but the fascinating possibilities have not been much discussed, probably because persons interested in language are rarely interested in technology." Similarly, some recent studies, most notably by James McAllister, are beginning to find that the use of aesthetic criteria in the sciences, engineering, and the arts are all virtually identical and that the notion of beauty in science may be as essential as a motivation for discovery and as a criterion for evaluating novel ideas as it is in the arts. Thus, there is, at present, no reason to believe that the process of discovery in the sciences differs in any substantial way from the process of discovery in other disciplines, despite obvious differences in the types of discoveries achieved.

IX. AN EVOLUTIONARY THEORY OF DISCOVERY

Evolutionary theory provides a unifying concept for understanding the process of discovery in all its manifestations. Kuhn, for example, has argued that an evolutionary model could be applied to science in his classic *Structure of Scientific Revolutions* and the argument has been elaborated since by Donald Campbell, David Hull, and the author, among others.

In order to apply evolutionary theory to discovery, one must make analogies between species and ideas. Standard Darwinian evolution requires three key elements: (a) a source of diversity among species or ideas, (b) a way for individuals to inherit differences, and (c) a nonrandom means of selecting among differences. The source of diversity is provided in part by nature, which generates the phenomena for scientists to observe, and in part by scientists themselves, who invent techniques for exploring nature and explaining it. Here it is important to remember that the vast majority of ideas and observations that scientists make are incorrect or only partially correct. There is as much waste in the intellectual realm as when species produce many more offspring than can survive.

The inheritance of variations occurs by means of learning and teaching in cultural evolution. Thus, ideas and information take the place of genes. Evolution, in consequence, is more Lamarckian than Darwinian. Lamarck maintained that species evolve by willing themselves to change, and went on to argue that alterations during their lifetimes could be transmitted genetically. Lamarck's mechanism has been completely dismissed as a means of biological evolution but may still apply to cultural evolution because people can, in fact, change their minds and transmit their altered ideas to the next generation of scientists.

Finally, evolution requires a nonrandom means of selecting between competing ideas. Here a combination of natural and artificial processes come into play. The touchstone of all science is nature itself. One compares observations and theories by means of tests with nature. Often, however, several explanations may account for existing observations equally well. In this case, other criteria, such as the compatibility of the various explanations with other scientific principles, the range of phenomena explained, its simplicity and usefulness, and aesthetic criteria come into play. The point is that selection does occur and, in fact, competition among scientists, their observations, and theories is very rigorous.

Evolutionary theory accurately describes several other elements of the discovery process. One is the literal growth of each new development in science from previous discoveries. Every discovery builds on previous discoveries. If necessity is the mother of invention, then existing discoveries are the fathers.

An evolutionary model also describes accurately the increasingly specialized nature of discoveries in science. If one looks at science since the 17th century, it has developed in almost perfect imitation of a taxonomic tree. As of 1670, there was one journal of science, and all of science as generally categorized under the heading "natural history." Over the next century, the number of practitioners grew exponentially, as Derek de Solla Price has so well documented, creating a need for new and more specialized journals. The specific sciences of astronomy, physics, chemistry, and biology were all recognized by the end of the 18th century. During the 19th century, exponential growth in the number of chairs of science, journals, practitioners, and papers all continued resulting in further specialization. Chemistry split into physical, organic, inorganic, and biochemistry, for example. At present, the discipline recognizes more than a hundred specialties in which doctorates can be obtained and papers published. Every scientific field has branched into similarly diverse specialties. Thus, from the trunk of natural philosophy have emerged the general branches of the basic sciences, followed inexorably by the twigs that have produced the current crop of thousands of leaves that represent the crown of science as it exists today. Scientists diverge and specialize just as do species.

Many aspects of the evolutionary theory of discovery remain unresolved, however. For example, standard evolutionary theory places primary emphasis on the random generation of extremely large numbers of variants from which the best adapted can be selected. The implications of this approach for discovering are that an investigator should try as many random ideas or processes as possible to optimize his or her chances of making a discovery. Philosopher Paul Fayerabend (*Against Method*) provided the most lucid support for this strategy in his writings. Physicist Henri Poincaré placed the greatest emphasis on the selection process. Anyone can, he argued, find two ideas, theorems, facts, or techniques that have not been synthesized before and do so. Most of the results will be useless or trivial. Poincaré therefore argued that what is most important is having an aesthetic sensibility that allows the discoverer to sort the wheat from the chaff: "To invent is to choose." Indeed, if we admit that discovery is a process and not an act, then choosing the best ideas to investigate can be critical, for every idea of any value needs a great deal of nurturing. The greatest discoverers have been those who saw the oak in the acorn or the giant in the baby and put in the 99% perspiration that Edison said is always needed to make the germ of an idea grow.

Another equally important difference between standard models of biological evolution and that characterizing cultures such as science concerns integration. Standard Darwinian evolution is portrayed as a tree that constantly branches. The most adapted new variants are the ones that survive through time. But much of scientific progress is characterized by the integration of previously separate lines of investigation. Many of the greatest breakthroughs in science are syntheses and scientists are all after their field's equivalent of a unified field theory. Thus, the trees that represent scientific discoveries not only branch, but they also meld back together, forming a dense network of interactions. Symbiosis or synthesis in science is, in other words, as important as speciation or specialization.

The constant interplay between the need for ever-greater specialization and the drive to unify existing knowledge creates the tension so essential to continued discovery. Those who are most likely to create the most important discoveries are therefore likely to be both analytical and synthetic. They are likely to be just as interested in how this dynamic process of discovery itself works as they are in the special knowledge in their particular area. For discovering, as we have seen, requires more than merely finding something new— it also requires knowing how to interpret its meaning within the broadest possible context of science and society.

Bibliography

Braben, D. (1994). *To be a scientist.* Oxford: Oxford University Press.

Diesing, P. (1971). *Patterns of discovery in the social sciences.* New York: Aldine.

Ferguson, E. (1992). *Engineering and the mind's eye.* Cambridge, MA: MIT Press.

Hadamard, J. (1945). *The psychology of invention in the mathematical field.* Princeton, NJ: Princeton University Press.

Harwit, M. (1981). *Cosmic discovery: The search, scope, and heritage of astronomy.* Brighton, England: Harvester Press.

Hughes, T. P. (1985, Fall). How did the heroic inventors do it? *American Heritage of Invention and Technology,* 18–25.

Krebs, H. A. & J. H. Shelley (Eds.). (1975). *The creative process in science and medicine.* Amsterdam: Excerpta Medica.

Kuhn, T. S. (1962). *The structure of scientific revolutions.* Chicago: University of Chicago Press.

Langley, P., Simon, H. A., Bradshaw, G. L., & Zytkow, J. M. (1987). *Scientific discovery: Computational explorations of the creative processes.* Cambridge, MA: MIT Press.

McAllister, J. W. (1996). *Beauty and revolutions in science.* Ithaca, NY: Cornell University Press.

Medawar, P. B. (1979). *Advice to a young scientist.* New York: Harper & Row.

Root-Bernstein, R. S. (1989). *Discovering.* Cambridge, MA: Harvard University Press; Replica Press (1998).

Rothenberg, A. (1979). *The emerging goddess: The creative process in art, science, and other fields.* Chicago: University of Chicago Press.

Siler, T. (1990). *Breaking the mind barrier.* New York: Simon & Schuster.

Zuckerman, H. (1977). *Scientific elite: Nobel laureates in the United States.* New York: The Free Press.

Distribution of Creativity

Herbert J. Walberg and Gretchen Arian

University of Illinois, Chicago

Performance Behavior ranked with respect to quality, quantity, or both.
Positive Skew Distribution A case of mass mediocrity and rare exceptionality.

This article describes the nature of the **DISTRIBUTION OF CREATIVITY** *and the causes for this statistical phenomenon. Almost by definition, creativity is uncommon because it implies originality. In using the term, people often want to suggest something rare, perhaps one of a kind or something done for the first time. In art, athletics, science, and other fields, perhaps one in a thousand or one in 10 million people exhibit top creative performance, and the number of their creative acts or breakthroughs are severely limited.*

I. STATISTICAL DISTRIBUTIONS

Of course, many physical objects and phenomena show normal distributions. Figure 1a shows, the most common or modal behavior is the average as well as the median, because half the cases are below and half above it. A plot of adult U.S. heights, for example, might show an average and many instances around 5 feet 7 inches. The largest number of cases are likely to be within 5 inches of the average, and very few would be less than, say, 3 feet or greater than 8 feet tall. As Figure 1a shows, the distribution is likely to be roughly symmetrical on either size of the average.

Intelligence, educational achievement, and personality test scores often show normal distributions like Figure 1a but mainly because they are intentionally constructed to exhibit this distribution. It is mistaken to think that most psychological behavior follows the normal curve. As illustrated in Figure 1b, many human and social phenomena exhibit positive or right skew. This means that most people are mediocre to slightly above average, but a few are exceptional, and very few are very exceptional. Income and wealth show this distribution: In 1977 Sloan noted that the top 1% of the U.S. population owns a third of the nation's wealth, the next 9% owns another third, and the other 90% owns the last third.

Copyright © 1999 by Academic Press
All rights of reproduction in any form reserved.

a

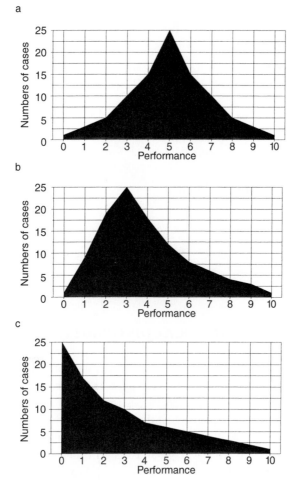

FIGURE 1 (a) Normal distribution; (b) right skew distribution; (c) Zipf distribution.

The Zipf distribution in Figure 1c forms a still more extreme curve in which nonperformance or the lowest level of performance is most common. The number of people in the world, for example, who speak a given number of words in English, Navaho, and Swahili would show this distribution; indeed, most people in the world could not speak a single word of any one of these or hundreds of other common and rare languages. The same appears true of performance in playing sports, running computers, and exhibiting expertise and creativity in many fields. Positive-skew distributions characterize many phenomena in education, linguistics, psychology, sociology, and the production of knowledge.

II. CAUSES OF POSITIVE SKEW

The positive skew distributions of expertise, creativity, and other learned accomplishments often result from the Matthew effect of the rich getting richer (named by Merton in 1968 after a passage in the Gospel of Matthew in the Bible). Merton described the stages in which distinguished scientific careers arise: initial talent advantages, study at distinguished universities, close work with eminent professors, early and frequent publication, job placement at famous laboratories, and citation and other recognition. These events and conditions multiply one another's effects to produce highly skewed scientific creativity. As few as a tenth of the scientists may account for nearly all the significant scientific work in a given field.

Though a few mavericks are exceptions, Nobel laureates and similarly distinguished scientists usually follow the Matthew pattern, which resembles wealth creation in that small initial advantages multiply over decades. In modern times, the very wealthy have often gained from initial wealth, expert knowledge, and social contacts that multiply and cumulate over time. In science and other creative fields, however, the driving incentive may not be wealth but prestige, excitement, competition, the pleasure of pursuing difficult goals, and the possible contribution of research to improving human conditions. In any case, creative accomplishments are strongly determined by talent and long, intense, and specialized experience. An advantaged start and long investment of hard work often lead to later opportunities. [*See* MATTHEW EFFECTS.]

III. MOTIVATION AND CREATIVE PERFORMANCE

Why should anyone work so hard over such a long period to reach the top levels of creativity or other kind of performance? As Figure 2 shows, more and more effort results in higher levels of performance but at diminishing rates. Because we can measure and think about physical performance more easily, consider runners: As shown on the performance curve, with more practice, those training for a marathon run at increasingly faster rates, especially those who have practiced

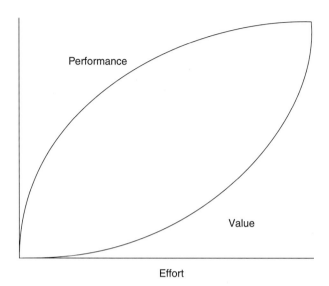

FIGURE 2 Effort, performance, and value.

little. Up to a point, however, each extra hour of practice per day in sports and other endeavors, other things being equal, yields a smaller rate increase. The time differences among top few marathoners may be measured in seconds.

In most fields, much of the fame, honor, and possibly gratification goes to the winners, especially those who come in first, as shown by Figure 2's value curve. Society tends to prize top performers and ignore others. Those at the top are often well compensated; those a few ranks down, though hardly different in performance, may be largely unknown except to aficionados. Of the thousands of good painters and physicists of this century, only a few are familiar names. Perhaps fewer than one in a thousand of all piano players have made a good living at it.

IV. MULTIPLICATIVE THEORIES OF CREATIVITY

Parallel to wealth accumulation and the development of scientific and other creative careers, Loehle suggested in 1994 that individual scientific discoveries are multiplicative products of cumulative events. For example, suppose a scientific discovery requires 20 necessary steps such as asking the right question, setting forth a researchable hypothesis, gaining financial support for the research, developing a detailed research plan, hiring capable assistants, supervising them, collecting data, analyzing it, drawing graphs, drafting a paper, submitting it to a scientific journal, and so on. Even if each step has an easy 90% probability of success, the multiplicative product (.9 × .9 × .9 . . .) or probability of project completion is only 12%. This poor overall success rate explains why many scientists rarely or never publish articles.

This cumulative, multiplicative theory draws together old and new ideas from several academic fields, and it apparently applies widely to behavior, education, and other fields. It is analogous, for example, to Darwinian evolutionary theory, which holds that plants and animals well adapted to their environments prosper, multiply, and "crowd out" poorly adapted organisms. Mutations (random genetic variations), moreover, that are further adaptive prosper still further.

Old and new cognitive theories extend such evolutionary theory to inventive thought. Campbell, in particular, pointed out that 2 years before Darwin's publication of the theory of natural selection, Alexander Bain, in 1855, used the term *trial and error* in analyzing creative thought. In this evolutionary insight, psychology preceded biology. Campbell held that "blind-variation-and-selection-retention is fundamental to all inductive achievements, to all genuine increases in knowledge, to all increases in fit of the system to environment" (p. 380).

In his view, therefore, three conditions are necessary for new ideas: "a mechanism for introducing variation, a consistent selection process, and a mechanism for preserving and reproducing the selected variations." The efficacy of rare new ideas depends on whether they can solve problems at hand. Those ideas that are useful, often those that succinctly express important phenomena or synthesize many particular instances, grow in their frequency of expression and consumption. Such successful ideas can be routinized and widely shared. They become increasingly frequent—even dominant.

V. DIFFUSION OF CREATIVE IDEAS

Once a creative idea proves successful, it can be widely adopted without endlessly re-creating or even understanding it. We hardly need think about electrons when turning on lights nor internal combustion when driving cars. In a humanitarian vein, Alfred North Whitehead (1864–1947) declared, "Civilization advances by extending the number of important operations which we can perform without thinking about them" (quoted in De Wolf, 1980, p. 281).

Psychological theories of B. F. Skinner and other behaviorists may be similarly construed. Like successful genetic mutations, rare random behaviors, when rewarded, become more frequent, even automated. They may become widespread when transmitted from one person to another through imitation and learning. Much of human life depends on such vicarious experience and socially transmitted abstract ideas; children, for example, need not figure all things out from raw experience.

VI. LEARNING, EXPERTISE, AND CREATIVITY

Creativity, however, usually requires expertise, which is itself rare and positively skewed. In intensive case studies of experts in various fields, Ericsson and Charness, in 1994, showed that expertise is a function of (a) carefully planning or goal setting, (b) daily hard work over long periods, and (c) continuous monitoring of progress—in short self mastery. Such conditions may outweigh initial ability; missing any single one results in less than expert performance. [*See* EXPERTISE.]

As many researchers have noted, studies on children's learning, creativity, and exceptional accomplishments suggest similar conditions are necessary, although parents, teachers and coaches may initially foster such propensities. In many fields, moreover, children's acquisition of exceptionality may proceed in stages. In 1985 Bloom, for example, emphasized early talent recognition, parental encouragement, and further encouragement from first teachers (though with limited deliberate practice), followed by elite teachers with increasingly demanding standards. Ericsson and Charness, in 1994, pointed to the crucial role of exposure to tough peer-group standards. From biographies of world leaders, Gardner, in 1995, identified general recurrent patterns of childhood experiences.

Talent, opportunity, hard work, luck, and other conditions for creativity may each be common. Combining and focusing these, however, for a decade or more is rare. Although many are called, few are chosen.

Bibliography

Bloom, B. S. (1985). Generalizations about talent development. In B. S. Bloom (Ed.), *Developing talent in young people.* New York: Ballantine.

Campbell, D. T. (1960). Blind variation and selective retention in creative thought as in other knowledge processes. *Psychological Review, 67,* 380–400.

DeWolf, A. S. (1980). *Bartlett's familiar quotations.* Boston: Little, Brown and Company.

Ericsson, K. A., & Charness, N. (1994). Expert performance: Its structure and acquisition. *American Psychologist, 49,* 725–747.

Ericsson, K. A., & Lehmann, C. (1996). Expert and exceptional performance: Evidence of maximal adaptation to task constraints. *Annual Review of Psychology, 47,* 273–305.

Fiske, A. P. (1991). *Structures of social life.* New York: The Free Press.

Gardner, H. (1995). *Leading minds: An anatomy of leadership.* New York: Basic Books.

Loehle, C. (1994). A critical path analysis of scientific productivity. *Journal of Creative Behavior, 18,* 33–47.

Merton, R. K. (1968). The Matthew effect in science. *Science, 159,* 56–63.

Simon, H. A. (19594). Some strategic considerations in the construction of social science models. In P. Lazarsfeld (Ed.), *Mathematical thinking in the social sciences.* Glencoe, IL: The Free Press.

Sloan, A. (1997, August 4). The new rich. *Newsweek,* 48–55.

Walberg, H. J., Strykowski, B. F., Rovai, E., & Hung, S. S. (1984). Exceptional performance. *Review of Educational Research, 54,* 87–112.

Walberg, H. J., & Tsai, S. L. (1984). Matthew effects in education. *American Educational Research Journal, 20,* 359–374.

Divergent Thinking

Mark A. Runco

California State University, Fullerton

Ideational Flexibility The number of themes or categories within an examinee's or respondent's ideation.

Ideational Fluency The total number of ideas given on any one divergent thinking exercise.

Ideational Originality The unusualness or uniqueness of an examinee's or respondent's ideas.

Ideational Pools These are constructed for each examinee or respondent and contain each of that individual's ideas. Judges can evaluate the pools rather than individual ideas.

Structure of Intellect J. P. Guilford's model, with 180 different kinds of intellectual processes and skills.

DIVERGENT THINKING is cognition that leads in various directions. Some of these are conventional, and some original. Because some of the resulting ideas are original, divergent thinking represents the potential for creative thinking and problem solving. Originality is not synonymous with creative thinking, but originality is undoubtedly the most commonly recognized facet of creativity.

To the degree that tests of divergent thinking are reliable and valid, they can be taken as estimates of the potential for creative thought. Not surprisingly, divergent thinking tests are among the most commonly used in creativity research. Divergent thinking tests are also used in numerous educational programs and in various organizational training packages.

I. BACKGROUND

J. P. Guilford is typically credited with distinguishing between divergent thinking and convergent thinking. (The latter is involved whenever the individual focuses on one correct or conventional idea solution. Convergent thinking is emphasized in most academic examinations and IQ tests.) He also argued cogently for creativity being a natural resource and is credited with initiating the empirical research on the topic in the 1950s and 1960s. Certainly he was the first to be explicit about the value of divergent thinking, and he did most of the early research on the topic, as part of his Structure-of-Intellect (SOI) model. (This model contained 180 cells, many of which represented divergent production, which was Guilford's own term for divergent thinking.) Several others before Guilford did, however, recognize the importance of divergent thinking—even if they did not call it that. Alfred Binet, for

Copyright © 1999 by Academic Press
All rights of reproduction in any form reserved.

example, had several open-ended questions that required his examinees to think divergently on his early tests of mental abilities. These tests were later adopted by Louis Terman of Stanford University and refined as the first IQ tests (i.e., the Stanford-Binet). Binet was working on his tests in the late 1800s.

Guilford's work represents the most comprehensive model of divergent thinking. Several other theories are, however, largely supportive of divergent thinking as an estimate of the potential for creative thought. In 1962, Sarnoff Mednick published his "Associative Basis of the Creative Process," and although he developed his own test—the Remote Associate Test, or RAT—the associative theory presented by Mednick also supported and encouraged the use of divergent thinking tests. This was especially the case because the RAT may be verbally biased. Individuals who do well on tests of verbal ability often do well on the RAT, and persons who do poorly on tests of verbal ability tend to do poorly on the RAT. [*See* ASSOCIATIVE THEORY.]

In associative terms people respond to problems by generating ideas. Often one ideas leads to another idea, which leads to another. Mednick discussed various ways that one idea could be associated with another idea, including acoustic similarity or functionality. Very importantly, he predicted that ideas found later in an associative chain are more likely to be original than those found early in that chain. This prediction has been supported a number of times—often with divergent thinking tests. This prediction from Mednick about "remote associates" is very important in a practical sense because it suggests that individuals taking a divergent thinking test or working on a problem that will benefit from creative insight should make certain that they invest some time into the task. Otherwise remote and original ideas might not be found.

II. TESTS AND EXAMPLE QUESTIONS

Guilford developed a large number of tests. Again, he was interested in the structure of the intellect and in distinguishing among 180 different kinds of thinking. (Most criticisms of Guilford's work are directed at his statistical methods, used to separate the different kinds of thinking. He often used factor analyses, for example, which required that subjective judgments be made by

the psychometrician.) The three most commonly used by Guilford were probably Plot Titles, Consequences, and Alternative Uses. Plot Titles required the examinee to think of a title for a story that was presented by Guilford. Consequences test questions asked examinees to list the consequences of some hypothetical situation (e.g., the world suddenly covered with water). Alternative Uses required the examinee to generate uses of some common object (e.g., a coat hanger or brick).

E. Paul Torrance developed the Minnesota Tests of Creative Thinking in the late 1950s, (published in 1966). It contained a wide variety of tasks. It was revised in 1974 as the Torrance Tests of Creative Thinking. Examples include Just Suppose, Product Improvement, Ask and Guess, Unusual Uses, Thinking Creatively with Words, and Thinking Creatively with Pictures. Torrance's work was extended in various directions. C. Woodruff Starkweather, for example, published materials describing the assessment of original ideation in preschool children. (The divergent thinking of young children can be assessed, though not with paper-and-pencil tests. Instead three-dimensional forms are given to them and they are asked to talk about all the things the form could be.)

III. DIVERGENT THINKING INDEXES

Divergent thinking tests are scored in different ways, although most of the time a Fluency score and an Originality score are calculated. These are surely the most common indexes of divergent thinking. Fluency represents the number of ideas given. Originality is scored in different ways. An objective score for originality might be calculated after determining the statistical infrequency of each idea. Highly infrequent ideas (e.g., those given by 5% of a particular sample) might be labeled original, each contributing to the Originality score. Unique ideas are sometimes viewed as original. Subjective scores have also been used, with judges rating the originality of ideas.

The next most common score is probably Flexibility. This is a very important score because (a) high flexibility precludes rigidity in problem solving, and (b) it guards against an artificially inflated originality score. Without a Flexibility score, one examinee could give a large number of unique ideas, all within the same category, and each would earn an Originality point even though they are not original compared to one another. If the examinee does this but Flexibility is scored, the Originality score will be high but the low Flexibility score will indicate that it is an inflated Originality score.

The various indexes of divergent thinking are usually highly intercorrelated. This has led some psychometricians to conclude that only one score is necessary. Unfortunately, when one score is used, Fluency is usually the one. It would make the most sense to use Originality since it is more closely associated with creativity in theory. Actually, it is probably best to use several scores because sophisticated statistical techniques (e.g., partialing unique variance and examination of interactions in canonical prediction equations) suggest that the different indexes may each contribute.

The scoring of the Torrance divergent thinking tasks involves Fluency, Originality, and Flexibility, defined in a way that is comparable to the definitions given above. Torrance also recommended an Elaboration index for some of the tasks. This is based on the examinee's ideation within a category or theme. A streamlined scoring system was developed for the Torrance tests in 1980. It uses a composite of the various indexes.

Not long ago Mark Runco developed a scoring system that uses "ideational pools." These pools are constructed for each examinee or respondent and contain each of that individual's ideas. They represent their entire ideational output. Judges then evaluate the pools rather than individual ideas. There are at least two advantages of this system. First is the amount of information available to judges. Second is the relatively low demand placed on their time. Judges have more information because they see everything any one examinee or respondent did—not just a small portion of it (i.e., one idea). The judges give one rating or judgment to each pool, rather than to each idea, so they need to invest much less time in the evaluations. This may preclude fatigue and allow them to concentrate better, and certainly it requires less of their time.

IV. TASK DIFFERENCES AND ADDITIONAL TESTS

The various tests differ in significant ways. The Similarities test, for example, is relatively constrained and not quite as open-ended as some of the other tasks. The Instances test seems to be wide open. The degree of openness is important in the sense that it can influence the order of test administration. If examinees have difficulty with divergent thinking, for example, which they might if they are in the midst of the "fourth grade slump" or simply have had little or no practice at generating a large number of ideas, it might be best to start with Similarities. Because of its structure and relative constraint, it might be the most familiar to these unpracticed examinees. After working on Similarities, they might be presented with a slightly less constrained task, such as Uses, and then eventually a completely unconstrained task, such as Instances. [*See* FOURTH GRADE SLUMP.]

If divergent thinking tasks are being used in a practical setting, as exercises, it is probably desirable that the skills or strategies they learn for divergent thinking generalize to the natural environment. For this reason realistic divergent thinking tasks might be given. These ask examinees to solve problems that might occur in the natural environment—but problems that are open-ended and allow fluency, originality, and flexibility. Mark Runco has developed a number of realistic tasks, such as these tasks for students:

Example problem 1

Your favorite TV show was on last night. You had so much fun watching it that you forgot to do your homework. You are about to go to school this morning when you realize that your homework is due in your first class. Uh-oh . . . what are you going to do?

For this problem, you could answer, "Tell the professor that you forgot to do your homework; try to do your homework in the car or bus on the way to school; ask your roommate, boyfriend, girlfriend, or classmate to help you finish your homework; do your homework tonight and turn it in the next time the class meets; or finish your homework first then show up late for class." There are many more answers to this problem, and all of them are legitimate.

Now turn the page, take your time, have fun, and remember to give as many ideas as possible.

Example problem 2

Your friend Pat sits next to you in class. Pat really likes to talk to you and often bothers you while you are doing your work. Sometimes he distracts you and you miss an important part of the lecture, and many times you don't finish your work because he is bothering you. What should you do? How would you solve this problem? Remember to list as many ideas and solutions as you can.

Example problem 3

It's a great day for sailing, and your buddy, Kelly, comes to your work and asks you if you want to go sailing. Unfortunately, you have a big project due tomorrow, and it requires a full day to complete. You would rather be sailing. What are you going to do? Think of as many ideas as you can!

There may be a trade-off with realistic tasks. They may motivate some examinees because they are realistic. Some examinees may not be all that interested in listing uses for a brick; but they might be more interested in listing excuses for not having completed homework! The trade-off arises because realistic tasks might be more constrained than the standard tasks, such as Instances or Uses. If this is the case the order of administration might be manipulated such that generalization to the natural environment is more likely. The order might begin with standard tasks, which are wide open, and then move to realistic tasks, which suggest that divergent thinking can be applied to problems found in the natural environment.

Runco has also developed divergent thinking tasks that reflect an examinee's ability to generate problems (rather than solutions). These are, then, problem discovery tasks rather than presented problems. This kind of task was developed because creative work often requires that the individual identify and define a problem before solving it. Problem generation tasks are open-ended and can be scored for Fluency, Originality, and Flexibility. They can be used in conjunction with standard divergent thinking tasks to obtain a more general profile of an individual's ideational skills.

Problem generation divergent thinking tasks are theoretically justified by the fact that creativity requires more than problem solving. Sometimes solving the problem is not the difficult aspect of the problem; defining it might be more difficult. And there are other important aspects of creative problem solving. Solution evaluation may be very important. Some persons seem to know an original idea when they have one, while others do not. [*See* PROBLEM FINDING.]

The problem generation scores derived from divergent thinking tests may be important for certain clinical predictions. For example, the interaction between problem generation and problem finding has been found to be highly related to suicide ideation. In particular, suicide ideation was related to the interaction between (high) Fluency scores on problem generation tasks and (low) Flexibility scores on the problem solving task. This interaction was expected because it indicates that the individual is aware of many problems (as seen in his or her Fluency) but not aware of many different solutions (as seen in the low Flexibility). Significantly, this interaction between problem generation and problem solving was more strongly related to suicide ideation than depression measures, which are typically quite respectable predictors of suicide ideation. [*See* SUICIDE.]

V. PSYCHOMETRIC ISSUES

The most critical psychometric issue is discriminant validity. This relates to the distinctiveness of divergent thinking. Is it distinctive or does it overlap with other forms of ability? Is it related to IQ? Can we predict divergent thinking ability from those measures of traditional intelligence?

Answers to these questions varied in the 1960s. In one seminal investigation Jacob Getzels and Philip Jackson found moderate overlap between their measures of creative potential, including divergent thinking tests, and measures of academic achievement. This brought the discriminant validity of divergent thinking tests into question. However, three years later, Michael Wallach and Nathan Kogan administered divergent thinking tests under conditions that were dramatically different from the conditions typical of testing. Indeed, they told the examinees—school children—that the divergent thinking tests were games, and they avoided referring to tasks as tests. They allowed a great deal of time and were explicit about the need to generate a number of responses (rather than one correct response). Under these conditions the divergent thinking tests did display more than adequate discriminant validity.

The issue of discriminant validity is important in

a practical sense because it indicates that divergent thinking tests provide information that would otherwise be unavailable. In behavioral terms it means that if we rely on tests of traditional ability we will overlook children who have outstanding divergent thinking abilities (but only moderate or even low IQs and academic aptitude).

The relationship of divergent thinking with IQ and traditional intelligence seems to vary at different levels of ability. There may even be a threshold of intelligence that is necessary for creative ideation. This would make sense because some basic information processing capacity is necessary for associative and divergent thinking. Additionally, many tests of divergent thinking require that the examinee has some basic knowledge, and that too suggests a modicum of traditional intelligence. [*See* INTELLIGENCE.]

The "threshold theory" suggests that some traditional ability is necessary for effective divergent thinking. The early estimates were an IQ of approximately 120, but this figure is probably just about meaningless, given that the average IQ in the population is on the rise, and given questions about the validity of the IQ. Still, the concept of a threshold does make good sense, even if we cannot pinpoint a specific IQ.

The threshold may be viewed graphically, as would be the case if divergent thinking scores were graphed as a function of IQ levels. When this is done a triangle of data points appears in the bivariate scatterplot. The top of the triangle is pointed at the origin of the graph, with the scatter of data spreading as IQ levels increase. If that same scatterplot is bisected perpendicularly to the X axis (and at the hypothetical threshold) and once perpendicularly to the Y axis, four quadrants are formed. Empirical studies find some persons in the first quadrant, with low divergent thinking and low IQ. There are also persons with high IQs and low divergent thinking. There are a few persons with high divergent thinking and high IQ, but no one with low IQ and high divergent thinking. This is because of the minimum threshold of IQ which is necessary but not sufficient for divergent thinking.

There are persons with high IQs and low divergent thinking, which again supports the discriminant validity of the divergent thinking tests. It also suggests that individuals who are extremely good at the convergent thinking and memorization required for exceptional IQs may be at a serious disadvantage for divergent thinking and creative thinking. [*See* GIFTEDNESS AND CREATIVITY.]

A second critical issue is that of the predictive validity of divergent thinking tests. Here again, results have been quite varied. This is not much of a surprise, however, given that creativity can be expressed in so many different domains (some of which may not depend very heavily, if at all, on the kind of divergent thinking that is tapped by tests of divergent thinking). Moreover, divergent thinking tests do not guarantee actual performance any more than any other controlled assessment. As noted above, divergent thinking tests are *estimates* of the *potential* for creative thought. The biggest obstacle is the "criterion problem." There is no widely accepted and universally applicable criterion of creative performance with which to give divergent thinking tests—or any other test of creativity—a fair evaluation. Divergent thinking tests have demonstrated only moderate, and sometimes disappointing, predictive validity. When fluency, originality, and flexibility are all taken into account, predictive validity coefficients have reached .55.

VI. CONCLUSIONS

Divergent thinking tests are grounded in sound theory. In particular, both associative theory and Guilford's own SOI model support their use. Divergent thinking tests have generated many interesting research findings. Divergent thinking has been used in studies of the fourth grade slump, for example, and in investigations of the relationship of creativity with suicide ideation. Much of this research is reviewed in other articles in this encyclopedia. The corpus of research is advantageous in the sense that the strengths and weaknesses of these tests are well known. Interpretations of test results are quite easy, given the large literature on divergent thinking. Another strength is the practicality of the tests. They can be used in various settings (e.g., educational, clinical, and organizational) and can be used as exercises or assessments. As noted above, when used as assessments, they are best viewed as estimates of the potential for creative thinking and problem solving.

Bibliography

Guilford, J. P. (1968). *Intelligence, creativity, and their educational implications.* San Diego, CA: EDITS.

Runco, M. A. (Ed.). (1991). *Divergent thinking.* Norwood, NJ: Ablex.

Runco, M. A. (in press). *Divergent thinking and creative ideation.* Cresskill, NJ: Hampton.

Diversity, Cultural

Giselle B. Esquivel and Kristen M. Peters

Fordham University

Cognitive Style The method in which an individual is able to process information, acquire knowledge, and evaluate experiences through mental activities, such as thinking, reasoning, and problem solving. There is a diverse array of cognitive styles as a result of individual differences, which are a product of genetic and environmental or cultural experiences.

Creativity A multifaceted human experience involving the interaction between predisposing genetic factors and environmental or sociocultural influences. All individuals have the potential for some form of creative expression. However, creativity is manifested in ways that are unique to the personality of the individual as well as consistent with his or her cultural context. Creativity may be studied in terms of personality characteristics, ways of processing, specific domains, and subjective outcomes and objective products. This article emphasizes the influence of culture on all of these aspects of creativity.

Culturally and Linguistically Diverse Individuals who are immigrants or who have attained varying degrees of acculturation, but whose traditional culture continues to exert an influence on their values and styles of thinking and behavior.

Culture Defined as the organization of values, ideas, and behaviors shared by a particular group of people. As a group, people use modal patterns for perceiving, interpreting, and relating to their environment.

Developmental Stages Developmental stages identify behaviors at particular age levels and attempt to account for gradual changes of an individual's behaviors (cognitive, emotional, motor, and social) by describing a progress based on a specific theoretical framework.

Divergent Thinking As defined by Guilford, divergent thinking is the generation of information from given information, where the emphasis is on the variety and quantity.

Diversity Cultural factors (and related linguistic and cognitive style differences) that influence the development and manifestation of creative abilities in individuals.

Linguistic Diversity Proficiency in a language other than standard English. The various stages of language proficiency may move from monolingual dominance of native language to incipient second language learning and may advance into balanced dominance of both native and host country language (English). Linguistic diversity is related to differences in style of creative expression (e.g., content and nature of verbal humor). Balanced bilingualism has been associated with cognitive and creative advantages.

Multiple Intelligences Gardner's theory of multiple intelligences is a multifaceted approach to describing intelligence. Gardner proposes that there are various types of intelligences including linguistic, logical–mathematical, spatial, musical, bodily kinesthetic, intrapersonal, and interpersonal.

Copyright © 1999 by Academic Press
All rights of reproduction in any form reserved.

Tests of Creativity The main uses of creativity tests are for identifying creatively gifted individuals for specific enrichment programs, for research purposes, and for career counseling. Formal evaluations of creativity that have been cross-culturally validated include the Torrances' Tests of Creativity and Mary Meeker's Structure of Intellect (SOI) (a measure based on Guilford's Model).

DIVERSITY, within the context of creativity, has been defined as the cultural factors and related linguistic and cognitive style differences that influence the development and expression of creative abilities in individuals. Attributing to the influx of immigrants to the United States from various countries, the definition of American cultural diversity includes those individuals who are from non-Western cultures and individuals of differing religions, customs, and languages. Typically, culturally diverse individuals have been referred to as being of "minority" status. However, throughout U.S. history, the "minority" label has changed perspectives. In the 1960s, for example, minority individuals were considered to be the "disadvantaged" group characterized by race, ethnicity, and socioeconomic status. More recently, minority individuals are divergent from the majority culture specifically in terms of their language and other social–cultural factors but are recognized as contributing to the American culture in unique ways. This article discusses the conceptual link between diversity and creativity, its implications for the identification and enhancement of creative abilities in individuals, particularly children, of culturally diverse backgrounds.

I. CREATIVITY AND CULTURAL DIVERSITY

The cross-cultural psychology literature has studied extensively the relationship between culture and various aspects of human behavior. In general, it has been well established that the concept of culture has a strong influence on a number of psychological variables. Furthermore, it has also been shown that some previously held assumptions about the universality of certain aspects of human behavior, such as developmental stages, may vary across cultural settings. [*See* DEVELOPMENTAL TRENDS IN CREATIVE ABILITIES AND POTENTIALS.]

In contrast, the study of culture specifically in relation to creativity has received limited attention. Creativity research has typically focused on examining individuals' psychological processes of creativity, while excluding such factors as social determinants of creativity. In effect, creativity, according to Csikszentmihalyi, should be considered as the dynamic between the person, the field, and the domain that is affected by the individual's social system and the culture. Currently, research is beginning to place more emphasis on examining bilingualism, and, linguistic and cognitive style diversity in relation to creativity.

Some major developments in this area may be originally attributed to E. Paul Torrance, whose pioneering work on cultural views of creativity led the way for future studies linking cultural diversity with creativity. Although creativity is manifestly a universal human experience, it is important to study how and to what extent culture influences its expression, without neglecting commonalties and within-group differences. An understanding of creativity from a multicultural perspective is critical, given the value that is placed on it and the desire to foster creativity among American youth in a democratic, pluralistic society.

II. THEORETICAL AND RESEARCH PERSPECTIVES

A. Culture and Creativity

The critical role of culture on creative abilities went unrecognized prior to the 1960s. Before that time, creativity was closely identified with the study of high intelligence, which, in turn, was attributed primarily to hereditary factors. The work of Francis Galton, as reflected in *Hereditary Genius,* published in 1869, emphasized the genetic aspects of individual differences in intellectual functioning. Similarly, Lewis Terman's longitudinal study of gifted children, begun in the 1920s, was based on a definition of giftedness and creativity as high performance on standardized tests of intelligence. The beginning of a shift from a unidimensional to a multidimensional perspective of intelligence may be attributed to Louis Thurstone, who posited in 1938 that there were multiple talents or primary abilities that could not be measured by a single test of intelligence. Furthermore, J. P. Guilford's structure of intellect model in 1956, which included the concept of divergent thinking abilities, provided an important turning point for viewing creativity as distinct from intelligence. [*See* DIVERGENT THINKING; INTELLIGENCE.]

The concept that creativity is a discrete construct was advanced by Getzels and Jackson in their 1962 landmark study. These researchers found that adolescents who were considered highly creative were not necessarily high academic achievers or the most intelligent. The role of nonintellectual factors on creative abilities, including sociocultural and environmental influences, continued to be studied in the 1960s by other researchers (e.g., Sato, Strang).

An often cited quotation from Torrance's writings, "What is honored in a culture will be cultivated there," concerns the influences of cultural differences on creativity. Torrance studied a number of diverse cultures and found differences in how creativity was defined, valued, and expressed. Based on his observations of economically disadvantaged black children, Torrance found that they exhibited unique creative characteristics. The creative positives of these children included the abilities to express feelings and emotions, improvise with commonplace materials, articulate effectively in role playing activities, engage in creative movement and dance, exhibit richness of imagery in language, figural fluency, and flexibility, and express enjoyment and skill in group problem solving. [*See* DEFINITIONS OF CREATIVITY.]

Other researchers, such as Baldwin, Bernal, and Kitano, have continued to focus their research on identifying gifted and creative characteristics among specific cultural groups. This research is of growing importance as analyses of gifted programs within the United States reveal an underrepresentation of minority groups as members of programs in the public school system.

Additional theorists, such as Robert Sternberg, have emphasized the contextual components of intelligence and the role of sociocultural environments on the human expression of abilities, including creativity. Howard Gardner's theory of multiple intelligences (i.e., linguistic, logical and mathematical, visual and spatial, kinesthetic, interpersonal, and intrapersonal) also has enhanced the concept that sociocultural factors that contribute to determining the diverse manifestations of intelligence and creativity. Further, contemporary em-

phasis is placed on how creativity is expressed in various specific domains rather than on the absolute level of creative ability. Specific attention is being given to the diversity of talents and distinctly different styles of creative problem solving (e.g., Kirton, Feldhusen, Treffinger, and Selby) and to specific forms of expression in culturally and linguistically diverse (CLD) populations (e.g., Bernal, Esquivel). Finally, it is important to consider the impact of individual diversity and culture, specifically in terms of language and cognitive style. [*See* MULTIPLE INTELLIGENCES.]

B. Bilingualism and Creativity

Research in the area of linguistic differences and bilingualism has taken a similar course in relation to the study of cultural factors on creativity Studies prior to the 1930s tended to perpetuate the view that there were negative effects associated with bilingualism and cognitive and academic functioning. However, beginning in the 1960s, studies by Pearl and Lambert, and others, began to reflect the opposite of the deficit view of bilingualism. Bilingual students showed a number of cognitive and creative strengths. In 1970 Landry examined creativity in bilingual children and found that when a second language was learned at a critical age, performance on measures of figural and verbal fluency, flexibility, and originality was significantly better than for the monolingual group. In 1974 Carringer studied divergent thinking in bilingual children for whom Spanish was their first language and found similar results. Earlier studies had failed to account for the different degrees of bilingualism resulting in methodological flaws. Furthermore, early studies may have utilized measures of functioning that were internally biased against individuals whose second language was English. Recent research has continued to substantiate the fact that students who become "balanced" bilingual or proficient in more than one language show higher metacognitive awareness, originality, divergent thinking, cognitive flexibility, linguistic humor (e.g., in the form of puns), and other signs of creativity.

Beyond the advantages of bilingualism, it is important to study the effects of linguistic style differences on creative expression. Catherine Collier suggested that some languages (e.g., romance) lend themselves to greater embellishment and elaboration, whereas others (e.g., Germanic) are more precise and direct. These differences may manifest themselves in ways of processing verbal information and in the quality of creative products. For example, creative writing of Hispanic students may be characterized by ornamentation. Additionally, humor, a creative characteristic, may vary across cultures based on cultural meaning and semantic differences. In general, research in psycholinguistics (e.g., Cummins, Krashen) points to a strong link with affective, cognitive, and creative processes. The study of bilingualism is increasingly relevant as the numbers of bilingual and ethnically diverse students increase in U.S. schools. [*See* PSYCHOLINGUISTICS.]

C. Cognitive Style and Creativity

Facets of diversity may also be examined through the interaction of culture and creativity in the area of cognitive styles. A cognitive style is the method in which an individual is able to process information, acquire knowledge, and evaluate experiences through mental activities such as thinking, reasoning, and problem solving. A cognitive style is a unique characteristic, or a personality trait that develops as a result of an individual's genetic inheritance and the experiences and interactions of the individual in the external environment and, more specifically, culture. Creativity is linked to cognitive style in the sense that creativity is an expression of the ways in which information in the environment is processed and manipulated.

Originally, the concept of cognitive style has roots in the cognitive-developmental theory of Jean Piaget. In the 1950s, Piaget's research focused specifically on mental intelligence and cognitive development. Piaget viewed development as a continuous process that begins when an individual enters the world and, thus, the environment and culture have an impact on the ways in which individuals perceive the world and interact within society. [*See* PIAGET, JEAN.]

Stemming from Piaget's work, further research began to examine the diversity of cognitive style and to define these styles primarily in terms of a bipolar continuum. Work exploring the polarity of cognitive styles began in 1958 with the work of Jerome Kagan. Kagan defined conceptual tempo as a specific cognitive style that was rooted in the notion of reflection (the tendency to reflect on alternative solutions) versus impulsivity (the tendency to respond impulsively without sufficient consideration of the problem). According to Kagan, it is conceptual tempo that can be considered a source of individual differences. Other work examining the polarity of individual differences in cognitive style continued throughout the 1960s and 1970s. In 1962 Herman Witkin and colleagues formulated the theory of field dependence versus field independence, which refers to how an individual utilizes the perceptual field in organizing information. Additional research by A. R. Luria, in 1973, examined how information is processed either simultaneously or sequentially. In 1975 Das and Moll found how the selection of the cognitive process is dependent on not only the type of task involved but the individual's preference for informational processing and the range and variety of past experiences. This early literature has attempted to define cognitive style as the methods in which an individual processes information from a dichotomous perspective.

Research in the 1980s and 1990s turned from evaluating cognitive style on a bipolar level to a multidimensional level, as cognitive processing began to be viewed as more complex in nature. Robert Sternberg's three facet model of creativity incorporates intelligence, cognition, and motivation. In 1988 Sternberg defined cognitive-learning style as a preferred way of utilizing abilities and not simply the possession of actual abilities. Preferences may be highly influenced by social learning and cultural differences.

Utilizing theories of individual differences within human cognition, research involving individuals of different cultures and ethnicity began to attempt to identify unique styles of cognition among culturally diverse populations. In Torrance's 1967 study comparing white and black children on divergent thinking, it was found that black children scored higher than white children on measures of figural fluency, flexibility, and originality. This study was further supported by Price-Williams and Ramirez in 1977. These researchers found that Mexican-American and black males scored higher than Anglo males on fluency and flexibility measures.

The emerging sociocultural perspective of the research literature in the area of cognitive style is based on the notion that there is a relationship between society, culture, learning, and development. This perspective is translated into studies by Rita Dunn and her associates, which established that there are numerous cognitive and social variables that influence learning in diverse populations. In 1990 Dunn, Dunn, and Price developed the comprehensive Learning Style Inventory (LSI) as a tool for understanding diversity in learning and cognitive style. According to Dunn and Dunn in 1993, cognitive style is composed of an individual's unique reactions to elements of instruction when learning information. These elements include the immediate environment, emotionality, sociological preferences, physiological traits, and cognitive-psychological inclination. In general, the construct of cognitive style has progressed from being viewed as a simple independent variable toward a conceptualization of style as part of a cultural process.

Research has been further stimulated by the high rate of academic underachievement among minorities in the United States and the assumption that culturally diverse populations learn differently. In 1990 Dunn and Griggs reported distinct cultural differences using the LSI in terms of preferred cognitive strategies. These researches analyzed the learning styles of at-risk high school students and found that these students utilize a processing style and instructional strategies that differ significantly from those who are more successful academically. Overall, differences in learning style, specifically the patterns of used and preferred strategies, have been found in the form of modal patterns, although there may be more within-group than between-group differences.

Furthermore, according to Collier, cultures tend to reinforce certain styles through socialization. For example, in the educational system, rewards are given for analytic rather than relational forms of learning. Students who do not exhibit analytic style in their academic performance and have an alternative style that may contrast with the teacher's style will be at a distinct disadvantage in the classroom. Societal influences affect development of particular cognitive styles and preferences for methods of processing information.

The role of culture also has been considered by Sternberg and Lubart, who believe that cognitive style is a component of creativity. Just as cognitive style may be influenced by socialization and environmental factors, so may creative style. Research by Darcy in 1989 focused specifically on the link between cognitive styles and creativity. In reference to Witkin's field dependence-independence theory, it was found that independent individuals were considered to be more creative, in that these individuals were better able to function independently of the perceptual field. Creative individuals have more cognitive flexibility in the ways in which they process information and solve problems. Additionally, Gary Davis promoted the perspective that life experiences and family structure can foster creative potential. Cultural blocks, such as rules, traditions and social norms, may hinder the expression of creativity and the development of flexible cognitive style.

Learning and cognitive style research is one approach to understanding individual differences and creativity. Currently, research needs to continue to explore cognitive style because the concept is quite relevant to psychological constructs. In particular, it is important to consider cultural diversity and the degree to which an individual identifies with his or her ethnic background in considering the relationship of individual differences to cognitive style and creativity. [*See* COGNITIVE STYLE AND CREATIVITY.]

III. IDENTIFICATION

A central assumption in the identification of creativity in culturally and linguistically diverse (CLD) individuals is that environmental, sociological, cultural, and linguistic differences affect the way in which creativity is expressed. Consequently, when attempting to identify creative ability in CLD students, there is a need to use approaches that are capable of tapping into the unique creative strengths and the ways in which creativity is manifested in diverse populations. These approaches, however, should be used with flexibility to avoid stereotyping individuals.

In general, CLD students, including blacks, Hispanics, Native Americans, and Asians of lower socioeconomic status, are underrepresented in programs for the creative and gifted. Reasons for this underrepresentation specifically include the narrow way in which creativity and giftedness have traditionally been defined, inappropriate methods and test procedures utilized, and the limited focus of the identification process itself.

More and more researchers are advocating that the identification of creativity should be based on a broad definition of what it means to be creative. In terms of CLD individuals, special consideration needs to be given to cognitive style and cultural factors that affect the expression of creative abilities. In essence, all individuals possess diverse creative abilities. Therefore, the aim is not to "identify" only the highly creative according to one set standard of what it means to be creative (e.g., high intelligence), but rather to assess in a suitable manner the diversity of creative abilities according to a variety of domains (e.g., visual and spatial, kinesthetic, mathematical).

Creativity within a multicultural perspective is more broadly defined as a multifaceted construct that may be exhibited through (a) diverse characteristics, (b) different ways of processing information and problem solving, (c) a variety of domains, (e.g., music, dance, or science), and (d) a wide range of subjective outcomes (e.g., sense of fulfillment and self-worth) and objective products (e.g., a painting, music score, or literary composition). Based on this definition, the assessment and identification process for CLD pupils will include multiple criteria, a variety of sources of nomination (e.g., bilingual and English as a Second Language [ESL] teachers, parents), and pluralistic assessment methods.

There are numerous ways in which creative characteristics may be assessed in CLD students, including the use of culture-specific behavioral observations in various settings, anecdotal reports from a number of sources, biographical inventories, acculturation scales, and sociometric measures, including same-culture peers as raters. The assessment needs to be accomplished with an understanding of the culture of the individual or group in question. For example, some cultures value personality characteristics of humor and cleverness in a social context over independent behaviors. Other cultures reinforce kinesthetic forms of expression (e.g., loud laughter, touching) that may be considered rude and disruptive, rather than creative channels, in mainstream culture. Some cultures (e.g., Oriental) show regard for quiet but influential leaders over assertive leadership styles. Current methods of identification could overlook these culturally different characteristics as signs of potential creativity.

In reference to past literature and research studies in the field, creativity and the creative process have been assessed in terms of divergent thinking, problem solving, cognitive flexibility, critical thinking, ideation, fan-

tasy, visual imagery, and other information-processing modes. The issue of preferences is also important to be considered in the realm of diversity and creativity. For example, some individuals are more creative (i.e., offer many ideas) in cooperative learning situations than in situations that are competitive in nature. Additionally, some individuals prefer to solve problems in a reflective and systematic manner, whereas others prefer a more intuitive and spontaneous approach. Learning style inventories may help determine the modalities of strength and the preferred cognitive styles and learning modes of the individual and of specific cultural groups. Very few paper-and-pencil tests are relatively free from cultural bias. However, the Torrance Tests of Creative Thinking have been effective in identifying creativity in CLD students. Bilingual administrations, untimed tests, and nonverbal forms of tests are useful for students with limited English proficiency. [*See* APPENDIX II: TESTS OF CREATIVITY.]

In addition, methods for assessing subjective outcomes and experiences may include personal and parental interviews and self-report measures. Again, it is important that this assessment be conducted with cultural sensitivity and understanding. Products, portfolios, and other objective outcomes in a variety of domains (e.g., art, creative writings, or science projects) may be reviewed and assessed by content experts who also have cultural expertise or by individuals with input from cultural consultants (individuals familiar with the culture in question). Consideration needs to be given to culture-specific aspects of the content and quality of outcomes. For example, there may be sociocultural difference in materials used (e.g., commonplace versus expensive), aesthetic values (e.g., choice of colors), manner of expression (e.g., poetic versus analytic writing style), functional utility (e.g., for the common good versus the individual advantage), or emphasis on process versus product (e.g., value on subjective versus objective outcomes). Criteria for what is considered creative need to incorporate cultural components. However, the intent is not to stereotype but to consider cultural factors with flexibility, showing respect for different levels of acculturation and individual differences.

In general, the identification process needs to be closely linked to intervention and implementation of enrichment programs. Caution needs to be taken in considering the role of diversity, particularly when implementing educational programs and identifying creativity in children. The main purpose of identification should be to provide students with opportunities for enhancing their creative development.

IV. EDUCATIONAL IMPLICATIONS

The assumptions that all individuals have the potential for creativity, that creativity may be expressed in diverse ways, and that creative abilities may be enhanced have implications for more comprehensive educational approaches than currently exist. Broader efforts in the area of intervention are represented by such models as Joseph Renzulli's schoolwide enrichment triad model and John Feldheusen's talent identification and development in education model, both of which attempt to reach a greater number of students in order to enhance their areas of strength. Donald Treffinger has emphasized the need for educators to develop and support independent learning methods and for instructional environments in the regular classroom to be more responsive to the development of talent and creativity in all students. Similarly, Ernesto Bernal has suggested that CLD students be provided with in-class accommodations and other diversified opportunities that are sensitive to their cultural and linguistic background. In addition, unique characteristics of learning style are found in the "gifted" as well as underachieving students, students in special education, and others at risk for school failure. For students to achieve at their potential, they should be taught in an environment and with the approaches that complement their specific talents, potentials, and learning styles.

There is limited research on creative development interventions specific to CLD students, but a number of researchers (e.g., Bernal, Cummins, De Avila, or Ortiz) recommend as effective those pedagogical approaches that incorporate bilingual interaction, a multicultural curriculum component, experiential methods, mentoring from cultural role models, special guidance, and parental involvement. Education in the United States should be sensitive to the cultural differences of the students and be flexible to enable all students to develop their creativity potential.

V. CONCLUSION

As a result of cultural plurality within the United States, research in the area of creativity has focused on determining the impact of cultural differences on creative expression. Different cultures view creativity along a variety of dimensions. The value placed on creativity may be attributed to the reward system and socialization process of the particular culture.

Although it has been supported that diversity in creativity and cognitive style exists between and among ethnic and cultural groups, research also suggests that there are as many within-group as between-group differences. Continuing research will focus on determining the universality of the creative process and the ways it is expressed in differing cultures and countries.

In general, as the understanding of creativity continues to grow, it is important to consider the diverse manifestation of creativity, including the role that culture plays in its expression. In essence, attending to cultural diversity in creativity is another way of being sensitive to the uniqueness of each individual.

Bibliography

Barkaa, J. H., & Bernal, E. M. (1991). Gifted education for bilingual and limited English proficient students. *Gifted Child Quarterly, 35,* 144–147.

Kessler, C., & Quinn, M. E. (1987). Language minority children's linguistic and cognitive creativity. *Journal of Multilingual and Multicultural Development, 8,* 173–186.

Lopez, E. C., Esquivel, G. B., & Houtz, J. C. (1993). Exploring the creativity skills of gifted culturally and linguistically diverse students. *Creativity Research Journal, 6,* 401–412.

Runco, M. A. (1993). *Creativity as an educational objective for disadvantaged students* (Creativity: Research-based Decision-Making Series, Report No. 9306). Storrs, CT: University of Connecticut, National Research Center on the Gifted and Talented. (ERIC Document Reproduction Service No. ED 363 074).

Treffinger, D. J., & Selby, E. C. (1993). Giftedness, creativity, and learning style: Exploring the connections. In R. M. Milgram, R. Dunn, & G. E. Price (Eds.), *Teaching and counseling gifted and talented adolescents.* Westport, CT: Praeger.

Domains of Creativity

John Baer

Rider University

Divergent Thinking A kind of thinking often associated with creativity that involves the generation of varied, original, or unusual ideas in response to an open-ended question or task.

Domain The set of representations that underlie and support thinking in a specific area of knowledge; also, any specific area of knowledge.

Domain Specificity A theory that argues that the skills, traits, or knowledge that underlie successful (or creative) performance in a given domain are largely unrelated to the skills, traits, or knowledge that underlie successful (or creative) performance in other domains.

Microdomain A subset within a larger domain, such as the microdomain of poetry within the larger linguistic domain.

Modularity A theory of domain specificity that claims there can be no exchange of representations among different domains—that information is encapsulated within its given domain.

Task Specificity A theory that argues that the skills, traits, or knowledge that underlie successful (or creative) performance in different microdomains within the same more general domain are different and largely unrelated.

Theories of domain specificity argue that cognitive development proceeds independently in different DOMAINS of knowledge—such as linguistic, artistic, musical, and mathematical knowledge—and that the skills and understandings that underlie successful performance in each domain are distinct and unrelated to the essential skills and understandings central to other domains. There is a growing body of evidence that suggests that creativity is domain specific. This article will explain what is meant by domain specificity, provide an overview of the evidence for domain specificity in creativity, and discuss the implications of domain specificity for creativity theory, testing, and training.

I. INTRODUCTION

Single-factor theories of creativity, like single-factor theories of intelligence, are very appealing in that they allow one to paint the full picture of creativity—or at least a large part of it—in a single brushstroke. If creativity were a general trait or a single set of cognitive skills that influenced creative performance of all kinds, it would be much easier to understand, train, and test creativity.

Although single-factor theories of creativity have

591

Copyright © 1999 by Academic Press
All rights of reproduction in any form reserved.

been popular, there is growing evidence that they may not explain creative performance across a wide variety of content domains as well as more narrowly defined, domain-specific theories. Just as the thinking of many psychologists about intelligence and cognitive development in general has moved in recent years toward more domain-specific and less all-encompassing theories (although the case is by no means closed), so it has been with creativity. In fact, there is considerable evidence suggesting that the skills underlying creative performance are not even so general as to span the many tasks that make up such common content areas as the verbal, mathematical, or artistic domains. This task-specific (or "microdomain") view of creativity argues that the skills that lead to creativity on one task in a broadly defined domain of knowledge, such as writing, are not the same (and show little overlap with) the skills that lead to creativity in another task within the same writing domain. Thus, for example, poetry-writing and story-writing creativity may not rely on the same set of cognitive skills.

Such a fragmented approach to creativity, in which every domain (or even every narrowly defined task within a domain) relies on its own unique underlying set of traits or skills, is naturally less satisfying than a grand, all-encompassing theory of creativity. The most widely held general view of creativity, which posits divergent thinking to be a general, domain-transcending skill applicable in all areas of creative endeavor, has been popular in creativity theory, training, and testing for many years. And despite doubts raised regarding the possible validity of *any* general theory of creativity by new research suggesting that creativity must be domain specific, divergent thinking theory continues to be used widely in both education and psychology (and especially in creativity testing, where it has virtually no competition).

After outlining the evidence for domains of creativity, this article will conclude by examining the implications of domain specificity of creativity for creativity theory, testing, and training. It will also consider how a newly emerging metatheory of creativity rooted in a modified divergent thinking theory and that incorporates a domain-specific view of creative-thinking skills can replace earlier general theories as a unifying idea in creativity theory, training, and testing.

II. DOMAINS AND DOMAIN SPECIFICITY

The concept of a domain as a set of representations underlying (a) comprehension of a specific area of knowledge and (b) performance of the tasks associated with that domain is, at the conceptual level, a fairly clear one. Applying this definition in a way that demarcates domain boundaries can be a much more contentious exercise, however.

In 1983 Gardner published *Frames of Mind: The Theory of Multiple Intelligences,* and the seven domains (or, as Gardner termed them, "intelligences") that he described have become familiar to many readers and quite influential in many fields, especially the education community. Gardner distinguished the following intelligences:

- Linguistic intelligence (abilities having to do with understanding and using the sounds, rhythms, and meanings of words and the functions of language)
- Musical intelligence (abilities having to do with understanding and employing rhythm, pitch, timbre, and musical expressiveness)
- Logical–mathematical intelligence (abilities having to do with finding logical and numerical patterns and producing chains of reasoning)
- Spatial intelligence (abilities having to do with understanding the visual-spatial world and transformations within that world)
- Bodily kinesthetic intelligence (abilities having to do with control of one's body movements)
- Interpersonal intelligence (abilities having to do with understanding and responding appropriately to the feelings, moods, and motivations of others)
- Intrapersonal intelligence (abilities having to do with understanding one's own feelings, moods, and motivations; with assessing accurately one's own strengths and weaknesses; and with drawing upon such knowledge to guide one's behavior)

Gardner's classification is based on such evidence as (a) the effects of brain trauma, such as strokes, that influence the functioning in one domain but not others; (b) the existence of prodigies and autistic savants who show extreme abilities in one domain but not others;

(c) psychometric evidence that suggests consistency among the skills that lie within a given domain and independence between the skills that fall in different domains; and (d) the existence of a set of core information-processing operations that can deal with specific kinds of input.

Gardner's seven intelligences (which have in his recent writing increased to eight with the addition of "naturalist's intelligence") are not the only way that domains have been conceptualized, but they will suffice as an illustration of the idea of broadly defined cognitive domains (and they are the most widely followed classificatory scheme at present). The term "domain" is often also used to refer to general fields of knowledge or ways of knowing without specifying boundaries between domains as clearly as Gardner has done, and the breadth of what may be properly called a domain is often not clearly defined. For example, a child's understanding of gravity may be viewed as a different domain of knowledge than her understanding of object permanence, number, animacy, and so on. Overall, as the idea that development is domain specific has increased in popularity among psychologists, the number of such domains has also tended to increase, and the breadth of the hypothesized domains has tended to shrink. [*See* MULTIPLE INTELLIGENCES.]

Some writers, such as Karmiloff-Smith (whose 1992 book *Beyond Modularity: A Developmental Perspective on Cognitive Science* is one of the clearest accounts available of the idea of domain-specific development), use the term "microdomain" to refer to subsets of skills that seem to go together and yet have somewhat separate developmental histories. The use of pronouns, for example, can be considered a microdomain within the larger linguistic domain, and counting skills can be thought of as a microdomain within the larger mathematical domain.

An important area of disagreement among those who argue for the significance of distinct domains of knowledge is the possibility of interaction among the skills and knowledge that make up the various cognitive domains. Some theorists argue for strict modularity; under such an interpretation, each information-processing module is encapsulated and cannot make use of representations from other modules. One oft-cited example of such an encapsulated module is the perceptual system, which is at least relatively immune from input from other modules (and thus one's beliefs or preferences cannot interfere, or can interfere at most only slightly, with what one sees or hears—and the fact that one does not want or expect to see an elephant in one's living room will in no way interfere with actually seeing or hearing an elephant if one should appear there!). Strict modularity is an extreme version of domain specificity, but modularity and information encapsulation are not essential features of theories of domain specificity.

III. EVIDENCE FOR DOMAINS OF CREATIVITY

Any evidence that there are different cognitive domains or "intelligences," even when that evidence is collected with an indifference to creative performance, is indirect evidence that creativity is domain specific. This is true for the simple reason that creative performance must occur in *some* content domain, and if the basic cognitive skills underlying performance in that domain are domain specific, this will necessarily have an impact on creative performance in that domain as well as the performance of more ordinary tasks in the domain (tasks unrelated to creativity).

The larger battle about domain specificity—which includes, for example, disagreements about the degree to which generic intellectual competencies exist and can be tested, as is assumed in standard IQ testing—is beyond the scope of this article. The evidence for domain specificity of creativity goes beyond the assertion that different content domains rely on different basic skills for performance of all kinds, however. Arguments for the domain specificity of creativity are based primarily on research into the creativity of actual creative products, such as works of art, and not on the testing of specific intellectual abilities associated with various content domains. This evidence suggests that levels of creative performance on tasks in one domain are essentially unrelated to levels of creative performance on tasks in other domains, and even that creativity in performing one kind of task within a broad cognitive domain may be unrelated to creativity in performing other tasks within the same domain.

A widely used technique in creativity research is to ask subjects to create something, and then to have groups of experts in that field evaluate the creativity of those products. This "consensual assessment technique," which Amabile developed and validated in 1982 and which has been used successfully in scores of studies since then, is based on the idea that whatever creativity may be, judgments of the creativity of work in a given field are most appropriately made by recognized experts in that field. Thus the creativity of poems is best judged by poets and poetry critics, and the creativity of cosmological theories is best judged by cosmologists. Although at the "cutting edge" of any field there may be many disagreements about the creativity of a particular work or idea, assessments of more "garden variety" creativity—the kind of everyday creativity that occurs in most psychological studies of creativity—tend to produce fairly uniform judgments among appropriate experts. Thus by asking a group of artists and art critics to independently evaluate the creativity of a group of collages, or a group of fiction writers and critics to independently evaluate the creativity of a group of stories, a researcher can obtain a reliable and valid measurement of the creativity of a group of creative products. [See CONSENSUAL ASSESSMENT.]

Several studies using subjects of diverse ages have shown that when subjects are asked to produce more than one creative product—such as collages, poems, stories, and mathematical puzzles—the creativity ratings of the products of each individual vary significantly. In fact, there is often little or no relationship between the creativity ratings a subject's various works of different types receive, despite the fact that the level of one's creative performance on a given task is highly predictive of performance on the *same* task, even when the second work is produced as much as a year after the first.

It should be noted that this lack of relationship among creativity ratings on different products is not only true across domains—such as the linguistic and artistic domains—but also, in at least some cases, within domains. A prime example of such within-domain task specificity is the lack of correlation between poetry- and story-writing creativity that has been observed in several studies.

Approaching the question of domain specificity of creativity from a creativity training perspective, it has also been shown that training in divergent thinking, which is the most common kind of creativity training exercise, can also be targeted to specific domains, or even to specific tasks within domains. For example, divergent thinking training using only poetry-relevant exercises—such as brainstorming words with similar beginning sounds (alliteration) or words that can stand for or represent a given thing or idea (metaphor)—tends to increase poetry-writing creativity far more than story-writing creativity. [See DIVERGENT THINKING.]

An important source of evidence *against* domain specificity of creativity—evidence favoring domain generality of creativity—comes from studies using self-report scales of creativity. When individuals are asked to rate their creativity across various domains, the levels of creative achievement they report in the various domains tend to be moderately correlated. Critics of this research point out (a) the questionable validity of self-report scales and (b) the response-set bias that may lead individuals to systematically under- or over-estimate their creative activities in all domains.

Although there is a growing consensus in the field that creativity is more domain specific than previously believed, creativity theorists and researchers are far from unanimous about how best to interpret the available evidence. They are in much greater agreement with the position that further research will be needed before such unanimity is likely to be achieved.

IV. CONCLUSIONS AND IMPLICATIONS

If creativity is domain specific, it means that a single theory of creativity—such as the theory that divergent thinking is a basic component of all creative thinking—cannot account for the diversity of creativity across domains. Creativity theories must either become domain specific themselves or find some general approach to dealing with these domain-based differences. Similarly, domain specificity of creativity means that creativity testing as currently practiced is necessarily inadequate and of limited validity. And finally, creativity training programs cannot be assumed to increase creativity across all domains simply because they successfully promote creativity in one domain.

In 1993, Baer proposed a divergent thinking metatheory of creativity that, although encompassing all domains of creativity in a single conceptual scheme, nonetheless took into account the domain specificity of creativity. According to this metatheory, divergent thinking *is* an important creative thinking skill, but the cognitive mechanisms underlying divergent thinking are different in each domain (or possibly even for each task within a domain). Thus there are many *different* divergent thinking skills rather than a single divergent thinking skill. Divergent thinking as a general class of thinking skills is still a useful construct, however, both (a) because it makes this wide range of skills more coherent and easy to conceptualize and (b) because it makes it simpler to postulate and identify the appropriate domain-specific divergent thinking skills that will be important within any given task domain. Thus in terms of what is happening inside a creative thinker's head, divergent thinking skill may actually be many unrelated, domain-specific cognitive skills; but in terms of how psychologists can understand these many diverse skills (viewing divergent thinking from the outside, as it were), divergent thinking is a coherent class of skills that bear a strong family resemblance.

Moving from the implications of domain specificity on creativity theory to its implications on creativity testing, a domain-specific understanding of creativity provides a very direct challenge to all existing notions of how to test creativity. Simply put, to the extent that creativity is domain specific, creativity testing becomes that much more difficult. If creativity is domain specific, what exactly is one to test? Creativity testers will necessarily have to determine in which domain(s) of creativity they are interested, because under a domain specific theory of creativity, "general" creative thinking skill becomes an empty construct. Tests of creativity in specific content domains—which might use the consensual assessment technique to evaluate the creativity of products, or might instead find simpler (perhaps paper-and-pencil) techniques for assessing domain-specific skills—would still be possible in principle, but they could be of only limited range and applicability. Major test developers are unlikely to support extensive test development efforts for tests of such limited potential use. [*See* TESTS OF CREATIVITY.]

Creativity training, on the other hand, can accommodate domain specificity of creativity rather easily. Most creativity training programs already use a wide variety of tasks, spread across various content domains, in the exercises they use to improve divergent thinking and other creative thinking skills. Creativity training programs aimed at a particular domain can easily limit their training exercises to ones connected to that domain, while programs aimed at increasing creativity in general—the vast majority of programs—can simply be careful not to limit their training exercises to just one or a few content domains.

Creativity theory has only recently begun to accommodate research evidence suggesting that creativity is task specific. General, domain-transcending theories—if true—would have far greater power than domain-specific theories that account only for creativity in a limited content domain. For this reason, and because creativity theories have historically been one-size-fits-all theories, domain-general theories of creativity continue to have great appeal.

It should be noted that the research evidence pointing toward domain specificity of creativity is fairly new, and, like the research that preceded it, this research may not tell the whole story. As already noted, self-report scales of creative behavior suggest more generality of creativity than do assessments of the creativity of actual creative products. It is quite possible that both domain specificity and generality are true, each in part and in its own way. More research will be needed to clarify the conditions under which generality or specificity of creativity is the more valid perspective. In the meantime, both views will continue to claim adherents among researchers and theorists.

Bibliography

Amabile, T. M. (1982). Social psychology of creativity: A consensual assessment technique. *Journal of Personality and Social Psychology, 43,* 997–1013.

Baer, J. (1993). *Creativity and divergent thinking: A task-specific approach.* Hillsdale, NJ: Erlbaum.

Baer, J. (1994). Divergent thinking is not a general trait: A multidomain training experiment. *Creativity Research Journal, 7,* 35–46.

Baer, J. (1996). The effects of task-specific divergent-thinking training. *Journal of Creative Behavior, 30,* 183–187.

Baer, J. (1998). The case for domain specificity in creativity. *Creativity Research Journal, 11,* 173–177.

Gardner, H. (1983). *Frames of mind: The theory of multiple intelligences.* New York: Basic Books.

Gardner, H. (1988). Creative lives and creative works: A synthetic scientific approach. In R. J. Sternberg (Ed.), *The nature of creativity* (pp. 298–321). Cambridge: Cambridge University Press.

Karmiloff-Smith, A. (1992). *Beyond modularity: A developmental perspective on cognitive science.* Cambridge, MA: MIT Press.

Plucker, J. (1998). Beware of simple conclusions: The case for content generality of creativity. *Creativity Research Journal, 11,* 179–182.

Runco, M. A. (1987). The generality of creative performance in gifted and nongifted children. *Gifted Child Quarterly, 31,* 121–125.

Runco, M. A. (1989). The creativity of children's art. *Child Study Journal, 19,* 177–190.

Dreams and Creativity

Stanley Krippner

Saybrook Graduate School and Research Center

Creativity The English word *creativity* is linked, historically and etymologically, with the Latin word *creare*, "to make," and the ecclesiastical Latin word *creator* (Creator); therefore, both refer to the concept of origin itself (consider the related term *originality*). One of several useful psychological definitions was given by Csikszentmihalyi in 1996; he suggested that the term *creative* could be applied to "any act, idea, or product that changes an existing domain, or that transforms an existing domain into a new one." A more subjective, but also useful, definition was given by Martindale in 1994 who said that a phenomenon is creative if it is novel and, in some manner, useful or appropriate for the situation in which it occurs. The noun *creativity* is used if a process or phenomenon is being discussed while the adjective *creative* is used if a behavior, an experience, a product, a person, a group, or an environment is being discussed. In all these instances, there is the assumption that something is both novel and culturally appropriate to a given task.

Dreams A series of images, reported in narrative form, that occur during sleep. These images are usually visual and kinesthetic, but they can also be auditory or even gustatory or olfactory. They can be recalled spontaneously upon (or somewhat after) awakening or can be evoked if someone is awak-

ened from REM sleep. Occasionally they are evoked following an awakening from non-REM sleep.

Dream Interpretation An attempt by someone (often the dreamer) to attribute meaning to the content of dream reports for purposes of counseling, psychotherapy, or personal/social growth. Various approaches to dream interpretation exist, some of them contradictory; and some investigators insist that dream content is essentially meaningless.

Electroencephalogram (EEG) A graphic depiction (voltage versus time) of the brain's electrical potentials recorded by scalp electrodes and usually delineated by ink tracings [as are the electromyograph (EMG) and electro-oculogram (EOG)].

Hypnagogia The condition immediately preceding sleep. Hypnagogic reports typically include imagery (visual, auditory, kinesthetic, etc.) but little narrative.

Hypnopompia The condition immediately preceding awakening. Hypnopompic reports typically include imagery (visual, auditory, kinesthetic, etc.) but little narrative.

Lucid Dream Reports Characterized by claims that the dreamer was aware that he or she was dreaming during the ongoing dream.

Nightmares Reports of anxiety-provoking dreams, marked by confusion, fear, or horror.

Non-REM Mentation Reports Given after awakening from non-REM sleep, these reports are characterized by narrative but little or no imagery. Similar reports are sometimes, but infrequently, evoked after awakening from REM sleep.

Non-REM Sleep Consists of four sleep stages that occur in a cyclical pattern. Stage 1 sleep occurs immediately after sleep

Copyright © 1999 by Academic Press
All rights of reproduction in any form reserved.

begins, with a pattern of low amplitude and rapid frequency EEG tracings; Stage 2 sleep has characteristic EEG tracings of 12 to 16 cycles per second known as sleep spindles; Stages 3 and 4 have progressive, further slowing of EEG tracings and an increased amplitude. Over a period of about 90 minutes after sleep begins, most people have passed through the four stages of non-REM sleep and have emerged from them into the first period of REM sleep. Non-REM sleep is also referred to as orthodox sleep or S-sleep (because of its characteristic synchronized EEG tracings).

Rapid Eye Movements (REMs) Conjugate, coordinated horizontal or vertical eye movements, occurring rapidly during sleep and, less frequently, during napping, daydreaming, hypnotic imagining, and other times when one's attention is turned inward.

REM Sleep A recurring stage of sleep, characterized by rapidly occurring conjugate eye movements, loss of muscle tonus, and desynchronized EEG brain wave activity. REM sleep is also referred to as Stage 1 REM sleep, Stage REM, D-sleep (because of its characteristic desynchronized EEG tracings), and paradoxical sleep (because its EEG tracings resemble wakefulness). REM sleep recurs in approximately 90 or 100 minute intervals in humans; it also occurs in nonhuman sleep, for example, among most mammals and—in short intervals—among birds.

Sleep The recurring period of relative physical and psychological disengagement from one's environment characterized by cyclical brain/body activity.

Sleep Terrors (or Night Terrors) Episodic conditions usually occurring during Stage 4 sleep, marked by panic, confusion, and poor recall. Characteristically, the reports of sleep terrors do not include imagery or narrative. They occur developmentally, peaking by 2 years of age.

Wakefulness The recurring period of relative physical and psychological engagement with one's environment and the presence of various types of conscious awareness.

This article explores the association between nighttime **DREAMS AND CREATIVITY,** *using English language terms that are hypothetical constructs (e.g.,* creativity*). Even the word* dream *is a social artifact, because dreams are viewed differently from culture to culture. What Westerners refer to as* dreams *and* visions *are referred to by a single word among many North American Indian tribes. The Australian aboriginal terms* Dreamtime *and the* Dreaming *have very different meanings than the same terms have in Western societies. For the purposes of this entry, dreams are series of images, reported in narrative form, that occur during sleep. Creativity and its equivalents in other languages is a fairly new term in the lexicon. Over the millennia, however, dreams have been linked with what is now called* creativity*, that is, with products and processes that are considered new, novel, and useful by individuals or by social groups. Because dreaming, at least in part, is a cognitive activity, its images and scenarios can serve as symbols and metaphors for unresolved life issues as well as their possible solutions. Examples from science, invention, business, sports, and the arts demonstrate how creative thinkers have reported insights occurring in their dreams. A variety of research studies gives tentative support to the association between creativity and dreams.*

I. CREATIVITY, DREAMS, AND CULTURE

From the perspective of Western psychology, *creativity* is a term that can be used to describe the process of bringing something new into being by becoming sensitive to gaps in human knowledge, identifying these limitations, searching for their solutions, making guesses as to a potential resolution, testing one's hypotheses (sometimes modifying and refining the result of these examinations), and communicating the final product. However, the creative process is imperfectly understood; these steps may be linear or may overlap, they may occur in a planned sequence or spontaneously, or they may be intentional or operate outside of one's awareness. It could also be said that people, groups, or cultures are creative during those periods of time when they exhibit activities, innovative for them, that yield concepts, objects, or behaviors that address human needs (e.g., for survival, for enhanced work performance, for enjoyment, for aesthetic satisfaction, for enriched quality of life) in ways considered valuable by a social group. These novel concepts, objects, and behaviors (e.g., a scientific discovery, a mathematical theorem, a philosophical insight, an artistic masterpiece, a technological product, a military victory, a diplomatic accomplishment) can be termed creative, although one social group might arrive at a different consensus than another group. In other words, the term *creativity* is a social construct used to describe various social outcomes.

The word *creative* has several possible meanings. To most observers, this adjective describes something new that has been brought into existence. For others it describes the psychological process by which novel and valuable products are fashioned. For still others, it describes the person or group engaged in the process. Finally, the press (or social milieu) in which the transaction took place can be described as creative. Definitions of *creative* and *creativity* range from simple problem solving to the full realization and expression of all an individual's unique potentialities. Thus, there are at least four aspects of creativity: the creative process, the creative product, the creative person, and the creative press (or situation). [*See* DEFINITIONS OF CREATIVITY.]

In 1962, E. Paul Torrance provided a definition of creativity that is congruent with what some investigators propose happens in dreams. Torrance stated that creativity is a process of being sensitive to problems, deficiencies, gaps in knowledge, missing elements, and disharmonies. The creative process identifies problems, searches for solutions, makes guesses, and formulates hypotheses about these problems. It then tests and retests the hypotheses, often modifying and again testing them, and finally communicates the results. One school of thought holds that dreaming is similar to Torrance's concept of the creative process because dreams also can identify problems, search for solutions, test hypotheses, and communicate the results to the dreamer. In 1996 I. Strauch and B. Meier discussed how the creative transformation of memories is an expression of human consciousness that can take place both during wakefulness and during dreaming. [*See* MEMORY AND CREATIVITY.]

Montague Ullman, in 1965, listed four reasons to explain why dreams partake in a creative process. All dreams are original; no two are alike. Dreams combine various elements to form new patterns. Like many creative processes, most dreams are involuntary experiences. Dreams contain metaphors and symbols that have creative potentials. Many non-Western societies have also appreciated the creative aspects of dreams. Among Australian aborigines, the Laws of the Dreaming were laid down during what they call the Creative Period. Each species has its own set of laws, and all of these laws are a part of the Dreaming, the ground of all existence. Humans can obtain new information (e.g., new songs and rituals) from the Dreaming at night. Thus the Dreaming is dynamic, not static, in nature.

In *The Tempest,* William Shakespeare wrote about "such stuff as dreams are made." Many of the images that appear in dreams can be symbolic in nature. Images are mental representations of objects or persons not physically present. Whereas an image directly represents the object it pictures, a symbol is an image that stands for something else. In much the same way, activities in dreams may be metaphorical, a metaphor being a narrative or an activity that stands for something else.

Sometimes dream content makes no sense if the dreamer presumes that the images refer directly to the people or objects they depict. In those instances, the dream might make more sense if allowances are made for the possibility that its images are referring to something other than themselves. Sigmund Freud complicated this issue by asserting that the symbols occurring in dreams differ radically from other symbols because dreams express, in disguised form, wishes the dreamer has repressed. However, this assertion implies a discontinuity in nature. Most current dreamworkers believe that the symbol-making process in dreams exhibits more commonalties than differences with the symbol-making process in waking life. This emphasis on the continuity between waking life and dreaming life can even be found in the writings of St. Thomas Aquinas who wrote, "Those things that have occupied a man's thoughts while awake recur to his imagination while asleep."

This continuous, cognitive-psychological position was also taken by Alfred Adler, Calvin Hall, and David Foulkes, who described dreams as meaningful but not as containing preplanned encoded messages that need to be translated the way a linguist would work with a foreign language. According to Foulkes, the dream is "knowledge-based" and "bound to reflect some of the ways in which the dreamer mentally represents his or her world." Indeed, almost all people awakened after a dream are able "to identify *some* events as having rough parallels in her or his waking experience." A body of research indicates that complex thinking processes can be found in dreams, and the differences between dreaming and waking cognition are more quantitative than qualitative in nature.

Yet some differences between waking cognition and dreaming cognition do exist. In 1979 Rycroft mused that if dreams are poetry, their creative efforts are imperfect. Poets and artists need to cast their meaning in metaphors and symbols that are a part of the shared legacy of their culture. But dream imagery tends to be too dependent on the dreamer's personal experiences to convert easily into works of art with wide appeal.

Some dream theorists urge the dreamer to accept dream images and stories as creative experiences in their own right. For example, in 1978 Boss and Kenny denied that a hidden, symbolizing agent lies within the dreamer. Writing from a neuroscience perspective in 1983, Crick and Mitchison proposed that dreams function to purge unnecessary, even parasitic, brain cell connections produced during wakefulness; dream content, therefore, is best forgotten.

However, Hobson, also taking a neurophysiological and neurochemical perspective, wrote, in 1988, that

> since dreaming is universal, it stands as testimony to the universality of the artistic experience. In our dreams, we all become writers, painters, and film makers, combining extraordinary sets of characters, actions, and locations into strangely coherent experiences. . . . I thus strongly object to any implication that the artistic experiences of waking or dreaming are fundamentally pathological, defensive, or neurotic.

Hobson added that the brain is so determined to find meaning, that it creates dreams out of images that have been randomly evoked by its own neurochemical activity.

It can be seen that dream specialists do not speak with one voice on the topic of creativity and dreams. But non-Western traditions lack uniformity as well. Among pre-Columbian Native American dream traditions, some saw dreams as having the same meaning for every member of the tribe, whereas others felt that dreams conveyed meanings personal to the dreamer; some believed that dreams served problem-solving functions, whereas others felt that they forecast the future; some believed that dreams dictated actions that needed to be taken in daily life, whereas others believed that dream events took place in the spirit world. In some tribes, dream messages were direct and undisguised, whereas for others they required inter-

pretation. However, few North American tribal groups neglected dreams; they were seen as sources of knowledge, power, inspiration, and what today would be called creativity.

II. RESEARCH ON CREATIVITY AND DREAMS

R. W. Weisberg, in 1986, stated that creative problem solving has occurred when a person produces a novel response that solves the problem at hand. He went on to debunk many highly publicized accounts of problem solving in dreams and other altered states of consciousness. A critical perspective needs to be taken not only in regard to anecdotal accounts but also regarding formal research programs. These phenomena are difficult to investigate for several reasons. Even if a useful definition of *creativity* can be implemented, an investigator never works with a dream, simply with a dream report. These reports, whether obtained from archives, from field research, or from laboratory research, are subject to so many vagaries of memory, unconscious distortion, and deliberate omission or elaboration as to pervade the field with a well-deserved sense of modesty when even tentative results are announced. [*See* ALTERED AND TRANSITIONAL STATES.]

A. Anecdotal Data

An often-cited anecdote is that the physicist Niels Bohr, in 1913, conceptualized the model of an atom following a dream in which he visualized the planets whirling around him just as, later, he pictured electrons circling the nucleus of an atom. William Dement wrote Bohr some 50 years later to obtain more details and Bohr not only denied that he ever had such a dream but responded that he had never received any practical idea from a dream in his life!

Many creativity researchers have discussed creativity within the framework of preparation, incubation, inspiration, and verification, although these four stages may not always develop in a predetermined order in creative work and problem-solving, and some stages may not occur at all. It has been suggested that when the problem solver's deliberate efforts to evoke solutions are abandoned during sleep, dreams can impart clues and novel approaches that elude individuals during wakefulness. Many researchers cast doubt on the credibility of anecdotal reports of this nature, noting that many of them were made long after the event, hence there is the risk of distortion and elaboration. Even in cases that appear to be credible, a period of considerable preparation is required; however, simply taking a break from the problem is a more likely explanation than unconscious processing because during the break people typically mull over a solution.

Many of the most frequently cited cases of dream creativity did not take place in dreams at all but actually took place in transitional states of consciousness, not sleep. Rarely do dreamers record their dreams and secure them in such a way that their creative potential can be assured.

B. Formal Research Data

Several investigators have used tests, questionnaires, and interviews to obtain information about creative problem solving in dreams. Some representative studies demonstrate the direction that formal research has taken; the journal *Dreaming* is an excellent resource for those who are interested in following developments in this field.

In 1979 Davé attempted to determine if dreams could facilitate creative problem solving on behalf of 24 people who were at an impasse in solving a creative problem. One group was hypnotized, hypnotic imagery was evoked, and the subjects were told that they would have nighttime dreams offering solutions to their problems. Another group was given instructions on how to solve their problems through activities emphasizing rational, cognitive thought exercises. The final group of participants simply were interviewed regarding their problems and served as a control group. Davé judged the treatment to be a success for six of the eight members in the hypnotic imagery group, for one member of the rational-cognitive group, and for nobody in the interview group.

Barrios and Singer, in 1982, queried 48 volunteer subjects about their creative impasses, finding that most had been blocked for more than three months. The subjects were divided into four groups and randomly assigned to one of four conditions: exposure to either a waking imagery or to a hypnotic induction procedure, participation in a focused and collaborative examination of their projects in which task-irrelevant thoughts were avoided, and a control group encouraged, in a nondirective fashion, to discuss their projects. Results indicated that the waking imagery and hypnotic imagery conditions were most effective in promoting the resolution of creative blocks.

An experiment reported by Brodsky, Esquerre, and Jackson in 1991 asked students, while they were awake, to apply an operational definition of dreaming to four problem-solving tasks. All proposed solutions were rated on a 5-point creativity scale by raters, working independently. No gender differences were noted, nor was frequency of dream recall associated with the creativity ratings. However, students who attributed considerable importance to their dreams received higher creativity scores, as did students who reported having had lucid dreams. It was suggested that dreaming consciousness is a permission-giving format for eliciting active imagination, bypassing typical goal-oriented thinking processes.

A series of experiments reported by Cartwright in 1984 demonstrated that problem solving in dreams is probably more successful when the material to be processed is emotionally or personally meaningful.

A different problem was approached by Koulack, Prevost, and de Koninck in 1985; they studied how dreaming could help one adapt to a stressful intellectual activity. They reported that subjects who incorporated elements from a presleep stressful event into their remembered dreams showed less adaptation on awakening than subjects who did not.

Other studies have shown that dream reports of more creative individuals exhibit more primary process thought than less creative individuals but also show greater symbolism and more unusual combinations of dream content elements.

Highly creative individuals also endorse beliefs that dreams have hidden and symbolic meanings, can produce inventions and artistic creations, can sometimes predict the future, and can be programed more so than less creative individuals. The creative group also claim to make a greater effort to remember their dreams than the other group. High creatives relax more easily, fall asleep more rapidly and more of them claim to be able to solve problems in dreams than do less creative individuals.

The association between nightmares and creativity has long been a matter of conjecture. A questionnaire survey of college students found that art majors report the most nightmares, whereas physical education majors report the fewest, with mathematics and science students in the middle. Furthermore, students with frequent nightmares tend to report more visual imagery during awakening, become easily absorbed in aesthetic stimuli, and score higher scores on a hypnotizability scale than do other students.

Other studies have found a close relationship between the frequency of nightmare reports and psychopathological scores on personality tests for dreamers reporting frequent nightmares. Furthermore, high nightmare individuals have more primary process material in their dream reports than low nightmare individuals.

C. Cross-Cultural Considerations

It is not the dream itself that is available for interpretation, but the individual's or group's report of the dream experience. The visual, sensory, and emotional aspects of a dream are often lost in Westerners' accounts of dreams, but indigenous dreamworkers generally consider these qualities to be among the most important.

Remembered dreams and performed myths are both forms of production that bridge the verbal, logical characteristics of rational thought with the visual-sensory-spatial-emotional images that reach their most elaborate level of integration in art. The recounting of a dream brings the nonverbal, nonrational imagery of a dream to awareness, and begins to link it with logical reasoning.

III. POSSIBLE MECHANISMS

Contemporary sleep and dream research has demonstrated the elaborate, entirely intrinsic mechanisms of *state* control. In other words, a change in the brain's state while asleep causes a change in the dreamer's mental state. Sensory input can be internally controlled so that even the transforming mechanisms do not operate alone to protect the system from overload. Three

features of the modern conception of the nervous system—its intrinsic plasticity, its autoregulation, and its creativity—give us a very different set of operating principles on which to construct a scientific psychology. This model depicts a nervous system that can turn itself on and off, regulate the flow of internal information in diverse ways, and control external information's access to the system. It is in the context of this model that the incorporation of presleep stimuli, dream incubation, and lucid dreaming assume importance for the understanding of creativity and dreams.

A. Incorporation of Presleep Stimuli

In 1979 Fiss described an experiment he conducted in which his subjects read a nautical story before going to sleep and were tested on it the following morning. If the story influenced their dreams, or even if their dreams were unusually vivid (with considerable emotion and color), the subjects recalled more details about the story. This study demonstrates the impact of presleep experience on dreams as well as illustrating some mechanisms behind the memory-serving function of dreams.

The influence of presleep stimuli in dream content has been successfully attempted in experiments using hypnosis, subliminal stimulation, emotionally arousing films, and real-life stress situations. The results indicate that it is relatively easy to influence dream content in predictable ways. It has been suggested that dreams may serve the purpose of assimilating emotionally arousing information into problem solutions that are already embodied in existing memory systems.

B. Dream Incubation

If it is possible for an experimenter to influence the course of a subject's dreams, then it should also be possible for dreamers themselves to influence their dream content.

Dream incubation was common among the American Plains Indians, ancient China among artists, and in the practices of ancient Egypt, Greece, and Tibet.

In more recent research, in 1977 Foulkes and Griffin moved from the anecdotal level to more rigorous types of inquiry, teaching 23 subjects "dream control" methods, and asking them to dream about randomly selected topics. The subjects kept daily records of their dreams for 10 nights. Judges attempted to match dreams with the suggested topics; their matchings did not exceed what would have been expected by chance. The same investigators designed a second study using 29 highly motivated subjects who claimed some previous success in dream control or an interest in the topic. They spent 10 nights attempting to dream about assigned topics, but in this case they were allowed to select the nights on which they felt they could successfully control their dreams. Again, judges were unable to match the dreams with the topics. Other studies have reported more encouraging results in projects in which incubated dreams focus not on abstract topics but on real-life concerns. Fiss has warned that some people expect too much when they assume their dreams will become springboards for feats of artistic creation. Nevertheless, dreams can help many people live more fully integrated lives and augment their capacity for adaptation and personal growth.

C. Lucid Dreaming

When a dreamer realizes that he or she is dreaming, the dream is considered to be lucid. The Tibetan Buddhist practice of "dream yoga" focused on the ability to remain aware and lucid during nighttime dreaming. However, the Hindu yogic dream tradition eschewed such dream manipulation in favor of a waking meditation practice described as "merging with the light." Aristotle wrote about lucid dreams, noting that when one is asleep, there may be something in one's awareness that declares what is presented is a dream: "The sleeper perceives that he is asleep, and is conscious of the sleeping state during which the perception comes before his mind." In the second edition to *The Interpretation of Dreams*, published in 1909, Freud noted that some people are clearly aware when they are dreaming and are able to direct their dreams.

Firsthand reports from lucid dreamers have produced a list of methods thought to be useful in facilitating the experience. Presleep reflection is frequently mentioned; in other words, one can often incubate a lucid dream. Asking such critical questions as "Is this a dream?" and "Am I dreaming?" during a dream will often produce lucidity. Some dreamworkers encour-

age people to ask these questions during the day at regular intervals, with the expectation that these questions will later arise during the night. External stimulation is sometimes incorporated into a dream and triggers lucidity; again, this can be deliberately programmed. Gackenbach has estimated that about 58% of the population experience a lucid dream at least once while about 21% report one or more per month. Instruction in lucid dreaming has been used therapeutically, especially to help people who suffer from chronic nightmares. Studies have shown that lucid dreaming can be "learned" by those who wish to use it for creative problem solving. There are anecdotal stories of more specific skills being learned as a result of lucid dreaming.

D. Neurophysiological and Neurochemical Mechanisms

Several studies with animals indicate that the frequency of time spent in REM sleep increases as a result of new learning, such as finding the way out of a maze. This relationship is evident in work conducted with cats, mice, rats, and newly hatched chicks. Therefore, REM sleep may play an important role in the consolidation of such cognitive activities as learning, memory, and problem solving for both humans and other organisms that engage in REM sleep. It has been proposed that REM sleep's purpose is to restore one's mental operations after the daily tribulations of wakefulness. REM sleep may do so by providing an opportunity for the neurochemical systems in the brain, which have become depleted while one is awake, to recuperate. Non-REM sleep, on the other hand, may play its role by restoring the physical effects of waking and preparing for the action of REM sleep.

The role of learning in REM sleep production may be connected to an underlying biological process. It has been suggested that new protein structures are being synthesized in the brain during REM sleep. Evidence indicates that the initiation of REM sleep does come from the brain stem, and then extends itself over the entire brain cortex. Because animal experiments indicate that protein synthesis is present in new learning, it has been hypothesized that it also takes place during REM sleep.

Some theorists have used computer analogies to describe REM functioning, as akin to "off-line processing." The acquisition of input information is placed in temporary storage, until processing components are available. Information about the day's events is gathered and stored until the onset of REM sleep when it can be "processed" (i.e., integrated with memories and formed into strategies for the future).

Winson has noted that the spiny anteater, or echidna, is an early mammal whose sleep pattern shows no REM activity. The echidna's brain has a large prefrontal cortex, presumably to integrate new experience with older experience. The mammals that evolved later were able to handle this task more efficiently during REM sleep; as a result, their brains were smaller— a more productive direction for evolution to follow. This problem did not exist in the earlier reptilian species; their behavior was largely reflexive and this activity was adequately handled by a small brain with a neocortex. Dreams, then, can serve as a window on the neural processes whereby—from early childhood on—strategies for behavior are being set down, modified, or consulted. This process and the mechanisms involved were termed the "unconscious" by Freud and can be used advantageously in the clinical setting by both Freudian and non-Freudian psychotherapists and other dreamworkers.

The model that has tried to be the most inclusive in regard to incorporating physiological discoveries about dreams is that proposed by Hobson and his associates, the activation-synthesis model. They propose that cells deep in the pontine area of the brain stem are *activated,* generating REM sleep and randomly stimulating the forebrain, which then *synthesizes* dreams by using stored memories to make sense of the incoming neural firing. On the one hand, Hobson has reduced dreaming to biochemical events in the brain, but on the other hand, he has a keen understanding of dreams as imaginative creative events.

Hobson pointed out that Freud insisted that wishes and repressed desires caused dreaming but that this notion has been discredited due to data that brain stem mechanisms during sleep cause dreaming. Once these mechanisms trigger REM sleep (and dreaming), wishes may be expressed and may even shape dream plots, but they are in no sense causative of the dream process. Hobson's reciprocal-interaction model proposes that REM sleep occurs when the REM-off neurological

activity in the brain stem has reached a low enough level to allow the inhibited REM-on neurological system to escape from its control. At this point, Hobson's activation-synthesis model takes over. It proposes that dream elements derive from a synthesis of information produced by activation of the brain's motor pattern generators and sensory systems. This internal information is linked and compared with information about the organism's past experiences, making the best possible fit of intrinsically chaotic data produced by the automatically activated mind/brain. This process reflects the creative imagination, which is an intrinsic part of the dream process.

Like other subjective experiences, dream material tends to be organized by the linguistic faculty of mind/ brains. Thus, Hobson concluded that dreams are not the result of an attempt to disguise repressed wishes but are a direct expression of a synthetic effort. That is to say, the brain is first internally activated and then synthesizes this information to form the physiological patterns of the dream experience. One's memories are scanned for images that will match these internally generated patterns. The activation-synthesis model sees dreaming as the preprogrammed running of an internal system. The bizarre features of the dream are naturally associated with the mode of operation of the system during dreaming sleep, and there is no need for a mechanism that would transform information. Since the system is capable of selecting what computer scientists would call the "store" or "no-store" modes, there is no need to postulate an active energy-consuming mechanism for the restoring of dream material in the unconscious. It can simply be the no-stored mode that is unremembered.

Once activated, the mind/brain synthesizes or constructs a unified conscious experience (the dream) by comparing the internally generated signals to perceptions, actions, and emotions in its memory bank. The rules of synthesis are as yet unclear but may involve such complex organizational processes as language (given the narrative structure of reports) and nonverbal symbolic operations (given the dream's elaborate scenarios), which are presumably a function of higher brain centers. The state of the art in cortical psychophysiology is so primitive even in the waking state that one must remain at least as vague and promissory in discussing dreaming. This is due to the fact that during REM sleep the mind/brain is off-line (input independent), movement free (output independent), and hence operating on its own terms. Hobson's theory ascribes the cognitive properties of dreaming to unusual operating features of the internally activated, auto-stimulated brain during REM sleep. This is the heart of his theory. For once, wrote Hobson, contemporary scientists can agree with Freud's assertion that dreams are the "royal road" to a scientific understanding of consciousness. Hobson's model is seen as unduly reductionistic by those researchers who hold that REM sleep and dreaming are two separate but related processes.

E. Further Research

Future research studies need to identify the genetic markers for creative behavior, reconcile personality and cognitive research data in creativity, evaluate the part played by the dreaming process in creative ideation, determine the role of mental illness in blocking or facilitating creative expression, and specify what home and school variables are key factors in the development of highly creative individuals.

It is apparent that individual differences exist in dream creativity, and that there are cultural differences as well. The vast preponderance of studies in the field are devoted to the neurophysiology and neurochemistry of sleep and dreaming as opposed to the psychosocial variables in dreaming, and, of the latter, only a handful concern themselves with creative aspects of dreaming despite the near-consensus of dream researchers that the two phenomena are linked in several ways.

The unanswered questions posed by existing research data are legion: for example, why is color spontaneously reported in the dreams of half of art students studied, 16% of the science majors, and virtually none of the engineering students? Why do subjects, in general, tend to report color in their dreams more frequently if they claim to place greater reliance on feelings than on thinking? In laboratory studies, why does recall of color in dreams disappear quickly if the investigator does not ask for it? What is the nature of dreams in which color is greatly intensified, radiating with phosphorescent hues? What is the nature of black and white dreams that a dreamer reports who almost always dreams in color? What are the mechanisms that determine shifts in dream color when people wear colored goggles during every waking moment for a week? Why do members of some cultural and social groups report more and different colors in dreams than do others? Why do children report more color in dreams than adults?

The answers to these questions can be sought from psychosocial, neurophysiological, and neurochemical investigations, as can answers to dozens of additional questions relating to creativity in dreams. In the meantime, for the Australian aborigines, the Amazon Kagwahiv, and other tribal people, the Dreaming still exists. They believe that if other human beings would begin to make their own dream journeys, reestablish their links with nature, and creatively invoke Dreamtime songs and dances, many of the world's current dichotomies and discontinuities could become accommodated and transcended. For both the mind/brain and the individual/group, this has been one of dream's creative functions over the millennia. The need for creative solutions to the world's many social, economic, and environmental problems reflects the importance of creativity and of the researchers and dreamworkers who see creativity in dreams as a critical frontier in understanding and assisting human development in a world—and a species—currently at risk.

Bibliography

Almansi, G., & Begun, C. (1986). *Theatre of sleep: An anthology of literary dreams.* London: Pan Books.

Barrios, M. V., & Singer, J. L. (1981/1982). The treatment of creative blocks: A comparison of waking imagery, hypnotic dream, and rational discussion techniques. *Imagination, Cognition, and Personality, 1,* 89–109.

Brodsky, S. L., Esquerre, J., & Jackson, R. R., Jr. (1990–1991). Dream consciousness in problem-solving. *Imagination, Cognition and Personality, 10,* 353–360.

Crick, F., & Mitchison, G. (1983). The function of dream sleep. *Nature, 304,* 111–114.

Delaney, G. (1990). Personal and professional problem solving in dreams. In S. Krippner (Ed.), *Dreamtime and dreamwork: Decoding the language of the night* (pp. 93–100). New York: Jeremy P. Tarcher/Putnam.

Fiss, H. (1979). Current dream work: A psychobiological perspective. In B. B. Wolman (Ed.), *Handbook of dreams:*

Research, theories and applications (pp. 20–75). New York: Van Nostrand Reinhold.

Foulkes, D. (1985). *Dreaming: A cognitive-psychological analysis.* Hillsdale, NJ: Erlbaum.

Gackenbach, J., & LaBerge, S. (Eds.). (1988). *Conscious mind, sleeping brain: Perspectives on lucid dreaming.* New York: Plenum Press.

Garfield, P. (1974). *Creative dreaming.* New York: Simon & Schuster.

Hobson, J. A. (1988). *The dreaming brain.* New York: Basic Books.

Krippner, S., & Dillard, J. (1988). *Dreamworking: How to use your dreams for creative problem-solving.* Buffalo, NY: Bearly.

Rycroft, C. (1979). *The innocence of dreams.* New York: Pantheon.

Stone, M. D. (1993). Creativity in dreams. In *Encyclopedia of sleep and dreaming* (pp. 149–151). New York: Macmillan.

Strauch, I., & Meier, B. (1996). *In search of dreams.* Albany, NY: State University of New York Press.

Ullman, M. (1965). Dreaming a creative process: Discussion. *American Journal of Psychoanalysis, 24,* 10–12.

Drugs and Creativity

Jonathan A. Plucker

Indiana University

Robert Q. Dana

University of Maine

Central Nervous System (CNS) Depressants Include alcohol and barbiturates and antianxiety drugs. These substances depress brain function.

Central Nervous System Stimulants Include nicotine and amphetamines. These substances increase brain activity. Cocaine is a topical anesthetic that mimics CNS stimulants.

Creative Achievement An estimate of creative productivity accomplished through the use of creative activity checklists.

Hallucinogen Include LSD and PCP. These substances disrupt the chemical and electrical balance in the brain to create a disorganized CNS. Marijuana is an hallucinogenic drug, though its effects are unique.

Substance Abuse Maladaptive pattern of substance use manifested by recurrent and significant adverse consequences related to the repeated use of substances. These include problems related to fulfilling social and occupational roles, family functioning, and psychological well-being. There is no clear pattern of tolerance or withdrawal in this syndrome.

Substance Dependence A cluster of cognitive, behavioral, and physiological problems associated with the continued use of a substance despite these problems. There is a pattern of repeated self-administration that typically results in tolerance, withdrawal, and repeated drug-taking behavior.

DRUGS *are addictive substances that produce physical, behavioral, and often psychological effects when consumed. Although drugs include illegal substances such as heroin, cocaine, marijuana, and LSD, common substances such as nicotine, caffeine, and alcohol are also considered to be drugs. This article describes the theoretical and empirical evidence on the relationship between drugs and creativity.*

I. POPULAR BELIEFS

Anecdotes about creative individuals who used or abused drugs are quite common. Ernest Hemingway, Edgar Allen Poe, Richard Burton, John Belushi, and several other writers and actors had well-documented problems with alcohol and other drugs, and the history of music is full of cases of musicians and entertainers who abused or became addicted to drugs (e.g., Janis Joplin, Charlie Parker, Kurt Cobain).

Over time, the addictive habits of these creative individuals have fostered a popular impression that drug

Copyright © 1999 by Academic Press
All rights of reproduction in any form reserved.

use enhances creativity. Indeed, when asked about the potential benefits of drug use, adolescents usually mention the enhancement of creativity as a positive aspect. Unfortunately, this belief is a moderate to strong predictor of future drug use. The conventional wisdom, shared both by children and adults, is that consuming drugs has a positive impact on creativity.

Surprisingly, this assumption has been tested infrequently by psychologists, physicians, and educators. Collectively, research paints a predominantly negative picture of the impact of drugs on creativity, but several significant issues have yet to be investigated thoroughly. The remainder of this article reviews theory and research regarding the relationship between specific drugs and creativity, discusses possible mechanisms through which creativity may lead to drug use, and explores areas in which more information is needed.

II. ALCOHOL AND CREATIVITY

The question of whether alcohol enhances creativity is a complicated one. Anecdotes of famous writers' and actors' use of alcohol while engaged in creative behavior are commonplace, yet many of their careers were cut short by their substance abuse. At first glance, the empirical evidence regarding the impact of alcohol use on creativity is equally contradictory.

For example, although many researchers have found that alcohol has no appreciable benefits for the creative process, several others believe that alcohol enhances creativity by reducing inhibitions (e.g., helps alleviate writer's block). This phenomenon, often referred to as the disinhibition hypothesis, is believed to be a mechanism through which alcohol positively influences creativity.

However, most studies that provide evidence in favor of the disinhibition hypothesis provide equally convincing evidence that alcohol has—at best—a negligible impact on other aspects of creativity: personality characteristics associated with creativity, locus of control, and creative achievement. In general, few studies suggest a uniformly positive alcohol-induced effect on creativity (a possible exception may be found in the work of Gustafson and Norlander, described later). Moderate consumption appears to have no better than

a negligible effect on creativity, and heavy consumption is usually associated with a negative effect. [*See* ALCOHOL AND CREATIVITY.]

III. TOBACCO AND CREATIVITY

The relationship between creativity and tobacco use (i.e., nicotine consumption) is rarely discussed, yet the addictive nature of nicotine and the health risks associated with tobacco use suggest that it may also have an impact on cognitive processes such as creativity. Nicotine consumption appears to result in certain cognitive gains in areas such as information processing speed and working memory function. However, a recent, exhaustive review of tobacco research did not find significant cognitive benefits from tobacco use, and two recent studies involving nicotine's effect on creativity found the relationship to be inconsequential. Given the current research, there is little reason to believe that creative processes are in any way enhanced or harmed appreciably by tobacco use.

A. Methodological Issues

A possible cause for the somewhat equivocal results of nicotine research is the presence of methodological inconsistency. The methodological issues associated with nicotine research are representative of those associated with drug research in general, with the main problem involving the comparison of inappropriate samples. For example, during smoking research a common practice is to determine the cognitive effects of nicotine on smokers versus nonsmokers. Nonsmokers are frequently defined as smokers who abstain from tobacco consumption for a given time before the research begins. In effect, any of the smokers' cognitive benefits may actually be withdrawal deficits for the abstaining smokers. Due to the withdrawal effects associated with most drug use, sample selection and comparison is the major factor limiting the generalizability of drug-creativity research.

A second issue involves a somewhat different aspect of sample selection. Because the possession of many drugs is illegal (e.g., marijuana, cocaine, LSD) or strictly controlled (alcohol, tobacco products), sample sizes are generally small and include only subjects older than 21 years of age. In addition, researchers often use post hoc causal-comparative designs. All of these factors limit the generalizability of drug research and should be considered when interpreting results.

Finally, investigations of the relationship between drugs and different aspects of creativity have traditionally involved writers, musicians, painters, and other people involved in the arts and humanities. Few investigations have considered how the relationship between drugs and creativity is manifest among scientists, engineers, mathematicians, businesspeople, laborers, and those who work in other vocations. This is probably due in part to the conventional wisdom about artists, writers, musicians, and alcohol and other drug use, which has arguably guided a majority of research on this topic. Fortunately, a majority of recent research has focused on general populations of college students and adults, which should help to correct this sampling oversight.

IV. MARIJUANA AND CREATIVITY

The use of marijuana to enhance creativity is usually associated with musicians, although once again anecdotes regularly circulate about a wide variety of creative individuals and their marijuana use. Few studies have explicitly focused on the impact of marijuana on creativity, with a majority limited by their anecdotal or post hoc nature. For example, at least one study has found that musicians report slightly higher percentages of marijuana use than other creative individuals, but determining whether marijuana use influenced creativity is not possible due to the retrospective, self-report nature of the research.

The few experimental studies that involve marijuana effects upon creativity provide both positive and negative evidence. Marijuana use apparently results in increased originality but has a negligible or slightly negative impact on creative achievement. Since marijuana use is associated with short-term memory degradation, text comprehension difficulties, and slowed reaction time on some cognitive tasks, the apparent advantages of marijuana use may be balanced or slightly outweighed by marijuana-induced, cognitive detriments.

V. OTHER DRUGS AND CREATIVITY

Because empirical investigations on the impact of the use of common drugs on creativity are limited, the reader should not be surprised that research involving creativity and less common (e.g., cocaine, hallucinogens) or less threatening drugs (e.g., caffeine) is almost nonexistent. The handful of studies that have involved use of these drugs suggests that, again in direct opposition to conventional wisdom, creativity gains no positive benefit from drug use. Indeed, long-term or heavy use of these drugs may have a detrimental effect on creative production.

VI. DOES CREATIVITY LEAD TO DRUG USE?

Although the evidence is mounting that drug use may have little if any positive impact on creativity, the issue of whether creativity *causes* drug use is yet to be established. Preliminary evidence suggests that college students' tobacco and marijuana use is correlated with past creative achievement, especially among young women. In contrast, alcohol use appears to be negatively correlated with past creative output.

Theorized mechanisms for creativity leading to drug use fall into three basic categories. First, the stress brought on by creative activity—nonconformity, risk-taking, specific psychological afflictions—may lead creative people to use drugs as a coping strategy. This line of investigation is best exemplified in the work of Gustafson, Norlander, and their colleagues, who have conducted several interesting studies of the impact of the creative process (i.e., Wallas' stages of creativity) on subsequent alcohol consumption. Their results suggest that intensive creative work may lead to increased alcohol use. Similar research involving tobacco, caffeine, marijuana, and other widely consumed drugs is not currently available.

Second, given the popular association of creativity and drugs, creative individuals may feel expected to engage in drug use. Because social comparison processes (e.g., peer pressure, identity issues) can dominate the lives of adolescents and young adults, creative people may experiment with and regularly use alcohol, nicotine, and other drugs because they feel that using such drugs is what creative people are expected to do. This mechanism suggests one of the most striking paradoxes in the creativity literature: creative individuals, usually assumed to be nonconformist, engaging in conformist behavior in order to be considered creative. Finally, the possibility exists that certain creative individuals use the myth of drug-enhanced creativity as a rationale for behaviors that they suspect are perceived negatively by society at large. Although each of these mechanisms is plausible, not enough empirical evidence has been gathered to support or refute any of them convincingly.

A. Impact on Audiences

One of the most important aspects of the drug-creativity relationship has yet to be explored. Although a limited amount of research has measured creativity using activity checklists that contain items involving recognition by others (e.g., concerts, awards, publications), the impact of substance use on audience perception of creativity has not been directly studied.

The audience issue is an important one, especially for those individuals who are actively engaged in trying to prevent the use and abuse of addictive substances. If alcohol and other drug use were found to have a negative impact on an audience's perceptions of a person's creativity, that individual (especially if his or her behaviors are influenced by social expectations) may be less likely to use the substances—even if she or he perceives the drugs to have a beneficial, short-term effect on creative production.

VII. FAMILY DRUG USE

Alcoholics' children differ negatively from nonalcoholics' children in terms of personality characteristics related to creativity. Divergent thinking test scores of the two groups of children are similar. Although the possibility exists that offspring compensate for the personality deficits and maintain productively creative lives in spite of the negative influence of parents' substance use, parent alcohol and drug problems do not

appear to have an appreciable effect on student's creative achievement through the undergraduate years. However, gender may influence the impact of family history on creativity, with male children experiencing a more detrimental impact than female children.

Most available research involves younger children and adolescents. Because the true effects of parent substance abuse may not be felt for several years, future research should investigate these issues with older offspring.

VIII. CONCLUSIONS

Even if one assumes a short-term creative benefit from drug use, the long-term impact appears to be at best inconsequential and at worst quite negative. The few drug-induced creative advantages are outweighed, both in the short- and long-term, by the negative effects of the drugs. Having a drug-induced advantage and using it to be creative are clearly different issues, with current research indicating that they may be mutually exclusive.

The lack of long-term benefit is not surprising. Addictive behaviors tend to overwhelm an individual's psychological, sociological, and physiological space. As these behaviors advance and develop, they may fully occupy a life space while narrowing a person's ability to function adaptively in his or her environment. The use of these substances can become all-consuming, allowing little time for creative activity. Consider the case of Rosa, a 37-year-old woman who played music and wrote poetry throughout college. She played her music with friends and in a small band that performed locally. She published two poems and was frequently asked by friends and acquaintances to write something for them.

After college, Rosa's use of marijuana and alcohol increased from occasional use and intoxication to almost continuous daily use of marijuana and heavy use of alcohol four to five times per week. As the duration and intensity of Rosa's use grew, she continued to play music and write. However, her ability to perform and create music and her ability to pen coherent poetry were seriously disrupted by declining motivation and the narrowing perspective caused by her intoxication.

Friends gradually became less moved by Rosa's

work, and Rosa became less interested in her friends and work and more interested in pursuing her "self-development" through expanding her consciousness and creativity through the use of substances. In pursuit of these goals, Rosa's use intensified, and an arrest for drunk driving coerced her into a substance abuse treatment setting. At the point of admission, Rosa was diagnosed with alcohol abuse and cannabis dependence, and she stated that music and writing were boring and that she was put off by her friends' and colleagues' lack of interest in her and her once creative output.

In educational and counseling settings, people should be made aware that the belief that a creative benefit from drug use exists is based on anecdotal and predominantly weak evidence. Although a great deal of research still needs to be done in this area, existing evidence suggests that any relationship between creativity and drug use may be due to people's expectancies and not to any direct pharmacological effect.

Bibliography

Goodwin, D. W. (1988). *Alcohol and the writer*. Kansas City, MO: Andrews & McMeel.

Gustafson, R., & Norlander, T. (1995). Effects of creative and non-creative work on the tendency to drink alcohol during the restitution phase of the creative process. *Journal of Creative Behavior, 29,* 25–35.

Heishman, S. J., Taylor, R. C., & Henningfield, J. E. (1994). Nicotine and smoking: A review of effects on human performance. *Experimental and Clinical Psychopharmacology, 2,* 345–395.

Kerr, B., Shaffer, J., Chambers, C., & Hallowell, K. (1991). Substance use of creatively talented adults. *Journal of Creative Behavior, 25,* 145–153.

Ludwig, A. M. (1990). Alcohol input and creative output. *British Journal of Addiction, 85,* 953–963.

Noble, E. P., Runco, M. A., & Ozkaragoz, T. Z. (1993). Creativity in alcoholic and nonalcoholic families. *Alcohol, 10,* 317–322.

Rowe, G. (1994). Group differences in alcohol-creativity interactions. *Psychological Reports, 75,* 1635–1638.

Eccentricity

David J. Weeks

Jardine Clinic, Royal Edinburgh Hospital

Kate Ward

University of Edinburgh

Curiosity Also known as the intrinsic motivation, the only intellect-orientated major motivation, it often involves strong needs to find out, as well as much exploratory behavior.

Elaboration A secondary component of the creative process, defined as the ability to improve upon an initial idea or applying it in other overlapping content areas.

Empathy The ability to take on the other's perspective, and to vicariously partake of, or more deeply experience, the emotional responses of the other.

Flexibility A component of the creative process, defined as a spontaneous willingness to attempt a variety of solutions and not being tied prematurely to any one solution.

Fluency A major component of the creative process, defined as the productive quantity of creative output.

Imagery The ability to visualize either imagined or previously perceived objects accurately and vividly.

Micropsychotic Episodes Symptoms of formal thought disorder, including those of delusion and hallucination, which are very mild, weak, intermittent, and of brief duration.

Nonconformity Not attending to, or not agreeing with, the consensually accepted patterns of thought or behavior, and acting accordingly.

Originality The major component of the creative process, de-fined as the uniqueness of a given response used to solve an artistic or scientific problem.

Schizotypal Personality A personality pattern distinguished by magical thinking, odd communication styles, suspicion, and mildly paranoid thinking.

ECCENTRICITY is a partly socially constructed concept used to describe the personality predisposition and behavior of individuals who are otherwise difficult to classify in terms of personality. Eccentric people are lifelong permanent nonconformists who, by and large, do not violate legal prohibitions but are oblivious to, or do not accept, some social norms and conventions.

I. DEFINITION

Eccentricity refers primarily to nonconforming individualists with strikingly unusual personalities. The persons in question, who feel that they single-mindedly are being true to themselves, are like this over the long term. While they do accept that they are different from most other people, some are not convinced of their eccentricity and will readily deny it, blaming this disparity on the misperceptions of others. They are

Copyright © 1999 by Academic Press
All rights of reproduction in any form reserved.

predictably unpredictable, especially in reference to the normative values and expectations of society. The development of society and of eccentricity can be viewed as interdependent; indeed, the wayward individual has an integral part to play in the shaping of society. [*See* CONFORMITY.]

However, although the different personality and behavioral patterns that eccentrics demonstrate may be odd, they themselves should not necessarily be considered to be pathological. Indeed, they show no higher rates of psychiatric disorder than would be found in equivalent random community population survey samples. Eccentric people are also statistically rare. Probably for these or other reasons, they are perhaps the last category of people to have escaped the scrutiny and investigation of the psychological sciences.

The question of definition is technically formidable. A few adjectives that have been popularly applied to eccentrics include nonconforming, rebellious, and whimsical. Some have been superficially described as loners. Different dictionaries have offered different definitions. Most mention nonspecific oddness of personality, unconventionality in reference to accepted patterns of social behavior, and singular ways of behaving in terms of its component actions or hypothetical goals. Other associated adjectives have included words like anomalous, irregular, peculiar, capricious, devious, and even slightly mad.

An operational definition of eccentrics is more helpful if it incorporates an empirical description of their behaviors and tendencies. In continuing studies in Great Britain, The Netherlands, Australia, New Zealand, Canada, and the United States (taking place between October 1984 and 1997) of eccentrics living in the community, the following 25 descriptor variables emerged (in descending order of frequency):

- Enduring non-conformity
- An enduring and distinct feeling of differentness from others
- Creative
- Strongly motivated by an exceedingly powerful curiosity and related intellectual exploratory behavior
- Idealism, wanting to make the world a better place and the people in it happier
- Happily obsessed with a number of long-lasting preoccupations

- Intelligent
- Opinionated and outspoken, convinced that they are right and that the rest of the world is out of step with their ideas
- Noncompetitive
- Not necessarily in need of reassurance or reinforcement from the rest of society
- Unusual in their eating habits and living arrangements
- Not necessarily interested in the opinions or company of other people, or of personal popularity
- Possessed of a mischievous sense of humor, charm, whimsy, and wit
- More frequently the eldest or an only child
- A poor speller, especially in relation to their above average general intellectual functioning
- Eccentricity noted in at least 36% of detailed family histories of eccentrics, usually a grandparent, aunt, or uncle (it should be noted that the family history method of estimating hereditary similarities and resemblances usually provides rather conservative estimates)
- Eccentrics prefer to talk about their thoughts rather than their feelings; there is a frequent use of the psychological defense mechanisms of rationalization and intellectualization.
- Slightly abrasive
- Midlife changes in career or lifestyle
- Feelings of "invisibility," which means that they believed others did not seem to hear them or see them, or take their ideas seriously
- Feel that other people can only take them in small doses
- Feel that others have stolen, or would like to steal, their ideas; in some cases, this is the reality
- Dislike small talk or other apparently inconsequential conversation
- A degree of social awkwardness
- Single

To summarize, eccentrics are exceptional individuals with insight into their differentness. They are personal and ideological loners. Their relative separateness comes about because of their integrity to themselves and to their principles. [*See* AUTONOMY AND INDEPENDENCE.]

II. PSYCHOPATHOLOGY

It is perhaps relevant to point out that in *every* psychiatric study conducted in this century, the most common trait seen in the well, nonpsychotic relatives of schizophrenic patients has been odd eccentric demeanor and behavior, usually, but less frequently, in combination with instability, social isolation, emotional coolness, and suspicion. Symptoms commonly associated with schizophrenia are prevalent among eccentrics studied, albeit in very mild forms, brief duration, and very infrequent occurrence. [*See* SCHIZOPHRENIA.]

However, their originality is statistically significantly correlated with the degree of their formal thought disorder ($p < .01$) and their repetitive thinking ($p < .01$). These symptoms can best be described as subtle *micropsychotic* episodes, as has been suggested in a different context by the clinical psychologist and methodologist Paul Meehl. Such episodes are seen as one of the several best diagnostic signs of either a preschizophrenic state or of schizotypal personality. However, in one large sample of eccentrics ($n = 130$), interviewed using the stringent research diagnostic criteria of the Personality Assessment Schedule, only 8% of these eccentrics fulfilled the criteria of either schizotypal or schizoid personality disorder. While this may be more than the proportion found in the general population, the data undercut previous clinical lore that these personality syndromes could be related to eccentricity.

Occurring as frequently as these are the kinds of minimal quasi-delusional beliefs that most would think of as merely irrationality rather than partial delusion. Many of these concerned either paranormal or mystical belief. In this occult tendency, the external agency assumes a universal spiritual dimension, and its bearer may contract the sense of shouldering an outwardly unwanted mission. Related to this is an acknowledgment of all-inclusive, encompassing cosmic verities. These primitive thought-feelings share many similarities with those experienced by mystics, Zen Buddhists, and artists, as well as delusional psychiatric patients. In these, normal time and space seem to become suspended, and there are relatively dramatic oscillations of mood. These very transitory, evanescent conditions could imply a release from the perceived encumbrances of ordinary common sense, and with that, a perceived increase in personal freedom.

Throughout all this, emphasis is placed on the forces of natural harmony, nature, and a cosmic order beyond the ability of expression by "mere" words. These forces are doing battle with, and finally vanquishing, society's false claims for conventional sufferance, thereby overcoming others' cynicism or demoralization and their belittling of idealism. To their eccentric bearers, these ideas are seen as natural rather than intrusive, though they can certainly recognize, through experience, how others might find them to be strange.

Eccentrics exult in their creative inspiration and ideas. This is sometimes accompanied by feelings of uncanniness and even weirdness. There are also some tendencies toward occult beliefs; in this, their impressions seem to them to augur something of universal significance. The spiritual or mystical content in this included all-encompassing transcend verities. Their cognitive experiences are acquiesced in by them, without any resistance. Their thoughts are usually *egosyntonic*. The possession of these beliefs is, however, significantly correlated with the eccentrics' observed degree of creativity and, as adjudged by others, their more distinctive quality of originality. The same individuals experienced more severely stressful life events, and there was more hostile expressed criticism in the parental family directed at them when they were children. In retrospect, they viewed the latter as precipitated by them, and therefore, at least in part, justifiably deserved.

Many eccentrics behave in inveterately unorthodox and challenging ways, carrying out their preoccupations with great enthusiasm, sometimes contrary to the well-meaning advice of others. That their actual behavior is often paradoxical, when viewed from the outside, may or may not be of great concern to them, but they are usually fairly resistant to external influences. What narcissism or egocentricity they show is reflected primarily in linguistic self-reference, either when talking about other people or neutral topics. This also comes out in almost compulsive speechifying, frequently interrupting other people's flow of speech.

III. CREATIVITY

A high proportion of prodigiously original people have been described by their contemporaries as being eccentric. If eccentricity is positively associated with the ability to conceive startlingly original artistic and technological breakthroughs, it behooves social scientists to attempt to understand the factors that may stimulate not only the lateral thinking itself, but also the conditions under which it may freely flourish. Perhaps because of their greater openness to novel experiences, eccentrics possess a great variety of seemingly unrelated interests, and are sometimes able to connect and use these manifold experiences to good effect.

Creativity encompasses effective empathic problem solving. The part that empathy plays in this formulation is that it represents an intuitive transaction between the creative individual and the problem to be confronted. The individual displaces his point of view into the problem by an imaginative leap, investing into it something of his own intellect and personality, while drawing knowledge from the nature of the problem. He or she no longer identifies the problem solely as an object, or with its qualities or attributes, but rather identifies himself with all the profound depths of the problem. The artist Georges Braque exemplified this when he said, "One must not just depict the objects, one must penetrate into them, and one must oneself become the object." The closer one comes to this ideal the better.

This total immersion into the problem means that there is a great motivational welling up of commitment to understand it at all costs. This involves the recognition of few limits and therefore leads to the concomitant shift in the individual's point of view. In some cases this is the intentional strategy employed, and can appear quite extreme as compared to more routine experimental methodological techniques. This general approach of "getting inside the problem," a special instance of participant observation, begins with the subjective internal state of the creator/problem solver and works outward from there.

To accomplish these ends, the eccentric creator exercises various component processes of creativity, as noted by many researchers in this field. These components are principally originality (the searching for a more unique response); fluency (the productive quantity of output per problem); flexibility (the spontaneous willingness to attempt and to modify various solu-

tions and not being prematurely tied to any one type of solution); and elaboration (improving upon the initial idea or applying it in other overlapping content areas). How these components are specifically utilized by any particular individual will partly be determined by that person's past experiences, previous social and learning environments, and the specific task demands of the problem and subject. [*See* FLEXIBILITY.]

Eccentrics are creative across a broad front and are represented in practically every modality. Most demonstrate clear insight into how to use their creative abilities. The fluency of their ideas, and the translation of these ideas into creative output, is prodigious. Their talents are not restricted to a specific medium, topic area, or mode of representation; about a fifth of eccentrics exhibit their skills in more than one modality. On average, a creative eccentric will retain a great deal of active intellectual interest in about five separate topics. They focus their imaginative tendencies to some degree; some have found ways to test out their frequently controversial ideas.

For some eccentric creators, a degree of empathy is involved in their imaginative approaches to greater understanding. This is used not only for problem solving and related technical matters, but also, somewhat less so, in the interpersonal domain. Despite this, it is a paradox that this is a factor that most eccentrics do not fully exploit, many usually preferring to be social loners, though not averse to a healthy argument. While being able to see several sides of an issue, they will not be swayed by external persuasion, and will quite adamantly press their points home with more regard for their apparent rightness than for the feelings of those mounting opposing propositions.

These attitudes, of conviction in their rightness and resistance in the face of opposition, color their approach in actuality. These are more likely to be encountered in eccentrics who have carried forward and expanded their childlike openness onto a more adult level. These creative eccentrics manage to preserve their more innocent sensory perceptions and "naive" intellectual responses to them, and do not easily succumb to orderly limitations imposed on their thinking by more accepted or customary methodologies. Eccentrics who use such highly personalized models are often reluctant to explain every relevant example or factual data point in terms of general rules or laws, or even necessarily in a consistently coherent way from one new instance to another. However, much of their creative behavior is conscious and deliberate, utilizing discernible strategies.

In preparation for the creative process, the individual tries to place herself in the requisite frame of mind. One distinctive tactic used is intentional indirection. In this, she may go off on a seemingly irrelevant tangent, but with the intent to return ultimately to the problem at hand. This indirect approach is also used at other stages in the creative process. There is also planning involved; in this, a range of contingency plans are modeled, considered, and elaborated in thought. This preference for planning out problem areas in detail, a predilection for troubleshooting at an early stage, is in the context of an habitual personal approach with an emphasis on long-range planning.

Growing out of the concomitant thinking involved in this is the apprehension of newly appreciated possibilities. The beginning elements in these ideas are most frequently poorly defined, nebulous cognitive experiences for which there might not even be words appropriate or available. Amid this a number of automatic subroutines may be generated, sometimes almost passing unnoticed in the turbulence and excitement of thinking the new thoughts. There is greater ease in forming permeable ideational associations, some of which are more remote; a certain fraction of these are innovative, and a smaller proportion still are innovative *and* feasible. [*See* INNOVATION.]

However, this ability to make remote associations, in eccentric creativity, is neither necessary nor sufficient. This particular facet may be more highly related to conventional verbal intellectual skills and to convergent, rather than divergent, thinking. However, it may also contribute to a fantasy life of singular intensity and what may appear to be irrationality. [*See* DIVERGENT THINKING.]

It is probable that the eccentric creator is only loosely repressed. Overtly, he would tend to reject repression as a concept; in practice, he is less inhibited, prefers informality and a bohemian lifestyle, and would be perceived by others as radical in his belief systems. Because of these personal factors, he can sometimes remove the remaining restraints on his partially semi-

conscious impulses. The related attitudes might be expected to be invaluable to those who unrelentingly challenge the conventional in society. The person may still be left with some inner repressions, but he is aware that his own ideas are at variance to the normative values of society.

The many refractory oppositions thus set up repeated frustrations within him. There are opportunities for emotional release from these pent-up frustrations, and these culminate in creative outbursts. This pattern of sporadic outbreaks forces the individual's creative process to be intuition-led and therefore unpredictable. This manifests itself in an apparently undercontrolled and sometimes indirect approach.

Such creative people, despite seeming to be temporarily emotionally erratic, unstable, and distracted, are still capable of using their instability effectively. They may not be "well adjusted" according to strictly psychological parameters or personological definitions, but they are adjusted in the broader sense of being socially useful and often personally happy, especially when caught up in their more purely creative pursuits. For some, the actual creative functioning becomes an autonomous end in itself, and so addictive that the eccentrics develop special specific techniques to regain their privileged access to these unique states of mind.

Eccentrics explore seemingly irrational ideas through their use of humor. For them, humor has the power to liberate them from more everyday worries. Adopting a humorous attitude frees up the eccentrics' views of mundane reality. Wit sometimes turns predictable ideas upside down, and a playful sense of fun can be an unquenchable source of delight. Wit and humor provoke new insights because a certain sense of incongruity is common both to humor and to creativity, and both of these also manage to help integrate apparently opposing elements. [*See* HUMOR.]

However, a good proportion of eccentric creativity is intentional, understandable, and derived from elegantly simple techniques. One of these is the appropriate use of meditational methods and techniques. In the case of eccentric creators, these are bound up with their tendencies to use vivid visual imagery. The eccentric's degree of conscious control over such imagery abilities is important to creativity. The images created are active, operating as used on other concrete and abstract ideas within the mind. In eccentrics, there are substantial variations in the clarity, flexibility, and the mastery attained over their visual imagery. Some images become transformed playfully into speculative hypotheses, while some enlighten with further understanding. [*See* IMAGERY.]

The most frequent aspect of imagery in eccentrics' detailed descriptions on interview was that of image vividness. This vividness amounted to well-preserved, near-eidetic imagery of sparkling clarity. Eidetic imagery is a mental representation of an object or event which has all the redolent characteristics of the original perception on which it is based. More accurately, it is the ability to imaginatively project upon a blank screen the duplicate of a picture, after its removal from view, and to focus precisely and at will on any of its details. This capacity is often well developed in young children but, as one grows older, it partly becomes less distinct for most people. It is thought that this happens in tandem with the acquisition of more abstract methods of processing information.

Imagery can work in other sensory modalities other than the visual. It need not necessarily be only a matter of passive reception, but can be actively worked on, manipulated, and changed. Eccentric creators can, with their eyes shut or open, clearly "see in the mind's eye" a play or story enacted as if it were being presented to them. They may appear outwardly passive or even pensive, as if watching a film. Due to their practice, perseverance, and experience, imagery-related skills can become more accurate over time.

The movement and action of the images can become extended to the point where sequences of them appear to fuse; they can precipitate, by associative actions, further images. They can also become blocked temporarily, and then, a little later re-fuse and produce further series in rapid succession, until the imagery is almost impossible to follow and "dances before the eyes." Just like some nocturnal vivid dreamers who, on awakening, attempt to make sense out of the images which come unbidden to them in sleep, so too do the eccentric creators attempt to interpret their diurnal images. They also attempt to produce further chains of thought or images from them. But just as dreams can only very rarely be well controlled, sometimes the tangential ideas flowing from some images can have an elusive quality.

Vivid daytime imagery and vivid nocturnal imagery in dreams share much in common. When REM (rapid eye movement) sleep, which is when most people dream, is experimentally suppressed, some people show an intensification of sporadic eye activity just at the onset of the delayed REM sleep state. These coincide with much more vivid dream imagery.

Recent electroencephalographic (EEG) brain-wave studies suggest that during visual dreaming the right and the left sides of the brain are far less well integrated. The electrical activity of the nerve fibers connecting these two hemispheres, known as the corpus callosum or cerebral commissures, is greatly reduced during REM sleep. This amounts to a partial functional disconnection; when this occurs the dominant language-orientated cerebral hemisphere (the left cerebral hemisphere for most right-handed people) is less able to affect what goes on in the opposite nondominant, perhaps more image-laden, cerebral hemisphere. Neurological patients who have sustained injuries to the nondominant (usually right-sided) cerebral hemisphere report that they can no longer experience dreams. There is other evidence that remote memories used in imagery are also used in recognition, and that dreaming and waking visual imagery share some common neuropsychological processes.

Dreams often continue on the main lines of previous waking thoughts, be they verbally or visually mediated. If a dream contains associations with waking experience, it can continue, albeit with interruptions, into periods of sleep, particularly processing those more salient parts of ongoing experience that are actively meaningful or have not as yet reached a satisfactory resolution.

Although the form of ideas and thoughts changes from primarily words to primarily images with sleep, whatever is of concern to the individual when she falls asleep may be carried forward into dreaming states. Sleep is not a total interruption, but a transition, in the form of the flow, and of the degree, of consciousness. In this light, dreams can be seen to vary as eventual by-products of cognitive function, personality, and lifestyle. [*See* DREAMS AND CREATIVITY.]

For eccentric and noneccentric people, there is a close relationship between positively vivid imagery and an absorbing style of imagination. People who shared these qualities also had diurnal images that contained happy emotional content. There is also a positive orientation toward imagination, introspection, daydreaming, and meditation for those who remember their dreams well, but not for those who recall them poorly. A similar relationship exists between dreams and imagery, particularly for eccentrics. Factor analytic studies revealed a separate and significant factor; this was composed primarily of overall creative productivity and vivid dreaming, but also included, to a lesser degree, the experience of conscious dissolution (eg., affirming test items and statements such as "My mind is dissolving"), diurnal imagery, and the overall degree of eccentricity itself. One of the pertinent points here is that eccentrics share, to a higher degree than others, excellent nocturnal dream imagery and diurnal waking imagery.

There is an unambiguous relationship between creativity and curiosity among eccentric creators. Eccentrics not only arouse the temporary curiosity of otherwise reserved people; they themselves are exceptionally curious. For many, this is their major motivation, viewed by many of them as more important than their desire to be different. This is somewhat at variance with cultural norms. The expression of curiosity by adults is often inhibited, due perhaps to fears of giving offense to others, social embarrassment, or appearing to be ignorant or naive.

Curiosity-related behaviors are said to be carried out "for their own sake," by which is meant that they are carried out for the sake of their internal rewarding associations and consequences. Curiosity is known as the "intrinsic motivation." This motivation is fundamental to the nurturing of creativity and to the genesis of authentic eccentricity. The creative insight is partly the end result of semiautomatic processes in the brain engendered by curiosity, but essentially these are maintained by brain work, both active and interactive. [*See* MOTIVATION/DRIVE.]

The novelty of what one produces is positively correlated to the degree of complexity of thought one can sustain, and to the readiness to explore not only the outer world but also what is going on internally, in concepts and by psychological self-analysis. Novel associations are preferred by creative people. Novel associations are also obviously preferred, and acted upon, by eccentrics. Curiosity, therefore, can best be described as a general condition analogous to the need to seek out new experiences—to extend one's knowledge into unknown frontiers. Although male eccentric creators tend to describe their personal creativity succinctly, female eccentric creators demonstrate more curiosity than do equivalent male eccentrics ($p < .01$). [*See* NOVELTY.]

Eccentrics are intellectually gifted in many ways—they are highly curious, full of vivid visual imagery while awake and while dreaming, and highly intelligent in terms of conventional measures of convergent intelligence (achieving above average IQs, mainly in the range between 115 and 120 on standardized test measures). A number had been identified early by teachers and educational psychologists as intellectually exceptional gifted children. They create, by synthesis, conceptual analysis, symbolism, and constructive conceptual modeling, new forms of information. [*See* GIFTEDNESS AND CREATIVITY; INTELLIGENCE.]

However, despite all this, some eccentrics' creative projects do misfire. There are several reasons for this, which are instructive. Problems with specific components of the creative process introduce further difficulties into some eccentrics' creative work. Endowed with high fluency, they have higher numbers of ideas per unit of time. For instance, one successful eccentric artist invented 25 different fictional personalities for himself, and then painted in the way demanded by that biography.

However, this much fluency causes further problems later because for some period of time after their ideas' conceptions, the eccentric creators are very attached to each and every one of them. Each of their ideas, testable and untestable alike, are greatly valued by them, as is the process of their achievement.

Their embarrassment of riches in the cognitive sphere can be the source of another problem; eccentric creators are often very uncertain about which of their early ideas to select as the primary focus to devote their energies toward further understanding. Often, as might be expected concerning intellectual nonconformists with a diversity of educational backgrounds, the ideas chosen are consensually adjudged by more conventional scientists as the least viable. This applies not only to those ideas which are perceived as counterintuitive, but also to those that others consider to be implausible if not impossible, for example, human levitation, perpetual motion machines, and squaring the circle.

Once having chosen a subject or concept, and

having posited one or several unorthodox theories about it, the eccentric creator cannot usually be dissuaded from pursuing his or her theory's contingent lines of inquiry with evident persistence. With high curiosity, eccentrics will go to great lengths to obtain as much information as possible. They will read every relevant primary and secondary source available, and many that are difficult to obtain. If possible, they will set up experiments. They will communicate with, and personally consult, eminent or well-known academics, preferring those who have themselves enunciated controversial views. If any of the expert opinions is at variance with the eccentric's hypothesis or approach, the eccentric will not usually be dissuaded from uncompromisingly following the initial tack. To the contrary, the more skeptical is the response, the more tenaciously will the eccentric creator redouble his or her efforts to pursue it further, sometimes for many years. Such resilience in the face of criticism is not always disadvantageous, but there are only so many blind alleys that any one eccentric is able to pursue.

At these stages, and in this way, some eccentric creators can be seen to be far from flexible. Clearly, without a flexible approach toward either the discarding of an incorrect idea, or toward considering changing it, intractable difficulties can be caused. Of course, the alternative interpretation of this is that the eccentric is nevertheless thereby retaining a coherent sense of willed integrity.

But the eccentric creator might also take the wrong notion even several steps further, usually earlier in the creative cycle than less eccentric individuals would in similar circumstances. He might overelaborate the idea prematurely. He might think how it could possibly work in other situations or environmental niches, and work out and propound further new applications for his untested original conceptualization.

If the eccentric creator does develop her proposition into a viable application, she may communicate it to potentially receptive audiences in decidedly quirky ways, which may range from simply ineffectual to wholly indecipherable. For example, there is a well-attested anecdotal case, unfortunately not apocryphal, of a highly respected university postdoctoral mathematician who invented a new and constructive equation which he believed would revolutionize the field of statistics. Upon being invited to present his theory and

formulas to a conference of his professional association, he spent the first three quarters of his lecture explaining in prodigious detail how his specific make and model of electronic calculator was the best tool for performing the type of work he had been doing. The time remaining to him was insufficient for presenting his thesis intelligibly. Follow-up questions were answered even more digressively, so that even his more forebearing colleagues were frustrated.

Another hurdle in the path of creative eccentrics with many ideas is that some find difficulties in bringing any of them to fruition. A minority of these eccentrics seem to specialize in concocting ideas and selling them on as incomplete ideas only. Other eccentrics seem to mass-produce book titles, opening chapters of novels, and unedited film script synopses, but have difficulties ever finishing an art or music work of any kind. There is always a work in progress, daydreams of what success might bring, and new future projects to do, "If only there were enough hours in the day."

Eccentrics are an invigorating reminder of everyone's intrinsic uniqueness. Eccentrics are examples of independent mindedness and a questing freedom of spirit. They do more than merely grapple with the existence of free will; they engineer their lives in such a way as constantly to force its limits. They ceaselessly assert their fundamental right to be what they want to be.

Eccentrics are living proof that one does not necessarily need to go through life with a rigid set of rules. They believe that they have attained greater awareness and perception; they believe that they see and understand things, including social arrangements, in depth. They do not accept mundane everyday objects at face value. Because of this, their lives are enriched. They see more, and in so doing, point to how much positive experience so-called "normal" people miss. By flouting norms of behavior that most of us never question, they remind us how much of our liberty we forfeit without thought, and how great our ability is, in fact, to forge our own identities and shape our own lives for ourselves.

Bibliography

Arnheim, R. (1969). *Visual thinking*. Berkeley, CA: University of California Press.

Barron, F. X. (1968). *Creativity and personal freedom*. Princeton, NJ: Van Nostrand.

Hall, J. A. (1984). *Nonverbal sex differences.* Baltimore, MD: John Hopkins University Press.

Kegan, R. (1982). *The evolving self, problems and processes in human development.* Cambridge, MA: Harvard University Press.

Kendler, K. S. (1985). Diagnostic approaches to schizotypal personality disorder: A historical perspective. *Schizophrenia Bulletin, 11*(4), 538–553.

Lenz, H. (1983). Belief and delusion: Their common origin but different course of developments. *Zygon, 18*(2), 117–137.

Meehl, P. E. (1972). A critical afterword. In I. I. Gottesman & J. Shields (Eds.), *Schizophrenia and genetics.* New York: Academic Press.

Morris, P. E. & Hampson, P. J. (1983). *Imagery and consciousness.* London: Academic Press.

Walker, E. L. and Heyns, R. W. (1962). *Anatomy for conformity.* Englewood Cliffs, NJ: Prentice-Hall.

Weeks, D. & James, J. (1995). *Eccentrics. A study of sanity and strangeness.* New York: Villard.

Economic Perspective on Creativity

Todd I. Lubart

Université René Descartes (Paris V)

Mark Runco

California State University, Fullerton

Benefits Something that increases well-being.

Buying Low Pursuing a new or undervalued idea that has growth potential.

Costs Resources expended in producing an output.

Demand Quantity needed or desired of a commodity or service.

Depreciation Loss in value of an asset over time.

Human Capital Skills, knowledge, and abilities that people possess and can use in a productive fashion; these personal assets result from initial endowment and education or training.

Investment Outlay of assets for future income or profit.

Marginal Utility Benefit obtained from one additional unit of a good.

Psychic Costs Intangible mental or social expenses, such as emotional stress.

Resources Available assets useful for production.

Selling High Releasing a novel production (such as an idea) on the market when it has gained value.

Supply Quantity available of a commodity or service.

Creativity theorists have used economic phenomena to develop and convey ideas about the nature of creativity.

This perspective was explored, in particular, by Robert Sternberg and Todd Lubart in their investment theory of creativity and by Daniel Rubenson and Mark Runco in their psychoeconomic approach to creativity. It was also explored by Herbert Walberg in his work on education and human capital. These proposals together with those of several other authors will be synthesized in the following description of THE ECONOMIC PERSPECTIVE ON CREATIVITY.

I. THE MICROECONOMICS OF CREATIVITY

In this section, the economic perspective is applied to creativity at the individual level. Microeconomic issues include the notions of investing in new ideas, human capital, the development of human capital by creativity training, and the costs and benefits of creative work at the individual level.

A. Investing in Ideas: The Principle of Buying Low and Selling High

Sternberg and Lubart proposed that creative people are like successful investors in the financial marketplace: They buy low and sell high. Buying low in the realm of creativity means pursuing new or undervalued

Copyright © 1999 by Academic Press
All rights of reproduction in any form reserved.

ideas that have growth potential—that may be successful for solving one's problem. Selling high means releasing a novel idea on the market when it has gained value and not holding an idea so long that others eventually have the same idea. This buy low–sell high principle is partly descriptive of what creative people do naturally and partly prescriptive of a strategy that people may try consciously to implement to improve their creativity. Engaging in buy low–sell high behavior may involve an analysis of the potential of ideas and of the marketplace for launching these ideas. Thus creators may use strategies similar to those employed by market analysts for choosing among several possible ideas. One strategy is fundamental analysis in which key elements of a new idea may be evaluated for their intrinsic originality, their appropriateness to the problem-solving goal, as well as other qualities such as the aesthetic appeal of the idea. This strategy can be seen in some accounts by inventors in which they debate the strengths and weaknesses of their ideas before fully engaging work on a project. An alternative strategy is technical analysis, in which trends in the problem domain may be examined in order to predict what will be considered by the target audience as novel, appropriate, or aesthetic. This strategy can be observed in some accounts of artistic creativity, including work in fashion design and advertising.

According to the buy low–sell high principle, people may fail to be creative because they (a) buy high, pursuing ideas that are already valued or known (perhaps to avoid risk); (b) buy low, pursuing ideas that do not have growth potential; or (c) sell low, exposing an idea before the audience is ready, before the idea has gained in value, or, inversely, holding the idea too long so that it becomes commonplace.

B. Human Capital: The Resources for Creativity

Capital refers to assets that enter into the productive process and lead to income. Although we think often of physical capital (e.g., land or machines) or financial capital (money), there is also human capital. Human capital can be defined broadly as the knowledge, abilities, and skills of workers as well as their time and energy. For creativity the necessary human capital consists of a set of cognitive and conative resources. These resources are specific intellectual abilities, cognitive styles, knowledge, personality traits (e.g., risk taking), and motivations. Individuals vary on the extent to which they possess each resource. For example, one person may be a risk taker whereas another person is rather risk avoidant. The resources are hypothesized to develop and change over the life span.

A large body of research in psychology has examined the precise nature of the intellectual abilities, cognitive styles, knowledge, personality traits, motivations, and environmental circumstances favorable to creativity. This work can be synthesized within the economic perspective on creativity: Each person possesses a portfolio of resources (skills and traits) relevant to creativity. This portfolio of psychological resources for creativity is part of a person's human capital, which may be actively invested in creative projects. From this perspective, the level of creative performance observed depends on (a) a person's level on each of the resources necessary for creativity, (b) the person's active engagement of his or her resources, and (c) the match between the portfolio of resources that a person has and the profile of resources required for creative work in a domain (or a task) (i.e., the market demands).

Some fundamental economic principles may account for observed nonlinear relationships between the resources and creative performance as well as lifespan changes in the resources. For example, some studies suggest that a greater and greater amount of certain resources is not always the best for creativity. Knowledge and formal education seem to show an inverted-U relationship to creativity with an intermediate level of education being preferable to a very advanced level. There may be a trade-off between two desirable but conflicting attributes. For example, knowledge is beneficial because it permits an individual to avoid reinventing existing ideas (which already have a high value) and to avoid errors that others have already made in trying to work on a problem. However, increases in knowledge toward an expert level tend to have a negative effect on another desirable attribute, namely flexibility of thought. Experts often get stuck into using certain techniques for attacking a problem. Indeed, they have spent so much time and energy acquiring these advanced techniques that it only makes sense to capitalize on their initial investment. In terms of intelligence and creativity, it has been often hypothesized that increases in intelligence contribute greatly to creativity initially, and then less and less. This is the phenomenon of diminishing returns. [*See* INTELLIGENCE.]

With regard to life-span changes in the resources for creativity, the well-known economic phenomenon of depreciation may be one of the processes at work. For example, knowledge acquired at a certain moment may become outdated (1 year later, 10 years later, etc., depending on the field of endeavor). The value of the initially acquired knowledge depreciates as a field advances and new advances are made. To the extent that one acquires a substantial knowledge base in one's field upon entry to the field, we may expect that the person's capital in terms of knowledge will gradually become devalued with age. The desire to avoid depreciation of one's existing knowledge may explain results showing that older scientists resist, in some cases, new theories more than younger scientists do. In addition to these explanatory insights offered by the economic perspective, this perspective brings into focus some aspects of creativity more than others (as is the case with any particular point of view). For example, the economic perspective places a special emphasis on risk taking, part of the personality resource for creativity. Risk taking is generally accepted as a key to investment decisions. Risk taking involves decision making in the face of uncertainty and opportunity costs. Concerning the pursuit of creative ideas, people may underinvest because the potential rewards of a new idea are somewhat ambiguous as compared to pursuing technically sound but mundane ideas for which the limited rewards are clear. Thus, one of the features of an economic approach to creativity is that risk taking is highlighted and explored in more detail than it has been in other approaches.

C. Investing in Creativity-Relevant Human Capital: Creativity Training

The resources for creativity can be enhanced, at least partially, through training. For example, a person may study creative thinking techniques through a self-help book or by participating in a training program. Most creativity training focuses on enhancing the cognitive resources for creativity. Training is possible with regard to the attitudinal and motivational resources for creativity, but this type of training is less common.

An investment in creativity training leads to an accumulation of human capital that can later be put to use. The investment in training depends on the marginal utility to the individual. Age and occupation are two variables that may influence decisions to pursue creativity training. Younger workers may derive benefits of training for a longer time than would older workers, thus increasing the utility of training for younger workers. Some occupations may demand creativity more than others, thus modulating the marginal benefits of training.

The benefits of creativity training, which may vary from person to person, include intrinsic rewards (e.g., personal enjoyment) and extrinsic rewards (e.g., increased job performance, earnings, and opportunities for job advancement). The costs of creativity training include book expenses, tuition for courses, and opportunity costs of work not accomplished during the time spent on creativity training. For some individuals, the costs are reduced because their company sponsors the training program.

The decision to pursue creativity training is based on the marginal utility of each unit of training. A person with little human capital for creativity will benefit more than a person who already possesses many resources for creativity. Each of these individuals, however, can be expected to benefit less and less from each additional unit of creativity training, which is the phenomenon of diminishing returns. At some point, the marginal cost of additional creativity training will exceed the marginal benefit and the individual will not seek further training. With regard to the choice of creativity training versus traditional education, people are more likely to invest in traditional education than in creativity-related education. The former has more predictable, less risky returns than the latter. Thus, even if people think that the effect of creativity training may be potentially more positive than traditional expertise training, the effects of creativity training are less certain than those expected with traditional education.

D. Costs and Benefits of Creative Activity

As the description of the economic perspective on creativity already implied, there are costs and benefits of creative work. Often, because creativity is a socially valued behavior, we tend to focus on the benefits of creative work. For an individual, there are both extrinsic benefits, such as recognition and financial gains, and intrinsic benefits, such as satisfaction with one's work, a feeling of accomplishment. However, there are costs to creative work. These include pecuniary costs (time and resources expended during the work) and psychic costs such as emotional wear and tear of overcoming the obstacles encountered often in creative work. Psychic costs may furthermore include social isolation for one's "deviant ideas." The initial negative reaction that often accompanies creative work may affect one's self-confidence or task motivation.

There are opportunity costs as well: the individual could have been pursuing other projects that may have given some positive results themselves. Finally, there are transaction costs—costs that the creative person pays to a third party to facilitate the exchange with the audience. These transaction costs may be tangible ones such as a commission paid to art gallery owners for displaying an artist's work or intangible costs such as limitations that one places on one's thinking to express ideas within the implicit rules of a discipline. In addition to the costs already mentioned, there are "taxes" that are collected after a creative success. For example, a scholar may be asked to review grant proposals or articles, which takes time from future creative work.

The decision to pursue creativity training (through self-help books or through a structured program) also is based on costs and benefits. These costs and benefits are subject to change, of course, with the amount of creativity training or the number of creative projects in which one is engaged. Notably, there may be diminishing marginal returns for each additional unit of creativity training but diminishing marginal costs for each additional creative idea that is pursued in solving a problem. The benefits of each unit of creativity training depend on the amount of training already received and on the value that a person assigns to creativity.

II. THE MACROECONOMICS OF CREATIVITY

In this section, we discuss how the economic perspective is applied to creativity at the societal level. This includes a discussion at the aggregate level of the supply and demand of creativity, investment in human capital, and the costs and benefits of creative work.

A. The Market for Creativity

At the aggregate level, there is a supply and a demand for creative activity. The supply of creativity refers to the number of novel, useful productions (ideas, inventions, artistic works, etc.) that the members of a social unit (such as an organization or a society) provide. The demand for creativity is the need or desire in a society for creative productions. This demand may vary across domains (art, science, business, etc.) and across time. The demand for creativity also varies from one place to another. Some societies value conformity and maintenance of the status quo more than others. Societies may choose to offer incentives or reduce incentives to influence the supply of creativity. These adjustments can be accomplished, for example, through grants to stimulate activity in certain domains, through educational initiatives, or through changes to the patent system.

With regard to the market for creativity, the economic perspective highlights the social consensual nature of creativity. The value of stocks on the stock exchange or other financial instruments depends on the extent to which those actively involved in the market value and collectively desire a stock. In a parallel way, the value of an idea depends on the audience and the extent to which the audience collectively values the idea. Thus ideas (or productions) can appreciate or depreciate in value with time or with a change of audience. We are able to therefore understand why some creative geniuses are "discovered" posthumously and other "greats" in their day disappear into oblivion.

B. Investing in Creativity-Relevant Human Capital

As mentioned earlier, societies may invest in creativity through grants, fellowships, and educational programs. In the United States, governmental agencies such as the National Endowment for the Arts and the National Science Foundation oversee many grants and fellowships. Societies tend to underestimate the need for creativity because they do not adequately take into account the long-term benefits of creative ideas and focus instead on short-term, immediate needs. This underestimation of the demand for creativity can result in occasional shortages of creativity, as was perceived in the United States in the 1950s upon the Soviet launch of *Sputnik*.

Investment in creative human capital is, of course, subject to diminishing returns. The marginal benefits derived from each unit of societal resources spent on enhancing creativity will initially be great and then will decrease in size. Eventually a point will be reached for which resources devoted to creativity may yield small increases but these resources could be better used to foster noncreativity-related endeavors.

Another dimension of the societal investment in creative human capital is the policy decision of who will receive this investment. For instance, there is a societal choice in terms of investing in the education of average children to increase the general level of creativity in the population versus investing in a smaller number of gifted children who could eventually achieve the highest levels in their fields of endeavor. To the extent that a society invests in those who have already succeeded in the past, there is a Matthew effect (the creatively rich get richer, and the creatively poor stay poor). This pattern of investment in human capital increases the probability that investments in creative human capital will yield some returns. However, some authors have argued that a society may derive a greater benefit from enhancing the creativity of the "average" person (through educational programs) rather than investing the same amount in a restricted group of highly creative people who may show a relatively small increment in their creativity. [*See* MATTHEW EFFECTS.]

C. Costs and Benefits

As discussed at the microeconomic level, there are macroeconomic costs and benefits to creative work. The costs include direct financial costs and the use of physical and human resources. The opportunity costs refer to foregone advancements on other activities of the society (e.g., maintenance of roads). Opportunity costs also include the foregone advances on alternative creative domains. For example, if scientific creativity is promoted, artistic creativity may suffer a lack of advancement.

The benefits of creativity include an enhanced quality of life for the society in general as well as possible stimulation in the economic sphere. Each creative idea may have a trickle-down effect in which new supplementary products and services result from an initial idea. For example, the invention of the microcomputer fostered the emergence of many new computer-related services that have enhanced economic growth in recent times.

III. CONCLUSION

The economic perspective highlights aspects of creativity at the microeconomic and macroeconomic levels of analysis. Microeconomic phenomena include the investment in ideas that are unknown or undervalued, human capital as an input in the creative process, the notion of actively increasing human capital through creativity training, and the costs and benefits of creative work for the individual. Macroeconomic phenomena include the market for creativity, the supply and demand for creativity, societal policies toward investing in creativity, and the costs and benefits of creativity at the aggregate level. It should be noted that for some authors taking the economic perspective, creativity is metaphorically similar to economic behavior, in that creative people are viewed as successful investors, whereas for other authors, creative activity is seen to be directly influenced by economic concerns.

Bibliography

Rubenson, D. L., & Runco, M. A. (1992). The psychoeconomic approach to creativity. *New Ideas in Psychology, 10*(2), 131–147.

Sternberg, R. J., & Lubart, T. I. (1991). An investment theory of creativity and its development. *Human Development, 34,* 1–31.

Sternberg, R. J., & Lubart, T. I. (1995). *Defying the crowd: Cultivating creativity in a culture of conformity.* New York: The Free Press.

Walberg, H. (1988). Creativity and talent as learning. In R. J. Sternberg (Ed.), *The nature of creativity* (pp. 340–361). New York: Cambridge University Press.

Walberg, H. J., & Stariha W. E. (1992). Productive human capital: Learning, creativity, and eminence. *Creativity Research Journal, 12,* 323–340.

Education

Arthur J. Cropley

University of Hamburg

Accommodative Thinking Thinking that responds to new experiences by building new concepts to adapt to them (contrast with *assimilative thinking,* which retains existing concepts).

Creative Personality A personality structure marked by possession of properties favorable to the emergence of creativity (see *Personal Prerequisites for Creativity*).

Creativity Program Special forms of school instruction that are aimed at fostering creativity (resource room, resource teacher, etc.).

Creativity Training Packages Sets of activities that are thought to foster the development of creativity (often published commercially).

Forcing The process of trying to make children develop unusually rapidly by compelling them to focus on special areas where they are thought to display high potential.

Metacreativity A concept of creativity that emphasizes not only thinking but also factors and processes that control or guide it.

Paradoxical Personality A personality structure marked by the coexistence of apparently contradictory characteristics.

Personal Prerequisites for Creativity Psychological properties of an individual that are necessary (but not sufficient) for the emergence of creativity.

Societal Filters Rules in a given society that block the emergence of novel behavior or thoughts.

The systematic fostering of creativity is part of a liberal/ humanistic approach to **EDUCATION** *that goes back to the ancient world. Creativity brings benefits both to society and to the individual, and the need to support it is accepted in principle by most teachers, even if there is uncertainty about what this means in practice. In modern discussions, creativity was initially conceived of as primarily a matter of thinking, especially divergent thinking. This approach was particularly attractive to educators, because it explained many behaviors seen in the classroom (it was plausible) and it generated simple suggestions for fostering creativity (it was practical). Various forms of creativity training were developed and applied in schools. However, despite its value, an approach limited to thinking is too simple. Creativity arises from a combination of cognitive, affective, motivational, personal, and social factors, but many creativity training packages fail to take this sufficiently into account. Special provision for fostering creativity such as building enrichment sessions into the curriculum are also less effective than they could be, particularly because they are isolated from regular classroom activities. What is needed are creativity-facilitating teaching and learning*

Copyright © 1999 by Academic Press
All rights of reproduction in any form reserved.

methods and approaches that permeate the entire curriculum in all content areas and at all age levels.

I. THE NEED TO FOSTER CREATIVITY IN THE CLASSROOM

A. Origins of Modern Interest

The upsurge of interest in fostering creativity in the classroom that started in the United States about 40 years ago was set in motion by concern that the nation's educational system was producing large numbers of graduates, but that most of these were trained simply to apply the already known in conventional ways. The perceived need was for graduates capable of inventiveness and originality. Several years earlier, psychological interest had been reawakened by influential criticism of the prevailing way of conceptualizing intelligence and the call for more emphasis on creativity, seen as involving branching out, generating alternatives, and making unusual associations. These two streams of interest merged in the idea that creativity should be fostered in the classroom.

This goal initially aroused controversy and opposition. It was argued that creativity is by its very nature mysterious and unknowable, and thus incapable of being promoted or fostered by mere mortals. A second argument was that because creativity is a special property found in only a few individuals, its promotion would lead to elitism. Finally, there was fear that fostering creativity would lead to forcing the development of children who would become the victims of creativity fanaticism among teachers and parents. At a more concrete level, many teachers and parents were uneasy about emphasizing creativity in school, because this might mean encouraging unruly, disobedient, careless, imprecise, or just plain naughty behavior. Others saw the call for creativity in the classroom as meaning that basic skills, standards, and principles, such as correct versus incorrect responses, would be abandoned.

Indeed, some studies have shown that children identified as creatively talented have sometimes been forced by ambitious parents into long hours of practice on, for instance, a musical instrument, in the hope that they would develop into creative musicians on the world stage. Such children have complained, among other things, of being robbed of their childhood or of having had their family life destroyed. Their "creativity training" took most of their time or turned their parents into slave drivers intent on living out their own frustrated ambitions through their children. Sometimes, an unremitting focus on the children forced the youngsters into a dominant role in which they had to behave like mothers and fathers to their own parents.

Promoting such circumstances cannot be the aim of efforts to foster creativity in the classroom. Most educational researchers and theorists interested in promoting creativity reject the elitist view, concentrating on aspects of creativity that they believe are present, at least as potentials, in everybody. In other words, appropriate learning conditions can promote some elements of creativity in all children. The central focus of fostering creativity in the classroom is not production of creative geniuses, and it is not necessary for teachers interested in fostering creativity to set their sights on achieving scientific, technological, literary, artistic, or other revolutions. Nonetheless, teachers may sometimes make a contribution in this direction—for instance, by sowing the seeds—and this possibility cannot be disregarded; research has shown that teachers have sometimes played a key role in the emergence, even years later, of widely acclaimed creative talents.

It is also important to emphasize that the desire to foster creativity is part of a liberal tradition in educational thinking going back at least to the Ancient Greeks. This tradition emphasizes that all children should be given the opportunity to develop their potentials to the fullest, and that education should help prepare young people for the richest and most productive life possible. Forcing children at the cost of their mental health is not part of this tradition, but giving them the best possible opportunity to develop to the fullest is. In this context it is also important to note that in the liberal tradition the purpose of both education and creativity is not self-aggrandizement or domination of other people, but the making of contributions to the common good. For this reason, discussions of the fostering of creativity should have an ethical element.

B. The Value of Creativity

Although the term *creativity* is strongly associated in everyday English with fine arts, literature, music, and the like, the original thrust of modern calls for fostering creativity in the classroom derived from fear that the then Soviet Union was gaining the upper hand in the arms and space races. In this article, creativity is understood as a complex of psychological characteristics that are needed to achieve effective novelty in all areas: artistic, literary, and musical to be sure, but also in science, engineering, commerce, government, and interpersonal relations. Ironically, the initial legislation emphasizing creativity in schools in the United States was the National Defense Act. A less bellicose but still related approach emphasizes the importance of creativity for keeping up with the competition in international trade. More recent thinking also emphasizes the necessity of creativity for national development in industry, commerce, transport, and communications in order to raise the standard of living—for instance, by easing the burden of manual labor. Modern life is marked by rapid technological advancement as well as rapid change in many other areas (e.g., social, political, and economic), and one important aspect of creativity is that it offers prospects not only of promoting change but also of turning it into progress—that is, helping to ensure that change leads to positive, healthy advances consistent with fostering human dignity and with responsible handling of the environment. In other words, creativity is seen as having an important role in the evolution of society.

At the level of the individual, it is evident that knowledge and skills have ever diminishing half-lives (the period of time within which 50% of what a person knows or can do will become incorrect or irrelevant). The knowledge and skills needed in the future may not even be known at the time a person attends school. As a result, the school cannot limit itself to the transmission of set contents and techniques, but must promote flexibility, openness, the ability to adapt the known or to see new ways of doing things, interest in the new, and courage in the face of the unexpected. These are central elements of a psychological definition of creativity. Such properties help the individual cope with the challenges of life, especially in the areas of change, uncertainty, adaptation, and the like, and they are closely connected with mental health. Thus, the fostering of creativity in the classroom is part of efforts leading to the development of healthy individuals.

It is also important to note that fostering creativity is not inconsistent with traditional school goals such as acquisition of knowledge and skills. Research has shown that learning activities, such as discovery learning, learning under playlike conditions, and learning with the help of fantasy, can be more effective than traditional methods, such as face-to-face lecturing or rote learning. Teaching and learning methods that emphasize creativity can also have strongly beneficial effects on pupils' motivation as well as their attitudes to school and their self-image.

C. Teachers' Support of Creativity

Surveys have shown that teachers overwhelmingly support creativity as something that should be fostered in the classroom—one study reported that 96% of them expressed this view. However, they often frown upon traits associated with creativity or even actively dislike characteristics such as boldness or the desire for novelty or originality. Preferred are courteousness, punctuality, obedience, and receptiveness to other people's (the teacher's) ideas. In the area of thinking, high skill in memorization and accurate recall are often preferred to critical thinking or independent decision making. Empirical findings have shown that students who scored highest on tests of creativity were rated by their classmates as the ones most often in trouble with teachers. It must be emphasized that punctuality, obedience, and consideration for others, on the one hand, or good memory, speed, and accuracy on the other, cannot be rejected in the name of creativity. It is obvious that these are important characteristics both for school and for life itself. However, when they are overemphasized to the point of the exclusion of discovering, branching out, speculating, experimenting, or innovating, it can be said that teaching has become excessively onesided.

A concrete example shows the consequences this can have. A grade 2 class was given the task of drawing a person's head. They worked away at their places for some time until one boy went to the teacher's desk with a problem. When he explained the problem the teacher realized that he was drawing the *inside* of a head! Her reaction was to fly into a rage. She made him hold up his drawing so that all the others could see it, then said, "Everybody look at what Mr. Clever has drawn. He couldn't draw a *proper* head, could he? Oh no. He had to be different from everybody else and draw the inside." She than had all the other children hold up their drawings for the offending boy to see. "There, Mr. Clever, you see what a proper head looks like. Everybody else got it right, all except you!" The other children took their lead from the teacher and looked shocked or pointed their fingers and jeered. The offender sat down with a red face. What this boy had learned was far more than how a "proper" head looks: He had been taught that unusual viewpoints are not wanted, that the right way is the way everybody else does things, and that it is very dangerous to reveal in public that you have (in this case, probably unwittingly) looked at something from a novel perspective.

It is not being suggested here that undisciplined, disruptive, defiant, ignorant, aggressive, or humiliating behavior should be accepted in the name of fostering creativity. The aim is not to replace one form of excessive onesidedness with another. The problem is recognizing immature creativity or creative potential. What teachers need are guidelines on what is meant by creativity in the classroom and on what to do to foster its further development.

II. WHAT SHOULD TEACHERS FOSTER?

A. Creativity as a Psychological Constellation

Early studies of creativity focused primarily on creative thinking. This involves appropriate skills and abilities, such as the capacity to recognize inconsistencies or to get ideas. However, it has become increasingly apparent that children only display creativity when, in addition to being able to, they also *want to* and *feel that it is safe to do so*. Creativity arises from a constellation of psychological characteristics including (a) cognitive aspects (knowledge, creativity-related skills and abilities), (b) motivation, and (c) personal properties such as self-confidence. Some writers have emphasized *metacreativity*. This is essentially a cognitive approach that conceptualizes creativity as not merely thinking, but as thinking plus control processes that activate, guide, and evaluate the thinking. An approach that gives more emphasis to personality conceives the constellation described here as defining the

personal prerequisites for creative behavior. Some of the elements are—at least in theory—easy to promote in schools, although school traditions and conventional classroom practice often make promotion more difficult than theory suggests it should be. Figure 1 summarizes the psychological dimensions of creativity. Within the individual, cognitive factors (thinking, remembering, knowing, reasoning) are applied to information. For this interaction to lead to creativity, the person must be motivated to seek the new, take the risk of being laughed at, or go without the security offered by sticking to the safe and well known, as against seeking a quick, safe, tried, and trusted solution. This requires appropriate personal properties such as courage (as in the example just given of the boy drawing the head), openness, or self-confidence.

Figure 1 presents an oversimplified view to demonstrate the main psychological dimensions. In fact, there are interactions within the elements of a psychological domain (e.g., thinking processes enhance the amount of information available, to take a single simple example) and also between domains (e.g., risk taking and openness combine to promote acquisition of information and to encourage divergent thinking).

These interactions occur within a social context, of which the classroom is most important for the present chapter. Properties of the classroom context, often referred to as the "classroom climate," affect all three intrapersonal areas (information and thinking, motivation, personal properties), as is shown in the figure. Thus classroom climate forms a fourth dimension. The relationship between creativity and the classroom environment is similar to that between creativity and any social environment such as family or place of work. The classroom can foster or inhibit the emergence of the personal prerequisites for creativity such as interest in the new, daring thinking, or openness, but it is also itself affected by the personal properties, thinking skills, and motivation of the students—openness, adventurousness, and the like are encouraged by an appropriate classroom climate but also contribute to the emergence of such a climate. [*See* CREATIVE CLIMATE.]

B. Cognitive Factors in Creativity

Perhaps the best-known definition of creativity emphasizes thinking. It arises out of the distinction between convergent and divergent thinking. Convergent

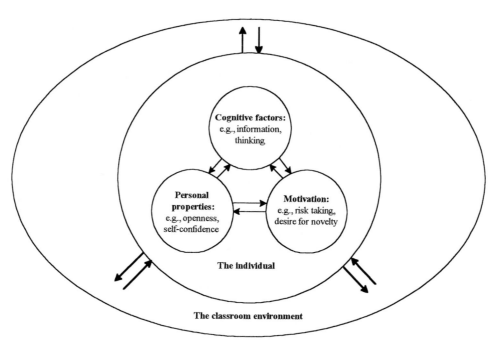

FIGURE 1   The interaction among personal prerequisites for creativity and classroom environment.

thinking involves applying conventional logic to a number of elements of information in order to zero in on the one and one only best answer implied by the available information—the answer that would in theory be arrived at by anybody who possessed the necessary information and applied the rules of conventional logic. Because the answer is unique and arises more or less inevitably from the available information, in a certain sense it already exists and must only be discovered. In practice, this usually means that the teacher already knows the answer and that students must find out what this answer is. By contrast, divergent thinking involves branching out from the available information (diverging), for instance, by seeing unexpected aspects that others might not notice. There are as many answers implied by a given set of information as human ingenuity can invent. Different students may come up with drastically different solutions that are theoretically of equal value. In practical settings where a genuine problem must be solved, of course, some ideas may prove more practicable than others. [*See* DIVERGENT THINKING.]

Effective application of divergent thinking requires information—that is, knowledge of a field. Otherwise the divergent thinking has no contents to which it can be applied. Some researchers have argued that the making of creative associations is a random process. A person with broad knowledge of a field possesses a large array of cognitive elements that can be combined with each other to form configurations until a novel and effective configuration (a combination of ideas that meets the requirements of the particular situation) occurs. However, blind associating, in the sense that all possible combinations of all possible kinds are carried out until one of them delivers the hoped for solution, would involve vast numbers of empty trials unless the person in question employed mechanisms that permitted shortcuts, for instance, by ruling out whole groups of associations that can be recognized as in principle blind alleys, or by indicating that certain lines of attack are very promising. Such mechanisms involve *metacognition*. They permit control, selection, and evaluation of one's own cognitions. One interesting study of creative writers showed that whereas most people orient metacognition to external criteria (i.e., to what the external world regards as correct, desirable, proper, and so on), creative people also make strong use of internal criteria. Researchers have suggested that creative information processing has special characteristics: (a) production of unusual associations, (b) recognition of analogies, (c) building of metaphors, (d) carrying out of transformations, (e) selectively applying attention to the essential, and (f) abstracting from the concrete. [*See* METACOGNITION.]

One approach, based on Piaget's research on cognitive development, differentiates between *figural, operational* and *executive schemata*. Figural schemata permit an accurate internal representation of information, operational schemata yield an abstraction and generalization of the information, and executive schemata consist of general principles for transforming information. Creativity is permitted by accurate figural schemata, abstract operational schemata, and flexible, complex, and differentiated executive schemata. A further approach to describing the thinking processes involved in creativity based on Piagetian principles involves a distinction between *accommodative* and *assimilative thinking*. This distinction is important for educators, as it emphasizes that fostering creativity involves both broadening and deepening the existing organization of knowledge in a process of enrichment (assimilative creativity), as well as fostering the building of novel ways of seeing the world (accommodative creativity).

Teachers should not go overboard for creativity; what is needed is rounded ability—originality and similar characteristics accompanied by accuracy and conventional thinking at appropriate times. Research has shown that for certain tasks such as the acquisition of facts, students who display high levels of divergent thinking unaccompanied by accuracy, speed, conventional logic, and similar properties may have particular difficulties. They are sometimes surpassed even by students who are poor at both convergent and also divergent thinking. On the other hand, those students who do best of all in the widest variety of situations are the ones who display a combination of creative factors accompanied by speed, accuracy, logic, and the like.

Teachers will be tempted to suppress divergent thinking, fantasizing, and similar processes in the justified interest of exam success, preferring to promote one-sided convergence that is often more favorable for this kind of task than one-sided divergence. Success in school in conventional terms (i.e., good grades) is valuable or necessary not only for factors such as admission to higher education but also for other aspects of life. In addition, knowledge of facts is often important. Even rote learning has its advantages: It is difficult to see, for instance, how the basic vocabulary of a foreign language can be acquired more quickly and effectively than by learning it by heart.

Present forms of evaluation of student performance largely reward conformity, conventionality, accuracy, orderliness, and the like. Although strict evaluation according to the conventional rules is often seen as anticreative, total failure to ask whether ideas are realistic or effective is not the best way to promote creativity. For this reason, teachers should continue to expose students' creative thinking to the rigors of the real world, for instance, by evaluating it. However, guided self-evaluation, rather than externally imposed correct-incorrect categories of judgment, is necessary.

What these findings on the cognitive aspects of creativity mean for teachers is that they should strive to promote the following characteristics in their students:

1. Possession of a fund of general knowledge
2. Knowledge of one or more special fields
3. An active imagination
4. Ability to recognize, discover or invent problems
5. Skill at seeing logical connections, overlaps, and similarities, drawing logical conclusions, and so on (convergent thinking)
6. Skill at making remote associations, branching out, seeing the unexpected, and so on (divergent thinking)
7. Ability to think up many ways to solve problems
8. A preference for accommodating rather than assimilating
9. Ability and willingness to evaluate their own work
10. Ability to communicate their results to other people.

C. Personal Properties

Some theorists have gone so far as to argue that creativity is, in the first instance, a particular pattern of personality rather than a set of cognitive factors. Many studies have investigated this view by studying people already acknowledged as creative, and have concluded that personal properties such as flexibility, sensitivity, tolerance, responsibility, autonomy, and positive self-image are related to creativity. Openness to the new has also been regarded as crucial for creativity. Openness involves an interest in novelty for its own sake; the open person simply likes to go beyond the conventional, is spurred on by the unexpected, and seeks alternative explanations for everything. Researchers have drawn attention to the fact that descriptions of the creative personality cross the boundaries of gender stereo-types: inspiration is thought of as stereotypically female, for instance, elaboration as stereotypically male. In a similar way, sensitivity and responsibility are regarded as female, autonomy and positive self-image as male. Thus, the creative personality is said to involve a mixture of stereotypically male and stereotypically female characteristics.

Although very recent studies on creativity and personal properties cast doubt on the possibility of identifying a consistent, standard creative personality, it seems to be true that creativity is related to a complex pattern of personal properties; according to one author, it results from a "paradoxical personality" that involves an integration of seven polarities: openness versus the forming of good gestalts; acceptance of the unconscious into the conscious; a distanced attitude versus being strongly engaged; a critical, questioning attitude versus constructive problem solving; egocenteredness versus altruism and empathy; self-criticism and self-doubt versus self-confidence; and relaxedness versus concentration. These findings underline the need to break away from gender stereotyping in school programs—for instance, by assuming that boys need to be trained to be critical and questioning and girls to be socially constructive, or that boys should be tough in imposing their own view and that girls should be altruistic and empathic. Because creativity requires integration of such polarities, the creativity of both boys and girls would benefit from crossing gender boundaries. Very recent research suggests that boys do not simply pick up empathy, altruism, consideration, and the like, but that such properties need to be deliberately fostered in males, whereas girls acquire them more or less effortlessly, for instance, by learning from models.

A major problem for educators is that many of the personal properties discussed are not conducive of order and discipline in the classroom. Independence, autonomy, and nonconformity associated with quick shifts of attention, fascination for the unexpected, and a constant search for alternative explanations may not only be disconcerting for the teacher but may be misunderstood by peers. As a result, children who display such properties may either act as a catalyst for disorderliness or be regarded by other youngsters as beneficiaries of playing favorites by the teacher, who may seem to peers to be tolerating behavior from one stu-dent that is not tolerated when classmates behave in (as they see it) a similar way. It is helpful for teachers to remember the distinction between genuine creativity, pseudocreativity, and quasicreativity, at this point, as this makes it possible to recognize and describe the difference between creativity and similar looking misbehavior.

D. Motivation

Research has shown that creative individuals differ from the less creative in motivational patterns too. Among other things, they seek to create new order out of chaos (to accommodate), whereas less creative people seek to return things to the way they were before (to assimilate). A further motivational characteristic of highly creative individuals is their fascination, almost obsession, with some tasks. They are willing to strive to their mental and physical limits. This requires a fascination with the field and a sense of invincibility, which is greatly strengthened when the drive comes from within—that is, when motivation is intrinsic. According to one summary, the motivational prerequisites for creativity are (a) curiosity, (b) willingness to take risks, (c) tolerance for ambiguity, (d) dedication, (e) stamina, and (f) fascination for the task. Of these, dedication and tolerance for ambiguity are crucial. Tolerance for ambiguity is so highly developed that it does not involve simply tolerance for two alternatives (ambivalence) but a willingness to see that anything could be combined with anything else (omnivalence). [*See* MOTIVATION/DRIVE.]

A major question is that of the effect of rewards on motivation for creativity. The dominant point of view is that praise, good grades, prizes, and the like cause children to concentrate on behaviors that led to such rewards in the past and to cease behaving when the rewards stop. Such a state of affairs is the antithesis of creativity, because it involves reproducing the already known under the direction of others. Under these conditions, children are said to experience *extrinsic motivation* and, as has just been explained, this form of motivation is thought to inhibit creativity. What is said to be necessary is *intrinsic motivation,* where children are motivated by their own curiosity and their fascination for an issue, events, a problem, or an activity and are thus encouraged to invent, innovate, and branch out on the basis of their own imagination, fantasy, and the like. Very recent findings indicate, however, that the effects of external rewards are not as simple to define as had been thought. Their effects are dependent on the exact situation and may differ between males and females. Some studies have shown that extrinsic motivation too can be applied in such a way as to encourage creativity. Participation in activities such as singing, drawing, painting, or acting showed that highly differentiated external rewards given only for high-quality performances increased participation rather than reducing it. "High quality" can be defined in terms of the child's own talents, abilities, and skills and need not involve sublime performances at the level of acknowledged creators. The point is that the child must know exactly what it is that is being rewarded: If creativity is to be facilitated by giving rewards, the children must have a concept of creativity (even if it is not given this label)—for instance, novel ideas, brave speculations, or promising fantasies.

Creativity research has scarcely concerned itself with the role of feelings and emotions in the process of finding effective novel solutions. However, one important study with creative engineers and physicists showed that a number of feelings such as fascination for the task, self-confidence, frustration when progress was blocked, excitement at the moment of illumination, and satisfaction upon successful verification played a major role. These are all aspects of what might be called "the joy of creating." Interestingly, the participants in this study made little mention of competitiveness or aggressiveness, perhaps because these feelings are socially undesirable. Creativity seems to be positively affected by feelings such as fascination or excitement, negatively by the feeling of stress. [*See* EMOTION/ AFFECT.]

The findings just presented suggest that teachers should value and promote in their students properties such as the following:

1. Task commitment, persistence, and determination
2. Curiosity and adventurousness
3. Drive to experiment and willingness to try difficult tasks
4. Tolerance for ambiguity
5. Independence and nonconformity
6. Self-confidence and willingness to risk being wrong.

E. Social Factors

It is important to bear in mind that creativity is influenced by the social setting, in this case the classroom. Various authors have pointed out that being creative means living your life your own way or displaying resistance to socialization. Studies in several different countries such as Israel, the Soviet Union (as it then was), and the United States. have shown, for instance, that a low level of control can facilitate creativity, although this must be accompanied by warmth and support, as it may otherwise be interpreted as aloofness and lack of concern for the child's well-being. Several authors have emphasized the role of social factors such as norms and conformity pressure in inhibiting creativity. Children learn that certain things are simply not done, and thus acquire general rules forbidding certain lines of action (e.g., "You shouldn't question what the teacher tells you"). As a result, whole classes of theoretically possible solutions are banned en masse. Society has filters through which certain behaviors, even certain thoughts, are blocked. [*See* CONFORMITY.]

Social factors can, however, also have a positive effect on creative achievement. Studies of creative people have shown that in many cases a single significant person played a crucial role in their childhood, for instance, by making the young person aware of his or her own potential. This was often done by a person in a fairly humble position, such as a grade-school teacher who demonstrated passionate interest in a topic and awakened fascination for it in the child, showed a creative youngster that he or she was not alone, or helped the student make contact with peers, experts, or other supportive adults. Despite this, a major aspect of social factors seems to be their powerful role as inhibitors. Thus, in fostering creativity teachers must seek not only to provide releasers but also to eliminate blockers.

An interesting finding in this regard is that some teachers tend to be more supportive of creative students, so that it is possible to speak of creativity-fostering teachers. These teachers often get along well with all students but are particularly effective with creative students. They provide a model of creative behavior; reinforce such behavior when students display it; protect creative students from conformity pressure from their peers; provide a safe refuge for the students when they are subjected to ridicule or criticism from peers, parents, or other teachers; and establish a classroom atmosphere that is supportive of creativity. They are those who exhibit the following behaviors:

1. Encourage students to learn independently
2. Have a cooperative, socially integrative style of teaching
3. Motivate their students to master factual knowledge, so that they have a solid base for divergent thinking
4. Delay judging students' ideas until they have been thoroughly worked out and clearly formulated
5. Encourage flexible thinking in students
6. Promote self-evaluation in students
7. Take students' suggestions and questions seriously
8. Offer students opportunities to work with a wide variety of materials and under many different conditions
9. Help students to learn to cope with frustration and failure, so that they have the courage to try the new and unusual
10. Develop a classroom atmosphere that is tolerant of unexpected answers, questions, suggestions, and so forth.

III. METHODS FOR FOSTERING CREATIVITY

A. Eliminating Blocks versus Actively Promoting Creativity

Many theorists believe that creativity is present in all people, especially children, at least as a potential, and that it emerges spontaneously if it is not inhibited or blocked. The basic idea is that children already know how to think divergently, fantasize, make remote associations, and the like. They are also naturally open to the new and flexible, and they have the courage to take risks, a drive to break away from the well known, and a fascination for the new. Fostering creativity is seen as eliminating learned blocks that make children hide these properties. The example of the boy who drew the head from inside certainly shows how children can be taught that an unusual approach is to be avoided. In this case, fear of being ridiculed a second time could easily block this boy's creativity. Typical blocks in the

child's own mind include (a) inability to break an existing set, (b) inability or unwillingness to relax control and let ideas flow, (c) inability to handle the flow of ideas, (d) excessive preference for analytical thinking, (e) excessive preference for verbal expression, (f) fear of letting the imagination loose, (g) fear of giving the wrong answer, and (h) desire to answer as quickly as possible. Other blocks are part of the social climate of the classroom. These include (a) exaggerated success orientation, (b) intolerance of questioning, (c) reliance on external evaluation, (d) exaggerated conformity pressure, (e) rigid maintainance of strict sex roles, (f) strict distinction between work and play, and (g) intolerance of differentness. For this group of theorists, fostering creativity is principally a matter of breaking down blocks.

The opposing point of view is that people are not naturally divergent and full of fantasy but need to be shown how to be creative. Some research suggests that the necessary instruction can be quite simple. For instance, merely giving students examples of unusual responses seemed to increase their scores on a divergent-thinking test. Other researchers reported higher scores on creativity tests brought about simply by allowing children to play with test materials, or to watch a video of a comedian, or to watch a film of a person solving a creativity test. Other authors have emphasized the need to learn special thinking techniques such as reversing the problem, considering the end result, focusing on the dominant idea, or discarding irrelevant constraints. Gamelike procedures exist for training specific thinking skills including producing, analyzing, elaborating, focusing, associating, combining, translating, breaking out, or recognizing the new.

B. Well-Known Techniques and Packages

Among the specific techniques that have become well known and are often available on a commercial basis are synectics, bionics, brainstorming, morphological methods, imagery training, and mind maps. Of these, brainstorming has assumed particular importance in business, where it has become probably the most widely practiced set technique. Reduced to the absolute minimum, brainstorming is a group procedure in which participants initially produce answers without particular attention to whether they are practicable or not, and other members of the group accept all ideas without criticism. Synectics has similar properties, although it involves special techniques for finding ideas, especially making the familiar strange and making the strange familiar; basically this is a procedure for encouraging unexpected associations. [See BRAINSTORMING.]

Many other procedures for training creativity have also been marketed. These may consist of specific, discrete activities, such as attribute listing, the idea matrix, and the creativity toolbox, that sometimes take the form of games: bridge building, idea production, or creative productions. Sometimes a series of activities are combined to form creativity facilitating packages or programs that are meant to be used regularly for creativity training, according to a schedule. It has become common to refer to such materials (both the discrete activities and the packages) as involving the technology of creativity training, in much the same way as the machines in a gymnasium constitute the technology of bodybuilding. The basic idea is that it is possible, with the help of this technology, to do mental workouts, just as athletes do physical workouts.

The U.S. Patent and Trademark Office compiled an extensive overview of relevant techniques and materials, listing about 25 packages aimed at promoting creative thinking—several hundred separate activities in all. About a dozen sets of the materials they listed were concerned with fostering critical thinking, once again encompassing hundreds of individual activities. Also listed were materials on fostering decision making, higher-order thinking skills, and problem solving. This publication is an invaluable source of information on creativity technology.

A number of better-known packages or programs for fostering creativity are listed in Table I. Particularly interesting for the present discussion are the psychological characteristics the programs aim to promote. As Table 1 shows, most programs give greatest weight to the cognitive aspects of creativity (getting ideas, combining elements of information, and the like), even those that do not specifically see themselves as focusing on creative thinking. Only one program focuses on aspirations and feelings, whereas another gives some weight to attitudes to problem solving.

There is only limited evidence that such approaches actually increase creativity, although it is widely ac-

cepted that they do have a positive effect, especially those that emphasize not only cognitive but also affective aspects (e.g., the courage to try something new or positive feelings about creativity). Deliberate attempts to increase creativity by means of formal training are more effective than simply reducing the level of formality in the classroom or exposing children to a wider variety of experiences (i.e., systematic promotion is superior to mere openness or tolerance). However, the results of creativity training are not simple and direct and are moderated by other factors, such as gender: Procedures that are effective with girls do not necessarily work with boys, and vice versa. The results of research on creativity training are also partly dependent on the research methodology, among other things, the conditions under which the criterion data are obtained.

Many creativity training procedures seem to improve performance only on activities that closely resemble the training procedures. An authoritative study of early research came to the conclusion that the effects of training are at their strongest when the criterion closely resembles the training procedure and are at their weakest when this similarity is low. In the case of personality, interests, and preferences (as against thinking skills), only limited effects are obtained. Many training procedures have little effect on attitudes, values, self-image, or motivation. There is even a danger that creativity training may have the opposite effect from the desired one. For instance, children could become aware that certain kinds of behavior are preferred by the teacher and could copy this behavior. As a result, they have learned to conform to teachers' wishes rather than to be original. Although children may be encouraged by the training to work hard on a variety of tasks, they may learn that it is easy to give original answers by engaging in hairsplitting, giving rambling answers without regard to accuracy or relevance, or offering unexpected banalities. Instead of becoming more creative as a result of offering ideas freely and without evaluation, people may simply become less self-critical.

A number of organizational forms have been adopted for incorporating various forms of creativity training into school curriculum. The traditional approaches involve various forms of enrichment. This frequently occurs outside the regular classroom, often involving special creativity sessions conducted by a specialist

TABLE I
Main Characteristics of Well-Known Creativity Programs [a]

Program	Age level	Material	Aimed at promoting
Imagi/Craft	Elementary school pupils	Dramatized recordings of great moments in the lives of famous inventors and discoverers	• The feeling that their own ideas are important • Widened horizons • Career aspirations of a creative kind
Creative Problemsolving	All levels	No special material; makes great use of brainstorming	• Problem finding • Data collection • Idea finding • Solution finding • Implementing of solutions
Talents Unlimited	All levels	Workbooks based on the idea of inventive thinking; aimed at problem solving with an emphasis on brainstorming	• Productive thinking • Communication • Planning • Decision making • Forecasting
Productive Thinking Program	Fifth- and sixth-grade pupils	Booklets containing cartoons	• Problem-solving abilities • Attitudes toward problem solving
Purdue Creative Thinking Program	Fourth-grade pupils	Audiotapes and accompanying printed exercises	• Verbal and figural fluency, flexibility, originality, and elaboration
Osborne-Parnes Program	High school and college students	No special materials	• Getting many ideas • Primary emphasis on brainstorming, with separation of idea generation and idea evaluation
Myers-Torrance Workbooks	Elementary school pupils	Workbooks containing exercises	• Perceptual and cognitive abilities needed for creativity
Khatena Training Methods	Adults and children	No special materials; simple teacher-made aids are employed	• Ability to break away from the obvious • Transposing ideas • Seeing analogies • Restructuring information • Synthesis of ideas
Clapham-Schuster Program	College students (engineering)	No special materials; • Relaxation exercises • Definition of creativity as involving combining ideas • Various exercises (brainstorming, synectics, etc.)	• Getting ideas • Understanding creativity • Metacognitive techniques (setting goals, expecting success, coping with failure

[a] Reprinted with permission from M. Runco (Ed.) (1997). *Handbook of Creativity,* Vol. 1, Cresskill, NJ: Hampton Press.

resource teacher and frequently in a special resource room, the "creativity center." In some countries, programs for fostering creativity outside the regular classroom involve visits, for instance, to art galleries, whereas special activities such as creativity weekends, creativity workshops, or creativity vacation camps are now offered, not only in North America but also in Germany and France, among others. Some schools incorporate creativity training into the regular classroom, for instance, by having creativity lessons or sessions once or twice a week in the homeroom. In these sessions, students are usually encouraged to work with unusual materials and to create nontraditional products, quite often in a problem-solving context—for instance to make a model of a rocket ship for mice out of cardboard, string, paper clips, and glue. The product may also be artistic in nature, for instance, to draw a picture of the child's nicest experience using paints, crayons, chalk, pencils, colored paper, and so forth. With older children the emphasis may be on creative thinking, and future problem solving is very popular. Such activities are often criticized as being no more than fun and games or situation-specific training that have little to do with the goal-directed, self-critical work of acknowledged creative people.

C. Differential Diagnosis of Creativity

The creativity enhancing enrichment in a resource room or in weekend seminars or vacation camps often involves only a small group of children who have been selected as showing particular promise. This raises the whole issue of selection: What instruments are to be used, how valid are they, do they discriminate against specific groups on the basis of sex, race, socioeconomic status, physical disadvantage, and the like? Even where selection procedures are technically sound, the whole

idea of selection contradicts the ideal of full development of all children and the view that creativity can be fostered in all children, as well as raising fears of forcing children to participate. Some authors have developed procedures for admitting children to creativity programs that deal with some of these issues, such as the revolving door approach (children pass into and out of the program according to interest, need, and success) or selection via performance (those who display creativity go into the program), or selection via motivation (all those children who wish to enter the program are admitted).

The psychological model of creativity presented earlier offers prospects of what can be called a *differential diagnosis* of creativity. It is seen as arising out of the interaction between a number of elements, each of which is necessary but not sufficient: knowledge, thinking skills, motivation, and personal properties. The classroom is seen as a social setting in which these properties can be fostered or inhibited. Table II shows the various combinations of properties that are theoretically possible. A plus sign indicates that the characteristic in question is strongly developed, a minus sign that it is weak. To focus the discussion, only situations in which the personal prerequisites are particularly strongly or particularly weakly developed are presented in the table. As a result, the 16 types shown are more or less stereotypes, but they serve here to demonstrate the point very clearly.

Column 1 refers to a child who possesses all four elements and represents "fully realized" creativity; column 2 refers to a child in whom the personal properties are absent—"stifled" creativity; column 3 refers to a child in whom only the motivation is missing— "abandoned" creativity; column 4 refers to a child who does not possess the necessary thinking skills— "frustrated" creativity; and column 5 refers to a child

TABLE II
Theoretically Possible Combinations of the Factors Involved in Creativity

	Possible combinations															
	1	*2*	*3*	*4*	*5*	*6*	*7*	*8*	*9*	*10*	*11*	*12*	*13*	*14*	*15*	*16*
Knowledge	+	+	+	+	−	−	−	−	+	+	+	+	−	−	−	−
Thinking skills	+	+	+	−	+	+	−	−	−	−	−	+	+	+	−	−
Motivation	+	+	−	+	+	−	+	−	−	+	−	−	+	−	+	−
Personal properties	+	−	+	+	+	+	+	+	−	−	+	−	−	−	−	−

who lacks knowledge—"naive" creativity. The patterns shown in columns 5 to 8 have in common that the child does not possess the necessary knowledge—that is, various forms of pseudocreativity. It can be seen that a child resembling the profile in column 3 (no motivation to be creative) needs a different kind of help from a child resembling the profile in column 2, where openness, flexibility, and self-confidence are missing.

Differential diagnosis of the kind just suggested can only occur if appropriate diagnostic instruments exist. This indicates the need for procedures—for instance, tests—capable of yielding a profile, rather than a global "creativity quotient" that attempts to sum up a child's creativity in much the same way as a global IQ summarizes intelligence but loses sight of special strengths and weaknesses. Such diagnosis has no point, of course, unless it leads to differentiated treatment. Thus, a challenge for the theory and practice of creativity in the context of education is the development of instruments capable of delivering profiles and of training procedures capable of fostering development in specific areas. This, in turn, opens issues in the developmental psychology of creativity and requires answers to questions about such issues as the timing of the necessary cognitive, personal, and social development; the reversibility of developmental defects; and the possibility of critical phases in both development and remediation.

D. Creativity Facilitating Teaching and Learning Methods

Various researchers have developed and tried out special approaches to teaching and learning that can be applied in the classroom in all disciplines and at all age levels and that focus not only on thinking skills but also on motivation, attitudes, and personal characteristics. These include the following:

1. *Discovery learning.* Working alone or in small groups, students examine contents to discover hidden or unexpected connections or structures, either physically or, more usually in the form of recurring regularities, categories, rules, or irregularities, incongruencies, problems, and the like. For instance, a physics class could tackle the following task: In what way are an electric motor and a prism similar?

2. *Play learning.* Play is free of the constraints of the strictly logical. Risks can be taken without fear of real life consequences, rules can be broken, the impossible can be tried out, fantasy can be given free rein. An example could be the following: Act out a scene showing what would have happened to the Plymouth Brethren when they reached America if the Viking settlement hundreds of years earlier had been successful. [*See* PLAY.]

3. *Learning via problem solving.* A gap, difficulty, or open question is the starting point for the learning. The problem has to be defined, relevant information collected, and solutions suggested. The suggestions can be developed in a playlike atmosphere with the advantages listed above, or they may be required to be strictly reality oriented. In the latter case, the relationship to reality must be managed in such a way that risk taking and the like are not inhibited by the stringent requirements. An example might be the following: How could you build a perpetual motion machine? [*See* PROBLEM SOLVING.]

4. *Learning via structural analysis.* A given situation has to be broken down into its constituent elements (in some ways the opposite of discovery learning) and the rules or principles of its structure identified. Suggestions, including fanciful ones, can then be made for ways of changing elements or their connections with each other. English students could be asked: How could you turn *Macbeth* into a comedy?

In all these suggestions, surprising, unorthodox, even apparently absurd suggestions are tolerable and can be pursued. However, the point is not to encourage blind guessing, random answers, and the like. A child who gave the answer "Eat more bananas" to the question "How could you build a perpetual motion machine?" could be asked to explain further.

IV. CLOSING REMARKS

If all children's creativity is to be fostered effectively in the classroom, it seems unlikely that narrow, limited exposure to cookbook creativity-facilitating exercises will achieve the desired effects. Although limitations of space preclude a detailed discussion here, this is especially the case with children from disadvantaged groups and children of low intellectual ability. What is needed is an approach in which all aspects of teaching and learning adhere to basic principles for fostering creativity. Children need contact with complexity, ambiguity, puzzling experiences, uncertainty, and imperfection. The task for teachers is to challenge children to be open to the novel, to give them courage to think for themselves and to seek the new, and to show respect for children and their achievements in order to foster in them self-confidence and high expectations. These tasks involve not only the intellectual but also the personal, motivational, emotional, and social aspects of creativity.

What is needed was put with great clarity about 100 years ago by the German educationist Rain (I have translated his words with a certain artistic license):

> You cannot become creative merely by reading books on creativity. However, simply daubing paint on canvas, making up doggerel or stringing notes together

does not make you creative either. Above all, two things are necessary: creative potential on the one hand and schooling that takes creativity seriously on the other.

Bibliography

Bloom, B. S. (1985). *Developing talent in young people.* New York: Ballantine.

Couger, J. D. (1995). *Creative problemsolving and opportunity finding.* New York: Boyd & Fraser.

Cropley, A. J. (1992). *More ways than one: Fostering creativity in the classroom.* Norwood, NJ: Ablex.

Fryer, M. (1996). *Creative teaching and learning.* London: Paul Chapman.

Starko, A. J. (1995). *Creativity in the classroom.* White Plains, NY: Longman.

United States Patent and Trademark Office. (1990). *The Inventive Thinking Curriculum Project.* Washington, DC: U.S. Patent and Trademark Office.

Albert Einstein

1879–1955

Theoretical Physicist, Philosopher

Discoverer of Special and General Theories of Relativity; Light
Quantum; Theory of Brownian Motion; Fundamental Criticisms
of Quantum Theory

Arthur I. Miller

University College London

*ALBERT EINSTEIN (1879–1955) is one of the greatest
scientists in the history of scientific thought and an icon
of the 20th century. His name is synonymous with genius, and exploring his scientific creativity is extremely
important toward understanding extraordinary minds.*

I. EARLY YEARS

Albert Einstein was born 14 March 1879 in Ulm,
Germany, where his father Hermann, age 32, owned a
featherbed business; his mother Pauline (née Koch),
was age 21. As a child Albert entertained himself,
doubtless due in no small part to difficulties with language learning. He did not speak well until 2½ years
and showed no early precocity. Albert's sister, Maja,
born 1881, later recalled that "those around [Albert]
were afraid he would never learn to talk."

Einstein's teachers considered him only moderately
talented, apparently owing to the length of time he
needed to mull over a problem. For the most part, during his childhood Albert was a solitary child, preferring
private games that required patience and perseverance,
like building elaborate houses of cards.

Einstein had more than moderate success with the

Albert Einstein. Used with permission from
AIP Emilio Segrè Visual Archives.

violin which he began at age 6, and really started to
enjoy at age 13 or 14 when he discovered Mozart's violin sonatas. Until then he had to tolerate teachers who
emphasized mechanical or rote learning, a mode of

Copyright © 1999 by Academic Press
All rights of reproduction in any form reserved.

learning that Einstein detested. Although playing Mozart's sonatas was beyond his technical competence as a teenager, Einstein practiced them repeatedly, but not systematically. He also stopped violin lessons at this time.

Einstein began his school career in 1886 at a public school in Munich where his parents had moved in 1880. In 1888 he entered the Luitpold Gymnasium, Munich, where the curriculum focused on rote learning of, for example, classics in Greek and Latin read in those languages.

About age 13 or 14 Einstein demonstrated the ability to solve difficult mathematical problems posed to him by his paternal uncle Jakob Einstein. These diversions, in addition to insightful recognition of young Einstein's talents by a medical student who boarded in the Einstein household, were necessary counterbalances to the disastrous situation he faced at school.

Some years later Einstein described his entire student career as a "comedy." The humor was found only in retrospect. Einstein recalled that the "teachers in the elementary school seemed to me like sergeants and the teachers in the [*Luitpold*] *Gymnasium* like lieutenants." These remarks were aimed at the rote learning demanded by authoritarian teachers. In what few science classes were available Einstein would sometimes ask a question that Herr Professor could not answer. Instead of admitting this, praising the student for asking such a question, and then promising to come back the next day with a reply, the teacher kept on trying for a solution, thereby exacerbating the situation. In the meanwhile the young Einstein sat with an ever-widening grin. A teacher of Greek told Einstein that he would never amount to anything—he never did in Greek. Another time the same teacher scolded him severely for something he was not at all involved in, asserting that "your mere presence in class destroys respect for me of the other students." Even though he was among the top students at the Luitpold Gymnasium in mathematics and physics, this tongue lashing was the last straw. Moreover, the prospect of military service was impending, which Einstein dreaded. If Einstein did not emigrate before age 16 then, according to German citizenship laws, he would have to serve in the army or be declared a deserter.

The electrical business owned by Einstein's father at this time failed and the family moved to Milan, Italy, where business prospects seemed better. (The feather-bed business had failed some years earlier.) They left Albert behind in Munich to complete his Gymnasium education. The parents' move gave Einstein the idea to resolve both the Gymnasium situation and the army problem. Einstein obtained a doctor's certificate to the effect that he was nervous and depressed. On 29 December 1894 at age 15, Einstein withdrew from the Luitpold Gymnasium without a diploma. He joined his parents in Milan as a high school dropout. The Luitpold Gymnasium was destroyed during World War II. Ironically, it was rebuilt and renamed the Albert Einstein Gymnasium.

Until the fall of 1895 Einstein traveled through northern Italy. As had been the case for Goethe some hundred years before, the Italian sunshine and landscape impressed the young Einstein, freeing him of the *sturm und drang* of the Munich years. During this period, however, Einstein did not neglect his love of science. By this time he knew integral and differential calculus, self-taught at about age 13. In the summer of 1895 Einstein wrote his first scientific essay, which he sent to his maternal uncle Caesar Koch. The essay demonstrates that Einstein was conversant with advanced topics in electromagnetic theory. Even so, there are no signs of genius in the essay. Yet in retrospect the perseverance and self-discipline needed to teach oneself difficult subjects is an indication of things to come. Einstein was an autodidact.

The influence of uncles and aunts is not to be overlooked. As we know these family members hold a privileged position with children at an impressionable age. Being siblings of the parents they can be seen as representing the nonautocratic and so exhibiting the more outgoing side of the parents' psyche. Bertrand Russell recalled an uncle who "did a great deal to stimulate my scientific interests."

As Einstein had promised his parents prior to withdrawing from the Gymnasium, he prepared himself for the entrance examination to the Eidgenössische Technische Hochschule (ETH), Zurich. Einstein failed the entrance examination to the ETH due to deficiencies in foreign languages, biology, and historical subjects, all of which require rote learning. Owing to Einstein's excellent grades in the mathematics and physics portions of the entrance examination, one of the school's most eminent professors, Heinrich Friedrich Weber, encouraged Einstein to attend his lectures if Einstein stayed in Zurich. Instead Einstein decided to take the advice of another professor to spend a year at a preparatory school in the Swiss canton of Aarau, in order to correct the deficiencies that had caused him to fail the entrance examination.

The strong impression made on Einstein by the cantonal school was due to its unpretentiousness and to its seriousness which was in no way dependent on a teacher's authority. The school also emphasized the power of visual thinking, a mode of thought to which Einstein found himself disposed. Sometime during his sojourn in Aarau during 1895–1896, Einstein realized a thought experiment in highly visual terms over which he would ponder tenaciously until, in 1905, he realized that it contained the "germ of the special theory of relativity." The experiment concerned the experiences of an observer who is trying to catch up with a point on a light wave. By 1905 Einstein was able to frame the observational-theoretical situation as a paradox whose resolution concerned his realization that time is a relative concept. Einstein flourished in Aarau, passing out with the highest grade average in his class and gained admission to the ETH.

II. UNIVERSITY YEARS

Einstein's educational experience at the ETH during 1896–1900 was bittersweet. Almost immediately difficulties arose. The role of visual thinking was deemphasized and the outdated physics curriculum focused on applications. Einstein liked neither the subject matter nor being coerced to memorize large quantities of what to him was unessential material. So at home in the evenings and during cut classes, he studied the masters of theoretical physics like Ludwig Boltzmann and Hermann von Helmholtz. From them he learned the kind of physics not taught at the ETH, as well as the importance of visual thinking in the making of a scientific theory.

Einstein's independence of thought was not appreciated by the professors at the ETH, particularly not by the eminent Professor Weber, with whom Einstein had many intense personality conflicts. The upshot was that Weber, the man who had encouraged Einstein to pursue studies at the ETH, tried to prevent him from graduating. Having failed, he refused Einstein any letter of recommendation upon graduation. Einstein was the only one of four students in his class who passed

the final examination to be refused a position as *Assistent* to a professor at the ETH. Einstein recalled that it took him a year to recover from the ETH and to reacquire his taste for scientific research.

During 1900–1902 Einstein had only intermittent employment and was denied positions as assistant to several major physicists. He was convinced that somehow Weber was behind this situation. As Einstein wrote to his girlfriend and wife to be, Mileva Maric, on 4 April 1901, "Soon I will have honoured all physicists from the North Sea to the southern tip of Italy with my offer." He persevered. In 1901 Einstein submitted a doctoral thesis to the University of Zurich which was rejected, but he succeeded in publishing his first paper in the prestigious German physics journal *Annalen der Physik*.

Finally, through intercession of the father of a college friend, Marcel Grossmann, Einstein obtained a position as technical expert third class (provisional) at the Swiss Federal Patent Office, Bern. In reply to someone's comment that he might be bored in this position, Einstein wrote to Mileva in February 1902, "certain people find everything boring—I am sure that I will find it very nice and I will be grateful to Haller [the Director of the Patent Office] as long as I live." And he was.

Einstein's personal life was even less settled. In 1902 he married Mileva, with whom he had a tumultuous love affair since 1899. Their published love letters attest to the passion of the relationship. Unfortunately, by around the time they were married the relationship had begun to cool down. They were divorced acrimoniously in 1919. Later that year Einstein married his cousin Elsa with whom he had had a liaison for some time. Einstein's love life is a complex and highly interesting topic, but this much seems to be the case—Einstein's liaisons may well have been an inspiration to his research, just like in the lives of artists, musicians, and writers. What other scientist can you think of whose love letters have been published?

III. BERN PERIOD

Einstein's Bern period (1902–1909) was the most creative of his life. While working at the Patent Office eight hours a day, six days a week, he published on the order of 50 papers. Although during 1901–1904 he had published five papers in the *Annalen*, there was no forewarning of Einstein's creative outburst in 1905. After all, in 1905 Albert Einstein was a 26-year-old middle-level junior civil servant with an academic record that was distinctive in retrospect only by its lack of distinction. His score on the cumulative final exam at the ETH was 4.91 out of 6, good but not superlative. He had failed once to obtain a Ph.D., and was denied letters of reference from his undergraduate school. To make ends meet for his wife and child Einstein gave private classes in physics. Yet at eight-week intervals, starting in March 1905, Einstein submitted three papers that were published in the September 1905 volume of the *Annalen*. The third one contains the special theory of relativity. Later in 1905 Einstein published a fourth paper in the *Annalen* which contained a result he had overlooked in the relativity paper: the equivalence of mass and energy, $E = mc^2$. These four papers changed the course of physics in the 20th century, not to say life itself on our planet.

IV. LATER YEARS

Einstein's early research results were at first appreciated, mostly for the wrong reasons, if at all, including the 1905 paper on special relativity. That Einstein had an annus mirabilis in 1905 became clear only in retrospect from the 1920s when *all* of his contributions from that year were duly acknowledged. Special relativity was not recognized as an achievement until 1911.

By this time Einstein had resigned from the Patent Office (6 July 1909) to take up a position as Associate Professor at the University of Zurich. During 1911–1912 he was professor at the German University in Prague. Einstein's reason for leaving was an offer he could not refuse. His old undergraduate school, the ETH, offered him a professorship. In 1914 he moved to the University of Berlin as a Professor with no teaching duties. There he remained until forced to leave in 1933. From 1933–1955 he was a Professor at the Institute for Advanced Study in Princeton, New Jersey.

In 1915 Einstein had a second annus mirabilis when he formulated the generalized theory of relativity. As was the case with the 1905 special theory of relativity, one of Einstein's key revelations came in the guise of the following thought experiment: Someone jumps off the roof of a house and also drops a stone. They fall side-by-side even though stone and person are accelerating toward the ground. Einstein's understanding this apparently "simple" phenomenon requires thinking of what it means for the falling person to imagine himself and the stone to be relatively at rest even though they are both accelerating toward the ground. This necessitates assuming the equivalence of acceleration and gravitation, a monumental step. Owing to experimental verification in 1919 of one of the spectacular predictions of Einstein's new theory—the bending of light in the vicinity of massive bodies—his name became worldwide known literally overnight, and synonymous with genius.

Although after 1915 Einstein spun no more grand theories, his contributions, for example, to quantum theory, remain of the deepest importance, spanning physics and its philosophy. His correspondence on scientific, philosophical, and social matters remains of the greatest interest today. And his creativity remains to be fathomed.

Bibliography

Holton, G. (1988). *Thematic origins of scientific thought: Kepler to Einstein.* Cambridge, MA: Harvard University Press.

Miller, A. I. (1981). *Albert Einstein's special theory of relativity: Emergence (1905) and early interpretation (1905–1911).* Reading, MA: Addison-Wesley. [To be reprinted in 1998 by Springer-Verlag, New York.]

Miller, A. I. (1996). *Insights of genius: Imagery and creativity in science and art.* New York: Springer-Verlag.

Miller, A. I. (1999). Einstein's first steps toward general relativity: *Gedanken* experiments and axiomatics, *Physics in Perspective, 1,* 85–104.

Renn, J., & Schulmann, R. (Eds.). (1992). *Albert Einstein, Mileva Maric: The love letters* (S. Smith, Trans.). Princeton: Princeton University Press.

Eminence

Dean Keith Simonton

University of California, Davis

Creative Achievement Scale An instrument designed by Arnold Ludwig to score eminent creators according to the magnitude of their contributions. This score considers such factors as originality, universality, versatility, influence, transcendence, and virtuosity.

Cultural Configurations The tendency for eminent creators to cluster into particular periods of history. The creators who constituted the Golden Age of Greece and the Italian Renaissance are classic examples. These periods of creative fervor are separated by others with much less creativity, at times descending into a Dark Age, in which eminent creators disappear altogether.

Space Measures The objective technique of assessing eminence in terms of the amount of space devoted to the creator in standard reference books, such as encyclopedias, biographical dictionaries, and histories.

Zeitgeist The German word for the "spirit of the times." The term indicates the broad milieu in which creativity takes place, such as the political, economic, social, and cultural environment. The zeitgeist appears to be responsible for the clustering of eminent creators into cultural configurations.

The noun **EMINENCE** *and the adjective* eminent *are derived from a Latin word that meant to "stand out" or "jut out." This original meaning still survives when we speak in English of a hill or rise of ground as an eminence. However, the terms are now more likely to be applied to persons who have attained high station, who can claim great achievements, or who have in some other manner reached a level of distinction or superiority. Such individuals are outstanding, rising "head and shoulders above the rest of the crowd" or "towering above the rest." They are the notables, the famous, the distinguished, the accomplished of a culture, society, tradition, or domain of achievement. When these terms are transported into the realm of creative activity, the application is straightforward. Eminent creators are those who have made a name for themselves—whose creative achievements have made history. They are the creators who have entries in the encyclopedias and biographical dictionaries. These are the persons who become the topics of college courses and doctoral dissertations. These are the individuals whose works fill the art museums, the opera houses, the concert halls, and the libraries. And, the most eminent of the eminent creators boast names that are easily recognized by most educated persons throughout the world. Indeed, such name recognition is often adopted as a criterion to decide whether someone can be considered a well-educated person. Who can*

Copyright © 1999 by Academic Press
All rights of reproduction in any form reserved.

claim to be a cultured and knowledgeable individual and not have at least an acquaintance with the achievements of, say, Galileo, Descartes, Shakespeare, Cervantes, Michelangelo, and Beethoven?

I. SIGNIFICANCE

One of the most urgent problems in the scientific study of creativity is precisely how to define the phenomenon. By what criterion does a researcher identify one subject as creative? The published literature is replete with rather diverse operational definitions. Most often, however, individuals are said to display creativity when they score sufficiently high on a so-called creativity test. Yet clearly, such an identification only begs the question: How do we know that the psychometric instrument actually measures creativity? Obviously the test must undergo some type of validation. For instance, the test might be validated by determining if those who score high on the measure can generate products or ideas that are judged creative by others. But this merely sweeps the problem under yet another rug. Who shall we rely on to perform these judgments? [*See* Tests of Creativity.]

One reasonable resolution to this measurement quandary is simply to say that individuals who have received broad acclaim for their creative contributions can be safely deemed creative. Such a definition seems sound on prima facie grounds. In the parlance of psychometrics, an eminence measure of creativity has "face validity." Note that creative eminence also solves a host of other methodological niceties as well. For example, another difficulty in the investigation of creativity is how to define different types or levels of the phenomenon. How does the researcher distinguish artistic from scientific creativity? How does the investigator gauge the magnitude of creativity? From the standpoint of the eminence criterion, the response to both questions is direct. Individuals who attained distinction for contributions to the arts are artistic creators, whereas those who earned applause for contributions to the sciences are scientific creators. Therefore Picasso exemplifies artistic creativity, whereas Einstein exemplifies scientific creativity. Similarly, the higher the level of fame achieved, the greater the presumed

level of creativity displayed. By this judgment, accordingly, Johann Sebastian Bach is deemed more creative than, say, Gebel, his exact contemporary and compatriot.

As the foregoing discussion suggests, the eminence criterion of creativity may be employed two distinct ways:

1. In the simplest usage, eminence is adopted as a sampling criterion. Individuals who exhibit sufficient excellence in a creative domain are selected for inclusion in the researcher's sample. For instance, when Ann Roe wished to understand the basis for scientific creativity, she sampled a group of 64 eminent scientists. Sometimes the eminence criterion is also used to single out subjects for the control group. A good example is the approach taken by researchers at the Institute for Personality Assessment and Research at the University of California at Berkeley. Wanting to understand the basis for creativity in architecture, the investigators recruited the participation of some rather renowned members of that profession. But the researchers also obtained the participation of far less successful colleagues who could provide the basis for comparison. [*See* Consensual Assessment; Institute of Personality Assessment and Research.]

2. The other role of eminence is as a continuous variable used to measure individual differences in creativity. Just as the amount of creativity may vary from person to person, so may the amount of eminence exhibit considerable cross-sectional variation. To the extent that the fame of creators is founded on the magnitude of creative achievement, the degree of distinction should be directly related to underlying creativity. Such an eminence indicator of creativity is employed three major ways in the published literature. First, the eminence measure may be studied alone. The researcher may focus on the degree of variation, the distribution, the stability across time or cultures, and so forth. Second, the eminence measure may be adopted as a dependent variable in a prediction equation. In such cases the goal is to identify the factors that predict historic creativity. This constitutes the most common use of this type of creativity measure. Third, but less frequently, eminence may be used as an independent variable, especially as a moderator variable in a

regression equation testing for interaction effects. For example, one study looked at whether the curves defining the relationship between age and creative productivity varied according to how illustrious were the creators. The interest was not in predicting eminence but in determining whether the same career trajectories held for all individuals regardless of the magnitude of accomplishment.

II. MEASUREMENT

What are the ways that researchers go about assessing the eminence of creative personalities? What are the psychometric properties of the resultant eminence assessments? These are the questions answered next.

A. Assessment Techniques

Once the investigator decides to use eminence in a particular study, the first issue that must be addressed is how to best assess the eminence of the individuals under investigation. Sometimes a purely informal procedure suffices. For instance, most psychobiographical studies of creative individuals select a particular case for study precisely because that person is obviously famous (and at the same time interesting in some other way). Thus, when Sigmund Freud did his analysis of Leonardo da Vinci, he felt no need to justify the choice of subject. The artist's eminence would be obvious to all. Similarly, when Howard Gardner selected the seven subjects for his book *Creating Minds,* he simply picked a 20th-century luminary who represented each one of the seven intelligences according to his theory of multiple intelligence. The resulting sample consisted of Albert Einstein, T. S. Eliot, Pablo Picasso, Igor Stravinsky, Martha Graham, Sigmund Freud, and Mahatma Gandhi. Even though someone else might pick a different set of representatives, the distinction of these seven figures is beyond doubt.

One difficulty with such informal sampling methods is that they permit the potential introduction of bias. Because there is so much latitude for subjectivity, it can happen that the eminent are unconsciously selected to be consistent with some perspective or hypothesis. An interesting illustration is the sample that Abraham Maslow collected to study self-actualizing personalities. Because, as a humanistic psychologist, Maslow believed that creativity was associated with superior mental health, it cannot have been mere accident that there are no cases of truly "mad geniuses" among the creators in his sample. Sometimes the avoidance of the psychopathological made him sample the less famous rather than the more famous. Why else would Maslow choose Camille Pissaro rather than van Gogh or Franz Joseph Haydn rather than Beethoven? [*See* MAD GENIUS CONTROVERSY; SELF-ACTUALIZATION.]

To avoid the potential introduction of bias, many investigators adopt more systematic and objective strategies for sampling eminent creators. Sometimes the researcher will study those individuals who have attained sufficient acclaim that they have biographies written about them or at least articles under their name in major reference works, such as encyclopedias or biographical dictionaries. Other times the investigator will rely on peer nominations. Experts in a particular domain will be asked to nominate those contemporaries who have made the most creative contributions. Still other researchers will adopt the criterion of the creator having received a major honor, such as the Nobel or Pulitzer.

So far the focus has been on the application of the eminence criterion as part of a sampling procedure. Yet as pointed out earlier, eminence often figures prominently as an individual-difference variable in its own right. Even among the notables of a particular creative domain, the variation in reputation can be quite substantial. The question then becomes how to best capture this dispersion in terms of reliable scores on some eminence measure. One of the oldest and most common solutions is to use standard reference sources to define some type of space measure. For instance, the investigator might count the number of pages or lines devoted to each creator in a biographical dictionary, encyclopedia, or history. Alternatively, the researcher might count the number of books or articles written about each individual in the sample. Such archival indices of eminence have the advantage of being highly reliable and objective.

However, some investigators prefer eminence assessments that allow more room for subjective considerations. A good example is the Creative Achievement Scale devised by Arnold Ludwig. This instrument requires assessments of an individual's contributions in terms of originality, universality, versatility, influence, transcendence, virtuosity, and so on. These assessments are based on biographical and historical information available about each eminent creator. Another approach is simply to ask experts to rate eminent creators on the global level of creativity realized. Sometimes such global assessments are carried out in the form of rankings.

In any case, these subjective measures have certain advantages over the objective measures mentioned in the previous paragraph. For one thing, the subjective indicators can help the researcher understand better what exactly is being assessed, especially when the components of creative eminence are made explicit in the design of the measurement scale, as is the case in Ludwig's instrument. In addition, the objective measures sometimes have biases that are not necessarily present in the subjective measures. For instance, archival assessments of eminence based on space measures often favor some forms of creativity at the expense of other forms. It is much easier to describe in words the contributions of writers and philosophers than it is to give a verbal account of the contributions of painters and composers. As a consequence, encyclopedias tend to devote more space to eminent individuals whose creativity took a verbal form than to those whose creativity required nonverbal means of expression. Fortunately, statistical procedures do exist that permit the introduction of the appropriate corrections, but these procedures necessarily make the data analysis more complicated.

B. Psychometric Features

It should be pointed out that eminence measures have been shown to have highly desirable properties from a psychometric perspective. In the first place, indicators of individual differences in creative eminence display quite impressive reliability coefficients, which signify that the amount of measurement error is relatively small. In fact, eminence measures are just as reliable as other, more commonplace measures in psychology, such as scores on intelligence tests. Second, alternative techniques for assessing individual differences in eminence yield quite comparable results. Not only do the diverse kinds of objective measures correlate highly with each other (and the various types of subjective measures intercorrelated highly as well), but in addition the objective and subjective assessments are in substantial agreement as well. Hence, a consensus exists on the relative eminence of creative individuals. Finally, this strong consensus on differential eminence is highly stable over time. Researchers have examined eminence ratings separated by a century or more and still obtain respectable correlations. Indeed, there appears no pronounced tendency for the agreement to decline as the temporal separation between two measures increases. This transhistorical constancy of eminence suggests that differential fame is tapping into some stable individual differences in creative accomplishment. If Mozart is consistently rated as more famous than one of his contemporaries, such as Türk, this contrast no doubt reflects to a very large extent their comparative creativity.

Admittedly, the correspondence between eminence and creativity is by no means perfect. Exceptions to the general rule do exist. Sometimes creators die before they receive the recognition they deserve (e.g., Gregor Mendel), whereas other times creators received far more contemporary fame than they will be granted by subsequent generations (e.g., Trofim Lysenko). Yet these occasions are too few and far between to seriously undermine the reliability and stability of eminence indicators.

It must also be confessed that it is the fairly irreversible fate of every luminary that his or her fame will decline with time. After all, as more and more creative products are added to the cultural store, the competition becomes ever more fierce. Each year there are ever more paintings to hang on gallery walls, compositions to perform in the concert halls, plays to be produced, books to be reprinted, and so forth. Accordingly, even the most illustrious creators are fated to see their market share gradually diminish. Yet that decline by itself does not attenuate the significance of eminence as a gauge of exceptional creativity. So long as the relative positions of eminent creators remain constant over time, the stability of eminence will persist. Hence, in the theater Shakespeare may have had to yield some ground to Shaw and other more recent playwrights, but so did Marlowe, Jonson, and other

Elizabethan contemporaries. Shakespeare's differential standing thus survives unscathed.

III. DETERMINANTS

Once eminence is accepted as a criterion of creativity, the researcher is tempted to ask: What are the predictors of creative eminence? How do famous creators differ from their less distinguished colleagues? And in what ways do creative luminaries contrast with the rest of us? These questions will be answered by giving an overview of some of the central empirical findings.

A. Individual Differences

The following four factors are most likely to differentiate the eminent from the noneminent as well as distinguish the comparative degree of eminence among those who have attained some acclaim.

1. Productivity

The single most important predictor of achieved eminence as a creator is the total lifetime output of creative products. At the very minimum, of course, it takes at least one successful creative achievement to secure a lasting reputation, but many creators are guilty of seeming overkill, creating hundreds if not thousands of works. Thomas Edison, for example, still holds the record for the number of patents granted to any one person by the United States Patent Office. Of course, such massive lifetime output is not really superfluous. A positive relationship exists between the total number of creative products and the magnitude of eminence attained. To be sure, some perfectionists attain fame on the basis of very few works, whereas some mass producers generate tons of totally forgettable creations. But these two classes of creators represent only a very small proportion of the population. In fact, quality (or creativity) of output is a positive function of quantity (or productivity) of output. Those creators who generate the most successful works also, on the average, produce the most unsuccessful works.

Two additional features of this lifetime productivity deserve mention. First, the total lifetime output is typically attained by beginning the career early, continuing the career until late in life, and maintaining exceptional annual rates of productivity. In other words, eminent creators exhibit productive precocity and longevity, and as well as being highly prolific in any particular unit of time. Second, the cross-sectional distribution of creativity is highly skewed, a small percentage of illustrious producers accounting for a lion's share of the total output. Often those creators who are in the top 10% in lifetime output will be responsible for 50% of everything produced in their fields. This lopsided distribution departs greatly from the normal curve that so often characterizes individual differences. [*See* PRODUCTIVITY AND AGE.]

2. Intelligence

It was Francis Galton who first argued that creative eminence had a firm foundation in individual differences in natural ability or intelligence. The first empirical study to address this issue directly was that conducted by Catharine Cox in her 1926 book titled *The Early Mental Traits of Three Hundred Geniuses*. After first using biographical data to calculate IQ scores for eminent creators and leaders, she then showed that (a) creative geniuses have higher IQs than average and (b) higher IQs are positively associated with the level of eminence attained. Subsequent investigators have replicated these findings, but only after imposing a serious qualification: Intelligence tends to operate as a necessary but sufficient factor underlying creative eminence. This means, first of all, that a certain minimum intellectual power is required to support the knowledge and skills that generate creative contributions. Yet a high, and even a genius-level intellectual capacity (i.e., IQ 140) by no means guarantees that an individual will exhibit any creative ability. Moreover, as intelligence increases beyond this threshold level, the potential for creative achievement increases, but again without any assurance that the full potential will be realized. Thus, an individual with an IQ of 200 has the potential of being more creative than an individual with an IQ of 130, but it may in fact be the latter person who turns out to attain the more impressive creative eminence. The lack of precise correspondence between intelligence and eminence simply reflects the fact that creativity has a great many determinants, intelligence alone only playing a small part. [*See* INTELLIGENCE.]

3. *Personality*

Among those additional factors, of course, are individual differences in certain personality traits. Highly eminent creators tend to exhibit a distinctive character profile in comparison to the less eminent colleagues or to control groups of noneminent professionals working in the same domain. The most important components of this profile are motivational in nature. To obtain a conspicuous degree of distinction in a creative activity requires an exceptional amount of energy, enthusiasm, determination, and persistence. The most eminent creators usually must struggle hard to overcome obstacles in their path, nor are they prevented from pursuing their creative visions by sporadic setbacks and failures. Along with this drive comes a host of other traits that largely shape how eminent creators interact with their fellow human beings. For example, they tend to be introverted, original, independent, nonconformist, sometimes even bohemian. In general, the profile seems to consist of traits that would best permit an individual to devote the considerable effort necessary to produce a profusion of original ideas. [*See* PERSONALITY.]

4. *Psychopathology*

One particular dispositional characteristic of eminent creators deserves special attention. For centuries thinkers have speculated on the possible connection between madness and genius. The general consensus favored the existence of a positive relationship, a relation that was thought to be especially strong for creative genius. The only major dissent from this opinion was that voiced by Maslow who, as noted earlier, thought that eminent creativity was associated with superior mental health. Nonetheless, more systematic investigations that have employed a variety of methods reveal that creative eminence bears a conspicuous link with mental illness. To begin with, the incidence rates of psychopathological symptoms are higher among eminent creators than among the general population. In addition, eminent creative contemporaries score higher on the clinical scales of various diagnostic instruments (such as the MMPI or the EPQ). Furthermore, higher psychopathology tends to be positively correlated with higher degrees of attained eminence. Finally, eminent creators are more likely to come from family pedigrees in which the incidence of mental illness exceeds that found in the general population.

The general conclusion that genius and madness are related must be tempered by four qualifications. First, eminent creators appear to exhibit subclinical levels of psychopathology. That is, their symptoms are usually higher than average without being so high as to cause debilitating distress. Second, the psychopathology is counterbalanced by other traits, such as ego strength and intelligence, which serve to lessen the adverse repercussions. Third, the magnitude of expected psychopathology varies according to the specific domain of creative activity. On the average, for example, eminent artists display more severe symptoms than do eminent scientists. Fourth, it is not entirely clear what are the causal linkages between illness and creativity. It may be that certain levels of psychopathology support the cognitive style and behavioral disposition necessary for creative activity. Yet it may also be that a highly creative life is much more challenging than an ordinary one, and that these challenges themselves can stimulate mental and emotional breakdowns. Even worse, these two possibilities need not be mutually exclusive, nor are other causal relationships yet ruled out.

B. Development

Eminent creators tend to come from rather distinct biographical backgrounds. The following six circumstances have perhaps received the most attention in the empirical research:

1. *Family Pedigrees*

Galton's 1869 classic *Hereditary Genius* was the first systematic study of the tendency for creative genius to run in family lineages. He specifically showed that eminent creators were far more likely to come from families that featured close relatives who attained distinction in the same general domain of creativity. Although others have replicated Galton's finding, the best substantive interpretation is more elusive. Galton believed that this showed that genius had a genetic foundation, but such speculation goes well beyond the data. Especially problematic is the fact that the inheritance appears to be so domain specific. It is very unlikely that a gene or set of genes exists that enables people to do creative science, for example. Hence, the relevance of family pedigrees may reflect more nurture than nature. Parents and relatives are more likely to provide support for talent development in domains in which a family history of distinction exists. Certainly such successful lineages will provide ample models for emulation by developing creative talents. The biological portion of the inheritance, in contrast, may be limited to more broad capacities, such as general intelligence and high energy levels. In line with what was said earlier, another component of this generalized genetic endowment may entail a certain proclivity toward psychopathology. [*See* FAMILIES AND CREATIVITY.]

2. Childhood Precocity

Prior to adulthood, the concept of precocious development is intimately related with that of intelligence. Indeed, the intelligence quotient, or IQ, was originally conceived as a ratio of mental to chronological age. Those who are highly accelerated in intellectual development exhibit higher than normal ratios and thus earn higher than average IQ scores. This linkage is evident in the IQs that Cox calculated for her 301 eminent personalities, because the scores were based on comparing their intellectual capacities in childhood and adolescence with what is normally expected of youths at the same age level. Nonetheless, it should also be pointed out that Cox's assessments were actually much more broad than are found in the typical IQ test, such as the Stanford-Binet. The most weight was given to precocity most directly related to the domain of adulthood achievement. Mozart, for example, was credited with a high IQ owing to his phenomenal musical precocity, both as a performer and as a composer. Yet musical ability is not even evaluated by a standard IQ test. Hence, Cox was assessing domain-specific precocious development far more than generalized intellectual precocity. In any case, subsequent investigations, using different samples and techniques, have arrived at the same conclusion: Eminent creativity is strongly associated with early manifestations of precocity within a particular domain of creative activity. For example, notable composers are far more likely to begin music lessons at a young age, to begin composition very early, and to experience their first genuine success early as well. [*See* PRODIGIES.]

3. Birth Order

In 1874, Galton was the first behavioral scientist to investigate whether ordinal position in the family bore any connection with eminence as a creator. His discovery that firstborn children are overrepresented among eminent scientists has been replicated many times since then. This robust finding is consistent with other studies showing that firstborns exhibit higher than expected frequencies among doctors, lawyers, professors, and other professionals. However, subsequent research also suggests that birth order is most relevant as a determinant of the domain and style of creative eminence. Firstborns are most likely to gravitate to those areas of creativity that impose greater constraints on the creator, whereas later borns are more prone to enter creative activities where the constraints are fewer and conformity to norms less expected. Within science, for example, revolutionary scientists who overthrow traditional paradigms are more likely to be later borns, whereas firstborns have a higher likelihood of making contributions that fit within the received scientific paradigm or tradition. Similarly in the arts: Where later borns are overrepresented among creative writers, firstborns are predominant among composers of classical music. Interestingly, this pattern parallels that observed among eminent leaders as well. Firstborns exhibit a propensity for becoming status quo or establishment leaders, whereas later borns display an inclination for becoming revolutionaries. This birth-order distribution holds for both political and religious leaders. [*See* BIRTH ORDER.]

4. Early Trauma

Eminent creators do not necessarily emerge from happy, stable, conventional home environments. On the contrary, they tend to suffer more than their fair share of trials and tribulations during childhood and adolescence. Their families may experience big fluctuations in financial well-being, and many grow up in minority or immigrant homes that must overcome prejudice and discrimination. Often future creators will have had to surmount some intellectual, emotional, or physical disability, as well as endure extreme loneliness and isolation. But probably the traumatic event that has received the most attention in published research is the experience of parental loss or orphanhood. Eminent people in general, and famous creators in particular, seem to have suffered this type of trauma at incidence rates noticeably higher than what is seen in the overall population. The parental loss rates are especially high for literary creators. At present we do not know how traumatic events contribute to creative development. Three main explanations have been offered. First, these experiences may disrupt the standard socialization process, and this disruption leaves enough freedom for the emergence of an independent, even iconoclastic intellect. Second, such encounters help the young talent to develop the robustness necessary to overcome the many obstacles and setbacks faced by adult creators. Third, such trauma may produce a "bereavement syndrome" to which creative achievement serves as a form of compensation or adjustment. It is hoped that once researchers discover exactly how trauma contributes to the development of creative genius, they will also learn why some distinguished creators do indeed manage to grow up in totally normal and pleasant home environments.

5. Role Models and Mentors

It is difficult if not impossible for creative talent to develop from nothing. To a very large extent creativity is a form of expertise that requires the imitation and emulation of other creators who have already made a name for themselves within a particular domain. This social learning process takes two main forms. First, a promising youth may assume a student, apprentice, or discipline relationship with an older teacher or master. This direct influence entails both instruction and modeling. Second, a developing talent can be actively influenced by creators at a distance, an indirect effect that involves modeling only. Not only may these influences not be known personally and only admired at a distance, but in addition these models of creativity may be deceased. The most dramatic illustration of this latter effect is the way that the artists of the early Italian Renaissance were inspired by the rediscovered masterworks of classic antiquity.

It should be pointed out that role models and mentors need not invariably have positive effects on the emergence of eminent creators. The influences can be negative as well. For instance, a student or apprentice may imitate a teacher or master too closely, and thereby become an intellectual clone incapable of original ideas. For this reason, creators are more likely to attain higher levels of eminence if they take inspiration from multiple models and mentors.

6. Formal Education and Training

The instruction may be more formal than what we have so far described. Besides working in a studio or laboratory, developing creators can actually enroll in regular courses at an academic institution or special school. Such formal education and training has a somewhat ambiguous relationship with the attainment of distinction as a creative person. On the one hand, a certain minimal amount of domain-specific knowledge and skills is essential for creativity, and a good proportion of this requisite may be acquired from formal course work and instruction. On the other hand, excessive formal training and education can severely narrow an individual's expertise, with negative consequences for the capacity for original thought. As a consequence, eminent creators are not necessarily outstanding students in terms of scholastic performance, nor are they always prone to seek the highest degree or diploma available in their field of creative activity. Indeed, sometimes the relationship between level of formal education and creative eminence may be described as a curvilinear, inverted-U function. At the beginning formal education enhances the development of creative talent, but after a certain optimum level, further amounts of education may undermine the emergence of creative potential. The precise location of this peak depends on the specific type of creativity. For the arts and humanities the optimum may be only a couple of years of undergraduate instruction, whereas for the sciences the optimum may appear in the first few years of graduate or professional school.

C. Sociocultural Context

One of the recurrent issues in the study of creativity has been the relative importance of individual and situation. How much is creativity a matter of genius, and how much is it a matter of the zeitgeist? Are so-called creative geniuses simply persons who were lucky enough to be born at the right place at the right time? Perhaps the most striking evidence for the causal significance of the larger milieu is the fact that eminent creators are not randomly distributed over history or across cultures. Rather, creators cluster into cultural configurations. That is, at particular times and places, certain peoples may exhibit an emergence or renaissance of creative activity, ascend to a Golden Age of achievement, only to descend into a Silver Age before disappearing into a Dark Age. This story of the rise and fall of civilizations and creative traditions is centuries old, and shows no evidence of ending in the future. Such culturewide cycles in creative activity suggest that the appearance of eminent creators is very much affected by massive societal forces. For convenience, we may divide these forces into the political, economic, cultural, and ideological. [*See* ZEITGEIST.]

1. Political

The creativity of even the most independent genius must take place in a particular political milieu, making it susceptible to some of the dramatic events that sometimes characterize the world of politics. Among the most conspicuous of such influences is international war, a circumstance that has been shown to depress creative output in a diversity of creative activities. Interestingly, even areas that are supposed to be encouraged by warfare are actually harmed. In particular, overall technological innovation is harmed, apparently because the war effort channels resources toward the development of military inventions, to the detriment of other technologies.

The effect of war is immediate, affecting the output of eminent creators during their active careers. Other political effects operate only after a considerable delay. The time lapse occurs because these circumstances determine the environment in which a talented youth grows up. Some of these long-term developmental effects are positive, such as the benefit of growing up under circumstances of political fragmentation. This is the condition in which a civilization area is divided into numerous nation-states, as was the case during the Golden Age of Greece and the Italian Renaissance. Closely related to this relationship is the beneficial impact of nationalistic rebellions and revolts. On the other hand, some developmental effects are quite detrimental to the eventual emergence of eminent creators. The best case in point is political anarchy, when the power elite is torn by internecine strife—when assassination, conspiracy, and coup d'état become the order (or disorder) of the day. The next generation will suffer the adverse consequences, at least in terms of the absence of eminent scientists, philosophers, and writers. [*See* POLITICAL SCIENCE AND CREATIVITY.]

2. Economic

A certain level of material well-being is a prerequisite for the appearance of historic creative activity. Creative genius rarely emerges in impoverished nations. In fact, a creative florescence in a civilization usually occurs when the economy becomes prosperous enough to generate sufficient surplus wealth to support creative inquiry, invention, and imagination. However, although economic prosperity is necessary, it is not a sufficient cause of creative eminence. Greece under the Byzantine Empire was far more prosperous than the Greece of Periclean Athens. Yet with the exception of Byzantine achievements in architecture and mosaic, it is the Classic Age that boasts the most impressive creative achievements. [*See* ECONOMIC PERSPECTIVE ON CREATIVITY.]

3. Cultural

Earlier it was pointed out that creative development is dependent on the availability of role models and mentors. Stated in generational terms, the number of eminent creators in one generation tends to be a positive function of the number of creators in the previous generation. One consequence of this intergenerational influence is the clustering of creative genius into cultural configurations—the periods of Golden and Silver Ages separated by Dark Ages. However, this generational continuity also raises a critical issue: If creative development is contingent on the availability of creative models, how do these cultural configurations get started in the first place? Somehow creativity has to get a booster shot to establish the basis for modeling and mentoring. One answer to this problem involves the influx of ideas from outside the nation or civilization. Research has found that when creativity stagnates in any given culture, it experiences rejuvenation if the culture opens itself up to the scientific and aesthetic ideas from foreign cultures. For instance, it was the Greeks' exposure to the culture of Persia, Egypt, and elsewhere that helped set the stage for the Classic Era of Greek civilization.

This alien input explains why eminent creators can begin to appear. But what happens at the other end of the cultural configuration? Once a civilization reaches a climax, the number of available role models reaches a maximum. So why does the level of creative activity decline rather than continue to increase indefinitely? Why must Golden Ages yield to Silver Ages and the latter to Dark Ages? Evidently, the answer lies in the fact that a given culture at a given time is usually confined to a particular paradigm, style, or ideology that sets the pattern for all creative endeavors. Eventually that cultural pattern becomes exhausted, making it ever more difficult to come up with good creative ideas. Decadence and decay eventually appear. It is interesting that the most eminent creators of a given cultural growth tend to appear when the civilization is experiencing an ascent, whereas those who appear after the climax has passed, being left with the residue or "cultural dregs," tend to be much less eminent.

4. Ideological

The general philosophical and moral zeitgeist plays a major role in the coming and going of eminent creators during the course of history. To begin with, creative activity in any civilization is more likely to appear during times of ideological diversity rather than during times when one single dogma monopolizes thought. In addition, the intellectual milieu helps shape the type of creative achievement that is most likely to appear in a particular time and place. For example, periods dominated by materialism, empiricism, determinism, and individualism tend to be more favorable to scientific eminence than periods dominated by idealism, rationalism, free will, and collectivism. Sometimes the prevailing ideology actually prevents certain kinds of creative talent from appearing at all. A good example is the way that Confucianist ideology—which maintains a very hierarchical view of the place of women in society—has been shown to be antithetical to the appearance of eminent female creators in Japanese culture.

These ideological influences are closely linked to political and economic circumstances. For instance, threatening conditions tend to encourage the emergence of authoritarian ideologies, which in turn favor the appearance of superstitious and occult activities at the expense of scientific rationality.

IV. EVALUATION

Like any methodological strategy in the study of creativity, the eminence definition has both advantages and disadvantages. The latter should be discussed first.

A. Disadvantages

The eminence definition of creativity has three major drawbacks.

1. By conceiving creativity in terms of an eminent elite, research on creators becomes far removed from more everyday forms of creative activity. A person does not have to be famous to engage in creative problem solving. Moreover, it is highly likely that the vast majority of creative acts take place at this lower level, where creativity is personal and anonymous. Yet how does the researcher know that what is found for exceptional creators also holds for more mundane forms of the phenomenon? One answer to this objection is to point out that there does appear to be some degree of continuity from the noncreative to the everyday creative to the eminent creative. That is, they seem to represent different points on an underlying individual-difference dimension. The relationship between psychopathology and creativity provides a good illustration. Everyday creators seem to have a higher level of symptomatology than noncreative individuals, but they also seem to have a lower level than seen in the eminent creators, who in turn fall below the level seen in institutionalized patients. Hence, insofar as there exists such dimensions, the study of eminent creators can shed light on the determinants of creativity.

2. Sometimes research on eminent creators suffers from inferior data quality. Historiometric studies, for example, are invariably retrospective and archival in nature, and therefore must rely on the biographical and historical record. This record may not always be up to the desired task. For instance, when Cox wanted to estimate IQ scores for creative geniuses of the past, she found it necessary to delete several important personalities due to the lack of sufficient data about early childhood and adolescence. Among the figures so omitted was William Shakespeare! Even psychometric studies of eminent personalities must contend with a large number of problems. It may be difficult to obtain the participation of eminent creators, and those who are willing may not constitute a representative sample. In addition, the retrospective information about early de-

velopmental experiences may be no more reliable for eminent contemporaries and for historic creators.

3. Eminent creators are not as easily studied as, say, schoolchildren or college students. Investigations into eminent contemporaries often require considerable expenses for travel, food, and lodging, and the logistics of interviewing even a relatively small sample of creators can be extremely difficult. Although historiometric studies of historic creators do not suffer from these problems, they have their own. Often it takes a considerable amount of time to gather all the biographical, historical, and content analytical data necessary for a given study. The statistical analyses required to control for the many potential artifacts in correlational research can also be quite laborious. Such labor may discourage many investigators from studying famous creators, past or present.

B. Advantages

Besides the face validity of the eminence definition of creativity, this approach has many unique assets. In the case of psychometric studies of eminent contemporary creators, one of the most important advantages is the ability to examine the extreme upper tails of the distribution of creativity. Famous creators are the intellectual analogs of the athletic champions, such as the Olympic medalists, and as such represent the best the human mind can achieve. Historiometric studies of deceased creators take this scrutiny one step further by examining those who have attained even more elite heights, the best of the best, the individuals whose creations have survived the tests of time.

Moreover, historiometric investigations have three assets besides those enjoyed by any other approach, including the psychometric inquiries of the famous:

1. Such studies feature *unit replicability,* that is, different investigators may study the same eminent creators over and over, replicating and extending earlier findings. For instance, several researchers have studied the 301 geniuses first studied by Cox, adding new variables and more sophisticated data analyses.

2. Because the creators are already deceased, it is possible to adopt a truly life-span developmental perspective on the phenomenon of creative behavior. Historiometric inquiries can examine the development of creative talent from the moment of conception (e.g., family pedigrees) to the moment of death (e.g., the swan-song phenomenon). No other method has this developmental scope.

3. The historiometric study of eminent creators facilitates the study of samples that are cross-culturally broad and transhistorically deep. A science of creativity must produce findings that transcend the idiosyncrasies of a given place and time. Because the history of creative behavior spans several world civilizations and extends back millennia, this desideratum can be easily attained. Some of the empirical results reported earlier in this article, in fact, have been shown to be valid for every eminent creator who ever existed, from Europe and the Americas to Africa and Asia, and from antiquity to modern times.

In light of these remarks, a science of creativity that did not choose to study creative eminence would be a very impoverished science indeed.

Bibliography

Eysenck, H. J. (1995). *Genius: The natural history of creativity.* Cambridge, England: Cambridge University Press.

Ludwig, A. M. (1995). *The Price of greatness: Resolving the creativity and madness controversy.* New York: Guilford Press.

Simonton, D. K. (1990). *Psychology, science, and history: An introduction to historiometry.* New Haven, CT: Yale University Press.

Simonton, D. K. (1994). *Greatness: Who makes history and why.* New York: Guilford Press.

Simonton, D. K. (1997). *Genius and creativity: Selected papers.* Greenwich, CT: Ablex.

Emotion/Affect

Sandra W. Russ

Case Western Reserve University

Affect A broad set of events and processes that includes moods, emotions, feeling states, and cognitive-affective structures.

Divergent Thinking The ability to generate a variety of associations to a word or solutions to a problem.

Mood Induction Refers to a research technique that stimulates a specific feeling state in the individual.

Pretend Play Play involving make-believe, the use of fantasy, and treating one thing as if it were something else.

Primary Process An early, primitive system of thought that is affect laden and not logical, such as in dreams.

EMOTION/AFFECT processes involve feeling or emotion as distinct from cognition. Affect and creativity form a very exciting area in the field of creativity today. Although creativity scholars have long recognized the importance of emotion and affect in the creative process, only recently has research investigated the role of affect in creativity. A creative act results in a creative product that is both useful (according to the criteria of the domain) and novel. A number of cognitive, affective, and personality processes are involved in a creative act. Researchers have reached a consensus about which cognitive and personality processes are important in creativity. There is less research about which affective processes are important in creativity, but there is some converging evidence. This article summarizes the current thinking in the field about what those affective processes are, how they relate to creative cognitive and personality processes, and how they are involved in different domains of creativity. The measurement of affect and manipulation of affect are both necessary to carry out good research. Both measurement and manipulation of affect are complex events that require careful procedures. The development of affective processes is important in the development of creativity. Children's play is one area where affective processes do develop, and therefore play is an important research area. The area of creativity and psychopathology also tells us about the role of affect in creativity. As we learn more about what kinds of affective processes are involved in creativity, how they work and how they develop, then we can apply these principles to fostering creativity in children and in adults.

Copyright © 1999 by Academic Press
All rights of reproduction in any form reserved.

I. DEFINITIONS OF EMOTION AND AFFECT

A. Concept of Creativity

A useful distinction in the conceptualization of creativity is that of the creative product as opposed to the creative process. The creative product is the output of the individual. This output is then judged according to criteria in a particular field as to its creativity. There is a consensus in the field that for a product to be judged as creative, it must be (a) original, unique, novel and (b) useful—that is, adaptive and aesthetically pleasing according to the standards of the particular discipline. [See CREATIVE PRODUCTS; DEFINITIONS OF CREATIVITY.]

Given these two criteria for a product to be judged as creative, the question is often asked, "Can children be truly creative?" Although children can generate new and useful products, the products are usually not at a level of sophistication necessary to truly contribute to an area. However, if one considers whether or not a product is new and good for that age group, then children can be considered to be generators of creative products. Even though a discovery or idea may have already occurred in a field, if it is new to the thinker, then it is a creative act. Thus, many adults generate creative products every day. Ruth Richards has called this kind of creativity *everyday creativity.* Therefore, children and many adults demonstrate creative acts on a daily basis, even though the creative products are not making major contributions to a discipline like art or engineering. This is an important point because it implies that we can study the processes important in creativity in children and in normal adult populations. [See EVERYDAY CREATIVITY.]

The creative act, which generates a creative product, can involve a number of underlying processes. A major question in studying creativity is "What are the processes that are part of the creative act?" What cognitive, affective, and personality processes are involved in the creative process and increase the likelihood that an individual will generate a creative product?

B. Concept of Emotion/Affect

It is important to define the terms *emotion* and *affect.* Affect has been described as a broader concept, with emotion as a subset of affect. Emotion is defined as a state of aroused feeling or agitation. Affect has also been viewed as a broad set of events that includes emotions and drives, and involves feeling states that are pervasive. Emotions have been described as interrupting events that are more specific in terms of stimuli and behavioral response than are broader feeling states. Moods are often defined as being of longer duration than emotions without a clear trigger or object. The term *affect* is used throughout this chapter, rather than *emotion,* because affect is the more inclusive concept. Affective processes refer to the different dimensions of affect, or types of affective events, that occur within the individual. Most theorists think that cognition frequently is involved in the affective processes, although they differ as to whether cognition is always involved, the degree of involvement, and the type of involvement.

C. Types of Affective Processes

Five affective processes have emerged that are important in creativity based on theory and the research literature. The five affective processes, briefly defined, are as follows:

1. *Openness to affect states.* This is the ability to feel the affects and specific emotions as they occur. Tellegen and others have found that different types of affect states can be classified as positive affect or negative affect. Individuals differ as to how much they can experience positive and negative affect states. These specific feeling states seem to function differently in the creative process.

2. *Access to affect-laden thoughts and fantasy.* This is the ability to think about ideas, images, and fantasies that include affect. Thoughts involving affect themes such as aggression, sex, affection, or anxiety illustrate this blending of affect and cognition. The psychoanalytic concept of primary process thinking, to be discussed in a later section, is an example of this type of affective process.

3. *Affective pleasure in challenge.* This process involves the excitement and tension that comes with identifying a problem or mystery and wanting to immerse oneself in the task. A combination of positive and negative affect could be involved.

4. *Affective pleasure in problem solving.* This is the

tendency to take a deep pleasure in solving a problem or completing an artistic production.

5. *Cognitive integration and modulation of affective material.* This process is the ability to control, think about, and regulate the affective events one experiences and not be swept away. Although this process is probably more cognitive than affective, it warrants inclusion because it involves both cognition and affect and it is so important in the creative process.

Three other types of affect systems important in creativity are often referred to as broad motivational systems. The whole area of motivation subsumes needs, drives, and affective processes. Drive refers to both primary and acquired drives. Three major motivational systems found to be important to creativity and that include affective components are intrinsic motivation, curiosity, and conflict-resolution/sublimation. [*See* MOTIVATION/DRIVE.]

6. *Intrinsic motivation.* This is the motivation that comes from within the individual to perform a task rather than coming from sources external to the individual, such as rewards or evaluation. Amabile has carried out a research program that has found intrinsic motivation to be especially important in creativity. Positive affect is an important part of intrinsic motivation, as Amabile and Hennessy have pointed out.

7. *Curiosity.* Curiosity is a motivational state found to be important in creativity. Berlyne has written extensively on this issue. He wrote in 1966 about his view of curiosity as reflecting the organism's striving to maintain an optimal level of arousal.

8. *Conflict resolution/sublimation.* This is the motivation that comes from the need to resolve an internal conflict or distress or, in the case of sublimation, to channel one's energy into a specific creative endeavor. The concept of an unresolved conflict or desire driving one to creative acts is a psychoanalytic one that has little empirical support, but has much clinical anecdotal material behind it.

These different affective processes and motivational states work in different ways in different areas of creativity and for different types of creativity tasks. As a field, we are just beginning to learn about the role of these processes.

II. THEORIES OF AFFECT AND CREATIVITY

Different theories of affect and creativity focus on different types of affective processes and different types of creativity. There is no one comprehensive theory that accounts for all variables and all research findings.

A. Psychoanalytic Theory

Historically, the first theory of affect and creativity was psychoanalytic. The key concept in the area of psychoanalytic theory and creativity is primary process thinking.

1. Primary Process Thinking

Sigmund Freud in 1915 first conceptualized primary process thought as an early, primitive system of thought that was drive laden and not subject to rules of logic or oriented to reality. A good example of primary process thinking is the kind of thinking that occurs in dreams. Dreams are illogical, are not oriented to rules of time and space, and frequently include affect-laden content and images. Affect is a major component of primary process thinking. [*See* DREAMS AND CREATIVITY.]

Access to primary process thought has been hypothesized to relate to creative thinking because associations are fluid and primitive images and ideas can be accessed and used. According to classic psychoanalytic theory, primary process thinking is characterized by mobility of cathexis—that is, the energy behind the ideas and images is easily displaced. In this mode of thinking, ideas are easily interchangeable and attention is widely and flexibly distributed. Therefore, access to primary process thinking should facilitate a fluidity of thought and flexibility of search among all ideas and associations. Flexibility and fluidity of thought are characteristic of two of the most important cognitive processes involved in creative thinking. [*See* FLEXIBILITY.]

Divergent thinking and transformation abilities are the major cognitive processes that are unique to the creative process. Divergent thinking refers to the ability to generate a variety of associations to a word or solutions to a problem. A typical item on a divergent thinking test would be "How many uses for a brick can you think of?" A high scorer on this test would generate a high number of different, acceptable uses for the object. Individuals who can use primary process and the fluidity of thought and breadth of associations inherent in it should be highly divergent thinkers. They should also score high on a second important cognitive process, transformation ability. This involves the ability to transform or revise what one knows into new patterns or configurations and to be flexible and break out of an old set. Again, the broad associations and flexible thinking characteristic of primary process should facilitate transformation abilities. [*See* DIVERGENT THINKING.]

a. Regression in the Service of the Ego

An important point in psychoanalytic theory is that it is controlled access to primary process thinking that is facilitative of creative thought. The concept of regression in the service of the ego postulates that creative individuals could regress in a controlled fashion and tap into primary process thinking. The creative individual could go back and forth between early, primitive primary process thought and more mature, rational, secondary process thinking. The creative individual could be distinguished from the individual with a thought disorder in that the creative individual was in charge of this regressive process and could critically and logically evaluate the loose, primitive associations and images.

Recently, a number of theorists have proposed that the concept of regression may not be necessary in understanding the relationship between primary process and creativity. Rather, we can think of primary process as a separate cognitive-affective process that one can have access to that then facilitates divergent thinking and transformation abilities. A separate ability to cognitively integrate and modulate primary process thinking would be important in the critical evaluation stage of creative thought.

In summary, the psychoanalytic model of primary process and regression in the service of the ego stresses the importance of two types of affective processes in creativity: (a) access to affect-laden thoughts and images and (b) cognitive integration of affective material. These processes are important in the facilitation of creative cognitive processes.

2. Empirical Evidence

Primary process has been found to relate to creative cognitive processes in the research literature. Most of the research has used the Rorschach inkblot test as a measure of primary process. In general, as psychoanalytic theory predicted, the ability to give good responses to the Rorschach that contained primary process content was significantly related to measures of divergent thinking and flexibility in problem solving. Using a different approach, good artists were found to have more primitive primary process content than poor artists and top ranked creative architects had more libidinal (sexual) primary process content than lower ranked architects.

Similar results have been found with children, although age, gender, and specific scores emerge as important factors. Primary process on the Rorschach significantly related to divergent thinking and to flexibility in problem solving for boys, but not for girls, independent of intelligence. These gender differences occur throughout the research literature with adults and with children.

In summary, affect-laden primary process thinking is related to cognitive processes important to creativity for males. For females, the results are mixed. A few studies found that pure access to primary process was related to creativity in females. One possible explanation for these sex differences is that females do not have as much access to primary process thought because of cultural taboos and socialization processes. Another explanation could be that the Rorschach is a more valid measure of primary process for males than for females. Indeed, when measuring primary process in children's play, Russ found that primary process related to divergent thinking for both boys and girls. There are many questions remaining to be answered in this research area. [*See* GENDER DIFFERENCES.]

3. Conflict Resolution and Sublimation

From a different perspective psychoanalytic theory has stressed the importance of unresolved conflicts and unfulfilled wishes in motivating the individual to engage in creative work. For example, unrequited love will be expressed in a poem or drawing. Resolving the loss of a loved one will occur as a result of composing a symphony. The motivating force of transforming one's own pain into artistic creations that have universal appeal is thought to be an important factor in creative work. Although there is little direct empirical evidence for this theory, there is indirect evidence from clinical vignettes from therapists and from descriptions from creative individuals.

B. Cognitive-Affective Models

A more recent approach to affect and creativity has been within a cognitive-affective interaction framework. Research has investigated very specifically how affect influences cognitive processes important in creativity. Much of the research within this framework has used a mood induction paradigm. A specific mood state is induced by having participants watch a film, receive a gift, or think about a memory that is happy or sad. Mood induction provides a way of altering affect states so that the effect on cognitive processes can be observed.

A growing body of research has found that induced affect facilitates creative thinking. Alice Isen has carried out a series of important, carefully controlled studies in the mood induction area. She and her colleagues found that positive affect induction resulted in more creative problem solving when compared to control groups. Other researchers have found similar results with a variety of creativity measures. Alice Isen concluded that the underlying mechanism is that positive affect cues positive memories and a large amount of cognitive material. This process results in defocused attention and a more complex cognitive context. This, in turn, results in a greater range of associations and interpretations.

What about negative affect? In general, induced negative affect has had no effect on creative problem solving. As the researchers pointed out, it is possible that the negative affect that was aroused (for example, by a film of the Holocaust) was too extreme, and that less extreme conditions of negative affect should be explored. A few studies suggest that milder forms of negative affect could facilitate some kinds of problem-solving tasks. Different types of affect may have different effects on various dimensions of problem-solving tasks.

An interesting theoretical model that explains how affect could influence cognition was provided by Isaac

Getz and Todd Lubart in 1996. In an emotional resonance model for generating associations, they described *endocepts* that represent emotions attached to concepts or images in memory. These emotional memories are partially interconnected and can activate one another. Endocepts attached to concepts resonate with each other. Endocepts that are stimulated trigger other memories and associations and influence creative problem solving.

The emotional resonance model is consistent with other cognitive affective models such as Bower's associative network theory. In this model, emotion is conceptualized as a memory unit that has a special node in memory. The activation of the emotion unit aids in the retrieval of events associated with it. It primes emotional themes for use in free association. When activated, it spreads activation through memory structures. [*See* MEMORY AND CREATIVITY.]

Primary process thinking might also be conceptualized as mood-relevant cognition, occurring when emotion nodes are activated. Primary process memories could be stored in emotion nodes. Primary process content has been proposed to be content around which the child had experienced early intense feeling states (e.g., oral, anal, or aggressive). Current primary process expressions could reflect these early encodings of emotion. Access to this primary process material would activate emotion nodes and associations, thus resulting in a broad range of associations for creative problem solving.

C. Intrinsic Motivation

Intrinsic motivation is conducive to creativity. Intrinsic motivation is defined as having to do with the intrinsic value of attaining the creative solution. Research has found that conditions extrinsic to the task, such as reward, evaluation, being watched, and restricted choice, all have detrimental effects on creativity. Intrinsic motivation is important for task persistence, for seeing a project through, and for ensuring exploration of solutions.

Intrinsic motivation is also accompanied by positive affect. The love of the task is an important component of creative work. The love of the work has been mentioned as crucial by most creative individuals. More research is necessary to explore the positive affect and intrinsic motivation link.

D. Tension and Creativity

Tension as an important factor in creativity has been conceptualized by Mark Runco. He presented a variety of ways in which tension could be involved in the creative process. The anticipation of the resolution of tension could be an important motivating force in creative problem solving. The tension could be an internal conflict, similar to psychoanalytic theory's idea of conflict resolution. For example, several researchers have found that creative individuals have come from families with problems or have themselves felt marginalized in the society. Tension could also develop from identifying a problem or sensing a gap in an area. Problem identification is important in creativity. Creative individuals could use the tension experienced in seeing the problem as both a cue and a motivator.

Affective pleasure in challenge could also be part of this process. There could be a mix of negative (tension) and positive affect in identifying a problem. The anticipation of the positive affect involved in solving the problem may act as a motivating force. However, there may be an inherent excitement in seeing the ambiguity in the situation that leads to problem identification, which is itself pleasurable. It may be similar to the pleasure that some children feel in discovering "what is wrong with this picture?"

The concept of optimal challenge is relevant here. An optimal amount of challenge is necessary for the experience of *flow* to occur. Flow is a total involvement in the activity, a deep sense of enjoyment, and optimal challenge. Creative activities involve this sense of flow. Perhaps optimal challenge involves the best mix of tension in seeing the problem and the anticipated pleasure of the creative act.

E. Curiosity

Although it is not clear whether or not curiosity has affective components beyond arousal, it is a motivational system important in creativity. Curiosity may be viewed as reflecting the organism's efforts to maintain an optimal level of arousal. Subjective feelings of pleasantness have been associated with the growth of the curiosity drive as a function of increasing stimulus intensity and arousal of the positive reward system. Curiosity may interact with anxiety to determine approach or avoidance behavior.

Curiosity is important to creativity because interest in novelty and exploration aids in problem identification as well as task persistence. Also, the highly curious and risk-taking individual is more likely to gain a wide variety of experience that would add to his or her knowledge base.

F. Integrative Model of Affect and Creativity

An integrative model of affect and creativity identified the connections among affect, cognitive, and personality processes important to the creative process. This model was based on the research and theoretical literature and attempted to be comprehensive and reflect the current state of knowledge (see Figure 1).

In this model of affect and creativity, the major cognitive abilities that emerge as unique to and important in the creative process are linked to related specific affective processes and to global personality traits. In some cases the personality traits are behavioral reflections of the underlying affective process. One assumption of this model is that these specific affective processes and personality traits facilitate creative cognitive abilities. Reciprocal interactions probably occur as well. [See PERSONALITY.]

This model summarizes all of the affective processes discussed in this article. Because there is no one comprehensive theory of affect and creativity, a variety of theories and underlying mechanisms are represented in this model. At this time, it appears that different mechanisms underlie different components of the creative process. For example, access to affect themes and affect states facilitates a breadth of associations. Intrinsic motivation should help the individual keep on task and explore alternative solutions. Good cognitive integration of affect should aid the critical thinking process necessary in the evaluation stage of creative work. An important point is that in any creative act, different processes and different mechanisms could be involved.

Future research should add to the empirical base for this model and answer the questions of what specific affective processes are important in creativity and

Affect and creativity / a model

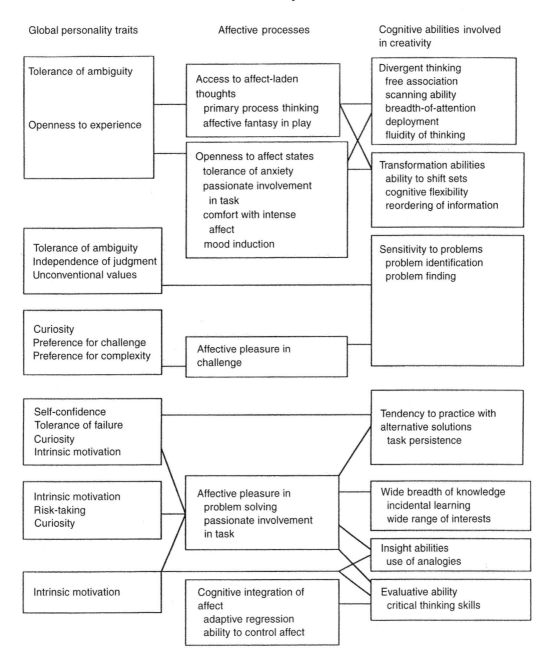

FIGURE 1   Affect and creativity model. In this model of affect and creativity, the major cognitive abilities that emerge as unique to and important in the creative process are linked to specific affective processes and to global personality traits. In some cases, the personality traits are behavioral reflections of the underlying affective process. One assumption of this model is that these specific affective processes and personality traits facilitate cognitive abilities. From Russ, S. (1993). *Affect and creativity: The role of affect and play in the creative process.* Hillsdale, NJ: Erlbaum.

how they are important. It is possible that a larger number of affective processes are involved than are currently recognized or that several of these processes are really the same process. For example, are affect-laden thoughts and mood states different dimensions of affect or are they really the same process? Do they function in the same or in different ways? Can the motivational systems of intrinsic motivation and curiosity be broken down into several affective components? (In this model, because of their global nature, both were classified under personality traits.) Future research will answer these important questions.

III. PLAY, AFFECT, AND CREATIVITY

Play is important in the development of many of the cognitive, affective, and personality processes important in creativity. The type of play most important to the area of creativity is pretend play. Pretend play involves make-believe, the use of fantasy, and treating one thing as if it were something else. Pretend play frequently involves affect. Children express both positive and negative emotion in play. In 1987 Fein proposed that the affect is represented in an affective symbol system. Information about affect-laden events and relationships is coded and stored in these symbols. These symbols are reflected in pretend play and are especially important for creative thinking. From a psychoanalytic perspective, play is a place where primary process thinking as well as other kinds of affect can be expressed. [*See* PLAY.]

A. Research Evidence

Research supports a relationship between affect in play and creative thinking that is independent of intelligence. A positive relationship has been found between playfulness (that included the affective components of spontaneity and joy) and divergent thinking in kindergarten children. Similarly, a relationship has been found between the amount of affect expressed in play and divergent thinking in several samples of first and second graders. In a recent longitudinal study, affect in play in young children predicted affect in play stories in older children. This longitudinal study suggests that affect in fantasy is a trait that has some stability over a 4-year period.

Play has been found to facilitate creativity in children, but there is no research that provides direct evidence that it is the affect in play that facilitates creativity. That question remains to be investigated.

IV. AFFECT, CREATIVITY, ADJUSTMENT, AND PSYCHOPATHOLOGY

Research has found that creativity relates to both adjustment and psychopathology. How can both findings be true? If we conceptualize creativity as evolving from a configuration of cognitive, personalty, and affective processes that set the stage for creative acts to occur, then the propensity for adjustment could go either way, depending on the mix of processes. If creative individuals are good divergent thinkers, have diverse associations, have access to primary process in a controlled fashion, are open to affect states, and are good critical thinkers, then one would expect them to be sensitive but relatively stable individuals, perhaps with periods of emotional instability. Some research studies are supportive of the hypothesis that creative individuals are adaptive and well adjusted. Many of the psychological traits that are related to creativity are also indicators of positive mental health. Other researchers have found a relationship between creativity and psychopatholgy.

In a study of British artists and writers, 38% of the sample sought treatment for mood disorders. Ruth Richards, based on her research, offered three major conclusions about creativity and mental health. She concluded (a) mild psychopathology may contribute to creativity (mild mood swings, especially, may carry advantages for creativity), (b) intermediate levels of variables may be most optimal for creativity, and (c) affect is important in creativity. She stressed the positive affect involved in creative accomplishment.

A. Positive and Negative Affect

Interestingly, the experimental work in mood induction, correlational studies on affect in fantasy and play, and studies on mood disorders all point to an association between positive affect and creativity. This converging evidence strengthens the theory that positive affect facilitates creative problem solving.

The results are less conclusive for negative affect. The mood-induction research usually finds no effect for negative affect on creativity but at times has found facilitative effects. The play and fantasy research finds that both positive and negative affect themes relate to creativity. A possible curvilinear relationship between negative affect and creativity has been proposed. Negative affect may facilitate creativity when it is of low to moderate levels. At those levels, such as in fantasy or in well-controlled play, negative affect may indeed trigger memories and associations just as positive affect does. In more intense negative affect states, such as in a depressed mood, other factors such as constriction of cue utilization may take over.

Negative affect also may function as a motivating force (tension reduction), an affect cue that a problem exists (problem identification), or as content to be worked with in artistic productions.

B. Artistic and Scientific Creativity

Affective processes play different roles in different domains of creativity. In general, scientists have been found to be better adjusted than artists. As reviewed earlier, a higher than normal proportion of artists have been found to have affective disorders. Research with scientists paints a different picture. A number of reseachers have concluded that creative scientists may be a more emotionally stable group than creative artists. [*See* ART AND ARTISTS; MAD GENIUS CONTROVERSY; SCIENCE.]

Why would this be so? The personality differences between creative artists and scientists may reflect the differences in the domains of creativity and the cognitive and affective processes that are involved. There are similarities. Divergent thinking is important in scientific problem solving as well as in artistic production. Breaking out of a set and creating new configurations is also imporant in both types of creativity. Affective processes would be expected to function in similar ways for similar creative tasks in artists and scientists.

One of the main differences between artistic and scientific creativity may be the importance of getting more deeply into affect states and thematic material in artistic creativity. This in-depth involvement in the affective processes themselves may not be so necessary in scientific problem solving. Some theorists think that art-

ists incorporate early traumas and conflicts into their artistic products. Many scientists do not need to face into and incorporate affect-laden material into their scientific problem solving. For the scientist, good divergent thinking ability, transformation ability, and a flexible cognitive style may be sufficient for creative work to occur. For the writer or the musician or the artist, the need to get to basic affective content, primay process material, or drive-laden material may be necessary in order to be able to get to the universal truths that transcend the individual.

One often hears artists and writers describe the need to get to this kind of experience. One can see how the need to live in that emotional state and to control that process may at times be disruptive, resulting in emotional instability and some personal agony. Writers in particular describe anxiety at uncovering primary process material. [*See* WRITING AND CREATIVITY.]

On the other hand, interviews with creative scientists indicate that scientists often feel very strong emotions during the creative process. In a study that gave artistic and scientific problems to art and science students and had them rate their intensity of emotions, art and science students experienced the same intensity of affect before and during insight, but art students reported more positive emotion after the insight than did science students.

It is logical to assume that each specific artistic and scientific domain will have cognitive and affective processes that are especially important in that area. Different creative profiles should emege for different fields. A dynamic (not static) nonlinear mode of affective-cognitive interaction has been proposed for artistic creativity. Creativity and psychopathology are ever-changing continua with a mixture of affect states. Only a dynamic model can capture the complexities of the interactions.

V. NEUROLOGICAL PROCESSES, AFFECT, AND CREATIVITY

As research on affect and neurological processes becomes more sophisticated, we should be able to learn about the interaction between affect and cognition. With the development of the CAT scan and PET technology, we can map cerebral activity and obtain a picture of brain involvement during problem solving. Eventually, we should learn about the actual neurological processes involved in creative problem solving.

Research by Klaus Hoppe has shown that the mutual interaction of the left and right hemispheres is important in creativity. The corpus callosum is involved in exchanging information between the hemispheres. The symbolization and visual imagery in the right hemisphere is available to the left hemisphere in creative functioning. Cognitive representation of emotion occurs in both hemispheres. [See SPLIT BRAINS: INTERHEMISPHERIC EXCHANGE IN CREATIVITY.]

Research on the neurological processes involved in affect processes has addressed several important questions in the area of emotion that have implications for the affect and creativity area. It has been concluded that different emotions have different neurological and physiological activity. It appears that there are different brain systems that mediate different affects. Therefore, we need to investigate specific emotions. This conclusion is consistent with findings in the affect and creativity area that different emotions have different effects on cognitive processes.

It has also been proposed that emotions are represented in memory. An important point is that these emotional memories appear to be stored in the amygdala. This is a different area in the brain than that which stores nonemotional memories, the hippocampus. Research suggests that emotional memories are organized differently than are nonemotional memories. The emotional can act independently of the cognitive system. It has been suggested that these precognitive emotions are functional in infants, during the early formative years. Behavior is affected, but we have no conscious memory of the event.

The concept of emotional memories functioning as a separate system appears to be consistent with theoretical explanations for why affect should facilitate creativity. If affect stirs a network of associations and emotion-laden memories, which in turn affects cognitive processes, then the organizational system of these emotional memories becomes very important. The rules that govern how this emotional memory system functions await discovery. These principles should help us understand the mechanisms that underlie the complex relationship between affect and creativity.

VI. CONCLUSION

During the past 15 years, there has been a resurgence of research in the area of affect and creativity. As it should be in any science, the research is theory driven, theories are being developed and tested, measures and methods are being refined, and new lines of investigation are opening. The field is interdisciplinary and what we learn in one field informs another. For example, what we learn about affective processes from neurophysiological research will be applied to affect and creativity research. Key concerns for the future in the affect and creativity area are (a) identifying specific affective processes that are most important for specific creativity tasks; (b) discovering the underlying mechanisms that account for the relationships between affect and creativity; (c) exploring differential effects of various types of affect, such as positive or negative affect, on creativity; (d) understanding how affect and creativity relate to psychological adjustment and psychopathology; and (e) understanding the developmental processes involved in affect and creativity. As research paradigms and measures of affect continue to be developed, we will continue to learn about this exciting area.

Bibliography

Ekman, P., & Davidson, R. (Eds.). (1994). *The nature of emotion.* New York: Oxford University Press.

Fein, G. (1987). Pretend play: Creativity and consciousness. In P. Gorlitz & J. Wohlwill (Eds.). *Curiosity, imagination and play* (pp. 281–304). Hillsdale, NJ: Erlbaum.

Feist, G. J. (in press). Affective states and traits in creativity: Evidence for nonlinear relationships. In M. A. Runco (Ed.), *Creativity research handbook,* (Vol. 2). Cresskill, NJ: Hampton Press.

Isen, A., Daubman, K., & Nowicki, G. (1987). Positive affect facilitates creative problem solving. *Journal of Personality and Social Psychology, 52,* 1122–1131.

Richards, R. (1993). Everyday creativity, eminent creativity, and psychopathology. *Psychological Inquiry, 4,* 212–217.

Runco, M. A. (1994). Creativity and its discontents. In M. Shaw & M. A. Runco (Eds.), *Creativity and affect* (pp. 102–123). Norwood, NJ: Ablex.

Russ, S. W. (1993). *Affect and creativity: The role of affect and play in the creative process.* Hillsdale, NJ: Erlbaum.

Russ, S. W. (Ed.) (1999). *Affect, creative experience and psychological adjustment.* Philadelphia: Brunner Mazel.

Shaw, M., & Runco, M. A. (Eds.). (1994). *Creativity and affect.* Norwood, NJ: Ablex.

Enhancement of Creativity

Jonathan A. Plucker

Indiana University

Mark A. Runco

California State University, Fullerton

Cognitive Processes Actions taken by the human mind to process information. At a relatively simple level, includes attention, perception, rehearsal, and encoding. More complex processes include higher-order thinking skills such as problem solving.

Constructivism Learning and cognitive theories that posit that knowledge is constructed, either individually or by groups.

Discretion Process by which potential actions and subsequent outcomes are identified, evaluated, and differentiated.

Functional Fixedness Reliance on traditional techniques and strategies for problem solving, even when conditions surrounding a problem diverge considerably from previously encountered conditions. Also, inability to consider alternatives when faced with problems, especially alternative uses for traditional problem-solving tools.

Information Stores In the traditional two-store model of human memory and information-processing, the locations where bits of information are stored either temporarily (working memory) or permanently (long-term memory).

Metacognition An individual's analysis of his or her own cognitive processes or, more colloquially, thinking about one's own thinking.

Rigidity Lack of flexibility in the application of cognitive processes, especially problem solving. This inflexibility is reinforced by the effects of prior experience.

Schema The organizational framework for information found in long-term memory. Schema theory posits that more complex schema are associated with more efficient recall and information processing.

Self-efficacy Belief in one's own ability. Usually applied to a specific subject area or task, such as mathematical or reading self-efficacy.

Social Constructivism Subset of constructivist learning theories that represent knowledge as being socially constructed, either within one's immediate environment or within the broader culture.

Vygotskian Theory Precursor to modern interpretations of social constructivism. Vygotsky was primarily concerned with the ways in which tools of knowledge are transmitted within cultures.

Creativity is highly valued, both as a personal characteristic and as a commodity. It may stimulate economic, artistic, academic, and personal growth. As such, the **ENHANCEMENT OF CREATIVITY** *is frequently the*

Copyright © 1999 by Academic Press
All rights of reproduction in any form reserved.

focus of curriculum, therapy, and in-service training. Efforts to enhance creativity are found in many schools, families, studios, and organizations.

I. CAN CREATIVITY BE ENHANCED?

In the not-so-distant past, the belief that creativity could not be enhanced was widespread. This notion about the unchanging nature of creativity could be found in academic circles as well as the media and popular press. Although perceptions have changed slightly over the past 20 years, a great deal of controversy still surrounds the nature-nurture issue as applied to creativity.

The relationship between nature and nurture is better conceptualized as a continuum and not as an either-or proposition. Those holding a radical nativist view assume that creativity cannot be enhanced. The extreme nativist view is rare, however, and current consensus holds that potentials can be fulfilled and maximized. It may be analogous to one's height: Each of us inherits a *range of reaction* within which our experiences have their impact. One person might inherit a range of potential height between 5 foot 6 inches and 5 foot 9 inches, and given specific developmental experiences (e.g., exercise, vitamins), end up being 5 foot 10 inches. This idea about a range of potential also applies to psychological constructs such as creativity and intelligence. Hence, in response to the question "Can creativity be enhanced?" the best answer is yes, because potentials can be fulfilled. Efforts to enhance creativity will not expand one's in-born potentials but can insure that potentials are maximized.

II. WHAT EXACTLY CAN BE ENHANCED?

When an attempt is made to enhance creativity, what is the exact focus? To answer this question, the multifaceted nature of creativity must be recognized with its cognitive, affective, attitudinal, interpersonal, and environmental components. Taken both collectively and individually, these aspects of creativity suggest specific targets for enhancement efforts.

Recent theory and research support the inclusion of such diverse components in models of creativity. Although each component has separately been the subject of significant theoretical and empirical investigation, the importance of collectively considering these aspects is reinforced by the recent predominance of systems, interactionist, and interdisciplinary (e.g., psychoeconomic) theories of creativity. We discuss enhancement by focusing on each of the components.

III. COGNITIVE COMPONENTS

Cognitive components are by definition intellectual. They reflect information-processing models and problem solving. Models of information processing generally include cognitive processes, transfer operations, information stores, and metacognitive components, all of which are important to consider when attempting to foster cognitive aspects of creativity.

Certain process strategies are very useful when looking for original ideas. As a result, creative process strategies for enhancing creativity are quite numerous and include teaching people to use cognitive heuristics such as lateral thinking, brainstorming, SCAMPER (substitute, combine, adapt, magnify/modify/minify, put to other uses, eliminate, reuse), analogical reasoning (e.g., synectics), and creative problem solving. Other frequently mentioned strategies include identifying and overcoming blocks to creativity, balancing the use of reflection and tinkering, encouraging playfulness, creative imagery or visualization, assuming multiple perspectives, questioning assumptions, and looking for patterns. Perhaps the most popular techniques over the past 50 years have involved the teaching of divergent thinking and general problem-solving heuristics. [*See* BRAINSTORMING; DIVERGENT THINKING; HEURISTICS; IMAGERY; PLAY.]

The role of information stores has received considerably less attention during discussions of creativity than that of cognitive processes, but the role may be no less important. Expert problem solvers tend to have better working and long-term memory skills than novices, although this distinction only applies to the memorization of situated knowledge (i.e., information that can be placed into an expert's existing schema) and not tangential or random knowledge. In addition, general knowledge may be very important during the creative process, and such knowledge depends on memory and information storage. Without well-organized information stores (i.e., schemas), knowledge becomes difficult to use and recall during the creative process. Constructivist approaches to learning, in which individuals construct their own schemas based on their personal experiences, should prove especially useful when helping people learn to retain, recall, and apply knowledge during the creative process. Jean Piaget, the well-known psychologist, titled one of his monographs, *To Understand and to Invent,* implying that true understanding depends on personal constructivism. Very often it is beneficial for students to relate new information to prior knowledge (i.e., existing schema), and activities should be based on realistic problems that require application of prior knowledge and new skills. Much new work on divergent thinking and creative problem solving relies on realistic problems. [*See* EXPERTISE; MEMORY AND CREATIVITY.]

The importance of prior knowledge can, however, be easily overstated. An individual or group that is embedded in a particular field of study or interest area may be reluctant to consider ideas and solutions that are uncommon, unpopular, or even antiparadigmatic within that context (or within one's personal experiences). This phenomenon is referred to as functional fixedness or rigidity. As a result, creative contributions in a given area are often made by individuals who are not necessarily experts within that field. A case in point is the numerous early paleontologists who had primary training in the arts. When painting and drawing illustrations of dinosaurs, they realized that the existing knowledge base was quite superficial and provided inadequate answers to many important questions. Their fresh perspective allowed them to move beyond existing paradigms and field-based constraints to make creative contributions to paleontology. Other examples include experts who retain flexible strategies while maintaining their expertise in certain domains.

Although many people believe that the exponentially increasing complexity of most disciplines has made creative contributions to fields other than one's own uncommon, this is probably an overstated belief. The ability to apply processes and use information from areas of interest other than one's own area of interest is clearly important. The tension between different areas of interest may stimulate creativity as well. When participating in creativity enhancement exercises, people should thus be encouraged to look across fields of study and areas of knowledge for potential solutions to their problems. This act of looking beyond the established parameters to obtain a solution to a problem has popularly become known in business circles as thinking outside of the box and in psychology as insight, moving beyond the problem space, or problem finding and redefinition. Other specific strategies in this area include forcing someone to assume a different viewpoint or perspective on an issue, which can be facilitated by a debate or role playing.

Experts tend to exhibit a greater degree of metacognition during problem solving than do novices. In this context, metacognition involves monitoring one's own cognitive processes in order to manage time effectively, assess progress accurately, and attempt problem-solving efforts efficiently. Suggested strategies for helping students develop metacognitive abilities include providing a variety of creative and problem-solving strategies, allowing students to practice using these strategies in a low-risk, constructive environment, encouraging self-assessment of the steps taken to solve a problem, and modeling metacognitive skills. [*See* METACOGNITION.]

IV. AFFECTIVE COMPONENTS

The affective component of creativity refers to one's emotions. Affect is quite important because creative work very likely has personal meaning. A technique used to enhance creativity should provide more than just a new strategy—it should provide a practical use for the strategy. Benefits to individuals or society should be communicated, and intrapersonal and interpersonal incentives described. [*See* EMOTION/AFFECT.]

Care must be taken, because—in contrast to the potential of incentives—the positive relationship between intrinsic motivation and creative behavior is well documented in the theoretical and empirical literature. But the question of whether external motivation (especially when created by external evaluations) is detrimental to creativity has yet to be answered. E. Paul Torrance suggested that freedom from evaluation during practice with a creative strategy resulted in more proficient use of that strategy over time, but he found this to be less true with older, late elementary students than with younger students. Other researchers have also called into question whether extrinsic motivation is truly detrimental to creativity, with a few theorists going so far as to say that constraint and external motivation are essential for creativity to emerge. Very likely both are potential influences, with the contribution of each varying across individuals and tasks.

Given the controversy surrounding external motivation, recommendations regarding evaluation and creativity can only be made hesitantly. At this point in time, it seems practical to expose people to reasonable amounts of evaluation, but only when the evaluators are trained in how to provide constructive criticism. [*See* MOTIVATION/DRIVE.]

V. ATTITUDINAL COMPONENTS

The individual's attitude toward creativity is very important, especially his or her creative self-efficacy. One's belief in his or her ability to create, defined broadly, forms the psychological foundation of creative achievement. Creative self-efficacy can be fostered by providing genuine praise and feedback about a person's creativity and avoiding discouraging statements (e.g., "You can't do that, you're not creative"). But some people may be challenged by competitive statements, again stressing the value of constructing enhancement efforts on a case-by-case basis.

The attitudinal enhancement of creativity may also involve modeling, which can be accomplished in a variety of ways. Individuals can be exposed to information about unambiguously creative individuals, perhaps via biographies or case studies. These can provide a glimpse into the more personal aspects of creativity and provide evidence that even eminent creators "are just human, like you and me." This kind of information can be reassuring and even inspiring, though it does not suggest specific ways to be creative. It is informational in the literal sense, providing factual rather than procedural information about creativity. In a similar vein, teachers, managers, parents, and others who are attempting to foster creative self-efficacy in others should model a can-do, enthusiastic attitude when confronted with problems and tasks that require creative solutions. By explaining their thought process as they tackle the problem, the creative process may be

further demystified and made more accessible to the observer. Working closely with a mentor may also help in this way.

VI. INTERPERSONAL COMPONENTS

Two types of interpersonal skills appear to facilitate the creative process: the ability to gain acceptance for one's creativity and the ability to work with others during the creative process. Although there is considerable debate about whether gaining acceptance for creativity (i.e., persuasion) is a vital component of everyday or only eminent creativity, the ability to market personal or group creative products can be a positive attribute. Students should be encouraged to share their creative work with others. It is hoped that they will receive and benefit from this positive and perhaps even mild negative feedback. This may help them to develop the ability to convince an audience of their creativity.

Working with others can both foster and inhibit creativity. Groups can serve as a detriment to creativity when members are simply told to "do well," when group goals are lacking, and when members do not have the freedom to work as individuals within the larger group. Conversely, groups tend to enhance creativity when members are socially comfortable with each other, when both the group and individual members are held accountable for clear performance standards, and when group tasks are meaningful. Recall also the potential impact of evaluation, which can also be interpersonal. [*See* GROUP CREATIVITY.]

A seldom mentioned aspect of group creativity is the intergroup interaction as each group solves similar problems. By allowing group members to interact with other groups, the informal sharing of information and ideas can help members of a group overcome any functional fixedness that has developed. This perspective, which is based on the work of social constructivists, suggests that intergroup communication should be encouraged.

Problem-based and situated learning is also relevant to the discussion of interpersonal components of creativity. These constructivist-inspired strategies, which allow students to learn content and process skills through the solving of real-life problems, place a strong emphasis on the application of information rather than on simple memorization of the information. Additionally, the realistic nature of problem-based and situated enhancement efforts fosters intrinsic motivation, which can be beneficial for creativity. Although situated learning makes sense in light of constructivist learning theories, situated approaches pose certain problems for the enhancement of creativity. Constructing knowledge and developing creative process skills may be more applied in a situated context, but they may be constructed and developed in a way that promotes functional fixedness. Problem-based learning activities should be designed so that students are required to apply factual and procedural knowledge in a variety of contexts, to interact with others as part of the learning process, and to engage in some abstract thought (i.e., nonsituated thought, which is frequently mentioned as a cognitive characteristic of creative individuals).

VII. ENVIRONMENTAL COMPONENTS

The assembled research from the past 50 years paints a clear picture of the characteristics of a creativity-enhancing environment. The key characteristics are tolerance, moderation, and availability of resources. Although these concepts may seem antithetical, they are (like many aspects of creativity enhancement) more applicable than they first appear. For example, a stimulating environment should be created, with a multitude of diverse materials (i.e., resources) available to stimulate ideas and create solutions. But the common tendency to provide predominantly verbal materials should be avoided, as many individuals prefer to express their creativity through several domains. In addition, given the importance of problem finding, it may be desirable to expose people occasionally to open stimulus environments, in which stimuli must be sought and problems need to be identified.

The environment should allow and even encourage reasonable risks to be taken, but irresponsible and physically dangerous risks (e.g., consumption of drugs) should be discouraged. Everyday uses of creativity and problem solving are fostered by the management of risk, not simply by taking any risk that presents itself. In more general terms, the creative environment fosters the use of creative discretion, which separates originality from psychotic ideation.

Deviance and ambiguity are tolerated in the creativity-enhancing environment. Individuals should be encouraged when they think outside of accepted procedures and customs and not criticized for ignoring cultural and experiential limitations. However, the environment should encourage self-regulation of creative processes so that even the most exhilarating dead ends can be self-identified and put aside. Divergent thinking needs to be linked with convergent thinking in the creative environment.

In general, the environment should be marked by balance: a mixture of structured and unstructured tasks that require divergent and convergent thinking, independent and group work, and procedural and declarative (factual) information. [*See* CONDITIONS AND SETTINGS/ENVIRONMENT; CREATIVE CLIMATE.]

A. Increasing Creativity Test Scores

Several researchers have investigated the possible impact of environmental conditions on creativity test scores. Conditions include practice with heuristics before administration, gamelike conditions, manipulation of instructions (e.g., telling students to be original when completing a divergent thinking [DT] test, verbal versus nonverbal instructions), allowing students to take the tests home to be completed, different types of tasks (i.e., abstract versus real-world, interesting versus uninteresting), timed versus untimed tests, presence of model before or during administration, stimulus-rich versus barren environments, high versus low structure, individual versus group completion, and playing musical or comedic recordings during administration. In general, testlike conditions appear to be associated with the most convincing evidence of reliability and validity, although actual performance effects vary considerably across age and grade levels. For example, although instructions to be original probably result in increased originality and decreased fluency scores on DT tasks regardless of a person's age, working with others appears to produce higher creativity scores than working alone for children after the age of 6 but not earlier.

VIII. DRUG USE

Conventional wisdom posits that the use of certain drugs (e.g., alcohol, marijuana, LSD) enhances personal creativity. Although certain aspects of creativity (e.g., affective, cognitive, interpersonal) may be positively influenced by drug use, research over several decades provides convincing evidence that—at best—moderate drug use has a negligible effect on long-term creative production and heavy use has a detrimental effect. Even in specific situations where a positive drug effect has been documented, the drug does not appear to encourage creative production. For example, several researchers have observed that alcohol consumption tends to lower a person's inhibitions, which is assumed to result in more flexible thinking and, therefore, greater creativity. However, this research has also shown that the disinhibition does not lead to enhanced creative production, rendering the effect of the alcohol moot with respect to long-term creative productivity. [*See* DRUGS AND CREATIVITY.]

IX. PROGRAMS DESIGNED TO ENHANCE CREATIVITY

Over the past few decades, several creativity training programs have been used to help people maximize their creative potential. These programs usually incorporate strategies that address multiple components of creativity.

Two types of programs have been designed to enhance children's creativity. The first involves modifications of the regular school curriculum, such as the Schoolwide Enrichment Model and Mentor Connection, the Talents Unlimited Model, the Cognitive-Affective Interaction Model, the SOI system, and the Purdue Creativity and Enrichment Models. The second includes extracurricular programs that may or may not be affiliated by educators attached to a child's school, including the Odyssey of the Mind and Future Problem Solving programs and numerous local, regional, and national invention programs. However, the distinction between these two types of programs is not universal, and programs frequently and successfully transverse this rather artificial boundary. [*See* TEACHING CREATIVITY.]

Within the business community, programs for enhancing creativity are quite popular. The increasing popularity of creativity in the business sector has led to an explosion in the number and type of programs aimed at this audience. In general, the components mentioned

previously in this article are included in these programs, with predictable changes in terminology.

X. CONCLUSIONS

Must all of the components be present in an effort to enhance creativity? As mentioned earlier, aspects of each component have been studied individually; similarly, intervention efforts occasionally focus on only one or two components. Research is mixed with respect to evaluations of the effectiveness of narrowly focused strategies. It may be helpful to think about these strategies in a manner similar to the way that many people describe different therapies: If you think a specific technique works for you, it does.

However, because each of the components is a necessary but not sufficient condition for creativity, enhancement efforts that consider the components collectively should be more effective than narrowly focused strategies. For example, if a person was to choose one component to exclude from enhancement efforts, which would it be: creating a supportive environment in which people are encouraged to take sensible risks, encouraging people to monitor their creative processes, or stressing the importance of interpersonal skills to creativity and the creative acceptance process? Each is clearly important and overlooking any of them (or any other aspect of creativity) would be difficult in light of the assembled research and theory. Although efforts to foster creativity need not focus on each and every component (and cannot do so effectively), well-designed programs consider all of the components and their interactions.

With the ideal that all facets of creativity should be represented in enhancement efforts, the following general guidelines appear to be reasonable.

1. Design activities that demand an individual's or group's attention. Capitalize on teachable moments such as current political, cultural, and community events.

2. Supply information about strategies and creators that is both useful and interesting. Information on the difficulties in building a canal or on intricacies of Einstein's general theory of relativity may not appeal

to a group of marketing specialists, but stories about Einstein's struggles to get his ideas accepted or about the political creativity involved with constructing sky-scrapers may appeal (and appear more pertinent) to this group.

3. Provide either the skills and information that will generalize to other settings (e.g., the home, school, workplace) or opportunities to apply the intro-duced skills and information to different settings and problems.

4. Remove excessive evaluation and supervision from the creative environment. Micromanaging is just as disruptive to young students as it is to corporate managers.

5. Attempt to alter attitudes about creativity and originality and encourage creative confidence (i.e., cre-ative self-efficacy) and risk taking.

6. Design activities that excite, stimulate, and in-crease curiosity and help people develop the intrinsic motivation to be creative.

7. Require problems to be solved individually and in groups. Have groups critically examine their own processes and attitudes (i.e., develop group metacog-nition) during and after the creative process.

8. Avoid making assumptions about students. Re-cent theory and research on intelligence, motivation, personality, and thinking and learning styles provide evidence that individuals vary tremendously in their abilities, preferences, and attitudes. This diversity ap-pears to be a critical element of creative production.

9. Similarly, introduce variety into enhancement ef-forts. This capitalizes on individual preferences and interests and promotes diversity in one's approach to finding and solving problems.

10. Consider the use of well-established programs that address multiple components of creativity and have already been field-tested and refined.

Bibliography

Adams, J. L. (1986). *Conceptual blockbusting: A guide to better ideas* (3rd ed.). Reading, MA: Addison-Wesley.

Davis, G. A. (1992). *Creativity is forever* (3rd ed.). Dubuque, IA: Kendall/Hunt.

Hennessey, B. A., & Amabile, T. M. (1987). *Creativity and learn-ing.* Washington, DC; National Education Association.

Renzulli, J. S. (Ed.). (1986). *Systems and models for developing programs for the gifted and talented.* Mansfield Center, CT: Cre-ative Learning Press.

Runco, M. A. (1993). *Creativity as an educational objective for dis-advantaged students* (Research Based Decision-Making Series 9306). Storrs, CT: National Research Center on the Gifted and Talented.

Sternberg, R. J., & Lubart, T. I. (1995). *Defying the crowd: Culti-vating creativity in a culture of conformity.* New York: The Free Press.

Sternberg, R. J., & Williams, W. M. (1996). *How to develop stu-dent creativity.* Alexandria, VA: Association for Supervision and Curriculum Development.

Ensemble of Metaphor

Stephen K. Sagarin and Howard E. Gruber

Teachers College, Columbia University, New York

Case Study Method Study of size $N = 1$ or a very small number. The aim is a deep and thorough description and understanding, not the relatively more shallow examination of a statistically acceptable number.

Ensemble of Metaphor Within the work of a creative person, a group of related metaphors that help to connect and unite a group of concepts.

Evolving System A single person may be seen as an evolving system that consists of three evolving subsystems: knowledge, affect, and purpose. Evolution implies change over time in a manner developmentally relevant to the subject or to the researcher. That this evolution is systematic implies that it is structured, that parts of it are interconnected, and that it is governed in part by recursive feedback loops.

Figure of Thought A description of cognition that includes percepts, concepts, and uniting metaphors. From a book title by the poet Howard Nemerov.

Heuristic A consciously chosen interpretive scheme or device that is ultimately unjustifiable without reference to itself.

Image of Wide Scope A single metaphor that unites or forms a body of thought or research. The idea of evolution is an image of wide scope.

Metaphor A symbolic or literary device that constructs or represents a qualitative relationship between two components or that constructs or represents one component in terms of the other.

Modality A particular pathway from perception through cognition to expression or representation. Modalities include written language, mathematical representations, dance, and painting. Modalities may be as general as those listed or as specific as necessary: a golfer's visual perception of depth, for example, or an acrobat's kinesthetic awareness.

Paradigm The communally shared and relatively uncontested theory or set of theories that governs discourse within a discipline at any given time.

Rhetorical Trope and Scheme Classically, the formalized devices of argument and persuasion. A trope is a figure of speech in argument—simile or synecdoche, for example—and a scheme is the mode effected by the use of tropes—romantic or ironic, for example.

Symbolic Function The cognitive process by which one thing is represented in terms of another or the cognitive capacity to effect such a process.

ENSEMBLE OF METAPHOR is a term originally coined by Howard Gruber to describe an avenue for understanding the symbolic function in scientific thought. It has since been expanded to include related figures of thought and perception within the context of a case study of a creative person at work. Examining ensembles of metaphors plays a significant role in the evolving systems approach to the study of the development of cre-

Copyright © 1999 by Academic Press
All rights of reproduction in any form reserved.

ativity. Each unique creative person, in the work of Gruber and others, is an evolving system that consists of three subsystems: knowledge, affect, and purpose. As part of the evolutionary change inherent in creative work, the creative person links concepts with metaphors or images, thereby creating a cognitive web with concepts at some nodes and metaphors at others. The collection of metaphors in this web is considered an ensemble *in that these metaphors unite a particular set of concepts.* [*See* EVOLVING SYSTEMS APPROACH.]

I. ENSEMBLE OF METAPHOR

An examination of ensembles of metaphor within the context of a case study allows for description of multiple, linked instances and multiple modes of perception and cognition. Such a study supplements Gruber's previous examination of *image of wide scope;* the concept of an image is singular and limited to one modality of thought and perception, most often visual.

Metaphor is used here in a broad and functional sense. It subsumes many rhetorical tropes and schemes and, depending on the requirements of the case at hand, may refer to such figures of thought as images, symbols, allegories, and analogies. It may even apply to so broad a concept as paradigm, although work in this heuristic usually treats collections of metaphors broader than those found within the work of one person. These broader collections of metaphors may be called *metaphors in a field.* The sense here is that the functions of metaphorical thought are to unite concepts through an implicit comparison. Further, metaphors may serve at least three functions: they may be descriptive, evocative or affective, or explanatory. It may well be that ensembles of metaphors are easier to study in scientists than in artists because in science metaphors serve, more often, descriptive and explanatory functions whereas in art they serve, more often, an evocative function. That is to say, metaphors that function as descriptions and explanations are often more clearly defined and therefore easier to catalog than are evocative metaphors, which may, for example, have fuzzy or even deliberately ambiguous meanings. This is not to imply that a metaphor functions in only one way; it seems possible that a metaphor may partake si-

multaneously of all functions but to different degrees, thereby presenting a particular profile.

Ensembles of metaphors may also be described according to function; they may be theory constitutive and theory generative. Understanding a theory may necessitate mastering an ensemble of metaphor, and creating an ensemble of metaphor may create a theory.

We focus on function rather than on definition because metaphor has so far proved difficult if not impossible to define. Recent philosophical explanations of metaphor have all focused on function rather than on attempted definition; what may not be pinned down may still be examined. Max Black, for example, saw metaphorical function as an interaction between semantic contents. A particular focus within a particular frame causes a listener to form a "parallel implicative complex" to make sense of the metaphor. "Every metaphor is the tip of a submerged model," according to Black. We would add that every submerged model may present several points of metaphor where it breaks the surface, thereby constituting an ensemble of metaphors.

The psychologists Sam Glucksberg and Boaz Keysar dismissed this and many other philosophical descriptions because they seem to be demonstrably wrong; they imply a first attempt at establishing a literal meaning for a metaphor followed by the construction or comprehension of metaphorical meaning only afterward. Glucksberg and Keysar claimed that cognitive processing does not take this route; we may comprehend a metaphor as swiftly as we comprehend a literal statement. (The dichotomy literal/metaphorical may, in fact, be false; there may be a sense in which all perception and cognition is metaphorical and a sense in which it is also literal. Such an argument, however, ranges beyond our present scope.) We do not generally have to reject a first, literal interpretation before we move on to a second, metaphorical one. Glucksberg and Keysar suggested that metaphors consist of specific groupings within an accepted context and hierarchy of meaning, groupings that may be fathomed as easily as any other more literal groupings, given the appropriate context and hierarchical implication.

All of these descriptions argue against the earlier Aristotelian substitution (or comparison) model, in which the predicate portion of a simple metaphor is to be substituted for or compared with the nominative portion. Nonetheless, almost all metaphors function adequately in this simple and ancient way, given the frequency with which questions of context and understanding may be taken for granted. When Darwin described evolution as a tree, we understood that in some way at least one quality of a tree, notably its branching, is like some aspect of evolution that Darwin wished to elucidate. We are not confused over whether or not bark texture is to be included, and we can even extend the metaphor to consider the fruit of the tree. In the work of a creative person, metaphors often help us to understand the novel, evolution by natural selection, with reference to the known, a tree.

An examination of ensembles of metaphor should not be confused with the problem solving by analogy approach to creativity or scientific thought. This approach is well represented by Nancy Nersessian, who stated bluntly, "the metaphor has blocked development of the historicized epistemology," but later claimed, however, that "analogies themselves do the inferential work and generate the problem solution." Nersessian claimed that operating on the level of paradigm or metaphor in a field distances us from the creative process, whereas examining the metaphorical processes of a creative person at work contributes to historical analysis. So far, we may agree, although we believe there is room in the field for worthwhile research at all levels. To the extent that not all metaphors function as analogical models, however, and to the extent that cognitive-historical analysis seems to create a chasm between the creative work of a scientist and the creative work of an artist, we disagree. To reduce creative work to problem solving, however historically scrutinized, diminishes the project of understanding creativity and places the project within an unnecessarily confining metaphorical box. [*See* ANALOGIES.]

II. FINDING ENSEMBLES OF METAPHOR

Identifying ensembles of metaphor is an interpretive act. We do not usually find them neatly packaged but must tease them from the body of work in which they are embedded. Some, like Darwin's, may be relatively easily identified, clearly drawn and labeled, whereas others may require more work to discover.

In particular, we must be sensitive to the context in which the metaphors occur; it is only there, *in situ,* that we can argue for their inclusion or exclusion from a particular ensemble. That is to say, we must relate the individual metaphors to each other in forming the ensemble and to the broader development of the creative person in constructing the context. Here we examine such questions as the mode or modes in which the subject worked, the subject's network of enterprise, and the broader historical context of the subject. To choose an example in the arts, metaphorical elements in Velázquez's *Las Meniñas* may only become apparent in context. Possible constituents of this context include the rest of Velázquez's work, his life in the court of Philip IV, and the iconography of European painting in the 17th century generally. Without this context, it is impossible to argue that an element of a painting— a mirror, for example—is or is not a metaphor; that is, that it does or does not have significance beyond its appearance as a mirror.

Constructing the context, like finding a metaphor, is also an interpretive act. There is room in every case for discussion and disagreement. There are likely to be *lumpers,* those who tend to find fewer, larger ensembles in a given body of work, and *splitters,* those who tend to find many smaller ensembles. We can say generally that an ensemble must have more than one metaphor in it, but that its actual size may be extraordinarily large. In 1935, Caroline Spurgeon published a book identifying around 6000 metaphors in the works of William Shakespeare. This may constitute one enormous ensemble, or many. If we live long enough, we can examine them all. Fortunately, it is not so much the actual ensembles as the quality of the arguments we make about them that validates our research.

Ensembles of metaphors can be seen to function within an increasingly broad spectrum that begins with a single metaphor, contains small families of metaphors, then larger ensembles of metaphors, and concludes with metaphors in a field, collections of metaphors from different creative people within the same discipline or field of endeavor. Examples of this last, examined next, include Robert Sternberg's collection of metaphors for intelligence and Stephen Pepper's "world hypotheses." *Smaller* and *larger* in this spectrum are left to the discrimination of the investigator.

The term *ensemble of metaphor* should be taken as a potential direction for appropriate improvisation, not as a strictly defined term. Each case study will suggest a use of the term appropriate to itself. The term ensemble of metaphor is itself a metaphor for particular descriptions of processes of development, descriptions that are themselves metaphors.

III. EXAMPLES OF ENSEMBLES OF METAPHOR

A. Ensembles of Metaphor

In early case studies the use of the concept of image or imagery is virtually synonymous with our use of the term *metaphor*. Two prominent cases are Jeanne Hersch's untranslated study of the relationship between Henri Bergson's imagery and his system of thought, published in 1932, and Spurgeon's study of Shakespeare's imagery.

1. Shakespeare's Metaphors and His Personality

Spurgeon examined and cataloged approximately 6000 images from the work of William Shakespeare. Her aim was to elucidate Shakespeare's "personality, temperament and thought." She did not make a developmental or evolutionary argument regarding her findings, but her primary questions were psychological rather than literary or historical. Among her conclusions was this: "For the rest of him, the inner man, five words sum up the essence of his quality and character as seen through his images—sensitiveness, balance, courage, humour and wholesomeness." [*See* SHAKESPEARE, WILLIAM.]

2. William James's Stream of Consciousness

Among the most thorough treatments of the concept of ensemble of metaphor is Jeffrey Osowski's examination of William James's ensembles of metaphor in the development of *Principles of Psychology*. This study was published in 1989. Osowski reviewed much of the literature outlined in examples here and gave a

thorough description of the "intricate hierarchic structure of *ensembles* of metaphor." He then demonstrated James's development and elaboration of the metaphor of consciousness as a stream, as opposed, for example, to consciousness as a chain or train of thoughts. "Through the *stream* family of metaphors, James was able to capture the concepts of continuity, constant change, direction, connectedness, pace, rhythm, and flow," wrote Osowski. Osowski examined several other ensembles of metaphor, including consciousness as the flight of a bird, as a fringe of felt relations, and as a herdsman. He concluded with a consideration of the functions of metaphor in creative thinking similar to ours.

3. Freud's Theory of Mind

Chantal Bruchez-Hall studied Freud's development of a theory of the unconscious by tracing the evolution of the ensembles of metaphor that relate to his model of the mind. Her work, published in 1996, examined seven of Freud's publications between 1892 and 1899, each demonstrating Freud's grappling with such concepts as consciousness, dreams, memory, psychotherapy, and psychopathology. Although the list of Freud's interests from this period is large the number of metaphors he uses to conceptualize his thoughts about these topics is relatively small. Bruchez-Hall showed how just two ensembles of metaphors, those having to do with control and those having to do with transformation, lead eventually to Freud's theory of mind involving the preconscious and the unconscious. This should not imply that a study of one facet of a creative person's work, metaphor, is part of a reduction of creative work. Ensemble of metaphor, rather, affords the opportunity to study as many facets as necessary to form a cogent understanding. [*See* FREUD, SIGMUND.]

4. Tolman's Ratiocinations of an Amazed Mind

A study by Laurence Smith from 1990 examined the work of the behaviorist Edward Tolman to show how even a pragmatic, positivistic scientist cannot escape the qualitative infusion of metaphor. Tolman's writings are rife with metaphors of mind as maze and mind as map. The metaphors Smith found in Tolman's work clearly function both to generate a theory of mind and behavior and to constitute this theory. That is, one cannot conceptualize Tolman's theory without such metaphors (or else it would be a different theory), and the metaphors themselves lead to further possible elaborations of the theory.

B. Metaphors in a Field

The number of works here is too large to include more than a smattering. The point is that metaphors, commonly accepted, provide, on the one hand, a conceptual framework for discussion within a field or discipline and, on the other hand, a fence that includes some conceptions of a phenomenon and excludes others. For the sciences, a seminal theoretical work here is Thomas Kuhn's *The Structure of Scientific Revolutions,* from 1962, which proposed that scientific research is guided by models, metaphors, or the overused and best avoided term *paradigm.*

1. Stephen Pepper's Root Metaphors

Stephen Pepper's *World Hypotheses,* published in 1942, regards philosophical metaphors in a field. Pepper argued that when we speak about the world we give evidence of a theory about it as well, a theory that is synonymous with our beliefs about the nature of the world itself. He identified seven "root metaphors," three of which—animism, mysticism, and eclecticism—he rejected for various reasons, and four of which—formism, mechanism, contextualism, and organicism—he acknowledged to be relatively equally persuasive or powerful. Pepper's argument is directed toward philosophical dogmatists, those who would hang all on only one metaphor or point of view when a reasonable person would acknowledge the equal validity of several. Clearly, Pepper's book is a response to the strife of the first half of the 20th century, strife he believed stemmed in large part from dogmatic adherence to indefensible principles.

2. Sternberg's Metaphors of Mind

In *Metaphors of Mind: Conceptions of the Nature of Intelligence,* published in 1990, Robert Sternberg ex-

amined seven metaphors for intelligence and related them to the questions we may pose about intelligence and the theories we may construct about it. These metaphors are presented not as an ensemble within the work of a creative individual but as a collection of principal metaphors that have supported various theories of intelligence. These metaphors are the geographic (cf. Tolman's map of the mind), the computational, the biological, the epistemological, the anthropological, the sociological, and systems metaphors. The first six generally enable examination of the relationship of intelligence to either the internal or the external world of an individual, but not to both. Sternberg favored the last, systems metaphor, as do we, because it enables us to examine both the internal and external worlds of an individual. The systems metaphor also enables us to examine, in context, the evolution or development of an individual's creative work with respect to that person's ensembles of metaphor. [*See* INTELLIGENCE.]

Bibliography

Black, M. (1979). More about metaphor. In A. Ortony (Ed.), *Metaphor and thought.* New York: Cambridge University Press.

Glucksburg, S., & Keysar, B. (1990). Understanding metaphorical comparisons: Beyond similarity. *Psychological Review, 97,* 3–18.

Gruber, H. (1980). Darwin on psychology and its relation to evolutionary thought. In R. Rieber & K. Salzinger (Eds.), *Psychology: Theoretical and historical perspectives.* New York: Academic Press.

Kuhn, T. (1970). *The structure of scientific revolutions* (2nd ed., enlarged). Chicago: The University of Chicago Press.

Nersessian, N. (1992). How do scientists think? Capturing the dynamics of conceptual change in science. In R. Giere (Ed.), *Cognitive models of science: Minnesota Studies in the Philosophy of Science,* (Vol. 15). Minneapolis: Minnesota University Press.

Osowski, J. (1989). Ensembles of metaphor in the psychology of William James. In D. Wallace & H. Gruber (Eds.), *Creative people at work.* New York: Oxford University Press.

Smith, L. (1990). Metaphors of knowledge and behavior in the behaviorist tradition. In D. Leary (Ed.), *Metaphors in the history of psychology.* New York: Cambridge University Press.

Sternberg, R. (1990). *Metaphors of mind: Concepts of the nature of intelligence.* New York: Cambridge University Press.

Everyday Creativity

Ruth Richards

Saybrook Graduate School,
University of California, San Francisco,
and Harvard Medical School

Eminent-Level Creativity This regards creative persons or their creative products where recognition has been awarded by society at large, or by relevant organizations, and may involve awards, honors, prizes, publication, performances, or other forms of distinction. Criteria may vary, and they may be implicit or explicit—the common factor here is social recognition. Such creators and their works are often thought to have exceptional qualities (although later generations might not agree). The term may also be applied to the creative process that generated these accomplishments.

Everyday Creativity This term regards the creative person or creative outcome (products, ideas, or behaviors) that involve day-to-day activities at work and during leisure time. These are characterized both by originality (involving new or unusual aspects) and meaningfulness to others. Beyond this, a great many manifestations of such creativity are possible, be this in office management, raising children, repairing a home, cooking a meal, or doing community service. The term may also pertain to the creative process which underlies this. Indeed, everyday creativity, viewed as a survival capacity, or motive for ongoing growth and development, should be applicable to virtually any domain of human endeavor.

Mood Disorders Families of mood disorders, or affective disorders, defined by multiple criteria in the American Psychiatric Association's *Diagnostic and Statistical Manual of Mental Disorders (DSM-IV)*. Disorders are characterized particularly by lowered or depressed mood (unipolar depressions), or by alternating mood elevations and depressions (bipolar disorders); such moods may alternate with significant and often extended periods of normalcy—particularly with adequate treatment. Genetic factors have been shown by twin and adoption studies to contribute in both types of disorder, although environment has a major (and so far incompletely understood) effect. Mood manifestations occur along a "spectrum" of qualitative and quantitative variants; for instance, a familial bipolar risk will manifest most often as a unipolar disorder (with presentation ranging from mild dysthymia to major depression), or at other times as an alternating mood disorder including bipolar I symptoms (with major mood elevations and depression), bipolar II symptoms (mild elevations and severe depressions), or cyclothymia (milder elevations and depressions, although cycling may be more rapid).

EVERYDAY CREATIVITY, or the originality of everyday life, is familiar to virtually everyone. It is vital for our flexible adaptation to life, and sense of personal well-being. Yet everyday creativity often goes unrecognized and unrewarded. Several reasons for this are considered. Everyday creativity is also distinguished from eminent and exceptional creativity, and is viewed in terms of cog-

Copyright © 1999 by Academic Press
All rights of reproduction in any form reserved.

nitive style or orientation, rather than specific abilities. Its multiple relationships both to personal difficulty and personal health (viewed as source and as outcome of creative efforts) are illustrated using a typology of direct and indirect effects. A "dark side" of creativity is acknowledged. Yet, in general, whether its origins are in pain or personal well-being, creativity tends to work in the service of health. In fact, everyday creativity can help one cope, increase physical and psychological health and well-being, and even further one's self-actualization and caring contributions to the world.

I. EVERYDAY CREATIVITY— UNRECOGNIZED AND UNREWARDED?

A. Eminent-Level Creativity

The type of creativity we are apt to most read about in the newspaper may be called eminent-level creativity. Here is the prize-winning playwright, the best-selling novelist, the distinguished artist, the groundbreaking scientist, or the Internet innovator with software that ties the world more closely together. Often these are accomplishments in the "traditionally creative" areas of the arts and sciences. Most often, these have also received some significant form of social recognition. [*See* EMINENCE.]

To many, such work is sure creative (defined in terms of the two most commonly employed criteria of *originality* and *meaningfulness* to others). Yet to some people, this is where creativity also ends. Such people may be equating creativity with the arts—or perhaps the sciences—and with unusual standards of excellence and recognition. [*See* DEFINITIONS OF CREATIVITY.]

B. Everyday Creativity

Meanwhile, the same people may be doing a great many innovative (original, meaningful) things they are not "counting." Examples include a sympathetic co-worker saving her friend from a breakdown, an at-home mother developing a thriving cottage industry, a high school teacher who inspires new involvement in social studies, or a marketer of canned goods who develops an engaging campaign. Examples of accomplishments include innovations in work and leisure, such as new approaches in home repairs, gourmet cooking, athletics, community service, correspondence, business planning, or a range of arts and crafts. Yet often this work is not recognized as creative. And if it is not recognized as creative, then it is unlikely to be rewarded as such, never mind encouraged and nurtured.

Nevertheless, authors and scholars have long seen creativity of everyday life as both a survival capability—representing the "phenotypic plasticity" that allow humans to adapt to changing environments—and a humanistic force in ongoing growth, personal development, and even transcendence. New research on creativity and health further underlines its potential as a force in survival and evolution.

Through another lens, creativity may be viewed as a hallmark of life's emergent systems (here using a term of nonlinear dynamics, or chaos theory)—of systems found everywhere from the working of our brains, to the weather, economic systems, and the rise and fall of governments. What is called creativity may involve a profound working out of a fundamental life force in our manifest reality.

If there is evolutionary value to creativity it would be at the level of everyday creativity, not eminent contribution. To be a reproductive or evolutionary advantage, creativity must happen at each level on a day to day basis. [*See* CHAOS THEORY IN CREATIVITY.]

C. One Creativity or Many?

J. P. Guilford postulated 120 different structure of intellect abilities; a subset of these, called "divergent production" abilities, 24 in number, were particularly linked with creativity, across verbal, visual, and other modalities. Howard Gardner has written about seven multiple "intelligences," including linguistic, musical, mathematical, spatial, kinesthetic, personal, and interpersonal capacities. Some people can be good at painting, some at mathematical problems, and some at modern dance. Whence comes "everyday creativity"? [*See* INTELLIGENCE.]

The notion of everyday creativity is not in conflict with the idea of discrete abilities or talents. Everyday creativity is not necessarily an ability, or *only* an ability.

For one thing, it appears to relate to personality factors found in highly creative people across fields. Originality is "habitual" with highly creative persons. Scientists do not turn their originality off when they leave the laboratory, nor artists when they leave the studio. They tend to encounter the world in more transforming ways than another person might do.

Everyday creativity, as a disposition or style, may be related to the "self-actualizing creativity" of humanistic psychologist Abraham Maslow (versus his "special talent" creativeness). Perhaps not surprisingly, self-actualization is at the top of Maslow's hierarchy of needs. Along different lines, research on everyday creativity and bipolar affective disorders indicates that higher creativity appears in connection with somewhat milder forms of bipolar disorders—not characteristically in the most severely ill—and is additionally high among normal relatives of bipolar individuals. This pattern appears despite subjects' areas of endeavor. There is also higher familial creativity in many cases, but it does not "run true" to a particular modality or interest. Hence creativity might come out for one person in art, one in schoolteaching, and one in business. [*See* AFFECTIVE DISORDERS; FAMILIES AND CREATIVITY.]

In the area of cognitive style (modes of thinking reflective of underlying personality trends), greater "overinclusive thinking" has been found among creative persons (and also, incidentally, among people with bipolar mood disorders, especially when hypomanic or manic—which is also consistent with tendencies toward "loose associations"). This has been a consistent finding both with eminent creators, and with everyday creators. [*See* COGNITIVE STYLE AND CREATIVITY.]

Studies have additionally found greater overinclusion among people in general who were in a mildly good (versus neutral) mood. This finding helps explain one way in which mild mood elevation is relevant to creativity. Whatever other mechanisms may also be involved, general style factors across special endeavors or "intelligences" may affect creativity.

D. Creativity Underemphasized and Discouraged

The estrangement of creativity from our day to day lives may be abetted by a number of phenomena, singly or in combination. These include (a) *idealization,* our tendency to glorify certain people—heroes, geniuses, and the like—who seem qualitatively different from us and can do (we think, or hope) what we cannot; (b) *the mystique of creativity,* coming from subterranean and irrational places we cannot all access (included here is the notion of creativity and illness—we may be weird or sick if we are creative, or encounter unnecessary pain, and do we really want that?); and (c) *false dichotomies* and our living within these, as a culture, and accepting various divisions of emphasis and commitment—whether these involve thought versus feeling, mind versus body, science versus art, or male versus female—rather than embracing the whole-person integration and freedom from stereotypes that allows us creatively to do what is needed; (d) *reactions to the nonconformist.* Creative people are sometimes difficult insofar as they may do what they want, break rules, and not value norms. Studies suggest that teachers in general do not greatly value creative students—and even those teachers who think they value creativity poorly tolerate some of the behaviors going along with it. If this is so in our schools, it is easy to see how this might also be true in our families, workplaces, and government. The complex solution here involves a greater societal valuing of creativity—and indeed of the trouble it may require to foster creativity. [*See* BARRIERS TO CREATIVITY AND CREATIVE ATTITUDES.]

II. FIVE TYPES OF RELATIONSHIP

Below are typologies for the complex and overlapping possible interactions between creativity and either illness or health, with both direct and indirect relationships. There is a basis for connecting creativity and mood disorders, most especially in the case of eminent creativity and accomplishments in the arts. However, this is only one pattern associated with creativity in the arts, and not the only one. There are many roads to creativity.

A. Typology: Creativity and Personal Problems or Pathology

Five general types of association are noted and illustrated below. Many situations may involve more than one type of phenomenon simultaneously. These categories are an oversimplification of patterns that may involve many simultaneously operating factors. [*See* FIVE-PART TYPOLOGY.]

1. *Direct effects of problems/pathology on creativity.* Personal problems might be transformed directly into artistic or other forms of work.

2. *Indirect effects of problems/pathology on creativity.* Personal problems could lead to patterns, styles, or choices of the individual and motivating energy that later end up influencing creative work.

3. *Direct effects of creativity on pathology/problems.* Creative efforts could unearth difficulties which could lead to a decompensation—or to greater mental health, if not suppressed or escaped, and if worked through under supportive conditions.

4. *Indirect effects of creativity on pathology/problems.* Creative efforts lead to either personal or social reactions that can bring about personal problems.

5. *Third factor which affects both creativity and pathology/problems.* A factor such as a vulnerability to a mood disorder might independently enhance creativity on the one hand, and personal problems on the other.

B. Typology: Creativity and Health

Creativity may facilitate psychological openness and health. This could continue to build on itself, through a cycle of positive feedback, health increasing creativity, and then creativity health. Creativity, whatever its origins, tends in most cases to work in the service of health. Here are some possible reasons.

1. *"Open minds"—Direct effects of health on creativity.* A healthy mind may yield higher creative potential related to psychological openness, lack of defensiveness, and access to material at the threshold of consciousness.

2. *"Integrated minds"—Indirect effects of health on creativity.* If a person keeps open channels for mental associations, however, charged the memories may be, there should be more lasting integration of affectively charged material in memory storage—and more raw materials for creativity.

3. *"Creative coping"—Direct effects of creativity on health.* Work on catharsis through creative writing is notable for subjects' increased well-being, their de-

crease in health-care visits, and increases on two biological markers of immune function. [*See* WRITING AND CREATIVITY.]

4. *"Positive snowball effect"—Indirect effects of creativity on health.* There are potential positive and healthy aftereffects of ongoing work on both creative *ability* and *motivation*. The creator may leave in his or her mental wake a more richly connected repository of memories, leading to greater openness and mental health in the future, both in the ability and in the motivation to access one's memory storage, possibly for further creating.

5. *"Amplifier or snowball effect"—Third factor affecting both creativity and health.* For example, young children at birth are temperamentally more or less prone already to be curious versus more fearful and reluctant. Curiosity in this sense, may be considered an "amplifier" to the extent that it encourages a would be inventor to try something out. In the case of mental health, curiosity may prove the impetus to put fears and self doubts aside.

Patterns such as the above, when they repeat, should increase the probability of creative response the next time around—it feels good, it works, and the person is more empowered.

III. IS CREATIVITY INHERENTLY HEALTHY FOR INDIVIDUALS AND FOR CULTURES?

A. A Dark Side of Creativity

Some people have brought their innovative abilities to particular domains of expertise for destruction, as in the creation of terrorist strategies or biological weapons. Creativity and its products are not always used toward positive ends. [*See* DARK SIDE OF CREATIVITY.]

B. Self-Actualization and a Greater Caring

In a more positive light, research has shown an association between creativity and self-actualization. It has been suggested that creativity may fulfill deficiency needs (e.g., love and acceptance) and may perpetuate the intrinsic motivation and satisfaction associated with that creativity or creative product. [*See* SELF-ACTUALIZATION.]

IV. CONCLUSIONS: MAXIMIZING OUR CREATIVE POTENTIAL

If everyday creativity truly functions as an adaptive quality of evolutionary significance, then one hopes such progress will occur frequently. It may be that innovation is driven by a fundamental need to progress and grow, to challenge, to become self-actualized, and to become "all one's potentialities." Yet we do not always become this, and we need to look carefully at ourselves and at our institutions to see what may be blocking our progress. Our everyday creativity, when fully enabled and nurtured, can bring to us, individually, new health, satisfaction, and purpose, and together, the means to address many challenges of a new millennium. [*See* FOUR PS OF CREATIVITY.]

Bibliography

Gruber, H., & Wallace, D. (Eds.). (1993). Creativity in the moral domain. [Special Issue]. *Creativity Research Journal, 6*(1, 2).

Montuori, A., & Purser, R. (1997–in press). *Social creativity: An exploration of the social, historical and political factors in creativity and innovation* (Vol. 1, 1999; Vols. 2 & 3, in press). Cresskill, NJ: Hampton Press.

Pennebaker, J. W. (Ed.). (1995). *Emotion, disclosure, and health.* Washington, DC: American Psychological Association.

Richards, R. (1981). Relationships between creativity and psychopathology: An evaluation and interpretation of the evidence. *Genetic Psychology Monographs, 103,* 261–324.

Runco, M. (Ed.). (1996). Creativity from childhood through adulthood: The developmental issues [Special issue]. *New Directions for Child Development, 72.*

Runco, M., & Richards, R. (Eds.). (1997). *Eminent creativity, everyday creativity, and health.* Greenwich, CT: Ablex.

Russ, S. (Ed.). (1998). *Affect, creative experience, and psychological adjustment.* Philadelphia: Brunner/Mazel.

Shaw, M., & Runco, M. (Eds.). (1994). *Creativity and affect.* Greenwich, CT: Ablex.

Special Issues on Creativity and Health. (1990). *Creativity Research Journal, 3*(3, 4).

Sternberg, R. J. (Ed.). (1988). *The nature of creativity: Contemporary psychological perspectives.* New York: Cambridge University Press.

Evolving Systems Approach

Howard E. Gruber

Teachers College, Columbia University

Pluralism An attitude guiding the investigator, welcoming and looking for the many rather than the one or two essentials. Thus: many metaphors, many insights, many mentors, many motives.

System The way in which the several elements comprising an entity are interrelated or organized into a functional whole. It is usually intended that the elements do not completely lose their identity when participating in such an arrangement.

Extrinsic and Intrinsic Motivation When the considerations impelling a person to do a certain project are inherent in the nature of the work, either as a process or as product, we speak of intrinsic motivation. When the motivating considerations are different in kind from the nature of the work—as monetary rewards for creative products—we speak of extrinsic motivation. The two kinds, although usually contrasted with each other, are not necessarily incompatible.

Facet Any aspect of a creative case that can be made sufficiently distinct to permit intensive study of it, whether regarding process, product, content, or context.

Initial Sketch The creative person frequently begins work on a project by making a quick and crude sketch of the work to follow.

Network of Enterprise Creative work can be viewed as organized so that enduring enterprises are composed of several projects, and to carry out a project requires engaging in several tasks. The whole assembly of a creator's enterprises is a network of enterprise.

The **EVOLVING SYSTEMS APPROACH** (ESA) is both a method and a theory for understanding the unique individual creative person at work. It involves no commitment to discovering generalizations one can make about all creative people. Its primary aim is to construct an account, both analytical and developmental, of each creative person considered and to arrive at what may be called a "theory of the individual." By "developmental" we do not mean an account starting with infancy, but one that starts wherever it is feasible. Fortunately, productive creators usually leave ample traces of their work. The evolving system comprising the creative person includes three major subsystems: knowledge, purpose, and affect. Creative acts are taken to be outcomes of the functioning of this system, and every episode and every facet of the process of creative work engages all three subsystems.

Copyright © 1999 by Academic Press
All rights of reproduction in any form reserved.

I. INTRODUCTION

What follows is a brief overview of the ESA to creative work. Although we mention many facets of the creative process, for reasons of space only a few are illustrated.

If we do no more than vary the starting point of each study, other changes follow so that each new starting point reveals new facets of the creative process. Consider two contrasting points of view: the psychobiographer approaches the case with the primary aim of understanding the historical and personal factors that set the stage for the creative process, without actually examining in any detail the creative work itself. On the other hand, the experimental psychologist interested in creativity, in order to have a manageable experimental design, narrows the focus of attention drastically and increases the number of subjects. The psychobiographer typically pays little attention to the process of creative work; the experimenter relaxes the criterion used in selecting creative subjects (e.g., the more creative half of an ordinary high school class) in order to have enough subjects to complete the experimental design. Taken to an extreme, the assumption underlying much of this experimental research is that everyone or almost everyone is creative in some degree, and we can consequently study the process in the less than great even if our aim is to understand the higher levels of creative endeavor.

One of the important facets of the case study is the initial sketch, which seems to occur in many if not all instances of creative work. For example, when Picasso began the monthlong effort that produced the great mural *Guernica,* his first move was a small, rather primitive sketch to which he referred repeatedly in the month that followed. Later, we will come to other facets of the creative case study. For the moment suffice it to say that each new starting point serves as a searchlight that reveals new configurations and as a gyroscope that keeps the creator pointed toward remote goals. In this way, selecting a new starting point permits the creator to maintain a freshness of his or her work. In practice, history and evolution guarantee that such new starts will recur incessantly.

By a system we mean a set of distinct components in specified relationships. A simple list of traits is a kind of theory because it proposes to say what is important,

but it is not a systemic theory. Only when we examine interrelationships of these members of the system can we begin to speak of systems. Systemic analysis is possible at many different levels, for example, the organism is composed of organs and society is composed or organisms. To choose as one focus of attention a particular level of analysis, or set of levels, need imply no denigration of other levels of their students.

II. ORGANIZATION AND ADAPTATION

In the present context, the idea that organization and adaptation are twin aspects of creative evolution could also be described as forces making for stability and forces making for novelty. In the study of creativity, as in all other living processes, there must be continuity and stability.

There is a loose confederation of scholars interested in creativity in different subgroups, such as genetic epistemologists, Gestalt psychologists, and system theorists. Of course, some workers in each camp claim superiority for their brand. More important, however, each of these approaches can be considered as highlighting some important aspects of the whole process, their totality providing the context for any one of them.

At any given moment in intellectual history several schematizations are available to the thinker, and they can be selected, composed, and arranged in different ways by different creators. One of the central ideas of the ESA can be called "pluralism": not one but several schematizations, not one but many metaphors, not one but many enterprises, and so on.

The field of psychology presents a puzzling spectacle. The same controversies seem to crop up in every generation, such as the conflict between wholism and atomism, or that between evolution and stasis, or that between sudden intuitive leaps and incremental change.

In 1937, the prominent personality psychologist Gordon Allport wrote,

> It is not upon the cell nor upon the single organ, nor upon the group, nor upon the species that nature has centered her most lavish concern, but rather upon the integral organization of life processes into the amazing

stable and self-contained system of the individual living creature. (1937, p. 3)

It may well be that these repeated controversies stem not from blind commitment to one or another ideology, but from the legitimate necessity to rework fundamental concepts as circumstances change. Allport argued emphatically and at length for the necessity of studying the single case and to point out the various tendencies, in the psychology of that period, to escape from the trap of atomistic, individualistic positivism.

III. FACETS

It is common in psychological research to distinguish between "how" questions and "why" questions. "How" addresses itself to the processes of creative work; "why" asks, what are the underlying reasons for doing it? To a large extent the failure to separate the two kinds of questions has led to profound neglect of "how" questions. An important movement in the study of creativity has been psychobiography—the application of personality theory, especially Freud's, to understanding creative people. A related effort, psychohistory, applies the same range of theories, not to understanding the individual creator, but rather to historical events for which a psychological theory is proposed. Insofar as these approaches delve deeply into the life of a creative person, they are of very great interest. Unfortunately, to a large extent psychobiography and psychohistory have been the occasion for neglecting "how" questions. Insofar as these approaches draw upon the early years of the creator they are forced into undocumented speculations. A third category of creativity research is the psychometric approach, in which tests are administered to large enough numbers of subjects to permit statistical analysis. For different reasons these three methods all avoid studying the creative person at work. On the contemporary American scene this has meant a shifting focus on:

- Birth order effects, in which the person becomes creative because of his or her special place in the developing family. [*See* BIRTH ORDER.]
- Bipolar disorder, where the anguish of private life

provides the stimulus for creative expression. [*See* MOOD.]
- Metaphor, where the ability to see and express commonalities between unlike things is the central ingredient of creativity. [*See* METAPHORS.]
- Great powers of visualization. [*See* IMAGERY.]
- Divergent thinking, the ability or propensity for thinking of unusual responses. [*See* DIVERGENT THINKING.]

All of these and many more have been singled out as the essence of creativity.

Paradoxically, in the ESA we avoid a singular focus by welcoming all such proposals into our toolshed. However, the uses to which the tools will be put vary from project to project and different creators may accomplish similar ends with different collections of tools. For example, the physicist Richard Feynman solved an important class of physical problems with theoretical tools quite different from those used by others in solving the same problem. Feynman's method was geometric and the others' was algebraic. While in this instance Feynman's method eventually prevailed, the work of the others was also creative. Moreover, the creator does not use one prefashioned tool but a collection of them, including some that are invented in the course of work on each project.

Looked at from the creator's point of view, a given facet or facets may be foremost in attention, the vast remainder being the background. The distinction between figure and ground is well known in the psychology of perception. A change in attention may be thought of as a figure–ground reversal. If the figures in question are cherished projects, the creator may experience mixed feelings upon switching—excitement at the new engagement together with regret at what is left behind. The ground, or context, is so complex and dynamic that new facets are continually appearing. For example, after Charles Darwin published the *Origin of Species* he took up with great vigor questions of physiological botany that had long lain fallow in his network of enterprise. This move brought a certain closure to his work: nearly a century before, his grandfather Erasmus Darwin had written much on botany. Of particular relevance was his long scientific poem, *The Love of the Plants,* which the young Charles Darwin greatly admired but never emulated.

For a second example, many scientists who are completely engrossed in their work are nevertheless aware of severe and chronic social disorders in the world around them. Even if they manage to shut that world out it may still cast a dark shadow on their lives.

IV. INSIGHT AND PROBLEM SOLVING

There is a widespread belief in the prevalence of sudden insights arrived at intuitively (i.e., inexplicably), such insights constituting the genuine article, a creative product. An often retold and celebrated story is August Kekulé's account of his discovery of the benzene ring, which he made while half asleep on a London bus. However, if his account is read carefully one can see that he had been moving in that direction for well over a decade, and the dance of the molecules that he described was not a unique event, but a mode of thought that he employed in his chemical thinking. [*See* INSIGHT.]

The reverie on the bus must be seen in its larger context, the general nature of Kekulé's thinking. Moreover, his thinking must be seen in the still larger context of the history of chemistry in the 19th century. Viewed in these lights, Kekulé's traumerei was not a miracle of intuition, but the product of protracted and directed work by an international network interested in structural chemistry.

If insight is not the cause or the embodiment of creative work, what is its role in the creative process? First it should be said that insight, when it does occur, takes a variety of forms. As the culmination of a protracted process it may be a sudden change in awareness or it may be a gradual shifting in point of view. With this in mind, there is no great need to define insight *a priori*: we study the record, note changes, and describe them (sudden or gradual, aware or unconscious, pursued immediately or bracketed for later attention).

V. PURPOSES AND MOTIVES

A distinction widely agreed upon is made between intrinsic and extrinsic motivation. The former refers to the satisfaction sought in actually doing creative work.

The latter refers to the satisfaction arising out of recognition, prizes, monetary awards, and the power that comes with fame. With regard to intrinsic motivation we ought to distinguish between the satisfaction deriving from doing the work and that derived from completing it. On the surface it might appear as though extrinsic motives correspond to "why" questions and intrinsic motivations to "how" questions. But if we take the creator's network of enterprise as a whole as reflecting the totality of his or her intentions, absorption in this set of tasks becomes a powerful motive.

Beginning work on a task sets up a kind of drive for completing it. The question remains open whether this drive is the same as the pleasure in actually doing the work. It may well be that in real creative work, both kinds of satisfaction are at work under the broad heading of intrinsic motivation. Meanwhile, it is reasonably clear that extrinsic motivation is also important. Nobel prizes and other blandishments are ever present and highly visible. A plausible hypothesis is that, for whatever reason, at moments when one is not engrossed in the work, extrinsic motivation drives the creator back into it; when he or she is engrossed, the very same extrinsic motives may be a distraction, even a pollutant: intrinsic motivation takes over. In Darwin's notebooks there are few passages indicating extrinsic motivation, but there are some. And it should be remembered that writing the notebooks was itself part of the work process, a record of activity governed by the task, not of activity governed by other considerations. On the cognitive side belief systems evolve throughout the life history, and on the intentional side motives evolve. [*See* MOTIVATION/DRIVE.]

Tasks are not undertaken singly. Each task becomes a member of one or more enterprises. These, taken together, form a *network of enterprises,* and this network can be thought of as the individual's evolving organization of purpose. This network of enterprise, once formed, serves to locate any given project within it; at the same time, it represents a large portion of the individual creator's self-concept. Every task may be said to have a history. A gap, disequilibrium, or unsatisfactory situation is observed; this leads to the undertaking of a task. Some subset of such tasks form an enterprise. Seen in this light, an insight need not be the solution to a problem, it may be the initial recognition that one exists. Often, the recognition of a problem unsolved, a voyage not yet taken, can produce the thrill of discovery that we usually associate with solution.

VI. SKILL

It is widely believed that astonishingly high levels of skill account for high levels of creativity. But we certainly can find examples of individuals with great skills who are not very creative. For example, among artists there are greatly skilled copyists and plagiarists who can successfully imitate at least one artist and sometimes many. Such individuals become the plague of museum curators, who for all their expertise sometimes fall victim to artistic fraud. So skill alone is not sufficient for creative work. On the other hand skill is certainly a virtue and it is attainable through practice.

VII. COLLABORATION

Growing out of the extreme individualism of modern Western society, the picture of the creator as a lonely genius is very widespread. But we are coming to see that various kinds of collaborative processes are also important. For example, there is the well-known case of Einstein and the Olympia circle, three young men who met every week over coffee to share ideas. Thus Einstein, during his years working in the Swiss patent office, was not, as is sometimes suggested, alone in his theoretical quest. He had important collaborative opportunities. Another example is the case of Picasso and Braque, who together invented and initiated the important movement in art of cubism.

Even in the case of the project that is conducted alone, one almost invariably finds that the individual creator is in some kind of fruitful relations with others. van Gogh, for example, sent his canvases to fellow artists all over Europe and received theirs, providing a rich language for aesthetic discourse, the work itself. Gauguin and van Gogh lived together for a while in Arles, working side by side and dreaming of a utopian artists' community. Thus even famously isolated creators such as Newton, Einstein, and van Gogh always seem to have profited from collaborative relationships. To these examples should be added informal groupings such as the Salon des Refusés—artists who were rejected by the French artistic establishment

but nevertheless managed to construct relationships of mutual defense and support. [*See* COLLABORATION AND COMPETITION.]

VIII. CONCLUSION

The evolving systems approach requires an accumulation of individual case studies. We need enough of them to get from the unique creative person at work to whatever generalizations may follow. We will not be in a position to present a well-founded theory until we can document our thinking with theories of individuals. It is possible to study an individual in detail without raising individualism itself to cult status. Unique people, which we all are, can work together. Creative work always takes place in a multiplex environment. There is no necessary conflict between respect for the individual and sensitivity to the social nature of all creative thought. [For other expressions of the evolving systems approach, *see* ENSEMBLE OF METAPHOR; CREATIVITY IN THE MORAL DOMAIN; PIAGET, JEAN; SHAW, GEORGE BERNARD; and VAN GOGH, VINCENT.]

Bibliography

Allport, G. (1937). *Personality, a psychological interpretation.* New York: Holt.

Csikszentmihalyi, M. (19939). *The evolving self.* New York: Harper Collins.

Franklin, M. B. (1994). Narratives of change and continuity: Women artists reflect on their work. In M. B. Franklin & B. Kaplan (Eds.), *Development and the arts, critical perspectives.* Hillsdale, NJ: Erlbaum.

Gruber, H. E. (1981). *Darwin on man: The psychological study of scientific creativity* (2nd ed.). Chicago; University of Chicago Press.

Gruber, H. E. (1995). Insight and affect in the history of science. In R. J. Sternberg & J. E. Davidson (Eds.), *The nature of insight.* Cambridge, MA: MIT Press.

Gruber, H. E. (1996). The life space of a scientist: The visionary function and other aspects of Jean Piaget's thinking. *Creativity Research Journal, 9*(2/3), 251–265.

Gruber, H. E., & Davis, S. N. (1988). Inching our way up Mount Olympus: The evolving systems approach to creative thinking. In R. J. Sternberg (Ed.), *The nature of creativity.* Cambridge, MA: Cambridge University Press.

Hammond, K. R. (1996). *Human judgment and social policy.* New York: Oxford University Press.

Wallace, D. B., & Gruber, H. E. (1989). *Creative people at work: 12 cognitive case studies.* New York: Oxford University Press.

Expertise

K. Anders Ericsson and Andreas C. Lehmann

Florida State University

I. Overview: Expertise and Expert Performance
II. Expertise as Innate Talent
III. Expertise as Acquired Knowledge and Skill
IV. The Structure of Expert Performance
V. Expert Performance and Creative Achievements

Deliberate Practice Structured activity, often designed by teachers or coaches with the explicit goal of increasing an individual's current level of performance. In contrast to other activities such as work and play, it requires the generation of specific goals for improvement and the monitoring of various aspects of performance. Furthermore, deliberate practice involves trying to exceed one's previous limit, which requires full concentration and effort. Consequently, it is only possible to engage in these activities for a limited amount of time until rest and recuperation are needed.

Domain Area of behavior with an organized set of activities where experts and an accumulated body of shared (teachable) knowledge are recognized. The most well-known disciplines or domains are those of the arts and sciences, medicine, sports, and games.

Expert Performer An individual who, by objective standards and over time, shows a superior and reproducible performance in representative (typical) activities of a domain. In contrast to the everyday use of the term *expert,* which is applied freely to any specialized individual, expert performers must display consistent superior performance in their respective domains.

Innate Talent Innate capacities that many believe are necessary for attaining the highest levels of performance in a specific domain. It is well known that most necessary component skills and attributes of expert performers require extended training for their acquisition—with the exception of talent. Talent is thought to be directly determined by genes, and it cannot be modified or improved through training. The associated abilities develop naturally without the need for any specific practice. Consequently, society tries to identify talented individuals during early phases of training and provide them with the best education and encouragement for the extended road to expert performance. The terms *talent* or *giftedness* are used in the text, despite the lack of firm scientific evidence supporting these constructs.

Novice A person who has received all the necessary knowledge and instruction to be able to perform independently in a domain. Novices represent the lowest level of attained skill for individuals who can still perform the basic tasks of the domain. They are therefore often used as a reference group for comparisons with the highest level performers in studies of expert-novice differences.

EXPERTISE *refers to the cognitive, perceptual-motor, and physiological mechanisms that allow experts to consistently attain superior levels of performance. Webster's dictionary defines an expert as "one who has acquired special skill in or knowledge of a particular subject through professional training and practical experience."*

Copyright © 1999 by Academic Press
All rights of reproduction in any form reserved.

Accordingly, typical experts are individuals such as medical doctors, accountants, teachers, and scientists who have been certified as professionals after extended training and have then accumulated experience in their specialty. More recently, the term expert *has been expanded to describe any highly skilled performer who exhibits superior achievement after instruction and extended experience in a field. Among those fields, which are called* domains, *are the arts (e.g., music, painting, and writing), sports (e.g., swimming, running, and golf), and games (e.g., chess, Othello, and bridge). Because we assume that the performance of experts in those various domains is mediated by mechanisms that share certain characteristics, we can apply a single concept, namely that of expertise, to performance in different domains. Also, we would expect expertise in various domains to be acquired and develop in a similar fashion.*

I. OVERVIEW: EXPERTISE AND EXPERT PERFORMANCE

The main task for researchers of expertise is to explain how some individuals attain the highest levels of achievement in a domain, and why there are only so few who reach such levels. To attain very high (expert) levels of performance in domains of expertise, both nature and nurture must be involved. Experts' performances often look effortless, and their most refined and insightful behavior is generated rapidly and naturally rather than being the result of prolonged deliberation. One is thus led to believe that experts excel in general basic characteristics, such as intelligence, memory, speed, and flexibility. It has traditionally been assumed that those characteristics are impossible to train and thus are determined to a large degree by genetic factors (nature). Everyone agrees, however, that experts must acquire at least some necessary domain-specific knowledge and skill (nurture). The relative importance of nature versus nurture for expert achievement has been discussed and argued since the origin of our civilization. A couple of questions have been the primary focus. First, how does expert achievement develop and what is the role of instruction and training? Second, are people born with certain characteristics to attain expert performance or are those characteristics acquired through development and training? This article briefly reviews the most important conceptions of expertise

spanning the past century, summarizes our current knowledge, and finally outlines the implications and connections of expert performance for creativity and genius.

II. EXPERTISE AS INNATE TALENT

A. Beginnings in the 19th Century: Sir Francis Galton

In his pioneering studies of excellence in 19th-century England, Sir Francis Galton found that a very large number of the most valued achievements were made by members of a small number of eminent families. Galton found that as the genetic bond to these families lessened, the likelihood that individuals had outstanding reputations also decreased. To explain how individuals from these eminent families could succeed in such diverse professions as politics, literature, and science, Galton claimed that instruction and training were beneficial, perhaps even necessary, and associated with large initial improvements of performance. However, with further experience these improvements in performance became increasingly smaller and soon a rather fixed upper bound for performance was attained. Galton thought that the upper bound on an individual's performance was limited by basic capacities that could not be modified through training and experience. The rare occurrence of expert performance could thus be explained by the small number of individuals engaged in the domain who were endowed with sufficiently superior basic capacities. Consequently, Galton and many other contemporary psychologists and educators developed psychometric tests to measure basic capacities of memory, perception, and thinking. In those tests the influence of knowledge and prior experience was minimized. Through extensive testing of children and adolescents, investigators hoped to identify innately talented individuals who, given the necessary resources of training and support, were most likely to achieve high levels of performance.

B. Is the Importance of Innate Basic Capacities Overrated?

Today, more than a century later, we can safely say that past efforts did not succeed in predicting future expert performance from individual differences in basic capacities. For example, when athletes or other experts are tested in the laboratory on how fast they can respond to the onset of a light (simple reaction time), they are not systematically faster than other subjects. The superior speed of a tennis player in returning a fast tennis serve must thus reflect an acquired ability to respond rapidly in representative situations rather than a general superiority of speed of neural impulses. Similarly, chess experts can recall nearly all the 24 chess pieces in a typical chess arrangement after a brief exposure, whereas beginners in chess can only recall around four pieces. Yet, if the chess pieces have been randomly arranged, then neither expert nor beginner can recall more than around four pieces of a position. Both the chess experts' and athletes' superior abilities are limited to their domain of expertise and therefore do not reflect basic capacities measured in the laboratory.

In a recent review, the major differences between experts and less proficient individuals were found to nearly always reflect specific adaptations acquired by the experts during their lengthy training. This holds true for many anatomical and physiological characteristics of athletes, such as the size of their muscles and bones and the flexibility of joints, and for the increased range of mobility of the limbs in ballet dancers and musicians. Some of these attributes, such as structural changes in the brains of musicians, are correlated with the length or early onset of training. Other adaptations—for example, the selected muscle growth only on the playing arms of tennis and baseball pitchers or the optimization of oxygen absorption of runners only at certain levels of running intensity—are so specific that self-selection of individuals in those domains appears highly unlikely. Finally, most physiological adaptations have been shown to revert back to the normal values once training was stopped, which is clearly an indication of their acquired nature. However, at least in one instance, namely height, we know for certain that genetic factors independent of experience can play an important role for the attainment of expert performance in domains, where more height constitutes either an advantage (e.g., basketball) or a disadvantage (e.g., gymnastics).

The incidence of expert achievement in some famous families, such as the Bach family which had many famous musicians, is frequently cited as proof for the genetic transmission (high heritability) of special talents. However, recent reviews of this evidence have questioned such claims. Instead, the early instruction of children by parents and access to networks and specialized training seem to offer sensible alternative accounts. Because expert performers are so rare, it is very difficult to conduct rigorous studies of heritability. So far, the small number of published studies on experts (i.e., Olympic athletes and musicians) have been unable to document any significant heritability. Heritability studies rely mainly on data from individuals who have shared the same environment during upbringing (adopted children) and from those who share genetic material (identical twins, fraternal twins, or siblings). Unfortunately, those individuals are surprisingly underrepresented in the expert population, making estimates of heritability of expert performance extremely difficult. [*See* FAMILIES AND CREATIVITY.]

III. EXPERTISE AS ACQUIRED KNOWLEDGE AND SKILL

A. Acquiring and Organizing Knowledge for Use in a Given Domain

One of the most significant advances in our understanding of expert performance resulted from a direct comparison of the thought processes of experts and less accomplished individuals. In his pioneering study conducted during the 1940s, researcher Adrian de Groot described the thought processes that allowed world-class chess players to consistently find better chess moves than less skilled players. He instructed chess players of each group to think aloud while they selected their next move for a given chess position. The transcriptions of these reports, so-called think-aloud protocols, revealed that all chess players were quickly retrieving promising moves from memory while examining the organization and structure of the presented chess position. Then, in the process of evaluating these potential moves by searching and planning, even better moves were often discovered. Neither de Groot nor other researchers found evidence that world-class players were more intelligent or that the speed of their planning or thoughts in general differed from that of less skilled chess players. The primary difference between the chess players was that the world-class players were better able to generate superior chess moves. The speed of generation indicated that the moves were directly retrieved from knowledge of similar chess positions in memory. Thus, with experience, experts acquire increasingly larger numbers of more complex patterns of moves and countermoves, which they can use when confronted with similar configurations.

Thus expertise is thought to be an extreme case of acquired skill. This view is in agreement with general theories of skill acquisition in which knowledge is first acquired and then organized into adequate procedures and actions. With continued practice, individuals become increasingly able to access more appropriate chess moves automatically through pattern-based retrieval. By recognizing complex configurations of chess pieces, an expert can retrieve good moves from his memory of related chess games. William Chase and Herbert Simon were the first to propose that the availability of stored complex chess patterns could explain why chess experts possess superior memory only for meaningful chess positions and not for random ones; new meaningful positions are the only type of material that adequately matches the body of already stored patterns. Finally, the expert's storehouse of chess patterns can also explain why good chess moves can be retrieved even more rapidly from memory when it is necessary, such as in speed chess.

Highly organized knowledge is also a key factor when it comes to more traditional, academic activities, such as solving textbook problems in physics. When physics experts read through a physics problem, they immediately retrieve a solution plan as part of their normal comprehension. In contrast, nonexperts (novices) typically look for the question at the end of the problem first and then retrieve formulas—one by one—and compute intermediate results by working backward from the requested answer. As one would expect, physics experts not only had more knowledge than novices, but they also had organized it around relevant theoretical principles of physics. This allowed the experts to retrieve plans for solving the problem directly as part of their understanding it. In contrast, the physics knowledge of the novices was poorly integrated and based on superficial appearance rather than deeper concepts. More generally, the superior ability of experts to reason appears to be specific to domain-related material in much the same manner as is their

ability to store and retrieve relevant knowledge. For example, studies have shown that experts in chemistry and social science lacked the special knowledge and strategies to successfully analyze a problem in political science; experts in experimental research were found to be able to design experiments of superior quality only within their specialty.

All these results support the general notion that experts' superiority is closely linked to their superior accumulation of knowledge. Could one use this knowledge to build computer programs, so-called expert systems, that almost behave like a human expert? A number of researchers have indeed taken this knowledge-based approach to expertise by designing methods to elicit the knowledge of experts, then describing the structure and organization of this knowledge in specific domains, and finally implementing it in complex computer models. However, the massive amount of relevant knowledge and methodological problems of extracting that knowledge from the experts remain major obstacles to the expert-systems approach to expertise.

B. Recent Challenges to the Knowledge-Based View of Expertise

Once psychologists had become interested in expertise, they went out and searched for domain experts. To their amazement, some experts with lengthy education and extended experience did not exhibit a performance superior to that of less experienced individuals or even novices. For example, professional stockbrokers were not found to be consistently superior in selecting investments when compared to statistical models or to completely random selection of stocks from investment indexes. Similarly, psychological therapists with Ph.D.s and many years of clinical experience were not more successful at helping clients than less experienced therapists with much less advanced training. The most impressive dissociation between level of expertise (indicated by the amount of schooling and experience) and performance has been demonstrated in many types of expert decision making and judgment. One review found that many types of expert judgments were surprisingly inaccurate and largely unrelated to the amount of experience of the person making the judgment.

With experience, individuals generally increase their performance for a limited time until they have reached an acceptable level of performance. Further improvements beyond this point are unpredictable. For domains such as medicine, computer programming, auditing, and sports, the number of years of work experience is a poor predictor of attained performance. Even if knowledgeable and experienced individuals do display slightly superior achievement in their domain of expertise, the vast amount of their experience stands in marked contrast to the small advantages that can be observed. Thus, it cannot be taken for granted that all individuals who are considered experts, based on their knowledge and experience, will actually exhibit superior performance. Objective evidence for their superior performance is therefore necessary.

C. True Experts' Control over Their Performance

How do we establish superior performance, if mere social recognition does not always yield scientifically reliable evidence for a person's expertise? If we assume that expertise consists of reliable superior performance in a domain, then the first step is to ensure objectively that all the studied experts actually exhibit this performance under controlled conditions. By defining expertise as a reproducible performance which is superior to that of most other individuals in the domain, it becomes an observable empirical phenomenon that can be measured independent of any theoretical framework. It now becomes possible to analyze the phenomenon experimentally and compare alternative theories of its structure and acquisition. For example, we can try to find out whether or to what degree the performance requires innate talent or if it can be explained with skills acquired through extended experience and training.

Objectively measuring performance of individuals is difficult, and most domains have developed and refined relatively standardized methods for assessing the level of achievement. Virtually every domain focuses on independent and reproducible performance of participants in the domain. In the most simple case, different performers perform the same task, such as athletes running 100 yards during a competition, and the performer with the best performance for an event wins. In other domains, such as chess and tennis, the outcomes of many pair-wise competitions allow one to rank all of the advanced performers in the domain. In the arts, sciences, and some sport events, a panel of experts or judges ascertains the quality of individual performances or specific achievements. The highest level of achievement in the latter domains is to have artifacts, such as paintings, compositions, recordings, books, or articles, recognized as master pieces or major creative innovations. In sum, the evidence from the measurement of expert performance shows a general superiority of experts that can be consistently reproduced under different conditions. Next this article will examine the findings—generalizable across domains—that underline the importance of experience and practice for attaining consistently superior levels of performance.

D. Need for Extended Domain-Specific Experience for Reaching High Levels of Performance

Recent reviews show that long-term engagement in activities of the domain is absolutely necessary to attain expert performance. When the skill development is studied over longer periods of time, as in longitudinal studies (see Figure 1), we find that there are no sudden increases in performance from one point of time to the next. For example, even child prodigies in chess display a performance that, measured by ratings that are

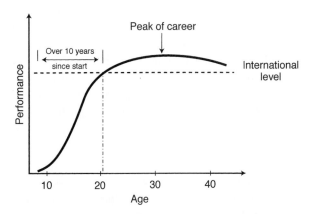

FIGURE 1 An illustration of the general performance trajectory of elite chess players as a function of age. The international level, which is attained after roughly 10 years of involvement in the domain, is indicated by the horizontal dashed line.

based on results of adult tournaments, show a gradual yet steady increase over time.

Also, expert performers continue to improve their performances long into adulthood. The age at which they typically reach the peak performance of their career lies in the mid to late 20s for many vigorous sports and in the mid to late 30s and 40s for the arts and sciences. The extended development past physical maturity, illustrated in Figure 1, shows that experience is essential for improving performance.

Finally, the most compelling evidence for the necessity of vast experience is how long it takes even the most talented individuals to reach an international level after their start of engagement in the domain (see Figure 1). In their influential theory of chess expertise mentioned earlier, Simon and Chase proposed a 10-year rule: no modern chess master has ever reached the international level in less than around 10 years of playing. Results from domains of expertise other than chess, such as music composition and a wide range of sports, science, and arts, support this 10-year rule. However, the vast majority of individuals who reach such high levels take considerably longer. In sum, the necessity of active engagement in domain-related activities in order to improve performance in a domain of expertise is well established.

E. Mere Experience Not Enough— The Role of Deliberate Practice and Teachers

When individuals start to engage regularly in a leisure activity, such as playing tennis or golf, or begin to work in a job/profession after finishing school, they initially go through a limited period of relatively rapid improvements. During this time obvious mistakes are corrected. Once they reach a satisfactory level of performance further increases are usually small. Most of us have experienced this phenomenon of minute improvement in spite of long-term active engagement in a domain. Not surprisingly, the length of experience in the domain has been found to be, at best, a weak predictor of current level of performance in a wide range of domains, such as sports, medical diagnosis, psychotherapy, and accounting. If additional experience does not automatically change individuals' behavior, what does?

When our actions and activities run smoothly, a change in the structure of performance is generally not necessary and hence would not be expected. Even if mistakes occur, such as when a tennis player misses a backhand volley during a game, there is typically no chance for corrections. Moreover, this shot is so rare that the next encounter with a similar shot may occur only weeks later for a recreational tennis player. Yet the same performance could easily be improved by special activities designed to improve performance. For example, a tennis player like the one mentioned could hit many consecutive backhand volleys under the supervision of a tennis coach, who could create backhand volleys of suitable difficulty. When first learning to master the basic stroke, the student would benefit from simple training situations. Later, the trainer could challenge the tennis player with less predictable and more difficult shots that are embedded in a representative game context. Optimal training involves exactly this design and presentation of situations that challenge the trainee. But at the same time, the trainee has to be able to master the challenge with full concentration or repetitions. "Deliberate practice" is the term used for such training activities that are designed by a teacher solely for the purpose of improving an individual's performance. Contrary to what one might think, active participants in domains rarely engage in deliberate practice. Although they recognize that engaging in it would improve their performance, they also find it so much more effortful and less enjoyable than regular recreation that its costs outweigh its benefits. Engaging in a domain activity is usually motivated by its inherent enjoyment (play) or external rewards (work). Yet these activities lack the essential prerequisites for efficient improvement that deliberate practice offers, including training goals, feedback and opportunities for gradual improvement through repetition. Active engagement in a domain does not invariably lead to improvement of performance once some initial acceptable level has been attained.

That mere engagement in activities of the domain is necessary but by itself not sufficient for attainment of very high (expert) levels of performance is well established. In most every domain, promising individuals are supervised by a teacher who instructs them and designs their practice from a very young age. In interviews with international level performers in mathematics, biochemistry, music, sculpture, swimming, and tennis, performers had studied with excellent (master) teachers. In fact, many of them or their families had even relocated to be close to a desired teacher or an excellent training environment. Virtually all of them had chosen teachers who either were international-level experts themselves or had successfully trained students to reach that level.

Why is it nearly impossible for individuals to guide themselves to expert levels of performance without the help of teachers? Moreover, why does the level of excellence of teachers appear to be so important? Whereas the general cognitive development in children is surprisingly invariant across very different environments and cultures, the development of expertise in domains of expertise, such as music, sports, and science, shows large differences across varying cultures and historical times. One of the primary reasons is that domains of expertise have over time extracted and accumulated a body of organized experience in the form of knowledge and produced artifacts. Through teachers, this body of externalized, written-down, and codified experience can be shared with subsequent generations. It is no longer necessary for each individual to rediscover pieces of knowledge and methods for doing things, and individuals are thereby able not simply to match but to surpass the level attained by pioneering predecessors. In the 13th century, for example, Roger Bacon argued that it would be impossible to master mathematics in less than 30 to 40 years by the then customary methods of learning, namely self-study; Bacon was talking about a material roughly equivalent to the mathematics that is today taught in well-organized and accessible form in high schools everywhere.

The necessary role of teachers in mastering any of the arts and sciences becomes apparent when one considers that the accumulation of knowledge and achievements is based on specific shared concepts, symbolic systems, technology (in a very broad sense, e.g., instruments, equipment, materials), and theories with efficiently organized knowledge. Generally, we take the increases in level of expert performance over historical time in science and sports for granted. Given the large changes in technology in these domains, it is difficult to make inferences about the actual changes in skill. Conversely, in domains with less changes in technology, such as performing music on the piano or

the violin, today's performers readily master music that was virtually unplayable by the best musicians in the 18th and 19th centuries. Similarly, in many sports with minimal equipment, such as running or swimming, the highest level of performance attained early in this century is now commonplace and matched by a most reasonably serious amateurs.

In all major domains there has also been an accumulation of effective methods for teaching the growing body of knowledge and skills. By going through the sequences of training tasks that teachers and coaches have developed over the past centuries, students eventually perform more complex tasks, which they thought they would never be able to master. Unlike the beginners themselves, the teacher can foresee future skill demands. They know with what method and to what degree of mastery the simpler tasks have to be learned to serve as a solid foundation for more complex future skills. If the simpler skills are not acquired properly, the student might have to completely relearn certain skills. The core assumption of deliberate practice is that expert performance is acquired gradually and that effective improvement of students' performance depends on the teachers' ability to isolate a sequence of simple training tasks that the student can successively master by repetition with feedback and instruction. As mentioned earlier, the individual training tasks have to be difficult enough to lie slightly outside the students' current range of skills, so that the students concentrate on critical aspects and gradually refine their performance through repetition in response to feedback. This requirement of focused attention to individual task components differentiates deliberate practice from both mindless drill and playful engagement. These latter two activities would at most merely strengthen the current structure of the performance rather than change it.

In many domains, promising children start training with teachers at very young ages. Because of the requirement of sustained concentration, the duration of training is initially quite short—typically no more than around 15 to 20 minutes per day. This leaves enough time for many other more playful but still domain-related activities. Many parents supervise their children's practice by helping them to concentrate during practice, by establishing regular practice patterns, and by encouraging them. With increasing age, domain-related activities, especially deliberate practice, occupy more and more room in the daily lives of future expert performers until by the end of adolescence the commitment to the domain is essentially full time. By using diaries and other methods to study how expert musicians spent their daily lives, Anders Ericsson and colleagues demonstrated the importance of deliberate practice for attaining expert performance. They investigated three groups of experts differing in their level of music performance. Although all experts from the three groups spent about the same overall amount of time with music-related activities each day, the better musicians spent more time in deliberate practice; the top two groups spent around 4 hours every day, including weekends, in solitary practice. Based on retrospective estimates of past practice times, the researchers calculated the number of hours of deliberate practice accumulated by the different groups of musicians (see Figure 2).

By age 20, the best musicians had spent more than 10,000 hours of practice, which was 2500 and 5000 hours more than the two less accomplished groups of expert musicians and 8000 hours more than typical amateur pianists of the same age.

A number of studies in chess, sports, and music have confirmed the relationship between performance and

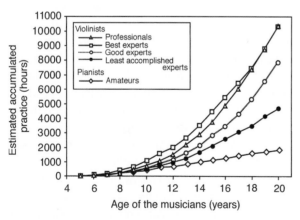

FIGURE 2 Estimated amount of time for solitary practice as a function of age for the middle-aged *professional* violinists (triangles), the *best* expert violinists (squares), the *good* expert violinists (empty circles), the *least accomplished* expert violinists (filled circles), and *amateur* pianists (diamonds). From "The role of deliberate practice in the acquisition of expert performance," by K. A. Ericsson, R. Th. Krampe, and C. Tesch-Römer, 1993, *Psychological Review, 100*(3), pp. 379, 384. Copyright 1993 by American Psychological Association. Adapted with permission.

amount/quality of deliberate practice. The broad range of known evidence suggests that individual differences in giftedness or talent, especially among children, can be attributed to differences in practice history rather than innate differences in talent. For example, higher achieving music students who showed faster improvements were found to have spent more time practicing each week than lower achieving students.

Some critics of practice incorrectly equate it with mere drilling to attain rapid and effortless automaticity. However, the next section will show that developing expert performance results in acquisition of unique mental mechanisms. Experts use those to reason and plan better and also to continue learning without a teacher, in essence becoming their own teachers.

IV. THE STRUCTURE OF EXPERT PERFORMANCE

The development of performance of most active individuals in the domain is often arrested once an acceptable level of performance has been reached. These individuals want to achieve effortless performance, similar to how they master most everyday activities, such as driving a car or typing. In contrast, future experts want to continue to improve important aspects of their performance with deliberate practice for years and decades. The key challenge for aspiring expert performers is thus to avoid a stagnation in their development and instead acquire mental mechanisms that can support continued learning and improvement. What these cognitive mechanisms are and how they mediate performance will be explained in the next two sections.

A. Cognitive Mechanisms That Mediate Superior Performance

By giving experts representative tasks that capture the essence of the expertise in their domains, it is possible to reproduce their superior performance in the laboratory. Figure 3 gives some examples of tasks for which an expert's performance in the laboratory would correspond closely to real-life measures of performance used in his domain.

In laboratory experiments we can instruct the experts to think aloud while or immediately after they

Domain	Presented Information	Task

Chess

Select the best chess move for this position

Typing

Type as much of the presented text as possible within one minute

Music

Play the same piece of music twice in same manner

FIGURE 3 Three examples of laboratory tasks that capture the consistently superior performance of domain experts in chess, typing, and music.

perform a certain task. Reviews show that in a wide range of domains experts' think-aloud protocols reveal precisely how their superior performance is mediated by preparing, planning, reasoning, and evaluating. The first example in Figure 3 illustrates a procedure, in which different chess players are asked to select the best move to a set of unfamiliar positions from published games of elite players. By presenting medical doctors with descriptions of a patient's symptoms and asking for a diagnosis, one can similarly study medical doctors' expertise. In both examples the correct solutions are known to the researcher: We know what move the chess master made, and we know what disease the patient had. The second example in Figure 3 illustrates how to reproduce superior typing performance in a controlled situation by instructing every typist to copy the same material. The final example shows how musicians can be asked to give multiple renditions of the same piece of music. All three types of expert performance are mediated by different types of acquired cognitive mechanisms. The mechanisms mediating chess and medical diagnosis have many similarities, but the mechanisms underlying expert typing and performing music differ and will be considered separately.

When highly skilled chess players select the best move for an unfamiliar position, they rapidly retrieve potential moves from among the many moves they have stored in memory. To select the best move, the players then examine the retrieved moves by planning out their consequences mentally. During this evaluation even world-class players can discover better moves than those they retrieved at first. Although chess experts can retrieve acceptable moves soon after being confronted with a new chess position, their move selection is further improved by planning, reasoning, and evaluation. This indicates that performance of experts is not completely automated but remains controlled by increasingly complex processes. The ability to anticipate what consequences a particular chess move would have several moves in the future increases slowly as a function of chess skill. Chess masters have perfected this type of planning to a point where they are able to play chess blindfolded—that is, without seeing a chessboard and relying entirely on their mental image of the chess positions. Experts from other domains reveal similar characteristics. The processes that mediate the performance of medical experts allow them to extract the relevant information about a patient better than less accomplished doctors. Also, they can entertain and reason through alternative diagnoses until they have found the correct one. Thus, at higher levels of performance, individuals have acquired the ability to mentally represent relevant information. This information is made accessible in a fashion suitable for supporting more extensive and flexible reasoning about an encountered task or situation. In most domains, better performers have acquired memory skills that allow them to rapidly encode and store relevant information for representative tasks. However, as mentioned earlier, their superior memory skills are limited to information related to their domain of expertise.

Even the rapid typing speed of expert typists appears to depend on acquired representations rather than mere speed of their finger movements. High-speed films of typing show that expert typists look ahead in the text beyond the words that they are currently typ-ing and make anticipatory finger movements toward upcoming keystrokes. In fact, the best predictor of individuals' typing speed is how far they look ahead. Accordingly, in experiments where typists were restricted in looking ahead, their typing speed was dramatically reduced. During the mastery of typewriting the expert typist has acquired the skill to look ahead in the text in order to prepare future keystrokes. Similarly, the rapid reaction of athletes such as hockey goalies, baseball hitters, and tennis players have also been found to reflect the ability to anticipate future events.

In many instances, the relevant information that performers extract and encode changes as a function of attained level of performance. For example, the primary reason that expert tennis players can so rapidly intercept and return a fast serve is the following: rather than looking at the actual trajectory of the ball once it is hit, they anticipate the ball's path from the preparatory body movements of the server, even before the server's racquet makes contact with the ball. Hence, the resulting shorter reaction times of experts (as compared to less accomplished individuals) in a domain of expertise are not caused by an innate basic speed advantage but by superior anticipation, preparation, and improved perceptual skills.

Finally, expert musicians are well known for their ability to vary their performance of a given piece of music to convey a different musical interpretation. This ability would be difficult to study if the performance changed every time the musicians performed. Laboratory studies have shown, however, that if expert musicians are instructed to play the same piece several times in as similar a manner as possible, they are able to reproduce their own performance very accurately from one rendition to the next. Expert artists have a high level of control along with a precise image of their own performance, allowing them to reproduce or vary a performance at their will or to satisfy external requests.

In sum, expert performance is not characterized by reduced cognitive processing and automatization. In fact, to reason about, anticipate, and plan alternative future actions, experts increase the control over their performance and their ability to internally represent it. This control is essential for experts to select appropriate behavior. In the case of athletes this could mean capitalizing on an opponent's weakness or taking into account the weather conditions; for the performing artists it may imply adapting to unfavorable room acoustics or synchronizing with other members of the ensemble. Imagine competitive domains, where newly discovered techniques or knowledge constantly change the status quo of a domain and where each tournament takes place with different opponents and in unfamiliar locals. If experts were not able to adapt to those conditions very effectively, others would immediately exploit the emerging weak points. Thus, to maintain high levels of performance despite any changes in the environment, experts need to possess a flexible, generalizable skill.

B. Cognitive Mechanisms That Mediate Learning

Attaining expert performance in a domain is not just a matter of shaping and gradually increasing the performance, but it appears necessary to acquire and refine mental representations. When the expert performers themselves can image and plan their desired performance and monitor and evaluate their own ongoing performance, then they have reached independence of their teachers and coaches. Developmental studies show that the improvement in representations goes hand in hand with increases in observable performance. Thus, a similar development of representations appears to be the key mechanism that allows students to be trained for adult independence.

The training of expert performers can be roughly broken down into three phases illustrated in Figure 4. After a brief period of playful engagement in a domain (Phase I) some children are introduced to systematic practice in the domain (Phase II). The teachers will present the beginners with simple training tasks and often explicitly guide their students to focus their attention on critical aspects and to make specific changes and corrections. Parents or teachers normally help the children, at least initially, to monitor their performances and to give feedback on how well the training goal was attained. As the complexity of the acquired level of performance increases, so does the complexity of the practice tasks and goals. With further increases in performance, some individuals reach a point where they decide to commit full time to the domain and make it their professional career (Phase III). Along with the improvement of observable performance, students

acquire improved representations to image the desired performance and to monitor their own performance, and they learn how to reduce discrepancies between the two. For example, musicians must be able to internally represent many different aspects of their music performance, such as how a given music performance should sound to an audience and how to play their instruments to achieve this goal. In this context, it does not matter whether the musician is in the practice room or performing in public. It seems unlikely that a musician who fails to acquire any of these representations would be able to perfect his or her music performance through solitary practice.

When the expert performers have finally assimilated most of the available knowledge and skills in the domain, they start their professional careers. During this fourth phase, the primary goal is to make a personal creative contribution to the domain. By making those major innovations that permanently change the conception of performance or training in the domain, some expert performers will be able to reach a new level of achievement in the domain.

With the help of their highly developed representations, skilled performers can organize their own training to further improve their performance. Studying

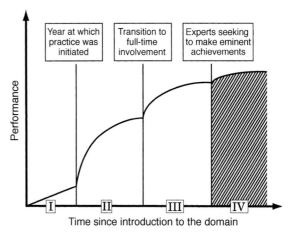

FIGURE 4 Bloom's three phases of acquisition of expert performance, followed by a qualitatively different fourth phase when, in order to make a creative contribution, experts attempt to go beyond the available knowledge in the domain. From "Can we create gifted people?" by K. A. Ericsson, R. Th. Krampe, and S. Heizmann in *The origins and development of high ability* (pp. 222–249), 1993, Chichester, UK: Wiley. Copyright 1993 by CIBA Foundation. Adapted with permission.

and analyzing the performances and achievements of masters in the field is one important way of doing this. For example, expert chess players collect books and magazines with published games of chess masters. Similar to the laboratory task mentioned earlier, they play through those games move by move and try to predict the next best move the master could have chosen. Any inconsistency between their own prediction and the chess master's actual move would imply that they overlooked some aspect of the configuration during their planning and evaluation. Serious chess players spend up to 4 hours every day with this type of solitary study. In general, this form of self-study is theoretically interesting because attempting to copy the model behavior of established masters allows the performers to gradually refine their own independent representations and expand their body of knowledge.

V. EXPERT PERFORMANCE AND CREATIVE ACHIEVEMENTS

Within the framework of expert performance, creative innovations represent the highest levels of expert achievement in any domain (see Phase IV in Figure 4). Here, experts go beyond and thus redefine the current boundaries of a domain of expertise. This view contrasts sharply with the popular view that creativity is reflected in children's spontaneous behavior and that education and extensive training tend to confine and suppress it rather than enable it. In fact, the expert performance view maintains that without training students do not acquire the necessary representations for imaging and creating their products and achievements. To even have a chance to make a major innovation that has not already been made by someone else, it is necessary to have assimilated the previously accumulated knowledge and be familiar with earlier, similar achievements. Only extended education will allow an individual to recognize a purposefully generated or accidentally encountered possible innovation as such.

As far as we know, the empirical evidence on creative achievement shows that individuals have not been able to make generally recognized creative contributions to a domain unless they had mastered the relevant knowledge and skills in the course of a long preparatory period. Even prodigious children seem to need extensive experience and training, and their creative achievements do not always compare well when judged by adult standards. Obviously, their performance is vastly superior to that of their peers. Not even in the cases of revolutionary innovations by individuals such as Einstein and Picasso did Howard Gardner find that the key creative innovations were generated until the creative individuals had completed their study and mastery of the existing techniques. Furthermore, careful analyses of extraordinarily gifted children have shown that the trajectory of development they follow is similar to that of normal children engaged in the same domains. The difference is that gifted children progress through the stages faster than less gifted children, attaining higher final levels of proficiency. Detailed analysis of the mechanisms mediating the very high level of performance of children in tennis and chess show the same types of acquired mechanisms as those of adults with comparable level of performance. This rules out qualitatively different mechanisms for talented children. In music, and also in other artistic domains, researchers have found that the higher achieving children tended to practice more on a daily basis than the lower achievers. This higher involvement along with motivational differences may account for the faster progress of some children over others. [*See* PRODIGIES.]

In conclusion, the training of expert performers should not stifle creativity but rather provide the tools to empower the experts to be more successful and effective in their daily work and their search for innovative ideas, especially those few that go beyond what is currently known and done. Equipped with the rich knowledge of other experts' creative achievements through extensive education, the artists, scientists, athletes, or other expert performers can explore possibilities and perhaps generate major innovations, thus making lasting contributions to their domain.

Bibliography

Bloom, B. S. (Ed.). (1985). *Developing talent in young people.* New York: Ballantine Books.

Chase, W. G., & Simon, H. A. (1973). The mind's eye in chess. In W. G. Chase (Ed.), *Visual information processing* (pp. 215–281). New York: Academic Press.

Chi, M. T. H., Glaser, R., & Farr, M. J. (Eds.). (1988). *The nature of expertise.* Hillsdale, NJ: Erlbaum.

de Groot, A. (1978). *Thought and choice and chess.* The Hague, Netherlands: Mouton. (Original work published 1946)

Ericsson, K. A. (Ed.). (1996). *The road to excellence: The acquisition of expert performance in the arts and sciences, sports, and games.* Mahwah, NJ: Erlbaum.

Ericsson, K. A., & Lehmann, A. C. (1996). Expert and exceptional performance: Evidence of maximal adaptations to task constraints. *Annual Review of Psychology, 47,* 273–305.

Ericsson, K. A., Krampe, R. Th., & Tesch-Römer, C. (1993). The role of deliberate practice in the acquisition of expert performance. *Psychological Review, 100*(3), 363–406.

Ericsson, K. A., & Smith, J. (Eds.). (1991). *Toward a general theory of expertise: Prospects and limits.* Cambridge, MA: Cambridge University Press.

Galton, F. Sir (1979). *Hereditary genius: An inquiry into its laws and consequences.* London: Friedmann. (Original work published in 1869)

Hoffman, R. R. (Ed.). (1992). *The psychology of expertise: Cognitive research and empirical AI.* New York: Springer-Verlag.

Proctor, R. W., & Dutta, A. (1995). *Skill acquisition and human performance.* Thousand Oaks, CA: Sage.

Starkes, J. L., & Allard, F. (Eds.). (1993). *Cognitive issues in motor expertise.* Amsterdam: North Holland.

Sternberg, R. S. (Ed.). (1982). *Advances in the psychology of human intelligence* (Vol. 1). Hillsdale, NJ: Erlbaum.

VanLehn, K. (1996). Cognitive skill acquisition. *Annual Review of Psychology, 47,* 513–539.

Wright, G., & Bolger, F. (Eds.). (1992). *Expertise and decision support.* New York: Plenum.

Families and Creativity

Barbara Kerr and Corissa Chopp

Arizona State University

Creativity The process by which a symbolic domain in the culture is changed. The result of the interaction of a system composed of three elements: a culture that contains symbolic rules, a person who brings novelty into the symbolic domain, and a field of experts who recognize and validate the innovation.

Eminence Achieved recognition and ranking by others who are highly knowledgeable and skilled in a similar area of expertise.

Family Climate The ways in which families relate to one another, contribute to personal growth of the individuals in the family, and maintain the household and the family system.

Tension Arousal, emerging from marginality, asynchrony of development, disequilibrium, conflict, change, or loss, which may motivate creativity.

Curiosity about the origins of creativity has often led biographers and scholars of creativity to try to understand what family characteristics and dynamics might give rise to creative accomplishment. Psychologists have tried several approaches to the study of FAMILIES AND CREATIVITY. Early scholars, interested in genetic ex- *planations of extraordinary creativity, explored family trees of eminent individuals, looking for patterns of creation over and across generations. Later, interest turned to family history, such as parental loss or illness, childhood trauma, and family crises and the effect of these historical factors on adult creativity. More recently, psychologists have tried, through both qualitative and quantitative measures, to understand more complex family variables such as family climate, parenting style, and interaction patterns and the relationship of these variables to the development of creative behavior.*

I. CREATIVE EMINENCE AND FAMILY TREES

Although studies of eminent individuals and their ancestors were very popular in the 19th and early 20th century, they never led to any clear evidence of heritability of creativity. This is partly because genetic variables cannot be separated from the influence of environmental variables in the study of families. It is just as likely that the accumulation of the knowledge and culture of a creative domain is given as a gift across generations as that the genetic material underlying creative behaviors is inherited. That is, what appears to be genetically transmitted characteristics may actually be behaviors learned in a creative family environment.

Copyright © 1999 by Academic Press
All rights of reproduction in any form reserved.

Nevertheless, early researchers were fascinated by the possibility of family pedigrees of creativity.

Galton, in his 1869 book, *Hereditary Genius,* used popular directories to collect the biographies of men he considered to be men of genius, which he defined as

> the qualities of intellect and disposition, which urge and qualify a man to perform acts that lead to reputation . . . a nature which when left to itself, will be urged by an inherent stimulus to climb the path that leads to eminence and has strength to reach the summit. . . . (p. 33)

Genius, he believed, arose from the genetic pool of the family. He found that half of the eminent people he studied had fathers or other close relations who were, in Galton's judgment, also creative geniuses.

Cox, in her 1926 study, *The Early Mental Traits of Three Hundred Geniuses,* located young people who had achieved creative eminence at an early age. She found that these young geniuses all had an "above average heredity," that is, parents of above average intelligence as evidenced by achievements, but that the inheritance of superior abilities was not sufficient to produce eminence. These young people, she said, also had superior advantages in their early environment. Therefore, it could not be said conclusively that these young geniuses had inherited their capacity for creative achievement.

Later studies tended to show, like Cox's work, the interplay of inherited factors and environmental nurturance of creativity. However, there were a variety of cases that were used to support the idea that creativity runs in the families: writer Aldous and biologist Julian Huxley, sons of scientist Thomas Huxley; the Brontë sisters; and the Bach generations of musicians. Nevertheless, the lack of any consistent data supports the idea that the tendency for creativity to run in the family is a result of both a complex set of inherited characteristics and a consistent family culture across generations.

Another approach to studying inherited creativity is to study possible heritable correlates of creativity, such as mental illness. There is a strong theme linking family history of mental illness with creativity. Several researchers have found extremely high incidences of schizophrenia and manic depression among writers and their families. Similarly, psychometric studies have found a correlation between inherited psychoticism and creativity. Therefore it may be possible that some personality or mood characteristics that have been correlated with creativity are indeed heritable. However, most manic depressive and psychotics are not productive or creative; therefore, it is possibly some adaptation to the bipolar personality or the presence of psychoticism which is a component of some forms of creativity. [*See* MAD GENIUS CONTROVERSY.]

II. FAMILY HISTORY OF CREATIVE INDIVIDUALS

Several researchers have found strong patterns of parental loss among creative men and women in both historical and case studies. It has been suggested that it is not the fact of orphanhood, but the way in which the young person receives and deals with the orphaning that determines whether that individual will become creative or destructive. Mark Runco makes the distinction between privation and deprivation; privation is when a child is unable to form an attachment to a particular caregiver, but deprivation describes situations where the child is able to form a bond with a caregiver, but the caregiver is lost at some point in the early development. Privation may lead to cognitive deterioration such as mental retardation. Deprivation, he says, is more characteristic of creative individuals; it may lead to affective effects such as insecurity and anxiety, which may in turn cause the individual to turn to creative work as a comfort.

Parental loss, particularly father loss, may play an important role in the development of creativity. Boys deprived of fathers may feel a tremendous sense of liberation as well as the burden of feeling they have to live up to their projections of what their father would have wanted them to be. It may be that the effect is different for girls, but research suggests, some form of separation from the mother seems to enhance girls' creativity. The significance of parental loss may lie in the fact that it reduces parent–child affiliation; it brings about an early psychological maturity; and it leads to a cognitive freedom which promotes creative productivity. The mere fact of coping with death at an early age may give a young person a broader perspective and arouse an anxiety which may lead to the need for a creative outlet.

The tendency of creative individuals to be firstborn is also a much observed phenomenon. Among active scientists, more than half are firstborn, as well as nearly half of creative mathematicians and creative writers. Several explanations have been suggested for these findings. First of all, the environment for firstborns involves more interaction with adults and therefore is a richer environment for language acquisition. Firstborns often act as teachers for younger siblings, making them more comfortable with a role as an authority and expert. It is also possible that parents may be more direct in communicating their aspirations and expectations for firstborns.

While typically family size for gifted children has been found to be smaller than average, findings on family size for creative subjects are mixed. A larger family size has been found to typify happy, moderately creative individuals. Therefore, it is difficult to say what size of family may be most conducive to a creative environment. However, the strong evidence for firstborn status would seem to indicate that a family size which allows for space and attention for the creative individual may be most effective in promoting creativity. [*See* BIRTH ORDER.]

Creative people come from all walks of life. However, it is clear that most creative people have the resources necessary not just for survival but for the growth of the imagination. Much is to be said for a bourgeois existence, in terms of providing stability and necessary resources. While most are born to the middle class, where there are opportunities for advancement and service to communities, creative people are apparently born to all social classes. However, conditions cannot be so aversive as to make the prosocial impulse impossible. A clear theme is that creative people learn through their families to transcend their own needs in creating something for the common good.

It appears that creative children often regard themselves as being "different" and experience early isolation and marginality from their peers. The majority of eminent women were isolated for much of their childhood years. Writers, in particular, sought less social companionship as children. However, while creative individuals may be loners, it does not mean that they are neurotic or unhappy.

Family attitudes toward creativity may also play a role in creative development. The families of creative individuals value and encourage cultural pursuits. Humor and play within the home seem to be very conducive to creative development. In addition, the homes of creative individuals seem to have had numerous materials and resources for the exploration of childhood creativity. Home environments that are enriched with materials reflecting various hobbies and interests allow for opportunities of creative expression. Yet, having an overabundance of such resources can lead to a desire for thrill seeking and novelty, rather than a desire for genuine problem solving. Therefore, it would seem that a home which provides the necessary tools and resources for creation, rather than constant, varied stimulation, may be most conducive to creativity.

Not only are the attitudes and behaviors within the home important in the development of creativity, but there have also been findings about the houses themselves. The families of creative persons typically live in houses that are unconventional in terms of style, location, and decor. Many had decorating that included various collections—from collections of teapots to collections of birds—and highly creative adolescents themselves who were living in such homes were more likely to have collections. The happy, moderately creative students have large, interesting homes as well.

III. FAMILY CLIMATE AND INTERACTION

Much of the literature on creativity discusses parenting styles and the effects upon the development of creativity. There is a great deal of controversy on this issue. An authoritarian parenting style demands conformity and restrains creative thought and activity. Unusual parenting styles, or ones that are less conventional, have often been found in the homes of creative individuals. Parenting styles that are less rigid and more flexible encourage freedom of expression, as well as more independence, allowing for originality. Furthermore, it appears that the homes of creative individuals tend to have fewer expressed rules, although there are implicit standards of behavior.

Some have argued that parenting styles that produce some distance between the parent and child are often found in the homes of creative individuals. "Distance" may be in the form of emotional space or a lack of over-protectiveness, which may encourage freedom to explore and independence. "Distance" may also refer to conflict or tension in the parent–child relationship, which may encourage the child to separate and become more autonomous and independent, thus allowing for the creative process. In fact, some theorists suggest that when parents are rejecting, it produces a rebelliousness within the child that results in independent thinking, whereas parents that are loving encourage children to be conforming. It is interesting to note that despite the degree of distance, the result seems to be independence and autonomy. There may be an optimal level of autonomy in parent–child relationships: one that allows the child to feel secure enough to explore and learn, but that provides at the same time opportunities to develop self-confidence.

Some research indicates that in the families of creative persons, the parental relationship is more egalitarian. In these homes there is less emphasis on sex-role stereotyping, allowing for more flexibility in roles. Creative individuals have been found to be less stereotyped in their sexual identities than less creative men and women.

Creative individuals typically come from more difficult and distressful family environments. The conflictual family may cause such disorder that certain tensions within the individual may develop that may foster independent thought and creativity. The sources of tension may be interpersonal and intrapersonal. Interpersonal tension refers to tension between individuals. Intrapersonal tension refers to tension between cognitions and affect. There may also be tension between ideas, tension as a result of lack of satisfaction with current conditions, and intrapsychic tension. When an individual experiences tension or recognizes a problem, he or she may then be motivated to overcome this problem or tension, and thus ensues the creative process. Over time, an individual learns to interpret such tensions differently, and to see them as a source of his or her creative power. The individual may even learn to appreciate such tensions and use them in his or her creativity. This process has been called "cathartic originality"—the artwork reflects and transforms the artist's discomfort.

Case studies give us some examples of the long-standing controversy in the literature of creativity which has centered around the question, what kind of families produce creative individuals? Is it the dysfunctional, conflictual family? Or is it the stable, content family?

The case study of Jochen Seidel is an example of creativity developing in an individual who struggled with a great deal of personal anguish and pain. Jochen Seidel was a talented German painter born in 1924 in an industrial town in Germany. Throughout his childhood his family was abusive, controlling, rigid, and cold. There was tremendous pressure placed upon him by his parents to achieve. He felt that he was a constant source of disappointment to them, despite academic success. When he was 10 years old, his father disappeared and was later found dead. It was speculated that his father had committed suicide, although some believed that it may have been the result of his involvement in the Nazi party. At the time of his father's disappearance, Seidel's mother abandoned him and his younger sister for a period of one month—initially leaving them in the care of neighbors and later with grandparents. His relationship with his mother would remain conflictual throughout his life. At 13, Seidel began displaying more emotional difficulties. He became chronically depressed and his academic performance deteriorated dramatically. He became increasingly rebellious and openly angry. At 17 he was drafted into the German army. While in basic training, his artistic talent was discovered. After the war, he entered the art academy and rapidly gained wide recognition. He was known to paint for up to 36 hours without stopping to eat or sleep. His style was obsessional, and he continued to have bouts of depression along with heavy drinking. He went through two failed marriages, and had minimal contact with his children from these marriages. His later life was plagued by numerous psychiatric hospitalizations and suicide attempts; he also had spurts of enormous creativity. In 1971, he hung himself. This gifted artist's life consisted of pain and loss in childhood and a lifetime of emotional turmoil.

Another example of a creative individual developing out of a life full of struggles and difficult experiences is that of Maya Angelou. She was born in 1928 and grew up in a poor, disjointed family—she and her brother moved back and forth across the country between her mother and grandmother. She had a distant and removed relationship with her father. Angelou experienced a great deal of pain and distress during her childhood and adolescence, including poverty, racism, and being raped by her mother's boyfriend. While living with her grandmother, there was a special woman who became a mentor for Angelou, encouraging her academically, emotionally, and socially. She excelled in school, even when she was one of only three black students. She also enjoyed drama and dance. Intellectual and artistic pursuits had always provided Angelou with an escape from the harsh realities of her own life. At 16, she became a single mother and found herself struggling to support her child and herself. She nearly succumbed to the despair and challenges—she had become involved in prostitution and almost began using heroin. Yet her strength and resilience prevailed and she returned to work, while also pursuing acting, singing, and dancing. Despite extreme circumstances and adversity in her young life, she went on with strength and dignity to pursue an illustrious career as a writer, dancer, and political activist.

These case studies illustrate the difficult and potentially devastating childhoods and family environments of these creative persons. However, there have been equally persuasive studies showing precisely the opposite conditions for the development of creative talent, indicating that eminent musicians, artists, scientists, and athletes came from what they perceived to be cohesive, intact families who nurtured the creative individual's talents.

Mihaly Csikszentmihalyi interviewed over 90 of the most creative and interesting people in the world, including artists, musicians, actors, writers, scientists, and businessmen, in order to find out how creativity has been a force in their lives. Csikszentmihalyi argued that, contrary to the popular image, the overall picture presented of creative people and their lives was "upbeat and positive." He does not assert that all creative persons are well-off and happy, but criticizes the literature which focuses only on the negative while "debunking" anything positive. He suggests that suicide and drug problems among creative individuals may be due to the artistic scene that promises much, gives few rewards, and leaves nine out of ten artists neglected.

In terms of familial influence, Csikszentmihalyi found that in most cases, it was the parents of these individuals who were responsible for stimulating and directing the child's interest. He discussed a variety of parental influences, not all of which were always positive, but he found only a few cases where parental influence appeared as a thoroughly negative force. It seemed that one of the most important parental contributions was in shaping character, and more specifically the value of honesty. He found that although 20% of creatively eminent females and 30% of male subjects had lost fathers, the vast majority of his subjects had families that supported and nurtured their children's self-confidence. Their families exposed them to a stimulating and rich environment, and instilled strong values. As a result, Csikszentmihalyi believes the stereotype of the tortured genius is a myth. [*See* MAD GENIUS CONTROVERSY.]

A frequent finding in studies of families of creative children is that creative children have a great deal of independence from parents, particularly mothers. Mothers of high creative children are significantly less involved and less overprotective with their children than mothers of less creative children. These mothers are also more self-confident and self-realized in their homes, have higher occupational levels, and are less likely to deny any hostile feelings (such as frustration).

A study exploring the family characteristics of adaptability and cohesion found no evidence that family cohesion per se was a critical indicator of creativity. Highest creativity scores were from families that were characterized as highly adaptable—those that demonstrate flexibility and freedom (almost to the point of being chaotic). Perhaps these families encouraged openness to experience and allowed enough autonomy for the individual to experience making their own mistakes as a learning process. The results of these studies indicate that mothers who are self-realized and are not overly involved or protective and family environments that are flexible encourage creativity.

While there are undeniably numerous cases that demonstrate conflict among families of artists, writers, and musicians, there are many exceptions to the unhappy family even among artistic individuals. Some of the artists, writers, and musicians with the longest and most sustained records of creative productivity come from happy, functioning families. When other fields besides the arts are considered, there is little evidence of unusual family dysfunction. Creative inventors, scientists, and mathematicians more frequently seem to have come from well-functioning, intact families. Of all the family lives of eminent individuals, inventors seemed to experience the least amount of family conflict, and creative scientists and mathematicians also seem to have more stable homes as children.

Finding information about creative individuals who had a happy childhood provides a bigger challenge—perhaps because these lives are less dramatic and do not make such interesting reading! Nonetheless, there are some notable case studies of individuals from happy, functional families.

Born in 1929 in an all-Jewish section of Brooklyn, Beverly Sills' life gives an example of a child growing up in a loving, supportive environment. From an early age her mother exposed her to music and dance, particularly opera. Her mother encouraged singing, dance, and piano lessons for Sills. Her father, an insurance executive, was primarily concerned about her overall education, although he remained supportive of her artistic endeavors. A vocal coach became a mentor and second mother to Sills, and helped her on the road to tremendous sustained success as a world-renowned opera singer. An impresario, Sills created many of her own roles, and after her acting and opera careers, she went on to direct the New York City Opera. While Sills did encounter personal difficulties during her life, including the death of her father and having two special-needs children, she displayed emotional strength and perseverance—characteristics that were first encouraged and supported in childhood.

Stephen Wosniak, the cofounder of the universally known Apple Computer grew up in Palo Alto, California, also known as Silicon Valley. He was raised in a happy family with supportive parents in a pleasant neighborhood full of engineers and electronics enthusiasts. From an early age, he loved electronics and enjoyed creating electronic gadgets. His parents were willing to make sacrifices and go to great lengths to make sure that he had the education needed for a mathematically talented child. In fact, they went to the State Board of Education to obtain an exception from the rule that children in California could not be dually enrolled in both vocational and gifted classes. Because of these efforts, he became the only child in California to take electronics and advanced math. Wosniak stated that without this opportunity he would never have been able to invent the microcomputer. It is interesting that by average society's standards, he would likely have been considered a "nerd," yet he described himself as popular and well liked. His parents were always supportive of him having only a few friends (with whom he would spend his Friday evenings comparing their circuit boards). His parents never forced him into interests or activities in which other kids his age were involved. Within this supportive and accepting environment, Wosniak gained confidence and was allowed to explore his interest and flourish.

Because the primary emphasis in the literature of both family functioning and creativity has been on dysfunctional families, and because the controversy described previously seemed so far from resolution, Kerr and colleagues decided to approach the problem of the link between family happiness and creativity from a different angle. Instead of questioning creative people about their families, people from happy families were questioned about their creativity in a series of three studies.

The first study was a quantitative study, assessing the personality characteristics of the participants and their perceptions of family environments. The second study was a qualitative study, in which students' responses to interviews were analyzed in terms of family characteristics and creativity. The third study was also a qualitative study measuring how counselors who interviewed the students perceived them.

The results of the quantitative measures seemed to show a group of young people whose pattern of needs did not necessarily match those predicted by the literature of creativity; yet they did not look like people who have been labeled in the literature as noncreatives, and they did indeed have creative lifestyles and moderate creative accomplishments for older adolescents. They perceived their families as close-knit and peaceable, and they saw themselves as part of a family actively involved in recreational, intellectual, and cultural pursuits. Of course, this picture of family happiness does not match the miserable and dysfunctional families often depicted in the literature of creativity, particularly in the arts. It is more similar to the descriptions of families of inventors and social activists.

A more in-depth picture emerged in Study 2 of openly affectionate, supportive people who are proud of their family's closeness. They lived in fairly large houses which were either neat and comfortable or cluttered and comfortable. Their houses were cheerful and interesting. They were large families by American standards, where mother and father were home a lot, and where creative activities were likely to be in progress. Children were encouraged to take risks, and were supported in their challenges.

The major conclusions drawn from the students' statements about their creative accomplishments were that, first, every student appeared to be multipotential, having talents in several areas; second, that spatial-visual works were most prominent among accomplishments; and third, that students seemed to have confidence that their experience was important. That is, they believed their life experiences were worth documenting and recording, and saw this activity as part of their general creative life. In addition, these students saw themselves as creative. The portrait of their creative life that emerged was one of gentle, sustained creativity in varied domains.

Study 3 amplified and confirmed the results of Study 2, as counselors attempted to summarize their impressions of the students. Counselors found the students to be "supported," that is, sustained and nurtured by their families, and perhaps as a result, resilient and optimistic. Perhaps also as a result of this strong system of support, they were family oriented. Counselors perceived the students to be modest about their own creativity and admiring of their siblings' and parents' creativity. However, these students seemed to the counselors to have a friendly relationship with their own creative powers, and a confidence in their futures as creative people. The counselors and the experimenters agree that there were only a few extraordinarily creative people in our sample, if extraordinary creativity is judged as that receiving recognition beyond one's own school and community. However, these were very young adults, at the beginning of their training for their life's work, and much accomplishment may lie ahead.

Perhaps the literature thus far has not taken into account the complexity of the relationship of family functioning to creativity. Csikszentmihalyi says, creative individuals seem to have had either exceptionally supportive childhoods or very deprived and challenging ones. What appears to be missing is the vast middle ground.

Perhaps, however, there is no middle ground. It is possible that there are two or more kinds of relationships between family climate and the creative development of children. Possibly, there is a tormented, dramatic creativity which arises from families that are themselves tormented and dysfunctional. Children from these families find that creativity is an escape from the madness they find within their families and often within themselves. On the other hand, perhaps there is another kind of creativity, with which we are actually more familiar: everyday creativity. This creativity, a more gentle, sustained creativity, leads to lives of productive and prosocial works, and may be the kind which is engendered by the happy family. Therefore, the controversy is by no means resolved. The origins of creativity in family life remains a rich and fertile field for researchers. Future studies of inherited correlates of creativity, family history, and family climate may clarify the contribution of the family to the development of creative lives. [*See* EVERYDAY CREATIVITY.]

Bibliography

Albert, R. (1992). *Genius and eminence.* New York: Pergamon.

Csikszentmihalyi, M. (1996). *Creativity: Flow and the psychology of discovery and invention.* New York: Harper Collins.

Olszewski, P., Kulieke, M., & Buescher, T. (1987). The influence of the family environment on the development of talent: A literature review. *Journal for the Education of the Gifted, 11*(1), 6–28.

Piirto, J. (1992). *Understanding those who create.* Scottsdale, AZ: Gifted Psychology Press.

Runco, M. A. (1994). Creativity and its discontents. In M. P. Shaw & M. A. Runco (Eds.), *Creativity and affect.* Norwood, NJ: Ablex.

Five-Part Typology

Ruth Richards

Saybrook Graduate School,
University of California, San Francisco,
and Harvard Medical School

I. Introduction
II. Five Potential Links: Creativity and Psychological Problems
III. Societal Health and Creativity
IV. Conclusions

Creative Product Concrete outcomes, ideas, or behaviors may be identified by two criteria: (a) originality, or relative newness compared to other outcomes (either in a larger society, for eminent creativity, or in a person's more immediate environment or experience, for everyday creativity), and (b) meaningfulness to others, which implies a potential understandability or usefulness of an outcome, while ruling out productions which are fully random or idiosyncratic.

Eminent Creativity Often applied to creators or their innovative outcomes in more "traditionally creative" fields, including the arts and sciences. The creator's work has received significant social recognition in the professional field or in society at large. Criteria may vary in different fields and for different purposes (e.g., the National Book Awards), although an important impact on a culture or field is generally implied. Criteria of originality and meaningfulness are often involved, explicitly or implicitly.

Everyday Creativity One may distinguish another type of creativity, or type of outcome, allowing more broadly for innovation in each one of us, which indeed can occur at any time or any place, at work or at leisure. This is everyday creativity, and it has been viewed as fundamental to our adaptation and even to our survival. Everyday creativity is not a new concept, going back even as far as Sir Francis Galton, who moved from the idea of unique genius by proposing that "natural abilities" were normally distributed. With everyday creativity, criteria of originality and meaningfulness can again be applied. One can do an innovative job, for example, of raising children, organizing an office, planning an advertising campaign, fixing a car, developing a new toothpaste, landscaping a property, or finding new ways to feed the homeless.

Health For a particular individual, this involves a state of physical, mental, and social well-being, and adaptability, and may be reflected by a variety of indicators related to the structure or functioning of the person in an environment. As with psychopathology, below, or as with abnormal function, what is considered healthy may be defined in part by culture or context (e.g., picture a loose and uninhibited comic actor versus a military officer, and then have them switch settings). A particular culture might also tentatively be characterized as healthy or less healthy, depending upon the function and structure considered adaptive to needs in a particular context (e.g., consider our health with regard to educational opportunity—or to the level of infant mortality).

Psychopathology Refers to study of abnormal human functioning, including behavior or experience, and issues of its manifestations, development, and causation, with attention to the *psyche,* or the faculty for thought, judgment, and emotion; included are both conscious and unconscious processes. At times, what is considered normal and hence abnormal may be quite culture bound. One mainstream reflection of abnormal psychological function in the United States is the

Copyright © 1999 by Academic Press
All rights of reproduction in any form reserved.

Diagnostic and Statistical Manual of Mental Disorders (4th ed.) (*DSM-IV*) of the American Psychiatric Association.

One often hears generalizations such as "creativity comes from solving problems." Yet, in fact, there are many roads to creativity. Some, but not all, of these involve personal difficulty. Even here, connections may be multiple and overlapping, and involve both direct and indirect effects. This is not surprising; creativity is an immensely complex construct. To simplify matters, a FIVE-PART TYPOLOGY of general relationships between creativity and psychopathology is presented here, along with extended examples. This framework simplifies the possibilities to a manageable number on the one hand, yet also reminds us not to be too quickly content with any one facile explanation on the other. One may also note relevance of concepts of health and pathology to groups and to cultures, and issues in addressing social health which are also considered using the five-part typology.

I. INTRODUCTION

This article presents a way to encompass the spectrum of relationships between creativity and psychological problems. Five categories of indirect and direct causation are presented which, singly or together, encompass a great many possibilities. There are many roads to creativity, including a vast and diverse number of healthy ones. Further, there are multiple patterns involving the presence of psychological problems. Creativity, after all, is among the most complex of human functions.

Plus, it is important to understand that having problems will not in themselves lead to creativity—although their presence at the right time or place, along with the right predisposing factors, may increase either creative ability or creative motivation.

An interaction of personal strengths and environmental advantage may be needed for effective "creative coping," or the resilient overcoming of adversity. Creative personality patterns are often complex and interacting. They may be associated with a range of biopsychosocial factors. Researchers studying predictors of psychological resilience, have also shown a complex

equation involving person and environment. Yet, having noted this complexity, we note too that there is some truth to the fabled link between creativity and certain mental health syndromes, and most notably certain affective disorders. A connection has been shown for both eminent creators and everyday creators. Within eminent creators there is a stronger connection between mood disorders and artistic rather than scientific creativity. Keep in mind that this link is far from a rule for every person with a mood disorder. Furthermore, a finding that many eminent artistic writers do have mood disorders does not imply that most people with mood disorders will be creative (never mind eminent, or indeed, writers); these are not simple and symmetrical two-way relationships. In any case, this creativity–psychopathology connection does make one think more deeply about how a society defines "normality" and "abnormality." [*See* AFFECTIVE DISORDERS.]

The five-part typology which follows is not distinct from such diagnosis-specific issues, but rather cuts across various pathologies, showing varied ways in which a connection with creativity might develop and manifest.

Below, examples of creativity–pathology connections are first provided at the level of individuals, where the five typology levels are demonstrated in some detail. Then, in a briefer concluding section, the focus turns to groups or societies, and application of the typology to challenges in creating a healthier world.

II. FIVE POTENTIAL LINKS: CREATIVITY AND PSYCHOLOGICAL PROBLEMS

One can talk about five general types of connection between aspects of creativity and psychopathology (see Table I). These involve direct and indirect (mediated) influences of one area on the other, or a connection between aspects of creativity and psychopathology through a mediator or third factor which affects the two areas independently. In Table I, the P's indicate some aspect(s) of pathology and C some aspect(s) of creativity. The arrows indicate the proposed direction of influence. The T signifies the third factor or mediator.

Note that this general typology could apply to any one of us, to some degree, and to a range of problems

TABLE I
Relations between Aspects of Creativity and Pathology or of Creativity and Health

Symbols for pathology (P) and creativity (C)[a]	Type of relationship[a]	Applied to health (H) and creativity (C)
P → C	1. Pathology contributes to creativity directly	H → C
P → T → C	2. Pathology contributes to creativity through a third factor	H → T → C
C → P	3. Creativity contributes to pathology directly	C → H
C → T → P	4. Creativity contributes to pathology through a third factor	C → T → H
C ← T → P	5. A third factor contributes to both independently	C ← T → H

[a] It is understood that some *aspect* of pathology influences some *aspect* of creativity, and so forth. Note that T stands for a separate third factor (or for multiple factors) which mediates an indirect relationship. In a particular person, relationships can be multiple and overlapping.

of living, and not just to people with formal psychiatric problems and diagnoses. The discussion below illustrates each category, through key examples, and also raises issues of how such creativity may ultimately move in the direction of health.

If five patterns of association and causal connection sound like a large number, consider the many potential factors which may operate: biological, psychological, and social. Usually, there will be more than one. There are also directional issues, for example, does creativity lead to psychological problems (or health), and/or does illness have an impact on creativity? Is this direct and/or is it mediated? The ultimate set of predictors in any one case may be complex and overlapping. Should we find it surprising then, with this most complex of human activities, that there may be many roads to creativity?

Note also that direct effects of pathology on creativity include influences on creative ability/potential; related outcomes are connected intrinsically to advances in the creative process. By contrast, effects on motivation which can lead to creativity—where pathology helps mobilize whatever creative talent is present—have been considered for clarity as indirect effects. Creative ability might or might not be increased, along with a willingness to use it; in addition, the motivation might at times be turned to a noncreative solution (e.g., "hiring someone else" to solve the problem).

Finally, it is reemphasized that not all roads to creativity involve pathology. You do not have to feel bad to be creative. Using your creativity is natural, commonplace, and typically good for you.

A. Example—Creative Writer: Direct Effects of Pathology on Creativity

Here are two instances in this psychopathology-enhances-creativity category involving both the content and the process of creative work. Consider a creative writer, let us say someone with a bipolar or unipolar mood disorder, who writes about the experience of depression, the ups and downs, the despair, and the lifting of the cloud.

As a second instance, consider now a creative writer who perhaps writes in a loose associative vein, an expressive style drawn (or learned somehow) from a hypomanic state of mind. In the first example above, pathology directly influenced the content of a writer's work; this time pathology influences the process, or the mode of expression, in writing.

B. Example—Coping with Trauma: Indirect Effects of Pathology on Creativity

Here we can find hope, perhaps. If the right "third factors," or mediating factors, can be found and encouraged, perhaps we can turn psychopathology more frequently toward creative outlets, and even thereby increase health. Note that motivation is classified here as a third factor or a mediator. It is a happy factor when indeed it can interact with pathology and bring about creativity (as the most preferred response), rather than something less productive, be it drug abuse, acting out, depression, despair, or lowered will to live.

Potential mediated effects of this sort could be

conscious or unconscious. Consider a traumatized war victim, a combat veteran, or survivor of domestic violence. She or he could write consciously and movingly about this traumatic experience, the conflicts, the fears, the destruction of civilized values, and the lasting devastation, perhaps to help master the personal trauma, or to share the cultural pain, or to inform and help ensure such a tragedy could never occur again.

She or he could alternatively write, somewhat less consciously, perhaps, and in general terms with the context more masked (let us say in children's literature), about the overcoming of fears, or empowerment of individuals to resist wrongdoing. In the context of science or social action, rather than art, this same person might be motivated, either consciously or unconsciously, to work for peaceful uses of energy sources, or to develop advanced methods of conflict resolution. These would represent creative responses to trauma, rather than perpetuation of conflict and violence. We need to know more about factors that increase the chance of creative coping and find out why some take this route while others (often in greater numbers) do not.

C. Example—"Knowing Thyself": Direct Effects of Creativity on Pathology

Although creativity may function, in general, in the service of health, it will not necessarily do this at every moment. Creativity may have its rough periods in the short run, and especially in the arts. In this example, we discuss both the short-term price and some potential long-term benefits of looking within.

Albert Rothenberg and others have written about high levels of anxiety which may occur in writers working through conflictual material. Many scholars of creativity have noted the characteristic openness to inner experience and nonrational elements which may be found as part of one's creative style. If you write (or draw, sing, tell, perform, advise, empathize with, or even lecture) about an experience persuasively, you're going to have to relive it. In the previous example, the creative person coped with acute and overwhelming trauma. This may represent one extreme of something which could occur for most of us less painfully, more naturally, and more continuously on a day to day basis. A creative person who is open to unconscious processes may receive frequent surprises, say in giving an account of an experience—"hmmm, she/he/I was self-serving, self-involved, inattentive, then overreactive." Such unwelcome insights about self or others must be valued (or at least accepted) as part of the whole, if the whole is not to be stunted in its development. This self-confrontation may come to occur more continuously and less pathologically, and in smaller and more routine self-confronting steps. Completion of these steps could be empowering instead of (or more than) traumatizing. [*See* WRITING AND CREATIVITY.]

Creative openness and catharsis may, in fact, be health-producing. Research has indicated that subjects who wrote about their buried traumatic experiences made fewer doctor's visits and reported increased feelings of well-being. There was even enhanced immune function. Such a cathartic process may be self-rewarding, providing health effects, richer internal access in memory storage, and benefits more valuable than protection of our egos through mental boundaries and psychological defense.

Finally, there is potential here for a culture of creativity. The acceptance of our frank divergence, and even bizarreness—may help us as a culture to broaden the acceptable limits of normality. By being more accepting of ourselves and each other, we could become a healthier culture and a more creative one.

D. Example—"Please Act Normal!": Indirect Effects of Creativity on Pathology

Here we see, as two examples, some negative effects when deviancy is *not* accepted by the greater culture or accepted as normal by the creator him- or herself. Remember that deviancy is not necessarily pathology. But what if it is treated as such? Without toleration of deviancy, the presence of creativity may raise the odds of psychological problems. Consider creative children. The research of E. Paul Torrance, Mark Runco, and others illustrates clearly how creative young children may have a hard time of it in schools and with their peers. Even teachers (or parents) who claim to value creativity often do not, and tend to favor the "good child" who is relatively more calm, controlled, compliant, and productive. Picture little Jane, in third grade, who wants to do the subtraction problem "my own way." "Just do it the way I showed you!" says the overworked teacher.

Creation of the new generally involves destruction of the old, or some part of it. Creative children (or adults) may seem at times like trouble—they challenge the status quo, overthrow teachers' (or parents') ideas, and come up with new means of doing things. With peers, too, some creative children can end up being rejected or ostracized. Some may withdraw or play the clown. Some may become troublemakers.

Let us not forget the adult innovator in society, either, who also can be a threat, may face various negative reactions, and may develop a unique style of coping (or defending). Furthermore, if the creator lacks a source of support—at home in the family, at work, or among friends—then the chance increases, not just for some stylistic oddities, but, as stress increases, for some sort of decompensation. This includes the risk of a mood disorder among vulnerable people, or anxiety disorders, adjustment disorders, and various chemical and other forms of escape.

We also briefly note another pattern: that of self-induced oddity, in an externally or "other-directed" image making focus that may pull people away from acceptance of who they are. This may occur more in the arts, where the creative artist may be seen as intrinsically eccentric and odd. Here, creators (and especially certain insecure would-be creators) might further cultivate such an image. Interestingly, as far back as the 16th century, "melancholia" was seen as a mark of eminent genius, characterized by qualities such as eccentricity, sensitivity, moodiness, and solitariness, even to the extent that emulating these qualities became a fad. This may still occur.

Now add to this another phenomenon, people who stop their treatment or medication for a mood disorder, for fear it will hurt their creative inspiration. They link inspiration to their symptoms. Where symptoms are concerned, they may assume "the more the better." Treatment can be extremely helpful, not only with the painful symptoms of mood disorders but in freeing the creative process. Yet evidence suggests a different picture.

E. Example—A Moody Family?: Third Factor Independently Affects Creativity and Pathology

Consider this time a biologically based example. Here are factors which may independently increase the likelihood of creativity, and at the same time of developing a psychiatric disorder. Let us take two ex-amples involving external and internal factors: (a) personal stressors, and (b) personality characteristics.

Take, as example 1, the fact of hard economic times. Now here is an individual who has lost a job and is unable to pay the bills. Socioeconomic stressors may lead, on the one hand, to pathology, including anxiety and varied adjustment disorders, or major depression in people carrying the vulnerability. On the other hand, it might (also) lead to creative coping efforts, perhaps including artistic expression, or direct coping with financial needs, through innovations such as entrepreneurship.

For a second example, take stylistic factors in personality. Let us assume a heightened sensitivity and fluidity of association, which may go along with bipolar disorder. Let us further assume that this pattern (which has also been found in their psychiatrically normal relatives) represents a more general and perhaps earlier manifestation of a familial risk for bipolar disorders.

Now let us assume that, in one person (someone with an enriched environment and supports conducive to creativity), this disposition manifests as heightened potential for unique ideas, unique sensitivity, and an innovative career. Here is a creative outcome. In another person, this disposition (along with certain risk factors in family and upbringing) results in amplified mood swings, and a severe bipolar disorder. This time, the result is pathology. In yet a third person, there is a mixture, involving both heightened creativity at some points, and severe mood swings at others (and the periods may or may not overlap).

This mechanism is hypothetical. Still, it illustrates how a possible "third" factor, a dispositional factor which is neither positive nor negative in itself, could interact with the environment, influencing creativity and/or psychopathology, and creating an apparent direct link between them.

III. SOCIETAL HEALTH AND CREATIVITY

We have looked at five ways in which creativity and pathology may interact at the level of individuals, directly and indirectly. The discussion is in no way inclusive of the many ways in which creativity and psychopathology may interact. It does, however, attempt to highlight five major patterns of association, patterns which may occur singly or together, and to highlight that the origins of creativity may be multiple and complex.

A. What Is Our Diagnosis, and Why Do We Ignore It?

A 1997 book, *Eminent Creativity, Everyday Creativity, and Health,* collects new and classic articles in this area, focusing on both individual and societal creativity. One lead article by Dean Keith Simonton highlights several societal pathologies with positive or negative implications for societal (and eminent level) creativity, on the average. Based on his historiographic research, Simonton identified, on the negative side, societal phenomena including international war, political instability (anarchy), and external threat. On the positive side, predicting for creativity in the next generation, were patterns of political fragmentation (subdivision into workable geopolitical units) and civil disturbance. One could debate mechanisms of direct and indirect (and delayed) influence of these conditions on individuals. We consider instead here other pathologies based in the individual, and yet supported betwixt us in our social groups. These are currently not only inhibiting societal creativity, but may be putting us greatly at risk.

B. What Is the Diagnosis? What Is the Treatment?

Consider group pathology as reflected in our generic helplessness and despair at a rapidly changing and endangered world. One might wonder what we as citizens can do in our own isolated domains. Is there any way we can be helpful? Quite frequently, people choose just to forget the danger, or else they suppress, repress, avoid, deny, or rationalize what might occur (e.g., community violence, international war, or toxins in the air). Our reaction may be marked by helplessness, hopelessness, guilt, despair, too much or too little "sleep" (including substance abuse and mindless media addictions), and even by a touch of global suicidality. Collectively it would seem we are *depressed.*

There are solutions we can enact together. Unfortunately, Western cultures of individualism, competition, zero-sum solutions, and self-centered shortsightedness may prevent creative solutions.

C. Five-Part Typology Applied to Awareness and Amelioration of Social Ills

How does this fit the five-part typology? Let us look at the five categories in a prescriptive sense, with a focus on awareness of or knowledge of the precarious situation we are in. Because this is what we first need to do—we need to wake up.

1. *(Knowledge of) pathology directly causes creativity.* As Rollo May said in *Courage to Create,* "If we let ourselves experience the evil, we will be forced to do something about it." To hang onto our awareness for any length of time, we may need 2, below, but as soon as awareness occurs, if it can be maintained and marshalled by means of strategies of creative coping, a blocked potential and motivation can become available.

2. *(Knowledge of) pathology indirectly causes creativity.* If we can raise awareness, and do so together, in the context of actions we can take, we may begin to find ways to join together, to develop and harness our creativity, and increase our sense of empowerment. Many schools are doing this profitably, at a realistic level for young kids, helping classrooms and individual creative youngsters contribute to the greater community, for example, through local environmental activism.

3. *(Knowledge of) creativity directly causes pathology.* Yes, it can, but this may (believe it or not) be good in the short run—plus, it gets better! An initial awareness of what must be done may yield anxiety, but this can abate considerably as greater hope and connectedness appear. Indeed there can be joy in working with others, and in the greater openness involved in finally facing things, rather than defending against them. After all, the problems were always there, and unconsciously, we may well have known it. Confronting them further frees creativity, and advances health as in earlier sections above. We can get outside of the box of assumptions that binds us and defenses that blind us, and look for real and innovative solutions. The knowledge of this is empowering.

4. *(Knowledge of) creativity indirectly causes pathology.* As one gets to work, there is certainly further pathology (if that is what it is)—in other words, the opening feelings of concern, anxiety, and compassion as the danger is faced—and alongside these the positives and healthy feelings of growth and progress. Cre-

ative people have particular power to assist here as Gruber and others indicate.

5. *(Knowledge of) third factor contributes to creativity and psychopathology.* Here we are back to awareness, the awareness that may stimulate more creativity in the first place, and which is fed by a creative mind-set. Here is the source of discomfort, pathology, and anxiety, yet also of our hope, health, and joy.

The healing power of creativity can be amplified greatly when we join together. More attention is needed to our creative and collaborative behavior as groups and how we can work together more effectively toward common goals. [*See* FOUR PS OF CREATIVITY.]

IV. CONCLUSIONS

Creativity is surely a complex construct, representing as it does, a wide range of possibilities in our lives—including many which have not yet arrived. (Indeed, in some views, creativity is the life force behind all of creation!) The spectrum of psychopathology is broad in turn, and complex. The five-part typology of direct and indirect relations between creativity and psychopathology is designed to (a) on the one hand, bring one form of structure and simplicity to this highly complex area and at the same time to (b) remind us that, with psychopathology and creativity, rarely can a situation be reduced to a single cause or explanation. Beyond this, any single explanation also represents a process in motion that can generate many possibilities

along the way. Consider Example C, in which healthy effects of greater openness to self through creative expression can generate even greater growth in a number of respects. Finally, this article reminds us that creativity and health are constructs with meaning at the level of groups and societies, as well as the level of individuals, and that we may apply the typology to our efforts here, as we work toward a healthier world. Here, in fact, lie some of our central challenges in a new millennium.

Bibliography

American Psychiatric Association. (1994). *Diagnostic and statistical manual of mental disorders* (4th ed.). Washington, DC: American Psychiatric Association.

Goodwin, F. K., & Jamison, K. R. (1990). *Manic-depressive illness.* New York: Oxford Univ. Press.

Gruber, H., & Wallace, D. (Eds.). (1993). Creativity in the moral domain. [Special issue]. *Creativity Research Journal, 6*(1, 2).

Ludwig, A. (1990). Alcohol input and creative output. *British Journal of Addiction, 85,* 953–963.

Ludwig, A. (1995). *The price of greatness.* New York: Guilford.

Pennebacker, J. W. (Ed.). (1995). *Emotion, disclosure, and health.* Washington, DC: American Psychological Association.

Richards, R. (1981). Relationships between creativity and psychopathology: An evaluation and interpretation of the evidence. *Genetic Psychology Monographs, 103,* 261–324.

Richards, R. (1998). Everyday creativity. In H. S. Friedman (Ed.), *Encyclopedia of mental health* (pp. 619–633). San Diego: Academic Press.

Runco, M., & Richards, R. (Eds.). (1997). *Eminent creativity, everyday creativity, and health.* Greenwich, CT: Ablex.

Shaw, M., & Runco, M. (Eds.). (1994). *Creativity and affect.* Greenwich, CT: Ablex.

Fixation

Rebecca A. Dodds and Steven M. Smith

Texas A&M University

Fixation A persistent block or impediment to successful problem solving.

Functional Fixedness Biased perception of an object that blocks the ability to use it in unusual ways.

Mental Set Persistent use of a previously successful method resulting in inadequate or failed problem solving.

FIXATION *refers to a persistent impasse in problem solving in which unwarranted assumptions, typical thinking, or recent experiences block awareness of the solution. Fixation can occur in several forms, including process, function, and perception. A rest period may allow fixation to dissipate and successful problem solving to occur.*

I. TYPES OF BLOCKS

Becoming fixated during problem solving is an almost universal experience. An inability to move beyond a block can occur when attempting to solve any problem. Most fixation can be classified into one of three types: process, function, or perception.

A. Process

A process fixation (also referred to as mental set) occurs when one persists in using an unsuccessful method of problem solving. Working with similar problems, the thinker develops successful methods. When the surface characteristics of a problem resemble those for which a method has been previously established, the established method will simply be reapplied, even when that established method is inappropriate. If failure to solve does not result in the creation of a new method, but instead, leads to further attempts using the old inappropriate method, the thinker is said to have become fixated.

Fixation has been demonstrated with the now-famous water jug experiments. Subjects were asked how they would measure various quantities of water given only three jugs (A, B, and C) of specified sizes. For instance, the problem might be to measure 40 oz. of water using three containers holding A = 4, B = 50, and C = 3 oz. In this example and several of the initial problems given to subjects, the answer can be derived using the algebraic formula B − A − 2C (e.g., 50 − 4 − 2 × 3 = 40). A critical problem was presented after numerous others that could be solved by the formula B − A − 2C. The critical problem (e.g.,

Copyright © 1999 by Academic Press
All rights of reproduction in any form reserved.

measure 20 oz. using A = 23, B = 52, and C = 3), however, could not be solved using the same formula. Instead, the simpler algorithm A − C was required. Despite the simplicity of the solution, subjects tended to get stuck on the critical problem, and were unable to solve it because they were fixated on the previously reliable process.

B. Function

In 1945, Karl Duncker introduced the phrase "functional fixedness" as a label for the inability to use familiar objects in unusual ways. In a series of experiments Duncker asked subjects to complete a task using an object in an ordinary manner (e.g., draw triangles on paper using a calligraphy pen and a bottle of ink with a cork stopper). Later the subjects were asked to solve a new problem that required them to use one of the previous objects in an unusual way (e.g., joining two rods by sticking the ends into the cork stopper). In one of Duncker's problems subjects were asked to mount a candle on a wall so that it would burn properly. The objects available included a box of tacks, a candle, and matches. An optimal solution requires the box to be emptied and affixed to the wall with the tacks as a shelf to hold the candle. Subjects in the experiment appeared unable to grasp the function of the box as a shelf, because they were fixated on seeing its usual function as a container.

In 1945, N. R. F. Maier also experimentally demonstrated the effects of functional fixedness. In his famous two-string problem, subjects are required to tie together two strings hanging from the ceiling. However, the strings are arranged to be so far apart that they cannot be reached at the same time. The solution requires the use of a pair of pliers as a weight so that one string can be set in motion as a pendulum. The swinging string can then be caught by the subject, who can wait for it while holding the other string.

Duncker listed several conditions that can lead to functional fixedness. If an object is commonly used in a certain way or a task is only completed with a given object (using a hammer to pound nails), fixation is likely to occur when one must use the object or complete the task differently. As in Duncker's 1945 experiments, recent use of an object in a familiar manner may decrease the likelihood of unusual use. Fixation may also result if an object must be altered before it can be used to solve a problem. Finally, one who knows a better object for solving a problem may be unable to substitute a less-satisfactory, although adequate, object.

C. Perceptual

According to Gestalt theorists, fixation can be caused by faulty perception. Maier stated that solving problems requires reasoning, which he defined as the ability to combine experiences. By using the Gestalt principle of similarity, humans are able to appropriately transfer skills learned in one situation to others. But, successful problem solving may require that when previously learned ideas are inappropriate, they must be modified or reorganized. Instead of merely relying on reproduction of previous thoughts, the thinker must produce new solutions by altering perceptions. Even though memories remain constant, perceptions may be altered by emphasizing different aspects of memory.

Duncker agreed that problem solving initially involves the abstraction of perceptual properties from one situation to another. If the central demands of the situation are not precisely delineated, transformation and problem solving become increasingly difficult. [*See* PROBLEM SOLVING.]

One example of perceptual fixation frequently occurs with the nine-dot problem. The dots are arranged in a square pattern.

The problem is to join the dots using four straight lines. Although there are no outer border lines, thinkers are often constrained by the assumption that they must draw only within the square boundary formed by the dots. This assumption based on visual perception of the dots must change before the problem can be solved.

II. RESULTS FOR CREATIVITY

For well-defined problems, fixation manifests itself as a solution failure. In creative endeavors in which no predetermined "correct" answer exists, the outcome of fixation is a decrease in originality. When blocked, thinkers tend to conform with past ideas and examples. This effect was demonstrated by S. M. Smith and colleagues who had subjects design novel toys or imaginary creatures. Those who saw examples before generating were more likely to include critical features of those examples in their own inventions. A follow-up experiment demonstrated that this conformity effect was not due to any intention of subjects to copy what they believed to be good examples; rather, the effect was unintentional, and could not be avoided even by subjects who were explicitly instructed to generate ideas different from the examples.

Less originality (increased conformity) was also evident in studies by D. G. Jansson and Smith of design fixation. In the experiment, engineering designers generated either measuring cups for the blind or spillproof coffee cups. Half of the subjects saw examples, which contained obvious design flaws, and half saw no examples. Despite explicit instructions not to copy the examples, more than 50% in the experimental group included features they had previously seen. Fixating on previous examples can constrain the creative process, just as fixating on previously successful solutions can prevent success in creative problem solving.

III. THEORY

S. M. Smith has offered a theory that explains fixation as a result of response competition in memory. The problem solver begins by searching memory for an appropriate response. Once found, the answer is brought into working memory and acted upon to solve the problem. However, in instances in which more than one answer exists, there is competition between the possible responses. Fixation results when an *incorrect* answer is stronger than the correct answer. The dominance of a possible response may be due to recent experiences in which the incorrect answer was used, contextual information that suggests the inappropriate response, or repetition of that response. Fixation occurs when the nondominant (but correct) response cannot be retrieved from memory to solve the problem.

Smith has suggested that fixation may be overcome when the thinker takes a break from active attempts to solve the problem. This period of time, an incubation period, allows time for the wrong answer to dissipate from memory. Experimental evidence from R. Adamson and D. Taylor provides support for Smith's hypothesis. After having subjects work with either a microswitch or a relay connection, subjects were given a break of 1 min, 30 min, 60 min, 1 day, or 1 week. Then subjects were asked to solve the two-string problem. Instead of supplying pliers as a pendulum weight as Maier did, available objects were the microswitch and relay. Functional fixedness was demonstrated by the greater than chance avoidance of the object that subjects had been working with in the first phase of the experiment. That is, those fixated on using microswitches or relays as electrical devices could not easily think of them as pendulum weights. In addition to showing that subjects who had used the microswitch in an electric capacity in the first half of the experiment were less likely than chance to use the switch as a weight for the pendulum (the same was true of those who used the relay), it was noted that fixation was not the same over the various delay groups. Subjects who had breaks of only 1 or 30 min clearly demonstrated functional fixedness. Fixedness slowly declined as the break period increased. For subjects who waited 1 week before solving the two-string problem, fixedness had completely dissipated.

IV. CONCLUSION

The same cognitive processes that allow practiced behaviors to become automatic are responsible for fixation. These processes create difficulty for problem solvers only when well-practiced behaviors are persistently used, despite a lack of success. Fixation can be seen in process, object function, and perception. Theoretically, fixation may be the result of response competition that fails to allow access to a correct solution. Incubation allows time for dominant, incorrect responses to dissipate, so that problem solving may be completed successfully.

Bibliography

Adamson, R., & Taylor, D. (1954). Functional fixedness as related to elapsed time and to set. *Journal of Experimental Psychology, 42,* 122–126.

Duncker, K. (1945). On problem solving. *Psychological Monographs, 58*(5), 270.

Jansson, D. G., & Smith, S. M. (1991). Design fixation. *Design Studies, 12,* 3–11.

Luchins, A. S., & Luchins, E. H. (1970). *Wertheimer's seminars revisited: Problem solving and thinking* (Vol. 3). Albany, NY: Faculty–Student Association, State University of New York.

Maier, N. R. F. (1945). Reasoning in humans. III. The mechanisms of equivalent stimuli and of reasoning. *Journal of Experimental Psychology, 35,* 349–360.

Smith, S. M. (1995a). Creative cognition; Demystifying creativity. In C. Hedley, P. Antonacci, & M. Rabinowitz (Eds.), *Thinking and literacy: The mind at work* (pp. 31–46). Hillsdale, NJ: Erlbaum.

Smith, S. M. (1995b). Getting into and out of mental ruts. In R. Sternberg & J. Davidson (Eds.), *The nature of insight* (pp. 229–251). Cambridge, MA: MIT Press.

Smith, S. M., Ward, T. B., & Schumacher, J. S. (1993). Constraining effects of examples in a creative generation task. *Memory & Cognition, 21,* 837–845.

Flexibility

Becky J. Thurston

University of Hawaii, Hilo

Mark A. Runco

California State University, Fullerton

Adaptive Flexibility To abandon conventional problem-solving methods that have become unworkable and to think of original solutions.

Androgyny Refers to persons who have higher than average male and female elements in their personalities.

Cognition Processes of knowing, including attending, remembering, and reasoning along with conceptualizaton, judgment, and information processing.

Divergent Thinking An aspect of creativity characterized by an ability to produce unusual, but appropriate, responses to standard questions.

Functional Fixity The belief that objects have only one purpose.

Spontaneous Flexibility To produce a diversity of ideas in a relatively unrestricted situation.

FLEXIBILITY is manifested and tied to creative behavior in several ways. Cognition can be flexible, for example, and this can facilitate creative problem solving. Individuals can be flexible in their attitudes as well, and attitudinal flexibility may in turn allow tolerance and adaptability.

Flexibility reflects a capacity for change—a change in the meaning, interpretation, or use of information; a change in understanding of the task; a change of strategy in doing the task; or a change in direction of thinking, which may mean a new interpretation of the goal. Flexibility as a personality trait allows the person to see the whole of the situation. It allows an individual to see all of the components in a problem and not just one of the parts. It allows the individual to see the parameters and boundaries of problems, and often it allows that individual to change the problem itself. This is because the flexible person is capable of redefining the problem. Flexibility is a kind of adaptability.

I. FLEXIBILITY AS COGNITIVE PROCESS

Flexibility is an important aspect of the cognitive process. In the well-known divergent thinking model, for example, creative thinking may result in fluency, with greater originality, and with more flexibility. Fluency is measured by presenting very simple tasks (e.g., list all the things you can think of that are solid, flexible, and colored), and the quantity of output determines the scores. Fluency has to do with the generation

Copyright © 1999 by Academic Press
All rights of reproduction in any form reserved.

of a quantity of ideas. Originality on divergent thinking tests means the production of unusual, far-fetched, remote, or clever sponses. Originality is manifested in novelty and in the statistical infrequency of responses. Flexibility, in contrast, is manifested when the individual moves from one ideational category or theme to another. [*See* DIVERGENT THINKING.]

One type of flexibility is spontaneous flexibility. It is termed spontaneous because the tests that measure it do not even suggest that the examinee be flexible. A participant can be asked to list all the uses for a common brick, and the total number of uses listed is a score for ideational fluency. But the participant can also be scored on the number of times he or she changes category of uses. For example, the person who responds with "build a home, build a school, build a factory," does not change class of uses. Another person who responds with "make a paper weight, drive a nail, make baseball bases, throw at a cat, grind up for red powder," etc., changes class with each new response. This person demonstrates much more flexibility.

A second kind of flexibility has been called adaptive flexibility because in tests in which it was first found, the examinee must make changes of some kind—changes in interpretation of the task, in approach or strategy, or in possible solutions.

Criticisms of the divergent thinking model focus on the moderate predictive validity of divergent thinking tests and ambiguous connections to creative performances occurring in the natural environment. It appears that while divergent thinking is not synonymous with creativity, divergent thinking tests are very useful estimates of the potential for creative thought. Recent research suggests that divergent thinking tests are the most useful and have the most impressive validities when flexibility is used for assessment and prediction.

II. FLEXIBILITY IN
INSIGHT PROBLEMS

Flexibility is required by the nine-dot problem, often used in studies of insight and creative problem solving. Nine dots are presented (see Figure 1), and the examinee is asked to connect all nine dots with four straight connected lines. (It is sometimes best to be more concrete and insist that the individual put their pen or

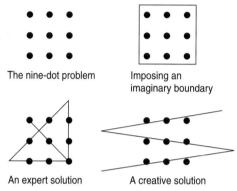

FIGURE 1   Conceptual blocks in the nine-dot problem.

pencil on the paper and leave it there until the dots are connected.)

Most individuals assume that a boundary is imposed by the eight dots making up the perimeter of Figure 1. No such boundary or constraint is given in the directions, but nonetheless it is very common for those attempting to solve the problem to stay within that self-imposed perimeter. This says something about the assumptions individuals may make and how these may constrain our thinking, and it also says something else about how we structure our perceptions toward gestalten, or complete figures. What is most relevant here is what the efforts say about flexibility—or lack thereof. Low flexibility is seen in the nine-dot problem when the examinee sticks with one approach to the problem. The individual who experiences such functional fixity will probably try various lines—all within the perimeter. Flexible thinking, on the other hand, would lead the person to try more varied approaches to the problem. Perhaps the first attempt was inside the perimeter; a flexible approach would take the next attempt outside. And indeed, that is the easy way to find solutions to the nine-dot problem (see Figure 1).

Clearly the benefits of flexibility, and the problems of fixity, can be seen in more than just the nine-dot problem. They might be seen in much real world problem solving—anytime the individual (or group) relies on one type of solution, rather than varying the approach. Surely flexibility is useful in insight problems, as well as in divergent thinking tasks.

III. FLEXIBILITY IN PERSONALITY THEORIES

There is some uncertainty about personality as the direct and primary cause of creativity, but it does seem clear that certain traits are intimately involved in the process. Evidence indicates that there are various traits that play a role in promoting creativity. These traits include stimulus freedom, functional freedom, flexibility, risk taking, preference for disorder, delay of gratification, and psychological androgyny. [*See* PERSONALITY.]

Flexibility may manifest itself as a perceptual tendency. Here it is the seeing of all the components in a problem, and not just fixating on one of the parts, that is much more likely to produce a creative solution. In early empirical work on the creative personality, Frank Barron found that writers as a class are significantly more flexible than most people, and that creative writers who have achieved renown are 84% more flexible than the general population. Donald MacKinnon found that creative architects, more often than those less creative, report turning to another activity when seriously blocked in a task and returning later to it when refreshed. Less creative architects more often report working stubbornly at a problem when blocked in their attempts at solution. [*See* WRITING AND CREATIVITY.]

IV. FLEXIBILITY AND DEVELOPMENT

Flexibility may be tied to developmental experiences which enhance creativity. Research has, for example, shown a connection between playfulness and creativity. Playfulness or the predisposition to engage in symbolic play has been linked to high levels of fluency in children. Children who have spent time playing tend to be more creative on tasks they do immediately afterward than children who go directly from one task to another. Based on studies of kindergartners, high school students, and adults, it appears that playfulness and the flexibility it supports become part of an individual's personality and are an essential ingredient in creative thought. [*See* PLAY.]

Flexibility is also tied to sex role identification which is learned first in families and then reinforced by school and work experience. Sex roles play a large part in a person's belief about whether or not she or he can be creative. A relatively new aspect of sex role identification has been identified that has ramifications for creative thinking. Known as psychological androgyny, it refers to those persons who have higher than average male and female elements in their personalities. Most importantly, androgyny is not seen merely as the midpoint between the two poles of masculinity and femininity. Rather, it is at a higher level of sex role identification than either of the more traditional roles.

Sandra Bem illustrated the relationship between androgyny and creativity. Bem concluded that rigid sex roles are costly to the personality (they are essentially a form of rigidity). Such rigidity frequently causes conflict and requires great expenditure of energy to deal with the stress brought on by the conflicts. Bem concluded that the androgynous role is far more functional because it fosters the search for the truly appropriate course of action. This is also more likely to cultivate creativity.

Another developmental issue involves open-mindedness, a personality trait generally associated with flexibility. It is the ability to receive new information without prejudice. Most people tend to view the new and different with a certain degree of fear. Creative persons differ in that they tend to treat the unknown or the unusual phenomenon as a challenge rather than a threat, and thus they are more likely to come to an insightful understanding of it. Why are some people genuinely open-minded? The style of parenting is probably a major part of the answer. When parents encourage adventurousness, the child develops a flexible personality. Individuals with more flexible personalities tend to be less rigid, less neurotic, and less anxious than most.

Finally, the research on attachment is also relevant in that securely attached children tend to explore their environments more than insecurely attached children. Such exploration will provide children with varied experiences and, perhaps, more flexibility.

V. CONCLUSIONS

Flexibility is an important aspect of the creative cognitive process as seen in the divergent thinking model and its role in insight. Very likely, the benefits of flexibility can be seen in real world problem solving. Varying the approach (flexibility) rather than relying on one type of approach (fixity) is much more likely to lead to interesting and valuable solutions—for example, when you need a new route home from work or school, when you have less time than your schedule seems to demand, or when the refrigerator lacks the ingredients for dinner that is one-half complete. In addition, flexibility as a personality trait plays a role in promoting creativity by allowing the individual to see all parts of a problem and by supporting open-mindedness. Individuals with flexible personalities tend to be less rigid, less neurotic, and less anxious than most.

Finally, flexibility may be tied to developmental experiences which enhance creativity. It may be that playfulness becomes part of an individual's personality and is an essential ingredient in creative thought. Psychological androgyny, a type of sex role identification which is learned in the home and reinforced by society, may be more functional and enhance creativity because it fosters flexibility and the search for the truly appropriate course of action. Parenting that encourages adventurousness appears to influence the development of a flexible personality. Research on attachment suggests that securely attached children tend to explore their environments more than insecurely attached children, providing these children with varied experiences and, perhaps, more flexibility.

Bibliography

Dacey, J. S. (1989). *The fundamentals of creativity.* San Francisco: Lexington Books.

Guilford, J. P. (1967). *The nature of human intelligence.* New York: McGraw–Hill.

MacKinnon, D. W. (1978). *In search of human effectiveness: Identifying and developing creativity.* Buffalo, NY: Creative Education Foundation.

Runco, M. A., & Albert, R. S. (Eds.). (1990). *Theories of creativity.* Newbury Park: Sage.

Taylor, C. W., & Barron, F. (Eds.). (1963). *Scientific creativity: Its recognition and development.* New York: Wiley.

Four Ps of Creativity

Ruth Richards

Saybrook Graduate School,
University of California, San Francisco,
and Harvard Medical School

Four P's of Creativity Four conceptual approaches to the study of creativity, originally introduced almost 40 years ago by Ross L. Mooney at the Utah Conferences on the Identification of Creative Scientific Talent. Since then, these perspectives have become widely adopted in study of creativity (see Mooney, and Sternberg, in bibliography). They are applied below to issues in innovative higher education, looking toward the world of the future, and stretching each conceptual area just a bit. The following order is observed: creative PROCESS, PERSON, PRODUCT, and PRESS of the environment.

Person, Creative These may include both ongoing *trait* characteristics and fluctuating *state* characteristics of the person, and may involve observable evidence as well as more inferred capabilities and personal traits. Consideration may include abilities, cognitive styles, affective and motivational patterns, underlying intentions, attitudes, and values, and many other features we may yet need to identify. In the educational illustration below, group issues are raised, including questions of valuing both individual uniqueness and collaborative ability in an institution, if one is to optimize creative power in education.

Press of the Environment Favoring Creativity In Mooney's view (1963), this involves discerning "what pattern of circumstances *around* individuals or groups accompanies what patterns of behavior in them. . . .circumstances necessary for releasing creative production" (p. 332). Note that one may well add issues of culture and subculture shaping perception and conceptions in the first place, either in the moment or over time. These can facilitate or restrain particular concrete outcomes or requisite processes the creator might have the capability to generate. With an open systems view, as found in the educational example below, the issue of what is "creator" apart from what is "environment" can become radically more debatable.

Process, Creative Includes ways in which creators think, feel, experience, motivate and direct themselves, and behave related to the generation of original and meaningful (creative) outcomes. Of particular interest are aspects of process which may be relatively unique, or necessary, even if not sufficient, to the generation of creative outcomes. In the educational illustration below, one considers the process of learning to learn — including learning about oneself, and the vital difference this may sometimes make — in a rapidly changing world.

Product, Creative Result or outcome of creative efforts, be this a concrete product, behavioral result or repetoire, set of ideas to be communicated or indeed a process one is attempting to influence. These products may be identified for the purposes of this entry by using IPAR's widely utilized criteria of originality and meaningfulness. (see IPAR). In the educational example below, one may go even further to ask if new products are (or change is) always good, or whether some characteristics should stay relatively more fixed, to optimize a creative educational outcome.

Copyright © 1999 by Academic Press
All rights of reproduction in any form reserved.

Creativity may be viewed from perspectives of person, process, product, and press of the environment: the FOUR Ps OF CREATIVITY. In this article, issues in innovative graduate education are explored, corresponding to these four perspectives. At times this can push the "4Ps" beyond their conventional application to isolated individuals viewed as fixed quantities. Here are multiple persons in flux, reflecting on their own process, in complex and ongoing interaction. Key issues for teaching and learning in a rapidly changing world include learning how to learn, learning about the learner, honoring uniqueness while learning to work together, going with the flow (sometimes), and taking an open systems view. Overall, in innovative education, whether working singly or together, there is relatively less emphasis on fixed learnings and more on an ongoing learning process.

I. INTRODUCTION

At the graduate level—and certainly in fields that follow the flux in our world, such as psychology and the social sciences—we are in certain ways, and at certain times, all teachers and all learners. This is true whether we are faculty or student—and one may note that among graduate students there are increasing numbers of midcareer learners. The world is changing rapidly, and we can hardly keep up with it; we must look to each other and our ways of accessing resources. There are also so many fields and proliferating areas of knowledge that even the hardiest generalist must choose.

We in particular who are committed to innovative and alternative education, and to letting our students (at least part of the time) pursue their special interests, to go where we might not know much, and to learn and discover in their own ways, will need be on the alert for ways to best serve their needs—and indeed the needs of this transforming society to which all we learners and teachers hopefully contribute. All the more, as we approach the millennium, one may ask, what can a community of educational innovators do to be a creative force in society, toward the overall humanistic objective of realizing our fullest human potential, both individually and together?

In this article, it is recommended that we start with what we do not *know*, as well as what we do know—

and know about ourselves as well as our world—to keep afloat in a time of rapid change. Perhaps not surprisingly, creativity is key. Four issues are presented below in the framework of the well-known "four p's of creativity," that is, (creative) process, person, product, and press of the environment. These constructs are widely used in the psychological study of creativity. In essence, the discussion addresses issues in: (a) learning for the future, and learning our limitations; (b) collaboration and creative eccentricity; (c) where to stand fast when all is in flux; and (d) factors in programs that remain receptive to innovation—programs which can catch, rather than miss, the passing waves.

Before proceeding further, we address the construct of "everyday creativity," which is central to issues of educational innovation.

II. EVERYDAY CREATIVITY— HOW RECOGNIZED? HOW VALUED?

Some people are amazed to hear the notion of everyday creativity, or the "originality of everyday life." Creative people, to them, tend to be artists, scientists, and a few other sorts of professional people; these figures are often widely known in their culture and celebrated for their accomplishments. This is a popular stereotype of the creative person. Meanwhile these same self-denigrating people may say of themselves, "I can't draw," or "I can't write"—even though they may have done so quite readily as children—and they therefore conclude that "I am not creative."

Yet without the flexible adaptiveness and daily improvisations we all have, we could not even shape a new sentence, never mind survive. Human beings are not creatures of instinct, following well-worn species templates for each activity during the day. Each of us presents our own variation on the theme of "human" in how we work, play, live, and thrive. The concept of everyday creativity, as discussed by Ruth Richards, Dennis Kinney, and associates, has been related to positions as diverse as Abraham Maslow's "self-actualizing creativity" (distinguished from his "special talent creativity"), involving our ongoing growth and fullest human potential, and the "phenotypic plasticity" revealed in the varied expressions of our DNA, as discussed by T. Dobzhansky, furthering our physical adaptation and survival in changing environments. Indeed, one would expect a broadly conceived "originality of everyday life" to touch down in more than one area of thought.

Various of the self-denigrating "noncreative" people above may in reality be extremely innovative at solving personal or organizational problems—as parent, coach, manager, friend, counselor, or teacher. They may design original clothes, do gourmet cooking, make clever home repairs, organize charitable and community activities, start new businesses, write copy for local newsletters, and do a great many other things which emerge to meet the needs of a moment in a way which has not occurred before.

Everyday creative products or outcomes (concrete products, ideas, or behaviors) are required to meet the two most widely accepted criteria for creative work, as formalized by Frank Barron and associates, namely, originality (new or unusual qualities) and meaningfulness to others (the outcome communicates; it is not random or idiosyncratic). Yet the products need meet only these. Beyond this, creative work can occur in virtually any area at work or leisure. Furthermore, creative persons can appear virtually anywhere; they are the ones who habitually do such work. With everyday creativity, it is not so much what you do as how you do it. [*See* EVERYDAY CREATIVITY.]

Perhaps this is where we, as educators, should take a closer look.

In these terms, a graduate faculty member could become highly creative as a curriculum designer, lecturer, group facilitator, online instructor, student adviser, catalyst of independent or group study projects, committee member, and so forth. An innovative or alternative program would also tend to seek students for such preferences, learnings, and, to be sure, past performance.

Just who then is one selecting? Interestingly, we can also talk about everyday creativity in terms of a disposition toward originality, a view supported by "core" personality traits and cognitive style features associated with creative performance across diverse fields of endeavor in the work of people such as Frank Barron, Donald MacKinnon, and Ravenna Helson at the University of California at Berkeley. "Characteristics such as what?" one might ask. Try independence, flexibility, nonconformity, openness to experience, and preference for complexity—sound familiar? And if so, what might this mean for a school so blessed.

Below, we turn to the so-called "4 Ps" of creativity, and in particular on the first two Ps as revealed in graduate education: the creative person, and aspects of the creative process which helps them (or helps us) to innovate. We shall then turn to the creative product which we hope will result, and the press of the environment which may facilitate or inhibit such a creative outcome.

III. THE FOUR Ps OF CREATIVITY AND FOUR ISSUES IN INNOVATIVE EDUCATION

A. Process—Not Only Learning to Learn, but Learning About the Learner

The creative person will need to be reflective and introspective here—how do we marshall, apply, and expand our creative and educational potential in the 21st century? What does this mean for our personal creative process?

As teachers, we do not know all the current problems, never mind the future! Yet we bring significant knowledge, resources, ways to help students approach problems, and powerful means of seeing how well we all did. But first, what exactly are we seeing, and what are we seeing with?

This is a world in rapid transformation. The details will change from one field of endeavor to another, and even within fields, depending upon context, guiding assumptions, and intentions. Two sets of three examples may help set the stage, focused here largely on the rapid flux of events around us. The first set highlights dramatic change in our culture and our world, sometimes welcome, and sometimes frightening. Yet if there is a constant, it is that things will be increasingly in flux. How do we cope?

The second set of examples illustrates certain human qualities which have not changed appreciably, qualities we do not normally think about, yet which may pose a problem in our creative coping with the future. Certain ingrained tendencies may not only keep us from seeing change around us, but may blind us to potential dangers. In a rapidly changing world, we must not only learn how to learn, but also address factors which may *keep us from learning*.

1. A World in Flux — Three Examples

These three examples involve health psychology, biotechnology, and the information revolution. Certainly other examples might have been chosen. Yet each of these affects multiple fields of endeavor and shows the underlying momentum of change and a question we all face: If we cannot possibly keep up with the necessary information, even at one point in time, what can we learn and teach others that may help us cope, and face the unknown?

1. *Advances in healing.* Fifty years ago, in medicine, it was the dawn of antibiotics. Now we are also finding, beyond the burgeoning multitudes of medications in the massive *Physician's Desk Reference* (the compendium of available medications), new and unsuspected sources of healing. Consider, for instance, group support, spirituality, and coping through expressive arts. Nor is this solely about feeling better subjectively; even our T-cells, our immune system, know the difference. We are seeing a major change in our Western views of health and healing.

Try a thought experiment: Health care ten years from now—what will things be like? How do we educate our students now so they can deal with, and contribute to, the explosion of health information?

2. *Rapid progress in genetic engineering.* Not long ago, we learned what DNA was and what a gene was. Now we are—and just think about it—designing organisms. We who know so little about ourselves are designing organisms. Should we not be thinking about some of the ethical issues as much as questions of DNA patenting?

Another thought experiment: Genetic engineering 10 years from now—how will the world look? Will modern bioscience pursue an exponential growth curve? What would, or would not, people do to have better vegetables or better milk? A cure for a life-threatening disease? What else might one unleash, whether driven by humanitarian motives, a profit motive, or something else? How do we see ourselves more consciously, as individuals and as cultures, and infuse our progress with emotional awareness and humanistic values?

3. *Promise of information technology.* These days we are sometimes painfully logging onto the Internet, using letters and nonsense syllables. In 10 or 20 years, we may log on with a nod to our wrist monitor, step into a nearby storefront, and be in instant virtual reality contact with people across the globe. It may be as if we were together in the same room. Consider a future faculty meeting—a future virtual meeting of the American Psychological Association.

Try this thought experiment: The world 10 years hence—how much of our lives may be "lived" in this new dimension? Might some people never leave home, either to do their work, or to see friends? Might those who are not part of the "online" culture be a highly disadvantaged group, in this country and abroad? Think too of people who have talked about "consciousness" on the Internet, and whole new metalevels of consciousness and awareness in general. Who are we, anyway, and who are these "others" of our possible creation—including such "thinking" offspring of our technology—whom we may so poorly understand?

Taking these three examples, and certainly others, how do we educate our forthcoming thinkers, leaders, and citizens to deal with change, and not a static set of data points at one time in history, which will quickly become obsolete?

Surely, one focus should be on *process*—on flexibility, openness, anticipation, and enjoyment of the new—and about *learning to learn.* Here is a place to turn directly to the literature of creativity—to challenging of the old, risking of the new, and the valuing of multiple viewpoints and possibilities. There is also rich ongoing work in the field of education, related to changing paradigms, postmodern (and post-postmodern!) thought, collaborative learning, diverse knowledge communities, mutual negotiation of knowledge, and a myriad of possibilities for innovative instructional goals, approaches, and venues. But whatever we do, let us not learn only about the so-called world without, but also look within, and learn about the learner. We can get in the way of ourselves a lot sometimes. Here, we focus on three ways in which this may occur, two of which involve distortions we may unconsciously permit.

2. Blindness to World or Self — Three Examples

Ironically, while things rush and change about us, there are human features which have changed little over hundreds of years, and not all of these are to our advantage. Here are three ways in which any of us may at times remain blind to our situation, personally or as a cultural group. There are other possible examples, but this selection—involving conceptions of society, individual frailties, and failure to adapt to changing conditions and knowledge structures—can illustrate the point. Although such limitations are longstanding in human history, there is now a notable amplification due to our human rate of "progress." Just think of how much more harm, as well as good, we can now do.

1. *A painful reality? POOF! and it is gone.* It is difficult for any of us to read it or to hear it: A child dies every other second. *Every other second.* The reasons include lack of medical care and malnutrition. If a starving little girl was in front of us right now, we would feed her. But she is not here, the problem is huge, it seems remote, and often people say, "there's nothing I can do" (or can do by our single isolated selves, one recalls.) It seems too much; we cannot stand it. *Poof* and it is gone.

Our fabulous defenses have done it again—they have aligned with our consensual delusion, which can also be our group psychosis. We decide together that we will not think about that problem or this problem. As a result, in our day-to-day world, and by mutual agreement, it does not really exist.

Another factor can join in—quite simply, what we are biologically more versus less apt to notice as a human organism. We read all about the local child who was killed—how terrible—but after all, we humans do react biologically and emotionally to stark contrast and change. We have evolved to notice such things—and how often we put them on the front pages of newspapers. Yet we are bad at slow and gradual transformations, such as those changes due to increasing drought and famine. We also have trouble appreciating numbers beyond our human scale. In one sense, 1,000 and one million can both seem "large"—so never mind how many tons of TNT the new weapons are equal to.

Then, with repetition, habituation may yet rear its head. If it was shocking the first time, it can get a little less so the second time: "We heard that one before. It's the same as it was yesterday." "Sorry, we've got other things to do." Or maybe a rationalization? "There must be some very good people working on this." Yet we

hear the crack of a pistol, and we whirl about. The adrenaline is pumping.

Let us be clear about our perceptual and conceptual limitations, and learn to listen for all the warning shots.

2. *We are who we want to be—and sometimes too much!* Think of the misperceptions about who we think we are that distort our thinking. This time, they distort everyone's thinking; this is a human issue. We often block out of consciousness what we cannot handle personally, as well as handle by our autonomous self in this Western world. Many times a day, we each block or distort material that threatens our idea of who we are. This may even be (and often unknowingly may be) be at the expense of others.

Has a parent ever been caught saying, "Me? I am not opinionated. Yes, of course I'm listening—of course I'm open to new ideas." But just ask their child! Kids are a real voice of honesty here. But how can we all give and accept feedback, and accept our own humanity?

3. *Misperceptions of global ground rules.* We live in a world of nonlinear dynamics, of chaos theory, from the beating of our hearts and the working of our minds, to the many manifestations of nature and human society around us. Yet we may be thinking of simple cause and effect, and little linear cases of "this causes that." Half the rain, and half as many crops? Or drought, mass starvation, and massive migration?

As they say, "it's all connected." Things may be simply determined and linear at times, but often they are not. A little change may lead to . . . who knows what? Think of the so-called "butterfly effect," where a butterfly flapping its wings over Moscow could (under the "right" conditions) cause a storm system to erupt over New York City.

Can we teach our students, and ourselves, to think more readily in a holistic, nonlinear, and sometimes unpredictable (and humbling) way? Imagine if we could appreciate that the waste we choose to recycle, rather than dump, today, lessens by X a possible climate change that will otherwise occur, which puts off the drought mentioned above, and the death of another child. How much more quickly one might put those tin cans by the curb.

Better yet, what if we could see our behavior as representative of what a large group of other like-minded people might do (or not do) at the same time, and acted accordingly. This is a bit like voting for candidate X, while knowing that others are doing so too. By contrast, consider an unknowing person, pushing his or her ecological theory, in a zero-sum environment (you win, I lose), and thinking mainly of self-interest and professional advancement. What if this person suspected that overpromotion of environmental idea A, in a competitive self-serving atmosphere, over someone else's idea B, could prevent the collaborative birth of idea AB. (Now imagine AB sitting just on the "edge of chaos"—on the threshold of just happening through a snowball reaction, or a butterfly effect.) Thus a collaborative decision, the empowerment of a consensus group, a lessened chance of drought, and the life of yet another child might be saved.

These problems all reflect human limitations—and we have not changed terribly over the last hundred years. Yet the price of our blindness, culturally, is rising dramatically. It is not as if there is nothing we can do. A dash of social awareness, a spot less personal defensiveness, a course in systems thinking, a push for collaboration—these would go a long way. But it will take a conscious effort for us to change how we think, and what we are willing to think about. Process, and reflection on process, should be very much our concern. Surely, our education should be as much about ourselves as human beings, including our strengths and weaknesses, and how they impact us from inside, as about the issues that may impact us from the outside.

B. Person—Both Honoring Our Uniqueness and Working Together

From the above, we can turn to collaboration, to creative collaboration, which can involve optimizing the value of individual differences and the creative power of groups. What does this tell us about the "creative person"?

In innovative graduate education, we have the chance to learn about, and to model for others, a "culture of creativity." Sobering issues such as the rapidity of change, and our blind spots as learners, suggest we think carefully about who can best thrive in a changing world. A culture of creativity could help. Yet creativity is not always easy to encourage. Indeed, "creativity is not always pretty." Noting that there are many complex strands, we consider the following data.

In schools, creative kids are often clowns, trouble-makers, or withdrawn, and are not the favorite of teachers, even when teachers say they value creativity. Surely we all need to face this: these risk-taking innovators are trouble. Yet here we are, those creative educators and students who are taking time now to ponder these issues. We are the creative nonconformists, gathered under our respective institutional roofs. Somehow we have made it to our institution, and we persist in showing up (and usually do so), without spontaneous combustion. We exist in a world that needs more creativity, not less, so how can we model more consciously a way to make this work for ourselves and for the greater world outside?

For us teachers and learners, as a creative group, one might posit the following cheerful possibility: Creativity in graduate education can mean being the *respected* voice of innovation (source of innovative ideas solidly studied and backed) in a process of cultural give and take. (This ongoing dialogue, and not necessarily a dialectic, between relatively more and less radical viewpoints has been called by Richards "cultural brainstorming.")

For us as creative individuals, I would suggest the following paired possibilities.

1. Creativity in graduate education will often mean honoring the individual you disagree with most—and, in valuing diversity, looking for some way for that individual to be heard.

2. Creativity in graduate education will often mean finding a way to work with others, and knowing when to put a larger goal before a personal preference.

The genius of innovative graduate education begins with the diversity of unique staff and students who have been attracted—on purpose!—to their unique alternative setting. Many perhaps represent a force for change in the counterculture. Whether as individuals or together, we are all open systems in a greater picture, and indeed many teachers and students have learned ways to influence it.

Consider what so many innovative academics and students—just think of the students and faculty in one's own institution—have accomplished in the larger community: professional leadership, organizational innovation, renowned research, journals edited, books written, papers published, and new directions spearheaded in diverse ways in diverse areas.

Why do students come to innovative graduate schools? *This* is why.

The issue now is whether there is any unnecessary friction, butting of heads, and wasting of time within the organization. After all, might not there be problems if creative people truly are such trouble? Well, of course there might be! If one is being honest, one might begin to acknowledge this as part of the fall-out, if not the excitement, and the well-worth-it price, when creative people all get together.

1. Optimizing a Working System of Eccentrics

Innovative teachers and academics are anything but sluggish when they are out in the world. Indeed, those creative educators and creative students reading this (that is, all of us), are surely able to reflect on ourselves a bit more, and avoid butting heads unproductively, as some have been known to do in their schools and departments. It takes making this a priority, and somehow providing each other—each creative other—a little slack. If one works with mindful awareness, and knows what one is doing, it is all the more possible to build up trust and mutual support from within, and take advantage of a more creatively flowing group process, to complement the strengths of individuals.

To this end, one needs to bend a little from time to time in acknowledgment of the delightful eccentricity (or outrageous behavior) we choose to value (or tolerate) in each other. Ruth Richards, Robert Albert, and David Schuldberg have discussed the importance of broadening what Richards called our "acceptable limits of normality" to increase our viability as a species, and our ability as humans to adapt to change. If our neighbor is a little unusual, well that will be okay with us! No harm done, and tomorrow it will be our turn. (Plus, you never know, this may be the beginning of tomorrow's conformity.) Meanwhile, somewhere out there, a remarkable new idea will have been tolerated long enough to take root and survive. If ever such toleration was needed, it is during these times of rapid flux. Wherever should it occur more readily than in our alternative educational institutions, where we strive to examine the possibilities, and educate our most creative and foresightful groups of individuals?

Yet what exactly is appropriate? One also needs norms for how to relate, and for cocreating the values that can celebrate a creative eccentricity, while still facilitating compromise and keeping a particular culture working. When exactly do we stand strong, when do we bend, and what are the greater values that guide this mix, and each decision? It is certainly not the intention of this brief article to produce such norms—which, after all, must also be worked out within each group. Here is a chance to use one's own creative environment, one's teaching and learning environment, as a laboratory, to learn how to work consciously and well, individually and together. How much better if this can then be modeled and then exported into the broader world. [*See* ECCENTRICITY.]

Yet there are also a few clues as to behaviors and characteristics of value, when applied in a group setting. Creative people might be particularly able to recognize those qualities involved in a creative "cognitive style," in others as well as in themselves, and celebrate these a bit more—even when in clear disagreement with someone. Such qualities help creators manage diverse information and a temporary lack of closure. What about applying them to the toleration of each other? Consider capacities such as "flexibility," "tolerance for ambiguity," and "preference for complexity," mentioned earlier as common features in creative people. [*See* COGNITIVE STYLE AND CREATIVITY.]

One might make an argument that creative people are in some ways "learning disabled," by virtue of the unique interpersonal dilemmas they raise and resources which may be required to help them (us). Yet one could argue as readily for ways in which creators can be "learning abled," and remarkably so. Creative people, at least, if not all institutions in society, must think this is a useful trade-off. If indeed innovative educators want to perpetuate creativity-related traits, to encourage them in future students, and to enhance creative change in society, such self-reflection is all the more worthwhile. Let us keep a focus on qualities that work within our own groups at home, and then study them in yet other contexts of change. After all, the world of the 21st century will need more creative persons, not less.

In a graduation address, Dean Maureen O'Hara of Saybrook Graduate School stressed the enormity of the educational task in this rapidly changing postmodern world and proposed that we will need a new psyche and a new consciousness as a model for the culture as a whole. An ambitious program indeed. Yet knowledge is not only shifting beneath our feet, but our feet help cocreate the knowledge; it is a function of the knower, the context, and the situation—indeed of all of us together and in our individual communities and interest groups. Nor does it end here, at one point in time, but stretches forward in time and space to affect generations to come. How do we help people learn, learn how to learn, and learn about the learner? Is the sand still shifting beneath us? Which sand do you mean? Will we need "tolerance for ambiguity"? Yes.

2. Welcome People Who Take Risks—But Then Evaluate Outcomes

There is also an evident need to take some risks. That is a major way that innovative education will progress. (Few of us have time to wait around for certainty to arrive.) Yet, at the same time, we should not just stand as educational innovators, out on a high diving board, hoping to dive and not to flop. We can also study what happens in our institutions—through ongoing evaluation of faculty and student experience and performance, and that of other constituencies, including alumni, staff, and administration. Mechanisms include the real-time in-process possibility of "action research" drawing data and perceptions from all constituencies as the system evolves, so that progress is known, problems are identified, and decisions are informed.

Within various departments or interest areas in many schools, students can be involved in this self-reflective way of thinking from Day One. This is often an aspect of the intended student experience in advanced education, and we can help encourage it in our students as an ongoing practice. Plus this is a further way of exporting our evolving successes into the world.

Surely we should preach no more than we practice. Our innovative programs in higher education can provide some ideal laboratories.

C. Product—Deciding What One Stands for, and What Stays the Same, While All Else Is in Flux

Let us say faculty agree that change in a program is fine. It is great, and it is long-awaited. No problem, they are willing to take some risks. Yet one cannot blow with every breeze; we do not necessarily want to change everything at once. Is there a semifixed point to depend upon? In any evolving school, or program, one is faced with many internal and external suggestions

about what to do. There are many pressures and directions. How does one identify and address certain needs within student populations, and within society, now and in the future, while drawing on the expertise of a faculty? What does one therefore do? Each graduate school may have its own specific variant of an answer, based on particular priorities and "core" subjects they have defined in their field. Let us look beyond this at an additional perspective on the *where,* the *what,* and the *how* of an innovative enterprise, and the linked *why?*

As stated, one major point may be to take risks, yet to see clearly in doing this, and then find out later what happened. Reflexive. Feedback-sensitive. Self-reflexive. Cannot we at a minimum bring excellence in clarity and method?

There are many *where*'s for the schools of the future—many contexts in which one's work may take place, as an innovative educational institution, including schools of different sizes, with different geographical recruitment and draw, and even potential for global participation and impact, as well as electronic campuses, summer institutes, community work sites, affiliated institutions, online support groups, networks for recruiting, practice in the community, placements, mentoring, colearning, group learning, and so on. The emphases are many and varied.

The *what* will depend very much upon one's area, but may hopefully include a range of initiatives which are sometimes surprising, and therefore may also be hard to predict. As stated, if we are any good, we cannot right now anticipate many of the questions that will occupy us in 10 years. But whatever they turn out to be, should not we stress that we be able to ask "most any (pertinent and open-minded) question" in graduate education, at least if we do it well? If not in our innovative schools, then where?

The *how* and the linked *why* are where one might put down the stake. Here is one potential fixed point, involving the process and its values, while so much else is in flux:

Goals should be addressed with rigor and excellence, with caring for all parties, and with values supporting innovation and risk-taking, diversity plus collaboration, and consciously knowing ourselves and our world. Why? In order to realize our fullest human potential, by ourselves and together.

D. Press of the Environment— That Is Us Too!

We have looked at rapidity of change, some of our limitations as learners, and ways to look more closely at processes of excellence and creativity in teaching and learning (which also means looking at ourselves, separately and together). Assume one can do this while preserving, at a minimum, the possibility of asking many types of questions, as an institution researching itself as well as the world. What then is left?

The last P in creativity research involves the press of the environment, notably the environment that facilitates creative process and product. Perhaps the reader has learned some of this the hard way, as has the author and many others—that harsh criticism can hurt, and that a valuing supportive environment can help, and particularly a setting that honors intrinsic motivation and creative involvement, which allows risks, tolerates deviancy, and does not demand perfection. These are well-researched conclusions and certainly make sense.

While we are at it, we should also question the zero-sum game which is all too common in education. In some schools, it is as prevalent as anywhere else. This is a highly competitive—and common—evaluative model which pits learners against each other; if you win, I lose, and vice versa. With some competition, how can we ever learn to work together, or appreciate the benefits of this? The colearner becomes an adversary. Much better, as Carl Rogers said about creativity, to be open and playful. Let us therefore frolic together. That way, the environment becomes a playground.

Are conclusions such as the above surprising? Perhaps not. Could we be more supportive of each other? One might think so.

Yet a final point, implicit in the sections above, is worth making explicit. This so-called environment is not a thing out there, like a tennis backboard, against which we play. Nor is it someone else, someone out there, who will be nice to us, or will not. We are not atoms of inert helium gas bouncing independently in a container—nor are we players against a fixed backdrop. Every statement above, whether about creative process, person, product, or press, is (also) a statement about the environment. And a statement about the environment is a statement about us, We are all open systems; we are of, in, and connected with the environment. Indeed, we are the environment.

Truly, we enable each other or we do not. In each moment, we cocreate a learning environment, be it conducive to our efforts or toxic. In an innovative graduate school in particular, the emphasis should be increasingly less on fixed learnings, and more on the ongoing learning process—both singly and together. Hence, among the four Ps, in our modern, postmodern, and transmodern world, this last P should remain of no less interest, and may be even more actively explored, as part of a more far-reaching open-systems form of inquiry. We as educators have the chance to make the environment for creative teaching and learning one of our proudest creations.

IV. KEY QUESTIONS BY WAY OF SUMMARY

1. Process. How do we learn to learn, and learn about the learner?

2. Person. How do we honor uniqueness and also learn to work together, so as a community of creative teachers and learners, we can play an innovative role in the greater society, indeed taking our risks more without, and not so much within.

3. Product. How do we stay open, yet decide what is relatively more fixed, including the excellence and values possible in alternative education?

4. Press. How do we get out of that tank of helium—of our inert and isolated roles—and see our roles together in this open system? We are the environment, and we are the individuals.

Bibliography

Gruber, H., & Wallace, D. (Eds.). (1993). Creativity in the moral domain. [Special issue.] *Creativity Research Journal, 6*(1/2).

Maslow, A. H. (1968). *Toward a psychgology of being.* New York: Van Nostrand.

May, R. (1975). *The courage to create.* New York: Bantam.

Montuori, A., & Purser, R. (in press). *Social creativity: An exploration of the social, historical, and political factors in creativity and innovation* (Vol. 1, 1999; Vols. 2&3, in press). Cresskill, NJ: Hampton.

Mooney, R. L. (1963). A conceptual model for integrating four approaches to the identification of creative talent. In C. W.

Taylor & F. Barron (Eds.) *Scientific creativity: Its recognition and development* (pp. 331–340). New York: Wiley and Sons.

Pennebaker, J. W. (Ed.). (1995). *Emotion, disclosure, and health.* Washington, DC: American Psychological Association.

Perkins, D. N. (1992). *Smart schools: From training memories to educating minds.* New York: Free Press.

Runco, M. A. (Ed.). (1996). *Creativity from childhood through adulthood: The developmental issues. New directions for child development* (Vol. 73). San Francisco: Jossey-Bass.

Runco, M., & Richards, R. (Eds.). (1997). *Eminent creativity, everyday creativity, and health.* Greenwich, CT: Ablex.

Sagor, R. (1992). *How to conduct collaborative action research.* Alexandria, VA: Association for Supervision and Curriculum Development.

Sternberg, R. J. (Ed.). (1998). *The nature of creativity. Contemporary psychological perspectives.* New York: Cambridge Univ. Press.

Fourth Grade Slump

Mark A. Runco

California State University, Fullerton

Conventionality Sensitivity to norms and expectations.
Internalization The process by which expectations and pressures in the environment become a part of a child's own values and way of thinking.
Maturation The unfolding of genetic material.
Postconventional Creativity Seen in individuals who are aware of conventions and norms but who make the decisions—including some that lead to original behavior—for themselves.

*E. P. Torrance, well known for his work on divergent thinking, described a **FOURTH GRADE SLUMP** in creative performances. First identified with cross-sectional comparisons, and then confirmed in longitudinal research, the fourth grade slump was apparent in all indexes of divergent thinking (i.e., ideational fluency, flexibility, originality, and elaboration). Torrance defined a slump as a drop of at least one-half a standard deviation in the standard scores. Actual mean scores dropped from 53 to 48 for fluency; from 53 to 47 for flexibility; from 50 to 47 for originality; and from 50 to 46 for elaboration. Some cross-cultural data have confirmed that this slump is not limited to students in the United States.*

I. EXPLANATIONS FOR THE SLUMP

At one point explanations for the fourth grade slump focused on the educational setting. This made some sense, given the pressures on children to conform—to sit in rows, raise hands before speaking, play only at recess, and so on. The curriculum often becomes more demanding in the third and fourth grades as well. These pressures might be internalized and peak in the fourth grade.

Then again, there are significant differences among different schools and teachers, so some variation would be expected. Moreover, children differ significantly in temperament and presumably in reactivity to the aforementioned pressures. Again, more individual differences might be expected given temperamental and experiential diversity.

Not surprisingly, more recent explanations focus on "maturation," which is defined as the unfolding of genetic material. Of course it is not specifically a slump that is genetically programmed. It is instead probably a more general sensitivity to conventions. This sensitivity is manifested as a kind of conforming behavior, and conformity precludes originality and the autonomy that characterize creativity.

Support for this view is provided by the range of conventional behaviors which all peak at around the same time. There is the fourth grade slump, with losses

Copyright © 1999 by Academic Press
All rights of reproduction in any form reserved.

apparent in divergent thinking. There is also a heightened conventionality in moral reasoning. Children move from a preconventional stage, where they do not know the rules or do not understand that rules are stable and useful, to the conventional stage, where they recognize rules and are often vehement about upholding them. This view of rules is quite apparent when children play games—younger ones often change rules as the game progresses and older children tend to stick carefully to rules—as well as in situations that require moral reasoning. [*See* DIVERGENT THINKING.]

Additional support for the role of conventionality is provided by research on children's artwork. Here again, young children often disregard conventions, drawing what they feel or like rather than creating realistic, representational, and conventional pictures. Only later do they become uncomfortable drawing things that differ from their experiences and expectations. [*See* CONVENTIONALITY.]

In the social domain, peer pressure represents a kind of conventionality. The rules involved differ from the guidelines found in games, but children do form clear expectations and share them. These are the conventions to which children often conform, especially starting around the fourth grade. [*See* CONFORMITY.]

Howard Gardner, in *Art, Mind, and Brain,* described a literal stage which corresponds to the fourth grade slump and the peak of conventionality. Children in the literal stage have difficulty with metaphor and idiom—with any nonliteral use of language. This is even apparent in the jokes, riddles, and puns they prefer. [*See* METAPHORS.]

Thus the evidence for the sensitivity to conventions can be found in moral reasoning, game playing, art, social behavior, and language. The slump in originality, demonstrated in the research using divergent thinking tests, may be explained in the same manner: Maturational processes allow children to recognize conventions very easily. They begin to rely on conventions rather than their own spontaneity. There is great value in this sensitivity: They learn important conventions,

and these conventions allow them to communicate and fit into a given culture. There is a drawback in that children may lose some of their originality, but many of them move on to a postconventional stage. Here they are aware of conventions but choose in a mindful way, for themselves, which conventions are appropriate for them, and which are not. [*See* DEVELOPMENTAL TRENDS IN CREATIVE ABILITIES AND POTENTIALS.]

II. CONCLUSIONS

There are two points to emphasize. First is that maturational processes do not guarantee a slump. Maturational processes do rely on genetic potential, but it is just that—potential. Potential requires experience to be fulfilled. In other words, the slump is just a potential slump. In this light it might be avoided by carefully guiding development.

The second point is that the evidence for the fourth grade slump is not overwhelming. Torrance found that between 45 and 61% of the children in his research show signs of a slump, depending on the divergent thinking index—but between 11 and 38% showed growth during the same period. This might be explained in the terms used in the paragraph above in that 61% of the children had pressures on them and were reinforced for conventionality, thus fulfilling that potential. The other 38% may have had very different experiences that did not fulfill the potential slump. Whatever the explanation, the figures given in Torrance's report suggest that a slump is far from universal.

Bibliography

Runco, M. A., & Charles, R. (1997). Developmental trends in creative potential and creative performance. In M. A. Runco (Ed.), *Creativity research handbook* (Vol. 1, pp. 115–152). Cresskill, NJ: Hampton.

Torrance, E. P. (1968). A longitudinal examination of the 4th grade slump in creativity. *Gifted Child Quarterly, 12,* 195–197.

Sigmund Freud

1856–1939

Psychiatrist

Author of *The Interpretation of Dreams*
and *Beyond the Pleasure Principle*

Alan C. Elms

University of California, Davis

SIGMUND FREUD was the creator of psychoanalysis.
*Psychoanalysis is a form of psychotherapy, a set of
methods for collecting data on human behavior, and
a system of psychological theories. Freud developed a
variety of concepts that have become central to the understanding of creativity, including unconscious motivation, sublimation, defense mechanisms, and the resolution of neurotic conflicts through creative activity.
Though Freud's ideas have been often modified, criticized, and challenged since his death, psychoanalysis
remains the most broadly influential approach to the
study of creativity.*

I. BACKGROUND

Freud was born on May 6, 1856, in Freiburg, Mora-
via (now Príbor, Czech Republic). His father Jakob was
a 41-year-old wool merchant who had two adult sons
from a previous marriage. Freud's mother, Amalia, was
21 years old at the time of his birth. Sigmund, her firstborn child, was followed by six more children, five of
whom survived to adulthood.

The Freud family moved to Vienna amid serious financial difficulties when Sigmund was nearly four. As

Sigmund Freud. Used with permission from Snark/Art Resource, NY.

Copyright © 1999 by Academic Press
All rights of reproduction in any form reserved.

Jews, they lived in the Jewish ghetto of a predominantly Roman Catholic city. Sigmund remained in Vienna for all but the final year of his life. Though he proclaimed his hatred for it, the city was a center of European culture, science, and politics. Sigmund was his mother's favorite child, whom she called her "golden Sigi." She often repeated a gypsy woman's prediction that he would be a great man. His father was not so optimistic; when the 7- or 8-year-old Sigi urinated inappropriately in the parental bedroom, Jakob Freud exclaimed, "The boy will never amount to anything!"

Sigmund soon began to fulfill his mother's expectations. In Vienna he attended a classical German-style *gymnasium* (an advanced secondary school), where he was inspired by the works of such great writers as Goethe and Wordsworth, plus scientists such as Darwin. His school performance was outstanding; at age 17 he entered medical school.

II. EARLY ADULTHOOD

As a medical student at the University of Vienna from 1873 to 1881 (with a year out for required military duty), Freud received not only a basic medical education but some of the best training in scientific research that Europe had to offer. The professors with whom he worked closely were distinguished in their fields, and Freud was expected to follow their paths in anatomy and physiology: Carl Claus, Hermann Nothnagel, Theodor Meynert and Ernst Brücke. However, in contrast to much of today's scientific training (especially in psychology), the research skills Freud developed there were not experimental or correlational but observational, mainly involving dissection and microscope work. Freud became a scientist without ever performing a controlled experiment. His initial interest was in physiological research; his first published paper answered a long-standing question by establishing the presence of testes in the male eel. His other research topics included the nerve cells of fish and crayfish. Freud was one of the first scientists to suggest the general outlines of the modern neuronal theory of the nervous system. Later in his life, long after he had abandoned physiological research altogether, Freud continued to compare his explorations of the deeper layers of the unconscious to the process of peeling away surface layers of skin or tissue—the kind of thing he had done as a physiologist when he was trying to get at a nerve cell.

Though Freud was regarded by his professors as a promising neurophysiologist, this was not a career in which he could make enough money to support a family. He had already fallen in love, not long after he completed his research training, with a young woman named Martha Bernays. Therefore his professors advised him to go into clinical practice, specializing in neurological problems. Getting the necessary clinical experience and establishing a practice took him four years beyond medical school, during which time he and Martha remained engaged though often apart.

Among the factors that frequently separated Freud from his betrothed was his continuing effort to obtain the most progressive training available. He traveled to Paris to observe the treatment of hysteria and other psychological syndromes by the great Jean Martin Charcot, and to Nancy (also in France) to study the hypnotic techniques of Hippolyte Bernheim. In his own early psychiatric work, Freud became an expert on aphasia (an assortment of syndromes involving the inability to speak) and a respected authority on childhood paralyses. When he began to treat patients whose main symptoms were evidently psychological rather than physical, Freud administered the latest therapies—such as electric shock and hypnosis—but found them unsatisfactory. Then he tried a technique developed by another prominent scientist, Josef Breuer, who was already a fatherly friend and mentor to Freud. Several years earlier Breuer had treated a friend of Martha Bernays, with some success. That patient later became a pioneering social worker under her real name of Bertha Pappenheim, but she has gone down in psychological history under the pseudonym of Anna O.

III. THE BEGINNINGS OF PSYCHOANALYSIS

When she came to Breuer for treatment, Anna O. was suffering from a variety of paralyses, aphasias, inhibitions, and periods of confused thinking. Breuer found that if he asked Anna under hypnosis to talk about the original circumstances associated with each of her symptoms, she reexperienced the circumstances vividly and her symptoms were thereby relieved. When Freud subsequently tried a similar procedure on his own patients, he soon gave up hypnosis. Instead, he simply (or perhaps not so simply) insisted that his patients tell him, as fully and with as little mental censorship as possible, what came into their minds whenever they began to think of their personal problems. Thus was born the practice of free association, the earliest element of psychoanalysis as a general therapeutic technique.

Over the next several years, Freud developed an array of techniques that became essential both to psychoanalytic psychotherapy and to Freud's accumulation of psychological data as a foundation for his development of psychoanalytic theory. While encouraging free association, Freud found that his patients were often more willing to free-associate to their recent night dreams than to events of the day. When he got them to free-associate to each element of a dream, he saw emerging patterns that revealed the patient's underlying motives and psychological conflicts. In the process of engaging in such dream interpretation, as well as having patients free-associate to slips of the tongue, to temporary forgetting of names or words, and to other psychological anomalies, Freud developed a general approach now known as the "intensive study of the single case."

Freud did not try to study large numbers of similar individuals at one time, as in the standard psychological experiment or survey. Instead, he closely examined one patient at a time. "Intensive study" has two meanings here. One is that Freud obtained a great deal of information on any particular individual. He typically saw each patient for three to six hours per week for anywhere from several months to several years. During the hundreds of hours of each patient's free associations, then, Freud could observe changes in the patient's behavior and memories, could double-check his developing hypotheses, and could alter those hypotheses as new developments emerged. The other meaning of "intensive study" is that Freud was not content to accept new information from a patient as it first appeared, or to categorize it in terms of superficial criteria. If certain information supplied by the patient seemed to have no immediate significance, Freud probed further into the patient's memories and free associations. He checked out possible connections with other material provided by the patient, and generally tried to relate the information to an organized and coherent picture of the patient's personality. Freud constantly evaluated the material's internal consistency — the omissions and contradictions evident in the patient's statements. He sometimes compared himself to the great fictional detective Sherlock Holmes, tracking down tiny clues that might lead to the solution of a crime — or in Freud's cases, tracking down clues that would lead to a fuller understanding of a patient's psychological problems.

In addition to dream interpretation, free association, and the intensive study of the single case, Freud developed two other techniques to obtain data salient to his theories. He was quite aware that his severely neurotic patients were not a random sample of the human race, and that he could not base a general theory of personality entirely on them. Neither, however, could he reasonably expect mentally healthy individuals to volunteer the most intimate information about their psychological functioning as part of a research study. Therefore Freud turned to other sources of data that were readily available: first, himself, and second, works of art.

His self-analysis was, according to his friend and biographer Ernest Jones, "one of the two great deeds of Freud's scientific life." (The other great deed was the development of the free association method.) The German researcher Hermann Ebbinghaus had already discovered several basic laws of learning and memory by studying himself as he learned and forgot emotionally neutral stimuli. Now Freud proposed to examine, as objectively as possible, his own memories of such highly unneutral topics as his love and hate toward his parents and siblings, his most repulsive desires, and his most shameful behavior, all the way back into early childhood. When Freud found the same kinds of emotional conflicts and irrational urges in himself that he had discovered in his most neurotic patients, he came to feel that his hypotheses about personality were essentially correct and broadly applicable.

Freud was aware, of course, that even adding himself to his sample of late-19th century Viennese patients did not provide sufficient basis for generalizing his conclusions to all humankind. But Freud also read and studied a wide range of the world's creative writers, from the ancient Greeks and Romans (especially

Homer, Sophocles, and Virgil), through more recent masters (including Shakespeare and E. T. A. Hoffmann), to such contemporaries as Mark Twain, Fyodor Dostoyevsky, Rider Haggard, and Arthur Schnitzler. Their work teemed with detailed depictions of psychologically complex characters, who exhibited much the same motives and behavior as Freud kept finding in his patients and himself. He saw such literary creations as valuable confirmation by other brilliant thinkers of his own hypotheses. When even mediocre writers offered characters who described their dreams and fantasies in detail, as in the German novelist Wilhelm Jensen's popular romance *Gradiva,* Freud took such works as additional instances of unconscious motives expressed in conscious behavior, both by the fictional characters and by the writer.

A core concept in Freud's early psychoanalytic theories is named after a literary work: the *Oedipus complex.* Freud's reference here is to Sophocles' play *Oedipus the King,* written 2300 years earlier. The play depicts what modern audiences typically perceive on first viewing as a strange set of events: a Greek king, warned by an oracle that his newborn son will eventually kill him, takes the baby into the countryside and leaves him to die. The infant Oedipus is saved by a shepherd and is then raised by adoptive parents. As a young adult, Oedipus finds himself in circumstances where, unaware of the family relationships involved, he kills his father the king and takes his mother the queen as his wife. Upon discovering that he has committed patricide and incest, Oedipus blinds himself in shame over his terrible acts.

Why, Freud asked, does this ancient play from an unfamiliar culture remain so disturbing to us? Because, as Freud answered his own question, Sophocles captured in the play's characters and symbolism a set of feelings that most of us experience in childhood but have driven deep into our unconscious: a desire to monopolize the body and the attention of our opposite-sexed parent, and to eliminate our chief competitor, the same-sexed parent. Freud saw a similar emotional pattern in the most powerful work of the greatest English-language writer, Shakespeare's *Hamlet.*

From early in his psychoanalytic practice, Freud had been aware of the power of sexual motivation, as well as of his patients' struggles to keep it under control. They often tried to avoid thinking about sex altogether, though without complete success. The repression of distressing childhood sexual experiences was so consistently a problem among his patients that Freud formulated what he called the "seduction hypothesis": the idea that severe neurosis always originates from a child's "seduction" or sexual initiation by an older sibling or adult. In repressing such memories of early sexual abuse, the child removes important aspects of his or her sexuality from conscious access, with various unfortunate impacts on later adult behavior and psychological functioning.

After several years of psychoanalytically rescuing these early memories of sexual abuse from repression, Freud began to doubt their literal truth in a number of cases. They were just too frequent, he felt, and in certain instances they appeared to be contradicted by other kinds of biographical evidence. Freud therefore gave up his initial seduction hypothesis in large part (though he never abandoned it completely, as some critics have charged). He turned instead to his newly formulated concept of the Oedipus complex.

Freud now argued that the child naturally comes to focus sexual and aggressive feelings on the most convenient and emotionally charged objects, his parents. He proposed that the four- or five-year-old child typically fantasizes about sexual or sensual contact with the opposite-sexed parent, and that the child as adult later recalls such fantasies as real events (under pressure from the eager psychoanalyst). Freud was thus the first person to recognize that some retrospective reports of abuse are actually signs of what is now called a "false memory syndrome," just as he had been the first person to pay serious attention to the long-term psychological effects of childhood sexual abuse. He has also been the only person to be criticized from both sides of the current controversy over such matters—that is, to be criticized both for treating his patients' reports of childhood sexual abuse as sometimes false, and for treating them as sometimes true.

During the course of considering the role of sexual motivation in personality development, Freud came up with another concept that remains important in discussions of creativity: the process of sublimation. Sublimation was not an entirely original concept with Freud, but he made it his own, and he considerably elaborated earlier and more casual uses of the term. According to Freud's initial conceptualization, sexual urges that are not permitted direct expression will go in one of two directions: they may be converted into anxiety and other neurotic symptoms, or they can be expressed in creative work and other culture-building acts. The process of redirecting sexual energy (as well as, to some degree, aggressive energy) into creative acts was what Freud called sublimation. It can never completely satisfy an individual's sexual desires, according to Freud; only actual sexual intercourse can do that. But he viewed sublimation as certainly a better way to gain indirect sexual satisfaction than through neurotic symptoms, and at the same time he regarded sublimation as the chief source of human cultural accomplishments.

Freud had personal reasons to consider the effects of incompletely expressed sexual urges at this time. He and his wife had quickly established a family; Martha gave birth to six children during the first eight years of their marriage. Sigmund and Martha Freud had attempted by various means to prevent the conception of the later children—especially the sixth, the daughter they named Anna—but every birth control method they tried had failed. Finally, after Anna's birth, husband and wife simply stopped having sexual relations. Sigmund was 39 at the time and Martha was 34. During the first several years after their sexual relationship ceased, Freud experienced an explosion of creative ideas. It is probably no accident that one of these ideas was his concept of sublimation as the creative transformation of unexpended sexual energy. (Certain of Freud's critics, beginning with C. G. Jung, have accused him of conducting an affair with his sister-in-law during this period, and have argued that the supposed affair may have influenced his ideas about sexual motivation and other matters. The evidence for such a relationship is highly speculative at best, and there are much clearer sources for Freud's principal theoretical concepts.)

IV. PSYCHOANALYSIS: THE MIDDLE YEARS

For Sigmund Freud, psychoanalytic theory was not a static body of ideas but a constantly growing and changing structure. Freud first conceptualized the personality as composed principally of consciousness, of a deep unconscious that contains our basic urges and repressed memories, and of a preconscious that includes temporarily forgotten or ignored memories. As

his theories developed, Freud began to differentiate aspects of the psychological structure more clearly: the id, a completely unconscious mass of primitive biological urges which insists on immediate sensual gratification; the ego, largely conscious but with unconscious components, mediating between the id and external reality; and the superego, the internalized representative of the parents' (and through them, of society's) moral standards. In this middle-phase formulation by Freud, the id controls most of the personality's psychological energy; the relatively weak ego struggles constantly to delay or redirect the id's demands, through repression and other psychological defenses; and the superego tries with limited means to block the id's more outrageous demands completely.

As his theories changed, Freud's therapeutic treatment objectives shifted as well. Where he had sought mainly to encourage the patient to express previously hidden memories and desires, he now began to analyze the patient's transference of early emotional patterns onto Freud himself. Freud had at first experienced such transferences as an annoyance and an embarrassment, since they often took the form of female patients falling in love with him and even throwing themselves at him physically. In time he came to recognize that he was serving these patients as a target of displacement for feelings originally aroused by parents and other figures from early childhood. (Freud's male patients redirected their emotional patterns toward him too, but they more often did so by making him the object of unreasonable hostility.) By bringing to a patient's attention the transference patterns expressed toward the therapist, and by working with the patient to develop an understanding of the patterns' origins and their current inappropriateness, Freud felt he was able to gain much more extensive and lasting therapeutic success than through his previous efforts.

It took him a while longer to recognize that in addition to each patient's transference of emotions onto him, Freud was engaging in a constant process of countertransference of his own long-established emotional patterns onto the patient. This recognition enabled Freud to overcome previously unacknowledged or uncontrolled difficulties in the therapeutic interaction. Finally in this sequence of new recognitions, Freud came to realize that transference and countertransference are not limited to the interaction of therapist and patient, but extend through all human social interactions beyond those of child and parent. With this recognition, Freud finally achieved what he regarded as a general psychology of human personality.

For several years before and after his 50th birthday, Freud felt that he had become creatively exhausted and was experiencing a decline into old age. During this time he revised his ideas about sublimation to say that only students were able to make effective use of unexpended sexual energy, and then only to fuel their studies; sublimation was of no use to creative artists or theorists. Then Freud experienced a brief resurgence of his own sexual urges, and at the same time he began to write his longest treatment of creativity, his psychobiography of Leonardo da Vinci. [*See* DA VINCI, LEONARDO.]

According to Freud, Leonardo as a child lived with his single mother, felt sexually aroused by her before he could deal effectively with such feelings, and at the same time strongly identified with her. In attempting to manage such complex emotions, Leonardo as an adult became a celibate homosexual, expressing his sexual desires both for his mother and for young boys mainly through his painting. Eventually his superego forced him to steer away from even the indirect artistic expression of these morally and socially unacceptable urges. Leonardo shifted his attention to focus for a while on his scientific research, a less obviously sexual use of his psychological energy. Then, at about the same age that Freud had reached at the time of writing, Leonardo experienced a rearousal of his repressed desires for his mother, stimulated by the woman now known as Mona Lisa. Leonardo thereby regained his artistic creativity in midlife, and maintained that creativity into old age. Freud too experienced new creative urges at this time in his own life, and over the next three decades he formulated further important revisions in psychoanalytic theory.

In addition to a degree of sexual renewal, Freud experienced another kind of psychological stimulus in midlife: the acquisition of a band of disciples, who endorsed Freud's ideas and who practiced therapy under his tutelage. The most important of these followers was Carl Gustav Jung, a Swiss psychiatrist who was Freud's closest friend and colleague from 1907 to 1912. Jung influenced Freud to give more weight, for a time, to ideas about inherited symbolic configurations and behavioral tendencies, which Jung called archetypes. But after 1912, Jung went off to advocate a distinctive version of psychoanalytic theory and therapy, in which creative activities were seen largely as variations on those inherited archetypes. Freud then reemphasized his own previous concepts of creative patterns as emerging out of the crucible of the individual's early family life.

V. PSYCHOANALYSIS: THE LATER YEARS

Though Freud continued to worry about the effects of age and illness on his own creativity, the years from his late fifties into his seventies were among his most productive. In terms of broad theoretical tendencies, he placed increasing emphasis on the power of the ego to control the unruly id, and on the psychological importance of the person's interactions with other individuals—emphases that were amplified and modified by later psychoanalytic theorists, who called themselves ego psychologists or object-relations theorists. In terms of his thinking about creativity, Freud moved from: (a) early concepts about artistic works principally as symbolic expressions of unconscious motives and conflicts, to (b) artistic works as also involving the artist's conscious manipulation of the audience's aesthetic responses, in order to lead the audience into close contact with potentially disturbing latent content, to (c) the artist as using his or her art to confront and creatively resolve the artist's own psychological problems. Freud discussed both Leonardo and Michelangelo as examples of the latter process, which has been referred to by later theorists as a restitutive or restorative use of art by the artist.

Freud's essay on Michelangelo's statue of Moses, in which Freud appears to identify strongly with Moses as a man who has reached an inner peace after the backsliding of his followers, was written on the eve of World War I. The war brought great physical deprivation to Freud and his family, as well as anxiety about his sons who were fighting in the war and distress over the deaths of relatives, friends, and expatients. Freud had already begun to elaborate his concepts of the id's basic drives, which he had originally conceptualized as including both self-preservative drives and species-preservative (sexual) drives. Now he perceived a new division, between the life instincts (self- and species-preservative drives together) and the death instincts (including self-destructive and other-destructive urges). The horrors of the war solidified the position of this new drive schema in Freud's theoretical system.

In his first postwar book, *Beyond the Pleasure Principle,* Freud proposed that a more basic urge than the desire for pleasure is the "compulsion to repeat" earlier states of being, even unpleasant ones—a compulsion that ultimately drives us to restore our original state of being, which is zero stimulation or nothingness. This theoretical postulate (or, as Freud described it, this "speculation") led Freud to his grimmest pronouncement: "The aim of all life is death." But in spite of his assumption that the death instincts will triumph within all of us in the end, he maintained the companion assumption that the life instincts will continue to struggle against the death instincts for as long as possible, and can give us considerable pleasure along the way.

In the 1920s, Freud achieved worldwide fame as the greatest psychological theorist of all time—much to the dismay of Jung and other theoretical dissidents. Freud's ideas had increasing impact on novelists, poets, painters, sculptors, and filmmakers, who incorporated Freudian dream symbolism or free-associational content into their work. As W. H. Auden put it in a famous poem, Freud was "no more a person / now but a whole climate of opinion / under whom we conduct our different lives."

But Freud's fame did not prevent the Nazis from targeting him as a Jew, or from burning his books. Freud narrowly escaped from Austria as the Nazis solidified their hold there in 1938. He and his daughter Anna moved to London, where Freud continued to write during the final year of his life—working especially to complete a speculative work that he first titled, *The Man Moses: A Historical Novel.* Translated into English as *Moses and Monotheism,* this book was not really a novel, but a creative consideration of the origins of the Jewish people. Had Moses really been born as a Hebrew slave and raised as Egyptian royalty (as the Bible says), or had he been born and raised as a member of the Egyptian royal family, who then adopted (and was adopted by) the Hebrews as their spiritual and politi-

cal leader? In proposing the latter answer to his own question, Freud developed a preliminary theory of charismatic leadership that has been elaborated by Saul Friedländer and others.

Freud died of cancer in 1939, in the midst of work on a final *Outline of Psychoanalysis.* After his death, his major ideas and certain minor ones have retained their power to stimulate the thinking of many other theorists and psychological practitioners—and to provoke what Freud called "continued resistance" to these ideas. (Others would call it criticism or hostility.) Though few psychologists and psychiatrists now wholeheartedly accept Freud's specific versions of theory and therapy, most current personality theories and psychotherapies incorporate his broad positions at some level. His influence is most strongly visible in two areas: first, in the academic practice of critical and cultural theory, plus psychobiography and psychohistory, and second, in our society's most widespread conceptions of personality, which include many "pop psychology" versions of unconscious conflict, the retention of the "inner child," psychological defenses such as denial and reaction formation, and the variously named contrasts between male (rule-oriented) and female (relationship-oriented) personality patterns. Every few years—sometimes every few months or even weeks—a new book or magazine article announces that Freud is dead and that his ideas are in total disarray. But such repeated insistence on his death suggests that Freud is still a very lively ghost, continuing to haunt our most anxiously and aggressively defended ideas of our own basic nature.

Bibliography

Elms, A. C. (1994). *Uncovering lives: The uneasy alliance of biography and psychology.* New York/Oxford: Oxford University Press.

Gay, P. (1988). *Freud: A life for our times.* New York: Norton.

Gay, P. (Ed.). (1989). *The Freud reader.* New York: Norton.

Holland, N. N. (1990). *Holland's guide to psychoanalytic psychology and literature-and-psychology.* New York/Oxford: Oxford University Press.

Spitz. E. H. (1985). *Art and psyche: A study in psychoanalysis and aesthetics.* New Haven, CT: Yale University Press.

Gender Differences

John Baer

Rider University

Associative Thinking Bringing together of ideas that are not typically associated with one another

Convergent Thinking Thinking that involves finding the single best answer to a problem or question.

Divergent Thinking A kind of thinking often associated with creativity which involves the generation of varied, original, or unusual ideas in response to an open-ended question or task.

Evaluative Thinking Making judgments or decisions about the quality of ideas.

*There is a considerable amount of evidence of **GENDER DIFFERENCES** in creative accomplishment in a wide variety of fields, including the arts, business, and science. This article will summarize research evidence regarding possible differences in cognitive abilities related to creativity and will outline prominent theories that have been offered to explain observed gender differences in creative achievement.*

I. INTRODUCTION

The question of gender differences in creativity is a complex and controversial topic. There is little doubt that in many fields of endeavor gender differences in creative achievement exist, especially if one focuses on the highest levels of creative accomplishment. It is not clear, however, what has caused those differences. In fields in which men have predominated, as in the sciences and many of the arts, it has been argued that the relative paucity of women's accomplishments is due entirely to societal constraints. Women have not been allowed to participate to the same degree as men, according to this argument, and have therefore naturally not been able to achieve as much as men.

It is certainly true that men have controlled access to many fields and limited participation by women in those fields. It is possible, but less certain, that a combination of such factors as (a) gender differences in the availability of schooling and other important resources, (b) different expectations and other common socializing experiences in the development of boys and girls, and (c) control by men of the standards by which individual accomplishment have been judged can provide a complete explanation for gender differences in creative achievement.

Copyright © 1999 by Academic Press
All rights of reproduction in any form reserved.

Although there have been notable exceptions, the study of gender differences in creativity has not attracted the sustained attention of cadres of creativity researchers over the years. Questions such as how or why men and women differ in their creative thinking or their creative accomplishments are both difficult to tackle experimentally and highly charged politically. This combination of difficulties has, in all likelihood, led many researchers who have considered doing research related to these questions to choose instead to investigate more tractable and less controversial research topics. Although there have been numerous studies comparing the divergent thinking abilities of girls and boys—abilities hypothesized to underlie creative thinking and achievement—investigations of gender differences in adult creative achievement have been relatively few in number. Research studies in this area have often been either very limited in their focus or quite speculative (and sometimes polemical) in their approach.

There is sufficient data to reach consensus on some issues related to gender differences in creativity, however. This article both explains those areas in which there is considerable agreement and maps out the key positions in those areas in which researchers and theorists disagree on how to interpret the available evidence. The article looks first at evidence that argues for or against the existence of gender differences in creativity. This evidence includes both tests aimed at measuring skills hypothesized to be important ingredients in creative thinking and measures of creative performance itself. This summary of the evidence for gender differences is followed by an outline of several theories that have been proposed to explain gender differences in creative accomplishment. The article ends with a brief summary.

II. EVIDENCE OF GENDER DIFFERENCES IN CREATIVITY

The evidence presented in this section comes from psychological studies of creativity. The first subsection looks at the results of creativity tests, which have been primarily (but not exclusively) divergent thinking tests. The second subsection examines gender differences in (a) creative performance in psychological studies that examine the creativity of actual products (e.g., poems, stories, and collages) that have been produced under controlled conditions; (b) self-assessments of creativity; and (c) assessments by others, such as peers and teachers, of individuals known well by the assessors.

This section does not attempt to document differences in actual creative achievement across a wide variety of domains. While the existence of such differences in real-world creative accomplishments is widely recognized, most research in this area has focused on explaining rather than describing such differences.

A. Creativity Tests

Divergent thinking tests have become widespread as measures of creativity, although it should be noted that there is a continuing and unresolved dispute among creativity researchers regarding the validity of these tests. The term "divergent production" was first introduced by J. P. Guilford in his Structure of the Intellect model of human intelligence in the 1950s. Divergent production (a term which has been mostly displaced by the more recent term "divergent thinking") referred to the production of different, varied, original, or unusual ideas in response to an open-ended question or task. Divergent production can be understood most simply by contrasting it to "convergent production," which is thinking aimed at finding the best answer to the kind of problem that has only a single best answer. Divergent production was one of five large categories of thought in Guilford's rather complex theory, and the one that has received the most attention. [*See* DIVERGENT THINKING.]

Guilford and many of his followers have argued that divergent thinking is an important part of creative thinking. Although most creativity theorists would agree that it is only one part of creative thinking, the fact that it is very different from the kind of thinking that is (a) used in other (noncreative) kinds of problem solving and (b) most frequently assessed in schools and workplaces (such as intelligence or achievement testing) has led divergent thinking to become almost synonymous with creative thinking among many people, including many educators. Divergent thinking testing is used as a way to assess individuals' creativity in many educational settings (such as entry to programs for creatively talented students) and in much psychological research. A typical question on a divergent thinking test might ask examinees to list as many different and unusual uses for empty egg cartons as they can, often within a limited time period. The most common divergent thinking tests are the Torrance Tests of Creative Thinking. [*See* APPENDIX II: TESTS OF CREATIVITY.]

Are there differences in the divergent thinking abilities (as revealed in divergent thinking test scores) of men and women? Scores of studies have tried to answer this question, and the results have been quite mixed. Depending on the study, women have sometimes scored higher than men, and men have sometimes scored higher than women. It is safe to conclude from the often contradictory outcomes that there are not consistent differences favoring one gender over the other in divergent thinking test scores.

This is true not only among male and female test takers in general, but also at every age level. Among preschool and elementary subjects, girls outperform boys more often than the reverse, but not so often that one can make a clear statement regarding the overall nature of gender differences in divergent thinking ability. Among middle and high school students the results are much the same: generally mixed, with both girls and boys scoring higher in several published studies, and with a slightly larger number of studies that favor girls. The same slight advantage favoring women oven men is found in studies of adult divergent thinking, although as with children there are studies in this area pointing in both directions, and when considered together they provide no clear and consistent message.

In one comprehensive review of recent research of gender differences in creativity, over 80 studies were reported that compared divergent thinking scores of males and females. Over half of these studies reported no difference, with about two-thirds of the remaining studies favoring women or girls and one-third favoring men or boys. No meta-analysis of these diverse studies has been reported, but if consistent differences could be uncovered by pooling these results, such differences would be necessarily quite small. It should be borne in mind that it is probable that studies in which one group outscores the other have a greater likelihood of being published than studies that find no differences, which makes the observed small difference in the numbers of studies favoring women or men even more suspect.

It should be noted that longitudinal validity studies of divergent thinking test scores have suggested that these tests are more predictive of creative accomplishment by men than women. Interpretation of this difference is not easy, in part because the validity studies themselves have been criticized sharply; however, one plausible interpretation offered by supporters of divergent thinking tests is that because men are more likely to have access to the resources necessary for creative productivity, it is more likely that differences in divergent thinking ability among men will result in differences in creative accomplishments.

It has been argued that divergent thinking is domain or task specific—that divergent thinking skill in one area, such as poetry writing, may be very different than divergent thinking in some other area, such as collage making. If this is the case, it may help make sense of the results of studies showing gender differences in divergent thinking. It is possible, for example, that girls may be better at divergent thinking in the verbal and artistic domains, while boys may be better at divergent thinking in the mechanical and scientific domains. There is some limited support for such an interpretation, but further study is needed. [*See* DOMAINS OF CREATIVITY.]

There have been only a handful of studies comparing male and female creativity using tests other than divergent thinking tests. In Guilford's Structure of the Intellect model, which includes the already-mentioned divergent and convergent production, there is a third kind of thinking termed "evaluation." Evaluative thinking refers to the ability to make judgments or decisions concerning the quality of ideas and their accuracy, appropriateness, suitability, or desirability in a given situation. In the only two reported studies of evaluative thinking that have compared male and female subjects (one of children and one of adults) there were no statistically significant gender differences.

One other kind of thinking hypothesized to be an important part of creativity is "associative thinking." In this theory, the creative thinking process can be defined as the association or bringing together of ideas that are different and often remote (in the sense of not typically being associated with one another), followed by an evaluation of the resulting synthesis for appropriateness in the context. This theory is similar to ideas that go back at least to John Locke. There is a test of this kind of thinking (Mednick's Remote Associates Test, or RAT) which, though far less widely used than divergent thinking tests, is used occasionally in psychological research. Two studies have compared the associative thinking abilities of male and female subjects using the RAT. In a study of adults, there was no significant gender difference, but in a study of adolescents, girls outscored boys.

In summary, research has not uncovered consistent differences in the kinds of thinking hypothesized to be significant contributors to creativity. Most studies have revealed no significant gender differences; however, in those studies in which one group outperformed the other, female subjects scored higher than male subjects more frequently than the reverse.

B. Creative Achievement

A number of research studies have looked for possible gender differences in creativity more directly. That is, rather than use some test designed to measure some skill hypothesized to be important in creative thinking, actual creative performances have been the criterion. This has been done in a number of ways.

One way to look at actual creative performance that is almost like a test is to ask subjects to create some product, such as a poem, a story, or a collage, and then ask experts (e.g., poets, short story writers, artists, or critics in each of these fields) to evaluate these artifacts for their creativity. Such studies, most of which have employed either children or college students as subjects, have generally uncovered no significant gender differences in creativity.

Using a rather different approach, some researchers have looked for gender differences in creative productivity by examining patterns of publication in specific academic journals. Unsurprisingly, the ratio of male to female authors has been fairly large (roughly three to one). In recent years this ratio has decreased, mostly as the result of an increase in the number of female authors (rather than a decrease in the number of male authors). However, there has been a tendency for these gains by women to reach a peak and then plateau.

Creativity researchers have also used general assessments of creativity, both self-evaluations of creativity and evaluations by knowledgeable others (e.g., teachers), in their search for gender differences. These studies have tended to find no significant gender dif-

ferences, which has been a fairly consistent theme throughout the psychological study of gender differences in creativity.

III. THEORIES OF GENDER DIFFERENCES IN CREATIVITY

Psychological studies have had little success finding gender differences in abilities hypothesized to underlie creativity, such as divergent thinking. They have likewise failed to find significant gender differences in subjects' performance on creativity-relevant tasks, such as writing poems or making collages.

Gender differences in creative accomplishment are real and significant in the world, however. Psychologists have on occasion measured such differences (as in the previously mentioned studies of authorship), but more often they have acknowledged such differences and sought biological, psychological, or sociocultural explanations to make sense of them. Some writers have also endeavored to explain why creativity testing has not uncovered the kinds of differences found in real-world creative achievement by disparaging the kinds of tests used to measure creativity, such as divergent thinking tests.

Some theories of gender differences in creativity weigh heavily on biological factors, while others stress environmental differences in the development of children and in the environment in which creative achievement is accomplished and evaluated. The theories in the first group stress the nature side of the nature–nurture debate in looking for biological differences between males and females that might explain gender differences in creative productivity. The theories in the second group take a very different approach in looking for cross-cultural differences to explain the same phenomenon. The last group of theories are developmental in their approach and consider gender differences in socialization that impact creativity in different ways at different ages.

A. Biological Theories

Gender differences in creative achievement vary considerably from field to field. In writing, musical performance, dance, and drama, the creative achievements of women are more on par with those of men than in such fields as science, musical composition, or painting. This imbalance led Vernon to argue in 1989 that social-environmental influences could not be the only causes of different patterns of creative achievement by men and women and that genetic factors must also play a role. In 1994, Simonton countered that active discrimination against women had often made it difficult or impossible for women to have access to the resources necessary for achievement in some fields. Thus, a woman might more easily succeed in a field like writing, where the necessary resources are few, than in musical composition or science, where lack of access to an orchestra or a well-equipped laboratory might make it far less likely that a woman could participate. Such differences, together with societal views toward success by women and men in a given place at a given time, might account for the unequal ratios of men and women who have had creative success in different fields.

Although there has been considerable speculation about genetic differences that might account for differences in creative behavior, there is very little research evidence regarding such differences. A few studies have investigated testosterone-related effects on brain development and speculated on possible differences in resulting patterns of hemispheric dominance and found limited support for such differences, but far more research is needed to support and clarify such hypotheses.

There is some evidence that androgyny, as measured by levels of salivary testosterone, is associated with higher levels of musical creativity. In one study a similar association with musical creativity was found for psychological androgyny. Psychological androgyny has not shown a consistent association with creativity, however. Studies correlating various indices of creativity with psychological femininity, masculinity, and androgyny have shown no consistent pattern.

B. Developmental Theories

Some theories of gender differences in creativity are connected to specific developmental stages. A number of theories have been tested experimentally, but none has received clear confirmation. One such theory proposed that boys tend to prefer accommodation and girls assimilation as ways to respond to new information. Because divergent thinking tests and other measures of children's creativity tend to favor novelty and innovation, this theory suggests they reward accommodation more than assimilation and therefore boys score higher than girls. This hypothesis contradicts the actual results of comparisons of boys' and girls' scores on divergent thinking tests, of course, in which boys clearly do not score higher. Independent tests of this hypothesis have failed to confirm it.

There is evidence that there are gender differences in the ways girls' and boys' creative performances are influenced by extrinsic motivation, such as praise and rewards. There is evidence, for example, that among middle school children, boys' creativity may be increased by such extrinsic constraints while girls' creativity may be significantly decreased. This difference appears to continue at least until college.

C. Sociocultural Theories

If gender differences in creative achievement are a function of sociocultural influences, one would expect to find cross-cultural differences in patterns of women's and men's creative achievements, as well as differences in those patterns as cultures change over time. In a 1992 analysis of almost 1400 years of creative achievement in Japan, Simonton found some evidence that supports the latter hypothesis. Although this study found that most of the contextual factors influencing creativity affected female and male creative achievement in similar ways, there were some factors, such as the level of importance in a given time period of two of the three predominant ideologies of Japan (Shinto and Confucianism, but not Buddhism), that appeared to work against female achievement in the arts but not against male success. [*See* CROSS-CULTURAL DIFFERENCES.]

Much of the evidence of cross-cultural influences that affect creativity differently in women and men has relied on creativity tests of one kind of another (primarily, but not exclusively, divergent thinking tests). In some non-Western cultures there is evidence that the process of Westernization leads to higher creativity test scores for girls and a narrowing or elimination of the gap between girls' and boys' scores. There is also evidence of what has been termed an "oversocializing" effect: The difference in creativity test scores which favors boys in traditional cultures (such as Arab culture) starts small and grows with increasing age. Girls in traditional cultures, according to this argument, are subject to "oversocialization"—a very inhibiting kind of socialization that restricts the development of creative thinking skill.

Perhaps the most interesting and significant theories are ones that have tried to explain why men have produced far more creative accomplishments than women. Helson argued in 1990 that cultural values, social roles, and sexist thinking explain the differences in creative achievement by women and men. As children, girls are less likely to be singled out as special by their parents. These early differences are then magnified by the rules, roles, and assumptions of cultures that expect men to seek power and women to be dominated, that encourage men to be independent and women to be dependent, and that see creativity as a male privilege.

In 1991, Piirto argued that girls do not show less creative achievement until after high school and college. This observation about the creative accomplishments of children and adolescents is in line with the results of comparisons of creativity test scores of children noted previously, in which girls score at least as well as boys. The crucial period for Piirto is the time following college. At this point creative people are making crucial life choices and resolving conflicts between their own goals and the expectations of others. Young women are pulled by their society away from the kind of intense commitment necessary for creative accomplishment. The roots of this difference in levels of commitment to a field of endeavor may be rooted in earlier decisions and influences—such as the role that parenthood will play in one's life, the importance of connectedness with others rather than separateness, and self-assessments of the quality of one's work—but Piirto argues that it is in early adulthood that decisions are made that pull more young men toward intense commitment to a field of creative endeavor and more young women away from such intense commitments.

IV. CONCLUSIONS

The consistent lack of gender differences in creativity both in creativity test scores and in the creative accomplishments of boys and girls make it difficult to build a strong case for innate gender differences in creativity. There may be innate gender differences—perhaps related, as some have suggested, to testosterone levels at crucial points in individual development—that relate to later differences in creative productivity, but thus far research in this area has not produced any hypotheses that have gained significant empirical support.

At the same time, the large difference in the creative accomplishments of men and women make simple environmental explanations inadequate, and the explanations we have thus far are at best incomplete. More research like Simonton's 1992 study of creative accomplishment of men and women over long historical time periods is needed to elucidate the major cultural influences that affect men and women creators differently. At the same time, large theories like those of Helson and Piirto need to be spelled out in detail in ways that will allow empirical testing of their various claims.

Bibliography

Abra, J., & Valentine-French, S. (1991). Gender differences in creative achievement: A survey of explanations. *Genetic, Social, and General Psychology Monographs, 117*, 235–284.

Baer, J. (in press). Gender differences in creativity. In M. A. Runco (Ed.), *Creativity research handbook* (Vol. 3). Cresskill, NJ: Hampton Press.

Barron, F., & Harrington, D. M. (1981). Creativity, intelligence, and personality. *Annual Review of Psychology, 32*, 439–476.

Feist, G. J., & Runco, M. A. (1993). Trends in the creativity literature: An analysis of research in the *Journal of Creative Behavior* (1967–1989). *Creativity Research Journal, 6*, 271–286.

Helson, R. (1990). Creativity in women: Outer and inner views over time. In M. A. Runco & R. S. Albert (Eds.), *Theories of creativity* (pp. 46–58). Newbury Park, CA: Sage.

Kogan, N. (1974). Creativity and sex differences. *Journal of Creative Behavior, 8*, 1–14.

Piirto, J. (1991). Why are there so few? (Creative women: Visual artists, mathematicians, musicians). *Roeper Review, 13*, 142–147.

Rejskind, F. G., Rapagna, S. O., & Gold, D. (1992). Gender differences in children's divergent thinking. *Creativity Research Journal, 5*, 165–174.

Simonton, D. K. (1992). Gender and genius in Japan: Feminine eminence in masculine culture. *Sex Roles, 27*, 101–119.

Simonton, D. K. (1994). *Greatness: Who makes history and why*. New York: Guilford Press.

Generativity Theory

Robert Epstein

United States International University
and Cambridge Center for Behavioral Studies

Automatic Chaining A process wherein a sequence of behaviors emerges when one behavior accidentally produces a stimulus that makes another behavior more likely. Also called auto-chaining.

Creativity Competencies Skills that are essential for the expression of creativity. The four core competencies for individuals are capturing (preserves new ideas as they occur), challenging (seeks challenges and manages failures), broadening (seeks diverse training and knowledge), and surrounding (makes frequent changes in the physical and social environments).

Extinction The cessation of reinforcement.

Frequency Profile A graph of overlapping frequency curves, each showing a moving sum or moving average of occurrences of various behaviors in small intervals of time.

Generativity Theory A formal theory of the creative process that suggests that new behavior is the result of an orderly competition among previously established behaviors.

Insight A cognitive process said to occur when the solution to a problem occurs to someone suddenly, without obvious precursors.

Probability Profile A graph of overlapping probability curves that shows how the probabilities of different behaviors in an individual change over time.

Reinforcer A consequence of behavior that strengthens that behavior.

Resurgence The reappearance of previously reinforced behaviors that occurs when a current behavior is no longer effective.

Transformation Functions A series of equations which, when employed iteratively in a state model, generate curves that can predict complex behaviors in an individual continuously in time.

GENERATIVITY THEORY *is a formal, predictive, empirically based theory of ongoing behavior in novel environments. Because it can be used to predict and engineer novel performances, it is also a theory of creativity. Generativity Theory suggests that novel behavior is the result of an orderly, dynamic competition among previously established behaviors. By using specific equations, called "transformation functions," in a state model, the theory can predict ongoing performances in individual subjects continuously in time. The theory has also been used to engineer novel, complex performances in both humans and animals. Management techniques derived from Generativity Theory have recently been applied in*

Copyright © 1999 by Academic Press
All rights of reproduction in any form reserved.

business and industry to enhance and direct employee creativity. Most recently, Generativity Theory has led to the development of tests that measure creativity competencies in both individuals and managers.

I. BACKGROUND

Generativity Theory has its origins in pigeon research conducted at Harvard University in the late 1970s and early 1980s. In a series of studies conducted by Robert Epstein, B. F. Skinner, and others, pigeons were shown to be able to behave in a variety of complex ways typical of human behavior. In the first of these studies, published in a satirical article in *Science* in 1980, pigeons appeared to demonstrate a form of "symbolic communication." The two pigeons, named Jack and Jill, were in adjacent chambers separated by a clear plastic partition. Jack initiated each exchange by pecking a sign labeled "What Color?" Jill, having seen this, thrust her head through a curtain where she could see one of three colors hidden from Jack's view—either red, green, or yellow. She then pecked the corresponding alphabet letter on her side of the partition—"R" for red, "G" for green, or "Y" for yellow. Jack, having observed this, rewarded Jill with food by pecking a sign labeled "Thank You," thus operating an automatic feeder in Jill's chamber. Finally, Jack pecked one of three colored disks on his side of partition which corresponded to the letter Jill had illuminated. Jack's feeder was then automatically operated, after which he initiated another sequence. Even though the colors behind Jill's curtain changed randomly at the beginning of each sequence, the birds were able to "communicate" with each other accurately for extended periods of time on more than 90 percent of the trials. Random selections of alphabet letters and colors would have yielded about a 33 percent rate of accuracy. Thus it appeared that the pigeons were able to communicate "messages" to each other using arbitrary symbols.

This study was conducted to demonstrate the power of operant conditioning techniques in establishing complex performances, reminiscent of an early study of Skinner's in which pigeons were taught to play Ping-Pong. It was intended in part as a form of criticism of current research on chimpanzees, in which it was common for researchers to "anthropomorphize"—that

is, to mistakenly attribute higher-order human cognitive abilities to animals, often ignoring simpler explanations for the human-like behavior they observed.

The Jack and Jill study was perhaps more of a political statement than a scientific study, but it soon led to a series of studies—with unlikely titles such as "The Spontaneous Use of Memoranda by Pigeons," "Spontaneous Tool Use in the Pigeon," "'Self-Awareness' in the Pigeon," "'Insight' in the Pigeon," "The Spontaneous Interconnection of Four Repertoires of Behavior in a Pigeon," and so on—which, over time, shed significant light on the laws that govern the emergence of novel, complex behavior in both animals and people.

II. "INSIGHT" IN THE PIGEON

In perhaps the most striking of these studies, published by Epstein and his colleagues in *Nature* in 1984, pigeons solved a classic problem—the so-called "box-and-banana problem"—first studied by Gestalt psychologist Wolfgang Köhler in the early 1900s. In one variation of the problem, a banana was suspended out of reach of a group of chimpanzees, and a wooden crate was placed on the floor a few feet away from the position of the banana. The chimpanzees' attempts to reach the banana by reaching and jumping proved fruitless. After a few tries, most of the chimpanzees did little else of interest in this situation. But one chimp, named Sultan, paced back and forth between the banana and the crate for several minutes, apparently confused and frustrated. Then, suddenly, he moved the crate into position beneath the banana, climbed onto the crate, and managed to jump from there and retrieve the banana. Köhler could offer no explanation for this remarkable performance other than to suggest that it demonstrated "insight." [*See* INSIGHT.]

In the *Nature* study, Epstein and his colleagues first gave pigeons various types of training and then confronted them with the box-and-banana problem. All of the pigeons received food for pecking a small facsimile of a banana when the banana was within reach. Subsequently all of the pigeons readily oriented toward and pecked the toy banana whenever it was placed nearby at eye level. Some of the pigeons were also taught to push a small box around the floor of their chamber. Still others were taught more precise pushing: to push the box toward targets placed at different locations along the base of the wall of the chamber. Some pigeons were also taught to climb onto a box and to peck the banana directly overhead, and some pigeons learned that jumping and flying in the direction of the toy banana when it was suspended out of reach did not produce a food reward; in effect, they learned to ignore the banana when it was suspended out of reach.

After training, each pigeon was confronted with the classic problem: The toy banana was suspended out of reach, and the box was placed elsewhere in the chamber. None of the pigeons had ever seen this particular arrangement before. Each pigeon behaved in new ways when confronted with this new situation, and the general finding was that the new behavior that emerged was systematically related to the training the bird had received prior to the test. For example, birds that had learned (a) to climb and peck, (b) to push the box directionally, and (c) to ignore the banana when it was suspended out of reach, solved the problem in a remarkably Sultan-like (and human-like) way. At first they motioned back and forth between the box and the banana in apparent confusion and then, suddenly, began to push the box toward the banana, sighting the banana as they pushed. When the box was beneath the banana, they stopped pushing, climbed, and pecked. The entire performance typically took about a minute to complete (Figure 1).

A bird that had not learned to ignore the banana when it was out of reach spent about 4 min jumping and flying toward the banana before finally solving the problem in a rapid fashion. A bird that had been

FIGURE 1 "Insight" in the pigeon. When faced with the box-and-banana problem for the first time (A and B), at first the pigeon looks back and forth between the banana and the box in apparent confusion; (C) then, suddenly, it begins to push the box toward the banana, sighting the banana as it pushes, and (D) stops pushing when the box is beneath the banana, climbs onto the box, and pecks the toy banana.

taught to climb and peck but that had never learned to push the box toward targets rarely looked up while pushing the box around the chamber. After 14 min of pushing, it happened to look up when the box was beneath the banana, at which point it immediately climbed and pecked—a performance one might label "trial-and-error." Birds that had never learned to push did not push the box during the test, and birds that had never learned to climb also failed to solve the problem.

The point is that a wide range of novel performances—from failures to trial-and-error performances to "insightful" ones—can be understood, at least in part, by looking at the particular training history of the animal. What's more, the authors offered a tentative moment-to-moment account of the emergence of the novel performances in terms of laws and principles that govern the transformation of previously established behaviors in novel situations. The account can be considered an early, informal version of Generativity Theory.

III. THE TWO-STRING PROBLEM

In a series of publications beginning in 1985, Epstein introduced a formal methodology for analyzing, predicting, and engineering complex novel performances in animals and people. In an application of this methodology with human subjects, Epstein showed that the behavior of people confronted with Norman Maier's classic "two-string" problem can be modeled using principles from Generativity Theory which have been cast into mathematical form. In the two-string problem, the subject is shown into a room in which two long strings are suspended from a high ceiling. The researcher points to an object, such as a pliers, which is positioned on table, and says, "Your task is to tie the ends of these strings together. If necessary, you may use this object to help you."

The subject immediately takes hold of one string and pulls it toward the other, only to find that the strings are so far apart they cannot be touched simultaneously (see Figure 2). Typically, and the laws of geometry notwithstanding, the subject then takes hold of the second string and pulls it toward the first. Some subjects repeat this pattern several times. Eventually, the subject

FIGURE 2   When faced with the two-string problem, subjects usually begin by pulling one string toward the other. After they find that they cannot reach the second string, they often pull the second string toward the first.

may try to use the object to extend his or her reach, but that does not work either, since the object is never long enough to allow contact with the other string. The solution to the problem is to tie the object to one string and to set that string in motion in a large arc—in other words, to construct a pendulum. Then the subject simply walks over to the second string, pulls it back toward the swinging string, and catches the swinging string when it swings within reach. With one string now in each hand, it is a simple matter to tie the ends together.

Epstein showed that outcomes in this performance can be systematically altered by changing simple features of the object on the table. For example, given a relatively long object (but not long enough to allow contact with the second string), subjects have enormous difficulty solving the problem; some cannot solve it at all, presumably because long objects are typically used for reaching, not for constructing pendulums. Given a relatively short object, subjects solve the problem readily—usually within a minute or two.

Of greater importance, Epstein showed that simple principles of behavior, instantiated in a computer model, can predict different types of performances under different stimulus conditions. In Figure 3, for example, overlapping probability curves are shown for a performance involving a short object. The curves show a fairly smooth transition from (a) pulling one string

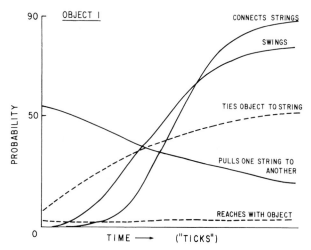

FIGURE 3 A probability profile generated by the transformation functions mentioned in the text (Figure 4), shown for five behaviors in the two-string problem. The *x*-axis is labeled "ticks," which are cycles of the computer algorithm. The profile was generated with parameters for the short object (Object 1), which produced rapid solutions to the problem and no irrelevant reaching. Note that pulling one string toward the other decreases steadily in probability and that other behaviors increase in probability in an orderly sequence. Tying the object to the string makes swinging more likely, which, in turn, makes connecting the strings more likely.

toward the other, to (b) tying the object to a string, to (c) setting one string in motion, and to (d) connecting the strings.

IV. REAL-TIME PREDICTION

According to Generativity Theory, novel behavior (including the verbal and perceptual behaviors we often call "ideas") is the result of an orderly and dynamic competition among previously established behaviors, during which old behaviors blend or become interconnected in new ways. If the process is so orderly, why does creativity seem so mysterious, and why do people often feel confused or frustrated before or during creative episodes? [*See* NOVELTY.]

The air of mystery surrounding creativity is probably due to several factors. For one thing, when behaviors are competing, the nervous system is in some sense overloaded, and we feel that overload as confusion

and frustration. It is difficult enough to experience this process and harder still to try to analyze it while it is occurring. The process of interconnection is also fairly complex—typically so complex that it takes the power of a computer to analyze the process. The computational complexity of the process alone is probably enough to make it seem mysterious. New ideas often seem to come out of the blue, mainly because we cannot track the antecedent events or processes.

Computer simulations model the interconnection process using a mathematical "state" system. In each cycle of the algorithm—in other words, each state of the system—several behavioral processes are assumed to be occurring simultaneously, with each operating on the probabilities of multiple behaviors. Each process is represented by a simple equation, called a "transformation function" (Figure 4), and each cycle is assumed to represent a very small interval of time. At the end of a cycle, the resulting probabilities are plugged back into the same equations to begin the next cycle. Surprisingly, with repeated cycling, the probabilities change in increments small enough to yield relatively smooth curves (Figure 3), which together comprise a "probability profile"—a graphical picture of how the various behaviors are expected to change over time.

The equations shown in Figure 4 are labeled with the names of empirically established behavioral laws, such as extinction (the decrement in responding that

(1) *Extinction:* $y_{n+1} = y_n - y_n * \epsilon$

(2) *Reinforcement:* $y_{n+1} = y_n + (1 - y_n) * \alpha$

(3) *Resurgence:* for $\lambda_{yy'} < 0$ and $y'_n - y'_{n-1} < 0$,

$y_{n+1} = y_n + (1 - y_n) * (-\lambda_{yy'}) * y'_n$

(4) *Automatic Chaining:* for $\lambda_{yy'} > 0$ and $y'_n - y'_{n-1} > 0$,

$y_{n+1} = y_n + (1 - y_n) * \lambda_{yy'} * y'_n$

FIGURE 4 Equations used to generate the probability profiles shown in Figures 3 and 5. y_n is the probability of behavior *y* at cycle *n* of the algorithm, y'_n is the probability of behavior *y'* at cycle *n* of the algorithm, ϵ is a constant for extinction (it determines the rate at which the probability of behavior *y* decreases over cycles of the algorithm), α is a constant for reinforcement (it determines the rate at which the probability of behavior *y* increases over cycles of the algorithm as a result of certain environmental events), and $\lambda_{yy'}$ is the constant of interaction between behaviors *y* and *y'*.

occurs when reinforcement is withheld), reinforcement (the strengthening of behavior that occurs when behavior has certain consequences), resurgence (the reappearance of old behaviors that occurs when current behavior is ineffective), and automatic chaining (the sequencing of behaviors that occurs when one behavior accidentally generates a stimulus that occasions another behavior). Other laws can easily be incorporated into this type of model, and equations can be refined so as to represent various laws more accurately.

Epstein has also developed a new method for plotting the behavior of an individual subject in graphical form. This type of graph, called a "frequency profile," yields overlapping curves that are similar to probability curves in some respects, and it can be generated in real time or post hoc. A frequency profile is generated by computing a moving average or sum across binary values that represent the occurrence or nonoccurrence of each of the individual's behaviors in small intervals of time. Comparing the curves of a probability profile to the curves of a frequency profile allows one to evaluate the accuracy of a simulation (Figure 5).

In recent years, Epstein and his colleagues have used this methodology to study and simulate the behavior of both adults and children performing a wide variety of tasks. Typically, a subject is asked to solve a problem using various toys or unusual objects. The performance is videotaped and later coded, which allows a frequency profile to be constructed and models to be generated. Most recently, subjects have been given problems to solve on a computer touch screen, so that both frequency profiles and probability profiles can be generated in real time. This methodology may soon allow relatively complex novel performances in individual human subjects to be predicted continuously in real time.

V. CREATIVITY COMPETENCIES

Generativity Theory suggests that the generative mechanisms that underlie creativity are universal. After all, variability is the rule in behavior; no one brushes his or her teeth the same way twice, and it is rare that we repeat the same sentence. We also negotiate our way through new supermarkets and malls reasonably

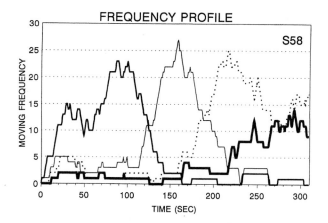

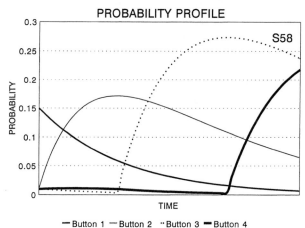

FIGURE 5 A frequency profile (top panel) and a corresponding probability profile (bottom panel) for an individual subject who is trying to solve a simple problem on a computer touch screen. Over a 5-min period, the subject gradually shifts from one strategy to another in an attempt to move a spot across the screen. Actual (top) and predicted (bottom) curves follow the same pattern.

well; in other words, novel stimuli reliably produce novel, fairly effective behaviors in just about everyone. We all solve problems, large and small, throughout the day. We all daydream, we all have fantastic dreams at night, and we all enter the fertile "hypnagogic" state— the odd semisleep state we experience just before we fall fully asleep. Moreover, generativity models seem to work well with everyone; only parametric changes are needed to accommodate different individuals.

But if generative mechanisms are universal, why do so few people express creativity? There are two principle reasons. First, as part of the socialization process that begins when children enter the first grade (at about age 6), children are severely discouraged from expressing new or unusual ideas, and daydreaming is strictly forbidden. In kindergarten, virtually all children are creative, whereas very few children express creativity by the end of the first grade. This is not because of some sudden change in the brain; it is due entirely to educational demands. Second, the expression of creativity depends on a set of "competencies"—particular skills and abilities that underlie successful performance. For obvious reasons, creativity competencies are not taught in our school systems. A small number of people manage to acquire some of these competencies by accident or through certain role models—the uncle who composes music, for example, or the inventor who lives down the street. The vast majority of people, however, have very few of the skills needed for the expression of creativity. Alas, the children who continue to express creativity throughout the school years are the ones who are difficult to socialize. In other words, our society inadvertently makes creativity the nearly exclusive property of antisocial personality types.

Generativity Theory suggests four core competency areas—capturing, challenging, broadening, and surrounding—that are critical for the expression of creativity in individuals, as well as eight competency areas that allow teachers and managers to elicit creativity in others. Validated tests, called, respectively, the Epstein Creativity Competencies Inventory for Individuals (ECCI-i) and the Epstein Creativity Competencies Inventory for Managers (ECCI-m) have been developed to measure both core and managerial competencies, and training programs now exist to boost competencies that are weak. The four individual creativity competencies are as follows:

1. *Preserves new ideas* ("Capturing"). The individual preserves new ideas as they occur and manages resources to aid in this process. The elite group of people we tend to call "creative" typically have superb capturing skills. Artists carry sketch pads compulsively; writers carry notebooks or tape recorders and keep such tools by their beds at night; and inventors record ideas on napkins, sleeves, or skin when proper writing materials are unavailable. It is easy to learn capturing skills and to surround oneself with the tools that make capturing likely.

2. *Seeks challenges* ("Challenging"). The individual subjects him- or herself to difficult and challenging tasks that require performance exceeding current levels of skills or knowledge. New ideas emerge when multiple repertoires of behavior compete, and one of the simplest ways to get multiple behaviors going is through the resurgence of old behaviors that occurs when current behavior is ineffective. When you are locked in a room, for example, every behavior that has ever gotten you through a closed door becomes more probable: jiggling the door knob, pounding on the door, kicking the door, shouting for help, and so on. From these various behaviors, new sequences or new blends emerge. Thus, learning to manage failure—and not to fear failure—is an important means of boosting creativity.

3. *Broadens skills and knowledge* ("Broadening"). The individual seeks training, experience, and knowledge outside of current areas of expertise. The more diverse the repertoires of behavior, the more interesting, frequent, and surprising the interconnections.

4. *Changes physical and social environment* ("Surrounding"). The individual changes his or her physical and social environments on a regular basis. Resurgence gets multiple repertoires competing, and so do unusual or diverse stimuli. A static environment is deadly for generative processes.

The eight creativity competencies for managers and teachers derive from the core competencies just listed, but additional skills are also required, because the manager's principle function is to develop and nurture the core competencies in other people. The eight competencies for managers are as follows: [*See* Corporate Culture.]

1. *Encourages preservation of new ideas.* The manager provides opportunities, encouragement, and resources that allow others to preserve new ideas as they occur. In the corporate setting, this can be achieved through training, by providing appropriate supplies or software, by establishing anonymous suggestion systems, and through many other methods.

2. *Challenges others.* The manager presents others with difficult and challenging tasks. One of the simplest ways to do this is by making sure that all tasks, goals, and assignments are stated in an "open-ended" form—a form that neither states nor implies boundaries or limits. A variety of "controlled failure systems" can be established to manage failure productively in organizational settings.

3. *Encourages broadening of knowledge and skills.* The manager provides opportunities for others to obtain training, experience, and knowledge outside of their current areas of expertise.

4. *Manages surroundings to stimulate creativity.* The manager changes the physical and social environments of other people on a regular basis.

5. *Manages teams to stimulate creativity.* The individual manages teams and workgroups to optimize creative output. For example, since creativity is fundamentally an individual process, the creative output of a team is greatly enhanced through a simple technique called "shifting": Team members are shifted in and out of the group so that they alternate between periods in which they work on the problem alone and periods when they work on the problem with others.

6. *Manages resources to stimulate creativity.* The manager seeks to provide others with adequate resources to allow them to develop new ideas.

7. *Provides feedback and recognition to stimulate creativity.* The manager interacts with others in ways that encourage creative thinking. This involves withholding judgment at certain times, providing incentives for the expression of new ideas, and so on.

8. *Models appropriate creativity-management skills.* The individual sets a good example by managing his or her own creativity skillfully, meaning that he or she has strong core competencies.

Through training, modification of the physical and social environments, the establishment of controlled failure systems, proper team management, appropriate evaluation systems, the proper use of incentives and feedback, and other means, the creative output of both individuals and groups can be both enhanced and directed toward desired ends.

VI. CONCLUSIONS

Generativity Theory provides a powerful framework for the scientific study and understanding of the creative process. The theory and related research have demonstrated that the creative process in individuals is orderly and predictable continuously in time. The theory also suggests that the generative processes that underlie creativity are universal and that, with appropriate training, almost anyone will display a high degree of creativity. Few people have the appropriate competencies necessary for the expression of creativity because our educational system does not teach these competencies and because society in general discourages most people from expressing creativity. Generativity Theory provides guidelines for identifying the necessary competencies, assessing current competency levels, and providing the appropriate training.

Bibliography

Epstein, R. (1985). Extinction-induced resurgence: Preliminary investigations and possible applications. *Psychological Record, 35,* 143–153.

Epstein, R. (1991). Skinner, creativity, and the problem of spontaneous behavior. *Psychological Science, 6,* 362–370.

Epstein, R. (1996). Capturing creativity. *Psychology Today, 29*(4), 41–43, 75, 76, 78.

Epstein, R. (1996). *Creativity games for trainers.* New York: McGraw–Hill.

Epstein, R. (1996). *Cognition, creativity, and behavior: Selected essays.* Westport, CT: Praeger.

Epstein, R., Kirshnit, C. E., Lanza, R. P., & Rubin, L. C. (1984). "Insight" in the pigeon: Antecedents and determinants of an intelligent performance. *Nature, 308,* 61–62.

Epstein, R., Lanza, R. P., & Skinner, B. F. (1980). Symbolic communication between two pigeons (*Columbia livia domestica*). *Science, 207,* 543–545.

Genetics

Colin Martindale
University of Maine

Cross-Fostering Method A twin study in which the twins were reared apart. The method allows one to rule out the possibility that monozygotic twins are more similar than dizygotic twins because they are treated in a more similar manner, spend more time together, etc.

Emergenesis A situation in which a trait will appear if and only if all of its component subtraits are present. Even if all of the subtraits are normally distributed, emergenic traits show a log-normal distribution. That is, they are extremely skewed with a very long upper tail: very few people show high levels of the trait.

Heritability The proportion of variance in a trait that can be attributed to genetic factors. In twin studies, heritability is computed as two times the difference between the intraclass correlation for monozygotic (identical) twins and dizygotic (fraternal) twins.

Intraclass Correlation The proportion of variance in a trait that is common to the twins in a sample.

Psychoticism After extroversion–introversion and neuroticism–stability, the third main dimension along which personality varies. According to Eysenck, psychoticism is a genetic trait predisposing people to psychosis, criminality, and creativ-

ity depending upon the degree to which it is present. Those having low degrees of psychoticism are conventional, tender-minded, and empathic; those having high degrees are cold, antisocial, and unempathic.

Twin Study The most common method of studying heritability. Monozygotic twins have identical genes, whereas dizygotic twins share only half of their genes. To the degree that monozygotic twins are more similar on a trait than dizygotic twins, we can infer that the trait has a genetic basis.

Genius-level creativity is an extremely rare trait. It is difficult to imagine environmental factors that could possibly produce the likes of a Newton or a Gauss. In fact, the early environments of Newton and Gauss were, if anything, impoverished. Other immensely creative people coming from environments that did nothing at all to encourage creativity include Michael Faraday and George Washington Carver. This leads us to expect that creativity must in large part arise from GENETIC FACTORS. However, if we examine the relatives of Newton, Gauss, Faraday, or Carver, we find that they are not at all creative.

Efforts to teach people to be more creative have been notably unsuccessful. When they have succeeded at all, they have amounted essentially to "teaching the test." If one is more or less told the correct answers to a test, it

Copyright © 1999 by Academic Press
All rights of reproduction in any form reserved.

is hardly surprising that he or she will do well on the test. However, teaching people to be creative on one test of creativity does not generalize to other tests of creativity. In a way, this is surprising. We have a fairly good idea of what is necessary in order to be creative, thus creativity is quite easy to teach. The problem is that it seems to be impossible to learn. If one cannot teach creativity, this suggests that it must be genetic, but early studies of the heritability of creativity were disappointing. They yielded heritability coefficients on the order of .20 or so. This contrasts markedly with studies of the heritability of intelligence, where virtually all properly conducted studies yield a heritability coefficient of around .70. [*See* ENHANCEMENT OF CREATIVITY; TEACHING CREATIVITY.]

Several lines of evidence have converged that shed light on the question of the genetics of creativity. A number of studies have shown very high levels of psychopathology, especially affective disorders, in eminently creative people. Because these disorders have a large genetic component, it is suggestive that creativity may also have a genetic component. It has been shown that there is a genetic relationship between creativity and schizophrenia. Creative people exhibit very low rates of schizophrenia, but the relatives of schizophrenics are markedly more creative than the relatives of people without a family history of schizophrenia. Such findings led Hans Eysenck in 1995 to propose that creativity and various forms of psychopathology have a common genetic basis which he labeled psychoticism. [*See* MAD GENIUS CONTROVERSY.]

It has become increasingly clear that creativity is an emergenic trait. That is, creative achievement will not occur unless all of a set of subtraits are present. These subtraits include the ability to think in a certain fashion, self-confidence verging on megalomania, love of novelty, special talents, capacity for and love of extremely hard work, and an obsessive interest in ideas (and a possible corresponding lack of interest in other people). This list is certainly not complete. The point is that if any one of these subtraits is absent, creativity will be absent. This is because the subtraits combine in a multiplicative rather than an additive fashion. Niels Waller and colleagues reported in 1993 on the most extensive study of the heritability of creativity. For identical twins, they found an intraclass correlation

of almost .60 for a creative personality scales but an intraclass correlation of essentially zero for fraternal twins. This makes sense if creativity is emergenic. If a large number of traits must be present before creativity emerges, the probability that all these traits would be present in fraternal twins is vanishingly small. Note that if heritability is computed as described in the glossary, these results give us a heritability quotient of 1.00 for creativity. This must be a bit of an overestimate, but it is certainly possible that creativity is about as heritable as traits such as eye color or height.

I. GENERAL CONSIDERATIONS

If one encounters an unmedicated psychotic in a florid state, it is impossible to imagine an environment so malign as to produce such a state of mind. By the same token, it is impossible to imagine an environment so benign as to produce a Newton or a Gauss. Genius-level creativity is extremely rare, but benign early environments are very common. Millions of children have been raised by wonderful parents who were warm, encouraging in every respect that the child fulfill his or her potentialities, provided every possible benefit, and—as probably the majority of parents of this sort—had the delusion that the child was a genius. Why, then, have there not been millions of geniuses?

In fact, the early environments of Gauss and Newton were not at all conducive to creativity. Gauss's father was a bricklayer and Newton's a farmer. Gauss's father did not encourage him; Newton's could not, as he died before Newton was born. George Washington Carver was the son of slaves. He did receive encouragement but from kind people with no great ability. Because of racist policies, he literally had to fight to get an education of any sort and was in large part self-educated. Yet, he became as productive as Thomas Edison, who in the 1920s offered him an unheard of, for those times, salary of $100,000 per year if he would work in Edison's laboratory. (He declined the offer because he did not think that he should accept money for his discoveries.) A number of studies have shown that eminently creative people tend to have childhood environments that should on the face of it be detrimental to creativity. For example, as compared with the general population, they tend to lose a parent during childhood or have antagonistic or domineering parents.

One can go to any large bookstore and find dozens of pop psychology books telling one how to become more creative. These books apparently sell rather well and give rather sound advice. Why, then, have we not seen an upsurge in creativity across the last several decades during which these books have been produced? It would seem that creativity is very easy to teach but impossible to learn. Thus, it would appear that genius must be born, and not taught. If such books succeed at all, they succeed in merely "teaching the test." That is, if one is told the correct answers to a test, then he or she will obviously do quite well on the test or very similar tests. There is no evidence showing that "teaching the test" will improve performance on creativity tests of another sort, let alone improve real-life creativity.

The preceding considerations suggest that creativity cannot be mainly due to environmental factors. Some other considerations point in the same direction but are not so clear-cut. Let us consider sex differences in creative achievement. No one denies that men outnumber women in most areas of creative endeavor by several orders of magnitude. The difference is greatest for the physical sciences; mathematics, where an honest estimate would give perhaps two or three genius-level women mathematicians; and music—an honest estimate would be around 12 women composers who we would want to label as eminent. There is not a single woman represented in the 120 most famous composers from the Renaissance to the present. The difference is large, but smaller, in the case of literature. One explanation is that women were formerly oppressed or not encouraged. Another explanation is that genetic factors may be involved.

Research on gender differences has found some consistent differences in abilities. For instance, men generally do better at right-hemisphere tasks, including music, whereas women usually do better at left-hemisphere tasks, including language. Women are also better at linguistic fluency than are men. This may explain why the discrepancy between great male and female writers is not as great as the discrepancy between great male and female composers. Interestingly,

women score higher than men on tests of creative potential; but historically have not actualized this potential. Women also score much lower than men on psychoticism, a trait that has been argued to be necessary for creative achievement. Another gender difference is that males are typically more interested in things, while females are typically more interested in people. Thus, though females may be talented, this talent will not be actualized if their interests are devoted to other people rather than to things and ideas. It remains to be seen the extent to which these gender differences are genetically or environmentally caused, but many researchers believe genetics to play an important part. [*See* GENDER DIFFERENCES; WOMEN AND CREATIVITY.]

II. EARLY STUDIES

The scientific study of the heritability of creativity began in 1869 with the publication of Sir Francis Galton's *Hereditary Genius*. Galton's thesis was that genius is a biologically transmitted trait. As such, it should run in families. In order to find out, he collected the family trees of hundreds of eminent men and made the argument that they did in fact have eminent relatives. In general, Galton did not make a very convincing case. His evidence for distinction in relatives of eminent men was often as flimsy as an aunt who liked to read a lot. For Beethoven, the best he could do was repeat the baseless rumor that he was the illegitimate son of Frederick the Great, who could play the flute rather well. In the case of Newton, Galton did come up with some fairly distinguished people, but it was not clear that they were really Newton's relatives. It has since been shown, using his own data, that Galton was wrong. Creativity does not run in families. Talent does seem to run in families, but high-level creativity does not.

In 1976, R. C. Nichols reviewed a large number of twin studies, including 10 in which divergent thinking, an aspect of creativity, was studied. The average heritability coefficient for divergent thinking was only .22. This was by far the lowest heritability for the 12 types of abilities surveyed. The average heritability for all 12 was .42. For six types of interests surveyed, the average heritability was .38. For the nine personality traits surveyed, average heritability was .38. These twin studies of divergent thinking can be criticized on several grounds. First, each used a small number of subjects. Second, the tests of divergent thinking used were not especially valid or reliable. [*See* DIVERGENT THINKING.]

III. GENETIC RELATIONSHIP BETWEEN CREATIVITY AND PSYCHOPATHOLOGY

In the 19th century, degeneration theorists argued that the rate of psychopathology among eminently creative people is extremely high. They attributed this to degeneration of higher nervous centers that was passed in a Lamarckian fashion from generation to generation. When it became clear that Lamarckian transmission does not occur, the baby was thrown out with the bath water, and degeneration theory as a whole was dismissed. By the 1950s, creativity was generally thought to be related to positive mental health. In the last several decades, matters have been clarified. Eminently creative people do in fact show extremely high levels of psychopathology. For example, a study of creative British writers and artists showed that 38% had been treated for mental disorder, in almost all cases of an affective sort. For the general population, the lifetime prevalence rate for bipolar disorder is 1% and for depression, 5%. In another study, 291 eminent individuals were diagnosed. Diagnoses of severe psychopathology were given to 18% of the scientists, 31% of the composers, 38% of the artists, and 46% of the writers. However, a diagnosis of psychosis was given to only 1.7% of the sample and none were diagnosed as schizophrenic. In this as in many other studies, the subjects were found to be high in ego strength or resilience. In the general population, ego strength and psychopathology are negatively correlated. Because most types of psychopathology, and especially affective disorders, are based upon genetic predisposition, the relationship between creativity and psychopathology suggests that creativity may be more heritable than earlier studies suggested.

There is a clear genetic relationship between creativity and schizophrenia. This was demonstrated in a study comparing schizophrenia-prone subjects (people with large numbers of schizophrenic relatives for the last several generations) with subjects not prone to schizophrenia (people with no schizophrenic relatives for the last several generations). The relatives of the schizophrenia-prone subjects were markedly more creative (as evidenced by production of books, poems, patents, etc.) than the relatives of those not prone to schizophrenia.

The family trees of schizophrenics are interesting in that they not only show large numbers of schizophrenics but also large numbers of criminals, creative people, and people suffering from affective disorders. This led Hans Eysenck in 1995 to propose that the genetic trait of psychoticism predisposes one to schizophrenia, affective disorder, criminality, and creativity. He argues that a moderate degree of psychoticism leads to creativity, whereas higher levels lead to criminality, affective disorders, and schizophrenia, in that order. People high in psychoticism are aggressive, cold, egocentric, impersonal, impulsive, antisocial, unempathic, and tough-minded. They also have wide associative horizons (give unusual responses on word association tests) and a tendency toward defocused attention. These are also traits found in creative people. Several studies have shown that creativity is correlated with psychoticism. This is especially the case for real-life creativity. Results using paper and pencil tests of creativity have generally yielded positive results but not in all cases. [*See* SCHIZOPHRENIA.]

Eysenck's argument is that psychoticism is a genetically transmitted trait. What is transmitted is relatively high levels of dopamine and low levels of serotonin. These lead to a lack of cognitive inhibition which in turn leads to creative potential. For actual creative achievement to emerge, other things—for example, intelligence, motivational and cognitive factors, special talent, and various sociocultural factors—must also be present.

IV. EMERGENESIS

Emergenesis is an important concept introduced by David Lykken in 1982. An emergenic trait is one that appears if and only if a number of independent traits are all present. Most genetic effects are additive. An example is height. One's height is determined by taking an average of the mother's and father's height. The intraclass correlation for height of identical twins is

.95. (It is not 1.00 because of minor environmental influences such as nutrition.) As would be expected, the intraclass correlation for fraternal twins is about .50 because they only share half of their genes. Emergenic traits are synergistic or multiplicative: all of the component traits must be present or the trait will not emerge, because multiplying anything by zero yields a result of zero. According to Lykken, high monozygotic twin similarities and low dizygotic twin similarities are strongly suggestive that we are dealing with an emergenic trait. This is because it is unlikely that dizygotic twins would end up with all of the necessary component traits. It is thus very unlikely that an emergenic trait would aggregate in a family. If creativity is an emergenic trait, then Galton's idea that creativity would run in families if it were genetic is wrong. If creativity aggregated in families, this would actually suggest environmental rather than genetic influences.

Creativity does seem to be an emergenic trait. That is, it depends upon the simultaneous presence of a number of traits. None of these traits is especially rare. What is extremely rare is to have all of these traits present in the same person. Some of the traits include tendency toward reverie, high intelligence, propensity for hard work, and extreme self-confidence.

Bibliography

Eysenck, H. J. (1995). *Genius: The natural history of creativity.* Cambridge: Cambridge University Press.

Galton, F. (1869/1978). *Hereditary genius.* New York: Friedmann.

Lombroso, C. (1894/1901). *The man of genius* (6th ed.). New York: Scribner's Sons.

Lykken, D. T. (1982). Research with twins: The concept of emergenesis. *Psychophysiology, 19,* 361–373.

Martindale, C. (1989). Personality, situation, and creativity. In J. A. Glover, R. R. Ronning, & C. R. Reynolds (Eds.), *Handbook of creativity* (pp. 211–232). New York: Plenum.

Nichols, R. C. (1976). Twin studies of ability, personality and interests. *Homo, 29,* 158–173.

Nordau, M. (1895). *Degeneration* (5th ed.). London: Heinemann.

Stein, M. (1974–1975). *Stimulating creativity* (2 vols.). New York: Academic Press.

Waller, N. G., Bouchard, T., Lykken, D. T., Tellegen, A., & Blacker, D. M. (1993). Why creativity does not run in families: A study of twins reared apart. *Psychological Inquiry, 4,* 235–237.

Giftedness and Creativity

John F. Feldhusen

Purdue University

Ability General capacity to meet the demands of daily life.

Aptitude Specific ability derived from factor analysis of a general ability test.

Creative Problem Solving Metacognitive skills that enhance or facilitate creative thinking processes.

Creative Productivity Creative activity that yields new ideas, products, devices, or works of art.

Creative Thinking The cognitive processes that yield new ideas, products, devices, or works of art.

Creativity Creation of new ideas, products, devices, or works of art that are seen as enhancing our lives.

Gifted Possessing special general abilities superior to those of the general population.

Giftedness A state of having superior general abilities.

Gifts Things given to us without remuneration. Here, especially abilities that enhance our lives.

Talent Superior aptitude or ability in a worthwhile line of human endeavor.

GIFTEDNESS *may be defined as a superior ability in any worthwhile line of human endeavor.*

The major definition of giftedness in the United States was presented in the Marland Report (p. 2) in 1972:

> Gifted and talented children are those identified by professionally qualified persons who by virtue of outstanding abilities, are capable of high performance. These are children who require differentiated educational programs and/or services beyond those normally provided by the regular school program in order to realize their contribution to self and society.
>
> Children capable of high performance include those with demonstrated achievement and/or potential ability in any of the following areas, singly or in combination:
> (1) general intellectual ability
> (2) specific academic aptitude
> (3) creative or productive thinking
> (4) leadership ability
> (5) visual and performing arts
> (6) psychomotor ability

While this model stresses a comprehensive view of giftedness, in practice the definition has often been limited to academic areas and abilities. [*See* DEFINITIONS OF CREATIVITY.]

In an update, that definition from the U.S. Office of

Copyright © 1999 by Academic Press
All rights of reproduction in any form reserved.

Education was revised in 1993 and is now stated as follows:

> Children and youth with outstanding talent perform or show the potential for performing at remarkably high levels of accomplishment when compared with others of their age, experience, or environment.
>
> These children and youth exhibit high performance capability in intellectual, creative, and/or artistic areas, possess an unusual leadership capacity, or excel in specific academic fields. They require services or activities not ordinarily provided by the schools.
>
> Outstanding talents are present in children and youth from all cultural groups, across all economic strata, and in all areas of human endeavor. (p. 26)

The definition is notable for its shift away from the term "gifted." The authors even suggest that "giftedness" denotes a mature power and should not be used to classify children as is common practice in schools. The definition also remains broad but school practice continues to be academic in its focus in programs for gifted youth, but creative areas were noted in the new definition and creativity is often stressed in school programs.

Definitions of creativity abound in the literature, ranging from relatively simple innovations or adaptive behaviors of children and adults to the kind of things that people do that change the world. The following definition summarizes and unites the several views and probably will serve best as a guiding conception in further efforts to understand and control the processes called "creativity":

> People of all ages are constantly confronted by problems and situations that require decisions and provide them with opportunities to improve the human condition and enable them to understand phenomena in their lives. Every day they must act or behave in new or different ways because they are unable to solve the problems or resolve the situations using their current repertoire of knowledge and skills. Thus, these problems and situations require creativity, that is, innovative or adaptive thinking and behavior.

While some systems for the identification of gifted students have included creativity as one criterion, most of the systems for identification have focused on youths' academic aptitudes and achievements. In schools throughout the United States it is common practice to administer tests of academic aptitude, to secure achievement test scores from existing files, to combine these with teacher ratings of their students' intellectual characteristics, to set local criteria for the gifted classification, and then to declare the candidates as "gifted" or "not gifted." There has been much criticism of these procedures.

I. HISTORICAL BACKGROUND

The concept of giftedness dates to ancient times. The gospel writer Mark tells us that we are born with diverse gifts that should be used or manifested accordingly. Later Shakespeare describes the scene in which Macbeth interviews prospective murderers and asks that they present their special gifts that qualify them to murder King Duncan. However, the definitive specification of the concept of giftedness came with the work of Binet at the turn of the century in the development of intelligence testing, and its culmination with Terman's development of the Stanford–Binet scale in 1916 and his pioneering research on gifted children. [*See* INTELLIGENCE.]

The phenomenon of creativity has also engaged the thoughts of men and women for many centuries. The opening chapters and verses of the Christian Bible describe the creation of human beings and the world in which they would live. Later the writers of the Bible would produce the first great record of the verbal, creative work of human beings. Subsequent written works of Greek, Roman, Islamic, and Oriental scholars recorded the evolution of civilization, but it remained for Gutenberg and his printing press to set the stage for the great ideational creativity of the Renaissance and for the computer to herald the creativity revolution of our own age.

While the early conceptions of giftedness said little about creativity, Terman's longitudinal follow-up of gifted youth, identified in 1920 and 1921 when they were 12 years old, focused on their later creative productivity in adulthood. Opinions differ as to the amount and quality of their creativity, but concern for the creative output of youth and adults who are identified as gifted and nurtured in special programs continues.

Creativity is a salient concern of professionals who work with gifted children and often a major part of the curriculum for gifted education programs. While the high intelligence score that is the major criterion for admission to programs for gifted students is often seen as representing convergent abilities, educational programs often place primary emphasis on divergent learning experiences, especially in the project work and creative problem solving activities that are stressed in school programs. The ultimate goals that are stated for gifted programs also commonly stress creative achievements in adulthood. [*See* DIVERGENT THINKING.]

II. EDUCATIONAL PROGRAMS

There is a major emphasis on creativity as cognitive skills and creative problem solving in school programs for gifted youth. This reveals itself in specific educational activities related to the development of fluency, flexibility, originality, and elaboration skills. It also is revealed in programs that stress creative problem solving, such as Odyssey of the Mind and Future Problem Solving. All of the much emphasized focus on projects in programs for the gifted also imply much creative originality in the conceptualization, conduct, and carrying out of major activities. [*See* PROGRAMS AND COURSES IN CREATIVITY.]

It is possible to enhance children's creative thinking abilities through systematic introduction of creativity instructional materials and learning experiences in the elementary school curriculum. Such programs can be highly effective in increasing children's basic divergent thinking abilities of fluency, flexibility, originality, and elaboration. [*See* ENHANCEMENT OF CREATIVITY; TEACHING CREATIVITY.]

III. PROGRAM MODELS

Models of gifted education that stress academics, acceleration of subject matter learning, and traditional curricula pay far less attention to creativity or view it as a capability that can only emerge after a solid grounding for gifted youth in the basic knowledge and skills of a discipline in which they have special talents. Creativity in these models is most often viewed as processes at the high end of the model proposed by Feldman, Csikszentmihalyi, and Gardner in 1994, namely, things that people do that change the world. The latter may mean discoveries in chemistry, solution of major classical problems in mathematics, formulation of a plan for a new social order, development of a new economic theory, or a linguistic breakthrough in understanding an ancient language. This conception contrasts sharply with the views of other theorists who see creative behavior and potential in the ideas and writings of young children. [*See* EMINENCE.]

Some models for gifted education programs have stressed creativity in both the identification process and the curriculum and instructional design. Several specialists in gifted education have developed models to serve gifted youth in the regular classroom where all levels of ability are represented and where creativity is often stressed. Milgram presented her own model and that of other leaders in gifted education in her edited book, *Teaching Gifted and Talented Learners in Regular Classrooms.* She stresses the need to customize, or we would say individualize, teaching–learning processes for each gifted student. All areas of the curriculum are treated in Milgram's volume. All of the models in this book advocate more or less of independent, creative activity, creative project work, and explicit attention to the provision of instruction in cognitive and creative or divergent thinking skills and creative problem solving.

H. Feldhusen presented a model to meet the needs of gifted students in her book, *Individualized Teaching of Gifted Children in Regular Classrooms,* which stresses engagement of gifted students in a wide variety of creative learning experiences. Children begin the school day by planning how they will engage or involve themselves in the various activities offered by the teacher or by their own design. They develop a learning agreement which the teacher will examine and, after possible counsel and discussion, will become their learning regimen for the day. Later in the school year they plan a week at a time, and some even plan for several weeks of learning activities.

In this model children attend to their learning in basic subject matters but move ahead to higher levels when they are ready. They also devote much time to creative writing, planning for and carrying out projects, conducting experiments, doing creative problem solving activities, designing the art to accompany projects, and writing project reports. Creativity is stressed in the use of divergent thinking activities that are often done both with the whole class and in all the individual and small-group work in which students are engaged.

IV. DEVELOPMENTAL ISSUES

There is no well-established model or paradigm for the development of divergent or creative thinking abilities, nor is there a developmental model for giftedness. However, both may be seen as developing within frameworks established by Piaget for general cognitive development.

Research shows that creativity grows through childhood but tends to slump at about the fourth-grade level, or at ages 9 and 10, and resumes growth again in high school and young adulthood if there are appropriately nurturing educational conditions. However, some researchers see creativity as an outgrowth of mastery of a field or discipline and propose that creative productivity emerges after intensive study in, and mastery of, a discipline. [*See* FOURTH GRADE SLUMP.]

The Bloom *Taxonomy,* which has been widely used as a guide to curricular and instructional practice in gifted education, is viewed as a hierarchical structure of cognitive activities with an implied developmental or growth order from the lower cognitive operations of knowledge or memory, understanding, and application to the ascending higher levels of analysis, synthesis, and evaluation. Convergent cognitive abilities are the major components of the lower three levels while divergent or creative abilities are clearly significant of synthesis activities, and to some extent they are involved in analysis and judgment or evaluation. Creative cognitions are probably enhanced by ability to see elements or components as implied in the Bloom analysis stage and by ability to judge ideas as potentially creative when they occur.

Feldman suggests that constructivist theory provides the best basis for understanding the development of creative abilities and giftedness in the individual. As individuals, through experience and interaction with the environment, we build interpretations, understandings, and theories about the world around us. We come to understand the world through activities, exploration, and interpretations, but the resultant cognitive schema are of our own construction. When those schema differ from the commonly held schema and are judged ten-

able, or valid, "creative" thought processes may have occurred. The creative individual, Feldman asserts, does not see existing bodies of knowledge or fields of endeavor as inimitable or fixed, but changeable. Feldman posits what he calls "the transformational imperative," the motivation to produce creative change. The transformational imperative grows in those who master the basic intellectual framework of a field but are also motivated to find new conceptual and creative linkages and schema that better explain or represent the field.

Bloom carried out a retrospective research study of highly successful artists, athletes, and scientists and concluded that development of talent and creative ability goes through at least three stages. In the first phase in childhood the individual develops strong interest in an area, topic, or field of study and becomes motivated to explore it. In phase two, adolescence, the individual engages in intensive study and acquisition of knowledge in a field. In the third phase, young adulthood, the individual is motivated to seek, to study with, and to emulate the masters, and to strive for the highest levels of creative achievement in the field.

It is clear that creative capacities grow in individuals as a function of their cognitive abilities, the intellectual structures they create, and the motivational patterns they develop. Creative adults are cognitively equipped and motivationally oriented to create. Gifted children develop a consistent and spontaneous capacity for creative thinking, and ideational originality and flexibility can be reliably and validly assessed in the gifted. It seems quite clear that gifted children have high potential for the development of creative processing skills.

V. PSYCHOLOGICAL BASES

Both psychological constructs, giftedness and creativity, have a substantial base of representation in psychological and educational research. Research on giftedness began with the development of procedures for the measurement of intelligence by Binet and Simon, and reached the first stage of fruition in the publication of *Measurement of Intelligence: An Explanation of and a Complete Guide for the Use of the Stanford Revision and Extension of the Binet–Simon Intelligence Scale* by Lewis M. Terman in 1916. It was then a relatively short time span to the beginning of Terman's *Genetic Studies of Genius,* which began in 1920 and culminated in the first publication of results in 1925. In the decades that followed a host of pioneer researchers began to focus their work on gifted youth.

Psychological sciences and research emerge with the advent of procedures for measuring psychological phenomena. While the beginnings are quite clear for intelligence, the construct of creativity and its measurement are far less clear. Mednick's *Remote Associates Test,* first published in 1962, surely generated a substantial body of research and evidence concerning the concept of creativity. His early publication in *Psychological Review* in 1962, "The Associative Basis of the Creative Process," set forth clearly his theoretical view that creativity was a process of discerning connections among otherwise disparate things and ideas. However, the work of Guilford in the late 1940s, 1950s, and 1960s heralded a substantial thrust of test development and research on creativity.

The next steps forward in psychological focus on creativity came with the work of E. Paul Torrance and his development of both the *Torrance Tests of Creative Thinking* and diverse educational programs to foster the development of children's and adolescents' creative thinking abilities. With the publication in 1966 of the *Torrance Tests of Creative Thinking* there was a mushrooming of research on the creative thinking abilities of gifted youth and on educational procedures for teaching creative thinking to the gifted. [*See* TESTS OF CREATIVITY.]

There followed then, during the decades of the 1970s, 1980s, and 1990s, a vast amount of research on creativity, much of it reported in two journals, *The Journal of Creative Behavior* and *The Creative Research Journal,* and others reported in books such as Isaksen's *Frontiers of Creativity Research* and Glover, Ronning, and Reynold's *Handbook of Creativity.* Research on creativity as a psychological phenomenon continues to engage many psychologists and educators.

VI. CONCLUDING DEFINITIONS

There is less agreement on definitions for "creativity" than for "giftedness" but both concepts have varying meanings. As a resolution of several conceptions we define creativity as cognitive processes and overt behaviors that result in new ideas, products, or performances and that are judged by some audience to be new, original, useful, and/or aesthetically pleasing. The milieu may be a home in which a teenager plans a summer outing for the family that is enthusiastically endorsed by all family members or a university setting in which a biological researcher develops a new theory of human evolution that is accepted and applauded by colleagues, with infinite variations between the two. Ultimately it is thinking that yields new ideas and new productions that come to be accepted by some audience or constituents.

Bibliography

Binet, A., & Simon, T. (1908). The development of intelligence in children. *L'Anneé Psychologie, 14,* 1–90.

Bloom, B. S. (1956). *Taxonomy of educational objectives, Handbook I, Cognitive Domain.* New York, NY: Longmans, Green.

Bloom, B. S. (1985). *Talent development.* New York: Ballantine Books.

Feldhusen, H. J. (1993). *Individualized teaching of gifted children in regular classrooms.* West Lafayette, IN: STAR Teaching Materials.

Feldman, D. H. (1994). Creativity: Proof that development occurs. In D. H. Feldman, M. Csikszentmihalyi, & H. Gardner (Eds.), *Changing the world: A framework for the study of creativity* (pp. 85–101). Westport, CT: Praeger.

Feldman, D. H., Csikszentmihalyi, M., Gardner, H. (1994). *Changing the world: A framework for the study of creativity.* Westport, CT: Praeger.

Gagné, F. (1993). Constructs and models pertaining to exceptional human abilities. In K. A. Heller, F. J. Monks, & A. H. Passow (Eds.). (1993). *International handbook of research and development of giftedness and talent* (pp. 69–87). New York: Pergamon Press.

Glover, J. A., Ronning, R. R., & Reynolds, C. R. (1989). *Handbook of creativity.* New York: Plenum Press.

Isaksen, S. G. (Ed.). (1987). *Frontiers of creativity research: Beyond the basics.* Buffalo, NY: Bearly.

Marland, S. (1972). *Education of the gifted and talented: Report to the Congress.* (Document 72–5020). Washington, DC: U.S. Government Printing Office.

Mednick, S. A. (1962). *Remote associates test.* Ann Arbor, MI: University of Michigan Press.

Milgram, R. M. (Ed.). (1989). *Teaching gifted and talented learners in regular classrooms.* Springfield, IL: Thomas.

U.S. Office of Education (1993). *National excellence: A case for developing America's talent.* Washington, DC: U.S. Government Printing Office.

Group Creativity

Paul B. Paulus
University of Texas, Arlington

Brainstorming A technique for increasing idea generation that emphasizes quantity of ideas and deferred judgment.

Competition Working for individual goals or to surpass the performance of others in a group.

Cooperation Working together collaboratively toward a common goal.

Cross-Functional Teams Work teams that involve individuals with different job skills or expertise.

Divergent Thinking Style A way of thinking that emphasizes the generation of unusual or atypical responses to problems.

Electronic Brainstorming Generating ideas as a group on a local computer network.

Intrinsic Motivation A strong interest in an activity for its own sake rather than for external rewards such as praise or money.

Leadership Style An approach to leadership that is typical of certain individuals, such as directive or participative.

Teamwork The organization of work in terms of groups that collaborate in performing work tasks.

Transformational Leadership Style A type of leadership enacted by one who has charisma, is inspiring, encourages innovation, and is sensitive to the needs of individuals.

GROUP CREATIVITY *is the creation, development, evaluation, and promotion of novel ideas in groups. This can occur informally in interactions among friends or colleagues or in more structured groups such as scientific research laboratories and research and development teams.*

I. CREATIVITY

Creativity is generally considered to involve the generation of novel but useful ideas that gain widespread acceptance. The development of novel ideas requires a certain degree of knowledge and experience, a willingness to take risks or take unique perspectives, and a style of bringing together diverse or previously unconnected domains. From the various ideas that are generated, the most useful ones must be selected and then promoted to gain social acceptance.

Most research and theory on these creativity processes focuses on individual creativity. The classic perspective is that creativity requires certain individual

Copyright © 1999 by Academic Press
All rights of reproduction in any form reserved.

characteristics and our culture tends to focus on individual geniuses. Yet creativity is essentially a social phenomenon and almost all creativity involves group processes. Geniuses such as Einstein and Freud were greatly influenced by the scholarship and mentorship of others. The development of novel ideas requires some basic knowledge in a variety of areas. This knowledge is often attained in group contexts through the role of teachers, mentors, and colleagues. These individuals may directly provide information or direct or motivate the knowledge acquisition process. Individuals may also learn to model the work and creative styles of key individuals in their group or social context. Colleagues and peers are used to obtain feedback on novel ideas or discoveries. Creative geniuses often encounter considerable resistance to their ideas but eventually their novel ideas may gain much acceptance and acclaim. Creative processes need to successfully go through these phases of generation, incubation, evaluation, and promotion to gain widespread acceptance for novel ideas. Only a small percentage do so successfully.

II. GROUP PROCESSES

Group interaction provides a basis for the exchange of information among group members. This information can be in the form of knowledge, skills, or new perspectives. Effective groups should have individuals with a diversity of knowledge and skills and be motivated for a full exchange of ideas. However, a number of factors inhibit groups from attaining this ideal. In their discussions, group members tend to focus on information and ideas they have in common rather than ideas that are unique to a particular individual. They also tend to evaluate ideas as they are presented and this may inhibit group members from presenting novel or unusual ideas that may receive critical reactions. In particular, group members may be hesitant to share ideas or perspectives that are contrary to the shared beliefs, values, or norms of the group. Groups tend to react negatively to those who deviate from their norms or values and often enforce conformity to norms. If group members share responsibility for a group product, some members may loaf or reduce their efforts and let others do most of the work. Unless group members are already strongly motivated to work on a particular task or project, the group context may lead to reduced motivation. If these various negative group factors are counteracted, groups have much potential to facilitate creativity.

III. GROUP IDEA GENERATION

Creativity requires that individuals take new or unusual approaches to problems. This is sometimes called a divergent style in which there is an emphasis on unique or atypical responses. This may require a somewhat random association of different domains, sets of knowledge, or ideas. Group interaction should be ideal for such a process. One can bring together people with diverse knowledge and skills and allow them to combine these in unique ways. Certainly such a group has a greater potential for developing unique conceptual combinations than a similar group of individuals working in isolation. However, experimental studies have demonstrated that groups generate fewer ideas and a lower quality of ideas than do similar numbers of individuals performing in isolation.

One problem with groups is the tendency toward conformity. Groups often have a strong tendency to seek consensus or agreement. Individuals who deviate from a group consensus or norm often receive negative reactions from group members. They may be criticized and rejected if they do not conform their ideas to those consistent with the group consensus. This type of reaction can be observed in creative and scientific domains as well as in areas of values and opinions. However, if conformity is the dominant force, how can innovation ever occur? Fortunately, highly motivated individuals who persist in promoting their novel ideas or perspectives with novel ideas may eventually gain group acceptance. Research on the influence of minority opinions in groups indicates that persistent minorities can have an impact on the beliefs of those holding the majority perspective. Furthermore, new generations that are not as committed to older paradigms are more likely to appreciate or accept these novel perspectives. Exposure to minority perspectives can even increase divergent thinking. Thus a critical factor in creative innovation is the persistent efforts by the creator to promote his or her ideas. [*See* CONFORMITY; DIVERGENT THINKING.]

A. Heterogeneity

A major benefit of group interaction is that it allows individuals with different educational backgrounds and expertise to exchange information and ideas. With the increasing complexity of different disciplines and areas of expertise, it is difficult for an individual to develop significant expertise in more than one area. As a result, creative advances that require the combination of information from different domains of expertise will require some form of group interaction or exchange process. Cross-functional teams in business and industry involve individuals with different job skills or expertise. Scientific research also often requires this type of diversity. Intellectually diverse groups should be more likely to develop unique or creative ideas because they have the ability to combine many different sets of knowledge. However such an outcome is not inevitable. Unstructured groups tend to focus on areas of expertise or knowledge that they have in common. Group members may have difficulty understanding ideas from an area where they do not have a grasp of some of the basic concepts or language.

Individuals from different backgrounds may also have different value systems. As a result, conflicts or disagreements in heterogenous groups are likely. Such conflicts can inhibit group productivity, but under the right conditions they can increase creativity. If conflicts stimulate individuals to reevaluate their assumptions or perspectives, group members may experience some intellectual growth. This is evident from studies where the majority viewpoint is challenged by a minority perspective. The group member presenting the conflicting perspective tends to produce negative reactions from other group members. However, if the group deviant persists in making a strong case for his or her point of view, the other group members may think more deeply about the issue and experience some degree of cognitive change. Exposure to minority perspectives in groups may even stimulate group members to take a more creative or divergent approach on other tasks or projects.

B. Group Brainstorming

Even though groups have much creative potential, they often do not attain it. In a desire to get along and please others, group members may avoid disagreements or self-censor any thoughts or ideas they feel might receive negative reactions. Groups are often formed on the basis of similarity of values, interests, or purpose. Individuals whose words or deeds conflict with the general group consensus are likely to elicit negative reactions from other group members, who will try to move the deviant member back into the group mainstream. However, conflict, disagreement, and exposure to disconfirmation of one's ideas are the seed of creativity in groups. Therefore, it is important to structure groups so that there is much tolerance of disagreement or deviant perspectives. This is the philosophy behind the brainstorming procedures developed by Alex Osborn. He noted that premature judgment of ideas shared in groups is a major inhibitor of creativity. He developed a set of rules and procedures to facilitate the exchange of ideas in groups. Groups are instructed to defer judgment of ideas in intensive idea-generation sessions. They are to express all ideas that come to mind, not to criticize ideas presented, to generate as many ideas as possible, and to build on the ideas of others. Thus there is an emphasis on the full and nonjudgmental exchange of ideas or information in a group. Only after such an exchange process will the group members or outsiders begin the task of evaluating the value or utility of the ideas generated. The brainstorming rules do seem to increase idea generation in groups, but groups often still generate fewer ideas than a comparable group of solitary brainstormers. [*See* BRAINSTORMING.]

Why do these groups underperform? It may be hard for group members to overcome a natural tendency to self-censor unusual or unique ideas, even in groups where there may be no overt negative evaluations. Even though no negative feedback may occur, individuals still do not want to make negative impressions. Individuals in groups may also tend to reduce their efforts or loaf if there is no individual accountability for the group's performance. This is most likely if other group members appear willing to take up the slack. The group interaction process also may inhibit one's ability to generate novel ideas. When others are talking, one cannot present ideas and it may be difficult to think of new ones. Groups may also get off on tangents or elaborations that limit the time available to generate new ideas.

These various problems can be counteracted in various ways. When groups use a writing or computer-based exchange process, their performance improves significantly. Various forms of electronic brainstorming are now available to facilitate the idea-exchange process. In electronic brainstorming individuals type ideas on computers and these ideas are shared with others who are typing their ideas at the same time. At the end of the brainstorming session, the ideas are often summarized and evaluated by means of computer voting. Conventional face-to-face groups can also significantly improve their performance if they receive some training in the efficient sharing of ideas. Groups composed of members who are positively disposed to social interaction (e.g., low social anxiety or high sociability) tend to be more productive in the generation of ideas in groups.

The major benefits of group interaction for creativity may come after the interaction process is completed. When individuals have some time to reflect or let the ideas incubate, additional creative insights may occur. Thus the most beneficial pattern may be one in which group interaction and solitary reflection are interspersed. This is, of course, typical of the ways many scientific and work teams function. There are also benefits of group brainstorming experiences beyond the ideas that are generated. Participants enjoy the experience and may use it to practice or develop their intellectual skills. Group brainstorming may also be viewed positively as means of impressing others and developing appropriate organizational norms such as openness to the ideas of others. [*See* INCUBATION; INSIGHT.]

IV. LEADERSHIP

An important factor in group effectiveness is leadership. Most groups have either an appointed or an informal leader. A major function of the leader is to motivate each group member to contribute effectively to the group. The style of the leader has a strong impact on group functioning. Some leaders tend to be very directive or production oriented. Their major concern is that the job gets done or the goal is achieved. Other leaders are more nondirective or person oriented. They are concerned with the personal well-being of the group members as well as goal achievement. The nondirective/person oriented style is consistent with a teamwork culture of participative management. Recent trends in teamwork have emphasized the importance of teams being autonomous or self-directed. This involves having team members with much freedom in the choice and conduct of their tasks. There is some evidence that these types of teams are most productive. Team autonomy should also be related to team creativity. Team members are more likely to be intrinsically motivated when they have a lot of choice in the conduct of their work. Intrinsic motivation exists when individuals have a strong interest in an activity for its own sake rather than as a means for external rewards such as praise or financial gain. Intrinsic motivation appears to be an important factor in the generation of creative products. A highly directive or authoritarian leadership style may inhibit or reduce such intrinsic motivation.

Participative or nondirective leadership is not inevitably better than directive leadership in enhancing group creativity. People can be motivated to work hard for both intrinsic and extrinsic reasons. Many artists and scientists reap significant financial rewards and worldly acclaim and continue to make creative contributions. Extrinsic rewards that reflect positively on one's competence may, in fact, increase the sense of efficacy that is required to take on the unusual challenges or risks that lead to significant creative accomplishments. Thus directive leaders who set high standards or goals and provide significant rewards for creative successes may significantly enhance the creative efforts of group members.

What then are the critical features of leader or supervisory behavior? Many of the important components are part of a transformational style of leadership, which motivates individuals to perform beyond expectations. Transformational leaders have charisma in the sense of being strong role models in terms of ability, standards, persistence, values, and willingness to take risks. They inspire by motivating followers to a shared vision, high goals, and a sense of optimism. They encourage innovation and creativity and refrain from public criticism. They are sensitive to the unique characteristics and needs of each group member and provide the appropriate level of directive or nondirective support. The type of leadership or management that is likely to inhibit creativity would be characterized by high levels of control, emphasis on external evaluation and criticism, lack of clear direction or vision, and lack of support for innovation. [*See* LEADERSHIP.]

V. COOPERATION AND COMPETITION

When people work together in groups there are tendencies for competitive or cooperative relationships to develop. Some group members or groups may emphasize the need for cooperating or working with one another to achieve their common goals. Cooperation may be the only way to function effectively when the unique skills of all group members are required for success. This would be the case for many complex scientific and technological enterprises. However, cooperation is also emphasized as a generally positive orientation by those who espouse the benefits of teamwork and collaborative learning. Participants in research and development teams cite a cooperative and collaborative corporate climate as being conducive for creativity. A cooperative atmosphere should enhance the willingness to take risks, to share ideas and information with others, and to compensate for the inadequacies of some group members. However, a system that ignores individual differences in the quality of contributions is not likely to motivate group members to optimum levels of performance.

Any system of reward that is sensitive to differences in contributions to the group may induce some sense of competition among group members. In competition the goal achievement of one group member may reduce the chance of goal attainment of other group members. In competitive situations, one group member's gain is another's loss as when only one can win a prize or get a big raise. Competition can be healthy in motivating group members to perform at high level, but it can also lead to conflicts and a reduced willingness to work cooperatively. This problem does not occur when competition is between groups, teams, or organizations. Fierce competition among top scientific teams to be the first with a certain discovery is quite common and provides strong additional motivation for creative efforts. Effective group leadership is required to develop the appropriate balance of cooperation and competition in groups. This is likely to vary with the phase of the innovation processes. In the discovery or generation phase, cooperation may be critical for a full exchange of information and views. Once a range of ideas has been proposed, there could be some healthy competition in the development and promotion of different alternatives. [*See* COLLABORATION AND COMPETITION.]

VI. TEAM INNOVATION

Today is the era of teamwork. Most organizations have structured their work so that individuals work together as a team on a particular project. Team members are often trained in multiple skills so that they can perform a range of tasks. It is presumed that teamwork will lead to higher job satisfaction and productivity. Teamwork is also common in scientific enterprises because the complexity of most scientific problems requires individuals with a variety of skills. So much of the creative work that occurs in the business and research enterprises occurs in a group context. Researchers have only recently begun to study creative processes in these types of groups. [*See* TEAMS.]

Studies of scientific research laboratories have shown that group interactions are important in facilitating important discoveries. These interactions often occur during regular laboratory meetings in which research findings are discussed. Creative laboratory groups are led by researchers who are willing to take risks and set challenging but realistic goals. They often may work simultaneously on a set of high- and low-risk problems to ensure that they will have some degree of success. They pay particular attention to unexpected or inconsistent results and use analogies to understand the implications of these and other findings. These analogies focus on the similarity between the ongoing research and prior research or research and concepts in other domains. Conceptual or creative change often involves the use of these types of analogies by highly expert researchers. Other important factors in the creative success of research laboratories are a diversity of expertise among the group members, a willingness to challenge one another's interpretations, and the posing of questions that stimulate group members to think about an issue in different ways. [*See* ANALOGIES; SCIENCE.]

Research on team innovation in organizations has led to a similar perspective. Innovation or development of new ideas in teams requires a supportive organizational context. Some important features of this context are explicit support by the organization of innovation, a participative leadership style, effective communication, and a cooperative atmosphere. Innovative teams often contain members with diverse backgrounds and skills who are inclined to make innovative suggestions. It is important for the team to be committed to a clear set of goals or objectives. Teams in which there is a high level of participation or communication, an open and frank exchange of conflicting ideas or opinions, and support for innovative ideas are most likely to develop innovations. [*See* BUSINESS STRATEGY.]

VII. PHASES OF GROUP CREATIVITY

Creative processes tend to go through a series of stages. A preparation stage involves the acquisition of knowledge, information, or ideas. It may take some time to digest these and to come up with some novel perspectives. This period of incubation often involves being focused on other activities. Most creative people are engaged in a variety of activities that allow for multiple incubation opportunities and potential combination of ideas from different domains. The incubation period may be followed by an experience of insight or discovery. After new ideas have been generated they have to go through a promotion or elaboration process. The creator needs to persuade colleagues and other consumers of ideas or products of the value or utility of the new ideas. This may involve considerable feedback from peers and experts in relevant domains as ideas are sharpened or elaborated. The social judgment process can be influenced by a variety of factors. Groups may not be particularly objective in this process. The prior reputation of the innovator, the apparent novelty of the ideas, and the consistency of the ideas with prior conceptual systems will likely influence this judgment process. Groups may be wrong in their judgments if they simply focus on developing a consensus. However, if there is a full exchange of perspectives, group interaction may increase the likelihood of making correct decisions. Groups can be helpful in catching logical or conceptual mistakes, especially if these can be clearly demonstrated.

Bibliography

Amabile, T. M. (1996). *Creativity in context.* Boulder, CO: Westview Press.

Bass, B. M. (1998). *Transformational leadership: Industrial, military, and educational impact.* Mahwah, NJ: Erlbaum.

Guzzo, R. A., & Salas, E. (Eds.). (1995). *Team effectiveness and decision making in organizations.* San Francisco: Jossey-Bass.

Levine, J. M., & Moreland, R. L. (1990). Progress in small groups research. *Annual Review of Psychology, 41,* 585–634.

Nemeth, C. J. (1992). Minority dissent as a stimulant to group performance. In S. Worchel, W. Wood, & J. A. Simpson (Eds.), *Group process and productivity* (pp. 95–111). Newbury Park, CA: Sage Publications.

Osborn, A. (1963). *Applied imagination: Principles and procedures of creative thinking.* New York: Scribner's.

Paulus, P. B., Brown, V., Ortega, A. (1999). Group creativity. In R. E. Purser & A. Montuori (Eds.), *Social creativity.* (pp. 151–176). Creskill, NJ: Hampton Press.

Paulus, P. B., Larey, T. S., & Dzindolet, M. T. (in press). Creativity in groups and teams. In M. Turner (Ed.), *Groups at work: Advances in theory and research.* Hillsdale, NJ: Erlbaum.

Sternberg, R. J., & Davidson, J. E. (Eds.). (1995). *The nature of insight.* Cambridge, MA: MIT Press.

Sternberg, R. J., & Lubart, T. I. (1995). *Defying the crowd: Cultivating creativity in a culture of conformity.* New York: The Free Press.

Sutton, R. I., & Hargadon, A. (1996). Brainstorming groups in context: Effectiveness in a product design firm. *Administrative Science Quarterly, 41,* 685–718.

West, M. A. (Ed.). (1996). *Handbook of work group psychology.* Chichester, England: Wiley.

Guilford's View

William B. Michael

University of Southern California

Contents The input dimension (stimulus material) of the structure-of-intellect model comprising four kinds of given information identified as figural, symbolic, semantic, or behavioral, any one of which is subsequently processed by one of five types of psychological operations to generate any one of six forms of products or new information (outputs).

Convergent Production The psychological function that generates from the memory storage new information (products) from given information (contents) for which the objective is to realize a unique product outcome; in creative problem solving, the product would represent a transformation of given information (input) into a product that is clever, original, novel, or innovative, as found, for example, in the invention of a new product for a defined use.

Divergent Production The psychological function that generates from the memory storage in an open-ended manner new information (output) from given information (input) with a large variety and quantity of outcomes from the same source; in creative problem solving, it is associated with abilities reflecting fluency and flexibility.

Implications One of six products (outputs) in which an extrapolation of outcome information occurs in the form of predictions, expectancies, inferences, suggested antecedents (or causes) of observed events, or specific consequences of an intervening activity as reflected in the creative abilities of sensitivity to problems or elaboration.

Operations The processing dimension of the structure-of-intellect model consisting of five types of psychological functions (cognition, memory, divergent production, convergent production, or evaluation), any one of which processes one of four kinds of given input information (contents) to generate any one of six types of products (output information).

Products The output dimension of the structure-of-intellect model embracing six forms of newly generated output information (units, classes, relations, systems, transformations, or implications) that have been achieved from one of five types of psychological operations having processed one of four kinds of contents (input information).

Structure-of-Intellect (SOI) Model A three-dimensional information-processing theory of intelligence conceptualized by Guilford in which any one of five types of psychological operations (cognition, memory, divergent production, convergent production, or evaluation) processes any one of four kinds of content, or given information (figural, symbolic, semantic, or behavioral), to generate any one of six forms of products, or new information (units, classes, relations, systems, transformations, or implications).

Structure-of-Intellect Problem-Solving (SIPS) Model An extension of the structure-of-intellect model specifically oriented toward solving problems associated with creative production in which the dynamic interaction of the constructs of the SOI model are portrayed in an ongoing iterative activity as one

Copyright © 1999 by Academic Press
All rights of reproduction in any form reserved.

would find in a computerized cybernetics model with evaluation being heavily emphasized.

Transformations One of six forms of products constituting newly generated information that represents a redefinition, modification, or marked change in the given or existing information that has been processed—a product of a novel, clever, unique, and innovative form often found in creative problem solving in mathematics, science, engineering, or invention.

Trigram An acronym comprising three letters to describe 1 of 120 hypothesized constructs in the structure-of-intellect model in which the first letter stands for one of five types of psychological operations, the second letter for one of four kinds of contents, and the third letter for one of six forms of products; for example, CMU would stand for the cognition (C) of semantic (M) units (U).

*Through his formulation of the structure-of-intellect (SOI) model and the structure-of-intellect problem-solving (SIPS) model, the late J. Paul **GUILFORD** provided a comprehensive theoretical framework of the constructs of human intelligence within which those pertaining to creative thinking and creative problem solving could be understood. The three-dimensional information-processing SOI model postulates four kinds of content or given information (figural, symbolic, semantic, and behavioral) that is processed by one of five types of psychological operations (cognition, memory, divergent production, convergent production, or evaluation) to generate any one of six forms of products, or new information (units, classes, relations, systems, transformations, or implications). Each of the constructs within this model is represented by one type of psychological operation processing one kind of content to yield one form of product. The SIPS model is an extension of the SOI model that is specifically directed toward an iterative process of creative problem solving in which a dynamic interaction of the constructs of the SOI model takes place. Selected constructs from these two models are involved in creative problem solving. In the instance of the creative ability of fluency found in written and oral communications, divergent production involving almost unrestricted variety and quantity of responses or outcomes occurs. On the other hand, creative problem solving in the sciences, mathematics, engineering, and invention often requires the convergent production of given information into a form portraying a major transformation as a product reflecting a novel, clever, unique, or innovative solution. In addition to the consideration of other creative abilities, numerous examples are presented in this article to illustrate each of the several constructs within the SOI model that have been hypothesized to represent creative thinking. Within the SIPS model, the interplay of the SOI constructs is explicated. Finally, a critique of the SOI and SIPS models is provided.*

I. HISTORICAL BACKGROUND

Professor J. Paul Guilford (1897–1987) stands out in the history of psychology as one of the great contributors to the study of creativity. Having obtained his Ph.D. degree in psychology at Cornell University under the tutelage of such renown scholars in the history of psychology as E. B. Titchener, Kurt Koffka, Harry Helson, and Karl Dallenbach, he became heavily involved in experimental psychology and in quantitative methods leading to the publication of the landmark volume *Psychometric Methods* in 1936. This work also reflected his interest in individual differences, a primary focus for the remainder of his professional career. Challenging Spearman's g-factor theory of intelligence, which postulates one overriding global attribute of cognitive abilities, Guilford was convinced that intelligence was a composite of many different abilities, many of which were relatively independent of one another. [See MULTIPLE INTELLIGENCES.]

His interest in the study of intellectual abilities and of the individual differences associated with them was greatly facilitated by his participation in the United States Army Air Corps during World War II where he was responsible for the preparation of numerous psychological tests reflecting a variety of abilities shown to be valid in the selection of pilots, bombardiers, and navigators. Much of his success in test development for the Air Corps rested on the application of factor analytic methodology that he had acquired earlier from study of L. L. Thurstone's *Vectors of Mind* published in 1934. Briefly stated, factor analysis as a statistical methodology allows one to identify in a matrix of intercorrelated variables (such as test scores) a relatively small number of mathematically derived dimensions that can account for the correlations of scores among a relatively large number of variables. In the instance of psychological tests, each measure registers on each of the dimensions its degree of association in the form of a correlation coefficient referred to as a *factor loading* (often designated as a structure or pattern coefficient). Determination of a psychologically meaningful definition or interpretation of a factor dimension constitutes an inference that rests on the presence of what appear to be common content and process characteristics of those groups of tests exhibiting relatively high loadings on (that is, correlations with) the dimension but displaying relatively small loadings on all or most of the remaining dimensions. Thus, clusters or groupings of tests that are moderately or highly interrelated with one another but not substantially correlated with other tests in the battery can be expected to define a factor by having loadings or weights on that factor. Many of these factors may be interpreted as reflecting creative abilities, particularly within a comprehensive theory of intelligence.

In the Air Corps, scores on criterion measures (indicators of success) and on test variables were intercorrelated and factor analyzed to determine those ability factors that were common to both the tests and the criterion measures. Thus, for subsequent selections of pilots, bombardiers, or navigators, a relatively small number of tests could be identified to duplicate as closely as possible those factors in the criterion measures that appeared to represent abilities needed for the particular subgroup of aspirants (pilot, bombardier, or navigator). At the end of World War II, about 25 different abilities had been quite clearly identified. At this stage of his research, Guilford had not identified in a systematic or comprehensive way those abilities associated with creative thinking, although he had formulated some tentative hypotheses.

Following his separation from the Army Air Corps, Guilford returned to the University of Southern California to teach and to conduct his continuing research on mental abilities. Shortly before 1955, Guilford noticed from his ongoing research that about 40 different abilities had been identified within which some interesting patterns or groupings of intellectual factors occurred. At an inductive level of theory building, he generated a taxonomy of mental abilities that led to the development in 1955 of a theory of intelligence to become known as the structure-of-intellect (SOI) model.

Guilford's SOI model initially consisted of 120 hypothesized abilities. The model was subsequently expanded to 150 abilities in 1985 and to 180 abilities in 1987. Within this model Guilford identified a number of abilities that he later hypothesized were related to creativity. In the following sections of this presentation, the SOI model is described at length, followed by a delineation of those abilities that were hypothesized to reflect creativity.

II. THE STRUCTURE-OF-INTELLECT MODEL

A. The Original 120-Factor SOI Model

As described at length by Guilford in his 1967 classic volume *The Nature of Human Abilities* and subsequently in 1971 in the book by Guilford and Hoepfner titled *The Analysis of Intelligence,* the SOI model is an information-processing one comprising inputs (*contents* represented by four kinds of information or stimulus material that the individual discriminates), processes (intellectually oriented psychological *operations* of five major types of intellectual psychological functions or activities that are needed to make discriminations in the given information or stimulus contents), and outputs (*products* revealed by six forms of increasing complexity that newly generated information can assume after the initial content inputs have been processed by one or more psychological operations). As Figure 1 illustrates, cross classifications of all possible permutations of facets or elements in the three dimensions (*contents, operations,* and *products*) expressed as geometric intersections of lines perpendicular to each of the three dimensions serve to generate a large cube or three-dimensional solid within which are $4 \times 5 \times 6$, or 120 different small cubes or cells. These cells are hypothesized to represent different and relatively independent abilities or constructs. Each small cube, or cell, indicates one type of psychological operation that has processed one kind of content (given information) to yield a product of typically new information. This taxonomic classification resembles in many ways the periodic table of chemistry, the empty cells of which in its initial formulation provided a stimulus to researchers to identify and to substantiate other elements

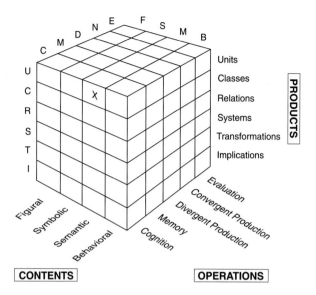

OPERATIONS

Major kinds of intellectual activities or processes; things that the organism does with the raw materials of information, information being defined as "that which the organism discriminates."

C— *Cognition* Immediate discovery, awareness, rediscovery, or recognition of information in various forms; comprehension or understanding.

M— *Memory* Retention of storage, with some degree of availability, of information in the same form it was committed to storage and in response to the same cues in connection with which it was learned.

D— *Divergent Production* Generation of information from given information, where the emphasis is upon variety and quantity of output from the same source. Likely to involve what has been called transfer. This operation is most clearly involved in aptitudes of creative potential.

N— *Convergent Production* Generation of information from given information, where the emphasis is upon achieving unique of conventionally accepted best outcomes. It is likely the given (cue) information fully determines the response.

E— *Evaluation* Reaching decisions or making judgments concerning criterion satisfaction (correctness, suitability, adequacy, desirability, etc.) of information.

CONTENTS

Broad classes or types of information discriminable by the organism.

F— *Figural* Information in concrete form, as perceived or as recalled possibly in the form of images. The term "figural" minimally implies figure-ground perceptual organization. Visual spatial information is figural. Different sense modalities may be involved, e.g., visual kinesthetic.

S— *Symbolic* Information in the form of denotative signs having no significance in and of themselves, such as letters, numbers, musical notations, codes, and words, when meanings and form are not considered.

M— *Semantic* Information in the form of meanings to which words commonly become attached, hence most notable in verbal thinking and in verbal communication but not identical with words. Meaningful pictures also often convey semantic information.

B— *Behavioral* Information, essentially nonverbal, involved in human interactions where the attitudes, needs, desires, moods, intentions, perceptions, thoughts, etc., of other people and of ourselves are involved.

PRODUCTS

Forms that information takes in the organism's processing of it.

U— *Units* Relatively segregated or circumscribed items of information having "thing" character. May be close to Gestalt psychology's "figure on a ground."

C— *Classes* Conceptions underlying sets of items of information grouped by virtue of their common properties.

R— *Relations* Connections between items of information based upon variables or points of contact that apply to them. Relational connections are more meaningful and definable than implications.

S— *Systems* Organized or structured aggregates of items of information; complexes of interrelated or interacting parts.

T— *Transformations* Changes of various kinds (redefinition, shifts, or modification) of existing information or in its function.

I— *Implications* Extrapolations of information, in the form of expectancies, predictions, known or suspected antecedents, concomitants, or consequences. The connection between the given information and that extrapolated is more general and less definable than a relational connection.

FIGURE 1   The structure-of-intellect model and definitions of its categories. From *The Nature of Human Intelligence* by J. P. Guilford (1967), New York: McGraw-Hill, with modifications. Copyright 1967 by McGraw-Hill. Reproduced by permission.

in the domain of chemistry. By 1967 Guilford declared that nearly 100 of the 120 hypothesized abilities had received empirical support from programmatic factor analytic research efforts carried out over about a 15-year period (1952–1967).

In the paragraphs to follow the key facets or elements of each of the three postulated dimensions of the SOI model are described. Following the input, process, and output characteristics of the information-processing SOI model, the sequence of description is with reference to the contents, operations, and product modalities. Each facet of a dimension is given a short verbal identification statement followed by an acronym in parenthesis to facilitate future reference to hypothesized factors.

1. Contents

The first dimension of *contents* comprises four categories (along with a letter symbol serving as an acronym) that are defined as follows:

Figural (F). Given information in concrete form often as visual-spatial images.

Symbolic (S). Given information in the form of denotative symbols that in and of themselves have no significance such as numbers, letters, codes, music notations, and isolated words.

Semantic (M). Given information in the form of meanings that typically are associated with words as reflected in verbal thinking and communication, but sometimes in pictures (e.g., comic strips) or mathematical equations (i.e., the requirements of a word problem expressed in the form of a formula or set of equations).

Behavioral (B). Given information essentially in a nonverbal form that occurs in social interactions where moods, attitudes, needs, desires, intentions of others, and one's self are interpreted often in association with body language and empathic feelings.

2. Operations

The second dimensions of *operations* consists of five components that are described as follows:

Cognition (C). To know, comprehend, recognize, or discern almost immediately information of various

kinds—information typically already in one's possession (i.e., recognizing the face of a friend or the sound of a fire alarm).

Memory (M). To retain information that has been placed in storage and that can be retrieved in essentially the same form as that in which it had already been committed to storage (e.g., remembering $8 \times 7 = 56$).

Divergent production (D). To generate from the memory storage in an open-ended manner new information from given information with a substantial variety and quantity of output from the same source (e.g., writing an essay, making a speech, or generating informal conversation).

Convergent production (N). To generate from memory storage new information from given information where the objective is to achieve a unique conventionally accepted outcome (e.g., obtaining the answer to an algebra word problem or the solution to a mathematical equation).

Evaluation (E). To reach a decision or to arrive at a judgment that meets specified criteria of the accuracy, appropriateness, adequacy, and desirability of newly generated information (e.g., a music critic affording a criticism of a symphonic performance or a literary critic judging the value of a newly published novel or biography).

3. Products

The third dimension of *products* is made up of six elements that are detailed as follows:

Units (U). Relatively discrete, circumscribed, delineated items of newly generated information that have a "thing like" quality or characteristic (e.g., words or numbers that exist independently without any common theme or central concept).

Classes (C). Conceptions central to sets of items reflecting newly generated information grouped in terms of their common properties (e.g., mammal for a human being, dog, cat, or whale or vehicle for automobile, bicycle, or motorcycle).

Relations (R). Connections between items of newly produced information often found in analogies or metaphors (e.g., hand is to glove as foot is to shoe).

Systems (S). Organized or structural sets of items revealing complexities of interrelated or interactive parts (e.g., a sentence consisting of words in an organized order or a repetitive pattern in linoleum or draperies).

Transformations (T). Changes assuming many possible forms as revealed in newly generated products that represent a redefinition, modification, or shifts of given or existing information and its functions, often found in creative problem solving (e.g., finding a new use for an old medication).

Implications (I). Extrapolation of outcome information in the form of predictions, expectancies, suggested antecedents (or causes) of observed events, specific consequences of an intervening activity, or concomitant occurrences—products less definable and more general than a relations product (i.e., possible consequences of a major hurricane or consequences of a risky investment).

4. Use of Trigrams to Describe Abilities

Consistent with the statement that a given type of operation processes a particular kind of content to yield a specified form of product, Guilford introduced the use of trigrams to designate the hypothesized ability or construct identified by a cell in the SOI model. For example, CMU would represent the cognition (C) of semantic (M) units (U)—an ability portrayed in a vocabulary test involving matching a given word with one of five alternative words, of which one is the correct synonym. In a reading comprehension test, a multiple-choice item requiring an examinee to interpret the intended meaning of two or three sentences in a paragraph could be hypothesized to represent the cognition of semantic systems as represented by the trigram CMS. Trigrams are to be employed subsequently in designating those cells that have been hypothesized to represent different abilities, but especially creative abilities.

B. The 150-Factor and 180-Factor SOI Models

In 1977 Guilford separated the figural part of the content domain of the original SOI model of 120 factors into two components of auditory and visual, as each one represents an aspect of sensory input. Thus, there resulted 150 different hypothesized abilities

(5 contents × 5 operations × 6 products). Shortly before his death in 1987, Guilford submitted his last manuscript to a professional journal that was published in early 1988. In this paper, he separated the operation of memory into two components that he described as memory retention (long term) and memory recording (short term). Thus, he created a revised SOI model of 180 abilities (5 contents × 6 operations × 6 products). Relatively little, if any, follow-up research has been undertaken within the framework of this 180-factor model. In fact, the original 120-factor model has been predominant in most research endeavors.

C. Strategies Used in Obtaining Empirical Support for the SOI Model

As mentioned earlier, factor analytic methodology was the primary approach that Guilford employed in his attempt to identify mathematical dimensions associated with hypothesized constructs in the SOI model. His essential strategy was to prepare a test battery in which approximately one-third of the test measures had been shown in many previous studies to have yielded consistently factors with almost the same factorial composition. These tests served basically as a form of experimental control so that the remaining two-thirds of the tests within the battery could have any portions of their score variance related to previously established clearly identified factors. Among the remaining measures within the battery the opportunity was afforded to construct typically sets of three or four experimental measures intended to operationalize each of a number of hypothesized constructs within certain regions or segments of the SOI model. The expectation was that each of these sets of three or four tests would define quite clearly one of the mathematically derived factors. Although a number of successes was realized, many occasions arose in which certain tests actually defined a factor different from the one that they had been intended to represent. Sometimes a given test would reflect substantial weights or loadings not only in the factor serving to define the construct intended to be represented by the test but also on another factor identified by a given set of tests that had been designed to portray a different construct. Such outcomes would suggest the (a) lack of definitive support for a hypothesized construct or (b) the need to revise the measure or to eliminate it from further consideration, especially if the reliability level of its scores was low. By a process of successive approximation, Guilford was able to improve on many of his measures and eventually to gain support for several hypothesized constructs in the SOI model.

It should be mentioned at this point, however, that Guilford's intention to achieve nearly factorially pure tests that would measure only one construct at a time was in many instances not a realistic objective because many psychologically related activities such as those portrayed in a given measure may require the simultaneous use of two or more abilities. In other words, one does not use one ability to the exclusion of another. This statement would appear to be particularly relevant in the instance of devising measures to assess various forms of creative endeavor. A further point to note is that Guilford's early emphasis on the independence of intellectual abilities was probably somewhat misleading in that within hierarchical arrangements of abilities one may find increasing levels of correlation or interplay among abilities in the form of what is called higher-order factors. In about 1985, Guilford recognized that certain abilities did tend to be intercorrelated and represented essentially components of a more generalized or higher-order ability.

D. Representation of Higher-Order Abilities in SOI Symbolic Notation

The trigrams already cited, such as CMS (cognition of semantic systems), would constitute a first-order ability with each letter representing an element from each of the three dimensions (operations, contents, or products). Among the higher-order abilities, a second-order one would be defined in terms of any two of the three dimensions being represented by just one fixed element (one letter) and of the remaining dimension being portrayed by two or more elements (two or more letters). For example, the symbol N•S would imply the convergent production of a system in which two or more kinds of content were to be processed, such as a sentence containing both numbers (symbolic content) and words (semantic content). A third-order factor would be one in which only one dimension would have a single element (letter) but in which the remaining two dimensions would be allowed to have two or more ele-

ments (letters) free to vary. For example, D•• would indicate the divergent production of two or more forms of products from processing two or more kinds of content. Contrary to the multidimensional conceptualization of intelligence favored by Guilford, the presence of three successive dots or bullets in a trigram would imply the presence of one general or super dimension within which all of intelligence could be conceptualized. Subsequently, attention is given to the potential presence of higher-order factors in the construct of creative abilities.

III. PORTIONS OF THE SOI MODEL REPRESENTING CREATIVE ABILITIES

A. General Overview

In 1971 Guilford formulated eight hypotheses that embraced the major characteristics of creativity that could be related to the constructs of the SOI model: (a) analysis, (b) flexibility, (c) fluency, (d) originality, (e) penetration, (f) redefinition, (g) sensitivity to problems, and (h) synthesis. Of these eight broad hypotheses, the five that appeared to be most important to creative endeavor as reflected by the frequency of the citation of constructs in the SOI model by research studies of the creative abilities in the SOI model were fluency, flexibility, redefinition, sensitivity to problems, and originality. Subsequently, Guilford added elaboration to this list of eight major components of creativity. Certain of these broadly conceptualized hypothesized components of creativity tended to focus on particular elements within the three dimensions of the SOI model. The several forms of fluency factors placed emphasis on divergent production of several forms of products from the processing of many kinds of content. Spontaneous flexibility also made considerable use of divergent production resulting in products of units or classes with an occasional transformation, whereas redefinition, also known as adaptive flexibility, was concerned with more difficult tasks in which an altered product portraying a transformation of given information was predominant. Another aspect of flexibility was that of closure in which typically the convergent production of one or more kinds of content would result in a transformation. [*See* FLEXIBILITY.]

The broad hypothesis of sensitivity to problems was closely linked to the product of implications, as was the subsequently suggested ninth broad hypothesis concerning elaboration. Implications essentially depicted the expectations of what might happen in the instance of a catastrophe or other significant events often posing a situation with risk. Thus one form of creative endeavor would be that of anticipating the consequences of an activity (sensitivity to problems) or the generation of many extrapolations, inferences, or hypotheses (elaboration) associated with a given problem situation.

Originality appeared to be even more complex and difficult to assess than were any of the other broadly stated hypothesized catagories of creativity. Originality was frequently operationalized in terms of the rarity of responses in answers to given items in a test or to the judged cleverness of the resulting responses to test questions describing a problem situation. Typically many different constructs within the SOI model occurring in conjunction with one another would be involved in measures indicative of originality—a broad construct of great complexity requiring the use of several abilities simultaneously.

B. Representative Creative Abilities with Illustrative Examples

1. Associational Fluency

Associational fluency could involve the divergent production of products indicating a common set of classes or relationships for any one of four kinds of content. In the instance of the factor of DMR or possibly DMC, an examinee might be requested to cite as many words as possible that have the same meaning as the word *soft*. The product could be considered as either one of classes (C) or one of relations (R), as there would be either conceptual or relational connections, respectively, among the item responses.

2. Expressional Fluency

Expressional fluency typically requires the divergent production of any kind of content into a product perhaps best represented by units, classes, relations, or systems. In the instance of the trigram DMS, one might be asked to restate a given sentence in several different ways. In carrying out a review of related literature on a topic, one might have to try to summarize in one's own words the major conclusions that had been reached by the contributing authors. Several alternative interpretations might have to be given.

3. Ideational Fluency

Ideational fluency tends to be associated with the rather rapid listing of as many items falling within a specified classification as one can cite in a short period of time. The tasks corresponding to this type of fluency tend to be relatively simple as in listing as many items as possible that are wearable, black, and comfortable. This ability could probably be represented by the trigram of either divergent production of semantic units (DMU) or divergent production of semantic classes (DMC) or by a higher-order factor designated as DM•. Actually, any one of four kinds of content could be represented in which the expectation is one of quantity rather than one of a high level of quality. Another illustration might be to suggest as many uses to which a picture of a bell could be adapted—a factor probably best described as being one of either divergent production of symbolic units (DSU) or divergent production of figural units (DFU) or as a higher-order factor of D•U.

4. Flexibility Factors Requiring Convergent Production

As portrayed by Guilford, flexibility factors involving the use of convergent production tended to correspond to tasks in which one needs to differentiate figure from ground as portrayed in Gestalt studies of perception. Typically one is given a highly complex set of stimuli that can be figural, symbolic, or semantic from which a particular element or characteristic has to be identified as a unique but often common product reflecting a transformation. In the figural domain one might need to find in a complex geometric design all triangles within the design or in a picture of the front lawn of a home all the hidden toys or all the concealed Easter eggs. This gamelike problem would be described as the convergent production of figural transformations (NFT), as the identified objects have been literally torn from a context in which they were blended with other objects within a unified whole.

In the symbolic domain, flexibility of closure could be illustrated by having an individual identify as many five-letter words that are nouns within four pages of running text or to locate as many three-digit prime numbers that are located in a section of a newspaper dealing with stock market quotations. This ability would be identified as the convergent production of symbolic transformations (NST).

Flexibility of closure with semantic content often involves the selection of one of several available stimuli or procedures that could be adapted to realize a specific objective or solution to a problem—particularly in the sciences, in inventive activities, or in household repairs. As an example, one might be given five stimuli (e.g., hammer, magnifying glass, alarm clock, yardstick, and knife) and asked to select the one that would permit the creation of a fire. The individual needs to process one kind of given information for content and to generate a form of product that represents new information (a unique solution). This process requires the transformation of one kind of content comprising familiar items to a substantially modified product in a foreign or altered context. The ability underlying this activity would be defined as the convergent production of semantic transformations (NMT).

5. Flexibility Factors Requiring Divergent Production

In the context of divergent production, Guilford endeavored to separate *spontaneous flexibility* from *adaptive flexibility,* or *redefinition.* Whereas spontaneous flexibility tends to be associated with tasks of relative simplicity and with easily interpretable products often in the form of classes, adaptive flexibility, or redefinition, occurs in relatively difficult tasks demanding a substantially modified product representing a transformation. For example, spontaneous flexibility could occur when one is asked to cite as many alternative uses as possible for such a familiar object as a knife, rubber band, or tin can. This ability would be categorized as the divergent production of either semantic classes (DMC) or as the divergent production of some other transformations (DMT) depending, respectively, on the commonplace nature of the products or their degree of uniqueness or novelty.

Two familiar kinds of adaptive flexibility are likely to be encountered in daily life involving either verbal or figural content. Frequently when one is asked to come up with a new slogan in a contest or a clever title for a

story or poem, the associated construct is one of originality that would be defined as the convergent production of semantic transformations. In the instance of figural content requiring the manipulation of concrete objects, one might be directed to arrange a complex pattern of marbles of assorted colors into a given number of specific patterns. The examinee might be asked to remove as many marbles as necessary so that only rectangles with a particular number of red marbles for their length and a specified number of blue marbles for their width could be created. This task would be categorized as the divergent production of figural transformations (DFT).

Another factor of adaptive flexibility to which Guilford gave minimal attention would be within the content element of behavioral. A possible example might occur in a situation of conflict resolution in which a mediator in a labor dispute or a foreign policy dilemma could create a number of alternative solutions quite different from any of those reached by previous committees in the negotiation process. The construct underlying this activity might be tentatively classified as the divergent production of behavioral transformations (DBT).

6. Sensitivity to Problems

Closely related to the activity described in the previous example of conflict resolution would be the broadly conceived construct of creativity referred to as sensitivity to problems. This construct is concerned with the ability of one to identify needs, deficiencies, or defects in a highly complex problem area or to perceive difficulties that could be encountered in trying to cope with this complex problem or situation. One might be in need of identifying potential difficulties or problems that could be faced in financing a planned new office building for a corporate organization or to foresee possible threats to the security of a community in the path of a river that could potentially overflow its banks. This particular ability would be referred to as the cognition of semantic implications (CMI). It is also conceivable that this ability on the part of an individual who is highly fluent in the number of creative responses could be classified as the divergent production of semantic implications (DMI). Probably the activity would require the use of several higher-order abilities—such as one represented by the trigram •MI.

7. *Elaboration*

The immediately preceding example also might fall within the broad creative area of elaboration which pertains to the creation of as many hypotheses, extrapolations, or inferences as possible from a set of complex stimuli associated with a potentially hazardous environmental accident. In this instance elaboration could be interpreted as being the divergent production of semantic implications (DMI). Another example would be to cite as many consequences as one could suggest regarding the potential damage to the environment from a catastrophic volcanic eruption or from the entry of an unusually large asteroid into the earth's atmosphere. In the figural realm, an example would be to require one to form as many possible geometric figures without any restraints from 20 pieces of wood that have been cut to different lengths. This ability would be classified as the divergent production of figural implications (DFI) or as the divergent production of figural transformation (DFT).

8. *Originality*

It would appear that the previously mentioned originality construct shows considerable overlap with those of redefinition and flexibility and that the realization of transformations constitutes a key component to originality. In addition, as said before, the relative infrequency of a response and the cleverness of a solution to a problem would to be a central characteristic of products associated with the process of doing original thinking. Originality is a complex activity that would require the simultaneous use of many different first-order abilities in creative problem solving. Particularly important to creative endeavor such as that found in originality would be the operation of higher-order factors that constitute the simultaneous application of moderately to highly correlated constructs. As stated previously, Guilford recognized this possibility and began to devote systematic efforts in his research efforts to identify such abilities. Unfortunately, he did not live long enough to see his modified point of view exert a substantial impact on the investigation of creativity.

Several of his former students and their students have applied new methodologies of confirmatory maximum likelihood factor analysis to previously obtained correlational databases. This new methodology affords in a rather exacting means to test empirically the viability of alternative factor models comprising both first-order and higher-order factors. From these alternative models, one can ascertain which ones are able to explain the greatest amount of covariation among the test variables. The mathematical requirements of the highly complex procedures are beyond the scope of this presentation.

IV. THE STRUCTURE-OF-INTELLECT PROBLEM SOLVING (SIPS) MODEL

In the 1960s Guilford began to conceptualize creative thinking as a mode of problem solving that led to an adaptation of the SOI formulation into one he named the structure-of-intellect problem solving (SIPS) model. He found the SIPS model to offer a more dynamic and meaningful way to interpret the process of creativity within the context of problem solving. The SIPS model is reproduced in graphical form in Figure 2.

As shown in this figure, the SIPS model sets forth the same psychological operations as those in the SOI model, although it should be noted that both convergent production and divergent production have been placed in a single classification of production. The memory component is reflected in an elongated rectangle toward the bottom of the figure and the repetitive evaluation operation has been placed in smaller rectangles just above the elongated rectangle. The four kinds of content or information are portrayed just above the title of the figure. In the outlining regions of the geometric portrayal of the SIPS model are representations of input of information and its filtering. At key points an opportunity exists for the problem solver to exit or leave the problem-solving process.

In a highly simplified fashion, the dynamics of the model may be explained as follows. Initially, the individual is able to use the process of cognition to sense and to structure the problem once initial input has been filtered in such a way as to arouse and direct attention. If the level of attention is insufficient to create any interest or meaningful cognition once there has been some evaluation of the input, the individual in his or her problem-solving endeavor may exit from the scene. On the other hand, if the level of attention and accompanying interest level after filtering, cognition, and evaluation are sufficient, the problem solver devel-

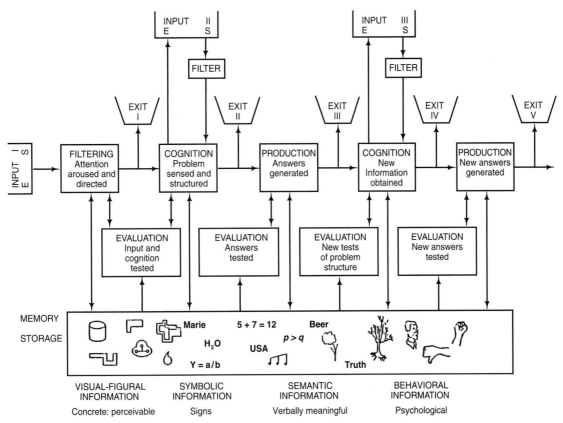

FIGURE 2 The structure-of-intellect problem-solving (SIPS) model. From *The Analysis of Intelligence* by J. P. Guilford and Ralph Hoepfner (1971), New York: McGraw-Hill. Copyright 1971 by McGraw-Hill. Reproduced by permission.

ops what Guilford termed a search model or strategy that may undergo many modifications in the process of problem solving. This search model typically contains several cues of an informational nature that show certain similarities in their distinctive characteristics to those found in one or more of the products occurring in the memory storage. During the beginning efforts of problem solving, this search model may take on additional characteristics new and unique in their nature from both the internal (typically affective or motivational inputs) and the external environment (often additional informational inputs) as well as from the memory storage. As this process takes place, there is continuous ongoing evaluation of all newly created information that will direct and facilitate future problem-solving activities. This process may continue for an indefinite period of time. Basically, the problem solver goes through a trial and error self-regulatory process that yields one or more tentative solutions to the prob-

lem that continue to be evaluated for relevance and appropriateness. Eventually the individual may select a solution and then exit from the scene.

It is apparent within this self-regulating process in which a considerable amount of filtering occurs that there is a marked amount of interaction or interplay of cognition, memory, evaluation, and production as displayed by the many two-way arrows in Figure 2. This process may be quite repetitive in what might be termed successive iterations with continual production of initially tentative and then increasingly refined solutions that are subject to an ever present evaluation as new information in being generated from the memory storage. As stated before, new information that may also be filtered from both the external and internal environment may be expected to result in modified cognitions, additional evaluation, and the ongoing production of alternative solutions. Constituting successive degrees of approximation to the solution of a problem, the repetitive cycles in some instances may lead to an unexpected or sudden insight of a solution that is interpreted to be adequate and pleasing to the problem solver or to his or her associates. It is evident that one may depart or exit from the field of endeavor at any time if the problem solver decides that the task is nonproductive or too demanding, if other immediate priorities override the need to solve the problem immediately, or if the answer obtained is judged to be satisfactory.

Another essential concept to creativity in the problem solving realm has been the construct of *transfer recall* that Guilford proposed in 1968. This particular construct appears to be especially relevant in problem-solving activities in mathematics, science, engineering, and invention. The products typically involve a transformation. From a positive point of view, transfer recall constitutes the retrieval of information from an incomplete set of cues in the memory storage and from the use of this information within a foreign or strange context in relatively novel ways. On the other hand, from a negative point of view, transfer recall is retrieval of information suggested by cues in relation to which the information has not been previously placed in the memory storage or has not become part of those relevant cues. The transformed employment of retrieved information is achieved primarily by flexibly redefining, reinterpreting, or reclassifying highly organized information within the memory storage in relation to the requirements of a well-defined problem. In contrast to what Guilford termed *replicative recall* in the context of associational learning that requires the retrieval of already stored information in its essentially original form, as in recalling the names of presidents in chronological order, transfer recall in the context of cognitive learning consists of and necessitates ongoing and active use of a *search model*. This employment of the search model in conjunction with transfer recall embodies the scanning of the domain of a highly rich memory storage to choose those kinds of information needed to meet the transformation requirements of a well-delineated problem.

It should be emphasized that the SIPS model is specifically directed toward problem solving, which Guilford considered to be the central approach to creative thinking. As already stated, the construct of transfer recall just considered is a key aspect to creative problem

solving whenever a transformation product is likely to occur. Moreover, a rich and comprehensive memory storage provides the foundation for which transfer recall can be more readily achieved, as it furnishes a substantial baseline against which ongoing evaluation can occur. The SIPS model also would seem to have implications for those teachers who are trying to encourage creative endeavor on the part of their students. Those who give instruction in metacognition would probably find the dynamics of this model to be particularly relevant in facilitating complex problem solving at a relatively high level of abstraction. Clearly, evaluation of tentative hypotheses and testing tentative solutions to a problem is a key component to reaching a final solution that is meaningful and relevant. Finally, as a matter of incidental interest, one may note that the ongoing iterative activity in the SIPS formulation is quite analogous to that found in a computerized cybernetics model in which evaluation also is heavily emphasized.

V. CRITIQUE OF SOI AND SIPS MODELS

In his formulation of a comprehensive theory of intelligence provided by the SOI model and of creative problem solving afforded by the SIPS model, Guilford made significant conceptual contributions to the understanding of the multidimensionality of intelligence of which creative abilities constitute an important part. He was able to integrate within his extensive framework key constructs for creative thinking. Although many psychologists may have raised questions regarding the adequacy of empirical efforts to validate the theory, most have come to the conclusion that intelligence as well as creativity is indeed multidimensional. Whereas many other researchers in the area of creativity have tended to emphasize fluency constructs based on divergent production as being the essential characteristics of creative endeavor, Guilford convincingly demonstrated the significance of transformations that in the disciplines of mathematics, science, and engineering are dependent on convergent production rather than on divergent production. He also introduced the construct of sensitivity to problems in which one has to be aware of implications posed by the problem situation, as in the instance of a major disaster or a risk-talking activity. His models have also been the source of scores of doctoral dissertations, hundreds of research studies and publications, the creation of tests of many diverse abilities, and instructional innovations both in the United States and in foreign countries. In short, Guilford will stand out in history as a major contributor to improved understanding of the creative process and to its implementation in the educational enterprise.

Most criticisms of Guilford's theories, as previously suggested, have been directed largely toward the questionable levels of empirical support for its many constructs. Many of these concerns have centered around the statistical methodologies that have been employed and the highly specific characteristics of his measures. In his use of exploratory factor analytic techniques, many have questioned the objectivity of his approach in that they thought that he had possibly forced his solutions to meet his own subjective expectations. Moreover, there was often a lack of clarity in the factor structures obtained and a failure to replicate the factor structures generated across diverse populations. Perhaps one of the most striking criticisms has been that he tended to minimize the significance of the amount of correlation among first-order factors that he considered to be quite independent and somewhat narrow in their test representation. Toward the end of his life, he did substantially modify his views and started to undertake an intensive study of higher-order factors that would necessitate the presence of at least moderate correlations among the first-order factors. Unfortunately, he did not live long enough to apply confirmatory factor analytic approaches that would have afforded considerable support for the presence of higher-order and correlated factors within his SOI model.

In addition to these largely statistically based criticisms, many expressed reservations about several of the SOI tests, the scores on many of which yielded relatively low reliabilities. Some have thought that the tests tended to represent somewhat artificial experiences that did not correspond to the realities of creative problem solving in real life. Others have been concerned that he neglected the affective and motivational aspects of creative experience that other researchers were considering. Certainly, future efforts need to be directed toward integrating both intellectual and affective constructs of creativity and toward developing reliable and valid indicators of the constructs associated with these two broad domains.

Despite these concerns, his models have continued to stimulate a vast amount of research and application both in the school environment and in the training settings of business and industry. Improved statistical methodologies, many of which have been applied in reanalyzing his databases, have provided useful information that can be expected to lead to the modification of his two theories with particular attention directed to the interdependence of the constructs of creativity. One point already made has been that individuals probably use simultaneously a number of psychological operations to process a variety of kinds of information content in a problem situation to generate more than one type of product, especially in a complex problem-solving situation. One can anticipate that his models will continue to provide a direction for future research that will yield an increased understanding of the properties of human intelligence and its creative characteristics as well as practical outcomes that can be applied to solving significant problems encountered in day-to-day living.

Bibliography

Guilford, J. P. (1967). *The nature of human intelligence.* New York: McGraw-Hill.

Guilford, J. P. (1968). *Intelligence, creativity, and their educational implications.* San Diego, CA: Knapp.

Guilford, J. P. (1981). Higher-order structure-of-intellect abilities. *Multivariate Behavioral Research, 16,* 411–435.

Guilford, J. P. (1985). The structure-of-intellect model. In B. B. Wolman (Ed.), *Handbook of intelligence.* New York: Wiley.

Guilford, J. P. (1988). Some changes in the structure-of-intellect model. *Educational and Psychological Measurement, 48,* 1–4.

Guilford, J. P., & Hoepfner, R. (1971). *The analysis of intelligence.* New York: McGraw-Hill.

Guilford, J. P., & Tenopyr, M. L. (1968). Implications of the structure-of-intellect model for high school and college students. In W. B. Michael (Ed.), *Teaching for creative endeavor* (pp. 25–45). Bloomington, IN: Indiana University Press.

Michael, W. B., & Bachelor, P. (1990). Higher-order structure-of-intellect creativity factors in divergent production tests: A re-analysis of a Guilford data base. *Creativity Research Journal, 3,* 58–74.

Handwriting and Creativity

Warren D. TenHouten

University of California, Los Angeles

Spoken words are the symbols of mental experience, and written words are the symbols of spoken words.

Aristotle

I. Creativity: Aspirations and Organization
II. Graphology, the Study of Handwriting
III. Creativity, Thought, and the Brain
IV. Dysgraphia and the Split Brain
V. Alexithymia, Creativity, and the Split Brain
VI. Graphology as Scientific Methodology

Creative Aspirations The interest in and the desire for the realization of a creation. Graphologically, creative aspirations are reflected in the height and elaboration of the upper zone of letters such as t, f, h, k, and l, and in many capital letters, and in the expressiveness of writing—in the totality of graphic movements sufficiently distinguished to differentiate one writer from another.

Creative Organization The deliberate and systematic production of ideas and methods that result in creation. Graphologically, the creatively organized person shows good organization, simplification of form, and originality of graphic expression. Good organization is reflected in the overall use of space and movement in time (ease of forward movement). Simplification is the use of economic shortcuts, finding econ-

omy of time and motion, and seeking what is essential. Originality refers to spontaneity and creativity in the handling of space, form, and movement.

Creativity in Writing The ability to produce new forms, to restructure stereotyped situations, to innovate, to redefine, and to improvise. Required is the aspiration to imagine and conceptualize creations, together with the organizational skills for turning such ideas into objective creations.

Graphology A study or description of handwriting in relation to changes from the ordinary which occur in some diseases, such as paralysis and alexithymia; the art or science of inferring a person's character, disposition, and aptitudes from the peculiarities of his or her handwriting.

Intentionality Creativity requires that a person is able to care about a state of future affairs (the realization of a creation), organize a program to realize this state, and stick to this program in spite of distractions and obstacles. On the other hand, the intention to solve a problem can lead to the deliberate and systematic production of ideas that result in creations.

Graphology, as art and science, in the interpretive analysis of HANDWRITING. In addition to communicating the meanings of written words, writing reveals much about a person's personality, mentality, and capability. It is possible, through graphological analysis, to make inferences about various "sectors" of personality structure.

Copyright © 1999 by Academic Press
All rights of reproduction in any form reserved.

Techniques such as the Roman–Anthony Graphological Psychogram make it possible to generate an overall view of the personality. One Psychogram sector is "intellectual aspirations and creativity." To interpret the specific graphic features constituting this sector, study has been made of a group of brain-surgery patients hypothesized to have a pathological lack of creativity and ability to symbolize. The cerebral commissurotomy (split-brained) patients—lacking direct connection between the right side of the brain's gestalt-synthetic thought and the left side of the brain's logical-analytic thought—have been hypothesized to lack creativity. Comparison of the handwriting of a sample of these patients and of a precision-matched normal control group indicates a lack of creative aspirations and of creative organization in the patients' scripts. Creativity requires that a person care about their idea of a future state of affairs as a potential creation (creative aspiration), organize a plan of action to realize this future state (creative organization), and possess the intentionality necessary to stick to such a plan in spite of obstacles and distractions. Many indicators of a lack of intentionality can be seen in handwriting: among the split-brain patients, the handwriting specimens indicated, for example, a lack of emotional energy directed to objects, coordination, rhythm, connectivity, alignment control, and slant consistency. Thus, in their handwriting the split-brained patients showed a lack of aspirations to create, a lack of organizational capability to create, and a lack of the will to create. These findings are consistent with other observations of these same patients, namely of a lack of praxis and productive engagement with the world—the mundane and taken-for-granted creativities of the everyday social world.

I. CREATIVITY: ASPIRATIONS AND ORGANIZATION

Creativity requires productive thinking. There is a "dialectical" aspect to creativity in that it often involves interaction of logical-analytic/propositional and gestalt-synthetic/appositional modes of thought). Thinking that integrates these two opposite yet complementary modes of thought is perhaps necessary for creativity, but alone is insufficient because of linkages between creativity and intentionality. On the one hand, creative ideas can be stimulated by the integration of analytic and synthetic thought. But creativity means more than an idea and an aspiration; also required is that something actually be created, a creation. Thus, willpower and intentionality are necessary for a person to be able to care about a state of future affairs and the realization of a creation, organize a program to realize this state, and stick to this program in spite of distractions and obstacles. On the other hand, the intention to solve a problem can lead to the deliberate and systematic production of ideas that result in creations. Thus, there exist dynamic, reciprocal relations between creativity and intentionality.

II. GRAPHOLOGY, THE STUDY OF HANDWRITING

Handwriting, as a psychomotor gesture, can be used to identify a creative personality and mind insofar as writing communicates not only the meaning of the words but also the personality structure of the writer. Handwriting is a process of gesturing, this gesturing externalizing and thereby giving creation to inner speech. Qualitative and quantitative graphological analysis enables us to make inferences about "sectors" or "constellations" of personality structure on the basis of detailed features of handwriting. One quantitative graphological technique, the Graphological Psychogram, was developed by K. Roman and given formalization and elaboration by D. Anthony. The objective of graphology in general, and the Psychogram in particular, is to represent an integrated and synthetic view of the personality. The 40 separate graphic indicators of the Psychogram (organization, rhythm, speed, rightward trend, pressure, etc.) are partitioned, on a conceptual, a priori basis, into eight sectors, the sector of immediate interest being "intellect, aspirations, and creativity." Roman cautions that no single component or feature of handwriting can be interpreted without reference to all the others, even though for purposes of analysis they can be set apart and considered separately, view each one technically by itself. A single feature as such is significant only in relation to the group to which it belongs.

The intellect–aspirations–creativity sector is operationally defined in the Psychogram by six graphological variables, commented upon by Anthony: (a) good organizational structure; (b) innovative simplification of form; (c) upper zone elaboration ("desire to form, build, or arrange," e.g., of the letters f, h, k, l, and t, and numerous capitalized letters); (d) upper zone height; (e) originality, and (f) expressiveness (indicated, most generally, by an overall consistency in effort and direction).

III. CREATIVITY, THOUGHT, AND THE BRAIN

Gestalt-synthetic, holistic thought (in the adult, right-handed person) is usually associated with the functioning of the right cerebral hemisphere (RH) of the human brain, and logical-analytic thought with the left hemisphere (LH). Intentionality, along with planning, monitoring, editing, commanding, controlling, and anticipation, is associated with the functioning of the frontal lobes of the brain.

The frontal lobes evolved out of, and remain closely linked to, the limbic system, which provides emotional response to images and models, and which, in combination with memory and information about the body and environment, enables the frontal lobes to carry out meaningful, goal-directed behavior in the interests of the self. The goal-directed behavioral programs of the frontal lobes extend to intentions and plans. These programs are complex results of social development and are formed with the participation of language, which plays an important role in abstraction, categorization, and generalization, and in the control and regulation of behavior. In order to act with intentionality, it is necessary that the frontal lobes are able to evaluate the results of one's own actions. The frontal lobes carry out a complex process of matching actions and initial intention to evaluate success and error, so that action can be corrected and modified as necessary given changing circumstances. Luria and Homskaya view *intentionality as a core responsibility of the frontal lobes,* according to which a person cares about the state of future affairs, develops a program, and carries this program through, overcoming distractions and obstacles.

We can understand creativity through the study of neurological patients with a pathological lack of integration of analytic and synthetic thought. Such a group of patients are the split-brain (cerebral commissur-

otomy, corpus callosotomy) patients who have had—as a treatment of last resort for drug-refractory epileptic seizures—the two hemispheres of their brains surgically divided through sectioning of the corpus callosum (including the anterior commissure, dorsal and ventral hippocampal commissures, and in some cases the massa intermedia), a structure containing some 200 million nerve fibers that directly join the hemispheres. Following this operation, patients are unable to integrate the workings of the two sides of the brain. [*See* SPLIT BRAINS; INTERHEMISPHERIC EXCHANGE IN CREATIVITY.]

IV. DYSGRAPHIA AND THE SPLIT BRAIN

In a remarkably simple but nonetheless crucial experimental study of the first eight patients undergoing this surgery, neurosurgeon J. Bogen discovered limitations in both their writing and their drawing abilities. Following the operation, the right side of the body is controlled by the LH and vice versa. Therefore, performances carried out by the right hand result from LH activity, and performances carried out by left are related to the activities of the RH. All patients experienced a reduced capacity to write (dysgraphia) with the left hand but not with the right hand. These patients also experienced a reduced capacity to copy figures (dyscopia) with the right hand, but not with the left. The dysgraphia–dyscopia phenomena is illustrated in Figure 1 by responses of one of the split-brain patients. To measure dysgraphia, a written model of the word "Sunday" was used. The patient copied the word with his right hand (and LH) but could manage only a crude "S A" with his left hand. His dyscopia is illustrated by his effort to copy a cross and a solid cube. He copied the figures quite well with his left hand (and RH) but not with his right hand (and LH).

V. ALEXITHYMIA, CREATIVITY, AND THE SPLIT BRAIN

Hoppe and Bogen found *alexithymia*—a cognitive-affective disturbance involving a lack of words for feelings—in 12 commissurotomized patients. The

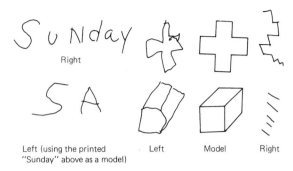

Right

Left (using the printed
"Sunday" above as a model)   Left   Model   Right

FIGURE 1

alexithymic has difficulty describing his or her feelings to other persons. There is a difficulty in verbally identifying feelings but also in distinguishing feeling from bodily sensations. There is a lack of symbolizations, termed "asymbollexia" by Hoppe in 1985, and an impoverishment of fantasy life, resulting in a utilitarian mode of thinking. The opposite of alexithymia, called "symbollexia" by Hoppe, is apt to be taken for granted in the everyday world but must be considered a form of creativity in its own right. According to interhemispheric transfer deficit theory, alexithymia results from a physical or functional disconnection of the two hemispheres, such that the cognitive representations of negative affects (of the RH) cannot be articulated in words (by the LH).

Bogen and Bogen have argued that an interaction between the modes of thought of the two sides of the brain is necessary for creative thinking. They suggest that "to demonstrate that division of the corpus callosum leads to a loss of creativity, we need some measure of creativity" (Bogen & Bogen, 1969, p. 201). Handwriting provided such a measure in a further alexithymia study carried out by TenHouten, which included 8 of the 12 split-brain patients of the Hoppe–Bogen study and 8 precision-matched control subjects. All 16 subjects were shown a 3-min videotaped film four times. The film depicted, with music and visual images, the deaths of a baby and of a boy. After the second showing of this film, all subjects were instructed to write four sentences expressing what they felt about the film.

Small samples of the handwriting of the subjects are shown in Figure 2. The commissurotomized patients, in comparison to controls, can be described by Psychogram variables as having less form and arrangement in the elaboration of their writing's upper zone and write in a less expressive way. They are relatively constricted in their expression of self, as their graphic gestures lack individual distinctiveness. Their script lacks rhythm and coordination of movements, organization, and trizonal dynamics. In addition to its arrhythmic quality, their handwriting lacks an effective articulation of the letters with connecting strokes, which according to Anthony indicates a lack of "creativeness of the graphic expression." Patients are infirm in their writing stroke (ductus) and show an arrhythmic alternation of pressure and release. Here they can be said to lack control of sensuous expression. Their writing lacks consistency in the slant of the letters. There is inadequate control over alignment and direction of lines and spaces between lines. And finally, there is a general irregularity in these patients' script.

The handwriting samples were scored on the Psychogram by a professional graphologist who was told only the age and sex of the writers (standard procedure in graphology). The six variables classified as indicators of creativity were intercorrelated, with the result that all correlations but that between Organization and Upper Zone Height were positive. A factor analysis of this correlation matrix resulted in a two-factor solution, meaning that there are two latent, abstract concepts which might explain the correlations.

A. Aspirations and Organization Measurement

The two upper zone variables—Upper Zone Elaboration and Upper Zone Height—joined Expressiveness in the first factor. Anthony defines "aspiration" as a desire for the realization of values—of "ideals, ambitious intellectuality, power, honor, excellence . . ." (1977, p. 3). He argues, "Graphologically, it is commonly reflected by the upper zone elaboration . . . and upper zone height (. . . interest and aspirations above the daily routine, the intellectual guiding principle)" (1977, p. 3). Anthony defines Expressiveness as "those graphic movements sufficiently distinctive to differentiate one individual from another. These can include a flair for dynamic design and spontaneous movements on the positive side or by a stultifying rigidity and static immobility on the negative" (1977, p. 3). This three-variable factor was named Creative Aspiration.

The second factor attracted the other three intellect–

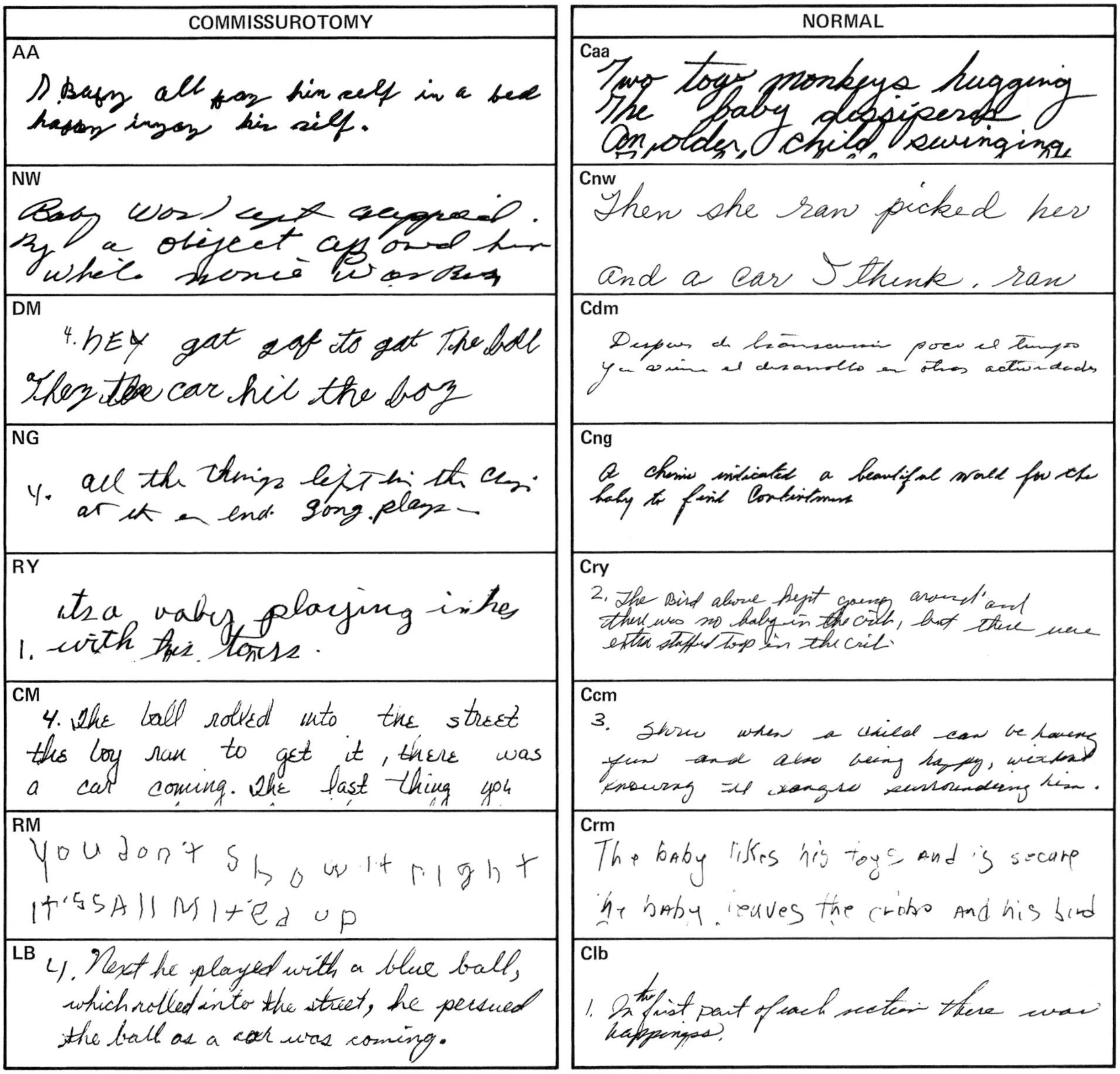

COMMISSUROTOMY	NORMAL
AA	**Caa**
NW	**Cnw**
DM	**Cdm**
NG	**Cng**
RY	**Cry**
CM	**Ccm**
RM	**Crm**
LB	**Clb**

FIGURE 2

aspirations–creativity sector variables: Organization, Simplification, and Originality. Organization refers to the writer's overall use of space and of movement in time (ease of forward motion). Here, the emphasis is on form and design, figure and ground, and unity, coherence, and coordination. If "creativity" is defined, as in Anthony, as "the ability to produce new forms, to restructure stereotyped situations, to invent or innovate, to redefine, to improvise" (1977, p. 3), then good organization can be interpreted as a rather global mea-

sure of creativity. Anthony states that "high scores for simplification and originality . . . are indicative of creativity" (1977, p. 3). Simplification of form means economic shortcuts in writing, seeking economy of time and motion, and seeking what is essential. Originality has the commonsense meaning of the term, here referring to "spontaneity . . . and creativity in the handling of space, form, and movement." The three variables forming this factor were together named Creative Organization. The person of high creative aspiration is apt to be known for his or her original ideas; the person of high creative organization not only has creative ideas, but possesses the methodological and organizational skills to turn such ideas into objective creations.

B. Intentionality Measures

The commissurotomized patients, as hypothesized, showed significantly lower scores for Creative Aspiration and for Creative Organization than did their precision-matched normal controls. They were lower than controls for overall measures of other sectors as well—for Goal Direction, Libidinal Energy, Expression of Feelings, Control, and script quality (Form Level and Functional Productivity). A "second-order" factor analysis, using six sector-level variables, led to the discovery of a possible lack of intentionality in these patients. In both alexithymia and in some psychosomatic disorders there is an impoverished level of relations to objects and goals, and a lack of dynamic energy in relation to these objects. This lack of intentionality degrades one's ability to sustain focus.

The data, while only exploratory and based on samples ordinarily considered inadequate for multivariate statistical analysis, suggest that a person predisposed to act with intentionality can be expected to show, in his or her handwriting, the following features: (a) an ability to integrate intentions with actions in a fluent and rhythmic manner; (b) good alignment control, indicated by parallel lines that are unwavering and straight—here reflected in a sense of direction and orderliness—and an effective use of time, all suggesting a functional integrity toward the fulfillment of objectives; (c) writing that shows a naturalness and spontaneity in voluntary control of size, pressure, form, and arrangement; (d) writing that is firm, with rhythmic alternation of tension and release in pressure and stroke (an elastic and flexible stroke shows meaningful functioning, the making of an effective "impression" on the world); and (e) contractions and release that are balanced and rhythmic in movement, distribution, and form, all of which indicate an ability to perform productively. Note in this description the importance of rhythm (the strongest single variable for commissurotomy–control group differences).

The commissurotomy patients' handwriting had as global features lack of coordination and rhythm, inten-

tionality, and goal-directedness. Graphological variables contributing to Intentionality included, in addition to three creativity variables (Upper Zone Elaboration, Upper Zone Height, and Expressiveness), Rhythm, Trizonal Dynamics (psychical energy, goal-oriented behavior), Firmness of Ductus (the control of meaningful functioning, or making an "impression" on the environment), Connectedness (ability to connect experiences purposefully), Fluctuation (which integrates intentions with actions in a fluent and rhythmic manner), Slant Consistency, Alignment Control (indicating functional integrity toward the fulfillment of objectives), and Regularity (movement and arrangement volitionally controlled by the writer, an ability to concentrate, and firmness and resolution). On the sector level, data analysis indicated that intentionality is primarily a joint function of two sectors, goal direction and emotional release. An overall measure of intentionality was positively correlated both with Creative Aspiration and with Creative Organization.

These results have implications for the study of creativity and of pathological lack of creativity. On the basis of other than graphological analysis, in the same study it was found that following the splitting apart of the left and right hemispheres of the brain, patients seemed to have a degraded experience of symbolization in 1985. TenHouten and colleagues found that the patients, in comparison to precision-matched normal control subjects, used few affect-laden words (a face-valid index of alexithymia); their relatively frequent auxiliary verbs suggested a passive and indirect personal style; and they used relatively few adjectives, suggesting speech that is flat, dull, uninvolved, and lacking in color and expression. Further, they were found relatively less apt to fantasize or imagine symbols (of the filmic stimulus). There was an overall lack of creativity in the contents of their spoken and written verbal productions; these patients have been described as dull, flat, colorless, unexpressive, passive, indirect, lacking fantasy, unimaginative, unresponsive to symbols, and describing circumstances of events rather than feelings about these events. The evidence suggests, albeit indirectly, a lack of creativity in the content of their spoken and written verbal productions. They symbolized in a discursive way, using mainly secondary-process thought as opposed to a presentational structure consistent with primary-process thought. Hoppe showed that there was a concreteness in their symbolizations, with an emphasis on stereotypic denotations.

The strongest result of the graphological study was that, for each of the eight pairs of subjects, patients showed less emotional release than did controls, which replicates the earlier finding of alexithymia following cerebral commissurotomy.

VI. GRAPHOLOGY AS SCIENTIFIC METHODOLOGY

Graphology, as a measurement methodology, is useful to the extent to which handwriting is an active and generalized symbolic system of gestures. Therefore, it can be used to measure personality characteristics or syndromes. The use of a graphological level of analysis was supported by the split-brain study's predictive and content validity; there was a consistency of results based on graphology and on other content-analytic measures.

The hypotheses advanced on the basis of graphological variables, distinguishing the handwriting of patients and controls, were consistently supported by other data. The split-brain patients showed a strong dysgraphia in their left hands. They also showed a strong dyscopia in their right hands. In addition, because the linear-thinking left hemisphere was not enriched by the right hemisphere's affective, expressive, and spatial creative mode of thought: This overall propensity can be thought of as an expression dysgraphia in the right hand. The split-brain patients did to some extent, however, express and symbolize emotions, primarily in a subconscious, negative way, through their handwriting. The alexithymia of these patients is a matter of degree, and their LHs are hardly devoid of affective expression, especially for positive emotions. Research with split-brained patients shows that their RHs are able to signal their LHs, possibly by means of brain-stem connections. In two of these patients researchers found an "affective aura" rapidly communicated from RH to LH. In 1987 TenHouten and colleagues also found, during the showing of the film, slightly higher interhemispheric electroencephalographic alpha-band coherences between each of four RH channels and the LH central (C3) sensory-motor channel for patients than for controls, possibly indicating brain-stem synchronization.

Bibliography

Anthony, D. (1977). *Psychogram guide book.* New York: Pantheon.

Bogen, J. E., & Bogen, G. M. (1969). The other side of the brain III: The corpus callosum and creativity. *Bulletin of the Los Angeles Neurological Societies, 34,* 191–221.

Hoppe, K. D. (1985). Mind and spirituality: Symbollexia, empathy and God-representation. *Bulletin of the National Guild of Catholic Psychiatrists, 9,* 353–378.

Hoppe, K. D., & Bogen, J. E. (1977). Alexithymia in twelve commissurotomized patients. *Psychotherapy and Psychosomatics, 28,* 148–55.

Luria, A. R., & Homskaya, E. D. (1964). Disturbances in the regulative role of speech with frontal lobe lesions. In J. M. Warren and K. Akert (Eds.), *The frontal granular cortex and behavior: A symposium.* New York: McGraw–Hill.

Roman, K. (1952). *Handwriting: Key to personality.* New York: Pantheon.

TenHouten, W. D. (1994). Creativity, intentionality, and alexithymia: A graphological analysis of split-brained patients and normal controls. In M. D. Runco, K. D. Hoppe, & M. Shaw (Eds.), *Creativity and affect.* Norwood, NJ: Ablex. [A substantial portion of this entry is extracted from this chapter.]

TenHouten, W. D., Hoppe, K. D., Bogen, J. E., & Walter, D. O. (1985). Alexithymia: An experimental study of cerebral commissurotomy patients and normal controls. *American Journal of Psychiatry, 143,* 312–316.

TenHouten, W. D., Walter, D. O., Hoppe, K. D., & Bogen, J. E. (1987). Alexithymia and the split brain. V. EEG alpha-band interhemispheric coherence. *Psychotherapy and Psychosomatics, 47,* 1–10.

TenHouten, W. D., Seifer, M., & Seigel, P. (1988). Alexithymia and the split brain. VII. Evidence from graphological signs. In K. D. Hoppe (Guest Ed.), *Hemispheric specialization, affect, and creativity* (Psychiatric Clinics of North America Series). Philadelphia, PA: Saunders.

Heuristics

Michael D. Mumford and Dwayne G. Norris

American Institutes for Research

Category A concept or schema capturing an organized body of information about a class of objects.

Declarative Knowledge Knowledge or information bearing on object characteristics or properties.

Expertise Experience solving problems in a domain.

Heuristic A set of rules or procedures for executing certain cognitive processes.

Ill Defined Goals, requirements, and operations are not clearly specified or easily identified.

Metacognitive Knowledge about cognition, such as when and how to apply heuristics.

Procedural Knowledge Knowledge about ways of applying or working with information.

Process A set of organized, directed mental operations performed in working with information.

*The term **HEURISTICS** has been used in different ways by different investigators. The most common definition* of a heuristic, however, is a set of rules or procedures applied in problem solving. Thus "means–end" analysis, or attempts to solve a problem by working backward from a goal, is commonly considered a heuristic. At first glance, it is not clear how such concrete procedures can prove of any great value in understanding creative thought when people must deal with novel problems where fixed rules simply do not apply. In recent years, however, it has become clear that creative problem solving involves certain key processes, or mental operations, used to reshape and reform existing knowledge as people attempt to generate new ideas. Some rules and procedures for executing these processes appear more useful than others in helping people generate creative ideas and solve novel problems. Accordingly, in this article we will examine the heuristics, or rules and procedures, that contribute to effective organization of certain key processes involved in creative thought. We will then consider what we know about the development and application of these heuristics.

I. CREATIVE PROBLEM SOLVING

Not all problems we confront in the course of our lives call for creative thought. Creative thought, however, is required when we are confronted with a certain type of problem. The kind of problems that call for

Copyright © 1999 by Academic Press
All rights of reproduction in any form reserved.

creative thought share three common characteristics. First, creative problems tend to be ill defined, or poorly structured, in the same sense that the goals and procedures applying to the problem situation are not evident. Second, the problem situation confronting the individual is novel, resulting in a situation where rote extrapolation from past experience is likely to prove of limited value. Third, and finally, these problems require people to reshape or reform existing knowledge to generate the new ideas and new approaches. [*See* PROBLEM SOLVING.]

To solve novel problems, one must have knowledge. Knowledge, however, is not simply an accumulation of discrete facts. Instead, expertise lies in the systematic, principle-based organization of information. The principle-based knowledge that characterizes experts in different domains has two distinct aspects: (a) declarative knowledge reflecting the content, characteristics, and organization of relevant objects or key exemplars, and (b) procedural knowledge reflecting the rules, procedures, or strategies for applying this declarative knowledge when solving certain types of problems. Heuristics can be viewed as a form of procedural knowledge. [*See* EXPERTISE.]

Of course, if we had only existing knowledge, either procedural or declarative, it would be impossible for people to create new ideas. Students of creativity, as a result, have tried to identify those general processes, or major kinds of cognitive activities, that allow people to work with extant knowledge in creating new ideas. Broadly speaking, the available evidence indicates that the generation of new ideas is based on the combination and reorganization of existing knowledge structures which gives rise to new features, or new ways of understanding the problem situation, thereby permitting people to generate new, alternative solutions.

As important as combination and reorganization is to creative thought, successful creative problem solving efforts are contingent on effective execution of a host of other processing operations. Over the years, scholars have proposed a number of models describing the processes likely to play a key role in people's creative problem solving efforts. These models show a high degree of convergence, at least with respect to conscious, active processing activities, and identify eight core processes.

Idea formation activities include processes such as

(1) problem construction, where the nature of the problem is defined and an approach selected; (2) information encoding, where people gather or retrieve information bearing on the nature of the problem; (3) category selection, where people organize information into concepts, or categories, and identify concepts that appear especially useful in addressing the problem, and (4) category combination and reorganization, where retained concepts are combined or restructured to generate new frameworks for understanding the problem. The second major set of activities consists of idea generation and implementation, which begins after new ideas, or new concepts, have been formulated, and includes processes such as (5) idea generation, where this new understanding is used to generate one or more potential solutions; (6) idea evaluation, where these potential solutions are appraised for likely success and workability; (7) implementation planning, where an approach for applying this idea in a situation is generated and executed; and (8) monitoring, where implementation is assessed, adjustments made, and further refinements identified through ongoing performance monitoring.

II. HEURISTICS IN CREATIVE PROBLEM SOLVING

The heuristics called for in creative problem solving depend on the processes that represent key determinants of performance and the type of procedures most likely to contribute to successful process execution. For example, encouraging people to think of alternatives is a heuristic commonly used to stimulate creative thought. As useful as this heuristic may be during idea generation, it is not likely to prove of great value during information encoding, where people expressly seek relevant information.

Not only are heuristics, and their value, specific to a given process, one will not be able to identify a single heuristic that always guarantees successful process execution. Creative problems are novel, complex, and ill defined. These characteristics of creative problems, in turn, imply that a number of different procedures might be applied in executing a given process leading to viable, but perhaps different, solutions. Thus, both broad-based and more focused goal-based searches can be used during information encoding. Of course, the potential availability of multiple heuristics implies that creative thought requires not only the ability to identify applicable procedures, but also the capability to shift from one procedure to another.

The availability of multiple heuristics and the need for people to select viable heuristics is related to studies examining people's preferences for using, and skill in applying, different heuristics. One finding that emerges from these studies is that people, when solving problems, often rely on intuitive, default heuristics. Those naive biases toward the application of certain intuitively appealing heuristics can occasionally prove useful. Quite often, however, these biases may inhibit creative thought. For example, when confronted with novel problems, people often use a heuristic referred to as means–end analysis, working backward from a preordained goal using a trial and error approach. Means–end analysis, however, is highly inefficient and resource-intensive, typically failing to produce much in the way of viable new ideas. Another heuristic that people seem to apply intuitively is satisficing—simply seizing on the first available approximation of a solution. Use of this heuristic is problematic when executing processes, such as problem construction and category combination, requiring elaboration and exploration.

Clearly, some heuristics are more useful than others when people are attempting to solve certain types of problems or execute certain processes. As people acquire experience working with problems in a domain, they also acquire procedures for executing different processing operations. One implication of this statement is that experts, in contrast to novices, will have a wider range of viable heuristics available. In fact, the available evidence indicates that not only do experts have more procedures and more effective procedures available, these procedures are linked to relevant processes and problems. Experts, moreover, appear better able to retrieve, select, and execute procedures, and are more likely to transfer appropriate procedures to related problems.

III. IDEA FORMATION HEURISTICS

Heuristics, of course, may or may not generalize across domains. By virtue of their definitional charac-

teristics, however, creative problems may call for the application of certain general heuristics likely to facilitate performance whenever people must apply the kind of processes called for in creative problem solving. In recent years, a number of investigators have initiated studies to identify the kinds of procedures people use in solving novel, ill-defined problems.

The design used in these studies was based on the proposition that heuristics are process-specific, although processes may evidence some generality. Accordingly, a series of problem solving tasks were developed where each task served to isolate a certain process. To measure problem construction, to cite one example, people were presented with a problem statement and were asked to redefine the problem in different ways, selecting 4 alternative definitions from a predefined list of 16 potential response options. These response options, however, were expressly designed to capture certain heuristics believed to contribute to more effective problem construction. The heuristics measures derived from those problems were then correlated with the indexes of the quality and originality of the products produced on two complex, realistic, creative tasks—one where people were asked to address certain management and public policy issues, and one where they were asked to devise advertising campaigns for a new product, the 3D holographic TV.

Problem construction is known to require active processing and to improve as a function of the time spent in problem construction. These findings suggest that problem construction requires a search for alternative ways of representing, or defining, the problem situation. This observation, however, poses a new question. Is creative thought enhanced by a search for representations, or alternative definitions, that display certain content characteristics? Research indicated that creative problem solving was related to the tendency to use problem definitions that reflected high-quality approaches and relevant restrictions. Use of problem definitions based on highly original material or high-quality goals and information was not as strongly related to performance. Apparently, use of relevant representations that provide viable, realistic approaches for problem solving contributes to effective problem definition.

Once a problem has been defined, people must search for information bearing on the nature of the problem situation. A variety of evidence indicates that people use different strategies in gathering information and may search for different types of information. To examine heuristics bearing on the types of information being gathered, researchers examined the time spent encoding certain types of information—information displaying certain content characteristics. The findings were consistent with earlier studies, in the sense that people who tended to focus on key factual information and anomalous observations were more likely to produce creative products (e.g., more original, higher quality advertising campaigns) than people who looked for other types of information, including information bearing on goals, principles, restrictions, or tangential facts. Thus, a targeted search procedure, taking into account discrepant or anomalous observations, represents a useful heuristic related to better performance in producing multiple creative products.

Unlike problem construction and information encoding, few attempts have been made to identify the heuristics involved in category selection. Research has indicated that people who preferred concepts reflecting long-term goals were more creative than people who preferred concepts based on abstract principals, goals, and interpersonal relationships. Thus to promote creative thought, people should retain categories, or concepts, that organize multiple activities in a flexible, pragmatic fashion.

A number of studies have examined the heuristics involved in the combination and reorganization process. For example, it has been found that performance is improved by mapping shared features among categories, identifying non-overlapping features, identifying key exemplars of the new category, elaborating the features of these key exemplars, and looking for cohesive coherent combinations rather than combinations with one specific application. When people are asked to combine categories, particularly diverse categories (e.g., birds and furniture), the tendency to look for metaphors (e.g., birds have feathers and feathers represent comfort) is a useful heuristic related to the tendency to produce creative products across different domains.

These findings provide us with some important clues about the kind of heuristics involved in the processes underlying initial idea formation, however, they also have some noteworthy implications for understanding how heuristics contribute to creative thought. First,

general heuristics linked to specific processing operations can be identified and measured by examining the procedures, or operations, called for during processes execution. Second, some heuristics are, in fact, more useful than others, and the tendency to apply useful heuristics is related to creative performance in multiple domains. Third, for any given process, multiple heuristics exist that are positively related to performance, suggesting that multiple procedures might be used in creative problem solving with different procedures being applied, depending on the nature of the problem and the processes that represent crucial influences on performance.

IV. IDEA GENERATION AND IMPLEMENTATION HEURISTICS

To this point, we have focused on the heuristics involved in the processes underlying initial idea formation. One cannot lose sight of the fact, however, that idea generation and implementation follow initial idea formation. Clearly, the rules or procedures involved in effective execution of these idea generation and implementation processes warrant some attention in their own right.

Of these implementation processes, the heuristics underlying idea generation have received the most attention due to their association with the kind of divergent thinking tests commonly used to assess creative potential. Broadly speaking, the results obtained in these investigations indicate that creative thought is enhanced by explicit instructions to search for new ideas. Instructional manipulations of this sort appear to affect idea generation by encouraging exploration of new ideas. Along related lines, heuristics such as an attempt to identify the indirect implications of ideas, an explicit search for new, alternative applications of an idea, and holding restrictions on idea implementation in abeyance also appear to contribute to creative thought during idea generation.

It is not enough to generate ideas. Ideas must also be evaluated. People employ different standards and procedures in evaluating new ideas, and the standards and procedures employed in idea evaluation have some important implications for the nature and success of people's creative efforts. It seems reasonable to hypothesize that the tendency to evaluate ideas based on their perceived popularity as well as the tendency to evaluate ideas with respect to immediate, concrete returns will tend to inhibit performance. In contrast, however, evaluations of ideas in terms of long-term workability and potential application in multiple venues tend to promote performance.

The heuristics involved in implementation planning and monitoring have received scant attention in the literature on creative thought. Nonetheless, various studies of planning and monitoring processes do provide some clues about the kinds of heuristics that might be involved in effective process execution. For example, in the case of implementation planning, there is reason to suspect that an open, flexible, opportunistic approach to planning, along with the development of plans expressly intended to identify and circumvent salient restrictions, or roadblocks, contributes to creative achievement. It appears, moreover, that attempts to develop long-term plans that can be integrated with other ongoing efforts also represents a useful procedure during implementation planning. In the case of monitoring it is more useful to focus on progress with regard to key marker events vis-à-vis an open, flexible implementation process that takes into account multiple, alternative indicators of performance. It is less useful to evaluate performance against fixed, absolute expectations or errors made in performance.

V. DEVELOPING HEURISTICS

Students of creativity are often interested in heuristics because one way to improve creative thought is to provide people with more appropriate heuristics for use in problem solving. The available evidence on expert performance, moreover, indicates that as people acquire experience, they tend to apply more appropriate, more effective, and less resource-intensive heuristics. Those observations, in turn, however, pose a new question. What instructional strategies might be used to accelerate the acquisition of viable heuristics?

A recent study by Michael Mumford and colleagues provides some clues about how one might answer this question. They were interested in determining whether training interventions could be devised that would facilitate the use of appropriate heuristics. Additionally, they wanted to determine whether certain types of training interventions were more effective than others,

and whether heuristics were, in fact, tied to specific processing operations. In the study they focused on the processes, and their associated heuristics, held to influence initial idea formation.

Two major types of training were examined in this study. In the heuristic acquisition condition undergraduates participating in this study were presented with a description of a process, its role in creative problem solving, the heuristics contributing to effective process application, and examples showing how use of a heuristic might influence creative thought. They were then asked to answer a series of questions about the instructional material applying to a given heuristic, proceeding to the next set of material only after they had answered three-quarters of the questions correctly.

In the heuristic application condition, undergraduates were presented with a two- or three-page description of current events in Russia and India. After reading through the background material, people were presented with a series of problems and asked to indicate whether a certain course of action would help or hinder the government. These questions were devised by five psychologists to illustrate effective, or ineffective, application of a certain heuristic. Feedback was provided after answering each question, intended to reinforce application of effective heuristics.

Performance during acquisition and application of the heuristics was correlated with the measures of processing skills as well as quality and originality ratings obtained from two creative performance tasks used as criterion measures. In the case of problem construction, simply acquiring knowledge about relevant heuristics was not related to problem solving performance or performance on the skill measures. Performance in application training, however, was related to problem construction skills and creative problem solving with heuristics such as avoiding satisficing, avoiding a focus on specific goals, and extending the search for additional representations all proving to be particularly useful heuristics. In the case of information encoding, performance during heuristic acquisition training and heuristic application training were both related to measures of encoding skills and creative problem solving. Here, the most important heuristic was searching for key diagnostic information.

For category selection, acquisition training was more strongly related to performance than application training. Moreover, acquisition of heuristics calling for retaining a variety of concepts, retaining related concepts, avoiding a search for one perfect concept, and avoiding superficial concepts all produced sizable positive relationships; thus it appears that retention of multiple well-organized concepts in category selection contributes to creative thought. In the case of category combination, performance during heuristic application yielded weak relationships with the skill and performance measures. However, performance during acquisition training was related to combination and reorganization skills, as well as performance on the two general creative problem solving tasks. Here, heuristics such as looking for features of the categories to be combined, searching for metaphors, and elaborating emerging ideas all appeared to be particularly useful.

The findings obtained in this study, of course, confirm some of our earlier observations about the kind of heuristics involved in the effective application of certain processes. These heuristics, furthermore, appeared to be process-specific in the sense that measures of heuristics for a process (e.g., problem construction) were more strongly related to performance on measures of the targeted processing skill (e.g., problem construction) than other processing skills (e.g., information encoding). Although these findings are noteworthy, the most important implication of this work is that viable experience with relevant heuristics, as indicated by performance during training, was in fact related to creative thought. Thus, it appears that training or educational programs might be devised to facilitate creative thought by exploring the application of requisite heuristics. In this regard, however, it is important to recognize that different types of interventions might be required for different heuristics and different processes—a point illustrated in the finding that knowledge about heuristics was more important for some processes while practice applying heuristics was more important for other processes. [*See* ENHANCEMENT OF CREATIVITY; TEACHING CREATIVITY.]

VI. APPLYING HEURISTICS

The fact that heuristics are specific to certain processes, and multiple heuristics, or procedures, are available for executing any given process, has an important, albeit often overlooked, implication. More specifically,

performance on creative problem solving tasks may be a function of having a wide range of effective heuristics available, and being able to identify the kind of heuristics or procedures most likely to prove useful in working through a particular problem. This observation, in turn, has led many scholars to conclude that metacognitive control mechanisms, those guiding the choice and application of certain heuristics, may also play an important role in creative thought. In fact, evidence showing that metacognitive awareness, as indicated by the appearance of procedure control statements in think-aloud protocols, is related to performance on creative problem solving tasks. Moreover, instruction in monitoring the application of heuristics appeared to contribute to improved performance on a series of creative problem solving tasks.

Of course, if multiple viable heuristics might be applied in creative thought, one would also suspect that effective application of these heuristics would require the ability to shift or change procedures as indicated by the processing demands imposed by the problem at hand. In fact, we have long known that cognitive flexibility is an important influence on creative thought. More recently, however, it has been shown that among gifted students, performance on creative problem solving tasks not only depends on the use of viable, systematic procedures and heuristics, but also on the ability of the individual to apply those heuristics in a flexible fashion, adjusting procedures in accordance with the nature of the problem. [*See* FLEXIBILITY.]

These observations about the importance of metacognition and flexibility when applying heuristics in creative thought have a somewhat more subtle, but notable, implication. More specifically, acquiring new procedures or new heuristics may represent a crucial determinant of creative thought. In fact, studies of creative achievement in the sciences indicate that the development of new methods or procedures, for example, procedures for recombining DNA, often make possible a host of new advances as these procedures are applied in new ways to new problems. Along related lines, one might argue that an important aspect of creative thought is essentially procedural in nature. In other words, the combination and reorganization of existing procedures may give birth to new heuristics that might be applied in solving a wide range of problems. Hopefully, future research will examine in greater detail the implications of new procedural combinations for creative thought.

VII. CONCLUSIONS

In this article, we have examined the role of heuristics in creative thought. Heuristics, or the rules and procedures for executing various processes, can make a contribution to creative thought. Further, although these rules and procedures appear tied to a particular process, it does appear possible to identify heuristics that contribute to creative problem solving across a wide range of problems. For example, avoiding satisficing, searching for key diagnostics, identifying overlapping features, and applying metaphors all appear of general value contributing to the more effective execution of certain key processes known to play key roles in solving the kind of novel, ill-defined problems that call for creative thought.

By identifying the kinds of heuristics or procedures that make possible the successful execution of these processes, it may become possible to develop a more sophisticated understanding of creative thought than has heretofore been possible. It is not enough to identify the processes involved in creative thought, we must know how people execute these processes in terms of the heuristics required. Not only will the identification of requisite heuristics serve to enhance our understanding of creativity, it may have some important practical applications providing guidelines for the development of educational interventions intended to enhance creative thought. Thus, by identifying the heuristics involved in different creative processes, we may find a vehicle for integrating theory and practice in the study of creativity.

Bibliography

Baxter, G. P., Elder, A. D., & Glaser, R. (1996). Knowledge-based cognition and performance assessment in the science classroom. *Educational Psychologist, 31*(2), 133–140.

Bull, K. S., Montgomery, D., & Bacoche, L. (1995). Teaching creativity at the college level: A synthesis of curricular components perceived as important by instructors. *Creativity Research Journal, 8,* 83–90.

Finke, R. A., Ward, T. B., & Smith, S. M. (1992). *Creative cognition, theory, research, and applications.* Cambridge, MA: MIT Press.

Jausovec, N. (1994). Metacognition in creative problem solving. In M. Runco (Ed.), *Problem finding, problem solving, and creativity* (pp. 77–98). Norwood, NJ: Ablex.

Kaizer, C., & Shore, B. M. (1995). Strategy flexibility in more and less competent students on mathematical word problems. *Creativity Research Journal, 8,* 77–82.

Mumford, M. D., & Gustafon, S. B. (in press). Creative thought: Cognition and problem solving in dynamic systems. In M. Runco (Ed.), *Creativity research handbook.* Cresskill, NY: Hampton.

Mumford, M. D., Baughman, W. A., & Sager, C .E. (in press). Picking the right material: Cognitive processing skills and their role in creative thought. In M. Runco (Ed.), *Critical and creative thinking.* Hillsdale, NJ: Erlbaum.

Mumford, M. D., Supinski, E. P., Baughman, W. A., Costanza, D. P., & Threlfall, K. V. (1997). Process based measures of creative problem-solving skills; overall prediction. *Creativity Research Journal, 10,* 73–85.

Pennington, N., Nicolich, R., & Rahm, J. (1995). Transfer of training between cognitive subskills: Is knowledge use specific? *Cognitive Psychology, 28,* 175–224.

Perkins, D. N. (1992). The topography of invention. In R. T. Weber & D. N. Perkins (Eds.), *Innovative minds: Creativity in technology* (pp. 238–250). New York: Oxford University Press.

Historiometry

Dean Keith Simonton

University of California, Davis

Content Analysis A method of measuring psychological variables by applying objective coding schemes to personal documents (letters, diaries, etc.) and creative products (poetry, musical compositions, etc.). Some content analytical methods have taken the form of computer programs that can directly extract measurements from the primary source material, most frequently written or transcribed text.

Multivariate Statistics A collection of techniques that permits the simultaneous analysis of numerous variables having a great variety of possible interrelationships. Examples include factor analysis, multiple regression, path analysis, latent variable models, and covariance structure analysis.

Nomothetic Research Investigations dedicated to the discovery of general laws, principles, or regularities that transcend the particulars of a given time, place, or person. To be distinguished from idiographic inquiries, which concentrate on discerning the distinctive features of a specific individual or event.

Quasi-experimental Designs A methodology that permits more powerful causal inferences than traditional correlational methods, but less powerful than conventional experiments. The most common quasi-experimental design in historiometric research is time-series analysis, which allows the inference that the variation in one variable precedes or follows variation in another variable.

Unobtrusive Measures Data gathered in such a fashion that the subjects' behaviors, thoughts, and feelings cannot possibly be influenced by the measurements. All measures based on archival data are unobtrusive (or nonreactive). In contrast, laboratory experiments and psychometric assessment techniques lack this quality, and can at least potentially alter the activities of those subjects under investigation.

Zeitgeist German word for the "spirit of the times," that is, the general political, social, cultural, intellectual, and economic milieu.

HISTORIOMETRY is the application of quantitative methods to archival data about historic personalities and events to test nomothetic hypotheses about human thought, feeling, and action. Because this definition is so complex, this article will make historiometry more intelligible by breaking it down into its component parts.

I. BACKGROUND

Historiometric research examines the big names and important happenings that can be considered historic

Copyright © 1999 by Academic Press
All rights of reproduction in any form reserved.

in the sense of "making history." For example, the subjects of historiometric studies may involve eminent artists, writers, or scientists (e.g., Leonardo da Vinci, Cervantes, or Einstein) or they may entail major acts of creativity such as musical masterworks or major scientific discoveries (e.g., Beethoven's Fifth Symphony and the heliocentric theory of Copernicus).

The database concerning these historic subjects is compiled from various archival sources, such as histories, biographical dictionaries, encyclopedias, anthologies, and collections. The data may also be derived from the content analysis of creative products, including the computer analysis of music and literature. Because historiometric research concentrates on individuals or products that are highly distinguished, the archival information on these cases is often extremely rich.

The goal of the study is nomothetic rather than idiographic. Nomothetic research involves the quest for general psychological laws or patterns, whereas idiographic research concentrates on those features that are unique to a particular individual or event. Thus, nomothetic research addresses such questions as whether creative development is enhanced when talented individuals are exposed to models of creativity. In contrast, idiographic research might address an issue such as the reason why van Gogh cut off his ear. Hence, in this sense historiometrics has goals comparable to other methods that psychologists use to study creativity, such as psychometrics.

In line with this focus, historiometric research favors multiple-case investigations. Only by obtaining a large sample of eminent personalities or important events can the researcher ensure that the findings are truly general rather than particular. It is rare for a historiometric inquiry to analyze fewer than a dozen cases, and sometimes the sample sizes may run into the thousands. Indeed, the largest number of cases ever examined in a single historiometric inquiry was 15,618—a very large sample size indeed!

Also consistent with the search for nomothetic results, historiometric research invariably entails quantification. Variables are first quantified from the available archival materials, and then these variables are subjected to statistical analysis. Because the number of variables studied will often be very large, the investigator usually must apply sophisticated multivariate statistics to tease out the complex interrelationships among the variables. The most commonly used statistics are mul-

tiple regression and factor analysis, but occasionally one sees studies using path analysis, latent-variable models, time-series analysis, and multidimensional scaling.

Needless to say, given the typical sample sizes and the complexity of the statistical analyses, historiometric studies almost invariably must be executed on a computer.

II. COMPARISONS

It is important not to confuse historiometric research with several alternative approaches. To begin with, historiometry differs substantially from psychobiographical and psychohistorical studies of creativity. The latter almost always employ qualitative rather than quantitative methods, and they tend to be idiographic rather than nomothetic in orientation. In addition, psychobiographical and psychohistorical inquiries are very often psychoanalytic in theoretical emphasis. These characteristics are evident in the classic psychobiography of Leonardo da Vinci that was published by Sigmund Freud. Historiometry, in contrast, is a method designed to test hypotheses that might be drawn from any theoretical framework, psychoanalytic or otherwise. An excellent example is Colin Martindale's book *The Clockwork Muse,* in which the author tests a formal model of stylistic change that has roots in psychoanalytic theories of creativity.

Another approach is sometimes confused with historiometry is the comparative. Comparative research takes a modest size sample of individuals or events and then tries to discern consistent patterns or regularities. Although the goal is often nomothetic, the method is qualitative, and the sample sizes typically much smaller. A good illustration is Howard Gardner's book *Creative Minds,* in which he carefully compares and contrasts the lives of seven eminent individuals. Comparative studies can lead to important insights about creativity and other phenomena but do not share historiometry's capacity for more precise model testing and prediction.

III. HISTORY

Surprisingly, historiometry actually represents the earliest scientific approach to the study of creativity.

In 1835 Adolphe Quetelet published a quantitative analysis of eminent English and French playwrights in which he established the relationship between age and creative output. The next important historiometric inquiry was the 1869 book *Hereditary Genius,* in which Francis Galton documented how eminent creativity (and leadership) tends to run in family lineages. Other pioneer historiometric investigations include Alphonse de Candolle's study of eminent scientists and Havelock's study of British geniuses.

However, none of these researchers explicitly identified their work as historiometric, for the term had not yet been invented. The word was not coined until the first decade of the 20th century, when Frederick Woods patterned the term after biometrics. Although Woods's own historiometric research focused more on famous leaders than creators, the term was adopted briefly by others. Most notably, Catharine Cox's 1929 study of the *Early Mental Traits of Three Hundred Geniuses* was explicitly labeled a historiometric inquiry. This monumental investigation, which constitutes the second volume of Lewis Terman's *Genetic Studies of Genius,* provided quantitative assessments of the intelligence and personality of famous creators and leaders. Cox's work inspired other historiometric studies, but unfortunately both the method and the term virtually disappeared from the research literature on creativity. Beginning in the mid-1970s, Dean Keith Simonton began to revive the technique and the name. At present, historiometry seems to represent a relatively rare but nonetheless acceptable approach to the study of creativity. Indeed, from time to time it has attracted the efforts of eminent psychologists whose primary contributions have employed very different methods. Among these holiday historiometricians are James McKeen Cattell, Raymond B. Cattell, B. F. Skinner, Lewis Terman, and Edward L. Thorndike.

IV. RESEARCH

One of the reasons that historiometric research may be here to stay is the tremendous amount of important empirical results it has generated. The great diversity of findings may be grouped into two inclusive categories: those concerning the creative individual and those concerning the creative product.

A. The Creative Individual

The largest proportion of historiometric studies of creativity examine those individuals who have achieved acclaim for their original contributions to some domain. These studies have tended to focus on the following three topics:

1. Individual Differences

Even among eminent creators, the cross-sectional variation in creative success is quite substantial. To appreciate the contrast, we need only compare Newton with William Higgins, Descartes with Henri Duroy, Shakespeare with Chatterton, Michelangelo with Hendrick Bloemaert, Beethoven with Anton Reicha—all pairs of individuals who have rubbed elbows in the same historiometric samples. Much of the contrast in differential reputation can be ascribed to differences in creative output. Accordingly, many studies have examined individual differences in lifetime productivity, including the peculiar skewed (or elitist) distribution of that output. Other studies have examined the personality and intellectual factors responsible for the cross-sectional variation in output and eminence. For example, Cox showed how success required a combination of both high intelligence and unusual motivational persistence. She also demonstrated how the distinctive personality profiles of eminent creators varies according to the domain of creative activity.

2. Life-Span Development

Rather than concentrate on individual differences, many historiometricians have studied how creativity develops and manifests itself across the life span. These developmental inquiries fall naturally into two distinct categories. In the first category are those that look for the early antecedents of adulthood creativity. For instance, researchers have examined the impact of such variables as family pedigree, socioeconomic class, childhood precocity, birth order, orphanhood, role models and mentors, crystalizing experiences, and formal education or special training. [*See* BIRTH ORDER; ENHANCEMENT OF CREATIVITY; FAMILIES AND CREATIVITY; PRODIGIES.]

In the second category are those developmental studies that scrutinize how creativity varies across the course of the career. Most of these studies are concerned with how the rate of output changes with age.

The expected age curves tend to vary systematically according to the specific type of creativity. For example, poets and mathematicians tend to produce masterworks at younger ages than do novelists and earth scientists. Other studies have examined the longitudinal relation between total quantity of output and the odds of producing a masterwork. Significantly, a creator's best work tends to appear in those periods of the career in which he or she is the most prolific overall. [*See* PRODUCTIVITY AND AGE.]

3. *Sociocultural Context*

Illustrious creators are not randomly distributed across history, nor are they evenly spread across the globe at any one time. On the contrary, creative genius is more prone to appear during "golden ages," less likely during "silver ages," and supremely unlikely during "dark ages." The Golden Age of Greece is a classic example. Such uneven distribution suggests that political, economic, social, and cultural forces may play a major role in the development and manifestation of creative talent. Historiometric investigations have specifically examined such factors as war, political system, ideology, and general intellectual ferment. These studies show that the "spirit of the times," or the zeitgeist, claims a crucial part in the origination of creative genius. The zeitgeist influences not only the number of eminent creators that appears in a given time and place, but also the particular domains in which creativity is most likely to be displayed. [*See* ZEITGEIST.]

B. The Creative Product

Because the eminence of a creator is very much contingent on the works he or she contributes to posterity, it is natural for historiometricians to investigate the characteristics of these artifacts of the act of creation. Some of this research has examined scientific discoveries and technological inventions. For example, several studies have been published on the multiples phenomenon where two or more scientists independently (and sometimes simultaneously) arrive at the same idea at about the same time. Classic illustrations include the proposal by Charles Darwin and Wallace of the theory of evolution by natural selection and the invention of the calculus by Newton and Leibnitz. Surprisingly, certain distinguishing features of these events—such as their timing and the number of participants—can

actually be accurately predicted using mathematical models. [*See* CREATIVE PRODUCTS.]

However, most inquiries into the creative product focus on the arts. Many of these studies are specifically devoted to the determination of the factors responsible for aesthetic effectiveness of compositions in literature, music, or the visual arts. For instance, the application of computerized content analysis to classical music has enabled researchers to predict the relative performance frequencies of works in the repertoire. Similar historiometric techniques have had comparable success in the prediction of the differential popularity of literary creations, such as poetry. In addition, several historiometric studies have been concerned with qualitative changes in the nature of the works produced over the course of a career. Of special interest are inquiries into the swan songs of classical composers and the late-period style changes in visual artists. The research shows that toward the very end of a creator's life the very nature of her or his creative output may undergo a dramatic transformation. [*See* ART AND AESTHETICS; OLD AGE STYLE.]

V. EVALUATION

The reason why the behavioral scientists have so many different techniques at their disposal is because no technique is perfect. Each enjoys certain assets, and each suffers from certain liabilities. Historiometry is no exception. It, too, has both advantages and disadvantages. Let us look at the latter before turning to the former.

A. Disadvantages

Any researcher interested in applying historiometric methods to the study of creativity must often confront one or more of the following four problems:

1. *Causal Inference*

Methodologists sometimes distinguish between internal and external validity of a technique. The former criterion concerns the security of the causal inferences the method permits. Laboratory experiments enjoy very high internal validity because the experimenter actively manipulates the independent variables and randomly assigns subjects to experimental and control groups. Historiometric research, in contrast, is inherently correlational in nature. The best the researcher can do is to determine how measured variables are associated. Because other unmeasured factors may contaminate the observed relationships, conclusions about causal influence are invariably insecure. Correlation never can be taken to prove causation. Thus, the internal validity of historiometric work is almost always inferior to that found in the experimental literature. For example, one of the oldest debates in the study of creativity is the relationship between genius and madness. What makes this issue especially irksome is the difficulty of determining which of three distinct possibilities is most likely to hold: (a) a proclivity toward psychopathology might make a positive contribution to creativity; (b) exceptional creative achievement might put exceptional strain on creative individuals, thereby making them more disposed to mental and emotional breakdowns; and (c) neither creativity nor psychopathology may have any direct causal relationship with each other but rather might be the consequence of some other factor or factors (e.g., traumatic or unconventional childhood experiences. [*See* MAD GENIUS CONTROVERSY.]

2. Data Quality

Because the historiometrician must rely so much on the historical and biographical record, sometimes the available information leaves much to be desired from a scientific standpoint. For example, when Cox attempted to calculate IQ scores for historic personalities, she lamentfully discovered that she had to exclude William Shakespeare from her sample. There exists very little data about the Bard's personal life and virtually nothing about his early years. Even when enough pertinent information could be found in the historical record for a particular individual, Cox found that the reliability coefficients for her IQ assessments could vary substantially from genius to genius. Moreover, when she wished to estimate 67 personality traits for her subjects, she was obliged to restrict her sample to the 100 famous people about which the most data were available.

3. Substantive Applicability

Closely related is the fact that some important issues in the scientific study of creativity probably cannot be addressed using historiometric methods. For instance, one of the central questions in the creativity literature is the very nature of the creative process. What is the role of intuition or unconscious processes? What is the function of logical analysis? Yet the biographies and published letters of eminent creators do not contain the necessary information in any systematic fashion, and when the records do, they cannot always be trusted as sources of solid data. For example, Samuel Coleridge's description of the creative process underlying the composition of "Kublai Khan" is inconsistent with his own unpublished manuscripts that contain the various drafts of the poem. It is now apparent that he distorted his narrative to render the episode more consistent with romantic notions of the creative process.

4. Labor Requirements

Perhaps the most prohibitive drawback of historiometric research is the sheer amount of work required to carry out a project. Collection of the raw data may require many trips to the library and special archives, followed by the arduous coding of qualitative information to get the data in quantitative form. Even after the content analytical, historical, and biographical data have been reduced to numbers, the statistical analyses may consume considerable amounts of time. Historiometric data sets often involve numerous variables with highly complex interrelationships that can only be teased out using the most advanced statistical techniques. As a consequence, it is not uncommon for a major historiometric study to require several *thousands* of hours of effort to produce a single journal article. That is a small payoff in comparison to, say, a laboratory experiment in the area of creative problem solving. Naturally, monograph-length investigations may demand even more time and effort. To offer one dramatic example, Frank Sulloway's book *Born to Rebel* represents the culmination of 26 years of intensive data collection and analysis.

These liabilities notwithstanding, it is essential to point out that often one or more of these problems can be alleviated if not entirely removed in well-conceived historiometric research. First, multivariate statistics and quasi-experimental designs have immensely increased the power of drawing causal inferences from correlational data. One especially potent inferential tool is time-series analysis. Second, data quality problems can often be handled by the introduction of more sophisticated statistical methods, such as latent-variable models. These permit the explicit incorporation of measurement error into the causal model. Third, the substantive applicability of historiometry can often be greatly extended if the investigator exercises care in selecting the optimal research site. For instance, sometimes a researcher may examine famous creators from non-Western civilizations precisely because the biographical and historical information is available regarding a particular set of variables. Fourth, if the investigator plans carefully and compiles a rich enough database, it is possible to generate more than one publication from a single data collection. For example, once a researcher decides on using a particular sample of Nobel laureates as the basis for the investigation, he or she can gather a great diversity of biographical, historical, and content analytical data that can be used to test a wide variety of hypotheses.

B. Advantages

Besides the extenuating circumstances just mentioned, researchers often have very strong reasons for adopting historiometric methods for a particular investigation. Five assets may be the most important from the standpoint of creativity research.

1. Criterion Validity

One of the main problems in studying creativity is how to measure the phenomenon. Some researchers may define creativity in terms of scores on a psychometric instrument, whereas others may rely on the judges evaluations of creative products. Although these conventional assessments have much to recommend them, they are also not without conspicuous limitations. For example, a measure cannot be called a "creativity test" without first validating the instrument against some more secure criterion of creativity. Perhaps scores on such tests have absolutely nothing to do with real-life creativity. Historiometric research circumvents this problem by studying those individuals who have made a name for themselves precisely for their creative achievements. If the investigator examines persons like Planck, Sartre, Joyce, Picasso, or Stravinsky, we have no other option but to assume that these individuals exhibit creativity. If we were to deny that attribution, the term *creative* would lose all meaning. Hence, historiometric methods take their point of

departure at those individuals who best exemplify the phenomenon under investigation.

2. Variable Accessibility

There are many important influences on creativity that for both practical and ethical reasons can only be examined using historiometric methods. If the goal is to determine the sociocultural milieu that best contributes to the development of creative development, it is hard to imagine a better method than to scrutinize the historical record with respect to the coming and going of creative genius. For instance, if we want to test the hypothesis that wartime conditions inhibit the expression of creativity, we probably have no other choice than to conduct a time-series analysis comparing the output of creative products against the magnitude of political violence. Even if the focus is on creative careers, the assets of historiometrics are paramount. The researcher can examine the emergence and manifestation of creative genius from the moment of conception (e.g., family pedigrees) to the moment of death (e.g., swan songs) and everything in between (e.g., birth order, childhood trauma, role models and mentors, education and special training, and career trajectory). Historiometry is thus truly life-span developmental in scope.

3. Unobtrusive Measurement

Ever since the advent of the Heisenberg uncertainty principle in quantum theory, physicists have learned that the very act of measuring a phenomenon may interfere with the phenomenon under scrutiny. A similar consequence often may be seen in many standard methods in the behavioral sciences. For example, the very act of studying the creative process in the laboratory may distort the observed behavior to such a degree that it becomes unrepresentative of what would happen under more natural conditions. Similarly, the application of psychometric measurement, surveys, and one-and-one interviews to samples of contemporary creators may produce expectancy effects, "guinea-pig" effects, and other kinds of artificial reactions. Historiometric measurement, in contrast, is totally unobtrusive. The subjects in historiometric inquiries do not know that they are under observation. Indeed, because the subjects are most often deceased, they will never find out the results. Accordingly, the phenomenon of creativity can be investigated without fear of inducing unnatural responses from the subjects of the study.

4. Cross-Cultural and Transhistorical Invariance

Behavioral scientists seek general laws or principles of behavior that transcend place and time. If an empirical relationship only holds for a particular culture or is merely valid for a single historical period, it cannot have the claim to universality that is the hallmark of all nomothetic science. For example, Newton's law of gravitation holds not only for apples falling from trees in 17th-century England but also for all massive bodies in the universe throughout the history of time. One great asset of historiometric research is that it can sample creators from all civilizations of the world and from every major historical period. Hypotheses tested on such diverse sample shave a much higher probability of claiming cross-cultural and transhistorical invariance. For instance, one historiometric investigation of literary creativity showed that poets produce their best works at younger ages than prose writers. Because the sample consisted of hundreds of literary figures drawn from all the world's major literatures from antiquity to the present day, we can have greater confidence that this result is not confined to, say, such 19th-century British authors as Keats, Shelley, and Byron.

5. Unit Replicability

One of the peculiarities of historiometric research is that the subjects who compose its samples can all claim a permanent and distinct identity. After all, the individuals under scrutiny have made a lasting name for themselves on the basis of their creative contributions to human culture. As a consequence, it is not uncommon for historiometric studies to identify their subjects by name, listing them either in a table or in an appendix. For instance, Cox listed all 301 geniuses whom she studied along with some of the basic information compiled about each, including the estimated IQ scores. Other times the researcher will give sufficient details about the sampling procedures—such as the precise biographical dictionaries used—that any reader can easily determine who were the famous personalities under investigation. In any case, because the subjects are identified or identifiable, subsequent investigators can study exactly the same individuals, adding new variables and altering the statistical analyses performed. For example, the eminent persons in the Cox study have been reexamined in several follow-up inquiries published over a 50-year period.

This asset of unit replicability allows the historiometrician to improve on previous results in a manner that can accelerate the accumulation of scientific knowledge. Most alternative methods lack this feature. A laboratory experiment can always be replicated in terms of method, but not in terms of subjects. As a consequence, when experiments fail to replicate a previously published finding, it is uncertain whether the contrast may be ascribed to the change of participants in the study. In contrast, when a historiometrician scrutinizes the exact same subjects as analyzed in a previous study and fails to obtain identical results, the cause of the discrepancy can be more easily isolated.

VI. CONCLUSION

Because historiometry has already been around in the behavioral sciences for more than 150 years, its use will likely continue in the future. The technique has already made considerable contributions to our understanding of creativity in its most historic manifestations. Moreover, the method enjoys many methodological advantages over other research strategies. Above all, it is the technique of choice for anyone who wants to test nomothetic hypotheses about history-making creativity. No alternative method features the same inferential rigor and quantitative precision. Moreover, despite various methodological disadvantages, many of these drawbacks are becoming ever less critical. Certainly statistics for analyzing correlational data are becoming increasingly sophisticated, permitting ever more powerful causal inferences. Even more important, the quality of the data about historic creators is becoming increasingly better with time. After all, creativity is not dead in the world, and each generation will usually produce a new crop of eminent creators that can serve as subjects in future historiometric research. Furthermore, there will probably be more and better information about these forthcoming creative individuals than holds for those born in earlier historical periods. Indeed, historiometric research has actually demonstrated that the reliability coefficients for many variables have increased over time.

In a sense, the situation for the historiometrician is very similar to that of the astronomer centuries earlier. The first astronomical measurements were rather too imprecise to support anything more than the crudest planetary theories. But as observations became more precise, the archival records collected by astronomers began to encourage the development of increasingly sophisticated theories. I predict that historiometry will enjoy the same historical trend with respect to its own phenomena. In fact, in some respects it has already done so. As mentioned in the section on the method's history, the first historiometric study ever published dates back to 1835. That investigation concerned the relationship between age and creative productivity. Since that pioneering inquiry, many investigators have scrutinized the same question using ever more precise measurement and statistical analysis. Now the cumulative body of evidence on this question has reached the point that researchers have begun to propose mathematical models that provide rather precise predictions about how creative output changes across the life span. Hence, in this substantive domain at least, historiometrics can indeed provide the foundation for scientific progress in our comprehension of creativity. The same progress should be seen with respect to other topics that attract historiometric inquiry.

Bibliography

Ludwig, A. M. (1995). *The price of greatness. Resolving the creativity and madness controversy.* New York: Guilford Press.

Martindale, C. (1990). *The clockwork muse: The predictability of artistic styles.* New York: Basic Books.

Simonton, D. K. (1990). *Psychology, science, and history: An introduction to historiometry.* New Haven, CT: Yale University Press.

Simonton, D. K. (1997). *Genius and creativity: Selected papers.* Greenwich, CT: Ablex.

Sulloway, F. J. (1996). *Born to rebel: Birth order, family dynamics, and creative lives.* New York: Pantheon.

History and Creativity

Colin Martindale
University of Maine

I. Evolutionary Theories
II. Reflectionist and Relational Theories

Adaptation Trap Extinction of a style occurring because its adaptive niche disappears. An example is extinction of Nazi art deco with the collapse of the Third Reich.

Aesthetic Evolution A theory involving the argument that art evolves in a predetermined way according to Darwinist or non-Darwinist rules.

End of Art Proclamations that art has ended because there are no possible continuations. Such proclamations date from Vasari up to the present. Like announcements of Mark Twain's death, they are probably "grossly exaggerated."

Evolutionary Trap Something causing the extinction of an artistic style.

Fitness In biological or cultural evolution, how well a species or style is adapted to its environment.

Greenberg Narrative The idea advanced by Clement Greenberg that the goal of painting is to exploit what is specific to painting (e.g., brush strokes) and that painting progressed as extraneous things such as realism were eliminated. With the collapse of abstract expressionism in the 1960s, this narrative came to an end.

Habituation The waning of interest in a stimulus that is repeated over and over again.

Hedonic Selection Selection of a stimulus because of its aesthetic properties. In biological evolution, this is usually called sexual selection. Mates are chosen on the basis of their beauty.

In both the arts and sciences, artifacts and equations are chosen on the basis of their beauty.

Historiometry The nomothetic and quantitative study of history. A method advocated by historians but mainly conducted by the psychologist Dean Keith Simonton.

Institutional Definition of Art The definition which states that anything the art community calls art *is* art (first proposed by George Dickie). Given that artists can present Brillo boxes bought in a grocery store as art, this definition means that anything can be art (see *End of Art*).

Law of Immanent Change First proposed by Pitirim Sorokin, the belief that the development of any genre or discipline is determined almost entirely by its prior history rather than by external forces.

Period Style A style found in various media during the same epoch. There is evidence for such styles, but only if the epochs are quite long.

Production Trap Extinction of a style because there is a gap in training. An example is loss of knowledge of how to depict linear perspective between the fall of the Roman Empire and the Renaissance.

Recapitulation of Ontogeny Theories Theories that artistic styles recapitulate ontogeny—that is, they have a birth, maturity, and decline.

Reflectionism The theory that cultural products reflect the zeitgeist of the time in which they are produced. Such theories are espoused only by writers of college textbooks and naive Marxists. Theorists as diverse as Trotsky and Martindale repudiate reflectionism.

Relationist Theories The theories that state that there is some

Encyclopedia of Creativity
VOLUME 1

823

Copyright © 1999 by Academic Press
All rights of reproduction in any form reserved.

relation, albeit indirect, between the content or style of art and what occurs when the art is produced.

Rule of Series Kubler's observation that innovations depend on one another. For example, the steamboat or locomotive cannot be invented before the steam engine has been invented.

Variation Trap Extinction of a style because of loss of variation on which evolutionary selection pressures can operate. Architectural examples include domes and Gothic fan vaults. A modern example would be abstract expressionism in painting.

Vasari Narrative The narrative of art history that the goal of painting is to depict in two dimensions a three-dimensional scene. The term is attributed to A. C. Danto. (See also *End of Art* and *Greenberg Narrative*.)

Zeitgeist The spirit of the times.

Any definition of a creative product includes the stipulation that the product be novel. Thus, the study of creativity is an intrinsically historical enterprise. To judge whether an idea or artifact is creative, we must be aware of the history of the domain in which it was produced. The fact that, to be judged creative, a product must be new has led a number of theorists to argue for evolutionary theories of the arts and sciences. That is, the continual pressure for novelty must push products produced within a given domain across time in one or another way. HISTORY AND CREATIVITY are also linked by reflectionist and relational theories of the history of art and science. Reflectionist theories of art history argue that art forms reflect the zeitgeist, or the spirit of the time, of the society in which they were produced. In the history of sciences, the zeitgeist argument is that certain discoveries become obvious at a certain point in time and so will be discovered at about the same time by a number of people. If true, this argument supports the idea that there is nothing special about creative genius: virtually anyone aware of the question and the facts at hand can make a creative discovery.

I. EVOLUTIONARY THEORIES

A number of evolutionary theories of sociocultural change have been proposed. Several theorists have proposed cyclical theories of art history in which artistic styles follow internally determined patterns of growth, flowering, and decay. This does seem to be the case, but these theories do not give a cogent explanation of why. A related type of theory argues that creative domains evolve in the sense of working out inherent possibilities or following an inner logic. For example, a rule of series posits that certain forms are logically dependent on others and so must be created later rather than earlier. For example, the invention of the steamboat could not possibly precede the invention of the steam engine. In his monumental *Social and Cultural Dynamics,* Pitirim Sorokin proposed that cultures oscillate between sensate and ideational values and that these values appear in everything from the philosophy to the sculpture of a society. Sensate values are empirical, deterministic, and extroverted. Ideational values are introverted, religious, and appeal to reason or intuition rather than empirical values. This implies that period styles exist. That is, philosophy, painting, literature, and so on produced during the same epoch should show the same style. There is some evidence for the existence of period styles, but only if very long epochs are considered. Modern reanalyses of the massive quantitative evidence that Sorokin gathered suggest that his theory was wrong in postulating period styles. His principle of immanent change—the history of any creative domain is mainly caused by the prior history of the domain—remains a viable concept.

In 1875 Hippolyte Taine proposed a Darwinian theory of the evolution of art forms. At any point in time, he held, art is a product of race, environment, and moment. By the last he meant the currently prevailing zeitgeist as well as what had already been done in the art form. By environment he meant both the physical and cultural environment. He argued that, to survive, an art form must fit the "moral temperature" of its times. Thus, pornography has low fitness in a puritanical society just as moralistic art has low fitness in a licentious era. [*See* ZEITGEIST.]

It would seem that a Darwinian perspective gives us a general framework for explaining art history. The three factors necessary for either biological or sociocultural evolution are (a) presence of variation, (b) consistent selection criteria favoring one type of variant over others, and (c) mechanisms for preserving the selected variants. At any point in time, a number of variants of a cultural artifact are produced, and the most useful or pleasing is chosen. Then, at the next point in time, there is variation of the new form and the process continues.

Before getting to details, we must ask exactly what is evolving. Do the arts evolve in synchrony or do they evolve independently? There is evolution in biology, but species generally evolve independently because it is impossible for members of different species to produce offspring. Are art forms analogous to species? Such an idea seems reasonable if we consider painting and music. They are members of the same genus (art) but cannot influence (the analogue of sexual reproduction) each other very directly because their content is so different. On the other hand, painting and sculpture could clearly influence each other. Nevertheless, a summary of empirical studies in this area all show a surprising independence in the evolution of art forms. For example, British poetry, painting, and music evolve in the manner described later—they show cycles in what is called primordial content—but the cycles are not in synchrony. By the same token, British, French, and American poetry all evolve but not in synchrony. To give a more extreme example, 19th- and 20th-century American short stories told in the first person versus those told in the third person show completely different trajectories. The two forms could influence one another but seem not to have done so. All art forms have several subtypes that have little to do with each other. For example, painting has high art versus low art or Kitsch. Within high art, there is now modern or abstract art and the tradition of realistic art, which did not die with Kandinsky but was increasingly neglected by art historians and critics.

In biology, a species must adapt to its environmental niche or become extinct. There is not just one niche but millions of them. In art, the analogue of the environmental niche is the audience. Clearly, there is not one general audience for all of the arts but a number of quite different audiences with quite different demands. In the low arts (e.g., popular music) the audience is large and can thus place severe demands on creators. In other words, the low arts exist in a harsh environment. The audience for the high arts is small. To take an extreme example, the audience for modern poetry is essentially other poets. The tiny external audience is more or less completely ignored. After all, it does not

make much difference if the royalties on a poet's latest book are $200 or $250. Thus, poetry could be said to exist in a very benign environment.

A. Aesthetic Variability

Many theorists have pointed out that if art is characterized by factors such as novelty or disruption of expectation, a necessity for change is built into it. If a work of art must be novel, each successive work of art must be different from prior works or it will not qualify as a work of art. The Russian and Czech formalists argued that poetic devices involve *estrangement* or *deformation*. What gives poetry its effect is the use of words in unusual or unexpected ways. The deformed word usages in poetry intensify perception and attract attention. With repetition, linguistic deformations and estrangements gradually become "automatized." They lose their effect. Several formalist theorists derived from this fact the hypothesis that literature must necessarily evolve. If aesthetic effects arise from deformations, and if deformations are gradually automatized, then there is a constant pressure on successive artists to produce new deformations. [*See* ART AND AESTHETICS.]

B. Selection Criteria

For evolution to occur, consistent selection criteria must be present. In the case of art, the most consistent selection criterion is that its audience must find it pleasing. Preference for any stimulus is based on the arousal potential or impact value of that stimulus. The arousal potential of a stimulus is determined by collative properties (e.g., novelty, complexity, surprisingness, unpredictability), ecological properties (signal value or meaning), and psychophysical characteristics (e.g., stimulus intensity).

Repeated presentation of a given work decreases that work's impact value, so that a work of art gradually loses its arousal potential. A work of art with optimal arousal potential will not keep on having optimal arousal potential forever but will gradually lose its capacity to elicit interest, liking, and attention. Thus, if a series of artists kept producing the same or very similar works of art, liking for their productions would decrease across time. To compensate for this habituation, it is necessary for successive works of art to have more and more arousal potential. In principle, this could be accomplished by manipulating any of the components of arousal potential. Successive composers could create louder and louder musical compositions or successive painters could paint larger and larger paintings. However, there are practical limits as to how loud a piece of music can be or how large a painting can be. In a medium such as poetry, it is impossible to compensate for habituation of arousal potential by increasing stimulus intensity. Arousal potential can also be increased by increasing the meaningfulness of an artistic work. There are several difficulties with this technique. People vary widely in what is meaningful to them. A poet cannot be sure that what is more meaningful for him or her will also be more meaningful for the audience. On the other hand, collative properties such as novelty or unpredictability are much freer to vary in all of the arts. Thus, the necessity to increase the arousal potential of aesthetic products over time eventually comes down to a pressure to increase novelty, incongruity, unpredictability, and other collative variables. Another way of saying this is that the second law of thermodynamics applies to the art world just as to the physical world: Entropy, disorder, or unpredictability must always increase and can never decrease.

The most important selection criterion in aesthetic evolution is analogous to Darwin's idea of sexual selection or hedonic selection rather than to his more well-known selection criterion of fitness to the environment first proposed in 1859. Both selection criteria operate on artistic products, but their effects are quite different. Selection on the basis of preference has been present ever since works of art were first produced, because habituation is a universal property of nervous tissue. Thus, hedonic selection has exerted a constant pressure in the same direction throughout the entire course of human history. On the other hand, fitness has varied wildly across time. Pornography has low fitness in a puritanical society, moralistic literature has low fitness in a licentious society, and so on. Thus, fitness has not exerted a consistent, unidirectional pressure on works of art.

Fitness does come into play in aesthetic evolution. An artwork has to conform to the moral temperature of its times. Morality no doubt evolves, but it pushes in different directions—puritanical versus licentious. Thus, it has not exerted a consistent, unidirectional pressure on works of art. It would seem that fitness is more important for the low arts than for the high arts. For example, the lyrics of American popular music do evolve—but in a rather sloppy fashion. They are also highly correlated with a number of extra-artistic time series such as unemployment and stock market prices. On the other hand, poetry evolves in a very clear manner, but its content is correlated with very few extra-artistic time series.

Fitness can also be considered as the degree to which an art form accomplishes what it is aiming to accomplish. In 1997 Arther Danto argued that painting has followed two narratives. What he calls the Vasari narrative is that the goal of painting is to render an accurate two-dimensional depiction of a three-dimensional object or scene. Attempts to reach this goal clearly exert a unidirectional pressure. Danto implied that the Vasari narrative ended when the goal was met in the middle of the 19th century. Apparently the goal was not completely met. The Vasari narrative continued with the 19th-century academic painters, a variety of 20th-century realists, and contemporary photographic realists.

What Danto called the Greenberg narrative (after the critic Clement Greenberg) is that the goal of painting is to develop what is specific to painting—flatness and brush strokes. Implicit in this view is that objects are a distraction and that the real goal of painting is to eliminate them. This narrative began with the impressionists and ended with the abstract expressionists. Critics thought that the Greenberg narrative would last as long as the Vasari narrative. The Greenberg narrative drove art not forward but into an evolutionary trap (discussed later).

Artists are not motivated solely by a quest for novelty. They are interested in accomplishing many other things besides making their works novel. However, what these other things are varies unsystematically, whereas the pressure for novelty is consistent. Thus, only the pressure for novelty can produce systematic trends in artistic form and content. This is true even if need for novelty is a comparatively *unimportant* motive for any given artist. [*See* NOVELTY.]

C. The Direction of Aesthetic Evolution

The formalist theorists agreed that their evolutionary theory could not explain the direction of aesthetic changes, but that it is necessary to look to extra-artistic social or cultural forces for such an explanation. How do successive creators produce ideas or artifacts that become more and more novel, original, or incongruous over time? To answer this question, it is necessary to ask how novel ideas or works of art are produced in the first place. Novel or original ideas arise from a biphasic process. An initial inspirational stage involving regression is followed by a subsequent stage of elaboration with a relatively less regressed mode of thought. Regression refers to a movement of thinking toward primordial thought. The conceptual-primordial continuum is the fundamental axis along which states of consciousness and types of thought vary. Conceptual cognition is abstract, logical, and reality oriented. Primordial cognition is concrete, irrational, and autistic. It is the thought of dreams and reveries.

Primordial cognition is free-associative. This increases the probability of novel combinations of mental elements, which form the raw material for a work of art. This raw material must then be put into final form (e.g., be made to conform to stylistic rules) in a rational or conceptual state of mind. Novel ideas could emerge in two ways from the inspiration-elaboration process: Holding the amount of elaboration constant, deeper regression toward primordial cognition should lead to more free-associative thought and thus increase the probability of new ideas. To produce a novel idea, one must regress to a primordial level. To produce an even more novel idea, one must regress to an even more primordial mode of thinking. Holding the amount of regression constant, decreasing the degree of elaboration can lead to statements that are original by virtue of being nonsensical or nonsyntactic in varying degrees.

If we define a poetic style as a lexicon of permitted words and a set of rules for combining them, a stylistic change must occur once all of the usable word combinations have been used. Hypothetically, stylistic change allows creators to return to word combinations composed of relatively close associates. In the case of poetry, this is accomplished either by changes in the poetic lexicon such that entirely new words are dealt with or by loosening the stringency of poetic rules so that previously forbidden word combinations are allowed. There should be a partial return from primordial toward conceptual cognition during periods of stylistic change: Because the rules have been changed, deep regression is not needed to produce novel ideas. Once such stylistic change has occurred, the process of increasing regression would be expected to begin again.

A very clear example of stylistic change can be found in the history of modern French poetry. Until 1900 French poets accepted the commonsense stylistic rule that the word *like* had to join like words. Thus, if a poet wanted to compose a simile, "A is like B," then "A" and "B" had in fact to be alike in at least some arcane way. By the end of the 19th century, a lot of French poets had written a lot of poetry. It had become very difficult to comply with the stylistic rule without repeating what someone else had already said. Around 1900 this rule was explicitly abrogated. It became acceptable poetic practice to combine unlike words with the word *like*. Thus, "the earth is blue like an orange," was perfectly good poetry. Surreal images tend to be composed of close word associates such as *blue* and *orange*. No great regression is needed think of *orange* given the word *blue*. There is quantitative evidence that successive 19th-century poets did in fact regress more and more up to about 1900, when the process was reversed and depth of regression decreased, presumably because of the loosened stylistic rules.

If this theory is valid, four predictions can be made about any series of literary products produced within a given tradition: Indices measuring collative properties such as novelty, complexity, and variability should increase monotonically across time. Indices of primordial cognition should increase over time; but there should also be cycles of increasing and decreasing density of words indicative of primordial cognition thought superimposed on this uptrend. Periods when primordial cognition content decreases should show evidence of stylistic change.

A number of studies have been conducted to test this evolutionary theory. Those concerning literature include investigations of 19th- and 20th-century French poetry, 14th- through 20th-century British poetry,

17th-century English metaphysical and nonmetaphysical poetry, 18th- through 20th-century American poetry, and an experimental simulation of literary change. In Colin Martindale's 1990 book, these as well as studies of the history of painting, architecture, music, and science are summarized.

As an example, Martindale divided the epoch from 1290 to 1949 into 33 successive 20-year periods. The British poets born during each period were ranked on the basis of number of pages devoted to them in the relevant Oxford anthology of English verse. The poets assigned the most pages were included in the sample. The final sample consisted of 170 poets. Once poets had been selected, the most complete and recent available editions of their poetic works were obtained and random samples of this poetry were taken.

Computerized content analysis was employed. To test the theory using a traditional humanistic or qualitative approach would have been impossible. The task of reading the works of 170 poets and deciding whether arousal potential increased in a monotonic fashion across time completely exceeds the capacities of human memory.

The first question of interest concerned the prediction that the arousal potential of British poetry has increased over time. Martindale constructed a Composite Variability Index to measure the collative properties of texts. The goal was to create an index of the degree of complexity, surprisingness, incongruity, ambiguity, and variability of texts. The index is composed of measures such as the Hapax Legomena percentage (percentage of words occurring only once in a document), mean word length, and the coefficient of variation of word frequency, of word length, and of phrase length. The Composite Variability Index is for the most part a measure of unpredictability or entropy. A text that is unpredictable should be surprising. The more unpredictable a poem is, the less certain we are of what the poet is going to say next. The Composite Variability Index gets at unpredictability on a very basic linguistic level.

The Composite Variability Index varies across periods in a highly significant way. As predicted, these differences are due to a monotonic uptrend over time. Arousal potential has been changing and accelerating according to the empirically derived equation since before Chaucer. It is speeding up in its rate of change,

but this has *always* been the case rather than being a modern phenomenon.

To test the predictions concerning trends in primordial content, we need a measure of the latter. Martindale constructed a computerized content analysis measure. His measure of primordial content rose over time, but a cyclical or oscillatory trend is superimposed on the uptrend. We find that 70% of the variation between periods is due to a monotonic uptrend. The other 30% of variation between periods is due to the quasi-periodic oscillations around the trend line. Presumably, the linear uptrend has occurred because more and more primordial cognition has been needed to think of useful word combinations. Theoretically, the oscillations indicate stylistic changes. Primordial content does tend to begin declining during periods commonly seen as involving initiation of new styles: Chaucerian, Skeltonic, Tudor, Jacobean, neoclassic, preromantic, romantic, postromantic, and modern. It begins to rise once the new style is established. Martindale presents quantitative evidence to support this contention.

D. Aesthetic Speciation

In biology, it is quite clear what a species is. If the concept is transferred to art or science, it becomes a very fuzzy set. Transferring the concept may be of some use though. Consider the definition of art. The dominant contemporary definition of art is Dickie's: Anything that a cultural community says is art *is* art. The problem with this definition is that *anything* can be art. Andy Warhol exhibited a Brillo box as art in the 1960s. Because it was accepted as art, Danto proclaimed the end of art. By this he meant not that art would no longer be produced but that anything could be represented as being art, so the Vasari and Greenberg narratives had come to an end.

We can look at things in quite a different way. If we look at painting and sculpture as genuses or even phyla, Warhol's Brillo box only destroyed some species of painting and sculpture—those of the modernist variety. Various species of representative art were not affected at all. This is because of the way that they are defined. Some include beauty (e.g., neoclassicism) in their definition, others include depiction of absolute realism (e.g., photographic realism). Art history books treat painting as a single species. Since 1860 they trace the history of painting from impressionism through postimpressionism and cubism to abstract expressionism. This makes as much sense as a book on biological evolution that treats elephants as the only existing species. In the case of painting, or any of the other arts, there are dozens of styles at any given point in time. There may be some cross-breeding, but each evolves in a fairly independent manner. Art history books tend to neglect all of these other styles or species.

Histories of literature have also been completely miswritten in that they treat poetry, for example, as a single species. Feminist and multicultural critics argue that women and minorities have been unfairly excluded from the literary canon, which they characterize as a set of works by rich dead white men and a few dead white women who wrote in the same style. Perhaps women and minorities should not *want* to be included in the dead-white-man canon but in their own canons, which may have followed quite different evolutionary trajectories. This is an empirical question better to be left to be resolved by scientific inquiry than by humanistic argumentation.

E. Stylistic Extinction

Styles and art forms, just like species, become extinct. This is because they become caught in what could be called evolutionary traps. An evolutionary trap is similar to what happens in biological evolution: An adaptive trap can occur when the ecological niche disappears. For example, Nazi art deco became extinct with the collapse of the Third Reich.

A variation trap involves a loss of variants. With no variation, evolution is not possible. Modern painting since Manet illustrates this. Every innovation did increase impact value but also cut down on the possibility of variation. For example, Manet's elimination of shading clearly eliminated one possibility. To jump to the abstractionists, there are infinite ways of more or less randomly putting paint on a canvas. The problem is that they all look about the same. Thus, there is essentially no variation at all. Creativity is related to primordial cognition in an inverted-U fashion. With extreme primordial cognition, ideas become vague and holophrastic. This cuts down on the number of available mental elements. This version of the variation trap involves artists moving too far toward primordial cog-

nition. Because of this, impact values or novelty falls rather than rises. There is quantitative evidence that late English metaphysical poets fell into this trap.

The production trap has no biological analogue. If there is a gap in training, a style may at least go into dormancy. The Romans knew how to paint using linear perspective. This knowledge was lost during the chaotic epoch following the fall of the Roman Empire, and it took painters around a thousand years to rediscover the rules.

II. REFLECTIONIST AND RELATIONAL THEORIES

Some theories explain art as a reflection of society and, hence, artistic change as a reflection of social change. Such theories can be traced back to Madame de Staël's maxim that "literature is the reflection of society." This approach is rare on the level of systematic theory. It is much more likely to be encountered as an assumption among those, such as compilers of college textbooks on art history or of literary anthologies who have not really thought much about aesthetic theory. Among such authors it is extremely common. A few Marxist theorists have held this view, but mainstream Marxist theorists of art explicitly argue that artists are so autonomous from social control that they are not reflectionist theorists in the real sense of the word. The ultimate conditioning of art by economic and social structures turns out to be so indirect in mainstream Marxist theory that, art is said to reflect society in more or less the same way an automobile might be said to reflect its raw materials.

At first glance, it may seem obvious that art reflects society. For example, a portrait painting almost always depicts a person dressed in the style of his or her day and perhaps surrounded by the furnishings of the time. A moment's thought reveals that such a painting reflects not society but other art forms—fashion and furniture. Of course, art may reflect nonartistic aspects of society. There are no medieval war stories in which atomic weapons are resorted to and no literary depictions of the events of World War II in which battles are settled by jousts between individual mounted and armored knights. However, reflectionist theorists are not concerned with such surface details. Rather, they aim to explain the deep structure of art. For example, Gothic cathedrals are explained as being due to the soaring and spiritual character of the medieval mind.

There are at least three problems with reflectionist theories. First, the social factors that art supposedly reflects are very often things that were inferred from art in the first place. Second, there is no very good reason why art should be expected to reflect society. Artists' attitudes and values are often at extreme variance with the general attitudes and values of the society in which they live and that the individuals recruited as artists are probably not very motivated by a need for consistency. Marxist theorists explicitly stress that the artistic motive of deformation prevents any straightforward reflection of social reality. Third, these theories are not parsimonious. There is often a sufficient explanation for aesthetic trends to be found on the level of purely artistic causes. This makes it quite needless to search for more remote causes.

Reflectionist theories seek some sort of one-to-one mirroring of society in art. Relational theories argue that there is a relationship between social change and artistic change but that it need not be a direct one. As implied earlier, mainstream Marxism is really a theory of this sort. There is no doubt that art and society may be related. For example, the originality or variability of musical compositions is lower during times of intranational civil strife and higher during times of international war. Why? Clearly, melodic originality does not directly reflect anything in this case. There is no obvious relationship between originality and war, riots, and rebellions. Rather, the relationship must be mediated by some third factor. [*See* HISTORIOMETRY.]

Bibliography

Danto, A. C. (1997). *After the end of art: Contemporary art and the pale of history.* Princeton: Princeton University Press.

Martindale, C. (1990). *The clockwork muse: The predictability of artistic change.* New York: Basic Books.

Simonton, D. K. (1994). *Greatness: Who makes history and why.* New York: Guilford.

Sorokin, P. A. (1937–1941). *Social and cultural dynamics,* 4 vols. New York: American Book.

Homospatial Process

Albert Rothenberg

Harvard University

Analogic Reasoning Drawing of inferences or conclusions based on likenesses and comparisons.

Association Meaning is given in consciousness by the associative compounding of ideas.

Blind Rating In an experiment, the practice of concealing or otherwise obscuring the identity or features of subjects in both test and control conditions.

Gestalt Term used for an organizational whole, therefore the perceptual organization of a whole visual space into foreground and background features. The term is used for a psychological theory and movement based on principles of the whole in mental processes.

Semistructured Research Interviews Use of predetermined questions and categories for eliciting interview information relevant to specific proconstructed hypotheses. These questions and categories are not presented in a set sequence but according to the flow and logic of the interview interaction.

Statistical Significance Method for assessing the operation of nonchance factors in an event or series of events.

The **HOMOSPATIAL PROCESS** *consists of actively conceiving two or more discrete identities occupying the same space, a conception leading to the articulation of new identities. The term derives from the Greek meaning of* homoios, *(i.e., "same"). In this process, concrete entities such as rivers, houses, and human faces, as well as sound patterns and written words, are superimposed, interposed, or otherwise brought together in the mind and totally fill its perceptual space—the subjective or imaginary space experienced in consciousness. Such a space is generally located in the* mind's eye, *but to describe the process accurately it is necessary to include the terms* mind's ear, mind's taste, *and the like because entities perceived in any of the sensory spheres may be involved: visual, auditory, tactile, kinesthetic, olfactory, and gustatory.*

I. INTRODUCTION

The homospatial conception of discrete entities occupying the same space is always a rapid, fleeting one. Discrete elements cannot remain unified for very long, even in the mind, and the diffuse initial conception soon leads to a separating out of various components. The important factor, however, is that the components

Copyright © 1999 by Academic Press
All rights of reproduction in any form reserved.

separated out of a homospatial conception are new ones, they are not simply aspects of the original discrete entities presented or considered in stepwise or analytic fashion.

Data regarding the homospatial process were derived from more than 2500 hours of semistructured recorded research interviews with 375 outstanding and neophyte creative persons and comparison subjects. Creative subjects were identified by independent judges. These interviews focused on the creative process in ongoing work in progress in art, literature, and scientific research. Hypothesis-testing experiments with creative subjects in literature and art and matching controls were also carried out. Examples in the following text are derived from both interview studies and primary source investigations.

II. CREATION OF POETIC METAPHORS

The homospatial process is a prime factor in the production of poetic metaphors. For example, a poet produced the metaphor "the branches were handles of stars" through the homospatial process as follows: sitting at his desk writing a poem, he was attracted to the words *handle* and *branch* because of their shared sound qualities—the assonance or shared "an" sound in the center of each—as well as the shared shapes of the wooden objects themselves, and he superimposed them in his mind's eye; he brought them together because he felt they *ought* to be together. Then, in the next fleeting moments, he asked himself when in reality they were the same, and also fleetingly experienced a vivid impression of the letter *a* overlapping in the two words. At that point the idea of stars was generated. Associational or analogical ideas of the country (or park) at night did not generate the metaphor; it was derived from the homospatial conception and provided both the real scene and the sound qualities that unified the words and their meanings.

Similarly, in the case of another type of metaphor, "the tarantula rays of the lamp spread across the conference room," a poet was sitting at a desk thinking about a vacation in the tropics and, among the various thoughts and words that came to mind, he became interested in the sound similarity between the words *tarantula* and *lamp*. He actively superimposed images of the spider and a light source together, along with images of the letters in the words, because he felt these ought to be together. Then, after mentally visualizing spidery light radiating out from a central source in the superimposed images, he thought of the metaphor, "tarantula rays of the lamp." Deciding to elaborate that fragment with a suggestive context, he next conceived of "conference room." Once the entire construction was created, he thought of overtones such as wars in the tropics, the idea of the slow crawl of a tarantula in contrast with the dazzling speed of light and, experiencing an awe-inspiring type of beauty, he was pleased.

In both cases using the homospatial process, the authors visualized a vague scene as well as found the answer in words. Later, they visualized more fully developed and vivid scenes similar to ones evoked by hearing or reading the completed metaphors. The fully visualized scenes did not, however, produce the metaphors; they mainly added to each poet's feeling of the aptness of his creation.

Commonly held associational or analogical views of such metaphor creation are based on people's experience of the impact of the perceived completed metaphor. Hearing or reading "the branches were handles of stars" brings up ways that branches look like handles topped by fiery stars and engenders awareness of previously unnoticed similarities and connections, an experience that is part of the aesthetic reaction. Effective literary metaphors are not, however, produced that way; the poet does not only notice similarities between different or disassociated elements that were previously unnoticed, have unusual associations, or undertake searches for comparisons and analogies to something he or she perceived.

Discrete elements may be brought together for many other reasons besides, or in addition to, similarities in their shape or in the sound of words. Rhythmic connections, verbal overtones and associations, emotional relationships, and conceptual formulations may stimulate the homospatial process. For example, the poet James Merrill developed an initial formulation of a horse as both beast and human simultaneously for the poem, "In Monument Valley," and that formulation was subsequently integrated into a central poetic metaphor (a *poetic image*) by a homospatial conception. [*See* Janusian Process.] A horse and human being were conceived as occupying the same space; that led to the construction of the following image in which a horse and a rider were virtually fused:

> One spring twilight, during a lull in the war,
> At Shoup's farm south of Troy, I last rode horseback.
> Stillnesses were swarming inward from the evening
>   star
> Or outward from the buoyant sorrel mare
> Who moved as if not displeased by the weight upon
>   her.
> Meadows received us, heady with unseen lilac.
>
> Brief, polyphonic lives abounded everywhere.
> With one accord we circled the small lake.

The resulting image was neither a centaur, a mythical entity that is part human and part horse, nor was it some other combination of horse and man. The homospatial conception leads to an integration in which the components interact and contribute to the whole; they are neither blended nor combined. This integration is an essential feature of effective metaphors.

Metaphorization is a prime element in poetic creation and it is also a crucial aspect of other types of creation as well, both artistic and scientific. Metaphors occupy a central place in the creations of painters, novelists, composers, sculptors, architects, and scientific theorists. For an example in science, the theory enhancing metaphor, "black holes in space" has been important in modern astrophysics. Such productive metaphors are characteristically produced by the homospatial process. [*See* ANALOGIES; METAPHORS.]

III. CREATIVE UNIFICATION IN ARTISTIC FIELDS

The process produces other types of creative unifications in the entire range of artistic fields. In literature it is a major factor in the creation and development of literary characters. Novelists, playwrights, and poets actively superimpose and interpose both images of persons they have known and images of themselves together with the developing image of the character they are creating. They do not simply add together or combine various characteristics of themselves and others, either consciously or unconsciously. Also, the homospatial process leads to effective literary double meanings and directly produces rhymes, assonances, and alliterations.

For the painter, sculptor, dancer, actor, and composer, the process brings aspects of foreground and background in the visual, kinesthetic, or auditory sphere into the same spatial plane, superimposed or interposed with one another. This leads to integrations and unifications of visual, movement, and musical patterns. For example, in 1937 Henry Moore indicated the crucial role of a homospatial process in the creation of sculptural works of art as follows:

> This is what the sculptor must do. He must strive continually to think of, and use, form in its full spatial completeness. He gets the solid shape, as it were, inside his head—he thinks of it, whatever its size, as if he were holding it completely enclosed in the hollow of his hand. He mentally visualizes a complex form from all round itself; he knows while he looks at one side what the other side is like.

In music, auditory metaphors and new musical patterns and themes develop from a homospatial process as in the following description by Ludwig van Beethoven: "[T]he underlying idea [of a musical work] . . . rises . . . grows, I hear and see the image in front of me from every angle, as if it had been cast." As Robert Schumann, regarding his composing process, also described, "certain outlines amid all the sounds and tones, . . . form and condense into clear shapes."

IV. HOMOSPATIAL PROCESS IN SCIENTIFIC CREATIVITY

A detailed instance of a homospatial conception leading to the achievement of an important mathematical discovery was described by the creative mathematician Hadamard. He conceived of a rectangle occupying the inside of a square, two discrete entities within the same spatial location, as follows:

> When I think of the example . . . [of the thought leading to the discovery of the valuation of a determinant] I see a schematic diagram: a square of whose sides only the verticals are drawn and, inside of it, four points being the vertices of a rectangle and joined by (hardly

apparent) diagonals—a diagram the symbolic meaning of which will be clear for technicians. It even seems to me that such was my visualization of the question in 1892, [when he made the discovery] as far as I can recollect.

Another mathematical example is Poincaré's mental conception of the coalescing of mathematical formulations, which led to the discovery of a crucial aspect of his famous Fuchsian functions and which he stipulated as follows:

> For a fortnight I had been attempting to prove that there could not be any functions analogous to those I have since called Fuchsian functions. I was at that time very ignorant. Every day I sat down at my table and spent an hour or two trying a great number of combinations and I arrived at no result. One night, I took some black coffee, contrary to my custom, and was unable to sleep. A host of ideas kept surging in my head; I could almost feel them jostling one another, until two of them coalesced, so to speak, to form a stable combination. When morning came, I had established the existence of one class of Fuchsian geometric series. I had only to verify the results, which only took a few hours.

In a semistructured interview exploration of scientific creativity, a Nobel Prize laureate microbiologist described his arriving at an important new idea after consciously visualizing himself superimposed on a living cell.

V. EXPERIMENTAL INVESTIGATIONS

Experimental assessment of the creative effect of the homospatial process has been carried out by means of an externalized concrete representation of the mental conception consisting of transilluminated superimposed slide images. In one experiment, the function of the process in literary creativity was assessed. Ten pairs of slide images, specially constructed to represent the range of predominant literary themes of love, animals, war, aging, and the like, were projected superimposed and side by side, respectively, to an experimental and matched control group of creative writers. An example of superimposition of one of the image pairs, consist-

ing of nuns in front of St. Peter's and racing jockeys, is shown in Figure 1. Subjects in both groups were instructed to produce short literary metaphors in response to each projected image of their designated

FIGURE 1 The first slide pair, separate and superimposed. (A) Photograph of color slides as projected superimposed onto the viewing screen. (B) and (C) Photographs of individual color slides.

type. Results were that metaphors produced in response to the superimposed images, representing externalizations of the homospatial conception, were blindly rated more highly creative on a statistically significant level by independent writer judges than the metaphors produced in response to the side-by-side images. By shortening the time of exposure of the projected images and encouraging mental imaging in another identically designed experiment with other creative writer groups, results were produced that supported the conclusion that creative effects were due to mental superimposition of imagery.

To trace the operation of the homospatial process through the connections between the visually stimulated homospatial conception and a visual creative result, and also to replicate the findings in artistic creativity, another experiment was carried out with visual artists. Subjects were asked to create pastel drawings in response to either superimposed or side-by-side slide images under the same experimental conditions as in the literary experiment. Judges, made up of independent artists and art critics, rated the products, and the superimposed image presentation again resulted in statistically significant more highly creative drawings. Also, measures of specific features of line, color, and composition of the drawings themselves gave evidence that they were produced from superimposed mental representations.

With highly talented award-winning artists, another experiment was carried out to assess whether results of the previous experiments could have been due to stimulus presentation effects. Single images were constructed to represent composite foreground-background (Gestalt) displays of the same slide pairs used in the transilluminated superimpositions. This experiment too showed significantly higher rated created products in response to the superimposed images. All the experiments together indicate a distinct connection between consciously constructed superimposed images representing the homospatial conception and the production of creative effects.

Bibliography

Handler, L. (1996). Object relations: Self, object and the space in between. *Contemporary Psychology, 41,* 385.

Merrill, J. (1972). In Monument Valley. In *Braving the elements* (p. 10). New York: Atheneum.

Rothenberg, A. (1979). *The emerging goddess: The creative process in art, science and other fields.* Chicago: University of Chicago Press.

Rothenberg, A. (1980). Visual art: Homospatial thinking in the creative process. *Leonardo: International Journal of the Contemporary Artist, 13,* 17.

Rothenberg, A. (1986). Artistic creation as stimulated by superimposed versus combined-composite visual images. *Journal of Personality and Social Psychology, 50,* 370.

Rothenberg, A. (1988). Creativity and the homospatial process: Experimental studies. *Psychiatric Clinics of North America, 11,* 443.

Rothenberg, A., & Sobel, R. S. (1980). Creation of literary metaphors as stimulated by superimposed versus separated visual images. *Journal of Mental Imagery, 4,* 77.

Rothenberg, A., & Sobel, R. S. (1981). Effects of shortened exposure time on the creation of literary metaphors as stimulated by superimposed versus separated visual images. *Perceptual and Motor Skills, 53,* 1007.

Smith, G. J. W. (1981). Creation and reconstruction. *Psychoanalysis and Contemporary Thought, 4,* 275.

Sobel, R. S., & Rothenberg, A. (1980). Artistic creation as stimulated by superimposed versus separated visual images. *Journal of Personality and Social Psychology, 39,* 953.

Humane Creativity

Andrei G. Aleinikov

Mega-Innovative Mind International Institute

Creative Linguistics A trend in contemporary linguistics exploring the interaction of creativity and language as well as explaining language innovative trends.

Creative Pedagogy A trend in contemporary education emphasizing creativity and innovation as the ultimate goal for individual development and aiming at creation of a creator, not just an informed and trained individual.

Humane Showing compassion, consideration, and sympathy for live beings as well as behaving according to or consistent with broad humanistic foundations of culture.

Humanism A generally progressive philosophical movement emphasizing the dignity, value, and uniqueness of every human being. Humanism started in the early Renaissance (15th century) and triggered a creativity explosion in arts, architecture, music, and literature as well as an overall blossoming of culture.

Humanistic Psychology A trend in psychology (20th century) emphasizing the inner ability of a human being for development and self-actualization (Abraham Maslow, Carl Rogers).

Self-actualization The ability, tendency, and activity of every individual to develop one's potential.

HUMANE CREATIVITY *is individual/social self-actualizing expansion through production of newness in the domain of humanity. Humane creativity includes any creative activity that promotes humane values and goals, humane communication and means, and humane products and processes. To comprehend the depth of the phenomenon called* humane creativity, *this article first outlines the concept of humane creativity, then analyzes the components of the term separately by exploring their origins and meanings as well as concepts and theories surrounding them, and, finally, synthesizes them to highlight the synergy such a synthesis brings.*

I. HUMANE CREATIVITY— WHAT IS IT?

Humane creativity is juxtaposed to inhumane creativity and to noncreative humanity, both of which are within the realm of human activity. Human activity as a whole first falls into humane activity and inhumane activity, the latter including acts of cruelty, violence, and so on. Second, the same human activity falls into creative activity and noncreative activity. Finally, with both fields put together, the overlap of creative activity and humane activity delineates humane creativity (Figure 1).

Copyright © 1999 by Academic Press
All rights of reproduction in any form reserved.

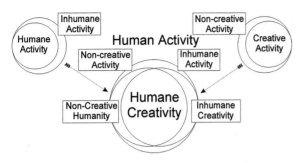

FIGURE 1 Schematic diagram of creativity and humanity relations.

Millions of creative acts form the humane creativity domain, embodying everything from a kindergartner's making a birthday card for his grandmother to Mother Teresa's activities on behalf of humanity. On the other hand, a specific orientation of education to creativity grows, too. The "quiet revolution" described by E. P. Torrance and K. Goff as bringing the dramatic change in education is, by all parameters, a humane revolution.

II. HUMANE, HUMANENESS, HUMANITY, HUMANITARIAN, AND HUMANISM

A. Origin and Meaning of the Term

Humane originates from the Latin word *humanus* and means "relating to human being or being human." However, the word *humane* somehow concentrated the best in the human and at present is certainly not equal to just *human* which is not always humane. The word *humane* is closely associated with ancient Greek and Roman culture. In the English-language texts, it first appeared much later—about 1500 A.D. The contemporary meanings of the word are (a) showing consideration, compassion, or sympathy for humans and animals and (b) characterized by or tending to a broad humanistic culture.

The first meaning can be further specified by numerous synonyms: *altruistic, benevolent, big-hearted, charitable, compassionate, concerned, considerate, cordial, friendly, generous, kind, loving, magnanimous, unselfish, tender, sympathizing, helpful,* and so on. Humane people are also described as acting out of deepest sympathy, devoted to human welfare, having fellow feeling or goodwill toward others, having one's heart in the right place, practicing the Golden Rule, or working for the public weal.

As the second meaning of humane implies, a humane person also tends to develop broad cultural horizons and to act with the vision of common regularities and laws. The word *humane* relates to *humanely, humaneness, human, humanity, humankind, humanism, humanist, humanistic,* and *humanitarian*—all positive words and historically important concepts.

B. Concepts and Theories

Modern primatologists studying primates, as humans' closest relatives in the animal world, have found strong evidence of sharing, sympathy, and mutual aid in their behavior. Animals certainly do not have morals and ethics, at least displayed at our level of understanding. Furthermore, they definitely do not have humanistic studies and humanistic philosophy. However, the conclusion of researchers is quite clear: Being humane (in the first meaning of the word) is not only confined to humans. Moreover, the origins of some behavior patterns (ethical and unethical, moral and immoral) can be traced to animal world. Examples are numerous: taking care of children, politeness (subservience) to older (or stronger) members of community, and even some democratic rules, such as "the majority is right." In the animal world, the latter is supported by the fact that being away from the herd (school, flock, i.e. the majority) sharply increases the probability of being terminated. Therefore, the evolution of these prehuman behavior patterns into highly developed theoretical and practical systems is the result of people's creative activity. This is just the specific creativity that comprises the field of humane creativity.

On the way from unwritten rules requiring humane behavior to codes and laws of modern times, historians usually mention Egyptian culture, Jewish culture with the Ten Commandments, maxims of Confucius, which became the ethical code, and, finally, Greek philosophers who since Pythagoras (6th century B.C.) theorized about moral behavior and developed Moral Philosophy (Socrates, 4th century B.C.). Aristotle first proclaimed that the highest good (as opposed to hedonism and Stoicism) is in the full realization of human potential. This idea later grew into a powerful movement called humanism and into humanistic psychology, which led to a new understanding of creativity itself.

Famous religious leaders like Christ, Mohammed, Buddha, as well as less famous ones, significantly contributed to the growth of humanistic values. The creation of religion was also a tremendous creative act by itself—it took more than 14,000 years. The development of religions from polytheism to monotheism obviously contributed to the growth of the individual's value versus commune (social) value—first in gods, then in humans—and that is why it led to humanism too. However, some of the most inhumane and destructive acts the world has ever seen (Jihads, crusades, the Inquisition, pogroms, etc.) are to this very day being committed in the name of religion (which is supposed to be humane).

Humanism, or humanistic philosophy, appeared in 15th century Italy during the early Renaissance and can be traced back to the famous Italian writers Alighieri Dante (1265–1321) and Giovanni Boccaccio (1313–1375). Humanism, emphasizing the dignity, value, and uniqueness of every individual, spread in Europe and helped establish new universities, academies, and schools. Via education and enlightenment, this trend positively influenced social development, thus causing a creativity explosion in fine arts, architecture, music, and literature as well as an overall blossoming of culture. No wonder a person studying languages, literature, and other creations of humanity was considered a humanist!

In the 20th century, a new research trend, *humanistic psychology* (Abraham Maslow), appeared as an intellectual opposition to behaviorism (Skinner) and Freudianism, named after the father of psychoanalysis (Freud). This trend paved the way to a contemporary understanding of human beings and humanity itself. The proponents of humanistic psychology emphasized the ability of a human being for development and *self-actualization*. Creativity was explained as the growth and expression of the individual's inner self, as the way to self-actualization. Thus, while the humanism of the Renaissance stimulated and strengthened creative activity in all spheres of life, humanistic psychology established firm foundations for further studies of creativity.

From the scientific point of view, the psyche of a human being is formed by a complex combination of genetic and social factors. This point of view is certainly as logical and acceptable as the earlier approaches, but it is also more humane because it allows a human being the right for humane choices and responsibilities. It also allows us to understand (but not condone) the inhumane behavior of some people. Humane behavior is reproducible. It carries on from parents and closest environment to be repeated by children and multiplied by descendents. Humane behavior is supported by the system of norms in ethics and morality. These norms from childhood sculpture personal views of social objects (human beings, groups, represented by the generic term *society*). So in addition to inherently present humane features, it includes the social environment (e.g., parents, relatives, friends, school, neighborhood, and the media) that influences the development or suppression of humane values, humane emotions, humane characteristics, and humane visions. Thus, it is important that the individual self-actualize in a humane versus inhumane environment. In a group built on humane principles, a person is not only treated with respect but also required to treat others with respect. The quality or state of being humane is, therefore, named humaneness (rare) or humanity. Humanity is the way of living in highly developed groups while maintaining the type of interpersonal relations in which a member of the group relates to others as if to self. Empirically, humane attitudes work as a constant identification of an individual with the other members of the group and society. In childhood, humane interrelations develop in mutual activities: first with adults and then with peers. These mutual activities create the commonality of emotions and attitudes that become the psychological basis of humane learning and behavior. The concepts of help, love, compassion, charity, and so forth are internalized and made a part of understanding, personal vision, and helping behavior. Direct demonstration of emotional responsiveness (such as cosuffering the hardships and coenjoying the successes) causes a child to inculcate indirect morality norms. Humane attitudes, communication, mental constructs, orientation, and activities are extremely important for the development of the fully developed personality.

In discussions and disputes going on for centuries, the views of philosophers and psychologists on humanity have changed, but there is absolutely no doubt that Socrates, if he were alive, could have a much better understanding of a modern humanist than Democritus would of a contemporary physicist.

III. CREATIVE, CREATIVENESS, CREATIVITY, AND CREATIVE ACT

A. Origin and Meaning of the Term

The word *create* originates from the Latin word *creatus,* the form of *creare* that means "to do, to make." In Greek, it can be traced in *kreinein* meaning "to fulfill."

Historical analysis shows that the concepts of creator and creation appeared at least 14,000 years ago in attempts to explain this world. However, in the relatively young English language, the word *creator* appears first only in the 13th-century texts. *Merriam-Webster's Collegiate Dictionary* states the earliest recorded use of the word *creative* is dated 1678, and the word *creativity* was not recorded until 1875. Despite the fact that Persians and Babylonians wrote of poetry and arts with admiration thousands of years ago, these dates show that creativity, as a generic phenomenon with a common essence for all these various activities, was not understood as precisely as it is now and certainly was not studied as broadly as it is now. The gaps between the dates also illustrate the intellectual difficulties of moving from *Creator* (uppercase) to a characteristic as an adjective (*creative*), then to the next level of abstract nouns *creativeness* and *creativity,* as an ability to be creative and, finally, down to *creator* (lowercase) as a creative person, regardless of profession. Actually, there is no match to our modern times when, according to some evaluations, more than half of all researchers deal with creativity in some form, including artificial intelligence.

In addition to the form change, the meaning of words *creator, creative,* and *creativity* has also changed. For example, in ancient and medieval history, only God was considered to be a Creator. Many, if not all, prominent figures of the past, while coming out with a new vision or some new product, used to think and say that it was God's idea—not their own idea or their own creation. They believed that it was God's decision or God's inspiration—the hand of God working through them. Humane explanation of creativity came much

later: in the 20th century. However, until now, the above-mentioned *Merriam-Webster's Collegiate Dictionary,* 10th edition, explains the contemporary meaning of the word *creative* as "marked by the ability or power to create." Marked by whom? If you contemplate deeply, you still may find a slight trace of being "marked" by God in the form "mark-ed."

B. Concepts and Theories

Since creativity was first explained and described as an understandable and achievable human activity, numerous terminological systems have been offered to explain the essence of creativity: psychoanalysis, Gestalt, associations, and even factor analysis. Maslow's humanism and self-actualization (1968) take a special place in this list.

There are thousands of books and articles on creativity, and even this encyclopedia is only a sign that creativity as a subject is important. Researchers state that various books and articles contain more than 1000 definitions of creativity. On the one hand, such a variety shows the complexity of the phenomenon and, on the other hand, it helps more or less adequately to explain it. With the ongoing attempts to reflect creativity, definitions and theories multiply. [*See* DEFINITIONS OF CREATIVITY.]

Among all the definitions, philosophical and psychological, simple and extravagant, one definition is used most frequently. It describes creativity as the ability or the process of producing something *new and useful.* This definition reflects the basic features of creativity in the first approximation, but it fades out in particular cases. Imagine, for instance, that a person shows high ability but is doing nothing. Is this creativity? Another person is always in the process; however, shows no results. Is this creativity? The third person, let it be a 1-day-old baby, produces a funny sound, very new and very useful. Is this creativity? Finally, maybe it is not a person at all: a spider produces a web, new and useful. Is this creativity? If not, then why do all these situations fit the definition? Thus, there is still a need to understand creativity in its philosophical significance.

Humanistic psychology has contributed to this. Both Maslow and Rogers mentioned the inherently present self-actualizing power, which allows the individual to expand. Expand, expansion: this is the internal natural pull reflecting the essence of creativity. Actually, by discovering (producing, generating) newness, an individual expands knowledge, experience, and, evidently, life because social memory depends on how creative and innovative this individual is. By generating newness and expanding one's own life, an individual also expands society's domain because after any creative act or innovative product, society knows more, understands more, *owns* more. A creative act, therefore, must end up with the society—it is a material action, not just a combination of thoughts, or an idea, or a flash of illumination. Creativity, as a process, may take place in deepest solitude. It may bring ideas and thoughts unshared with others at the moment, but a creative act will be completed only when these ideas are manifested in sounds, letters, paintings, mechanisms, and so on, and given to other people. One clapping hand produces no clapping.

A simple model, offered by Andrei Aleinikov in the late 1980s to explain sign, language and language consciousness, was also extrapolated to a creative act in the early 1990s. This model (Figure 2) helps visualization of the philosophical essence of creativity.

A creative act (and creativity) is a complex essence embodied within four absolutely necessary and sufficient aspects, or elements: individual (A), society (B), instrument (C), and reality (D). An individual (A) produces some newness (expansion) in reality (D) with instruments (C) and gives it to society (B). The double line arrow (AB) in the model stands for a material action: utterance, implementation, or any other form of

giving back. Rejected discoveries, inventions, pieces of art, and performances are all unconsumed products that some individual produced but society did not accept. Giordano Bruno, for instance, was burned during the Inquisition. That was the form of rejection. Galileo Galilei, who is known as a symbol of fighting against the authority for the freedom of inquiry was compelled to abjure his work and was sentenced to life imprisonment (changed later into home arrest). His book was ordered to be burned, and the sentence was publicized in all the universities. Nevertheless, both Bruno and Galilei stayed in the book of history: everybody knows them. It means the society of the past rejected them, but the society of the future (from their point of view) accepted them and moved to the new heights, like space exploration. Creativity, therefore, is an individual/ social self-actualizing expansion realized through producing newness.

In reality, though, it is society that teaches individuals. It does this first through parents and school; it explains reality, gives instruments, and incorporates goals. Then, the individual moves where nobody yet has reached, thus expanding oneself and society to the new space. In addition, an individual deed is not and cannot be absolutely new. Part of the deed is common for both society and individual (language, culture, etc.). Moreover, an individual, even the smartest one, acquires only a tiny fraction of what is known to society. So if everything known to society is depicted by a sphere, then the preceding three statements will result in the picture of a creative act depicted in Figures 3

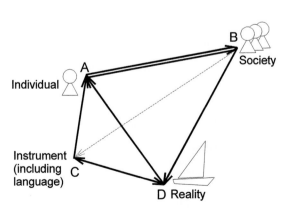

FIGURE 2 Model of a creative act.

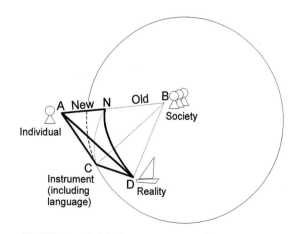

FIGURE 3 Model of a creative act in relation to society.

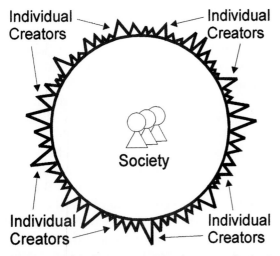

FIGURE 4 Model of society expanding by means of individual creative acts.

and 4. The volume of the "new" that the individual discovers and brings to society may be different, and that is why the configuration of the new (in this case ACDN) may vary as well. Taking the model into consideration, individuals can do the following:

- Discover new reality (new continent, new planet, for example)
- Produce a new instrument, make an invention
- Express themselves more eloquently than others
- Find new facts in the history of the society or social structure

This all expands D, C, A, and B. Usually, it is not one element that is changed, but two, three, or even four. For instance, the description of discovered newness in reality (D) requires new words, new grammatical structures, and so on, which also helps to explain why the word *creativity* appeared so late. This also expands the instrument (C) because language is an instrument. So the four elements can grow either in turn, or in groups, or all together.

As a result, with the help of individual creators getting new knowledge, experience, and so on, society expands step by step. In the same manner as individuals progress and expand (biologically and psychologically), society lives through progression and expansion (socially). In any certain moment, society with individual creators expanding its space looks like Figure 4.

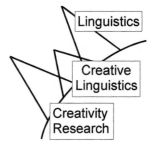

FIGURE 5 Creative linguistics appearing in the gap between two other research domains.

If the gap between two neighboring peaks is large, some new field of research pops up, like biochemistry or *creative linguistics* (Figure 5). On the other hand, several small peaks form the base for a larger peak, as in the case with *creative pedagogy*. This trend in science generalizes and explains everything from music and art classes to creatively oriented courses so thoroughly gathered and precisely described by Alex Osborn in 1965 (Figure 6). Thus, this model, as an heuristic tool, helps to illustrate and develop new trends in creativity research.

Andrei Aleinikov's creative pedagogy introduces new methodologies of creativity formation, which lead to raising more creative and, therefore, more humane people. It also generalizes Maslow's hierarchy of human needs and S. J. Parnes' model of creative problem solving into a universal five-level model explaining everything from a single speech act to the human and nature development in general. This five-level model, when applied to research in humane creativity, paints

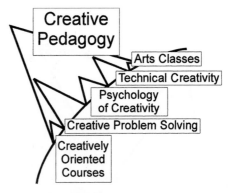

FIGURE 6 Creative pedagogy appearing as a generalization of five different creative education trends.

a vivid picture of different levels. Consequently, creative pedagogy symbolizes the synergy of humanity and creativity research leading to innovative results.

So, if creativity is the expansion of the individual human being in particular and of human society in general, then humane creativity is individual/social expansion through the production of newness in the domain of humanity.

IV. HUMANE CREATIVITY: PAST, PRESENT, AND FUTURE

Humane creativity manifests itself in creative acts within the humanity domain. First of all, everything presently available in this domain is the result of humane creativity of the past. Second, humane creativity of the present includes diverse human activities directed at the development of the following:

- Humane values (attitudes, emotions, beliefs)
- Humane communication (creative versus non-creative communication)
- Humane tools (moral and ethical concepts and theories, humanistic philosophy, social sciences, medicine, education theories, etc.)
- Humane social agencies, institutions, organizations, movements (hospitals, schools, courts, associations, foundations, humane societies and shelters, environmental groups, peace and justice organizations, social reform movements, etc.)
- Humane innovative products (performances, books, movies, videos, etc.; for example, humanist manifestos, and even a virtual humanist Web site on the Internet, spreading humane views internationally, etc.)

Third, any currently unknown but possible activity expanding the domain of humanity will constitute the humane creativity of the future.

How does it all work? Parents, teachers, writers, producers, and so on create situations to awaken humane attitudes and emotions. These attitudes and emotions form the foundation of humane values. The emotional (existential) level includes cofeeling in which a person feels "as if" or "like" the other person. Such cofeelings include empathy, sympathy, compassion, concern, consideration, as well as cogladness, cohappiness, coanger, and so forth.

The emotional level, however, is internal and mostly unobservable until it manifests itself in helping or assisting behavior. The primary level of humane behavior is humane communication. The communication level, or humane communicative behavior, includes nonverbal communication and verbal communication. Nonverbal humane communication comprises sympathetic smiles, eye contact, sighs, postures, touches, pats, intonations, voice tone and volume, as well as joining in laughter, joining in sorrow, and other variations of behavioral empathy. Verbal humane communication includes all utterances and texts containing words and phrases of sympathy, love, respect, and so on.

The communication level, especially the verbal, needs a well-developed vocabulary for naming attitudes, emotions, mood nuances, and so on. It needs instruments—concepts, theories, models, and so on—which all together form the instrumental level. This instrumental ("instru-*mental,*" conceptual) level includes knowledge and understanding of humanity with all its derivative notions. It deals with the historically developed principles of equality and justice, with notions of altruism (as opposed to egoism and egotism), as well as with the other concepts explaining humanity.

The instrumental level, as well as the emotional and communication levels, exists to solve social problems. Humane concepts, theories, words and phrases, and the rest serve the interests of humane society and manifest themselves in the acts of physical help to people in need, as well as physical participation in their lives. Sharing joys and sorrows is the essence of this participation. Rituals and traditional gatherings during holidays (holy days), weddings, funerals, and anniversaries make good examples of humane responsiveness and the sharing of both grief and joy. Social institutions such as temples, churches, hospitals, schools, courts, and even states are created to preserve and promote humane behavior and constitute the orientational (or social problem-solving) level. Associations, foundations, societies, and groups taking a humanistic stance complement these social entities.

Finally, the achievement of new results and the creation of all new products and processes constitute the innovative level of humane creativity. These new material results liberate human beings from dangers and hardships of the environment, such as houses and shelters, food and water facilities, or medical and educational equipment. They also promote humane values, such as books, journals, newspapers, movies, and so on.

Understandably, some of these material things, products, and processes, as well as institutions, have stopped seeming new to us because their invention took place long ago. However, they were definitely invented, for at one time they did not exist. Once they caused inspiration, they were thought through, dreamed about. They may be misused or may have outlived themselves, but they were created thanks to humane emotions and values, humane communication, humane tools, and humane activities with humane goals.

Religious and secular educational institutions are intended to promote humane compassion and love. The world's art masterpieces create or depict humane ideals as the way to follow. This all is a part of the system, which inculcates humane values and, by doing so, solves the problems of a humane and prosperous future. Being humane is a constant fight against that inhumane part that exists in all human beings (i.e., against cruelty, blood thirst, egotism, narcissism, aggressiveness, and their manifestations in violence, crime, and war).

All of this notwithstanding, the world of the present is definitely much more humane than the world of the past. However, the human psyche of the present is still like the battlefield between the biologic past with no or very little humane features and the social future with a highly developed dream of the better—more humane—world. Peace efforts, global societies for hu-

manism and humanity, human rights movements, and so on give us a hope, which no terrorism act can destroy. We build a more humane world for our children and for children of our children to live. Humane activities foster creativity. Creativity, in its turn, works for humanity. Humane creativity is a producer of civilized achievements. The whole civilization as we know it now is the result of humane creativity, and the humane being, an individual creator, is the product of this breathtaking and lifesaving activity in the past, present, and future.

Bibliography

Aleinikov, A. G. (1994). Sozidolinguistics for creative behavior. *The Journal of Creative Behavior, 28*(2), 107–123.

Aleinikov, A. G. (1995). An approach to innovative education [editorial]. *International Journal of Innovative Higher Education, 11,* 5–7.

Maslow, A. H. (1968). *Towards a psychology of being* (2nd ed.). New York: D. Van Nostrand.

Meadows, B. D., & Rogers, C. R. (1973). Client-centered therapy. In R. Corsini (Ed.), *Current Psychotherapies* (pp. 119–166). Itasca, IL: F. E. Peacock.

Millar, G. E. (1995). *E. Paul Torrance: "The creativity man."* Northwood, NJ: Ablex.

Osborn, A. F. (1992). The creative trend in education. In S. J. Parnes (Ed.), *Source book for creative problem solving* (pp. 39–62). Buffalo, NY: Creative Education Foundation Press. (Distributed in 1965)

Parnes, S. J. (1997). *Optimize the magic of your mind.* Buffalo, NY: The Creative Education Foundation, Inc., and Bearly Limited.

Torrance, E. P., & Goff, K. (1989). Quiet revolution. *The Journal of Creative Behavior, 23*(2), 136–145.

Humor

Karen O'Quin

SUNY College at Buffalo

Peter Derks

College of William and Mary

Bisociation Arthur Koestler's name for thinking which connects two or more planes. Perceiving a situation or idea in two self-consistent but habitually incompatible frames of reference. An idea is linked to two associative contexts.

Humor Appreciation Understanding jokes, amusing situations, witticisms, etc., and finding them funny.

Humor Production Creating jokes, stories, amusing situations, witticisms, etc., that other people find funny and/or laugh at.

Incongruity Pairing of ideas or situations that are not usually paired.

Meta-analysis A set of statistical techniques for combining the results of many different studies to summarize them.

Psychoticism On H. J. Eysenck's Personality Inventory, a trait which involves being insensitive to others, impulsive, aggressive, etc.

Resolution In creativity, the idea that to be creative, an idea, act, or product needs to be appropriate, to be valuable, to solve a problem, or to fit the requirements of the situation. In humor, resolution of an incongruity means "solving the problem," or figuring out how two different ideas are related.

*The production and appreciation of **HUMOR** have been said to involve the same kinds of thinking required for*

creativity. This article will review both theory and research which examine the link between humor and creativity. It will examine cognitive, emotional, social, and behavioral similarities, how a humorous atmosphere can facilitate creativity, and methodological problems which obscure our understanding.

I. INTRODUCTION

Arthur Koestler's triptych of creativity, first published in 1964, was an important milestone in the recognition of relationships between humor and creativity. Koestler noted that the structural pattern was the same in art, science, and humor, that is, "the discovery of hidden similarities." He characterized the outcome of that discovery as the "aah" of art, the "aha" of science, and the "haha" of humor. A sudden change in the angle of vision on reality is the key to the humorous way of thinking, as well as to the type of thinking that leads to creativity in the scientific and artistic fields. Koestler thought that these three domains of creativity shaded into each other without sharp boundaries.

Since Koestler's time, there has been considerable research on the humor–creativity link. In 1997, Karen O'Quin and Peter Derks completed a review of the empirical literature on creativity and humor which forms the basis for this article.

In order to understand the similarities between hu-

Copyright © 1999 by Academic Press
All rights of reproduction in any form reserved.

mor and creativity, it is helpful to narrow the broad concept of "humor" down to two different activities: understanding humor (humor appreciation) and creating humor (humor production). Of course, the difference between understanding and producing humor is partly artificial. A person cannot intentionally produce humor unless he or she is capable of appreciating humor. However, the opposite is not necessarily true; there are people who claim that they do not or cannot produce humor, even though they are quite capable of appreciating the humor of others.

At the other endpoint are professional humorists or comedians. William Fry and Melanie Allen studied eight such individuals. They noted two different extremes: the common humor discovery experience which happens to many people, and the much less-common experience of the humor inventor. This differentiation parallels the distinction between humor appreciation and humor production.

The bulk of the creativity literature in humor deals with humor appreciation. However, there is now a fair amount of theory and research examining humor production, as well. This article will consider both of these types of humorous activities. Note that it will neither attempt to address "humor" in the broadest sense, nor provide a theoretical description of why people laugh and smile. Rather, this article will examine the humorous behaviors and cognitions that have been related to creativity.

II. SIMILARITY OF DEFINITION

The parallels in the definitions of humor and creativity are readily evident. Both experts and laypersons agree that one of the delineating characteristics of creativity is originality. Similarly, originality (or its close cousin surprisingness) is also frequently suggested to be characteristic of humor. The jester must say or do something that is new, and the success of her original, unexpected act is typically measured by how funny it is. Funniness is often said to be related to surprise.

However, simple originality is not enough for the definition of creativity, and surprise is probably not enough for humor once a person is past the "peek-a-boo" stage. Something else is needed. In the creativity field, that second dimension has been given many

names, perhaps the most consistent of which is "resolution," or the idea that to be creative, an idea, act, or product needs to be appropriate, valuable, or fit the requirements of the situation. To make more clear the relationship of creativity to humor, we might call it relevant originality.

Similarly, in humor appreciation and production, the simply bizarre will not do. Instead there must be a balance governed by a departure from one idea with the introduction of another idea, different but somehow related and appropriate: a relevant incongruity. The resolution of an incongruity (figuring out how two different ideas are related) can make a significant contribution to funniness. Frank Wicker has also noted that the appropriateness of the joking context appears to be synonymous with the resolution, or "fit," of a joke. Wicker suggested that an inappropriate context might detract from its funniness.

A. Similarity of Cognitive Processes

An important way in which humor and creativity are similar lies in the cognitive processes involved. The classic incongruity theories of humor say that humor arises from the pairing of ideas or situations that are not usually paired. Information-processing models of humor focus on the resolution of incongruities.

For example, in tying together humor and creativity, Arthur Koestler coined the term "bisociation" to describe the mixing of ideas involved when a person abruptly perceives as similar two habitually incompatible contexts. Koestler gave as an example the following venerable joke which had been quoted by Freud:

> The Prince, travelling through his domains, noticed a man in the cheering crowds who bore a striking resemblance to himself. He beckoned him over and asked: "Was your mother ever employed in my palace?" "No, Sire," the man replied. "But my father was." (1964, p. 84)

Koestler noted that the mild amusement afforded by the story is partly derived from oblique hints that readers must complete on their own. Understanding the joke requires some transformation or reinterpretation of the given data. "Higher" forms of comedy or satire pose more of a challenge to a person's intelligence, for example, "Psychoanalysis is the disease for which it pretends to be the cure" and "Philosophy is the systematic abuse of a terminology specially invented for that purpose."

Other names have been used for the same basic idea that Koestler named bisociation. For example, in the creativity field, Sarnoff Mednick called it "remote association," and D. N. Perkins called it "contrary recognition."

It has been suggested that humor comprehension and creativity should be similar because both require the ability to link disparities. Humor often depends upon unexpected or unusual associations, so a person's ability to generate and understand humor would seem to depend, at least partly, upon ideational fluency (the ability to produce many ideas to fulfill certain requirements, such as thinking of possible uses for a brick). Ideational fluency has been said by Michael Wallach to be the essence of creativity.

J. P. Guilford used similar concepts in his multidimensional theory of the structure of intellect. He proposed that there are five different types of mental operations, among them convergent and divergent thinking. In his theory, divergent thinking is defined as producing a variety of responses in which the product is not completely determined by the information given to the respondent. Guilford considered that semantic transformations (puns) are evidence of divergent thinking, as well as one important source of wit and humor. He said that such transformations do not necessarily produce humor, but they often produce delight as well as surprise—an "aha" moment or a "eureka experience."

Over time, divergent thinking has come to be considered almost synonymous with creativity. Tests have been devised to measure divergent thinking, the most widely used of which are the Torrance Tests of Creative Thinking. Such tests are often considered to be measures of creativity, and adults and children who score high on them are considered to be "creative." As will be discussed, several of these creativity tests assign points for humor, as Guilford did. [*See* DIVERGENT THINKING.]

Convergent thinking has received somewhat less attention in the creativity literature. Sarnoff Mednick's Remote Associates Test is sometimes considered to be a measure of convergent thinking, and standard intelligence tests are similarly believed to measure convergent thinking. There has been some evidence that humor production is more strongly related to divergent thinking, whereas humor appreciation might be more strongly related to convergent thinking.

B. Emotional Similarities

In both the creativity and the humor fields, emotional themes of delight, surprise, and enjoyment are found. For example, as already noted, J. P. Guilford discussed the delight and surprise that often accompanied divergent thinking in the form of semantic transformations.

Frank Wicker has stated that enjoyment of humor is in part an aesthetic enjoyment of a creative product, and the joker often shows individual creativity by engaging in a bisociative process to play an incongruity-resolution game. Wicker suggested that even if incongruity resolution fails as a general account of why people laugh, it may still provide a good description of the creative element in humor.

Arthur Koestler said that bisociation required a kind of emotional tension. Although he discussed some of the more negative emotions, such as aggression, he also noted the joy and merriment of humor and the happy emotion which can accompany aesthetic appreciation of an artistic product.

Mary Murdock and Rita Ganim identified 11 categories of theories of humor, and then reduced the number of categories down to 3 important types. "Release and relief" theories were one of the 3 important types they identified. Several classic theories, including Freud's, emphasized the relaxing and emotion-relieving characteristics of humor. Unfortunately, these theories are typically not consistent in whether they refer to the humor producer, the humor appreciator, or both. But in any case, relaxation, emotional release, or "liberation" from the bounds of rational thinking seem to be consistent themes in classic humor theories.

Thus, the joy of discovery seems to be a fairly common emotional theme in both humor and creativity. As noted by Don L. F. Nilsen, humor and creativity are linked by "ah," "ah ha," and "ha ha." The discovery can be tiny or grand, but is typically accompanied by some delight, surprise, or enjoyment.

C. Social Similarities

Avner Ziv discussed the possible relationship between humor and creativity in several presentations. In talking about intentional humor (humor created by a person in order to be enjoyed by other people), he emphasized that humor is a form of communication. The communicator is the humorist (humor creator), the message is the joke or story (the creative product), and the listener is the humor appreciator.

The jester must typically utilize information more quickly than the scientist or the artist for the product to be successful. Not only must the incongruity be recognized, but the immediate interests and the intellect of the audience must be considered in formulating the proper form of communication. A successful new joke requires making a product and communicating that product in such a way as to allow someone else to appreciate its "artistry."

Interestingly, Freud himself perceived successful joking to be a process involving the audience. He said that jokes are the most social of all the mental functions that aim to yield pleasure; the completion of a joke requires the participation of someone else in the mental process.

Since the time of Freud, many theorists and researchers in the field of humor have noted the importance of considering the audience in understanding the phenomenon of humor production. Research has been facilitated because the success of a humorous creation can be readily and immediately identified by audience laughter. Some classic studies, such as those of Jacqueline Goodchilds, have measured wittiness with the Observer Wit Tally, in which observers credit a subject with a successful witticism when at least two other group members laugh. In 1972, Goodchilds asked whether the "puzzling trio—creating, creating humor, and creating humorously" (p. 187) were similar. She suggested that persons who are spontaneously humorous are also spontaneously creative. In addition, some researchers have found that extraversion, or the extent to which a person is socially outgoing, is correlated with self-reported "sense of humor," measured as a personality variable.

In creativity, social factors are sometimes not considered to impinge upon the scientist or the artist; nonetheless, scientific and artistic products must be recognized by others to be considered successful. The editors of scientific journals, peer reviewers, teachers, gallery and museum directors, theater goers, the art-buying public, etc., all serve as audiences to the creative products of scientists and artists. Thus, the social dimension in creativity lies in the implicit or explicit evaluation of the creative idea or product. In a broader sense, social factors are part of the "press," or environment, in which creativity takes place.

D. Behavioral Similarities

As previously noted, Murdock and Ganim reviewed the theoretical literature on humor and creativity. Of the three important categories of theories they identified, one was play/spontaneity. Play, although not synonymous with humor by any means, is related to humor through its association with lighthearted behavior, laughter, etc. Josefa Nina Lieberman, who formulated perhaps the most influential measure of play in children, explicitly considered humor to be one part of play.

In the creativity literature, it is common to find the theme of playfulness mentioned as being characteristic of creativity or creative people. Both researchers and theorists have noted that play and creativity have much in common. In particular, play often involves symbolic transformations in which objects and actions are used in new or unusual ways, similar to the novel, imaginative combinations of ideas involved in creative thinking. [*See* PLAY.]

III. SURVEY OF RESEARCH

A. Humor as a Form of Creativity

In surveying the humor–creativity literature, it is clear that several authors of studies of the humor–creativity link have assumed that humor is simply a type of creativity without examining the basis for that assumption. In fact, some studies of creativity have used the production of captions for a cartoon, drawing, or picture as the *only* measure of creativity.

"Sense of humor" has been included in several measures which attempted to assess creative personality or creative potential. Classic theorists in the field of creativity have often mentioned humor as being a characteristic of creativity or creative persons. For example, E. Paul Torrance noted that the work of creative children is characterized by humor and playfulness. Scoring instructions for the Torrance Tests of Creative Thinking include assigning a point to humor in assessing the Originality and Interest scores. Other tests of creative potential, such as Urban's Test for Creative Thinking–Drawing Production, include humor as one of the evaluation criteria. Getzels and Jackson have noted that creative children tend to rank the importance of a sense of humor more highly than less-creative children.

Murdock and Ganim concluded that creativity and humor were so highly integrated that humor should be considered a subset of creativity. However, they surveyed only a selected literature, that is, theories in the creativity field which explicitly included humor.

B. Humor as a Correlate of Creativity

Many researchers have recognized the multifaceted nature of both humor and creativity Therefore, attempts to predict creativity from humor (or vice versa) have often employed tests of both constructs. O'Quin's comprehensive meta-analysis of the empirical literature in which measures of both humor and creativity were used showed a moderately sized average correlation of .34 between humor and creativity measures. The standard deviation was small enough to conclude that the relationship between humor and creativity across many studies was indeed higher than zero.

In examining the humor and creativity literature, it is important to notice the wide variety of ways in which both humor and creativity have been measured. Humor has been measured by such things as appreciation tests (usually rating cartoons or jokes for funniness), writing cartoon captions which are judged for funniness, teacher ratings of sense of humor or humorous attitude, writing humorous definitions, completing jokes, peer nominations, humor knowledge, humor reasoning ability, observer ratings of laughs/smiles/behavioral attempts at humor, judges' ratings of how clever or humorous a product was, and sense of humor tests.

Creativity has also been measured in numerous ways, for example, the Torrance Tests of Creative Thinking

(the most commonly used), the Remote Associates Test, Guilford's Plot Titles, teacher ratings, word atypicality, the Asymmetrical Preference Test, observer ratings, Wallach and Kogan's ideational creativity, Getzels and Jackson's Word Association Test, infrequency, and the originality subtest of the Comprehensive Aptitude Test Battery. [*See* APPENDIX II: TESTS OF CREATIVITY.]

Obviously, there is little agreement about how best to measure either humor or creativity. Despite this lack of agreement on measurement, however, meta-analysis showed a fairly consistent tendency to find modest positive relationships between measures of humor and measures of creativity.

Many studies have been conducted on the humor–creativity relationship. A frequent humor measure used, whether alone or in conjunction with additional tests, is nomination by others for being funny. This nomination is often made by teachers or peers of students, and the students vary from preschool age to college undergraduates. Sometimes, however, teacher ratings of humor frequency correlate less with observer ratings of laughter production (in other words, the focal child produced an event at which someone else laughed) than peer nominations of the funniest in the class.

Several studies have tested both male and female subjects, and similar results are found for both sexes; however, there is a slight tendency for the correlation between humor and creativity to be higher for females. Perhaps the slight female advantage occurs because they are more verbal and/or better liked by the teachers. The rowdy class clowns may have been ignored.

The most mature group of subjects studied in the literature was a sample of participants chosen from survivors of Terman's study of gifted children. An interviewer rating of "altruism, humor or sublimation as a major defense" correlated highly with lifetime creative productivity for participants in their late seventies. In this study, however, the measure of humor was especially nonspecific, so no strong conclusions can be drawn.

C. Comparing Humor Production and Humor Appreciation

When looking specifically at studies assessing the production of humor, the correlations with creativity are also moderate. Many of these experiments tend to use samples of young adults (most often college students), but even preschoolers have been studied. For example, in 1980, Paul McGhee asked observers and teachers to rate the verbal and behavioral attempts at humor production in young children. The creativity measure was observers' ratings of overall amount of creativity. Results showed that creativity ratings were significantly positively related to humor initiation after the age of 6 (but not before).

These studies have used a variety of measures of humor production (such as making up humorous captions for Thematic Apperception Test (TAT) cards, a Make-A-Joke test, funniness of slogans, cartoon captions, observer or teacher ratings of humor production), and several measures of creativity, although Remote Associates Test scores have been the most frequently employed. To summarize the results of several studies, the size of the correlations between humor production and a variety of creativity measures is about the same moderate size as the correlation of other measures of humor, such as appreciation, with creativity.

Relatively few studies have specifically examined the relationship between humor appreciation and creativity. Some studies have found that those nominated for having a good sense of humor have higher creativity scores than those who do not. Although there are some inconsistencies, people who score highly on creativity tests tend to get higher humor appreciation scores. The size of the humor appreciation–creativity relationships is quite similar to the size of the humor production–creativity relationships.

Although several authors have suggested that humor appreciation is not as close to the rigorous definition of creativity as humor production, there is little difference in the size of the statistical relationships. Why? Humor production seems conceptually closer to the concept of creativity than humor appreciation. Perhaps this conceptualization is simply wrong. Another possibility is that the wide variety of measures used for both humor and creativity has obscured true differences in the size of the relationships. Perhaps the correlation between humor appreciation and creativity comes about more indirectly, maybe through humor's facilitation of a relaxing "game-like" atmosphere. Let us look further at the latter possibility.

D. Humor as a Producer of Creativity

Traditionally and theoretically, humor should have two related effects on thinking that would facilitate creativity. First, the cheerful mood associated with humor should reduce tension and anxiety. In a state of relaxation, individuals would show less fixation and rigidity in their responses to problem-solving situations. Second, beyond the reduced rigidity, there might also be a wider range of options that could be considered. The cognitive network could be expanded due to priming by the incongruous.

There is research evidence that both these factors can contribute to a relationship between humor and creativity. Six research reports in the humor–creativity literature actually manipulated humor as an independent variable. In all six studies, exposure to humor (typically in the form of cartoons, comedy films, or records) facilitated creativity or problem solving in some form (for example, remote associates, unusual word associations, unusual uses, or word atypicality).

A question left unanswered by these studies on humor as a producer of creativity is the duration of the effect. All the tests reported above were immediate; a humor experience was followed right away by creative tasks or problems to be solved. It is possible that popular workshops or conferences that evoke humor to enhance creativity would be a good testing ground for a longer-lasting effect.

E. Group Research

If a humorous atmosphere aids individual originality by increasing freedom and breaking boundaries, then it should also be helpful to groups. A study found that groups trained in creative problem solving produced more ideas while showing more signs of humor. However, inferring causality is a problem because students who choose to take creative studies courses (who formed the basis for this study) may be more humorous to begin with than those who choose alternative courses.

Other research showed that production and divergence seem to relate to a jovial group, but not necessarily problem solving. For groups, then, the value of humor is not as clear as for the individual. A sensible speculation is that humor, while it may "break the ice" and relax the atmosphere in a group, may also consume time, distract group members from the task, etc. More research will help us understand the effect of humorous interaction on group creativity tasks. [*See* GROUP CREATIVITY.]

F. Methodological Issues

A problem for the comparison of creativity and humor, and an indication of their relevance to each other, is the recurrent inclusion of humor or funniness as an element in the scoring of creativity tests. When humor is one of the ways to get points on a creativity test, such as the widely used Torrance Tests of Creative Thinking, it is easy to see how that may inappropriately inflate the humor–creativity relationship.

There is also evidence that alerting respondents to the possibility of humorous answers may positively affect their creativity scores. Avner Ziv has found that instructions to "be funny" do, in fact, improve performance and originality on tests of unusual uses. Wallach and Kogan also suggested that a game-like, rather than a test-like, atmosphere would improve creativity test scores.

A second important methodological issue for both the humor and the creativity literatures concerns validity of measurement. Although reliability of tests is typically high, several authors have criticized commonly used creativity measures, such as the Torrance Tests of Creative Thinking, for lacking validity. For example, Avner Ziv pointed out that people who score highly on tests of divergent thinking do not necessarily create products generally associated with the work of creative people such as artists, musicians, and writers. Only two studies in the entire creativity–humor literature examined actual creative products rather than spur-of-the-moment creativity tests.

The state of affairs with regard to validity in the humor literature is somewhat better; at least criteria such as laughter and smiling are relatively objective. Humor production can be measured by the simple and obvious criterion of creating something judged by others to be humorous. Despite this relative advantage, however, the wide variety of humor measures chosen by researchers reveals that there is little agreement as

to exactly what constitutes humor production, sense of humor, and humor appreciation.

IV. DISCUSSION

A. Unresolved Questions

There are several questions that cannot be answered based on the current theoretical and empirical knowledge base. First, can the effects of humor be more simply explained by positive affect or good feelings? Michael F. Scheier and Charles S. Carver have shown that optimism and positive thinking are related to a number of beneficial physical and psychological outcomes in health psychology, and it seems a short cognitive leap from optimism to good mood and humor. Is humor simply a stronger laboratory manipulation of positive mood than most laboratory manipulations, or does humor make some unique contribution? Avner Ziv has noted that creativity seems best fostered in a relaxed, positive mood. A "game-like" atmosphere seems to facilitate optimal creative performance. Humor and laughter can certainly lead to such a relaxed, positive, game-like state. The roles played by positive affect and general optimism in the humor/creativity relationship are likely to be important, and deserve greater attention in future research.

Second, to what extent is humor appreciation different from humor use or humor production? It seems that one can certainly be an appreciator of humor without also being a producer, but the reverse does not seem at all likely. It is hard to imagine a humor producer who is not also capable of humor appreciation. However, comedians do not necessarily respond when comedic events are produced by others. To the best of our understanding, humor appreciation can exist without production, but humor production is less likely to exist without appreciation. Logically, humor production should be more closely related to creativity than humor appreciation, but the research literature is not particularly supportive of this proposition. Perhaps the type of measurement of creativity is important. It is possible, although research evidence is inconclusive, that humor production is more strongly related to divergent thinking, whereas humor appreciation might be more strongly related to convergent thinking. More research is needed.

Third, to what extent is humor truly separate from creativity? Murdock and Ganim concluded, after reviewing theories that addressed both humor and creativity, that humor was sufficiently integrated to be considered a subset of creativity. However, our review of the broader empirical literature leads us to disagree with their conclusion. Rather, humor and creativity seem to be two interdisciplinary areas which overlap most clearly in the area of humor production. While it is possible to argue, based on the literature, that humor appreciation itself requires some creativity, humor production is logically more directly related to creativity. In 1980, Paul McGhee summarized our view when he said, "as with all great discoveries, then, a higher level of creativity should be required to create a joke, cartoon, or other humour situation, than simply to understand the same event when it is initiated by another person" (p. 122).

However, another possibility is that humor and creativity are related because of their mutual correlation with another construct, such as intelligence or verbal ability. Some newer measures of humor have been created which will allow better tests of this possibility.

Another possible candidate for one of the links in the relationship between humor and creativity is personality. For instance, research has shown that cartoon caption production, but not humor appreciation, showed low but significant positive correlations with extraversion and "psychoticism" on Eysenck's Personality Inventory. H. J. Eysenck has suggested that psychoticism is related to creativity, and other authors have pointed out that some forms of psychopathology seem to be more frequent among highly creative people.

B. Summary and Suggestions

We believe that Koestler was on the right track, but not exactly right. If creativity can be defined as "successful originality," then Eliot Oring's definition of humor as "appropriate incongruity" seems a plausible parallel. For creativity the problem is to define success and originality. For humor, "appropriate" relates to the experience, personality, and circumstances of the individual and/or the group. "Incongruity" plays a cog-

nitive role similar to originality. A creative product is not always (or even usually) funny, and a funny idea is creative only in a very special way, involving originality and a resolution that takes social, human factors into account.

Granted, humor and creativity share similar cognitive, behavioral, and emotional processes that give the two parallel psychological implications. Creativity requires flexible examination of the connections among ideas, and humor depends on the selection and evaluation of different associations at different levels of analysis. However, an original idea that does not solve a problem is usually not considered creative. A joke that leaves the incongruity unresolved is nonsense, but might still be funny. Production of ideas is necessary for both humor and creativity, and evaluation of those ideas is critical (although not always acknowledged) for both. Creativity and humor do require similar cognitive processes. The specific applications are, however, different.

As previously discussed, a major problem in investigating the humor–creativity link is a lack of clarity of the two constructs. Humor is sometimes considered to be a form of creativity. Creativity measures sometimes assign points for humor or include tasks that involve humor. Such confounds must be removed before the "true" nature of the relationship between the two constructs can be thoroughly examined.

In addition, there still remain problems with basic definitions and theories. Many years ago, authors bemoaned the lack of a single and widely accepted theory of creativity to focus research. Despite a tremendous surge in creativity research between the mid-sixties and the mid-eighties, no absolute consensus or overarching theory of creativity has yet been reached.

Similarly, there is no single theory of humor. Murdock and Ganim pointed out that the word "humor" describes a complex multifaceted phenomenon which is often misused to name only one part of it. As noted in this article, even basic differences such as those between humor appreciation and humor production have not always been made clear by either theorists or empirical investigators.

Finally, there still remain problems with the interface between the fields of humor and creativity. For example, Murdock and Ganim noted limitations on the way the concept of humor has been treated by creativity researchers, and suggested a broader examination of the humor literature by creativity researchers. We strongly concur with their conclusion. Similar criticisms might be made of the creativity measures chosen by humor researchers. Sometimes, experts in one domain impose their own ways of thinking on another domain, which may yield insights which are original, but are not high in resolution.

Perhaps one day, a general unified theory of cognition will encompass both humor and creativity. Until then, we need more precise definitions. Rather than simply saying "humor," researchers and theorists must be more clear as to what, in the broad array of cognitions and behaviors that can be encompassed by that term, they mean. In the short run, rather than trying to come up with a grand and complete theory of humor, we need more "mini-theories" to help explain individual phenomena. Similarly, in the creativity literature, researchers should be more aware that a vast amount of humor research exists, only a small part of which overlaps with "creativity."

We believe that consideration of the cognitive, emotional, behavioral, and social aspects of both humor and creativity need to be weighed in understanding the two phenomena. Complex issues sometimes demand complex answers.

Bibliography

Fry, W. F., & Allen, M. (1976). Humour as a creative experience: The development of a Hollywood humorist. In A. J. Chapman & H. C. Foot (Eds.), *Humour and laughter: Theory, research and applications* (pp. 245–258). London: Wiley.

Goodchilds, J. D. (1972). On being witty: Causes, correlates, and consequences. In J. H. Goldstein & P. E. McGhee (Eds.), *The psychology of humor: Theoretical perspectives and empirical issues* (pp. 173–193). New York: Academic Press.

Koestler, A. (1964). *The act of creation.* New York: Macmillan.

McGhee, P. E. (1980). Development of the creative aspects of humor. In P. E. McGhee & A. J. Chapman (Eds.), *Children's humour,* (pp. 119–139). Chichester, UK: Wiley.

Murdock, M. C., & Ganim, R. M. (1992). Creativity and humor: Integration and incongruity. *Journal of Creative Behavior, 27,* 57–70.

O'Quin, K., & Derks, P. (1997). Humor and creativity: A review of the empirical literature. In M. Runco (Ed.), *Creativity research handbook volume 1* (pp. 223–252). Cresskill, NJ: Hampton Press.

Ruch, W. (Ed.). (1996). Measurement approaches to the sense of humor [Special issue]. *Humor: International Journal of Humor Research, 9*(3/4), 239–250.

Scheier, M. F., & Carver, C. S. (1992). Effects of optimism on psychological and physical well-being: Theoretical overview and empirical update. *Cognitive Therapy and Research, 16,* 201–228.

Wicker, F. W. (1985). A rhetorical look at humor as creativity. *Journal of Creative Behavior, 19,* 175–184.

Ziv, A. (1989). Using humor to develop creative thinking. *Journal of Children in Contemporary Society, 20*(1/2), 99–116.

ISBN 0-12-227076-2